The McGraw-Hill Illustrated Dictionary of Personal Computers

Fourth Edition

Michael F. Hordeski

McGraw-Hill, Inc.
New York San Francisco Washington, D.C. Auckland Bogotá
Caracas Lisbon London Madrid Mexico City Milan
Montreal New Delhi San Juan Singapore
Sydney Tokyo Toronto

© 1995 by **McGraw-Hill, Inc.**

Printed in the United States of America. All rights reserved. The publisher takes no responsibility for the use of any of the materials or methods described in this book, nor for the products thereof.

pbk   2 3 4 5 6 7 8 9 FGR 9 9 8 7 6 5
hc   1 2 3 4 5 6 7 8 9 FGR 9 9 8 7 6 5

Library of Congress Cataloging-in-Publication Data

ISBN 0-07-0304092
ISBN 0-07-0304106 pbk.

Acquisitions Editor: Roland Phelps
Editorial Team: Joanne M. Slike, Executive Editor
             Margaret Myers, Book Editor
Production Team: Katherine G. Brown, Director
             Brenda S. Wilhide, Computer Artist
             Janice Stottlemyer, Computer Artist
             Jeffrey M. Hall, Computer Artist
             Wanda S. Ditch, Desktop Operator
             Nancy K. Mickley, Proofreading
             Linda L. King, Proofreading
             Lorie L. White, Proofreading
Designer: Jaclyn J. Boone
        Katherine Stefanski, Associate Book Designer

DICT
0304106

Acknowledgments

I want to thank those who have helped with this project: my reviewer and editor, Dee, who kept moving the project along; Patrick Rockwell, who provided many useful suggestions for definitions; the good folks at Rockwell International and Fairchild Camera and Instruments, who allowed me to use some of their illustrations; and all those who have contributed to the literature and the use of new terminology.

List of Contributors

Marianne Krcma
Marianne Krcma Technical Services

Jessica Keyes
Techinsider

Carla Rose

John Mueller
Owner, DataCon

Stephen J. Bigelow
Dynamic Learning Systems

Michael O. Stegman

Introduction

The third edition of *The McGraw-Hill Illustrated Dictionary of Personal Computers* (then titled *The Illustrated Dictionary of Microcomputers*) was more comprehensive than earlier editions, with the addition of many popular hardware and software products. This fourth edition continues that trend by addressing the latest topics in personal computers and microcomputers, including networks, desktop publishing, and alternative input and output devices.

Since the third edition, terms such as *open systems interconnection* (OSI) and *interleaving* are used more frequently, and network terminology is much more common and of interest to most users. Advances in these and other areas since publication of the last edition are incorporated here. New and revised topics include those related to bulletin boards, computer communications, CD-ROMs, distributed systems, embedded systems, groupware, fiber-optic products, hypertext products, modern programming, local area networks, Macintosh computers, programming loops, mouse products, network protocols, PostScript products, relational databases, software prototyping, user interfaces, videodiscs, windowing environments, and workstations. There is an extensive treatment of major terms in NetWare and other networks, as well as world-recognized international standards and terms. Highlights of this new edition include additional illustrations and improved, extensive cross-references.

Every time a new process is developed or a committee is established, another abbreviation or acronym appears. While this proliferation of terms reflects an expanding technology with a high level of productivity, it can hamper communications. From a systematic evaluation of major national and international publications, more than 2,400 new terms have been added in this edition. Coverage is extensive in the areas of abbreviations and acronyms, including those related to conventional electronics and particularly microcomputer electronics and data processing.

To be included in this dictionary, entries should be used widely enough to be both timely and interesting. In addition to updating with new terms, an analysis of the existing terms and content was performed regarding the clarity of the definition, the usefulness of any illustrations, and the quality of cross-references. Of course, the decision to add and delete terms is a subjective one. In some cases, older definitions that apply to outmoded equipment have been retained because much of this equipment is never discarded, but is recycled or in some form of storage waiting for a suitable application. Other terms and technologies remain because they have historical significance in the development of the microcomputer.

How to use this book

The following conventions have been used in this book:

- Terms are listed alphabetically without regard to spaces.
- Terms that begin with numerals are alphabetized as though they were spelled out, except where numerical order is more natural, such as in a list of part numbers (e.g., Intel 80286, Intel 80386, Intel 80486).
- *See* is used to refer the reader to the full definition of a term. *Also see* is used to refer the reader to a related term. *Contrast with* is used to direct the reader to an opposing term.
- Cross-referenced terms are indicated in small capitals when they appear elsewhere in the book as separate entries.
- Synonyms and variants are indicated in italics when they do not appear as separate entries.
- Terms are listed under their acronyms and abbreviations, as well as their spelled-out counterparts. The full definition will appear with whichever usage is most common.
- Older terms and technologies are indicated with (*o.t.*).

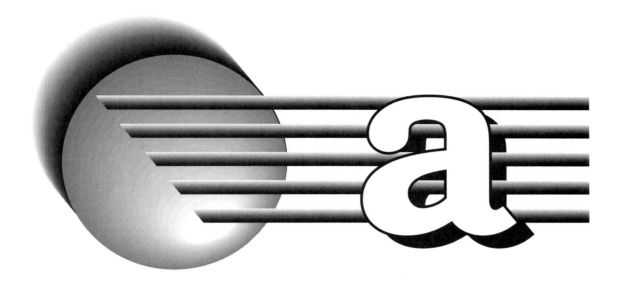

A 1. Symbol for *accumulator*. 2. Symbol for *ampere*. 3. Symbol for *angstrom*.

AAAS Acronym for *American Association for the Advancement of Science*.

A and not B gate A binary logic coincidence (two-input) circuit used to complete the logic operations of A and not B. The result is true only if statement A is true and statement B is false.

a-axis A is an angle defining rotary motion around the x-axis. Positive a is in the direction to advance a right-handed screw in the positive-x direction. The standard coordinate system gives the coordinates of a moving tool with respect to a stationary workpiece. Used in CAD/CAM systems.

abbreviated addressing A process of shortening the address in the direct addressing mode by using only part of the full address. This process provides a faster means of processing data.

ABC-AB switch A variation of the basic RS-232C ABC switch, as shown. In addition to the basic ABC operations of switching two devices (A or B) between a common device (C), this switch also allows connection A-B to be selected. The ABC-AB is internally wired as a null modem across the A-B connection, permitting direct connection of two DTE devices. Some ABC-AB switches have a selection labeled "TEST." The test feature loops data back to the devices on switch positions A and B. It is useful for self-testing.

ABC-Centronics switch This switch supports the 36-pin Centronics interface used by Centronics, Printronics, Data Products, Epson, Star Micronics, and many other printer manufacturers.

ABC classification The classification of the items in inventory in decreasing order of annual dollar

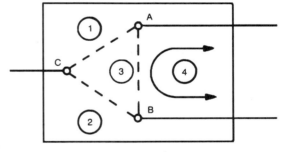

ABC-AB switch

volume or other criteria. This array is then split into three classes called A, B, and C class. The A class contains the items with the highest annual dollar volume and receives the most attention. Class B receives less attention, and class C, which contains the low dollar volume items, is controlled routinely. The ABC principle says that effort saved through relaxed controls on low-value items will be applied to reduce inventories of high-value items.

ABC-current loop switch A switch that transfers either a single four-wire circuit or two two-wire circuits from A to B. An ABCDE-current loop switch transfers a single four-wire circuit or two two-wire circuits to A, B, C, D, or E. An X-current loop switch makes two different current loop circuits change partners.

ABC database A public-domain, user-friendly data filing system that accepts up to 1,500 records with up to 12 fields in each record. It can be used to handle customer files, mailing lists, daily schedules, or technical cross-references.

ABCDE switch A switch that allows you to connect four different compatible devices to a fifth device and switch among them. For example, it can enable up to four workstations to share one printer, four terminals to share a single modem, or four printers to operate from one computer, as shown. *Also see* AUTOMATIC DATA SWITCH.

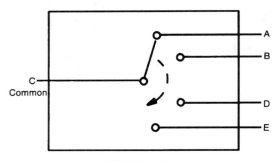

ABCDE switch

ABCDE-25 switch A switch that is equipped with five DB25S connectors to connect and switch up to five RS-232 devices. The switch may be ordered in three configurations to switch 4, 12, or 24 leads of the RS-232 interface.

ABC Flowcharter A Windows-based flowcharting program from Micrografx. You can point and click to draw shapes; type in text to fill shapes; move shapes; simplify procedures by linking shapes to subcharts, and attach notes or code to shapes. It also includes full font support, snap grids, text search, custom shape, and import capability.

ABC Fun Keys A program that teaches the alphabet to children ages two through five using four games. It requires at least a CGA monitor.

ABC switch A switch that allows switching among three compatible devices, as shown in the figure. For example, it can connect two terminals to one modem, two microcomputers to one printer, or one word processor to two different peripherals.

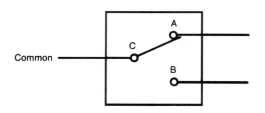

ABC switch

ABC-25 An ABC switch that is equipped with DB25S (female) connectors to enable the connecting and switching of devices that conform to the popular RS-232 interface specification, the most common interface in the world. Users outside of North America know it as CCITT V.24.

ABC-25 monitor This switch performs the same function as an ABC-25 switch but has the additional feature of monitoring the active connection with LEDs. Six leads are monitored: 2 (TX), 3 (RX), 4 (RTS), 5 (CTS), 6 (DSR), and 20 (DTR). The LEDs are interface-powered so the switch requires no external power supply.

ABEND unrecoverable An error condition that results in abnormal termination of a program. *Contrast with* RECOVERABLE ABEND.

ABL Abbreviation for *atlas basic language*.

ABLE Acronym for *activity balance line evaluation*.

abnormal preamble A package error that occurs when the preamble does not match the legal eight-byte Ethernet synchronization pattern.

abort connections A diagnostic in NetWare that shows the number of times (since SPX was loaded) that applications have called SPX abort connection.

abort flag A print service in NetWare. If nonzero, it deletes a capture file rather than queuing it for printing.

abort timer A unit designed to continuously monitor dial-up (DDD) modems for received data traffic, as shown in the figure. If, after a call is established, data is not received within an adjustable, preset period of time, the abort timer will disconnect the call by dropping DTR (data terminal ready) to the modem. The modem then becomes available for other users. This product may be used with either a terminal/modem or a computer port/modem. Use of the abort timer can lower telephone toll costs as well as aid in a more efficient use of computer resources.

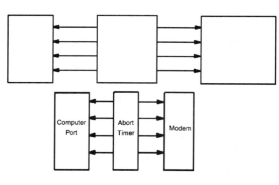

Abort timer

AboveBoard This was the first product to allow a DOS-based program to access more than 640K of memory and support the Lotus-Intel-Microsoft expanded memory specification. This board is particularly useful to users of older PCs running DOS-based programs that require all data to be memory-resident, such as Lotus 1-2-3, Symphony, and Framework. With it you can access up to 2M additional memory on a PC and 4M additional memory on an AT or higher, enabling you to create documents up to 15 times that available under normal DOS constraints. The software that comes with this board provides a RAM disk, print buffer, and menu-driven configuration program. If you expect to be running DOS-based software that requires expanded memory, either consider buying this product or use a memory manager like DOS's EMM386 to simulate expanded memory. *Also see* LIMM.

ABR Abbreviation for *automatic baud rate detection*, in which the receiving device automatically senses the baud rate of an incoming message and sets its own baud rate accordingly.

absolute accuracy Accuracy as measured from a reference that must be specified.

absolute address An identification of an exact location where information is stored in a computer system.

absolute assembler A type of assembly language program that produces binary (object) programs in which all addresses and address references are absolute addresses.

absolute code A code that specifies the memory location where an instruction operand is stored; a code that uses absolute addressing and lists the exact location where the operand is to be found.

absolute coordinates In computer graphics, a pair of values that specify the location of a point with respect to the origin of the coordinated system. *Contrast with* RELATIVE COORDINATES.

absolute dimension A dimension expressed with respect to the arbitrary origin of a coordinate system.

absolute element An executable computer program written in a source language, which is compiled and then the addresses are assigned for use during the execution of the program. The resulting element is termed *absolute* because the program can only be executed in a specific space in memory. This is to be distinguished from a *relocatable element*, which can be run in any memory space.

absolute error The amount or value of an off-tolerance state, expressed in the same unit of measure as the quantity being monitored or measured.

absolute loader A program loader used to load programs and associated data in absolute address format into memory for execution.

absolute maximum ratings The published limiting values for the operation and environmental conditions of electronic equipment. Absolute maximum ratings should not be exceeded in order to maintain the expected reliability of the equipment.

absolute path The complete name of a directory, showing all the directories the operating system must access to reach it, starting with the root directory.

absolute programming The use of a machine language, in contrast to a symbolic language.

absolute readout A display of the true position as derived from the position commands to a control system.

absolute system A numerical control system in which all positional dimensions, both input and feedback, are measured from a fixed point of origin.

absolute value Value without respect to algebraic sign.

absolute-value machine A computer that processes all data using full values of all variables at all times. Absolute-value machines operate in a contrasting mode to *incremental machines*.

absolute-value transducer A device that produces an output proportional to the input, but always of the same polarity. The output does not change polarity and remains at the absolute value of the input proportion.

absorption The deposition of a thin layer of gas or vapor particles onto the surface of a solid. The process is also known as *chemisorption* when the deposited material is bound by a chemical bond.

absorption current The current flowing into a capacitor following its initial charge, due to a gradual penetration of electric stress into the dielectric. Also, the current that flows out of a capacitor following its initial discharge.

ABSTAT A flexible statistics package that can be used in a variety of applications. It is command-driven, fully interactive, and has a wide range of report formats. Data can be input from a dBASE file, an ASCII file created by another program, or by the ABSTAT editor. A set of transformations allows you to define your own equations or access the mean, standard deviation, and case number of each variable. ABSTAT is flexible in interpolating missing values. It provides descriptive statistics, analysis of variance, chi-square, correlations, cross-tabulations, and multiple regressions.

abstract syntax A description of a data structure that is independent of machine-oriented structures and encodings.

-ac A suffix meaning *automatic computer*, as in ENIAC, SWAC, UNIVAC, etc.

ac *See* ALTERNATING CURRENT.

ACC and DEC Abbreviation for *acceleration and deceleration*. An increase or decrease in velocity (tool feedrate); it provides smooth changes in velocity for machine tool slides. It may be provided for in hardware or software.

acceleration time The total elapsed time between the application of a read or write instruction, and the transfer of the acted-upon information to its storage medium.

accelerator board A board that delivers additional processing power to a microcomputer, typically by adding RAM and a processor or coprocessor. For example, one half-size accelerator card provides AT-class processing speed to IBM PCs, XTs, and compatibles by providing a 10-MHz 80286 processor and 16 bytes of cache memory. For added flexibility it retains the PC's original 8088 processor, allowing the user to toggle, via a software-controlled hot key, between turbo mode (10 MHz) and regular PC speed (4.77 MHz). Support is also provided for an 80287 math coprocessor.

accelerometer quartz array Isolator quartz accelerometers employ a unique compression mode quartz array that maintains a stable output signal in the presence of thermal transients or base strain even at low frequencies. Typical units have a 50 m V/g, low-impedance output signal.

acceptance test A test to show compliance of purchased equipment or services with the purchaser's stated requirements, specifications, or conditions of purchase.

acception An atom in a doped semiconductor crystal that accepts an electron or gives up a hole.

Access A professional, Windows-based database application developed by Microsoft Corporation.

access The process of obtaining data from or placing data into a storage device or register.

access control byte The byte following the start delimiter of a token or frame that is used to control access to a token-ring network.

access control list *See* ACL.

access line The connection between the public network and a subscriber's facility.

access method A set of rules that a LAN uses to govern network traffic. The access method determines the major classification of the LAN: either carrier-sense multiple access with collision detection (CSMA/CD) or token passing. *Also see* CSMA/CD.

access mode A file protocol service that defines how the call opens a target file.

access priority The maximum priority that a token can have for the adapter in order to use it for transmissions.

access rights Refers to the use of a mask of the calling station's privileges for accessing a specified file or directory.

access time The total time required to deliver data after the initiation of a command to retrieve it. Internal data storage usually provides the fastest access time, but tends to increase system costs. Processing with internal storage can be done in less than a microsecond, while external random access processing is typically expressed in terms of milliseconds. The ideal access time would of course be zero, and for many purposes the nanosecond speeds of some internal storage units appear to be virtually zero. When this is the case, it is called *immediate access* or *simultaneous access*.

access unit A unit that gives multiple attaching devices access to a token-ring network at a central point. Such a device is sometimes also referred to as a *concentrator*.

Accumaster A UNIX-based workstation under AT&T's Unified Network Management Architecture (UNMA) that collects information from network components including T-1 lines, LANs, PBXs, and mainframe computers.

Accumaster integrator A network management station under AT&T's UNMA.

accumulator A temporary storage register in a processing unit where the results of arithmetic or logic operations are held. The accumulator may operate on one word length, one word and one character, two words, or two words and two characters. Sometimes it is made up of two registers that function at double-word length.

accumulator address An address used when the operand is in an accumulator. For example, the 6800 uses two accumulators: a primary (A) and a secondary (B). Therefore, the instruction

```
ASL A ; (shift A left)
```

shifts the contents of register A to the left by one bit length.

accumulator extension register The accumulator extension register in some microcomputers can be used for serial input and output. The extension register will function as a serial shift register using an instruction. The serial input and the serial output are controlled by an instruction, which shifts the contents of the register right by one bit.

accumulator register That part of an arithmetic unit in which the results of an operation remains, and into which numbers are brought to and from storage.

accuracy 1. Conformity of an indicated value to a true value, an actual value, or an accepted standard value. 2. A measure of the difference between the actual position of a machine and the position demanded (in control systems). The accuracy of a control system is expressed as the deviation or difference between the ultimately controlled variable and its ideal value, usually in the steady state or at sampled instants.

accuracy rating Refers to the limit, usually expressed as a percentage of full-scale value, not exceeded by errors when the equipment is used under reference conditions.

ac/dc Describes electronic equipment that is capable of operating from either alternating current (ac) or direct current (dc) sources. *Also see* ALTERNATING CURRENT, DIRECT CURRENT.

ac dump The removal of alternating current from a unit either intentionally, accidentally, or conditionally. An ac dump results in the removal of all power from a unit unless special provisions are made for a backup system.

achieved reliability Refers to reliability that is determined on the basis of actual performance or on operations based on standards or benchmarks under equal or equivalent conditions and circumstances. Also known as *operational reliability*.

ACIA Abbreviation for an *asynchronous communications interface adapter*, an adapter unit that provides the data formatting and control to interface asynchronous communications data to organized systems. The interface can include such functions as select, enable, read/write, interrupt, and the logic for data transfer. The parallel data from the bus is transmitted in the serial mode using the ACIA. Error checking and variable word lengths are allowed with this adapter.

ACK Abbreviation for an *affirmative acknowledgement*. ACK, as used in block data transmission, signifies that a previously transmitted block has been accepted by the receiver and the receiver is now ready to accept the next block of data.

acknowledgement A response sent to indicate receipt of a particular message or portion (block) of a message.

acknowledgements sent Refers to a count of acknowledgements sent by a network server. An acknowledgement is sent when a workstation repeats a request that is already being serviced.

acknowledge number Refers to the sequence number of the next packet expected to be received.

ACL Abbreviation for *access control list*, a network security technique. Most network security systems operate by allowing selective use of services. An ACL is the usual means by which access to, and denial of, services is controlled. It is simply a list of the services available, each with a list of the hosts permitted to use the service.

ac line plug-in surge protector *See* SURGE PROTECTOR.

ACM Abbreviation for *Association for Computing Machinery*, a professional and technical society whose publications, conferences, and activities are designed to help advance the art of computing, as regards machinery and system design, language and program development, and other related areas. It is a member of the American Federation of Information Processing Societies (AFIPS).

ac modem surge protector *See* MODEM SURGE PROTECTOR.

ACORN Acronym for *automatic checkout and recording equipment*.

acoustic coupler An electronic device used in conjunction with a modem for transmitting data via a standard telephone handset. This is done by *coupling* via sound waves (acoustically) the handset and the modem.

acousto-mechanical mice Mice that use the change in resistance in a strain gauge to determine direction and a piezoelectric transducer to determine the velocity. There are no moving parts, no maintenance, and the mouse can track motion on almost any surface; however, the resolution (counts per inch) depends on the type of surface on which the mouse is used and on the downward pressure placed on the mouse.

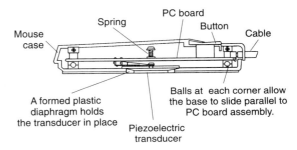

Acousto-mechanical mouse

acquisition time The time a sample/hold circuit takes to acquire the input signal to within the stated accuracy. It may include the settling time of the output amplifier. Since it is possible for the signal to be acquired and the circuit switched to hold before the output is settled, the user must be certain that the output amplifier is settled before accepting the results as meaningful.

ACRE Abbreviation for *automatic checkout and readiness equipment*.

ACS Abbreviation for *asynchronous channel splitter*, a unit that attaches to most asynchronous and synchronous modems and splits the main channel into two asynchronous subchannels. Each of the resultant channels must operate at half the modem data rate; for example, two 2400-baud channels can be derived from one 4800-baud modem.

ACT! A popular integrated software application emphasizing contact/client management and tracking. Originally developed by Contact Software International and now marketed by Symantec.

ACS In-Control A software system for relating activities to prospects. It can summarize dollars spent for any activity or group of activities, for a prospect, for any period of time. In-Control has search capability, Rolodex features, appointment schedules and graphics, label management, 50 context-sensitive online help screens, a built-in telephone dialing system, and a built-in proposal and invoice generator. The program can function as a prospect and activity tracking system; a bank loan recovery/collections tracking system; a time, billing, and activity tracking system; and an appointment scheduler. It comes with a tutorial to help you get started. An options menu is used to adapt In-Control to a particular business.

active element **1.** An element in its excited or in-use state. **2.** A transistor or other device that is on or alive rather than off, dead, or in a ground state. **3.** A file, record, or routine that is being used, contacted, or referred to. Computing components are active when they are directed or excited by the control unit.

active filter A filter consisting of an amplifier and suitable tuning element, usually inserted into a feedback path. Active filters have a number of advantages over passive filters. They can eliminate inductors with associated saturation and temperature-stability problems. The response of an active filter can be set by temperature-stable capacitors and resistors. They overcome the problems of insertion loss and loading effects through the use of operational amplifiers.

A typical active filter is shown in the following figure. It is manufactured with thick film hybrid technology. It uses the state variable active filter principle to implement a second order transfer function. Three operational amplifiers are used for the second order function, while a fourth uncommitted op amp may be used as a gain stage, summing amplifier, or buffer amplifier, or to add another real pole. Two pole low-pass, bandpass, and highpass output functions are available simultaneously from three different outputs. Notch and allpass functions are available by combining these outputs in the uncommitted op amp. To realize higher order filters, several devices can be cascaded. Q range is 0.1 to 1,000 and resonant frequency range is 0.001 Hz to 200 kHz. Frequency stability is 0.1% per degree centigrade. Frequency tuning is done by two external resistors and Q tuning by a third external resistor.

active **1.** Operational. **2.** Pertaining to a file, page, or program that is in main or memory, as opposed to a file, page, or program that must be retrieved from auxiliary storage. **3.** Pertaining to a node or device that is connected or is available for connection to another node or device.

active hub An ARCnet component used to connect network workstations into a star topology.

active indexed files Refers to a count of files that are currently active, open, and indexed.

active interrupt Refers to the state of an interrupt level that is the result of the CPU starting to process an interrupt condition. *Also see* INTERRUPT.

active matrix A technology used in color monitors, especially for notebook (portable) computers. It produces a high-quality picture, but draws a considerable amount of power.

active monitor A computer on a token-ring network that acts as the controller for the ring. The active monitor regulates the token and its performance characteristics.

active monitor present Refers to a packet issued every three seconds by the active monitor on a token-ring network.

active session The session in which a user is currently interacting with the computer.

active star A network topology in which a controller establishes active links to other star networks.

active storage Data storage locations that hold the data actively being processed. *Also see* BUFFER STORAGE.

active transducer Any transducer in which the applied power controls or modulates locally supplied power.

activity ratio The ratio of the number of records in a file that are used or modified during some time period to the total number of records in the file.

Actor An object-oriented Windows development environment that allows you to quickly design and program Windows applications with considerably less code than a traditional language. It includes an extensive class library, the ObjectWindows library for simplified Windows programming, and an assortment of tools including a class browser, inspector, and debugger. The included "Read Me First" tutorial book provides a good understanding of object-oriented programming techniques.

Actor Professional A complete tool for Windows development. In addition to features of Actor, it includes additional classes and links to easily access popular databases such as Paradox, dBASE, and SQL Server. Actor Professional also includes the ObjectGraphics class library for easier graphics programming and the Whitewater Resource Toolkit, a visual tool for creating and editing Windows resources.

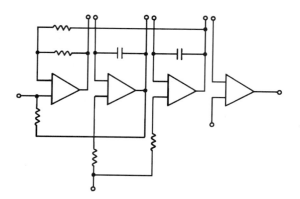

Typical active-filter IC

actual maximum bindery objects In NetWare, refers to the maximum number of bindery objects that have been used concurrently since the file server came up. This field is only meaningful if the previous field is set. *Also see* BINDERY.

actual maximum indexed files In NetWare, refers to the number of indexed files the server has had active simultaneously since it was brought up.

actual maximum open files In NetWare, refers to the number of files open simultaneously since the server was brought up.

actual maximum simultaneous transactions In NetWare, refers to the highest number of transactions that have occurred simultaneously since the server was brought up.

actual maximum used directory In NetWare, refers to the most directory slots ever used at one time on a volume.

actual maximum used routing buffers In NetWare, refers to the maximum number of routing buffers that have been in use simultaneously since the server was brought up.

actuator This mechanism in the hard drive positions the drive head, moving it to a specific track of data. A voice-coil actuator is generally faster than a stepper motor actuator. A voice coil can quickly position the head to a specific location, while a stepper motor steps from track to track to get a specific track.

ACTV Abbreviation for *advanced compatible television*, a set of techniques for advanced television transmission. ACTV I is a channel-compatible, receiver-compatible system utilizing different techniques to add widescreen panels and increase horizontal and vertical resolution. ACTV II adds improved resolution and sound.

ACU 1. Abbreviation for *address control unit*. **2.** Abbreviation for *automatic calling unit*.

A/D Abbreviation for *analog-to-digital*.

ADA Abbreviation for *automatic data acquisition*.

adapt Acronym for *air material command developed APT*, a computer-aided numerical control programming language and processor. It is a subset of APT (automatically programmed tools) with limited capabilities compared to APT. It has been essentially limited to two axis contouring and has been implemented and supported on small and medium-size computers.

adapter A device that allows operation between different components of a microcomputer system.

adapter address The hexadecimal digits that identify a LAN adapter.

adapter board *See* ADAPTER CARD.

adapter card A circuit card that plugs into one of the expansion slots in a microcomputer. Adapter cards are used for most I/O functions, including the LAN interface.

adapter plug A fitting designed to change the terminal arrangement or size of a jack, socket, or other receptacle so that electrical connections other than the original are possible.

adaptive equalization A process in a receiver in which received symbols are used to continuously update the settings of a filter used for equalization.

adaptive packet Refers to the use of large data packets when the channel is relatively error-free and smaller packets when conditions worsen.

adaptive routing A method of routing packets of data or data messages in which a system's intelligence selects the best path. This path can change with traffic patterns or link failures.

adaptive session-level pacing A form of session-level pacing in which session components exchange pacing windows that can vary in size during the course of a session. This allows transmission within a network to adapt dynamically to variations in availability and demand on a session-by-session basis. Session-level pacing occurs in independent stages along the session path according to local congestion at the intermediate nodes.

ADC *See* ANALOG-TO-DIGITAL CONVERSION.

A/D converter *See* ANALOG-TO-DIGITAL CONVERSION.

A/D converter controller When several analog inputs are connected to an analog-to-digital converter through an analog multiplexer, the controller selects an analog channel for conversion by the A/D converter. When conversion is complete, the end-of-conversion signal is issued. The converted signal's binary value is then read into the controller for processing. Errors are tested for, and out-of-circuit checks are performed on the digital representation of the analog signal.

add 1. The mathematical operation of summing. **2.** The command to perform a summing operation.

addend In a summing operation, the contents of a storage register addressed for addition with the augend. The result is the sum. *Also see* ADDITION.

addend register The addend register serves as an addend store. When it stores both addends and answers, it is called the *accumulator register*.

adder A device that outputs the sum of two or more numbers presented as inputs, as shown. The adder is the main arithmetic element of the ALU (arithmetic and logic unit) in some computers. The adder can perform addition, subtraction, multiplication, and division with the help of the accumulator and other storage registers.

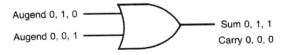

Using the OR gate as an adder

adder-accumulator In some systems the adder is a parallel binary adder with an internally connected carry for implementing precision arithmetic operations. The adder then operates with the accumulator to form the arithmetic logic unit (ALU) section of the central processing unit (CPU). Functionally, the CPU has ten or more microinstructions dedicated to arithmetic and logical operations. All can be one-cycle instructions and can enable direct arithmetic operation between the accumulator and the data in RAM or ROM storage. In addition to its arithmetic functions, the accumulator is the primary working register in the CPU and is the central data interchange point for most data transfer operations occurring in the system. During the internal data transfer, the accumulator is the interfacing data register for both RAM and ROM. For external data exchanges (input/output), the accumulator is the source of the output data and the receiver register for the input data. *Also see* CPU.

adder, two input A logic element that performs addition by accepting two digital input signals, a digit of a number and an addend or a carry, and that provides two output signals, a carry digit and a digit for the sum.

addition The summing of two or more numbers. Addition is always performed in a microcomputer by summing two numbers at a time, the AUGEND and the ADDEND. The augend is usually the contents of the accumulator, and the addend is the contents of a storage register that is addressed. A typical microprocessor contains a number of data registers. One of these registers functions as the accumulator with all arithmetic and logic operations being performed in it; the other registers hold temporary results and provide the operands of instructions to control the accumulator. When the operand is stored, for example, in register D, the instruction

```
ADD D ; (A = A + D)
```

adds the contents of the register D to the accumulator and stores the result in the accumulator.

Another type of microprocessor uses one register (A) as a primary accumulator and another (B) as a secondary accumulator; in this case the operand is likely to be stored in memory. To add the contents of the memory location to the accumulator, you can use extended addressing and write the following instruction:

```
ADD B $212 ; (add the contents of M (212) to B)
```

The symbol $ indicates to the assembler that 212 is a hexadecimal number.

address A label identifying a location where information is stored. An address can be represented by characters or bits that name, label, or number a location, a part of storage, a data source, or a destination. Also, an address can be that part of an instruction that identifies the location of the operand of that instruction.

A location in a city can be located if one knows the street address; similarly, if you know the computer storage medium's address for a desired piece of information, this information can be located in the storage unit. When the information is put into the storage unit, an address is assigned to each word; then when a particular word is desired, the address is used to find it.

Storage locations in a microcomputer can be thought of as being similar to a set of post office boxes, message boxes at hotel front desks, or stockroom bins, as shown in the following diagram.

00	01	02	03
04	05	06	07
08	09	10	11
12	13	14	15

Storage assignments

All the storage locations are identified by a specific label and the locations are capable of holding various items. The contents of the locations change, but the locations and the location numbers remain the same. However, while post office boxes and storage bins can hold many different items at any one time, an address in a computer unit stores only one unit of data at a time.

If the storage unit had 2000 locations, then the addresses would be numbered from 0000 to 1999. Each of these numbers identifies a unique location; it says nothing about the contents of the location. Instructions deal only with address numbers; for example, let $144 be stored in address 1888. To have the machine print this amount, you would instruct it to print 1888. The microcomputer will interpret this to mean that the contents of 1888 be displayed, resulting in the printout of $144.

A simple payroll program might have the following English instructions:

1. Start the machine.
2. Read the employee's payroll data into storage for processing.
3. Multiply hours worked by the hourly rate to find gross earnings.
4. Multiply gross earnings by the withholding percentage to find the tax deduction.
5. Add the hospitalization insurance deduction to the amount from step 4 to compute the total deduction.
6. Subtract the total deduction from the gross earnings to find the take-home pay.

7. Print a check for the amount of the take-home pay with the employee's name and identification.
8. Stop the machine at the end of processing for the last employee.

The storage locations for such a program can be assigned as shown in the accompanying illustration. In this example, the payroll data is stored in locations 00 to 04; location 05 is used for temporary storage, and the instructions are assigned to locations 06 to 17 (which become the program storage areas). The first instruction sets the location of the payroll data as 00 to 04. (The location of this data is arbitrary.)

00 Store employee name	01 Store hours worked	02 Store hourly rate	03 Store withholding percentage	04 Store hospitalization deduction	05 Temporary storage area
06 Read data into 00, 01, 02, 03, 04	07 Write contents of 01 into arithmetic unit	08 Multiply contents of arithmetic unit by contents of 02	09 Store result of D8 in 05	10 Multiply result of 08 by contents of 03	11 Add result of 10 to contents of 04
12 Subtract result of 11 from contents of 05	13 Store result of 12 in 18	14 Print check for contents of 18	15 Make check payable to contents of 00	16 If 00 empty stop	17 Go to 06
18 Store take-home pay	Storage assignments				

Payroll program storage locations

Address Book A public-domain personal or business address-book program written in BASIC. With it, you can create your own address file, which can be edited, printed, searched, and sorted. Mailing labels can be prepared, and birthdays or other user-defined notes kept. WordStar and WordPerfect mailmerge files also can be created, as can subdirectories of the main directory. Function keys are used extensively in this program, and a RAM disk may be used for more speed.

address bus The original 8-bit IBM PC microprocessor had a set of 16 pins to carry the binary numbers called *addresses*. These pins (there may be more than 16 today) are called the address bus. The address bus carries information out from the microprocessor to ROM, RAM, or I/O chips. Signals on the address bus are used to select a certain memory or I/O chip and to select a particular location inside that chip. *Also see* BUS.

address connections Refers to how the ROM and RAM are wired to the address bus. Bits A11 and A1 are the chip selects. The RAM uses A7 through A0 and the ROM uses A9 through A0. The address bus is used to select a location within a component. To perform this function, two selections must be performed: First, the device must be selected, then the location within the device must be selected.

addresselope An envelope-addressing utility for PCs that provides automatic address capture from within a word processor; extended printer support; support for up to eight fonts; compatibility with most word processors; ten predefined return-address and four envelope formats; single-envelope, batch, and bulk envelope formats; and single-envelope, batch, and bulk envelope printing. Designed for direct-mail, most features such as address positioning, envelope size, and fonts are user-definable.

address field The instruction segment that stipulates a specific memory location where an information element may be accessed.

addressing capabilities Much of the power of microcomputers is derived from wide ranges of addressing capabilities. Addressing modes include sequential forward or backward addressing, address indexing, indirect addressing, 16- or 32-bit word addressing, 8-bit (byte) addressing, and stack addressing. Variable-length instruction formatting allows a minimum number of bytes to be used for each addressing mode. The result is efficient use of program storage space.

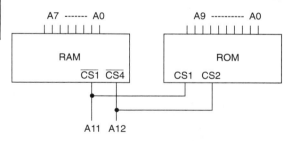

RAM and ROM address connections

addressing, symbolic A fundamental procedure or method of addressing using a symbolic address. The symbolic address is chosen for convenience in programming. The symbolic address must be translated into an absolute address before it can be used in the microcomputer.

address modification An alteration to the address portion of a program instruction that results in an internal transfer to a new memory location when the original address is called for after the first time in an iterative routine.

address resolution Conversion of a logical address into the corresponding physical address.

Address Resolution Protocol A protocol used to dynamically discover the low-level physical network hardware address that corresponds to the high-level address for a given host.

address space A collection of addresses that form a unified collection such as an internetwork.

add/subtract time The time required for a circuit, system, or machine to perform addition or subtraction operations. The add/subtract time does not include the time required to obtain the numbers from storage, nor does it include the time involved in placing the answers into storage.

add time The time required to acquire from memory and execute one fixed-point add instruction using all features such as overlapped memory banks, instruction lookahead, and parallel execution. The add is either from one full word in memory to a register or from memory to memory, but not usually from register to register.

adjacent In a network, pertains to devices, nodes, or domains that are directly connected by a data link or that share common control.

adjacent link station A link station directly connected to a given node by a link connection for network traffic.

adjusted ring length The transmission path length for a ring architecture when a node or segment fails and the ring wraps to provide network service without interruption.

administrative domain A collection of hosts and routers, and the interconnecting network(s), managed by a single administrative authority.

admissible mark Any one of the elementary units or basic symbols in a symbol system, such as the letters of the English alphabet, or the digits 0 through 9 in the decimal number system; a character.

Adobe Illustrator A program that can be used to trace over and enhance blueprints, photos, logotypes, and art files from compatible software. It can be used for technical publications, textbook art, medical illustration, product illustration, fashion layouts, editorial art, parts catalogs, comics, logos, business graphics, and brochure art.

Adobe Photoshop A 32-bit color image-processing program that includes drawing, painting, and darkroom capabilities. Users can scan a color or grayscale image and then rotate the image, combine it with other photos, alter the colors or gray levels, touch it up, make it transparent, and so on. Available in both Mac and Windows versions.

Adobe Type Library A set of typefaces, each with its own personality designed to communicate a different message. The package includes screen fonts for use at any point size. You can use a Mac or PC desktop publishing system, a PostScript printer, and Adobe downloadable fonts for newsletters, reports, proposals, or documents.

Adobe Type Manager Abbreviated ATM. A utility available for Mac, Windows, and even some DOS (i.e., non-Windows) systems that allows the user to view type on the screen with the highest possible resolution the user's monitor will allow, regardless of type size.

ADP Abbreviation for *automatic data processing*; the process of obtaining input information in machine language as close to the point of origin as economically possible, processing the information by computer and other machines without human intervention (as far as economically justified), and having the output information produced in accordance with the needs of management and the techniques of data processing.

ADR *See* ADDER.

advanced BASIC A form of BASIC with such features as extended color graphics commands; event trapping for communications adapters, joysticks, and special function keys; and light pen and music support.

Advanced NetWare A local area network operating system for PC networking.

Advanced NetWare for PS/2 A NetWare operating system that supports the IBM Personal System/2 (PS/2) as a file server. You can bridge your PS/2 network through the file server to token ring and PC network LANs. You can also bridge through a workstation to any LAN supported by NetWare. The package lets you use either a nondedicated or dedicated file server on PS/2 models 50 and 60. The nondedicated option lets the model 50 or 60 file server operate simultaneously as both file server and workstation.

advanced peer-to-peer communications *See* APPC.

advanced peer-to-peer network *See* APPN.

Advanced Program-to-Program Communications A protocol used for peer-to-peer communication in IBM's System Network Architecture. *Also see* SNA.

Advantage A multifunction expansion board that uses the IBM PC-AT's 16-bit data bus and extended memory addressing capabilities. It allows up to 3 megabytes (M) of parity checked memory and several I/O functions in a single expansion slot. It is compatible with either 64K or 256K RAM chips, and the user-upgradable memory expansion capability permits both types of chips to be mixed on the same board. Using 256K chips, the Advantage main board provides up to 1.5M of memory. An additional 1.5M may be added by installing a piggyback board, for a total memory expansion of 3M.

Advantage disassembler A memory-resident program that gives programmers the ability to disassemble executable files (.EXE and .COM files) to produce assembly language source code. The programmer can add additional comments; make changes to code; define labels for subroutines, data areas or I/O port addresses; check conflicts in memory; or add more code before reassembling. It supports Intel math coprocessors and includes two tutorials providing examples for the disassembly of .EXE and .COM files.

Advantage network DEC's network strategy that supports its own propriety protocols and international standards.

Advantage Premium A multifunction board with a six-pack of premium features for PC-AT systems. It can add up to 2M of expanded memory so you can create 2M-sized spreadsheets and databases. It comes with DESQview multitasking software so you can run up to nine programs at the same time and view them in windows. The board comes with 512K and is expandable to 2M using 256K chips. For the other 1M, you add a 512K piggyback board that expands to 1M. Adding three additional RAMpage boards will take you to the 8M EMS (expanded memory specification) limit.

adventure A class of computer game involving an exercise in logic, concentration, and memory recall, frequently using a fantasy background of caverns, dwarves, and giants.

ADX Abbreviation for *automatic data exchange*.

AFP Abbreviation for *AppleTalk Filing Protocol Services*.

AFP directory path In the AppleTalk Filing Protocol Services, this specifies at least the target AFP directory name, and optionally the names of one or more parent directories. The field is 1 to 255 bytes long.

AFP entry ID In the AppleTalk Filing Protocol Services, this is the four-byte Apple equivalent of a NetWare directory handle, with an exception: a NetWare directory handle points to a file server volume or directory, while an AFP entry ID points to a file server volume, directory, or file.

After Dark A series of Windows-based screen-saver products developed and marketed by Berkeley Systems.

Agenda Time-management software from Lotus Development Corporation.

agent A device under the Simple Network Management Protocol that can report alarm information to a manager. *Also see* SNMP.

aggregate A function in a query language used to perform an operation on several rows of data. Sum is an example of an aggregate.

AI Abbreviation for *artificial intelligence*, the branch of computer science devoted to developing a machine that can improve its own operations or can perform functions normally associated with human intelligence such as reasoning, adapting, or learning. The strength of an AI system is based on the rules and protocols that make it. A *strong AI* might use an expert system created from the input of hundreds of experts. It would also incorporate heuristics and neural nets, enabling the system to adjust its rules to meet the needs and habits of the user. A *weak AI* uses hard-coded rules that would remain the same and provide limited flexibility to the user of that AI.

AIFF Abbreviation for *audio interchange file format*, a Macintosh file format.

alarm systems, microprocessor CPUs scan input or output points at preselected intervals, checking against alarm limits. Critical deviations from normal operating conditions are detected and alarms are sent to the control/acknowledgment terminal. The CPU at the terminal formats and routes the alarm data to an operator's display panel. The operator on duty observes the detected alarm and takes the necessary steps to correct the problem. Alarms corresponding to "crisis" situations can be detected directly by limit switches, circuit continuity breaks, or the manual depression of a button. Crisis conditions require immediate attention and would therefore be assigned as priority vector interrupts in the CPU.

algebra Mathematical operations in which letters and other nonnumeric characters are used to represent variables and constants.

Algebrax An algebra tutor program that provides different skill levels from the beginning student to the advanced. The program keeps track of progress as the student completes each lesson so that he or she can concentrate on any difficult areas. It requires CGA and DOS 3.0 or higher.

ALGOL Acronym for *algorithmic language*, an internationally defined arithmetic language designed for scientific applications that involve computer processing of numerical procedures (algorithms). It includes a number of special features such as unrestricted nesting of conditional statements and the intermixing of real and integer identifiers. ALGOL is used more extensively in Europe than in the U.S.

algorithm A precisely defined set of rules or a structured procedure that provides the solution to a problem in a finite number of steps. For example, suppose that it is desired to compute the value of a polynomial of the form

$$f(x) = ax^n + bx^{n-1} + cx^{n-2} \ldots$$

For $n = 5$ you can write the following algorithm:

$$f(x) = (((((a) x + b) x + c) x + d) x + e) x + f$$

This algorithm indicates that the computation can be done by repeating a multiply-and-add step five times.

algorithmic language program conversion Refers to the steps involved in converting a program in a high-level language to a machine language program. Among these are decomposition of syntactic structure, allocation of storage, production of target program, editorial and optimizational function, and diagnostic provisions.

algorithm, transfer A specific type of algorithm used in a demand-fetching system to determine the order in which segments demanded by concurrent processes are transferred from a backing store to an internal memory.

aliasing Also called *stairstepping* or *jaggies*. In sampling, a flaw is produced when the input signal contains frequency components higher than half of the sampling rate. It typically produces jagged steps on diagonal edges. *Contrast with* ANTI-ALIASING.

aliasing distortion An error in reconstructing a sampled analog signal when it is sampled at a rate that is less than twice the signal bandwidth. Also called *foldover distortion.*

align To set the position of an annotation by a point on the annotation.

alignment The process of adjusting components of a system for proper interrelationship. The term is applied especially to the synchronization of components in a system.

alignment error Refers to a packet that has not been synchronized correctly.

alignment pin Any pin or device that will ensure the correct mating of two components designed to be connected.

allCLEAR A software package that automatically creates presentation-quality flowcharts, tree-charts, procedure diagrams, decision trees, and organization charts from plain English descriptions. You can import files from a word processor or Lotus spreadsheet and output to a screen, printer, or desktop publishing system.

All-in-One DEC's office automation shell, consisting of a menu driver, a mail user interface, a calendar manager, and a file manager.

allocate Refers to assignment of storage in a computer to main routines and subroutines, thus fixing the absolute values of symbolic addresses.

allocate cannot find route In NetWare, this is the number of times (since the shell was activated) that the shell, asked by an application to establish a connection with a file server, could not find a route to the destination network.

allocated stock **1.** In an inventory system, an allocated item is one for which a picking order has been released to the stockroom but not yet sent out of the stockroom. It is an "uncashed" stockroom requisition. **2.** A process used to distribute material in short supply.

allocate no slots available In NetWare, this is the number of times (since the shell was activated) that the shell, asked by an application to establish a connection with a file server, could not do so because the file server's connection table was full.

allocate server is down In NetWare, this is the number of times (since the shell was activated) that the shell, asked by an application to establish a connection with a file server, could not establish the connection because the target file server was down.

allocation A concept used in the NetWare SPX transport layer protocol. An allocation is the amount of unacknowledged traffic that may be outstanding at one time.

allocation number In NetWare, this is the number of listen buffers outstanding in one direction on the connection. SPX manages this field; clients need not be concerned with it.

allocation unit Refers to disk space that is allocated to files in blocks.

alloy A composition of two or more elements, of which at least one is a metal. It may be either a solid, solution, a heterogeneous mixture, or a combination of both.

all points addressable mode A graphics mode in which the programmer can control each dot on the screen.

all-routes broadcast frame A frame transmitted to all network nodes.

all-station broadcast frame A frame with all destination address bits set to one.

Aloha network A radio-linked local area network developed at the University of Hawaii.

alphabet code A set of letter-character abbreviations for computer instructions, which can be interpreted by a computer as the instructions themselves.

alphabetic character A letter of the alphabet.

alphabetic coding A system of abbreviation used in preparing information for input into a computer. Information can then be reported in the form of letters and words as well as in numbers.

alphabetic-numeric *See* ALPHANUMERIC.

Alpha database manager An older, menu-driven, DOS-based file manager with features that include full two-way integration with Multimate, Visicalc, Multiplan, dBASE, and ASCII files; support for searches and reports with Boolean operators and wildcards; and Soundex-phonetic matches. It allows the user to define up to 26 input screens for a file. Because of its ability to consolidate multiple files into a target file, it can be used for many multi-file applications despite the fact that it is not a relational database. It has a mailing label feature and a report writer that allows for titles, footnotes, calculations, page numbering, page breaks, and control breaks.

alphameric A contraction sometimes used for *alphanumeric.*

alphanumeric Characters that include the letters of the alphabet, numerals, and symbols used for punctuation and mathematical operations.

alphanumeric instruction An instruction containing both letters and numbers.

alphanumeric mode A graphics mode for text only.

alphanumerics display, gas discharge A gas-discharge display that produces a light output that exceeds 300 microcandelas, which makes characters easy to read and viewable in high ambient light. These displays are suitable for point-of-sale and moving-message applications, and are used in large audience information systems.

alpha radiation errors A potential problem in memories that occurs when positively charged alpha particles cause "soft errors" in dynamic RAMs. The phenomenon has also been observed in some static RAMs. As signal levels inside memory and logic devices continue to shrink, other noise sources (thermal noise, for example) may be isolated as error generators, but the assumption is that not all errors can be prevented, which has sparked new interest in correction and detection schemes. Simple parity checks can spot single-bit errors, while more elaborate schemes such as the Hamming code can correct single-bit errors and detect double-bit errors.

The Hamming code is gaining popularity in 16-bit microprocessors since the percent of overhead needed to perfom the correction declines as word size increases. Five extra bits are required for an 8-bit word, while only six bits are needed to correct a 16-bit word. Error correction systems are a trend, and the logic necessary to perform this correcting is available in more and more integrated circuits.

alpha release A very early release of a software product for testing purposes, in which distribution is very limited.

ALRP Abbreviation for *APT long-range program*, an organization of private companies and government agencies who have pooled their funds for the purpose of developing a numerical-control computer-aided programming language called APT (automatically programmed tools). The management and development contractor hired by the organization is the Illinois Institute of Technology Research Institute.

alternate buffer A memory area set aside to receive data when the primary buffer is full so that data transmission is not interrupted.

alternate mark inversion coding A bipolar line-coding scheme in which spaces are encoded as zero signal levels and marks are encoded as nonzero levels that alternate between positive and negative for successive marks.

alternate routing A routing scheme usually less preferred than the normal routing, but delivering an identical end-product.

alternating charge characteristic Refers to the functions, under steady-state conditions, of the instantaneous values of the alternating component of transferred charge to the corresponding instantaneous values of a specified periodic voltage applied to a nonlinear capacitor.

alternating current Electric current whose flow alternates in direction; the time of flow in one direction is a half period, and the length of all half periods is the same. The normal waveform of ac is sinusoidal, which allows a simple vector algebraic treatment.

alternation Refers to one half of a cycle, when an alternating current goes from either positive to zero or negative to zero.

alternative denial Concerns a logical operation applied to at least two operands that will produce a result according to the bit patterns of the operand.

alter switch An alter switch, when toggled, causes its contents to be copied into the register selected by the display switch or the memory location contained in the program counter if the display is so set.

Alt key A key found on many microcomputers, typically used to enter an ASCII character code directly from the keyboard. The key is held while the digits are typed on the numeric keypad.

ALU Abbreviation for *arithmetic and logic unit*, the part of the microcomputer that performs arithmetic, logic, and related operations. Calculations are performed and logic comparisons are made in this part of the chip set.

For example, a program involving a simple series of payroll calculations might have the following instructions:

07	08	09	10	11
Write contents of 01 into arithmetic unit	Multiply contents of arithmetic unit by contents of 02	Store result of 08 in 05	Multiply result of 08 by contents of 03	Add result of 10 to contents of 04

Typical payroll calculation

The first instruction requires that the contents of address 07 be written into the arithmetic and logic unit. The ALU must have the capability to store temporarily the data contained in address 01. Typically, registers would be used to store this data. The number of registers and the data flow pattern vary among microcomputers and this results in differences between arithmetic and logic units.

aluminum gate and silicon gate differences An intrinsic determinant of the threshold voltage is the choice of gate electrode and substrate materials. This relates to the physics concept of work function, which represents the binding energy of an electron in a particular material. When polycrystalline doped silicon is used as a gate electrode instead of aluminum, the work function changes in such a way as to cause a lower threshold voltage. This is the basic difference between aluminum gate and silicon gate processes.

AM 1. Abbreviation for *auto/manual*. **2.** Refers to a process by which a constant frequency is varied in amplitude by a signal or an information frequency. In this manner, the envelope of the constant frequency bears a direct relationship to the signal or information frequency. **3.** A form of modulation in which the level of the baseband information affects the level of the carrier. The carrier frequency remains unaltered by the process.

ambient conditions The conditions of the surrounding medium (pressure, noise, temperature, etc.).

ambient noise Acoustical or electrical noise existing in a room or other location.

AMD 2901 The Advanced Micro Devices (AMD) 2901 is a 4-bit slice unit that uses TTL technology. It is designed for use as a high-speed element in controllers and other applications. The 2901 uses a 40-pin package and consumes 925 mw at 5 volts. Instruction word size is 9 bits, and the chip uses a single phase clock with clock speeds of to 20 MHz. The basic structure for the 2901 is shown in the following figure. The 2901 uses a 16-word, 4-bit RAM, a high-speed ALU, and the Q register along with associated shift, decode, and multiplex circuitry. The microinstruction word is organized in three groups of three bits each, which are used to select the ALU source operands along with the function and destination registers.

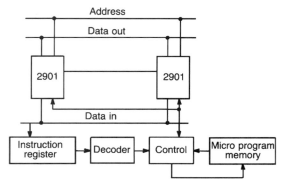

Bit-slice system

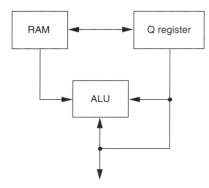

2901 Structure

AMD 2901 system The architecture of a 2901 bit slice system is shown in the following figure. The complexity of the external control required to build such a system has been decreasing with the introduction of new control devices. The main use of bit slice devices has been in building large CPUs using components that reduce the parts count over other types of logic. Bit slices have become the major design tool for fast CPUs. A typical CPU implemented with the 2901 bit slice device can achieve speeds of 300 nanoseconds for 32 bits.

American Federation of Information Processing Societies Abbreviated *AFIPS*, an organization of computer-related societies. Its members include the Association for Computer Machinery, the Institute of Electrical and Electronic Engineers Computer Group, Simulation Councils, Inc., and the American Society for Information Science. Its affiliates include the American Institute of Certified Public Accountants, the American Statistical Association, the Association for Computational Linguistics, the Society for Industrial and Applied Mathematics, the Society for Information Display, and the Association of Data Processing Services Organizations.

American National Standards Institute *See* ANSI.

American Standard Code for Information Interchange *See* ASCII.

American wire gauge A standardized system for the specification of wire sizes.

America Online Consumer-oriented online service with approximately 2 million members. Its graphical interface and aggressive marketing led to a dramatic surge in the number of users during 1994. AOL, as the service is commonly known, offers an easy onramp to the Internet's newsgroups, and other features (but not, as of this writing, the World Wide Web).

Amiga A series of personal computers manufactured and marketed by Commodore Business Machines in the 1980s and early 1990s. Now discontinued, the Amiga remains very popular in graphics, video, and animation applications.

Ami Pro A word-processing program from Lotus Development Corporation that offers tabbed dialog boxes, thumbnail previews, and the ability to copy formatting by clicking on a section of text and pasting the format to another section. It has been one of the popular Windows-based word processors.

AM modulation One of the methods of inserting information into a carrier. In this case, the amplitude of the carrier is varied at the rate of the carrier signal.

ampere A unit of electrical current or rate of flow of electrons. One volt across one ohm of resistance causes a current flow of one ampere. A flow of one coulomb per second equals one ampere. When an unvarying current is passed through a solution of silver nitrate of standard concentration at a fixed temperature, a current that deposits silver at the rate of .001118 grams per second is equal to one ampere, or 6.25×10^{18} electrons per second passing a given point in a circuit.

amplification, power 1. The amplification of an

input power to give a larger output power, as contrasted with voltage amplification. **2.** The difference between output and input power levels of an amplifier, expressed in decibels.

amplifier A device for controlling power from a source so that more is delivered at the output than is supplied at the input. The source of the power can be of any type, including mechanical, hydraulic, pneumatic, and electric. Electric amplifiers may be classified as follows:

1. Valve or tube, which operates on voltage
2. Repeater, especially used for telephone circuits
3. Transistor, which operates on current
4. Magnetic, which operates on very low frequency currents
5. Solid state, which is operated by transistor action in a single semiconductor block

amplifier output ratings The output voltage and current ratings of an amplifier imply a minimum value for the load resistor. In an inverting amplifier, the feedback resistor is a load for the output, and the current through this resistor must be subtracted from the amount of current still available at the output. Most operational amplifiers can be shorted to ground without damage, but shorting to a voltage can destroy some of the circuitry.

amplifier slew rate A measure of how fast the output can change, comparable to rise or fall time in a digital circuit. If an amplifier output could go from zero volts to 10 volts in two microseconds, it would have a slew rate of 5 volts/sec.

amplifier, transistor A type of amplifier that uses transistors as the source of current amplification. Depending on impedance considerations, there are three types: base, emitter, or collector grounded.

amplifier, tuned A type of amplifier that contains tuned circuits, and therefore is sharply responsive to particular frequencies.

amplitude The magnitude of a simple wave or simple part of a complex wave. Amplitude is quantified in terms of the largest, or *crest*, value measured from zero.

amplitude distortion A condition that occurs in an amplifier or other device when the output amplitude is not a linear function of the input amplitude. Amplitude distortion should be measured with the system operating under steady-state conditions and with a sinusoidal input signal. When other frequencies are present, the term *amplitude* applies to the fundamental frequency only.

amplitude modulation Refers to a process by which a constant frequency is varied in amplitude by a signal or information frequency. In this manner, the envelope of the constant frequency bears a direct relationship to the signal or information frequency. *Also see* AM.

amplitude-shift keying *See* ASK.

amplitude ratio The ratio of peak height of an output signal to the peak height of a related input signal.

AMPS Abbreviation for *automatic message processing system.*

AM-Tax A public-domain software product designed to assist you in the preparation of federal tax returns. It will do most calculations for you and, where possible, check to see that information entered is consistent and valid. The software allows you to try out various what-if situations; you can change an income or deduction figure and instantly see the result on your tax balance or refund. In addition to the 1040 form, many other commonly used forms and schedules are supported. Information entered or calculated for a supporting form is automatically transferred to the appropriate line that it supports. All the forms can be printed and filed directly with the IRS.

analog A continuous direct current level of voltage or current, the magnitude of which is usually proportional to an unrelated parameter or function being monitored or measured.

analog amplifier In some analog/digital systems, the analog amplifier performs two functions. First, it supplies the dual-delayed sweep comparators with the proper direct-current levels. Second, it accepts the direct-current level from the vertical channel, processes this level, and provides two pieces of information for the processor through the input interface. The two pieces of information are polarity of the direct-current level and whether the level is greater or lesser than some reference. If it is greater, the processor increases the reference until it is within one lower sideband of the unknown. Conversely, if it is lesser, the processor decreases the reference until it is within one lower sideband of the unknown. In both cases, it displays the reference level that is now equal to the unknown.

analog and digital I/O boards These boards plug directly into an expansion slot within the computer. All connections are made through a connector that extends out the rear of the computer. Field wiring can be connected to a mating connector or a screw terminal board that brings all connections out.

analog channel In an analog computer, a channel in which transmitted information can have any value between the defined limits of the channel.

analog computer A computer that represents variables by physical analogies; any computer that solves problems by translating physical conditions such as flow, temperature, pressure, angular position, or voltage into related mechanical or electrical quantities and uses mechanical or electrical equivalent circuits as an analog for the physical phenomenon being investigated. It uses an analog for each variable and produces analogs as output. An analog computer measures continuously, while a digital computer counts discretely.

analog feedback Feedback in amplifier circuits is usually obtained by means of a resistor from output to input. An important property of this type of amplifier is that if a suitable capacitor is used in the feedback path instead of a resistor, the output will be the derivative of the output. Thus, the operations of the calculus can be performed with the amplifier.

analog function circuits Special-purpose circuits used for a variety of signal conditioning operations on signals that are in analog form. When their accuracy is adequate, they can relieve the microprocessor of time-consuming computations. Among the typical operations performed are multiplication, powers, roots, nonlinear functions such as those used for linearizing transducers, root mean square measurements, the computation of vector sums, integration and differentiation, and current-to-voltage or voltage-to-current conversion. Many of these operations can be purchased in available devices as multiplier/dividers, log/antilog amplifiers, and others.

analog interfacing Refers to the necessity in many systems to provide an interface for analog devices such as transducers for pressure, temperature, or other variables. The output of the transducer can be a voltage or current that may or may not require amplification for interfacing. The transducer output is converted into a digital word to be used by the microprocessor.

analog I/O A capability required in many industrial systems. To provide analog input/output functions, a digital-to-analog converter is used for digital-to analog-conversion and one or more analog-to-digital converters are used for analog-to-digital conversion.

analog loopback In telecommunications, loops transmit data at a modem's analog (leased line) interface back to the terminal; an analog loopback also loops received line signals back to the remote modem.

analog module testing A binary-coded-decimal digital-to-analog converter module that can be used to test any analog-to-digital module. Another way of testing an analog-to-digital module is by supplying 0 volts direct current through 10 volts direct current and observing the binary equivalents using light-emitting diodes; in this case, a power supply is needed. Digital-to-analog converter modules can be tested using a scope.

analog multiplexer A device that allows the time sharing of analog-to-digital converters between a number of analog information channels. An analog multiplexer consists of a group of switches arranged with inputs connected to the individual analog channels and outputs connected in common, as shown in the figure. The switches can be addressed by a digital input code. MOSFET switches are generally used and can be con-

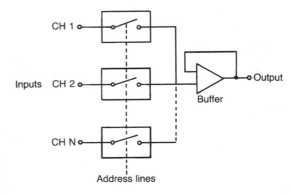

Analog multiplexer

nected directly to an output load, if it has a high enough impedance, or to an output buffer amplifier that provides a high impedance to the switches.

analog multiplier An analog circuit or device that can be used either to compute power by squaring voltage or current signals, or to multiply two or more inputs together, as shown in the figure.

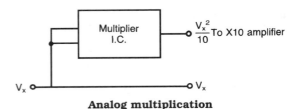

Analog multiplication

analog network A circuit or circuits that represent physical variables in such a manner as to permit the expression and solution of continuous mathematical relationships between the variables or permit the solution directly using electric or electronic means.

analog output As opposed to digital output, the output quantity is continuously proportionate to the stimulus, the proportionality being limited by the resolution of the device.

analog signal An electronic signal that varies continuously over a range of voltages or frequencies. Analog signals vary continuously as they are sent. Modems use analog signals. *Also see* DIGITAL SIGNAL.

analog switches A switching device that will only pass signals that are faithful analogs of transducer parameters. Many analog switches are available in electromechanical and solid-state forms. Electromechanical switch types include relays, stepper switches, cross bar, and mercury-wetted and dry-reed relay switches. The mechanical switches provide high direct-current isolation resistance, low contact resistance, and the capacity to handle voltages up to one kilovolt. Multiplexers using mechanical switches are suited to low-speed applications as well as those having high resolution requirements. They interface well with the slower analog-to-digital converters, like the integrating dual slope types. Mechanical switches have a finite life, usually expressed in number of operations.

analog-to-digital conversion The process of representing precisely a varying voltage or current by a series of discrete pulses when the varying voltage or current itself is an analog of some other form of information. Analog-to-digital conversion techniques are required to convert any information that is in analog form into the digital form required by the microcomputer. Analog data is frequently encountered in data acquisition as voltage from a transducer, potentiometer, or other sensor of physical data.

Most methods of conversion involve division of the signal conversion device into two sections. The analog section contains all analog functions of the converter, and the digital section contains the digital functions of the converter. A major part of the digital conversion can be done with microcomputer software, if software is available for this purpose. The software can control the analog section, determine the digital value of the input of the analog section, and perform calculations with the data. If a multiplexer is used in the data acquisition system, the software can perform the function of a controller for channel selection, end-of-conversion flags, and error checking.

Successive-approximation conversion is widely used and can provide both serial and parallel outputs. The conversion system uses a digital-to-analog converter in a feedback loop that generates a known analog signal, as shown in the figure. The unknown input is compared with this signal and then sensed by the digital section.

The successive-approximation register is implemented in the software of the microprocessor. Successive approximation provides medium conversion speeds when used in this arrangement.

analog transducers Sensing devices that output either voltages in the 1–5, 2–10, 5–25, or 10 volt ranges for currents in the 1–5, 4–20, or 10–50 milliampere ranges.

analog transmission A transmission using varying, continuous waveforms to represent information, values of which must be interpreted by the receiver, which estimates the values by approximation.

AnalytiCalc A public-domain integrated program, combining spreadsheet, database, graphics, and word-processing functions. Written in For-

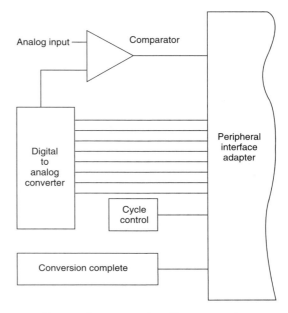

Successive-approximation converter

tran, it is quite fast and has some attractive features. The author's goal was an inexpensive, highly integrated package. The complete system comes on three disks. Disk one is the primary disk for a computer that is limited to 256K memory. Disk two is the supplemental disk with documentation and extra files. Disk three is the primary disk for a computer with more than 320K memory. This is a complex package, and the user should read the documentation before using it.

analytic relationship The relationship that exists between concepts and their corresponding terms.

analyzer A routine to analyze a program. The routine usually consists of summarizing references to storage locations and tracing jump sequences.

analyzer, electronic differential A form of analog computer that uses interconnected electronic integrators to solve differential equations.

ancillary equipment Refers to all types of input/output, communication, and interface equipment. *Also see* PERIPHERAL DEVICE.

AND A logic operator that has the property that if A and B are both statements, then *A AND B* is true if both statements are true, but it is false if either is false or both are false. Truth is usually expressed by the value 1, while 0 is used to indicate a false state. The AND operator is usually represented by a centered dot, as in *A • B*, or by no sign, as in *AB*. An inverted u is sometimes used to denote the logical product:

$$A \cap B$$

Finally, the standard multiplication sign may be used to express the AND function:

$$A \times B$$

AND element One of the basic logic elements (gates or operators) that has at least two binary input signals and a single binary output signal. The answer or variable that represents the output signal is the conjunction, in set theory, of the variables represented by the input signals.

AND gate A circuit that performs the AND function. The AND gate is a signal circuit with two or more input wires, in which the output wire gives a signal if and only if all input wires receive coincident signals. Also called an *AND circuit*.

AND instruction A microprocessor instruction that causes the contents of the accumulator to be modified depending on the contents of the addressed memory location. If there is a 1 in the corresponding bit positions of both words, then that bit position in the accumulator is retained as 1. Any other combination in that bit will result in 0 in the corresponding bit position in the accumulator as shown:

```
11001100 = Contents in the accumulator
01100110 = Contents in the memory location
01000100 = Logical AND result in the
           accumulator
```

AND operator *See* AND.

angle modulation A general category of modulation techniques that includes both phase modulation and frequency modulation. *Also see* FM, PM.

animation software Animation packages for multimedia presentations come in 2D and 3D versions. Both are available in a range of prices and corresponding capabilities, although 3D products have the greatest sophistication. Macintosh is especially strong in this area of graphics. Windows packages, however, tend to be more integrated. Amiga has the advantage of built-in output to video, while UNIX programs are able to exploit that platform's high-powered, multitasking hardware for effects such as particle animation, where an object dissolves into pieces.

Path-based animation programs let you dictate the path for the animated object to follow. If *keyframes* are used, single frames of the sequence are defined to look a certain way and the software then determines how to achieve that look for an animated object. *Cameras* are the viewpoint through which the animation is observed and *timelines* are sequences simulating movement over time.

There is more to 3D animation than movement. Such packages also include a modeler and/or renderer, either integrated or in separate modules. *Modelers* are the tools to build the object. Most can turn a 2D shape into a 3D solid. The surface of the object can be changed through shading, texture, and reflection mapping. Light sources are defined along with the object's movement (animation). The final product is a result of all of this.

annotation Any text, line shape, or symbol added to a chart using the draw/annotate command in a presentation graphics package.

anomalous propagation A propagation condition that results from abnormal changes with altitude in the atmospheric index of refraction.

anonymous FTP An Internet technique that allows a user to retrieve documents, files, programs, and other archived data from anywhere in the Internet without having to establish a userid and password. By using the special userid of "anonymous," the network user bypasses local security checks and has access to publicly accessible files on the remote system.

ANSI Abbreviation for *American National Standards Institute*, a nonprofit, nongovernmental organization that acts as a clearinghouse for standards involving computers, electronics, and communications. ANSI establishes standards for character sets such as ASCII, high-level languages such as Fortran and BASIC, and data communications protocols such as X.25.

answer-back ID Automatic terminal identification that operates with most asynchronous terminals, as shown in the diagram.

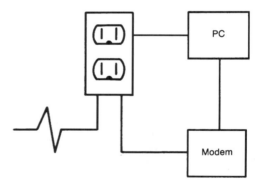

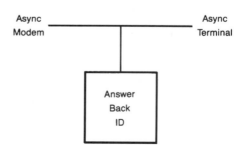

Answer-back ID

anti-aliasing The process of reducing the visibility of aliasing (a jagged effect on diagonal lines) by using grayscale pixel values to smooth the appearance of jagged edges.

anticoincidence unit A binary logic coincidence circuit for completing the logic operation of exclusive-OR. The result is true when A is true and B is false, or when A is false and B is true. The result is false when A and B are both either true or false. Also known as a *difference gate*, *nonequivalence gate*, *distance gate*, *diversity gate*, *add-without-carry gate*, *exjunction gate*, *nonequality gate*, *symmetric difference gate*, *partial sum gate*, and *modulo-two sum gate*.

anti-static devices Mats, cloths, pads, and other materials designed to protect a computer and media from static, usually through the use of a grounding cord and protective resistor, as shown in the figure. These devices ground destructive charges instantly and help prevent memory loss or alternation, video wipe-out, program errors, and most static-related malfunctions.

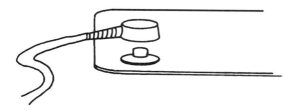

Anti-static pad

anti-static spray A spray specially formulated to eliminate static-related problems, computer memory loss, distorted data and unnecessary downtime. It is designed for use on high-friction surfaces such as carpeting, clothing, chairs, workstations.

anti-static wipes A disposable nonwoven cloth moistened with staticide, designed to clean and eliminate static from monitor screens and desktops. Each wipe is individually foil-sealed.

anti-streamer See AS.

AOC Abbreviation for *automatic output control*.

APA mode See ALL POINTS ADDRESSABLE MODE.

APCHE Abbreviation for *automatic programmed checkout equipment*.

aperture As applied to television, the specific size and shape of the point of the electronic beam in a camera or picture tube. When the beam does not come to a unique point, it affects the area around it by reducing resolution.

API Abbreviation for *application programming interface*, software that provides certain functions to application software and makes programming the application software easier. APIs help software to look and work similarly across various types of applications.

APL Abbreviation for *a programming language*, a language in which an extensive set of operators and data structures are used. It is considered to be one of the most flexible, powerful, and concise of the algorithmic/procedural languages.

APP Abbreviation for *auxiliary power plant*.

apparent power The product of the root mean square value of the current and the root mean square value of the voltage.

APPC Abbreviation for *advanced peer-to-peer communications*, a standard programming interface from IBM that allows applications running on different systems to communicate with one another. APPC builds programs whose various parts run on different machines simultaneously. It governs how these parts communicate with each other over a network.

Apple compatible cables These are cables designed to connect Apple personal computers to the Imagewriter printer or a personal modem.

Apple Multimedia Although Windows-based multimedia PCs are more plentiful due to their many manufacturers, Apple was first in graphics-based applications for both education and business, using its QuickTime system with built-in CD-ROM drives and integrated DSP (digital signal processing).

Apple's AV (*audio-visual*) class of machines, which originally included Centris and Quadra, features integrated audio-visual capabilities. The 660AV and 840AV machines have CD-quality stereo sound and 16-bit, full-motion video both in and out. When you use these multimedia systems, you just plug in your sources and go. Built-in CD-ROMs are also available.

The AV models use Trinitron CRTs with two built-in, 2.5-inch stereo speakers in the front and a unidirectional microphone on top. These machines are useful for videoconferencing and collaborative work with remote screen-sharing, since they enable users to give commands by voice with the computer responding by voice.

Apple's LC machines use 68040 processors with built-in CD-ROM drives, speakers, and microphones. Several of the color PowerBooks can also be considered multimedia machines; they have LCD screens that can keep up with motion video, along with built-in speakers and microphones.

AppleShare A program that allows different kinds of computers to provide or take advantage of AppleTalk resources, such as printing.

applet In Windows, Mac, and some other operating systems, a small application that comes bundled with the system, such as the Windows Paintbrush.

AppleTalk Apple Computer's LAN software for linking Macintosh computers over a network. It uses CSMA access protocols and transmits data at 230K bits per second. It supports up to 32 devices. *Also see* LOCALTALK.

AppleTalk filing protocol The protocol in AppleTalk used for remote access to data.

AppleTalk session protocol The AppleTalk session layer protocol for the OSI model. *Also see* OSI MODEL.

AppleTalk transaction protocol AppleTalk transport layer protocol for the OSI model. *Also see* OSI MODEL.

Apple IIc compatible cables These cables will connect an Apple IIc to the Imagewriter. They have a 5-pin din connector on one end and an 8-pin mini din connector on the other. *Also see* DIN CABLE.

application 1. The system or problem to which a microcomputer can be devoted. Applications range from the computational type (in which arithmetic operations predominate) to the processing type (in which data-handling operations are the major function). **2.** A set of computer programs and/or subroutines used to solve problems and perform specific tasks in a particular application.

application fit Refers to the relative efficiency of an application program in solving a particular problem or improving a worker's output; for example, a word-processing program would be good fit for a typing task.

application note A published paper, usually from a product or device manufacturer, that offers suggestions, recommendations, or instructions for using the manufacturer's product or device in a specific manner or for a specific purpose.

application process A program residing within a specific application.

application program The ordered set of programmed instructions by which a computer performs an intended task or series of tasks. *Contrast with* MICROPROGRAM.

Application Programming Interface *See* API.

applications layer The portion of the ISO/OSI model that is concerned with the interface between the applications software and the presentation layer. *Also see* OSI MODEL.

application software *See* APPLICATION.

application study The detailed process of determining the system and set of procedures for using a microcomputer in a particular application. This involves establishing the definite functions and operations of the machine, along with developing specifications and machine and peripheral selection criteria.

applications support Applications support packages assist users in several ways:

- Evaluating the operation of a microcomputer in an actual application
- Reducing the engineering time and development costs required to develop and construct prototype systems
- Comparing different software and firmware programs
- Reducing the time required to evaluate and debug system hardware, software, and firmware
- Providing a working prototype of a microcomputer system

application transaction program A program written for or by a user to process the user's application.

APPN Abbreviation for *advanced peer-to-peer network*. An advanced peer-to-peer network provides the same communication methods and uses the same technology as a standard peer-to-peer network. However, it also adds other capabilities normally associated with a full-fledged dedicated network, like e-mail and broadcasting. This network also provides a more robust security scheme.

APPN end node A type 2.1 end node that provides full SNA end-user services. It supports sessions between its local control point (CP) and the CP in an adjacent network node, and can dynamically register its resources with the adjacent CP (its network node server) to send and receive directory search requests and obtain management services. It can also attach to a subarea network as a peripheral node.

APPN intermedia routing The capability of an APPN network node to accept traffic from one adjacent node and pass it on to another, with an awareness of the session for controlling traffic flow and outage notifications.

APPN intermediate routing network The section of an APPN network consisting of the network nodes and their connections.

APPN network A type 2.1 network having at least one APPN node.

APPN network node A type 2.1 (T2.1) node that offers full SNA end-user services, provides intermediate routing services within a T2.1 network, and provides network services to its local LUs and attached T2.1 end nodes in its domain. It can also attach to a subarea network as a peripheral node.

Approach A professional, Windows-based database product developed by Lotus, Inc.

APT Abbreviation for *automatically programmed tools*, a special computer language for programming the operation of numerically controlled machine tools.

APU Abbreviation for *automatic program unit*.

AQ Abbreviation for *any quantity*.

AQL Abbreviation for *acceptable quality level*.

ARAGO dBXL A database management system compatible with dBASE III and IV. It provides extensive help facilities, a test coverage analyzer, a panel painter, and other tools for both first-time users and advanced developers.

ARAGO Professional A dBASE IV compatible development environment that includes versions of ARAGO dBXL and ARAGO QuickSilver. With it you can create dBASE programs and also generate .EXE files for unlimited distribution. It requires DOS 3.1 or higher, an IBM PC or better with a hard disk, and at least 640K RAM.

ARAGO QuickSilver A software package for compiling ARAGO dBXL or dBASE IV applications into stand-alone executable files that do not require distribution royalties. The resulting .EXE files are small, run fast because they are created in machine code, and protect application source code.

aramid yarn A strength member element used in Siecor cable to provide support and additional protection of the fiber bundles. Kelvlar is a particular brand of aramid yarn.

arbitrary function generator A specific function generator (analog) that is not committed by its design function exclusively, so that the function which it generates can be changed by the operator or programmer.

ARC Abbreviation for *automatic ratio control*.

arc clockwise An arc in the clockwise direction with respect to the workpiece when viewed from the positive direction of the perpendicular axis. Used in automatic machining.

arc counterclockwise An arc in the counterclockwise direction with respect to the workpiece when viewed from the positive direction of the perpendicular axis. Used in automatic machining.

Archetype Designer A page-composition package for highly designed documents, combining typographic tools with a simple and intuitive user interface. This program can be used from the design stage through production. Features include scaled outline display fonts; hyphenation by rules and an exception dictionary; user-definable kerning pairs; editable width, kerning, and track kerning tables (five levels); automatic column-to-column text flow; multiple text streams; template storage for page styles; point and set sizes in $\frac{1}{100}$-point increments; optional loose-line flagging; and WYSIWYG screen font display. An interactive status line allows you to change point size, line size, or fonts on screen. Archetype Designer also outputs pre-separated continuous-tone and line art for color printing.

ARCHIE A public-domain program that teaches the elements of structured BASIC programming.

Archie An Internet utility for locating files.

architecture The way hardware and/or software is structured; the structure is usually based on the design philosophies. Architecture deals with the fundamental elements that affect the way a system operates, and thus it defines the system's capabilities and limitations.

archival Refers to placing computer information in an archive.

archive As a verb, to copy data and programs onto a low-cost storage medium such as tape for long-term retention. As a noun, a collection of such media. Also, an archive is a compressed file on disk or tape consisting of one or more other files, either data or programs. They are packed into the archive to save storage space and must be unpacked (taken out of the archive) to be accessed.

archive attribute An indicator stored in a file's directory entry that shows whether or not the file has been changed since the last time it was archived or backed up.

archive site A machine that provides access to a collection of files across the Internet. An anonymous FTP archive site, for example, provides access to material via the FTP protocol.

ARC-monitor A unit that analyzes an ARC LAN, performs passive and active diagnostic procedures, and alerts the user to hardware failures and traffic overloads. Complete diagnostics are available to test individual workstation interfaces and individual cards for cable, memory, or communications controller failure. The ARC-monitor also identifies nodes experiencing intermittent failure or causing reconfiguration. The case histories of individual nodes can be viewed to locate intermittent or transient failures.

ARCnet A local area network technology characterized by a 2.5M-per-second throughput and token passing access. The token passing feature makes ARCnet viable for large networks of up to 50 to 75 users—more if the demand on the LAN by each user is low. ARCnet is known for its reliability. It operates over RG62 A/U coaxial cable and has a low cost per user. Its distributed star topology makes it easy to install, expand, and modify.

ARCnet fragmentation layer A sublayer between the ARCnet medium access control and the network layer (NetWare's IPX), allowing packets that are larger than the 508-byte ARCnet maximum packet length to be submitted.

ARCnet Plus A 20M-per-second version of ARCnet.

area chart A graphic chart that represents a quantity by the area under a line. Each series in an area chart is represented by a layer, the base of which is the previous series.

arelem Acronym for *arithmetic element*, a section of the APT (automatically programmed tools) processor that calculates cutter locations based on the motion commands that were input and the canonical forms of the geometry input. *Also see* APT.

argument An independent variable that identifies the location of a number in a mathematical operation. The argument can determine the value of a mathematical function when substituted; it can be the operand in operations on one or more variables.

arithmetic and logic unit *See* ALU.

arithmetic game Refers to an educational program that is involved in some way with basic arithmetic skills. Examples include Rockets, Number Chase, Fact Track, and Discovery Machine.

arithmetic instructions Microprocessor instructions that perform internal arithmetic operations, as shown in the following table.

Command	Meaning	Action
ADD	Add	The result of the binary addition of the contents of the accumulator and the contents of RAM currently addressed replace the contents of accumulator.
DCC	Decimal correction	A binary correction is added to contents of accumulator. Result is stored in accumulator.

Typical arithmetic instructions

The Add and Add With Carry-in instructions are among the most common arithmetic instructions. The Add instruction may be used to initialize the adding operation for the first word of a multi-word number to be added. It also may be used for additions that do not extend the basic word length for the microprocessor. The DCC instruction adds a fixed constant to the accumulator. Addition of a constant will convert binary arithmetic operations to decimal arithmetic. This instruction is used to correct the sum in the accumulator to a binary-coded-decimal. Decimal subtraction can be performed when the subtrahend is loaded into the accumulator and complemented. Multiplication and division instructions are available in the 8086 family.

arithmetic logic register stack A basic building block in some microcomputer chips. It often contains a four-bit arithmetic and logic unit, an eight-word-by-four-bit RAM with output latches, an instruction decode network, control logic, and a four-bit output register. Eight arithmetic and logic functions can be implemented in the ALU by the input data, and a second four-bit operand can be supplied internally from one of the eight RAM words.

arithmetic mean The arithmetic mean is found by summing a series of numbers and then dividing by the number of entries in the series.

arithmetic operation A mathematical manipulation of numbers or symbols performed for the purpose of solving a problem as stated by a prescribed formula.

arithmetic overflow 1. The generation of a quantity beyond the capacity of the register or location that is to receive the result; the information contained in an item that is in excess of a given amount. 2. The portion of data that exceeds the capacity of the allocated unit of storage. Overflow develops when attempts are made to write longer fields into a field location of a specific length; for example, a 12-bit product will overflow a 10-bit accumulator.

arithmetic progression Any sequence of numbers in which the difference between two adjacent numbers is constant, for example, 5, 10, 15, 20, etc.

arithmetic register Microprocessor register on which arithmetic and logic functions can be performed. The register can be a source or destination of operands for the operation. Registers that can supply but not receive operands for the ALU are not normally considered as arithmetic registers. *Also see* ALU.

arithmetic section That portion of computer hardware in which arithmetic and logical operations are performed.

arithmetic shift Any shift that does not affect the sign position. An arithmetic shift results in the multiplication of a number by an integral power of the radix.

arithmetic unit *See* ARITHMETIC AND LOGIC UNIT.

armed interrupt An interrupt that can accept and hold the interrupt signal. A *disarmed* interrupt ignores the signal.

armed state The state of an interrupt level in which it can accept and remember an interrupt input signal.

armoring Refers to additional protection between cable jacketing layers to guard against severe outdoor environments. Armoring is usually made of plastic-coated steel and may be corrugated for flexibility.

Armstrong oscillator An oscillator in which the feedback is achieved through coupled plate and grid circuit coils. *Also see* OSCILLATOR.

ARPANET One of the earliest packet-switched networks; developed and funded by the Advanced Research Projects Agency (ARPA).

ARQ Stands for *automatic repeat request*, a technique used for error-checking such that a signal detected as being in error automatically initiates a request for retransmission.

array 1. A group of devices, components, or numbers arranged in a logical or meaningful pattern. 2. A matrix.

artifact In video systems, something unnatural or unintended observed in the reproduction of an image by the system.

artificial intelligence *See* AI.

artificial language A language designed for a particular application area that has not evolved through long usage into a natural language.

ARU *See* AUDIO RESPONSE UNIT.

AS Abbreviation for *anti-streamer*, a unit that is designed to be inserted between a modem and a terminal in a multidrop polled network, as shown. With an AS, network maintenance is performed by monitoring the Request to Send (RTS) lead and shutting it down when the duration of signal exceeds a predetermined time limit. This permits the rest of the interconnected devices on the network to continue to function. Automatic reset is accomplished by removing the RTS signal.

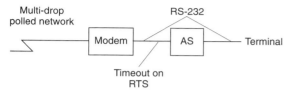

Anti-streamer

ASCII Acronym for *American Standard Code for Information Interchange*, usually pronounced "ASK-key," a standard data transmission code that was introduced to achieve compatibility between data services. Widely used for information interchange in data-processing systems, communication systems, and associated equipment, it consists of seven information bits and one parity bit for error-checking purposes, thus allowing 128 code combinations. If the eighth bit is not used for parity, 256 code combinations are possible. Table on page 24.

ASCII/Baudot converter A unit that can provide a bidirectional communication link between asynchronous data terminal equipment and five-level Baudot equipment. The unit features full- or half-duplex operation on both ports. The ports can be programmed to different word structures and data rates for flexibility.

ASCII keyboard A computer keyboard laid out in a specific format and containing the character symbol buttons and function switches required to generate signals representing the 127 different character variations of ASCII. One implementation of an ASCII keyboard is shown below.

ASCII keyboard

ASD Abbreviation for *automatic synchronized discriminator*.

As-Easy-As A Lotus 1-2-3 compatible shareware program. Its features include storage of up to a 8192-row-by-256-column spreadsheet; pop-up or panel menus; over 100 macro programming commands; over 80 math, statistics, finance, logic, string, and data functions; and spreadsheet linking.

Ashton-Tate Original maker of the dBASE and Framework data management products.

ASI Abbreviation for *asynchronous/synchronous interface*, a unit that provides an interface between an asynchronous CPU and a synchronous modem, as shown. Placed into the communication system, the ASI provides the proper interconnection to allow the async terminal to operate within the timing control of the sync modem or SME. The data format is that of the asynchronous terminal, i.e., ASCII (a start bit, eight intelligent data bits, and a stop bit interval of one or more bits) or IBM seven-level code (strap selectable).

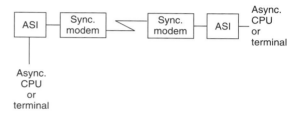

Asynchronous/synchronous interface

ASK Abbreviation for *amplitude-shift keying*, a form of amplitude modulation in which the amplitude of the carrier must assume one of several discrete levels.

ASM (*o.t.*) The assembler used in the CP/M operating system.

ASM Checker A set of software tools to automatically locate potential problems in assembler source code. Similar to LINT for C programmers, ASM Checker locates and explains potential logic errors in assembly source code.

ASM-86 (*o.t.*) The assembler used in the 8086 version of the CP/M operating system.

ASN Abbreviation for *average sample number*.

ASN.1 Abbreviation for *abstract syntax notation 1*, the language used by the OSI protocols for describing abstract syntax. This language is also used to encode SNMP packets. ASN.1 is defined in ISO documents 8824.2 and 8825.2. *Also see* PRESENTATION SYNTAX.

ASP *See* APPLETALK SESSION PROTOCOL.

aspect card A card containing the accession numbers of documents in an information retrieval system.

aspect ratio The ratio of the width of an image to its height, sometimes expressed as two numbers separated by a colon. For broadcast television, the standard aspect ratio is 4:3.

aspirated thermocouple A thermocouple with a means for achieving a gas velocity past the junc-

24 ASCII code

Character or Symbol	Binary Code	Decimal Equiv.	Hex. Equiv.
NUL	0000 0000	0	0
SCH	0000 0001	1	1
STX	0000 0010	2	2
ETX	0000 0011	3	3
EOT	0000 0100	4	4
ENQ	0000 0101	5	5
ACK	0000 0110	6	6
BEL	0000 0111	7	7
BS	0000 1000	8	8
HT	0000 1001	9	9
LF	0000 1010	10	A
VT	0000 1011	11	B
FF	0000 1100	12	C
CR	0000 1101	13	D
SO	0000 1110	14	E
SI	0000 1111	15	F
DLE	0001 0000	16	10
DC1	0001 0001	17	11
DC2	0001 0010	18	12
DC3	0001 0011	19	13
DC4	0001 0100	20	14
NAK	0001 0101	21	15
SYN	0001 0110	22	16
ETB	0001 0111	23	17
CAN	0001 1000	24	18
EM	0001 1001	25	19
SUB	0001 1010	26	1A
ESC	0001 1011	27	1B
FS	0001 1100	28	1C
GS	0001 1101	29	1D
RS	0001 1110	30	1E
US	0001 1111	31	1F
Sp	0010 0000	32	20
!	0010 0001	33	21
"	0010 0010	34	22
#	0010 0011	35	23
$	0010 0100	36	24
%	0010 0101	37	25
&	0010 0110	38	26
'	0010 0111	39	27
(	0010 1000	40	28
)	0010 1001	41	29
*	0010 1010	42	2A
+	0010 1011	43	2B
, (Comma)	0010 1100	44	2C
-	0010 1101	45	2D
. (Period)	0010 1110	46	2E
/	0010 1111	47	2F
0	0011 0000	48	30
1	0011 0001	49	31
2	0011 0010	50	32
3	0011 0011	51	33
4	0011 0100	52	34
5	0011 0101	53	35
6	0011 0110	54	36
7	0011 0111	55	37
8	0011 1000	56	38
9	0011 1001	57	39
:	0011 1010	58	3A
;	0011 1011	59	3B
<	0011 1100	60	3C
=	0011 1101	61	3D
>	0011 1110	62	3E
?	0011 1111	63	3F
@	0100 0000	64	40
A	0100 0001	65	41
B	0100 0010	66	42
C	0100 0011	67	43
D	0100 0100	68	44
E	0100 0101	69	45
F	0100 0110	70	46
G	0100 0111	71	47
H	0100 1000	72	48
I	0100 1001	73	49
J	0100 1010	74	4A
K	0100 1011	75	4B
L	0100 1100	76	4C
M	0100 1101	77	4D
N	0100 1110	78	4E
O	0100 1111	79	4F
P	0101 0000	80	50
Q	0101 0001	81	51
R	0101 0010	82	52
S	0101 0011	83	53
T	0101 0100	84	54
U	0101 0101	85	55
V	0101 0110	86	56
W	0101 0111	87	57
X	0101 1000	88	58
Y	0101 1001	89	59
Z	0101 1010	90	5A
[	0101 1011	91	5B
\	0101 1100	92	5C
]	0101 1101	93	5D
^	0101 1110	94	5E
_	0101 1111	95	5F
`	0110 0000	96	60
a	0110 0001	97	61
b	0110 0010	98	62
c	0110 0011	99	63
d	0110 0100	100	64
e	0110 0101	101	65
f	0110 0110	102	66
g	0110 0111	103	67
h	0110 1000	104	68
i	0110 1001	105	69
j	0110 1010	106	6A
k	0110 1011	107	6B
l	0110 1100	108	6C
m	0110 1101	109	6D
n	0110 1110	110	6E
o	0110 1111	111	6F
p	0111 0000	112	70
q	0111 0001	113	71
r	0111 0010	114	72
s	0111 0011	115	73
t	0111 0100	116	74
u	0111 0101	117	75
v	0111 0110	118	76
w	0111 0111	119	77
x	0111 1000	120	78
y	0111 1001	121	79
z	0111 1010	122	7A
{	0111 1011	123	7B
?	0111 1100	124	7C
}	0111 1101	125	7D
~	0111 1110	126	7E
DELete	0111 1111	127	7F

ASCII code

tion higher than that of free stream. This increases the heat-transfer rate from the gas to the junction and lowers the response time.

ASR Abbreviation for *automatic send-and-receive*, a terminal that has the capability to send and receive messages without an operator.

assemble 1. To integrate subroutines into the main routine by adapting or changing relative or symbolic addresses to absolute addresses. **2.** To prepare an object language program from a source language program by substituting machine operation codes for symbolic operation codes and absolute or relocatable addresses for symbolic addresses. *Also see* ASSEMBLER.

assembler A computer program that is used to translate symbolic language into machine language. A typical program supplied by a microcomputer manufacturer is loaded and then executed using the same type of microcomputer to perform the assembly operation. The following is an example of an assembler program:

Source program (symbolic language) LD AC$,@. + 10 (load register AC$ through the address resulting from adding octal 10 to the current value of the program counter, shown on the object tape below)

```
10 000 9109 LD AC$,@. + 10
```

Where:
    10 = line number on source tape in assembly language program.
    000 = location of instruction.
    9109 = hexadecimal equivalent of 16-bit machine language word.
    LD AC$,@. + 10 = the statement in assembly language written by the programmer.

Object tape (machine language) 1001 0001 0000 1001

Assemblers also control the assembly of instructions into machine language. These assembler instructions can save programming time and reduce errors while allowing modifications to be processed more easily. Assembler instructions can typically help in the following areas:

- *Numbering* For example, *B* can be used to signify that literals in operand fields be interpreted as binary numbers, while *O* and *D* can be used to signify octal and decimal values.
- *Origins* To store the next instruction at location 112 decimal, the statement *ORIGIN 112D* can be used; consecutive locations follow 112 until a new origin statement appears.
- *Comments* To add comments in English in the source file, use symbols such as the solidus (/), comma (,), semicolon (;), or colon (:). The assembler ignores whatever follows these symbols on each line of the source text, at the same time reproducing the comments for the final list file.
- *Equals* For labeling registers, equal signs (=) can be used; thus either the original label or a more descriptive term can be used interchangeably as names for the register. Equal signs can also be used to set the contents of a register in either binary, decimal, or octal.
- *Tables and other sets of data* By using a statement such as *TABLE D 23, 37, 41*, three data words (in decimal) can be stored in successive locations in memory starting at a location labeled TABLE.

Another feature of assemblers is the ability to detect and flag errors. Syntactic errors—those that result from misuse of the language—are the only type that can be detected unless special routines are used; logic errors and errors of intent will be passed by. Statements containing errors are printed in the list file with *flags* (code letters signifying the error) or an entire error message. Errors that are easily detected include duplicate address labels, undefined address labels, undefined instruction mnemonics (misspelled operation codes), undefined operand field labels, incomplete numbers of operands, and invalid numbers or numbers from an incorrect number system. The following shows an assembler program with error messages, and its corrected version:

Program with errors:

```
              NUMBERS OCTAL
              ORIGIN 0
      ENTRY 1 LOAD R1, MEM 1
              LOAD R2, MEM 2
error         'LOAD' IS UNDEFINED
                OP-CODE*
      ENTRY 1 COMPARE R1, R2
error       * DUPLICATE
                ADDRESS LABEL*
              JCOND PLACE
error       * 'PLACE' IS UNDEFINED
                ADDRESS LABEL*
error       * OPERAND MISSING*
              JUMP FINISH
              STORE R1, MEM: IF
              R1 GREATER THAN
              R2, EXCHANGE
      FINISH  HLT
error       * 'HLT' IS UNDEFINED
                OPERATION*
              MEM 1 = 1732
              MEM 2 = 1840
error       * NUMBER IS INVALID
                OCTAL*
              END
```

Program with corrections:

```
NUMBERS OCTAL
ENTRY 1              ORIGIN 0
                     LOAD R1, MEM 1
                     LOAD R2, MEM 2
             ENTRY 2 COMPARE R1, R2
                     JCOND GREATER,
                       PLACE
                     JUMP FINISH
             PLACE   STORE R1, MEM 2; IF
```

```
                    R1 GREATER
                    THAN R2,
                    EXCHANGE
             FINISH HALT
             MEM 1 = 1732
             MEM 2 = 2040
                    END
```

Macro capability, a feature sometimes found in assemblers, can be very useful when similar but slightly different sections of coding are used over and over again. The differences in the coding do not allow the use of conventional subroutines for repeating.

The macro is defined in parameters such as data values, addresses, labels, or instructions. Once the macro is defined for the assembler, a single statement produces an expansion of the macro for all the parameters. The statement begins at the location the expansion is desired and contains a listing of the values of the parameters.

assembler development system A software development system. Some development systems permit the use of full macro capabilities, which means that a programmer can define special pseudo-instructions in the main program during the assembly process.

assembly A group of subassemblies and/or parts that are put together; the total unit constitutes a major subdivision of the final product. When two or more components or subassemblies are put together by the application of labor or machine hours, it is called an assembly. An assembly may be an end item or a component of a higher-level assembly.

assembly language A hardware dependent, low-level source language employing crude mnemonics that are more easily remembered than their object language equivalents, which are "words" consisting solely of zeros and ones.

assembly language processor A language processor that accepts words, statements, and phrases to produce machine instructions. It is more than an assembly program since it has compiler powers. A macroassembler may permit segmentation of a large program so that sections can be tested separately. It also provides program analysis capabilities to aid in debugging.

assembly-level languages Programming languages that use a mnemonic or symbolic representation of the binary code for the particular microprocessor. Assembly-level languages can produce very efficient user programs, but the proper use of an assembly language requires manipulating the registers to achieve program optimization in terms of code and memory usage. A good understanding of the structure of the computer system is required for the optimization of the program.

assembly list A printed list that occurs as a byproduct of the assembly procedure. The assembly list shows the instruction sequence with all details of the routine using coded and symbolic notations. The list is very useful during debugging operations.

assembly system A software system that includes a language and machine-code programs that perform such programming functions as checkout and updating. An assembly system has two main elements, a symbolic language and an assembly program, that translate source programs written in the symbolic language into machine language.

assembly testing The testing of a group of functionally related programs to determine whether or not the group operates according to specifications. The programs may be related in that they have access to common data, occupy high-speed storage simultaneously, operate under common program control, or perform an integrated task.

assembly unit 1. Any device that performs the function of assembly. **2.** A portion of a program which is capable of being assembled into a larger program.

assignable cause A definitely identified factor that contributes to a variation in quality.

Association for Computing Machinery *See* ACM.

associative storage registers Various registers that are not identified by their name or position but are known and addressed by their contents.

astable multivibrator An oscillator that generates desired shapes of signals, normally of the relaxation type. Operation depends on two interacting devices, such as two transistors connected in such a manner that one governs the operation of the other. One device causes the charging of a capacitor, resulting in a rise in voltage, which triggers the other to discharge the capacitor, causing an output voltage pulse.

astronomical unit The mean distance of the earth from the sun: 92,907,000 miles.

Asymetrix ToolBook Multimedia Kit A collection of extensions to ToolBook that link to and control multimedia hardware and software using the Microsoft Windows Multimedia extensions. It includes DLLs (dynamic link libraries) and drivers that enable you to access multimedia devices like CD audio, wave audio cards, animation software, video disk players, and MIDI sequencing devices. It also includes a runtime version of the Microsoft Windows Multimedia extensions. *Also see* TOOLBOOK.

asynchronous Refers to a system in which each event or operation starts as a result of a signal that the previous operation is complete and the microcomputer is now ready for the next operation. Synchronous machines have a master clock that sends pulses for timing to all critical circuits. Asynchronous machines do not use a master clock system for overall control; some timing circuits may be used for local control, but overall control is provided by the completion of a switching operation that serves to initiate the next operation.

asynchronous channel splitter *See* ACS.

asynchronous communication A data transmission that takes place using short, defined groups of bits. *Contrast with* SYNCHRONOUS COMMUNICATION.

asynchronous communications adapter Refers to the circuits or circuit board used to provide asynchronous serial communications between a microcomputer and other devices including modems and printers. The adapter is usually placed in one of the microcomputer's expansion slots.

asynchronous computer A computer that operates primarily in the asynchronous mode. In an asynchronous computer, the performance of each operation starts as a result of a signal either that the previous operation has been completed or that the parts of the computer required for the next operation are now available. *Contrast with* SYNCHRONOUS COMPUTER.

asynchronous data transfer Data communications can be either asynchronous or synchronous. Asynchronous data transfers usually occur in short bursts, while synchronous data transfers are suited for long streams. Asynchronous messages are preceded by a start signal, which synchronizes the transmitting and receiving circuitry, as shown in the diagram.

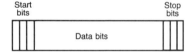

Asynchronous data

asynchronous data transmission An operating mode in which there is no intentional bit synchronization between the transmitting and receiving devices. Start-stop operation is the most common form of asynchronous transmission, where start and stop bits are used to indicate the beginning and end of each character.

asynchronous event An event in a system that cannot be predicted based on previous events.

asynchronous gateway In an Ethernet network, a unit that lets a computer terminal, printer, modem or other asynchronous device talk to other devices on an asynchronous network. The number of devices you can connect is only limited by the number of six-port asynchronous gateways the Ethernet trunk can support.

asynchronous machine Any machine with a speed of operation that is not proportionate to the frequency of the system to which the machine is connected.

asynchronous memory capability A control function that allows a microprocessor to wait for memory or I/O (input or output). A small system in which all components are access-time compatible may not require asynchronous memory access, but as soon as users mix memory types and speeds, the need for this type of access becomes more obvious.

asynchronous modem eliminator A unit that replaces two modems when connecting asynchronous devices together over short distances, as shown. It is small and very economical. The unit operates within EIA RS-232C specifications. Sometimes abbreviated *AME*.

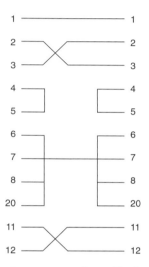

Asynchronous modem eliminator

asynchronous/synchronous interface *See* ASI.

asynchronous transmission A transmission in which each group of code elements corresponding to a character signal is preceded by a start signal, which serves to prepare the receiving mechanism for the reception and registration of a character, and is followed by a stop signal, which serves to bring the receiving mechanism to rest in preparation for the reception of the next character. *Contrast with* SYNCHRONOUS TRANSMISSION.

Async Plus A set of Pascal routines that for building asynchronous communications and solving the problems of serial communications. You can set port options, capture data reliably, command modems, transfer files using Xmodem and Ymodem file transfer protocols, and control up to four ports simultaneously. It supports Turbo Pascal 4.0 or later.

Async Professional A Turbo Pascal library of asynchronous communications functions for programmers working in the DOS environment. It includes object-oriented and procedural programming interfaces, buffered I/O up to 115K baud, buffered UART support, file transfer protocols including Zmodem and Kermit, built-in tracing and debugging, terminal emulation, and modem control. Full source code is included. It requires Turbo Pascal 5.5 or 6.0.

ASYST A scientific workstation software package comprised of four integrated modules. The System/Graphics/Statistics module establishes the ASYST environment and provides arithmetic operations and special functions, statistical functions, a text and array editor, poly-nomial mathematics, synthetic division, integration and differentiation, shifting and root extraction, matrix inversion, eigenvalues, regression analysis, frequency analysis, data smoothing, peak detection, convolutions, and filtering. A data acquisition module allows data acquisition using the personal computer (this requires that an I/O board be installed in the PC). Another module allows the user to read or write data to IEEE-488 controlled equipment. The software allows communications on a number of levels.

ASYSTANT A data acquisition/analysis and graphics software package that runs on the IBM-PC and compatibles. It is menu-driven and supports functions such as FFT, power spectrum, matrix inversion, and smoothing, as well as basic arithmetic and trigonometric functions. Other menus support automatic waveform generation, curve fitting, presentation graphics, statistics, polynomials, differential equations, and file I/O.

AT 1. Abbreviation for *automatic ticketing*. 2. Abbreviation for *advanced technology*, the IBM 286-class personal computer that performs 16-bit data processing. The AT was intended for higher-performance applications than the PC/XT while using PC-compatible serial ports, keyboards, RAM and ROM, and a bus compatible with all PC/XT expansion cards.

AT commands A set of auto-dialing commands used by the computer to control a modem. These commands were developed by Hayes Microcomputer Products and have become a standard for modems.

ATM Abbreviation for *asynchronous transfer mode*, a method for the dynamic allocation of bandwidth using a fixed-size packet (called a cell). ATM is also known as *fast packet*.

ATP *See* APPLETALK TRANSACTION PROTOCOL.

AT serial modem cable A cable that connects the AT DB9S (female) to the modem DB25P (male).

AT serial printer cable A cable that connects an AT-class PC to a standard RS-232 serial printer or other digital device. The interface is DB9S (female) to DB25P (male).

attach during processing In NetWare, a part of the File Server Environment Services that contains the count of indexed files ready for indexing but not ready for use.

attached indexed files In NetWare, a part of the File Server Environment Services that contains the count of indexed files ready for indexing but not ready for use.

attach while processing attach In NetWare, a part of the File Server Environment Services that contains the number of times a request to establish a connection from a workstation was received when the server was already processing a request to establish a connection with that workstation.

attendant message A control-panel display message, such as on a printer, requesting that the user perform some task before continuing.

attendant phone In a central dictation system, a phone that allows the word originator to communicate with an aide in the word-processing center or other remote recorder location.

attenuation The decrease in amplitude of signal (current, voltage, or power) during its transmission from one point to the next. It may be expressed as a ratio or in decibels.

attenuation characteristic As a signal propagates on a cable, it gets weaker, or attenuates. The attenuation characteristic of the medium is the rate at which it gets weaker.

attenuator A circuit of resistors, capacitors, or other elements, which introduces a known attenuation into a measuring circuit or line.

AT&T ISN AT&T's Information Systems Network, an office-communications architecture based on twisted-pair wiring. The network uses AT&T's Premises Distribution System (*PDS*) as the signaling medium. PDS can support voice, data, video, and facsimile, and can be used with almost any PBX switch product, as shown in the following figure. An adapter on the ISN packet controller supports IBM synchronous communications.

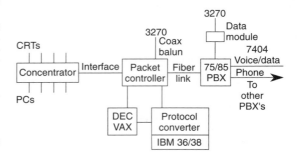

AT&T ISN

AT-to-HP LaserJet printer cable A cable that connects the AT DB9S (female) to an HP LaserJet printer DB25P (male).

atto A prefix for the numerical quantity of 10^{-18}, e.g., *attovolt*.

attribute In the context of graphics, a graphical display feature or characteristic, such as shade or background.

attribute code A control byte used in some microcomputers to control a video feature, such as the intensity of a character or the darkness of the display background or foreground.

AT/XT CMOS CPU A CPU intended for high-performance, embedded control applications. It has a PC-compatible serial port, keyboard port, speaker port, calendar/clock, 2M of DRAM, and ROM-DOS. The card is an instant DOS system that can be programmed either through the serial port from your PC, or by adding a keyboard, monitor, floppy drive and drive cards. The unit is compatible with all expansion cards, and performs 16-bit data processing in memory and 8-bit I/O processing on the bus.

auctioneering device A specific device designed to automatically select either the highest or the lowest input signal from among two or more input signals. Also known as a *high or low signal selector*.

audio CD support Refers to a CD-ROM drive's ability to read and play audio CDs.

audio drivers Several types of audio outputs are available from personal computers. The sounds are usually created in software. The IBM PCs and most clones have their own speaker and audio circuits. The audio circuit that responds to the program usually employs four chips, as shown in the figure. The speaker is typically driven by a 75477 relay driver chip. This chip amplifies the incoming bit signals so the signals can be applied to the speaker cone. Controlling the frequency of the movement produces a range of sounds; for example, BASIC can be used to produce sounds up to about 1000 Hz, while machine language can be used to produce sounds up to 3000 Hz.

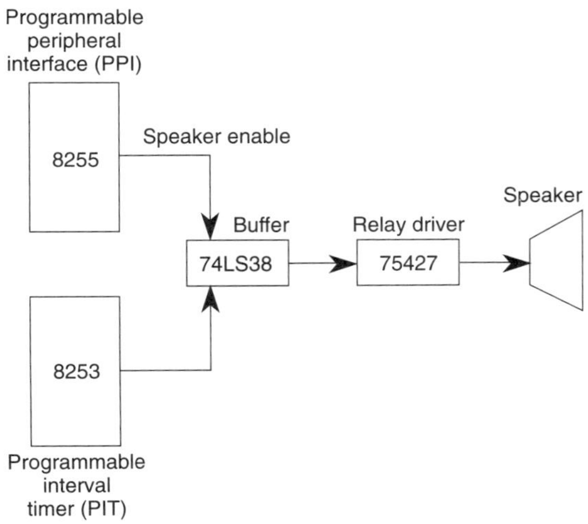

audio-editing software Any of the sound-editor programs that serve multimedia producers. Packages range from the basic to professional level. Such programs edit digital audio files by presenting a graphical display of a file for editing, which can be zoomed in for detail work. Most provide sound mixing, ranging from simple to sophisticated multi-file, multi-track capabilities.

Features include nondestructive editing, which does not affect the file until you save; a range of effects like fade, crossfade, flange/chorus (thickening), delay/echo, reverb, and distortion; open dialog audition, which plays a sound file before opening it; playback looping; and the ability to edit only the left or right channel of a stereo signal. *Also see* DIGITAL AUDIO FILE.

audio response A form of output that uses verbal replies to inquiries. A computer can be programmed to seek answers to inquiries made on-line by using a special audio-response unit that elicits the appropriate prerecorded response to the inquiry. Inquiries must be of the nature for which the audio response output has been prepared.

audio-response calculator A calculator that announces each entry and the results of every calculation using a synthesized voice stored in memory. It is used for vocational education of the blind and as an audio reinforcement of basic math concepts for sighted students.

audio-response unit A device that connects a computer system to a telephone to provide a verbal response to inquiries; abbreviated *ARU*.

audio system Relates to the various types of special equipment that have the capabilities of storing and processing data obtained from voice sources, either recorded or transmitted.

AUDIT Acronym for *automated data input terminal*, the handheld terminals that stockbrokers use to key in stock transactions.

audit A systematic examination of records, documents, and other evidence for determining the following:

- The legality of transactions
- If all transactions have been recorded
- If transactions are reflected accurately
- Assets and liabilities
- Compliance with set procedures
- The effectiveness of the accounting system

The audit can be an effective means of examining new procedures and systems in an organization.

audit trail A system for tracing items of data, step by step. The audit trail begins with the recording of the transaction, follows through the processing steps and any intermediate records that

Audio driver circuit

might exist, and ends with the production of output reports and other generated records. A representative sample is chosen of previously processed source documents and an audit trail is traced through the system to test the adequacy of procedures and controls.

augend In a summing operation, the contents of the accumulator addressed for addition with the addend. The result is the sum. *Also see* ADDITION.

AUI cable The attachment unit interface cable that connects a workstation to a transceiver or fan-out box. Also called a *drop cable*.

authentication A process that determines whether a user is authorized to transmit and receive packets.

autoboot ROM A ROM chip that enables diskless workstations to boot automatically from the file server.

AutoCAD A two-dimensional, general-purpose, computer-aided drafting and design system from Autodesk, Inc., suitable for a variety of applications including architectural and landscape drawings; drafting for mechanical, electrical, chemical, structural, and civil engineering; and printed circuit design. AutoCAD's ability to create user-defined screen menus and to define parts libraries simply by drawing them makes it easy to gear the system to specific requirements. Not only is AutoCAD useful for engineering drawing, but it is also often used for flowcharting, organizational charting, and office layout.

AutoCAD requires little computer knowledge. It acts like a word processor for drawings, allowing the user to interactively create and edit drawings of any size and to any desired scale. It uses previously created drawings, as well as basic elements such as any-width lines, circles, arcs, and solid filled areas. Drawings can be stored on disk or output on a plotter or printer; they may be annotated with text of any size inserted in any position or orientation. Drawings can be entered by keyboard, light pen, touch pen, digitizing tablet or mouse. AutoCAD provides optional support of the 8087 family of math coprocessors in order to increase the speed and precision of mathematical calculations.

Drawing and editing features allow you to move, copy, modify, dimension, scale, mirror, hatch, rotate, fill, and erase objects in a drawing. Repetitive patterns such as brick walls, memory arrays, or office components can be generated automatically. Colors and an unlimited number of layers may be used, allowing selective viewing of plotting or drawings as if on transparent overlays. The full bidirectional zoom facility allows work at any level of detail. The ratio between the largest and smallest objects in a drawing may be over a trillion to one. An alignment grid may be displayed. Distances and areas can also be calculated and displayed.

autocode A programming aid used with some IBM computers.

autodial The ability of a modem to originate and dial an outgoing call without a telephone. The call can be initiated remotely by keystrokes at a terminal or by a computer.

AUTOEXEC.BAT On a PC, an automatically executing batch file that contains instructions to DOS regarding the location and execution of other software. It is one of the most important files on a PC, and one of the first loaded into memory when the computer is turned on.

Autofile A public-domain, free-form database program. Data is stored as an 80-column by 20-line page, indexed and searchable by up to 42 keywords. It is a useful program for keeping track of information that might not be handled as well by a conventional database program.

auto-indexing In programming, refers to the ability of the index register to be automatically incremented or decremented each time it is used. This is useful in program loops.

Auto-Intelligence Decision-making software that works by identifying rules based on the user's weighting of attributes. Applications include medical and systems diagnosis, financial investments, loan approval, and risk analysis.

auto loader A program that allows program loading to be initiated automatically, remotely, or from a front panel switch.

auto log-on The ability of an autodial modem to cycle through a handshaking procedure with a remote computer automatically.

automata theory A theory that relates the principles underlying the operation and application of automatic devices to various behaviorist concepts and theories.

automated data input terminal *See* AUDIT.

automated factory A factory that is capable of bringing together all materials required for processing and returning a final product.

automated production management Management using the assistance or under the control of data-processing equipment that relates to production planning, scheduling, designing, or changing, and the reporting of output.

automatic Refers to a process or device that has the ability to guide and control itself during the course of its operation for a finite period of time without human intervention. In the case of a computer, once the human operator has set up the machine to operate, it will function by itself within definite prescribed limits. The machine will digest the input data, perform the processing function, and produce the output data. The functional operation is predetermined during the setup of the system and preparation of the program. The program is stored, but not built into, the machine.

automatic calling unit A unit that dials telephone calls automatically.

automatically executing batch file A disk file that a microcomputer runs automatically when it is turned on. This type of capability is also referred to as *turnkey*. *Also see* AUTOEXEC.BAT.

automatic code A code that allows a machine to translate symbolic language into machine language.

automatic coding Refers to a technique by which a computer is programmed to perform a significant portion of the coding of a problem.

automatic computer A machine that manipulates symbols according to given rules in a predetermined and self-directed manner; more specifically, a high-speed, automatic, electronic, digital-data-handling machine.

automatic data processing *See* ADP.

automatic data switch A switch that lets up to four personal computers share a single printer. They are available in two versions, two-way and four-way (shown), to suit the system requirements. They require no operator intervention and feature fully automatic operation with manual reset when needed. These units constantly scan all of the PCs and lock on to one until transmission of the data to the printer is complete. Users save time, because there is no manual switching, and the printer is utilized with maximum efficiency.

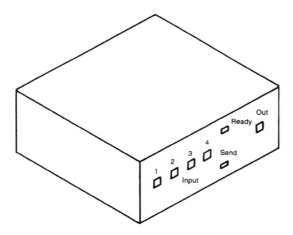

Automatic data switch

automatic dialing unit A modem or device that is capable of automatically generating dialed digits.

automatic dictionary A translating device that provides word-for-word substitution from one language to another. An automatic dictionary is used in automatic searching systems for substituting codes for words and phrases during encoding.

automatic forward reset In telephone dictation, a feature that enables the recorder to continue in playback mode to the end of recorded dictation, even though the person reviewing the dictation has disconnected. The next dictator can thus begin recording on an unused part of the medium.

automatic hold Refers to the attainment of a hold condition automatically through comparison of a variable or through an overload condition.

automatic interrupt 1. An interruption caused by program instruction as contained in some executive routine. **2.** An interruption not caused by the programmer but due to hardware devices. **3.** An automatic program-controlled interrupt system that causes a hardware jump to a predetermined location. There are at least five types of interrupts:

- Input/output
- Programmer error
- Machine error
- Supervisor call
- External, such as an alert button on a console

Unwanted interrupts such as an anticipated overflow can be masked out on some computers. *Also see* INTERRUPT.

automatic loader A program usually implemented in ROM that allows loading of at least the first record or sector of a mass storage device. The program is equivalent to a bootstrap loader plus a binary loader. When an automatic loader is installed, it is seldom necessary to key in a bootstrap program to load any other programs. *Also see* BOOTSTRAP LOADER.

automatic loader diagnostic A program aid that reads out and verifies the contents of the automatic loader ROM. It verifies the proper sequencing when the automatic loader switch is selected.

automatic programming A method of programming where the computer is used to translate the programming from a language that is easy for humans to write to a language that is efficient for a computer to operate with. Examples of automatic programming include assembling, compiling, and editing.

automatic queue A specific series of events or registers designed to implement either a LIFO or a FIFO queue without program manipulation. For a FIFO queue, new entries to the queue are placed in the last position and automatically jump forward to the last unoccupied position, while removal of the front entry results in all entries automatically moving forward one position. *Also see* PUSHDOWN LIST *and* PUSHUP LIST.

automatic remote switch This easy-to-install unit, abbreviated *ARS*, allows switching between three RS-232 devices or three telco RJ-45 devices at local or remote locations, as shown. The unit is designed to switch a standby modem online. Three switching control options are built in and can be strap selected:

- TTL input control (DB9 connector)
- RS-232 lead control via pin 12 of the RS-232 terminal port
- Manual switch control

The ARS switches leads 2 through 6, 8, 12 through 17, 19 through 22, and 24 of the RS-232 interface. Four leads of the RJ-45 interface (pins 3, 4, 5, and 6) are switched when analog switching is selected.

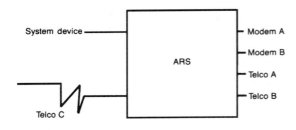

Automatic remote switch

automatic repeat key A key that continues operating as long as the key is depressed. Most keys on microcomputer keyboards are automatic repeat keys.

automatic repeat request *See* ARQ.

automatic reset **1.** A function that returns a control to its home position when a circuit fails to energize within a given time. **2.** The function of an overload relay that restores the circuit as soon as the cause of the overload is corrected.

automatic routine A set of instructions that is executed independently of any manual operations. An automatic routine is usually triggered in response to certain conditions that are set within the program.

automatic selector In telephone dictation, a connection method that automatically links the handset to the first free recorder available.

automatic stop The automatic halting of processing as a result of error detection by built-in checking devices.

automatic switchover An operating system that has a standby machine capable of detecting when the online machine is faulty and, once this determination is made, taking control.

automatic tape transmitter A device that senses data on magnetic tape. It includes mechanisms for holding, feeding, controlling, and reeling up the tape, as well as sensing the data on the tape. It can be used as a computer input device to drive printers or plotters, or to send information over a communications line.

automatic voltage regulator A device or circuit that maintains a constant voltage, regardless of variations of input voltage or load.

automatic word recall In dictation systems, an adjustable feature that enables the word originator or the transcriptionist to replay a measured portion of the previous dictation.

automation Implementing a process such that human intervention is minimized. For example, the microcomputer can be useful in automating the manufacture of almost any product. The microcomputer can be programmed to operate milling and drilling machines, turret latches, and other machine tools with more speed and accuracy than is possible with human operators. A part or process can be inspected using suitable transducers as shown; data from the transducers can be used by the microcomputer to control and adjust the machine tool or valve.

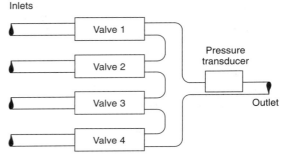

Automation example

automaton Pronounced "ah-TOM-ah-tawn," a robot-like machine designed to simulate the operation of high-order living beings.

Automenu A public-domain DOS-based program that creates a plain-English menu system for access to programs, batch files, and DOS commands. It can be used with or without a mouse.

automonitor A microcomputer's record of its functions; also, a program or routine written for this purpose.

autonomous system A collection of routers under a single administrative authority using a common Interior Gateway Protocol for routing packets.

autonomous working **1.** A specific type of concurrent or simultaneous working; i.e., the carrying out of multiple instructions at the same time. **2.** The initiation and execution of a part of a computer or automation system independent of other operations being performed on other parts of the system. The independent set of operations on various data are often monitored.

auto six-shooter A unit that automatically scans six computer ports for data that is ready to print. It does this by sequentially removing BUSY signals from the computer's port. If the computer starts to send a DATA STROBE signal, the unit locks onto that channel until that computer stops sending data. This unit has a selectable PRIORITY/SEQUENTIAL scanning option, as well as two built-in selectable timers.

auxiliary equipment The peripheral equipment not in direct communication with the central processing unit. All auxiliary equipment must be interfaced with the CPU through a peripheral interface adapter. *Also see* PERIPHERAL.

auxiliary function In automatic machining, a function of a machine other than the control of the coordinates of a workpiece or cutter, usually on-off types of operations.

auxiliary memory Additional storage beyond the capacity of the main memory. Most computers accumulate large amounts of information. Not all the accumulated information is needed by the processor at the same time. It is more economical to use lower-cost storage devices to store the information that is not currently in use. The memory that communicates directly with the central processing unit is called the *main memory*; the devices that are used to provide the backup storage are called *auxiliary memory* or *auxiliary storage*. Auxiliary memory devices may include magnetic disks and tapes.

auxiliary processor A specialized processor, such as an array processor, a fast Fourier transform (*FFT*) processor, or an input/output processor (*IOP*), generally used to increase processing speed through concurrent operation.

auxiliary PROM module A programmable read-only memory (PROM) unit that is often treated as an input/output module. Data stored on these PROMs can be accessed only as data; they cannot contain control programs to run the microcomputer.

auxiliary routine A routine designed to assist in the operation of the computer and in debugging other routines.

auxiliary storage *See* AUXILIARY MEMORY.

available blocks In NetWare, a directory service that is the number of unused blocks on a volume.

available directory slots In NetWare, a directory service that is the number of unused directory slots on a volume.

available indexed files In NetWare, a part of the File Server Environment Services that contains the count of file indexes that are available for use.

available inventory The on-hand balance minus allocations, reservations, backorders, and (usually) quantities held for quality problems.

available machine time The number of hours the computer is available for use. The available machine time is the time the machine is under power, when no maintenance is being performed, and the machine is known or believed to be operating correctly.

available power The maximum power obtainable from a given source by suitable adjustment of the load.

available SPX connection count In NetWare, a part of Communication Services that shows how many SPX connections are available to an application. *Also see* SPX.

available work Work that is actually in departments as opposed to scheduled work not yet on-hand.

avalanche Refers to a rapid generation of a current flow with reverse-bias conditions as electrons sweep across a junction with enough energy to ionize other bonds and create electron-hole pairs, making the action regenerative.

avalanche breakdown In a semiconductor diode, a nondestructive breakdown caused by the cumulative multiplication of carriers through field-induced impact ionization.

avalanche conduction A form of conduction in a semiconductor in which the charged particle collisions create additional hole-electron pairs.

avalanche diode Also called a *breakdown* or *zener diode*, an avalanche diode switches the current through it rapidly whenever the applied voltage increases beyond a certain point (the zener voltage).

avalanche-induced migration *See* SHORTED-JUNCTION DEVICES.

avalanche noise A phenomenon in a semiconductor junction in which carriers in a high-voltage gradient develop sufficient energy to dislodge additional carriers through physical impact.

average **1.** The typical value representative of any one of a group of values related to the same source; also called the *median* or *median value*. **2.** The arithmetic mean.

average access time In a disk drive, the amount of time, measured in milliseconds, that it takes the drive, on the average, to move a track and read data.

average effectiveness level A percentage computed by subtracting the total machine downtime from the total performance hours and dividing this difference by the total performance period hours. Downtime is usually measured from the time the defect has been reported to maintenance to the time the equipment is returned to the user in proper operating condition.

average inventory When demand and lot sizes are expected to be relatively uniform over time, the average is projected as one-half the average lot size plus the reserve stock. Historically, the average can be calculated as an average of several inventory observations taken over several historical time periods, i.e., period-ending inventories may be averaged. When demand and lot sizes are not uniform, the stock levels versus time can be graphed to determine the average.

average letter In word processing, a piece of correspondence of 92 to 115 words with from 18 to 23 lines of 12-pitch typing.

average transfer rate The transfer rate of blocks of data over a long enough time to include gaps between the blocks, words, or records. Regeneration time and other items not subject to program control are included. Programmed control items such as starting, stopping, and searching are not included.

average transmission rate The rate at which data is transmitted through a channel over an extended period of time to allow for gaps between words, blocks, records, files, or fields. Starting, stopping, rewinding, searching, or other operations subject to program control in the case of magnetic tapes and disks are excluded.

AWG Abbreviation for *American wire gauge*, a standardized system of copper wire size and other properties.

axis 1. A principal direction of movement of the tool or workpiece in automatic machining. **2.** One of the reference lines of a coordinate system.

axis inhibit A feature in automatic machining that prevents movement of selected slides with the power on.

axis interchange The capability of inputting information concerning one axis into the storage of another axis.

axis inversion The reversal of normal plus and minus values along an axis, which makes possible the machining of a left-handed part from right-handed programming and vice versa. Same as *mirror image*.

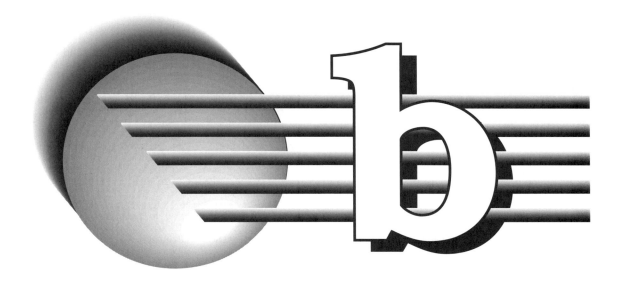

BA **1.** Abbreviation for *binary add*. **2.** Abbreviation for *bus available*.

babble The crosstalk from a large number of channels in a system. Also, the disturbing sounds in system operation resulting from such crosstalk.

babbling When a LAN workstation is transmitting meaningless data into the network channel due to a defect. This condition can cause severe performance degradation.

Baby Driver A printer interface library for C and C++ developers needing to provide integrated printer support from an application. The library supports over 300 printers and allows printing of text and graphics on any supported printer. It also allows you to control scale, rotation, position, palette, and dithering. The Presentation Graphics Option adds a graphics primitive library for producing high-quality graphics images at the maximum resolution of any printer. This option gives you EMS/XMS support, 8-bit color support, HP soft font capabilities, and more.

BAC Acronym for *binary asymmetric channel*.

backbone A LAN, a WAN, or a combination of both dedicated to providing connectivity between subnetworks in an enterprise-wide network. Subnetworks are connected to the backbone via bridges and/or routers and the backbone serves as a communications highway for LAN-to-LAN traffic.

backbone bridge A topology where a backbone is directly connected to several bridges. This topology is particularly useful in multifloor buildings.

backbone circuit In data communications, a single circuit running from a computer to one or more remote devices, each of which has branch circuits. A backbone circuit is like a river with many tributaries.

backbone network A section of the network whose primary function is to deliver messages between network segments. Systems and servers are, generally, connected to local network segments which are then connected by bridges and repeaters to the backbone.

back coupling A form of coupling that permits the transfer of energy from an output circuit to an input circuit. *Also see* COUPLER.

back-end Usually refers to a database management application where several different user interfaces can communicate with a common database processor. The back-end is sometimes called the *engine* or *server*. It performs all storage and retrieval functions for the front-end.

backfill To supplement the amount of memory from the computer system board with memory from another board in order, for example, to fill DOS to the 640K limit.

background The area that surrounds a subject. In particular, the part of the display screen surrounding a character.

background aged writes In NetWare, a part of the File Server Environment Services that represents the number of times the background disk write-process wrote a partially filled cache block to disk.

background dirty writes In NetWare, a part of the File Server Environment Services that represents the number of times a cache block that was written to disk was completely filled with information.

background noise 1. Extra bits or words that must be ignored or removed from data at the time the data is used. **2.** Errors introduced into data in a system. **3.** A disturbance tending to interfere with the normal operation of a device or system.

background processing Automatic execution of lower-priority programs when higher-priority programs are not using the machine. Batch processing, such as inventory control, payroll, and housekeeping, is often treated as background processing and can be interrupted on orders from terminals or inquiries from other units.

background program 1. In multiprogramming, the program with the lowest priority. Background programs execute from batched or stacked job input. **2.** In time sharing, a program executed in a region of main storage that is not swapped. *Contrast with* FOREGROUND PROGRAM.

backing memory Those units whose capacity is relatively larger when compared to working (scratchpad or internal) storage, but which have longer access times; their transfer capability is usually in blocks between storage units. Also referred to as *auxiliary memory*.

backlash A property of many regenerative and oscillator circuits by which oscillation is maintained with a smaller positive feedback than is required for inception.

backlog In materials requirement planning, this refers to customer orders booked and received but not yet shipped. Sometimes referred to as *open orders*.

backplane The connecting slots available for microcomputer circuit boards. A typical bus-oriented backplane is used as the "data highway" between logic, memory, and process input/output modules. Some backplanes are configured to give each plugged-in module its own unique address. As a result of this *card address* design, users can interchange memory and input/output modules throughout the chassis. One typical backplane has in each chassis three control slots, one terminator slot, and 16 multipurpose addressable slots. Since only three of the 16 are used in many basic systems, 13 slots are available for users to plug in any additional memory or interfacing required.

backplane testing Refers to the testing of the backplane connections. Wiring error rates on backplanes may run between 0.1 percent and 5 percent depending on the type of wirewrap equipment used. Manual wiring produces the highest error rates, between 2 percent and 5 percent. These errors are usually due to missed connections, misplaced wires, and loose solder. Semiautomatic connection errors run between 0.1 percent and 1 percent, with most errors resulting from machine malfunction, operator mistakes, and broken wires. Using completely automatic wrapping equipment, error rates seldom are above 0.2 percent. Newer solid-state-switched systems connect to the backplane via daisy-chained *fixture cards* to minimize the interface wiring.

back-porch effect The prolonging of the collector current in a transistor for a brief time after the input signal (particularly if it is large) has decreased to zero.

backspace code A key-operated instruction that backspaces the carriage or carrier of some word-processing equipment without backspacing the storage medium. It is used, for example, in underscoring.

back-to-back devices Refers to two semiconductor devices connected in parallel but opposite directions so that they can be used to control current without introducing rectification. Also referred to as an *inverse-parallel connection*. *Contrast with* RECTIFIER.

backup A system, device, file, or facility that can be used as an alternative in case of a malfunction or loss of data.

backup date A part of the AppleTalk Filing Protocol Services that shows the date of the last backup of the specified directory or file.

backup path In an IBM token-ring network, an alternative path for signal flow through access units and the main ring path.

backup server A program or unit that copies files so up-to-date copies always exist.

backup system 1. A system that combines several error-detection and -correction techniques to spot and correct equipment and transmission errors. **2.** A system that takes over when the primary system is down for various reasons.

backup time 1. The time it takes to complete a disk backup. **2.** The date of the last backup of a specified directory or file.

backup utility Any of the many backup programs available for hard disk users, such as MS-Backup in DOS versions 6 and higher. These programs allow you to save files from your hard disk to floppy diskettes so you will have backup copies of the files. Once the files are copied to the diskettes, most backup utilities will not copy over them unless you select a special function. During the backup procedure, most backup utilities tell you which diskettes to insert and how long it will take to perform the backup. As you are storing the files to diskettes, the utility creates a catalog of all the files just as they appear on the hard disk. This catalog is usually stored on both the hard disk and the backed up diskettes.

Most backup utilities can be set to do a periodic backup of files. This feature tells you when it is time to do a backup and gives you the necessary prompts. Because some backup utilities condense the files to save space, you have to reinstall the whole system in order to read them. However, with others the files can be read directly from the diskettes.

backward scheduling A scheduling technique that starts with due date for an order and works backward to determine the required start date. This can generate negative times, thereby identifying where time must be made up.

bad incoming packets In NetWare, a part of the Diagnostic Services that shows the number of times (since SPX was loaded) that SPX has received and discarded a packet because the connection ID in the packet was wrong. *Also see* SPX.

bad logical connection number In NetWare, a part of the File Server Environment Services that shows the count of all request packets with invalid logical connection numbers, which are those numbers not supported by a file server.

bad send requests In NetWare, a part of the Diagnostic Services that shows the number of times (since SPX was loaded) that applications have incorrectly called SPX Send Sequenced Packet by passing an invalid connection ID, or bypassing the address of an ECB that indicates a packet header size of less than 42 bytes. *Also see* SPX.

bad sequence number packets In NetWare, a part of the File Server Environment Services that shows the count of request packets where the server received from a connection where the sequence number in the packet did not match the current sequence number or the next sequence number. Packets with bad sequence numbers are discarded.

.BAK In many file-naming schemes, an extension that indicates a backup file.

balance In NetWare, a part of the Accounting Services that shows an object's account balance.

balanced circuit A circuit with two sides electrically alike and symmetrical to a common reference point, usually ground. These circuits may be terminated by a network whose impedance balances the impedance of the line so that the return losses are infinite.

balanced instrumentation amplifier system A system in which the output of the signal source appears on two lines as shown, both having equal source resistances and output voltages in relation to ground or the common-mode level.

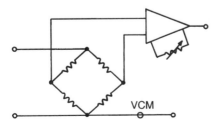

Balanced system

balanced line A transmission line consisting of two conductors; in the presence of ground, it is capable of being operated in such a way that the voltages of the two conductors at all transverse planes are equal in magnitude and opposite in polarity with respect to ground; the currents in the two conductors are equal in magnitude and opposite in direction.

balanced line system A system consisting of a source, balanced line, and a load adjusted so that the voltage of the two conductors at all transverse planes are equal in magnitude and opposite in polarity with respect to ground.

balanced network A network arranged for insertion into a balanced circuit and therefore symmetrical electrically about the midpoints of its input and output pairs of terminals.

balanced oscillator A type of oscillator in which the impedance centers of the tank circuits are always at ground potential and the operating voltages between either end and the centers are equal at all points and opposite in phase.

balanced system A system in which the number of CPU operations being performed is equal to the number of I/O operations being performed.

balanced-to-ground The state of impedance on a two-wire line when the impedance to ground as measured from one side of the line is equal to the impedance to ground as measured from the other side of the line.

balanced transmission A method for the transmission of baseband data in which each signal circuit consists of a pair of conductors, and the signal consists of a differential voltage between the two conductors. The voltage with respect to ground on one conductor of the pair will be mirrored or balanced by a voltage of equal magnitude of opposite polarity on the other conductor.

balanced voltages On the two conductors of a balanced line, balanced voltages are the voltages relative to ground, which are equal and opposite in polarity at every point along the line. Also referred to as *push-pull voltages*.

balanced-wire circuit A circuit with two sides that are the same electrically and symmetrical to ground and other conductors.

balancing capacitor A capacitor that impedes the flow of direct current in a circuit without affecting the flow of alternating current.

baluns Impedance matching devices comprised of a transformer that connects a balance line (twisted pair) to an unbalanced line such as a coaxial cable.

BAM Acronym for *basic telecommunications access method.*

band 1. A range of frequencies or the frequency spectrum between two limits. **2.** A continuous recording track on a storage device such as a magnetic drum or disk. The surface of the drum or disk is divided into more or less equally spaced rings, called bands, each with its own read/write head for reading in or writing out data (or both).

band-edge energy The band of energy between two defined limits in a semiconductor. The lower limit corresponds to the lowest amount of energy required by an electron to remain free, while the upper band is the maximum permissible energy of a free electron.

band-elimination filter A filter having a single attenuation band with neither of the cutoff frequencies being zero or infinite, such as a filter to eliminate 60-cycle noise pickup from electrical power devices.

bandpass filter A filter that gives a "tuned" output consisting of frequency components of a signal within a specific range.

band printer A high-speed printer in which the type moves on a band or chain. Not commonly used in microcomputer systems because of their expense.

band splitter A multiplexer designed to split the available bandwidth into several independent narrower band subchannels, each suitable for data transmission at a fraction of the total channel data rate.

bandwidth A frequency range between minimum and maximum frequency points of stated attenuation. The attenuation limit is usually 3 decibels (half power) at the bandwidth limits.

bandwidth-distance product The product of bandwidth and distance that is used to specify a limit on a transmission media, such as an optical fiber's bandwidth and repeater spacing.

bank A unit of memory starting at a round address, often 256K bytes. RAM chips are generally sold and installed on the memory board as banks. For example, an expansion board for the PC-XT/AT might hold eight banks of memory, or up to 2 megabytes of RAM. *Also see* SIMM.

Bank Link A software package used for electronic banking.

bank select Refers to the ability to turn internal system components on and off with electronic control signals. For example, some computers have several banks or blocks of memory under the control of the CPU. Only one memory bank may be active at a time, so control is accomplished by bank selection (electronically waking up) of the desired memory via signals sent by the CPU.

Bank Street Writer A word processor designed for the user who writes a quick, occasional memo. It was originally designed for children, so the program is extremely easy to learn. Bank Street Writer has very few commands or codes; most functions are executed by using the Tab and Return keys. Instructions and command choices are displayed at the top of the screen at all times, so reference to the manual is rarely necessary.

This program does not have the advanced features of other word processors such as multiple formats or advanced cursor movements, so it should not be used for complex documents. Experienced operators might find it slow and tedious to use. It is not a powerful program; some versions will not access a hard disk nor allow the program to be copied onto the hard disk.

bank switching A technique used by expanded memory managers to swap expanded memory into addresses with DOS's 1M address limit. *Also see* EXPANDED MEMORY.

banner text 1. Large-font text used to print banners. **2.** In NetWare Print Services, a flag that contains the text of the bottom half of a banner. This is an uppercase, 13-character ASCII string. The default is the name of the file to be printed.

Banyan The manufacturer of Vines, a competing network to Novell NetWare.

BAR Acronym for *buffer address register*.

barcode Optical binary code, often used on merchandise in retail stores.

Bar Code Labelmaker A software program that lets you create barcode labels for products, pallets, cartons, shelves, signs, and other material you need to label by following the program's label profile and data entry screens.

Bar Code Library A programmer's library, written in C, that generates and prints barcodes from within your own program. It can print over one dozen barcodes and supports several languages such as Clipper, C, QuickSilver, and QuickBASIC. It supports most printers.

barcode reader Abbreviated *BCR*, a device for reading barcodes. It is a fast method for reading price and product data. Using your IBM PC or compatible, you can quickly enter data for inventory control, manufacturing, or other repetitive coding applications.

bare board A printed circuit board that has conductors on it but no electronic components. It is often provided with electronic hobby kits and also sold separately for engineers and fabricators who wish to build a design of their own.

barrel connector A double-sided male coupling that interconnects coaxial sections.

barrier layer A double electrical layer formed at the surface of substances that have differing work functions; there is a diffusion of electrons up this work-function gradient.

.BAS A filename extension that indicates a BASIC program file.

base *See* RADIX.

base address The number in an address that serves as the reference for subsequent address numbers.

baseband A signalling technique in which the signal is transmitted in its original form, not changed by modulation.

baseband data The normal or unmodulated form of a data signal as generated by digital circuits.

baseband LAN A local area network that transfers data in baseband form only. *Contrast with* BROADBAND LAN.

baseband transmission A transmission method that uses low frequency starting at 0 Hz, and carries only one transmission at a time. This method utilizes no carrier.

base bandwidth The amount of bandwidth required by an unmodulated signal, such as video or audio. In general, the higher the quality of the signal, the greater the base bandwidth required.

baseline Refers to the horizontal or vertical line formed by the sweep of the electron gun as it moves across the CRT screen. *Also see* CRT.

base material An insulating material used to support a conductive pattern. The material used most often is a copper-clad laminate.

base memory Refers to the amount of RAM the system unit or printer is equipped with. The more memory the system or printer has, the quicker and more powerful it is.

base metal The metal substrate on which one or more coatings of other materials or metals are deposited, as in printed circuits or connections.

base notation A notation consisting of a decimal number written as a subscript suffix to a number, indicating the base or radix of the number. For example, 10_2 indicates the number *10* has a binary base, and 11_8 indicates the number *11* has a base of 8.

base number The radix of a counting system that indicates the quantity of characters available for use in each of the digital positions. For example, with a binary number, only the characters *0* and *1* are used, and the base is two.

base register A register that extends a limited address to a larger address. The base register is used to point to a region of memory where the displacement takes place. In one simple technique, the data memory is divided in half and an instruction is provided which will select bank A or bank B. This, in effect, provides two base registers with an implied selection. Base registers also provide a technique for program segment relocation (the binding of the program segments into an absolute address).

base time A precisely controlled function of time by which some particular process is controlled or measured.

base voltage The voltage between the base terminals of a transistor and the reference terminal.

BASIC An algebraic programming code developed at Dartmouth College. The name is an acronym formed from the initial letters of *beginners' all-purpose symbolic instruction code*. BASIC is a conversational type of programming language using English-like statements and mathematical notation. A BASIC program is made up of lines of statements that contain instructions for the interpreter or compiler. A program can be saved, listed, retrieved, or executed using the commands available in BASIC.

In the *immediate mode*, it is not necessary to write a complete program in order to use BASIC. This mode is useful for debugging and desk calculation problems. Program loops are allowed, as shown in the table of square roots.

```
FOR L = 1 TO 9: PRINT L, SQR (L): NEXT L
1    1
2    1.41421
3    1.73205
4    2
5    2.23607
6    2.44949
7    2.64575
8    2.82843
9    3
```

BASIC is not the fastest, nor the most powerful, nor the most elegant of programming languages. However, it has been in use for some time, and much code has been written in it. Many people are familiar with BASIC and its many versions, and feel comfortable writing programs using it. It meets the needs of many applications, but it does have problems.

The most critical problem with BASIC for some control or monitoring applications is its speed, even in the compiled version (usually BASIC is interpreted) and even when the BASIC programs can call assembly language subroutines. The slow execution is compensated by fast I/O calls.

basic control system Abbreviated *BCS*, a system used in computer satellites that is interrupt-oriented, providing fast execution of dedicated programs, without any time-scheduling capability.

basic disk operating system *See* BDOS.

basic input-output system *See* BIOS.

basic linkage A program linkage that is used repeatedly in one routine, program, or system and that follows the same set of rules each time.

basic telecommunications access method *See* BTAM.

BASIC Tutor A BASIC tutorial program that teaches the user to write or modify BASIC programs. It requires BASIC.

BASICXREF A public-domain BASIC cross-reference utility used as a programming aid for the serious BASIC programmer on the IBM PC. Its use facilitates the programming and debugging of BASIC source language programs. The utility provides the following output:

- A complete listing of all program line numbers, showing all references by other statements in the program
- An alphabetic listing of all reserved words showing the line numbers in which they appear
- An alphabetic listing of all program variables, and I/O-related variables that are neither reserved words nor program variables
- A listing of the BASIC source program with top and bottom page margins, page headings, and formatting of program statements for improved readability

.BAT In many file-naming schemes, an extension that indicates a batch file. *Also see* BATCH FILE.

batch An assortment of data items that can be processed during a single computer program run.

batch control A way of apportioning predetermined quantities of work to users at regular intervals.

batch file A text file that contains operating system commands and program commands. Batch files tell the computer to perform a string of commands, with the user only having to type in one command to start the batch file. They are used for standard procedures that are performed repetitiously.

batch mode A computer mode in which the program is submitted on disk or some other medium and the results returned hours or days later.

batch processing A method of processing in which a number of items are grouped for processing during the same machine run. Batch processing systems usually do not require immediate updating of files, since data is gathered up to a specific cutoff time and then processed.

batch total The sum of certain quantities, related to batches of unit records, used to verify the accuracy of a particular batch. For example, in a payroll calculation, the batches could be employees and the batch totals would be the number of employee hours per each employee or the total pay per employee.

batten system See *cordonnier system.*

battery backup A backup power system for IBM compatibles and other computers that uses a lifetime-rechargeable sealed battery that continuously charges while the system is on.

battery pack A unit that provides backup power to support components such as RAM, particularly for portable computers and peripherals.

BauBloc A development tool that provides a graphical user interface and a mechanism for the integration of other development tools. It graphically supports the overview and organization of development platforms, programs, and files, and offers integration of the development tools. It is particularly well-suited for software development on a LAN.

baud A unit of signaling speed derived from the length of the shortest code element. The speed in baud is equal to the number of code elements per second transmitted. It is also the unit of modulation rate, with one baud equal to a rate of one unit interval per second, and the modulation rate equal to the reciprocal of the duration in seconds of the unit interval. The modulation rate for a unit interval of 20 milliseconds is 50 baud.

Baudot A data-transmission code in which five bits represent one character. The use of letters/figures and the Shift key enables 64 alphanumeric characters to be represented. Baudot is used in many teleprinter systems with one start bit and 1.42 stop bits added.

Baudot code A communications code that contains five binary symbols. The correct interpretation depends on knowing the previous history of the message, for example, whether an upper- or lowercase character was last struck. If a sixth bit, called the *case bit*, is used, the Baudot code can be uniquely identified. Some examples of the code are shown in the following table.

Keystroke	CASE	1	2	3	4	5
A	0	1	1	0	0	0
B	0	1	0	0	1	1
S	0	1	0	1	0	0
Y	0	1	0	1	0	0
4	1	0	1	0	1	0
&	1	0	1	0	1	1
8	1	0	1	1	0	0
0	1	0	1	1	0	1
:	1	0	1	1	1	0
;	1	0	1	1	1	1

baud rate A measurement of data flow in which the number of signal elements per second is based on the duration of the shortest element. When each element carries one bit, the baud rate is numerically equal to the bits per second (*bps*).

bayonet A type of connector that uses a quick-release mechanism rather than a threaded sleeve. This type of connector is widely used with coaxial cable in a LAN.

B-box A register that contains a quantity used to modify an address; an index register.

BBS Abbreviation for *bulletin board system*, an on-line computer service that subscribers use, as they would use a traditional bulletin board, to post and circulate messages. These services operate through modems, which connect the subscriber's microcomputers to the information network. Users connect with a BBS using a modem to download and upload files, and leave messages for each other.

BC *See* BINARY CODE.

BCC Abbreviation for *block check character*, the result of a transmission-verification algorithm accumulated over a transmission block, normally appended at the end for the purpose of error detection.

BCD Abbreviation for *binary-coded decimal*, a method of coding in which each decimal digit is coded into a separate four-bit word. For example, the binary coded decimal number for 9 is 1001. For 8 it is 1000 and for 10 it is 0001 0000. BCD is also known as the *8421 code* due to the weight assigned to each four-bit word.

Decimal	BCD	
	8 4 2 1—Weight	
0	0 0 0 0	
1	0 0 0 1	
2	0 0 1 0	
3	0 0 1 1	
4	0 1 0 0	
5	0 1 0 1	
6	0 1 1 0	
7	0 1 1 1	
8	1 0 0 0	
9	1 0 0 1	
10	0 0 0 1	0 0 0 0
11	0 0 0 1	0 0 0 1
12	0 0 0 1	0 0 1 0

BCFSK Abbreviation for *binary-code frequency-shift keying*.

BCO Abbreviation for *binary-coded octal*.

BCR *See* BARCODE READER.

BCS *See* BASIC CONTROL SYSTEM.

BCW Abbreviation for *buffer control word*.

BDOS Acronym for *basic disk operating system*, a part of the CP/M operating system.

BDU Abbreviation for *basic display unit*.

beacon A token ring packet that signals a serious failure on the ring.

beating the shift A typing action in which a very fast or erratic typist causes a character to misprint following or preceding a shift.

beginners's all-purpose symbolic instruction code *See* BASIC.

being processed count In NetWare, a Diagnostic Service that shows the number of times (since the shell was activated) that the shell has received a "being processed" reply from a file server. A file server sends this reply to a shell when the server, while processing the shell's request, receives duplicate requests from the shell for the same service.

bel A nondimensional unit used for expressing the ratio of power units (P_1 and P_2).

$$N = \log_{10} (P_1/P_2) \text{ bels}$$

A bel is ten times the size of the more frequently used term *decibel*. In Europe, *neper* is used instead of bel.

Bell 103 (*o.t.*) A family of 300-bps FSK (frequency-shift keying) modem standards developed by the Bell System.

Bell 113 (*o.t.*) Same as Bell 103, but provided originate-or-answer capability only.

Bell 201 A family of 2400-bps four-level DPSK (differential phase-shift keying) modem standards developed by the Bell System.

Bell 202 A family of FSK modem standards developed by the Bell System. These modems operate at 1200 bps on dial-up lines, at 1400 bps on leased lines with C1 conditioning, and at 1800 bps on leased lines with C2 conditioning.

Bell 208 A family of 4800-bps eight-level PSK (phase-shift keying) modem standards developed by the Bell System.

Bell 209A A 9600-bps modem standard developed by the Bell system. This modem uses a combination of PSK and ASK (amplitude-shift keying) called *quadrature amplitude modulation*.

Bell 212A A 1200-bps four-level PSK modem standard developed by the Bell System. This modem can also operate in a 300 bps mode, which is compatible with the Bell 103 standard.

Bell 43401 A Bell publication that defines requirements for data transmission over limited-distance dc-continuous private metallic circuits supplied by the telephone company.

BEMA Acronym for *Business Equipment Manufacturers Association*.

benchmark A test criterion used for measuring the performance of a product. Microprocessors, for example, can be evaluated using a benchmark program to compare different types. A flowchart in assembly language can be used to test each type with respect to execution time, accuracy, and other critical parameters for a particular application.

benchmark comparisons Comparisons that show the results of a benchmark test using a sample program. The results may reflect tests of available microprocessors, as shown in the graph. In this task, microprocessor C requires the least amount of processing time and uses the smallest amount of memory for the benchmark program. Microprocessor D, on the other hand, uses more memory and requires the most processing time.

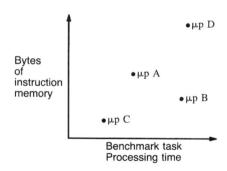

Typical benchmark test results

Benchmark results using microprocessors may be based on a program that consists of the movement of a block of data using a sequence like the following:

```
SET UP    MOV;    move data to register A
          MOV;    move data to register B
          MOV;    move data to register C
                  (character move)
LOOP      MOV;    ; combine data in
```

```
LOOP 1                    register A with B
                          ; loop to register C
EXIT
```

Other criteria can consist of interrupt servicing, arithmetic operations, searching, or monitoring.

benchmark problem A routine used to evaluate the performance of computing machines and software. A typical problem might be to perform nine complete additions and one complete multiplication, and measure the time to complete all operations, which include operation acquisition from storage, performance of the operation, storage of the result, selection of the next instruction, and instruction execution.

benchmark program A sample program, routine, or operation mix typically used to compare the performances of different processors or programs. Since processors utilize different instruction sets, the benchmark programs are specified using flowcharts, such as the one shown here, designed to test or poll a peripheral device. The blocks of the flowchart represent machine functions in this example. From the flowchart, a program for the particular microprocessor can be coded and run, and a timing memory size analysis can be computed based on execution times and instruction bytes. The key performance parameters obtained in this example are the number of memory bytes occupied by the program or task and the speed of execution of the program or task. The relative importance of these parameters depends on the application, but a benchmark can establish a quantitative measurement for making a comparison.

A complex program or actual operational application may contain many routines, so conclusive information cannot always be drawn from simple benchmarks. Also, it is not always easy to establish a single benchmark. Therefore, you must use judgment, or if time and resources are available, actual simulation.

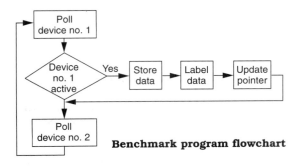

Benchmark program flowchart

bend radius The amount that a cable can bend before the risk of breakage or increase in attenuation.

BER Acronym for *bit error rate*, expressed as the number of bits encountered before one erroneous bit is found. The BER for CD-ROMs is one bad bit in 10^{12}, or as a frequency of erroneous bits, 10^{-12}.

Bernoulli box A removable-cartridge, high-speed, high-capacity form of data storage. It allows access to information quickly and delivers performance that often exceeds hard disks. It is available in many different storage capacities, from 10M to 90M or more.

BERT Acronym for *bit-error rate test*.

beta release A version of a software product released for testing purposes after the alpha release. Distribution, although still limited, is wider than for the alpha. *Also see* ALPHA RELEASE.

BESS Acronym for *binary electromagnetic signal signature*.

BestChoice A software program designed for alternative analysis. It is useful for determining design specifications, product evaluation, purchase considerations, and personnel reviews.

best-effort delivery service In NetWare, a network module, such as the network layer IPX, will attempt to deliver data but will not try to recover if there is an error such as a line failure.

BEV Abbreviation for *billion electron volts*.

Bezier curve A probe that is calculated mathematically to connect separate points to form a smooth, continuous curve. Since only a few points are needed to define a relatively complex curve, Bezier curves are extremely useful in CAD and illustration programs.

BFO Abbreviation for *beat frequency oscillator*.

bias 1. A term that denotes an electrical, mechanical, or magnetic force or voltage applied to a relay, transistor, vacuum tube, other electrical device to establish an electrical or mechanical operational reference level. **2.** The amount by which the average of a set of values departs from a reference value. **3.** In teletypewriter applications, the uniform shifting of the beginning of all marking pulses from their proper positions in relation to the beginning of the start pulse.

bibliographic retrieval service A type of subscription database service offered to microcomputer users with the proper equipment.

BIC Abbreviation for *bus interface circuit*.

biconic A type of connector for a fiber-optic cable.

bidirectional Capable of operation in two directions; for example, toward the input and toward the output. A bidirectional operation saves time and provides easy access to stored information.

bidirectional buffer Since some chips cannot drive a heavily loaded data bus, it is sometimes necessary to buffer the data bus to this chip. This can be done as shown in the figure.

bidirectional bus A bus that accepts both input and output signals on a single line. *Also see* BUS.

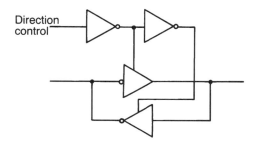

Bidirectional buffer

bidirectional bus driver A power driver that can operate with bidirectional signals.

bidirectional lines Bus lines with bidirectional and asynchronous communications. These lines permit devices to send, receive, and exchange data at their own rates. The bidirectional nature of a bus allows utilization of common bus interfaces for different devices and simplifies the interface design.

bidirectional printer A device capable of printing from right to left as well as from left to right, thus reducing wasted motion during operation. Also called a *reverse printer*.

bidirectional pulses Signal pulses that rise in one direction and repeat in the opposite direction.

bidirectional signal A signal that appears to be symmetrical about an axis or bias.

bidirectional transistor A type of transistor in which the emitter and collector can be used interchangeably. Either terminal can be used as the input or the output.

bidirectional waveform A waveform that shows a reversal of polarity, such as the waveforms produced when a bidirectional pulse generator produces both positive and negative pulses.

bifurcated contact A contact that is forked or pronged.

bifurcation A condition under which two, and only two, outcomes can occur, such as on or off, or 0 or 1.

big-endian A format for storage or transmission of binary data in which the most significant bit (or byte) comes first. (The term comes from *Gulliver's Travels*; the Lilliputians, being very small, had correspondingly small political problems. The Big-Endian and Little-Endian parties debated over whether soft-boiled eggs should be opened at the big end or the little end.)

BILE Acronym for *balanced inductor logic element*.

billi A prefix that designates the quantity one billion; synonymous with *kilomega*. *Billibits* means one billion bits; *billicycle*, one billion cycles per second.

binary Countable using two digits, 0 and 1. The basic requirement of a computer is its ability to represent numbers and to perform operations on the numbers represented; since any number can be represented by an ordered arrangement of ones and zeros, most computers use this system of counting. In the binary number system, the carry is used with the two digits. The numbers used to count to ten are as follows:

DECIMAL	BINARY
0	0
1	1
10	2
11	3
100	4
101	5
110	6
111	7
1000	8
1001	9
1010	10

A weighting table can be used to convert any binary number to its decimal equivalent. Each digit is multiplied by its position coefficient and the results added to obtain the decimal number.

2^3	2^2	2^1	2^0	Binary weight
1	0	1	0	Binary number
8	0	2	0	Decimal equivalents

Binary-to-decimal conversion

The table can be extended to the left as far as desired. The 1 in the far left position is always called the most significant bit (*MSB*); the digit in the far right position is called the least significant bit (*LSB*).

binary arithmetic Mathematical operations performed using the binary digits, 1 and 0. In the binary number system, there are four addition rules:

$$0 + 0 = 0$$
$$1 + 0 = 1$$
$$0 + 1 = 1$$
$$1 + 1 = 0 \text{ and carry a } 1$$

These rules are demonstrated in the following example of adding the binary equivalents of 10 and 14.

```
carries    →111
            1010   = 10
          + 1110   = 14
           11000   = 24
```

A microcomputer program could add these numbers by using three registers (A, B, and C).

The program could have the following steps:

1. Load numbers to be added, 1010 and 1110, into registers A and B.
2. Clear C to remove any bits stored there.
3. Transfer the contents of A to C (they now hold the same value).
4. Add the contents of B to C, using the addition rules, and store in C. The sum is now stored in C for transfer to another location or readout.

Multiplication has a similar set of rules:

$$0 \times 0 = 0$$
$$0 \times 1 = 0$$
$$1 \times 0 = 0$$
$$1 \times 1 = 1$$

An example of multiplication follows:

```
  1010    = 10
× 101     = 5
  1010
 1010
 110010 = 50
```

Multiplication can be done in a microcomputer by multiple additions, multiple shifts, or a combination of both. A shift to the left results in a multiplication by two. In the above example, 1010 is shifted left twice for a multiplication of four, and then 1010 is added to the result to give a multiplication by five.

Subtraction is usually done by *complementing*, which involves changing all ones to zeros and all zeros to ones in a binary system. To perform binary subtraction, follow these steps:

1. Complement the subtrahend.
2. Add it to the minuend.
3. Move the digit from the most significant position and add it to the value of the least significant position, performing the end-around carry.

For example, to subtract 1011 from 1100:

1. Complement 1011 = 0100
2. Add to the minuend:

```
  1100
+ 0100
 10000
```

3. Perform the end-around carry:

```
 10000
   ↘
 00001
```

Division is accomplished with binary numbers by repeated shifts and subtractions, as shown in the following:

```
         101
    101 )11010
         101
          110
          101
            1 ← remainder
```

binary cell An elementary unit of storage that can be placed in one of two possible stable states.

binary chain An entire series of separate binary circuits, each capable of existing in one of two states. They are arranged so each circuit can affect or modify the condition of adjacent circuits.

binary code A code in which every element has only one of two possible values, which may be the presence or absence of a pulse, a one or a zero, or a high or a low condition for a voltage or current.

binary-coded decimal See BCD.

binary counter A counting circuit that produces an output for every two input pulses, producing a division by two.

binary counter transistor A combination of flip-flops and gates in which a pulse train or clock changes a flip-flop according to the zero or one condition of the inputs. When a set of these flip-flops is connected, a binary counter is obtained. As successive pulses enter into the first trigger or clock input, the zero or one condition of the flip-flop change.

binary digit A numeral in the binary system of notation. Usually known as a *bit*, the digit may be a one or a zero.

binary dump A portion of a program that allows for printing or displaying a binary copy of a portion of memory.

binary lookup Relates to techniques designed for finding a particular item in an ordered set of items by repeatedly dividing in half the portion of the ordered set containing the sought-for item until only the sought-for item remains. Binary searching is more efficient than sequential searching, even when the number of items is small.

binary number system A number system having 2 as its base and expressing all quantities using the numerals *0* and *1*. The two-state character of the binary number system makes it especially suitable for a digital computer that operates most conveniently on a bistable basis. *Also see* BINARY.

binary object program A program that can be directly executed by a digital machine. It substitutes the actual addresses in place of the symbolic ones and substitutes the actual binary encoding of the data along with the binary code of instructions in place of the mnemonics.

binary pair An electronic circuit having two stable states, two input lines, and two corresponding output lines such that a signal exists on either one of the output lines if and only if the last pulse received by the flip-flop is on the corresponding input line. A binary pair can store one binary digit (bit) of information, since it is a bistable device.

binary point 1. A point located half the distance between the integral powers of two in a binary number. **2.** That point in a binary number that separates the integral from the fractional part. It is analogous to the decimal point for a decimal number.

binary search A method for locating an item in an ordered set of items by dividing an ordered set of items into two parts, one of which is rejected; the process is repeated on the saved part in an iterative routine that ultimately results in the retrieval of the desired item. Also called a *dichotomizing search*.

binary signaling A method of communications in which information is transferred by the presence or absence of the two state variations of the signal.

binary synchronous A mode of transmission in which the synchronizing of binary characters is controlled by signals generated at the receiving and sending stations. Also known as *bisynch*.

binary synchronous communication A half-duplex, character-oriented synchronous data communications protocol originated by IBM in the 1960s for transmission of binary-coded data between stations in a data communications system. Abbreviated *BSC* or *bisync*.

binary-to-decimal conversion The process of converting a binary number to its equivalent in decimal form.

binary-to-Gray code conversion A conversion between the two codes that takes place as follows: when the binary most significant bit (*MSB*) is zero, the Gray code MSB will be zero. Then, going from the MSB to the LSB (least significant bit), each change produces a 1, each nonchange a 0. A circuit in which binary to Gray code conversion may be achieved is shown in the figure. *Also see* GRAY CODE.

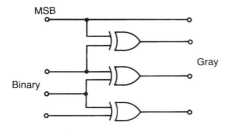

Binary-to-gray code conversion logic

binary tree *See* BTREE.

bindery A file on the NetWare operating system used to store management information such as user passwords.

bindery files NetWare's security information, kept in special, hidden files in the SYS:SYSTEM directory. All of the user information, Trustee Assignments, group information, and print server information is stored in these files. NetWare 286 has two files: NET4BVAL.SYS and NET$BIND.SYS. NetWare 386 has three files: NET$OBJ:SYS, NET$PROP.SYS, and NET$VAL.SYS. Backup systems must be able to back up these files.

binding A concept used in remote procedure calls. Two remote programs bind with each other by starting a connection and then exchanging command requests.

bionics The application of biological techniques to the design of electronic hardware and systems. Bionics uses the knowledge gained from the study of living systems to create hardware that functions in a manner analogous to the biological systems being studied. The result sometimes creates hardware that strongly resembles the characteristics as well as the functions of living systems.

BIOS Acronym for *basic input-output system*, a collection of subprograms that control the transfer of characters between the microprocessor and other devices in the microcomputer system such as the printer, video display, and keyboard.

biosensor A sensor or mechanism for detecting and transmitting biological data from an organism in a way that permits processing, display, or storage of the results.

biphase coding A line-coding scheme in which 1 is represented as a high-to-low signal transition occurring in the middle of the bit cell, while 0 is represented as a low-to-high transition. This is also referred to as *Manchester II coding*.

bipolar Having two polarity levels. Bipolar transistors are configured as npn or pnp "sandwiches," as opposed to the controlled channel construction of field-effect devices such as MOS (metal-oxide semiconductor) transistors and integrated circuits. Since bipolar devices have low capacitance, switching time (the time required to turn them on and off) can be very short, resulting in very fast computer operations.

Bipolar integrated-circuit devices tend to have a higher surface area per unit volume compared to MOS, which tends to keep the cost of fabrication high for complex chips. Another disadvantage of bipolar construction is the requirement of isolation barriers between adjacent devices, which adds to fabrication costs. Bipolar devices also dissipate more power than MOS, since they operate on current rather than voltage.

The first bipolar microprocessor chips to appear were 10 times faster than the MOS microprocessor available at the time. With a machine-cycle time of 200 nanoseconds, the architecture of the bipolar chips was a two-bit slice approach and the instruction set was microprogrammable. The device was designed for products in which it would be tailored for a specific application.

Later bit-slice bipolar chips used sets of four-bit chips, each chip consisting of a register file read by two address multipliers. Data in the registers passed through a set of latches. One of the chips contained the arithmetic logic unit and provided data-routing control. An internal register was used for temporary storage of results and double-precision arithmetic storage. Bit-slice microprocessors are now being produced with Schottky-TTL logic, integrated injection logic (I^2L), and emitter-coupled logic (ECL), all of which are bipolar.

Bipolar microprocessors offer a building-block approach from which complex processing systems can be constructed, using various hierarchies or levels of control memory. Both microinstruction and macroinstruction programming can be used in these systems.

Many bipolar chip sets that use the slice approach do not have fixed instruction sets. The user must develop these and store them in microprogram memory. Then the various peripherals, including additional memory, can be connected with the chip set to form a microcomputer, and additional programs are developed and stored as the design proceeds.

bipolar coding Refers to line-coding schemes that involve both positive and negative voltages referenced to ground. This is in contrast to unipolar coding, which uses either all-positive or all-negative voltages.

bipolar CPU slice A type of chip that provides many of the speed advantages of discrete logic and all of the processor-oriented advantages of a microprocessor. It does require another level of system design: users must build their own instruction set (macroinstructions) using techniques like those used to create microprogrammed CPUs.

bipolar current-switching D/A conversion A converter that uses offset binary or two's complement codes. An offset current equal and opposite to the most significant byte current is added to the converter output. This can be a resistor and a separate offset reference, but usually it is derived from the converter's basic reference voltage, to minimize drift with temperature. The gain of the output-inverting amplifier is doubled in order to double the output range, from 0 to 10V to +10V, as shown in the figure.

bipolar fabrication Refers to the fabrication of bipolar devices. Bipolar fabrication typically requires 12 masking steps and four diffusion steps, versus five masking steps and one diffusion step for n-channel and p-channel MOS devices. Bipolar fabrication is complex because of the need for isolation rings around each device, and because a number of alternating diffusion steps are required to create the n-p-n-p layers.

bipolar mask bus A mask bus, unique to bipolar systems. The mask bus provides a mechanism for supplying constants to a central processor array and permits additional functions in the system.

bipolar microprogram The microprogrammed approach is useful for bipolar microcomputers because complex macroinstruction sets can be realized as sequences of relatively primitive microinstructions. The logic of the final macromachine remains relatively simple, with most of the complexity being represented by the contents of the control memory. When used with a CPE (central processing element) slice, the basic microinstruction functions are established, although additional logical elements drawn from standard TTL families may be added, which may alter or enhance the microinstruction set.

bipolar N-zero substitution See BNZS.

bipolar RAM Bipolar random access memory used in high-speed buffer memories and as replacements for high-speed core memories in older systems. The memories are generally organized with an 8-bit binary address field and separate data-in and data-output lines. Some memories have three active LOW chip select inputs and a three-state output or open collector output. Inputs are generally buffered to present an input load of 0.5 TTL (transistor-transistor logic) unit loads. Read/write operations may be controlled by an active LOW write enable input. When the write enable is LOW and the chip is selected, the data on the data input is written into the location specified by the address inputs. During this operation the output floats, allowing the data bus to be used by other memories or open collector logic elements that are tied to the inverting data output. Reading is accomplished by having the chip selected and the write enable input HIGH. Data stored in the locations specified by the address inputs is read out and appears on the data output inverter.

Bipolar RAMs use bipolar transistors arranged as flip-flops in the basic cell configuration shown below. The memory, with its multiple emitter transistors, may be bit-orga-

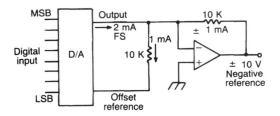

**Bipolar current-switching
D/A converter connected for offset
binary or 2's complement codes**

nized or word-organized. If it is bit-organized, only one data bit is provided for each address. In a word-organized system, the flip flops are tied together in groups to obtain the desired word length. The address decoding circuits are usually included as a part of the chip.

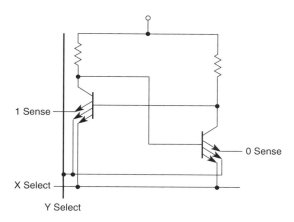

Basic TTL memory cell

bipolar ROM A read-only memory of bipolar transistors. Standard features permit the efficient use of ROM for subroutine programming. An installed ROM in some systems covers a corresponding area of main memory and contains a window into the main memory at each ROM location containing a zero data word. A read or write operation into a zero ROM location will cause an operand to be read from or written into the corresponding main memory location. In particular, subroutines can be programmed into the ROM based on the fact that return addresses are automatically stored in and retrieved from main memory when the first location of a ROM subroutine contains a zero word.

Bipolar ROMs are typically set up as 512 eight-bit words with an access time of 70 nanoseconds and are used for lookup tables, microprogram storage, code conversion, and function and character generation.

bipolar semiconductor A semiconductor device fabricated with bipolar processes. The basic processes depend on the type of logic circuit built with the process, such as TTL (transistor-transistor logic) or ECL (emitter coupled logic). All bipolar technologies are similar, being based on the formation of silicon layers with different electrical properties. The major difference is the number and sequences of diffusion operations required to manufacture the device.

bipolar transistor One of the two basic types of components that can be fabricated using inte-grated circuit technology. Bipolar devices have two types of charge carriers, while unipolar devices only have one type of charge carrier. Bipolar technologies used in microprocessors include TTL, ECL, and I²L. A cross sectional view of a bipolar transistor is shown in the following figure.

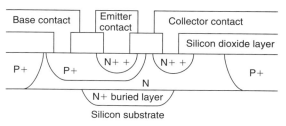

Bipolar transistor

The contacts are usually made of aluminum using an evaporation process. The buried layer is used to provide a more conductive path between the collector, base, and emitter regions. The figure shows only one transistor; a microprocessor or memory circuit would have thousands of these transistors connected together to form the logic elements required.

bipolar violation A mark that has the same polarity as the previous mark in the transmission of bipolar signals.

biquinary coding A method of coding that uses two parts of a binary code to represent a decimal number; one of the parts has the value of decimal zero or five, and the other part has the value of zero through four, as shown in the table.

Decimal	Biquinary	Decimal Interpretation
0	0 000	0 + 0
1	0 001	0 + 1
2	0 010	0 + 2
3	0 011	0 + 3
4	0 100	0 + 4
5	1 000	5 + 0
6	1 001	5 + 1
7	1 010	5 + 2
8	1 011	5 + 3
9	1 100	5 + 4

This system is used in the hand-manipulated abacus and soroban. A modified biquinary system was used in some early computers such as the IBM-650. Sometimes abbreviated *quinary*.

bistable Having the capability of assuming either of two stable states in a circuit or circuit element. A typical bistable circuit is a flip-flop or bistable multivibrator, which can store one bit of data. All computer operations are carried out by setting and resetting bistable elements. The action of bistable elements is such that if the circuit is in a stable state with a zero output, a change of the input produces a change of the output to a one state; and if it is in a stable state with a one output, a change of the input produces a change in the output to a zero state. The change in the input can be a pulse of limited duration, which allows a series of bistable elements to function as a counter or register.

bistable circuit A circuit capable of assuming either of two stable states. *Also see* FLIP-FLOP.

bistable component A component that can exist in one of two states: if the bistable component is in stable state *A*, an energy pulse will drive it to state *B*; if the bistable component is in stable state *B*, an energy pulse will drive it to state *A*. Thus, a bistable component can represent the number 0 or 1:

- Stable state A = 0
- Stable state B = 1

A group of bistable components can be used to represent any number.

bistable latch A flip-flop circuit that can be enabled to store a logical one or a logical zero. One bistable latch device is required for the storage of each bit.

bistable multivibrator An electronic circuit having two stable states, two input lines, and two corresponding output lines such that a signal exists on either one of the output lines if and only if the last pulse received by the flip-flop can store one binary digit (bit) of information. *Also see* FLIP-FLOP.

bistable relay A relay that requires two pulses to complete one cycle composed of two conditions of operation. Also referred to as a locked, interlocked, or latching relay.

bistable trigger circuit A circuit that can be triggered to adopt one of two stable states.

bisync *See* BINARY SYNCHRONOUS COMMUNICATIONS.

BIT Abbreviation for *built-in test*.

bit A blend formed from *binary digit*, a unit of information equal to one binary decision. It can be a single character in a binary number, a single pulse in a coded group of pulses, or a unit of information capacity.

When used as a unit of information capacity, the capacity in bits is equal to the logarithm to the base two of the number of possible states available. In a memory, for example, each element is capable of representing a zero or a one at any instant, and the total number of ones and zeros at any instant is the capacity of the memory.

bit-bender Slang for a computer hobbyist.

BitBlt Abbreviation for *bit boundary block transfer*, a data transfer function that moves a rectangular region of pixels within or between bitmaps. This function often is used for displaying pop-up windows, cursors, and text.

bit check A manual or machine-conducted examination of a word or bit group to verify the presence of a parity bit in its prescribed position.

bit count integrity Refers to the preservation of the precise number of bits (or characters or frames) that originated in a message or unit of time.

bit density The number of bits of digital data that can occupy a given volume or area of storage medium.

bit error rate The ratio of the number of bits incorrectly received to the total number of bits transmitted.

bit interleaving A method of time-division multiplexing in which each channel is assigned a time slot corresponding to a single bit. *Also see* TDM.

bit location **1.** A storage position capable of storing one bit. **2.** The position of a specific digit in a binary number.

bitmap **1.** A screen display in which each pixel location corresponds to a unique main-memory location accessible by the CPU. **2.** An image intended for display on this type of display system.

bitmapped A graphics term in which all bits of a display are controlled. *Contrast with* CHARACTER DISPLAY.

bitmapped font A character set in which each character is made up of a unique pattern of dots. Also called a *raster font*. *Contrast with* OUTLINE FONT.

bitmapped graphic In graphics and desktop publishing, a graphical image that is formed by rows and columns of small dots, rather than as a collection of objects. Also called a *paint*, *pixel*, or *raster graphic*. *Contrast with* OBJECT-ORIENTED GRAPHIC.

Bitnet An academic computer network that provides interactive electronic mail and file transfer services, using a store-and-forward protocol based on IBM's Network Job Entry protocols. Bitnet-II encapsulates the Bitnet protocol within IP (Internet protocol) packets and depends on the Internet to route them.

bit-oriented protocol A type of data-link control protocol that does not use control characters. The data need not even be in character form, because its nature is completely transparent to the data-link control protocol.

bit parallel A method of simultaneously moving or transferring all bits in a contiguous set over separate wires, one wire for each bit in the set.

bit parity The condition of an output group of bits when a check bit is used to parity-balance the total value for the purpose of error-checking. A specific bit is used to indicate if the sum of ones in a series of bits is odd or even. The series of bits can be a word or a series of words, and the check bit must be separated from the counting operation. In a typical system, if a 1 parity bit indicates an odd number of ones in a series, then a 0 parity bit indicates an even number of ones. If the total number of ones, including the parity bit, is always even, the system is called an *even-parity system*. If the total number of ones is odd, the system becomes an *odd-parity system*.

bit plane In a digital video display, hardware that has more than one video memory array contributing to the displayed image in real time. Each memory array is called an *image plane*, but, if the arrays have only one bit per pixel, they may be called *bit planes*.

bit position A specific location in memory, space, or time at which a binary digit occurs or is located.

bit rate The number of individual data bits processed in a given period of time (usually in one second).

bit serial A method of sequentially moving or transferring a contiguous set of bits one at a time over a single wire, according to a fixed sequence.

bit sign The value of a binary digit used to indicate the polarity of data representing a number or quantity, such as an angle. The binary digit carrying this value is called the *sign bit*.

bit slice An approach in structuring microprocessors such that the resulting microcomputers are put together using a building-block technique. A typical processor using bit-slice chips might use four 4-bit microprocessor chips. The bit-slice approach allows the user to configure the microprocessor and requires the development of a specialized instruction set during the initial design phase. For example, a 16-bit processor can be built up with two dozen or less chips. The processor consumes only about 10W of power, with an instruction time of about 1 nanosecond and a cycle time of 300 nanoseconds.

bit-slice devices Large-scale-integration components that implement some of the functions of central processing units (CPUs). Popular usage labels these components as microprocessors, but they cannot be properly classified as such, since they are not complete CPUs.

The bit-slice device is a section of an arithmetic logical unit (ALU) along with its data paths. It may include registers, the ALU, multiplexers, and buses. It does not include the control section; this part of a bit-slice system is implemented with other devices and is generally microprogrammed as shown in the figure. The complete microprocessor requires a significant number of devices that make bit-slice systems larger and more expensive than single-chip microprocessors.

The usual size for bit-slice devices is four bits. Bit slices are used for building the most powerful processors in use.

bit-slice processor An approach that allows microcomputer organizations of variable word sizes, with processor units separated into two, four, or eight bit slices on a single chip. These devices can be paralleled to yield an 8-, 12-, 16-, 24-, or 32-bit microcomputer when assembled

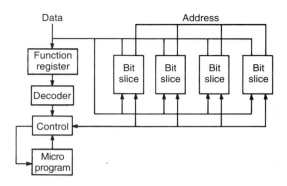

Bit-slice structure

with the other necessary components of the system. Sixteen-bit microprocessors constructed from these components can be assembled into microcomputers that perform in the minicomputer class.

bits per pixel The number of bits used to represent the color value of each dot (pixel) in a digitized image. *Also see* PIXEL.

bit stream Refers to transmission methods in which character separation is accomplished by the terminal equipment, and the bits are transmitted in a consecutive line without regard to groupings by character. The term is often used in connection with synchronous transmission and the devices operating in this mode.

Bitstream scalable typeface package A collection of font libraries. Each library in the series provides fonts of 2 to 144 points, complete character sets for European languages, and support for most laser, dot-matrix, and PostScript-compatible printers.

bit string A string of binary digits in which the position of each binary digit is considered as an independent unit.

bit stuffing See *pulse stuffing*.

bit time The time for a network to transport 1 bit of data.

BIX 1. Acronym for *binary information exchange*. **2.** Acronym for *Byte Information Exchange*, an online service from McGraw-Hill, Inc.

black box Any functional electronic unit, such as the central processing unit of a microcomputer, that converts data from one format to another or changes the data or signal in any way.

Blakbook An address-book program that allows conversion to and from dBASE, PC-File, and text files. This database program can print pocket-sized address books and mailing labels.

blank 1. A location in a storage medium (character or space) that is used to provide a method of checking the accuracy of the operations. **2.** A quartz plate.

blanking The process, and period of time when it takes place, when the beam from the electron gun in a video display is turned off. Blanking is used to prevent the beam from being visible on the screen when it resets from right to left or bottom to top of the screen; also that portion of the time that a video signal is transmitted when it is at or below blanking. These time portions can be divided into a *horizontal blanking interval* (HBI) and a *vertical blanking interval* (VBI). The blanking intervals are used for descrambling codes, text transmission, time code, and text and reference signals.

blanking level In a video signal, the signal level during the horizontal and vertical blanking intervals, typically representing zero output.

blank, switching *See* DEAD BAND.

blank transmission test In database management, a feature that allows checking of the data field for all blank positions. Used as a control measure, a blank transmission can prevent destruction of existing records in storage, indicate when the last item in a record has been processed, and instruct the computer to skip a calculation when a blank is encountered.

blastable ROM Fusible read-only memory, which provides a nondestructive memory in applications in which the contents of memory do not change.

Blinker A dynamic overlay linker for C, C++, ASM, BASIC, QuickBASIC, Fortran, Pascal, Clipper, and other languages with an integrated memory swap function to save time and memory. It uses EMS/XMS memory to save the currently executing program.

blinking An intentional, regular change in the intensity of a character on the screen.

blitter A blending of the term *bit-block transfer*, usually it is a chip that does graphics routines like drawing circles or lines, freeing the CPU to do other tasks. The CPU tells the blitter what it needs drawn, and the blitter sends the information to screen memory.

blitting Also known as *bit blitting*. The technique of moving large quantities of graphic data to the video board.

BLOB Acronym for *binary large object Borland*, a term for nontext objects in a database file.

block 1. A group of words considered as a unit. On magnetic media, a block (also called a *physical record*) is considered to be any group of words, recorded in the serial mode, that is separated by intervening blank spaces. Each block is considered to be made up of one or more records. The records can be reduced to blocks to decrease acceleration and deceleration times. 2. On magnetic tape, blocks are ten or more words in length and separated by enough blank spaces to allow the tape to start and stop accurately before read or write operations are attempted. 3. Geometric figures in block diagrams to show basic functional relationships, such as a part of a circuit or a part of a program.

block check character *See* BCC.

block delete A feature that permits selected blocks of data to be ignored or removed at the discretion of the user.

block diagram A graphic representation of any operational circuit or system in which each functional element is presented as a box or block, and the relationship of each element to other elements is depicted by connected lines depicting a hierarchy.

blockette A subdivision of a block that is treated as a unit, particularly during input and output transfer.

block gap *See* INTERBLOCK GAP.

blocking The combining of two or more records into one block.

blocking oscillator A tuned oscillator that has more than sufficient positive feedback for oscillation, but in which a condition periodically causes a suspension of normal oscillation. As the cycle is continuously repeated, it produces sawtooth and pulse waveforms. *Also see* OSCILLATOR.

blocking rights NetWare directory rights cascade to downline directories. Blocking rights are created by making a Trustee Assignment of No Rights in a downline directory. Assigning No Rights blocks the cascading rights from applying to downline directories.

block input A group of words to be transferred from external storage to internal storage (input).

block length The number of characters, bits, or words comprising a defined unit word or character group.

block marking Refers to special marks or characters for the beginning of a block of text.

block mode A mode in data transmission where the data keyed in at a terminal is stored until a particular key (such as Enter) is pressed, then all the data is sent as a block.

block move In word processing, refers to moving a block of text in one operation either with the mouse or with a keystroke combination.

block output A group of words to be transferred from internal storage to an external destination.

block parity An error-detection scheme using more than one code together, such as LRC and VRC, to permit the precise location of a single bit error within a block of data. *Also see* LRC and VRC.

block sort A sort of one or more of the most significant characters of a key to serve as a means of making workable-sized groups from a large volume of records.

block transfer The conveyance of a word or character grouping from one register or device to another.

blown fuse, polysilicon Refers to semiconductor memory in which a formed fuse is blown with a pulse train of successively wider pulses, with a current of 20–30 mA typically needed to blow the fuse. During this operation, which determines the bit pattern in the read-only memory, temperatures close to 1400°C are reached in the notch of the polysilicon fuses. At these temperatures, the silicon oxidizes and forms an insulating material. The use of silicon eliminates conductive dendrites and the existence of conductive materials in the fused gap.

blue book In networking, refers to the proprietary specifications for Ethernet issued jointly by Xerox, DEC and Intel, and now largely supplanted for new products by the IEEE 802.3 standard.

blue-ribbon Adjective used to describe a program that is handwritten and designed to run properly the first time. The blue-ribbon program is carefully written and debugged to remove all program errors before running (also known as a *star* program).

blue sheet A term sometimes used for a machine-language operator instruction sheet.

blur 1. A state of reduced display resolution. Blur can be a picture defect, as when a photograph is indistinct because it was shot out-of-focus or the camera was moved during exposure. 2. A picture improvement, as when an unnaturally jagged-edged diagonal line or jerky motion is blurred to smoothness. *Also see* ANTI-ALIASING.

BM Abbreviation for *Buffer module.*

BMT Abbreviation for *beginning of magnetic tape.*

BNC Abbreviation for *Bayonet-Neil-Concelman*, a type of connector that uses a quick-release mechanism rather than a threaded sleeve. This type of connector is widely used with coaxial cable in a LAN.

BNZS Abbreviation for *bipolar N-zero substitution*, a form of bipolar transmission in which all strings of *N* zeros are replaced with a special *N* bit sequence of bipolar violations.

board 1. A panel that can be changed by adding or deleting external wires. Also called a *jumper board, plugboard,* or *panel.* 2. A circuit board.

BOBCAT A public-domain database of small-business computer information. Reviews, tutorials, general articles, buying guides, and ads for products that apply to small businesses are listed. The database may be searched by any combination of category, subject, form, product, or company name. BOBCAT is distributed as user-supported software in PC-File format; it needs PC-File or a similar program to sort and print information in a usable format.

bode diagram A plot of log amplitude ratios and phase angle values on a log frequency base for a transfer function. This can be a control-element, output, or loop-transfer function.

bode plot A method of plotting control-element transfer functions that uses logarithms of gain or phase angles versus the logarithm of the frequency of the plotted function. For closed-loop system control, it is desirable to obtain the maximum gain while retaining control-loop stability.

The higher the gain of the system, the faster the system response and the better the control of the controlled variable.

Analysis of a closed-loop control system usually begins with an assessment of the frequency response of each component in the system. If this information is not known, frequency-response tests are conducted. From the characteristics of the frequency response, the maximum gain for loop stability can be calculated using a bode plot.

In the bode plot, the gain and phase of the control component are plotted as a function of the log frequency, as shown in the figure.

The frequency at which the phase is -180 degrees is called the *critical frequency*; the gain at this frequency must be less than one for loop stability.

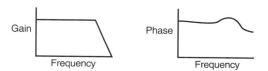

Gain and phase in a bode plot

Bode plots have the following advantages for control system analysis:

- Since logarithms are used, the expressions for gain are additive.
- For many electronic elements, the shape allows representation of the exact plot by straight-line asymptotes.
- Since the bode plot is easy to construct, it provides a convenient starting point for more complex methods of control analysis.

body text In word processing, refers to "plain vanilla" text that is not a heading, list, or other special style, and has no level assigned to it.

BOI Abbreviation for *branch output interrupt.*

boilerplate Text that is used over and over without change, such as a return address, a copyright notice, or even whole sections of papers or reports. Some word-processing programs allow boilerplate text to be stored in a separate file, often called a *glossary.*

Book One A software tool that allows PC users to create their own interactive graphics applications such as sales presentations, educational and training programs, point-of-sale and point-of-information displays, simulations and games, online tutorials, and interactive demonstrations.

bookkeeping Maintenance of accounting ledgers, either manually or by machine. Bookkeeping represents an application area for microcomputers that involves variations of inventory control and general accounting. For a general accounting operation, the typical end-products are income statements and balance sheets with supporting documents.

Boolean algebra A deductive system or process of reasoning named after George Boole, an English mathematician who lived from 1815 to 1864. This system of theorems uses symbolic logic to denote classes of elements, true or false propositions, and on-off logic circuit elements. Symbols are used to represent operators such as AND, OR, NOT, EXCEPT, IF...THEN, etc. When Boole introduced his system in 1847, one purpose was to provide a shorthand notation for the system of logic originally set up by Aristotle. Aristotle's theorems dealt with statements that were either true or false, never partially true of partially false. Boolean algebra likewise consists of single-valued functions with only two possible output states.

For a long time Boole's system lay dormant, almost forgotten; however, it is now recognized as an effective method of handling single-valued functions with two possible output states. When Boolean algebra is applied to binary arithmetic, the two states become 0 and 1; when applied to switching theory, the two states become open and closed.

The convention normally used in switching theory is 0 for an open or low state, and 1 for a closed or high state, as shown in the figure here.

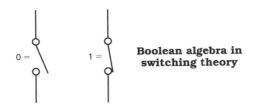

Boolean algebra in switching theory

The AND function occurs if two or more gates are placed in series; the resulting configuration is called an *AND gate*, shown in the following figure. This arrangement will transmit information if and only if all series gates are closed. The equivalent equation in Boolean algebra is as follows:

$$AB = C \ (A \text{ and } B \text{ equals } C)$$

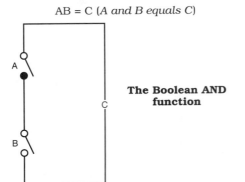

The Boolean AND function

Also, the following truth table can be written:

A	B	C
0	0	0
0	1	0
1	0	0
1	1	1

Truth table for AND function

The result is called an *OR gate*, and transmission occurs when one or more gates are closed. This is shown in the following circuit.

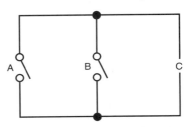

The Boolean OR function

The equivalent equation in Boolean form is

$$A + B = C \ (A \text{ or } B \text{ equals } C)$$

and the truth table is as follows.

A	B	C
0	0	0
0	1	1
1	0	1
1	1	1

Truth table for OR function

The NOT gate occurs when two gates are connected such that a single signal will close one gate while opening the other. The NOT gate forms the complement of its input; thus, a 1 on the input to the gate results in a 0 on the output, and a 0 on the input results in a 1 on the output. If the input is labeled A, the output is labeled $\overline{A}$ (referred to as A not, or not A). An entire function can be complemented. For example, if

$$A = B (C + D)$$

then

$$\overline{A} = \overline{B (C + D)}$$

The commutative and associative laws apply in Boolean algebra:

$$AB = BA$$
$$A(BC) = (AB) C = ABC$$

Some other identities are as follows:

$$1 + A = 10 + A = A$$
$$1A = A \quad 0A = 0$$
$$A(B + C) = AB + AC$$
$$A + A = A \quad A + \overline{A} = 1 \quad \overline{\overline{A}} = A$$
$$AA = A \quad A\overline{A} = 0$$

Also, De Morgan's laws, which only apply to Boolean algebra, can be verified as:

$$\overline{A + B + C + \ldots N} = \overline{A}\,\overline{B}\,\overline{C} \ldots \overline{N}$$
$$\overline{ABC \ldots} = \overline{A} + \overline{B} + \overline{C} \ldots \overline{N}$$

Boolean calculus Boolean algebra modified to include the element of time.

Boolean operator An operator (gate) used in Boolean algebra as applied to logic units of computer architecture; the result of any operation is restricted to one of two values, generally represented as 1 or 0.

Boolean variable The use of two-valued Boolean algebra to assume either one of the only two values possible. Examples are true or false, on or off, open or closed. All digital computers use two-state or two-variable Boolean algebra in construction and operation.

booster response An automatic controller technique in which there exists a continuous linear response between the rate of change of the controlled variable and the position of the final control element. Also called *rate action*.

boot To turn on the computer's operating system. If you boot from a hard disk, the basic system commands are on the hard disk, so you boot up by turning the power switch on. To boot from a floppy disk, you must insert a system or boot diskette in the floppy drive, and then switch on your computer.

boot disk A floppy disk containing the operating system that the PC uses to boot, or start, from. In LAN environments, this diskette also contains the programs needed by the PC to connect with the network.

BOOTP The *bootstrap protocol* used for booting diskless nodes.

boot record A sector at the beginning of a disk that tells DOS about the makeup of the disk and may contain a program to boot the computer.

boot sector A sector on the disk containing enough information defining the disk's layout and programming code to load the BIOS programs used to boot or start the disk.

bootstrap A technique designed to cause a circuit, stage, or operation to bring itself into a desired state by means of its own action. The name is taken from the impossible situation of a person lifting him- or herself off the ground by pulling on his or her own bootstraps. Used as a machine routine, the bootstrap technique involves loading the first few instructions into storage; these instructions are then used to bring in the rest of the routine—usually by entering a few manual instructions or by using a special keystroke combination.

bootstrap loader A program that enables users to enter data or a program into RAM from a keyboard and execute the program. The loader usually is a PROM that plugs into the system board.

border 1. A line or double line automatically connected to a paragraph of text. A border can be on the left, right, top, or bottom of a paragraph. A border can also be drawn around a paragraph. **2.** In desktop publishing, a graphical element that is repeated around the margins of a page or box.

Borland C++ A development system for applications with full support of ANSI C and C++ 2.1, a global optimizer, and templates, used for creating code in either the Windows or DOS environments. Creating Windows applications from within Windows can be done with the Windows IDE, which includes "speed bars" for quick access to common functions. The WinScope utility makes debugging easier, and the Resource Workshop allows you to visually draw Windows resources. The package includes Turbo Debugger, Turbo Profiler, the object-oriented Turbo Assembler, and other tools.

Borland C++ & Application Frameworks A software development package for creating Windows or DOS applications. It uses ready-made user interfaces that can be tied into the application with just a few lines of code. ObjectWindows for Windows or Turbo Vision for DOS can be used for user interfaces with pulldown menus, dialogs and mouse support. The package includes the Resource Workshop, Turbo Debugger, Turbo Profiler, the object-oriented Turbo Assembler, and other tools.

BOT Acronym for *beginning of tape*.

bounce The return of a piece of e-mail because of an error in its delivery.

boundary A special register that selects the upper and lower addresses for each user's memory block in a multiprogrammed system.

box 1. Any box or enclosed area that is used to represent a function, circuit, stage, or element graphically. **2.** The symbol used in flowcharting to indicate a choice or branch in the path of the flow. The diamond-shaped decision box always has one entrance line and two exit lines, or branches, as shown in the figure.

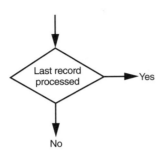

The decision-box flowcharting symbol

The exit paths are determined by a yes or no, or other comparison test. In the example given, the condition to be determined is if the last record of a stack has been processed. If the answer is yes, the program is allowed to branch away from the loop that it has been following. If the answer is no, then the processing of the records continues until completion.

bps Abbreviation for *bits per second*; for serial transmission, bps is equal to the speed at which a device or channel transmits characters. *Also see* BAUD.

BR Abbreviation for *break request*.

branch The selection of one or more paths in the flow of data or signals through a system or stage. Selection of a path is based upon some criterion that allows a decision to be reached. The instructions used to mechanize the selection are sometimes called *branch instructions*. Transfer of control and jump operations are also used in this context. In a microcomputer program, branching is done on the basis of computed results causing modification of the function or program sequence. The usual modification can be classed as either a change of the program direction or a departure from the normal sequence.

Very few programs do not take advantage of the microcomputer's ability to determine the direction that a program should take based upon intermediate results. For testing a condition and providing alternative paths for the program, microinstructions, sometimes called *conditional skip instructions*, are used.

A transfer of control can be handled in a microprocessor as follows:

```
AAA:      ; (stack address)
    .JMP BBB ; (go to BBB,
              then return)
```

Control is transferred in this sequence to BBB; when that routine is completed, control goes back to AAA, the address at the top of the stack.

branch circuit In a wiring system, the branch circuit is the portion that extends beyond the final overcurrent device that protects the circuit.

branch impedance In a passive branch, the impedance obtained by assuming a driving force across and a corresponding response in the branch, assuming that no other branch is electrically connected to the one under consideration.

branch instructions An instruction that, when executed, causes the ALU to obtain the next instruction from some location other than the next sequential location. A branch may be one of two types: *conditional* or *unconditional*.

branch-on A term used to mark indicators or switches on a control console to indicate when branching is taking place. A branch-on indicator is used to show that conditions for a particular group of registers are such that branching will occur for the next block of data. Branch-on switches are used to control the use of certain memory locations or index registers. The setting of the switch determines if the program is to branch at that location.

branchpoint The location in the program where one or more choices is selected, depending upon the character of the most recent data processed.

breadboard An initial or experimental model of a process, program, or device. Temporary arrangements of early electronic circuits used modifications of kitchen breadboards. These evolved to the many types of boards available for prototype work today, but the name held up and is still used today. Specialized breadboards are available for designing custom microcomputer interfaces. A typical board allows for data transfer over the data line using program control with or without interrupts. Board area is allowed for 14-, 16, 24-, 36-, and 40-pin integrated circuits along with discrete components. Power and ground buses are provided, as well as edge connectors for input/output cables or card interconnections.

breadboard construction A temporary arrangement of electronic components fastened to a board for experimental work.

breadboard kit A circuit kit that usually comes with an assortment of sockets for custom circuitry. A number of circuit kits allow the user to add special functions to the modular microcomputer system. Designed for insertion into a breadboard, they include a collection of parts and sockets, and full instructions.

break 1. An open circuit. **2.** An interruption that usually allows transmission from the user at the other end of the transmission system.

breakdown impedance Small signal impedance at a specified direct current in the breakdown region of a semiconductor diode. Also referred to as *avalanche impedance*.

breakdown voltage The voltage at which a marked increase in the current through an insulator or semiconductor occurs.

break-out boxes Devices designed to allow the enabling/disabling, jumpering, crossing over, and busing of interface signals. They are a standard tool for configuring nonstandard devices to function in a standard environment or to allow two DTE or two DCE devices to communicate. One of the most common uses are crossing pins 2 and 3 of the RS-232 interface to allow two terminal devices (DTEs) to communicate. DTE devices have transmit data (TX) on pin 2 and receive data (RX) on pin 3; a crossover between the two devices must be made to allow transmit data of device A to be received on the receive data of device B and vice versa. These jumpers allow devices that require these signals for operation to supply the signals to themselves merely by requesting them. Some devices provide the additional feature of connector-gender matching.

breakpoint A point in a program that allows a conditional interruption to permit visual checking, printouts, or other analysis. Breakpoints permit debugging and are usually indicated by a breakpoint flag or controlled by a breakpoint switch on the console. With a breakpoint in the program, the user has an opportunity to check, correct, and modify the program before continuing its execution.

breakpoint instruction An instruction that tells the machine to either transfer control or stop and take some special action. The breakpoint instruction is usually triggered by some specific conditions placed into the program.

breakpoint switch A manually operated switch that controls conditional operation at breakpoints, used primarily in debugging.

b-register A register that can store words used to change an instruction before it is executed by the program. The b-register (also called the *index register* or *b-box*) is sometimes used to extend the operation of the accumulator during multiply and divide operations.

Some machines use many index registers, their basic function being to add a number to part of an instruction after the instruction leaves storage on its way to the control unit and before it goes into the instruction register. The instruction entering the instruction register does not have to be identical with the one read from storage, since the contents of the index register may be added to it before it reaches the instruction register. B-registers allow changes to be made in the program just before program execution.

bridge 1. An inadvertent solder connection on a circuit board between two conductive paths. **2.** A full-wave rectifier composed of four diode legs. **3.** A circuit used in some data acquisition transducers to compensate for extreme temperatures and other error-inducing conditions. The system is derived from the Wheatstone bridge, a widely used method for the precision measurement of resistance. In strain gauge transducers used for pressure or stress measurement, a bridge circuit is required to display the small resistance change that occurs. The strain gauge is placed in one or more arms of the bridge as shown in the figure.

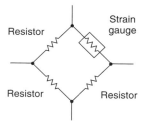

A bridge circuit

bridge circuit A circuit of elements arranged so that, when an electromotive force is present in one branch, the response of a detecting device in another branch can be zeroed by adjustment of the electrical constants of other branches.

bridge driver In NetWare, a Diagnostic Service that specifies the target bridge driver (0, 1, 2, or 3) within the target node. The target bridge drive corresponds to the target LAN board (0, 1, 2, or 3).

bridge label A hexadecimal number that the user can assign to each bridge.

bridge limiter A unit intended to prevent a variable from exceeding specified limits. A diode bridge that is used as a limiter is also called a *bridge limiter*.

bridge network *See* LATTICE NETWORK.

bridge number The bridge identifier that the user specifies in the bridge program configuration file to distinguish between parallel bridges.

bridge tap In a telephone-line local loop, a length of unused wire attached to one of the conductors (usually from an unused connection) that affects the characteristics of the line.

bridging connection A parallel connection in which some of the signal energy in a circuit may be withdrawn with little effect on the normal operation of the circuit.

bridging contacts A set of electrical contacts in which the moving contact touches two or more stationary contacts simultaneously during operation.

Brief An editor for PC programmers that features mouse support, EMS caching, re-do and undo. It allows you to program faster and more productively with multiple windows, built-in support for 42 compilers, template editing, smart indenting, search/replace, editable keystroke macros, and a C-like macro language with source-level debugger.

broadband In data communications, any bandwidth greater than the 4 kHz of voicegrade channels. Loosely, any relatively wide frequency bandwidth.

broadband LAN A local area network that handles modulated data signals, in which use of the links is shared through frequency-division.

broadband noise A noise distribution that is relatively uniform over a wide spectrum of frequencies.

broadcast To send information to all users of a particular service. An Ethernet broadcast, for example, sends an Ethernet packet to every address on the network.

broadcasting A fax board or machine's ability to transmit faxes to many destinations at once.

broadcast message A message sent from one station to all other stations on the network.

broadcast packet A packet that has a destination address that contains the hexadecimal character *F* in the entire field. All LAN protocols use this to denote that this packet is addressed (broadcast) to all workstations. All workstations process the packet and respond accordingly.

broadcast storm An incorrect packet broadcast onto a network that causes multiple hosts to respond all at once, typically with equally incorrect packets, which causes the storm to grow exponentially in severity.

broadcast television Conventional, common, television broadcasting.

broker workstation A specialized personal computer used to calculate the type and number of stock transactions a broker would need to make at a certain market price.

brouter **1.** A program on the NetWare operating system that manages Btrieve access among multiple computers. *Also see* BTRIEVE. **2.** Abbreviation for *bridge/router*, a device for forwarding messages between networks at both the network and data-link levels.

bridge/router *See* BROUTER.

BRS Abbreviation for *break request signal*.

brownout A condition where the utility company transmits low voltage.

BS Abbreviation for *binary subtract*.

BSAM Abbreviation for *basic sequential access method*.

BSC *See* BINARY SYNCHRONOUS COMMUNICATION.

Bserver A program on the NetWare operating system that retrieves data for Btrieve users. *Also see* BTRIEVE.

BSI Abbreviation for *British Standards Institute*.

BTAM Abbreviation for *basic telecommunications access method*, a technique used in IBM equipment for data communications between terminals.

b-tree An abbreviation of *binary tree*, a storage structure with a dynamic index used for environments with frequent updates to data.

Btrieve A Novell program that allows use of the btree access method to retrieve data from servers. It is a complete, key-indexed record manager design for file handling and improved programming productivity. It can be accessed from any standard programming language and allows you to create applications that will run in stand-alone or distributed environments under NetWare, DOS, OS/2, or Windows. You can also share data with Novell's other data management products.

Btrieve Developer's Kit Complete toolkit that allows developers to write applications with Btrieve, Novell's key-indexed record manager. You can write applications for either the client-server or client-only versions of NetWare Btrieve without changing data management code. It supports BASIC, C, Pascal, Fortran, Modula-2, COBOL and Assembler. Also included are development utilities for creating and manipulating Btrieve files. It is available for DOS, OS/2, and Windows environments.

bubblejet A computer printer that produces images by "spraying" droplets of ink onto the page surface. Droplets are ejected from the ink print head by heating the ink in each channel. As the ink is heated, a bubble is formed. When the bubble "pops," the ink droplet is ejected, and more ink is drawn in from the reservoir.

bubble memory A type of mass memory storage that uses nonvolatile magnetic bubbles generated from a single-crystal sheet to store data. The bubbles are generated when two magnetic fields are applied perpendicular to the single-crystal sheet. A constant field is used to strengthen the field region, and a pulsed field is used to break up the field regions into small bubbles. The bubbles are free to move within the plane of the sheet. The presence or absence of bubbles indicates a binary 1 or 0. The bubbles are created by a bubble generator in the memory and converted to electrical signals by an internal detector as the data is read. An external rotating magnetic field propels the bubbles through the film. No mechanical motion is required.

Metallic patterns, or chevrons, are deposited on the film to move bubbles in the desired direction. Transfer rates average about 20,000 bits per second. The bubbles are circulated past a pickup point where they become available to external connections and in this way the operation can be compared to a tape recorder. However, in a tape, the stored bits are stationary on a moving medium, while in a bubble memory, the medium is stationary and the bits are dynamic. If power fails, the bubbles and the data they represent are maintained in the film. When power is restored, the data is still accessible.

Reliability and ruggedness are the primary advantages of bubble memory, while cost is the major disadvantage. Bubble memories offer a high tolerance to dust and dirt, shock, vibration, temperature, and humidity; with some units, an MTTF (mean time to failure) in excess of 20 years is possible. In the early years of bubble memories, it was believed that they would eventually become less expensive per-bit than semiconductor RAM; however, the popularity of PCs dropped the cost of RAM faster than expected. Bubbles are now used mainly in military and industrial applications where the levels of heat, dust, humidity, shock, and vibration would damage floppy or hard disk drives. Bubble memories are available in the form of expansion boards or cartridges that emulate a disk drive in an IBM PC or compatible.

bubble memory operation Since the presence of a bubble is read as a one and its absence as a zero, data can be written by the selective formation of bubbles. This is accomplished by applying a weak external magnetic bias to the film, which in its normal state contains an equal mix of oppositely polarized magnetic regions. The external-bias field groups regions of opposite polarity to the field into bubbles. By lining up and moving the bubbles via a magnetic overlay around a closed loop, a type of shift register is formed in a manner like that employed by charge coupled devices (CCDs). An essential difference between bubbles and CCDs is that bubbles, being magnetic rather than electronic, are nonvolatile; their bit pattern is retained if power fails.

bubble shift registers A shift register is the simplest bubble memory application, but it is not the only type of memory that can be made using bubbles, nor is bubble technology limited to memory applications. The properties of magnetic bubbles, related to their deformation or annihilation as a function of the bias field strength, also allow switching and logic applications. *Also see* BUBBLE MEMORY.

bubble sort In database management, a technique for sorting a list of items into sequence. Pairs of items are examined, and exchanged if they are out of sequence. This process is repeated until the list is sorted.

bucket An expression used to indicate a portion of storage reserved for accumulating data or totals of information. Buckets are labeled *1, 2, 3*, etc., and are commonly used during initial system planning.

bucket brigade A continued shifting of data bits in a given direction.

buffer A device or unit that serves as an isolator or interface between two dissimilar elements. It is used to match impedances, speeds, or other characteristics while maintaining isolation between matched elements. Buffer storage involves the following:

- A synchronizing element between different forms of storage, usually internal and external
- An input device for assembly of information from external or secondary storage for transfer to internal storage
- An output device that copies information from internal storage for entry to external storage
- Any device for temporary storage during data transfer

As a register, a storage buffer serves as an intermediary storage point between two registers or data-handling systems with different access times or data formats. In a typical communications interface, buffering provides asynchronous communications between Bell 103 or 202 data sets at speeds up to 9600 baud.

buffer box A unit that provides an asynchronous communication channel with a memory buffer. A typical unit may contain two individually programmable ports with a user-allocatable buffer between the ports. It might utilize either DTR (data terminal ready) or XON/XOFF flow control. *Also see* DTR.

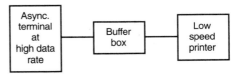

Buffer box

buffer capacitor A type of capacitor connected across the secondary of a transformer to suppress surging voltages that could cause damage to other circuit parts.

buffer circuit In a keyboard system, an electronic circuit that allows an operator to type ahead of the data output.

buffered computer A computer system that allows input and output data to be stored temporarily to match transfer speeds of the input and output devices with the speed of the computer. To accommodate a difference in speed changes, a buffer is used to accept the data at one speed, hold the data, and then release it at the required rate.

For example, a printer might be printing data at about 200 characters per second, and yet this data might be put into its buffer at a rate of several thousand characters per second. Part of the buffer operates at the higher speed and temporarily stores the data until it can transmit it at the lower speed.

Some amount of buffering is required for all input and output equipment because of the translation needed in going from one language to another. Buffers are found in a variety of equipment functions, including controllers, synchronizers, electronic amplifiers, transmitters, selectors, adapters, and communicators. They may perform time-sharing code changes, speed changes, mode changes, format changes, and checking. Format changing might include the following:

- Rearranging data
- Duplicating data
- Generating code
- Inserting and deleting data

buffered parallel-to-serial interface An interface that is available for parallel interfaces. The unit comes with a special adapter cable. Switch selections can include baud rate, word structure, and self test.

buffered serial-to-parallel interface An interface that is available to convert RS-232 serial data to parallel data. A 1K version and a 2K version are both available with either a Centronics or Data Products compatible parallel interface. Any parallel device with a compatible interface may be adapted. Switch options are provided for baud rate, word structure, busy or inverted busy, parity, XOFF/XON control, and self test.

buffered timing A form of timing used with independent clocks in which buffers compensate for the differences in clock rates between pieces of equipment.

buffering 1. A protective coating extruded directly on an optical fiber coating to protect it from the environment. **2.** Extruding a tube around the coated fiber to allow isolation of the fiber from stress on the cable.

buffering, simple A technique for allowing simultaneous input/output operations and computation. This method involves associating a buffer with only one input or output file or data set for the entire duration of the activity on that file or data set.

buffer length 1. The size, usually in kilobytes (K), of a printer or other peripheral's buffer. Most printers have expandable buffers that can be increased via a proprietary expansion board or the addition of memory chips. **2.** In NetWare, a Value-added Process Service that represents the length of an input buffer and cannot be greater than 80.

bug 1. A usually elusive error in a program, circuit, or machine. **2.** A DIP integrated circuit, so named because of the insect-like appearance of the device. *Also see* DIP.

bug patch A temporary circumvention of a program element or automatic routine through manual control. Bug patches are worked out and inserted to fix the errors. After a number of patches are made, they are incorporated into the source program, which is reassembled to complete the documentation of the changes.

building block A self-contained element that can serve as a stage or subsystem by interconnection with other such elements. This concept of construction provides an approach to system and hardware design that allows expansion of a system using a modular technique.

build-up charts In presentation graphics, a series of charts that gradually reveal more information until a complete chart is displayed.

build-virtual-machine A modeling process whereby a machine program duplicates an actual defined system configuration. A build-virtual-machine program allows the user to structure programs that will fit the limits of the memory of the actual system.

built-in check A system, usually implemented in hardware, for verifying the accuracy of information transmitted, manipulated, or stored in any part of the computer system. Also called an *automatic check*, *built-in automatic check*, or *hardware check*.

bulk encryption A process in which two or more channels of a telecommunications system are encrypted by a single unit of cryptographic equipment.

bulk memory A memory device for storing large amounts of data, such as a hard disk or magnetic tape unit.

bulletin board system *See* BBS.

bunched frame structure A TDM (time-division multiplexing) scheme in which the frame alignment signal occupies contiguous bit positions. Also called *burst frame structure*.

bundle Many individual fibers or other wires within a single cable jacket or buffer tube. Also, a group of buffered fibers or wires distinguished in some way from another group in the same cable core.

bundling The lump-sum pricing of computer equipment and software along with associated systems analysis and support services, in contrast to an "unbundled" arrangement in which each of these products or services is priced separately.

buried layer A heavily doped (N+) region directly under the N-doped epitaxial collector region of transistors in a monolithic integrated circuit used to lower the series collector resistance.

burn-in 1. The operation of an item to stabilize its failure rate. **2.** Refers to an image or pattern appearing so regularly on a computer screen that it ages the phosphor and remains as a ghost image even when other images should appear. Screensaver programs are designed to prevent this by regularly changing the image on the screen.

burst A sequence of signals counted as one unit using a specified criterion. In burst transmission, messages are stored for a time period, then released at a much faster speed for transmission. The received signals are recorded and then slowed down for the user.

burst error Errors detected in consecutive data bits on CD-ROMs, often caused by scratches, fingerprints, or other physical irritants to the disk. Burst errors cause more data loss in optical memory. Error-correction codes are designed based on the anticipated frequency and duration of burst errors.

burst frame structure See BUNCHED FRAME STRUCTURE.

burst mode A high-speed data transfer involving the movement of a continuous bit stream between devices until an interruption or completion of the stream occurs. It is a feature of Intel's microprocessors starting with the 486.

bus A circuit used as a high-traffic path for data or power transmission. A bus often is used as a common connection between a number of locations or switching points and is sometimes called a *trunk* or *trunk line*. Buses are used in microcomputers to speed data flow, and for addressing and control. A single bus can be used at different times for data, addresses, and control signals.

Multibus systems use a dedicated bus for data and another for addressing. Control may or may not be on a dedicated bus. The multibus system allows data and addresses on the same cycle without the serial delays found in a common-bus system. Some of the features found in data and address buses used to minimize package count and improve performance include the following:

- Multibus systems to eliminate multiplexing and latching
- Three-state output buffers to minimize the use of bus drivers
- Separate output-enable logic to allow bidirectional signal flow

Typical bus cycles found in microprocessors are

- Data word transfer in, followed by word transfer out
- Data word transfer in, followed by byte transfer out

Data transfer on the bus is sometimes interlocked so that communications can be independent of the length of the bus and response times. Asynchronous operation allows each device to run at maximum speed without the need for clock pulses.

Bus organization is an important part of a system's architecture. Many microcomputers use a single bus for address, data, and control information; others use a memory bus for data transfer between CPU and memory, and another bus for data transfer between the CPU and peripheral devices. A typical data bus may have 60 or more signal lines transmitting information.

The single-bus system acts as a universal interface connecting all parts of the system, while the dual bus treats the CPU as a focal point with separate interfaces to memory and peripheral units.

Buses are usually designed on some form of backplane with a bus motherboard to handle words up to 32 bits long. Bus construction requires control and power lines, variable- and fixed-frequency clocks, and connectors to peripheral devices.

Bus program counters are incorporated as counting registers on chips; one can be used for program location and another for stack counting. The counter contents are sent out on the address bus to allow the memory to fetch the correct instructions; the processor then increments the program counter after each use of the instructions.

Voltage levels and impedance at the bus interface allow rapid transmission and minimize effects due to noise. A number of units can share the bus without excessive loading. In some systems, a bus protocol allows a vectored interrupt. Device polling is not required for interrupts, which reduces processing time in cases where many devices are connected to a common bus. Usually, an interrupt vector is passed to the processor; the vector points to addresses for a new status word and the start of the interrupt service routine.

A priority structure is used to determine which device has control of the bus. Each device on the bus is assigned a priority number so that when two or more devices request use of the bus, the device with the higher priority receives control first.

A typical microprocessor bus system is shown in the figure that follows. *Also see* PCI BUS.

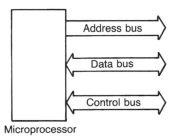

Microprocessor bus system

bus available A control line that is normally in a low state until the microprocessor stops and the address bus becomes available.

bus driver A power device designed to supply signals to all devices on a bus without signal degradation.

bus extender module A module that provides the capability to extend the bus for the purpose of signal tracing.

Business Kit A software package with two programs designed for small businesses: the Simple Bookkeeper and the Billing Statement. The Simple Bookkeeper is a single-entry bookkeeping system that tracks income and expenses for a year and produces three different reports. The Billing Statement is an intuitive, easy-to-use program for creating standard billing forms on plain or letterhead stationery. It produces two different reports. Neither of these programs requires any accounting experience.

bus interface A circuit or device designed to match a peripheral with a bus.

bus interlocked communication Data transfer on the bus can be interlocked so that communication is independent of the physical bus length and the response time of the slave device. An asynchronous operation precludes the need for synchronizing with, and waiting for, clock impulses. Thus, each device is allowed to operate at the maximum possible speed. Full words of information can be transferred on many buses between a master and a slave. The information transfer occurs when the processor, as master, is fetching instructions, operands, and data from memory, and storing the results into memory after execution of the instruction.

bus master The device controlling the current bus transaction in a bus structure in which control of data transfers on the bus is shared between the central processor and associated peripheral devices. *Contrast with* BUS SLAVE.

bus mastering Refers to a controller board taking over the bus to transfer a large block of data.

bus motherboard A connecting board that handles bus resources such as control and power supply lines, frequency clocks, and plug-in connectors with provisions for auxiliary devices.

bus mouse A mouse with a special card that you install into one of the computer's expansion slots. A bus mouse can be either mechanical or optical. *Also see* MOUSE.

bus-organized structure A structure for the input/output of data and control information. Often in these bus systems, information can flow in both directions, and generally more than one talker and listener share a single interconnecting wire. The voltage levels and impedances at the bus interface are set to allow the transmission of information with minimum errors due to noise and to allow a number of units to share the bus line without excessively loading it.

bus priority structure Since many buses may be used by processors and I/O devices, there must be a priority structure to determine which device gets control of the bus. Every device on the bus that is capable of becoming the bus master is assigned a priority. When two such devices request use of the bus simultaneously, the device with the higher priority position will receive control.

bus program counter Usually a 16-bit counting register used for program location counting. The program counter contents are sent out on the address bus for use by memory modules in fetching the appropriate instructions; the processor increments the program counter by one after each use.

bus slave The device currently receiving or transmitting data from or to the bus master in a bus structure in which control of data transfers on the bus is shared between the processor and peripheral devices. *Contrast with* BUS MASTER.

bust Slang for the bad performance of a programmer or machine operator.

bus-to-peripheral interface An interface in some systems in which the interrupt control logic has separate interrupt sections. These provide interrupt requests to the CPU through unique vector addresses. Any specific vector addresses and bus request levels can be selected using wire-wrap jumpers on the interface. An interrupt request can initiate a bus request sequence on a selected bus request line. A resulting bus grant signal then causes logic to issue a command to indicate that the interrupt sequence has begun and the interrupt request may be removed. Interrupt control logic executes the rest of the sequence, issuing control signals and causing the related vector-select signal to gate the jumper-selected address into specific data lines.

bus topology A LAN structure in which the output drivers and input receivers of every node are connected directly to a linear bus. In a bus topology, each network node is connected to a central wire. Bus topologies are often associated with the Ethernet network architecture. Peer-to-peer LANs often use this topology.

bus transceiver A type of bidirectional buffer intended for bipolar or metal-oxide semiconductor microprocessor applications. Such a device may consist of D-type edge-triggered flip-flops with a built-in two-input multiplexer on each. The flip-flop outputs are connected to four open-collector bus drivers. Each bus driver is internally connected to one input of a differential amplifier in the receiver. The four receiver differential-amplifier outputs drive four D-type latches that feature three state outputs.

busy token A unique bit pattern used in token-passing access control schemes to indicate that a data packet or message immediately follows.

bypass A shunt or parallel path around a circuit, device, or unit. A bypass filter, for example, provides a low-attenuation path around the unit to be bypassed, as in the case of a carrier-frequency filter used to bypass a telephone repeater station.

bypass capacitor A type of capacitor used for providing a low-impedance ac path around some other circuit, equipment, or device.

byte A term developed to indicate a measurable number of consecutive binary digits (bits) that are usually operated upon as a unit. Bytes of eight bits representing either one character or two numerals are most often encountered.

byte addresses Some computer words are divided into a high byte and a low byte. In most systems, the word addresses are even-numbered. The byte addresses can be either even- or odd-numbered. Low bytes are stored at even-numbered memory locations and high bytes are at odd-numbered memory locations.

byte manipulation Refers to an ability to manipulate, as individual instructions, groups of bits such as characters.

byte mode The movement of one byte at a time between devices, separated by an interrupt and the release of channel control. Used in multiplexing, the byte mode permits the handling of data from several low-speed devices simultaneously.

byte multiplexing The processing of data in sequential chunks, by the assignment of time slots to individual input/output devices. Bytes, one after another, are then interlaced on the channel going to or from the main memory.

bytes read In NetWare's File Server Environment Services API, the number of bytes a logical connection has read since the workstation logged in.

bytes written In NetWare's File Server Environment Services API, the number of bytes a logical connection has written since the workstation logged in.

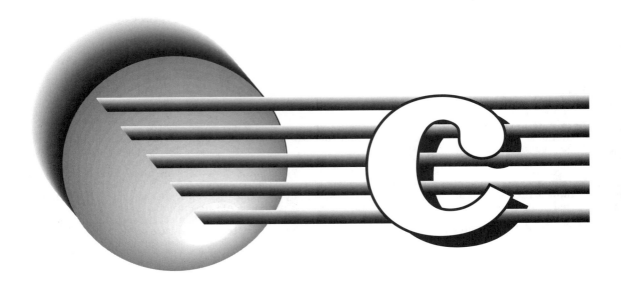

C A high-level language developed in the early 1970s. It is a general-purpose language that allows the programmer to create additional commands called *functions*.

C++ A development system based on the C language, used for creating object-oriented programs. *Also see* BORLAND C++.

cabinet An enclosure for rack-mounted equipment.

cable analyzers/testers Units that permit a cable to be attached and then tested, sometimes referred to as *CATs*. CATs are available in both bench and portable models, and provide a continuity indication with LEDs.

cable bend radius During installation, the term implies that the cable is experiencing a tensile load. *Free bend* implies a lower allowable bend radius, since it is at a condition of no load.

cable loss The amount of signal (amplitude) lost (attenuated) while it travels on a network.

cable matchers Handy tools that quickly match wrong-sex equipment or cables. They are made with back-to-back ribbon connectors, joined and made rigid with metal standoffs.

cable rack One of the many types of racks designed for holding conductors with or without connectors or terminal strips. The cable rack is particularly useful in applications where the number of input and output lines is large.

cable scanner A unit with a TDR function to locate cable faults. *Also see* TDR.

cable tester A testing tool to verify the integrity and performance of coaxial cable and twisted-pair wire.

cable through The capacity of an information system that allows multiple workstations to attach to a single cable.

cable, twisted pair A cable formed by twisting together two thin conductors, each separately insulated. This arrangement reduces their intercapacitance.

cabling The medium that connects devices on a network, or peripherals to a system unit.

cache Pronounced "cash," memory set aside in RAM for holding data that has been retrieved in anticipation of user needs. Data could be held because the user has used it earlier or because of an algorithm that predicts future needs based upon past use.

cache allocations In NetWare, a part of File Server Environment Services that shows the number of times a cache block was allocated for use.

cache block scrapped In NetWare, a part of File Server Environment Services that contains the number of times a cache block is scrapped due to the following scenario: A process was put to sleep because it needed a cache block and the least-recently used block had to be written to disk before it could be reused. When the process awoke after the block had been written and freed, the process checked and discovered that while it was asleep another process had come in, allocated a different block, and read into it the information that the sleeping process was seeking. In this case, the newly awakened process must free the cache block, and use the block that already contains the sought information.

cache buffer count In NetWare, a part of File Server Environment Services that shows the number of cache buffers in a server.

cache buffer size In NetWare, a part of File Server Environment Services that shows the number of bytes in a cache buffer.

Cache86 A small disk-cache program that uses conventional, XMS, extended, or expanded memory. On hard-disk intensive applications, it can significantly increase the speed of an older PC. In expanded memory, the cache driver uses less than 1K of conventional memory. Cache86 is compatible with Windows, DOS 5.0 or higher, DR DOS, and SCSI drives, and can be loaded high with memory managers.

cache full write requests In NetWare, a part of File Server Environment Services that shows the number of times the cache software was instructed to write information that exactly filled one or more sectors.

cache get requests In NetWare, a part of File Server Environment Services that shows the number of times the cache software was requested to read information from the disk.

cache hit on unavailable block In NetWare, a part of File Server Environment Services that shows the number of times a cache request could be serviced from an available cache block but the cache buffer could not be used because it was in the process of being written to or read from disk.

cache hits In NetWare, a part of File Server Environment Services that shows the number of times cache requests were serviced from existing cache blocks.

cache misses In NetWare, a part of File Server Environment Services that shows the number of times cache requests could not be serviced from existing cache blocks.

cache partial write requests In NetWare, a part of File Server Environment Services that shows the number of times cache software was instructed to write information that did not exactly fill a sector.

cache read requests In NetWare, a part of File Server Environment Services that shows the number of times the cache software was asked to ready data.

cache write requests In NetWare, a part of File Server Environment Services that shows the number of times the cache software was asked to write data.

CA-Clipper An application development system for PCs offering network support, user-extensibility, a replaceable database driver, and executable file generation. It is an open architecture system with a robust language, preprocessor, compiler, linker, virtual memory manager, editor, and debugger. It allows the development of applications that are larger than available memory.

CA-Cricket Draw A Mac program designed to assist artists and graphic designers in creating camera-ready art. A range of special effects is provided, including *fountains* (graded tints from 1% to 100% in 1% increments) and shading. Advanced text-handling functions offer full rotation, tilting, and placement of text on any path. Drawing tools include Bezier curves, gradient fills (linear, logarithmic, and radial), polygons, and more. A PostScript editor is provided.

CA-Cricket Graph A Mac program for making presentation-quality graphs. The program handles data sets of up to 100×2700 elements; produces special polar, double-Y, and quality-control charts; and creates column, stacked column, bar, pie, area, line, scatter, linear, logarithmic, and semi-log graphs. The graphs can incorporate scientific notation, including double-precision floating point notation.

CAD Acronym for *computer-aided design*, a technique for using the computer for drawing and problem-solving in architecture, engineering, systems design, and other technical fields. CAD techniques are used whenever conventional design methods prove excessively time-consuming.

Several CAD programs are available for the design of integrated circuits, including ECAP, NET-1, CIRCUS, PREDICT, NASAP, and SCEPTRE, all of which handle lumped-parameter elements. Depending on the external construction of the device, sometimes frequency-response characteristics can be used to describe a device accurately. The response characteristics are obtained experimentally without regard to the internal structure of the device. This is known as the *black-box method*, and it offers the following advantages for integrated circuit design:

- The model is able to accept experimental or analytical data.
- The complete circuit is enclosed in a black box for repetitive analysis of a complete system.
- Model parameters can be lumped or distributed.
- Problem-solving can be done in sections using small computers.

CADPO Abbreviation for *communications and data processing operation*.

CADpower A drawing package designed for creating architectural designs, technical drawings, office layouts, or line drawings that can be combined with text to form illustrated reports or documentation. It can be used for just about any type of report that includes both drawings and text. CADpower is popular in Europe, where it goes by the name of *Doodle*. This name, picked with the familiar British understatement, implies the product's ease of use.

A complete set of commands is available for creating and manipulating drawings. Using cursor keys, a mouse, or a digitizer tablet, you draw by adding shapes such as lines, arcs, arrowheads, grids, parallel lines, and filled areas. Six different line types are available with a choice of color and width. Shapes may be manipulated either individually or in groups by using commands such as move, scale, rotate, repeat, mirror, shear, stretch, and fill. You can zoom in or out to see either greater detail or a drawing overview. Text may be added in a choice of five different fonts and manipulated by choosing text direction, justification, character width, height, rotation and slant. Up to 199 layers may be used, with shapes assigned to specific layers. *Layers* are similar in concept to transparent sheets superimposed one upon another. By turning layers off or on and by manipulating individual layers, it is easy to accomplish what-if scenarios with different designs.

Although CADpower is command-driven, its commands are mnemonic for ease of learning. Commands may be sequenced as macros that are executed automatically, a useful feature for automating repetitive drawing operations, creating dynamic (moving) displays, or automating printing of a sequence of drawings. CADpower supports many popular printers and plotters. When drawings are combined with word processor documents, output is available on dot-matrix printers only.

C Adventure An adventure game written in the C programming language. Not only can the game players have fun, but hackers can make changes to suit their interests. It features a fairly good English parser, and can save or restore a game in progress.

cafeteria plan A series of options that can be selected on an individual basis rather than as a whole.

cage, card game A unit that recesses the circuit card frame. It may be equipped with wings for 19-inch rack mounting. The system cage may also include a hinged front door panel for mounting controls and indicators. Some card cages are designed with extended depth to accommodate a middle component chassis allowing special components to be mounted within the standard chassis. *Also see* CARD CAGE.

CAI Abbreviation for *computer-aided instruction*, the use of a computer to assist in the instruction of students. CAI systems may involve a dialog between the student and the computer that informs the student of errors and offers guidance.

CAL Abbreviation for *Cornell Aeronautical Laboratory*.

CALC (DB) Extends CA-Clipper 5.0 dialect to include spreadsheet and calculation capabilities.

calculator 1. A data processor especially suitable for performing arithmetical operations that requires frequent intervention by a human operator. **2.** A device for carrying out logic and arithmetic digital operations of any kind. Data and instructions are usually, but not always, inserted manually. A calculator can be used with a microcomputer, or a microcomputer can be used as a calculator. Early digital machines were used primarily for calculations and were considered special-purpose calculators.

Present-day calculators are small, highly specialized computers with a memory structure composed of a fixed and variable section. The fixed section is in the form of a ROM and provides the control for changing instructions in a limited fashion, called *firmware*. This contrasts with general-purpose computers programmed by software and random logic systems that use hard-wired circuitry.

The simple four-function calculator can be used to do advanced operations such as square roots, squaring, summing of products and quotients, trigonometric calculations and exponents. This is done by altering the order of computations and adding a few extra steps.

The scientific programmable calculator is typically used for complex scientific and engineering problems. These units can be used as portable scratchpads for problem-solving and typically have a 10-digit display that operates in scientific notation. Results are computed in degrees or radians, and some calculators have 15 or more scientific functions, including trigonometric, inverse trigonometric, hyperbolic, exponential, and logarithmic. Some units offer 64 or more steps or programming using eight or more registers. Decimal points systems supported include floating-point and exponential with scientific notation to 10^{99}.

Calculators typically operate in a sequential mode, working on one program step at a time. Following power-on initialization, the input data is strobed through a multiplexer as fast as the system clock will allow. Numbers representing one of the four functions are entered in a similar manner; at the conclusion of the equation, a number representing the equals operation is entered. The output is then provided either to a display or as latched outputs to external equipment.

calculator chip An integrated circuit dedicated to calculator use. A typical calculator chip might have the following characteristics:

- Five basic math functions (+, −, ×, ÷, %)
- Eight-digit display
- Percent discount and percent add-on calculations
- Memory with automatic accumulation
- Algebraic keyboard with full chaining
- Automatic constant factor on five functions
- Floating decimal mode with decimal wrap-around on overflow
- Automatic power-on clear with leading zero suppression
- Square root, entry, percentage mark-up, and percentage difference calculations
- Register exchange, change sign, and fixed decimal point with 5/4 rounding
- Conversion of liters/gallons, kilograms/pounds, and centimeters/inches

calculator circuit test unit A unit designed to test calculator chips. It will reject devices on the basis of failures in substrate continuity, logic functions, input or output tests, power drain, and bounce delay. Data for test voltages, limits categorization, input stimuli, and output results are stored in a random-access memory. To minimize setup time, plug-in units containing the device adapter, pin assignment, level shifting, and special circuitry required for a particular device can be used. Test programs are generated and edited by means of a separate keyboard unit.

calculator I/O Refers to a specific I/O circuit used in calculators that provides a general-purpose time/impedance buffer between the MOS instruction/data bus and TTL logic signals.

calculator, remote Refers to the use of a desk calculator that can access online computing services. In a time-sharing system, the terminal can be a remote calculator that provides direct, remote access to the computer. Remote connections can be made via standard telephone channels, through the common user dial networks. Answers are shown on the remote calculator display panel.

calculator terminal A desktop calculator with microcomputer-compatible inputs and outputs, designed for interactive computations. Terminals designed around desktop calculators can handle such applications as inventory control, order processing, payroll, and account maintenance with the help of the BASIC language.

Other desktop calculators allow time-sharing for many users from their home or office. Remote connections are made through standard telephone channels, and the remote keyboard has all the functions and symbols required for the application. Answers are flashed back to the remote display, and many features of powerful minicomputers are available as options.

Calculators are also used to communicate calculated data directly to large batch computers for additional processing and storage. The batch computer can then send a final message based on the data for display at the calculator. The batch terminals are usually used in an organization where centralized processing stations are required and large amounts of data are transferred between two or more points.

A typical calculator terminal may have the following characteristics:

- 2000 bps transmission speed, with ranges from 1200 to 9600 available
- Half-duplex mode, with full-duplex available
- 80-column or 32-column display width

calendar age Age measured in terms of time since the object was manufactured.

calendar life That period of time, expressed in days, months, or years, during which an item can remain installed in an operating environment and be expected to perform satisfactorily and reliably. The item should be removed at the expiration of the designated time for repair, overhaul, or other maintenance action.

calendar of conversion A schedule prepared for the implementation of a new or different system.

calibration accuracy The limit of error in the finite degree to which a device can be calibrated. It is influenced by sensitivity, resolution, and repeatability of the device itself and of the calibrating equipment. Usually it is expressed in as a percent of full scale.

call To bring a computer program, routine, or subroutine into effect, usually by specifying the entry conditions and jumping to an entry point.

calling macro A macro that calls or invokes another macro during its execution.

calling sequence The basic set of instructions used to begin, initialize, or transfer control to and return from a subroutine.

call scheduling In telecommunications, a software option of scheduling a fax or other transmission to be sent at a specific time.

CAM 1. Acronym for *content-addressable memory*, a special type of RAM in which the addresses of data can be retrieved on command. Programming is usually done by writing into the unit using a separate addressing and control line. CAM also allows a normal read/write across rows, which makes it useful for applications requiring quick data searches, correlation checking, and sorting. The higher cost and low bit densities of CAM means it has limited applications. Costs are high compared to conventional RAM because of the additional space needed for the equal-access system and the additional pins required for the dual control system. Fast CAMs find application in large virtual-memory systems or in applications like airline reservation systems, where searching for items like flight numbers, destinations, and departure times makes up a large part of the processing task. **2.** Acronym for *computer-aided manufacturing*.

CAM-cache memory In some systems, when the CPU requests a word from memory, it checks a CAM (content-addressable-memory) for the location of the data. If the word is already in cache, it is sent to the CPU. If not, it is retrieved from main memory and sent through the cache to the CPU. Simultaneously, the cache is loaded with the addressed word plus the words from the adjacent memory locations. Because programs tend to be sequential in nature, the next location requested is likely now to be in cache. If requested, that word will then be transmitted to the CPU. In some systems, each memory board contains its own local cache, so the ratio of cache to memory remains constant no matter how many memory boards are used. This allows easy memory expansion.

camcorder A camera-recorder used to add motion video to multimedia presentations. An add-in card external device converts the recorded material from analog to digital format. There are dozens of camcorders from which to choose, but some lend themselves more easily to the needs of multimedia producers.

The type of camcorder is defined by the videotape format it uses: 8mm is adequate, but Hi-8 has better quality. Other formats are used for professional-level quality, like NTSC broadcasts. Some camcorders can also be used for still-images because of their snapshot function, which allows the user to freeze and capture a single frame of video. Other camcorders are designed for videoconferencing.

camp-on A PBX or LAN operation that allows a caller (user) to wait on line if the called station is busy.

CAN The cancel character instruction, which is used to indicate data that is in error and should not be accepted.

cancel To stop or abort a process or selection in progress.

cancel hold amount In NetWare, a part of Accounting Services that should be the same as the amount specified in the corresponding Submit Account Hold call. If no Submit Account Hold call was made prior to providing the service, the hold amount should be zero.

CANCL A status word used to indicate that the remote system has deleted information previously transmitted.

canned cycle A preset sequence of events (hardware or software) initiated by a single command.

cannibalization A maintenance modification or repair method in which the required parts are removed from one system or assembly for installation on a similar one.

cannot cancel ECBs In NetWare, a part of Diagnostic Services API that is the number of times (since IPX was loaded) that IPX has been unable to find and cancel an event control block. *Also see* IPX.

cannot find route In NetWare, a part of Diagnostic Services that is the number of times (since IPX was loaded) that IPX has been unable to find a route to a requested network address. *Also see* IPX.

Canvas A draw program that allows you to create drawings using an unlimited number of layers. You can use color objects, bitmaps, or text in one of 16.7 million colors. You can also create multipoint Bezier curves, specify gray levels in 1% increments or customize arrowheads with auto-dimensioning on lines or arches. *Also see* DRAW PROGRAM.

capacitance The property that permits the storage of electrically separated charges when potential differences exist between the conductors. The capacitance of a capacitor is the ratio between the electric charge that has been transferred from one electrode to the other and the resultant difference in potential between the electrodes. The value of this ratio depends on the magnitude of the charge.

$$C \text{ (farad)} = \frac{Q \text{ (coulomb)}}{V \text{ (Volt)}}$$

capacitive pressure transducers A device that converts one quantity into another quantity, specifically when one of the quantities is electrical. A capacitive pressure transducer employs a metal diaphragm, with a metal plate positioned on one side of the diaphragm. Deflection of the diaphragm changes the capacitance between it and the fixed plate. An ac signal across the plates is used to sense the change in capacitance, or the capacitance change is used to alter the frequency of an oscillator circuit.

The advantages of a capacitive transducer are its small size, high-frequency response, and high temperature operation. It has the ability to measure both static and dynamic quantities. Shortcomings are a sensitivity to temperature variations, high impedance output, and complexity of associated circuitry. Capacitance transducers must be reactively as well as resistively matched. Long lead lengths and loose leads can cause a variation in capacitance. It is usually necessary to locate a preamplifier very close to the transducer.

capacitor 1. An electronic component consisting of two metal plates separated by a nonconductor. Also referred to as a *condenser*, but capacitor is the preferred term. A capacitor consists of two conductors, *A* and *B*, each having an extended surface exposed to that of the other, but separated by a layer of insulating material called the *dielectric*. The dielectric is designed so the electric charge on conductor *A* is equal in value but opposite in polarity to the charge on *B*. The two conductors are usually called the *electrodes* or *plates*.

capacitor storage A device that uses the electric field in an insulator held between conductive plates to store digital or analog data. Also called *condenser storage*.

capacity The measurement of computer storage, usually in terms of megabytes.

capture in progress In NetWare, a part of Print Services that is a flag set when the first character is sent to the specified LPT device. The flag is cleared when the capture is ended, canceled, or flushed.

Carbon Copy A data communications software package that allows you to control a remote PC. Carbon Copy Plus has a background file transfer capability and a "universal graphics translator" function that supports CGA, EGA, VGA, SVGA, Hercules, and PS/2 Model 30 Extended CGA graphics cards. There is also an advanced and novice user mode, error-checking to verify keystrokes, moving "chat windows," terminal emulation (VT-100, VT-52, TVI-920, and IBM 3101), ability to access remote mainframes and minicomputers, password and call-back security, access to local area networks, remote printing, data compression, Xmodem and Kermit telecommunications protocols, and backward compatibility.

carbon set A multi-ply form manufactured with carbon paper interleaved between the original and tissue copies. Only impact printers (usually dot matrix) can be used to print a carbon set.

card 1. (*o.t.*) An information storage medium of paper stock. Data was typically stored in the form of magnetic ink characters or punched slots in ordered positions on the card face. Such cards were typically 3¼ × 7⅜ inches. 2. A plug-in circuit board containing printed-circuit connections and components. Circuit cards are designed to hold the integrated-circuit packages and other components that make up the electronics of a functioning microcomputer system.

card address backplane A microcomputer's printed, card-connecting plane, which serves as the bus and assigns an address to each card or module. Users can assemble nearly any combination of memory and interfacing modules, plug them into the standard backplane, and still have a system that requires no hard wiring.

card cage The structure that holds the various printed-circuit cards required by the microcomputer. The card cage includes one or more output connectors and may be prewired to hold a minimum number of circuit cards such as the CPU, memory, and output controller. Expansion is allowed by connecting card cages together. The card and card cage system are modular in design, offering

- Simple assembly
- Easy access for checkout and troubleshooting
- Choice of output connections

card chassis A chassis designed to accommodate circuit cards or boards.

card deck (*o.t.*) A pack of punched cards.

card frames A connector and guide assembly for printed-circuit cards. Up to 40 cards may be mounted with some card frames. Frames can be supplied assembled with connectors, with bused power terminations with connectors, and with bused power terminations with connector options.

card hopper (*o.t.*) That part of a punched-card processing machine that held the card deck during processing. The card *hopper* held the cards to be processed, and a card *stacker* typically held the cards that had been processed.

card modules, microprocessor The functional modules that are provided on printed wiring cards, such as the following:

- *CPU module*, comprising the central processing unit, bus interface logic, and sockets for ROM and RAM.
- *Memory modules*, which may contain memory timing and control logic as well as storage chips.
- *Interface modules* containing the interfaces needed by the system. There may be one card devoted to each interface function.
- *Protyping cards*, blank cards that are generally drilled to accept wirewrap pins and sockets. These cards are used for the development of special interfaces and other nonstandard circuits.

Carets & Cursors A Windows utility from Instant Replay Corporation for improving visibility of both the mouse cursor and the keyboard caret. It comes with a large library of creative, "designer" carets and cursors, all menu-selectable. The library can be expanded and customized with any resource toolkit.

carriage The control mechanism for a typewriter or printer, which is usually automatically controlled for such operations as paper feed, spacing, skipping, and ejecting. The term *carriage* was assigned in the typewriter's early days, when the sheet being typed upon was physically carried back and forth in front of a stationary impact printer.

carriage return The keystroke operation that causes the next character in a series to be printed at the first position on the next line, usually by pressing the Enter or Return key.

carriage-return character *See* CR.

carriage width In a printer, the width of paper that can be fed through, measured in columns. An 80-column printer accepts paper up to 8½ inches wide, and a 132-column printer accepts 11-inch or 14-inch wide paper.

carrier A radio-frequency signal of a specific wavelength, usually modulated with frequency or amplitude variations that represent intelligence to be conveyed.

carrier board A circuit board that offers the versatility of modular construction. The basis of the system is a carrier board with supporting chip sets for onboard RAM capacity, and the interface to an I/O module which carries the fixed disk and standard floppy disk controllers. The I/O module may also include two serial ports and a Centronics-compatible parallel printer port. The carrier board has provisions for adding "personality modules" to define the processor characteristics of the system.

carrier detect An RS-232 interface modem signal that indicates to the attached terminal that the modem is receiving a signal from a remote modem. Same as *received line signal detector*.

carrier detection In telecommunications or networking, refers to monitoring the channel to determine if a carrier signal is present. Also called *sensing* or *carrier sense*.

carrier, exalted Refers to the addition of a synchronized carrier before demodulation, to improve linearity and to reduce the effects of fading during transmission.

carrier frequency The frequency of the modulation signal.

carrier noise Noise that is produced by variations of a radio frequency signal in the absence of any intended modulation. Also referred to as *residual modulation*.

carrier sense *See* CARRIER DETECTION.

carrier-sense multiple access with collision detection *See* CSMA/CD.

carrier system A means of obtaining a number of channels over a single circuit or path by modulating each channel with a different carrier frequency and demodulating at the receiving point to restore the signals to their original form.

carrier transmission A communications system in which a signal of one frequency (the carrier) may be modulated by signals of other frequencies to convey intelligence over many channels. The signals are demodulated at the receiving end to recover the original information signals.

carrier wave The basic frequency or pulse repetition rate of a signal with no intrinsic intelligence. It is modulated by another signal that does have intelligence. The carrier may be amplitude-, phase-, or frequency-modulated.

carry The operation required when the sum of two digits equals or exceeds the base of the number being used as in adding:

$$\begin{array}{r} 1110 = 14 \\ +\ 1010 = 10 \\ \hline 11000 = 24 \end{array}$$

Four carry operations are required for this addition in binary notation. A carry within a computer results in a forwarding or transferring of the digits to a new digit place. When a carry into a digit place results in an additional carry and the normal adding circuit is bypassed, the carry is called a *high-speed* or *standing-on-nines carry*. If the normal adding circuit is used, a *cascaded carry* results, which produces a partial sum numeral and a carry numeral; these are added together until no new carries are produced.

The *partial carry* results from forming the partial product during multiplication. If the partial carry is propagated to completion, a *complete carry* results. The *end-around carry* occurs in multiplication and other operations, such as the addition of two negative numbers in nines-complement notation. In subtraction operations, a carry results when the difference between the digits is less than zero. This type of negative carry is usually called a *borrow*.

carry-complete The signal used by parallel adders to indicate that all carries have been generated and propagated to completion for an addition operation.

carry look-ahead generator A unit used in some systems to provide a fast carry in arithmetic operations, considerably improving system throughput.

carry time The time required to perform a carry operation. The carry time consists of the time required to transfer a carry digit to a higher position and add it, or the time required to transfer all the carry digits to higher positions and add them to all the digits in the number.

Cartesian coordinates A coordinate system in which the position of a point can be defined with reference to a set of axes at right angles to each other.

cartridge A container of magnetic tape, usually self-contained and generally larger than a tape cassette.

cartridge fonts Fonts that are permanently encoded on cartridges that plug into the printer. Also known as *hard fonts*.

CAS 1. Abbreviation for *code activated switch*, an asynchronous RS-232C device designed to switch, under code control, a master port among four subordinate ports, as shown in the figure. The master device (a CPU or terminal) can select any of the four other ports by transmitting the proper arming and switching code. The CAS can also be set up to additionally allow any of the subordinate devices to select the master device. The CAS permits locking out any further channel changes with a special locking/unlocking character. **2.** Abbreviation for the Intel/DCA (Digital Communications Associates) *communications application specification*.

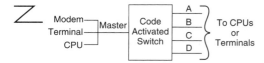

Code-activated switch

cascade connection Refers to two or more similar components or devices arranged in tandem; the output of one device is connected to the input of the next.

cascade control An automatic operations-controlling system in which control units are linked in such a way that each element regulates the input of the next succeeding unit.

cascaded bridges Refers to several bridges linked together in a sequential order.

case The form of a letter of the alphabet, either capital (uppercase) or small (lowercase).

CASE Acronym for Computer-Aided Software Engineering or Computer-Aided Systems Engineering, the use of computers to assist, perhaps ultimately to automate, all phases of the software development process.

The traditional programmer's toolkit—editor,

compiler, debugger, and version control (make) utility—are the very simplest form of CASE, the alternative being to create programs directly in machine code by hand. The thrust of "CASE" as the term is used today, however, is toward applying software tools to all phases leading up to the actual writing of the program, and the maintenance of it afterwards. Full CASE implementation also encompasses computer-assisted documentation, not only generation of the end-user manuals, but also maintenance of internal records of the software project as it evolves.

case-sensitive, case-insensitive Refers to whether it matters if letters are typed upper- or lowercase. For example, if a user wants to search for the acronym "CAD" in a document, as opposed to "cad," he or she would need to use a *case-sensitive* search string.

CASE:PM for C, C++, or COBOL A tool for developing OS/2 Presentation Manager applications in standard languages. CASE:PM includes a high-level prototype to visually design the GUI (graphical user interface) of the application. CASE:PM generates the exact C, C++, or COBOL source code framework required for the prototyped interface. Programmers integrate their application logic into the code generated by the CASE:PM. No runtimes are required.

CASE:W Corporate Edition for OWL A code generator for Borland's ObjectWindows C++ library that cuts the time it takes to learn and develop Windows applications. CASE:W CE for OWL includes a WYSIWYG designer that allows the programmer to "draw" the interface of a Windows application and generate the Windows GUI code in Borland C++. CASE:W generates fully documented, expert-level C++ code. This tool is highly recommended for developers new to Windows programming.

CASE:W Knowledgebase for C An add-on to the CASE:W Corporate Edition of OWL or MFC code generator. The CASE:W C Knowledgebase enables CASE:W to generate expert-level C code using the traditional Microsoft Windows C API, and is compatible with CASE:W CE 4.0 or later.

cassette A magnetic-tape housing that contains a tape of a specific length. The cassette includes the supply reel, take-up reel, head pressure pad, and a slot for the capstan drive.

cassette diagnostic A test for the functions of a cassette controller.

Casual.lib A software library that allows you to fax from within CA-Clipper programs. The routines in this library let the user fax any number of telephone numbers at any desired time; track when a fax is sent and the phone time used; continue working while fax processing is done in background; and set page size, font size and resolution for each fax. A fax card supporting the CDA/Intel CAS interface, like Intel SatisFAXtion, is required.

CAT 1. Acronym for *computer of average transients*. 2. Acronym for *computer-aided testing*. 3. Acronym for *cable analyzer/tester*.

catalog *See* DIRECTORY.

catastrophic failure A change in the operation of an item resulting in a complete lack of useful performance of the item.

catenate To join two strings of text together end-to-end.

cathode ray The stream of negatively charged particles (electrons) normally emitted from the surface of the cathode in a rarefied gas.

cathode-ray tube *See* CRT.

CATV Abbreviation for *community antenna television*, a method of delivering television by taking signals from a central antenna and delivering it to homes via a coaxial cable network. These same components can be used for a broadband LAN.

C-axis Part of the standard coordinate system that coordinates a moving tool with respect to a stationary workpiece. C is an angle defining rotary motion around the Z-axis. Position C is in the direction to advance a right-handed screw in the + direction.

CAW Acronym for *channel address word*, the instruction that selects a specific device on a dataphone digital service (DDS) communications line. The communication channel uses a T-1 protocol. Each T-1 line normally carries 24 channels of digitized information. Also, a computer instruction that selects a specific channel for the next address in a multiprocessing system.

CBT Abbreviation for *computer-based training*, software where people type answers to training questions provided by the software's interactive window and get immediate feedback on their choices.

CC 1. Abbreviation for *carriage control*. 2. Abbreviation for *code converter/speed converter*, a unit that can be programmed, via EPROMs (erasable programmable read-only memory), to convert almost any common data code to another, bidirectionally. Conversion tables that already exist include Transcode, EDCDIC, ASCII, and Baudot.

C-Call Caller/Called Software that can be used to produce a tree diagram to show the caller/called hierarchy of functions within a collection of C or C++ files. It also produces a function-versus-files table of contents, and creates summaries and detailed cross-references of function definition and usage.

CCD Abbreviation for *charge-coupled device*, a memory medium that uses carrier movement between potential wells to store digital information. The carriers are stored in the potential wells under electrodes biased in the depletion mode. Pulsing of the electrodes moves the carriers from one electrode to the next. The electrodes are located very close to each other in order to allow the potential wells to couple and move the carriers between them. Two types of structures are used in CCDs:

- The surface-channel type, which uses the surface of the substrate for storage and data transfer
- The buried-channel type, which uses both the surface and the bulk of the material for storing and transferring data

The primary differences between the surface channel and buried channel are that the surface channel has a higher total charge carrying capability, a lower charge transfer efficiency at extremely high charge transfer rates, and a simpler fabrication process. Charge transfer efficiency is defined as the percentage of the total charge packet (data) that is actually shifted or transferred per shift. The efficiency is typically greater than 99.9 percent per shift.

CCDs offer high speed, high packing density, and low power requirements. Experimenters have operated CCD shift registers at frequencies greater than 100 MHz; however, their useful range for memories is probably closer to 10 MHz, since the peripheral units are usually in that range.

A CCD memory simulates the operation of a rotating drum signal in the absence of any intended modulation. This is also referred to as *residual modulation*.

CCIRN Abbreviation for *Coordinating Committee for Intercontinental Research Networks*, a committee that includes the United States FNC and its counterparts in North America and Europe. Co-chaired by the executive directors of the FNC and the European Association of Research Networks (RARE), the CCIRN provides a forum for cooperative planning among the principal North American and European research networking bodies.

CCITT Abbreviation for *Consultative Committee for International Telegraphy and Telephony*, an international consultative committee that sets communications standards.

CCITT V.21 *See* V.21.
CCITT V.22 *See* V.22.
CCITT V.23 *See* V.23.
CCITT V.24 *See* V.24.
CCITT V.26 *See* V.26.
CCITT V.27 *See* V.27.
CCITT V.28 *See* V.28.
CCITT V.29 *See* V.29.
CCITT V.32 *See* V.32.
CCITT V.42 bis *See* V.42 BIS.
CCITT X.25 *See* X.25.

C-Clearly Software that formats C programs to your personal or corporate style. C-like templates are included for several common styles. Listings can also be created with optional highlights, line numbers, flow lines, and headers and footers. It automatically processes files and preprocessor statements.

CCM 1. Abbreviation for *constant current modulation*. **2.** Abbreviation for *controlled carrier modulation*.

C-CMT Comment Blocks Software that creates a comment block for each function, showing each function and the identifier usage within it. It can automatically insert these comment-blocks back into the source code at the beginning of each individual function. It can then be re-run at a later date, and will update its comment-blocks, while leaving any user-generated comments alone.

C Communication Toolkit Software that features a C and C++ communications library for Microsoft Windows development. It adds communications to Windows applications in the following protocols: ASCII, Xmodem/CRC/1K, Kermit, Ymodem, Ymodem-g and Zmodem. It has flow control and support for Hayes compatibles, Telebit, and Racal-Vadic modems.

C connector A type of bayonet-locking connector for coaxial cable.

CCR Abbreviation for *central control room*.

CD Abbreviation for *compact disc*.

CDC 1. Abbreviation for *command and data handling console*. **2.** Abbreviation for *code directing character*.

CDCE Abbreviation for *central data conversion equipment*.

CD-I Abbreviation for *compact disc interactive*, a compact disc format that includes the capabilities of reflective optical videodiscs in the 4.75-inch compact-disc medium, or features of the compact disc-interactive format, plus full-screen, full-motion video. Also called *CD-IV* (compact disc-interactive video).

C-DOC Software that allows automated documentation of C and C++ programs. C-DOC is a set of tools which need no source code changes, and which produces ASCII output files for a printer or word processor. These tools save time in documentation and debugging, since they produce documentation automatically. C-DOC is an integrated version of five component programs: C-CALL, C-METRIC, C-REF, C-LIST, and C-CMT. The C-DOC program comes with both a DOS and a protected-mode OS/2 version.

CDP Abbreviation for *checkout data processor*.

CD-R Abbreviation for *compact disk, recordable*, a drive that allows you to master and play your own audio, video, or data CDs. Double-speed CD-R drive mechanisms record a disc in about 30 minutes. CD-R can be used to create final multimedia titles for small production runs, to premaster and test CD-ROMs before a large run, and to archive data.

Drives should support multisession recording. The hard disk feeding the CD-R drive must be fast and maintain a steady rate; if the rate shifts, the resulting disc becomes useless. Some CD-R drives can also serve as ordinary CD-ROM drives for playback.

Software that supports multiple formats, including ISO 9660, High Sierra, HFS for Macs, and Red Book audio (for audio CDs), is important for multimedia developers. Other formats such as CD-I, Kodak Photo CD, and mixed mode are usually options. Those developing master discs for large runs need DAT disc-image support to put a disc's image (its content and file structure) on tape. CD pressing plants expect the master to be in DAT or Exabyte format. *Also see* WORM.

CD-ROM Acronym for *compact disc read-only memory*, a compact disk standard intended to store general-purpose digital data for personal computers. It provides 556M of storage at 10^{-13} corrected BER, compared with 635M at 10^{-9} for the audio CD standard. Also known as the *Yellow Book standard*.

CD-V Abbreviation for *compact disc-video*.

CEIP Acronym for *communications electronics implementation plan*.

cell The input box in a spreadsheet. Cells can be filled with labels, numeric values, or formulas.

cell animation A moving picture produced by displaying a series of complete screen images in rapid succession.

cell relay Refers to several bridges linked together in a sequential order.

cellular cable A type of cable that puts more conductors into less space than standard cable configurations. It consists of a series of woven conduits (cells) that are attached side-by-side.

central configuration Refers to the files required to tell an operating system or environment how to configure itself to interact with the user's workstation. This file might also contain user preferences like screen colors or macros. Usually, these files appear on the local hard drive of each user's workstation. However, in a central configuration, the files appear in one place in the file server's hard drive.

centralized network A network in which data is processed at individual workstations but stored on a central, or *dedicated*, file server. Centralized networks are typically larger, more powerful, and more expensive per unit that distributed networks. Also called a *server-based LAN*.

central member The center component of the cable. It serves as a strength member or an anti-buckling element to resist temperature-induced stress. The central member is comprised of fiberglass or glass-reinforced plastic.

central processing element *See* CPE.

central processing unit *See* CPU.

centrex A service of a phone company that provides PBX-like connections from the local exchange. *Also see* PBX.

Centronics busy condition A busy condition occurs when the printer is given a command to print the line in the print buffer (carriage return), or when a vertical tab, form feed, line

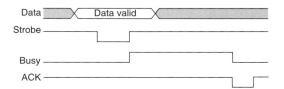

Timing diagram for the Centronics parallel-interface busy condition

feed, delete, bell, select, or deselect character is sent. The receipt of one of these special characters causes the printer to perform some mechanical operation that takes considerably more time than a few microseconds. In these cases, the handshake changes to busy condition timing, as illustrated in the figure.

Centronics handshaking sequence See the following figure. This is called *normal data-input timing*.

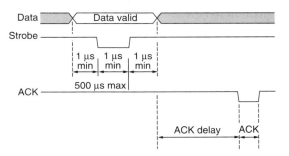

Centronics interface normal data-input timing

Centronics parallel interface A 36-pin interface that transmits bits simultaneously in groups of eight. It has become a widely accepted standard for computer/printer communications. The interface has eight lines that carry their respective binary bits in parallel. The transmission of these data bits is controlled by the computer-supplied strobe pulse. Handshaking (flow control) is achieved by asserting or deasserting either the ACKNOWLEDGE or BUSY leads. All Centronics parallel logic levels are transistor-transistor logic (TTL).

Centronics printer interface An 8-bit parallel connection with relatively simple handshake signals. This interface does not support device addresses, so only one device can be connected to the host output port. The typical timing chart is shown in the figure.

ceramic package A standard high-reliability package, made of three layers: Al_2O_3, ceramic, and nickel-plated refractory metal. In some types, the cavity is sealed with a glazed ceramic lid, using a controlled, devitrified, low-temperature

72   ceramic package • chain code

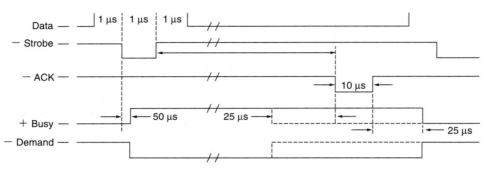

* Depends on the program loop time.

Typical Centronics timing

glass sealant. Package leads are of Kovar, which is nickel-plated and solder-dipped for socket insertion or soldering.

Certified NetWare Administrator See CNA.
Certified NetWare Engineer See CNE.
Certified NetWare Instructor See CNI.

.CFG In many filenaming schemes, an extension that indicates a configuration file, which saves the details of a program's settings.

CGA Abbreviation for *color graphics adapter*, a video adapter that provides low-resolution color adequate for some older DOS-based applications. It requires the same type of circuits as a mono-chrome card, plus the color and graphics circuits needed. IBM's CGA card is shown in the figure. A 6845 CRT video processor is used to control the input from the computer. The video RAM is dynamic rather than static. A CGA monitor is also known as *RGB* (red-green-blue).

CGB Abbreviation for *convert gray to binary*.

CGI Abbreviation for *computer graphics interface*, an ANSI/ISO graphics standard which specifies how to interface directly to graphic devices. The standard describes commands for such things as drawing lines, curves, and text. Originally called the *VDI* (virtual device interface).

CGM Abbreviation for *computer graphics metafile*, an American and international standard that specifies the format for storing a picture. Originally called the *VDM* (virtual device metafile).

.CGM In many filenaming schemes, an extension that indicates a CGM graphics file, especially one for use with Microsoft Windows.

CGS system A coherent system of units for expressing the magnitude of electrical and magnetic quantities. The fundamental units of these quantities are the centimeter, gram, and second.

chain 1. The invoking or running of one program from another with the variable remaining intact. **2.** A set of items that are serially linked together in specified segments that are processed in tandem, with only one allowed in the processor at any given moment. The items may be records or files that are dependent upon one another, and each may have access to previously executed segments. Chained files allow open-ended sequential data-handling and consist of data blocks with forward and backward pointers.

chain code A cyclic sequence of words that are related by one bit position from the left or the right. A word must not be repeated before completion of the cycle. An example of a simple chain code is the following:

```
000   111
001   110
010   100
101   000
011
```

IBM color graphics adapter layout

chained files Files that consist of a series of data blocks chained together with forward and backward pointers. They are used for open-ended sequential data-handling.

chained list A list of items in which each item has an identifier to locate the next item in the list.

chaining search A technique that uses an identifier to locate the next item in a search.

CHAMPION Acronym for *compatible hardware and milestone program for integrating organizational needs.*

change dump A dump triggered by those storage locations whose contents have recently changed.

change size In NetWare, a part of Diagnostic Services that specifies a value to increase or decrease the size of the next packet. This feature allows a packet size to vary during a diagnostic test.

channel A data pathway for the transmission of signals and data. In a communications system, a channel connects the message *source* with the message *sink*. In a storage unit, a channel may be the track or band that is connected to the read or write circuits. Also called *circuit, line, facility, link,* and *path*.

channel, analog A channel on which the information transmitted can take any value between the limits defined by the channel. A voice channel is an analog channel.

channel bank A device used by a broadband network to divide the bandwidth into separate channels and to control those channels.

channel capacity The maximum number of bits or characters that can be handled in a particular channel at any time. Also, the maximum transmission rate through a channel at a specified error rate. Channel capacity is usually measured in bits per second (for local media) or bauds (for data communications by wire or radio).

channel gain queuing RAM Random-access memory that allows a list of amplifier channel/gains to be sampled to be created in a sequence. A typical sequence is shown in the table that follows.

Sample	Channel#	Gain
0	0	X1
1	5	X100
2	1	X10
3	5	X100
4	2	X1
5	5	X100
.	.	.
.	.	.
.	.	.

channelizing The subdividing of wideband channels into a number of channels with narrow bandwidths.

channel logic The logic of functions between the transceiver cable and the data link layer, which supports the defined interface between the system and the hardware.

channel number In NetWare, a part of File Server Environment Services that shows the number of the disk channel to be queried.

channel pulse A pulse used to represent intelligence on a channel by virtue of its time or modulation characteristic.

channel service unit *See* CSU.

channel state In NetWare, a part of File Server Environment Services that shows the state of a disk channel:

- 00h (channel running)
- 01h (channel being stopped)
- 02h (channel stopped)
- 03h (channel nonfunctional)

channel synchronizer A synchronizer, often housed in the peripheral control unit, that provides the proper interface between the central computer and the peripheral equipment. Other control functions of the channel synchronizer include primary interpreting of the function words, searching by comparing an identifier with data read from a peripheral unit, and providing the central computer with peripheral-unit status information.

channel vocoder A voice encoder in which the vocal tract filter is estimated by samples taken in contiguous frequency bands within the speech signal.

chaos The use of "chaotic attractors"; patterns that appear complex, but are driven by very simple mathematical equations. Used to create stunningly intricate images.

character A letter, numeral, or other symbol that is used to express information. A character is usually part of an ordered set.

character-based interface A menu or other application system that uses only ASCII characters to display information, rather than using the display adapter's graphics mode. *Also see* USER INTERFACE.

character boundary As used in character recognition, the largest rectangle having a side parallel to the reference edge of the document.

character check A verification that characters have been formed correctly.

character code An ordered pattern of bits assigned in a particular system to represent characters. Baudot and ASCII are character codes.

character device A device designed to do character I/O in a serial manner, such as a printer.

character display A device that allows the display of characters on a screen. A simple system for a television monitor is shown in the figure that follows. Typically, the bit patterns for the characters are stored in a ROM. A television set in the United States operates with 525 lines, scanned at a rate of 30 frames per second. This corresponds to 64 microseconds for each picture line. For a display with 64 characters in each line, we must provide one character every

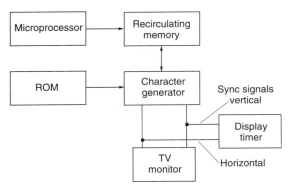

Character display system

microsecond. Shift registers or other recirculating memories are used to allow a character, which is written on the screen, to be continually rewritten or refreshed.

The radio-frequency section of the display consists of circuits for generating the correct rf signals to be supplied to the television monitor. The bit pattern is used to generate a modulating signal to modulate the rf output of an rf signal generator. The display pattern is a series of dots or scanning segments across a picture line.

The arrangement shown is not limited to generating characters. Graphics and other images can be generated and displayed by the use of a programmed ROM. A game can be created by providing the means for moving images across the screen with a joystick or other device. In the control unit, the joystick movement is translated into delayed pulses from the horizontal and vertical sync signal generators, and the delayed pulses are applied to a coincidence gate to modulate an rf signal that is applied to the television monitor.

character element 1. A basic information element as transmitted, printed, displayed, or used to control communications, when used as a code. **2.** Groups of bits, pulses, etc. occurring in a time period normally representing that for a character or symbolic representation.

character fill The insertion of specific characters, usually all ones or all zeros, to delete unwanted data.

character interleaving A method of time-division multiplexing in which each channel is assigned a time slot corresponding to a single character. Also called *word interleaving*. Also see TIME-DIVISION MULTIPLEXING.

character-oriented protocol A data link control protocol that uses special characters to frame the data characters and to control their exchange between communicating stations.

character parity An error-detection scheme in which an extra bit is added to each character. The value of the extra bit is set so that the total number of one-bits in each character is either always even or always odd.

character printer (*o.t.*) A class of printer, such as a daisywheel, that prints one letter at a time. Because they are much slower than line printers that print a line of characters at a time and are incapable of handling software fonts, they have become obsolete in most organizations.

character reader *See* SCANNER, 1.

character recognition The process of reading, identifying, and interpreting printed characters and converting them into a machine-language form for computers.

character set The complete group of representations used as characters. Examples include

- The letters of the alphabet
- The binary digits 0 and 1
- The complete set of signals used in Morse code
- The 128 ASCII characters

More generally, a character set may refer to any group of letters, numbers, punctuation marks, and symbols that a computer or peripheral can recognize and use. Each character in a set is mapped to a numeric code which, in almost every instance, can be represented by a single byte; this allows for a maximum of 256 characters in a character set, coded 0 through 255.

The most common coding scheme is the American Standard Code for Information Interchange, or ASCII. So-called "standard" ASCII uses only the first 7 bits of each byte, defining a 128-character range from 0 to 127. Both the IBM PC and Macintosh architectures define an additional, nonstandard, 128-character "extended ASCII" character set ranging from 128 through 255; the actual characters mapped, however, differ radically between the two platforms.

A similar but unrelated coding scheme is EBCDIC (Extended Binary Coded Decimal Interchange Code, pronounced "EBB-see-dick"). EBCDIC is a true 8-bit coding scheme found primarily in IBM mainframe computers and in equipment that must communicate with them.

A related concept is the *symbol set*, which could be viewed as a variation on a computer's basic character set that can tailor it to a specific use or context. The most common example would be a foreign-language symbol set that retains all the alphanumerics and punctuation of the standard character set, but substitutes the currency symbols, accented vowels, etc., appropriate to the country where the machine is to be used. Many symbol sets have been defined by the International Standards Organization and assigned standard designations such as ISO-57.

The increasing internationalization of computing, creating the need for many differing symbol sets, has underscored the inadequacies of the traditional 8-bit coding schemes. A number of alternatives, notably Unicode, currently are under investigation.

character shift **1.** A code-extension character used to terminate a sequence that has been introduced by the shift out character. **2.** A code-extension character that can be used by itself to cause a return to the character set prior to the departure caused by a shift-out character.

character string A group of connected characters associated by coding, keying, or other programming techniques.

character subset Selected characters from a character set that have a specified common feature. For example, the digits 0 through 9 are a subset of the ASCII character set.

charactron (*o.t.*) A cathode ray tube (CRT) that is capable of displaying only alphanumeric characters and other symbols.

charge A quantity of electricity associated with a body with an excess or deficiency of electrons.

charge amount In NetWare, a part of Accounting Services that shows the amount a server charges for the service it provides.

charge-coupled device *See* CCD.

Charisma A graphics program for Windows with 44 chart types, 40 fully editable fonts, drawing tools, and clip art. A slide-show utility provides onscreen graphics presentations.

chart A drawing containing text or a graph.

chart box The section of the screen on which you create drawings.

chart name The name used to store a chart and retrieve it from a disk. In Harvard Graphics, a chart name is equivalent to a DOS filename and must conform to DOS rules for filenames.

chassis assembly An assembly in many systems that provides mounting locations for the processor, power supply, and interface cards. The chassis assembly is usually designed using a printed circuit backplane for all interconnecting wiring.

chat Messages sent between users on a LAN using software that permits peer-to-peer communications.

chatter The rapid closing and opening of contacts on a relay that reduces its life.

Cheapnet A CSMA/CD LAN similar to Ethenet that uses less-expensive cabling in exchange for a smaller maximum network size.

check Verification of equipment operation and the progress of desired operating conditions along with the correctness of resulting calculations.

check, arithmetic An operation performed by the computer to reveal any failure in an arithmetic operation. It may also be used to determine whether or not the capacity of a register has been exceeded after an operation.

check, automatic Refers to various provisions usually constructed in hardware for verifying the accuracy of information transmitted, manipulated, or stored by any unit or device in a computer. Synonymous with *built-in check*, *built-in automatic check*, and *hardware check*.

check, balance Refers to an analog computer control state in which all amplifier summing junctions are connected to the computer zero reference level (usually signal ground) to permit zero balance of the operational amplifier.

check bit A binary verification digit inserted with other digits as an automatic machine function. A parity check bit, for example, is inserted when the sum of a group of ones is odd, thus keeping the parity always even. When an output contains an odd number of ones, an error is indicated.

check character A character used to perform a checking operation.

check digit A digit used to perform a check. A check digit is carried as a part of a machine word to report on the other digits of the word. When an error occurs, the check is negative and an alarm is initiated. One or more check digits can be used with either batch processing or real-time computing operations. Data with the check digits can be periodically regenerated and compared with the source data.

check indicator A device that indicates that a checking operation has uncovered an error. A check indicator may use either visual or audio to call the operator's attention to the error.

checking routine A diagnostic program that examines programs or data for the most obvious errors. A typical checking routine will discover errors in misspelling and typing, but usually does not execute the program to detect programming errors.

checklists In structure programming, lists that can be used with flowcharts. The programmer checks that each variable has been initialized, that each flowchart element has been coded, that the definitions are correct, and that all paths are connected properly. A good checklist can save time, but manually checking long or complicated programs should not be used, since the programmer may be more likely to make additional mistakes when checking the program. Some loops and sections of programs can be checked to see that the flow of control is correct. In the case of loops, the programmer can always check to see if the loop performs the first and last iterations correctly. These are the sources of many loop errors. The program can also be checked for the trivial cases, such as tables with no elements. Program checking and debugging should always be done systematically; one cannot assume that the first error found is the only one in the program.

Checkmate A checkbook management system that supports an unlimited number of savings and checking accounts and thousands of user-defined transactions.

check number A designated number composed of one or more digits and used to detect equipment malfunctions in data transfer operations. If a check number consists of only one digit, it is synonymous with *check digit*.

checkout The use of diagnostic tests during debugging to verify the correctness of machine and program operation. A checkout routine may consist of storage and printout subroutines.

checkpoint A place in a program or routine where a check or a restart can be performed. The checkpoint allows the storage of sufficient information to allow restarting, or it records the information so that the step can be restarted at a later time.

checkpoint and restart A program-verifying technique that allows processing to continue from the last checkpoint rather than from the beginning of the run following an error detection or other interrupt. The checkpoints are determined based upon a desired number of transactions out of the total number required.

check problem A test to detect errors in programming or machine operation. The check problem results in an error indication when it is not solved correctly.

check register A register used to store information for checking with the result of a succeeding transfer of data. The check register stores the information until a second transfer of the same information verifies that the information agrees.

check reset A key that is used to acknowledge an error and reset the program for restart.

checksum A summation of bits or digits used for checking purposes. Checksums are usually specified by an arbitrary set of rules fitted to the application. They provide a redundant checking method in which groups of digits are summed, usually without regard for overflow, and that sum checked against a previously computed sum to verify accuracy.

checksum error count In NetWare, a part of Diagnostic Services that specifies the number of checksum errors that have occurred while receiving packets (since the last reset or initialization).

check, unused command A check, usually automatic, that tests for the occurrence of a nonpermissible code expression.

Checkwrite A small-business accounting package that can do checkwriting and printing, budgeting, profit and loss, accounts payable and receivable, bank account management, cash forecasting, loan tracking and analysis, tax planning, and business reporting. The program can help set up a personal budget, reconcile bank accounts, manage credit cards, analyze loans, forecast cash, plan for taxes, and print a loan amortization schedule.

chemical deposition Refers to the process of depositing a substance on a surface by means of the chemical reduction of a solution.

chemical etching In printed-circuit manufacturing, a process in which dielectric and copper foil are sandwiched, and a circuit pattern is imaged on the copper with a material that is resistant to etching chemicals (the *resist*). The rest of the copper, which is not intended to be part of the circuit, is then removed by chemical etching.

child A subdirectory branching off from another directory called the *parent*.

chip A silicon slab selectively doped with impurities so that passive and active devices, circuit paths, and device interconnections are formed within the solid structure. Thus, a chip is the integrated circuit inside an IC housing.

Microprocessor chips typically utilize large-scale integration (LSI) techniques. Up to 10,000 transistors have been placed on chips of 6 mm square. The chips are usually mounted in dual-inline packages which may have up to 40 pins for mounting on circuit boards.

A microprocessor chip usually includes the arithmetic logic unit (ALU), general purpose registers, and bus controls. The microprocessor chip or chips are combined with memory and input/output chips to form a microcomputer system that will fit on a single circuit board.

chip architecture Refers to the functional structure of the microprocessor chip. The chip architecture generally includes the arithmetic logic unit (ALU), the general purpose registers, and the control bus structure. The architecture is to some degree dependent on the partitioning of the processor between one or more chips, the number of pins each chip has, the chip size, the off-chip memory, and the input/output bus structure.

chip, circuit Usually refers to an integrated circuit, a single device composed of transistors, diodes, and other interconnected components. It usually has been cut from a larger wafer, usually of silicon.

chip material Refers to the kind of substrate to be used, its doping concentrations, the choice of silicon or aluminum for the gate electrode, and the parameters of the chip materials.

chip selection To select the proper ROM chip, the proper address lines must be wired to the ROM's

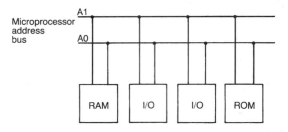

Chip selection interface

chip-select inputs. ROMs generally have four chip-select inputs, which means that some external AND gates may be required, as shown in the figure.

chip system Refers to a multiplicity of chips, together with addressing logic, interfacing circuits, and sometimes the power supply, in a convenient form for use in a microcomputer system.

chip technology, LSI Refers to the large scale integration (LSI) technology used to build microprocessor chips, which centers around metal-oxide semiconductor (MOS) devices. Chip densities on MOS devices range to over 100,000 transistors per chip. The chip's size typically ranges from 0.25 inches square to 0.45 inches square. The n-channel MOS (NMOS) devices have been the predominant technology for most of the newer microprocessors. NMOS has become the preferred approach by many of the integrated circuit manufacturers.

CHKDSK A DOS command that displays how storage space on the PC is being used. It can diagnose and report a variety of potential problems with your files, such as any damaged sectors. It also lets you know how such space is taken up by files, and how much memory is present and available. It has been superseded in recent versions of DOS by the SCANDISK command.

chroma The characterization of a color quality without reference to its brilliance or hue (saturation only).

chroma crawl Refers to "crawling" dots at the edges of saturated colors in an NTSC picture. Chroma crawl is a form of cross-luminance, a result of a television set decoding color information as high-detail luminance information (dots). *Also see* NTSC.

chroma resolution The amount of color detail available in a television system, separate from any brightness detail. In most television schemes, chroma resolution is lower than luminance resolution. Horizontal chrome resolution is 12 percent of luminance resolution in NTSC. *Also see* NTSC.

chrominance signal In an image-reproduction system, the signal that contains color information about the image, such as hue and saturation. A black-and-white image will have chrominance values of zero. In the NTSC television system, the I and Q signals carry the chrominance information. Also called the chrome signal or color signal. *Also see* NTSC.

CI Abbreviation for *call indicator*.

CIM 1. Acronym for *computer-integrated manufacturing*, the use of computers in manufacturing applications. **2.** Acronym for *computer input microfilm*, the process of reading microfilm data via a scanning device and then transforming it into a form a computer can use. **3.** Acronym for *CompuServe Information Manager*.

cipher text The apparently random text that results from encrypting a message.

circuit 1. A closed communications path between two or more points. A circuit may have individual high paths and return paths, or the return path may be shared between many circuits. *Also see* CHANNEL. **2.** A group of electronic components interconnected to perform specific functions upon application of proper voltages and signals. **3.** A closed path of current sources and sinks.

circuit analyzer Equipment that may consist of one or more test instruments controlled by a microprocessor, used to measure one or more quantities or verify performance of a circuit. A typical circuit analyzer is capable of a variety of functional tests on TTL, DTL, MOS, CMOS, and HTL devices using either combinatorial or sequential logic. The equipment may consist of constant-voltage and constant-current supplies, pulse generators, comparators, and a connection matrix. Power-supply levels, pulse levels, and comparator limits are all programmable, and the matrix is used to connect the measuring and the forcing connections with any lead of the device under test.

circuit, anticoincidence Refers to a specific logic element that operates with binary digits and is designed to provide signals according to specific rules; for instance, one digit is obtained as output only if two different input signals are received.

circuit, astable Refers to a circuit that continuously alternates between its two unstable states. It can be synchronized by applying a repetitive input signal of slightly higher frequency.

circuit, bistable trigger A type of binary circuit that has two states, each requiring an appropriate trigger for excitation and transition from one state to the other. Also called *binary pair*, *trigger pair*, and *flip-flop*.

circuit breaker A resettable fuse device for opening a circuit path, usually when overcurrent conditions are exceeded. A circuit breaker may also be used to control and protect circuits from conditions of excessive heat, noise, vibration, voltage, radiation, and other parameters.

circuit capacity The information capacity and the number of total channels that can be operated in a given circuit at any one time, usually measured in baud or bits per second.

circuit, closed Refers to a complete circuit through which current can flow when voltage is applied.

circuit components Refers to the fundamental circuit parts connected by metallic conductors. Attached to the conductors may be coils, resistors, diodes, capacitors, transformers, integrated circuits, and other parts or devices.

circuit hole The component-mounting hole that appears within or partially within the conductive lines of a printed circuit board; it may or may not be a through-the-board conductive path.

circuit, integrated. *See* IC.

circuit, interlock A circuit that originates a signal

that is in the ON condition only when all the following conditions are met: its internal circuits are arranged for signaling on a communication facility, and it is not in any abnormal or test condition that disables or impairs any normal function associated with the class of service being used.

circuit limiter A circuit of nonlinear elements that restricts the electrical excursion of a variable in accordance with some specified criteria. *Hard limiting* is a limiting action with negligible variation in output in the range where the output is limited. *Soft limiting* is a limiting action with appreciable variation in output in the range where the output is limited.

circuit, linear A circuit whose output is an amplified version of its input, or whose output is a straight-line variation of its input.

circuit load The electrical load due to equipment current drain, usually expressed as a percentage of total circuit capability under specific operating conditions for a specific operating time.

circuit noise Erratic and random electrical impulses generated by electrical switching in a circuit; these impulses, when interpreted by circuits as legitimate signals, cause errors and improper data timing.

circuit parameters The values of the physical quantities associated with circuit elements, such as the resistance (a parameter) of a resistor (the element), or the inductance per unit length (a parameter) of a transmission line (the element).

circuit reliability The percentage of time that a circuit meets specified operating conditions. The reliability figure is determined from the testing of enough parts to cause a desired number to fail based on the total population and the circuit application. The number of failures is then subtracted from the total number tested to obtain the circuit reliability.

circuit single-shot Refers to a circuit arranged to perform signal standardization to convert an imprecise input signal into one conforming to requirements.

circuit-switched routing A communications technique in which a circuit connection between the communicating parties is established and maintained for the duration of the conversation or data exchange. Packet-switching and message-switching are alternative techniques.

circuit switching A type of network in which the communications path is a physical circuit. The circuit exists as long as the two devices are communicating. Each time a device talks to another device, the path or circuit may be different. Telephone systems use circuit switching.

circuit tuned Refers to a circuit with an inductance coil and a capacitor in series or in parallel that offers a low or high impedance, respectively, to alternating current at the resonant frequency.

circuit, two-way A bidirectional channel that operates in both directions.

circuit video A circuit capable of handling non-sinusoidal waveforms involving frequencies in the order of several megahertz.

circular interpolation In computer-integrated manufacturing, a mode of contouring control that uses the information contained in a single block to produce an arc of a circle. Shorter lengths are possible when circular interpolation is used instead of linear interpolation.

circular shift *See* ROTATE.

circulating register A shift register operated as a closed loop with the data outputs circulated back to the input.

circulating storage A storage system that operates as a closed loop. Information is stored as a train or pattern of pulses; the pulse train at the output is usually sensed, amplified, and shaped before being inserted at the input.

CISC Acronym for *complex instruction set chip* (pronounced "sisk"), a processor architecture that maximizes the number of instructions performed by the processor. A CISC system places more of a burden on hardware rather than software. Also called *complex instruction set computing*.

cladding The coating on the fibers of a fiber-optic cable.

claim token The signal propagated by a station which determines that a token is overdue, lost, or corrupted.

clamping voltage The sustained voltage held by a clamp circuit at a desired level.

Clarion LEM Maker Software tools that help you create language extension modules for Clarion programs using the Turbo C compiler and libraries. It contains the components LM, CLA, LM.LIB, and MATRIX/DSPFILE. You can use any assembler that is source-code compatible with Microsoft's MASM.

Clarion Personal Developer Software that allows you to create and run your own custom programs. It gives you relational capabilities, functions, utilities, and a development environment. The programs and data files are upwardly compatible with the Professional Developer, and it imports/exports dBASE, Lotus 1-2-3, and ASCII files.

Clarion Professional Developer A full development system for producing PC applications. It includes an applications generator for creating screens, windows, tables, menus, and reports. Features include built-in LAN support, links to C and Assembler, and an .RTLink for generating overlaid .EXE programs.

Clarion Report Writer Software that offers the ability to use fields in data files for the generation of ad-hoc queries and reports. It performs calculations and filters on data and presents results; joins separate files; and reads Clarion, dBASE, DIF, and BASIC files. The program is menu-driven and features logical printer support. Online context-sensitive help is also provided.

cldata abbreviation for *cutter location data*, the input to the post-processor in some automatic machining systems. It consists of such items as XY coordinates and postprocessor commands. The actual data is contained in a clfile or cltape.

cleaning solution A static dissipative solution for the cleaning of screens and peripheral surfaces.

clear The placing of storage locations into a desired state, usually a zero or empty condition.

clear area As used in character recognition, the area that is to be kept free of any markings not related to reading the character.

cleared condition A destructive read operation that results in placing storage locations into cleared states. The cleared condition is usually permanent and is also called the *zero condition*.

CLEAR for C Software that helps C developers understand and document code by automatically producing program flowcharts, multilevel tree charts, formatted source listings, function cross-references, and prototype files. While it processes C applications, it analyzes a program's logic and reports logical inconsistencies and syntactical errors. It supports Microsoft C, Turbo C, and generic C compilers.

CLEAR for dBASE Software that helps dBASE developers understand and document code by automatically drawing program flow charts, multilevel tree charts, and formatted source listings. While processing applications, it analyzes a program's logic and reports logical inconsistencies and syntactical errors. It supports dBASE, FoxBASE, FoxPRO, Clipper, QuickSilver, and dBXL.

clfile In computer-integrated manufacturing, abbreviation for *cutter location file*, the storage medium name for the cldata.

click To press and release a mouse button in one nonstop motion.

ClickArt EPS A package of high-quality PostScript images created by professional artists using Adobe Illustrator. The images can be used in business presentations, newsletters, reports, and other published documents.

client Refers to a workstation in a client-server network, where the server acts as a host.

client ID In NetWare, a part of Accounting Services that represents the bindery object ID of the client being charged for a service.

client ID number In NetWare, a part of Queue Services that returns the object ID number of the station that placed a job in a queue.

client layer A term used to refer to the data-link and physical layers of the OSI model. *Also see* OSI MODEL.

client-server model A software mode that distributes the processing load between a front-end processor (FEP) and a back-end processor (BEP). It is most commonly used for database applications, where the FEP runs on the user's PC and the BEP runs on a central server. The FEP provides the user interface and various functions, but the BEP handles data storage and retrieval, including sorts, indexes, and queries.

client-server protocol A protocol that establishes how workstation software interacts with software running on a server. Client-server applications require that software modules running at the workstation and the server work together to provide an integrated application. The workstation and the server each performs a portion of the overall task.

client station In NetWare, a part of Queue Services that shows the connection number of the station that placed a job in a queue. This station has read-write access to the job entry's associated file.

client task number In NetWare, a part of Queue Services that represents a field containing the number of the task active on the workstation when the job was placed in the queue.

clip art A collection of pre-drawn images used in desktop publishing. Clip art provides a way for users who are not artistic to create documents with professional-looking graphics.

clipboard A Windows feature that acts as a temporary storage area allowing data from one Windows application to be recovered and used in other Windows applications.

Clipper A software product for developing database applications. *See* CA-CLIPPER.

clipper A circuit that removes the portion of a waveform that would otherwise extend above or below a specified level. This is usually accomplished by diodes and capacitors.

clipping 1. The removal of a portion of a waveform at a particular level. **2.** A condition in audio recording and playback where the first part of a word is not recorded or played back because of a hardware problem.

Cliptures A collection of clip art that includes business images, people, cartoons, objects, symbols, and graphics. Cliptures includes high-resolution EPS graphics created in Adobe Illustrator. They can be modified with either Illustrator or Aldus Freehand, and their EPS format allows them to be resized without losing detail.

C-LIST Software that lists programs with optional page titles and/or line numbers. It creates graphic action diagrams of the logic/control structure within functions, and can reformat source programs into standardized formats.

clock The controlled timing signal of a precise frequency that is used to time events within a piece of equipment. The clock is the basic method of generating periodic signals for synchronization in electronic equipment, including computers. A clock may be a shift register that changes its contents at specified intervals to mark time, or it may be a data communications clock that controls and limits the number of bits in a data stream.

clock battery The battery that powers clock circuits. The newer lithium battery assemblies provide the cure for clock-battery failure problems. A typical UL-listed battery replacement unit features no load voltages, 6.4 volts, capacities of 1.2, and a Velcro fastener system.

clock/calendar module A module for PCs that uses no expansion slots. It makes daylight savings switchovers easier and installs under BIOS EPROM with a 10-year warranty.

clock counter A memory location that records the progress of real time, usually by accumulating counts produced by a clock count pulse interrupt.

clock frequency *See* CLOCK RATE.

clock generator An oscillator, usually crystal-controlled, that provides all timing signals within a computer system. A typical clock generator provides the multiphase signals using only one external crystal and internal dividers for signals that are MOS (metal-oxide semiconductor) or TTL (transistor-transistor logic) compatible. ROMs are used with counters for generating clock phases in systems requiring complex clocking.

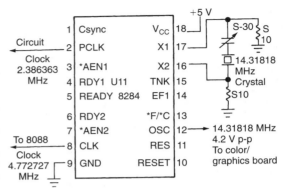

Real-time clock module

clock rate 1. The number of pulses per unit time that are generated by a clock. The clock rate is typically measured in bits per second or hertz (cycles per second). A standard IBM XT runs at a clock rate of 4.77 MHz. Also called the *clock frequency* or *clock speed*. 2. The rate at which bits or words can be transferred between elements within a system.

clock signals The pair of signals on an integrated circuit whose condition or change of condition controls the admission of other inputs and thereby controls the output. Two timing signals to generate the phases are shown in the following figure. By outlining the two instruction periods of influence, you can see that the instructions are overlapped in order to make better use of the bus system.

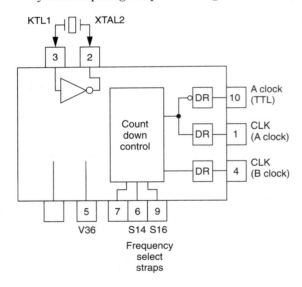

Clock generator

clock module, real-time A unit that provides programmable time bases. The time base reference is usually a crystal-controlled oscillator. Upon completion of a time interval, the microcomputer will receive an interrupt from the module if enabled. See the following figure.

clock pulse A signal provided for synchronization of events.

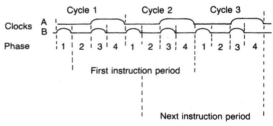

Typical microprocessor timing

A new instruction is obtained every clock cycle, and a single cycle instruction is completed every clock cycle. The actual time to complete an instruction depends upon the specific instruction being executed. Even though there might be variations in the actual instruction times, these variations are transparent to the programmer and the system user.

The clock signals perform two functions:

- Permit data signals to enter the chip
- After entry, direct the circuit to change state accordingly

Some circuits permit data entry when the clock goes to 1 and then causes the circuit to react to the data when the clock goes to 0, while others use the inverse of these signals.

clock speed See CLOCK RATE.

clock track The track upon which a pattern of signals has been cut or traced to provide a reference for the recording of time.

clone Usually refers to a microcomputer not made by IBM, but which is functionally identical to one of IBM's PCs (such as the XT, AT, or PS/2).

closed architecture Also called a *closed system*, a computer system in which the vendor has limited the ability of other vendor's products to interface with it. Thus, the user is limited in his or her ability to add expansion cards and special interfaces to the basic computer. All peripherals must be connected through I/O ports provided by the manufacturer. The limits are imposed by using proprietary designs and by not disclosing technical information. Many Macintosh computers have closed architectures. *Contrast with* OPEN ARCHITECTURE.

closed loop A circuit, system, or device in which the output is continuously sampled by the input for comparison and control purposes. Closed-loop or feedback-control systems are used to control many industrial processes.

closed-loop program A program in which there is no exit other than by intervention from outside the program. A closed-loop program is used when a group of indefinitely repeated instructions is required.

closed shop A computer facility that uses programming specialists for programming rather than using the originators of the problems, or one that uses full-time operators rather than user/programmers as operators.

closed subroutine A subroutine that can be stored in one place and connected to the main routine. A closed subroutine is usually entered by a jump operation and is forced to return control to the main routine at the end of the operation. The instructions related to the jump and return are known as *linkages*.

closed system See CLOSED ARCHITECTURE.

Close-Up A package that allows you to view and operate PCs from miles away via modem. You can run office PCs from home or on-the-road via a laptop and automate file transfers at night or on weekends.

clprint In computer-integrated manufacturing, **1.** An automatically programmed tools statement that calls for the listing or printout of a clfile. **2.** A clfile listing.

cltape In computer-integrated manufacturing, abbreviation for *cutter location tape*, the storage medium name of the cldata. It is common to store this on magnetic tape.

cluster DOS's basic unit of file organization. Clusters are composed of one or more sectors depending on disk type and DOS version.

cluster controller a device that serves as an interface between the host computer and many peripherals.

clustering In indexing, the grouping of elements within a table caused by equal hash indices.

CM Abbreviation for *computer module*.

CMOS An acronym (pronounced "see-moss") for *complementary metal-oxide semiconductor*. This technology employs integrated field-effect transistors in a complementary symmetry arrangement, which simulates a push/pull operation because of the placement of opposing-polarity devices (p-channel and n-channel FETs).

The characteristics and advantages of CMOS technology are in between those of NMOS and PMOS. CMOS is faster than PMOS, but slower than NMOS. Because it uses two transistors rather than one, CMOS offers less density than standard MOS. As a logic family, CMOS offers the following advantages:

- Low power requirements (about 1.5 volts)
- Excellent noise immunity
- High fan-out to other CMOS circuits
- High tolerance to power supply variations, allowing low-cost power supplies
- High temperature range

Since both n-channel and p-channel transistors are required, however, there is the disadvantage of having more processing steps involved in the manufacturing operation (two additional diffusions and photomasking steps). Also, more real estate is required for what are basically two separate MOS transistors. CMOS technology is suited for avionics, aerospace applications, and other systems that require portability and/or a very low power consumption.

CMOS circuits A circuit that includes CMOS components. In standard MOS circuits, the upper transistor, which acts as a load, accounts for a significant amount of the power dissipation. In CMOS circuits with p- and n-channel devices as shown in the figure, a complementary inverter is formed by applying an input to the gates of the two opposite polarity transistors. When a logical one is applied to this circuit, the upper channel transistor is off, while the lower n-channel device is conducting. The output is shorted to ground, and current from the supply is only the leakage through the p-channel device after the load capacitance is charged. When a logical zero is applied to the input, the upper transistor is on, while the lower device is off. The output is at +V, and the current will be a function of the load. If a similar high-impedance MOS device is the load, the current will remain small.

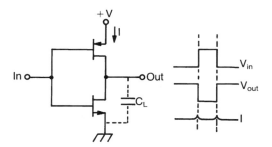

CMOS operation

CMOS IC contamination CMOS ICs are subject to greater yield problems than other digital ICs. Contamination and mask registration problems are more critical, and moisture has an important influence. Water is the vehicle that makes ions form, makes them mobile, and then puts them where they can do damage. Water and ions can create contamination problems for the devices with the smallest geometries and most sensitive parameters.

CMOS interface When a CMOS is operated with a 5-volt power supply, the interface to transistor-transistor logic (TTL) is straightforward. The input impedance of CMOS is very high, so that any form of TTL will drive CMOS without loss of fan-out in the low state. Most TTLs, however, have an insufficient high state voltage (typically 3.5 volts) to drive CMOS reliably. A *pullup resistor* (1K to 10K) from the output of the TTL device to the 5 V power supply will effectively pull the high state level to 4.5 V or above.

CMOS logic A logic family that can reduce power-supply costs and noise immunity. When operated with a 10-volt power supply, it has a worst-case noise immunity of 3 V. Even when operated at 5 V, ac and dc noise immunities are superior to those of other logic. The power dissipation is essentially zero at dc, climbing to that of lower-power TTL at a few MHz. The low power-regulation requirements allow power supply costs to be cut significantly.

CMOS propagation delay Compared to TTL, CMOS devices are slow and very sensitive to capacitive loading. Later devices use advanced processing (isoplanar) and improved circuit design (buffered gates) to achieve propagation delays and output rise times that are superior to junction-isolated CMOS designs. Silicon-on-sapphire (SOS) can achieve similar performance, but at higher costs. Isoplanar processing achieves lower parasitic capacitances, which reduce the on-chip delay and increase the maximum toggle frequency of flip-flops, registers, and counters. Buffering all outputs, even on gates, results in lower output impedance and thus reduces the effect of capacitive loading. Propagation delay is affected by three parameters: capacitive loading, supply voltage, and temperature.

The temperature dependence of CMOS is much simpler than with TTL, where three factors contribute: increase of beta with temperature, increase of resistor value with temperature, and decrease of junction forward voltage drop with increasing temperature. In CMOS, essentially only the carrier mobility changes, thus increasing the impedance and hence the delay with temperature. For some devices, this temperature dependence is less than 0.3 percent per degree Celsius—practically linear over the full temperature range.

CMOS structure The CMOS structure requires a more complex fabrication process than other devices, as shown in the following figure. The p-channel device is formed directly from the n-type substrate. A p-doped tub must be created for the n-channel device, which adds to the processing steps. Also, channel stops are required between the device, to prevent extraneous current flow between devices.

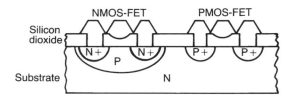

CMOS IC structure

CNC Abbreviation for *computer (computerized) numerical control*, a numerical control system in which a dedicated, stored-program computer is used to perform some or all of the basic numerical control functions.

coalesce The combining of two or more files into one.

coaxial cable A cable consisting of one conductor, usually a small copper tube or wire, within and insulated from another conductor of larger diameter, usually copper tubing or copper braid. A coaxial line has no external field and is not susceptible to external fields from other sources. Also referred to as *coaxial line, coaxial transmission line,* and *concentric line.*

COBOL Acronym for *Common Business-Oriented Language,* a programming language that makes use of English-language statements and was designed by a committee to serve two purposes:

- Provide a specific language for the business data processing industry

- Provide a language to help these users achieve program compatibility

The committee was sanctioned by the U.S. Department of Defense and the language was released for publication in 1960.

There are two types of COBOL words: *reserved* and *supplied*. Reserved words such as SELECT, ASSIGN, and READ have a special meaning to the COBOL compiler and must be used according to COBOL rules. Supplied words are created by the user and have meaning exclusive to the program without violating any of the language rules.

A COBOL source program has four basic divisions: identification, environment, data, and procedure. The *identification division* identifies the program, the program author, and the dates when the program was written and compiled. The *environment division* is used to describe the specific equipment being used. The *data division* has two sections: a file section and a working-storage section. The file section is used to describe all information that enters and leaves the CPU storage unit; the working storage section is used to specify the locations needed during proc-essing to hold intermediate results, record descriptions, and items such as reserved words. The *procedure division* specifies the steps that the computer must use to process the program. The steps of this division make use of the names of records and items defined in the data division.

Codan A C source-code analyzer that includes a database, built-in reports, and interfaces to most editors for source browsing. The database includes information about functions, variables, files, and declarations.

CODAS Acronym for *computer-based oscillograph and data acquisition system*, a hardware/software package that can be combined with an analog input board to form a data acquisition, storage, and real-time display system. A waveform scroller board included with the CODAS system makes possible real-time data display at speeds faster than software alone can provide. CODAS allows continuous data streaming to floppy or hard disk and simultaneous display to the screen at sample rates of 2000 samples per second on 4.77 MHz machines.

CODASYL Acronym for *Conference on Data Systems Language*, the assemblage that developed COBOL as a viable language.

code 1. A system of rules and ordered characters used to represent symbols and characters from a different character set. *Also see* BAUDOT CODE and GRAY CODE. 2. The act of writing or generating a computer routine, as in "code a program."

code activated switch *See* CAS, 1.

CodeBase A database and screen-management C library for programmers who need dBASE/Clipper file compatibility. You can maintain several index files per database, set relations and filters, and access dBASE memo files. It runs on DOS, OS/2, or Windows and supports most popular implementations of C and C++.

codec Abbreviation for *coder/decoder*.

CodeCheck A programming tool for analyzing all C and C++ source code on a file or project basis. It is input compatible with K&R, H&S, and ANSI C and C++. It is designed to solve portability, maintainability, complexity, reusability, quality assurance, style analysis, library/class management, code review, software metric, standards adherence, and corporate compliance problems.

code conversion The process of changing the bit grouping for a character in one code to the corresponding grouping in another code. ROMs and other storage elements are useful for code conversion.

code converter *See* CC, 2.

code, cyclic binary *See* GRAY CODE.

coded mark inversion A two-level code in which binary zero is coded so that both amplitude levels are attained within the bit duration, each for half the interval. Binary one is coded by either of the amplitude levels for the full bit duration in such a way that the levels alternate with each occurrence of a one.

coded program A program in its final form, ready for entry into the machine.

code extension character The control character that indicates that one or more of the succeeding code values is to be interpreted using a different code.

code generator An application that accepts a program description or specification as input and writes the appropriate computer instructions in a given language as output. *Template-based code generators* allow the programmer to produce the same program in more than one language by exchanging one template for another. Most code generators allow the programmer to modify the output by changing the contents of the template file. Code generators provide the means of writing generic or boilerplate code quickly, but the programmer must still write all customized or specialized code manually.

code-operated six shooter A unit that lets you select one of six printers by sending a two-character switching code. The code-operated six-shooter sends ACK signals back to the computer port when it receives the characters. The user then defines the control character for the switch. This character will usually be set as the EOT character. The next character received by the code-operated six shooter directs the switch to the selected printer.

CodePad Editor A programmer's editor for Microsoft Windows. It allows you to edit multiple source files in overlapping windows, and provides browsing, interactive search and replace, undo, and a match trace command.

code segment In NetWare, a part of Value-Added Process Services which represents the code segment of a new process.

code set The complete set of representations defined in a code, for example, all of the three-letter international designations for airport identification.

Code Transistor Software that automatically translates dBASE programs into C programs. The resulting C code will correspond directly to the original dBASE code. Variables are named the same, and dBASE commands are converted into calls.

code, unit distance A code format in which each characters is represented by some or all of the different words of n bits arranged in a sequence such that the signal distance between consecutive words is one.

coding The process of converting program flowcharts into the desired language, or the use of codes to represent characters.

coding line A line on a coding form that is reserved for an instruction.

coding scheme The rationale behind a code, the understanding of which could prove helpful in determining character codes in the absence of explanatory data.

coding, skeletal *See* SKELETAL CODING.

coding tools Hardware and software aids that are used in the various phases of microcomputer design, including techniques to simplify the designer's task. Some basic tools are assemblers, editors, loaders, and compilers. In addition, there are hardware or software simulators for program testing and error locating.

codirectional timing A form of timing for synchronous transmission in which the timing is provided along with data by the data terminal equipment.

COGO Acronym for *coordinate geometry*, a language used for solving coordinate geometry problems in civil engineering. COGO falls into the general group of production or process-control language along with APT and STRESS.

coherent detection Detection using a reference signal that is synchronized in frequency and phase to the transmitted signal. Also called *synchronous detection*.

COHO Acronym for *coherent oscillator*.

coincidence Refers to the property of a circuit or device in which an output is produced only when two or more inputs are received within a specified time period.

coincidence AND signal A circuit with two or more input wires in which the output wire gives a signal if and only if all input wires receive coincident signals.

coincidence circuit A circuit that produces a specified output pulse only when a specified number (two or more) or combination of input terminals receives pulses within a specified time interval.

COL Acronym for *computer-oriented language*.

cold boot A verb meaning to start up the computer after it has been off for at least fifteen seconds, or a noun signifying that act. *Contrast with* WARM BOOT.

cold start To start running a program at the beginning as though it had never been run before. A cold start does not attempt to pick up a program where it left off from a previous run.

collapse In word processing, the ability to make subheadings and body text invisible below the selected level. This is temporary, allowing you to see the structure of the document at a glance.

collate To combine items from two or more similar sets to produce another similar set. The collated set may or may not be in the same order as the original sets.

collating sequence The order that is assigned to a set of items, such that any two sets in the order can be collated.

collation operation A basic logic element (gate or operator) that has at least two binary input signals and a single binary output signal. The answer or variable that represents the output signal is the *conjunction*, from set theory, of the variables represented by the input signals. In set theory, the output is 1 only when all input signals represent 1.

collector capacitance Refers to the depletion-layer capacitance associated with the collector of a transistor.

collision 1. In networking, a bottleneck of simultaneous transmissions on the same shared medium. **2.** In indexing, two elements with the same hash index. A hash index is the initial estimate of the location of an entry within a table.

collision avoidance The process by which a station attempts to avoid collisions on a network. Avoidance techniques depend on the protocol. In CSMA (carrier-sense multiple access) LANs, it is done by listening to the channel to make sure it is idle before transmitting. In token passing LANs, the station must wait for a free token before transmitting. *Also see* CSMA/CD.

collision detection The ability of a transmitting node to detect simultaneous transmission attempts on a shared medium.

color adapter signal A television service scope can be used to check the output signals of a color adapter. The typical output traces that should be observed under normal operating conditions are shown in the following figure.

color balance In a color video system, the process of matching the amplitudes of the red, green, and blue signals so that the mixture of all three makes an accurate white color.

color bars A test pattern composed of eight rectangles of different colors: white, yellow, cyan, green, magenta, red, blue, and black.

color corrector A unit of equipment for adjusting the color values of a color video signal. Color

color corrector • color processing

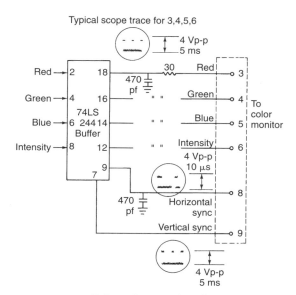

Color adapter signals

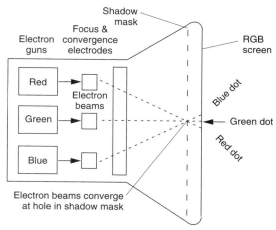

Color tube operation

correction usually is required for the proper reproduction of images from motion-picture film.

color depth The number of bits per pixel. One bit per pixel allows two colors (often black and white) to be displayed, two bits per pixel allow four colors, three bits allow eight colors, and in general, n bits allow 2^n colors.

color display device The basic display device that can be used with an adapter such as a television, a high-resolution monitor, or an RGB color monitor.

color electron gun Three electron beams are sent from the electron gun, as shown in the figure. One beam controls the red dots, another the green dots, and the other controls blue dots. The three colors are additive and produce the colors needed for a color image. In higher-resolution monitors, the color dot patterns are closer to each other, producing a more natural color display.

color graphics adapter See CGA.

colorimetry The characteristics of color reproduction, including the range of colors that a system can produce.

color information In color scanners, the amount of color information that the scanner detects and records. For example, 8 × 3 means that eight bits (256 different shades) of color are detected for each dot for each of the three basic colors (red, green, and blue). These three colors are mixed to produce other colors.

color monitor A color CRT display unit.

color noise The random interference in the color portion of a composite video system. Because of reduced color bandwidth or color subsampling, color noise appears as long streaks of incorrect color in the image.

color palette The total number of colors a video board can display. For example, a video board might allow 256 different colors onscreen and have a palette of 16.7 million colors. Those 256 colors can be any combination of colors from the 16.7 million color palette.

color processing In a color card, the three color outputs, the color burst, and clock signals are combined using a 74LS151 multiplexer chip, buffered with a 74LS244 or similar chip and then sent to the RCA jack, as shown in the following figure.

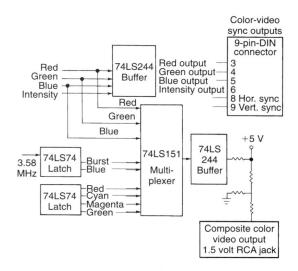

Color graphics card block diagram

color scanner A scanner that performs three individual image scans, each recording the light reflected from the object in one of three ranges of wavelengths. The wavelengths correspond to the colors red, green, and blue. The intensity of color per pixel is recorded for each individual pass. Eight bits (256 levels) are typically used per pixel to represent a color's intensity. At three passes per image, this amounts to 24 bits-per-pixel of information, or 16.8 million possible colors.

color subcarrier A subchannel created by the second NTSC (National Television Standards Committee) to carry color information within the original NTSC's black-and-white signal with minimal interference to black-and-white sets. The color subcarrier, an interlaced carrier at 3.579545 MHz, is quadrature modulated with a wideband (I) and a narrowband (Q) signal.

color table A table of color values that are displayed in an indexed color system.

color value The three numbers that specify a color. *Also see* PIXEL VALUE.

Colpitts oscillator An oscillator in which two resonant circuit capacitors with a tap between them are used. *Also see* OSCILLATOR.

ColRTrax A presentation-quality color screen-print routine for the HP PaintJet and DeskJets. The screen can be printed from 40 × 25 text mode up to 1024 × 76 × 256 color graphics mode. It lets the user adjust the hue weights (red, green, and blue), contrast, color saturation, brightness, and size of output images.

column A vertical arrangement of characters, bits, or other data on a page or screen.

column chart A chart containing one or two vertical bars in which each column is divided into slices by horizontal lines.

column parity A parity system that is applied to all bits in the same bit position in a block or to all bits in the same column. The parity bit is calculated by modulo-2 addition. The combination of row and column parity can detect all 1-, 2-, and 3-bit errors, all odd number of bit errors, and some even number of bit errors in the block.

COM 1. Acronym for *computer output microfilm*, an output device capable of producing high-quality text at 5000 lines or more per minute. A COM printer transfers the output of the computer in use onto microfilm. 2. A serial communications port.

.COM In many filenaming schemes, an extension indicating a small program file.

comb filter An electrical filter designed to deal with periodic signals (signals that are repetitive), such as scanning lines or frames. Comb filters are so named because a chart of their effect on a signal appears similar to the teeth of a comb. They are often used to separate luminance and chrominance signals in NTSC.

combi-lock system A locking system that prevents unauthorized moving of computer, printers, and other equipment. The equipment is held in place by a high-strength steel woven cable through a steel plate, which is permanently bonded to the case.

combinatorial logic Circuits or devices in which the outputs are completely determined by the present state of the inputs. Combinatorial logic includes AND, OR, NAND, NOR, and other circuits that do not rely on previous states to determine the present state.

command Usually refers to an instruction that signals the machine to start, stop, or continue a specific operation.

command button An item in a dialog box that causes an immediate action to take place.

command buffer A segment of memory used to temporarily store commands. The command buffer only holds a copy of the last command issued.

command, channel An instruction that directs a channel, control unit, or device to perform an operation or set of operations.

COMMAND.COM A file that makes up part of DOS. It loads and runs programs, and handles any interrupts, disk-error problems, and end-of-program housekeeping that might occur.

command console processor (*o.t.*) A section of the CP/M operating system, abbreviated *CCR*, where programs were loaded.

command control Refers to a type of program that handles all user-generated console commands sent into the system.

Commander A popular DOS utility from Symantec that integrates file management, file viewers, application launching, PC-to-PC file transfer, and e-mail into one user interface. You can navigate through directories and directory trees, perform DOS operations with one keystroke, or scan the contents of data files.

command field A space on a command menu, often preceded by a field name and a colon, where you specify further information about how a command should work. Most command fields contain a proposed response; you can replace or edit this response to fit your needs.

command key A key that is used to enter a particular command into a system.

command language A source language that consists mainly of process operators. Each operator in a command language is capable of executing a particular function or command.

commandpatch keypad An intelligent keypad that stores commands as individual keystrokes. It includes a 32-key microprocessor-based mini-keyboard with custom template and expanded version of keyworks software that enables you to create your own macros.

command processor The command interpreter section of DOS.

command word A word that controls device operation. For example, a command word may function to stop a motor or change a transmission rate.

comments Lines in a program whose only purpose is to document the program for debugging and maintenance. In general, comments should accomplish the following:

- Explain the purpose of the instructions or instruction sequences, not just define the instruction codes.
- Be clear and brief without involving shorthand or obscure abbreviations. A complete sentence structure is not required, but phrases should be complete enough to be well understood.
- Be limited to the more important sections of the program flow. Too many comments can make the program difficult to follow. Common sequences do not need to be explained unless they are used in an uncommon way.
- Always be placed close to the statements to which they apply, in order to avoid confusion.
- Be kept up-to-date. Comments that refer to previous versions of a program should be deleted.

common carrier A multiple-user communications system licensed and regulated by the Federal Communications Commission to provide services to all users at regulated rates. AT&T is one common carrier.

common field A field that can be accessed by independent routines.

common hardware Refers to hardware items having multiple applications in a number of functionally different systems.

Common-Link Software that allows SUN SPARC, IBM, RS, HP Interactive, and SCO Unix systems to read, write, and format Mac and DOS diskettes. No cable or external hardware is needed.

common memory A shared storage medium that many microcomputers can access.

common mode range Refers to the common mode rejection signal that usually varies with the magnitude of the input signal swing, which is usually determined by the sum of the common mode and the differential voltages. Common mode range is the range of input voltage over which the specified common mode rejection is maintained. When the common mode signal is ±5V and the differential signal is ±5V, the common mode range is ±10V.

common mode rejection The ability of a circuit to reject the effects of voltages applied to both input terminals simultaneously. It is usually expressed either as a ratio (CMRR = 10^5) or as $20 \log_{10}$.

common mode rejection ratio The ratio of the common mode voltage to the common mode error referred to the input; generally expressed in decibels.

common-mode shielding Refers to reducing common-mode errors by the use of a shield, as shown in the figure. In this circuit, no part of the common-mode signal appears across the line capacitors, since the shield is driven by the common-mode source. The shield also provides some electrostatic shielding to limit coupling to other lines in close proximity. It is important that the shield be connected only at one point to the common-mode source signal and that the shields be continuous through all connectors. The shield is carrying the common-mode signal, so it should be insulated to prevent it from shorting to other shields or ground. A return path must exist for the bias and leakage currents of the differential amplifier unless it has transformer or optically coupled inputs.

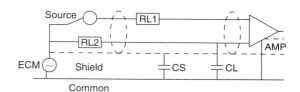

High-frequency common-mode rejection using a shield

common programs Programs that have common or multiple applications for more than one system. Programs in the following classes can be used for several routines if they are written in a language common to the computers:

- Sorting routines
- Report generation
- Code-conversion programs

common user access *See* CUA.

CommTools A telecommunications programming library for dBASE, CA-Clipper, FoxBase, FoxPro, and QuickSilver. CommTools supports file transfer protocols, terminal emulation, and fax boards. It allows the user to communicate with other systems in both terminal emulation mode and file transfer modes.

communication buffers In a network like NetWare, an area of the file server's RAM where the file server receives incoming packets and builds outgoing packets. These are also called routing buffers by Novell.

communication channel A channel or circuit path reserved for transmitting and receiving. Microcomputers can handle full-duplex communication between a printer or RS-232 device and the CPU with the interface provided by a UART (universal asynchronous receiver/transmitter). To receive data, the UART converts the asynchronous serial characters from the printer or RS-232 device into a parallel format for transfer to the CPU bus. During transmission, the parallel characters from the CPU bus are converted into a serial mode for the serial unit. The data transfer is independent, allowing the system to achieve simultaneous two-way data communication.

communication control character The character used to control the transmission of data over communication channels. A communication control character can be used to control printer operation by causing a backspace or line skip.

communication interface circuit A peripheral device programmed by the CPU to operate using almost any serial data-transmission technique currently in use. It can be used for synchronous operation or asynchronous operation, as follows:

$$CMMR = 20 \log \frac{V_{cm}}{e_{cm}}$$

where V_{cm} is the common mode voltage and e_{cm} is the common mode error referred to the input. CMRR is an important parameter of differential amplifiers. An ideal differential amplifier would respond to voltage differences between its input terminals without regard to the voltage level common to both inputs. In practice, there is a variation in the balance of the differential amplifier due to the common mode voltage, which results in an output even when the differential input is zero. *Also see* USART.

communication link The means of connecting one location to another for the purpose of transmitting and receiving information. A communications link may be a circuit, channel, or system of equipment that connects the two locations.

communication modules, microcomputer Modules that allow the use of devices such as printers and modems. Some modules permit serial communications over a current loop with optical isolation for distances up to several miles.

communication, real-time A real-time system combines data processing and communications between remote locations to allow data to be processed while the transaction is actually taking place. For example, airline-reservation systems are real-time systems.

communications The process of enabling computers to "talk" to each other. Just as people often have difficulty understanding one another, computers cannot communicate without properly matched hardware and software. Getting two computers to communicate is an involved process. First, the sender's software must convert data into a special format and insert control codes and error-checking information. The message is then sent to communications hardware (a modem) that converts computer bits into electronic signals. The signal then travels over telephone lines, twisted-pair wire, or coaxial cable to another modem, which converts the signal back into computer bits and sends it to the receiver's software.

The receiver's software strips off any control codes inserted by the sender and checks for errors. The receiver then can send back codes indicating the quality of the message received or its readiness to receive another signal.

Personal computers can communicate with other personal computers, minicomputers, main-frame computers, a public database like Dow Jones News/Retrieval or The Source, or members of a network containing any combination of the above. You can send many types of information from your personal computer: documents, programs, graphics—even sound and video files.

communications control device Data devices that can be attached directly to the system channel via a control unit, designed to perform character assembly and transmission control. The control unit may be either a data adapter unit or the transmission control.

communications executive The program or routine that provides the handling and protocol management for the system of communication links and equipment.

communications processor A microprocessor used as an interface or front end to the host processor, as shown in the figure. Some of the functions of the microprocessor are scheduling, data compression, polling, buffering, data link control, code conversion, and formatting.

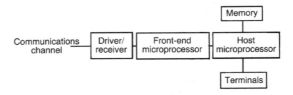

Typical communications processor applications

communications protocol The rules that set the sequence in which the data is to be transmitted, the structure of the message, the method of synchronization for the transmitter and receiver, and the error-checking procedure. Examples of protocols are IBM's binary synchronous communications (BISYNC), DEC's digital communications message protocol (DDCMP), and IBM's synchronous data line control (SDLC). The use of communications protocols has simplified many of the problems of data transfer between digital devices.

communications server A type of LAN gateway that translates the packets of a LAN to the asynchronous signals that a minicomputer or mainframe requires. The gateway can also handle various protocol types and allows LAN workstations to share host connections or modems. It is usually a PC with specialized hardware or software for performing protocol conversions.

communications software The means for a user to send instructions to the modem from either menus or a set of commands typed in at a prompt.

communication statements Statements used to link a subprogram to a main program. The *procedure call* communication statement is used to transfer control from a calling program to the called subprogram. Usually specific procedures are defined and used in this statement. The *return* communication statement is used to return control to the calling program from the subprogram.

communications terminal A point in a system or network at which data can be transmitted or received. A large amount of data communications is done over ordinary telephone lines using terminal devices and interfaces. Several leased lines are sometimes linked to improve the bandwidth and allow a heavier flow of traffic than is possible with single voice-grade lines.

communications test set Refers to test equipment that can do the following:

- Automatically or manually determine baud rate and parity settings on computers, printers, and modems
- Generate "quick brown fox" test patterns to troubleshoot equipment and cables
- Perform cable integrity tests to determine the maximum error-free data transmission rate on cables, even those installed in the walls
- Perform cable loopback tests to identify unknown or mismarked cables as well as testing the integrity of the data lines in the cable

Some units have their own rechargeable battery pack with ac charger so you can use it in the field. Operation can be simple: just select the test you want and push the start button. It will automatically go through the test, and LED indicators will show baud rate, parity, pass or fail, and the occurrence of errors. The error indicator is especially useful for long-term detection of dropouts and hits on the data line.

communications word The partial set of characters used as a unit to store or transmit information in a communications system.

commutator pulse A reference pulse that is used to mark, clock, or control a particular part of a word or a series of words.

compact disc-interactive *See* CD-I.
compact disc read-only memory *See* CD-ROM.
compact disc write-once (CD-WO) *See* WORM.
compaction The methods used for reducing space, bandwidth, and costs in the transmission and storage of data. Compaction techniques tend to eliminate repetition and remove irrelevant operations and steps in coding data.

companding The process of compressing a signal at the transmitter and expanding it at the receiver to allow signals with a large dynamic range to be sent through a device with a comparatively limited range.

comparator A device or method used for checking two or more items for precise degree of similarity, equality, relative magnitude, or order.

comparator check A check made to compare original data and printed data. The originals and the new data are run through a comparator check to uncover any errors made during processing operations.

compare between limits In some systems, it is possible to do a comparison between upper and lower limits quickly and simply using only two compare memory and skip instructions.

comparing unit A device used to compare two groups of time pulses and signals, on either an identity or a non-identity basis.

compatibility The ability to interface without special adapters or other devices. The term relates to the ease of the transfer of data or programs between systems.

compatibility, microprocessor Refers to the electrical compatibility of microprocessors with other logic circuitry as required in most applications. Most microprocessors offer some degree of transistor-transistor logic (TTL) compatibility. The speed of metal-oxide semiconductor (MOS) circuitry frequently degrades as more loads are paralleled, requiring the addition of buffers even within portions of MOS-only systems.

compensator A circuit used to alter the frequency response of an amplifier.

compilation time The time required to compile or translate a program, as opposed to the time when the program is actually being run.

compile To translate a program written in a high-level language into a machine-readable binary file (object code), as follows:

- Use the overall logic structure of the program
- Generate more than one machine instruction for each symbolic statement
- Perform the function of assembly

compiler A coding or programming system that inputs source language data and outputs a program either in assembly or machine language. (Source languages used in compilers include Fortran, COBOL, APL, ALGOL, PL/1, Pascal, and others.)

The compiler provides a language that requires fewer statements for algorithm-writing and eliminates the requirement for detailed coding to control loops, access data structures, and write complex formulas and functions. Below is a compiler statement with its equivalent in assembly language for the 8080 microprocessor.

The compiler statements are in PL/M, a subset of PL/1:

```
DECLARE (X, Y, Z) BYTE; IF X greater than Y
    THEN Z = X - Y + 2;ELSE Z = Y - X + 2
```

The equivalent assembly language statement for the 8080 would be:

```
                ORG 4000
       BEGIN    LLI LOW X
                LHI HIGH X
                LAM;
                LLI LOW Y
                LHI HIG Y
                LBM;
                SUB;
                ITS LOC2
       LOC1     ADI 2;
                LLI LOW Z
                LHI HIGH Z
                LMA
                JMPFINISH
       LOC2     LCI 377
                XRC;
                ADI 1;
                JMP LOC1
       FINISH   HLT
       LOW X    EQU 70
       HIGH X   EQU 10
       LOW Y    EQU 71
       HIGH Y   EQU 10
       LOW Z    EQU 72
       HIGH Z   EQU 10
                ORG 4070
       LOC X    DEF 0;
       LOC Y    DEF 0;
       LOC Z    DEF 0;
```

Source languages provide instructions that are much easier to read, understand, and write, but sometimes at the cost of excessive storage space and slow execution times. A compiler produces assembly language code to make programs smaller and more efficient. *Also see* INTERPRETER.

compiler, consolidate The final stage of compilation, in which subroutines implicitly or explicitly called by a source program are inserted from a library file into the program being compiled.

compiler-level languages High-level languages that are normally supplied with computers by the computer manufacturer. APL, ALGOL, COBOL, BASIC, and Fortran are compiler-level languages.

compiling program A program that translates from one programming language into another programming language. Also called a *translator*.

complement In any radix system, the difference between any given digit and its base raised to the next higher power. For binary, the complement of 1 is 11. To check the accuracy of a complementing operation, add the number to be complemented with the complement to get the base or the next higher power of the base. Thus, to verify that 11 is the binary complement of 1, add 1 and 11:

$$\begin{array}{r} \text{carry} \searrow 1 \ \ 1 \\ + 11 \\ \hline 100 \end{array}$$

In binary, $100 = 2^2$.

The complement C can be obtained by subtracting the given number from the base raised to the power represented by the number of digits in the quantity, or

$$C = B^D - N$$

where B is the number base, D is the digits in the number, and N is any number.

complementary codes Codes such as natural binary or binary coded decimal (BCD) in which bits are represented by their complements. In a 4-bit complementary binary converter, 0 may be represented by 1111, half scale (MSB) by 0111, and full scale (less 1 LSB) by 000. In a similar manner, for each quad of a BCD converter, a complementary BCD is obtained by representing all bits by their complements; thus, 0 is represented by 1111, and 9 is represented by 0110. The equivalents for 1 through 4 in the complementary binary and complementary BCD (with an over-range bit) are shown in the following table.

Decimal	Number	Natural Binary	Complementary Binary	BCD	Complementary BCD
0 BIN	DEC.	0000	1111	00000	11111
1, 1/16	1/10	0001	1110	00001	11110
2, 2/16	2/10	0010	1101	00010	11101
3, 3/16	3/10	0011	1100	00011	11100
4, 4/16	4/10	0100	1011	00100	11011

complementary metal-oxide semiconductor technology *See* CMOS.

complementary operator A logic operator that produces the complement of any given logic operator (the NOT operator).

complementary tracking A system of interconnection of two regulated supplies in which one (the master) operates to control the other (the slave). The slave supply voltage is made equal (or proportional) to the master supply voltage and of opposite polarity with respect to a common point.

complementation An operation that results in the reverse significance in each digit position in a series of digits. For example, if the word is 0101100, then complementation gives 1010011.

complementing The use of complements to produce the negative equivalent of a number.

complete carry A technique used in parallel addition in which all carries are allowed to propagate to completion.

complete operation A computer operation that includes the following steps:

1. Obtaining all operands from storage
2. Performing the desired operation
3. Returning the results to storage
4. Obtaining the next instruction

complex bipolar Refers to a technique used to produce memories significantly faster than standard transistor-transistor logic (TTL) or emitter-coupled logic (ECL). It involves an extra diffusion that results in smaller resistors, low base and collector resistance in the transistors, and two layers of aluminum interconnections that reduce interconnection resistance. This technique produces fast memories, but at higher cost. Since speed is the prime requirement, the ECL circuit form is used. These ECL memory components can easily be made TTL-compatible.

complex instruction set chip *See* CISC.

complexity A figure of merit, or measure of the quantity, of related parts or circuits. The total number of electronic parts is often used as the measure, and complexity units are sometimes used as a preliminary and approximate measure.

compliance voltage The output voltage range of a dc power supply operating in constant current mode. Compliance voltage is the voltage range required to sustain a given value of constant current throughout a range of load resistances.

component A functional part of a circuit, module, or system. A component can be a self-contained element or a combination of elements, parts, or assemblies.

component density The volume of a circuit assembly divided by the total number of discrete circuit components utilized.

component error Concerns the various errors related to a specific component, such as the input and feedback impedances of an operational amplifier.

component position In NetWare, a part of Diagnostic Services that shows the position of the target component within the IPX configuration, in the format *Response Packet (00h = first position, 01h = second position, etc.)*

component stress The particular factors of usage or test, such as voltage, power, temperature, and frequency, which tend to affect the failure rate of electronic parts.

component video The three color video signals that describe a color image. Typical component systems are RGB, YIQ, or YUV.

composite cable A cable in which conductors of different gauges or types are combined in one sheath.

composite conductor A conductor in which strands of different metals are used in parallel.

composite filter Relates to the combination of a number of filter sections or half-sections all having the same cutoff frequencies and specified impedance levels.

composite link The line or circuit connecting a pair of multiplexers or concentrators; the circuit carrying multiplexed data.

composite signal The data signal on the trunk side of a multiplexer. This signal is a combination, or composite, of a number of individual user data signals that have been combined by the multiplexer.

composite video The signal for a CRT consisting of picture signal, blanking, and sync pulses.

composite video signal The complete color television-picture signal, including all blanking and sync signals. Typical composite television standard signals are NTSC, PAL, and SECAM.

composition analyzers Microcomputers can be employed as processors in many intelligent instrumentation systems. Among these are systems used for composition analysis. In a mass spectrometer, charged particles of different atoms are separated by their mass-to-charge ratios. The separation normally takes place in a high vacuum to eliminate collision with other molecules. A sample is taken and ionized under reduced pressure by an electron beam. The charged particles then pass through a magnetic field to determine the mass to charge ratios. Spaced collectors then pass the charges to an electrometer, where they are amplified into voltages proportional to the compositions. A closed-loop control system is used to compensate for any variations in sensitivity.

The use of a microcomputer allows the system to be self-calibrating and able to operate automatically.

compound logic Logic that furnishes an output that is a function of many inputs.

compound modulation Modulation of signal that is already modulated, resulting in double modulation.

compress 1. To reduce certain parameters of a signal while preserving the basic information content. Compressing usually reduces a parameter such as amplitude or duration of the signal to improve overall transmission efficiency. **2.** To move fragmented data into a contiguous region of memory, leaving other regions free for other data. *Also see* PACK.

CompuServe An online information service that provides users with a wide variety of services including forums (i.e., bulletin boards), conferencing, weather forecasts, e-mail, news stories from wire services, such as the Associated Press, online publications, and access to the Internet. Owned by H&R Block, CompuServe is the oldest and largest of the "Big Three" online services (which also include AMERICA ONLINE and PRODIGY). It caters to professional and business users, although in early 1995, the company indicated that it would more aggressively target the home-based user of online services. CompuServe has approximately 2.5 million members.

compute bound The limiting of output rate due to delays caused by computing operations. Also called *compute limited* or *process bound*.

computer A data processor that performs computations, including arithmetic and logic, usually without intervention by a human operator during the processing run. Its basic architecture is shown in the following diagram.

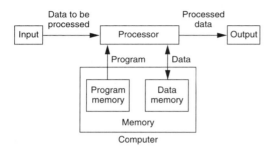

Basic block diagram of a computer

computer-aided design See CAD.
computer-aided instruction See CAI.
computer-aided software engineering See CASE.
computer-aided systems engineering See CASE.
computer, analog See ANALOG COMPUTER.
computer architecture The structure of the main computer components. Some modern computer architectures are patterned after the Mark I calculator, developed by Howard Aiken of Harvard University in the 1940s. This machine provided the architecture concepts of what is known as the *Harvard machine architecture*. It accepted programs on punched paper tapes, which controlled the electromechanical calculator.
computer, asynchronous See ASYNCHRONOUS COMPUTER.
computer circuits The circuits used in the construction of digital computers, including storage circuits, triggering circuits, gating circuits, inverting circuits, and timing circuits. In addition, there may be other circuits used, such as amplifiers for driving heavier loads, indicators, and output devices; amplifiers for receiving signals from external devices; and oscillators for obtaining the clock frequency.
computer clock The computer clock acts as the timekeeper for all processing. It runs at an assigned frequency, and all operations are done in step with the clock. The clock consists of a crystal-controlled oscillator circuit. A crystal oscillator produces a continuous sine-wave output. This sine wave is converted to a square wave for the digital circuits that need to use it. The square wave pulses provide the quickly rising and falling edges needed to trigger events. The faster the clock frequency, the faster the data will be processed. The processing frequency is derived from the clock frequency.

In the IBM PC the clock components are part of the clock generator chip. This chip divides the crystal frequency to provide the frequencies needed. The crystal used in the original IBM PC was cut to run at 14.31818 MHz. When power is applied to the crystal, the effect of the voltage across the crystal causes it to oscillate at this frequency, called the *master frequency*. The clock generator circuitry divides this master frequency by three, producing the system operating frequency of 4.772727 MHz for the original IBM PC. Computers that run at a faster frequency use a faster crystal.

computer code The machine language or code used within a computer system.
computer configuration A group of hardware units interconnected and arranged to operate as a system.
computer-dependent programs Programs written using the specific language and/or features of a particular computer.
computer instruction A machine instruction used with a specific computer system.
computer interface The type of connection port used between the computer and external devices such as printers or modems, or the computer compatibility of these devices. *Also see* PORT, 2.
computer network A system consisting of two or more interconnected computers. In addition to a host computer, a computer network usually contains the following elements:

• User communications interfaces
• Communications facilities
• Network-control hardware and software

Also see LAN.
computer (computerized) numerical control See CNC.
computer output microfilm See COM, 1.
computer part program In computer-integrated manufacturing, the definition of the workpiece geometry, motions, and commands in a numeric/control (N/C) part programming language such as APT or Adapt. The computer part program is the input to the N/C language processor; the processor translates this input into cldata, and the postprocessor in turn translates this data. *Also see* CLDATA.
computer program See PROGRAM.
computer run The processing of a batch of transactions or the performance of one routine or several routines that are linked to form an operating unit. During a computer run, manual operations are usually not required from the human operator.
computer, synchronous See SYNCHRONOUS COMPUTER.
computer virus See VIRUS.

computer word *See* MACHINE WORD.

COMSAT Acronym for *Communications Satellite Corporation*, the privately owned U.S. communications carrier in charge of commercial communications satellite deployment.

concatenate To link together in a series. A concatenated data set is one formed by combining the contents of several data sets in a specific sequence.

concatenation An operation that joins two strings together in the order specified, forming a single string with a length equal to the sum of the lengths of the two strings.

concentrated data transmission A form of data transmission that employs store and forward techniques for handling messages. These techniques include message-switching and packet-switching.

concentrator A processor used in communication systems that performs the following services:

- Polling of local lines
- Formatting of messages
- Error correction and flags to operator

concentricity A measurement of the centering of a conductor within the insulation.

concentric stranding A technique used in stranding wire in which the final wire is built up in geometric layers so that the inner diameter of the succeeding layer is equal to the outer diameter of the underlying layer.

concordance A type of program that uses alphabetic lists of words and phrases with references. Concordance programs sometimes use a free-form assembler to produce the alphabetized listings, which are referenced by line numbers.

concurrency Refers to multiple users accessing the same information at the same time.

concurrency control Programming methods that allow multiple users to access the same data simultaneously without data corruption or disruption to the other users. Record locking and file locking are common concurrency-control techniques.

concurrent The occurrence of two or more events or activities within the same time period. Concurrent operating allows several programs to share a computer at the same time. Job processing is allowed to continue while the computer performs inquiry or utility operations using time-sharing or multiprogramming.

concurrent operating control Refers to operating systems that provide the ability for several programs to share the computer at the same time. Concurrent operations include task processing while performing inquiry or peripheral utility operations.

concurrent processor A machine capable of operating on more than one program at a time; a *multiprocessor*.

CONDEN A public-domain set of DOS utilities. The major program can save disk space by removing excess blank lines and titles from text files. An associated program produces multiple-page-across listings using a wide-carriage printer. Other useful programs allow you to set screen colors from DOS and generate a cross-reference of your program listings.

condenser storage *See* CAPACITOR STORAGE.

conditional breakpoint A point in a program that causes the computer to stop because of a specified condition. The routine is continued from the breakpoint as coded, or another instruction is used to force a jump to another point.

conditional code Used to define a group of program instructions such as carry, borrow, and overflow. Conditional code instructions are important to program execution and are usually listed in a *condition code register*.

conditional implication A Boolean algebra operation defined by the following truth table:

Operand		Result
A	B	C
0	0	1
1	0	0
0	1	1
1	1	1

conditional jump A jump that occurs only if specified criteria are satisfied. A conditional jump instruction may result in obtaining the correct addresses for the next instruction that produces a transfer of control. The next instruction can be dependent on the specified criteria to determine whether a jump or skip to another instruction is called for.

conditional operators In some word processors, merge instructions included in a main document that tell the word processor to check the text in fields of a data document to see if that text meets certain conditions. If the conditions are met, the word processor will include the text from the field, or other text that you specify, when it prints form documents.

conditional stop A program stop that is dependent upon specified conditions. Conditional stops can sometimes be controlled by the operator.

conditional transfer A transfer of control that occurs only if specific conditions are met. If these conditions are not met, the program continues its normal sequence.

condition code register The condition code register in the 6800 is an 8-bit register used to indicate the results of an ALU operation such as negative (N), zero (Z), overflow (V), carry from bit 7 (C), and half carry from bit 3 (H). These bits are used to test conditions for conditional branch instructions. Bit 4 of the condition code register is used as the interrupt mask bit (I). Unused bits of this register are always ones. These bit positions are shown in the figure.

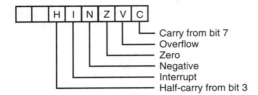

6800 status register

condition codes Codes that are used to contain information about the results of the last CPU operation, such as the following:
X = 1, if the result was zero
Y = 1, if the result was negative
Z = 1, if an overflow resulted

conditioned diphase A two-level code in which diphase is applied to a conditioned NRZ signal. *Also see* DIPHASE.

conditioned line A privately owned or leased telephone circuit that has been tuned to improve its performance for data communications applications.

conditioned NRZ A two-level nonreturn-to-zero code in which the presence or absence of a level change is used to signal a binary number.

conditioning The processing of signals to make them more intelligible or more compatible in a given application. Signal conditioning may include pulse shaping, clipping, digitizing, and linearization.

conditioning signal A signal used to process the form or mode of data so as to make it intelligible to or compatible with a given device.

conductance The physical property of an element, device, branch, network, or system that allows it to conduct electricity through a closed circuit.

conductor That part of a passive circuit path that carries electrical current.

conduit A hollow tube for holding wires of cables.

Confidant A shareware security program that encodes sensitive data in order to keep it confidential. The program allows a choice of two encryption procedures: the national Data Encryption Standard (DES) provides very high security, while a faster, somewhat less-secure procedure provides encryption where speed is important.

confidence interval A statistical range surrounding the average value.

confidence level A measure of the degree of confidence of a device's or system's operation, usually expressed as a percentage of the probability of success.

CONFIG.SYS On a PC, a file containing commands that configure the DOS environment and loads device drivers. It is found in the root directory of the disk drive from which the PC is booted. It is one of the most important files on a PC, and one of the first loaded into memory when the computer is turned on.

configurable array processor A system in which the processors are arranged in an array for processing data that have some geometrical relationship to each other. A two-dimensional array processor might operate on a two-dimensional representation of the data to be processed, such as calculations with respect to a set of grid coordinates. If the two-dimensional representation is changed to a different configuration of grid points, the system would reconfigure itself to another more suitable array configuration for the new task.

configuration A group or system of machines that are connected and programmed together.

configuration description In NetWare, a part of File Server Environment Services that contains an ASCII string indicating the channel's current I/O driver configuration.

configured maximum bindery objects In NetWare, a part of File Server Environment Services that shows the maximum number of bindery objects that the file server will track.

configured maximum open files In NetWare, a part of File Server Environment Services that contains the number of files the server can open simultaneously.

configured maximum simultaneous transactions In NetWare, a part of File Server Environment Services that shows the most transactions the server can track simultaneously. It is set with the Install/Netgen utility.

conjunction The logic operation that uses the AND operator and results in the logical product. The AND function occurs when two or more gates are placed in series and follow the truth table below:

Gate or Operand A	Gate or Operand B	AND Output C
0	0	0
0	1	0
1	0	0
1	1	1

The conjunction of the two operands is written as AB or $A \cdot B$ or $A \times B$.

connection/address mismatch count In NetWare, a part of Diagnostic Services that shows the number of times (since the shell was activated) that the shell has received an error code from a server indicating that the connection number in a shell's request packet did not match the shell's connection number in the server tables.

connection box An electrical distribution panel similar in purpose to that of a plug-board, which permits distribution or altering of the destinations of signals.

connection control In NetWare, a part of Communications Services that contains four single-bit flags used by SPX to control the bidirectional flow of data across a connection.

connection count In NetWare, a part of Message Services and File Server Environment Services that contains the number of logical connections to receive a message (0 = broadcast to all workstations).

connection flag In NetWare, a part of Value-Added Process Services that determines whether the created process is to be connected with a file server. If zero, then the created process receives a default connection with a file server; if nonzero, then no connection is established.

connection ID In a NetWare Queue Print Job, a flag containing a value (from one to eight) indicating the position in the workstation's Connection ID Table of the server receiving a print job.

connectionless operation A mode of operation where a logical connection is not established between communicating devices. Protocol data information is sent independently throughout the network.

connectionless packets NetWare uses a suite of protocols known as IPX/SPX. IPX (Internetwork Packet Exchange) protocols do not require a response from the recipient. SPX (Sequenced Packet Exchange) packets do require a response and therefore establish a virtual connection with the recipient. As a result, IPX packets are sometimes referred to as connectionless packets.

connection list In NetWare, a part of Message Services that specifies the connection number of each station to which a message is sent. Each byte in a connection list field has a corresponding byte in a Result List field.

connection number In NetWare, the number assigned by a file server to a workstation.

connection state In NetWare, a part of Communication Services that shows the state of the specified connection.

connectivity The ability of two units to be connected together and transmit data to each other. It does not imply that the devices understand each other.

connector 1. A means of converging lines on a flow diagram. A flowchart connector can be used to represent a break in a flowline, or the divergence of a flowline into several lines. 2. A terminal designed for easy mating with a complementary terminal or adapter, as on a cable.

connect time The time period during which a remote terminal is connected to a time-shared system, usually marked by a *sign-on* and *sign-off*.

Connectware A board that transforms a PC into an IBM 3278 terminal model 2, 3, or 4, or a 3279 model 2A or 3A. It allows native-mode connection to a 3270 network without requiring modems, telephone lines, or additional 3705 communications line support. The board has a microprocessor that operates independently of the PC's processor. A terminal program lets you use your PC as a terminal even while running a DOS application, and utilities are included to help write programs that automate access to corporate databases. A workstation facility provides menu-driven file-transfer capabilities between the PC and the IBM host computer system. The unit operates with both channels attached and remote to a 3274 or 3276 controller (either BSC or SNA/SDLC). It consists of a board that will mount in any expansion slot to connect your PC via Category A coaxial cable to any 3274 or 3276 controller.

consecutive The occurrence of two sequential events without the interference of any other event.

consecutive sequence computer A computer in which all instructions are executed in a defined sequence unless specified to enter a jump operation.

console The part of a computer system used for communication between the computer operator and the central processing unit.

console debugging Refers to systems that permit the programmer to debug at the machine console or at a remote console by slowly stepping the machine through each instruction and observing the contents of appropriate registers and memory locations.

constant A fixed value or an item of data that does not vary. Constants are those quantities or messages that are available as data for the program and are not subject to change with time. A constant can be one character or a group of characters that represent a value and are used to identify, measure, or compare.

constant area That part of storage selected to store the invariable quantities required during processing.

constant impedance multiplexer A multiplexer in which the input resistor is terminated in a real or virtual ground as shown; thus, the input resistance is almost constant regardless of the channel selected.

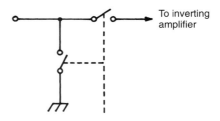

Constant impedance multiplexer

constant luminance principle A rule of composite color television that states any change in brightness should not have any effect on the brightness of the image displayed on a picture tube. The constant luminance principle is generally violated by existing NTSC encoders and decoders. *Also see* GAMMA.

constants, primary Refers to those parameters of a transmission line such as capacitance, inductance, resistance, and leakage of a conductor to earth, per unit length of line.

constraints Limitations, or tasks that cannot be accomplished by the computer or associated hardware and software available.

constructs Detailed construction drawings produced using a patented process employing a computer and a plotter. Constructs allow human intervention when required and are commercially available through Control Data Corporation.

contact The part of a relay, switch, or connector that allows circuits to be closed by physically touching a similar part on a current carrying line. Circuits are opened by breaking the physical connection.

contact alignment Refers to electrical contacts and the sideways movement or play in mating contact pins or other devices for plug or other contact insertions or surfaces.

contact area The common area between two conductors through which an electric current flows.

contact, bifurcated Contacts used in printed circuits with slotted flat springs that increase flexibility of the spring and provide extra points of contact.

contact float Refers to the amount of give, movement, or side play that a contact has within the insert cavity to allow self-alignment of mated contacts and easy insertion of the plug or other contact surface.

contact sensing Refers to the techniques used to monitor and convert field switch contacts into digital information for input to a computer. Contact points are usually scanned at programmed intervals.

contact separating force Refers to the exertion or force necessary to separate or remove pins from sockets or connectors.

content addressable memory *See* CAM, 1.

contention The conflict that arises when two or more data sources simultaneously attempt to put data onto the same physical medium. This will cause the loss of data if not detected, and can cause damage to driver and receiver circuits if they are not designed to withstand the increased voltage or current levels that can occur.

context-switching 1. A technique for managing memory. A dedicated, 8-bit register points to the stack in the zero page of RAM. An instruction loads this stack pointer with a value to establish the location of the stack in RAM. This type of context-switching instruction increments or decrements the stack pointer as required.

Context-switching can also be used with registers that are in memory and are pointed to by the contents of a workspace pointer. The context switch is initiated by an interrupt to fetch a new workspace pointer and program counter values from the interrupt vector. The current workspace pointer, program counter, and status register value are stored in a new workspace region. This type of stacking into successive workspace regions can go to any depth in memory. **2.** *See* MULTIPROGRAMMING.

contingency interrupt An interrupt that occurs due to one of the following:

- Operator requests use of the keyboard
- Character typeout
- Operator requests program stop
- An overflow occurs
- An invalid code occurs

continuity checker A tester as shown in the following figures that emits a visible indication or a 70-db tone for a connection, and is quiet for an open. Continuity checkers operate with AAA batteries and test for the presence of voltages from two to 500 volts ac or dc.

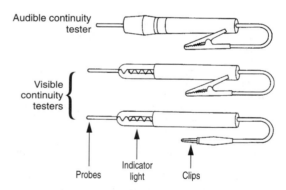

Continuity testers that will test for the presence of voltages from 2 to 500 volts ac or dc

continuously variable-slope delta modulation *See* CVSD.

continuous-path operation The controlling of the motion of a machine tool in space as a function of time such that the machine travels through the designated path at the specified rate. This generally requires the ability to simultaneously move more than one machine axis at coordinated rates.

continuous simulation A type of simulation represented by continuous variables scanned at regular intervals. Continuous simulation can be used for either linear or nonlinear differential equations.

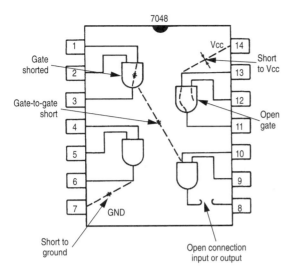

**Typical failures in a
small, four-gate integrated circuit**

contradirectional timing A form of timing for synchronous transmission in which the timing of the DTE (data terminal equipment) is slaved to the timing from the DCE (data circuit terminating equipment).

contrast enhancement An image-processing technique that increases the range of brightness levels in an image. Increasing contrast can, for example, enhance detail or help correct for improper exposure in photographs.

contrast ratio Refers to the difference between absolute black and white. The better contrast ratios are found in high-resolution desktop monitors, gas plasma displays, and fluorescent backlit models. They have contrast ratios of approximately 20 to 1, similar to the printed page.

control block The circuitry that performs the control function of a CPU. In a typical microcomputer, the control block decodes instructions and generates all control signals required for operation.

control bus A data pathway in a computer system that is used to regulate system operations. Control bus signals tend to operate like traffic signals or commands. They may originate in peripheral equipment and be under control of the bus register for access to the bus.

control, cascade Refers to a control system in which the various control units are linked in sequence, each control unit regulating the operation of the next control unit in line.

control character A character that initiates, modifies, or stops a control operation. A control character is generally not a graphic character, but it may have a graphic representation. A typical control character is used for nonprinting functions such as carriage return or line feed, or to control other operations such as recording, interpreting, transferring, and transmitting.

control circuits Circuits used to carry out program instructions in the correct sequence. Control circuits also interpret the program instructions and send the control signals through the system.

control code A one- or two-character key combination used to run a macro.

control, common area Refers to a memory control section used to reserve a main storage area that can be referred to by other modules.

control counter A device used to record the location of the current instruction word. The control counter is sometimes used to select storage locations.

control data Any data item that is used to identify, select, modify, or execute an operation, routine, record, or file.

control field A location where control information is placed, usually constant and usually as a sequence of similar items.

control function Any action that affects the recording, processing, transmission, and interpretation of data such as starting and stopping, carriage return, or font change.

control instruction An instruction that performs one of the following processes:

- Move data between the main memory and the control memory
- Prepare main memory storage areas for processing
- Control the instruction sequence and interpretation

controller A unit that operates automatically to regulate the performance of a controlled variable or system. Controllers use the data from the input and the output of a device to obtain the maximum and most efficient control of the device or process. Controllers are also used in computer systems for generation of signals to interface the CPU with memory and peripheral equipment. A typical controller chip performs all the control functions required for the flow of data at the interface, and is shown in the figure on page 98.

controller drive number In NetWare, a part of File Server Environment Services that shows the drive number of a disk unit relative to a controller number.

controller number In NetWare, a part of the File Server Environment Services that contains the address on a physical disk channel of the controller that controls the disk.

controller type In NetWare, a part of File Server Environment Services that contains the number identifying the type (make and model) of a disk controller.

controlling process In NetWare, a part of Value-Added Process Services that returns the VAP header segment of a VAP that has console control.

control logic The logic that operates the sequence of operations within the microprocessor. It controls the various cycles and data transfers through the internal bus system and provides external signals to let other modules know the status of the microprocessor at any particular time. During a fetch cycle, the microprocessor generates a status signal to request an instruction from memory. During an execute cycle, the microprocessor may be in a memory read, memory write, or input output status. The bidirectional bus buffers are controlled by the status request. When the microprocessor is requesting data from the external environment, the bidirectional bus is placed in an input mode. When it sends data to the external environment, the bus buffers are placed in the output mode and the information is placed on the data bus.

Controllograph A data logger program that supports type J, K, and T thermocouples and includes cold-junction compensation and linearization. Engineering unit conversions or arithmetic functions can be configured. The program outputs to a file in Lotus format.

control loop Refers to the implementation of an algorithm that will regulate a control system output as a function of the inputs.

control operation Any action affecting the recording, processing, transmission, and interpretation of data.

control panel A component of some data-processing units that permits the user to change the operational characteristics of the computer using switches or the insertion of pins, plugs, or wires into sockets, and thus making electrical interconnections that may be sensed by the data-processing machine.

control program A sequence of instructions that guides the CPU through the various operations or tasks programmed. Most often this program

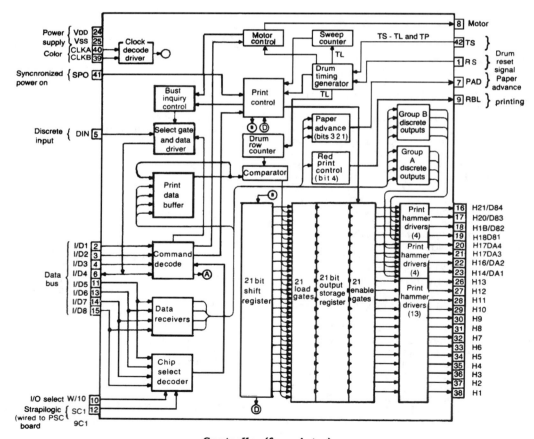

Controller (for printer)

is permanently stored in ROM, where it can be accessed but not erased by the CPU during operations. *Also see* CROM.

control ratio The required change in control resistance to produce a one-volt change in the output voltage of a power supply. The control ratio is expressed in ohms per volt.

control read-only memory *See* CROM.

control register The register that stores the current instruction to control the CPU for the next cycle. Also called the *instruction register*.

control routine A primary routine that controls the loading and rerouting of other routines. Control routines are used in automatic coding and are sometimes considered as a part of the machine itself as opposed to another program. Sometimes called *monitor routine, supervisory routine*, or *supervisory program*.

control section The sequence of instructions within a program that can be replaced from outside the program segment that contains it. A typical control section is exchanged with control sections from other segments in many microcomputer systems.

control sequence The normal order for the selection of instructions for execution. The control sequence can be specified by an address in each instruction, or it may be consecutive except for jumps and transfers.

control statements Instructions that direct the program flow and convey control information to the CPU. Control statements may cause transfers dependent upon specified conditions, but they do not cause the development of machine-language instructions.

control store An address register that allows the user to monitor the program point at which program operation is stopped. The control store register aids debugging and is usually monitored through the front panel of a ROM simulator.

control system A system that controls, analyzes, monitors, or measures a process or other equipment. Computers are integral parts of many modern control systems.

control unit The section of a computer that directs the sequence of operations, interrupts instructions, and sends control signals to other units in the computer system. Sometimes called the *control section*. A typical microcomputer has two control units: the CPU and the external logic control unit.

conventional memory On a PC, the first 640K bytes of memory, which is the only area of user memory that DOS can access directly.

conventions Standard or accepted procedures in programming and system analysis, which may include symbols, abbreviations, and characters with special meanings.

conversational Descriptive of a program or system that can carry on a dialog with the user. In the conversational mode, the system accepts input and then responds in real time. A conversational system can provide guidance to the user about the form and content of the response needed and is used in many teaching devices.

conversational language A computer language that uses a character set similar to English to aid communication between the user and the computer. BASIC is an example of a conversational language.

conversational mode A real-time communication mode in data transmission where a device talks to another device character-by-character. Each entry from the first device requests an immediate response from the second, enabling the first device to control, interrogate, or modify a task within the second. *Contrast with* BLOCK MODE.

conversion The act of changing data or information from one form to another without changing the content of the data. For example, numerical data can be converted from binary to decimal. Conversion equipment and software is used in many systems for transposing data from one form to another in order to make it acceptable as input for another device or program.

conversion device A piece of peripheral equipment that converts data from one form into another form or medium without changing the data content or information. A modem is one example of a conversion device.

conversion time The time required to perform a conversion, such as a code conversion or a conversion from analog to digital data.

converter A device that changes the level of a dc supply voltage to a higher value for powering hardware or peripherals.

convex programing A type of nonlinear programming used in operations research. The function is maximized or minimized to constraints that are convex or concave functions of the controlled variables.

coordinate dimensioning A system of dimensioning in which a point is defined as being a certain dimension and direction from a reference point as measured with respect to defined axes.

coordinate dimension word A word defining an absolute dimension.

coordinate indexing An indexing method in which all descriptors are correlated and combined to indicate interrelationships.

coordinates Numbers that identify a location on the display.

coordinate storage Storage in which all elements are arranged in a matrix so that any location can be identified using two or more coordinates. Examples of coordinate storage include cathode-ray storage and core storage, which uses coincident-current techniques.

Coordinator A workgroup productivity software product for businesses with small or large LANs. If a business has more than one network, it lets you join networks. The base package supports up to 50 users.

coprocessor A special-purpose processor chip that works in conjunction with a primary CPU to speed up time-consuming operations.

copy To reproduce data while leaving the source data unchanged. The physical form of the data may change, as when a hard disk is backed up onto magnetic tape. A *hardcopy* refers to any printed form of machine output, such as reports and listings.

copyholder A unit that positions copy at an optimum 20 degree viewing angle for quick, accurate keying. Both the arm and copyholder rotate 360 degrees.

core allocation The use of core memory (RAM and ROM) as allocated in a system. Since this memory is usually limited, core allocation is concerned with the division of memory for:

- Programs to be permanently stored
- Temporary storage of programs
- Data to be permanently stored
- Temporary storage of data
- Working storage

CorelDraw A Windows-based graphics and desktop publishing program. The current version has hundreds of fonts, thousands of pieces of clip art, and dozens of photographs. It supports most import and export standards, including TIFF, PCX, PIC, EPS, PIF, and Windows Metafile. The program's text-manipulation and freehand drawing capabilities make it a useful illustration program for the PC.

core memory 1. *See* MEMORY. **2.** (*o.t.*) A storage device that used ferromagnetic toroids in matrix arrays for storing binary digits.

Cornerstone A flexible database system that is completely menu-driven and designed for nonprogrammers. It gives an almost infinite flexibility in the structure and presentation of data. The system allows for simple construction of complex interrelationships between files, as well as detailed selection criteria and reporting structures. All operations are initiated through a series of menus. There is no command language, nor does it support keyboard macros. The menu orientation, while good for people who do not program, makes the system difficult to use for production-type tasks. To print a regularly required report, for example, you must go through more than a dozen menu levels.

The program includes some features that make database design simpler. For example, text fields do not require a preset field length; instead, an expected field length can be set but is disregarded if the data exceeds the expected length. Another feature of the product is date and time arithmetic; it understands "last monday" and "this quarter," for example.

All this flexibility does create some problems. The system's many modes can be very confusing, and first-time users will have difficulty just keeping track of where they are. The nomenclature and command structure of the system are also confusing. The program is good for people who are used to working with computers but who do not want to write a program to create a sophisticated database system.

correction routine A routine designed to be used after a failure, malfunction, or error. The routine is inserted at a point before the error, during a run or rerun of the program.

corrective maintenance Maintenance designed to eliminate existing faults. Corrective maintenance may occur as a part of emergency maintenance or deferred maintenance, and should not be confused with *preventive maintenance*, which is designed to prevent failures. Corrective maintenance time may be scheduled or unscheduled.

correspondence center 1. A word-processing center. **2.** A secretarial group performing typing activities.

correspondence secretary A secretary responsible for typing activities and assigned to a correspondence center; a word processor operator.

correspondence study A survey that identifies typing activities, including sources of input, and measures the volume of typing in an organization.

corrugated diskette mailer A mailing package designed to provide economical, durable protection in transporting diskettes.

corrupt To destroy or alter information so that its validity is dubious. When a program calls the operating system, for example, it must first save the contents of important registers because the registers are corrupted when control returns from the operating system. The contents of the registers might be different than before the call, leading to unpredictable results.

COS Acronym for *compatible operating system*.

cost-effectiveness A constructed or designated measure of performance for the evaluation of systems, products, or procedures. It is most often expressed as a ratio of some reference measure of cost and performance.

Costimator A software package used to estimate the cost of machining, assembly, sheet-metal work, and other processes related to the metal working and manufacturing fields. It offers a library of precalculated time elements.

coulomb The quantity of electricity that passes any point in an electric circuit in one second when the current is maintained constant at one ampere.

Coulomb's law The law that states that the force of attraction or repulsion between two charges of electricity concentrated at two points in an isotopic medium is proportionate to the product of their magnitudes and is inversely proportionate to the square of the distance between them. The force between the unlike charges is *attraction*, and between like charges *repulsion*. Also called the *law of electrical charge* or the *law of electrostatic attraction*.

counter A device used to measure and represent the number of occurrences of a specific event, also known as an *accumulator*. Some types of counters can be set to an initial value and then increased or decreased (as an *up-down counter*). Others may be used as address counters or registers in which address data is loaded to specify the location where the next block of data is to be transferred.

A counter may be used as an index register that can be set to any number from storage, incremented by a certain number, and then tested against another number in storage. Index registers are used for address modifications and in programs involving repetitive steps.

Counters used as *cycle index counters* measure the number of times a cycle of instructions has been repeated. A cycle index register can be used to determine the number of repetitions required in a loop at any given time.

counter-comparator conversion A type of analog-to-digital converter; the counter-comparator converter, as shown in the following figure, is analogous to the single-ramp type, except it is independent of a time scale. The analog information is compared with the output of a D/A converter, and the digital input of the D/A is driven by a counter. At the start of a conversion, the counter begins the count, which continues until the D/A output exceeds the input value. Then conversion stops and the converter is ready for the next conversion, once the counter is reset to zero.

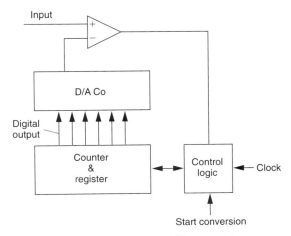

Counter-comparator A/D converter

counter, program *See* PROGRAM COUNTER.
counter timer interface board A type of expansion board that offers the user general-purpose 16-bit counters. Various frequency sources and outputs may be chosen as inputs for individual counters with software-selectable (active-high or active-low) input polarities. Each counter may be gated by hardware or software.

counting, sample-hold *See* SAMPLE-HOLD COUNTING.
couple, chip-select decode Refers to the use of chip-selects of memories to achieve a partial decode of the high-order addresses. For small systems, this can be sufficient to discriminate among all memory locations.
coupled circuit A circuit that contains only resistors, inductors, and capacitors with more than one independent mesh.
coupler A device that transfers signals and has its input and output isolated electrically. Also known as an *isolator*, a coupler usually consists of a light-emitting diode (LED) and a light sensor. The input signal activates the LED, which in turn forces current through the output light sensor. When the two devices are separated by an air gap rather than glass or plastic, the coupler can be used to sense motion and encode cards, plates, and slotted disks.
coverage A percentage of the completeness with which a braid or shield covers the surface of the underlying insulated conductors.
COZI Acronym for *communications zone indicator*.
CNA Abbreviation for *Certified NetWare Administrator*, Novell's entry-level certification. It is for the person who needs to administer a network on a day-to-day basis. Usually these people work for one company and perform the administrator tasks in concert with their other duties.
CNE Abbreviation for *Certified NetWare Engineer*, Novell's intermediate-level certification. This certification is for people who require a higher level of expertise than a system administrator. Many people who obtain the CNE certification are consultants, system integrators, or employees of companies that need a person with considerable NetWare expertise to help maintain the overall network.
CNI Abbreviation for *Certified NetWare Instructor*, is Novell's advanced-level certification. This certification is for the individual who wants to teach certified NetWare courses. These courses are taught at Novell Authorized Education Centers (NAECs) and use the Novell courseware.
CPA-Ledger A public-domain, menu-driven, general ledger and financial statement program. It is designed for nonmanufacturing businesses that offer products or services for sale. You must have a knowledge of double entry bookkeeping to operate this package. Any general ledger entry may have up to 30 debits and 30 credits, with total values of up to 999,999,999.99. Also, you may use any combination of 1 to 30 characters to identify the payee of a check.
CPE Abbreviation for *central processing element*, an element of a bit-slice microprocessor that

contains all of the major processing circuits necessary to build processors of longer word lengths. CPEs can be cascaded to form a processor of any desired word length. Multiple bus structures allow functions to be executed in a single microcycle instead of several cycles.

CP/M (*o.t.*) Abbreviation for *control program for microprocessors*, one of the first popular disk operating system for microcomputers, developed by Digital Research, Inc.

C Programmer's Toolbox A program that contains 12 tools that work with Microsoft C, Borland C++, ANSI C. The tools allow you to reformat your source code into your programming style; determine and graph program, function, and file organization and hierarchy; identify unused functions and runtime library usage; and profile program execution, including BIOS interrupts and DOS system-call usage.

CPS Abbreviation for *characters per second*, a standard unit of measurement for printer output.

CP switch A unit used to interconnect a CRT (or microcomputer), a modem, and a receive-only serial printer. The switch provides you with four options:

1. A bidirectional connection between the CRT and the modem
2. A receive-only connection between the modem and printer
3. A direct connection between the CRT and the prints
4. A simultaneous connection of both the CRT and the printer with the modem

The operation of the unit is controlled by three switches, a line/local switch and two receive on/off switches, as shown in the diagram. The line/local switch selects the modem or printer connection for the CRT (line for modem and local for printer). The two receive switches select the receiving device when in line mode—either CRT, printer, or both.

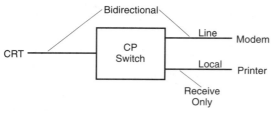

CP switch

CPU Abbreviation for *central processing unit*, a primary unit of the computer system that controls the interpretation and execution of instructions. A CPU typically consists of registers, computational circuits such as the ALU (arithmetic and logic unit), control circuits, and input/output ports. The registers may include accumulators, index registers, and perhaps stack registers. All registers are treated as internal memory.

CR The carriage-return character, which causes the print position to be moved to the first (usually flush-left) space on a new line.

cracker An individual who attempts to access computer systems without authorization. These individuals are often malicious, as opposed to hackers, and have many means at their disposal for breaking into a system.

CRC Abbreviation for the *cyclic redundancy check character*, a redundant character used for error detection in various modified cyclic codes. *Also see* CYCLICAL REDUNDANCY CHECKING.

CRC-12 A 12-bit cyclic redundancy-checking scheme that uses $X^{12} + X^{11} + X^3 + X + 1$ as the generator polynomial.

CRC-16 A 16-bit cyclic redundancy-checking scheme that uses $X^{16} + X^{12} + X + 1$ as the generator polynomial.

creation date In NetWare, a part of File Services and Directory Services. This and the Last Access Date are specified in two bytes. The Last Update Date and Time and Last Archive Date and Time are in a four-byte format, as shown in the figure.

credit A flow-control mechanism used in DEC'S LAT network protocols. A node is allowed to send a packet only if it has a credit available. If not, it must wait for the remote node to send one.

credit limit In NetWare, a part of Accounting Services. It is a minimum balance that must be maintained in an account.

```
   Year            Month         Day
+------------+  +---------+  +------------+
:7 6 5 4 3 2 1: 0:7 6 5  : :  4 3 2 1 0 :
+------------+--+---------  - ------------+
   Byte1                       Byte2


+------------+------------+------------+
:   Hour     :  Minute    :  Second    :
:7 6 5 4 3  2 1 0: 7 6 5   4 3 2 1 0   :
+------------+------------+------------+
   Byte3                       Byte4
```

Four-byte format of NetWare creation date

C-REF Software that creates summary or detailed cross-references of local; global; define; and parameter usage. It also creates a class-hierarchy tree diagram for C++ classes.

crimp To secure the buffer tubing of a fiber cable to the tabs on a connector, or to secure the shield of a coaxial cable to a connector.

crimp connection A method for joining a connector to a wire in which the connector is crimped around the wire to provide electrical contact and mechanical strength.

crippled leapfrog Refers to a variation of the leapfrog tests to discover computer malfunctions. The crippled leapfrog tests are done from a fixed set of locations rather than the changing locations used in the leapfrog tests. *Also see* LEAPFROG TEST.

criterion A value used for testing, comparing, judging, or determining whether a condition is plus or minus, true or false; also, a rule or test for making a decision.

critical path A scheduling system that uses milestones to check the progress of the task.

CRO Abbreviation for *cathode ray oscillograph*.

CROM Abbreviation for *control read-only memory*, a type of ROM designed and microprogrammed to decode control logic. The CROM is a major component of many two-chip microprocessors. One chip contains the CPU and the other a CROM that accesses the correct routine for each instruction, sequences through the routine, and provides the data control signals to the CPU. In general, the instructions are basic and have a short execution time, which makes it practical to use a large number of them in the program.

cross assembler An assembler translates a symbolic representation of instructions and data into a form that can be loaded and executed by the microprocessor. A cross assembler is an assembler executing on a machine other than the microprocessor that generates object code for it. Initial development time can be significantly reduced by taking advantage of a larger scale computer's processing, editing, and high-speed peripheral capability. Some systems consist of a simulation program, which enables the computer to simulate the operation of a microcomputer, and an assembly program used to program the microcomputer.

cross compiler A program that prepares a machine-language program on one computer for another computer. A cross compiler can replace a cross assembler in many high-level language applications to allow extra convenience to the programmer.

cross-coupling The usually unwanted, inadvertent transfer of signals and signal components between circuits or channels.

cross-linked file When two files overlap on a disk, they are said to be cross-linked. Cross-linked files both claim to have data stored in the same cluster.

cross modulation A form of signal distortion found in multiple-carrier systems, also called *crosstalk*. Cross modulation may be caused from the effects of the envelope of one carrier upon the other due to nonlinearity in the common transmitting medium. The source of the energy is called the *disturbing circuit*, and the circuit receiving the energy is called the *disturbed circuit*. *Far-end crosstalk* propagates in the same direction as the signals, and *near-end crosstalk* propagates in the opposite direction.

crossover cable A null modem cable for asynchronous applications where a DTE device is cabled to another DTE device. For short-distance applications, the cable eliminates the need for modems or modem eliminators.

Crossref A set of user-supported BASIC programming tools. One tool produces a cross-reference listing of variables referenced in a BASIC program, with line numbers. Another provides a user interface for any BASIC application, by creating a library of small modules which set up the screen, display menus, and ask questions. These tools help give a uniform, professional look to programs.

cross-16 A table-based absolute cross-assembler using the manufacturer's mnemonics. It produces a listing and Intel, Motorola, or binary hex file from an assembly language source file. It supports all of the processor families included in XDASM plus: 37700, 50740, ADSP-2100, NEC7500, PIC16C5x, TMS3201x, TMS370, TMS7000 and TMS9900. It is user-configurable for other processors.

crosstalk Contrast with CROSS MODULATION. 1. The undesirable energy transferred from one circuit to another. The source of the energy is called the disturbing circuit and the circuit receiving the energy is called the disturbed circuit. *Far-end* crosstalk propagates in the same direction as the signals, and *near-end* crosstalk propagates in the opposite direction. 2. (initial capital) A flexible data communications program that links a personal computer to virtually any other computer including other personal computers, minicomputers, mainframes and subscription information services. Available for most modems, Crosstalk works as a smart terminal. It has full support for autodial and auto-answer modems. It can transfer data and programs with error-checking. Incoming data can be routed to any display, printer, or disk. Data can be sent from the keyboard or a disk file.

The program has a retro-capture facility that lets you store data that has already scrolled off the screen. It stores and automatically transmits log-on information and commands to a remote system. It supplies extension help for the novice user yet has a command interface for the experienced user.

The program can emulate IBM 3101, DEC VT100, ADDS Viewpoint, and Televideo 910 and 920 terminals. It is one of the most popular communications programs for the IBM PC.

cross validation The verification of results by replicating an experiment under independent conditions.

CRT Abbreviation for *cathode-ray tube*, a large vacuum tube with a viewing face, in which an electron beam is focused and controlled to form characters and other images. The beam and pattern are easily varied to produce almost any desired information format.

CRTs are used for both display and storage in computer systems. As a display, the CRT can be operated in the point mode to allow points to be established and displayed on the screen. CRT storage uses the electron beam to sense the presence or absence of spots on the CRT screen.

A typical application of a CRT is in drawing display systems, where a designer uses a special stylus to draw on a sensing tablet; as the designer draws, the information is sensed and displayed on the CRT screen. Quickly sketched lines are displayed straight, and rough corners appear precise on the display screen. Changes and modifications are easily made and lines are erased with simple stylus movements.

CRT display microprocessor Refers to a display built around a microprocessor controller. The microprocessors controls both information read-out by the operator and the setting methods.

CRT screen cleaner kit A kit with nonaerosol pump-spray CRT screen cleaners, lint free wipes, and antistatic cloths to clean and control static charges on the surface of a CRT screen.

CRT storage The (usually) electrostatic storage characteristic of cathode ray tubes in which the electron beam is used to sense the data.

cryogenics The study and use of properties of materials at temperatures approaching absolute zero. Cryogenic elements offer high-speed storage from the superconductivity that occurs at near-zero temperatures. Since superconductors have no resistance, they also have the ability to store currents permanently.

cryotron A device operated at low temperatures to allow changes in small magnetic fields to control large currents; the cryogenic equivalent of an electron tube.

cryptographic equipment Scrambling devices based on digital logic for encrypting communications.

Cryptanalysis Helper A program that is designed to aid in the decoding of simple substitution aristocrat ciphers; it suggests translations based on a comparison of letter frequencies, with the frequency of the first letters of words, all letters, last letters, and one-letter words in a message. It matches words with some letters decoded in its dictionaries, which are written in C.

crystal The device that provides the timing for all computer functions, shown in the following figure. Suppose your computer comes with a 30 MHz crystal. Since most computers run at one-

Typical crystal package

half or one-third of their crystal speed, your computer will run at 10 or 15 MHz. If the crystal is dead, the rest of the circuitry will not run at all, and you might need to change the crystal. You might be able to even change to a faster crystal like a 36 MHz, speeding the system up to 12 or 18 MHz. The crystal looks like a little tin pellet on two wires. One side is usually attached to the system board by an adhesive pad. *Also see* COMPUTER CLOCK.

CS Abbreviation for *channel status*.

C-scape Development software from Interface Management System that supports DOS extenders including Ergo Computing OS/286 and OS/386 DOS Extender, Phar Lap 286 and 386 DOS Extender SDK, and Rational Systems DOS 16/M DOS Extender. It includes data entry and validation, windows, menus, text editing, context-sensitive help, mouse and graphics support. Programs written with C-scape can exceed the DOS 640K memory limitation, and are portable between DOS, OS/2, UNIX, VMS, and the X/Windows system. It supports Borland Turbo C, MetaWare High C 386, Microsoft C, and Watcom C 386.

CSMA Abbreviation for *carrier-sense multiple access*, a contention technique that allows multiple stations to gain access to a single channel. *Also see* CSMA/CD.

CSMA/CD Abbreviation for *carrier-sense multiple access with collision detection*, an access-control technique that allows multiple stations to successfully share a broadcast channel. Each station monitors the transmission medium for the presence of a carrier signal from another location. If none is detected, the station can begin transmitting its message, while simultaneously monitoring the channel to ensure that the message does not collide with messages from other stations that might have begun transmitting at approximately the same time.

Upon detection of a collision, all transmitting stations cease transmission, wait for a random length time interval, and then—if the channel is available—retransmit the aborted message. By requiring each station to wait for a random time interval before attempting to retransmit, one station will usually begin before the other(s), and they will sense the busy channel and postpone their own retransmission attempts, thus minimizing the probability of repeated collisions.

CSU Abbreviation for *channel service unit*, used to terminate a DDS (dataphone digital services) communications line. Terminating the line reduces noise and signal variances that could interfere with communications. A CSU is used for T-1 communications.

c-terp A C interpreter that provides a professional debugging and development environment. It features K&R support with ANSI extensions; a full-screen, built-in, reconfigurable editor; fast semi-compilation; multiple module support; automatic make file; global search; 8087 support, a preprocess facility; a system shell; and trace, batch mode, and full-screen source-level interactive debug facilities.

CTS Abbreviation for *clear to send*, a modem interface-control signal from data communication equipment (DCE) that indicates to the data terminal equipment (DTE) that it may begin data transmission.

CTS-10 A broadcast receiver that automatically links your PC to the world time standard, Coordinated Universal Time. Using a 10-MHz radio receiver and digital signal processing, it receives and decodes time and data information transmitted on a 10-MHz carrier by the National Institute of Standards and Technology (NIST), formerly known as the National Bureau of Standards (NBS). These radio signals are synchronized to the national atomic standard and have been providing a recognized time standard for over 60 years.

CUA Abbreviation for *common user access*, a technique for creating application menus in such a way that applications requiring similar functions use similar menus. For example, according to CUA, the file menu on every application will contain a Quit option. CUA also determines the order in which entries appear. For example, the File menu is always the first menu on the left side of the menu bar, while Help is the last menu on the right side of the menu bar.

cue The action made by the calling party in a communications mode, which serves as the signal for a subsequent series of events to begin.

cumulative graph A graph chart in which each point represents the sum of all values up to that point.

current The rate of flow of electrical carriers past a given point, usually measured in amperes.

current attenuation The loss of current in a device or circuit or along a line, usually expressed as the ratio of output to input current in decibels.

current balance Refers to a form of balance that measures the force required to prevent the movement of one current carrying coil in the magnetic field of a second coil carrying the same current.

current changed FATS In NetWare, a part of File Server Environment Services that contains the number of current FAT sectors the file system has modified.

current charge rate multiplier In NetWare, a part of Accounting Services that is multiplied by units of service (connect time, requests made, blocks read or written), and the result divided by the current charge rate divisor to calculate a charge against a user's account.

current charge rate divisor In NetWare, a part of Accounting Services that is used after the current charge rate multiplier is applied to units of service (connect time, requests made, blocks read or written) to calculate a charge against a user's account.

current density The amount of current passing through a given area of a conductor, usually expressed in amperes per square centimer (A/cm^2).

current directory The default directory for each drive on a computer system. This is the directory that the operating system searches if you enter a filename without a path specification.

current entries In NetWare, a part of Queue Services that shows a count of the jobs in a queue.

current gain In a transistor, the ratio of change in a collector current at constant voltage, resulting from a change in emitter current.

current instruction register A register that contains the instruction presently being executed.

current loop The electrical interface to a magnetic bubble memory. At specific points within a bubble track, conductors are deposited under the permalloy element in the form of single loops. Passing a pulse of current temporarily alters the level of the bias field under the permalloy element.

current loop cable A 24 AWG, four-conductor, twisted-pair cable with an overall shield for current loop applications. These cables may be ordered with Mate-N-Lok or DB25 connectors.

current loop interface converter A device that typically allows a 20 or 60 mA current loop to interface with an RS-232 device. Some of these devices have a power supply to drive the current loop (active converters), others require another device or external power supply to power the loop (passive converters). Interface converters also require component operating power, which may come from the interface converter (ac plug) or from the attached RS-232 interface.

currently used routing buffers In NetWare, a part of File Server Environment Services that shows the number of routing buffers that are being used by a server.

current multiplexer In a current multiplexer, the input resistor is removed to allow the multiplexing of current output transducers, as shown in the figure. When current output switching is used, the transfer accuracy is relatively unaffected by variations in line and connection resistance.

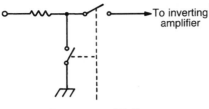

Current multiplexer

current open files In NetWare, a part of File Server Environment Services that contains the number of files the server has open. It reflects files that workstations have open and any internal files, such as the bindery, that the file server has open.

current servers In NetWare, a part of Queue Services that shows the number of currently attached job servers that can service a queue.

current shunt instrumentation amplifier Since instrumentation amplifiers can measure voltage differences at any level within their range, they are useful in current measurements. Typically, they measure and amplify the voltage appearing across a low resistance shunt, as shown in the figure.

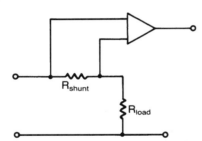

Instrumentation amplifier

current-switching sample-hold A sample-hold circuit that has an advantage in that the capacitor does not load the input source, which may either oscillate or lack the current to charge the capacitor fast enough. For faster charging at close to a linear slew rate, a diode bridge is used, as shown in the figure. The current sources are switched on to charge the capacitor. If the bridge and current sources are balanced, current flow into the capacitor stops when the capacitor voltage is equal to the input voltage. *Also see* SAMPLE-HOLD DEVICE.

current-switching D/A converter A digital-to-analog converter in which the switches and resistors are grouped as quads, with repeated 2R,

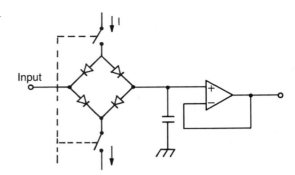

Current source sample-hold

4R, 8R, and 16R resistance values and 8:1 maximum range for bit currents. The less significant bit currents are attenuated in the output line, as shown in the figure. With the quad structure, there are only four different current values, which eases current matching. The attenuation allows the tolerances on the resistor values and transistor tracking in the less-significant quads to be relaxed. In the monolithic quads, the switching transistors have emitter areas with a power-to-two relationship to maintain a constant current density and equal tracking of V_{BE} and beta. The reference transistor, on the same chip, is usually identical to one of the switching transistors.

current-to-voltage converters Converters that use current outputs or voltage outputs directly from resistive ladders can be considered as voltage generators with series resistance or current generators with parallel resistance. They can be used with operational amplifiers in either an inverting or the noninverting mode, as shown in the figure. Some types use internal feedback resistors for output voltage scaling. These track the ladder resistors to minimize temperature variations. The gain-determining feedback resistances do not track the converter's internal resistors, only one another.

current tracer A current probe device that can be used to detect an ac current. It has a small magnetic pickup coil in its tip; when this coil is close to the magnetic field produced by an ac current, an indicator light glows. The tracer can be used to trace the path of or detect a continuous pulse train. The sensitivity is adjustable, and the detectable current range typically ranges from a few hundred microamps (a very dim indication) to a few milliamps, which lights the bulb to full brightness. The current path must be in line with the pickup coil; if the current flow is at an angle of 90 degrees there will not be enough coupling for the pickup to work.

The current tracer is useful when a circuit

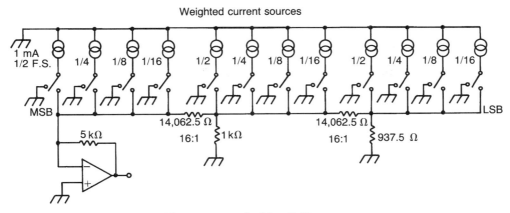

12-bit current-switching D/A converter

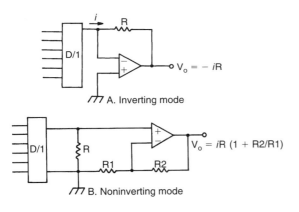

A. Inverting mode
$V_o = -iR$

B. Noninverting mode
$V_o = iR(1 + R2/R1)$

Current-to-voltage conversion

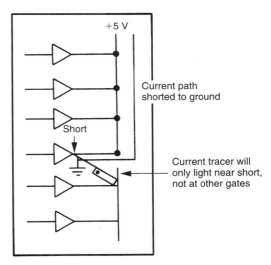

A current tracer, helpful when many parallel paths exist

has several parallel branches and a problem, like a short, could be in any one of the branches. In order to isolate the branch with the short, each branch would have to be disconnected and tested separately. This would require cutting or desoldering each branch to separate them and then resoldering to connect them. The current tracer allows you to test the current in each branch.

current transaction count In NetWare, a part of File Server Environment Services that shows the number of transactions in progress.

current unidirectional A current that, on the average, maintains the same direction in a circuit. It can fluctuate or go negative.

current used bindery objects In NetWare, a part of File Server Environment Services that shows the number of bindery objects currently in use on the server.

current used dynamic space In NetWare, a part of File Server Environment Services that shows

the amount of memory in the dynamic memory area that is currently in use.

cursor A manually controllable pointer used as a position or location indicator in a display. A cursor is usually employed to indicate a character to be changed or corrected, or a position where data is to be entered via the keyboard. The cursor may take the form of an underscore, a caret, an arrow, a rectangular block, or some other character.

custom ROM Refers to mask-programmed read-only memory, in which the manufacturer places the binary information into the memory as specified by the user. Custom-programming of ROMs is expensive when only small quantities are ordered. To reduce the high cost of small quantities of ROMs, one can use the field-programmable ROM, or PROM. The user can program information into the PROM by blowing selected on-chip fuses. The fuses are blown open by passing a specific amount of current through them.

custom variable In NetWare, a part of Diagnostic Services that is a word-length field that specifies information pertinent to the particular driver. These fields are optional.

cut and paste In word processing, a command that allows a user to move text from one part of a file to another or to a completely different file.

C Utility Library A library of over 400 C functions for both the experienced and novice C programmer. It includes pulldown and pop-up memos, windowing, and list and file boxes with shadows. Other features include EMS 4.0 support, a window editor/file browser, and file backup utilities.

cutter diameter compensation A method in automatic machining by which the programmed path may be altered to allow for the difference between actual and programmed cutter diameters.

cutter path The path described by the cutter in order to generate the desired part configuration in automatic machining.

cutter radius offset The distance from the part surface to the radial center of a cutter in automatic machining.

C++/Views An application development framework for building Windows programs using the C++ language. It comes with 65 C++ classes for Windows. These classes compose a library of parts supporting windows, views, menus, dialogs, controls, bitmaps, printers, and graphics. The package includes a class hierarchy browser supporting single and multiple rooted hierarchies, adding and deleting class, application management, library management, automatic make-file generation, and automatic class documentation.

C-Vision Software designed to analyze, understand, and maintain C source code. A cross-referencer provides detailed symbol descriptions including usage, data, type, arguments, return type, and full test of macros. A tree diagrammer can show different views of your code.

CVSD Abbreviation for *continuously variable-slope delta modulation*, a type of delta modulation in which the size of the steps of the approximated signal is progressively increased or decreased to make the approximated signal closely match the input analog wave. *Also see* DELTA MODULATION.

C-Worth User Interface A development system that allows you to build and test your interface onscreen without coding, recompiling, or relinking. It includes a message librarian for faster interface design.

cyan The color obtained by mixing equal intensities of green and blue light. It is also the proper name for the subtractive primary color often called blue.

cybernetics The science of communication and control in living organisms and the corresponding simulation through the use of

- Integration of communication and control technology
- Systems engineering development
- Hardware and software application development

The field of cybernetics has aided technology forecasting and assessment, systems modeling, policy analysis, pattern recognition, and artificial intelligence development.

cyberspace A term coined by William Gibson in his fantasy novel *Neuromancer* to describe the "world" of computers, and the society that gathers around them.

cycle One complete revolution in a repetitive sequence of revolutions; the operations are allowed to vary, but the sequence must retain a regular pattern. A computer cycle refers to a non-arithmetic shift in which digits are taken from one end of a word and moved to the other end, or to the repetition of a set of operations a required number of times. Cycling may include the supplying of address changes using a cycle counter to measure the number of times the cycle is to be repeated. An *action cycle* is the complete cycle operation performed on a block of data, including origination, manipulation, and storage.

cycle availability That specific time period during which stored information can be read.

cycle counter A mechanism or device that measures the number of times a specified cycle is repeated.

cycle criterion The total number of times the cycle is to be repeated; also, the register that stores that number.

cycled interrupt A change of control to a specific operation, usually in a predetermined manner such as a specific sequence or operation cycle.

cycle index An index of the number of times a cycle has been executed or is to be executed. A cycle-index register can be set to the number of cycles desired; then, each cycle shifts the register down by one until it is empty and the cycle series is complete.

cycle stealing A method of delaying execution of a program to allow an operation that would normally require a complete cycle for completion. A cycle-stealing data channel will allow the storage of a data word without changing the processor logic. After the word is stored, the program can continue as though never stopped. A cycle steal is different from an interrupt in that it does not change the contents of the instruction register.

cycle time The interval between calling for and delivery of information from storage, or any regular sequential time interval such as required to complete specific operations or execute instructions. Cycle time is one parameter that allows a comparison of speeds. Because other factors, such as the instruction set and cycles per instruction, affect computer speed, benchmark programs similar to the inquired application program should be used to compare speeds.

cyclic binary code See GRAY CODE.

cyclic check A cyclic method of error detection that is used to check the $x + n$ bit where $n = 1, 2, 3,...$ The cyclic check is usually preferred over horizontal, vertical, or combinational checks.

cyclic code Any code that differs by only one bit between numbers, such as the Gray code and cyclic decimal code.

cyclic decimal code A four-bit binary code word in which only one digit changes state between any two sequential code words, and which translates to decimal numbers. This code is one of a group of unit distance codes.

cyclic memory A memory that can be accessed only at multiples of the cycle time.

cyclic polynomial An error-detection method that uses division by a polynomial to check for errors. A cyclic polynomial check is a good test for single, double, and odd numbers of errors. If, after the division process, a remainder occurs, an error is present. The division can be done using a shift register, which also provides the checksum. A cyclic sum check results if the checksum data from the shift register is fed back through the register again.

cyclic redundancy An error-detection method that uses redundant check bits. A cyclic redundancy generator is used to generate a stream of check bits that are divided by the same polynomial as the data bits; a nonzero remainder indicates that an error has been detected.

cyclic redundancy check character See CRC.

cyclic redundancy checking An error-detection scheme that treats an N-bit message as an Nth-order polynomial, and divides it by a generator polynomial to produce a quotient and a remainder. This remainder is then appended to the message and transmitted. At the receiver, another remainder is computed from the received data bits and compared to the received remainder. If errors have occurred during transmission, the two remainder values will not agree.

cyclic shift A shift in which data is moved from one end of a word in a register to the other end. For example, if the register holds 00110011, then a cyclic shift of two bits gives 11001100. This is also called a *circular shift*, *end-around shift*, *logical shift*, *ring shift*, *nonarithmetic shift*, and *cycle shift*.

cyclic storage A storage system that operates as a closed loop; sometimes called *circulating storage*.

cyclic storage access Descriptive of a storage unit that allows access only during specific, equally spaced intervals. Cyclic access is found in units such as magnetic drums.

cycling The periodic change allowed on a variable or function by a control system or controller.

cycling control A fundamental machine control that programs the machine using a dial or plugboard input.

cylinder A term used primarily with hard disks to refer to the number of tracks on a disk drive that can be accessed without repositioning the recording heads. Each side of a diskette or platter that holds information is considered a cylinder.

cylinder line printer (o.t.) A printer that used a single-hammer system and a cylinder with a series of raised letters.

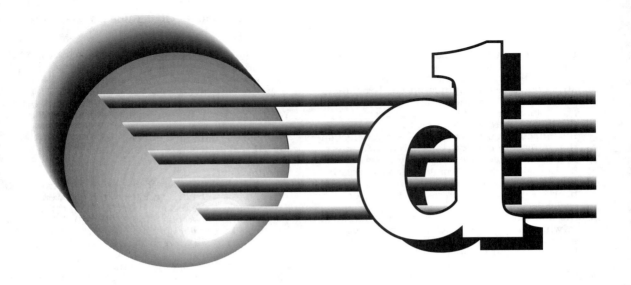

DA Abbreviation for *destination address*.

D/A 1. Abbreviation for *digital-to-analog conversion*. **2.** Abbreviation for *data acquisition*. **3.** Abbreviation for *discrete address*.

DAA Abbreviation for *data access arrangement*, an interfacing unit required between privately owned and common-carrier equipment on a direct-dial network. The DAA equipment is furnished or approved by a common carrier (such as Bell), permitting attachment of privately owned data terminal and data communications equipment to the common carrier network, normally the dial network.

D/A converters Abbreviation for *digital-to-analog converter*, a device for converting digital signals into continuous analog signals. Digital-to-analog converters usually buffer the input so that the output remains the same until the input changes. Units are available with up to 16 channels that can operate at 10,000 samples per second with a 100-microsecond conversion time.

The basic D/A converter circuit consists of a reference, a set of binary weighted precision resistors, and switches, as shown in the figure. In this circuit, an operational amplifier holds one end of all the resistors at zero volts. The switches are operated by digital logic. Each switch that is closed adds a binary weighted increment of current E_{REF}/R_j through the summing bus at the amplifier's negative input. The output voltage is proportional to the total current, which is a function of the value of the binary number. In an application that required 12-bit D/A conversion, the range of resistance values needed would be 4,096:1 or up to 40M for the least significant bit.

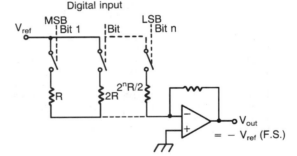

Basic D/A converter

DAC 1. Acronym for *digital-to-analog converter*. **2.** Acronym for *data acquisition and control*.

daisy-chain bus A bus that is similar to a party line, except that the units are interconnected and signals are transferred are made in serial fashion. Each unit is allowed to accept one interruption input, and the chips closest to the CPU have priority when requesting service. Each unit may modify the signal before passing it on to the next device. This approach is used mainly for signals related to interrupts or polling circuits. Whenever a device requires service, it blocks the signal. A priority is thus established, since the devices that are closest to the microprocessor usually have the first chance to request service.

daisy-chain polling An I/O polling method that is software driven, with the help of additional hardware, and uses a linked chain to identify the device, as shown in the figure. After preserving the registers, the microprocessor generates an interrupt acknowledge, which is gated to device A. If device A generated the interrupt, it places an identification number on the data bus, where it is ready by the microprocessor. If it did not generate the interrupt, it will propagate the acknowledge signal to device B. Device B will then follow the same procedure.

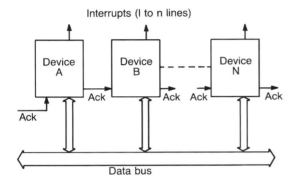

Daisy-chain polling technique

daisy-chain structure A bus structure in which the information passes through each system element until it arrives at the correct device. Each device acts as both a source and acceptor on the bus. *Also see* DAISY-CHAIN BUS.

daisywheel printers (*o.t.*) An impact printer with a steel or plastic disk that rotates in a circle, moving the proper "petal" of type to the area where the print hammer can strike it. Typical printing speeds for daisywheel printers range from 30 to 80 characters per second. Because they cannot handle software-based fonts or graphics, they are no longer common.

DAM Acronym for *data acquisition and monitoring*.

damping The reduction of oscillatory conditions in control devices and systems to improve stability. Damping may be done to electrical and mechanical components, and generally falls within three classifications:

- *Critically damped*—no overshoot or undershoot occurs (optimum response)
- *Underdamped*—overshoot occurs (excessive oscillation)
- *Overdamped*—no overshoot or undershoot (response too slow)

DANAL A graphically oriented data analysis tool that provides a quick means of manipulating and processing data files as if they were continuous functions. This program, coupled to a data acquisition system, would be especially useful to scientists and engineers, mathematically oriented businesspeople, those tracking the stock market, and academics.

DANCAD3D A graphics program that lets you do complex tasks like stereoscopic 3D wireframe animation or draw simple things like a letterhead. DANCAD3D involves drawing with lines, either on a plane (2D drawing) or in space (3D drawing). These lines can be formed into both simple and complex "elements," which can be saved, loaded, magnified, rotated, flipped, offset (moved), and used over and over again. Because the elements are separate, they can be moved and displayed repeatedly to simulate the effects of motion on the objects you have drawn. You can put a list of elements, their position, and the viewpoint from which they are to be displayed in a macro (ASCII text file), so DANCAD3D can run itself without you having to enter the commands manually through the menus and keyboard.

DAP Acronym for *data access protocol*, a file transfer protocol developed by Digital Equipment Corporation (DEC).

DAR Acronym for *data access register*, a register used in some microcomputers for RAM stacking address arithmetic. A typical register system uses three registers: a program counter, a stack pointer, and the operand address. Sixteen instructions allow decrement/increment and register transfer within a single clock cycle.

Darlington A monolithic circuit consisting of two direct-coupled transistors connected to function as one. A Darlington circuit provides high current gains, which makes it useful as a driver circuit in computer applications.

DARPA Acronym for *Defense Advanced Research Projects Agency*, an agency of the U.S. Department of Defense responsible for the development of new technology for use by the military. DARPA (formerly known as ARPA) was responsible for funding much of the development of the Internet as it is known today, including the Berkeley version of Unix and TCP/IP.

DART Acronym for *data analysis recording tape*.

DASD Acronym for *direct access storage device*, pronounced "DAZ-dee."

DAST Acronym for *Division for Advanced Systems Technology*.

DAT Abbreviation for *digital audiotape*, tape designed for use in systems that employ digital, rather than analog, recording technology. DAT cassettes are more compact than conventional audiocassettes and are used for data and image storage as well as audio.

data The graphic or textual representation of facts, concepts, numbers, letters, symbols, or instructions suitable for communication, interpretation, or processing. Data may be *source* or *raw data*, which is then refined to suit the user by processing. Data is the basic element of information used to describe objects, ideas, conditions, or situations.

data above voice A hybrid transmission scheme that places a data signal above the voice spectrum in a cable or radio system. Also called *data over voice*.

data access arrangement See DAA.

data access protocol See DAP.

data access register See DAR.

data acquisition The collection and processing of data for any or all of the following purposes:

- Storage for later use
- Transmission to another location
- Processing to obtain additional information
- Display for analysis or recording

Data can be stored in raw or processed form. It can be retained for short or long periods, transmitted over long or short distances, or displayed on a digital panel or a cathode-ray tube, as shown in the figure.

data acquisition and control The system used to collect or gather data and prepare it for further processing. Data acquisition and control equipment may include transducers, transducer amplifiers, multiplexers, and data converters, as well as logging units such as magnetic tape, disks, printers, and plotters. A typical system samples analog voltages, scales them, and converts them to digital format for recording or printout.

data acquisition and control board A board that uses data conversion and output components to provide a form of economical data acquisition and control. These boards often come with a complete software package and instructions. Many are designed to plug directly into a microcomputer expansion slot.

data acquisition module A typical module for data acquisition might have eight differential input channels and 16 single-ended input channels for 12-bit data acquisition in a 72-pin package. Acquisition and conversion time combined are 20 microseconds, giving a throughput rate of 50 kHz. The 12-bit binary data can be transferred out in three 4-bit bytes, by the three-state data bus drivers. Output coding is straight binary in unipolar operation and offset binary in bipolar operation.

The data acquisition circuit shown in the following figure includes a multiplexer, programmable amplifier, sample-hold circuit complete with hold capacitor, 10-volt buffered reference, and a 12-bit A/D converter with three-state outputs along with digital logic.

data acquisition system board A typical data acquisition system board might be capable of a 110 kHz throughput rate with 12-bit resolution. In this system, a sample-hold is used with a high-speed hybrid 12-bit A/D converter and a monolithic analog multiplexer. The basic config-

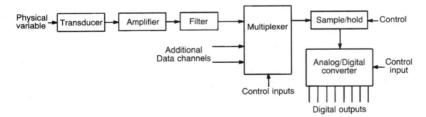

Typical data acquisition system

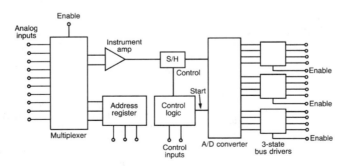

Data acquisition module

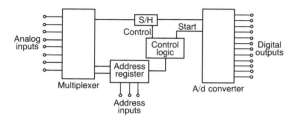

Data acquisition system board

uration is shown in the figure. The sample-hold might have a one microsecond acquisition time while, the A/D converter does a conversion every eight microseconds.

data, analog A physical representation of information such that the representation bears an exact relationship to the original information.

database A collection of data, usually larger than a file, that is sufficient for a given purpose in a data-processing application. For example, an invoice might form a *record* in an application, a set of records forms a *file*, and the collection of files becomes the database, also sometimes called a *data bank*.

Database Graphics Toolkit A software package that provides imaging support for over 10,000 applications running under 32 different languages. It retains your text as a graphic, then superimposes a miniature copy of the image onto the screen.

database management system *See* DBMS.

database manager A program that can be tailored to manage a set of data for personal or business purposes.

database protocol Refers to database access rules used for information storage and retrieval, in which the host commands what specified data fields will pass between the host and the controller according to set procedures.

database server A computerized database system for a network in which the workstation and host system divide up the processing. This technique distributes the processing load and reduces the communication load on the network, since it eliminates parsing the entire database through the workstation when all records need to be evaluated. If a database has no server, the entire database must be parsed through the workstation for operations that require all records. Typical operations that require all records are sorting, indexing, and selecting records according to a criterion.

Database Toolkit A package to be used with KnowledgePro. The Database Toolkit lets you read and write dBASE or Lotus 1-2-3 files from within a knowledge base. The data is returned to KnowledgePro as a list, permitting seamless integration of data with the KnowledgePro topic structure. *Also see* KNOWLEDGEPRO.

DATABasic Database design software for BASIC users. It has hash-key indexing, multiple keys per file, multiple fields per key, no packing, and automatic index updates for up to four gigabytes of files. This design tool works with Quick-Basic, VisualBasic and PDS.

data bits The bits in an asynchronous character that are actually data. In ASCII, there are typically seven data bits. There is also a start bit, one or two stop bits, and perhaps a parity bit.

DATABOSS A public-domain database manager with report generation and import/export capabilities. It runs in BASIC and needs DOS 3.0 or higher and a hard disk for full functions.

data broadcast *See* DB.

data bus A bus used in many microprocessor systems for transferring data to and from the CPU and the storage and peripheral devices. A typical microprocessor uses three buses: a data bus, a timing bus, and a control bus. The data bus is independent of the processor and handles all communications between any pair of devices connected to the bus.

data bus enable A control line that removes the data bus from a high impedance condition.

data bus system In most microcomputers, all communication between modules in the system occurs over the system data bus. This bus is usually independent of the processor and handles communications between any two devices connected to the bus. In order to transfer information over the bus, a device first requests access through the bus priority network of bus control. If no higher priority request is present, control of the bus is granted, and the device then becomes bus master for one bus cycle. During this cycle, the master may address any other bus-connected device (which becomes the slave) and may command a transfer of data to or from the slave.

data capture, direct *See* DIRECT DATA CAPTURE.

data cartridge case A case with a security lock for standard data cartridges or mini data cartridges.

data cartridge cube A case for ten data cartridges in original protective cases. The selected unit tilts out for retrieval.

data cartridge head-cleaning kit A kit for oxide build-up on drive heads, which can cause read-write errors and excess wear to data cartridges. A cartridge head-cleaning kit will correct both problems. You apply the cleaning solution to the cartridge-shaped unit and inset it like a data cartridge.

data chain A combination of two or more data elements in a sequence to provide meaningful information. For example, a data chain called *date* would consist of the data elements *year*, *month*, and *day*.

The sequence of chaining ranges from low to high or high to low for machine processing.

Data chaining is used for gathering or scattering information within one record from or to more than one region of memory.

data channel A bidirectional data path or bus between input/output devices and the main memory, which usually allows concurrent operations.

data code A set of numbers, letters, characters, or symbols used to represent a data item such as a record, file, or word.

data collection stations Units on production floors used to collect employee payroll data and other information, for entry into computer systems.

datacom Abbreviation for *data communications*.

data communication The transmission and reception of data generally using some form of electrical transmission. Data communication can be aided by using a data communications control unit, which scans the central terminal for messages and then transfers them to the processor. Another technique involves using a data station as a remote terminal for communication with a central computer. When not in use for transmission, the data station can be used for data preparation and editing tasks.

Data communication functions that can be performed by microcomputers include the following:

- *Message switching* by the processing and communication of messages over limited channel-capacity systems
- *File management* through the remote updating of a centralized file, or other file handling and processing functions from a remote location
- *Inquiry/response* systems, in which a remote station makes inquiries of a centralized file but does not change that file
- *Data collection* through the use of a remote station that provides updated or current information to a centralized file

data communications equipment *See* DCE.

data compaction The methods used to reduce space, bandwidth, generating time, and other factors that add to the cost of data storage and transmission. Compaction methods tend to eliminate needless repetition and other irrelevancies.

data compression The methods used to increase unused storage space by eliminating gaps, redundancies, and unnecessary data, and shortening the length of records, fields, and blocks.

data contesters Units that can function as monitors, breakout boxes, or test sets, but are especially designed to perform intensive testing of any async/sync RS-232 device. Data contesters can perform bit error-rate testing (BERT) and block error-rate testing (BLERT), and can be switch-configured as data terminal equipment (DTE) or data circuit terminating equipment (DCE).

data, continuous Continuous measures are those that may be found at any point along a continuous scale. Examples are thermometers, speedometers, and analog sensing devices. Sometimes used in a broad sense to indicate all quantitative data.

data control clerk A person who coordinates information flow through a computer center by checking users' data and sending resulting reports back to the user.

data conversion line The channel used to transfer data elements between data banks.

data converter Devices that convert analog data to a digital format or vice versa. Converters are available in either hybrid or monolithic form.

data delimiter A flag character that ends or bounds a series or string of bits or characters; the delimiter is thus not a part or member of such a string unless it is the first or last member. Certain special patterns of data are also used as markers and end-of-message signals.

data descriptor An identifier used to describe a data area by pointing to one or more data locations in storage.

data dictionary A file that lists all the data formats, files, and relationships in a database.

data document A document that contains pieces of text to be merged into a main document to create form documents and other merge documents. The data document includes a header record and data records. The header paragraph lists the categories of text stored in the data document, and the data records store the actual text.

data element A set of related data items. For example, *Monday* is a data item denoted by the data element of *weekday*. Data elements can always be broken down into subcategories of data, usually data items.

data element dictionary *See* DED.

data encryption The process of transferring information into a random stream of bits to create a secret code for data security.

data encryption key A string of characters used for the encryption of message text and for the computation of message integrity checks. Also sometimes called a *signature*.

data encryption standard *See* DES.

Data Entry A specialized library and CASE tool for creating data entry menus. Features include data conversion, realtime data checks, dBASE picture strings, immutable characters, exit conditions from any field, context-sensitive help, range-checking shortcut keys, multiple title lines. It provides an on-screen WYSIWYG environment for creating form menus with automatic code generation.

data entry The transferal of information into a computer for processing. Special data-entry methods can be designed for specific applications in payroll, accounts receivable, and other areas.

data entry procedure Rules to follow for correct and complete input of data.

data file A file created by the user of a program to contain information, such as a budget created with a spreadsheet program or the contents of a mailing list created with a database program.

dataflow A type of computer architecture involving a number of processors that are freed from any serial form of processing. Instead, each processor goes to work as data becomes available from other processors and shares the results of its work with other processors when it has finished.

data fork size In NetWare, a part of the AppleTalk Filing Protocol Services (AFP) that is the data size of a target AFP file. If the AFP directory/file path specifies an AFP directory, the data fork size field returns a zero.

data format The rules and procedures defining the system used to show the data used in records, files, or words. Data formats are usually defined by statements that can instruct the assembly program in the area of constants, spaces, and punctuation.

data grade line A specially constructed telephone line that uses higher-quality media and less multiplexing than a normal line, to reduce overall line noise and increase reliability. Data grade lines usually use fiber-optic connections to ensure minimum disruption from external signal sources.

datagram A packet that includes a complete destination address specification, which is usually provided by the user, along with the data it carries. Its one-way construction is similar to a telegram.

data-handling system 1. A system of automatic and semiautomatic devices used in the collection, transmission, reception, and storage of information in digital form. **2.** A system in which data is sorted, reduced, or stored in a particular form.

data hierarchy The structure of data consisting of sets and subsets of data in an ordered sequence. Each subset of data is of lower rank than each set of data.

data input bus A single-bus structure used in some microcomputers. The processor, memory, and input/output devices all share this common bus. A switch register is used to transfer address codes and data between units.

data integrity A performance measure based on the rate of undetected errors.

data in voice A hybrid transmission scheme that places a data signal in the middle of the voice spectrum in a cable or radio system.

data item An individual member of a set of data, usually classified under a data element. For example, *Tuesday* is a data item of the data element *weekday*.

Data Junction A software tool that translates data files to and from different file formats. Files can be filtered while being converted. You can sort, extract, edit or enter records, fields, and characters. You can also split, merge, move, or delete fields. Script files allow for automatic batch-mode operation and perform case translation and search/replace by column. Data Junction provides automatic parsing of name and address fields.

data librarian A person who identifies, maintains, and stores tapes and disks for a large computer center.

data line monitor *See* DLM.

data link The communications circuits, lines, and other equipment used in the transmission of information between two or more stations.

data link control *See* DLC.

data link control layer The second layer of the ISO-OSI model, an architectural model for data communications established by the International Standards Organization (ISO). The second layer coordinates the flow of data and the structure of data messages. It is concerned with the establishment of an active link between stations, control of byte synchronization, block framing, error detection and correction, and the regulation of the data flow rate over the link. *Also see* OSI MODEL.

data link escape character A communication control character used to form an escape sequence allowing supplementary communication control operations. Only graphic characters along with communication control characters are allowed to construct an escape sequence.

data link layer *See* DATA LINK CONTROL LAYER.

data logging The recording of data concerning events that occur in a time sequence. Data logging equipment ranges from simple visual readout devices to complex systems using microprocessors. Data logging applications include the following:

- Process monitoring
- Environmental monitoring and pollution measurements
- Product research and development engineering
- Structural testing for strength, stress, strain, and vibration

data-manipulation language A series of commands that control the database program, allowing manipulation of files and data.

date medium The method used to transport or hold data or information. A data medium may be magnetic tapes, floppy disks, CD-ROMs, or other physical methods that can be varied to represent data.

data migration The movement of data from online or offline as determined by the system or requested by the user.

data model A plan used by the computer for storing and accessing data items from a database.

data movement, microprocessor In microprocessor-based systems, data movement is an important aspect of system operation. As new systems evolve, users must evaluate microcomputers with a critical eye toward input/output transfer. The number of instructions is less important than the nature of the instructions and usable addressing modes. There is a need to know how quickly the CPU can respond to a peripheral interrupt and how the interrupt is managed as well as what is available in the way of interface devices. The list of questions depends on the needs of the user.

data name An identifier for an item of data.

data over voice See DATA ABOVE VOICE.

data PBX A unit that establishes and disconnects connections between computers and peripheral devices as needed.

Dataphone A product trademark of AT&T used to identify the data sets manufactured and supplied by the Bell System for transmitting data over the telephone network.

Dataphone Digital Service See DDS.

data processing The execution of systematic operations performed on data using sets of defined rules and procedures. Data processing has evolved as a general term for using computers in business and other applications.

data processor A device used to perform data processing. A data processor may be a calculator, a microcomputer, a minicomputer, or a large-scale computer. Also called a *processor*.

data purification The reduction of errors in data prior to using the data in the processing system.

data rate See DATA TRANSFER RATE.

data record A collection of data elements grouped together and considered as an entity.

data reduction The transformation of raw data into a more useful form using such methods as smoothing, scaling, or ordering.

data reliability A ratio used to measure a degree to which data is error-free.

data segment In NetWare, a part of Value-Added Process Services that is the data segment of a new process, or designates a segment to be used by the error handler.

data set 1. A set of data elements. The data set is a potential combination, and all elements are not required to be present to complete the set. A *symbolic* data set is a data set used for coding a program; the *actual* data set is determined at a later time during a particular execution of the program. 2. The electronic device used to provide the interface for data transmission to remote stations (as, for example, a modem).

data service unit See DSU.

Datashuttle A software utility for moving data between different file formats including ASCII (standard and field delimited), SIF, DIF, dBASE, SYLK, and Lotus. ASCII file manipulation is flexible; field-delimited ASCII files can be processed automatically, while more complex files can be converted by defining a typical record mask in an editing window. Transfers to Lotus-compatible spreadsheets can be controlled using a set of transfer commands.

data sink A device in a communications system used for accepting signals from a transmission device. A data sink may also check these signals and generate error control signals.

data source A circuit or device in a communications system used for originating signals for a transmission medium. A data source may also accept error-control signals.

dataspeak Voice data communications that involve a teleprinter input and an audio output from a remote computer.

data storage and retrieval Keeping data in an organized file and later accessing it for processing.

data stream The serial data that is transmitted through a channel from a single read or write, or other specific operation.

datastream type In NetWare, a part of Communication Services that indicates the type of data found in the packet.

data switches Data switches feature precious-metal plating on all contacts to provide long life reliability (25,000 operations). Shielded switches feature thicker plating for even longer life (50,000 operations), and a black steel-clad case to prevent EMI/RFI interference problems. They are used for long-distance and high-bps data transfers. Both styles are available in a variety of configurations to meet any application. The two-way (shown in the figure) and four-way switches are most often used to share one printer among two to four computers. Crossover switches allow two computers equal access to two printers. When you flip the switch, the computers are cross-connected to the opposite printers.

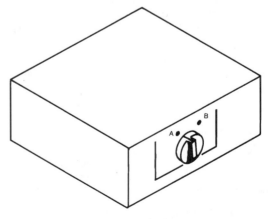

Data switch

data system The combination of personnel efforts, procedures, tools, media, and facilities that provide the means for recording, processing, and communicating data. The data system may be fully or partly automated. Also called an *information system*.

data terminal The equipment that provides a complete data sink and/or source. A typical video data terminal combines data entry and display and has its own storage and character generator for selected displays of up to 480 characters on the screen.

data terminal equipment *See* DTE.

data throughput The maximum speed at which data flows from the hard drive into the hard disk controller.

data transfer As used in microcomputers, an instruction that provides the ability to break the normal sequence of control. Three types of data transfers are used:

- *Programmed transfers*—the easiest and most direct method
- *Interrupt transfers*—peripheral devices initiate the transfer
- *Direct-memory-access transfers*—the fastest method

A data transfer controller can be used to provide the signal sequences to allow data transfers through the bus system; a data transfer register can simplify the movement of data for transfers. The data transfer register is also called a *memory data register (MDR)*.

data transfer rate The speed, measured in bits or bytes per second, that a device like a disk drive transfers data to the computer system. For example, the data transfer rate of a single-speed CD-ROM is 150,000 bytes per second.

data transmission The sending of data to one or more stations or locations.

data transparency An environment provided by a data link control protocol in which any arbitrary sequence of data bits can be sent without interfering with normal link operation. Data transparency is required when the data to be transmitted might contain bit sequences which could be interpreted as communications control characters. In character-oriented protocols, transparency can be provided by means of escape sequences or fixed-length frame structures.

data type In NetWare, a part of Accounting Services that contains the data types of a record. Data types larger than a LONG should be described as series of BYTE, WORD, and LONG FIELDS. Valid types are as follows:

Value	Type
1 (BYTE)	An 8-bit value
2 (WORD)	A 16-bit value, hi-low order
3 (LONG)	A 32-bit value, hi-low order
4 (TEXT)	A length byte followed by a string of printable characters

data under voice A hybrid transmission scheme that places a data signal under the voice spectrum in a cable or radio system.

data vac A lightweight vacuum to keep computer equipment clean. Features may include a triple filtration system, disposable bag, permanent cloth bag, and a fiberglass filter to keep the machine free of dust and paper.

data validation The checking of data for compliance with requirements. Data validation can be determined with tests such as the *forbidden-code check* to verify reliability and validity.

daughterboard A generic term usually referring to a sub-board that plugs into or connects with a larger board. A typical expansion board is sometimes referred to as a daughterboard since it must plug into a main board (a motherboard).

days charge occurs mask In NetWare, a part of Accounting Services. It contains a bit mask that specifies the days of the week for which a charge rate applies.

Dazzle/VB A program to display images in Windows with an image library for VisualBasic. You can fade and widen your pictures using one of the special effects, and zoom, pan, and adjust colors in your picture using custom controls.

DB Abbreviation for *data broadcast*, which refers to a standalone or rackmount junction panel that allows interconnecting of up to nine asynchronous RS-232C devices. It allows fan-out from the master device to eight slave devices.

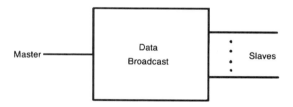

Data broadcast

dB Abbreviation for *decibel*, a unit of measure representing a power ratio between two power sources or sinks. One decibel represents the ratio multiplied by 10 times its common logarithm. By extension, voltages and current can be similarly compared (in which case the multiplier must be doubled). A doubling or halving of power represents a 3 dB difference. An order-of-magnitude power difference is 10 dB.

dBASE II (o.t.) The first true relational database management system for microcomputers. When you started dBASE II, only a period appeared (the "dot prompt"). English-like commands allowed you to retrieve information through queries, or you could write a program to allow untrained personnel to run complicated applications.

dBASE III (*o.t.*) The successor to dBASE II, rewritten to make it easier to use and to take advantage of the 16-bit microprocessor found in the IBM PC. The major advantages over dBASE II were:

- Up to ten databases open at the same time (dBASE II limit was two)
- Records of up to 4000 bytes (dBASE II limit was 1024)
- Up to 1 billion records per database
- Computational accuracy of 15.9 digits
- Improved browse and list procedures, improved index updating, temporary joins, and full access to DOS subdirectories

dBASE III contained context-sensitive help and an Assistant package which helped the user set up dBASE procedures. dBASE III provided a 40-to-1 improvement in speed for a sort compared to dBASE II.

dBASE IV The successor to dBASE III that does away with many previous limitations of dBASE. New features of dBASE IV include the structured query language (SQL) and query by example (QBE).

dbcs Abbreviation for *double-byte character set*, a 16-bit replacement for the standard ASCII character set. It is used for languages like Chinese and Japanese that use pictograms in place of letters.

dbFAST Windows A standalone dBASE/XBase development language for Windows. You can use it to create graphical applications. It has over 200 extensions to the dBASE language, and includes an interactive editor, compiler, and linker.

dBm 1. Power level in decibels relative to one milliwatt. **2.** *See* DECIBEL METER.

DBMS Abbreviation for *database management system*, a set of programs that allows the creation, maintenance, and manipulation of a database on a computer system.

dbPublisher A program for the automatic production of database documents. By modifying the content or layout of a report, you can utilize database publishing techniques for catalogs, directories, and price lists. It accepts data from all major databases, spreadsheets, word-processing programs, and graphics programs, including those running on mainframes and minicomputers. It provides advanced typographic controls, barcode generation, SGML-style markup tags, and supports more than 1,000 fonts.

DBS Abbreviation for *direct broadcast satellite*, a distribution scheme involving transmission of signals directly from satellites to homes. It does not carry common broadcasting's restricted bandwidth and regulations. DBS is the most effective delivery mechanism for reaching most rural areas, but it is relatively poor in urban areas and in mountainous terrain, particularly in the north. Depending on frequency band used, it can be affected by factors such as rain.

DBS-KAT A disk-cataloging program intended for people who use floppy disks for backup/archival purposes. Its central database can catalog the contents of 9,999 diskettes containing 16,000,000 files. There is a savings of 20 to 40 percent on hard disk space because of this capability.

DBU 1. Abbreviation for *dial back-up unit*. **2.** Abbreviation for the internal *designation bus* in a microprocessor CPU, from the ALU to its registers.

DbxSHIELD An inference engine and library that eliminates the need to write complex dialog boxes. It supports formatted/validated edit fields using picture masks and expanding dialog boxes.

dc 1. Abbreviation for *direct current*, current that flows only in one direction at an essentially constant value. **2.** Abbreviation for *direct coupled*. **3.** Abbreviation for *digital computer*. **4.** Abbreviation for *direct cycle*. **5.** Abbreviation for *data conversion*. **6.** Abbreviation for *device control*, a category of control characters primarily used for turning on or off a subordinate device.

DCA Abbreviation for *Digital Computer Association*.

dc coupling 1. Transmission with a modem using a steady stream of pulses. **2.** Direct coupling using components other than capacitors so as to avoid loss of direct current.

DCD Abbreviation for *data carrier detect*, an RS-232 signal to a device connected to a modem that indicates the modem is receiving a signal. Usually carried on pin 8.

dc dump The removal of any constant-sign voltage (and thus power) from a computer system.

DCE Abbreviation for *data communication equipment*, or more specifically, *data circuit-terminating equipment*, equipment that provides transmission connection. As used in EIA RS-232-C and related documents, this normally refers to modems or other equipment fulfilling a similar role. A DCE is sometimes required to couple the data terminal equipment (DTE) into a transmission circuit or channel and from a transmission circuit or channel into the DTE. *Also see* DTE.

DCFEM Abbreviation for *dynamic crossed-field electron multiplication*.

dc leakage current The current that flows through a capacitor when the rated dc voltage is applied.

DCS Abbreviation for *distributed computer system*.

DCTL Abbreviation for *direct-coupled transistor logic*, a logic system that uses only transistors as active circuit elements, as shown in the figure.

DD 1. Abbreviation for *double density* diskette. **2.** Abbreviation for *digital display*.

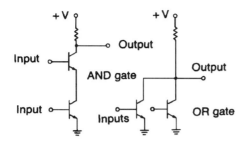

Direct-coupled transistor logic (DCTL)

DDA (*o.t.*) Abbreviation for *digital differential analyzer*, an early type of computing machine.

DDAS Abbreviation for *digital data acquisition system*.

DDCMP Abbreviation for *Digital Data Communications Message Protocol*, a byte-oriented synchronous data protocol originally developed by Digital Equipment Corporation that supports half-duplex or full-duplex modes, and either point-to-point or multipoint lines in a DNA (Digital Network Architecture) network.

DDD Abbreviation for *direct distance dialing*, the switched dial-up network that enables a telephone user to specify subscribers outside the originator's local area.

DDE Abbreviation for *dynamic data exchange*, a technique that helps ensure that device communication and information sharing is both regular and reliable.

DDL Abbreviation for *dynamic data library*, a technique similar to DDE, but with better error-checking and multitasking capabilities.

ddMap A mapping program that adds graphical location display to relational database applications development. It combines images onto a common grid coordinate system and then lets the user overlay database records as icons onto these images. It can be used for creating a graphical location inventory system for people, equipments, and events.

DDP 1. Abbreviation for *digital data processor*. **2.** Abbreviations for *Datagram Delivery Protocol*, an AppleTalk network-level protocol.

DDR Abbreviation for *data direction register*. Also see PERIPHERAL BUS.

DDRR Abbreviation for *directional discontinuity ring radiator*.

DDS Abbreviation for *Dataphone Digital Service*, a communications service of the Bell System in which data is transmitted in digital rather than analog form, eliminating the need for modems.

DDT Abbreviation for *dynamic debugging technique*, a sophisticated, online program debugger.

dead band A range of inputs for which no change in output occurs. A dead band is usually expressed in percent of span; resolution sensitivity can be defined as one-half dead band. When the output is at the center of the dead band, it denotes the minimum change in the measured quantity required to initiate a response. Also called *dead space* and *dead zone*.

dead front Concerns the act of joining a connector that is designed in such a way that the contacts are recessed below the surface of the connector's body, in order to prevent accidental short circuits and to keep the contacts from touching other objects.

deadlock A situation in which two software systems that exchange messages are hung up, both waiting for a message from each other. Also called *deadly embrace*.

dead mirror table In NetWare, a part of File Server Environment Services. It is a 32-byte table containing the secondary physical drive that each logical drive was last mapped to. The dead mirror table is used in conjunction with the drive mirror table. If the drive mirror table shows that a drive is not currently mirrored, this table can be used to determine the drive that previously mirrored the logical drive. This table is used to remirror a logical drive after a mirror failure.

dead time The interval between initiation of a stimulus change and the start of the resulting response.

dead zone *See* DEAD BAND.

debug To detect and remove errors and malfunctions from a program, routine, or machine. Debugging usually involves the running and checkout of programs to detect the errors. One typical method of debugging includes running a similar problem with a known answer through the system for checkout. Debugging aids are available to allow quick development of microcomputer programs. These aids allow the user to

- Print register contents
- Modify memory and register contents
- Use breakpoints for start and stop
- Search memory

Debug commands are allowed in some systems for tracing errors, and a class of software known as *debuggers* features programs that can be stopped and examined while slowly stepping the machine through the instructions.

To facilitate a successful system debugging operation, the user should be able to start, stop, and single-step the system clock. If the system is microprogrammed, there must be a way to set the contents of the control store address register and lock this register so that it cannot be advanced by the system clock or jump instructions. These controls over the register allow the user to select the starting point for coding and repeat a single instruction many times in order to completely debug that instruction. Monitoring the control store register is required to allow the user to know where the program is during debugging. This can be done in many microcomputer systems using the ROM simulator and the console control panel.

debugger A diagnostic aid that allows the user to analyze a program. The debugger allows the programmer to insert breakpoints and obtain register and memory dumps at desired points of the program execution. When the program detects an error, some debugger programs allow the user to make a modification and let the program continue to run.

debugging statements Statements that are often part of debuggers. They provide a variety of methods for manipulating the program in question, in an attempt to identify program errors or bugs. Debugging statements permit the user to

- Start and stop the program selectively
- Insert and delete control statements
- Print value changes as they occur
- Transfer control
- Cause printout of cross relationships among names and labels, and dynamic exposure of partial or imperfect execution

debug macros Refers to aids built into a program by the applications programmer, in addition to those supplied by the supervisory program.

DEC Digital Equipment Corporation, a major U.S. manufacturer of computer hardware and software.

decade A group or assembly of ten units.

decade switching The use of a series of switches, each with ten positions with the values of 0 through 9, in which adjacent switches have a ratio of values 10:1.

decay time The time in which a voltage or current pulse will decrease to one-tenth of its maximum value. Decay time is proportional to the time constant of the circuit.

decentralized processing Processing of data by individual subdivisions of an organization at different geographical locations.

decibel *See* DB.

decibel meter An instrument that is calibrated in decibels and used for measuring power levels above a usually arbitrary reference level, where the reference is 1 mW across 600 Ω. In audio equipment, 1 dBm equals 1 volume unit (1 VU); 0 VU or 0 dBm is the 1 mW reference. Sometimes abbreviated *dBm.*

decimal The number system that uses 10 as the radix or base.

decimal code A code in which each allowable position has one of ten possible states. The conventional decimal number system is a decimal code.

decimal notation A fixed-radix notation that uses the characters 0 through 9 and the radix of 10.

Using decimal notation, the number 601.2 is expressed as

$$(6 \times 10^2) + (0 \times 10^1) + (1 \times 10^0) + (2 \times 10^{-1})$$

decimal tab In word processing, a function that provides for automatic vertical alignment of decimal points at predetermined locations.

decimal-to-binary conversion The process of converting a number written in base 10 into the same number written in base 2.

decimal-to-hexadecimal conversion The process of converting a number written in base 10 into the same number written in base 16.

decision In computer systems, usually a comparison to determine the existence or nonexistence of a specific condition before taking a specific succeeding action. The action may involve a conditional jump or transfer of control. The comparison may take place between words or numerical characters in registers or other temporary storage.

decision box A rectangle or other symbol used on a flow diagram to mark a choice or branch in a program.

decision circuit A circuit such as a decision gate that performs a logical operation on binary information.

decision feedback equalizer An equalizer that uses a feedback loopback operating on the detector outputs to cancel intersymbol interference due to previous symbols.

decision gate A specific type of decision circuit that uses the states of two or more inputs to make a decision and provide the correct output indication.

decision instruction An instruction that causes the selection of a branch of the program, as, for example, a conditional jump instruction.

decision integrator A digital integrator used in incremental computers. The decision integrator provides an increment that is maximum positive, maximum negative, or zero, depending upon the input values.

decision level The signal amplitude that serves as a reference for determining the output of a comparison circuit. If the input signal is less than the decision level at the time of sampling, the output of the comparison circuit is negative or zero; if the input is greater than the decision level, the output is positive (with a binary 1 indication). Also called the *decision threshold* or *slicing level.*

decision symbol A diamond-shaped flowcharting symbol indicating where in a program a logical decision is made. In BASIC it is shown as the IF...THEN statement.

decision table A table that contains all aspects of a problem along with the actions that could be taken. Decision tables can be used in place of flow diagrams and are usually arranged in a matrix or tabular format. The upper part of each column can list all conditions to be considered for the problem, and the lower part can list the action to be taken for each set of conditions.

decision threshold *See* DECISION LEVEL.

declarative operation A coding sequence consisting of a symbolic label, a declarative operational code, and an operand. The declarative operation is used to write labels and codes for data and constants.

DECnet Digital Equipment Corporation's proprietary LAN operating system, which uses Ethernet protocols and is derived from Microsoft's PC-Net OEM LAN operating system.

decode The act of applying a set of data rules to restore a previous representation or to reverse a previous encoding operation.

decoder A device that determines the meaning of a set of data and usually initiates some action based on the meaning. A decoder may be a matrix of switching elements used to select one or more channels according to the combination of input signals. Many decoder chips can be expanded so that each decoder drives eight or more other decoders for large system applications.

In decoded addressing, the lines are connected to a decoder that linearly selects the components. An 8205 decoder appears in the following figures. It accepts three inputs and selects one of eight possible outputs. The 8205 can be used to select an 8708 ROM or a pair of 8111 RAMs that provide 8-bit words.

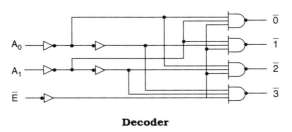

E	A0	A1	0	1	2	3
L	L	L	L	H	H	H
L	H	L	H	L	H	H
L	L	H	H	H	L	H
L	H	H	H	H	H	L
H	X	X	H	H	H	H

H = High voltage load
L = Low voltage load
X = Level does not effect output

Decoder

decode range In NetWare, a part of Diagnostic Services. Following a memory address, the decode range is the number of paragraphs in the block. Following an I/O address, it is the number of ports to be decoded.

decollate To separate the parts of a multipart form or document.

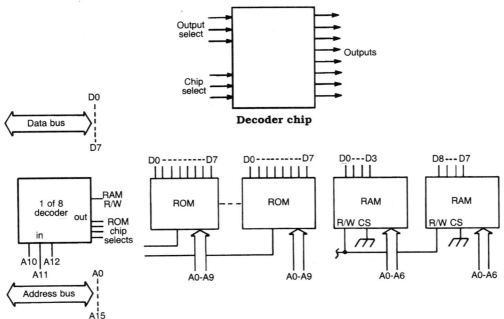

Typical ROM-RAM memory interface

decouple A gateway process (at the OSI application layer) to notify an application that transmission will not be completed within the roundtrip delay limitations protocol. Instead, a completion message (for transmission success or failure) is given at some later time. This feature is important in wide-area networks, heterogeneous networks, and enterprise-wide facilities.

decrement A device or instruction used to reduce, usually by one unit, the contents of a storage location and also the quantity by which the contents are decreased. Usually the decrement is a specific part of the instruction word.

decryption The process of converting encrypted data to its original (or non-encrypted) form.

DED Abbreviation for *data element dictionary*, an organized listing of data elements and their associated information in a given system.

dedicated Descriptive of machines, programs, or procedures that are designed, tailored, or reserved for specific uses.

Dedicated Advanced NetWare A network operating system that gives compatibility with DOS 3.1 and later. This allows multiuser software applications developed for DOS to run unmodified on NetWare. You also get internal bridging that permits up to four supported networks to bridge through the file server. NetBIOS emulation allows software applications written for IBM networks to run on any hardware that supports NetWare.

Because Advanced NetWare is a multitasking operating system, the file server allows for maximum utilization of processing power when responding to several different requests from users. Advanced NetWare uses such techniques as directory hashing, disk caching and elevator seeking. Advanced NetWare is fully compatible with NetBIOS and most software and hardware developed for the IBM PC and token-ring networks. It also has a security system to prevent unauthorized access to network information.

dedicated channel A specific channel that has been reserved or set aside for a very specific use or application.

dedicated circuit A communications circuit or channel that has been committed or allocated for a specific user or use.

dedicated computer A computer that is devoted to a singular processing activity. For example, a microcomputer used in a computer-aided-manufacturing system might be dedicated to machine tool activity.

dedicated line A service offered by the common carriers in which a customer may lease, for exclusive use, a circuit between two or more geographic points.

dedicated microprocessor techniques Specific tasks that are assigned to the microprocessor to maintain its productivity. Instead of the processor waiting for external interruption, it is put to work analyzing the external situation, continuously scanning and testing for inputs. The processor has complete command of the operation, knowing when to accept or ignore inputs. These simple but effective techniques reduce the need for expensive and complex interrupt structures.

de facto standards Standards popularized by the fact that they are from a large company, that there are a large number of users, or by default in that there are no others. Standards set by IBM are an example. *Contrast with* DE JURE STANDARDS.

default A value, parameter, option, or attribute that is assigned by the program or system when another has not been assigned by the user.

default drive The drive on which the disk operating system searches for the presence of a program, if no specific drive has been selected.

deference The process where an Ethernet controller delays its transmission when the channel is busy to avoid contention with an ongoing network transmission.

deferred address *See* INDIRECT ADDRESS.

deferred entry/exit An asynchronous event can cause a deferred entry by passing control of the CPU to a subroutine or to an entry point. This transfer causes a deferred exit from the program having control previously.

deferred maintenance Scheduled maintenance intended to connect an existing fault. Can only be used for faults that do not affect the successful completion of a project or program.

definition A measure of output appearance synonymous with *resolution* or *quality*.

deflection yoke The ring around the neck of a cathode ray tube that contains the deflection coils.

defragment The process of rewriting files on disk stored in discontiguous blocks into contiguous format to improve disk performance.

degauser A device that neutralizes magnetic charges; a device used to erase magnetic tape without removing it from the reel.

degauss A procedure that demagnetizes a magnetic tape. A coil is momentarily energized by an alternating current that disarranges the impulses on a magnetic tape when it is placed close to the coil.

degeneracy Refers to a condition in a resonant system when two or more nodes have the same frequency.

degenerative feedback Refers to techniques designed to be used to return part of the output of a machine, system, or process and to input it in a way that causes a larger quantity to be deducted from the input.

degradation 1. A gradual decline of quality or the loss of ability to perform within inquired limits. **2.** A special condition under which a system operates at reduced levels of service.

degradation factor Refers to various measures of the loss in performance that results from the reconfiguration of a data-processing system, e.g., a slow-down in runtime due to a reduction in the number of central processing units.

deionization The process by which an ionized gas returns to its neutral state after all sources of ionization are removed.

de jure standards Official standards set by groups such as IEEE, CCITT, ISO, and ANSI.

DEL In ASCII, the delete character.

delay The amount of time an event is retarded. Delays can be generated by special circuits, devices, elements, units, or lines.

delay circuit A specific circuit that can delay the passage of a pulse or signal from one part of a circuit to another.

delay counter A device that can temporarily delay a program long enough for the completion of an operation.

delay device, digit See DIGIT DELAY DEVICE.

delay distortion The distortion of a waveform made up of two or more different frequencies, caused by the difference in arrival time of each frequency at the output of the transmission system.

delayed access Refers to an access that is delayed because of procedures relating to processing or to the speed of input/output or storage devices.

delayed dialing The capability of programming in a fax/modem to send a document at a later specified time, also known as *timed dialing*.

delay element Refers to circuitry or electronic devices that accept data temporarily and emit the same data after a specific interval.

delay flop A monostable multivibrator; a circuit that holds information for a fixed period of time. This period is determined by the nature and arrangement of the circuit components.

delay line 1. A device capable of retarding a pulse of energy between input and output, based on the properties of materials, circuit parameters, or mechanical devices. Delay lines may use material such as mercury (in which sonic patterns may be propagated in time), lumped constant electrical lines, coaxial cables, transmission lines, and recirculating magnetic drum loops. **2.** A line or network designed to introduce adesired delay in the transmission of a signal, usually without appreciable distortion. **3.** A sequential logic element with one input channel, in which an output channel state at any one instant, T, is the same as the input channel state at the instant $T - N$, where N is a constant interval of time for a given output channel. **4.** An element in which the input sequence undergoes a delay of N time units.

delay unit A device in which the output signal is a delayed version of the input signal. If the input signal is $f(t)$, the output signal is $f(t - T)$ where T is the delay introduced.

delete A nonembedded command that permits removal of previously recorded material from the recording medium.

delimiter A flag or character that is used to separate and organize items of data. As a character, a delimiter is used to limit a string of characters, but it can never be a part of the string. A delimiter flag character can be used to mark the end of a series of bits or characters.

delimiter, data See DATA DELIMITER.

delni unit A type of fan-out box or wiring concentrator in DECnet.

Delphi Recently acquired by Rupert Murdoch's News Corporation, Delphi is a second-tier on-line service. It received much attention in the early 1990s for being the only online service to offer complete access to the Internet. Delphi has a loyal following, but is likely to remain second tier until it debuts its long-awaited graphical front-end, and follows through with an aggressive marketing campaign. It appeals to a mix of business and home users.

delta 1. A Greek letter (Δ) representing any quantity that is much smaller than any other quantity of the same unit appearing in the same problem. **2.** In a magnetic core, the difference between the partial select outputs of the same cell in a one state and in a zero state. **3.** An increment.

delta clock A clock used for timing subroutine operations. A delta clock can be used to restart a computer with an interrupt after a fault forces the machine into a closed programming loop or causes a halt. The interrupt can be programmed to alert the operator that a fault has occurred.

delta encoding/decoding A method of reducing a signal's bandwidth by storing or transmitting the differences between consecutive values rather than the values themselves.

delta modulation A type of digital speech encoding. Delta modulation uses a comparison of the input analog signal with a reference signal on a periodic basis. Depending on the result of comparison, a 1 or 0 is transmitted. The reference signal is typically obtained by a feedback loop from the previous input signals. The basic delta modulator has a limited dynamic range; a number of techniques are used to overcome this limitation. Most of these techniques increase the range by increasing the step size of the magnitude of the reference level each time a comparison results in an answer similar to the one previously obtained. If the first comparison reference signal is less than the input signal, the reference level is increased by a certain step. On the next comparison, if the reference level is still less than the input signal, the step again is increased. This type of delta modulator is called a *variable slope delta*(VSD) modulator. The *continuously variable slope delta* (CVSD) modulator is a variation of the VSD type in which the comparison signal (which is an indication of the slope of the analog input signal) is sent through a low-pass filter with a bandwidth of 25 to 35 hertz.

delta noise The difference between the 1-state and the 0-state; a half-selected noise condition.

delta T Delta time, a sniffer network analyzer indication of time elapsed between consecutive packets on the network, as opposed to *relative time*, which is the time that has elapsed since a particular anchor packet was sent.

demand An input/output coding method in which read/write operations are initiated as the need for them occurs.

demand fetching A memory multiplexing design in which segments are kept in external storage and only placed in internal storage when required.

demodulate To recover the information carried by a modulated signal. Demodulation recovers the signal from the modulated wave so that it has the same essential information characteristic as the signal before modulation. Various demodulators are used to receive tone signals and convert them into digital bits for acceptance by computer circuits.

demodulator-modulator See MODEM.

demultiplexer See MULTIPLEXER.

density An indication of disk storage capacity expressed in terms of the compactness of the information stored or the number of tracks per inch. The most common types are double- and high-density disks. Double-density disks formatted for a PC can store 360K (on a 5¼-inch disk) or 720K (on a 3½-inch disk) of data. High-density disks formatted for a PC store up to 1.2M (5¼) or 1.44M (3½) of information.

deny read count In NetWare, a part of File Server Environment Services that shows the number of logical connections that have denied other stations read privileges.

deny write count In NetWare, a part of File Server Environment Services that shows the number of logical connections that have denied other stations write privileges.

departure frequency In frequency modulation, the amount of variation of a carrier frequency or center frequency from its assigned value. Also known as *frequency deviation*.

dependent logical unit See DLV.

derivative action A type of response found in control systems, the output response of which is the derivative of the input.

DES 1. Abbreviation for *digital expansion system*. 2. Abbreviation for *data encryption standard*, a standardized technique for encrypting data which is supported by the National Bureau of Standards for use throughout the commercial and nondefense areas of the government.

descending order The order of sort that begins with the highest value and descends to the lowest.

description strings In NetWare, a part of File Server Environment Services that contains the following four ASCII strings:

- *Company Name* of the organization that distributed this copy of NetWare

- *Revision* (NetWare version and revision)
- *Revision Date* in the form of mm/dd/yy
- *Copyright Notice*

descriptor See KEYWORD.

design aids Special software or hardware elements that are intended to assist in implementation of a data-processing system. Design aids for microcomputers range from prototyping cards to software development systems. A prototyping card can reduce circuit design and fabrication time during the early development stage; the card usually contains the microprocessor, system clock, and input/output circuits. (Additional cards may contain RAMs and ROMs along with peripheral controllers.)

Design CAD A computer-aided design system that is easy to learn and use. It is compatible with over 100 printers and 50 plotters and with most graphics adaptors, digitizing tablets, and mice.

design cycle The complete cycle of development for complex products. In the case of computer manufacturing, this might include breadboarding, prototyping, testing, and production planning. After each phase, the requirements are refined and the specifications modified to reflect everything that has been learned up to that time.

Designer See MICROGRAFX DESIGNER.

Designer QuickWindows A companion CAD program for QuickWindows Advanced. You can use a mouse or keyboard to lay out windows, dialog boxes, and data-entry screens. When you are finished, Designer writes BASIC source code for that screen and merges it into your program. *Also see* QUICKWINDOWS ADVANCED.

design proof test A test that verifies that the design specification has met the overall functional requirements of the finished product.

desk check Analysis of a program for errors in logic or syntax without using any equipment or electrical design aids.

DeskPaint A Macintosh paint program for creating TIFF, MacPaint, and PICT graphic images. You can work with bitmaps up to 4,000 dots-per-inch and edit large scanned images. This desk accessory allows you to create or import and edit bitmapped images at any time without having to leave your page layout or word-processing program. It can be used for tracing bitmaps to use as polygons in DeskDraw (or MacDraw) or for converting MacPaint clip art and other bitmaps into quality objects without jaggies.

Desktop A Lotus 1-2-3 worksheet featuring a menu-driven appointment calendar and telephone directory. It is particularly useful for consultants and people who need to keep track of time and expenses. Desktop is sophisticated and relatively easy to use.

desktop publishing See DTP.

desktop utility software Programs that simulate common office procedures or items such as phone directories, calendars, calculators, and so on.

despiking The process of removing voltage spikes on power lines.

DESQ A DOS shell that allows you to have several different programs active at one time, so that you can switch easily from one program to another and transfer data between programs. DESQ has a learn facility that allows you to program repetitious tasks by creating macros that work across programs or within a program. This feature allows you to create a command shell so that each application uses the same set of commands. With DESQ, a user can build a multi-application environment to suit his or her work habits, or a programmer can create a complete operating environment for less-sophisticated users.

DESQview Software that lets you run multiple programs at the same time. You can print a spreadsheet, work on a graphic program, and sort a list, all at the same time. DESQview works with Microsoft Windows, so you can run Windows at the same time as nonWindows programs.

destination address The part of a data communication message that indicates the recipient of the data message. In a LAN, the destination address consists of the network ID and the station ID.

destination connection ID In NetWare Communication Services, a number assigned by SPX at the packet's destination.

destination network In NetWare Communication Services and Diagnostic Services, the number of the network on which the destination node resides. NetWare network numbers are 4-byte values given to servers on the same network segment.

destination node In NetWare Communication Services and Diagnostic Services, a 6-byte field that specifies the physical address of the destination node. The number of bytes depends on the LAN hardware used.

destination socket In NetWare Communication Services and Diagnostic Services, the socket address of the packet's destination process. Sockets route packets to different processes within each node.

destructive read A read operation that also erases the data from the source.

destructive testing Testing of any sort that drastically degrades the item tested.

detab *See* DECISION TABLE.

detach during processing In NetWare File Server Environment Services, the number of requests to terminate a connection from a workstation while previous requests were still being processed for that connection.

detach for bad connection number In NetWare File Server Environment Services, a count of requests to terminate a connection where the connection number is not supported by the server.

detail diagram Part of a HIPO chart that gives a detailed listing of what is contained in each program module. *Also see* HIPO CHART.

detailed report Document that lists, in report form, each record of a file.

detector (primary element) The first system element that performs the initial measurement operation and responds quantitatively to the measured variable.

deterministic simulation A type of simulation in which a given input always produces the same output.

DEV Abbreviation for *data exchange unit*.

development processor module Some development systems are constructed on a modular basis, with a number of boards for memory, I/O, and other functions. A block diagram of a typical development processor module is shown in the figure. The various peripheral devices required can be connected to the I/O interface. This interface would not be used in the final system; it is only used to develop software for the system. The usual interface is to a keyboard and cathode-ray tube terminal, which allows online programming and editing. The modular development system is popular, since the user may insert or delete modules from the system at will.

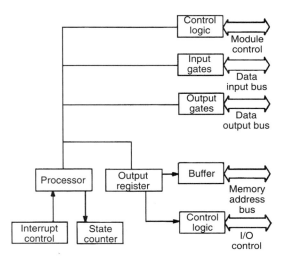

Processor module structure

development system A software design aid that enables the user to check and debug program quickly. A typical development system allows the user to compose and edit programs, run them in realtime in the system environment, diagnose problems, program modifications, and document the required changes. The development system console may furnish program control signals such as STOP/STOP ACKNOWLEDGE, INTERRUPT/INTERRUPT ACKNOWLEDGE, and RESET IN/OUT. The user can then halt, interrupt, and reset the resident CPU through the console interface. The console also allows the operator to manually write the data into memory, monitor bus contents during subcycles, and step the program to verify data flow.

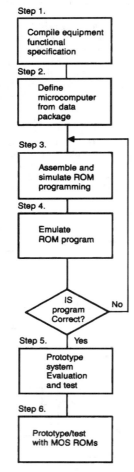

Development system

development time That part of operating time used for testing and debugging new routines and hardware.

Development ToolsKan A development toolkit for Windows composed of five modules in the program: table, status bar, ribbon/icon bar, and field validation. These are custom controls designed to be used as regular windows. All modules are written in Microsoft C.

deviation ratio In a frequency modulation system, the ratio of the maximum frequency deviation to the maximum modulating frequency of the system under specified conditions.

device A mechanical, electrical, or electromechanical contrivance or appliance. Commonly used in reference to peripherals such as printers, CRTs, and disk drives.

device control character A control character used for switching various devices in and out of data processing and telecommunications systems.

device dependence Refers to the organization of a computer system such that each device is expected to know how to interact with the applications. DOS is a device-dependent operating system. Due to device dependence, applications that need to use special features of a device must have software that interfaces with the device rather than the operating system.

device driver A program that interfaces input/output to a device.

device independence Refers to the ability to request I/O operations without regard to the characteristics of specific types of input/output devices.

device number A number assigned to a peripheral device that identifies it to the computer.

device selection check A check to verify that the correct device was selected during a program instruction.

device status word See DSW.

DF Abbreviation for *describing function*.

DFG Abbreviation for *diagnostic function generator*.

DFT Abbreviation for *diagnostic function test*.

DFT table An area of main storage that serves as a logical connector between the user's problem program and a file. This table can also be used to provide control information for transfers of data other than for diagnostic purposes.

dGE A database graphics package with graphing functions that include pie, high-low-close, polar, time series, 3D bar, and Cartesian charts. It supports dBASE III/IV, Clipper, QuickSilver, FoxBase+, dBFast, Eagle, and Microsoft, Turbo, and Quick C.

DI Abbreviation for *digital input*.

diagnosis, breakpoint conditions A variety of breakpoint conditions can be specified to stop a program: memory read, memory write, I/O read, and I/O write. These conditions may be further qualified by prototype logic operations, combined with such functions as stack operations or instruction fetch. For example, you can monitor a device such as a flip-flop and specify a breakpoint halt when it is set and a specific stack address is being accessed. This enables you to make sure the flip-flop is set at the proper point in a control, data processing, or interrupt-handling routine.

diagnostic program A program that facilitates testing through detection and isolation of malfunctions or mistakes. A diagnostic program might have a menu with the following choices:

- Floppy or hard disk tests that analyze each hard or floppy disk drive
- Extended tests including printer, memory, video, and communications.
- Individual test selection to help isolate a problem to a specific device

diagnostic routine A routine designed to locate a malfunction in the computer, a mistake in coding, or both. Diagnostic routines for programming mistakes are service-oriented; routines for detecting mistakes in data are much more specific. Many of the latter can be implemented from control store to test small portions of the system.

diagnostics Techniques employed for detection and isolation of malfunctions and errors in programs, systems, and devices. Diagnostics in microcomputers usually involve the use of ROMs. Small systems can store their diagnostics in ROM control. If a compiler is used, diagnostics are available in the following forms:

- *Precautionary*—Print warning and continue
- *Correctable*—Correct error, print message, and continue
- *Uncorrectable*—Print message, reject statement, and continue
- *Catastrophic*—Terminate compilation

diagnostic software Software that may be provided on ROMs that are plugged into the system. This software or firmware can check the operation of a program and provide an error message when a failure is detected. A monitor program that can place Trap instructions at specified addresses can be used for diagnostics.

diagnostic trace A program used to perform diagnostic checks on other programs. The output of the trace program can include the instructions of the program being checked along with the results of those instructions arranged in sequence.

DialogCoder A software tool for prototyping dialog boxes, which are a major user interface component of any graphical application. It provides a development environment with a built-in dialog editor, custom controls, a code generator, and a DLL builder. It allows edit-field validation, custom code support, commented source code, and a built-in test environment. It supports conditional control states, automatic code regeneration, color, and fonts.

dial network A network that is shared among many users, any one of whom can establish communication between desired points using a dial or push-button telephone.

dialog box A feature of a user interface that produces a specialized "window" in order to solicit a needed response from the user. For example, a dialog box may be displayed to request a filename when saving a new file.

dial-up The use of the standard telephone network (PSTN) by dialing.

dial-up lines Refers to communications through normal dial or touchtone telephone lines.

DIB Acronym for *data input bus*.

dibit A group of two bits. As used in some modulation systems, such as the Bell 201 data set, each dibit is encoded as one of four unique carrier phase shifts: 00, 01, 10, or 11.

dicap storage Storage using an array of diodes to control current directed to storage capacitors.

diced element Subminiaturized component part formed by deposition techniques on a substrate in checkerboard fashion and then separated by a slicing process.

dichotomizing search *See* BINARY SEARCH.

dictionary A list of code names used in a system or routine along with their intended meaning in that system or routine.

die A single piece of silicon that has been cut from a slice by scribing and breaking. It can contain one or more circuits but is packaged as a unit.

dielectric 1. The insulating material separating the two plates of a capacitor. Dielectrics can be made of impregnated paper, plastic, mica, or ceramics. The dielectric provides a medium capable of recovering all or part of the energy required to establish an electric field. The field, or voltage stress, is accompanied by displacement or charging current. **2.** A nonconducting material through which induction of magnetic lines of force may pass. It is a medium in which an electrical field can be maintained.

dielectric amplifier A type of amplifier that operates through a capacitor, the capacitance of which varies with the voltage.

dielectric current The current that results when a changing electric field is applied to a dielectric; it may consist of a displacement current, an absorption current, and a conduction current.

dielectric diode A capacitor sandwich whose negative plate can emit electrons, so that current flows in one direction. CdS crystals have this property.

dielectric dispersion Refers to the variation of dielectric constant with frequency.

dielectric fatigue The breakdown of a dielectric subjected to a repeated electric stress, which is insufficient to break down the dielectric if applied only a few times.

dielectric guide The possible transmission path of high-frequency electromagnetic energy functionally realized in a dielectric channel, the dielectric constant of which differs from its surroundings.

dielectric heating Radio frequency heating in which energy is released in a nonconducting medium through dielectric hysteresis.

dielectric isolation An integrated circuit electrical isolation that is obtained by insulating each pocket with a dielectric layer. Normally, thermally grown silicon oxide is used as the dielectric material. It is used when the parasitic junction capacitances or leakage currents associated with the junction isolation methods may not be acceptable.

dielectric polarization A polarization due to the formation of doublets (dipoles) of a dielectric under electrical stress.

dielectric relaxation Refers to the time delay arising from dipole moments in a dielectric when an applied electric field varies.

dielectric strength The electric stress required to puncture a dielectric.

dielectric viscosity The condition in which the polarization lags behind the changes in the applied field, depending on its rate of change.

difference of potential Refers to the voltage of electrical pressure existing between two points, which can result in a flow of electrons between the two points.

differential analyzer An analog computer that uses interconnected integrators for solving differential equations.

differential delay The difference between the maximum and minimum frequency delays occurring across a frequency band.

differential instrumentation amplifier An amplifier used to reject common mode signals, bias out the direct-current offsets, and scale the input as illustrated.

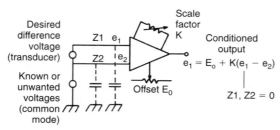

Differential amplifier used as signal conditioner

differential multiplexer A two-wire differential multiplexer may be constructed with pairs of switches, as shown in the figure. The output amplifier is usually an instrument amplifier with a high common mode rejection. This rejection can only be achieved if the input lines are identical, so that twisted pairs for cabling and matching the parameters of the channels and switches are required. Integrated circuits and dual field-effect transistor switches can allow the matching required. Switch leakages and thermal electromotive forces may introduce errors in the low-level inputs, and drift is a problem.

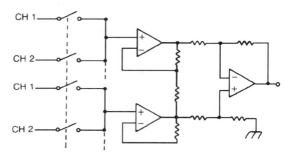

Differential multiplexer

differential phase-shift keying See DPSK.

differential pulse code modulation See DPCM.

differential transducer A transducer that is used to measure two separate parameters and provide a single output that is proportional to the difference between them.

differentiating amplifier A type of amplifier whose output current is proportional to the derivative with respect to time.

differentiating circuit A circuit whose output function is proportional to the derivative, or the rate of change, of its input function with respect to one or more variables. A differentiator circuit accepts square waves and produces a spiked or peaked wave of the same rise time and frequency.

differentiator A circuit or device with an output function that is proportional to the derivative of the input.

diffused alloy transistor A transistor constructed by combining diffusion and alloy techniques. First, the semiconductor water is exposed to gaseous dissemination to produce the nonuniform base region. Then, alloy junctions comparable to a conventional alloy transistor are formed.

diffused semiconductor strain gauges Strain gauges based on the technology of integrated circuits. These gauges have high gauge factors and give relatively high outputs at low strain levels. A sensing element is made by diffusing a four-arm strain-gauge bridge into the surface of a single-crystal silicon diaphragm whose diameter and thickness is varied according to pressure range and application. The silicon has excellent mechanical properties, being elastic and free from hysteresis. This basic sensor is built into an encapsulated transducer or transmitter using manufacturing techniques such as electrostatic or thermal compression bonding, and electron beam welding.

Operational ratings such as those for shock, vibration, and overload are typical of high-quality microcircuit devices. The combined linearity and hysteresis accuracy is typically less than 0.06%. The low-mass silicon diaphragm gives fast response and minimum acceleration sensitivity.

diffusion The process used in the production of semiconductors to introduce impurities into the substrate material. The diffusion process allows the impurities to spread throughout the masked area.

diffusion capacitance The rate of change of injected charge with the applied voltage in a semiconductor diode.

diffusion constant The ratio of diffusion current density to the gradient of charge carrier concentration in a semiconductor.

diffusion length 1. The average distance traveled by current carriers in a semiconductor between generation and recombination. **2.** A length significant in neutron diffusion theory. This length squared (termed the *diffusion area*) is one-sixth of the mean square distance traveled by a thermalized neutron.

diffusion theory Refers to a current-carrier migration theory based on Fick's law or the more detailed transport theory.

digit Any symbol that represents a positive integer smaller than the radix of a number system. In the decimal system, a digit is any one of the characters from 0 to 9; in binary, a digit is a 0 or a 1.

digital Employing discrete integers or voltage levels to represent data and information. A digital format can be used to represent any and all information required for problem solution.

digital audio file A computer file that stores sampled sound. Digital audio files are generally known as .WAV files on the PC, and AIFF files on the Mac. They can comprise a mix of music, voice, ambient sound, and special effects. They can be either mono or stereo and sampled at any frequency; the higher the sample rate, the better the quality. Digital audio files are highly transportable and sound basically the same on any audio card, unlike MIDI files. They are easily imported into digital video files and can be accurately synchronized with the action on-screen.

digital audiotape *See* DAT.

digital channel bank Refers to the PCM multiplexer equipment used in the North American digital hierarchy.

digital circuit A circuit that operates in the manner of a switch; that is, it is either on or off. Also called a *binary circuit*.

digital clock A system clock that operates in a digital mode and produces precisely timed voltage pulses of fixed duration. The output signals have a digital representation and allocate time as set by the system priorities.

digital computer A computer that processes data using combinations of discrete or discontinuous data representations, and that can perform arithmetic and logic operations on data as well as on its own stored program.

digital control *See* DIRECT DIGITAL CONTROL.

Digital Darkroom A program that allows you to retouch images on the computer screen, as done in many photographic labs. You can slice a shape out of the background, make a composite image, blend images together, or dissolve one image into another using slider controls.

digital data Refers to quantities or variables expressed in digital form.

Digital Data Communications Message Protocol *See* DDCMP.

digital differential analyzer *See* DDA.

digital filter A device that produces a predetermined digital output in response to a digital input. Digital filters find applications in telephone, radar, and signal processing, and thus are an important area for the application of microprocessors. A digital filter may consist of elements for multiplication, addition, delays, and storage in order to obtain the desired transfer function.

digital integrator An integrating device in which digital signals are used to show increments in input variables x and y and an output variable z.

digital logic Refers to the common types of logic families used for digital integrated circuits and systems, such as:

- TTL (transistor-transistor logic)
- ECL (emitter-coupled logic)
- HTL (high-threshold logic)
- I^{2}L (integrated injection logic)

digital loopback Loops receive data at the modem's digital (terminal) interface back to the line, it also loops the terminal's transmitted data back to the terminal.

digital modem Provides the necessary modulation, demodulation, and supervisory control functions to implement a serial data communications link over a voice-grade channel utilizing frequency-shift keying (FSK) techniques.

digital multiplexing For systems with small numbers of channels, medium-scale integrated digital multiplexers are available in the TTL and MOS logic families. The 74151 is a typical example. Eight of these integrated circuits can be used to multiplex eight A/D converters of 8-bit resolution onto a common data bus.

The digital multiplexing example shown in the figure offers few advantages in wiring economy, but it is lowest in cost, and the high switching speed allows operation at sampling rates much faster than analog multiplexers. The A/D converters are required only to keep up with the channel sample rate and not with the commutating rate. When large numbers of A/D converters are multiplexed, the data bus technique shown reduces system interconnections.

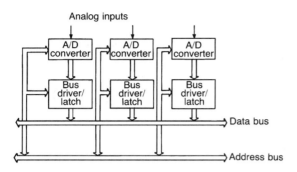

Digital multiplexing into the microcomputer bus system

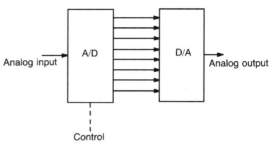

Digital sample-hold

is approximately equal to the sum of the A/D converter's conversion time and the D/A settling time. If the D/A output of a successive approximations A/D is used, a separate D/A converter is not required and the acquisition time is equal to the conversion rate. *Also see* SAMPLE-HOLD.

digital multiplier A circuit or device that generates a digital product from the representation of two digital numbers, usually by additions of the multiplicand in accordance with the value of the digits in the multiplier. It is necessary only to shift the multiplicand and add it to the product if the multiplier digit is a one, and shift the multiplicand without adding if the multiplier digit is a zero, for each successive digit of the multiplier.

Digital Network Architecture *See* DNA.

digital numbers Units of information represented by the presence or absence of fixed voltage levels. These bits or unit of information are binary; each will have one of two possible states.

digital pressure transducers Transducers that offer the accuracy and readability of digital readouts. Some use sensors such as bellows as the primary sensing device with analog-to-digital conversion circuitry. Others may use a boudon-coil pressure-sensing element and an optical encoder. These are mounted on a common shaft that rotates 270 degrees in proportion to applied pressure providing a direct binary-coded-decimal or serialized output to a readout device that displays pressure in digital form. The outputs are compatible with microcomputers as well with the monitoring and recording equipment in many chemical, paper, or similar industrial applications. By using selected transducers, engineers can produce high-performance instruments that can be used to calibrate other pressure transducers or gauges. Such instruments can be designed to produce digital displays in any pressure units.

digital sample-hold A sample-hold that uses an A/D converter and a D/A converter, as shown. When averaging is desired, the A/D converter used is an integrating type. The acquisition time

digital signal A signal that can have only two specific values (on or off, high or low), rather than varying continuously. Data normally exists in this two-state binary form and is transmitted as a series of pulses of discrete size in which the transmission medium is switched between the high and low values. Information may also be stored in digital form.

digital speech interpolation *See* DSI.

digital subset A collection of data in a specific format. The format is usually set by control information to which the system has access.

digital termination system A form of local loop or local distribution in which digital radio is used to connect users to a long-haul communication network.

digital-to-analog converter *See* D/A CONVERTER.

digital transducers Sensing devices that fall into two basic groups:

- Those that incorporate a sensing unit as part of an oscillator circuit and determine the frequency of that circuit as a function of the measured quantity
- Those that detect the position of a primary sensor and convert that quantity into a coded digital word

digital transducer input interface Digital transducers or encoders can simplify the system interface. For minimum software, connect each of the parallel outputs of a digital transducer to a corresponding power amplifier line in a peripheral-interface adapter. Unclocked, the transducer outputs present a word, which the microprocessor can sample at almost any desired rate. Even for a relatively long sampling period, only the least significant bits will change during the measurement of most parameters. This configuration uses the software to define the connections as inputs, and the sampling rate is under main program control.

To achieve minimum hardware usage in an interface for a digital transducer, use a software-oriented interface as illustrated in the figure. A digital transducer with a serial output requires only two connections.

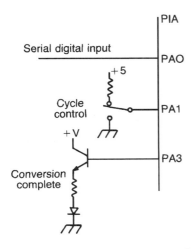

Digital transducer input interface

digital transducer interface program A program that simulates the serial-to parallel-register that the digital transducer interface requires. This interface with a peripheral-interface adapter is shown in the flow diagram that follows. The serial inputs and an output are defined to control a conversion-finished light-emitting diode. You can eliminate this output by making the conversion a subroutine of a larger control program. A cycle loop causes the microprocessor to wait until the cycle control switches to high; then it clears a memory location to use as a pointer that tracks bit processing. The routine rotates the carry bit and resets the conversion-finished line. It uses a conditional branch to determine when all bits have been tested. Then the program sets the carry bit to signify that all bits have been checked. It uses another branch for bit testing and pointer control and prepares the bits for the microprocessor.

digital up/down counter module A module that provides event-counting capability for the microcomputer or external peripheral device. It detects counter overflow and sets a corresponding flag. All count parameters and resets are program-selectable. The counter may be incremented or decremented at a 20-kHz rate. It provides up to 50 VDC input for external event counting.

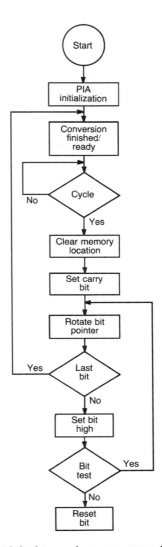

Digital transducer program flow

digital video Video in which all the information representing images is in some kind of computer data form that can be manipulated and displayed.

digital video interactive See DVI.

digital voltmeter 1. A type of indicator that provides a digital readout of a measured voltage as opposed to a pointer indicator. 2. An indicator that indicates a voltage by its nearest numerical magnitude.

digit delay device A logic device used to postpone digit signals and to achieve the effect of a carry from one digit location to another in arithmetic circuits.

digitize To convert an analog signal to a digital representation. Digitization creates steps at distinct levels of the analog signal.

digitizer The device that converts an analog quantity to a digital format. Also called a *quantizer*.

digit place As used in positional notation, the site where the digit is located in a word. Also called *digit rank* or *symbol rank*.

dimension A Fortran statement used to define arrays; used in assembler programming as the maximum number of values that can be assigned to the *set* symbol representing an array.

diminished-radix complement A complement obtained by subtracting each digit from one less than the radix; for example, the nines' complement in decimal notation and the ones' complement in binary notation. Also called *radix-minus-one* complement.

DIMS Abbreviation for *distributed-intelligence microcomputer system*, a multiprocessing method in which the tasks assigned to the distributed system remain fixed. In a multiprocessing environment, the tasks are allocated by software algorithms. With the DIMS, each processor may be assigned a fixed combination of the following tasks:

- Input/output controller activity
- Data concentration
- Information processing
- Remote communication

Distributed intelligence is used in some modular instruments, POS terminals, networks of remote sensors, and scientific computers.

din cable A cable with connectors that meet the Deutsche Industrie Norm (DIN) standards. On the PC, a din cable usually connects the keyboard to the base unit.

diode A usually solid-state electrical valve that permits current flow in one direction and inhibits flow in the other direction.

diode amplifier A parametric amplifier that uses a special diode within a cavity to amplify signals at frequencies as high as 6,000 MHz.

diode arrays Multiple diodes, usually on a single chip and connected in some kind of matrix.

diode function generator A device with the capability of generating an arbitrarily specified diode function or family.

diode ROM A semiconductor ROM that uses diodes. Diode ROMs are characterized by small volume, low cost, and nonvolatility. Like a RAM, the ROM can be addressed in a fixed time interval, regardless of location.

The figure shows a simplified arrangement of ROM elements. The circuitry is much less complex than read/write memories and is ideally suited to MOS or bipolar manufacturing processes. Data storage is indicated by the presence or absence of a diode at the intersection point of the X and Y lines. Thus, any crosspoint can be identified as a 0 or 1 by making the X line positive and the Y line negative. A diode at the crosspoint will conduct, thus providing the readout. Both discrete or monolithic diode arrays can be used in ROMs.

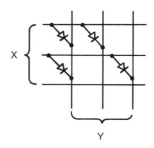

Diode ROM

To program MOS arrays, the manufacturer uses a custom mask operation (with the mask being computer-generated) to produce the required pattern of stored bits. ROM manufacturers provide forms on which users state the required contents. The data on these forms is translated into a computer program for automatic mask programming. There is also a variety of specialized ROMs for use in recurring applications. A block diagram of the organization of a typical ROM is shown.

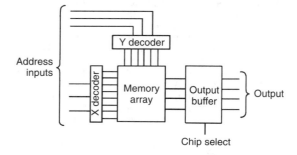

ROM organization

diode-transistor logic *See* DTL.

DIP Acronym for *dual inline package*, a popular type of IC package that has double parallel rows of leads for connection to circuit boards. This configuration allows standardization, low-cost manufacturing, and a degree of second-source replaceability. DIPs are available in plastic for economy, or ceramic for high humidities and temperatures. Also known as *bugs*.

diphase A two-level code generated by the modulo-2 addition of an NRZ signal with its associated clock signal.

dipole modulation The representation of binary digits in magnetic medium in which part of each cell is magnetically saturated in one of two opposing senses. The rest of the cell is magnetized as background and remains fixed.

DIP switch A DIP housing a group of small adjacent switches designed to be mounted on a PC board.

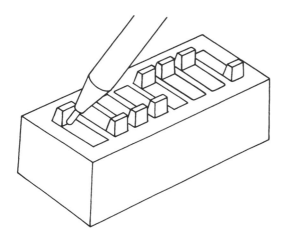

Changing DIP switch settings with a ballpoint pen (or equivalent instrument)

Direct Access A menuing and security package for DOS and Windows users. It is designed to simplify the use of a hard disk and protect files and programs from unauthorized use by providing customized menus. The package allows you to set various levels of password-protection for different users, providing limited access to the menu maintenance function as well as to potentially destructive DOS commands such as Format and Delete. There is also an option to monitor user activities. *Also see* WATCHDOG.

direct access A type of storage in which the access time is effectively independent of the location of the data. The items of data can be addressed or accessed in the same amount of time for each location, and program access is independent of any previous accessed location.

direct-access queue A group of message-segment chains of queues residing on a direct-access storage device. The group may include destination and process queues.

direct acting Refers to a specific and defined operation of a final control element directly proportional to the control output.

direct address An address that specifies the location of an operand. Direct addressing is a basic addressing method used in many microprocessors. It is designed to reach any point in main storage directly without using other registers. For example, a direct addressed instruction for the 8080 is

```
LDA 2132H; load A with 2132₁₆
```

This instruction loads the contents of location 2132 (hexadecimal) into the accumulator and is stored in memory as 3A2132.

direct binary programming Programming in direct binary code or in the hexadecimal equivalent requires the least amount of supporting hardware and software. This method is often used on simple systems that do not require much coding and where the coding must be very compact. The user communicates with the system through a hexadecimal keyboard and a light-emitting diode (LED) display. The instructions and data are transferred into the system using the keys in a hexadecimal format. For example, to select the larger of two numbers from memory, and store it in a third location, requires the following 8080-family hexadecimal code:

```
3A
FF
01
21
D3
00
EE
```

The direct coding technique is cost-efficient in terms of the hardware, but is very slow and tedious from the programmer's viewpoint.

direct broadcast satellite *See* DBS.

direct coding *See* DIRECT BINARY PROGRAMMING.

direct-connect modem A modem connected to telephone lines through the wall jack, instead of a phone receiver. It is often housed within the computer itself.

direct-coupled transistor logic *See* DCTL.

direct coupling The coupling of circuits by resistance or inductance so as to allow direct current to pass through the coupling.

direct current *See* DC, 1.

direct-current balancer Refers to the coupling and connecting of two or more similar dc units or machines such that the conductors connected to the junction points of the machines are maintained at constant potentials.

direct cutover System conversion involving stopping the old system and bringing on the new with no overlap.

direct data capture A technique used for cash sales, using sales slips on which customer account numbers, the amount of the purchase, and other information are automatically recorded, read by an optical reading device, and sent to the computer to be processed. Its use permits the generation of more timely and accurate transaction data.

direct data transmission The use of a single line or channel for the transmission of data. This system is the simplest type and is suitable for handling a predetermined volume of messages.

direct digital control Descriptive of the use of computers and other digital devices for the control of manufacturing processes. A typical direct digital controller might handle up to eight industrial control loops with more flexibility and options than would be possible with analog controllers.

direct distance dialing See DDD.

direct formatting The process of assigning a format directly to selected text by using predefined key combinations or format commands.

direct impression A term applied to printers in which each character is struck onto the paper, as in conventional typing.

direct insert subroutine A subroutine that is inserted into a routine at each place that it is used. Also called an *open* subroutine.

direct instruction An instruction that contains the operand for the operation specified by the instruction. *Also see* DIRECT ADDRESS.

direction keys The Up, Down, Left, Right and related keys on a keyboard. They can be used to move a block, highlight text, or select from lists of choices.

direction of lay The lateral direction in which the strands of a cable run over the top of the cable as they recede from the observer, expressed as *right-* or *left-hand lay*.

directive command As used in an assembler, a command that allows the user to generate data words and values for specific conditions in assembly time. Mnemonics are assigned to each instruction operation code in order to describe the hardware function of that instruction.

directive statements Statements that are used to define the program structure. Directive statements do not generate executable code. Examples of directive statements are ORIGIN STATEMENT, PROCEDURE STATEMENT, PROGRAM STATEMENT, and END STATEMENT.

direct memory access See DMA.

direct memory access controller See DMAC.

direct memory access I/O Some I/O devices must transfer large amounts of data too quickly to be controlled by a microprocessor. In this case, information can be transferred directly between the device and the memory of the microprocessor system using direct memory access (DMA). The transfer is controlled by a direct memory access controller (DMAC), a dedicated circuit or chip that can operate independently of the microprocessor. In a DMA data transfer, the DMAC takes over the control of the microprocessor memory in one of several ways. An external control line will stop the microprocessor after the current instruction is completed, as shown in the figure. The microprocessor memory control signals are disabled, and the DMAC initiates the data transfer. After the DMA transfer is completed, the controller resets the halt line, and the microprocessor resumes execution of the next memory access instruction.

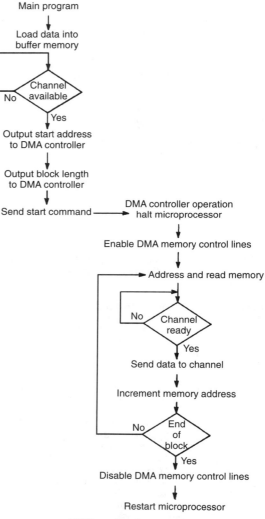

DMA control program

direct network connection In Internet, this refers to the means of a private user high-speed connection. A direct connection can range from a T-1 connection to a major node (at 1.44M per second) to a 56K fractional connection. By default, a direct connection becomes a node in the network and must have an IP (Internet Protocol) number. A direct connection also requires a level of administration, and there is the risk of unauthorized network access to your local system. This can be reduced using a technique called *firewalling*, which limits the activities that can penetrate the network.

The cost of a direct connection is more or less proportional to the bandwidth (bits per second) of the channel you require for connection. Connection options include a packet-on-demand scheme (where you pay for packets transmitted or received) ATM (asynchronous-transfer-mode, a high-speed twisted pair network), and ISDN.

direct numerical control *See* DNC.

directory The list of files on the storage media, together with their attributes and the information needed by the computer to keep track of their physical locations on the media. Directories are given names like files and organized into a hierarchy, called a *directory tree*. In DOS, a directory can be given a name up to eight characters long, plus an optional three-character extension, just like a filename. The directory name cannot include the following characters: *,?,:, \,/. Directory names longer than 12 characters are generally truncated. Sometimes also called a *catalog* or *folder*.

directory caching A performance-enhancing technique in which a disk's directory information is loaded into RAM so the system will be able to locate files in the directory faster.

directory entry In NetWare File Server Environment Services, an offset into file server's Directory Entry Table for the volume.

directory handles In NetWare Directory Services and Queue Services, directory handles are used in most calls. A handle is the index into the Directory Handle Table, which contains a pointer to the Directory Table and a pointer to the Volume Table. Directory handles calls are used to find handles given drive numbers, to set handles to different directories, and to save and restore handles.

directory hashing A performance-enhancing technique in which NetWare builds a special table in the file server's RAM to locate files in the directory quickly, without having to read the entire directory until the file is located.

directory path In many operating systems, the full name of a directory, including all of its higher-level directories up to the *root*. In some operating systems like NetWare, it can offset to a directory handle. If no handle is specified, the volume name must be specified in the format *volume:directory\subdirectory*. If a directory handle is specified, the path can be used as an offset to it.

direct reference address A type of virtual address that is not modified by indirect addressing. It can be modified by indexing.

direct-view A CRT or projected image that is watched directly, as opposed to a hardcopy print.

dirty cache buffers In NetWare, a part of File Server Environment Services that shows the number of cache buffers containing data that has not been written to disk.

dirty power Electricity that contains impure elements, such as power spikes or noise. These impure elements can damage computer equipment by momentarily driving the component beyond its specified limits. *Spikes* usually occur as the result of motor starts and stops. Switches and other devices that change the flow of electricity can also cause spikes. *Noise* usually comes from electrical lightning, transformers, or other devices that produce radio-frequency signals.

DIS Abbreviation for *Draft International Standard*, a specification that has passed both the working paper and draft proposal steps toward becoming an international standard.

disable 1. A state of the central processing unit that does not allow certain types of interrupts to occur; also called a *masked state*. **2.** As used in communications, a state that does not allow a device to accept incoming calls.

disarmed A state used to define an interrupt level in a system that cannot accept an interrupt input signal.

disassemble To translate a program from machine language into assembly language so that it is easier for a human to understand. Contrast with assemble.

disassembler A program that disassembles machine language.

disaster dump A dump that occurs as a result of a nonrecoverable error in the program.

disc Alternate spelling for *disk*. Also, the accepted spelling to indicate a CD or CD-ROM.

disc generator A capacitive charge type of voltage generator.

discrete Individual and separate, as opposed to integrated.

discrete circuits The various electronic circuits that can be built of separate, individually manufactured diodes, resistors, transistors, capacitors, and other specific electronic components.

discrete data A representation for a variable that may assume any of several distinct states. These variables are usually coded.

discrete media A term applied to recording media that are individually distinct and can be filed, mailed, moved, and otherwise separately handled.

discrete programming A class of procedures used in operations research for locating the maximum and minimum values of a function. All variables must have integer values or similar constraints. If only integer values are used, the programming is called *integer programming*.

discrete simulation A type of simulation where all major components and events are identified individually and used at irregular intervals. Also called *event-oriented simulation*.

discretionary replace In word processing, substituting each occurrence of text with a new text only upon the user's approval.

discrimination 1. The skipping of selected instructions as developed by the programmer. Usually, in discrimination, if a conditional jump is not used, the next instructions are allowed to follow in a normal sequence. **2.** The process of demodulating an FM signal.

disjunction The logical operation that uses the OR operator and results in the logical sum. In Boolean form, the operation is written as:

A + B = C (A or B equals C)

and follows this truth table:

A	B	C
0	0	0
0	1	1
1	0	1
1	1	1

disk A circular plate with magnetic material on both sides. This plate rotates for the storage and retrieval of data by one or more heads, which transfer the information to and from the computer. The computer readable information may be placed on a floppy or rigid (hard) disk, which may have information on one or both sides. *Also see* HARD DISK *and* FLOPPY DISK.

disk accessing The process and methods used to transfer data in and out of a disk file. Access is usually accomplished by direct addressing, symbolic addressing, or keyed-record addressing.

disk cache A type of smart buffer that anticipates the disk data that is most likely to be read next.

disk card An expansion card that places the controller and hard disk drive on a single board, allowing you more room for other hard disks.

disk channel table In NetWare, a part of File Server Environment Services. It is a 5-byte table showing which disk channels exist on a server and what their drive types are. (Each channel is one byte). A nonzero value in the disk channel table means that the corresponding disk channel exists in the file server (1 = XT drive type, 2 = AT drive type, 3 = SCSI drive type, 4 = disk coprocessor drive type, 50 to 255 = value-added disk drive types).

disk controller An adapter board used to connect disk drives to the computer's internal circuitry, as shown. Many manufacturers make disk drives that can be used with the IBM PC family. Some drives are external to the system unit and have their own enclosure.

In the IBM PC a disk controller card plugs into one of the expansion slots. The disk con-

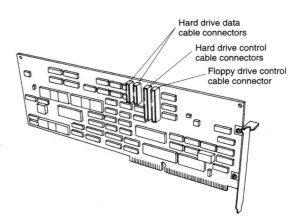

Drive controller board

troller card has a ribbon data cable that connects to the disk drive. A typical controller card can support four disk drives.

The data that moves between the disk and the processor is usually controlled by an 8237 DMAC on the main board, as shown. It controls the data transfer operations and is used to move data.

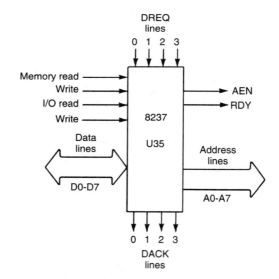

DMA controller

disk crash When the disk drive unit's recording head makes destructive contact with the recording media. Also, a disk drive malfunction.

disk density *See* DENSITY.

disk directory A list on a disk of all the files kept

on it. This list is updated and available every time the disk is used.

disk drive The piece of hardware that holds the motor, read/write heads, and electronics for use with a disk. The disk is inserted into the drive, which in turn is responsible for the communications between the disk surface and the computer. *Also see* FLOPPY DISK DRIVE and HARD DISK.

disk drive system A complete unit that consists of a disk drive, power supply, cooling fan, buffer, and addressing electronics.

DiskDupe A program designed to duplicate, format, and compare disks. It copies high-density disks in a single drive with no swapping and automatically formats and detects bad disks. It offers pulldown menus or command line control.

diskette *See* FLOPPY DISK.

diskette case A case for shelf, drawer, or briefcase storage of 5¼-inch or 3½-inch diskettes. Some use a color-coding system for diskette reference.

diskette mailer A sturdy cardboard or padded paper mailing case that holds up to four 5¼-inch diskettes.

diskless workstation A microcomputer that has no disk drives and is connected to a LAN. These are used in security-sensitive environments to prevent data from being copied. They are also popular in environments where there are a lot of airborne contaminants such as dust, or where there is a great deal of vibration that would harm disk drives. A special ROM chip on the LAN adapter card allows the workstation to load the operating system directly from the network file server.

disk operating system *See* DOS.

disk optimizer Software that rearranges the data stored in files into adjacent clusters (storage locations) on the hard disk. This rearrangement is called *optimizing* or *defragmenting* the disk and speeds up disk operation.

disk pack Portable direct-access storage units that use magnetic disks. Disk packs are mounted on disk storage drives for read and write operations.

disk partition table A data structure stored in the boot sector of DOS that describes how information is laid out on the disk.

disk speed adjustment There is a small resistive control on some floppy disk drives that can be adjusted with a screwdriver. A method of measuring the drive rpm is needed so the adjustment can be made at the proper speed. There are two ways the drive speed can be measured.

On the bottom of many drives is a marked pulley with timing marks. The outer marks are designed to be used with a 60-Hz light. To use these timing marks, you shine a 60-Hz light on them. The timing marks should appear to be stationary when the disk is running at the desired speed, as shown in the figure.

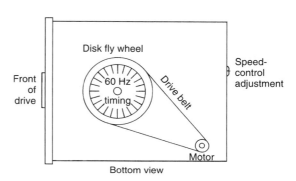

Disk drive speed adjustment

If the timing marks appear to be rotating during the test, then the resistive control needs adjustment. The marks could be rotating in either one direction or the other. They can be stopped by adjusting the speed control until the marks appear stationary. This is the speed that is desired.

Another technique is to use a disk drive speed program disk. You run the speed test program and the display shows the current speed setting. You can then adjust the speed control until the display shows the speed at 300 rpm. See the following figure.

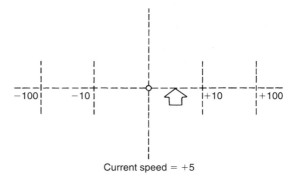

Typical disk drive test program display

disk track One of the concentric circles on a disk holding data as a stream of bits.

disk unit An electromechanical assembly containing a flat disk coated with magnetic material. Both sides of the disk may be used, and several disks can be stacked on a spindle. The disks rotate together at high speed. The bits are stored on the magnetized surface in spots along concentric circles called *tracks*. The tracks are divided into *sectors*. One sector is usually the minimum quantity of information that can be transferred. The division of disk into tracks and sectors is shown in the figure that follows. Some units use a single read/write head for each disk. In the unit shown, address bits are used to move the head to the specified track position before a read or write. In other systems, separate read/write heads are used for each track on each disk. The address bits then select a particular track with a decoder circuit. This kind of unit is more expensive and is used in larger systems.

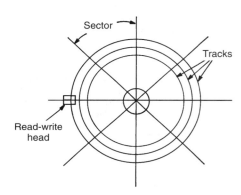

Magnetic disk memory configuration

Timing tracks are used to synchronize the bits and recognize the sectors. A disk is addressed by bits that specify the disk number, disk surface, sector number, and the track. As the read/write heads are positioned on the specified track, the system waits until the rotating disk places the specified sector under the head. Information transfers then starts once the beginning of a sector is reached. Some units have multiple heads for the simultaneous transfer of bits from several tracks. A track near the circumference is longer than a track near the center of the disk. If bits are recorded with equal density, some tracks will contain more bits than others. In order to make all the records in a sector of equal length, a variable recording density may be used with a higher density on tracks near the center than on tracks near the circumference.

disorderly closedown Stopping of a system due to an equipment error when it is not possible to shut down in an orderly manner. Special steps are usually taken to prevent the loss or duplication of data.

dispersion Refers to the variation of delay with frequency.

displacement transducer A device used to measure linear position or displacement and provide an analogous electrical output.

display A visual representation of data, which may take the form of numerals (as on the calculator shown in the figure), alphanumeric characters, or graphics. A display unit can provide viewing access into the operation of the microcomputer system.

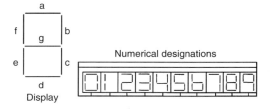

Numeric display

A microcomputer *video-terminal display* unit (a CRT) might use a dot array of 1024 × 1024 dots for character generation. A bright dot can be produced anywhere on the screen, and a series of dots can be used to indicate lines on a graphical display. Data on the CRT display screen can be highlighted by blinking, underlining, use of a different color, increased intensity, or a combination of methods.

Gas discharge displays have a pleasing color (orange or green) and large character size, but they are difficult to interface because of the high voltage required for ionization of the gas.

Light-emitting diode displays are compatible with TTL levels, but they have limited sizes and color selection.

Liquid-crystal displays (LCDs) require very little power and are compatible with MOS logic, but they produce no light themselves and are hard to see except under direct-lighting conditions.

Incandescent and *fluorescent displays* can produce high brightness with large character size, but because of costs and power requirements, they are used mostly in specialized applications.

display adapter An adapter unit that controls the transmission of data, control and status information, and the sequencing and synchronizing of the display units in the system. In general, the digital data received from computer storage is formatted for deflection commands for a CRT device.

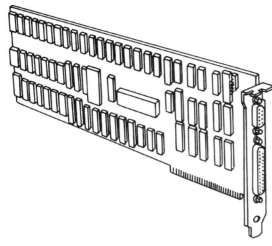

Display adapter

display adapter slots The display adapter installs in one of the expansion slots, as shown in the figure. Most are designed for 8-bit slots but there are some 16-bit display adapter cards. Many older display adapters are not designed to run reliably at the higher MHz speeds, so this can be a problem if you run at high speeds.

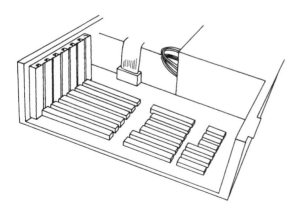

Expansion slots in a typical computer, one of which will hold the display adapter

display font In desktop publishing, a font useful for headlines and other attention-demanding applications. Sometimes also used to mean a screen font, as opposed to a printer font.

display highlighting Refers to a feature that enables the user to distinguish or emphasize data on a CRT display by reversing the field, making it blink, underlining it, changing its color, changing its light intensity, or some combination of these.

display list A set of structured graphics commands that a presentation device executes to draw an image on the screen. You can animate a display by having the presentation device read only changes to the list.

display list processing A CAD-specific video board feature that stores the screen generation commands in memory on the video board to increase the drawing speed.

display modes The various modes used in a display system to denote the points on the screen such as vector, increment, or character point.

display register A register with corresponding indicators on the display panel; used to display the contents of the register selected by the display switch.

display slide switch Some computers have a slide switch on the system board that determines whether the system boots up in color or monochrome mode. You must refer to the manual for the correct switch setting. Often, a display adapter will have several different display modes, which are set jumpers or DIP switches. It is important to use the correct switch settings for the system board, since you can damage some monitors by attaching them to a display adapter configured for the wrong mode.

display switch Switches used to select the register that is to be shown on the display panel.

display time The length of time a chart is shown on a computer screen.

display tube An indicating type of vacuum tube (such as a CRT) used to display data in a form recognizable to humans.

DisplayWrite An older, DOS-based word-processing system that handles a wide variety of documents.

dissector A mechanical or electrical transducer that detects in sequential order the light intensity of an illuminated space. The dissector is utilized in optical character recognition. Also known as an *image dissector*.

dissipation, module Refers to the power dissipation of a module calculated from the voltage current product, with an allowance for dissipation for load currents being supplied to other modules.

Distinct TCP/IP This program gives you TCP/IP connectivity without consuming DOS memory. It allows multiple concurrent Telnet sessions, drag-and-drop file transfer (FTP), and the ability to drop remote files onto a local printer.

distortion Any variation in a reproduced waveform that was not present on the original waveform.

distortion delay The distortion that results when the phase angle of the transfer impedance is not linear with a frequency within the desired range, thus making the time of transmission or delay vary with frequency in that range. Also called *phase distortion*.

distributed control Distributed control differs from distributed processing, in that it makes use of remote multiplexing. The processors communicate with field-located multiplexers, and each processor is usually dedicated to performing the same task in an online environment.

distributed database A database that looks to the user like a single database but is in fact a collection of several different data repositories.

distributed data processing A method of sharing the processing load on multiple computers with each one performing different functions. A communications channel connects the computers.

distributed environment See *distributed system*.

distributed file service A DEC product to make files on the network all appear local. It is similar to the Network File System.

distributed frame structure A time-division multiplexer (TDM) frame structure in which the frame alignment signal occupies noncontiguous bit positions.

distributed-intelligence microcomputer system See DIMS.

distributed naming service A network-based service to allow a user to find the current address of a given resource, such as a printer or file system.

distributed network In a distributed network, the file server can also be used as an individual workstation. Distributed networks are less powerful than centralized networks but are less expensive per unit and easier to install than centralized networks. *Also see* PEER NETWORK.

distributed processing Systems that use intelligent input/output controllers and direct memory access control to free the CPU of the details of block transfers. Distributed processing makes use of complex LSI chips similar to those used in microcomputers. These chips allow low-cost intelligent controllers for keyboards, displays, printers, modems, and floppy disks.

distributed-queue dual bus See DQDB.

distributed system An arrangement in which a number of computers at separate locations work cooperatively. The system may use one large computer and several smaller machines, with the central files located at the larger machine and the smaller computers calling on the files when required. Distributed systems can provide fast response to local events, maximum availability for single failure modes, and simplified system programming with good user access.

distribution cable An electrical conductor that feeds several branch circuits to distribute power or signals.

distribution diskette The original diskette that you get with the application program on it. Most distribution diskettes should be copied and put safely away while a copy is used.

distribution frame A point where several cables converge and signals are redistributed among them.

dithering A bitmapped graphics technique that expands the number of colors shown or printed by using small blocks of primary colors to simulate otherwise nonreproduceable colors. Dithering is analogous to the process of creating halftones in printing.

divide by zero An error message normally associated with applications written in assembly language or C. The message usually indicates a critical application error that results in data loss and other forms of damage. This error literally means that the application tried to divide some number by zero, resulting in an indeterminate result.

divide exception An exception created when the signed number resulting from a division would cause overflow.

division In word processing, a section of a document with a single-page format (for example, the table of contents). A document can have one or more divisions. Divisions may be separated by some sort of division mark, such as a single horizontal line.

division circuits A circuit that can be used to do division. A simultaneous type of circuit for numbers of larger than 8 to 10 bits involves a large number of gates and subtracters. These circuits are used where speed is essential. But since division, like multiplication, can make use of existing adder/subtracter circuits, most microcomputers do not use straight dividing circuits.

DLC Abbreviation for *data link control*, the data communications control characters that initiate a connection between two locations, check for errors, and terminate the transmission of data.

DLL Abbreviation for *Dynamic Link Library*, a library in OS/2 or Windows that contains the actual instructions for an API's (application programming interface) functions.

DLM Abbreviation for *data line monitor*, a card that allows an IBM PC to double as a data line monitor and data communications protocol analyzer. This half-size board plugs into an IBM PC or compatible to test and monitor lines in a number of synchronous or asynchronous protocols—X.25, HDLC, SDLC, NRZI, and BSC. It features a full-screen graphics presentation of the data on the lines, and standard PC printers are supported for hardcopy analysis. See the following diagram.

DLV Abbreviation for *dependent logic unit*, a logic unit controlled by an SNA host system.

DM Abbreviation for *data management*.

DMA Abbreviation for *direct-memory access*, a method used to obtain direct access to the main memory without involving the CPU. Sometimes known as the *data-break technique*, DMA permits transfers to take place without CPU intervention on a cycle-stealing basis. The approach usually taken bypasses the registers for direct access to the memory bus. The CPU is essentially disabled during DMA data-transfer operations; the CPU is only used to set up the transfer, and the transfer rate is limited only by the bandwidth of the memory and peripherals. DMA is the preferred data transfer method for high-speed applications, sometimes improving instruction times by as much as an order of magnitude.

The following tasks are required for DMA transfers:

- Address selection
- Interrupt control
- Bus control
- Word counting
- Input/output data buffering

Also see DMAC.

DMA boards DMA is used in high-speed analog and digital interface boards for IBM-compatible computers. These full-length boards install in an expansion slot and turn the PC into a high-speed, high-precision, acquisition and signal analysis instrument. These boards use a multilayer construction with integral ground plane to minimize noise and crosstalk even at high sample rates.

DMAC Abbreviation for *direct memory access controller*, a block-transfer processor that implements automatically at hardware speed the transfer process, which would normally be executed by a program in the microprocessor. Instead of sending an interrupt to the microprocessor, the I/O devices send the interrupt to the DMAC. The DMAC then suspends the microprocessor by putting it in a "hold" mode and takes over the operation of the system, transferring the words between the memory and the I/O device as shown in the following diagram.

DMA cycle-stealing A DMA technique used for high speed transfers. The DMAC transfers data on a cycle-stealing basis directly between the memory and the external device, bypassing the central processor.

DMA is used In NetWare, a part of Diagnostic Services that tells if the DMA line field value is valid. The following values can appear in a DMA Is Used field:

00h	No DMA line defined
FFh	DMA line defined for exclusive use
EEh	DMA line defined for a particular LAN board, but can be shared by others of the same type

DMA line 1. The wire used for the DMA control signal. 2. In NetWare, a part of Diagnostic Services that returns the value of the DMA line used by the LAN board.

DME Abbreviation for *distance measuring equipment*.

DMED Abbreviation for *digital message entry device*.

DNA Abbreviation for *Digital Network Architecture*, DEC's implementation of an architecture that allows large networks of computers to be connected together.

DNC Abbreviation for *direct numerical control*, the connecting of a set of numerically controlled machines to a common memory for part program or machine program storage, with provision for on-demand distribution of data to the machines.

DO Acronym for *digital output*.

dock A device containing ports, disk drives, and possibly other peripherals that converts a portable computer into the system unit of a desktop computer.

Doctor Data A mailing-list management program with user-friendly pulldown menus, up to 1 billion records per database file, 23 database fields available for each record, and ability to accept international as well as domestic addresses.

document 1. Any representation of data that can be interpreted by humans or machines, as well as the process of creating the same representation. 2. A paper voucher, form, report, or other record containing stored information; the information is usually recorded by the originator of the processing information and is usually more concerned with input information rather than output.

document cameras In multimedia, these cameras are called *video imagers* or *visualizers*. Document cameras mount a small video camera over a baseboard with light to display physical objects, such as notes or transparencies. Document cameras let presenters point out parts of an object or document. Some units may also simultaneously record the camera's output on videotape. Resolution ranges from 370 to 470 lines.

documentation The presentation, organization, and communication of information about a par-

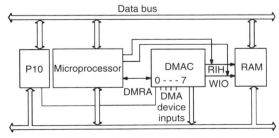

DMA controller application

ticular program or system. Documentation may include the programmer's detailed flowcharts, coding sheets, a listing for each program module, a list of the parameters and definitions, memory and I/O maps, hardcopy or online user instructions, and comments embedded in the program. Documentation is best generated during the design, coding, debugging, and testing stages of software development.

documentation techniques The techniques most used for program documentation are flowcharts, program listings with comments, memory maps, and parameter and definition lists. Structured programming and some of the other design techniques have developed their own documentation forms.

Flowcharts act as visual aids for program documentation. A general flowchart may serve as a pictorial description of a program, while a more detailed flowchart can be invaluable to the user who must use or maintain the program.

Comments are an important part of program documentation. A program with a clear structure and well-chosen names can be almost self-documenting.

document reference edge As used in character recognition, a specified edge of a document to which all alignment of characters is referenced.

Dolphin C Toolkit A program with over 225 functions. Data functions convert between calendar dates and perform data arithmetic. Disk functions include type and number of disks and disk drives. There is a spooler interface and many string and file functions. It supports Borland/Turbo C/C++ and Microsoft C.

domain In communications, an area within which a particular service is performed. In a messaging domain, a message transfer agent for that domain is able to deliver a message. Splitting a namespace into domains allows easier management.

domain tip A type of memory device that uses thin films to create magnetic domains for storing digital data. Thin aluminum layers are deposited on a glass substrate, and channels are etched into the aluminum and filled with a thin magnetic film which is used to form the domain regions. Costs are below core memory; applications include backup memories for microprocessors in areas like point-of-sale terminals, numerical control, and data logging.

dOneTwoThree A library of functions that allows access to Lotus 1-2-3 spreadsheets from within a Clipper program.

donor Refers to those elements that enter or are introduced in small quantities as impurities to semiconducting materials and which have a negative valence greater than the valence of the pure semiconductor.

donor ion An atom that gives up an electron in a doped semiconductor crystal.

dopant An impurity added to a semiconductor to increase its ability to conduct electricity.

dope additive A specific impurity added to a pure semiconductor to give it the required electrical properties.

doped junction A semiconductor junction created by adding an impurity during crystal growth.

doping 1. Increasing the level of impurities of semiconductors in order to make N or P types. **2.** The process of adding alien elements to a semiconductor crystal to supply it with the proper characteristics.

doppler A shift in the observed frequence of a signal caused by variations in the path length between the source and the point of observation.

dorfed up Slang; refers to damage to a file that renders its contents useless, or at best questionable. Such a file is said to be "dorfed up." Also called *hosed up*.

DOS 1. Acronym for *disk operating system*, a memory system using disks or diskettes that is designed to assemble, edit, and execute programs. A typical system includes an intelligent disk controller, a drive system, and a software system. Programs can sometimes be assembled, edited, and executed in seconds. Using the disk operating system requires the adding of additional memory to the executive. DOSs allow the efficient use of ROMs for initial loading and storage of frequently used mathematical routines such as numerical integration, statistical test data, and math functions (powers, logs, sine, cosines). **2.** Specifically, the term *DOS* often refers to the operating system usually used on IBM PCs and compatibles. Although Mac System 7.x, OS/2, Windows NT, etc. are also disk operating systems, they are not considered DOS in this sense. Microsoft's version of DOS is often called *MS-DOS*.

Following is a list of DOS versions, when each was introduced, and the primary features, changes, or corrections:

1.0	1981	Supported single-sided 5¼-inch diskettes with 8 sectors per track, formatting to 160K. File management through CP/M-like *file control blocks*.
1.05	1981	Bug fixes.
1.1	1982	Added support for double-sided, 8-sector 5¼-inch diskettes formatting to 320K.
2.0	1983	Added support for double-sided, 9-sector 5¼-inch diskettes formatting to 360K, and for 10MB fixed disks with the FDISK command. File control blocks superseded by management system based on *file handles*, which made possible Unix-like hierarchical directory structure and I/O

Version	Year	Description
		redirection. Added support for installing device drivers at boot-up via CONFIG.SYS file.
2.1	1983	Added support for IBM PC*jr* features, plus bug fixes and support for international symbol sets.
3.0	1984	Added support for IBM PC AT, including 20MB fixed disk and 5¼-inch, 1.2MB diskettes. Some commands added, as well as the RAM disk driver, VDISK.
3.1	1985	Added the beginnings of network support, notably the SHARE command, plus bug fixes and the SUBST and JOIN commands.
3.2	1986	Added support for 3½-inch, 720K diskettes, plus additional commands, notably XCOPY.
3.3	1987	Added support for IBM PS/2 line, and for 3½-inch, 1.44MB diskettes. Added commands, improved batch-file directives.
4.0	1988	Added support for fixed-disk partitions larger than 32MB, and improved handling of extended and expanded memory. Also added the DOSSHELL pull-down menu system, with mouse support.
4.01	1988	Bug fixes.
5.0	1991	Improved support for enhanced, extended, and expanded memory, and added ability to load MS-DOS and other drivers into memory above the 640K ceiling. Extended fixed disk partition support to 2GB. Improved the DOSSHELL menu, and added utilities such as a command stacker, UNDELETE, and UNFORAT.
6.0 6.1	1993	Introduced many disk-, memory- and configuration-management utilities, as well as virus detection, advanced laptop support, and on-the-fly disk compression. Microsoft's version (6.0) and IBM's (6.1) differed in detail and in the utilities, but were essentially variations on a theme.
6.2	1994	Applied numerous bug fixes to DoubleSpace disk compression utility (MS-DOS). Added disk scan/repair facilities and safety features for compressed disks.
6.21	1994	Removed DoubleSpace disk compression (MS-DOS), in response to court decision that some code infringed on patents held by Stac Electronics.
6.22	1994	Restored disk compression (MS-DOS) with fully legal DriveSpace utility, added safety features to other commands and utilities.
6.3	1994	PC DOS 6.3 added support for commas in large numbers, interactive batch processing, file overwrite protection for MOVE, XCOPY, and COPY commands. CD-ROM support, a no-swap DISKCOPY command, and improved boot procedures also were included.

DOS/ODI workstation shells Workstation software modules that NetWare 386 users may use to connect their workstation to the LAN. These modules can be used for supporting multiple protocols simultaneously, such as IPX and TCP/IP, with one set of programs. (ODI stands for *Open Datalink Interface*.)

DOS prompt The signal that DOS is awaiting a command. The prompt is usually displayed as the current drive letter, the directory path, and the greater than symbol (>). Thus

C:\>

is a DOS prompt with c: representing the hard drive, and the backslash with no directory path indicating the root directory.

DOS reserved word A filename extension that is only used for DOS system commands.

DOS shell A program that supplements standard DOS functions to make DOS easier to use. Typically, it displays menus or graphics of the operating system functions available, files and subdirectories on the current disk, time, date, space left on the current disk, status of the Capslock and Num keys, and other information relevant to the operation of the PC.

DOSUTILS A public-domain set of utility programs for performance analysis, low-level formatting, defect management, diagnostics, data recovery, and file maintenance.

DOS workstation shells Workstation software modules that Novell has used in NetWare 286 and 386 to connect a workstation to the LAN. These programs only support NetWare's IPX/SPX protocols and IBM's NETBIOS protocols.

dot 1. Pellet-shaped components inserted into holes in a punchboard-type of printed circuit board. **2.** Slang for the period (.) that separates elements in many filenaming schemes.

dot leader A word-processing command that automatically places a series of periods between two items on a line.

dot matrix printer A hardcopy device that creates characters using a series of wires that produce dots. Two stepper motors drive the print mechanism: one is used for moving the print head,

144 dot matrix printer • double precision

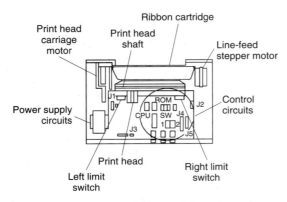

Typical layout of dot matrix printer

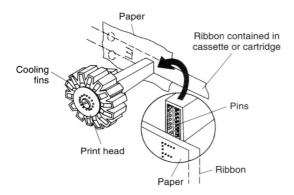

Dot matrix print head

while the other is used to advance the paper. The two motors operate independently and are controlled by a microprocessor.

Two methods of paper feeding are used, either a pressure roller driving the paper with friction, or tractors, as shown in the figure. Paper can be fanfold (with or without tractor holes), rolls, or single sheets. Optional roll-paper holders and single-sheet feeder assemblies are available for many machines. The inked ribbon is usually self-contained in a cartridge and is easily replaced by opening a lid on the printer case.

Some high-density dot matrix printers use up to 126 dots to form a character, which has a sharp, fully formed appearance. Although they are cost-effective, the characters from the lower density printers are usually not satisfactory for business correspondence.

dot pitch *See* DPI.
dots per inch *See* DPI.
double-byte character set *See* DBCS.
double bus system A bus system that uses one bus for data and instructions and another for addresses. Control information may or may not have a special bus. In a double bus system, data and addresses can be transferred back and forth simultaneously in the same cycle without waiting for the sequential use of a common bus. A multiple bus requires a larger number of pins in the IC microprocessor package.
double-density recording A technique by which the density of bits on a magnetic storage medium, such as disk or tape, is doubled by modifying the frequency and amplitude of the write signal.
double-doped transistor A particular type of transistor created by growing a crystal and adding P- and N-type impurities while the crystal is being grown.
double-entry polyethylene container Containers that offer front and back access, as well as environmental and impact protection, to sensitive rackmounted equipment. These reusable containers are rotationally molded as one-piece seamless units and equipped with aluminum rack frames welded to withstand heavy loads under shock and vibration.
double length *See* DOUBLE PRECISION.
double-length numeral Refers to a specific numeral that contains twice as many digits as ordinary numerals, and that usually requires two registers or storage locations. Such numerals are often used for double-precision computing.
double-level polysilicon The double-level polysilicon process, as shown in the following figure, helps maximize RAM cell capacitance while cutting the bit sense line in half to reduce its capacitance. A sense amplifier is usually located in the center of the sense line and senses the differential voltage between the two halves of the line.

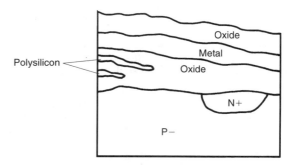

Double-level polysilicon RAM structure

double precision Descriptive of the use of two computer words to represent data. Double-precision arithmetic uses two words to represent numbers in order to obtain greater accuracy than is possible with a single word. If the normal word length is eight bits, then in double-precision arithmetic 16 bits are handled by breaking each number into two parts. Each part is handled separately, but in a manner that allows carries between them. Double-precision processing allows the system to operate as if its registers were twice as large, but operating at a slower speed. Sometimes called *double-length processing*.

double-pulse recording A type of recording in which each memory cell uses two regions magnetized in opposite polarities with neutral regions on each end. Zeros and ones are represented by the sequence of opposite polarities in the cell.

double rail A type of self-timed asynchronous logic circuitry that uses twin lines and three states: high, low, and undecided.

double resistance-capacitance phase shift converter A synchro-to-digital converter that eliminates at least two of those error sources that limited the performance of the single RC circuit. In this approach, V_A and V_B have equal but opposite phase shifts with respect to V_{re}, as shown in the figure. By measuring the time interval between the zero crossings of V_A and V_B and then using it to gate a clock pulse into a counter, the count can be scaled directly in degrees of Θ at one-half the clock frequency used in the single RC design.

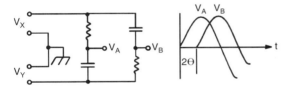

Double RC phase-shift configuration

double sideband signal A signal that contains both the upper and lower sidebands produced by the modulation process. This is in contrast to single sideband or **vestigial sideband**, in which one of the sidebands is either completely or partially removed.

double word Two adjacent words used to store more data than can be represented in one word.

DO-WHILE In programming, a looping structure as in *DO WHILE X*, where *X* is a logical expression and *R* is a routine with the permitted structures. The processor checks *X* and executes *R* if *X* is true; then it returns to check *X* again. The processor executes *R* for as long as *X* is true. An example of the structure for DO-WHILE is shown in the following code fragment:

```
INDEX = 1
DO WHILE INDEX ≤ MAX
   BLKA (INDEX) = BLKB (INDEX)
   INDEX = INDEX + 1
   END
```

This structure moves the number of elements specified by MAX from memory locations in one array (BLKA) to the memory locations in another array (BLKB).

download 1. To transfer data stored in a large computer to a storage device in a microcomputer. **2.** To copy files from a bulletin board or online service to a microcomputer. *Contrast with* UPLOAD.

downloadable font *See* SOFT FONT.

downsizing The replacement of computer equipment and the operating environment with a less expensive version; especially, replacing mainframe or minicomputer equipment with microcomputers.

downtime The time interval when a system is malfunctioning or not operating correctly and is thus not being used. Downtime differs from *available time*, *idle time*, and *standby time* because in all of these the system is functional.

DP Abbreviation for *data processing*.

DPCM Abbreviation for *differential pulse code modulation*, a process in which a signal is sampled, and the difference between the actual value of each sample and its predicted value (as derived from previous samples) is quantized and converted, by encoding, to a digital signal.

DPI Abbreviation for *dots per inch*. Letters and images on the monitor and on a printed page are rendered by an arrangement of black dots. The greater the number of dots per inch, the better the resolution. At low resolutions, the dots can be visible to the naked eye. At higher resolutions, the dots can be detected only through a magnifying glass. Also called *dot pitch*.

DPMA Abbreviation for *Data Processing Management Association*.

DPMA certificate A certificate given by the Data Processing Management Association indicating that a person has a certain level of competence in the field of data processing. The certificate is obtained by passing an examination that is offered annually throughout the United States and Canada.

DPS Abbreviation for *data processing system*.

DPSK Abbreviation for *differential phase-shift keying*, a method of phase-shift keying in which each symbol is a change in the phase of the carrier with respect to its previous phase angle.

DQDB Abbreviation for *distributed-queue dual bus*, a protocol used by an IEEE 8026 MAN. It describes a dual-bus topology with traffic traveling in opposite directions.

dQuery An interactive query management system and report writer for dBASE, Clipper, FoxBase, and Lotus 1-2-3 users. It supports QBE and dBASE programming constructs. It is designed for developers as well as end-users who need to get information out of data files quickly for analysis, interpretation, and reporting. It can import and export ASCII files.

DRA Abbreviation for *dead reckoning analyzer*.

draft A rough and unedited version of a document.

Draft International Standard *See* DIS.

draft-mode speed The fastest speed at which the printer can print text, usually by reducing the print quality from standard or presentation mode. It is measured in CPS (characters per second) or PPM (pages per minute).

drain 1. The current taken from any voltage source. 2. The load device that absorbs the current or power taken from the voltage source.

drag-and-drop A feature of graphic user interfaces that allows elements of the interface to be selected and moved about the display, then placed in another location.

DRAKE Testing Center The only company authorized by Novell, IBM, Banyan, and Microsoft to administer their certification examinations. This company specializes in providing quiet and comfortable test centers that cater to a wide range of specialties, including CPAs, registered nurses, and airline pilots.

DRAM Acronym (pronounced "dee-ram") for *dynamic random access memory*, in which data is stored capacitively and must be refreshed, or it will be lost. DRAM offers high bit densities, low cost, input/output compatibility with TTL levels, and speed compatibility with many microprocessors.

draw program A graphics program such as Adobe Illustrator or CA-Cricket Draw that produces object-oriented graphics. Traditional drawing packages are 2D, usually using layers (objects) to achieve depth and complexity. Each object is considered a discrete element and can be manipulated separately. *Contrast with* PAINT PROGRAM.

DR DOS A fully compatible operating system for all Intel-type PCs. It can be used in all PCs from 8088-type XTs to high-performance Pentiums. It provides a security system for data integrity, and is easy to use. The ease of use stems from the online help and the DOSbook command, a hypertext, online manual. In addition, data can be shared using FileLINK with other PCs over a serial cable. It is fully Windows, DOS, and network compatible. The system contains undelete, disk caching, file compression, memory management, task switching, and uninstall. It has a memory management scheme where files, buffers and network drivers are loaded into upper and high memory, freeing up to 628K, even in 286 and older PCs.

DREAM A relational database program like dBASE, for creating custom database applications. It can provide reports, sorting, query and data entry and retrieval without writing code. DREAM comes with over 200K worth of online and manual documentation that leads the user step-by-step through the program. DREAM can handle over 32,000 records per data file with over 1,500 characters per fixed record length.

Dr. Halo A desktop presentation package that lets you create your own graphics. In text mode, characters can be filled, unfilled, underlined, or drawn with drop shadow to give labels and titles depth. It includes math and scientific symbols and a polygon font for organizational charts, flowcharts, and diagram.

DRI Acronym for *data reduction interpreter*.

drift Refers to change in the output of a circuit, which takes place slowly. It may be caused by changes in environmental conditions.

drift-corrected amplifier A high-gain amplifier that has been separately equipped with a means for reducing drift, thereby preventing drift error.

drift stabilization Refers to the various methods used to minimize the drift of a dc amplifier.

drift voltage equivalent A voltage measurement or equivalent voltage that must be applied to the input of a high-gain amplifier to account for drift and to bring the output voltage to zero. This is a hypothetical voltage when applied to the input of the usual equivalent circuit of the amplifier.

drive cluster A group of one or more drive sectors. A cluster is the minimum number of sectors that the drive can access.

drive cylinders The number of physical cylinders on the disk drive.

drive definition string In NetWare, an ASCII string containing the make and model of a drive.

drive heads The magnetic recording heads on a disk drive.

drive mapping table In an operating system like NetWare, a table containing the primary physical drive that each logical drive is mapped to.

drive number This number corresponds to an index in a drive handle table. Drive A is 0, drive F is 5, etc.

driver 1. A small program used to execute other programs. 2. A circuit or device used to power or control other circuits or channels.

drive removable flag A flag used in some operating systems like NetWare that indicates whether a disk is removable.

driver mirror table A table used in some operating systems like NetWare containing the secondary physical drive that each logical drive is mapped to.

driver modules Modules that allow output signals to be power-amplified by bus drivers to allow them to drive a heavy circuit load.

drive name In DOS and similar operating systems, a single letter followed by a colon (as in C:) that identifies a real or simulated disk drive to the operating system.

driver type In some operating systems like NetWare, a number indicating the type of disk driver software installed on a disk channel.

driver workspace In NetWare, a part of Communication Services that is a 12-byte field reserved for the network driver when IPX is using an ECB. It can be used by applications any other time.

drive sector One allocation unit of memory on a hard disk drive. There are usually 512 bytes of memory associated with each sector on a PC drive. Most PC drives access sectors in groups called *clusters*.

drive size The size of the physical hard drive, usually in megabytes or gigabytes. In NetWare, the size is in blocks (1 block = 4,096 bytes) and the drive size does not include the portion of the disk reserved for "hot fix" redirection due to media errors.

drive slots Openings in the computer case for the disk drives, as shown in the figure.

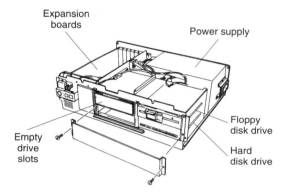

PC with floppy drive over hard drive and two additional drive slots

drive type Most IBM compatible computers have a table of compatible drives listed in their BIOS chips. To install a drive, it is necessary to match that drive's specifications to a specific number listed in the drive type table.

DRO Abbreviation for *destructive read out*.

droop A drifting of an output at an approximately constant rate. It may be caused by the leakage of current out of a capacitor.

drop The connection on a circuit, a cable from a distribution panel to a faceplate.

drop cable A cable that connects a PC to the network's main cable, a trunk, or backbone cable in a bus or tree topology LAN. Drop cables normally use either twisted-pair or coaxial media.

drop-dead halt A type of halt from which there is no recovery. A drop-dead halt may be programmed deliberately to shut down the system, or it may be the result of an error in the program. Sometimes called a *dead halt*.

drop-in The reading or recording of a spurious signal with an amplitude greater than nominal by a specified percentage.

dropout A temporary loss of transmission or the failure to read a bit from a magnetic storage system. In transmission, a dropout is usually due to noise or a malfunction. Dropout in a magnetic storage system is mainly caused by an output too low to be detected.

DRP Abbreviation for *Digital Routing Protocol*.

drum plotter A plotter using paper rolled around a drum. The drum rotates while the pen moves across it.

dry contact Refers to a part of a circuit containing only contact points and resistive components.

dry reed contact Refers to encapsulated units containing metal contacts that act as the contact points of a relay.

dry run A checking of the program flowchart, coding, and all program documentation before putting the program on a computer.

DS Abbreviation for *double-sided floppy diskettes*, where both sides of the flexible media are used to record data.

dSALVAGE A program that diagnoses, repairs, and edits DBF data files. You can use it to check the file and find how it is damaged, then fix the damage with a few keystrokes. dSALVAGE contains header/record/byte-stream editors that allow you to search, modify, and move data in ways not possible from within dBASE. It supports dBASE (all versions), FoxBase, and dBXL.

DSAP Abbreviation for *destination service access point*, the address for the destination user of a service. A remote IPX process would be considered the DSAP from the point of view of the local data link module.

DSE Abbreviation for *data storage equipment*.

DSI Abbreviation for *digital speech interpolation*, a form of digital multiplexing for voice that uses speech interpolation.

DSL Abbreviation for *deep scattering layer*.

DSR Abbreviation for *data set ready*, a modem interface-control signal from the DCE indicating to the attached terminal equipment that the modem is connected to the telephone circuit.

DST A Sniffer network analyzer abbreviation for the *destination address*.

DSU Abbreviation for *data service unit*, a device similar to a modem that connects a computer or terminal to a DDS (dataphone digital service) communications line. One end of the DSU connects through the CSU (channel service unit) to the four-wire DDS line. A DSU is used for T-1 communications.

DSW Abbreviation for *device status word*, a word used to indicate the status of devices such as registers in a computer system.

DTE Abbreviation for *data terminal equipment*, equipment consisting of digital devices that convert the user information into data signals for transmission, or reconvert the received data signals into user information.

DTL Abbreviation for *diode-transistor logic*, the earliest form of integrated circuits combining diodes as input and transistors as inverting amplifiers in a monolithic structure.

DTMF Abbreviation for *dual tone multifrequency*, the ordinary tone dial.

DTP Abbreviation for *desktop publishing*, a class of software that incorporates text and graphics to produce page layouts electronically. Also, the process of using such software for page or graphic design.

DTR Abbreviation for *data terminal ready*, a modem interface-control signal from the data terminal indicating to the modem that the terminal is ready for transmission.

D-type flip-flop A type of bistable multivibrator shown in the following figure that is triggered on the leading or positive edge of the clock pulse. D-type flip-flops are typically used for buffer and shift registers, and ripple counters.

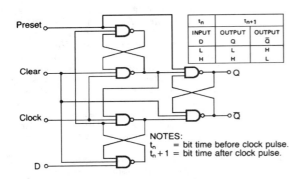

D-type flip-flop

dual diode A combination tube consisting of two diode sections in a single envelope. Dual diode refers to monolithic dual diodes intended for use in applications requiring low leakage currents. Applications include coupling with reverse isolation, signal clipping and clamping, and protection of low-leakage FET differential and operational amplifiers.

dual inline package *See* DIP.

dual media A term applied to equipment that is capable of utilizing two different types of media, such as tape and diskettes.

dual operation The negation of the result of the original operation. The dual operation is found by replacing all zeros with ones and all ones with zeros in the truth table of the original operation. The dual operation for a logical OR is the NOR operation.

dual-porting Making a disk drive available to two different computers, as done in SFT Level III in NetWare.

dual protocol stack Refers to computers that contain two different protocol stacks so that both can run.

dual ramp A/D conversion A type of analog-to-digital conversion, shown in the following figure. In the dual ramp or slope type of A/D converter, the input signal is applied to an integrator, and a counter is started, counting the clock pulses. After a predetermined number of counts fixes the period of time, T, a reference voltage with an opposite polarity, is applied to the integrator. At this time, the charge on the integrating capacitor is proportional to the average value of the input over the period T. The integral of the reference is an opposite slope ramp with a slope V_R/RC. Now, the counter starts counting from zero. When the integrator output is zero, the counter is stopped and the analog circuit reset. Since the charge is proportional to $V_{IN}T$ and the charge lost is proportional to $V_R\Delta/t$, the number of counts relative to the full period is proportional to $\Delta t/T$, or V_{IN}/V_R. The output of the binary counter is therefore a binary representation of the input voltage. When the input is attenuated and offset by half of the reference voltage, the output is an offset binary representation of a bipolar input.

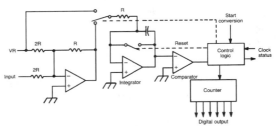

Dual-ramp A/D converter

dual ramp conversion interface The dual ramp method uses an integrating technique to cancel out many of the drift problems that occur with successive approximation. The two ramps occur from a ramp time when the input voltage has been integrated for a fixed number of clock periods; then the input voltage to the integrator is switched to a reference voltage, and the ramp time required for the integrator to decrease to the level of the original input voltage is counted. The ramp times are compared to allow the calculation of the unknown transducer voltage. The interface and converter hardware for a dual ramp are shown in the figure.

dual ramp conversion program The program for the 6800 family first requires instructions to initialize the input and output ports of the peripheral interface adapter (*PIA*). The ramp control is then set and the comparator tested. This ensures that the comparator output is below the reference voltage level at the beginning of

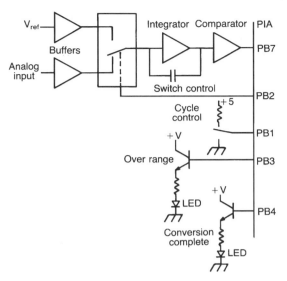

Dual-ramp conversion interface

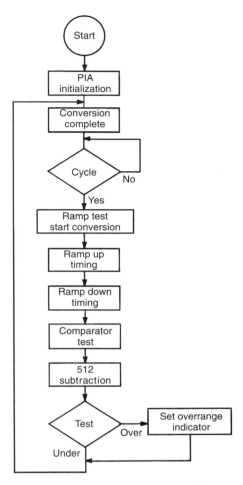

Dual-ramp conversion program flow

conversion. Then a conversion-finished flag is set, and the microprocessor enters a loop as shown in the flow diagram. This loop used the PBI cycle input from the PIA, and resets the conversion-finished flag when the ramp control goes low to stall a new cycle.

The index register is loaded and then decremented to provide the ramp-up timing. As the ramp crosses the threshold level, the comparator output is switched, causing the microprocessor to enter the ramp-up cycle. The index register is decremented until empty. Then the ramp control switches to high and the index register is incremented. A dummy statement equalizes the count for the ramp periods. As the ramp-down period ends, the contents of the index register are stored. The offset counts are obtained, and an overrange test then checks the contents of a location for a value.

dual system A system configuration in which two computers are used for processing and the results compared for accuracy. Identical inputs and routines are used. The dual system is employed for applications requiring a high degree of reliability.

dual-tone multifrequency signaling The generic name for the tone signaling method used on push-button or touchtone telephones.

dual Y-axis A bar/line chart with two Y axes: Y1 and Y2.

dub A copy of a video or audio tape recording made by replaying the original tape and simultaneously recording the signal onto a new tape, which becomes the dub. Also used as a verb meaning to copy a tape.

Duette A utility that can transfer files in either direction between any IBM-compatible laptop, portable, or desktop computer. It eliminates the need for additional hardware; only a null-model cable is required. The use of RAM disks is also supported.

dumb terminal A terminal that has no processing capability.

dummy A nonfunctioning item used to satisfy some format or logic requirement or to fulfill prescribed conditions. A dummy may be an artificial character, statement, address, or instruction usually inserted to complete format conditions, such as fixed word length.

dummy argument In a macro definition, a variable prototype field that will be replaced with a parameter (quantity or symbol) when the macro operation is used. Also called a *dummy definition*.

dummy instruction Refers to an artificial instruction or address inserted in a list of instructions. It is used to fulfill certain conditions, such as a word or block length, without affecting the operation.

dummy load 1. The act of transfer to storage of a program without execution in order to determine if all specifications and requirements have been met. **2.** A resistor that simulates electrically a sink for an electric current.

dump A transfer in operation or contents of a computer system. A power or *dc dump* results in the removal of power from the computer. Power dumps can result in the loss of operations and data unless specific measures are taken to prevent losses. *Binary* and *change* dumps cause a printout or output into binary form, or a printout or output only, for locations that have changed since the last dump. A dumping program usually has a restart provision to allow the program to start again at the last dump point if an interrupt such as that caused by a machine malfunction should occur.

Dump commands such as the following are used to transfer the contents of memory between two specific locations to a specified output format:

```
D x, y; (dump memory between locations x and y)
```

dump and restart Refers to software routines for taking program dumps at specified times and restarting programs at one of these points in the event of program failure.

dump, binary A printout of the contents of a memory unit in binary form onto some external medium such as paper or disk.

dump, change A printout or output recording of the contents of all storage locations in which a change has been made since the previous change dump.

dump check A check to verify data being transferred during dumping. One method adds all of the digits during dumping and checks the sum when retransferring.

dumping resistor A resistor that drains charge from a capacitor for safety purposes.

dump point The point in a program where it is desirable to have a transfer operation. Dump points are usually designed to protect against machine failure.

dump, power The removal of all power accidentally or intentionally.

duobinary A three-level coding scheme that uses controlled amounts of intersymbol interference to achieve transmission.

duodecimal Relating to the number system with a radix of twelve.

duplex Containing two sets of operational elements that may or may not operate simultaneously. In communications, a duplex system is one in which data may be received and transmitted over the same lines simultaneously.

duplex cable A type of cable constructed of two insulating stranded-wire conductors twisted together. They may or may not share a common insulating covering.

duplex channel A channel providing simultaneous transmissions in both directions.

duplexed operation A mode of operation in which a primary processor performs the control task. If a failure occurs, a backup processor takes over. The primary processor is then taken offline, repaired, and returned to service without interrupting control of the process. Duplexed processors provide twice the computing capacity, since either processor may control the process. This excess power can often be used for other optional tasks.

To guarantee higher reliability, the entire system should be examined for the consequences of each possible failure. Also, software for the duplexed processors must be designed to achieve the higher potential reliability of the duplicated hardware.

Duplexed operation allows the selection of two processors to take advantage of special characteristics. One may be designed to perform fast floating point calculations; this would be its function during normal operation of the system.

In order for the backup processor to keep up-to-date, it must have access to the current process status information. With a shared file interconnection, the information is maintained in the shared file. With channel-to-channel connections, the primary processor periodically posts the process status information into the memory of the backup computer.

duplexed system A system with two distinct and separate sets of facilities, each of which is capable of assuming the system function while the other assumes a standby status. Usually both sets are identical.

duplex fiber-optic cable This cable is available with a 50, 62.5, or 100 micron core. The cable design consists of two buffer tubes, each containing a single optical fiber. High-strength Kevlar is stranded around each tube to provide tensile strength. Each tube is then shaped with a PVC jacket, and coded for channel identification. The outer cable jacket is flame-retardant PVC.

duplex fiber-optic modem A modem as shown in the figure that allows asynchronous RS-232 equipment to transmit over fiber-optic lines. It is used in environments where electrical interference immunity is necessary. There is complete electrical isolation between the RS-232 equipment and the fiber-optic cable. Transmission distances of up to 6,562 feet at 19.2 Kbps are allowed with excellent security characteris-

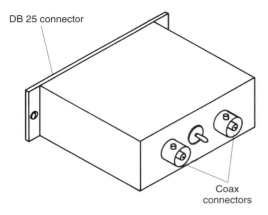

Duplex fiber-optic modem

tics. It cannot easily be tapped into without detection.

duplex operation A simultaneous operation of transmitting and receiving apparatus at two separate locations.

duplicate 1. To copy such that the result is in the same form and indistinguishable in content from the original, such as copying all of the contents of one disk to another. **2.** A copy of an original document or program.

duplicate packets 1. Copies of existing packets made for backup reasons. **2.** In NetWare Diagnostic Services, the number of times that SPX has discarded inbound packets because they were duplicates of previously received packets.

duplicate replies sent In NetWare, a part of File Server Environment Services that shows a count of request packets for which a server had to send duplicate replies. Duplicate replies are only sent for requests the server cannot process.

duplication check A check that requires that the results of two independent operations be identical. A duplication check may be performed at the same time on different equipment or at different times on the same equipment.

durability index A measure of the durability of a tape expressed as the number of passes that can be made before a significant degradation of output occurs divided by the corresponding number that can be made using a reference tape.

duration, character Refers to the time required for all of the pulses that are associated with a specific character to pass a given point on a communication channel.

duty cycle A specified operating time of a unit plus a specified time of nonoperation.

DVI Abbreviation for *digital video interactive*, a technology that allows real-time compression and decompression of graphics and full-motion video for recording on CD-ROM, videodiscs, magnetic disks, or other digital storage media.

dVOICE A dBASE-like programming language that allows for the creation of applications that speak and can be accessed through touchtone telephones. It provides built-in digitized text-to-speech. Preprogrammed applications include voice mail, order entry, inventory status, and account balances. Single-, two-, four-, eight-, 12-, and 16-line versions are available.

Dvorak simplified keyboard A rearranged typewriter keyboard; advocates of this keyboard claim that it permits 35 percent faster output than conventional keyboards. Patented in 1932 by Dr. August Dvorak of the University of Washington, Seattle.

DVST Abbreviation for *direct view storage tube*.

DW Abbreviation for *data word*.

dwell A programmed time delay of variable duration. A dwell is not sequential or cyclic, nor is it an interlock.

dwell time reset Refers to time spent in reset. In cycling the computer from reset to operate to hold and back to reset, this time must be long enough to permit the computer to recover from any overload and voltage changes.

DXC Abbreviation for *data exchange control*.

DXPERT Abbreviation for *machine diagnostic expert*, a DOS-based program that uses AI techniques to solve vibration-related rotating machinery problems. DXPERT has six general knowledge bases from which to solve machinery problems: pumps, motors, gearboxes, turbines, fans, and compressors. Users can create their own knowledge bases from specific plant-history data.

dyad An operator indicated by writing the symbols of two vectors with no symbol or other sign between them.

dyadic operator A Boolean operator with two operands. Dyadic operators include AND, OR, NAND, NOR, and exclusive-OR. *Also see* DYAD.

dye sublimation A method of color printing that uses a thermal head and a controlled spreading of the dye image to achieve a smoother blend of dyes. Sometimes abbreviated *dye-sub*.

DynaComm Asynchronous A communications program with 14 terminal emulations, seven file transfer protocols and LAN support. It provides automated logons to eight online services and a scripting language to automate tasks and construct new Windows front-ends.

dynamic Occurring at the time of execution.

dynamic adaptive routing Automatic rerouting of traffic based on a sensing and analysis of current actual network conditions.

dynamic check A test of any function or process that is conducted by subjecting the device, process, or function to the rigors of its anticipated operational environment.

dynamic data exchange See DDE.

Dynamic Data Manager A program that can monitor steady-state dynamic vibration data upon alert or danger alarm conditions on different types of rotating machinery. The data may be used immediately or accessed later for predictive maintenance.

dynamic debugging The debugging of routines at full system speed. The routines are first checked using the single-step mode; only when they are completely debugged at low speed should dynamic debugging be undertaken.

dynamic dump A dump that is performed during program execution.

dynamic gain The magnitude ratio of a steady state output to a sinusoidal input signal.

Dynamic Link Library See DLL.

dynamic memory See DYNAMIC STORAGE and DRAM.

dynamic MOS RAM A kind of metal-oxide semiconductor random-access memory in which the memory cells must be electrically refreshed periodically to avoid loss of held data. A three-transistor dynamic MOS cell uses a shared read or write select line and separate read and write data bit lines. The device capacitance (shown in the figure in dashed lines) is charged and discharged as a function of the write line. This type of MOS memory is relatively inexpensive to produce, but it requires additional circuitry for the refreshing operation.

MOS dynamic RAMs of 1024 bits were the first semiconductor memories to gain wide acceptance. Built from p-channel MOS technology, these chips made large, solid-state memory arrays possible. These dynamic memories used capacitive storage to hold each bit value and required periodic refreshing to retain data since the charge held in the capacitors leaked away. A three-transistor cell was used for each bit stored, and the 1024 bits were housed in about 20,000 square mils of silicon. This density first promised to displace core memories and make large semiconductor systems simple to implement. But it was not until even higher-density products were introduced that the takeover began occurring. The first of the higher-density devices, the 4096-bit dynamic RAM, provided quadruple the density. To make those higher-density and higher-speed RAMs possible, p-channel technology was abandoned and n-channel processing was used. N-channel allowed the low threshold voltages needed for TTL compatibility and its speed was greater. It also permitted device densities to grow larger. Along with n-channel processing came a new cell design that permitted a bit to be stored with a single transistor and a capacitor.

dynamic passwords One-time-only passwords generated by a special device.

dynamic programming Programming that allows a number of decisions for each stage of a multistage problem. Dynamic programming seeks to optimize the problem solution by the integration of the cumulative effects of each stage toward the overall goal.

dynamic RAM See DRAM.

dynamic relocation A program that can be moved to a different location in a partially executed state without affecting its ability to complete the processing.

dynamic response The specific behavior of the output of a device as a function of the input, with respect to time.

dynamic router A router that uses special algorithms to route packets to the optimal path at the moment.

dynamic storage A type of memory, usually semiconductor, in which the stored data gradually leaks away and is lost, unless it is refreshed periodically by special circuitry. Contrast with STATIC STORAGE.

dynamic subroutine A subroutine that has a skeletal form with regard to certain parameters that are selected later as the processing proceeds. These parameters may include the number of repetitions, decimal point position, or item size. The computer can be used to derive these parameters during program execution.

dynamic worksheet A program such as Lotus 1-2-3 that allows "what-if" analysis for financial or planning analysis. These programs automatically recalculate any entries on the sheet that change as a result of a directed change.

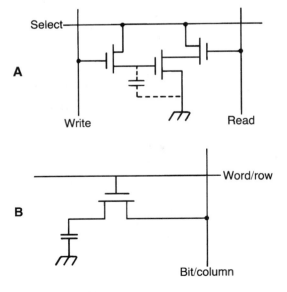

Basic dynamic (A) and single-transistor (B) MOS RAM cells

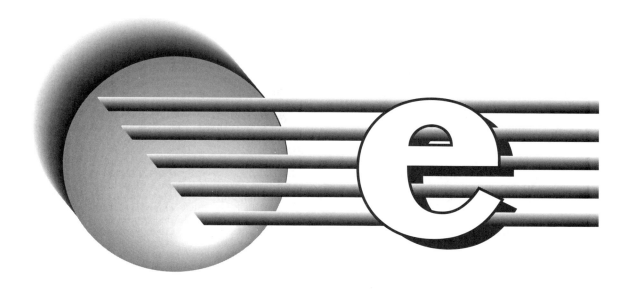

EA **1.** Abbreviation for *effective address*. **2.** Abbreviation for *extended attribute* file, an OS/2 system file that stores the icon and other descriptive information about the particular data file or application. Extended attributes include long filenames and the position within the workplace shell as well. Damage to the EA file usually results in a lack of descriptive information, but no loss in application functionality.

EAE Abbreviation for *extended arithmetic element*, a central processor element that is implemented with hardware to multiply, divide, and normalize functions.

early failure period An interval immediately following the final assembly during which the failure rate of certain items is relatively high. Also sometimes referred to as *infant mortality period*.

EAROM Acronym for *electrically alterable ROM*, a specialized random-access read/write memory that is programmed by writing into the array and used as a ROM. Read cycle time is 10 to 20 microseconds and writing takes about one millisecond. The contents can be erased in one operation. EAROM costs tend to be relatively high due to low production yield and the long test times required to check the data patterns. EAROM testing may take up to 30 minutes per unit, while testing of conventional RAMs can be done in 30 seconds. *Also see* EEPROM.

earth stations Refers to communications ground terminals that use antennas and associated electronic equipment to transmit, receive, and process communications via satellite. Future networks may be able to interconnect by domestic communications satellites, creating regional and national networks.

earth, virtual Refers to a live input terminal of a directly coupled amplifier that remains approximately at earth potential although not connected to earth.

EAS Acronym for *extended area service*.

EASI Abbreviation for *elastic asynchronous/synchronous interface*, an interface as shown in the figure that allows asynchronous equipment to use synchronous modems. It also adjusts the baud rates.

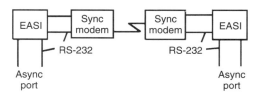

Elastic asynchronous/synchronous interface

EASIswap Software that enables virtually any DOS-based software package to become a terminate-and-stay-resident (TSR) application. You can swap between programs with a key-stroke. It requires less than 5K and will use expanded memory (if available) or the hard disk as needed to store programs during swapping.

EASY Loose acronym for *efficient assembly system*.

EASYBILL A system in which meters for industrial, commercial, and utility use can be monitored by computer. A standard interface is used which can be accessed by a PC. Software functions include meter polling and report printing.

EasyCASE A full-featured CASE tool. Its IBM SAA/CUA-complaint GUI (graphical user interface) supports a mouse and provides pulldown menus, dialog boxes, icons, and scrollbars. A click-and-drag approach is used for the selection and manipulation of chart objects.

EAX Acronym for *electronic automatic exchange*.

EBCDIC Acronym (pronounced"EBB-see-dick") for *extended binary-coded-decimal interchange code*, a data code developed by IBM that uses a set of eight bit-coded characters. EBCDIC is used for representation and transmission in data-processing systems, communications, and associated devices. Some examples of the EBCDIC code are shown in the following table. EBCDIC is used for IBM mainframe computers.(*Also see* CHARACTER SET.)

EBCDIC Symbol	Code
1	1111 0001
2	1111 0010
3	1111 0011
4	1111 0100
5	1111 0101

EBCDIC Symbol	Code
A	1100 0001
B	1100 0010
C	1100 0011
D	1100 0100
!	0101 1010
$	0101 1011
*	0101 1100
)	0101 1101

EBICON Acronym for *electron bombardment induced conductivity*.

Ebone A pan-European backbone service for telecommunications.

EBR Abbreviation for *electron beam recording*.

EC Abbreviation for *error correcting*.

ECAC Abbreviation for *Electromagnetic Compatibility Analysis Center* of the Engineering College Administrative Council.

ECAP Abbreviation for *electronic circuit analysis program*, a language for modeling and analyzing electrical networks. ECAP allows the synthesizing of device models using function generators or tables of functions in conjunction with passive components.

ECB Abbreviation for *event control block*.

ECB address In NetWare Communication Services, an address that points to an IPX event control block.

ECC Abbreviation for *error checking and correcting*, a term that originally referred to the self-diagnostic and self-correcting techniques used for RAM. The term now includes the same type of diagnostics provided with tape, hard disks, and floppy disk drives. In all cases, the device uses some type of microcode contained in a peripheral chip to detect and correct soft errors in the data stream.

Eccles-Jordan trigger (*o.t.*) A once-common tube-type bistable multivibrator in which the output of one section was directly coupled into the input of the other section. The circuit was capable of storing one bit of information.

ECCM Abbreviation for *electronic counter countermeasure*.

ECD *See* ELECTROCHROMERIC DISPLAY.

echo The return of a sufficient portion of a transmitted signal to be recognized due to reflection. An echo is usually received as interference, but in an echo check, the received echo data is compared with the original for accuracy.

echo check An error-control technique in which the receiving terminal or computer returns the original message to the sender to verify that the message was received correctly.

echoplexer A unit that allows an attached terminal to receive an echo of transmitted data, as shown. With an echoplexer, you communicate with your system in half-duplex, with an echo provided to the terminal that requires full-duplex operation. Sometimes abbreviated *EP*.

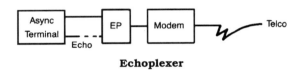

Echoplexer

echo-print To display on the screen or printer what is being input as data.

echo suppressor A device built into telephone circuits that prevents echoes of transmitted signals from returning to the sending device and being interpreted as received data.

Eckert, J. Presper Codeveloper with John W. Mauchly of the all-electronic computer (ENIAC) and the first commercial computer (UNIVAC I).

ECL Abbreviation for *emitter-coupled logic*, a logic family that uses signal coupling directly into the emitters of transistors. ECL is very fast, requires only a 1 volt of signal swing in 3 to 4 nanoseconds, and inherently generates little noise. Power requirements tend to be higher than other logic families. Microprocessors have been implemented with ECL using the bit-slice approach.

ECL microprocessor A microprocessor that uses emitter-coupled logic. A typical ECL microprocessor set contains five chips: a 4-bit slice, a control register function, a timing function, a slice memory interface, and a slice look ahead. The various chips may be used as building blocks to construct a microprocessor with capabilities larger than four bits.

ECM Abbreviation for *electronic countermeasures*.

ECMA Abbreviation for *European Computer Manufacturers' Association*, a group that is active in preparing and promoting standards for the performance and safety of computer data links, including LANs. ECMA inputs to IEEE 802 have been significant in the formulation of international LAN specifications.

ECNE Abbreviation for *Enterprise Certified NetWare Engineer*, Novell's advanced intermediate-level certification. This certification is a continuation of the CNE program. A person who becomes an ECNE usually has some special requirements or interest in the advanced or specialized areas of networking. For example, a consultant or a network administrator might need to connect NetWare and Unix using TCP/IP and NFS or create a wide-area network using Novell's dial-in/dial-out products.

ECONFIG A Novell utility that forces NetWare drivers to conform to the standard operation of Ethernet.

Ecstasy A full Xbase compiler for UNIX, OS/2, and Windows. It is a totally open system for Xbase and includes C sources to libraries. It creates a C version of the application, directly calling the system C compiler. It provides the characteristics of Xbase variables, including macro expressions with UDF calls and type reassignment. It supports the features of dBASE, Clipper, and FoxBase.

ED-Beta Abbreviation for *extended-definition Betamax*, a consumer/professional video recording format developed by Sony offering 500-line horizontal resolution and Y/C connections.

EDC Abbreviation for *external device code*.

EDDC Abbreviation for *extended distance data cable*, a cable specially constructed to extend the transmission of the RS-232 specification beyond 50 feet. Maximum distance depends on data rates; at 9600 bps, EDDC is operational up to 500 feet.

Extended-distance data cable

EDGE Acronym for *electronic data gathering equipment*.

edge A boundary in an image. The apparent sharpness of edges can be increased without increasing resolution. *Also see* SHARPNESS.

edge enhancement An image-processing technique for sharpening the edges of objects in an image, removing blur, or bringing out obscured detail.

edit To modify the form or format of data, such as inserting or deleting characters or decimal points.

edit commands Refers to specific commands used with an editor. In some systems, edit commands are implemented as single-, double-, or triple-letter mnemonics followed by optional command parameters. Commands are usually terminated by typing a carriage-return character, such as Enter.

editing 1. The act of revising and correcting text or a program prior to its production as a final document or publication. **2.** The act of operating the function and alphanumeric keys of an editor in a word processor or computer.

editor An interactive system or a program that allows users to prepare programs or text and to make changes using simple commands. Some time-sharing services offer such editor systems. Using the time-sharing programs, users can prepare assembly-language programs and correct them quickly. They can also add and store documentation as well as combine and retrieve programs. Editors typically allow the following functions:

- Character replacement
- Insertion and movement of characters, words, and blocks
- Batch balancing
- Check-digit verification

An editor allows the microcomputer designer to prepare the original assembly language programs and correct them using simple commands. Commands may be typed in at any time during the edit process in place of a source statement.

edits Any revision or formatting changes to a program listing, chart, document or stylesheet.

edit statements Statements entered from the keyboard that can be placed into an internal edit buffer. Each statement can be preceded by a statement number that specifies the relative order of the statement in relation to all the others.

EDIX A multiple-window, full-screen text editor for DOS, OS/2, UNIX, and VMS systems. It provides subprocess execution with automatic output capture, compiler support, keystroke record and playback, and a search-and-translate capability.

EDP Abbreviation for *electronic data processing*, data processing performed largely by electronic devices. EDP includes the functions of entering, classifying, computing, and recording information—and the devices such as internally stored program computers and disk drives.

EDP auditor An auditor who specializes in reviewing a company's financial records and procedures that are kept on a computer.

EDP controls Procedures used to prevent any illegal or accidental misuse of any component of a computer system.

EE designer A PC-based CAE/CAD software package for printed circuit board (PCB) prototyping.

This integrated system includes capabilities for schematic capture, analog and digital circuit simulation, and PCB layout. The PCB prototyping system is capable of producing two-sided prototype circuit boards.

EEPROM Acronym for *electrically erasable programmable read-only memory*, a PROM that can be electrically erased in one second or less and electrically written into. This alterability allows in-circuit programming where the device can be erased, written, and read without being removed from the circuit. A typical EEPROM is organized as 512 words of two bits each, and it can be erased and reprogrammed as many as one million times. The two types of devices are metal nitride-oxide semiconductors (MNOS) and floating gate. The floating-gate EEPROMs (shown in the diagram) are similar to ultraviolet EPROMs with the addition of a control gate; there is no quartz lid to allow erasing. EEPROMs are also known as *EAROMs* (electrically alterable ROMs).

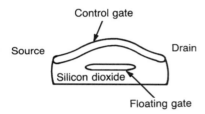

EEPROM structure with control gate

EEPROM programmer A device that provides a means of programming a single EEPROM or an EEPROM module using an integral hexadecimal keyboard and display. EEPROMS are electrically erasable and therefore need not be removed from the module or socket to be erased and reprogrammed.

effective address An address derived by indexing or indirect addressing techniques that is actually used to identify the current operand.

effective earth radius The radius of a hypothetical earth for which the distance to the radio horizon, for rectilinear propagation, is the same as that for the actual earth assuming a uniform vertical gradient refractive index.

effective instruction A method used to modify a presumptive instruction using a stored program computer. The method uses modifier or index words that are added to the original instruction to produce the effective instruction.

effective rights The rights that a NetWare user has in a directory. Effective rights are a combination of the user's Trustee Assignments, the Maximum Rights Mask, and any group membership rights.

effector A device used to bring about a desired response to a change in its input from another device where the end result is required.

EFTS Abbreviation for *electronic funds transfer system*, a computerized means of transferring funds and financial information from one location to another, as well as for the clearing and settling of accounts.

EGA Abbreviation for *enhanced graphics adapter*, a PC display standard that specifies 640 × 350 pixels with 16-color capability from a palette of 64 colors.

EHF Abbreviation for *extremely high frequency*, 30 to 300 gigahertz (FCC).

EIA Abbreviation for *Electronic Industries Association*, an organization of electronics manufacturers that sets industry technical standards, disseminates market data, and maintains contact with government agencies affecting the electronics industry. The EIA has interface standards that cover signal characteristics, voltages, currents, and time periods; connections to modem units; and the physical dimensions of hardware. The EIA also has standards for character codes and coding.

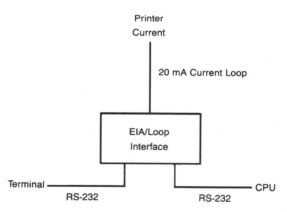

EIA loop interface

EIA current loop interface A unit designed to enable the interconnection of a current loop interface with an RS-232 interface, as shown in the diagram. Coupling is provided for both transmit and receive data. Some units permit the alternate selection of either an RS-232/20mA current loop connection or a straight-through RS-232/RS-232 connection. They may be ordered in active or passive models.

EIA RS-449/422 cable A cable designed for use with an EIA RS-449 interface. It is a 37-conductor cable with RS-449-type connectors.

EIA RS-232 The standard port used by most personal computers to talk with an external device like a modem or mouse.

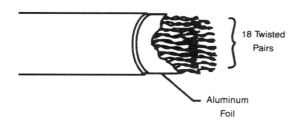

EIA RD-449/422 cable

EIA standard code A code or coding system conforming to any of the standards established by the EIA.

eight-level code Refers to a distinct code designed with eight impulses used to describe a single character, but with additional start and stop elements often used for asynchronous transmission.

80x86 *See* INTEL 8086, INTEL 80286, INTEL 80386, INTEL 80468, INTEL PENTIUM.

80/20 rule Programs tend to obey an 80/20 rule: 80% of the time is spent executing 20% of the code. To speed up a program, find that 20% and recode it. Often, significant improvements in performance will result. This 20% can usually be found in the inner-loop portions of the program. The recoding of selected subroutines can cut the running time approximately in half.

EIS Abbreviation for *end interruption sequence*.

EISA Acronym for *Extended Industry Standard Architecture* (pronounced "EE-sah").

EISA bus The Extended Industry Standard Architecture bus, a 32-bit bus used in PC systems starting with the 386.

EISA bus extender An expansion board with signal impedance matched to EISA specifications, so it is compatible with EISA backplanes and prototyping boards. Test points are available to facilitate diagnosis/repair operations, and accommodate test probes or wrapped wire.

EISA motherboard A system board that allows a data acquisition and/or control system. It includes an industrial BIOS that permits the system to boot without a video adapter or keyboard installed, once the other feature cards have been installed. A memory capacity of 64M on-board permits the use of any PC-compatible operating system such as Windows, QNX, SCO Unix and VM-386 for multi-user and multitasking capabilities. EISA expansion slots permit the use of new expansion cards such as SCSI disk controllers, ESDI disk controllers, specialized video adapters, and networking boards.

EISA prototyping board A prototyping board with a bus master interface chip and glue logic installed and connected. The board's design allows solder and wire-wrap connections and accepts components such as DIP, PGA, and PLCC.

elastic asynchronous/synchronous interface *See* EASI.

elastic buffer A storage device designed to accept data timed by one clock and deliver it timed by another clock.

electric Refers to any phenomenon that depends essentially on a peculiarity of electric charges.

electrical contacts Refers to paths, joints, or touchings of the two halves of a connector or contacts at points joined in electrical connections.

electrical degrees The angle, expressed in degrees of phase difference of vectors, representing currents or voltages arising in different parts of a circuit.

electrical element Any of the individual building blocks from which electronic circuits are constructed, such as conductors, resistors, capacitors, and inductors.

electrical heating Heating by an electrical means, such as current flow through a resistance, induction currents in a conductor, or displacement currents in a dielectric.

electrical impulse Any momentary transient voltage, whether inadvertent or intentionally produced.

electrical interference Interference due to the operation of electrical apparatus other than that arising from actual transmissions.

electrically alterable ROM *See* EAROM.

electrically erasable programmable ROM *See* EEROM.

electrical quantity Usually denoted by Q, it is the amount of electric charge, the practical unit being the coulomb.

electrical reset Restoration of a device, such as a relay or circuit, usually by a reset signal.

electrical schematic A diagram that represents all circuit elements using symbols and interconnecting lines.

electric axis The direction in a crystal that gives the maximum conductivity to the passage of an electric current; the X-axis of a piezoelectric crystal.

electric circuit A continuous closed path consisting of wires and elements for the flow of current.

electric delay line A delay line that uses lumped or distributed capacitive and inductive elements.

Electric Desk An integrated system that combines word processing, database management, spreadsheet, analysis, and communications. Its most important characteristics are its simplicity of use and its low price. It has appeal for both novice and advanced users.

electric doublet A system with a definite electric moment, mathematically equivalent to two equal charges of opposite sign at a very small distance apart.

electric field A region in which attracting or repelling forces are exerted on any electric charge present.

electric flux Refers to the electric field intensity

normal to the surface. The electric flux is conceived as emanating from a positive charge and ending on a negative charge without loss.

electricity A fundamental quantity consisting of two oppositely charged particles, the *electrons* being negatively charged, and the *protons* positively charged. A substance with more electrons than protons is said to be *negatively charged*; conversely, one with more protons than electrons is *positively charged*.

electric motor Any device for converting electrical energy into mechanical torque.

electric oscillations Electric currents that periodically reverse their direction of flow at a frequency determined by the constants of circuit or source.

electric polarization The dipole moment per unit volume of a dielectric.

electric potential A measure of the energy of a unit's positive charge at a point, expressed relative to that at infinite distance or at the surface of the earth (zero potential).

electric susceptibility A measure of the relative permittivity of a dielectric path, such as found in a transmission line.

electric transducer A device that converts non-electric energy into electric energy, such as the microphone, solar cell, or strain gauge.

electrochromeric display A type of display abbreviated *ECD* that uses materials that change from transparent to opaque under the control of an electric field. A field can be used to turn the ECD on, and it will hold that state until a field of opposite polarity switches it back to its original state.

electrode The conducting element in an electronic tube or semiconductor that emits or collects electrons or ions and/or controls their movement by means of an electronic or electric field.

electrode admittance The admittance measured between an electrode and earth when all other potentials on electrodes are constant.

electrode conductance The in-phase or real component of an electrode admittance.

electrode current The net current entering or leaving an electrode.

electrode impedance The ratio of a sinusoidal voltage on an electrode to the corresponding sinusoidal current, all other electrodes being maintained at constant potential.

electrodeposition The deposition electrolytically of a substance on an electrode, as in electroplating or electroforming.

electrodynamics The science dealing with the interaction or forces between currents, or the forces on currents in independent magnetic fields.

electrofluor A transparent material that has the property of storing electrical energy and releasing it as visible (fluorescent) light.

electrokinetics The science of electric charges in motion, without reference to the accompanying magnetic field.

electroluminescent screen A type of flat-screen technology, also called *ELD*, that is sturdier than a gas-plasma display and produces a better picture than either plasma or LCDs. However, ELDs are also more expensive because they must be coated with a smooth, very thin film.

electrolysis The chemical change, generally decomposition, effected by a flow of current through a solution of the chemical; the solution can be in its molten state. The process is based on ionization.

electrolyte strength A measure of the strength or extent towards complete ionization in a dilute solution. When concentrated, the ions join in groups, as indicated by lowered mobility.

electrolytic dissociation The splitting up (which is reversible) of substances into oppositely charged ions.

electrolytic ion A charged current carrier formed by dissociation of an ionic compound such as water.

electrolytic polarization A change in the potential of an electrode when a current is passed through it. As the current rises, polarization reduces the potential difference between the two electrodes of the system.

electrolytic sensors Tilt sensors to measure angles of 0.02 arc sec through +60 degrees from a true horizontal. They offer excellent repeatability; rigidness through vibration, shock, and temperature extremes; small size and light weight.

electromagnet A ferromagnetic core surrounded by a current-carrying coil, which exhibits appreciable magnetic effects only when current passes through it.

electromagnetic delay line A delay line whose operation is based on the time of propagation of an electromagnetic wave through the distributed or lumped capacitance and inductance.

electromagnetic field The field of influence produced around a conductor by the current flowing through it; it is a moving electric field and its associated magnetic field, the latter perpendicular to both the electric lines of force and their direction.

electromagnetic flowmeters Flowmeters that follow Faraday's Law that relative motion, at right angles between a conductor and a magnetic field, induces a voltage in a conductor. This voltage is proportional to the relative velocity of the conductor and the magnetic field. The flowmeter is made with a nonmagnetic tube and uses a conductive liquid. On the tube are magnetic coils that, when energized, provide a magnetic field through the frill width of the tube. As the liquid moves through the magnetic field, a voltage is generated proportional to the flow rate.

electromagnetic induction The transfer of electrical power from one circuit to another by varying the magnetic linkage.

electromagnetic inertia The energy required to stop or start a current in an inductive circuit.

An electrical inductance behaves like a mass in a mechanical system.

electromagnetic interference *See* EMI.

electromagnetic relay An electromagnetic switching device having multiple electrical contacts that are operated by an electrical current through a coil.

electromagnetic wave The radiant energy produced around a wire or other conductor when current passes through it.

electromechanical relay accessory board An expansion board equipped with relays and contacts; optional power can be wired to the board to assist the IBM bus under capacity loading. The board's LED status indicators monitor the relays.

electrometallurgy The branch of science concerned with the application of electro-chemistry to the extraction or treatment of metals.

electromotive force The force that causes electricity to flow when there is a difference of potential between two points. The unit of measurement is the volt. Electromotive force is abbreviated *emf.*

electron One of the natural elementary constituents of matter, which carries a negative electric charge of one electric unit and has approximately $1/1840$ the mass of a hydrogen atom, or 9.107×10^{-28} gram.

electron affinity The tendency of certain substances, notably oxidizing agents, to capture an electron.

electron avalanche A chain reaction that is started as one free electron collides with one or more orbiting electrons and frees them. The free electrons then free others in the same manner, as the reaction continues.

electron beam A narrow stream of electrons moving in the same direction under the influence of an electric or magnetic field.

electron conduction The conduction that arises from the drift of free electrons in metallic conductors when an electric field is applied.

electron device A device that depends on the conduction of electrons through a vacuum, gas, or semiconductor.

electron discharge The current produced by the passage of electrons through air or vacuum.

electron drift The actual transfer of electrons in a conductor as distinct from energy transfer arising from encounters between neighboring electrons.

electron emission The liberation of electrons from a surface.

electron gun An electron source, with the necessary anodes, which accelerates electrons in a given direction while focusing or diffusing them, as required in a cathode ray tube.

electronic Descriptive of any circuit or network employing solid-state or vacuum-tube active devices.

electronic beam recording The use of an electron beam to store and read information on a target. Targets are usually silicon dioxide, and the data is sorted as electrostatic charges or magnetic bubbles on materials like vitrium iron garnet.

electronic camera A generic term for a device that converts an optical image into a corresponding electric current directly by electronic means, without the intervention of mechanical scanning.

electronic configuration The arrangement of electrons or atoms in their various states or orbits in a molecule or crystal.

electronic control The general use of electronic devices for industrial and consumer control applications.

electronic data processing *See* EDP.

electronic efficiency The ratio of the power at a desired frequency, delivered by an electron stream to a circuit, to the average power supplied to the stream.

electronic flash Refers to a device that charges a capacitor, the latter discharging through a tube containing neon (stroboscope) or xenon (photography) and producing a burst of light when triggered.

Electronic Frontier Foundation A foundation established to address social and legal issues arising from the impact on society of the increasingly pervasive use of computers as a means of communication and information distribution.

electronic funds transfer system *See* EFTS.

Electronic Industries Association *See* EIA.

electronic mail *See* E-MAIL.

electronic mailbox The personal file or area on disk used to store messages in an electronic mail system. *Also see* E-MAIL.

electronic multiplier An all-electronic device for forming the product of two variables.

Electronic Numerical Integrator and Calculator *See* ENIAC.

electronic oscillations Oscillations of high frequency generated by moving electrons; the frequency is determined by the transit time.

electronic packaging Refers to the mechanical characteristics and features of an electronic assembly.

electronic pen *See* LIGHT PEN.

electronics The branch of science and engineering that deals with the phenomena associated with the flow of electrons in devices and the utilization of these devices.

electronic spreadsheet *See* SPREADSHEET PROGRAM.

Electronic Still Camera Standardization Committee *See* ESCSC.

electronic storage Refers to memory units that utilize electronic charges or conduction, such semiconductor read/write memory (RAM) and read only memory (ROM). The microcomputer's main or internal memory may be divided into RAM and ROM. RAM electronic storage is power vulnerable and is lost if there is any interruption of power to the microcomputer.

electronic switch A usually solid-state device that provides an automatic on/off switching action and functions primarily as an electronic circuit element.

electronic tuning The changing of the operating frequency of a system by changing the characteristics of a coupled electronic system.

electronic voltmeter A voltmeter that depends on the amplifying of the input signal.

electron jet A narrow stream of electrons, similar to a beam, but not necessarily focused.

electron lens A composite arrangement of magnetic coils and charged electrodes to focus or divert electron beams in the manner of an optical lens.

electron microscope A microscope that uses a tube in which electrons emitted from the cathode are focused by suitable magnetic and electrostatic fields.

electron octet The valency electrons (a maximum of eight) in an outer shell of an atom or molecule, which is characterized by great stability, in so far as the complete shell around an atom makes it chemically inert.

electronogen A photosensitive molecule that may emit an electron when illuminated.

electron pair Two valence electrons shared by adjacent nuclei, forming a nonpolar bond.

electron scanning The scanning or establishing of an image by an electron beam in a cathode ray tube, normally using a rectangular raster with horizontal lines.

electron stream A stream of electrons moving with the same velocity and direction in neighboring paths and usually emitted from a single source, such as a cathode.

electron trap An acceptor impurity in a semiconductor.

electroplating Deposition of one metal on another by electrolytic action when a current is passed through a cell. Metal is taken from the anode and deposited on the cathode through a solution containing the metal as an ion.

electropolar Possessing magnetic poles or positive and negative charges.

electrosensitive-matrix printer A printer that uses an aluminum-coated paper, which changes color when a voltage is applied. The printhead contains electrodes that are pulsed on when a dot is to be formed, as shown in the figure. The electric charge goes through the paper to a metal plate behind the paper. The plate is at ground potential and it completes the current path.

electrostatic adhesion The adhesion between two substances or surfaces due to electrostatic attraction between opposite charges.

electrostatic bonding The valence linkage between atoms arising from the transfer of one or more electrons from the outer shell of one atom to the outer shell of another. The transfer leads toward near-completion of the outer shells of both atoms.

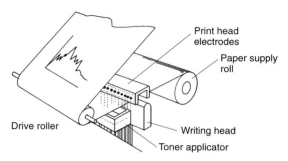

Electrosensitive printing

electrostatic printer A printer that uses a special metalized paper and sends an electric charge through the paper, thus creating the characters. These printers are principally used for draft work.

electrostatic shield A metal mesh used to screen one device from the electric field of another.

electrostatic storage A type of memory based on capacitor principles, in which a dielectric sandwiched between a pair of electrodes holds electrostatic charges representing information.

electrostatic units Refers to the units for electric and magnetic measurements in which the permittivity of a vacuum is taken as unity, with no dimensions in the centimeter-gram-second system.

electrostatic wattmeter A wattmeter that utilizes electrostatic forces to measure ac power at high voltages.

electrostriction The change in the dimensions of a dielectric accompanying the application of an electric field.

electrovalence The chemical bond in which an electron is transferred from one atom to another, the resulting ions being held together by electrostatic attraction.

elegant A buzzword popular chiefly with advocates of structured programming. It indicates more dignity than the similar slang terms *slick* or *nifty*.

element 1. One of the basic substances of matter that cannot be decomposed by simple chemical analysis. 2. A component of a circuit, such as a resistor or capacitor.

element, delayed A circuit or mechanism that accepts input, temporarily retains it, and emits it.

elevated CPU floor stand A stand that vertically positions a CPU at an elevation of about nine inches for easy access to the disk drives, as shown. The housing, with removable, ventilated panels at both ends, serves as a storage location for cables. As an alternative to using a floor stand, many computers can be ordered already housed in a tower configuration.

elevator seeking A NetWare term that describes how the disk read/write heads move in relation to the disk drive on a NetWare file server. Rather

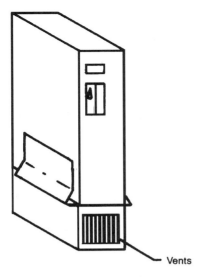

Elevated CPU floor stand

than randomly moving back and forth based on FIFO (first-in, first-out) disk access requests, NetWare sorts disk read and write requests into track order so that the movement of the read/write mechanism is in one direction until it reaches the innermost or outermost track.

ELF Abbreviation for *extremely low frequency*, electromagnetic radiation below 300 Hz. Sources of this form of radiation include computer power supplies and monitors. Some medical experts claim that ELF radiation produces adverse effects in the human body. Many countries have laws that severely restrict the amount of radiation a computer component can produce.

elite 1. The smaller of two common nonproportional typeface sizes, the larger being *pica*. **2.** A standard of nonproportional font spacing, 12 characters to the horizontal inch. Also called *12 pitch*.

elliptic polarization Refers to the polarization of an electromagnetic wave in which the electric and magnetic fields each contain two unequal components, at right angles in space and in phase quadrature.

ELS Abbreviation for *entry-level system*, a Novell term for less-expensive versions of NetWare, which are restricted in the number of users that can be logged into the file server. ELS Level I supports four users; ELS Level II supports eight users logged into the file server.

ELSE 1. An operation such as disjunction, OR, or inclusive-OR that is programmed to take place when conditions are not explicit. The ELSE conditions are handled as "don't care" or left blank. In a program, ELSE conditions usually cause a halt that must be covered to allow recovery for continued processing. **2.** An instruction that can be included with an IF instruction in many popular macro and programming languages. *Also see* IF INSTRUCTION.

ELSEC Acronym for *electronic security*.

EM The ASCII *end-of-medium* character, a control character used to indicate the physical end of a data medium. The character usually gives ample warning to allow the user to make changes in the system operation. In 7-digit ASCII, the EM is represented by a binary 25: 1001 1001 (the first character given is an even-parity indicator).

Emacs Programmer's Editor An application development environment that can be used by programmers, technical writers, and other professionals who need power and flexibility. It has built-in support for SunView, NEWS, XWindows, and hypertext. It provides a multi-window, full-screen, enhancement-packet text editor, automatic management of the compiling process, and databases with descriptions of keywords and language constructs, which makes it easy to develop software and run jobs through language-specific editing modes. It uses shell windows to give full access to system operations and tools.

e-mail Abbreviation for *electronic mail*. In an e-mail system, letters, memos, or text are typed into a terminal and transmitted to a receiving terminal or terminals, where the messages can be displayed at the viewer's choice of time or at a prearranged time.

EMAR Acronym for *experimental memory-address register*.

embedded command A word-processing instruction generally affecting the format of text, but not its content.

embedded computer A hard-wired microprocessor that operates within another machine and usually performs only a single task or several simple tasks.

embedded hyphen In word processing, a program instruction entered to ensure that the hyphen is not omitted. Also called a *required hyphen*.

embossment As used in character recognition, the distance from the distorted surface of a document to a specified part of a printed character.

emergency power system See EPS.

emergency procedure Rules users should follow when a computer crash occurs.

EMI Abbreviation for *electromagnetic interference*, a broad designation for any kind of unwanted electrical energy or noise induced in the circuits of a device due to the presence of electromagnetic fields.

EMI/RFI resistant hood A metallic hood cover that uses clear zinc chromate to shield connectors from both electromagnetic interference and radio frequency interference. They should only be used with shielded cables.

emission The release of electrons from atoms on absorption of energy in excess of the normal average, which can arise from any of the following:

- Thermal (thermionic) agitation, as in x-ray and cathode-ray tubes
- Secondary emission of electrons, which are ejected by impact of higher energy primary electrons
- Photoelectric release on absorption of quanta above a certain energy level
- Field emission by the actual stripping from atoms by a high electric field

emissivity The ratio of the amount of energy radiated by a body at some particular wavelength to that emitted by a black body of the same temperature and at the same wavelength.

emittance The power per unit area radiated by a source of energy.

emitter bias The bias voltage applied to the emitter of a transistor.

emitter-coupled logic *See* ECL.

emitter current The current flowing in the emitter circuit of a transistor.

emitter follower Refers to a circuit that resembles a cathode follower but uses a transistor rather than a vacuum tube and an emitter rather than a cathode. The base also substitutes for the grid.

e-monitor A unit that reviews packet transmission on a LAN and presents findings through graphs and displays. It informs the user about the percent of the time the LAN is active (nodes are transmitting data), the amount of data (in kilobytes) being transmitted, and amount of data corrupted due to collisions.

emoticon *See* SMILEY.

empirical That which is based on actual measurement, observation, or experience versus that which is based on purely theoretical determinations.

EMS Abbreviation for *expanded memory specification*, a technique developed by Lotus/Intel/Microsoft that allows compatible software programs to use memory above the DOS limit of 640K. Expanded memory is slower than extended memory, but it is compatible with more software. Expanded memory tends to provide better MS-DOS performance than extended memory, although it provides a more restricted utility. Expanded memory is usually found on add-in boards, but computers with extended memory can also use it. *Also see* EXTENDED MEMORY.

EMT Abbreviation for *electrical metallic tubing*.

emulate The process of using one system to imitate another such that the imitating system accepts the same input and achieves the same results as the imitated system. Emulation, which involves the software techniques used to imitate the other system, can minimize the impact of conversion from one system to another during program development.

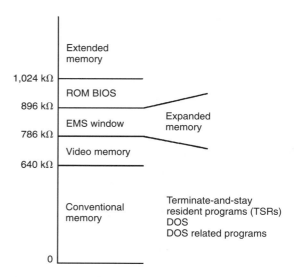

Memory map showing conventional, expanded, and extended memory

Emulation of a number of devices can sometimes be done using a single general-purpose unit. The general-purpose device, adapted to several different configurations through microprogramming, becomes a host serving the more specialized devices. One in-circuit emulator system uses two processors—one to execute commands and control peripherals, and the other to interface directly with the user's prototype system, as shown in the figure. Emulation allows custom instructions through microprogramming, which permits software designed for larger machines to run on microprocessors. The user is also allowed to run programs and integrate hardware and software very early in the development cycle.

emulsion Refers to a light-sensitive chemical coating on materials, commonly used on photographic film.

emulsion laser storage A storage system that uses a controlled laser beam to expose small sections of a photosensitive area.

enable To permit, either automatically or under manual control, the operation of a specific function.

Enable/OA An integrated program for spreadsheets, database management, word processing, graphics, and communications from Enable Software, Inc. All elements have the power to stand by themselves. Unlike other integrated systems, Enable does not center around a single component or metaphor. Each component tends to be optimized; for example, the spreadsheet is memory-resident for speed, while the relational database stores to disk.

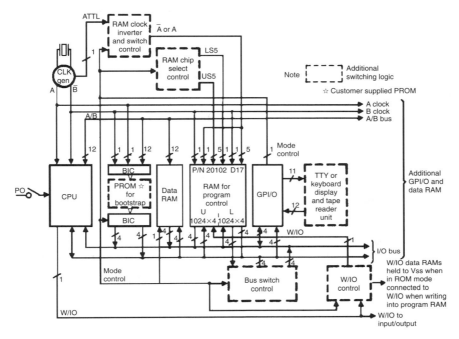

Emulation of ROM with CPU-loaded RAM

Enable's spreadsheet is a reverse-engineered version of Lotus 1-2-3. The menus, keystrokes, and functions are virtually identical.

The word-processing system offers most of the features of the powerful word processors, including embedded rules, advanced header and footer creation systems, and automatic footnoting. It has the ability to create indexes and tables of contents, and a simple calculation function is available. Graphics, spreadsheets, or database information can be incorporated into a word-processed document with a simple command.

The telecommunications module offers standard asynchronous communications protocols. It lets you create and save specific information to connect to computers or networks, and supports the Hayes Smartmodem with autodialing.

The database system is full-function and fully relational. The query system allows full Boolean searches on any field. Similar power and flexibility exist in the report writer, which has its own language.

Moving between applications requires a simple keystroke, and data can be moved between applications without complex reformatting. Each application is in a window that can cover the entire screen or overlay one another like other windowing systems.

enable flag A control line or signal used to allow (enable) a certain condition or mode to occur.

Encarta A Windows-based multimedia encyclopedia product developed by Microsoft Corporation.

encipher *See* ENCODE.

enclosure, microcomputer An enclosure specifically designed to house a microcomputer system. The enclosure may be ventilated and often includes an air blower, air filter, power disconnect, card chassis, power supply, bus terminator, and termination panel with terminal strips.

encode To apply a code to represent data or information that scrambles or otherwise alters data so that it is not readily usable unless the changes are first undone. Encoding may be done for convenience or to hide the meaning of information from others. *Also see* ENCRYPTION.

encoder Any device or circuit that provides an enabling code to permit an otherwise unusable system or device to be used in an environment where the code is required. In a selective calling communications system, an encoder may be a simple tone oscillator of a specific frequency.

encryption A means of securing data by transforming it into what appears to be a random sequence of characters.

end In braiding operations, the number of fibers or wire per carrier.

end-around carry A carry from the most significant digit position to the least significant position.

end instrument The final device in a communications loop. End instruments include all generating and loop-terminating units at receiving and transmitting stations.

end item A final combination of end products, component parts, and materials that is ready for its intended use.

end-of-data marker A character or code word that indicates that the end of all data held in a storage unit has been reached.

end-of-file See EOF.

end-of-medium character See EM.

end-of-message See EOM.

end-of-program A miscellaneous function indicating completion of a workpiece in automatic machining. It stops the spindle, collant, and feed after completion of all commands in the block. It is used to reset control and/or the machine.

end-of-run A type of routine used for housekeeping just before a run is completed. For example, an end-of-run routine may be used for printing out totals.

end-of-text character See ETX.

end-of-transmission-block character See ETB.

end-of-transmission character See EOT.

end point An extremity of a span of measurement points.

end sentinel A character whose only purpose is to signify the end of a message or record.

end use The way a device or program is used by its ultimate consumer.

end-user computing Applications in which the user is responsible for all aspects of processing: data entry, operations, and using the output.

energize To apply the rated voltage to a circuit or device in order to activate it.

energy band In a solid, the energy levels of individual atoms interact to form bands of permitted levels with gaps between. Normally, there is a valence band with a full complement of electrons, and a conduction band, which is empty. When these overlap, metallic conduction is possible. In semiconductors, there is a small gap and intrinsic conduction occurs only when some electrons acquire the energy necessary to surmount this gap and enter the conduction band. In insulators, the gap is large and cannot normally be surmounted.

energy levels Electron energies in atoms are limited to a fixed range of values termed *permitted-energy levels* and represented by horizontal lines drawn against a vertical energy scale.

engine A computer-processing platform such as a PC or Macintosh computer.

engineering data Data contained in an original source document prepared under a design activity. Engineering data may include configuration description, performance specifications, reliability and maintainability goals, and operational practices and procedures.

engineering improvement time Time that is set aside for installing and testing modifications to the computer system. Engineering improvement time is a part of the total time necessary for servicing. Engineering time includes preventive servicing, repair time, and testing following repairs. Time spent to improve reliability without improving the facilities is called *supplementary maintenance time*.

enhanced graphics adapter See EGA.

enhanced mode A Windows operating mode that supports the capabilities of 80386 and higher processors to run in protected mode. This mode also fully supports the virtual memory capabilities of the 80386, which means the size of the hard disk's swap file plus the amount of physical RAM determines the amount of memory available for applications. You also receive the full multitasking capabilities of the 80386 using this mode.

enhanced small device interface See ESDI.

enhanced statistical multiplexer A statistical multiplexer that provides menu-driven multiplexing for up to 16 channels with security features, individual configuration for each end of each channel, and full diagnostics. It can be custom-tailored for the DEC, DG, Prime, Tandem or HP ENQ/ACK protocol.

enhancement An improvement in either hardware or software.

ENIAC (*o.t.*) Acronym for *Electronic Numerical Integrator and Calculator*, the first all-electronic computer. It was built by John Mauchly and J. Presper Eckert.

enlarger printer A unit that projects an enlarged image from microfilm, and develops and fixes the image on a hardcopy medium.

ENQ Abbreviation for *end of enquiry*, a transmission-control character used as a request from a remote station.

ENQ/ACK A unit that permits an RS-232 asynchronous data source device (host computer) using an ENQ/ACK (end of enquiry/affirmative acknowledgment) asymmetric protocol to interface to an asynchronous receive-only device using either DTR lead control or XON/XOFF flow control. The host sends an ENQ to the ENQ/ACK unit, which responds with an ACK if the buffer can accommodate the data block. If the buffer is full, no response is given. On the receive-only side, the ENQ/ACK unit interacts with the receive-only device (printer) with either DTR RS-232 lead control or with XON/XOFF protocol.

enquiry character A control character used to request a response from a remote station. The ENQ character is usually for station identification or status data.

Enter A key or a command to allow data or a command sequence to be input into a program.

Enterprise Certified NetWare Engineer See ECNE.

entity An object.

entropy 1. The measure of unavailable energy in a system. 2. The unavailable information in a set of documents. 3. An inactive or static condition (total entropy).

entry block A block of main memory storage assigned for receipt of each entry into the system and associated with that entry for the life of the system.

entry conditions The initial conditions required to be satisfied for the execution of a given routine.

entry instruction The first instruction to be executed in a subroutine. The entry instruction may have several entry points at different locations of the subroutine.

entry point A place where control can be transferred, other segments of the program can reference, and where the program can be activated by the operator or the system.

enumerator A concept used in AppleTalk Name Binding Protocol searches. The enumerator value is used to distinguish among several instances of an entity on a single socket.

envelope The configuration of a modulation waveform in which the carrier may be seen as a different and more complex configuration.

envelope delay The propagation time between two fixed points of the envelope of a modulated wave. When the delay is variable over the frequency range of transmission, a distortion known as *envelope delay distortion* (also called *group delay distortion*) results.

envelope detection A form of demodulation in which a detection is based on the presence or absence of the signal envelope.

environment The operating conditions in which a computer system is designed to operate, such as a multiprogramming or multiprocessing environment.

environmental conditions External conditions of the surrounding environment such as heat, pressure, moisture, vibration, and temperature.

EOF Abbreviation for *end-of-file*, the termination or completion of a quantity of data, usually indicated by EOF marks.

EOM Abbreviation for *end-of-message*, a character or group of characters that indicates the termination of a message or record.

EOT Abbreviation for *end-of-transmission*, a control character used to indicate the conclusion of transmission. In ASCII, the EOT character is symbolized by a binary 4.

EP See ECHOPLEXER.

EPBX Abbreviation for *electronic private branch exchange*.

EP cartridge An electrophotographic cartridge that contains a photosensitive print drum and a supply of toner used in the printing process. The cartridge, which is used in laser printers and copies, is disposable.

EPISTAT A statistics package that contains a set of routines for use in analysis of small data sets. This is a complex program meant to be used by a person versed in math and computer operations; it is not recommended for the casual user.

epitaxial film A type of film with a single-layer semiconductor material that has been deposited onto a single-crystal substrate.

epitaxial growth The process of manufacturing semiconductor material by depositing a vapor on a seed crystal. The deposited layer can then continue to "grow" a larger, single-crystal structure.

epitaxial planar transistor A transistor in which a thin collector region is epitaxially deposited on a low-resistance substrate, and the base and emitter regions are produced by gaseous diffusion with a protective oxide mask.

epithermal Having energy just above the thermal agitation level; comparable with chemical bond energy.

EPROM Acronym for *erasable programmable read-only memory*, a ROM in which the data pattern written in may be erased to allow a new pattern to be used. Some EPROMs use a transparent lid to expose the chip to ultraviolet light for erasure; then a new pattern is written into the device. The chip is supplied in the erased condition with all bits in the zero state. EPROMs allow fast turn-around times during the microcomputer development stage.

EPS Abbreviation for *emergency power system* (or *supply*), a unit like the one shown in the figure that protects computer data and equipment, telephone systems, and other critical systems from potentially disastrous power interruptions. They can provide from 10 minutes to 3 hours reprieve during a power failure. They monitor the line voltage for outages, sound an alarm, and switch to a backup system when power fails or drops to an unsafe level. EPSs recharge automatically and plug into a standard wall outlet.

Emergency power system

.EPS A filenaming extension that indicates an encapsulated PostScript file. Encapsulated PostScript is a graphics description language and storage method used to describe a picture. The advantage of a graphics description language over a vector- or raster-based image is device independence. The major disadvantage is the large image size.

Epsilon Programmer's Editor An advanced editor for programmers that has an Emacs-style command set, automatic C, indenting, full undo/redo, a C-like extension language, and source code to all commands. *Also see* EMACS PROGRAMMER'S EDITOR.

EQ Abbreviation for *equalizer*.

equalization Circuit and techniques employed to compensate for the detrimental effects of methods used to reduce frequency and phase distortion in transmission lines. Equalization may involve the use of compensating networks to reduce delays due to frequency and phase shifts.

equalizer delay A corrective network that is designed to make the phase or envelope delay of a circuit or system substantially constant over a desired frequency range.

equation solver A technique used to solve systems of equations.

equation statement A statement used in high-level languages that appears as mathematical equations, but that might not have any mathematical validity. For example, in Fortran, BASIC, or PL/1, an instruction such as the following:

G = D/2 + G (replace G with D/2 plus G)

might not be valid algebraically, but is a valid equation statement.

equipment failure Refers to a fault in the equipment that prevents the accomplishment of a scheduled task.

equivalence The logic operator that states if P is a statement, Q is a statement, and R is a statement, then the equivalence of P, Q, and R is true if P, Q, and R are all true or all false.

equivalence element Any logic element that performs the following equivalence operation:

Inputs		Output
A	B	C
0	0	0
1	1	1
0	1	0
1	0	0

equivalent binary digits The number of digits required to express in binary notation a number expressed in another number system.

equivalent network A network identical to another network either in general or at some specified frequency. The same input applied to each would produce outputs identical in both magnitude and phase, generated across the same internal impedance.

equivalent resistance The value that the resistance of an equivalent circuit must have in order that the loss in it represents the total loss occurring in the actual circuit.

equivalent sine wave A sine wave that has the same frequency and the same root mean square value as a given wave.

ERA Abbreviation for *electronic reading automation*.

erasable programmable read-only memory *See* EPROM.

erasable storage 1. A storage device whose data can be altered during the course of a computation. 2. An area of storage used for temporary storage. 3. A storage medium that can be erased and reused repeatedly, such as magnetic tape or disk.

erase To clear or obliterate information in a storage medium. Erasing results in the replacement of all digits with zeros in magnetic storage. Erasing in some EPROMs is done with a specified level of ultraviolet light.

eraser A function in some graphics programs that allows the user to erase parts of a drawing on a screen.

eratosthenes sieve A method for calculating all the prime numbers within a given range. Although it may appear to be a pointless exercise in itself, it is a useful benchmark program for comparing the execution speeds of different computers or different languages.

ergonomics The science and art of designing machines for use by human users, taking into account the inherent limitations and psychological or physiological needs of the users. Some key elements of ergonomics for personal computers include the size of the screen; the number, shape, and size of the characters on the screen; the color and appearance of the screen; the arrangement of the keyboard; and the sound of the keyboard. Also called *human factors engineering* or *human engineering*.

error Any discrepancy between the observed or measured quantity, and the true or specified value. An error may be an incorrect step, process, or result in a data-processing system; it may be attributable to a machine malfunction or a human mistake. Errors can tend to average out, producing a *balanced error* that might have no system effects.

Boundary errors can occur in a system when the processing arrives at a limit condition. This is a common type of error occurring in incompletely tested programs when untested overflow procedures are exercised for the first time, or when unanticipated concurrent conditions complicate an overflow or boundary-handling procedure that has been tested only for a simple case.

error ambiguity A gross error that occurs in the reading of certain digital codes as the parameters represented by the codes change. Error ambiguity is common in analog-to-digital conversion because of imprecise digit positions. It is usually transient if the parameter continues to change. Anti-ambiguity circuits can be used to minimize this condition.

error budget A tool for establishing tradeoffs for the performance requirements of a system. The error budget can be used for predicting the overall expected error. A worst-case summation, a root-sum-of-the-squares summation, or a combination of the two may be used.

error burst A grouping of errors in a short period of time compared to error activity before and after the occurrence. In some transmission systems, a burst may be defined by a specific criterion, such as three consecutive correct bits or words after any errors to terminate the error burst.

error checking and correcting See ECC.

error condition The state that results from an attempt to execute programs or instructions that are invalid or that operate on invalid data.

error control The various methods used to detect and correct errors. Errors can be corrected by operating on the detected errors or by retransmitting from the source. An error-control character can be used to indicate if the data with it is to be disregarded or corrected; this character is also called an *accuracy-control character*.

error controller A device that eliminates the inconvenience of restarting or rerunning transmissions because of errors and the risk of having errors go through undetected. It does this by sending data in blocks and checking every block for errors, as shown in the diagram, automatically retransmitting any block that is not received error-free.

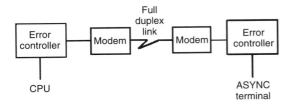

Error controller

error-correcting code A code in which expressions must conform to specific rules of construction. The code may define equivalent expressions that are not acceptable so as to allow the correction of errors. Some codes may use retransmission for correction.

Error-detecting codes may use similar methods for detecting without correcting errors. The code may be arranged so that single errors produce forbidden or impossible code combinations. Errors may be deleted or printed out for user correction.

Some compilers will continue through a program using error diagnostics; the errors are then listed along with the final printout.

error correction/error rate If there is any distortion or noise in the transmission path for data, the data may be corrupted and received incorrectly. The proportion of bits incorrect when received is known as the *error rate*; for example, an error rate of 1 in 10,000,000 means that on average one bit in every million is received incorrectly. Well-designed systems are able to cope with the occurrence of transmission errors by means of error detection and correction routines are built into the equipment and its programs.

error-detecting code A code in which each acceptable term conforms to certain rules such that if transmission or processing errors occur, false results can be detected. Error-detection codes have been effectively used in many bus-oriented systems. The information transfers are conducted with one or more added parity bits to provide error detectability through the use of parity-checking circuits that are placed strategically in the microprocessor system. The parity circuits are used to count the number of ones or zeros in the data word.

error diagnostic The listing of a program error and, possibly, a suggested correction. Also known as an *error message*.

error dump The dumping of a program into a medium so that the cause of an error interrupt can be analyzed.

error-free blocks A measure of error performance based on the percentage or probability of data blocks that are error-free.

error-free seconds A measure of error performance based on the percentage or probability of seconds that are error-free.

error message See ERROR DIAGNOSTIC.

error range The range of all possible values of the error of a particular quantity. Also, the difference between the highest and the lowest of these values.

error ratio The ratio of the number of units of data in error to the total number of data units.

error-receiving count In NetWare, a part of Diagnostic Services that is the number of times (since the shell was activated) that IPX has indicated an error even though a packet was received on the socket. This usually indicates an overrun error.

error-recovery procedure Rules to be followed after processing errors occur.

error service message A control-panel display message that shows when a device, such as a printer, has encountered some difficulty.

error signal The feedback signal used in a closed-loop control system for correcting the output.

ERwin/ERX A program that adds import/export capabilities to ERwin/SQL. It can build a model by importing existing SQL DDL scripts. This type of reverse-engineering capability can help maintain and enhance an existing database or migrate applications from one DBMS to another. It also adds support for Novell's NetWare/SQL database.

ERX Abbreviation for *electronic remote switching*.

Esc The escape character, a control character that signals a change in meaning for characters following it or forms an escape sequence for the development of additional operations. Usually not a printable character, instead it is used as a command code for a device. In ASCII, Esc is symbolized by the binary 27 (0001 1011).

ESCAPE A laser-printer library for CA-Clipper developers. It allows users to control Hewlett-Packard laser printers from within application written in Clipper. It supports soft and cartridge fonts.

escape character *See* ESC.

escape codes A series of characters that begin with the Esc character. These commonly control the various modes of a device, such as a printer or a monitor.

escape sequence Another term for *printer commands*.

ESCSC Abbreviation for *Electronic Camera Standard Committee*, a committee of over 40 corporations established in the late 1970s to create standards for the still video format.

ESDI Abbreviation for *enhanced small device interface*, a hard disk interface that provides a link between the disk drive and the system bus.

ESI Abbreviation for *externally specified indexing*.

ESIE Abbreviation for *Expert System Inference Engine*, an artificial intelligence shell that allows the user to build a custom knowledge base for assistance in making decisions. It operates by loading in a knowledge base and building inferences out of the rules contained therein. This shell is a good introduction to expert systems and building knowledge bases.

ESR address In NetWare, a part of Communication Services that contains the address of an application-defined event service routine (ESR) IPX can call when it is done sending or receiving.

ESS Abbreviation for *electronic switching system*.

Essential B-Tree A set of small, easy-to-use functions for database manipulation. It is written in C and can be compiled with just about any C compiler. There is support for single or multiple keys, fixed or variable-length records, automatic file and record locking, floating-point keys, and re-use of deleted records. It includes the option to combine the data and index files or keep them in separate files. Utilities are provided to convert to/from dBASE databases.

Essential Communications An asynchronous communications library designed for reliability and ease of use. It supports interrupt-driven communications on both the receive and transmit sides at speeds up to 115,200 baud. It includes support for up to 34 ports with buffers to 500K. It provides support for V.32, MNP, and Hayes-compatible modems as well as XON/XOFF Xmodem (CRC and checksum), Xmodem 1K, Ymodem, Kermit, and Zmodem protocols. It also provides ANSI and VT 52/100 terminal emulations.

establish connection failures In NetWare, a part of Diagnostic Services that shows the number of times that calls to establish connections have failed.

establish connection requests In NetWare, a part of Diagnostic Services that shows the number of times (since SPX was loaded) that applications have issued calls to SPX to establish connection.

estimated roundtrip delay In NetWare, a part of Communication Services that indicates in clock ticks the time that the local SPX waits. Eighteen clock ticks equal approximately one second.

ETB The ASCII *end-of-transmission-block* character, which indicates the end of a block of data being transmitted. The ASCII value of ETB is binary 23, or 0001 0111.

ETCG Abbreviation for *elapsed time code generator*.

etched circuit Refers to integrated circuits and the particular construction of a geometric design or pathing arrangement to form active elements by an etching process on a single piece of semiconducting material.

etched printed circuit A specific type of printed circuit formed by chemically or electrolytically (or both) removing the unwanted portion of a layer of material bonded to the base.

ETH Abbreviation for *Eidgenossishe Techische Hochscule*, Zurich.

EtherLink The basic building block for an Ether-Series network. It is the component that must be added to add a single workstation to the network. The EtherLink circuit board fits into a full-size slot of any PC. The package includes a card, user software, and documentation needed to add an additional PC onto an Ethernet network.

EtherMail Software used to deliver messages among the members of an Ethernet network. The product is installed in each server on the network, and only one copy is needed for each server in the entire network. The EtherShare server is the post office and postmaster, and the PC is the mailbox. Messages are automatically dated and stamped with the time, and the originator is told if a message is undeliverable. An attached file can contain text, programs, or data, and can be sent with any message. EtherMail includes a message editor.

Ethernet A baseband local area network specification developed jointly by Digital Equipment Corporation, Xerox, and Intel to interconnect computer equipment using coaxial cable and transceivers. An Ethernet LAN provides ten million bits per second of capacity for high-speed terminal-to-computer communication or computer-to-computer file transfer. A formal Ethernet standard has been published by the IEEE

Committee which is responsible for LAN standards. It is known as the IEEE-802.3 Standard for CSMA/CD (carrier-sense multiple-access with collision detection).

Ethernet card A card that provides a low-cost data link to an Ethernet LAN. The card fits into either a half- or full-size slot in any PC. The Ethernet card performs all functions to support high-speed transmission and reception of network data.

Ethernet controller A device controller that gives the computer access to Ethernet services. Typically, the CSMA/CD protocols are built into the controller so the CPU does not need to consider the details of the protocol. *Also see* CSMA/CD.

Ethernet line monitor A diagnostic tool for Ethernet and IEEE 802.3 users. It plugs in at the workstation, measures all signals in the transceiver (or AUI) cable, and indirectly monitors the signals on the coaxial cable. The unit comes with cable and connectors, providing a plug-in connection to the network. LEDs monitor the Ethernet signals.

Ethernet local module A unit that lets you attach an Ethernet segment to the network bridge via a standard 15-pin AUI connector or a BNC thin net coaxial connector. The unit is protocol-transparent and supports DECnet, TCP/IP, XNS, and IPX.

Ethernet spine cable A shielded coaxial cable that is the backbone of the LAN. The maximum length of each spine segment, in accordance with Ethernet specifications, is about 1640 feet (500m) for standard Ethernet.

Ethernet transmission cable A shielded coaxial cable that connects all the nodes on the LAN. The maximum distance between nodes, per Ethernet specifications, is approximately one mile.

Ethernet type In NetWare, a part of Diagnostic Services that is used for Ethernet drivers using the Ethernet protocol and not the IEEE 802.3 protocol. Xerox assigned a value of 8137h to Novell, where 81 is the high-order byte and 37 is the low-order byte. Only drivers with identical Ethernet types can communicate.

EtherPort SE A direct-connect internal card that supports all AppleTalk compatible software (such as TOPS or NetWare), and provides full access to high-speed Ethernet LANS. It also supports other protocols, including TCP/IP, so a Macintosh can communicate with other computing environments on the LAN.

EtherPrint A unit that allows for the sharing of printers on the network. When information to be printed is received, EtherPrint stores it on disk temporarily. If the printer is busy, the files are queued, then spooled to the printer as soon as it is available. Each EtherPrint PC server can support up to two parallel and one HP LaserJet serial printer for shared use. An EtherSeries network can handle multiple EtherPrint servers. EtherPrint can be used with graphics output and will support printers with sheet feeders. A direct-print mode is also supported, which allows a user to take control of the printer for special-purpose applications, such as printing on a form.

EtherShare Software that allows a PC with a hard disk to act as a shared resource among the members of the network. A menu-oriented control interface assigns space (volumes) to users and manages users' requests for access to the disk. A volume is labeled as a disk drive to the user (such as C or D). User names and passwords provide security. Data can be private, public, or shared. (Private data belongs to a single user; public data is shared for reading only; shared data allows complete access by multiple users.) Database software must be designed specifically to work with shared data on EtherShare.

EtherTalk Ethernet allows connections for standard AppleTalk-based software. EtherTalk allows popular packages for file and disk service, multiuser database systems and service, and electronic mail among Macintosh users to run unmodified. It can be based upon AppleTalk protocols, TCP/IP, or DECnet.

ETV Abbreviation for *education television*.

ETX The *end-of-text* character, a control character used to denote the end of a text. In ASCII, the ETX character is symbolized by a binary 3.

evaluation system A group of parts from a specific microcomputer family, mounted on a circuit board to allow the user to become familiar with the parts in a typical configuration. The user can run simple programs and connect the module to peripheral devices for operational tests. The evaluation module is usually interfaced with peripherals using a peripheral adapter for connection to keyboards, printers, displays, or other devices. A typical evaluation module may contain a CPU, RAMs, a clock generator, power-on initialization circuitry, and various I/O ports, as shown on next page.

even parity check A technique for detecting when bits are dropped by adding one bit to all odd numbers of bit patterns to signify a character; thus, all characters would be represented by an even number of bits. A failure to have such representation would be a *parity error*.

event An occurrence or happening. Some versions of BASIC refer to the events tested by ON COM(n), ON PEN, ON PLAY(n), ON STRIG(n), and ON TIMER.

EVGA Abbreviation for *extended visual graphics adapter*, an adapter that offers simultaneous display of 256 colors from a palette of over a quarter million in 640 × 400 pixel solution. All 17 VGA modes are implemented in the hardware. EVGA can perform with any software written for the VGA standard. Several 132-column modes are also available to view wide spreadsheets and reports. The analog PS/2 monitors, as well as multifrequency, EGA, CGA, and mono-

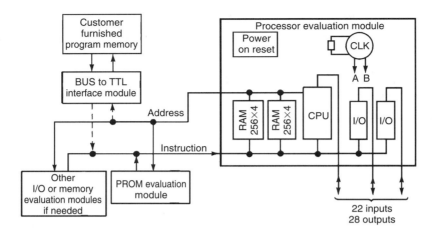

Evaluation system

chrome are supported. Formats include 800 × 600 × 4 and 1280 × 600 × 2 resolution.

evoke module A module containing hardwired circuits used for dedicated automatic control systems. Evoke modules are used where changes to the program are not expected. Up to 100 instructions are feasible, and the system can be very fast, since fetching and decoding are not required. A low-cost system can be built using evoke module control, but if program changes are ever required, expensive rewiring must be done.

Evolve An editor that can be used for Clipper or dBASE. It includes auto-templates, smart indenting, a function writer, a code formatter, a function/object locator, and a browser. You can view database structures and create comment blocks from them. It allows block commenting and uncommenting, and includes a source code report writer and online help.

EX Abbreviation for *exclusive OR*.

exalted carrier A method used for receiving amplitude- or phase-modulated signals. The carrier is first separated from the sidebands, filtered, amplified, and combined again with the sidebands for demodulation.

Excel *See* MICROSOFT EXCEL.

except gate 1. A logic process designed for exception; if *P* and *Q* are two statements, then the statement *P EXCEPT Q* is valid only if *P* is true and *Q* is false. **2.** A gate in which the specified combination of pulses producing an output pulse is the presence of a pulse on one or more input lines and the absence of a pulse on one or more other input lines.

exception reporting A reporting of only the exceptions, such as values over limits, changes, or deletions.

excess noise Interference that results from the passage of current through a semiconductor material or any current-carrying substance other than a metallic conductor.

excitation trigger A circuit with two stable states requires excitation triggers to cause a transition from one state to the other. The excitation may be caused by one and then the other of two inputs, by alternating two signals, or by causing the excitation of a single input.

EXCH Abbreviation for *exchange*.

exclusion gate 1. A logic operator having the property if *P* and *Q* are statements, then *P EXCLUSION Q* is true if *P* is true and *Q* is false; *P EXCLUSION Q* is false if *P* is false or *P* and *Q* are both true. Exclusion can be represented by *P AND NOT Q* or *P NAND Q*. **2.** A binary logic coincidence (two-input) circuit for completing the logic operation of *P AND NOT Q*; the result is true only if statement *P* is true and statement *Q* is false.

exclusive lock A lock on data that prevents other users from accessing it. It is used for write operations, in contrast to a shared (read) lock.

exclusive-NOR A logic operation that has a true output if the input statements are the same, and a false output if they are different. The exclusive-NOR function is shown in the following table.

Inputs		Output
A	B	C
0	0	1
1	0	0
0	1	0
1	1	1

exclusive-OR A logic operation that has a true output only if the input statements are different or odd. The exclusive-OR operation is shown in the following figure.

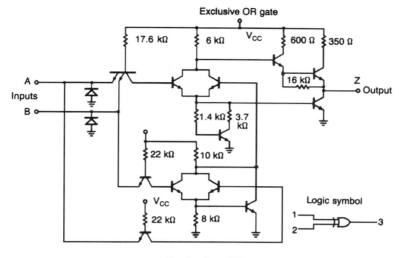

Exclusive-OR

Inputs		Output
A	B	C
0	0	0
0	1	1
1	0	1
1	1	0

exclusive-OR instruction In a microprocessor, an instruction that causes the appropriate bit in the accumulator to be set to 1 only when the corresponding bit positions in memory are different. This is shown below:

  11001100 = Contents in accumulator
  01100110 = Contents in memory location
  10101010 = Exclusive-OR result

EXE The command that tells a computer to execute a specific program or a part of a program.

EXEC An abbreviation for *executive statement* or *executive system*.

executable image A program that is ready to run on an operating system. A program starts as source code and gets compiled to generate object code. The object code is then linked to form an executable image.

execute To perform a computer instruction or program.

execute phase The part of the computer operation cycle when a command is performed.

execute statement A job-control command that designates the load module to be executed along with the specific job steps.

execution cycle That part of the machine cycle when the execution of instructions is taking place. Divide and multiply operations may require a number of execution cycles to complete an operation. The execution cycle is usually the same as the clock period, which can vary from a few hundred nanoseconds to a few milliseconds.

execution time The time required to complete an instruction, procedure, or cycle. The execution time is the portion of an instruction cycle when the actual operation is taking place, such as decoding and executing an instruction. It is usually expressed in terms of clock cycles.

executive A program, routine, or system that has supervisory control over others. Executive instructions are designed and used to control the execution of other routines and programs. The executive command language should be open-ended to allow easy expansion for additional features and functions. Statements may be of variable length.

An executive program usually consists of controlling loaders, an editor, an assembler, a Fortran (or other) compiler, a debug monitor, input/output devices, and a library of routines. After the executive program is loaded into memory, all operations are executed using typed commands to the executive, editor, and debug programs. The executive program coordinates and controls the running of all other programs and is essentially the key element that converts a collection of software into an operating system. The object programs rely on the executive and the library utilities for I/O and mathematical functions.

Parts of the executive program are resident in the memory at all times. The main tasks of the program include job scheduling, storage allocation, and output control. The executive is also called the *supervisor* or *monitor*. Also see REAL-TIME EXECUTIVE.

executive cycle Refers to a specific period of time during which a machine instruction is interpreted and the indicated operation is performed on the specified operand.

executive diagnostics A part of the executive system in an integrated system of diagnostic routines designed to provide the programmer with information of maximum utility and convenience in checking out programs. The programmer can select what is to be printed and may receive diagnostic listings with source code symbolics collated with the contents of both registers and memory. Both dynamic (snapshot) and postmortem (PMD) dumps of registers and memory may be provided.

Executive Filer A word-oriented database that can be used for a wide variety of applications. It is useful for storing and retrieving textual information that does not easily lend itself to the restrictions of predetermined field names and field lengths in a conventional database. You can enter any kind of data (such as a memo, price list, or name and address file) on an index card, then create an index list of up to ten keywords that can be used in a search for that card. Cards may even include graphics or data from another program, provided that the other program has the capability of creating a print file on disk. *Also see* EXECUTIVE WRITER.

executive instruction Similar to a supervisory instruction, this instruction is designed and used to control the operation or execution of other routines or programs.

executive routine An automated computer procedure used to control the loading, relocation, scheduling, and execution of other routines. The routine usually maintains control of the computer at all times and returns control from all functional operations back to the executive routine upon completion.

Executive Writer A word processor for use with Executive Filer. If you use your computer primarily for other applications but occasionally need word-processing capability for short documents, this can be a cost-effective product. It supports a full range of block operations, numbered footnotes, and onscreen underlining and bold. You can insert another file into your document, obtain a file directory while editing, and insert graphics from other programs into the body of the text. Long documents can be difficult to work with, however, because the program does not show page endings on screen.

exit A method used to interrupt or leave a repeated cycle of operations in a program.

exjunction A reasoning element applied to two operands that will create a result depending on the bit patterns of the operands.

EXORciser development system A system development tool for the 6800 microcomputer family. It can be tailored to meet the user's need in the design and development of the system. It reduces the time required to develop a system and, at the same time, provides flexibility in configuring the system hardware for the application. The EXORciser's firmware, through its debug and program control features, minimizes the time required to develop the user's programs. EXORciser functions include displaying the contents of registers, stepping through user's programs, dynamically tracing through user's program, stopping the user's program on a selected memory address, triggering an oscilloscope on a selected memory address, aborting from the user's program at any time, and reinitializing the system at any time.

EXP Abbreviation for *exponential*.

expand In word processing, to make visible any headings and text that were collapsed below a heading in an outline.

expanded memory *See* EMS.

expander transducer A transducer designed for a given amplitude range of input voltages that produces a larger range of output voltages. One type of expander uses the information from the envelope of speech signals to expand their volume range.

expansion board A printed circuit board that adds features or capabilities beyond those basic to the computer. Examples are color cards for video monitors and memory boards for extra memory.

expansion slot A place on a computer's bus for plugging in an expansion board, as shown in the figure.

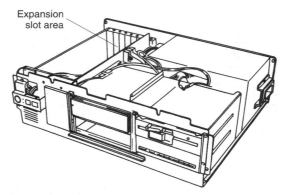

Expansion slots located in the left rear section of the AT system box

EXPERT Abbreviation for *expanded program evaluation and review technique*. *Also see* PERT.

Expert Help A hypertext system with access to over 100 topics using just 1K of memory. Features include auto-lookup, VGA and mouse support, text pasting, and global searching. There are also tools that let you create your own help files or modify existing ones.

expert system A computer system containing a knowledge base and inference engine that can draw new conclusions from data and add them to the knowledge base. Also known as a *knowledge-based system*; the process is sometimes called *knowledge engineering*.

explicit address An address reference that is specified as two absolute values, one of which supplies the displacement value. The explicit address values are assembled from object code by a machine instruction.

exploded pie chart A graphical pie chart in which one piece is separated from the whole for emphasis.

exponential delta modulator A type of delta modulator that uses an RC circuit as an integrator to provide an exponential response to a constant input. *Also see* DELTA MODULATION.

export To save a file, document, or chart in such a way that it can be used with a program other than the one in which it was created.

EXPRESSCALC A Lotus 1-2-3 clone with the capability of handling small spreadsheets (up to 64 columns by 256 rows). The program requires only 256K RAM and DOS 2.x or higher. Like Lotus 1-2-3, it can be used in a wide variety of applications ranging from business forecasts to financial analysis to simple database management.

EXPRESS GRAPH A package that turns raw data into business graphics.

expression A notation that has a value. Usually, a combination of variables, constants, and operators, such as $x - 3$.

Expressionist A Macintosh application/desk accessory that lets you create any type of equation or mathematical expression. It is fully compatible with TEX, and you can paste equations or expressions into any word processor or page-layout document using PICT or text format. Features include equation numbering structure, two-way TEX interface, optional integral styles, tweak feature for pixel-by-pixel adjustments, thin-space character for fine spacing preferences, box enclosures, independent matrix column widths, guide and magnify modes for ease of editing, online help, adjustable subscripts and superscripts, matrices up to 50 × 50, spreadsheet-style matrix selection, hierarchal tree structure, overstrikes, Tensor structures, adjustable structures through preference file, a customizable tool palette, customizable macros, polymorphic equation structure, and WYSIWYG. It is also MultiFinder compatible.

extended address Addressing that allows the widest possible selection of locations. In the 6800 microprocessor family, extended addressing allows access to any of the 65,536 locations in the memory space. For extended addressing, the operand is specified by the memory location of the second and third bytes of the instruction. The location's address is always stored with the most significant byte first. For example, in this extended address instruction for the 6800:

```
Add A $1256 (add the contents of M(1256) to A)
the $ indicates that 1256 is a hexadecimal number to the assembler.
```

extended addressing An addressing mode designed to reach almost anywhere in the memory system.

extended arithmetic element *See* EAE.

extended attribute file *See* EA, 2.

extended binary-coded decimal interchange code *See* EBCDIC.

extended character set An ASCII character set that uses all the 256 different characters that can be defined in an 8-bit word, as opposed to the standard ASCII character set, which uses only 128 characters. Different manufacturers use different extended character sets for printers and monitors; this can be a source of incompatibility. The IBM extended character set is a *de facto* standard used by many manufacturers.

extended distance data cable *See* EDDC.

extended file attributes In DOS, file attributes are bit fields in a byte that reside in the directory entry of each file. The DOS file attributes are read-only, hidden, system, or archive. NetWare extends the DOS file attributes to include four network-specific ones: the transaction bit, the index bit, and the read and write audit bits.

extended framing format A framing format for 1.544 Mbps digital channel banks introduced by AT&T.

extended graphics array *See* XGA.

extended memory Linear memory extending beyond DOS's 1M limit. Extended memory is only available on 286 and higher machines. Microsoft Windows and some application software can be loaded into this memory when special memory-access software is installed.

extender card kit A kit that allows all cards on the bus to be extended out of the card rack for easy maintenance.

extension In DOS filenaming, refers to a one- to three-character suffix used with a filename, usually to denote the file's usage. For example, an .EXE extension indicates an executable file, while an .XLS extension indicates a spreadsheet created with Microsoft Excel.

extension register A register that provides expansion for the accumulator register or the quotient register.

external clocking A type of clocking used in synchronous communication in which the bit timing signal is supplied from a modem.

external copy A copy of a separate text file within the current file being word processed.

external data representation A presentation-layer protocol developed by Sun Microsystems as part of its Network File System.

external delays Lost system time due to causes beyond the control of operators and service crews.

external device code An address code for an external device that specifies the operation to be performed. The code is used in systems with common bus lines for a number of external devices. The external device code addresses a particular device, and only that device will respond to the instruction that is part of the code.

external event module A module used to detect power failures and control interrupts, and processor start-up and half functions. The module will implement the system priority scheme in the event of any power loss.

external icons Icons from non-Windows application or ones you create.

external interrupt An interrupt caused by an external event, such as a device requiring attention.

external label A label defined in one program that is used in another. Usually the programs are assembled independently and executed together.

external memory See AUXILIARY MEMORY.

external modem A modem that has its own enclosure and is connected to the computer using one of the computer's serial ports. External modems typically have status lights to indicate what activity is occurring. They might also require their own power source.

external reference synchronization A form of network synchronization in which the timing or frequency reference is obtained from a source external to the communication network.

external register A register that can be referenced by the program, located in control storage as specific addresses. Also known as a *location register*.

external storage Storage that is separate from the computer unit, such as magnetic tape or floppy disks. Also called *offline storage*.

external symbol A symbol that is used in several program modules, or in a program module dictionary.

extracode Machine instructions that are used to provide increased capability for machine software. For example, an extracode may provide floating-point arithmetic for a machine that does not already have floating-point capability. Extracodes are stored within the system or in ROMs.

extract **1.** To remove from a set of items all items that meet a particular criterion. **2.** A procedure used to replace the contents of certain columns of data with the contents of other columns.

extract instruction An instruction that requests the formation of a new expression from selected parts of another expression. A typical extract instruction might remove the first, second, fifth, and sixth bits from an 8-bit word and combine them to form a new word.

extremely low frequency See ELF.

extrinsic properties The properties of a semiconductor, modified by impurities or imperfection within the crystal.

extrinsic semiconductor A semiconductor whose electrical properties depend on its impurities.

eye pattern An oscilloscope display of a digital signal used to examine performance.

E/Z Abbreviation for *equal to zero*.

EZ FORMS A form-generating program that allows you to generate custom forms. Using the menu-driven design process, you can create a new form or revise a master (one of the supplied forms).

EZ-INSTALL A package that produces installation routines for software products. It steps the developer through installation options, generates the installation configuration, and creates distribution disks.

EZ-SPREADSHEET A spreadsheet program designed to be fast and compact, being just 512 columns by 64 rows, which is enough for many users. In most cases, you can just use the worksheets supplied and enter your own data. Applications worksheets supplied for the home include calculating budgets, loans, and savings plans. Business applications include simple loan calculations to complete financial statements.

EZ-VU Development A package that allows you to create panels (screens) to help programs communicate with the user. Examples of panels are menus, fill-in forms, and help screens. It was written by the same IBM programmers who developed the mainframe product ISPF. Users who are familiar with ISPF will find it easy to learn. The two products, however, are not compatible; panels created on one will not transfer to the other.

EZ-VU Runtime This program, sometimes referred to as the *Interactive System Production Facility Runtime*, is a dialog manager. A dialog is the conversation between the user and the program, so a dialog manager monitors the interaction between what is displayed on the screen and how the program interprets it. EZ-VU Runtime is used to get input from panels created by EZ-VU Development. It then checks and interprets that information and transfers it to the applications program.

FA 1. Abbreviation for *frequency agility*. 2. Abbreviation for *final address*.
FACE Acronym for *field alterable control element*, a chip in the control logic unit of a field development system. Functionally similar to a CROM (control ROM), the FACE chip uses external memory for the microprogram store. It is used in low volume applications. The system employs a writeable control store, a control logic unit, and a display and debug unit.
facsimile *See* FAX.
facility Refers to a WAN connection provided by a common carrier (such as MCI or AT&T).
FACT Acronym for *fully automatic compiler translator*.
fade A phenomenon represented by more or less periodic reductions in the received field strength of a station or device, usually as a result of interference between reflected and direct waves from the source.
fade margin The amount by which a received signal level can be reduced without causing the system or channel output to fall below a specified threshold.
failsafe Descriptive of a system, circuit, network, or component with built-in protective measures that preclude system failure. Failsafe systems usually allow some degradation of performance that does not prevent proper system operation.
fail-soft A method of system implementation that prevents the loss of data and facilities due to an outage in some part of the system. Degraded performance usually results from a failure, but the system may continue to run. Fail-soft techniques can promote a progressive shutdown or idling mode of the system, rather than a complete loss when one of the components fails.
failure The inability of an item to perform its required function.
failure logging A procedure used in some systems to record the system state following the detection of an error. A section of the monitor using machine-check interrupts logs the data that is stored for diagnosing errors at a later time.
failure, mean time to *See* MTTF.
failure prediction The methods and techniques used to determine when failures are most likely to occur in specific parts and equipment. Failure prediction attempts to allow a schedule for the replacement of parts and equipment before failure occurs. Failure-prediction methods are used to determine the *mean time to failure* (MTTF) and *mean time between failures* (MTBF) for a part, based on test data that calculates the average time that the part will operate under normal conditions before failure occurs.
failure rate The average rate at which failures can be expected to occur throughout the useful life of an item.
Fairchild F-8 A multichip NMOS microprocessor system designed around a bus architecture. The heart of the system is the CPU chip. When the CPU is combined with the program storage unit (*PSU*) that contains a masked ROM, along with timing and interrupt control, a minimal system configuration is obtained that may be used as a simple controller. A memory interface unit contains the memory address regis-

ters and address bus, which are not in the CPU unit. The CPU recognizes inputs from the control panel keyboard and sensors located on the controlled item and produces output signals for motor control use. The PSU provides the control program storage along with the interface for the display unit. A DMA chip has the hold and wait circuitry required for direct memory access. The basic device family is shown in the figures that follow.

sor along with a 2K ROM. It consumes less power than the F-8, using a 5-volt supply instead of a 12-volt supply. Besides the 2K of ROM, the device has 64 bytes of scratchpad RAM, a programmable timer, and 32 bits of I/O.

The 3870 structure is shown in the figure. The instruction register receives the operation code of the instruction to be executed from the program ROM over the data bus.

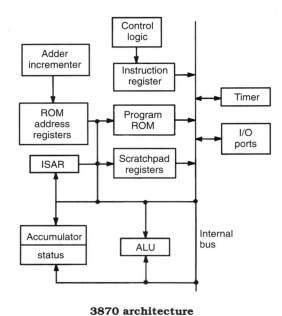

F-8 architecture

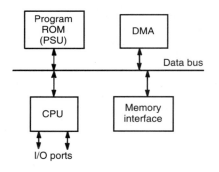

F-8 family

Fairchild F-8 CPU The Fairchild F-8 CPU chip contains 64 bytes of scratchpad memory, which may eliminate the need for RAM in simple control applications. The scratchpad can also serve as a workspace for simple calculations without transferring the data to external memory. The F-8 CPU contains a single accumulator, an ALU, an address register, an instruction register, and two bus transfer gates.

Fairchild 3870 The single-chip microcomputer version of the F-8; it uses the F-8 microproces-

3870 architecture

Fairchild 3870 registers The 3870 accumulator is the principal register for data manipulation. It provides one of the inputs to the ALU for all operations, and then the result of the operation is stored there. The status register holds the five flags shown in the figure. An interrupt

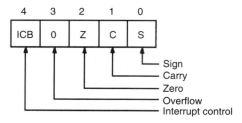

3870 status bits

control bit is used to enable interrupts. If this bit is set and an interrupt request is made to the CPU, the interrupt is acknowledged and processed when the first nonprivileged instruction is complete.

Fairchild 3870 timer An 8-bit binary countdown unit, which is programmable in one of three modes: interval, pulse width, or event. If there is both a timer interrupt request and an external interrupt request, the timer request is given priority.

Fairchild 9440 A 16-bit microprocessor fabricated with the Isoplanar I²L process (I³L) housed in a 40-pin DIP, as shown in the figure.

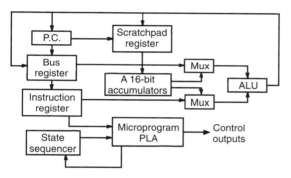

9440 architecture

FairCom SQL server An ANSI X3.135 1986 level 2 SQL engine with multi-thread design and the ability to link the SQL server directly into an application. SQL system functionality is available through both the interpreter and the programming interface.

fallback A condition in which substitute hardware is employed for malfunctioning systems. Fallback is used to increase capacity for malfunctioning systems or take over completely in the case of total system failure.

fallback procedure A procedure used to circumvent equipment faults. The fallback may give degraded service and may include switching to an alternate computer or to different output devices.

fallback switch *See* FBS.

fallthrough A software "step" that results in machine cycling to the operation represented by the next lower block on a flowchart.

false add To form a partial sum without carries.

FAMOS Acronym for *floating-gate avalanche-injection metal-oxide semiconductor*. A type of EPROM that uses ultraviolet light for erasing and an avalanche transport mode. The FAMOS device uses silicon-gate field-effect transistors with no connection to the silicon gate. Memory operation depends on charge transport by avalanche injection from a source or drain.

fanfold paper Paper that has sprocket holes on the sides and perforations between sheets. Also called *continuous paper*.

fan-in The number of inputs connected to a specific logic device or function.

fan-out The number of output circuits that are connected to a specific logic device or function. A device must be capable of driving the number of devices specified in the fan-out specification.

fan-out box A device that provides the capability to connect multiple workstations to a single transceiver. It also allows the construction of local area networks without coaxial cable, or the construction of concentrated clusters on a coaxial cable. Also referred to as *delni*, *multiport*, or *multitap*.

FAP Abbreviation for *File Access Protocol*, a file transfer protocol that allows parts of a file to be transferred. Also used as a generic term for the transfer portion in a File Transfer Protocol (FTP).

FAQ Acronym for *frequently asked questions*, a file on an online service or bulletin board containing typical questions and answers about a particular subject.

FAR Acronym for *failure analysis report*.

farad The capacitance of a capacitor in which a charge of one coulomb produces a change of one volt in the potential difference between its terminals. The farad is the unit of capacitance in the meter-kilogram-second-ampere system.

faraday A unit equal to the number of coulombs (96,500) required for an electronic reaction involving one electrochemical equivalent.

Faraday cage An earthed wire screen in which a number of parallel wires are joined at one end, which is earthed. It completely surrounds a piece of equipment in order to shield it from external electric fields, so that there can be no electric field within. Also called a *Faraday shield*.

Faraday's laws of electrolysis 1. The amount of chemical change produced by a current is proportional to the quantity of electricity passed. **2.** The amounts of different substances liberated or deposited by a given quantity of electricity are proportional to the chemical equivalent weights of those substances.

Faraday's law of induction The electromotive force induced in any circuit is proportional to the rate of change of the number of magnetic lines of force linked with the circuit, a principle used in every motor. Maxwell's field equations involve a more general mathematical statement of this law.

far-end crosstalk *See* FEXT.

Fat Memory Manager Software that allows error-free use of all memory in the first 640K. It provides dynamic allocation of blocks and multidimensional arrays, does array-bounds checking and allows extensive error detection. Memory operations can be recorded in a debugging log. It supports Turbo C/C++ and Microsoft C.

Fastback A fast hard-disk backup program that can eliminate the need for tape backup systems. Fastback allows you to make an incremental backup, in which only files that have changed since the last backup are backed up.

Fastgraph A high-performance graphics library suitable for writing games, educational software, scientific and business applications, and home entertainment products on DOS-based systems. The library includes over 170 functions, ranging from simple to complex. Fastgraph supports 22 video modes and works with most C/C++, BASIC, Pascal, and Fortran compilers.

FASTOPEN An external DOS command that lets it quickly access files that are several levels of subdirectories deep. FASTOPEN is available in DOS 3.30 and later versions.

fastpacket A T-1 enhancement that permits special T-1 multiplexers to allocate bandwidth dynamically.

FastPath A standalone device that acts as a high-speed gateway between LocalTalk and Ethernet networks and gives all connected Macintosh computers access to any computer on the Ethernet LAN. FastPath works with both standard Ethernet and ThinNet.

fast poll A 9600 bps modem (sometimes abbreviated FP) designed for use on multipoint networks over Bell specification 3002 unconditioned lines. An 8-millisecond RTS/CTS relay is made possible by the FP's capability to determine line characteristics for each modem drop, and thereby shape the remote modem's transmitter. The modem's train-on data feature allows you to place additional slave modems on the network without interruption of network operators. The unit will operate with 4800, 7200, or 9600 bps modems and employs an anti-streaming feature to prevent network jams.

FASTslot technology An architecture that allows two FASTslot cards to provide accelerated bus operations while remaining AT-compatible.

Fast Trax A program that optimizes hard and floppy disk performance by consolidating scattered pieces of files and subdirectories. The program places most files within disk cylinder boundaries, eliminating track-to-track seeks when accessing these files. You can also assign frequently used programs and data to the "fast tracks" of your disk (near the FAT), while placing rarely used files at the opposite end of your disk, effectively improving your disk's average seek time.

FAT Acronym for *file allocation table*, a table of numbers that correspond to cluster addresses on the disk, which tells DOS where to find a file. When you or a program you are using requests a file, DOS checks the addresses in the FAT to find out where a file's clusters are stored on disk, and then goes to the disk to get the cluster of information.

fatal FAT write errors In NetWare, a part of File Server Environment Services that contains the number of disk write errors that occurred in both the original and mirrored copies of a FAT sector.

fatbits In graphics, a function that allows the user to examine and change each bit in the drawing.

FAT scan errors In NetWare, a part of File Server Environment Services that contains the number of times an internally inconsistent state existed in the file system.

FAT write errors In NetWare, a part of File Server Environment Services that contains the number of disk write errors that have occurred when writing FAT sectors to the disk.

fault Any physical condition that causes an element of a system to fail or malfunction. A fault may be a broken wire, an intermittent device, or a failed element.

fault-location program A type of program used for identification or information regarding equipment faults. The fault-location program is designed to identify the location and type of fault and is usually an important part of the diagnostic routine.

fault tolerance An attribute of a computer system that reflects its degree of tolerance to hardware and software failures while continuing to run.

fault-tolerant computer A computer with duplicate processors, memory, and disk drives so that it remains available, even during a crash.

fault-tolerant systems Systems that find their major application in high reliability systems, such as communications and telephone processing applications. These systems must perform error detection, restriction of error propagation, and recovery from the fault or error. The system must reconfigure itself such that all data flows around the particular unit that is at fault once that unit has been localized as the source of an error.

fax Acronym for *facsimile*, a system used to convert images to electrical signals for transmission to remote points. The image is scanned, and the information is converted into signal waves for transmission to remote locations. The information is usually duplicated on hardcopy for final use and documentation. Facsimile transmission involves scanning the image with a revolving drum and using of photoelectric sensors to create the electrical signals.

fax board An expansion board that allows you to

transfer text and graphics files from your microcomputer to a facsimile machine, LAN, or another microcomputer. That document, or a response, can be sent back to you without ever printing a word. The fax board also sends and receives documents without interfering with what you are working on. It can operate unattended, permitting you to send documents at any hour (to take full advantage of lower telephone rates).

FaxFacts Fax-on-demand software that offers software and hardware DID (direct inward Dial) and remote image-update capabilities. It also includes password system entry, inbound/outbound call scheduling, fax-broadcast ability, and area code restrictions on callbacks.

FaxPress A fax gateway for the Message Handling Service made by Castelle.

FaxRight A program that allows end-users to send faxes directly from any Windows application, as well as receive faxes in the background, schedule fax transmissions, export fax images, and view and print faxes. The program uses integrated, dBASE-compatible phonebooks. Supported fax modems are EIA TR-20.3 Class II and EIA 578 Class I standards, as well as many fax modems that use the Sierra SendFax protocol.

FaxTones An interactive voice/fax system that allows callers from a touchtone telephone to choose documents to be faxed. The program includes dVOICE, a dBASE-like programming language that allows the creation of custom, interactive voice/fax applications. It works in either polled fax or FaxBack modes. It requires at least a 386SX with 1M RAM and an Intel SatisFAXtion or compatible fax board.

FBC Abbreviation for *fully buffered channel*.

FBS Abbreviation for *fallback switch*, a switch designed to be placed into a data communication circuit between a computer port and two modems, as shown in the figure. The FBS may be manually switched between the two modems or placed in the auto position for automatic switching.

Automatic switching occurs in the FBS when the alternate modem (B) raises DSR (data-set-ready) pin 6 and the FBS switches to connection B-C. Lowering of modem B's DSR releases the FBS to return to the primary modem connection A-C. All required leads of the RS-232 interface for asynchronous or synchronous operations are switched (a total of 12).

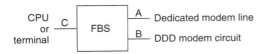

Fallback switch

FC Abbreviation for *frame control*, a token ring field that indicates whether the packet is a MAC-layer management packet (i.e., a token, beacon, AMP, or SMP) or is carrying LLC data.

FCC Abbreviation for *Federal Communication Commission*.

FCC Rules Part 68 The section of FCC rules concerned with data access arrangements.

FCS Abbreviation for *frame check sequence*, an error-checking mechanism like a CRC or checksum that guarantees the integrity of a packet of data.

FDC Abbreviation for *floppy disk controller*, the integrated circuit that controls and communicates with the floppy disk drive.

FDDI Abbreviation for *fiber distributed data interface* or *interchange*, a set of standards for using fiber-optic cable in networks based on the ANSI X3.139, X3.148, X3.166, X3.184, X3.186, and XT9.5 specifications. It is specified for transmission speeds of 100M bits per second using a token-passing communications protocol and ring topology with a maximum circumference of 4 kilometers, although copper-based (CDDI) hardware is an option. It is compatible with the physical layer of the OSI model.

FDM Abbreviation for *frequency-division multiplexing*, a type of multiplexing in which a communications channel is divided into a group of independent, lower-frequency channels. Each channel is assigned a slot for its unique pair of transmission end frequencies, and channels are easily cascadable (allowing low costs in many applications). FDM is used on voice-grade lines, where it provides asynchronous transmission speeds of up to 150 bits per second. *Also see* FREQUENCY-DIVISION MULTIPLEXER.

FDMI Apple's floppy disk drive that can read disks created by DOS or OS/2, found in Macintosh computers such as the SE30, IIx, or IIex.

FDX Abbreviation for *full-duplex*. In communication systems and devices, refers to simultaneous two-way independent transmission, in which transmission and reception occur mutually and on a noninterference basis.

FE Abbreviation for *format effector*, a control character used for control of the layout and position of information in printing and display devices.

feasibility study A preliminary system analysis to aid decision-making. A feasibility study may be directed at the suitability, capability, or compatibility of a new system or modifications to present systems and equipment.

FEB Acronym for *functional electronic block*.

feedback Refers to the return of a part of the output to the input. As used in a closed-loop control system, feedback provides the information about the condition under control. Feedback is used in analog amplifiers using various feedback elements. Negative feedback is used in most amplifiers and control systems to stabilize the output and reduce distortion generated within the stage. Positive feedback in an amplifier increases gain, but causes instability and accentuates distortion. Positive feedback is not always undesirable, however, as an oscillator depends on positive feedback for its operation.

feedback amplifier An amplifier that uses the feedback principle to perform operations on signals, by using some function of the output signal as part of the input signal.

feedback circuit A circuit for producing current or voltage feedback from the output to the input of an amplifier.

feedback control A type of system control obtained when a portion of the output signal is operated upon and fed back to the input.

feedback control loop A closed transmission path that includes an active transducer and consists of a forward path, a feedback path, and one or more mixing points arranged to maintain a prescribed relationship between the loop input and output signals.

feedback device An element of a control system that converts motion to an electrical signal for comparison to the input signal, such as a resolver, encoder, or inductosyn.

feedback element An element in a control system that changes the feedback signal as a response to the controlled variable.

feedback impedance The amplifier impedance between the input terminals and the output terminals that provides a feedback path, as shown in the figure. This impedance substantially defines the relationship of the input signals to the output signals.

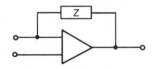

Feedback impedance

feedback loop A closed signal path in which outputs are compared with desired values to obtain the correct commands, as shown in the figure.

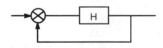

Feedback loop

feedback resolution The smallest increment of dimension that the feedback device can distinguish and reproduce as an electrical output.

feedback sample-hold A sample-hold circuit with a closed loop around the capacitor and a high loop gain for tracking accuracy, shown in the following figure. In this circuit, the usual input follower amplifier is replaced by a high-gain difference amplifier. As the switch is closed, the output represented by the charge on the capacitor is forced to track the input, as a function of the gain and the current driving capability of the input amplifier. The common-mode and offset errors in the output follower are compensated by the charge on the capacitor.

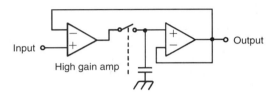

Low-frequency sample-hold with feedback

feedback sample-hold integrator A sample-hold integrator in which a current amplifier is used with an integrator, permitting the switch to operate at ground potential and thus easing the leakage problem, as shown in the following figure.

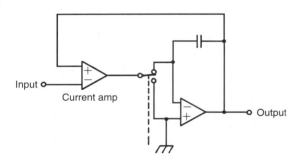

Low-frequency sample-hold with integrator feedback

feedback signal The measurement signal indicating the value of a directly controlled variable, which is compared with a setpoint to generate a correction command.

feedback transducer A transducer that generates a signal depending on the quantity to be controlled. A potentiometer, synchro, or tachometer might be used, giving proportional, derivative, or integral signals respectively.

feedforward A type of control action in which conditions that can disturb the control variable are minimized or converted into corrective actions.

feedforward control A technique in which the magnitude of the error is anticipated and corrective action is taken prior to the occurrence of an error.

feedforward/feedback control The combining of both feedforward and feedback concepts, resulting in an error anticipation and corrective action followed by readjustment. Feedforward/feedback control is illustrated in the following figure.

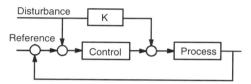

Feedforward/feedback control technique

feedrate bypass A function directing the control system to ignore programmed feedrate and substitute selected operational rate.

feedrate number A coded number that describes the feedrate function. Sometimes referred to as the "F-word."

feedrate override A variable manual control function used to reduce or increase the programmed feedrate.

feedthrough The fraction of the input signal that appears at the output of a sample-hold in the hold or off mode, caused primarily by capacitance across the switch. It can be measured by applying a fullscale sinusoidal input at a fixed frequency and observing the output.

F-8 See FAIRCHILD F-8.

female connector In electronics, plugs and connectors are commonly referred to as male and female. Most powered connectors are non-exposed female.

femto Prefix for the numerical quantity of 10^{-15}; for example, *femtovolt*.

FEP Acronym for *front-end processor*, a software-operated controller that offloads overhead functions such as polling devices off the host.

FEP plenum cable Cables designed for use in buildings with suspended or dropped ceilings. They are fire-resistant, produce little smoke, and confirm to the National Electric Code (1978) standards. FEP plenum cables are low capacitance to enable use for distances beyond 50 feet (15.24m).

Fermi level A point of a level of energy on a diagram that corresponds to the top of the Fermi distribution; the energy level in a semiconductor for which a Fermi-Dirac distribution function has a value of 50 percent, or half.

ferric oxide Chemical symbol Fe_2O_3, a red, iron-oxide coating used for magnetic recording in the form of a dispersion of fine particles within the coating.

ferroelectric A phenomenon in certain materials which exhibit spontaneous electric polarization along with dielectric hysteresis.

ferromagnetic Descriptive of the ability of certain materials to be highly magnetized and exhibit hysteresis. Ferromagnetic materials such as iron, nickel, and cobalt alloys have marked hysteresis properties and are used for storage in computers.

ferromagnetic oxide parts Specific parts that contain primarily oxides and display ferromagnetic properties.

ferrous oxide One medium used to contain encoded information on magnetic tape and disk.

ferrule A short tube used to make solderless connections to a coaxial cable or stronger, wear-resistant shoulders or other protective devices on multiple contact connectors.

FET Acronym for *field-effect transistor*, a type of transistor that uses conduction due to a field in a channel between depletion layers. The resistance of the channel can be altered by appropriately altering the applied gate voltage. The field is set up in a channel of semiconductor material that is made more or less conductive, depending on the applied gate signal.

Among the advantages of FET power devices are freedom from second voltage breakdown and thermal runaway, and reduced distortion in amplifiers. In some circuits, the major advantage of FETs is that they are turned on and off by voltages rather than currents. The voltages can be quite low, making FET switches compatible with digital ICs. Because FETs are majority carrier devices, they are essentially resistive when they are conducting. Also, they can be operated symmetrically, with the control voltage near ground potential, by using a second power supply.

A *depletion-type FET* has an appreciable channel conductivity for zero gate-source voltage. The channel conductivity can be increased or decreased according to the polarity of the applied gate-source voltage.

An *insulated-gate FET* has one or more gate electrodes that are electrically insulated from the channel.

A *tetrode FET* (also called a *dual-gate FET*) has two independent gates, a source, and a drain. An active substrate terminated externally and independently of other elements is considered to be a gate.

fetch 1. To locate and load a program from storage, as in bringing a program phase into main storage for execution from the memory library. **2.** That portion of a computer cycle from which the location of the next instruction is obtained. A fetch can also be used to retrieve phases of a program and load them into main storage, or transfer control to a system loader. A typical fetch routine includes the following:

- Obtaining the requested phase of the program
- Loading into main storage
- Transferring control to the phase entry point

fetch instruction The instruction or procedure used to locate and return instructions that have been entered in the instruction register.

FEXT Acronym for *far-end crosstalk*, crosstalk propagated in a disturbed channel in the same direction as the propagation of a signal in the disturbing channel. The receiving terminals of the disturbed channel and the energized terminals of the disturbing channel are usually remote from each other.

FF 1. The form-feed character. **2.** *See* FLIP-FLOP.

fiber 1. A thin filament of glass. **2.** An optical waveguide consisting of a core and a cladding which is capable of carrying information in the form of light.

fiber distributed data interface *See* FDDI.

fiber-optic cable Cable that uses either a glass or plastic fiber as a communication medium and light as the carrier instead of electricity. Light emitting diodes (LEDs) or lasers modulate the light source as it travels through the fiber. Fiber-optic cable has advantages over traditional copper wire in that its diameter is smaller, its data capacity (bandwidth) is larger, and it is not susceptible to electrical interference or inductance. It costs about the same as high-grade coaxial cable.

fiber-optic hub A unit that allows you to interconnect remote copper segments by forming a central fiber hub for the star connection of inter-repeater fiber links. Each copper segment is connected to the hub with a *fiber-optic repeater*.

fiber-optic local module A module that allows a point-to-point fiber attachment between two multiple segment LAN locations. Four modules can be used in one network bridge to form the hub of a star configuration supporting multiple segments in multiple locations. The fiber types supported are 50/125, 62.5/125, and 100/140. The maximum allowable mode separation from the network bridge chassis is 1.6 miles (2.5 km).

fiber-optic transceiver A unit that allows you to connect a variety of DTEs or PCs to a fiber-optic baseband 10 Mbps CSMA/CD LAN. These tranceivers are designed to meet ISO, IEEE, and ECMA international standards, give high-level data security, and detect fiber breaks or low light levels. They have two optical ports (transmit and receive) that connect the to duplex fiber-optic cable with any of these diameters: 50/125, 63/125, 85/125, or 100/140. An AUI (DB15) interface connects the transceiver to the DTEs or other devices that have standard AUI interfaces.

Fibonacci search A dichotomizing search in which the set or remaining subset is divided, using successively smaller numbers in the Fibonacci series. The Fibonacci series contains integers in which each integer is equal to the sum of the two preceding integers. If the number of items in a set is not equal to a Fibonacci number, then it is assumed to equal the next higher Fibonacci number.

Fick's law The rate of molecular diffusion is proportional to the negative of the concentration gradient. This law holds for mass and energy transfer and also for neutron diffusion.

field 1. A group of characters that can be treated as a single unit, or a specified area that is used for a particular category of data. Code fields can be assigned by source statements of the assembler or assembly program. Typical code fields include label, operand, comment, and operator. Fields are also used for data storage procedures: 8-bit words can be divided into two 4-bit fields, or eight 1-bit fields. **2.** In databases, the smallest meaningful amount of information, such as *last name* or *part number*.

field count In NetWare, a part of Accounting Services that contains the number of fields in a record type.

field density The number of lines of force passing normally through a unit area of an electric or magnetic field.

field discharge The passage of electricity through a gas as a result of ionization of the gas; it may take the form of a brush discharge, an arc, or a spark.

field-effect transistor *See* FET.

field-enhanced Refers to electron emission when a very strong field is effective at the emission surface.

field-free Refers to electron emission when there is no electric field at the emitting surface.

field name The name of a general category of information in a document or data set.

field of force Principle of action at a distance, such as mechanical forces experienced by an electric charge, a magnet, or a mass, at a distance from an independent electric charge, magnet, or mass, because of the fields established by these objects, which are described by uniform laws.

field-protected A display field in which the user is not allowed to enter, modify, or erase data from the keyboard.

field rate The number of fields per second.

field strength 1. The amount of magnetic flux produced at a particular point by an electromagnetic or permanent magnet. **2.** A vector representing the quotient of a force and the charge (or pole) in an electric (or magnetic) field, with the direction of the force; also called *field intensity*. **3.** An electromagnetic wave in volts-per-meter, which induces an electromotive force of one volt in an antenna of one meter effective height. Usually measured by a loop antenna.

FIFO Acronym for *first-in-first-out*, a priority basis used in many computer registers and storage elements. In a FIFO system, the data to be written in memory is stored in the next available location, and the read operation advances the outputs to the next memory word. Once the read is advanced, the previous word cannot ordinarily be used again. The main advantage of a FIFO system is the absence of external addressing; since control is automatic, the system requires only data inputs, read outputs, and clock lines. A FIFO system is useful for system applications where it is desirable to read out data in the same order that it was written. However, excessive read time in a FIFO system may cause delays in communication rates. FIFO read and write operations should be completely independent of each other and system timing.

FIFO memory A first-in-first-out memory scheme. These memories operate with a minimum of addressing logic; their separate write and read address inputs eliminate critical timing problems.

FIFO queue *See* PUSHUP LIST.

FIFO stack register A first-in-first-out stack register in which the register outputs are sequentially read in the same order that data is entered. A FIFO simplifies many information-handling operations such as high-speed compiling and code conversions.

FIFO storage A storage system that uses the FIFO technique. One method of FIFO implementation uses shift register circuits to ensure the proper first-in-first-out order. When data is entered, it is shifted to the last register stage. The next data entry is shifted to the next-to-last register stage; this is repeated until the register is full. A status register is used to identify full locations so that data is shifted only to the last empty stage.

FIFO up/down counter A minimum FIFO can be made using only the specified register files as storage elements and two binary counters for address control. Memory status indicators, however, are desirable to ensure that memory capacity is not exceeded. The usual indicators are memory empty and full, although a half-full indication is sometimes used. Many FIFO designs employ an up/down counter to produce the required status indicators. This approach, however, introduces serious timing problems with asynchronous data entry. Some systems overcome these problems by replacing the up/down counter with a binary subtractor, a circuit that reads the difference between the numbers in the two address counters. When this difference is zero, the FIFO must be either empty or full.

fifth-generation computer A computer of the generation characterized by VLSI (very large scale integration) microprocessors, parallel and multiprocessor architectures, and by the ability to understand verbal communication, produce verbal messages, and use artificial intelligence.

file A collection of related records or data sets that are used as a unit. A line or an invoice may be an item, a complete invoice may form a record, and a complete set of records may form a file. A *permanent* file is one maintained with new data perpetually being updated; such as a name and address file. A *working* file is a temporary collection of data sets that is destroyed once the data is utilized or transferred to another form.

file allocation table *See* FAT.

file attributes In NetWare, a part of File Services that contains information about a directory entry. A user must have modify rights to change these bits.

file cache A memory area for keeping portions of heavily used files. When the computer requests data in the cache, it eliminates the need to refetch it from the much slower disk drive.

file capture In NetWare, a part of Print Services that is a flag set when a capture filename has been specified. Data to be printed is then sent to the file, rather than being queued for printing.

file compression board A board that can squeeze more data into every bit you transmit or save. Using a built-in dictionary, the board translates every word or phrase into a short binary number. Then, after about a one-second-per-page interval, the board compresses the data into an information block less than one third its original size. The resulting transmission is three times faster, and disk storage is three times greater than the original.

File Express A database management system that is menu-driven and easy to use. A mailing list and report generator are included in the system.

file gap The area of a data medium used to indicate the end of a file or the start of another. A file gap may also be used as a flag to indicate the beginning or end of a particular group of data.

file handle In NetWare, a part of Locking and File Services that acts as the DOS file handle of the target file. The programmer can obtain it through the DOS Create File call or the DOS Open File call.

file locking A technique used by a computer system to help ensure data integrity. When a user locks a file, other users cannot update the file until it is unlocked. This prevents two users from attempting to add records simultaneously.

file maintenance Any activity required to keep a file up-to-date by changing, adding, or deleting data.

File Maintenance Protocol *See* FMP.

file management system A series of programs that control and manage flat files. *Also see* FLAT-FILE DATABASE.

file manager An online executive program that is used to create, delete, and retrieve programs by name from storage. A file manager can be used with disks, CD-ROMs, or cassettes in systems with as few as 4000 words.

filename In DOS and similar operating systems, the first part of a file's name, often followed by a period and then an extension. For example, in a DOS file named *LETTER.TXT*, *LETTER* is the filename, and *TXT* is the extension. *Also see* EXTENSION.

file path *See* PATH.

file protection Any device or technique used to prevent accidental erasure of data from a file.

file separator An information separator used to identify the boundary between adjacent files.

file server In a local area network, a mass storage device that holds programs and data accessible to and shareable by multiple work-stations connected with the network.

file service packets buffered In NetWare, a part of File Server Environment Services that shows the number of times file-service-request packets were stored in routing buffers.

FileShare Software available on a Macintosh running System 7 that enables network users to make all or part of their hard disk available to other users.

file sharing The ability of at least two users to share common data program files that usually reside on a file server.

file size The size of a file associated with a specified job or application, usually measured in bytes.

filespec Short for *file specifier*, a string of characters that tells DOS which file or set of files is wanted. A filespec might include a drivename, a path, a specific or global filename, and a specific or global extension.

file statistic Facts about one or more files on the network. These statistics can include the creation and last update dates, the author name, the date when someone last accessed the file, who has access to it, and which user last updated it. Other statistics might include the number of file accesses and any security restrictions.

file system The portion of an operating system that is responsible for storing and retrieving data onto a storage medium such as a disk.

file transfer The movement of long strings of data, such as the text of a memo, from one DTE to another. Often this is done a central data store to the user's station, requiring a high transmission rate to achieve an acceptable fast transfer. An Ethernet LAN has particularly good performance for this type of task because of its 10M data rate and ability to transmit relatively long packets.

File Transfer Protocol *See* FTP.

Filing Assistant An easy-to-use program for storing and retrieving information. It is integrated with other programs in the IBM Assistant Series. You can merge Filing Assistant data into spreadsheets, graphs, form letters, and reports created by Planning Assistant, Graphing Assistant, Writing Assistant, and Reporting Assistant.

fill In graphics and desktop publishing, to display or draw a character in solid color rather than an outline, or to draw a shape with a center that is a solid color or pattern.

fill bucket A graphics function that allows the user to fill an enclosed area of a drawing with a single color or pattern.

film resistor A type of fixed resistor having a resistance element made of a thin layer of conductive material on an insulated form. Some type of mechanical protection is usually placed over this layer.

film ribbon A printer ribbon made of mylar or polyethylene.

FILO Acronym for *first-in-last-out*, a push-down register in which the most recent entry is retrieved first. *Also see* STACK.

filter A device or program that "sifts" signals, data, or other materials according to specified criteria, with the purpose of separating the usable portions from the unusable. An electrical filter may contain inductors, capacitors, and resistors that allow it to select desired frequencies in communication channels or to provide a path to ground for noise signals.

filtering When a microcomputer has access to a large number of samples over a period of time, the input can be filtered to eliminate spurious indications and to obtain a more precise result. This filtering can be done in software. For example, if a digital multimeter samples 10,000 times every second, the simplest filtering is averaging 10,000 measurements, which are added together and then divided by 10,000. The result is the filtered or averaged voltage. Any unreasonable values would be averaged out, and the resulting measurement would have a higher precision in this programmable filter.

final copy A correct, finished document.

finder *See* MACINTOSH FINDER.

finder information In AppleTalk, the 32-byte finder information structure associated with each AFP directory or file.

Findfile A menu-driven DOS utility for hard-disk users that searches through subdirectories to find a file you have lost. It includes several support routines to help you manage your files. It provides a tree display and single or multiple file operations.

Finesse A desktop publishing program designed for reports, newsletters, memos, letters, invitations, brochures, and other documents. The package includes Bitstream fonts and Logitech's Image Library with high-resolution images for a range of subjects, including business, recreation, and holidays. There are also page-layout templates for memos, newsletters, and other documents.

finger An Internet program that displays information about a particular user, or all users, logged on the local system or on a remote system. It typically shows full name, last login time, idle time, terminal line, and terminal location (where applicable). It may also display plan and project files left by the user.

firewall A mechanism to protect network stations, subnetworks, and channels from complete failure caused by a single-point problem.

firmware That part of software that cannot be easily changed once it is implemented. Firmware might consist of those microprograms that are contained in ROM, and may be an extension to the basic instruction package for creating microprograms for a user-oriented instruction set. If the extension is done in read-only memory instead of software, it is called firmware. The ROM is used to convert these extended instructions to basic instructions for the computer.

Firmware tends to have a hardware compatibility while offering software-type implementation techniques. However, firmware generally is limited to moving data through the data paths and functional units already present; it is able to effectively process only the instruction formats, data types, and arithmetic modes that are defined for the hardware. Attempting to use firmware for new formats, types, and modes can be awkward and result in poor performances.

firmware building blocks Standard programs in PROMs that may include utilities such as a macroassembly language interpreter, I/O control system, and disk file manager. For program development, the user can write, simulate, and debug programs using these building blocks.

first DMA channels used In NetWare, a part of File Server Environment Services that lists the DMA controllers a disk driver uses to control a disk channel.

first DMA channels used in use flag In NetWare, a part of File Server Environment Services that provides a flag for a DMA channels-used field.

first generation 1. In the numeric control industry, the period of technology associated with vacuum tubes and stepping switches. **2.** The period of technology in computer design utilizing vacuum tubes, electronics, offline storage on drum or disk, and programming in machine language.

first-in-first-out *See* FIFO.

first-in-last-out *See* FILO.

first interrupt numbers used In NetWare, a part of File Server Environment Services that contains interrupt numbers for a disk driver to communicate with a disk channel.

first interrupt numbers used in use flag In NetWare, a part of File Server Environment Services that provides a flag for the first interrupt numbers used.

first IO address used In NetWare, a part of File Server Environment Services that contains addresses that a disk driver uses to control a disk channel.

first IO address used length In NetWare, a part of File Server Environment Services that contains the lengths of the addresses a disk driver uses to control a disk channel.

first-level address *See* DIRECT ADDRESS.

first shared memory address In NetWare File Server Environment Services, a field that a disk driver uses to control a disk channel.

first shared memory address length In NetWare File Server Environment Services, the length of shared memory addresses.

FirstSQL C An embedded precompiler for PCs that allows direct access to database files from C programs by using SQL statements. Database applications can be created using the precompiler and other compiler and development tools. High-level SQL commands for database access are placed directly in the program source code.

FIX An integrated process-monitoring and control system providing data acquisition and interactive graphics for the PC. Scanning, alarm, and control are performed in a background mode, so that other programs can be run online. Up to 50 programs can be run at once, including an online spreadsheet program. FIX connects to a variety of process I/O subsystems, data highways, and programmable controllers. The system has options such as direct database access from user-written programs, historical archiving with trend playback, and the ability to monitor up to 2,000 I/O points.

fixed area That part of main storage occupied by the resident section of the control program.

fixed block format A format in which the number and sequence of words and characters appearing in successive blocks is constant.

fixed capacitor A type of capacitor with a specific capacitance that cannot be adjusted.

fixed cycle A type of computer operation cycle in which a specific amount of time is used for each operation. Fixed-cycle operation involves clocking so that all events occur as a function of measured time.

fixed data Data that is not likely to change or affect the results, date, operator, designator, or dump format. Also known as *housekeeping data*.

fixed disk *See* HARD DISK.

Fixed Disk Organizer A DOS-based menu system to organize your hard disk into subdirectories. Files can be grouped together logically into related subdirectories or menus so that they can be accessed with only a single keystroke. You can password-protect for each menu. You can also create a menu of commonly used batch commands so that it is necessary only to press a single key rather than type a complex series of commands.

fixed expenses A category in many accounting and tax programs for costs that remain constant over time, such as rent or insurance payments. *Contrast with* VARIABLE EXPENSES.

fixed heads Rigidly mounted reading and writing transducers for bulk memory devices.

fixed length Refers to records, words, or other elements that always contain the same number of characters, bits, or fields. A fixed length may be a restriction due to equipment or a requirement to simplify and speed processing operations.

fixed-point 1. A type of arithmetic in which the computer does not consider the location of the radix point. In a desk calculator using fixed-point arithmetic, the operator must keep track of the decimal point. In a computer, the location of the decimal point is the programmer's responsibility. **2.** A type of arithmetic in which the operands and the results of all operations must be scaled to have a magnitude between certain fixed values. The following instructions may be used for the manipulation of fixed-point numbers:

```
MUL; (multiply)
DIV; (divide)
ASH; (shift arithmetically)
ASCH; (arithmetic shift combined)
```

Operand formats are allowed for 16-bit single words or 32-bit double words.

fixed-point constant Numerical data that contain a decimal point.

fixed program Instructions that are wired in or stored permanently in the computer. In a fixed-program computer, the instructions are not changed except by rewiring or changing the storage locations.

fixed resistor A type of nonadjustable resistor designed to introduce a predetermined amount of resistance into an electrical circuit.

fixed sequence format A means of identifying a word by its location in a block of information. Words must be presented in a specific order, and all possible words preceding the last desired word must be present in the block.

fixed storage Storage in which contents are not changed by computer instructions, as in CD-ROMs. Also known as *read-only storage*, *permanent storage*, and *nonerasable storage*.

F/L Abbreviation for *fetch/load*.

flag An indicator used to signal the occurrence of a specific condition. A flag may be a specific bit that indicates a point of demarcation such as a carry, overflow, of interrupt. Also known as a *mark*, *sentinel*, or *tag*.

flag bit A specific information bit that indicates a type or form of demarcation has been reached. This may be a carry, overflow, or interrupt. Generally the flag bit refers to special conditions, such as various types of interrupts.

flag object In NetWare Bindery Services, a byte identifying an object as either static (0) or dynamic (1).

flame A strong opinion and/or criticism of something, usually phrased as a frankly inflammatory statement, in an electronic mail message.

Flash Graphics A graphics generator that supports Borland, Microsoft, and several other C/C++ compilers. There is a debug library to catch errors and a standard library for speed and minimum code.

flash ROM A type of read-only memory, pioneered by Intel, which allows high-speed reads and moderate-speed writes. Some portable computers use flash ROM to create solid-state hard drives.

flat-bed plotter A plotter that uses a pen movable in four directions across a flat surface of paper.

flat-card resolving potentiometer A type of potentiometer that uses an element that is a square slab or card wound with resistance wire.

flat fading Fading in which all components of the signal change in the same way at the same time.

flat-file database The simplest type of database, so named because you can only maintain one file at a time. *Contrast with* RDBMS.

flat pack An integrated circuit package that has leads extending from the package in the same plane as the package so that leads can be spot welded to terminals on a substrate or soldered to a printed circuit board. The small size and low profile of the flat pack allows high-density circuit packaging.

flat-panel display An electronic display with a package thickness that is a small fraction of the display's height or length.

FLBIN Acronym for *floating point binary*.

flex circuits A type of fine-line flexible circuit for aerospace, medical and other uses. Flex circuits are available in single-, double-, multi-layer, and rigid-flex circuits, all certified to MIL-P-50884C.

flex life Resistance of a conductor to fatigue when repeatedly bent.

FLF Abbreviation for *flip-flop*.

flicker A visible fluctuation in the brightness of an image, often a problem in CRT displays if the vertical scan rate is lower than about 50 Hz.

FLIP Acronym for *floating instrument platform*.

flip-flop A circuit that is capable of assuming either one of two stable states; a *bistable multivibrator*. The flip-flop will assume a given state depending upon the previous history of the inputs. For a flip-flop with two inputs, the state of the outputs will correspond to the past and present conditions of the two inputs. Flip-flops can be coupled to other circuits with capacitors, or the circuits within the flip-flop can be coupled with capacitors, permitting operation only for alternating currents. Flip-flop circuits have a variety of configurations, including D, J-K, R-S, T and R-S-T.

D flip-flops perform a delay function, since the output will be the input which appeared one pulse earlier. If a 1 appeared at the input, the output after the next clock pulse will also be a 1.

J-K flip-flops have a J input and a K input following the clock pulse; a 1 on the J input and a 0 on the K input will set the output to 1. A 0 on J and a 1 on K will reset the output to 0. Where a 1 appears on both inputs, a change of state results, regardless of any previous states; a 0 on both inputs inhibits any change of state.

R-S flip-flops operate like two NAND gates that have been cross-connected. The circuit has a reset (R) input and a set (S) input. A 1 on the S input and a 0 on the R input will clear or reset the output to 0. A 1 on the R input and a 0 on the S input will set the output to 1. If 1s are on both inputs, the output will remain the same; a 0 on both inputs is not considered.

T flip-flops have only one input. A pulse on the input causes the output to change states. T flip-flops are used for ripple counters.

R-S-T flip-flops have three inputs labeled R, S, and T (for reset, set, and trigger). The circuit operates like an R-S flip-flop except that the T input is used to change the state of output.

Flip-flops can be strung together so that the state of one can be transferred to another. Then a number stored in one string can be transferred to another, allowing numbers to be transferred in computer systems. Flip-flops are used to form storage registers, counters, and controls for interrupt-level signals. Level-enable flip-flops control the interrupt level from a waiting state to an active state.

flip-flop, a-c coupled A type of flip-flop circuit in which the active elements are coupled with capacitors.

flip-flop equipment Electronic or electromechanical devices that cause automatic alternation between two possible circuit paths. The term is often applied to any mechanical operation that is analogous to the principle of the flip-flop.

flip-flop level enable A specific flip-flop signal that partially controls the ability of an interrupt level to advance from the waiting state to the active state.

flip-flop string A computer property in which the state of one flip-flop can be transferred to another by means of triggering circuits. A number stored in one string of flip-flops can be transferred to another string. In this way, numbers can be transferred from place to place in a computer. Many flip-flop circuits include a pair of triggering circuits for this purpose.

Flipper A graphics function library that integrates graphics into Clipper applications. It has XY, pie charts, 3D, and area graphs. A CAD interface for drawing maps and other vector images with automatic axis-scaling and multiple graph types per screen are provided. Support is provided for CGA, EGA, VGA, and Hercules displays.

flippy (*o.t.*) A type of floppy diskette used on single-sided disk drives. Two sets of write-protect notches and index holes allowed the diskette to be turned over and information recorded on both sides.

floating address An address that can be easily converted to a machine address by indexing, assembly, or some other means.

floating defects Defects on a disk due to the drifting alignment of the drive heads. These defects may not have been detected previously because they were located between tracks.

floating point A native data type on most operating systems which allows numbers after the decimal point.

floating-point arithmetic A type of arithmetic in which the computer keeps track of the decimal point. Floating-point arithmetic uses the floating-point notation to eliminate carrying the great number of digits that may occur in many calculations. Seven or eight digits are retained along with a two-digit characteristic, as shown:

Number	Scientific Notation	Floating Point Notation
0.024	2.4×10^{-2}	.24E – 2

Some floating-point subroutines for conversion include the following:

- Floating-point to ASCII
- ASCII to floating-point
- Floating-point to integer
- Integer to floating-point

These routines may be used to simulate floating-point operations on a computer with no built-in floating-point hardware.

floating-point calculation A specific number representation system in which each number, as represented by a pair of numerals, equals one of those numerals times a power of an implicit, fixed positive integer base, where the power is equal to the implicit base raised to the exponent represented by the other numeral. *Contrast with* VARIABLE-POINT REPRESENTATION.

floating-point number A noninteger number, real or imaginary, that uses the floating point representation. *Contrast with* INTEGER.

floating symbolic address A label used to identify a word or other item in a routine independent of the location of the information within the routine.

flooding A routing scheme in tree topology LANs in which each intermediate node repeats each received message onto all of its outbound branch links.

floppy disk drive A subsystem that consists of a disk controller board, a single spindle that is turned by the drive motor, and a read/write-head carriage assembly moved by one stepper-motor/lead-screw combination. The disk controller is used to connect the disk to the CPU. The controller may be a separate expansion board as shown in the figure, or it can be part of the main system board.

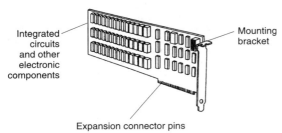

Typical floppy disk controller board

The disk drive has two sensors that detect when a diskette is installed in it. These sensors also look at the write-protect notch or tab on the side of the diskette's protective cover to see if the diskette is write-protected. A floppy disk drive is shown in the following figure.

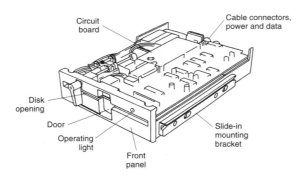

Floppy disk drive

floppy disk A magnetic storage medium that uses flexible disks coated with metal oxide (see the figure) and housed in a protective plastic jacket. Each floppy disk can provide random access storage for anywhere from 360K to 1.44M or more bytes. These disks or diskettes provide mass storage, data exchange, and file backup capabilities. Also called a *diskette*.

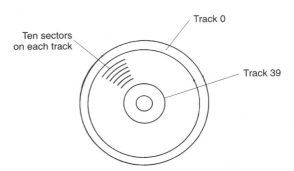

Floppy disk

floppy disk testing Floppy disk drives can be tested with a diagnostic disk. Typically, you insert the diagnostic disk and select the floppy tests from a menu, like the one in the figure.

Title	Floppy tests – Drives A and B
Runtime messages	Drive to be tested? select drive Remove diagnostic disk and insert formatted disk Warning contents of diskettes are destroyed!!! Number of tests – 11
This area may scroll as new messages are added	Test 1 – Internal register test Test 2 – Head load test Test 3 – Loopback test Test 4 – Restore test Test 5 – Step test Test 6 – Motor test Test 7 – Seek test Test 8 – Forced write errors test Test 9 – Write sectors test Test 10 – Forced read errors test Test 11 – Read sectors test
Error messages and status	Rewriting sectors used in test 9 End of tests. Insert diagnostic disk Controller board – Head load timing failure Enter P to proceed or L to loop on error

Floppy disk test menu

flowchart A graphical representation of the definition or solution of a problem, in which symbols are used to represent functions, operations, and flow. A flowchart might contain all of the logical steps in a routine or program in order to allow the designer to conceptualize and visualize each step. It defines the major phases of the processing, as well as the path to a problem solution. A standard set of flowchart symbols is shown in the following figure.

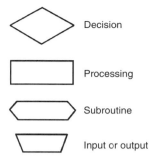

Flowchart symbols

The flowchart can contain logical operations by using symbolic notation to describe the arithmetic operations in terms of inputs and outputs. Functional flowcharts define all operations sequentially, but do not contain enough detail to allow program coding, as shown in the diagram that follows. Detailed charts are derived from combining the functional flowchart with command codes. The detailed charts include

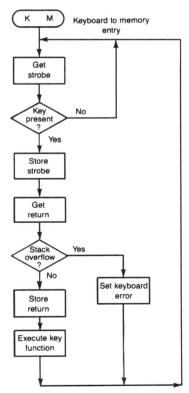

Flowchart for a keyboard-to-memory routine

every operation that must be performed during coding in step-by-step form. At that point, the programmer is only required to translate the steps into the programming language. Also called a *data flow diagram.*

Flow Charting A charting program that allows you to create flowcharts, data flow diagrams, process control, and organizational charts. These charts can be portrait or landscape, multi-page charts. Import/export capabilities, and international character support are also included.

flowcharting template A design tool that allows a nonartist to use standard symbols to represent program or system design icons.

flow control The control of incoming data to a buffer or similar device that stops the data before the buffer overflows. It can involve a signal, such as an XOFF character, to stop the transmitting device.

flow line The line providing the connecting path between flowchart symbols. Flow lines are used to indicate the sequential processes of the operation they represent.

flow process diagram A graphic representation of the work in a process. The major steps of work are defined by symbols that represent documents, equipment, or operations.

FLPL Abbreviation for *Fortran list processing.*

fluorescent screens Screens that use small fluorescent tubes with a diffuser so you cannot see the outline of the tubes through the screen.

flush capture on device close In NetWare Print Services, a flag that tells whether to flush a print job capture.

flush capture timeout count In NetWare Print Services, a flag that starts counting down when an application prints any data.

flux A type of material used to promote the joining of metals in soldering, such as rosin. Also refers to the flow of particles crossing a unit area per unit time, most commonly referred to in units of cm^2/sec. Integrated flux, after an exposure of time T, is equal to the total number of particles that have transversed a unit area during time T.

flux guidance Directing the electric or magnetic flux in high-frequency heating by shaped electrodes or magnetic materials.

fluxmeter An electrical instrument for measuring the quantity of magnetic flux linked with a circuit; it consists of a search coil placed in the magnetic field under investigation and a detector.

flying capacitor multiplexer A low-level multiplexer used for combating common-mode interference. The flying capacitor multiplexer is a two-wire sample-hold type, as shown in the figure. Switches X and X' are turned on with Y and Y' off to acquire the input signal. When the capacitor is fully charged, all switches are momentarily turned off; then Y and Y' are turned on to transfer the signal to the output amplifier. No common-mode voltage is transferred across the switches, and the output amplifier may be single-ended and noninverting. This is effective in eliminating common-mode voltages, but if normal mode interference is present as well, better rejection of both normal mode and common-mode interference can be obtained with a straight multiplexer and a floating-input integrating converter. An integrating converter used with the flying capacitor multiplexer will integrate the sample of the input rather than the input, and the sample will include variations from normal mode interference.

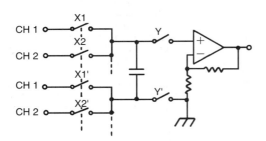

Flying capacitor multiplexer

flying-spot scanner A device in optical character recognition that uses a moving spot of light to scan each character's space. The difference in light levels as the light moves over dark lines and white spaces denotes the character printed.

FM Abbreviation for *frequency modulation*, a method of modulating a radio-frequency carrier of fixed amplitude, in which the instantaneous frequency deviates from the center frequency at a rate that corresponds with the signal. The amount of deviation is proportional to the *amplitude* of the modulating signal, but the *frequency* of the deviation is proportional to the frequency of the applied signal.

FMI Abbreviation for *failure mode indicator*.

FMP Abbreviation for *File Maintenance Protocol*, a generic term for some of the higher level functions of File Transfer Protocol (FTP), such as directory management and renaming.

FO Abbreviation for *fast operation*.

focal point Under IBM's network management program, a focal point receives information from entry points located on various SNA network addressable units (NAUs).

FOIL Acronym for *file-oriented interpretive language*.

foil thermocouple A thermocouple consisting of a thin foil junction and lead wires embedded between two thin layers of laminate insulation, with an overall thickness of 0.006 inches.

foldover distortion *See* ALIASING DISTORTION.

font The family or group of characters of a given style. The characters in the text of this book are from one font; the characters on the cover are from others.

Fontastic Plus A program that provides font editing with three levels of magnification, four levels of undo, background editing, and the capability to edit several fonts at once. Editing tools include pencil, eraser, line, filled box, and filled oval or circle. Character-styling abilities include bold, italic, outline, shadow, underline, expand, condense, and invert. Font size can be as large as 127 points, with independent vertical and horizontal scale factors.

font cartridge A printer cartridge that contains additional fonts. Cartridges can be installed in the printer so that a variety of fonts can be selected for printing.

font characteristics The characteristics that distinguish a printed font, including orientation, character height, style, stroke weight, and typeface.

Font Editor A program for special fonts, letterheads, accented symbols, logos, and foreign language characters. You can use up to five windows at once. It allows multi-segmented lines of varying widths, smooth curves of specified widths, circles, ellipses, boxes, fill, rotate, enlarge, reduce, slant, copy/move, invert, and boldface.

Fontographer A program that allows you to create new typefaces or add to an existing typeface. You can also make a picture font using line art as a tracing template, or combine multiple characters into a single keystroke for logos or foreign characters. Three independent drawing layers are provided for each character: foreground, background, and guideline. It includes a full set of editing tools and three types of windows: a font window, a character editing window, and a character metric window. Fonts from 1 to 127 points are generated automatically. PostScript printer resolutions from 300 to 2540 dpi are supported.

Fontrix A software tool for designing and printing type and graphic images. It is a combination of three different programs: a graphic writer, a font editor and a graphic printer. The graphic printer features include independent horizontal and vertical magnification, 90° rotation, justification, and negative images. Fontrix is useful for designing business forms, logos, reports, floor plans, newsletters, and circuit diagrams. Symbolic fonts make it possible to output music, equations, and foreign languages, as well.

Fontshare A software-based font server for Macintosh networks that works with fonts the way AppleShare and TOPS work with applications and files. It allows networked Macs to share laser fonts. It is compatible with network file servers such as TOPS, MacServe, and AppleShare.

font size The height of characters in a font, often measured in points or characters-per-inch. Fonts are often referred to in terms of size and name, for example, 16-point Helvetica.

Font-Tools A program for creating, editing, and using fonts within a graphics application. It includes a mouse-drive, graphics-based font editor and utilities for resizing, modifying, viewing, converting, and downloading fonts to laser printers. There are 100 sample font and icon files and a font function library with over 40 functions. It uses the GEM font format.

FontWINDOW A program that provides a MetaWindow-compatible bitmap font and icon editor with over 2M of additional fonts for use with Metagraphics MetaWindow. It allows you to create foreign-language fonts and combine characters from multiple fonts to create a new font. You can also create icons and animation fonts as well as bold, italic, and rotated font sets.

footer In word processing, text than can appear at the bottom of every page. Many word processors can automatically position footnotes.

footnote In word processing, text placed at the bottom of a page or at the end of a document or chapter to give a reference for, or add information about, a topic discussed in the main text of the document. Many word processors can automatically place and number footnotes.

footprint The amount of space that a computer or peripheral occupies on your desktop. If space is at a premium, look for a device with a small footprint.

forbidden combination A combination of characters, bits, or other items that is not valid in a given operation, according to specified criteria.

For_C A program that converts Fortran-77 into ANSI C. It supports MILSPEC and VAX extensions including Structures. It is available with C runtime library source code for portability or with binary runtime.

force flag In NetWare, a part of File Server Environment Services that indicates whether the file server should force itself down even when files are open.

force reduction A method where the performance of slow application code is improved by simplifying algorithms or using hardware-based solutions. A typical example is applying an index to a file that is otherwise sorted, or replacing multiplication operations with bit shifts.

foreground program The computer program in a multitasking or time-sharing machine that has the highest priority.

foreground processing A type of programming in which top-priority programs are processed, usually through the use of interrupts, into other programs of lower priority.

foreign attachments Any non-common-carrier connected directly to a commercial telephone wire pair.

Forge A Turbo Pascal and dBASE programmer's aid. It allows the programmer to design data input forms or help screens; it then generates the Turbo Pascal or dBASE source code for those forms. Forge was written entirely in Turbo Pascal, but only the .COM file is provided. Turbo Pascal and dBASE are not required to use Forge, but are required in order to make use of the files produced by Forge. The source code produced by Forge can then be compiled and used as-is for data entry, or it can be included as a procedure within a larger, more comprehensive program. Because this is a utility for Turbo Pascal and dBASE, a working knowledge of these programming languages is assumed.

Forge allows you to do with the forms for data input what most word processors do with text. You can fill an area on the screen with color without affecting the characters already on the screen, insert or delete lines from the screen, define areas on the form for entering data, define data entry areas as string, integer, or real data types, and use graphics characters to draw and use blinking characters.

forged detach requests In NetWare, a part of File Server Environment Services that shows a count of requests to terminate connections where the source addresses did not match the address the server had assigned to the connection. The detach request is ignored.

fork indicator In NetWare, a part of AppleTalk Filing Protocol (AFP) Services that tells whether the returned AFP Entry ID points to a data fork (0) or to a resource fork (1).

form A predesigned document used for recording, transmitting, and summarizing data. Forms may be printed or reproduced in other manners; they usually contain spaces for the insertion of information.

formant vocoder A vocoder in which the vocal tract filter is estimated by the frequencies and amplitude of the spectral peaks, or formants. *Also see* VOCODER.

format A predetermined arrangement of data, words, letters, characters, files, etc.

format classification A means by which parts, dimensional data, type of system, number of digits, and other functions for a particular application can be denoted.

format designator The letters and symbols used in instruction words to specify and establish a given format.

format detail Describes specifically which words of what length are used by a specific system in a format classification.

format effector *See* FE.

format length In NetWare, a part of Accounting Services that contains the length of the format control string used to print comment records associated with the Charge or Note record.

formatted capacity The capacity in megabytes of a disk after it has been formatted for use. The final formatted capacity can vary slightly due to differences in format structure.

formatting instructions In word processing, the instructions in a style that specify what enhancements to make to the text to which the style is applied.

format utility A DOS utility that initializes disks.

form document A printed document created by merging a main document with a data document. Standard text from a main document is combined with varying data or text from a data document; the result is the customized form document. Form letters and mailing labels are two common examples.

form factor The physical size of a drive. For example, a 3.5-inch drive has a smaller form factor than a 5.25-inch drive.

form-feed The format effecter that controls the movement of the printing position to the next form or page. In ASCII, this is the FF character represented by the binary 12 (0000 1100).

FormGen A collection of predesigned business forms. There are purchase orders, invoices, expense forms, accounting forms, inventory, applications, and work orders. You can customize them to your specifications.

form lock clutch A clutch that overcomes the chatter problems of conventional bidirectional clutches operating under overhauling loads. When operating under overhauling load conditions, such as turning a ball screw in the direction in which it is loaded, the energy-absorbing capability of the form lock decelerates the output rather than stopping it suddenly, enabling the clutch to operate without chatter. The clutch absorbs and dissipates energy, so there is no trapped, or locked in, torque to break loose after backstopping.

form name In NetWare, a part of Print Services that is a flag containing the name of a form to be mounted in a file server. This field is only for reference.

Formtool A software package used to create any form, any size. It automatically draws single or double lines vertically and horizontally. It supports a variety of laser and dot matrix printers and has a merge facility that is compatible with dBASE and ASCII files.

form type In NetWare, a part of Print Services that is a flag containing the name of a form to be used.

formula In a spreadsheet, calculations that can be entered into a spreadsheet cell and replaced by the result.

Form:view A software package that provides low-cost, dynamic viewing and annotation on minimally configured, graphics equipped, networked XTs and ATs or compatibles. Form:view's on-screen viewing capabilities permits any authorized workstation on the LAN to access documents for display purposes. *Form:redline* adds annotation capability to Form:view. It permits a user to mark up a technical document in order to note a potential or apparent problem, highlight a particular feature or provide written remarks.

FOR...NEXT In BASIC, a statement that allows a series of instructions to be repeated a number of times with a variable taking on specified beginning, ending, and incrementing values.

FOR_STRUCT A program that transforms "spaghetti" Fortran into structured code. GOTO and IF-GOTOs are replaced with IF-THEN-ELSE, DO-WHILE, and DO-ENDO constructs. The original logic is retained, and code is not duplicated. The dead code can be removed. There are structures to F-77, VAX F-77, or to FAX F-77 with Fortran-90 control statements.

Forth A programming language developed primarily for microcomputers.

FORTLIB A program with functions to handle keyboard, video, RS-232, disk drives, directories, files, system time and date, strings, memory allocation, data conversion, data sorting, system, and printer services. The functions are similar to the C standard library.

Fortran Blending of *formula translator*, one of the most widely used languages for scientific and business problems. Fortran requires a compiler for each particular model of computer. It is well-suited for problem-solving with mathematical and English-language conventions. Statements, used as sentences in the language, do the following:

- Define the arithmetic steps for the processor
- Provide the control required during program execution
- Define the required input and output operations
- Define such additional areas as dimensions of variables.

Arithmetic statements appear as equalities; the right side can involve parentheses, operation symbols, constants, variables, and functions. These are combined using a set of rules similar to ordinary algebra. The following operation symbols are used in arithmetic statements:

+ (Addition)
− (Subtraction)
* (Multiplication)
/ (Division)
** (Exponentiation)

An example of an arithmetic expression as it would appear on a Fortran coding sheet is as follows:

$$A**B*C + D**E/F - G + H$$

which is interpreted as:

$$A^B C + D^E/F - G + H$$

Besides the ability to indicate constants, variables, and operations, Fortran also allows you to use functions such as the following:

ABSF (X) (Absolute value of x)
SQRTF (X) (Square root of x)

SINF (X) (Sin *x*)
COSF (X) (Cos *x*)
ATANF (X) (Arctan *x*)

Input/output statements such as the following bring data into the processor and output the results:

```
READ 1,A,B,C; (Read the next record and the
numbers stored in locations A, B and C.)

PRINT 2, ROOT; (Print the number identified as
the variable ROOT in storage.)
```

Control statements are used to state the flow of the program. Any statement that is referred to by another is given an identifying number, which allows branching from one part of the program to another. Some examples of control statements are the following:

```
GO TO 3; (The next statement to be executed is
number 3.)

GO TO (3, 18, 20) K; (The next statement to be
executed depends on the previous value of k; if
k = 1, the next statement is number 3.)

IF (A*B) 3, 18, 20 ; (One of three alternate
instructions is executed if the value of a times
b is less than, equal to, or greater than zero.)
```

Fortran IV is an upgraded version that provides more power for interfacing with more complex configurations, greater flexibility, improved accuracy, and a more powerful instruction set. The Fortran IV compiler permits intermixing between assembly language and Fortran statements to produce an object listing for diagnostics. Programs are compiled in the operating system or as task modules under real-time executive control. The extended features of Fortran IV include the following:

- N-dimensional arrays
- Mixed-mode expressions
- Unformatted inputs and outputs
- Alphanumeric stringing
- Conditional compiling
- Tracing and debug facility
- Inline assembly language capability

Many microprocessors use Fortran IV assembly and simulators, which allow the use of large general-purpose computers for developing microcomputer programs.

Fortran variables Variables used in Fortran, which are restricted to integer values, consisting of one to six alphanumeric characters.

forward Describes the action a bridge takes when it sends a packet on to the next bridge.

forward bias Refers to a voltage applied to a P-N junction such that the positive terminal of the voltage is applied to the P section and the negative to the N section.

forward collator tray A tray for laser printers that snaps in place of the standard output tray. The paper will automatically be collated in the proper order. A capacity of 200 sheets makes it useful for form letters or long print runs.

forward current The current that flows through a semiconductor junction when a forward bias voltage is applied.

forward direction The direction in which the resistance to current flow through a semiconductor is lower.

Forwarn A program for Fortran that contains a static analyzer to detect programming errors, such as incorrect parameter lists, mismatched common blocks, and misspelled variable names. It summarizes routine and variable usage and prints cross-reference listings and calling-tree diagrams to aid documentation.

four-address An instruction format that contains four address parts.

4GL Abbreviation for *fourth-generation language*, a high-level programming language that uses nonprocedural techniques to help users specify program requirements. Also known as *program generators*.

Fourier analysis A method used to determine the harmonic components of a waveform, based on the theory that any waveform can be constructed using the appropriate number of selected harmonics from a sinusoid of a given frequency.

Fourier transform A mathematical technique for computing the frequency spectrum of a time-limited periodic signal. Also called a *Fourier series*.

four-phase modulation A digital type of modulation designed for the carrier to shift between four distinct phases; the four possible phases serve to encode the bits.

four-plus-one address An instruction that contains four operand addresses and one control address.

fourth generation In the numeric control industry, the change in technology of control logic to include computer architecture.

fourth-generation computer Computers with processing hardware characterized by VLSI (very large scale integrated) circuits such as a microprocessor. The fourth generation is used in data communication networks.

fourth-generation language See 4GL.

four-wire A two-way communications circuit that uses two discrete paths for transmission. Data is transmitted in one direction only on one path and in the other direction on the other path. The circuit may or may not use four wires, but the effect of a 4-wire system is achieved in that no crosstalk or intercoupling exists between the two circuit paths.

Fowler-Nordeim tunneling A mechanism used to write and erase data. The device erases and writes by causing electrons to tunnel across a 200 Angstrom layer of silicon dioxide. The cells hold their charge in the same way as conventional EPROMs. Maintained at 125°C, they retain data for years. Operation is fully static and refreshing is not required, regardless of read frequency. Byte erase/write or chip erase requires application of a 21-volt pulse for 10 milliseconds. Any 2K of the device can be erased and rewritten in 20 milliseconds. The tunnel structure is shown in the following figure.

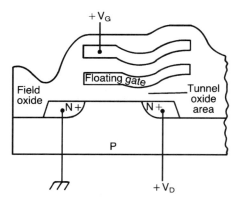

Floating-gate tunnel oxide EEPROM structure

fox box A handheld, battery-operated message generator for ASCII, EBCDIC, or Baudot testing of asynchronous RS-232 devices. Up to 16 messages, each from 1 to 128 characters long, can be programmed into the unit's EPROM. Character formats of 5 to 8 bits, one or two stop bits, and even or odd parity may be intermixed throughout the 16 messages.

FoxGraph A presentation graphics program for PCS that allows the creation of custom 2D and 3D graphs for screen display and printing or export to a paint program or desktop publisher. Utility programs allow data created with FoxPro, FoxBase, dBASE, or dBXL to be passed directly to FoxGraph for plotting.

fox message A standard message used to test communication systems, since it contains all of the alphanumerics and many of the function characters, as follows:

THE QUICK BROWN FOX JUMPS OVER THE LAZY DOG
1234567890 (*station name*) SENDING

FoxPro A DOS relational database management system with a mouse-driven interface and 4GL tools. Query optimization is used to perform queries faster. The industry-standard Xbase language is used with extensions for the development of object-oriented, event-driven applications.

FP *See* FAST POLL.

FPLA Abbreviation for *field-programming logic array*, an array that uses fusible links for programming the logic configuration. High current is passed through the links to achieve the desired logic design. FPLAs offer 50-nanosecond speeds along with editing compatibility and good flexibility. In typical FPLAs, product terms can be added or deleted from any output function, input variables can be deleted from any output function or product term, and programmed active-high outputs can be reprogrammed to active-low.

A typical device may provide eight output functions and 48 products terms; all outputs can be programmed active-high true or active-low true, which allows complements to be implemented using fewer product terms. FPLAs are used with a small auxiliary memory to repair core memory systems as an alternate to restringing methods.

FPLA core patch Refers to broken or marginal cores found in core planes that are not repaired by "restringing" methods. An alternate, dynamic repair technique is afforded by an FPLA in conjunction with a small auxiliary memory (RAM).

FPLA fast multibit shifter Computer performance can be increased by incorporating hardware capabilities for executing fast multibit shifts. Two FPLAs are sufficient to execute both arithmetic and logic shifts of an 8-bit byte any number of places, either left or right, within 35 nanoseconds.

FPLA priority resolver and latch A tristate FPLA can be configured as a priority resolver and latch, which is useful in asynchronous multiport systems. It can be extended to implement a vectored interrupt system in a typical microprocessor application.

FR Abbreviation for *fast release*.

fractal A term originated in 1975 by the mathematician Benoit Mandelbrot to explain a class of irregular shapes that appear to define a regular pattern. This characteristic allows graphic designers to use fractals to create natural-looking images such as landscapes, forests, clouds, and so on.

fractional frequency difference The algebraic difference between two normalized frequencies. Also called *relative frequency difference* or *normalized frequency difference*.

fractional programming Programming that deals with optimizing the ratio of two linear functions subject to linear constraints.

Fractional T-1 Service *See* FT1.

fragmentation header The sublayer on ARCnet networks between the ARCnet header and the IPX header. It is used to allow IPX to transmit packets of 576 bytes, which is larger than the 508-byte ARCnet maximum.

fragment count In NetWare, a part of Communication Services that is the number of buffers from which a packet is formed for sending or into which it is split when received; it must be greater than zero.

fragment descriptor In NetWare, a part of Communication Services API that contains the address and size of the buffer to or from which a packet is sent or received.

fragmented file A file whose contents are scattered through non-neighboring sectors of a disk at random instead of in adjacent (contiguous) sectors.

fragmented write occurred In NetWare, a part of File Server Environment Services that shows the number of times a dirty cache block contained noncontiguous sectors of information to be written, and the skipped sectors were not preread from the disk.

frame acquisition mode A mode of operation in the time-division multiplexer frame synchronization in which the frame alignment signal is detected. Also called *frame search mode*.

frame acquisition time The time that elapses between a valid frame alignment signal being available at the receiver terminal equipment and the frame alignment being established. Also called *frame alignment recovery time*.

frame alignment The state in which the frame of the receiving equipment is correctly phased with respect to that of the received signal.

frame buffer Memory that can be viewed directly on the display surface. Also called *display memory*.

frame connector A portion of metal or plastic that surrounds a multiple contact connector that has a removable body or insert. The frame supports the insert and permits mounting the connector to a panel.

frame check sequence *See* FCS.

frame control *See* FC.

frame grabber Hardware that takes the analog signal from a TV and digitizes the image into RAM. A single video field or frame can be captured by a frame grabber.

frame grounding circuit A conductor that will be electrically bonded to the machine frame and/or to any conducting parts that are normally exposed to operating personnel. This circuit may further be connected to external grounds as may be required by applicable codes.

frame maintenance mode A mode of operation in TDM (time-division multiplexing) frame synchronization in which the frame alignment signal, after detection, is continuously monitored to ensure that frame alignment is maintained.

frame reacquisition time The time that elapses between a loss of frame synchronization and the recovery of the frame alignment signal.

frame relay A Data Link Layer protocol that defines how variable data length frames can be assembled using fastpacket technology.

frame search *See* FRAME ACQUISITION MODE.

frame status *See* FS, 2.

Framework A DOS-based integrated software package with word processing, spreadsheet, graphics, and database functions. It also allows you to run other DOS programs without leaving Framework. This function is useful if there are functions external to Framework that are used frequently, such as project management or communications.

Current activities are all stored within Framework's outlines. Then, as you develop your ideas into word processed documents, spreadsheets, or graphs, the outline expands and tracks everything that is relevant. The outline can also perform like an idea processor. You create a frame for elements in your outline. A frame is a self-contained display of information on the screen that you can freeze and use either to develop the idea further or to save while you work on another function. A frame can be resized or relocated anywhere on the screen. There is no limit to the number of frames that can be active in the system simultaneously.

Included with Framework is FRED, a structured programming language for initiating the program's functions through commands. Advanced Framework users can use FRED to develop customized turnkey applications.

free buffer enquiry An ARCnet packet type used by a node to ensure that there is buffer space available on the receiving node before sending the data packet. It reduces the possibility of a deaf controller as in Ethernet.

Freelance Graphics A program with presentation management, charting, and drawing/editing tools for creating professional-looking documents, color 35mm slides, and color or black-and-white overheads.

freenet A community-based bulletin board system with e-mail, information services, interactive communications, and conferencing. Freenets are funded and operated by individuals and volunteers, somewhat like public television. They are part of the National Public Telecomputing Network (NPTN), an organization based in Cleveland, Ohio, devoted to making computer telecommunication and networking services as freely available as public libraries.

free oscillations Oscillating currents and voltages that continue to flow in a circuit after the voltage has been removed. This is due to the interchange of electromagnetic and electrostatic energy and is a function of the time constant of the circuit.

freeware Software that is distributed by its author without charge.

FREEWAY PAYROLL A payroll management system built expressly for the European businessplace. The program can accommodate weekly, fortnightly, four-weekly and monthly pay frequencies. The programs provide payment lists, check printing, internal pension schemes with fixed sum or percentage contributions, additional voluntary contributions, and up to 99 departments each with a coin analysis and cost of payroll total. The system accommodates statutory sick pay, and password protection. The user may change tax rates and bandwidths, as well as earnings brackets.

freeze mode An operational mode whereby the computer is stopped with all values held as they were when the interrupt occurred.

frequency The number of occurrences of a periodic phenomenon within a specified period of time, usually one second. The *clock frequency* refers to the master frequency of the periodic pulses used to schedule the operation of a computer.

frequency accuracy The degree of conformity to a specified value of frequency.

frequency deviation *See* DEPARTURE FREQUENCY.

frequency distortion A type of distortion in which certain frequencies are lost or discriminated against.

frequency diversity A method of radio transmission used to minimize the effects of fading, where the same information signal is transmitted and received simultaneously on two or more independent carrier frequencies.

frequency divider **1.** A circuit that reduces the frequency of an oscillator. **2.** A counter with a gating structure that provides an output pulse after receiving a specified number of input pulses.

frequency-division multiplexer A device that divides the available transmission frequency range into narrower bands, each of which is used for a separate channel. *Also see* FDM.

frequency modulation *See* FM.

frequency response analysis A method of analyzing systems based on introducing cyclic inputs and measuring the resulting output at various frequencies.

frequency response characteristic The amplitude and phase relation between the inputs and the resulting sinusoidal outputs.

frequency selective fading Fading in which not all frequency components of the received radio signal vary simultaneously.

frequency shift keying *See* FSK.

Fresnel zone A cigar-shaped shell of circular cross-section surrounding the direct path between a transmitter and a receiver. For the first Fresnel zone, the distance from the transmitter to any point on this shell and on to the receiver is one half-wavelength longer than the direct path. For the second Fresnel zone, it is two half-wavelengths, and for the third it is three half-wavelengths.

frictional error As applied to telemetering pickups, the difference in values measured in percent of full scale before and after tapping, with the measurand constant. Friction causing this type of error is known as *coulomb* or *dry friction*.

FRINGE A language for information file processing that provides report generation.

fringing In a color display, the effect caused by incorrect superimposition of the red, green, and blue images. Incorrect colors appear at the edges of objects in the image. Also called *color fringing*.

FROM Acronym for *fusable read-only memory*, a ROM that is programmed by deliberately blowing fusible links. Fusing is done by the customer or at the factory; FROMs cannot be changed after fusing to allow errors to be corrected. FROMs require little tooling to generate a pattern, but their cost per bit is high compared to conventional ROMs; this tends to make them more suitable for low-volume, low-capacity applications.

front-end A program or hardware with which a user interacts. The front-end usually sends off requests to the back-end for data.

front-end processor *See* FEP.

Front Office A program for prospecting, sales management, sales order processing, job costing, and profit analysis. It is designed for a direct sales business but can be adapted for other types of business.

FS **1.** Abbreviation for *file separator*, an information separator used to identify the boundary between adjacent files. **2.** Abbreviation for *frame status*, a token ring field that indicates if the address on a packet has been recognized by a station and if the data has been copied.

FSK Abbreviation for *frequency-shift keying*, a form of signal transmission in which the 1 and the 0 are represented by two distinct frequencies (tones). Frequency is made to vary at significant times by smooth, as well as abrupt, transitions. Typically, a 1-bit is represented as one frequency, and a 0-bit as another frequency. Also called *frequency shift signaling*.

FSM Abbreviation for *frequency-shift modulation*.

FSR Abbreviation for *feedback shift register*.

FT1 Abbreviation for *fractional T-1 service*, the division of T-1 bandwidths into fractional units such as one-eighth (192K), one-fourth (384K), or one-half (768K), which are sold to customers at a much lower rate than a full T-1 service.

FTM77/386 A compiler that executes 100,000 lines of Fortran in five minutes on a 386/33. It conforms to the ANSI Fortran77 standard and offers additional extensions (for VAX). It includes a built-in profiler, full-screen debugger, a make utility, and a library with over 230 routines for windowing and graphics.

FTP Abbreviation for *File Transfer Protocol*, a network protocol for moving files from one host to another.

full adder A circuit or device that performs complete addition with carry operations, shown in the following figure. Many adders can be cascaded to increase word-length capability.

full card An expansion card that takes up all the allotted space in the expansion slot. *Contrast with* HALF CARD.

full-character printer *See* LETTER-QUALITY PRINTER.

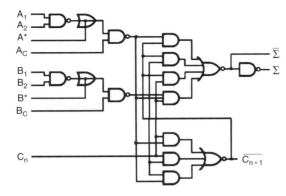

Full adder

full-duplex See FDX.
full-page display A large-screen CRT that can display one 8½ × 11 vertical page at full size. A full-page display system is useful for WYSIWYG desktop publishing, word processors, or CAD systems, since you really can see what you are going to get with a vertical page of more than 60 lines.
full-proportional servo A system with complete proportionality between output and input.
full-range floating zero A characteristic of numerical machine-tool control permitting the zero point on an axis to be shifted readily over a specified range. The control retains information on the location of the permanent zero.
full-read pulse As used in coincident current selection, the result of partial drive pulses that are applied at the same time.
full shift The capability of having more than just a single-place shift instruction. Full-shift includes single or multiple-place, left or right, or logical or circular shift instructions.
full-travel keyboard Keyboards that provide tactile feedback, desirable when the amount of programming or operator interfacing is great.
full-wave power supply A power supply using two diodes that draw current during both the positive and negative half-cycles of the input ac voltage.
full-write pulse The result of partial-write pulses that are applied at the same time in coincident-current selection.
fully connected mesh A network topology in which every node has a direct connection to every other node.
FUNCky An enhancement library for Clipper and C compilers including Microsoft, Turbo C, Turbo C++, Borland C, Watcom, and Zortech. The independent library is a core library to which surface libraries are added. It has over 1,000 functions.
function The purpose of an entity or its action, such as a machine action for carriage return or line feed.

functional address In IBM network adapters, a group address where each ON bit represents a function performed by the station.
functional diagram A diagram that represents the functional relationships of a circuit, device, or system in a logical sequence.
functional interleaving The technique of having input/output operations and computing operations proceed independently of one another, but share the memory.
functional partitioning A method of microprocessor partitioning directed toward user microprogramming. Microprogram storage is separate from the CPU and also from macroprogram storage. It is usually implemented in ROM, PROM, or RAM. Microinstruction address generation and internal register storage (along with all arithmetic processing) are also separated to allow a very flexible configuration.
function code In NetWare, a part of File Services that indicates the current lock mode or the mode to be set with Get Lock Mode and Set Lock Mode.
function digit A coded instruction used for setting a branch order for linking subroutines into the main program.
function element The smallest building block in a computer system that can be represented by logical operators using symbolic logic. Typical function elements include AND, NAND, OR, and NOR gates.
function generator A circuit or device capable of generating sine, square, and triangular waveforms. Some analog function generators provide arbitrary output waveforms that can be changed at the discretion of the operator; others may follow a curve drawn on a surface to generate the waveform function automatically.
function key A key on a keyboard that sends out a unique string of characters representing a code (to the computer), a set of data, or a command to activate a peripheral. A function key might cause a carriage return, query the system, or have it perform a specific operation. Specialized function keys are used in airline consoles, badge readers, stock quotation systems, and other applications.
function library A set of subroutines used to perform common mathematical functions using floating-point arithmetic. A function library might include square roots, exponentiation, logarithms, and trigonometric functions.
function multiplier A device for changing the values of the product of two varying functions.
function table 1. The arrangement of two or more sets of data such that an entry in one set selects one or more entries in the remaining sets, providing a tabulation of the values of a function for a set of values of the variable. 2. A hardware device that decodes multiple inputs into a single output, or encodes a single input into multiple outputs.

fuse A protective device that melts and breaks a circuit when current exceeds rated capacity.

fused connection A circuit using components interconnected by a fusion or hot metal flow technique.

fuser roller A roller in a laser printer that bonds toner to the page.

fusible link A type of PROM integrated circuit in which bit patterns are formed by being fused open by a destructive current or being left intact.

fusible link devices Refers to ROMs that are programmed by fusible links, as shown in the figure. Fusible link devices are completely nonvolatile, and once they are programmed they cannot be erased. Continued improvements in fuse technology have resulted in the following types of fuse material: nichrome, platinum silicide, polycrystalline silicon, and titanium tungsten. The fuse material is deposited as a thin film link to the column lines of the PROM. The memory cell is constructed as a transistor switch. The fuses are blown during programming by saturating the transistor through the selection of the row and column by the decoding circuit. When the cell's transistor base is high and the column line near ground, a large current is switched through the transistor and through the fuse in the emitter leg. The emitter fuse link is open circuited by the current, resulting in the programming of the bit location.

A historical problem encountered in the use of metal link PROMs has been the regrowth of opened fused links over a period of time. In the regrowth process, cells go from a programmed state back to the unprogrammed (closed) state.

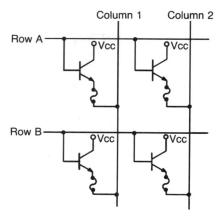

Fusible link bipolar PROM

Manufacturers, however, have refined the process of programming metal link devices to achieve improved yields as well as reliability.

fusible read-only memory *See* FROM.

fuzzy logic A concept in artificial intelligence that deals with the use of imprecise measurements as expressed by everyday terms such as *very*, *mostly*, and *somewhat*, enabling the computer to make human-like decisions about real-life situations without being confined to a strict rule of thumb. For example, being able to make a medical diagnosis without depending upon exact norms for body temperature and heart rate involves fuzzy logic.

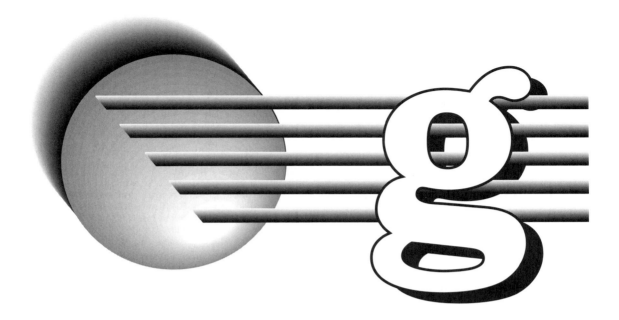

G Abbreviation meaning one billion. *Also see* GIGABYTE.

GA Abbreviation for *go ahead (cue)*.

gain The ratio of signal-level increase between the output and the input of a circuit or device.

galley proof In desktop publishing, a preliminary printout for checking purposes.

gallium arsenide A crystalline material, abbreviated *GaAs*, used in making high-grade semiconductors. It is superior to silicon, allowing electrons to flow six times as fast as silicon does, and thus has applications in optoelectronics. It is also harder to refine than silicon, and thus is more expensive.

galvanometer An instrument used to measure electric current by measuring the mechanical motion produced by the electromagnetic or electrodynamic forces generated by the current.

game theory A mathematical process of selecting an optimum strategy in the face of an opponent who has a strategy of his or her own.

gamma In video systems, refers to the grayscale reproduction or amplitude characteristic of the system. It is a measure of how much a graph of display-brightness versus scene-brightness varies from a straight line. Picture tubes have gammas of more than one or so; cameras use gammas of less than one, which allows the overall brightness-in/brightness-out characteristic to be linear (a straight line). Most CRT gammas do not match those in the NTSC standard, creating *nonlinear gamma*.

gamma correction The process of correcting the amplitude transfer characteristics of a video system so that equal steps of brightness or intensity at the input are reproduced with equal steps of intensity at the display.

gamma ferric oxide An oxide used to coat magnetic tapes for recording.

gamma release The final testing version of a software or other product before general and public release.

Gantt chart A method of displaying information commonly used in industry for the presentation of project status and resource utilization. Gantt charts are used as a graphic means of displaying schedules.

Gantt package A group of project management aids that produce presentation-quality Gantt charts from a list of dates and times on file. These programs have four primary applications:

- Producing Gantt chart transparencies for meeting displays
- Directly driving a video projector from a personal computer for meeting displays
- Creating Gantt charts to be inserted into the text files of word processors
- Directly viewing project status

gap A space or interval that appears between items of data. A *magnetic gap* refers to the airspace in the magnetic circuit. A *head gap* refers to the separation between the pole pieces of a magnetic recording head. A *data gap* may appear as an interval of space or time indicating the end of a word, record, or file on tape, or it may be the complete absence of information for a length of time or space on the recording medium.

gap digit A special character used to mark the beginning and end of gaps in some variable-word-length machines.

gap length The dimension of the gap of a reading and recording head measured from one pole face to the other. In longitudinal recording, the gap length is defined as the dimension of the gap in the direction of tape travel.

gapless Descriptive of a magnetic tape on which raw data is recorded in a continuous manner. The data is recorded onto the tape without word gaps, but it may still contain signs and marks in the gapless form.

gapped Refers to a magnetic tape on which blocked data is recorded. Gapped tape contains all of the flag bits required; the format can be read directly into a computer.

garbage Slang for unwanted and meaningless information in a computer system.

gas discharge A type of display that uses the glow produced by ionized neon gas to illuminate segments of alphanumeric display characters. Gas-discharge displays can be viewed in bright sunlight and have lifetimes in excess of 200,000 hours. Their main disadvantage is the high voltage required to operate them and the interfacing circuitry required for computer applications.

gas plasma Refers to a type of laptop screen having orange letters on a black screen. *Also see* PLASMA.

gate A circuit or device having one output and one or more inputs, with the output state completely determined by the previous and present states of the inputs. A gate can also be a trigger used to allow the passage of other signals through a circuit. Logical gates can take many forms, some of which are shown in the following table.

Gate type	Operation
Conditional Implication	A OR NOT B. (output is false only if A is false and B is true)
EXCEPT	A EXCEPT B. (output is true only if A is true and B is false)
Exclusion	A AND NOT B. (output is true only if A is true and B is false)
IF-THEN	A OR NOT B
IF-THEN-NOT	A OR NOT B
Implication	A OR NOT B
Inclusion	A OR NOT B
Inclusive-OR	OR
Majority	Implements the majority logic operator
Negation	Reverses the signal or state into as alternate or opposite
NOT-IF-THEN	AND AND NOT B
AND	Output true if all inputs are true
OR	Output true if one or more inputs are true
OR-NOT	A OR NOT B
NAND	Negative AND
NOR	Negative OR
Coincidence	Any gate that depends on the input history
Sheffer stroke	NAND

Logical gates

Gates can be implemented in software, individual hardware devices, or large gate arrays using integrated circuits.

gate, AND *See* AND CIRCUIT.

gate, B OR NOT A A binary (two-input) logic coincidence circuit for completing the logic operation of B OR NOT A, the reverse of A OR NOT B. The result is false only when A is true and B is false. Also called *implication*, *inclusion*, *IF-THEN* or *IF-THEN-NOT* gate.

Gate Capture Playback A tool used for testing software. You can use it to record and playback keystrokes, mouse events, and screen information to editable ASCII files. It allows the dynamic comparison of graphics and text screens during playback. Information on text screens can be masked, which causes the program to ignore those fields during comparison. You can use it to find bugs with automatically generated status reports. It has an adjustable playback speed and includes a programming language for writing and enhancing text scripts.

gate circuit An electronic circuit with one or more inputs and one output, with the property that a pulse appears on the output line, if and only if, some specified combination of pulses occurs on the input lines. Gate circuits provide much of the logical operations in a computer.

gate, EXCEPT *See* EXCEPT GATE.

gate, exclusion *See* EXCLUSION GATE.

gate, IF-THEN *See* IF-THEN GATE.

gate, IF-THEN-NOT *See* GATE, B OR NOT A.

gate, ignore *See* IGNORE GATE.

gate, implication *See* IF-THEN GATE.

gate, inclusion *See* IF-THEN GATE.

gate, majority A circuit designed to implement the majority logic operator.

gate, NAND *See* NAND GATE.

gate, negation A device with the capability of reversing a signal, condition, state, or event into its alternate or opposite.

gate, negative AND *See* NAND GATE.

gate, OR *See* OR GATE.

gate, Shaffer stroke *See* NAND GATE.

gate, time A circuit that gives an output only during certain time intervals.

gateway A special node that interfaces two or more dissimilar networks, providing protocol translation between the networks. Also used to describe the hardware and software used to provide this node.

gating The selection of a part of a waveform due to its time interval or amplitude, or the operation of a gating circuit when a signal is allowed to pass during a specific interval.

gating circuit Any circuit that operates in a selective manner, allowing conduction only under specified conditions.

gating pulse A pulse that permits the operation of a gating circuit.

Gaussian Refers to a distribution that is encountered when a large number of samples is collected. The Gaussian distribution is characterized by equal probabilities of values at equal positive and negative deviations from the mean. Also called *normal distribution*.

Gaussian noise Noise in which the particular voltage distribution is specified in terms of probabilities related to a normal curve. Gaussian noise occurs when unwanted signals are distributed in a Gaussian or normal manner.

Gaussian response A response for a transient impulse, which, if differentiated, matches the Gaussian distribution or normal curve. Some amplifiers are designed to furnish a response that can be differentiated with respect to time to match a Gaussian distribution curve.

Gauss meter A device that measures the strength of a magnetic field.

Ga-YIG Abbreviation for *gallium-substituted yttrium iron garnet*, a material useful in some specialized electronic applications. For example, small polished YIG and Ga-YIG spheres act as resonators at microwave frequencies.

GB *See* GIGABYTE.

G-code A command used in manufacturing process control that changes the mode of operation, as for example, from positioning to contouring.

GCR Abbreviation for *group code recording*, a block-oriented algebraic error-correction code that enables recovery from burst errors. It is used, for example, in the 6250 bpi half-inch nine-track magnetic tape on which computer data commonly is premastered for CD-ROM.

GD Abbreviation for *gate driver*.

GE information services A commercial network implemented to make available computing services. The network encompasses over 300 cities in North America, Japan, Australia, and Europe, making it international in scope. The communications network allows a user to make a local phone call that will then connect to the main computing facilities in Cleveland, Ohio, providing services ranging from light computation to remote batch processing. The network has the capability of connecting customer in-house computers to GE network service computers for the purpose of exchanging files. The GE network is a centralized hierarchal network. Topologically, all communications paths lead to the central facility.

GEM Artline A program for creating illustrations and tracing scanned images. Drawings and text can be modified and enhanced to provide a wide range of special effects. You can copy or scale drawings, merge them with other elements, or rotate them. Eight typestyles and a clip-art library are included. It is compatible with Ventura, PageMaker, and GEM Desktop Publisher.

GEM Desktop Publisher Page-composition package for producing a wide variety of professional-quality publications. The package includes automatic hyphenation, built-in graphics for line art, document reformatting across a single paragraph or multiple pages, nine standard typefaces, kerning, and tracking.

gender changer A cable-matching set used to mate connectors, as shown in the figure.

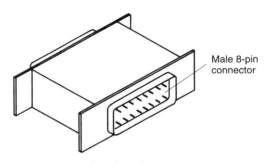

Gender changer

General Instruments 1600 A 16-bit NMOS single-chip microprocessor that uses ion implementation. Ion implanting produces a device with a cycle time of 400 nanoseconds and the capability to add two 16-bit numbers in 3.2 microseconds.

The architecture of the 1600 is shown in the figure. The chip is organized around a 16-bit bidirectional internal bus. Connected to the bus is the instruction register, the ALU, the input/output buffers, and eight 16-bit general-purpose registers.

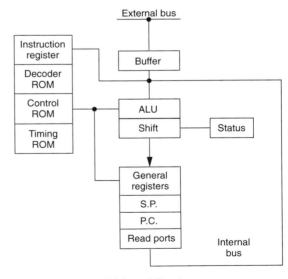

1600 architecture

General Instruments 1600 assembler/simulator Assembler/simulator routines for the 1600 are available on larger machines. These will accept assembly language statements to produce relocatable, linking object code. The microprocessor environment, which includes all input and output operations, can be simulated on the host machine to allow debugging and testing before the system is committed to hardware.

generalized routine A routine used to solve a general class of problem. The generalized routine is used to solve specific problems by inserting the appropriate values into the program.

general numerical control language processor A computer program developed to serve as a translating system for a parts programmer to develop a mathematical representation of a geometric form with the use of symbolic notation.

general-purpose computer A stored-program computer designed to solve a wide variety of problems and to be adapted to a large class of applications.

general-purpose data concentrator A low-cost statistical multiplexer designed to allow two, four, or eight terminals to share a single communication path. Originally designed for use with DEC computers, these data concentrators are also suited to many other asynchronous XON/XOFF computer applications. They require no changes to existing hardware or software, and they provide each terminal with an apparent direct connection to its host computer, as shown in the diagram.

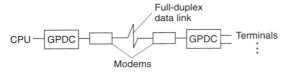

General-purpose data concentrator

general-purpose register file *See* GPR.
general-purpose system simulation *See* GPSS.
general register A register used for arithmetic operations and to compute and modify addresses. General registers perform such operations as addition, subtraction, multiplication, and division. They are used in place of special registers such as accumulators in many microcomputer systems.

A typical CPU might contain eight 16-bit general registers serving as accumulators, index registers, autoincrement registers, autodecrement registers, or stack pointers. Arithmetic operations are performed from one general register to another, one memory location to another, or between memory locations and registers. A general register unit may also serve as "scratchpad memory" for a microprogram and provide a skeletal interrupt system to allow microprogram emulation.

generate To create or produce; especially, to formulate a program by selecting subsets from a set of skeletal coding under the control of specific parameters. Also, to produce assembly-language statements from model statements of macro definitions when called for by a macroinstruction.

generated address The number or symbol that is generated by instructions and becomes part of the address.

generating routine A compiling routine that performs a generating function.

generator 1. A program or compiling routine that allows the computer to write other programs automatically. **2.** An electronic device that produces a tone, pulse, or other signal.

generator polynomial In cyclic redundancy check character (CRC) schemes, the polynomial that is divided into the message polynomial to produce the quotient and remainder. *Also see* CRC.

generator, voltage Refers to the concept of a total signal source, often with no internal impedance.

generic mode A mode that allows asynchronous "no frills" terminals and data-entry devices to communicate to the host. The full-screen formatting features of the terminal are not supported.

Genesis A software package for process modeling; control system design and checkout; operator training; real-time data acquisition or control; and plant or process information management.

GEnie The General Electric Network for Information Exchange (GEnie), like Delphi, is a second-tier online service. Despite fairly aggressive marketing, it never achieved the stature of PRODIGY, AMERICA ONLINE, and COMPUSERVE. As of this writing (1995), it appears that GEnie was reassessing its long-term strategy. GEnic is primarily geared to consumers, although it offers forums and other services that would interest more professional and business users.

genlocking The process of synchronization to another video signal. It is required in computer-capture of video to synchronize the digitizing process with the scanning parameters of the video signal.

GEOGRAF A graphics library of subroutines callable from within a program. You can create real-time graphics using 13 fonts and variable line types. It supports Microsoft QuickBasic 4.5, Microsoft C, Microsoft Quick C, Borland Turbo C, and Borland C++.

germanium A semiconductor material with properties similar to silicon. Germanium is used primarily for the manufacturer of special-purpose diodes and transistors where sensitivity is a criterion, as in communications detectors and passive front-ends.

germanium diode A type of rectifier or detector made from a germanium crystal.

get To locate, fetch, and transfer an item from storage, as the activity required to develop or make a record from an input file available, or to obtain or extract a coded value from a field. The GET command might be used to obtain a numerical value from a series of decimal digits.

Getit An events library and system enhancer for Clipper. It has asynchronous event-trapping functions to let you call user-defined procedures based on time interval, keyboard inactivity, COM port activity, and mouse clicks. Events can be nested, giving your program modularity and event scoping.

GFA BASIC A graphical user interface for DOS applications. It includes 500 systems commands and functions and several hundred commands and functions for developing GUIs.

GFX Graphics A graphics routines library that provides drawing functions, moveable viewports, C source code, setting of graphics modes, autoscaling, and color control.

GFX Screen Dump A program that dumps the graphics screen to a printer. It supports dot matrix, laser, and color printers. It stretches the output to adjust for differences between video and printer resolutions.

G-gradient The radial difference in g-force from inner to outer radius points of a test article.

gibberish A term used for totals or accumulations of records or data. The totals have no meaning or particular sense on their own, but are useful for control purposes. An example would be the cumulative account number for a customer's accounts-receivable total.

GID Abbreviation for *group identification*.

gigabyte Approximately one billion bytes of data. Abbreviated *GB* or *G*.

gigacycle One kilomegacycle, or one billion cycles.

gigahertz A term for 10^9 cycles per second, used to replace the more cumbersome *kilomegacycle*.

gigawatt One thousand megawatts (10^9 watts), abbreviated *gw*.

GIGO Acronym for *garbage-in, garbage-out*, a term used to describe the reason for meaningless computer output data: improper input.

GIRLS Acronym for *generalized information retrieval and listing system*.

GKS An ANSI standard that specifies a complete computer-graphics generation and storage system. Oriented toward object-oriented graphics, it provides some support for bitmaps as well. The specification (ANSI X3.124-1985) works on the program-interface level rather than on an application or user level.

glare guard A CRT screen that can block 90% of CRT glare and improves screen contrast, bringing text into sharper focus for reading comfort. A chemical coating is used to trap light before it strikes the screen and causes glare.

glitch A short-term voltage transient that usually occurs too fast for detection, but which causes improper machine operation because it is interpreted as a legitimate signal.

global That part of an assembler program that contains the body of any macro definition called from a source module and the open-code portion of the source module.

global change The ability of an editing system to change a word or other text element everywhere it appears in a document, with one instruction. Also called *global search* and *repetitive correction*.

Globalink Translation System A PC-based foreign-language translation program. It gives true morphological translations on whole files or blocks of text with up to 90% accuracy. You can modify or add to the general dictionary of over 60,000 terms. The product handles idiomatic expressions and multiple translations of a word based on parts of speech. Versions are available for Spanish-to-English, English-to-Spanish, German-to-English, English-to-German, French-to-English, and English-to-French translation.

global filespec A file specification containing wildcard characters (* and ?, in DOS) in the filename and/or extension to cause more than one file to be selected for an operation. *Also see* WILDCARD.

global replace Refers to the replacing of one text string with another throughout a document.

global resource Hardware, software, server, or resource generally available to all processes and users on a network.

global variable Any variable with a name that is accessible by the main program and all its subroutines.

global variable symbol A variable symbol used in assembler programming to communicate values between macro definitions and open-code sections.

GLOCOM The acronym for *global communications system*.

glossary In some word processors, a place where you store text you intend to use repeatedly. Each piece of stored text is a glossary entry and is assigned a unique name. You can save a glossary permanently in a glossary file on disk.

GLUDRAW A graphics generation software package with online help and sample drawings. It is a simple, easy-to-use program.

GM Abbreviation for *mutual conductance*.

GND Abbreviation for *ground*.

Go-Back-N ARQ A technique that utilizes the data unit sequence numbers provided by the logical link control layer. The receiving node indicates a specific number of data units that need to be retransmitted.

Go-Back-N Continuous An error-checking method in which a station receives several frames before replying with NAK or an ACK.

gold A metallic element of very high density used as a conductor in integrated circuits.

gold doping A process sometimes used in the manufacture of integrated circuits in which gold is diffused into the semiconductor material, resulting in higher operating speeds.

Goldstein, Adele Programmer for the ENIAC.

gone west A slang term used when a computer has entered an endless loop.

goof sheet A form on which personnel can write down suggestions to one another for improving service and avoiding problems.

Googol Math An educational program with graphics for math concept presentation. The user can drill and test math skills in addition, subtraction, multiplication, or division.

Gopher A distributed information service that makes available hierarchical collections of information across the Internet. Gopher uses a simple protocol that allows a single Gopher client to access information from any accessible Gopher server, providing the user with a single "Gopher space" of information.

GOSIP Acronym for *Government Open Systems Interconnection Profile*, which defines specifications for the purchase of network systems in government agencies. All federal agencies had to start using GOSIP standard products as of August 15, 1990. This meant updating the TCP/IP protocol, which had been the previous government standard.

go to A multilanguage statement that directs the computer to leave the current sequence of instructions and begin operating at another point in the program. For example, a typical Fortran go-to instruction might be

GO TO 5;

(The next statement to be executed is number 5). In some languages such as BASIC, the space between the words is omitted, so the statement takes the form *GOTO*.

GPC Abbreviation for *general-purpose computer*.

Gpf Abbreviation for *GUI Programming Facility*, a second-generation WYSIWYG Presentation Manager C code generator. It has its own integrated window/dialog box editor which provides support for GUI objects, user buttons, icons, bitmaps, and font/color presentations. You can link help messages at link or control level or fill list boxes from SQL databases.

GPIB/IEEE 400 interface boards These boards are designed to plug directly into an I/O expansion slot inside a PC or compatible. A standard IEEE-488 connector extends out the rear of the PC and connects to any standard IEEE-488/GPIB cable. The software driver/interpreter for the 488 board handles initialization and protocol conversions required for access to all functions covered in the IEEE-488 specification. The software may be designed as a DOS-resident driver, which simplifies interfacing the routine to higher-level languages.

GPSS Abbreviation for *General-Purpose Systems Simulation*, a problem-oriented language used to develop simulation systems.

GPR Abbreviation for *general-purpose register* file, a file usually made up of 2 to 16 registers for holding temporary memory data and addresses. GPRs are also used for calculating memory addresses and combining and moving memory data.

Grabber A memory-resident program that can save a screen image to a file. You can use the captured images to create a slideshow or illustrate documents.

graded-index fiber An optical fiber that has a refractive index that gets progressively higher toward the center, causing light rays to be continually refocused inward.

GRAFLIB A graphics library that supports CGA, EGA, VGA, and Hercules graphics cards, and Epson, HP LaserJet, and PostScript-compatible printers. It contains routines to draw arcs, circles, eclipses, and polygons, as well as linear, log, polar, smith, bar, and pie charts. It is available for C, Fortran, BASIC and Pascal.

GrafPRINT for Graphoria 2.0 A software package that supplements the Lahey Graphoria Graphics package by providing high-resolution output on most dot matrix, laser, and inkjet printers. This printer utility allows for complete control of the printer. GrafPRINT includes GrafFONTS, which provides seven vector font sets with functions for scaling, spacing, italicizing, mirroring, orientation, justification, changing text color, and bolding.

Grammatik A writing analyst program designed to help improve the user's grammar and usage. It uses writing guides like Strunk & White's *Elements of Style* and Gunning's *The Technique of Clear Writing*. It is included in recent versions of WordPerfect.

grandfather cycle A term used to indicate the time for magnetic records to be retained before they are rewritten, to allow records to be reconstructed in the event of losses or errors.

grant rights mask In NetWare, a part of Dictionary Services that contains the rights to be granted to a directory's maximum rights mask.

granularity The density with which a viewing surface is divided into physical areas such as pixels in an image or grains of emulsion in film.

graphic 1. Any assembly of symbols or characters that is used to denote any concept, configuration, or idea nontextually. **2.** Any symbol produced by printing, drawing, handwriting, etc.

GraphiC A set of C-callable routines that can be used to create publication-quality scientific and engineering graphics. Output files can be converted to PIC, GEM, PostScript, TIFF, or HPGL formats. It includes routines for creating linear, log, semi-log, contour, polar, 2D and 3D bar, and error function plots. Smith, bar, and pie charts, 3D routines, mathematical functions, labeling, 22 fonts, and PostScript are supported.

graphical user interface *See* GUI.

graphic character A character represented using a graphic rather than a control character.

graphic display A nontextual display that reproduces data on a video screen, panel, or page.

graphic panel The master control panel used in automated control systems that displays all the relationships and functions of the control equipment using colored block diagrams.

graphic plotter A plotting machine used as a computer output device. Graphic plotters can provide high-quality graphics in several different colors for displaying complex patterns.

graphics card A peripheral device that allows a computer to process and display graphics. A monochrome graphics card allows only a single color display. A color graphics card enables a color display.

graphics editing software A program that allows the creating and editing of graphic faxes and scans.

graphics mode A display mode in which a word processor shows a document on the screen just as it will be printed, with correct fonts, graphics, enhancements, etc. Your computer must have a graphics adapter installed to use graphics mode.

graphics package An application program that allows a user to present data as graphs or charts and do original drawings.

Graphics Server A chart and graph development toolkit for windowing applications. It provides automatic graphing, 2D and 3D graphs and charts, 2D and 3D pie graphs, area, Gantt, scatter, polar, log-linear, lined X-Y, and statistic applications.

Graphics Workshop A software package for manipulating and adding special effects to graphics. It has low-level graphics primitives, pulldown and vertical menus, and input routines that operate in graphics mode.

GraphiC-Win A library of C-callable routines that can be used to create publication-quality scientific and engineering graphics in the Windows environment. The same features provided in the DOS version of GraphiC are used. In addition, Windows metafile and bitmap screen-capture output formats are provided. Microsoft and Borland compilers are supported.

Graphing Assistant A product for basic business graphics that allows you to organize your data into pie, bar, or line charts, display the charts on your monitor, and output the charts to a printer or plotter. The program is part of the IBM Assistant series.

Graphtime A business presentation graphics package that does line, column and pie charts. The charts can be printed or plotted, viewed individually, or set up to run as an unattended slideshow on the monitor. Online help information is available. Graphtime accepts data from dBASE and Lotus 1-2-3, or you can enter data directly. There is a font editor and macro editor, math functions including moving averages, and an undo function. A mouse is recommended.

Graphwriter A program designed for those who use graphics frequently and need extensive capabilities and a variety of formats. It provides bar, pie and scatter and other types of business-oriented graphics, text/word charts, organization charts, tables and Gantt charts. Graphwriter is similar to Tell-A-Graf, ISSCO'S presentation-quality graphics package for mainframes.

A menu-driven and fill-in-the-blanks program, Graphwriter starts with templates specific to the type of graph chosen. It allows you to change the size, color, font, and location of each chart element. Graphwriter repositions and resizes the other components so there is no overwriting or crowding. Its menu-driven input format helps you through the process of setting up the graph. You can preview what you have done on the screen before plotting. The program comes with specification forms to help you plan your chart, and it includes some examples.

The package tends to be clumsy to use when you are experimenting with different graph types. If you want to see your data as a bar graph instead of a scatter diagram, you have to reenter the data.

Gray code A code in which sequential numbers are represented by expressions that differ only in one place and in that place only by one unit. The Gray code is very useful in positional systems, since the maximum error between positions is never greater than the least significant bit. A comparison of the Gray code with natural binary is shown in the table on page 206. In the Gray code, as the number value changes, the transitions from one code to the next require only one bit change at a time. The bits that change are underlined. Gray-to-binary code conversion can be implemented as shown in the following figure. Also called *cyclic binary code*.

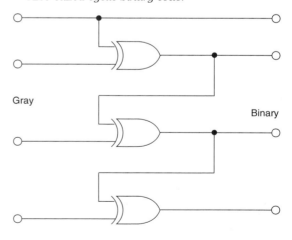

Gray-to-binary code conversion logic

Decimal	Cyclic Binary (Gray)	Binary
0	0000	0000
1	0001	0001
2	0011	0010
3	0010	0011
4	0110	0100
5	0111	0101
6	0101	0110
7	0100	0111
8	1100	1000
9	1101	1001
10	1111	1010
11	1110	1011
12	1010	1100
13	1011	1101
14	1001	1110
15	1000	1111

gray level Refers to one particular representation for a shade of gray in an image. Since image scanners can represent only a finite number of grays and there exists an infinite number of shades of gray, the scanner performs a one-to-one correlation between its internal set of gray-level increments and the actual gray intensity that it detects. The grayscale of a scanner is composed of a series of gray-level representations.

grayscale Refers to the number of shades of gray a device such as a scanner can represent. Typically, a scanner represents an image as an array of closely spaced dots. Each dot bears information pertaining to the gray level (the shade of gray) detected at the corresponding location in the scanned object. Often, the scanner's gray-level detection ability is cited in terms of the amount of bits of information used to code the gray level of each pixel. As the amount of information pertaining to the gray levels increases, the more closely the scanned image will represent a black-and-white reproduction of the original object. Typical grayscale representations used by scanners include 4-bits-per-pixel of information for 16 gray levels, 6-bits-per-pixel for 64 gray levels, and 8-bits-per-pixel for 256 shades of gray.

Greenleaf Comm++ A class library for interrupt-driven asynchronous communications. Classes are provided for serial ports, modem controls, file transfers, and check values. There are classes that support the hardware-dependent features derived from the base class. It supports up to 35 ports at baud rates to 115K baud in DOS, Hayes Smartmodems, Xmodem, Kermit, XON/XOFF, and VT52 and VT100 (subset) emulation. Support is included for DOS, Windows, and OS/2.

Greenleaf Financial MathLib++ A C++ class library supporting Zortech C++ and Borland Turbo C++ that includes math and logical operators. Decimal, decimal/array, date degree, radian, and other classes provide hundreds of member functions and operators to speed the development of commercial and financial programs.

grid **1.** As used in optical character recognition, two mutually orthogonal sets of parallel lines used for specifying or measuring character images. **2.** The lines that mark the unit of measurement horizontally (and sometimes vertically) across a bar or line chart.

grid ban The grid bias voltage required to produce anode current cutoff.

grid bias The dc negative voltage applied to control the grid.

grid bypass A capacitor that bypasses the signal from the grid.

grid leak A grid resistor through which dc grid current flows.

grid spaced contacts A type of electrical contact, usually spring types, pins arranged in parallel, or equally spaced rows and columns on a connector or the edges of printed circuit boards.

grommet Plastic or rubber edging used around cable and pigtail entrances to holes such as termination centers.

gross error In a measurement, an error may be expressed in units and a fraction (decimal) error; the gross error is that which is in the units but not in the fraction or decimal.

ground The point considered to be at zero potential voltage and to which all other potentials in the system are referred.

ground absorption The energy loss in radio frequency waves due to absorption.

ground plane The common ground electrical path for power and/or signals.

ground start A telephone signaling method where a station determines that a circuit is grounded at the other end.

groundstat monitor A unit that verifies static ground, shown in the following figure. An LED indicates proper ground.

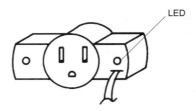

Ground static monitor

group **1.** In frequency-division multiplexing, a number of voice channels (generally 12) occupying a 48 kHz frequency band. **2.** On a network, to combine workstations to facilitate operations and improve support.

group address In a LAN, a locally administered address assigned to two or more adapters to allow the adapters to copy the same frame.

group code recording *See* GCR.

grouped record The combining of two or more records into single sections of information. Grouped records tend to decrease the time required for a storage medium's acceleration and deceleration and conserve storage space. Also known as *blocked record*.

group mark A mark that identifies the beginning or end of a set of data, such as words or blocks.

group SAP A single address assigned to a group of service access points (SAPs).

group separator An information separator, abbreviated *GS*, used to identify the boundary between groups of items.

GROUP 3 The most often-used standard for fax machines and modems, in which a connection of 9600 bps is made, and a page is transmitted in about one minute. Sometimes known as *V.29*.

groupware Application programs designed to increase productivity and cooperation among groups of coworkers.

grown diffused transistor A transistor made by combining diffusion and double doping techniques. Suitable n- and p-type impurities are added simultaneously while the crystal is being grown. The base region is formed by diffusion as the crystal grows.

grown junction The boundary between p- and n-type semiconductor materials, produced by varying the impurities during the growth of the crystal. These junctions have good rectifying properties.

grp Abbreviation for *group*.

GSS Graphics Development Toolkit A package that provides a portable and device-independent graphics programming environment for PCs. It has high-level graphics routines for application development. It supports DOS and OS/2, C, Fortran, Pascal, and BASIC.

guard band 1. The frequency band left vacant between two communications channels to prevent overlapping and mutual interference. **2.** The unused area that isolates components on a printed-circuit board.

guard bit A bit used to indicate the status of words or groups of words of memory. A guard bit can be used to indicate to hardware units or programs if the contents of a memory location can be changed by a program, or if a core or disk memory word is to be filed or protected.

guard digit The hexadecimal zero attached to each operand fraction in a single-word floating-point addition or subtraction operation.

guard ring An auxiliary electrode used to avoid distortion of the electric (or heat) field pattern in a working part of a system as a result of the edge effect, or to bypass leakage current to earth.

guard ring capacitor A capacitor consisting of circular parallel plates with a concentric ring maintained at the same potential as one of the plates to minimize the edge effect.

guard signal A signal that allows values to be read only when all values are not in a changing state. The guard signal is usually an extra output generated when all operations are completed.

GUI Pronounced "gooey," an acronym for *graphical user interface*, a user interface that uses bitmapped or vector graphics on the screen rather than character-based images. GUIs require more processing overhead than character-based interfaces; also, as screen resolution increases, more bytes are needed to present the information on the screen. However, GUIs are generally easier for new users to master than character-based interfaces.

gulp A term for a small group of bytes processed as a unit.

gun The group of electrodes constituting the electron beam emitter in a CRT.

gun current The total electronic current flowing to the anode, part of which forms the beam current.

Gunn effect The production of high field intensity domains in a semiconductor diode, usually by charges formed across a depletion layer, although other processes, such as charge accumulation, can produce similar effects. These domains are used in negative-resistance microwave semiconductor oscillators.

Gupta Technologies Maker of a database server that competes with Novell's NetWare SQL.

gutter The inner margins on facing page of a document. Often these margins must be wider than the outside margins to allow extra space for binding.

GVM Abbreviation for *generating voltmeter*, a voltmeter that uses an induced field, rotating vane, and a stator device.

GX Effects A program that allows you to use special effects without being restricted by an editor or slideshow program. It supports Hercules, CGA, EGA, VGA, and most extended VGA adaptors. There are fades, wipes, splits, and smooth scrolling routines along with a music definition language with 40 song examples.

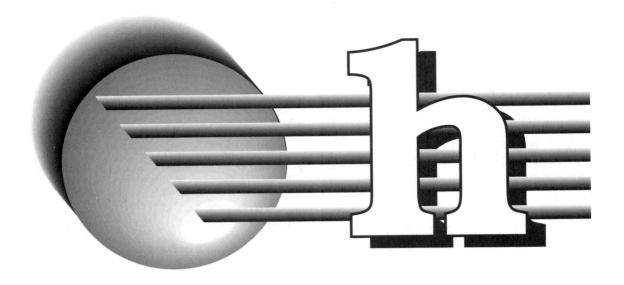

H 1. Abbreviation for *halt*. **2.** Abbreviation for *henry*, the unit of inductance in the International System of Units (SI) equal to the inductance present when a current change of one ampere per second produces one volt of potential in a closed circuit.

hacker Slang term for a computer enthusiast; more specifically, one who tries to gain access to another's networks and programs.

half-add An instruction that performs bit-by-bit half-adder operations. Half-add can be done using an exclusive-OR operation without carries.

half-adder A circuit that has two input and two output channels that operate according to the following table, where S = sum without carry, and C = carry. Two half-adders can be combined to perform binary addition.

Inputs		Outputs	
A	B	C	S
0	0	0	0
0	1	0	1
1	0	0	1
1	1	1	0

where S = sum without carry
C = carry

half-adjust 1. A type of numerical rounding in which the value of the least significant digit of a number determines whether or not a 1 will be added to the next higher significant digit, or in which the two least significant digits determine whether or not a 1 is to be added to the next higher significant digit. If the least significant digits represent less than half, nothing is added to the next higher significant digit; if the least significant digits represent half or more than half, a 1 is added to the next higher significant digit. **2.** To round by half of the maximum value of the number base of the counter.

half card An adapter board that only takes up half the space provided in a full-sized expansion slot.

half-card modem A modem that plugs directly into the card slot of a PC.

half cycle The time interval for the operating frequency to complete half, or 180 degrees, of its cycle.

half-duplex *See* HDX.

half-duplex channel A two-way channel used to transmit or receive at any one time.

half-duplex circuit A communications system, or portion of a system, with single loops to terminals for two-way, non-simultaneous operation.

half-duplex operation A communications mode in which transmission and reception take place, but not at the same time. Operating modes may be defined by the following:

- S/O—Send only
- R/O—Receive only
- S/R—Send or receive

Also called *half-duplex transmission*.

half-height Refers to how much space a disk drive takes up. A half-height drive takes up about half the space allotted for an externally accessible drive. A full-height drive occupies the entire space, about three inches.

half-shift register A type of flip-flop used in shift registers; it requires two half-shift registers to make one stage of a shift register. *Also see* FLIP-FLOP.

half sinusoid The complete positive or negative portion of a single cycle of a sine wave.

half splitting technique A circuit-tracing method in which tracing begins at a point where a fault is equally likely to exist ahead of or behind this point in the circuit path. The faulty half is found and then split in half again until the fault is isolated. The tracing from input to output can be time-consuming and costly. Half splitting is faster and can be used for automatic board testers.

halftime emitter A device that produces pulses halfway between two other pulses.

halftoning In printing, the capability to represent shades of gray with a dithered pattern of dots, creating halftone images.

half-word A continuous sequence of bits or characters that make half a computer word and are capable of being addressed as a unit.

Hall constant The constant of proportionality R in the relationship:

$$Eh = R \times J \times H$$

where Eh is the transverse electric field (Hall field), J is the current density, and H is the magnetic field strength. The sign of the majority carrier may be inferred from the sign of the Hall constant.

Hall effect The development of a voltage between the edges of a current-carrying metal strip when it is placed in a magnetic field perpendicular to the faces of the strip.

Hall mobility The mobility, or mean drift velocity per unit field, of current carriers in a semiconductor as calculated from the product of the Hall coefficient and the conductivity.

HALO Desktop Imager A desktop image-processing program that allows users to match each image to their printer, print test strips for a preview of work, and even create wall-sized posters. It provides input and display, file conversion, and image enhancement.

Halo Desktop Publishing Editor A desktop publishing program that can be used to merge text and graphics. It can handle newsletters, flyers, and other documents of ten pages or less. For longer documents, DPE can be used in conjunction with word-based desktop publishing programs such as Ventura Publisher. Features include WYSIWYG display, 20 typefaces, text rotations, and support for EMS memory boards. It supports most popular scanners and is compatible with Microsoft Windows, Ventura, and PageMaker.

HALO F/X A DOS-based grayscale image-editing software package. The windowed interface allows access of up to 10 images simultaneous. It supports all popular scanners, display devices, and printers. Functions include interactive, real-time editing of images, cut, paste, sharpen, rotate, warp, distort, posterize, and ditto.

HALO Professional An implementation of the popular HALO graphics library for professional developers. It is faster and supports SVGA, 8514/A, TIGA, TARGA, and XGA displays. It offers complete control over color mapping, portrait or landscape orientation, and print to file.

halt A condition occurring after the sequence of operations in a program stops. A halt may be due to a halt instruction, an unexpected halt, or an interrupt. The program would normally continue after the halt unless a drop-dead halt occurs, from which there is no recovery. *Also see* DROP-DEAD HALT.

halt indicator An indicator on the console or panel that shows whenever the processor is in the halt mode.

halt switch A switch on the console or panel that causes the processor to stop executing instructions.

Hamming code A general term for a data code that is capable of being corrected automatically. The Hamming code contains four information bits and three check bits.

Hamming distance The number of digit positions in which two corresponding digits of two binary words having the same length are different. Also called the *signal distance*.

handle A number used to refer to a file or directory that is being remotely accessed on a network.

handshaking A term that implies an initial exchange between two units or items in a system connection. Handshaking usually requires a matching at an interface, as when signals are exchanged between data set devices when a connection is made. A typical handshaking procedure takes place when a connection between a modem and an asynchronous communications interface adapter (ACIA) channel is established, as follows:

1. Local modem is enabled from the ACIA Request to Send signal.
2. Remote modem answers the call and sends back its carrier frequency.
3. Local modem detects this carrier and enables its Clear to Send output, which is detected by the computer.

handshaking protocol A sequence in a program that greets and assists the programmer in the use of procedures of the system. Handshaking in input/output control allows interfacing between peripherals with different response times. Control flags and jumps can be used to reduce decoding and software.

hands-on A descriptive term for actual operating experience of hardware and equipment, as opposed to theoretical or tutorial knowledge of that equipment.

hand-wired numerical control A numerical control system wherein the response to data input, data-handling sequence, and control functions is determined by the fixed and committed circuit interconnections of discrete decision elements and storage devices. Changes in the response, sequence, or functions are made by changing the interconnections.

hanging indent In word processing, outdenting a line in a paragraph (usually the first); that is, positioning it to the left of the remainder of the paragraph.

hangup A condition in which the central processor performs an illegal operation, keeps repeating the same routine, or stops execution. A hangup may be caused by the inability to escape from a loop, the improper coding of an instruction, or the use of an improper or nonexistent code. Also called simply a *hang*.

hangup prevention The design of a program such that no sequence of instructions can cause a halt or a nonterminating condition. Hangup prevention may include nonterminating indirect addressing and an infinitely nested execution of instructions.

hard break In word processing, refers to forcing a new page or a new line by pressing a key combination. *Contrast with* SOFT BREAK.

hardcard A hard disk expansion board only one inch thick that contains a complete hard disk subsystem. It can be installed in any expansion slot in a PC.

hardcopy A printed record of a machine output, such as printed reports and program listings.

hardcopy input Images from hardcopy (slides, film, photographs, drawings, or transparencies) scanned into the computer. *Also see* SCANNER.

hardcore section A portion or kernel of the processor tested by an external processor or other hardware and then used for the validation of another small portion of the system. The process is expanded until each successively larger level is validated.

In order to minimize the hardware in the hardcore portion, a portion of the diagnostic program is kept in ROM to avoid bootstrapping all the diagnostics from I/O devices. The hardcore section then includes only that hardware required to load the diagnostic.

hard disk A disk made of a rigid material, usually metal, with a magnetic coating, as shown in the following figures. These disks spin at 3600 rpm or more and are contained in a sheltered environment to prevent damage from dust particles. Hard disk capacity is usually measured in the millions of bytes (megabytes), and sometimes in the billions of bytes (gigabytes). The heads fly over the disk surface at a distance less than the diameter of a human hair. They may be vertically stacked in groups called *cylinders* to allow hundreds of megabytes of storage. Hard disk drives come in two types: removable disk drives (sometimes called *Winchester disks*) and fixed disk drives.

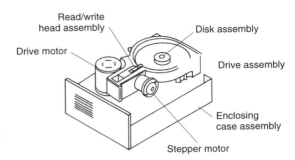

Typical hard disk drive

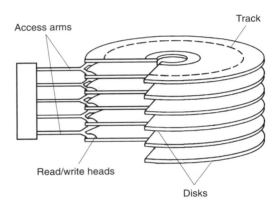

Sealed components of hard disk drive, side view

hard disk controller The expansion card that relays information from the computer to and from the hard disk.

hard disk driver motor Many drives use a stepper motor for moving the heads from track to track, as shown in the following figures. The stepper motor circuit is an open loop, which means there is not a type of signal indicating that the stepper motor has reached the track to which it was sent. Instead, a calculation is made by the processor to determine the amount of time that the stepper motor needs to position the read/write heads above the proper track.

hard disk interleave A system for minimizing the time to read consecutive sectors from a single track of the hard disk. In a 1-to-1 interleave, the sectors are numbered consecutively. In a 2-to-1 interleave, every other sector is numbered consecutively.

hard disk menu system A DOS shell that allows the user to create a menu of macros for loading and running software or performing common

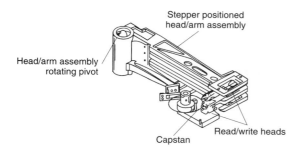

Radial arm of hard disk drive

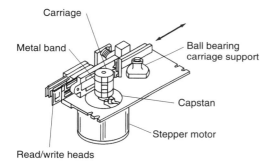

Hard drive components, top view

DOS functions. User-defined variables and parameters can be used to create complex command sequences. Passwords also can be set up to prevent unauthorized access to any (or all) menu selections or functions. Programs such as Direct Access and Norton Commander are examples of this class of software.

hard drop The malfunction of a RAM memory location. A hard drop causes an individual RAM bit location to freeze in either a one or zero mode; replacement of the defective RAM chip is required.

hard font A printer font permanently written on ROM. There are two types of hard fonts: *resident fonts*, which are embedded in the printer, and *cartridge fonts*, which are removable.

hard-limited integrator A type of integrator in which the inputs cease to be integrated when the output tends to exceed specified limits. Unlike the output from soft-limited integrators, output from hard-limited integrators does not exceed the limits.

hard limiting A circuit that restricts the excursion of a variable with a very small variation of the limited output.

hard return A code entered into the text by the user, usually by pressing the Enter key, that forces a word-processing program to move to the beginning of the next line.

hard-sectored Designates a floppy disk in which holes mark the boundaries of each sector. Space is not needed on the disk for records of those boundaries.

hardware The physical components of a computer system, including all electronic and electromechanical devices and connections.

hardware assembler An assembler that usually consists of PROMs mounted on simulation boards. A hardware assembler allows the prototype unit to assemble its own programs.

hardware check A check performed by built-in equipment. Also called a *built-in check* or an *automatic check*.

hardware interrupt Any interrupt that schedules input/output equipment. A hardware interrupt allows input/output operations to be performed simultaneously with processing.

hardware interrupt number A number that usually ranges from 0 to 15, specifying which hardware interrupt is to be installed in a network or other application.

hardware priority interrupt An interrupt that resolves priority when several events occur at the same time. Hardware priority interrupts can provide automatic vectoring and fast response to events. The routines are usually easy to write and take less memory than polling methods.

hardware selection Hardware considerations begin with the microprocessor system functions of data, addressing, timing, and control. The bus system depends on the type of microprocessor chosen, the application, and the need for flexibility and expandability. Smaller systems can take advantage of microprocessor family components, which use the bus for nothing more than the microprocessor's data, control, and address outputs. Larger systems can use the basic bus structure of the CPU chip, but to such systems users must add buffer elements or additional decoding logic to connect more functions to the system bus.

hardware standardization Standardization is critical in engineering, particularly in instrumentation and control. Without standards, there tends to be a greater flexibility, but also much duplicated effort. The lack of standards can be a serious problem. Most companies struggle to establish some kind of standards for computer hardware, either in each department or corporate-wide. Although there are many microcomputers available, most standardize on a particular IBM-compatible PC. This might not always provide the best functionality available, but it does diminish concerns about the proliferation of different brands and models.

hard-wired numerical control A numerical control system in which the response to data input, the data handling, and the control functions are determined by the fixed and committed circuit interconnections of discrete decision elements

212 hard-wired numerical control • harmonic oscillator sampling S/D converter

and storage devices. Changes in the response, sequence, or functions are made by changing these interconnections.

hard-wire logic Any system of logic elements that uses formed or wired connections. Hard-wire logic includes hand-wired diode-matrix boards and any logic board that cannot be easily reprogrammed.

harmonic A sinusoidal wave whose frequency is an integral multiple of the fundamental waveform. The *second harmonic* is twice the frequency of the fundamental, although logically it is the first actual harmonic (multiple) of that signal.

harmonic oscillator sampling S/D converter This type of synchro-to-digital converter is illustrated in the figure that follows. The resolver format input signals are first sent to phase-sensitive demodulators, with dc output levels

$$Vx = K \sin \theta$$
$$Vy = K \cos \theta$$

where K is a constant and θ is the shaft angle to be digitized. The dc levels are sampled at the proper time to set the initial conditions of the integrators in a harmonic oscillator converter. The rest of the circuit has two major sections:

- A two-integrator-and-inverter chain in a positive feedback loop. This loop, under the command of the control logic, will oscillate at a frequency determined by the integrator time constants.

- A clock-pulse-generator counter circuit that is on when the oscillator is on and off at the positive-going zero crossing of the voltage at the second integrator.

Initially, the loop is prevented from oscillating by the control logic, which also applies the sampled dc levels (Vx and Vy) as initial conditions to the two integrators. As the integrators stabilize at the initial conditions, the oscillation begins, and simultaneously, clock pulses are sent to the counter. When the positive-going zero crossing (point X) is reached, the counting stops. At this point, the total stored in the counter is the digitized value of θ, the shaft angle, provided that the clock frequency has the correct relationship to the integrator time constants.

At point X, the positive zero crossing that stops the counting process, the following relationship will hold:

$$\sin\left(\frac{t}{RC} - \frac{2\pi}{360°}\right) = 0$$

or

$$\frac{t}{RC} - \frac{2\pi\theta}{360°}$$

If the clock rate is proportional to some convenient number of pulses like 3600, these are produced in 2π RC seconds and the count at point X will be:

$$\frac{3600}{360\theta}$$

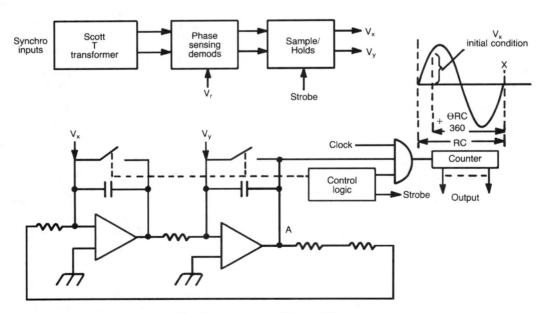

Sampling harmonic oscillator S/D converter

Then the total stored in the counter represents the angle θ to a resolution of 0.1° (1 part in 3600). Any desired resolution can be obtained within the stability and accuracy limits of the system.

hartley A unit of information content equivalent to 3.32 bits. The hartley is defined as the equal of one decadal position, or the designation of one of ten possible and equally likely states or values.

Hartley oscillator A type of oscillator characterized by a feedback element consisting of a split inductance. *Also see* OSCILLATOR.

hartley principle The principle that the gross information content is the number of bits or hartleys required to transmit a message in a noiseless system with a specified accuracy, without regard to redundancy.

Harvard architecture Refers to a computer in which the program memory and the data memory are separate. This separation of instruction storage and data storage gives the microcomputer designer flexibility in word-size selection. The major advantage of this architecture is that it permits an overlapping of the instruction and data accesses, which tends to increase performance for a given technology over single-memory von Neumann architecture.

Harvard Graphics A charting, drawing, and presentation management package. As you enter data, Harvard Graphics automatically sets options, such as text size and chart colors. It has advanced text-handling capabilities like word wrap, shrink text to fit, and truncate. It allows 160 chart types and has 32 preset color palettes.

Harvard Project Manager A package for developing project plan graphs to better understand relationships among tasks, times, and costs. Harvard Project Manager uses graphics and windows to input and display tasks and milestones. It makes project management concepts easier to grasp and visualize. The program's what-if capability helps evaluate contingencies by displaying and adjusting relationships. CPM (critical path method), PERT (program evaluation and review technique), and Gantt charts are supported for analyzing, planning and scheduling projects. The program produces both PERT and Gantt charts.

Although this program does time and cost calculations, it will not help you schedule or keep track of resources, nor will it automatically schedule tasks based on durations and dependencies; when creating a plan for the first time you must determine the schedule yourself. The program handles up to 200 activities in an individual project and can link up to 200 subprojects.

Harvard Total Project Manager A project management system for both the planning and control phases of a project. Although it is from the same company as Harvard Project Manager, this product has advanced project management functions such as resource allocation, the ability to allocate resources across projects, and planned versus actual results on the same display. Like its predecessor, however, this program does not automatically create a plan based on duration and dependencies of tasks.

The initial display is like a roadmap that shows task and milestone relationships. Simultaneously, a Gantt chart is created that displays each activity on a timeline. The project's critical path is shown on the roadmap with highlighted double lines. PERT charts can also be produced. A user-defined calendar allows you to customize the scheduling to meet specific needs. Schedules can be set and viewed in units as small as an hour.

Harvard Total Project Manager has a cross-project resource-allocation feature that allows you to assign an unlimited number of resources among all projects. This feature warns you when a resource is overscheduled and graphically shows how much of a particular resource is being used. What-if scenarios may be utilized to ensure the optimal assignment of resources.

Once started, projects may be monitored using both cost-tracking and schedule-tracking. A potential drawback of this program is the great number of menus, which makes it somewhat difficult to use.

hash 1. Electrical interfering noise arising from vibrators or commutators. **2.** Electrical noise that causes interference or unwanted and meaningless information to be carried in memory.

hashing A method of inserting and finding elements in a table. Some function is applied to each key, and the outcome of that function determines the location of that key in the table. If two keys hash to the same location (a collision), a collision-resolution routine must be employed.

hashing routine A formula used in relative files to convert a record's key to its disk location.

hash total A sum formed for error-checking purposes by adding fields or other items that normally are not related, such as the total of invoice serial numbers.

Hayes AT compatible Refers to a modem that recognizes the industry-standard Hayes set of AT modem commands and will work with Hayes-compatible software.

HC Abbreviation for *handling capacity*.

HDLC Abbreviation for *hierarchical data link control*, a structured set of standards governing the means by which unlike devices can communicate with each other on data communications networks.

HDMenu A hard disk utility that allows you to put all of your programs on a menu for quick access. HDMenu has security features, unlimited menus, and a telephone dialer.

HDTV Abbreviation for *high-definition television*, a high-resolution, wide-screen-television broadcasting with digital sound. Until an international standard exists for HDTV, improvements in the quality of equipment used to receive standard broadcasts are referred to as improved-definition television (IDTV) or extended-definition television (EDTV).

HDX Abbreviation for *half duplex*, a communications arrangement that permits alternate one-way transmission between two given points at any one time.

head A device used to read, write, or erase data in a storage medium. A head can be the small electromagnet for reading, writing, and erasing data on magnetic disks or tapes.

head actuator The device that moves read-write heads across a disk drive's platter. Head actuators are usually stepper motors or voice-call actuators.

head-cleaning diskette A specially treated floppy disk for cleaning floppy disk drive heads.

head crash A malfunction of a disk drive, where the read/write head touches the surface of a hard disk.

head end A central point in broadband networks that receives signals on one set of frequency bands and retransmits them on another set of frequencies, viewed as a central hub.

header 1. The initial part of a message, which contains information such as routing, addressee, destination, and time of origin. 2. In word processing, text than can appear at the top of every page. Also called a *running head*.

header file A file containing a header record to be used when creating form documents. A header record is a list of field names that correspond to the field names included in a main document and to the fields of varying text stored in data records. It is convenient to use a header record in a header file rather than in a data document when the records for the data document are created from a database.

header label A block of data at the start of a magnetic tape that contains information to identify the file. A header label may include the following:

- The date when recorded
- File name and number
- Reel number
- Retention time

header record A list of field names (or categories of information) stored in the first paragraph of a data document. The field names of a header paragraph match the field names placed where you want varying text in a main document. During printing, specific pieces of varying text listed under the field-name categories are merged into the appropriate places in each copy of a form document.

head gap The space between the pole pieces of a magnetic recording head.

heading 1. The sequence of characters preceded by the *start of heading* character, which is used as address and routing information. 2. In word processing, a major title in a document, which may be identified with a particular style.

head meters Certain flow-sensing elements, so-called because the differential pressure across two points can be equated to the head or the height of the liquid column. The elements are characterized by a constant area of flow passage. The Venturi tube, flow nozzle, orifice plate, pilot tube, and other restricted sections are included in this group.

head-to-tape contact The degree to which the surface of the magnetic coating of a tape approaches the surface of the record or relay heads during normal operation of a recorder. Good head-to-tape contact minimizes separation loss and is essential in obtaining high resolution.

heap A storage structure for data where data is not placed in any particular order, requiring a scan of the entire table for every retrieval.

heat of emission The additional heat energy that must be supplied to an electron-emitting surface to keep its temperature constant.

heatsink A device used to dissipate heat away from a component or chassis.

Help A program or system of files that provides assistance to the programmer or user of software and hardware.

HelpDOS A software package for learning and using the commands and functions of DOS. It consists of menus, reference information, a technical dictionary and a cross-reference feature. A Hints menu shows categories of actions you can take with DOS. For example, when you select the Hint category "Print," HelpDOS gives a menu of the ways you can print information with DOS.

help mark In some software packages, the question mark that is always displayed at a particular place on the screen or window. Point to the question mark with the mouse and click either button to see lists of Help topics.

Helpme Diagnostic A set of more than 300 diagnostic tests for PCs and LANs. Common problems involving hardware and software installation and performance are identified and, when possible, corrected with a single keystroke. Designed to aid in the support of other PC products, the utility identifies system configuration (including accessories), deviations from the IBM standard, and the current use of memory and interrupts. Help screens and several other functions are included for the less-experienced PC user.

help screen A window or section of the display screen that assists the user.

henry *See* H, 2.

Hercules color card An older color graphics card. It includes a parallel printer port and will fit in the short slot of an XT. It is completely compatible with IBM's color card software, runs text mode as well as color graphics mode, offers graphics resolution of 320 × 200 for four colors, and is compatible with the AT.

Hercules graphics card An older graphics card that replaced the IBM MDA (monochrome display adapter) in a PC. The Hercules card uses the standard IBM (or other) monochrome display already in the system and includes a standard parallel printer port and software to allow the use of BASIC graphics commands. It will not drive a color monitor.

hermaphroditic connector The connector whose mating parts are identical at their mating face; those which have no female or male members but still can maintain correct polarity sealing, and mechanical and electrical couplings.

hertz The SI (International System of Units) unit of frequency equal to one cycle per second, abbreviated *Hz*.

hertzian wave The electromagnetic radiation that carries a radio signal through space.

heterodyne To beat or combine two sinusoidal waves with a nonlinear device (such as a mixer) to produce sum and difference frequencies.

heterodyne interference Interference resulting from the simultaneous reception of two signals whose wavelengths are separated by a frequency difference in the audio range.

heterogeneous Different.

heterogeneous network A network consisting of different network protocols or kinds of computers. Specifically, a network combining SNA and DNA protocols, using an SNA gateway to connect the two is a heterogeneous network.

heuristic Refers to exploratory methods of problem-solving in which solutions are found by evaluating the progress toward a final result.

heuristic routine A routine that uses a trial-and-error method and a learning technique rather than a direct algorithm approach.

hex Abbreviation for *hexadecimal*.

hexadecimal Pertaining to the use of character sets with 16 possibilities, or number systems with a base or radix of 16. In hexadecimal, the first nine digits are 0–9 and the last six digits are represented by the letters A–F.

hexadecimal conversion A conversion system of the bit patterns and the hex letter/number codes, as shown in the chart. Note that the first four-bit patterns begin with 00; the next with 01; the next four with 10, and the last four with 11. This is the sequence for a two-bit binary number: 00, 01, 10, 11. Also notice that the groups of four (going down the table) start with 0, 4, 8, and C. Then the last two bits of each pattern go through the same sequence 00, 01, 10, 11—as you go through the set 4, 5, 6, 7. Next, look at the first two bits to get the starting point 0, 4, 8, or C. Then use the last two bits to sequence from there. So 1011 is in the group that starts with 8, and it is the last one in that group, so it is 11.

Starting with the letter/number code, first note the group, then write the first two bits; note where it is in the group, then write the last two bits. You can easily convert from an address like 23FF to its binary equivalent, 0011 0011 1111 1110.

0 0 0 0	0
0 0 0 1	1
0 0 1 0	2
0 0 1 1	3
0 1 0 0	4
0 1 0 1	5
0 1 1 0	6
0 1 1 1	7
1 0 0 0	8
1 0 0 1	9
1 0 1 0	A
1 0 1 1	B
1 1 0 0	C
1 1 0 1	D
1 1 1 0	E
1 1 1 1	F

Hexadecimal conversion chart

hexadecimal notation A notation system that uses 16 integers represented by the numerals 0–9 and the letters A–F, as shown in the table that follows. Sometimes called *sexadecimal notation*.

Binary	Octal	Decimal	Hexadecimal
0000	0	0	0
0001	1	1	1
0010	2	2	2
0011	3	3	3
0100	4	4	4
0101	5	5	5
0110	6	6	6
0111	7	7	7
1000	10	8	8
1001	11	9	9
1010	12	10	A
1011	13	11	B
1100	14	12	C
1101	15	13	D
1110	16	14	E
1111	17	15	F

Hexadecimal and equivalent numbers

hex format A technique that puts addresses in hexadecimal form with a base of 16. The 16 bits are broken up into four groups of four bits each; then a code of one letter or number is used to represent each group, as shown in the figure. An address that is 16 bits long can be given as four of these codes: for example FA34 or 05DC. These codes are easier to work with and remember. It is also easy to convert back and forth from the bit patterns.

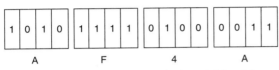

Hexadecimal representation of a 16-bit address

HF Abbreviation for *high frequency*.
HF/DF Abbreviation for *high frequency direction finder*.
Hg delay line A sonic or acoustic delay line in which mercury is used as the medium of sound transmission, with transducers on each end to provide electrical signal. Related to acoustic delay line.
hi-band A recording format for still video that allows resolutions of up to 500 horizontal TV lines from the original format of 360 lines. The recording heads and processing circuits are improved to increase the luminance frequency response.
HICAPCOM Acronym for *high capacity communication system*.
HICard A short-slot 256K RAM card that expands an IBM PC or compatible to 896K. The card works with EGA, all memory maps, hard disk drives, and ROM-based expansions. Flexible addressing provides configurations from zero to 640K.
hidden text A character format that allows you to show or hide designated text. It is used for annotations or nonprinting characters and for table of contents and index codes.
hierarchical database A database that structures data as a top-down hierarchy instead of in tables. You navigate the hierarchy to retrieve a particular row of data. Access to data is only made from the top down. This can be cumbersome when repeating operations. *Also see* IMS, 2.
hierarchical data link control *See* HDLC.
hierarchical networks Networks that use a multilevel master-slave configuration. Various levels in the hierarchy are assigned responsibilities for certain functions. The highest level in the hierarchy makes all major decisions, and the lower levels have the responsibilities for specific operations.
hierarchical routing A routing method based on domains. Interdomain routers are responsible only for getting data to the right domain. An intradomain router takes responsibility for routing within the domain.

hierarchical simulation A simulation technique that combines both gate level and functional simulation with several levels of detail. Gate-level models can be used, for example, at functional interfaces or for critical internal faults. In some systems, it is useful to simulate only critical sections that are known to cause most of the faults.
hierarchical storage controller *See* HSC.
hierarchical system A system that uses a master processor and two or more slave processors in a hierarchically ordered relationship, as shown in the diagram. The master processor controls or supervises the operation of the slave processors in either a tightly or a loosely coupled manner.

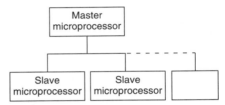

Hierarchical (master-slave) microprocessor system

hierarchy A structure that consists of ranked sets and subsets. A hierarchical file system can eliminate the requirement for a separate database definition language.
hierarchy chart A programming design technique that shows each module as a block or box with its logical relationship to all other modules in the program. It is similar to an organizational chart for a company. Also known as a *structure chart*.
high Refers to the higher voltage or the most positive level in a two-level logic system. Usually, true states are represented by a high (relative to the alternate state) voltage, a binary 1, and a closed switch; false states are denoted by a logic low, a binary 0, and an open switch.
high definition television *See* HDTV.
high-density bipolar N A form of bipolar transmission that limits the number of consecutive zeros to N by replacing the $(N + 1)^{th}$ zero with bipolar violation. Sometimes abbreviated *HDBN*.
high DOS The area of RAM located between 640K and 1002K. This 384K of memory is usually reserved for video memory and network interface cards. Memory manager utilities can utilize some unused portions of high DOS for programs such as TSRs. *Also see* EMS.
higher-order software technique A software design technique developed on NASA projects as a means of defining reliable, large scale, multiprogrammed multiprocessor systems. This method is based on rules that define a hierarchy of soft-

ware control; here the control is the specified effect of one software object on another. The rules are as follows:

- A module controls the operation of functions at only its immediate, lower level.
- A module is only responsible for elements of its own output space.
- A module controls the access rights to a set of variables that define the output space for each immediate, lower level function.
- A module can reject invalid elements of only its own input set.
- A module controls the ordering of the tree for only the immediate, lower levels.

high frequency Any frequency falling between 3 MHz and 30 MHz.

high-frequency heating Heating (induction or dielectric) in which the source of current is from rotary generators up to 3000 Hz and from electronic generators in the 1 to 100 MHz range.

high-frequency transformer A transformer designed to operate at high frequencies. In these units, the self-capacitance becomes important.

high-gain amplifier A voltage amplifier having little if any feedback.

high-information delta modulation A form of delta modulation in which the step size is doubled for consecutively identical bits at the coder output, and halved for consecutively opposite bits at the coder output. *Also see* DELTA MODULATION.

high-level compiler A compiler for high-level languages.

high-level language A computer language that uses English-like statements for instructions. In high-level languages, each instruction or statement corresponds to several machine-code instructions. Tests using microprocessors show that such languages require considerably less time for programming and debugging than assembly language.

high-level modulation A level of modulation produced in the output circuit of an AM transmitter system that permits 100% modulation.

high-level multiplexer A multiplexer designed to operate with input signals greater than 1 V. The most common type uses a bank of switches connected to a common output bus, as shown in the figure. The bus output can be buffered by a noninverting amplifier as shown. The configuration is simple, and with an output amplifier, it offers a high input impedance.

Depending on the switching device, this multiplexer can operate over a wide variation of input voltage. With solid state switches, the input voltage excursion is limited to about +20 V. Most multiplexers are designed for the standard analog range of 10 V; but some that use high threshold switches can be used for only ±5 range.

highlight On a video display, to call attention to an item by increasing the intensity of the characters, making them blink while others remain steady, or reversing the background and the character images (black characters on a white background, for example). Most video displays have software controls to accomplish this on a selective basis.

high memory area *See* HMA.

high-noise-immunity logic *See* HINIL.

high-order digit A digit that occupies a significant or highly valued position in a notational system.

high-pass Descriptive of a circuit or device (such as a filter) that permits the passage of all electrical signals above a certain critical frequency and shunts all other signals to ground.

high-pass filter A filter that freely passes signals of all frequencies above a reference value known as the *cutoff frequency*.

high-performance file system *See* HPFS.

high-record offset A term used in NetWare. Record offset is a Long value expressed in two words containing the offset from the beginning of the file where the record begins. The programmer must place the more significant word in High Record Offset and less significant word in Low Record Offset.

high-resolution graphics The display of graphic output using a large number of pixels per screen area, making it more effective for drawing precise lines and curves.

high-speed bus A set of wires that provides a path to transfer the electrical pulses that represent data and instructions to the various registers in the microcomputer.

high-speed digital input/output interface boards Expansion boards that use 8- or 16-bit DMA (direct memory access) capability to obtain data transfer rates of 250K per second on the original 4.77MHz PC, and higher speeds on faster machines. Normal processor I/O transfer may also be made through the data ports. An on-board counter/timer allows the user to set data transfer rates, or the transfer may be triggered externally.

Applications include interfaces to high-speed peripherals, high-speed memory transfers from other computers, digital I/O control, printer/plotter interfaces, and interfaces to external high-speed A/D and D/A converters.

high-speed logic A logic family such as ECL that offers relatively high switching speeds.

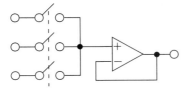

High-level multiplexer

high-speed printer A machine that operates in excess of 300 lines per minute with 100 characters per line.

high-speed storage loading A I/O port option on some systems that adds a high-speed input/output path to ROM. This option permits high-speed transfer between the ROM and external devices such as disk drives. Through the I/O port, a microcomputer's storage, line printer, and keyboard are available to store assembled programs, obtain program listings, and examine and modify specific locations in ROM.

high-split A broadband cable system in which the bandwidth utilized to send toward the head-end (reverse direction) is approximately 6 to 180 MHz, and the bandwidth utilized to send away from the head-end (forward direction) is approximately 220 to 400 MHz. The guard band between the forward and reverse directions (180 to 220 MHZ) provides isolation from interference.

HiJaak Pro A graphics utility suite from Inset Systems, Inc., that can translate among a wide variety of graphics file formats, including PostScript. The newest release (HiJaak Pro 3) includes draw and paint tools in addition to the basic capture and translation functions.

HiNIL Acronym for *high-noise-immunity logic*, a logic family designed especially for applications in which transients are likely to occur and create a noisy environment. HiNIL can be used directly with CMOS to protect the CMOS circuits from static electricity and transients during turn-on. HiNIL is also compatible with many analog circuits. HiNIL offers a dc noise immunity almost ten times greater than TTL (transistor-transistor logic) and will block transients large enough to cause TTL malfunctions.

HIPO chart Acronym (pronounced "high-po") for *hierarchy input-processing-output*, a program-design tool that includes a visual table of contents, overview diagram, and detail diagram for a program.

hi-pot Acronym for *high potential*, which commonly refers to a device used for testing insulation breakdown or leakage with high voltage. *High-potting* is the verb.

Hi-Res Rainbow A paint package that features pulldown windows, icons, and multiple device inputs (joysticks, mouse, keyboard, or tablet). Features include connecting lines, erase, draw, spray, fill, arc lines, connecting arcs, and undo.

histogram A stepped bar chart that shows a frequency distribution.

historical data Any data accumulated from prior periods, such as the productivity of a device.

hit A momentary electrical disturbance in a circuit or system.

hit ratio The ratio of the number of times data are successfully located in main memory to the total number of attempts over a given period.

.HLP In a filenaming scheme, an extension that indicates a help file. Such files contain the documentation associated with specific operations for a software product. They are not necessarily readable from outside the associated program.

HMA Abbreviation for *high memory area*, the first 64K of extended memory in PCs located just above the 1M memory boundary.

HNIL See *HiNIL*.

hold A condition that suspends operation of a system or circuit for a specified time (as, for example, to allow the user to study the parameters).

hold button A button used in analog computer consoles that allows the operation to be temporarily stopped for observation by the operator. All integrating capacitors are disconnected during a hold to maintain the correct charges.

Hold Everything A software product that allows programmers to swap out currently executing programs and return to DOS with almost all of the available memory ready to be used. It provides a method of saving active memory to disk or EMS in one function. This allows you to run another program and then return back to the calling program, where it left off.

holding beam A diffuse beam of electrons for regenerating the charges stored on the dielectric surface of an electrostatic memory tube or cathode-ray tube.

holding time The total time during which a given channel is occupied for each transmission or call. Holding time consists of both operating time and text or conversation time.

hold instruction An instruction that causes data called from storage to be retained after it is called out.

hole A mobile void in a transistor that is quickly filled by an electron and which gives the illusion of movement in a direction opposite that of electron flow.

hole current Current caused from the movement of electrons into holes, creating new holes in semiconductors.

hole density Refers to the density of the current-carrying holes in a semiconductor.

hole injection The creation of mobile holes in a semiconductor by applying an electric charge using a metallic point or other method.

hole mobility The ability of a hole to travel easily through a semiconductor.

hole trap An impurity in a semiconductor that can release electrons in the conduction or valence band and so trap a hole.

Hollerith code (*o.t.*) A punched-card code that uses 12 rows per column and usually 80 columns per card. It is a 12-level code that represents the alphabet plus the digits 0 through 9, using zone bits and data bits. The Hollerith code lends itself readily to error-detection methods.

hologram A type of imaging that uses lasers instead of lenses.

home On a video display, the position in the upper-leftmost corner where the first printable character is usually placed.

home directory 1. A user's personal directory on a file server, where they are permitted to store files. 2. The directory where a particular piece of software was installed.

homeostasis A steady-state condition in a system where the input and output are precisely balanced.

Homeware A package of miscellaneous household routines for tracking a household inventory, automobile expenses, meals, shopping, names and addresses, and hobbies. The package is written in C.

homogeneity A state or condition of similarity of nature, kind, or degree.

hooks Refers to a programming technique that allows a programmer to add new code to an existing program. The existing program has hooks that execute any additional code.

hop A single data link. The link could be a dial-up line, an Ethernet, an X.25 virtual circuit, or other mechanism that will move data for the network layer.

hopper The portion of a printer that holds the paper to be processed or the printed copies.

Hopper, Grace A mathematician and programmer for the MARK I computer.

horizontal blanking interval The period of time when a scanning process is moving from the end of one horizontal line to the start of the next line.

horizontal chart Typically, a bar chart in which the bars run horizontally and the uses of the X and Y axes are reversed. Also, a line chart (or bar/line combination) where the lines for each series run vertically.

horizontal delta encoding A method of data compression that stores the changes in value of a digital signal sampled along a horizontal plane. *Also see* DELTA ENCODING/DECODING.

horizontal resolution The specification of resolution in the horizontal direction. It shows the ability of the system to reproduce closely spaced vertical lines, or detail across the screen. It is usually specified as the maximum number of alternating white and black vertical lines (lines of resolution) that can be individually perceived across the width of a picture, divided by the aspect ratio. This number usually is expressed as *TV lines per picture height*. Dividing by the aspect ratio and expressing the result per picture height allows one to compare horizontal and vertical resolution.

Horizontal chroma resolution is measured between complementary colors (rather than black and white) but can vary in some systems (such as NTSC), depending on the colors chosen. Horizontal resolution in luminance and/or chrominance can vary in some systems between a stationary (static resolution) and moving (dynamic resolution) picture. It is usually directly related to bandwidth.

horizontal retrace period The time during which a CRT screen's line scan returns from the end of one line to the start of another.

horizontal scan frequency The rate at which the monitor updates the screen image. Higher horizontal scan frequencies correspond to higher screen resolutions. Monitors that have multiple scan frequencies or that can multisync and lock-in on a range of horizontal scan frequencies are compatible with multiple video standards.

horizontal scroll To move horizontally within a document that is wider than the window, so that parts of the document to the right or left of the window come into view.

horizontal tabulation character *See* HT.

host 1. The primary or controlling computer in a multiple computer installation; the computer system to which a network is connected. 2. A computer used to compile, link, edit, or test programs for use on another computer or system.

host node 1. A node where a host computer is located. 2. In SNA, a subarea node that contains an SSCP.

hot A terminal or conductor that is connected, alive, or energized, but is not at ground potential.

hot fix area An area of a disk installed on a NetWare file server that the file server uses to keep track of bad blocks that have developed since the disk was formatted. Also known as the *hot fix redirection table*.

hot fix blocks available In NetWare, the number of redirection blocks that are still available. This field is only meaningful with SFT NetWare I or above.

hot fix disabled In NetWare, this indicates whether Hot Fix is enabled or disabled (0 = enabled). This field is only meaningful with SFT NetWare Level I or above.

hot fix table size In NetWare, the total number of redirection blocks set aside on the disk for Hot Fix redirection. Some or all of these blocks may be in use. This field is only meaningful with SFT NetWare Level I or above.

hot fix table start In NetWare, the field indicating the first block of the disk hot fix area. This field is only meaningful with SFT NetWare Level I or above. *Also see* HOT FIX AREA.

hot key A key or key combination on a keyboard that has been designated for a special purpose by the user. The hot key engages the particular user-defined function without the user having to press Enter or Return.

hot wire anemometers A flow sensor that has a wire element, which is heated electrically, perpendicular to the flowing stream. Cooling by the flow changes the resistance of the wire as a function of the flow velocity. Other forms maintain the wire temperature constant and measure the current required to maintain the temperature; this current is then a function of the flow. Such instruments can measure mass flow as long as the product of the thermal conductivity, specific heat, and density remain constant. This is true for many gases at low pressures; thus this meter has the greatest application in the measurement of low flow rates of gases. They are also used for gas velocity determinations. They are sensitive to flow changes but tend to be expensive. Anemometers are widely used in air conditioning, in weather stations, and around cooling towers.

Some types of anemometers use the deflection of vanes measured with strain gauge bridges in a limited number of designs. The vane in these flowmeters is usually installed perpendicular to the flow. A wedge-shaped vane anemometer with strain gauges has been used for air turbulence measurements.

hot zone In word processing, the area, adjustable in width, for controlling the right margin of text. When a line of typing goes outside this zone, the program will either start a new line or pause so the operator can make a hyphenation decision.

housecleaning An operation in which a program compresses space by collecting all its useful data and frees up unused areas of memory that may have been used for strings of data.

housekeeping Any operation in a routine that does not contribute to the solution of the problem, but which is required for machine operation (such as setting up constants and variables). Housekeeping operations must be performed before actual processing begins, and may include the following:

- Establishing controlling marks
- Reading the first record
- Setting up auxiliary storage units
- Initializing parameters

housekeeping routine Initial instructions that are executed only once, such as clearing storage locations or initializing instruction addresses.

HP 1. Abbreviation for *high position*. **2.** Abbreviation for *Hewlett-Packard*.

HP DeskJet A family of inkjet printers from Hewlett-Packard, including several that print in color.

HP DeskManager Hewlett-Packard office automation software.

HPF Abbreviation for *highest possible frequency*.

HP font cartridge A single cartridge that includes all of the HP font library, which plugs into a slot on a laser printer. There are 8 symbol sets, 100 fonts (including bar codes) and a variety of different typestyles.

HPFS Abbreviation for high-performance file system, the method of formatting a hard disk drive used by OS/2. While it provides significant speed advantages over other formatting techniques, only the OS/2 operating system and applications designed to work with that operating system can access a drive formatted using this technique.

HP LaserJet A family of laser printers from Hewlett-Packard, including the HP III, 4L, and 4P.

HS 1. Abbreviation for *half subtractor*. **2.** Abbreviation for *handset*.

HSC Abbreviation for *hierarchical storage controller*, a standalone disk and tape controller. Most HSCs use a modified computer that has been optimized as a mass storage controller.

HT The ASCII horizontal tabulation (HT) character, designated by a binary 9 (0000 1001), that causes the printing or display position to be moved to the next series of positions along the display or printing line.

HTL Abbreviation for *high threshold logic*.

hub 1. A receptacle into which an electrical lead may be connected in order to carry a signal. **2.** The common connection point for a group of PCs in a LAN. Star and ring topology LANs use hubs to interconnect the PCs. The hubs in a token ring are called *multiple access units* (MAUs). In some LANs, the file server acts as a hub.

hue The color of a point, such as red, green, yellow, or violet.

Huffman coding A type of data coding scheme used to achieve data compression by using short code words to represent frequently used characters and longer code words to represent rarer ones.

human-factors engineering *See* ERGONOMICS.

Hungarian notation A form of program-code variable documentation that relies on prefixes to define the purpose of each variable. For example, a variable named *aNames* would contain an array of names. The original system, created by Microsoft employee Charles Simonyi, has been modified to meet the needs of a variety of programming languages.

hunt group A series of telephone numbers in sequence that permits the calling part to connect with the available line.

hunting 1. A condition in which a system appears to seek a state of equilibrium continuously. **2.** Repeated oscillation to limits above and below a desired value.

HVAC Acronym for *heating, ventilation, and air conditioning equipment*.

hy Occasional abbreviation for *henry*.

hybrid circuit A circuit fabricated by interconnecting circuits of different classes, such as transistor discretes and ICs, or thin-film and thick-film ICs.

hybrid coil A set of transformers connecting a two-wire local telephone line to a long-haul four-wire channel. Modems are often engineered for a two-wire line but data circuits usually have separate paths for transmit and receive. The hybrid coil resolves this problem by placing the transmit and receive sides of the channel on the same pair of wires for connection to the modem.

hybrid computer A computer that uses both analog and digital representations. Hybrid computers are used in many simulation applications in which a close relationship with the physical world is required.

hybrid integrated circuit An integrated circuit that uses a combination of technologies or components interconnected on a common substrate or package. *Also see* IC.

hybrid interface An interface for connecting analog and digital devices together.

hybrid system A system where a small computer is used for immediate quick-response processing and a larger, remote machine is used for off-site processing of large blocks of data.

hybrid topology A network arrangement containing some combination of star, ring or bus topologies.

hybrid transmission A type of transmission that carries FDM (frequency-division multiplexing) voice and digital data on the same medium.

HYCOL Acronym for *hybrid computer link*.

HYCOTRAN Acronym for *hybrid computer translator*.

HYDAC Acronym for *hybrid digital-analog computer*.

hyphen drop A feature of word processing in which a hyphen that originally appeared at an end-of-line word break is automatically dropped if the word later appears in the middle of a line.

Hypercard A user interface for the Macintosh that greatly expands its capability.

hypereditor An editor program, such as one used in a dynamic worksheet environment, that automatically recalculates results when changes are made.

hypergame A computer game that uses the characteristics of a familiar game such as dice or cards.

hyperkaleidoscope Refers to a computer game that automatically produces patterns or random events that allow the game to continue.

hyperspace Refers to higher-dimensional spaces, such as the four dimensional universe of time and space.

hypertext A nonsequential body or index of information that allows knowledge to be treated as accessible in any order.

HyperWord A multi-window hypertext word processor and development system. It can be used to create interactive tutorials and reference systems. It includes context-sensitive help, multi-level undo, pulldown menus. You can create program mock-ups, automatically display subroutine from any reference, and interrelate program source files. It has full WYSIWYG word-processing features and a 120,000 word dictionary.

hyphenation help A word-processing feature that allows users to choose whether the program should automatically hyphenate words too long to fit on a line.

hysteresis 1. A lagging in the response of a signal or property, which may depend upon the past history of the signal or device being observed. **2.** The difference between the turn-on threshold of a device or circuit and the turn-off threshold of that same device after turn-on.

hysteresis distortion The distortion of waveforms in circuits that contain magnetic components. It is due to the hysteresis of the magnetic cores.

hysteresis error The difference in readings obtained in a system with and without hysteresis present.

hysteresis loop The loop or closed curve that results when parameters are plotted for devices exhibiting hysteresis.

Hz Abbreviation for *hertz* (cycles per second).

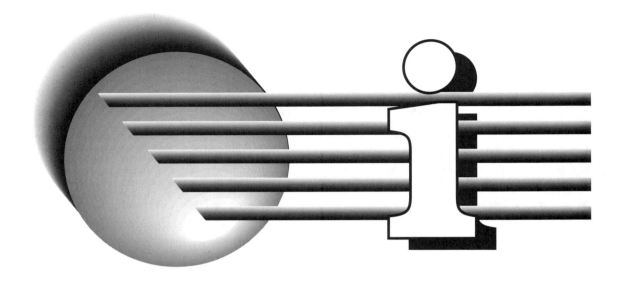

I Symbol for current.
IA *See* INDIRECT ADDRESSING.
IAC Abbreviation for *integration, assembly,* and *checkout.*
IAGC Abbreviation for *instant automatic gain control.*
IAR Abbreviation for instruction address register, the register that holds the address of the instruction to be executed next in the program sequence without regard to branching or interrupts. Also called *program counter.*
IBM Abbreviation for *International Business Machines Corp.,* the world's largest computer manufacturer.
IBM C Set/2 An IBM software product that includes a 32-bit SAA C complier with runtime libraries that have an integrated, source-level Presentation Manager debugger.
IBM Developer's Toolkit for OS/2 An IBM software product with language-independent tools and code samples for building OS/2 programs. It includes a System Object Module (SOM) compiler, resource compiler with dialog box editors, and debug support.
IBM 8228 A multistation access unit (MAU) sold by IBM. *Also see* MAU.
IBM Extended Services for OS/2 An IBM product with communications and database functions over those offered in the IBM Extended Edition.
IBM LAN Server IBM's LAN operating system based on the IBM/Microsoft OEM LAN Manager software. LAN Manager is based on OS/2 as the underlying operating system for the PC that acts as the file server. The LAN Server runs as a session on OS/2.

IBM OS/2 *See* OS/2.
IBM OS/2 extended edition *See* OS/2 EXTENDED EDITION.
IBM PC LAN IBM's network operating system.
IBM PC network A CSMA/CD network that uses a bus or star daisy-chain topology. It can be operated as a broadband network on coaxial cable and as baseband on twisted pair, as shown in the figure.

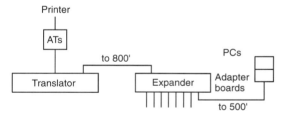

IBM PC network

IBM PC parallel printer adapter cable A cable that connects an IBM PC/XT or AT to a Centronics compatible printer. The cable may have a DB25P (male) connector on one end and a male Centronics-type connector on the other.
IBM PC/XT/AT Refers to the original IBM family of personal computers. The original PC series was a floppy-disk-based machine with the 8088 microprocessor. The XT is the hard-disk version and the AT (advanced technology) series is based on the 80286 microprocessor.

IBM token ring Refers to the IBM token-ring network. *Also see* TOKEN RING.

IBM token-ring adapter The token-ring controller card sold by IBM.

IBM WorkFrame/2 An IBM software product that features a project organizer that allows you to set up, combine, and associate application development projects.

IC Abbreviation for *integrated circuit*, an electronic self-contained assembly fabricated on a single chip of semiconductor material. An IC usually starts out as a schematic diagram, then a layout drawing that is 20–100 times larger than the final product. Mixtures of paste-like inks are used for conductors, and for each type of ink used a separate mask is produced by reducing the layout drawings. When the inking is completed, the chips are placed in a furnace, where the temperature is controlled and diffusion is used to achieve the proper resistivity of the semiconductor. *Laser trimming* can also be used for producing resistors with fine tolerances. *Etching* is used for trimming and removing unwanted paths on the chip.

icand register A register that contains the multiplicand during a multiplication operation (from the last two syllables of *multiplicand*).

ICC Abbreviation for *international computer center*.

IC chip packages Most older PCs used ICs with a DIP (dual inline package). The pins on the DIP package are placed in holes in the circuit board, then the pins are soldered to the circuit tracks on the board. The pins are numbered counterclockwise from the top, as shown in the figure. The marks may be half circles, dot indentations, or painted dots. Plastic DIPs are usually found in PCs. The pins are 0.1 inches apart. The plastic DIP usually has tin-plated pins; 60/40 solder works well.

Surface-mount devices (SMDs) use solder pads. Chips can be mounted on both sides of the board. The SMD package is smaller since four sides can have pins. The SMD can be made 40% to 60% smaller in surface area than a DIP containing the same chip. One type of SMD is called the *chip-carrier package* (CCP). These devices use pins that are bent over and resemble feet. These feet are designed to be soldered to pads. When the boards are manufactured, the feet are positioned over the pads and the board is heated. The solder melts and the feet become attached to the pads. This connection provides both a physical and electrical bond. Surface-mount technology is both cheaper and faster to manufacture than using DIPs. Two of the SMD foot styles used include the gull-wing and J-shape, as shown in the following figures.

IC DIP package Abbreviation for *integrated circuit dual-inline package*, a molded IC package generally available in 8-, 14- or 16-lead versions. It is somewhat larger (0.25 × 0.75 inches) and easier

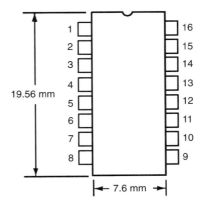

Dual-in-line (DIP) package

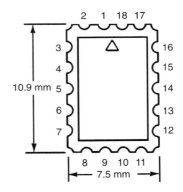

Surface-mount-device (SMD) package

IC chip packages, top view

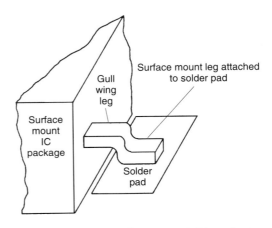

Gull wing leg on surface-mount IC package

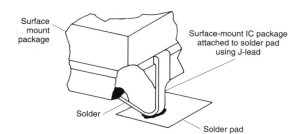

J-lead leg for an SMD, which provides a stronger solder joint than the gull wing

to handle than a flatpack. The inline bent structure makes it convenient for plugging into circuit sockets or for automatically assembling onto printed wiring boards. Its thermal resistance is comparable to that of a TO-5 transistor package.

IC dopant impurities Controlled amounts of dopant impurities introduced into preselected parts of the silicon surface through the diffusion windows in the oxide layer. Solid-state diffusion of these dopants into silicon at high temperatures results in the formulation of a pn junction within the single crystal silicon. Since the diffusion of impurities proceeds sideways as well as downward from the diffusion windows at the surface, the resulting junction edge is not exposed to air on the surface, but is protected by the surface oxide layer.

ICE An *in-circuit emulator* that is plugged directly into the user's system in a realtime environment. An in-circuit emulator allows early system control by using the emulator in place of the processor. ICE is used to control, interrogate, revise, and completely debug a user's system in its own environment.

IC electrical contact Electrical contact to semiconductor regions formed by depositing thin metal films of high electrical conductivity, such as aluminum, over the windows cut in the oxide. These conductive films can then be etched into desired interconnection patterns on the surface of the silicon wafer, thus completing the monolithic circuit structure.

IC fabrication In the actual fabrication of a single transistor, the silicon wafer is manufactured by cutting a single crystal of silicon in the proper direction (for example, direction 111 of the lattice). A layer of oxide is then deposited on the silicon.

The first mask is used to define the p-zones in the silicon. They are the source and drain areas of the transistor. Doping, using thermal diffusion, is then performed on the exposed areas, which allows p-type impurities into the silicon.

Next, a layer of oxide is grown on top of the silicon, as shown in the figure. Then, a mask is used to define the areas to be metalized. The oxide is then removed in these locations. Another oxidation for the gate is performed in order to grow a thin layer. A final oxide removal is performed to expose the source and the drain areas, which are then connected to the rest of the circuit during metalization.

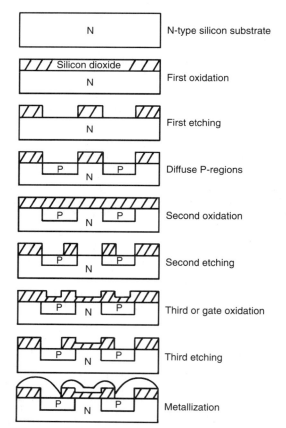

Integrated circuit MOS transistor manufacture

IC impurity diffusion For digital integrated circuits, controlled amounts of interstitial impurities such as gold, copper, or nickel introduced into a silicon lattice to reduce the minority carrier lifetime.

ICM Abbreviation for *inverted coaxial magnetron*.

icon In a graphical user interface, a small symbol or picture on the screen that represent a program or device.

icon-driven operating system An operating system that works when the user enters or points to an icon, rather than typing in commands. *Also see* GUI.

Iconic Query A program with a visual database interface. It allows database access by using the WYSIWYG ("what-you-see-is-what-you-get") query approach. It allows users to point and click at visual scenes instead of using a query language.

Icon Tools A standalone graphics tool that allows you to create, edit, display, and manipulate icons from a graphics application. It has an icon editor, icon modifier utility, and icon view/print utility, with a function library and a set of sample icons. The function library includes functions for loading and drawing icons, drawing and processing icon menus and for animation. Mouse support for graphics environments is also included.

IC photomasking The step in integrated circuit manufacturing that transfers the pattern to be etched through the oxide onto the wafer's surface. The wafer surface to be masked is initially coated with a photosensitive coating known as *photoresist* or *resist*. The resist-coated wafer surface is then brought into contact with the masking plate and exposed under an ultraviolet light. The portions of the photosensitive resist not covered by opaque portions of the mask polymerize and harden as a result of this exposure. Then, the unexposed parts of the resist can be washed away, leaving a photoresist mask on the wafer surface.

ICT Abbreviation for *insulating core transformer*, a type of high-voltage generating device with high-voltage/low-current capabilities and compact design.

IC tester Abbreviation for *integrated circuit tester*, a type of automatic test instrument that interrogates the parametric and functional performance characteristics for a wide variety of integrated circuits. The instrument may display pass or fail information during the test cycle, detect out-of-specification supply current, and identify each input or output pin at which a parametric or functional failure is detected. The entire test sequence may be performed within milliseconds.

ICU Abbreviation for *instruction control unit*. Those parts of a computer that allow the retrieval of instructions in the proper sequence with the interpretation of each instruction and the application of the proper commands to the ALU and other parts in accordance with that interpretation. A typical ICU contains a ROM in which the microinstructions are stored along with the address control logic for microprogram branching.

IDA Abbreviation for *incoming data alert*, a signal to a computer operator that incoming data is arriving. IDA fastens to the side of your terminal with double-stick foam tape. A double-ended DB25 connector plugs it into your computer. All power is derived from pin 20 (DTR).

IDAPI Abbreviation for *independent database application programming interface*, a Borland product for database development.

IDEAL Acronym for *interactive data environment for an application's life*, a program designed for building database management systems.

ideal filters Filters that have flat response, infinite cutoff attenuation, and linear phase response. In practice, you can choose a cutoff frequency, and an attenuation rate and phase response based on the number of poles and filter characteristic.

idealized system A conceptual system that is often used as a standard to measure the performance of other systems.

idealized value An expected or desired value of a parameter. The idealized value may be assumed to exist even though it is impossible to determine.

ideal noise diode A type of diode that has an infinite internal impedance and in which complete shot noise fluctuations are suppressed.

ideal sample-hold A sample-hold in which tracking is error-free, acquisition occurs instantaneously with zero settling times, and hold time is infinite with zero leakage. Commercial units are specified in the ways in which they depart from the ideal. *Also see* SAMPLE-HOLD.

Idea Tree A thinking tool that gives you control over the examination and expansion of your thoughts on any subject. It lets you structure your ideas as a tree, as a graphic representation of the decomposition of your thinking into levels of detail. You can add ideas to the tree and then rearrange and reorganize them. It can be used for job descriptions, writing, and problem structure.

identification systems Systems that are used to monitor or control the location of moving ob-

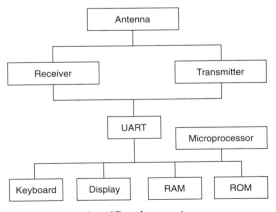

Identification system

jects, such as parts or vehicles, from a central location. The operator may issue commands to control the flow or direction to groups of parts or to a specific part or vehicle on the basis of the information that has been forwarded to the control station. A simplified block diagram of the system is shown in the following figure. This diagram shows the system for communicating with the central control station. A receiver and transmitter are shown, but a transponder could be utilized equally as well. Communications are conducted through a UART and the I/O interface to the data bus of the microcomputer system. Identification systems are an important industrial area for microcomputers.

identifier Any symbol that is used to tag, name, or indicate data.

identifier word A full-length word used in search or search-and-read operations. The identifier word may be stored in a special register and then compared with each word in the suspected sequence.

identity element A logical element that provides a true output when all inputs are the same. The term is usually used for circuits with only two inputs, while identity gates and units may have more than two inputs. Also called *equivalence element*.

identity gate An N-input device or circuit that yields a specified output signal only when all N-input signals are the same, as shown in the following table. Also called an *identity unit*.

Inputs			Output
0	0	0	1
1	0	0	0
1	1	0	0
1	1	1	1
0	1	0	0
1	0	1	0
0	1	1	0

IDF Abbreviation for *integrated data file*.

IDI Abbreviation for *improved data interchange*.

idle signal A signal on a communication channel indicating that the channel is not busy. For modems, the high-frequency tone is used. The idle signal indicates that the connection is still valid, even though no data is being sent. Otherwise, a communications device might think that the connection has been terminated.

idle time That portion of available time when the hardware is not being utilized. Idle time may be the time between runs when no work is scheduled.

IDN Abbreviation for *integrated digital network*, a network in which connections established by digital switching are used for the transmissions of digital signals.

IDP Abbreviation for *integrated data processing*, a data-processing approach in which all stages of processing are carried out using a coherent systems approach, such as a business system where data for orders and buying are combined to accomplish the functions of scheduling, invoicing, and accounting.

IDS Abbreviation for *integrated data storage*.

IDTV Abbreviation for *improved-definition television*, a term that refers to improvements restricted to television sets.

IDX See NDX.

IEC Abbreviation for *International Electrotechnical Commission*.

IEEE Abbreviation for *Institute of Electrical and Electronic Engineers* (pronounced "eye-triple-ee").

IEEE 488 A parallel bus standard also known as the general purpose interface bus (*GPIB*), the Hewlett-Packard interface bus (*HP-IB*), or ANSI bus (*ANSI MC11978*). The standard was originally developed by Hewlett-Packard for interfacing programmable electronic test equipment. The standard was later adopted by the IEEE and the American National Standards Institute.

There are many IEEE 488 bus-compatible devices, including computer peripherals. The IEEE 488 bus supports data transfer rates as high as one megabyte, and most microcomputer peripherals. Some personal computers use a 488 bus to interface with floppy disks.

The IEEE 488 bus uses a 24-pin wide cable for the sixteen signals: eight parallel data lines and eight control lines, as shown in the figure. Devices that interface to the bus always use a male plug. The bus cables have both male and female plugs at each end to allow multiple devices to be connected in a daisy chain. As many as 15 devices may share the bus. Devices may

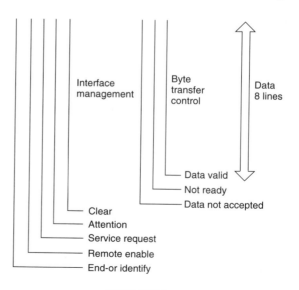

IEEE 488 bus

talk, transmit data, listen, receive data, and/or control the bus. Devices can be separated by 20 meters, but for maximum speeds, cable lengths should be limited to one meter for each device. Every device on the bus is assigned a control address. A listener can respond only to messages addressed to it. A control device can cause a talker to send data to a desired listener by issuing the correct address. Thus, peripheral devices can transfer data among themselves without involving a host computer.

IEEE 488 cables Cables compatible with devices equipped with the standard IEEE-488 interface. You can interconnect up to 15 programmable instruments in star or daisy chain networks with these cables.

IEEE 488 printer adapter An adapter that allows a printer with a Centronics-compatible parallel interface to be attached to the IEEE 488 or HP-IB bus, as shown in the figure. DIP switches are built-in for user programming of a 0 to 31 device address.

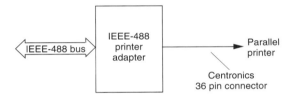

IEEE 488 printer adapter

IEEE 488 tester/exerciser A portable GPIB bus tester designed to test and monitor bus operations. The unit supports all of the IEEE 488 command mnemonics with dedicated keys on the front control panel; the unit's microprocessor automatically performs the necessary mnemonic-to-hex conversion. The unit has hex displays for data lines (488 mnemonic and data characters on the bus), and two columns of LEDs for displaying control handshake lines (five control and three handshake). A serial output port is included to allow the connection of a monitoring CRT for the identification of data transmission problems when the unit is in the listening mode.

The unit can function as a controller and can configure other devices as talkers and listeners via a series of keystrokes. A canned massage is resident in the unit for test (other messages can be specially programmed). The 488 tester is also capable of performing a serial poll and sending the results to an attached monitor.

IEEE 802 Standards for the interconnection of LAN (local area network) equipment. The IEEE 802 standard deals with the physical and link layers of the OSI model. *Also see* OSI MODEL.

IEEE 802.2 A standard that describes the data link control layer of a LAN and how the data connection is made over the physical cable media.

IEEE 802.3 A standard that describes the physical layer of a LAN using CSMA/CD access methods on a bus or tree topology. Both Ethernet and AT&T Starlan use a subset of this standard.

IEEE 802.4 A standard that describes the physical layer of a LAN using token passing access methods on a bus topology. ARCnet does not use this standard, even though it is a token passing, bus topology LAN.

IEEE 802.5 A standard that describes the physical layer of a LAN using token passing access methods on a ring topology. IBM uses this standard with their token ring products.

IEEE 10Base2 An IEEE standard for thinwire Ethernet: 10 Mbps/baseband/200 meters.

IEEE 10Base5 An IEEE standard for twisted pair Ethernet: 10 Mbps/baseband/twisted pair.

IER register A register that holds the multiplier during a multiplication operation (from the last two syllables of *multiplier*).

IF Abbreviation of *intermediate frequency*, the signal in a superheterodyne receiver that appears at the output of the first detector.

IF instruction A command for conditional searching. For example, consider a print-merge instruction included in a main document that tells a word processor to check the text in fields of a data document to see if that text meets certain conditions. If the conditions are met, the word processor includes the text from the field (or other text that you specify), when it prints form documents. IF instructions are also used in many programming languages. *Also see* ELSE INSTRUCTION.

IFIP Abbreviation for *International Federation of Information Processing*.

IF-THEN A logical inclusion or implication operator that states if A and B are statements, IF A THEN B is false if A is true and B is false; IF A THEN B is true if A is false and B is true or A and B are both true.

IF-THEN gate A gate that performs the IF-THEN operation. An IF-THEN gate may be implemented in hardware or software.

IF-THEN, NOT A logic operator possessing the property that if A is a statement and B is a statement, the NOT IF A THEN B operator is true if A is true and B is false, false if A is false and B is true, and false if both statements are true.

IF tube An inclined field acceleration tube designed for use in particle (Van De Graaff) accelerators, invented by Dr. Robert Van de Graaff.

ignistor A device composed of a transistor and a matched zener diode, integrated into one package.

ignore 1. A typed character used to indicate that no action should be taken. **2.** An instruction to inhibit execution.

ignore gate A gate with the Boolean logic A IGNORE B or B IGNORE A. *Also see* BOOLEAN ALGEBRA.

ignore gate, negative A gate with the Boolean logic negative A IGNORE B or negative B IGNORE A. *Also see* BOOLEAN ALGEBRA.

illegal character A character or character code that is not valid according to specified criteria. Illegal characters can be detected to indicate machine malfunctions.

illegal code A symbol that is not a true member of a defined code or language.

illegal operation An operation that cannot be performed or an operation that is performed with invalid results.

Illiac (*o.t.*) One of the world's earliest computers. Designed and built at the University of Illinois, it was the only one owned by a university in 1952. It was retired from service in December, 1962 after 10 years of 24-hour-a-day operation.

IM Abbreviation for *integral modules*.

image dissector *See* IMAGE SENSOR.

image enhancement In graphics and scanning, techniques for increasing apparent sharpness without increasing actual resolution. This usually takes the form of increasing the brightness change at the edges.

image file A file of data that represents an image.

ImagePress A desktop publishing program that supports predesigned page and document templates, allows you to mix up to 1,000 landscape and portrait-oriented pages in a file. You can also import spreadsheets and create lines, circles, rectangles, and text with different width and shade patterns. It includes a true word processor and a spelling checker, will create indexes and table of contents automatically, and supports both LaserJet and PostScript-compatible laser printers.

ImagePrint A program that enables you to produce high-quality characters on a dot matrix printer. Embedded backslash (/) commands in text files are used to select bold, underlining, double-width, italics, superscript, subscript, half-high, ten or twelve characters per inch, compressed, and proportional characters. Text can be formatted (with the program's formatting capabilities.

image processing Refers to techniques that manipulate the pixel values of an image, sometimes to the point where it hardly resembles the original, for some particular purpose. Examples are brightness or contrast correction, color correction, changing size (scaling), or changing the shape of the image (warping). Applying a *filter* to an image, or a piece of it, also changes its look in some way; for example, to resemble an Impressionist painting. Also referred to as *image manipulation*.

image program 1. A drawing, illustration, and/or paint package. Capabilities of some image programs include the ability to emulate real-world tools, such as pencils or charcoal, to break a drawing into layers (objects) that can be manipulated separately. *Also see* PAINT PROGRAM, DRAW PROGRAM. **2.** A COM program, in that it uses the same addresses when loaded as those that appear in the program when viewed on the disk.

image sensor 1. A type of light-intensity transducer that can detect differences in light within a sample space. One type of image sensor uses silicon chips in a continuous array. **2.** As used in optical character recognition, any transducer that detects the light intensity in different areas of a sample space.

imagesetter A typesetting device that ran handle graphics files, as well as text.

Image Studio An image editing and grayscale paint program for the Mac that lets you produce camera-ready halftones and incorporate them into desktop-published documents. It offers up to 256 levels of gray. It is useful for editing or processing continuous-tone images that have been digitized using a gray-level scanner. Selective filters are provided to sharpen, blur, or diffuse all or part of an image.

ImagingObjects A C++ imaging toolkit that allows you to write applications that enlarge, rotate, reduce, cut, copy, and paste. You can perform bitwise operations, sharpen, smooth, and extract edges.

IMC Abbreviation for *image motion compensation*.

imitation 2D A technique of circuit fabrication using a thin-film board containing a lattice of holes into which dot-type circuit elements are dropped.

immediate access store A store operation with an access time that is very small compared to other operating times.

immediate address An instruction in which the address contains the value of the operand. Sometimes called a *zero-level address*. In the 8080 microprocessor, the operand is provided by the second byte of the instruction, as shown in the following example:

$$SBI\ 4;\ (A = A - 4)$$

This operation subtracts the instant 4 from the accumulator.

immediate addressing A form of addressing in which the operand contains the value to be operated on. Immediate addressing requires address reference, since the operands and instructions are in the same location. Almost all microprocessors use immediate addressing for jump and call instructions.

immediate instruction An instruction that contains the operand itself rather than an address. The use of immediate instructions allows only half as much memory to be required since instruction and operand are contained in the same word. Immediate instructions include addition, subtraction, load, and compare in some microprocessors.

IMPACT Acronym for *implementation planning and control technique*.

impact printer A device in which the typing element directly strikes the paper to produce a character or symbol, such as a dot-matrix printer.

IMP computer In the Advanced Research Projects Agency net, small computers that handle the store-and-forward communications of the packet network, and also have the capability of collecting message-handling statistics.

impedance The ratio of voltage to current in alternating-current circuits. Impedance contains a resistance term and a reactance term, and is expressed in ohms.

impedance bridge A circuit used for the measurement of resistance, capacitance, and inductance.

impedance compensator A network used in a transmission path to obtain a desired characteristic over a specific frequency range.

impedor The physical realization of an impedance, as in an inductor, capacitor, or resistor.

imperative statement A statement defining an action in a symbolic program that is converted into machine language. Imperative statements consist of verbs and operands, and usually express a complete unit of procedure.

implementation The phase following final approval of a system, during which the details of the system are developed and carried out.

implication A logical IF-THEN operation that says if A and B are statements, A INCLUSION B is false if A is true and B is false. A INCLUSION B is true if A is false and B is true, or A and B are both true.

implication gate *See* IF-THEN GATE.

implicit address An address reference used in assembler programming that is specified as one absolute expression. An implicit address is converted into explicit form before it can be assembled into object code.

implicit differentiation A procedure used in analog computers in which functions are derived implicitly. For example, if the output is the square of the input, then the input is the square root of the output; if the output is the integral of the input, then the input is the derivative of the output.

implicit reference A motor-control technique suitable for implementation with a microcomputer. Usually, an external reference source, such as a series of programmable counters, furnishes a clock train that the motor locks onto. With the implicit scheme, the processor calculates the desired rotation period and then forces the motor to conform. No phase angle is used.

implicit rights Rights that a NetWare user has inherited from some other source, such as group membership, downline directories, or security equivalence.

implied indirect addressing A form of microprocessor addressing where the data memory is addressed by a register. Any instruction that references the memory uses the address that is pre-established in the register. There are instructions to load, increment, and test the address register. In some systems, incrementing of the address register occurs automatically and concurrently with some of the instructions. The probability of the next location containing the desired data is high, so these compound instructions can save code space and execution time.

import To get either data or graphics files created outside the particular system or application, into the system or application.

imprinter A device for marking characters onto a form, such as impact printers, presses, pressure plates, and stamping machines.

impulse 1. A pulse that begins and ends within so short a time that it may be regarded mathematically as infinitesimal. The change in the medium, however, is usually of a finite amount. **2.** A change in the intensity or level of some medium, usually over a relatively short period of time. **3.** A shift in electrical potential of a point for a short period of time compared to the time period.

impulse excitation 1. Excitation in which the current is allowed to flow for only a very short period during each cycle. **2.** The maintenance of an oscillatory current in a tuned circuit by pulses synchronous with free oscillations or at a submultiple frequency.

impulse generator A circuit providing a single pulse or a continuous series of pulses, generally by capacitor discharge; shaping is accomplished through the charging of capacitors in parallel and the discharging of them in series.

impulse inertia A property of an insulator in which the voltage required to cause disruptive discharge varies inversely with its time of application.

impulse noise A type of noise characterized by high amplitude and short duration, sometimes occurring as a group of impulses or burst. Impulse noise is a common source of error, originating from switching equipment or electrical storms.

impurity A material added to semiconductor crystals to produce excess holes or electrons. Excess holes are produced by acceptor impurities, and excess electrons are produced by donor impurities.

impurity level The energy level in a material due to the addition of impurity atoms.

IMS 1. Abbreviation for *Institute of Management Sciences*. **2.** (*o.t.*) Abbreviation for *Information Management System*, old database software from IBM based on the hierarchical data management model.

IMU Abbreviation for *inertial measurement unit*.

IN Abbreviation for *input*.

inaccuracies, systematic See SYSTEMATIC INACCURACIES.

in-band signaling Telephone system signaling that is transmitted over the same path and within the same frequency band used for the voice signal.

inbound packet In NetWare Diagnostic Services, the number of times (since IPX was loaded) that a node's driver has given an incoming packet to IPX.

INCH Abbreviation for *integrated chopper*.

incipient failure A degradation failure that is just beginning to exist or appear.

in-circuit emulator See ICE.

in-circuit test The testing of individual integrated circuits by checking their outputs. With an in-circuit test, logic inputs can be programmed while the outputs are measured to isolate pins stuck at zero or one, along with solder splashes and open connections.

in-circuit tester An automated test unit, such as the one shown in the figure, for performing in-circuit tests on mounted components. Some in-circuit testers can prescribe repairs and test simple components such as resistors in less than six milliseconds each.

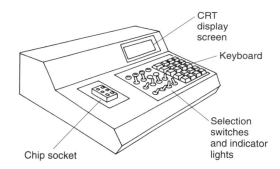

A device for programming an in-circuit test

inclusion See IF-THEN.

inclusion gate A circuit or device that performs the inclusion operation.

incoming data alert See IDA.

incoming packet discarded In NetWare File Server Environment Services, the number of incoming packets that were received in a routing buffer that needed to be transferred to a DGroup buffer so the socket dispatcher could transfer the packet to the correct socket. If no buffers are available, such packets are lost.

incoming packets In NetWare Diagnostic Services, the number of times (since SPX was loaded) that a node's driver has given an incoming packet to SPX.

inconnector A connector used in flowcharting to indicate the continuation of a broken flow line.

increment To move ahead by one step at a time; refers to a software operation used with stacks and stack pointers. The stack pointer is used to hold the addresses of information stored in the stack register. The pointer is incremented after each byte is removed from the stack and decremented (moved back one step) as each byte is added to the stack.

incremental An arrangement of outputs used in rotating sensors. The outputs are arranged such that the phase shift is 90 degrees apart, which allows the direction of rotation to be determined.

incremental backup A method of backing up only those files that are new or have been changed since the disk was last backed up.

incremental compaction A data compaction method that uses only the initial value and changes in storage for transmission. Incremental compaction allows a saving in time and space because only changes at specific intervals are processed.

incremental computer A computer that mainly uses an incremental representation of data; a special-purpose computer designed to process changes in variables as well as the absolute values of the variables.

incremental data Data that represents the change from the value of the data that just preceded it; each data word or value is referenced to the prior position.

incremental dimension A dimension expressed with respect to the preceding point in a sequence of points.

incremental induction Refers to one half of the algebraic difference between the maximum and minimum magnetic induction at a point in a material that has been subject simultaneously to a polarizing and a varying magnetizing force.

Incremental integrator A digital integrator that has an output that is maximum positive, zero, or maximum negative when the input is maximum positive, zero, or maximum negative.

Incremental representation A representation of a variable in which the changes in the variable are represented, rather than the variable itself.

incremental system A system in which each coordinate or positional dimension is taken from the last position.

IND Abbreviation for *indicator*.

indent In word processing, to bring a line or lines of typing in from the margin, as at the start of a paragraph.

independent clock synchronization A form of network synchronization based on the use of clocks that are independently timed or constrained within certain limits of accuracy.

independent heterodyne An oscillator, electrically separate from the detector, used for supplying local oscillations in heterodyne reception applications.

independent program loader A program that allows the system user to load nonsystem programs from operating system file devices.

independent software A program capable of using only the data designed for it.

index 1. A symbol or number used to identify a specific quantity in an array of similar items. **2.** An ordered reference list of the contents of a file with keys for identification of the contents and the action required to prepare such a list. **3.** In numerical control, the movement of a machine part to a predetermined location.

index address register See PROGRAM COUNTER.

indexed address An address that is modified by the contents of an index register or similar technique. As used in the 6800 microprocessor system, the operand will be in a memory location with an address formed by adding the second byte of the instruction to the value contained in X, such as the following:

```
ADD A 3, X ;(add X + 3 to accumulator A)
```

This instruction adds the contents of the memory location referenced by the contents of X + 3 to accumulator A. This instruction becomes the same as direct addressing if X contains zero. Sometimes called a *variable address*.

indexed addressing A form of addressing in which the address contained in the second byte of the instruction is added to the index register.

indexed files A file structure consisting of a series of pointers to data blocks throughout the disk. Indexed files are used for applications with a large amount of random-access data. They have the open-ended characteristic of chained files with a much faster access time. *Also see* CHAINED FILES.

indexed-sequential access method See ISAM.

indexed-sequential file An indexed file in which records are maintained in key field order for both sequential and direct access.

index entry In word processing, a term or phrase preceded by an index code to be included in an index.

indexing A programming technique developed to compress the coding. It allows a program loop to address data by adding a value to the address in the instruction. This value is then incremented or decremented to access the data array. The indirect or implied indirect address registers can also be incremented, decremented, and tested for zero or some value, and no address in the instruction is needed, only the index value in the indirect address register.

Some microprocessors combine the indirect address register scheme with indexing. An instruction such as *DECREMENT REGISTER AND JUMP ON REGISTER NOT ZERO* provides the dual functions of an indirect address register and the index.

index of refraction The ratio of light velocity in a vacuum to its velocity in a given transmission medium.

index register A register used to hold the addresses of information subject to modification prior to or during the execution of an instruction. The index register contents are available for loading into the stack when required. Modification may be either by addition or subtraction, yielding a new effective address.

index sensing A method in which an index hole is punched in the floppy disk to mark the beginning of the first sector. The hole is detected by a photosensing circuit.

index value A desired preset value of a controlled quantity used as a target value for an automatic control system.

index word register A register that stores a word used to modify addresses under the direction of the control section of the computer.

indicator A device that registers conditions resulting from computations.

indicator chart A chart or table used by a programmer to record items concerning the indicators in the program. The indicator chart can be a useful part of the program documentation, since indicators are often used to vary the sequence of operations within the program.

indirect address An address that specifies a location that contains either a direct address or another indirect address. Indirect addressing is any level of addressing other than the first level of direct addressing. It forms a system of computer cross referencing. Also called *multilevel address* or *deferred address*.

indium phosphide A semiconductor compound used in LEDs (light-emitting diodes) and other optoelectronic applications.

individual test menu A menu that allows you to run tests one at a time. It may allow you to run tests that check the communications port and the printer. The section can help isolate a problem to a specific device, as shown in the following figure.

Individual test selection
1. RAM test
2. RAM arbitration test
3. Video controller test
4. Floppy diagnostic test
5. COMM port test (no loopback plug)
6. COMM port test (loopback plug)
7. Printer port test (loopback plug)
8. Printer confidence test
9. Synchronous COMM test
10. System test
11. Video alignment pattern
12. Private RAM test
13. Keyboard test
Type selection number and <ENTER>

Individual test selection menu

induced Produced by the influence of an electric or magnetic field.

induced charge An electrostatic charge produced by the electric field surrounding a nearby object, such as that produced on a conductor as a result of a charge on a nearby conductor.

induced current The current that flows in a conductor that is moved perpendicularly to a magnetic field or that is subjected to a magnetic field of varying intensity.

induced environment The environment of shocks, vibrations, temperatures, accelerations, and pressure that are imposed upon a system due to the operation or handling of the system.

induced failure A failure essentially caused by a physical condition or phenomenon external to the failed item.

induced noise Noise that arises because of sufficiently high frequencies in the area in space close to a conductor.

induced voltage Voltage that is produced in a conductor when the conductor is moved through the magnetic field of a second conductor, or when the field varies in intensity and cuts across the conductor space.

inductance The property of a metallic conductor or circuit element containing metal that opposes changes in the current flowing through the circuit.

inductance bridge An instrument, similar to a Wheatstone bridge, for measuring an unknown inductance by comparing it with a known inductance.

induction coil A device that used induction for transforming a direct current into an alternating current.

induction noise The noise produced when two circuits or conductors are inductively coupled together.

inductive That property of an electric circuit or device that tends to prevent changes.

inductive coupling Coupling between circuits and conductors due to mutual inductance and a source of potential interference.

inductive neutralization A condition in which the feedback susceptance of the capacitance of the circuit elements is balanced by the equal and opposite susceptance of an inductor.

inductive potentiometer A type of toroidally wound autotransformer with one or more adjustable sliders.

inductive pressure transducer A transducer that uses pressure to move a mechanical member that alters the self-inductance of a single coil. The inductance is changed by the relative motion of a core and inductive coil as shown in the figure. Inductive single coil transducers have been used in L-C tank circuit oscillators, where they formed the frequency control. Their use has diminished because of difficulties in compensating for temperature effects, which required a matching of core and windings materials for temperature versus permeability characteristics.

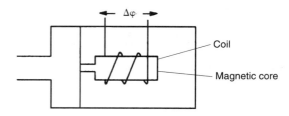

Inductive pressure transducer

inductive resistor A wirewound resistor having appreciable inductance at the frequencies in use.

inductosyn scale A precision data element for the accurate measurement and control of angles or linear distances, utilizing the inductive coupling between conductors separated by a small air gap.

industrial control The control of machines, processes, and systems involved in manufacturing operations.

industrial control communications Communications equipment designed for industrial control applications.

industrial control modules Electronic control modules designed primarily for industrial control applications. Examples include analog multiplexers, transducer amplifiers, analog-to-digital converters, sample-and-hold devices, and digital-to-analog converters.

industrial microcomputer A special version of a microcomputer designed specifically for industrial applications such as pollution control, utility control, machine tool control, and material control systems. These microcomputers are specially modified to withstand the environment found in a process or manufacturing application. They are usually incorporated into *industrial workstations* designed to provide various levels of protection, and with a built-in industrial keyboard and monitor.

industrial PCs PCs designed for industrial applications, available in four different configurations:

- Table or desktop
- Portable, battery-powered
- Rack-mounted
- NEMA (National Electrical Manufacturers Association) enclosured

A typical configuration for control devices in U.S. plants is rack mounting, as shown in the figure. NEMA enclosures are generally required by plants with corrosive environments.

industry standard architecture *See* ISA.

inequivalence A Boolean exclusive-OR operator, which produces a true output if only one of the

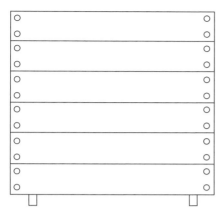

Rack-mounting industrial PC

two input variables it connects is true, as shown in the following table.

Inputs A B	Output C
0 0	0
1 0	1
0 1	1
1 1	0

inequivalence gate A device or circuit that performs the inequivalence operation.

inference engine The software for an expert system that processes new data, reports possible decisions, and increases the knowledge base. *Also see* EXPERT SYSTEM.

infinite loop A loop that, due to an error in the writing of a program, continues to execute until it is stopped by the operator or the time allotted to it expires.

infix notation A method of forming one-dimensional expressions, arithmetic or logical, by alternating single operands and operators. Any operator performs its indicated function upon its adjacent terms, which are defined subject to the rules of operator precedence and grouping brackets that eliminate any ambiguity.

Infobase A forms-driven database management system with mailmerge capabilities. You can use it to create forms that match preprinted forms, such as IRS forms. These forms can then be used to create or access databases.

information The aggregation of data that produces a whole idea, condition, or situation. Information may be a set of symbols that indicates alternatives for a situation.

information bits Any bits that are generated by the data source and not used for error control. Information theory provides that all information can be represented by some collection of bits, regardless of the complexity of the information.

information center An organization designed to support end-user computing and provide decision support.

information content A measure of transmission, divided into two types. *Gross information content* is the number of bits needed to transmit a message over a noiseless system with a specified accuracy, regardless of redundancy. *Net information content* is the minimum number required for essential information only.

information feedback system An information transmission system used in telecommunications that utilizes an echo check to verify the accuracy of the transmission.

information heading That portion of a message that contains control information such as the identification of originating station, the identification of a sending device or system, message priority, and message routing information.

information processing The execution of a systematic sequence of operations performed on data or information. In a typical microprocessor system, the processor accepts data, interprets it, and outputs the results. Information-processing activities include routing, arithmetic, and diagnostic operations. In most microcomputer systems, these operations will be performed by one processor or a single arithmetic processor and another processor for routing and diagnostics.

information retrieval The methods and procedures required for recovering specific information from stored data. Information retrieval may involve the cataloging of data so that all or part may be called out at any time.

information separator *See* IS, 2.

information society A society strongly dependent on the flow of information.

information system The network of all communication methods within an organization.

Information Systems Network *See* ISN.

information theory A branch of science involved in the likelihood of accurate communications and transmission of information. Information theory uses mathematical analysis to determine the efficiency of communications techniques.

information utility A company that provides references and consumer information at standard rates to individuals and companies. *Also see* ONLINE SERVICE.

informed user A computer user who is aware of the components of a system, knows what it is capable of doing and not doing, and is comfortable using computers to solve problems.

Informix A relational database management system.

Info-XL An easy-to-use personal information manager that interactively combines, links, and stores both structured data (records) and

freeform text. Six active windows permit users to outline ideas, store structured data, create and print reports, view time-sensitive calendaring events, schedule activities, or locate and retrieve information from their entire information base.

Ingres A relational database management system that runs on a variety of operating systems. It is one of the more powerful database systems.

inherited error An error that is carried forward from a previous step in processing. An inherited error produces an initial error or offset for the next processing step.

inhibit A computer operation, signal, or pulse that prevents another operation from taking place. An inhibit might be used on a bus system to disable a channel to give another channel control of the bus.

inhibit gate A circuit used as a switch and usually placed in parallel with the circuit it is controlling.

inhibiting input A computer gate input that can prevent outputs that might otherwise occur.

INI file Short for "initialization," an ASCII text file used by Windows or Windows applications to configure operating parameters. For example, the Windows operating system relies on five INI files: CONTROL.INI, WIN.INI, PROGRAM.INI, WINFILE.INI, and SYSTEM.INI. Other applications will likely have an INI file associated with them.

INIT A label used to denote an *initialization* signal in an IC pin or bus line.

initial condition mode A mode in analog computers in which all integrators are inoperative and the required initial conditions are applied to the system.

initialization packet A token ring packet used when a node joins the network.

initialize To perform the preliminary, nonrepeating steps for a routine, such as setting counters and addresses to zero.

initial program load *See* IPL.

initial review The first presentation to management on a systems development project covering users' specifications and general recommendations of the analyst.

injection logic, C³L (complementary constant-current logic) A form of bipolar logic for the TTL (10 to 50 nanoseconds) application range. This logic form is complicated by five Schottky devices in each gate, but it allows compact processor circuits. C³L processor slices were first built at the end of 1975.

injection molding The manufacturing process for making CD ROMs in which molten plastic is squirted into a mold.

injector grid A grid that injects a modulating voltage into the electron stream of the first detector of a superheterodyne receiver.

inkjet printer A nonimpact printer that sprays ink through an electrostatic field and onto paper to form the intended characters and symbols.

inline A method of processing in which all individual transactions are completely processed in the sequence in which they arrive, without the records being grouped or arranged.

inline assembly A mechanical assembly operation in which a line of assembly heads inserts electrical components into circuit boards.

inline package *See* DIP.

inline procedures A set of statements used in COBOL for controlling the program operations.

inline subroutine A subroutine inserted directly into the operational sequence of processing. Inline subroutines are recopied at each point at which they are required in a routine.

inner macroinstruction A macroinstruction nested inside a macrodefinition. The opposite is called an *outer macroinstruction*. *Also see* MACROINSTRUCTION.

in-phase Refers to two waves of the same frequency that pass through their maximum and minimum values of like polarity at the same instant.

INPOST A utility program in the Message Handling Service (MHS) used for transferring messages from an application to MHS.

input A device or set of devices used to bring data into another device; for example, a keyboard or mouse. An input may be a channel for impressing or inserting a state or condition on another device, or a device or process involved in an input operation. *Input* is often used as an all-encompassing term for input data, input signal, or input terminal when such usage is clear within a given context.

input area Internal storage area into which data from external storage is transferred. Successive groups of data can be compared for the correct format and are held until signaled for by the program.

input block A section of internal storage reserved for data from external storage (concerning processing and storage operations).

input buffer **1.** In a printer or other device, a buffer that holds characters in memory until they are ready to be printed or processed. **2.** In NetWare, a pointer to a buffer up to 80 characters long that returns the string typed in by the user.

input buffer register A register that receives data from input devices such as disks at one speed and then transfers it to internal storage at a different, usually much higher, speed.

input channel A channel for impressing a state or condition on a device or circuit.

input converter An analog-to-digital converter packaged for process control applications.

input editing Operations done on input data to convert the format for more convenient processing and storage. Input editing may also check the data for proper format, completeness, and accuracy. Many times, the input data has been formatted for the convenience of humans and must be reformatted for efficient machine usage.

input impedance An impedance that is measured

at the input terminal of a device, usually under no-load or other specified conditions.

input module A packaged functional device or unit used for conveying data into another device.

input/output See I/O.

input/output control system See IOCS.

input/output processor See IOP.

input/output, simultaneous See SIMULTANEOUS I/O.

input program A routine to direct or control the reading of programs and data into the computer system. Input programs may be internally stored or wired and may use a bootstrap operation for housekeeping and control operations.

input reference A value used to compare the deviation or error of a measured variable. The input reference is a selected value and is also known as the *set point* or *desired value*.

input resolution The smallest increment of dimension that can be an input to the system.

input signal The control loop signal when it enters a data block.

input stream The sequence of job control statements submitted to an operating system on an input unit. Also called *input job stream* or *job input stream*.

input symbol A flowcharting symbol, shaped like a parallelogram, indicating where in a program data must be input.

input transformer A transformer for isolating a circuit from any other circuit.

input translator A section or a program that converts a programmer's instructions into operators and operands for the computer. A translator can also check the input for errors of syntax.

input work queue A waiting line of job control statements from which jobs and job steps are selected for processing.

inquiry The interrogation of the contents of storage from a local or remote point by keyboard, keypad, or other device.

inquiry processing A type of processing in which inquiries and records from a number of terminals are used to interrogate and update one or more master files maintained by the central system. Also called *inquiry and transaction processing*.

inquiry station A remote terminal from which interrogation into computing or data-processing equipment is made. A reply to the inquiry is displayed on the screen until the operator desires to erase the display using an erase button on the console. Also called *inquiry terminal*.

INS Abbreviation for *instrument*.

insert 1. A word-processing function that allows the introduction of new material within previously typed text. 2. A key in the cursor movement section of many keyboards that toggles the user between insert and overwrite typing modes.

inserted subroutine A subroutine that must be relocated and injected into the main routine at each place it is used.

in-service testing A form of testing in which operational traffic is not interrupted.

instability A measure of the fluctuations or irregularities in the performance of a variable, circuit, device, or system.

INSTALIT An installer program with extensive system/environment/network sensing. An automatic master-diskette builder adds transparent CRC checking with state-of-the-art compression ratios and speed for multi-volume disk sets. A script language provides procedural control flow through internal and user-defined procedures and can run other programs. It edits system and binary files and provides easy generation of menus and dialog boxes.

INSTALL A set of tools that automates the installation of any product distributed on diskettes or CD-ROM. INSTALL is configured using a script file (an easy-to-learn "installation language") that gives complete control over the installation process. INSTALL handles all end-user errors, reduces disk costs by compressing data, detects the target computer's environment, modifies system files, and updates prior versions.

installation The systems or network development step involving the set up and testing of a new package, system, or network.

installation time Time required for installing, connecting, and testing either hardware or software (or both) until acceptance is complete.

InstallBoss An installation program generator for DOS-based applications. You can create .EXE installation programs without the need for programming or the use of script files. It includes compression utilities and allows for modification of CONFIG.SYS and AUTOEXEC.BAT with a selective installation re-boot option, greeting, and copyright messages.

INSTALL PRO A superset of INSTALL which includes a ddb utility to perform the following additional functions: automatically format disks, build or modify script files, compress files, and split large files across multiple diskettes. The ddb utility has a full-screen point-and-shoot interface to build distribution disk sets automatically. It also creates a configuration file, which can be used to quickly generate new distribution disk sets for updates.

instantaneous companding A form of companding used in delta modulation in which changes in step size are made at a rate equal to the sampling rate. *Also see* DELTA MODULATION.

instantaneous power In a circuit or component, the product of the instantaneous voltage and the instantaneous current. This may not be zero even for a nondissipative system because of stored energy, although its time integral must be zero.

Instant-C A programming environment that integrates the edit-compile-link-test cycle with one high-performance programming tool. It offers C programmers significant productivity gains by combining an incremental compiler and linker with automatic static and runtime error detection. It provides use of uninitialized pointers, source level debugging, interactive C expression evaluation (including macros, cross referencing and browsing), single function or partial program execution, and support of programs up to 16M. Instant-C is compatible with Microsoft C source and libraries, allowing programmers to develop using Instant-C and then produce production code using Microsoft C. Instant-C is compatible with commercial object code libraries.

Instant Prototyper A program for designing data-oriented applications. You can build demos for users of DOS or Windows without programming and make changes based on their feedback. It supports data entry and validations including mandatory, protected, picture, range checks, and lists. CUA-compatible objects include main windows, dialogs, mouse, menus, buttons, hypertext, scrollbars, list boxes, directories, text editor, and spreadsheet-like scrollable tables.

Instant Recall A memory-resident, free-form database program with its own word processor. Data can be entered in whatever form you like without worrying about field sizes, and can be recalled without worrying about keywords.

Instant Replay Professional An authoring/development software system for the creation of demo disks and software ads, computer-based training materials, and professional presentations (either laserdisk or computer-based). It manages the capture of audio, video, graphics, animations, and compressed video for incorporation into your presentation.

in string In NetWare Value-Added Process Services this occurs either when Enter is pressed or the input buffer length is reached.

instruction A statement containing information that can be coded and used as a unit in a computer to command it to perform one or more operations. An instruction usually contains one or more addresses and may specify arithmetic operations, such as addition or multiplication, or control operations for data manipulation. Instructions can be grouped as follows:

- Data transfers between registers and memory
- Branching operations
- Input/output control
- Loading and storing accumulators
- Restoring registers and accumulators
- Jumps and stack-pointer operations
- Binary and decimal arithmetic
- Set and reset interrupts
- Increment and decrement registers and memory

instruction address An address that must be used to fetch an instruction.

instruction address register *See* IAR.

instruction area That part of storage selected to store the group of instructions to be executed. The instruction area normally is used to hold the microcomputer program.

instruction characters Characters used as code elements to initiate, modify, and stop control operations. An example is the CR (carriage return) character.

instruction code All of the symbols and definitions used to systemize the instructions for a given computer or executive routine.

instruction control unit *See* ICU.

instruction counter A counter used to indicate the location of the next instruction to be interpreted.

instruction diagnostic A device using hardware and software that completely tests all CPU instructions, including interrupts, in all modes.

instruction execution logic The logic that allows each instruction to be retrieved or fetched from memory, decoded, and executed. The instruction execution logic may involve program counters, address registers, instruction registers, and the general-purpose register, along with many transfers between these units and memory.

instruction formats All instruction formats use an operational (OP) code that defines the basic operation. In general, all instructions must also address one or more elements to be operated on. The addressing is either implied by a unique OP code or it specifies the desired elements. The elements to be operated on may be internal registers or bits, or external memory or I/O. The number of elements that can be operated on by an instruction is related to the architecture of the processor and the instruction word size.

The two architectures that determine the instruction formats are *register-oriented processors* and *memory-oriented processors*. Register-oriented processors use the instruction formats to address internal registers; memory-oriented processors use the instruction format to select the modes for addressing memory. The 8-bit microprocessors, which have a limited instruction word size, have to choose between the two architectures. The 8080 favors a register architecture, and the 6800 favors a memory architecture. The 16- and 32-bit microprocessors have an instruction word size large enough for both architectures.

instruction modification An alteration in the operational code of a command or instruction such that if the routine is repeated, the computer will perform a different operation.

instruction operations A typical microprocessor processes instructions that are used to provide the solutions to processing tasks. Instructions and programming techniques used in microprocessor systems fall into seven basic functional groups:

- *Data transfer*, the methods of moving data from one point to another or organizing it for processing
- *Arithmetic operations*, which may include binary or binary coded decimal, or decimal manipulations
- *Logical operations*, including the methods for manipulating data as bits and the methods for obtaining logical functions of these bit combinations
- *Data address modifications*, the methods of modifying addresses in registers to facilitate data manipulation
- *Control transfers*, the techniques such as interrupts for modifying the normal sequence of the program for conditional and unconditional branching
- *Register manipulation*, the methods for storing data along with the manipulation of registers and individual segments of data within registers
- *Input/output operations*, the methods of using input/output instructions

Subroutine usage including the techniques for calling routines, setting up data addresses, returning from subroutines, and nesting subroutines may be used in conjunction with the other operations.

instruction pointer 1. In a microcomputer, a pointer in a register that points to or holds the current instruction. **2.** In NetWare, a created process's instruction pointer.

instruction register *See* IR.

instruction repertoire The set of operations represented in a given operational code.

instruction set The total structured group of characters and definitions to be transferred to the computer as operations are executed. Usually the instructions are listed in alphabetical order and include binary and decimal arithmetic along with logic, shift, store, rotate, load, branch, interrupt, and stack operations. Instruction sets can be encoded in binary, octal, or hexadecimal, with the names of operations in mnemonic form using combinations of letters and numbers.

instruction time The portion of an instruction cycle during which the control unit is analyzing the instruction and setting up to perform the indicated operation.

instruction word The grouping of letters or digits into a single unit that defines operations to be performed by the computer. The instruction word may be a complete computer word or part of the computer word that is executed as an instruction.

instrumentation Devices for measuring, recording, and controlling physical processes and quantitative phenomena.

instrumentation amplifiers A type of amplifier that may contain operational amplifiers, but is distinguished from op amps in that it is a committed device with a definite set of input/output relationships in a fixed configuration. Instrumentation amplifiers are designed for a high common-mode rejection ratio (CMRR), low noise and drift, moderate bandwidth, and a limited gain range, (usually 1 to 1000) programmed by a fixed resistor.

instrumentation calibration A procedure to ascertain, usually by comparison with a standard, the locations at which scale graduations should be placed to correspond to the series of values of the quantity that the instrument is to measure, receive, or transmit.

instrumentation correction The calculated difference between the true value and the indication of the measured quantity; a positive correction denotes that the indication of the instrument is less than the true value.

insulated Separated from other conducting surfaces by a nonconductive material offering a high, permanent resistance to the passage of current.

insulator material A material on or through which essentially no current will flow, used to confine the flow of current within a conductor or to eliminate the shock hazard of a bare conductor.

Int Abbreviation for *interrupt*.

integer One of the whole numbers 0, 1, 2, 3, etc. that does not have a decimal point.

integer programming *See* DISCRETE PROGRAMMING.

IntegrAda An Ada programming support environment for DOS and POSIX. It has a language-sensitive editor, libraries, automatic code generation and error checking tools, validated compiler, and pop-up training tools. It was chosen by the U.S. Air Force as the standard Ada product for the Desktop III contract.

integral action limiter A program or device that limits the output value of a signal due to integral action at a predetermined value.

integral boundary A location in main storage at which a fixed-length field must be positioned. The integral boundary may be a half word or a double word; its address is a multiple of the length of the field.

integral control action A control action in which the rate of change of output is proportional to the input.

integrated amplifier 1. An analog-computer amplifier that has an output voltage proportional to the area under a time-curve plot of a variable between a reference time and any arbitrary point in time. **2.** A high-fidelity stereo amplifier that includes an integral preamplifier with all necessary controls.

integrated circuit *See* IC.

integrated component A single structure with a number of elements that cannot be separated without destroying the function or functions of the device.

integrated data processing *See* IDP.

integrated digital network *See* IDN.

integrated emulator An emulator program whose execution is controlled by an operating system in a multiprogramming environment.

integrated injection logic An integrated circuit logic (abbreviated *IIL* or I^2L) that consists of interconnected bipolar transistors of both polarities. A cross section of an I^2L chip consists of an npn transistor operated in a vertical mode, while a lateral pnp transistor is used as a current source and a load for the preceding stage, as shown in the figure. Isolation is automatically accomplished between the collectors, allowing high packing densities. Besides high packing density, it offers a good speed-power product along with versatility and low cost.

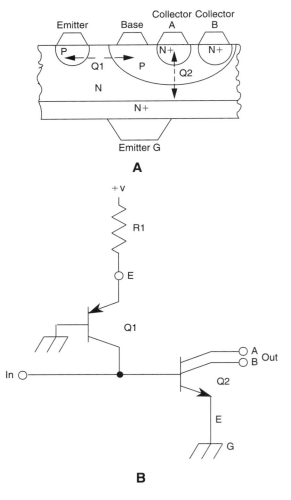

I^2L structure (A) and basic I^2L circuit (B)

integrated manufacturing Refers to systems that use CAD, CAM, robotics, materials resource planning and/or data communications to manufacture goods.

integrated monolithic circuit *See* IC.

Integrated Services Digital Network *See* ISDN.

integrated software Programs that incorporate the functions of several different application types, such as word processing and spreadsheeting, and can share data among the different functions.

integrated system **1.** Programs that allow the introduction of new or allied data into an existing set without having to reenter the previous data. Thus a customer name need not be reentered for use with both accounts receivable and inventory control. **2.** Hardware that works together without further need of additional circuits to allow communications between devices.

integration A/D converters Analog-to-digital converters that perform an indirect conversion by first converting to a function of time and then converting the time function to a digital quantity by using a counter. A dual ramp converter is one example.

integrator A unit or device that performs the mathematical function of integration, usually with reference to time. Integrators include circuits that integrate signals over a period of time and any system with an output proportional to the input.

integrator capacitor A device that may be shunted by a resistor to permit the zero balance of an integrator.

integrity Preservation of data for its intended purpose; data integrity exists as long as accidental or malicious destruction, alteration, or loss of data is prevented.

INTEK C++ A 32-bit C++ compiler that produces standardized C++ output. It is designed to allow the user to move code from different environments in both binary and object code formats. It allows users to continue to work with their existing code and technology (C compilers and related utilities) while they move up to the C++ language.

Intel 386 versus 486 The differences between an 80386 with a 387 math coprocessor and an 80486 lie in the architecture and the speed with which the integrated 486 carries out the same operation as the separate 386/7 chips. The 486 has an on-chip floating-point unit and 8K primary cache, since it is faster to move data about on one processor than it is to shuffle it between two chips.

The 386 also uses two clock cycles to transfer date to or from the main processor. Its 32-bit data bus can transfer two bytes of data per clock cycle, which produces a 66M per second data-transfer rate, as shown in the table that follows.

486	386
32-bit CPU	32-bit CPU
32-bit address bus	32-bit address bus
32-bit data bus	32-bit data bus
33 MHz crystal used for	66 MHz crystal used for
33 MHz clock speed	33 MHz clock speed
Up to 4GB physical memory	Supports 4GB physical memory
Up to 64TB virtual memory	Supports 64TB virtual memory
Maximum data transfer rate—106MB per second	Maximum memory data transfer rate—66MB per second
Average 1.2 instructions/clock cycle	Average 0.3 instructions/clock cycle
1.2 million transistors	270,000 transistors
Integrated floating point unit	External 80387 chip needed
Integrated 8K cache	External hardware cache needed
RISC integer core	CISC integer core
5 stage pipelining	2 stage pipelining
Fast burst bus	No burst mode
Demand paging	Demand paging

When the 486 reads data into the processor, it uses burst mode to fill both the cache and the processor. With the burst mode, the first read operation takes two clock cycles, but subsequent data reads take one clock cycle whether they are 8-bit, 16-bit, or 32-bit transfers. On each clock cycle, the burst transfer reads double data from memory and feeds it to the cache and the processor's instruction pre-fetch queue.

Pipelining allows program instructions to be executed as a series of smaller operations. The 386 uses two-stage pipelining, while the 486 offers five-stage pipelining, allowing sections of five instructions to be executed at one time.

In memory-handling, the 386 and 486 act the same since the same architecture is used for both chips. Demand paging and flat addressing are used for feeding data to the processor at the speeds it needs. The 386 uses these features, but since it is a less efficient processor, it is not able to use them as often as the 486.

Demand paging and flat addressing allow the efficient implementation of virtual memory up to the 64T (terabyte) limit for both chips. Flat addressing allows the processor to treat large areas of virtual memory as one contiguous area, ignoring the earlier constraints of 64K segments and the problems of addressing extended or expanded memory. These features make memory-intensive applications like Windows more efficient.

When the processor needs to work on a memory location that cannot be found in physical memory, a virtual memory swap file is made by the operating system, and the address is read into memory from disk. In a 16-bit segmented system, memory acts like a series of blocks with up to 64K. Data objects that are larger than this will overlap between these 64K segments. When a program like Windows must do this, it slows performance.

In flat addressing, memory can be treated as a single contiguous area. The processor is not tied up loading segments and converting virtual addresses into physical addresses. Flat memory addressing treats physical and virtual memory as one area and the memory decoding is such quicker than reading and converting 64K segments, so data is transferred to and from the processor much faster.

Intel 3002 (*o.t.*) An early two-bit slice microprocessor that used Schottky bipolar technology to achieve the first fast cycle times. The 3002 central processing unit was combined with the 3002 microprogram control unit to form a two-chip microprocessor system based on user-generated microcode stored in the microprogram memory. The two components were combined with memory and peripherals for the first high-speed controllers and processors. Each 3002 represented only a two-bit slice, and devices were connected in parallel to form processors of the desired word length. The basic architecture for the 3002 is shown in the illustration.

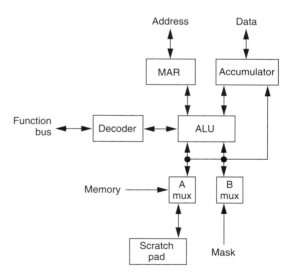

3002 architecture

In the 3002, the microfunctions were controlled by a function bus that instructed the decode unit to select the ALU functions to be performed, generate scratchpad register addresses, and control the A and B multiplexers. A microfunction action could be a data transfer, a shift, an increment or decrement, a test for a specified condition, an initialization for a specified condition, an addition or subtraction in two's complement, a bit mask, or a program counter operation.

Intel 4004 (o.t.) The Intel 4004 was the first microprocessor. It was designed as the processing element of a desk calculator and introduced in 1971. The 4004 was never designed to be a general-purpose computer. Its shortcomings in this area were soon recognized. It was, however, the first general-purpose computing device in a chip to be on the market. Many other chips introduced at about the same time were called microprocessors, but were in fact only calculator chips. Many of them used serial bit-by-bit arithmetic.

Intel 4040 (o.t.) An improved version of the Intel 4004, which was the first true microprocessor. In order to preserve the software investment of the 4004, the 4040 instruction set was made compatible with the 4004. The 4040 offered a number of improvements. It had an interrupt capability and a larger number of internal registers, allowing a fast interrupt response. When an interrupt occurred (provided there were no more than two interrupt levels), one could switch from one bank of registers to the other. The program counter and the status word were not repeated within the register banks, which required additional instructions to be executed for switching. The basic architecture of the 4040 is shown in the figure that follows. A 4289 memory interface was used with a 1 of 8 decoder for connecting a ROM. As a 4-bit microprocessor, the 4040 was intended for applications such as calculators, games, appliances, and simple control applications.

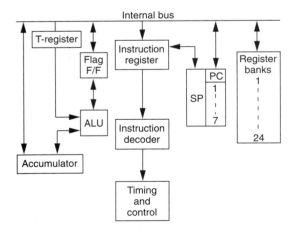

4040 microprocessor architecture

Intel 4116 (o.t.) The 4116 RAM chip, used in some early PCs, was a 16K-bit chip, as shown in the following figure. The actual memory matrix had 128 rows and 128 columns. Among the 16 address bits, the two most significant bits were used as the chip select, the next seven most significant bits were used to address the 128 rows, and the seven least significant bits addressed the 128 columns. Each bit cell could be addressed by first addressing a row and then addressing a column.

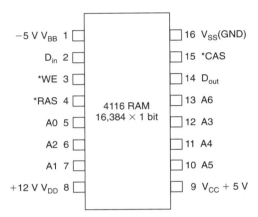

4116 RAM chip, which uses a 16-pin DIP housing

The 4116 chip was used in groups of eight, wired in parallel. Each byte was spread over the eight chips, with one bit in a corresponding location in all eight chips. The array of eight chips provided a total of 16,384 total bytes, or 16K. The eight chips were usually numbered 0 through 7.

Both TTL logic circuits and MOS logic circuits were used on this chip. The TTL circuits were used for input and output functions, while the MOS circuits were used in the memory matrix to store the logic states.

Intel 4164 A more-dense replacement for the 16K 4116 RAM chip. The 64K 4164 (shown in the following figure) uses the same 16-pin chip as the 4116, but the 4164 uses a 256×256 bit cell matrix and has only two power pins (8 and 16); four power inputs (1,8,9, and 160) are used in the 4116. Pin 1 is not connected and pin 9 is used as an additional address pin, A7 for the 64K bits.

Intel 41256 The 41256 chip has 262,144 bit cells. This fourfold density increase is achieved by doubling the numbers of rows and columns with a matrix of 512 rows and 512 columns, as shown.

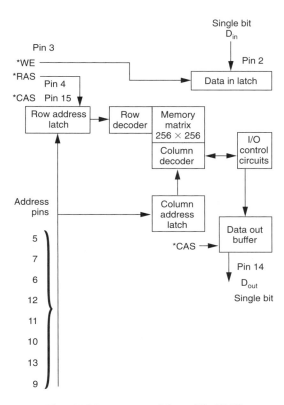

The 4164 memory chip, with *RAS to strobe the row address into a latch and *CAS to strobe the column address into another latch

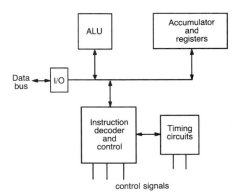

The RAM cell arrays in the dynamic chips use amplifiers for refreshing

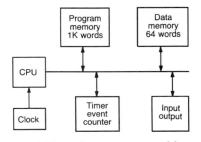

8008 architecture

8021 microcomputer chip

Intel 8008 (*o.t.*) A first-generation 8-bit microprocessor introduced in early 1972. It was the second of the first-generation processors, following the 4004, which was introduced in late 1971. The 8008 was fabricated using the PMOS process. It was packaged in an 18-pin DIP, and thus was compact for an 8-bit microprocessor.
  Address information was multiplexed over the 8-bit bidirectional data bus as shown in the following figure. At the beginning of each machine cycle requiring a read from or write to memory, the address information was put on the data bus. The address had to be saved or latched by external circuitry.

Intel 8021 (*o.t.*) An 8-bit parallel microcomputer chip in a 28-pin package. The n-channel silicon gate chip contained a $1K \times 8$ program memory, a 64×8 data memory, an 8-bit timer/event counter, 21 input/output lines, and oscillator and clocking circuitry. The block diagram for the 8021 is shown in the previous figure. The chip had a bit-handling capability and performed either binary or BCD arithmetic. The 8021 program memory was mask programmable with no provisions for external expansion. All locations in the data memory were indirectly addressable, with eight locations being directly addressable.

Intel 8022 A member of the Intel group of single-chip 8-bit microcomputers. It is designed for low-cost, high volume applications that involve analog signals, capacitive keyboards, and/or large ROM space. The 8022 addresses these applications by integrating on the chip additional functions such as analog-to-digital conversion, comparators, and zero cross detection.

The 8022 includes 2K of ROM, 64 bytes of RAM, 28 I/O lines, an on-chip A/D converter with two input channels, an 8-bit port with comparator inputs for interfacing to low voltage capacitive touchpanels or other non-TTL interfaces, external and timer interrupts, and zero cross detection capability. In addition, it contains an 8-bit interval timer/event counter, oscillator, and clock.

The 8022 can be a controller as well as a basic arithmetic processor. It has bit-handling capability plus binary and BCD arithmetic. The instruction set consists mostly of single-byte instructions and has extensive conditional jump and table lookup capability. The 8022 contains an on-chip hardware implementation of an 8-bit analog-to-digital converter with two multiplexed analog inputs. The A/D converter uses the successive approximation technique and provides an updated conversion once every 40 microseconds using a minimum of software.

Intel 8048 family The 8048 is a self-sufficient 8-bit parallel computer fabricated on a single chip using the n-channel silicon gate MOS process. The 8048 has a 1K × 8 program memory, a 64 × 8 RAM data memory, 27 I/O lines, and an 8-bit timer/counter with oscillator and clock circuits. For systems that require extra capability, the 8048 can be expanded with standard memories, but expanding the memory affects the hardware configuration drastically. The 8048 was designed for single-chip applications and does not suffer from having to be compatible with more powerful predecessors. The 8035 is the equivalent of an 8048 without program memory.

Three interchangeable pin-compatible versions of this microcomputer exist: the 8748 with user programmable and erasable EPROM for prototype and preproduction systems, the 8048 with factory-programmed mask ROM program memory for low-cost, high volume applications, and the 8035 without program memory for use with external memories.

The 8048 has bit-handling capability as well as facilities for both binary and BCD arithmetic. The instruction set consists mostly of single-byte instructions, with no instructions over two bytes in length.

The 8048 uses a register-oriented architecture with two banks of 8-bit registers in the 64 × 8 RAM. The selected bank operates with the accumulator, using a somewhat incomplete set of instructions. Incompleteness is due to a lack of compare and subtract operations. There is a full set of increments and decrements, and all of the registers, except the accumulator, may be decremented with a JUMP IF NOT ZERO instruction.

Intel 8051 family The 8031, 8051, and 8751 are standalone single-chip computers fabricated with depletion load, n-channel, MOS technology.

The 8051 and 8751 contain a nonvolatile 4K × 8 program memory; volatile 128 × 8 RAM data memory; 32 I/O lines; two 16-bit timer/counters; a five-source, two-level, nested interrupt structure; a serial I/O port for multiprocessor communications; a full duplex UART; and an on-chip oscillator and clock circuits. The 8031 is identical, except it lacks the program memory. It can address 64K bytes of external program memory in addition to 64K bytes of external data memory. The 8051 can be expanded using standard TTL compatible memories.

The 8051 microcomputer, like its 8048 predecessor, was designed as a controller or a basic arithmetic processor. It has facilities for binary and BCD arithmetic, as well as bit-handling capabilities. The instruction set consists of 44% one-byte, 42% two-byte, and 15% three-byte instructions. With a 12 MHz crystal, 58% of the instructions execute in one microsecond and 40% in two microseconds; multiple and divide require four microseconds. Among the other instructions added to the 8048 instruction set are subtract and compare.

Intel 8080 The 8080 is an 8-bit n-channel MOS device that is packaged in a 40-pin DIP. It is based on the older 8008 architecture, but it is capable of much more sophisticated applications. The architecture of the 8080, like the 8008, is organized around an 8-bit internal data bus as shown in the figure.

One of the limitations of the 8008 was its limited stack depth. The use of an external stack in the 8080 provides improved design flexibility, and the direct memory access feature allows peripheral devices to access the busses for direct memory data transfers without interfering with processor operation.

Intel 8080 status decoder The decoder shown in the figure that follows is necessary to synchronize the operation of the 8080 with the rest of the system.

Intel 8085 The 8085 is a faster version of the 8080. It has an on-chip clock along with a system controller to provide cycle status information. It is software-compatible with the 8080,

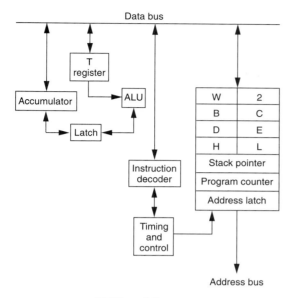

8080 architecture

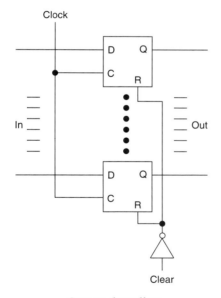

Status decoding

and it operates with a 1.3 microsecond instruction cycle for the A configuration.

The major value of the 8085 lies in the special chips that are available for a minimal 8085 system. These are memory and I/O combinations that connect directly to the 8085 without the need for any additional components. They allow a complete 8085 system to be assembled with just three chips. The limitation of the system involve the amount of memory contained in these memory and I/O combinations, 2K words of ROM, and 256 words of RAM.

Intel 8086 A 16-bit microprocessor based on the 8080. The 8086 uses silicon gate HMOS technology for faster performance and an expanded 8080 structure. Basically, it is an improved, 16-bit version of the 8080, with the 8080 multiplexed bus expanded into a 16-bit external bus. Like the 8080, the instructions are byte oriented.

The basic structure of the 8086 is shown in the figure. The 8086 consists of two separate processing units, an execution unit (*EU*), and a bus interface unit (*EIU*), connected by a 16-bit ALU data bus and an 8-bit Q bus. The EU obtains instructions from the instruction queue, maintained by the bus-interface unit (*BIU*), and executes instructions using the 16-bit ALU. Execution of instructions involves maintenance of the status and control logic, manipulation of the general registers and instruction operands, and manipulation of segment offset addresses. The EU accesses memory and peripheral devices through requests to the BIU, which performs all bus operations for the EU. This involves generating the physical addresses from the segment register and offset values, reading operands, and writing results.

The execution unit and the bus interface unit operate independently of each other, enabling the 8086 to overlap instruction fetch and execution. While the 8086 is decoding the current instruction, BIU fetches the contents of the next sequential memory addresses and loads them into the queue. If the current instruction

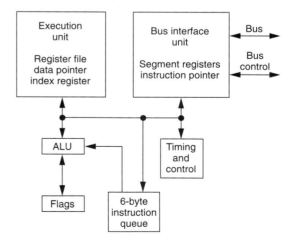

8086 architecture

is not a branch instruction, the next instruction is available to the processor's EU upon completion of the current instruction without the need for a memory access. If the current instruction is a branch instruction, the next instruction is fetched from memory. The queue decreases address bus/data bus idle times by prefetching data, thus increasing processor speed.

The 8086 register structure is similar to the 8080's. The execution unit contains four 16-bit point and index registers and four 16-bit data registers, addressable on a byte basis. These eight registers are used to provide compact coding at the cost of flexibility. The BIU contains one 16-bit instruction pointer, which holds the offset of the next instruction to be fetched. This pointer is updated by the BIU but is not directly accessed by the program. The BIU also contains four 16-bit segment registers for segment base addressing, which allows access of up to four 64K segments at a time. The EU also contains 1-bit status flags and three 1-bit control flags.

Intel 8086 addressing The 8086 computes a memory address by summing a displacement, a base register, and an index register. Segmentation and addressing mechanisms are based on 16 bits. The 8086 has 95 basic instructions, some of which are only eight bits long. In the 16-bit instructions, only the first eight bits are used for operation codes and the additional byte specifies the data displacement.

Intel 80286 A microprocessor with a 16-bit external data path, up to 16M of directly addressable physical memory, and up to 1G of virtual memory space. In the virtual address mode, 32-bit pointers are used for a 16-bit selector and offsets. In the real address mode, physical memory is a contiguous array. The selector portion of the pointer is interpreted as the upper 16 bits of a 20-bit address, and the remaining four bits are set to zero. This mode is compatible with the 8088 and the 8086. The chip has three programmable timer/counters controlled by an Intel 8254. The ROM subsystem is usually a 32K × 16-bit arrangement consisting of two 32K × 8-bit ROM/EPROMS. The RAM subsystem starts at hex address zero of the 16M address space. It may consist of either 512K, 640K, or 1M.

Eight DMA channels can be supported by the system. Two Intel 8237-5 DMA controller chips (four channels in each chip) can be used, with the DMA channels assigned as shown in the following tables.

Channels 0 through 3 are contained in DMA controller 1. Transfers of 8-bit data, 8-bit I/O adapter, and 8-bit or 16-bit system memory are supported by these channels. Each of these channels will transfer data in 64K blocks throughout the 16M system address space. Channels 4 through 7 are contained in DMA controller. To cascade channels 0 through 3 to the microprocessor, channel 4 is used. Transfers of 16-bit data between 16-bit adapters and 16-bit system memory are supported by channels 5, 6, and 7. DMA channels 5 through 7 can transfer data in 1238K blocks throughout the 16M system address space. These channels will not transfer data on odd-byte boundaries. DMA channel addresses do not increase or decrease through page boundaries(64KB for channels 0 through 3 and 128KB for channels 5 through 7).

The I/O channel supports the following:

- Refresh of system memory from channel microprocessors
- Selection of data accesses, either 8 bit or 16 bit
- 24-bit memory addresses (16M)
- I/O wait-state generation
- I/O address space hex 100 to hex 3FF
- Open-bus structure, allowing multiple microprocessors to share the system's resources, including memory
- DMA channels

Intel 80286 system interrupts Sixteen levels of system interrupts can be provided by the 80286 NMI and two 8259A interrupt controller chips. The following table shows how the interrupt-level assignments are typically set in decreasing priority.

Intel 80286 system timers The 80286 system has three programmable timer/counters controlled by an Intel 8254-2 timer/counter chip. These may be called channels 0 through 2 and connected as shown in the table. The 8254-2

CTRL 1	CTRL 2
Ch 0 — Spare	Ch 4 — Cascade for CTRL 1
Ch 1 — SDLC	Ch 5 — Spare
Ch 2 — Diskette	Ch 6 — Spare
Ch 3 — Spare	Ch 7 — Spare

Assignment of eight DMA channels in the 80286

Page register	I/O hex address
DMA channel 0	0087
DMA channel 1	0083
DMA channel 2	0081
DMA channel 3	0082
DMA channel 5	008B
DMA channel 6	0089
DMA channel 7	008A
Refresh	008F

Addresses for the page register in the 80286

Level	Function
Microprocessor NMI	Parity or I/O channel check
Interrupt controllers	
CTLR 1 CTLR 2	
IRQ	Timer output 0
IRQ 1	Keyboard (output buffer full)
IRQ 2	INTERRUPT FROM CTRL 2
IRQ 8	Realtime clock interrupt
IRQ 9	Software redirected to INT OAH (IRQ 2)
IRQ 10-12,15	Reserved
IRQ 13	Coprocessor
IRQ 14	Fixed disk controller
IRQ 3	Serial port 2
IRQ 4	Serial port 1
IRQ 5	Parallel port 2
IRQ 6	Floppy disk controller
IRQ 7	Parallel port 1

Interrupt levels in the 80286

timer/counter is treated by system programs as an arrangement of four programmable external I/O ports. Three are treated as counters; the fourth is a control register for mode programming.

Channel 0	**System timer**
GATE 0	Wired on
CLK IN 0	1.190 MHz OSC
CLK OUT 0	8259A IRQ 0
Channel 1	**Refresh request generator**
GATE 1	Wired on
CLK IN 1	1.190 MHz OSC
CLK OUT 1	Request refresh cycle
Channel 2	**Tone generation for speaker**
GATE 2	Controlled by bit 0 of port hex 61 PPI bit
CLK IN 2	1.190 MHz OSC
CLK OUT 2	Used to drive the speaker

Timer/counters in the 80286

Intel 80386 The first 32-bit version of Intel's 80x86 series. The SX version of the 386 has a 16-bit data bus. There are plug-in modules for DX versions: 25 MHz and 33 MHz modules without cache RAM, and 25 MHz and 33 MHz versions with 128K cache RAM.

Intel 80486 An improved 32-bit chip architecture available in many configurations, including 25, 33, and 50 MHz, with varying amounts of cache RAM. These plug-in modules are System upgrades and are easily accomplished by switching the BIOS ROM and the personality module to go from non-cache to cache. An SX version of the 486 offers the 32-bit addressing capabilities of the 80486DX but eliminates the built-in math coprocessor function to reduce cost. *Also see* INTEL 386 VERSUS 486.

Intel 80586 *See* INTEL PENTIUM.

Intel 80x86 The family of microprocessors made by Intel used in the PC line, including the 16-bit 80286, and the 32-bit 80386 and 80486 chips.

Intel 8257 A controller for the 8080 system, requiring an external latch to preserve the eight-address bits. A typical configuration of the 8257 appears in the figure. It shows four DMA levels for controlling four different disk units, each connected to its own DMA level.

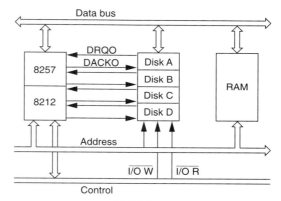

8257 DMA

Intel 8259 interrupt controller A priority interrupt controller chip whose structure is shown in the figure that follows. The 8259 provides interrupt management including priorities, interrupt mask, and automatic vectoring. It is imple-

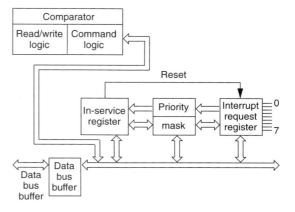

8259 interrupt controller

mented in an NMOS 28-pin package. The chip can be cascaded with up to eight other PICs to manage 64 separate interrupt levels.

Intelligence/Compiler A software compiler that allows you to develop multi-paradigm applications in an intelligent programming environment. It has object orientation, user-definable dynamic hypertext windows, rule-based programming, database management, and automatic interface generation to increase productivity.

intelligent bus interface A technique that reduces some of the costs required during the development of special-purpose interfaces. The intelligent interface, as shown in the figure, consists of a microprocessor system specially designed with a limited instruction set to emphasize I/O control and interface operations instead of the usual general-purpose instructions. The interface has a bus that is compatible with the host microprocessor system and extensive I/O facilities along with on-chip data and program memories. The system can be programmed to perform the interface functions required by the particular I/O device.

intelligent disk storage A disk system that does its own database management; only commands from the host computer and data field information need to be passed to the system controller. All indexing, searching, and deblocking are done on the disk system controller.

intelligent hub An ARCnet device used for the connection of computers.

intelligent interface card A microprocessor-based product designed to perform intelligent operations in addition to its designated interface conversions. Several models are dedicated to IEEE-488 interface conversions, as shown in the figure. An IEEE-488 serial interface converter is available with or without an IEEE-488 bus controller. IEEE-488-to-parallel and IEEE-488-to-analog interface conversions are also available.

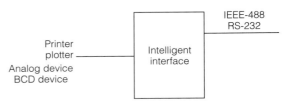

Intelligent interface card

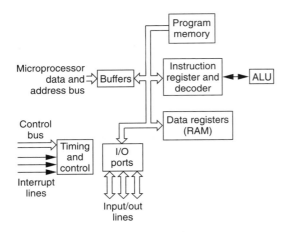

Intelligent interface

intelligent cable An interfacing system that allows input and output operations along with word and byte transfers to occur in any mix on all channels concurrently. An intelligent cable provides a low-cost parallel interface while freeing the designer from costly development time involved in interfacing the peripherals. Some features of intelligent cables include the following:

- TTL compatibility with low-power Schottky circuits
- Handshaking and strobing capability
- Multiple device control
- Microprogrammed interface control
- Standard ribbon cabling

intelligent keyboard system A keyboard system that performs all alphanumeric and numeric operations for keying, editing, calculating, storing, compressing, and printing.

Intel Pentium A 64-bit microprocessor architecture available in many configurations, including 60, 66, 90, and 100 MHz, with varying amounts of cache RAM. The Pentium is effectively the successor to Intel's 80486, but Intel decided against the *80586* designation as a result of a copyright battle with rival chip manufacturers.

INTELSAT Acronym for the *International Telecommunications Satellite Consortium*, established under a pair of international agreements originally signed by 14 nations in August 1964 as an international joint venture created to establish the global communications satellite system.

intensity level The level of power as expressed in decibels above an arbitrary zero power level.

interacting simulator A simulator that precisely duplicates the timing of the microcomputer to allow the user total interactive control to execute and alter the program.

interaction factor A factor allowing for insertion loss due to the connection between source and load. This vanishes when the impedance of a network equals that of the load or source.

interactive Refers to the point at which two systems, two devices, or a person and a device come into contact with each other.

interactive mode 1. In BASIC, a method of accepting data through a keyboard or from a data file one item at a time using BASIC's INPUT statement. **2.** Refers to a computer system that allows user input at any time. *Contrast with* BATCH MODE.

interactive multiprocessor system A multiuser system used for the simultaneous processing of a large number of jobs with different characteristics. The system may reconfigure itself by partitioning itself into independently operating units, on a space or time-division multiplex basis.

interactive processing A type of processing that involves the constant involvement of the operator.

interactive software *See* CBT.

interactive television Television that allows viewers to use control buttons to input responses to questions posed on the television screen.

Interactive Terminal Interface *See* ITI.

interbase current The current flowing between the two base connectors in a junction-type tetrode transistor.

interblock gap The area on a data medium used to indicate the end of a block or record. Also called *block gap*.

interconnection line A transmission line connecting two systems or networks that allows energy to be transferred in either direction. Also called *tie line*. A large interconnection is called a *giant tie* or *regional interconnection*.

interface 1. A common or shared boundary between instruments, devices, or systems, which is functionally compatible with connected units. Interfaces such as those shown in the figure enable devices to exchange information among devices and implies a connection to complete the interchange. **2.** The specification required for the interconnection between two systems. For example, the EIA interface is a standard set of signal characteristics including voltages, currents, and time durations for communication terminals.

interface bus A bus that provides the interface connectors and timing to interconnect different types of peripherals to a computer to form a complete system.

interface card Circuit boards or cards that permit the connection of various instruments and peripherals to the CPU.

interface converter A device that allows you to adapt mismatched equipment, such as a serial computer port to a parallel printer. The parallel side is a standard Centronics interface, and the serial side is RS-232 compatible with equipment that uses RTS/CTS handshake control along with DTR/DSR sensing.

interface debugging Some microcomputer interfaces can be checked out in part by writing short programs that test portions of the interface. Suppose you wished to check out the interface to a tape backup-storage unit. A short loop could be written that advances the tape and checks for data. This loop could be executed in a single-step mode. The final routine for driving the tape unit would be more complex, because it would have to time-out the interval between characters. The short routine determines that the circuits are working. In this way, the problem of determining whether the bugs are in the program or in the circuitry can be solved.

interface exerciser A device that performs an active test of the interface it is monitoring. Message generation and other intelligent operations distinguish these exercisers. The exerciser is usually configurable for such things as baud rate, word structure, and signal configuration.

interface module A hardware unit that provides the interface between a bus and the user's peripheral or instrumentation. Integrated circuits mounted on the module provide logic for address selection, interrupt control, and byte input/output transfers. Interface modules for industrial microcomputer systems may include power switches, analog-to-digital and digital-to-analog converters, time-keeping clocks, and pulsers.

interface standard A format that allows matching the characteristics of two or more units, systems, or programs so that they can be easily joined together.

interference Electrical or magnetic disturbances that cause unwanted responses or effects (usually voltage spikes or transients).

interference fading The fading of signals because of interference among the components of the

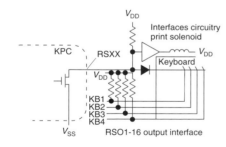

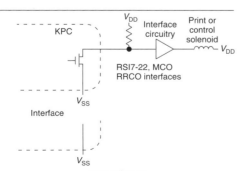

Interfaces

signals that have taken slightly different paths to the receiver.

interference trap A means of reducing interference, such as a tuned-rejecter circuit for a single steady transmission, or a bandpass filter that will reduce the accepted band of frequencies to a minimum.

interferometer An instrument that uses light interference techniques for the determination of wavelength, spectral lines, indices of refraction, and small linear displacements.

interlace 1. To assign successive storage location numbers to physically separated storage locations on a magnetic drum to reduce access time. **2.** In monitor technology, to superimpose two raster scans so that the lines formed by one scan appear as alternating lines of the other.

interlaced memory A memory with sequentially addressed locations occupying in physically separated positions in the storage media.

interleaved status checking A technique to free up processor time. In a program, the status check may be repeated continuously until I/O device is ready. This loop effectively stalls the program execution, which can use too much processing time. To avoid this, one can interleave the status check with other microprocessor operations, as shown in the following figure.

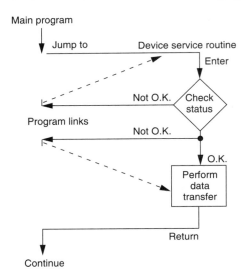

Interleaved status checking

interleaving 1. The inserting of segments of one program or read cycle into another to allow the two to be executed essentially in a simultaneous mode. **2.** A process of splitting memory into sections to speed processing. Interleaving allows a second word to be read during the half-cycle when the previously read word is being written back into the memory. **3.** A technique of skipping sectors when reading disks.

interleaving multiprocessing Relates to various techniques or processes of addressing adjacent storage modules in an even/odd fashion. It significantly reduces storage-access conflicts in a multiprocessor system, thereby increasing overall system performance. With interleaving, the modules are divided into even and odd locations (although the addressing structure within the modules themselves remains unchanged). Thus, in a fully expanded eight-module system, modules 0, 2, 4, and 6 are referenced for even addresses, while modules 1, 3, 5, and 7 are referenced for odd.

interlock To arrange the control of machines or devices so that their operation is interdependent in order to assure their proper coordination.

interlock bypass A command, device, or circuit, used to temporarily circumvent a normally provided interlock.

intermediate block character See ITB.

intermediate cycle An unconditional branch instruction that may address itself.

intermediate frequency oscillator An oscillator used in heterodyne reception that is coupled with the output of the intermediate amplifier for demodulation in the second or final detector.

intermittent control A control system in which the control variable is monitored periodically with an intermittent correcting signal supplied to the controller.

intermittent error A sporadic error that might not be detected when diagnostic programs or routines are run.

intermodal dispersion See MULTIMODE DISPERSION.

intermodulation distortion Amplitude distortion in which the intermodulation products are of greater importance than the harmonic products, as in audio amplifiers for high-quality reproduction.

internal arithmetic Computations performed by the arithmetic and logic unit.

internal font See RESIDENT FONT.

internal interrupt A control signal that diverts the attention of the computer to consider an extraordinary event or circumstance. An internal interrupt causes the control of the program to be transferred to a subordinate, which then corresponds to the stimulus. Internal interrupts are used primarily to synchronize the program with the termination of input/output transfers, and to signal the occurrence of errors.

internally stored program The set of instructions stored in internal memory, as opposed to those stored on disk or CD-ROM.

internal memory Addressable storage directly controlled by the CPU. Internal memory is the total memory or storage accessible to the CPU and forms an integral part of the microcomputer. Also called *internal storage*.

internal modem A modem installed inside the system unit of a PC. Modems are used to connect computing devices over the telephone system network. *Also see* MODEM.

internal storage *See* INTERNAL MEMORY.

internal timer An electronic timer that facilitates the monitoring or logging events at predetermined intervals.

international electrical units Values of the practical units ohm, watt, amp, volt that were adopted internationally until 1947, when MKSA (meter-kilogram-second-ampere) units were employed. The international watt differs by 16 parts in 10^5 from the absolute watt (1 J/sec).

International Standards Organization *See* ISO, 1.

Internet A collection of networks that share the same namespace and use the TCP/IP protocols. The Internet is a packet-switching, decentralized network that grew out of the efforts of the Advanced Research Projects Agency of the Pentagon. In the fall of 1969, the first node was installed in UCLA. By December of 1969, there were four nodes on the infant network, which was then called ARPANET, after its Pentagon sponsor. The four computers could transfer data on dedicated high-speed transmission lines and be programmed remotely from the other nodes. This gave scientists and researchers access to one another's computer facilities.

In 1971, there were fifteen nodes on ARPANET; by 1972, thirty-seven nodes. By the second year of operation, the main use of ARPANET evolved from computer sharing to a high-speed electronic mail system. Next came the use of the mailing list, a broadcasting technique in which an identical message could be sent automatically to large numbers of network subscribers. During the 1970s and 1980s, other organizations with computers linked up to this growing network, which began to be called the Internet.

Since the software used, TCP/IP, was public-domain, and the basic technology was decentralized, it was difficult to prevent connecting to the Internet. Each node was independent, and had to handle its own costs and technical requirements. The network became more valuable as it grew larger.

In 1984 the National Science Foundation took over the network. Its Office of Advanced Scientific Computing linked newer supercomputers using thicker, faster links. (The ARPANET name was dropped in 1989.) The Internet was upgraded and expanded in 1986, 1988, and 1990. Other government agencies that are also tied in include NASA, the National Institutes of Health, and the Department of Energy.

The nodes in the network are labeled in different ways. Most foreign computers and some U.S. sites use their geographical locations. Others use the six basic Internet labels: *gov, mil, edu, com, org,* and *net*. The government, military, and educational nodes were the first, since ARPANET had been started as a secure network needed for national security. Commercial institutions joined later, along with nonprofit organizations. The *net* label is used for computers that serve as gateways between networks.

There are now four hundred networks and tens of thousands of nodes on the Internet in over forty-two countries. Millions of people use the network, and it is growing faster than cellular telephones or fax machines. The number of host machines with direct connection to TCP/IP has doubled every year since 1988. The Internet has moved from its original base in military and research into schools, public libraries, and commercial sites. Also called *the net*.

Note: The Internet should not be confused with the generic term *internet*, which refers to all networks that have a path between them.

Internet address An address that uniquely identifies a node on the Internet, for example, *mari@unc.edu* (pronounced "mari at u-n-c dot e-d-u").

Internet Architecture Board The technical body that oversees the development of the Internet suite of protocols.

Internet Assigned Numbers Authority The central registry for various Internet protocol parameters, such as port, protocol and enterprise numbers, and options, codes and types. To request a number assignment, contact the IANA at iana@isi.edu.

Internet e-mail If you have Internet access via a commercial provider, you already have electronic mail available to you. You can send messages along Internet's "electronic highway" to any location on the globe. Commercial e-mail packages add features such as varied fonts, underlining, boldface, and sometimes audio and graphics transmission. In the Unix environment, various e-mail programs were developed in the 1960s. Most prevalent of these are the pine mailer and the elm mailer.

Internet Relay Chat *See* IRC.

internetwork A collection of data links and the network layer programs for routing among those data links.

internetwork address An address consisting of a network number and a local address on that network. It is used by the network layer for routing packets to their ultimate destination.

Internetwork Datagram Protocol The network layer protocol in XNS (Xerox Network System).

internetwork packet exchange *See* IPX.

Internetwork Protocol The network layer protocol in TCP/IP. *Also see* TCP/IP.

interoperable Refers to the ability to exchange one device for another without any modifications to the software. Many hardware devices are compatible but not interoperable. For example, most NICs (network interface cards) of the same types, such as Ethernet, are compatible but not interoperable. Different NICs require different software drivers even though they use the same transmission protocols.

interpolation The process of finding a value between two known values, and the procedure for determining values of a function between known and observed values.

interpolator A device that is part of a numerical control system and performs interpolation.

Interpress Page A page-description language from Xerox, used in XNS for driving laser printers.

interpret To translate or decode, as in converting nonmachine language into machine language.

interpret program A program that translates and executes each source language statement before operating on the next statement.

interpreter A routine that translates a stored program expressed in a code into machine code and performs the indicated operations, using subroutines as they are translated.

The interpreter is used like a closed subroutine that operates successively on the sequence of instructions and operands. It is usually entered as a closed subroutine and left with an exit instruction. Because the interpreter operates on the instructions one-by-one, and executes each statement before starting on the next, it tends to be slower than other methods of translation. *Contrast with* COMPILER.

interpreter operation Refers to a routine that, as the computation progresses, translates a stored program expressed in some code into machine code and performs the indicated operations, by means of subroutines, as they are translated.

interpretive translation program A program designed to translate each instruction of a source language into computer instructions and allow each one to be executed before translating the next instruction. If the program allows programs written for one type of computer to be run on a different type, it is often called a *simulator program*.

interprocess communication Refers to the communication between two processes by passing parameters and return values. Remote calls are a special case of an interprocess communication mechanism.

interrecord gap An interval of space or time left between recording portions of data or records. Interrecord gaps like the ones shown in the figure are used to prevent overwrite errors and permit tape start-stop operations.

interrupt To temporarily disrupt the normal operation of a routine by a special signal from the computer. Usually the normal operation can be resumed from that point at a later time. As the peripheral units interface with the CPU, inter-

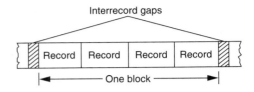

Interrecord gaps

rupts occur on a frequent basis. Multiple interrupt requests require the processor to delay, to prevent further interrupts, or to break into a procedure to modify operations.

With the use of interrupts, throughput increases because the processor is allowed to perform calculations concurrent with input/output operations. The major characteristics of interrupts include the following:

- *Latency*, the time to recognize the interrupt and branch to the service routine
- *Response*, the time to identify the interrupted device and begin execution of the device service code
- *Software overhead*, the time required to get to the service routine and return to the main program

An example of interrupt usefulness occurs in printer buffering. Serial printers tend to be slow and to print a line of characters without interrupts; a microprocessor transfers a character to the printer and then waits until that character is printed until it transfers the next character. Character transfer takes only microseconds, while character printing may take up to 100 milliseconds per character; the microprocessor spends most of the time waiting for printing completion. A program interrupt can eliminate this waiting time, so that when the printer is busy, the microprocessor can be involved in other tasks and return only when required to transfer a character. The flow of interrupt control is shown in the following figure.

interrupt-controlled I/O When the polling technique for input/output (I/O) does not provide a fast enough response, or uses too much microprocessor time, interrupts can be used. In the interrupt-driven scheme, the devices have the initiative for requesting service. An extra line is used as an interrupt line, which is connected to the microprocessor unit. Each of the devices is connected to this line and has the option of using it to request service. A device that requests service generates an interrupt pulse or level on this line. The microprocessor then detects the presence of interrupts on the line and manages them as illustrated in the diagram.

interrupt count pulse An interrupt level that is triggered from pulses provided by the clock.

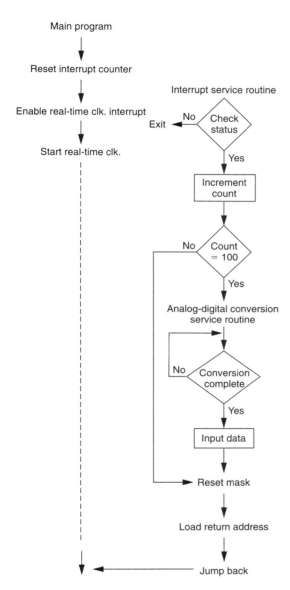

Interrupt-controlled data acquisition system

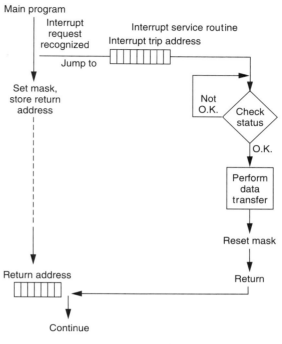

Interrupt-controlled I/O

Each pulse causes an instruction in the count-pulse location to be executed.

interrupt device The external device requesting an interrupt, such as a communications unit or timing signal.

interrupt enable and disable Instructions used to set and reset an interrupt-control flip-flop.

interrupt freeze mode A condition in analog computers under which all computing action is stopped and all values are held as they were when the interrupt occurred.

interrupt identification Identification of the device and channel causing the interrupt, often stored as a program status word (PSW). In addition, the status of the device and channel is stored in a fixed location in memory.

interrupt input lines Signal channels used for inputs that set the interrupt flags of the control registers.

interrupt is used In NetWare, a part of Diagnostic Services that indicates whether the value in the following interrupt line field is valid.

interrupt mask bit A specific bit used to prevent the CPU from responding to further interrupt requests until cleared by execution of programmed instructions. It can also be manipulated by specific mask-bit instructions.

interrupt mask word A word used to enable or disable interrupts in a system. Each bit of the word is interrogated to enable or inhibit a specific device interrupt.

interrupt module A device that acts as a monitor for a group of field contacts and notifies the computer when an external priority request is generated.

interrupt priority logic The priority scheme used in managing interrupts. Most hardware interrupt handlers use a masking register as shown in the illustration of basic interrupt-management logic, which does not include priority-encoding or a vectoring facility.

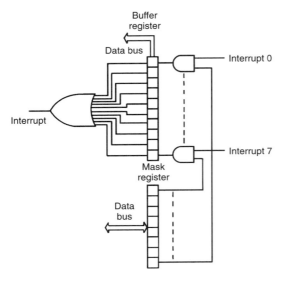

Interrupt priority logic

This circuit, which is on the right of the diagram, manages eight interrupts. The mask register appears at the bottom. When the contents of a bit of the mask are 0, propagation of the corresponding interrupt signal is blocked toward the left of the circuit. The interrupt level is then masked. The presence of a 1 in the mask register allows the interrupt to propagate toward the left. When all interrupt lines are used, or allowed, the mask register contains all ones. If interrupt line 2 is not allowed, then bit 2 of the mask register is set to 0. The interrupt levels that are not masked out will set a bit in the interrupt register. The contents of this register can be read out of the circuit via the data bus.

This register allows the implementation of the software priority decoding. An exclusive-OR of the lines of this register provides the final interrupt signal shown on the left of the circuit. This interrupt request line is connected to the microprocessor interrupt line.

interrupt request See IRQ.
interrupt response time The elapsed time between an interrupt and the start of the interrupt-handling subroutine. The difference between the total time elapsed and the actual execution time is the *overhead time*.
interrupt signal feedback A signal indicating that the interrupt signal has advance to the waiting or active state. The signal is not present once the interrupt level is reset to the disarmed or armed state.
interrupt vector 1. An interrupt channel reserved for the highest priority external function; in many cases this is a real-time interrupt from the 60-Hz line source. **2.** A polling scheme in which the highest priority device or devices are hard-wired to achieve fixed-priority encoding. The encoded value is then used as a system address to transfer control to the interrupt response routine.
intersymbol interference The extraneous energy from the signal in one or more signaling intervals that tends to interfere with the reception of the signal in another signaling interval.
interval marker In NetWare, a value between 0 and 65,535 representing one clock tick ($\frac{1}{18}$ of a second).
interval polling timer A control program that keeps track of the time of day in order to interrupt the system periodically as required.
interword gap The time or space allowed between words on a tape or disk. The interword gap allows the medium to be switched and is used for the control of individual words.
Interwork Concurrent Programming Toolkit A C program library that lets you write programs as a set of cooperating concurrent tasks. It is useful for real-time applications, simulation, and parallel programming. It has context switching, time-sliced or optional non-preemptive task scheduling, intertask communication facilities (shared memory and semaphores), interrupt and trap handling, and debugging facilities. The DOS version is compatible with Borland Zortech C/C++ and Microsoft compilers.
intra-application area A 16-byte area in low memory starting at address H4F0, reserved for use by any application.
intrinsic conduction Conduction in a semiconductor when electrons are raised from a filled band into the conduction band by thermal energy, thus producing hole electron pairs. Intrinsic conduction increases rapidly with rising temperature.
intrinsic mobility The mobility of electrons in an intrinsic semiconductor.
intrinsic semiconductor A pure crystal of germanium or silicon that conducts electric currents due to the presence of mobile holes and electrons, but is not as efficient a conductor as is copper, silver, gold, and aluminum, in which the carrier density is much greater. Since the property is that of a pure crystal, it is called *intrinsic*.
intruder detection Refers to techniques that are used to detect and lock out a computer system when someone attempts to access it with an incorrect password.
in-use flag In NetWare, a flag used in workstation

calls, where it displays the state of whatever activity the shell is performing.

invalid connection packets In the NetWare File Server Environment, a count of all request packets with invalid logical connection numbers. A connection packet is invalid if it contains a logical connection number that has not been allocated, or if a source address that does not match the address the file server has assigned to the logical connection.

invalid reply header count In NetWare Diagnostic Services, the number of times (since the shell was activated) that the shell has received a reply packet header whose checksum was −1 or whose packet type field indicated that the packet was not a file server reply.

invalid sequence number count In NetWare Diagnostic Services, the number of times (since the shell was activated) that the shell has received a file server reply packet specifying an incorrect sequence number. This usually indicates that the reply was unnecessary.

invalid slot count In NetWare Diagnostic Services, the number of times (since the shell was activated) that the shell has received a file server reply packet with an incorrect connection ID.

invert 1. To place in contrary order, as to exchange the numerator with the denominator in a fraction. 2. To reverse the polarity of any voltage or signal, whether dc or pulsed.

inverter 1. A circuit or device that takes in a positive signal and outputs a negative one, or takes in a negative signal and outputs a positive signal. 2. A device such as a rectifier that changes direct current to alternating current, with or without a voltage level change.

inverted R-2R ladder A network used in data conversion to give an unattenuated noninverting output by connecting the output to a high impedance load, such as the input of the follower amplifier shown in the figure. The MSB (most significant bit) output is ½ V (2R − 2R divider). Since the entire network may be considered as an equivalent generator having an output voltage NV (where N is the fractional digital input) and an internal resistance R, the output may be scaled accurately by connecting precision resistors to ground.

inverting amplifier An amplifier with an output voltage that is equal in magnitude to the input, but opposite in sign.

inverting current switch multiplexer For switching as much as several hundred volts with solid-state speed, this multiplexer (or *MUX*) can be used as shown in the illustration. Because switching takes place at the summing junction, with the protective diodes to ground, the switches are not subjected to the high voltages. This MUX has a high immunity to transient voltages and a constant but low input resistance while conducting; it assumes a safe state when power is removed. Each channel can be adjusted for gain. This multiplexer is rugged and suited to industrial system control.

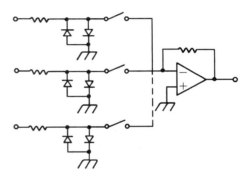

Inverting current switch multiplexer

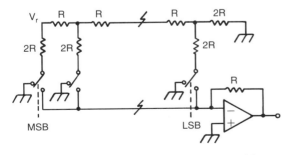

Inverted R-2R ladder for current switching

invitation to transmit *See* ITT.

INVOICE-IT A program designed for the small to medium-sized business to help keep track of invoices, merchandise, vendors, and customers at the point of sale. A perpetual inventory system helps keep track of inventory as well as providing look-up.

involuntary interrupt An interrupt that is not caused by the object program, but affects the running of the object program. An example is the termination of a peripheral transfer that causes the operating system to stop the object program while the interrupt is serviced.

INWG Abbreviation for *International Network Working Group*, IFIP Working Group 6.1.

I/O Abbreviation for *input/output*; refers to either input or output or both.

I/O address The address in memory where a CPU transfers data to or receives data from an I/O device. No two devices can have the same I/O address within a microcomputer.

I/O architecture A microcomputer's I/O architecture generally breaks down into these areas:

transfer techniques, instruction formats, buses, bus structures, interrupt schemes, and memory-access techniques. Most microprocessors allow three types of I/O transfer techniques: programmed transfer, interrupt program control, and hardware control. In the first two cases, found in most simple applications, the microprocessor controls the transfer. In the third case, system hardware controls transfer.

I/O bound Refers to programs that require a large amount of input/output operations, resulting in a large amount of CPU waiting time.

I/O bus A bus that provides parallel lines for data, command, device address, status, and control information. It makes interfacing easier, faster, and less expensive.

I/O cable A bus connecting various input/output devices to the microcomputer.

I/O card An input/output board that may be optionally mounted in the system unit at any time as an upgrade. The board may include RS-232 serial ports and a parallel printer interface with a Centronics-compatible parallel port. External connections to these ports may be available at the board mounting bracket for COM1 and LPT1, with a connector on a second mounting bracket for COM2.

I/O channel A circuit path that allows independent communication between the processor and external devices. Input/output channels may transfer data between memory and external interfaces in blocks of any size without disturbing working registers in the processor. Multiple channels are allowed to operate concurrently with hardware priority control of each channel. Transfers are in full words, with automatic packing and unpacking allowed in some systems.

I/O controller A control unit with the necessary logic circuitry to interconnect one or more peripheral devices with the input/output interface, usually required for devices having complex time-dependent mechanical operation. The controller may incorporate a processor that receives instructions and also executes them. The controller will implement the control sequence required by the I/O device. It might advance a mechanical linkage, perhaps using a stepping motor in a specified number of steps. These device controllers can range from simple circuits to complex boards. Device controllers are available in LSI chips for the most common I/O devices. Many controllers can operate multiple devices as long as they are the same type.

IOCS Abbreviation for *input/output control system*, a group of macroinstruction routines for handling the transfer of data between main storage and external devices. The routines can be divided into two parts: physical and logical.

I/O device A unit such as a modem or terminal designed for manual, mechanical, electronic, video, or audio entry to and output from the computer.

I/O device polling In the process of I/O device polling, the interrupt causes a jump to the service program by using the interrupt trap address. The interrupt service program checks the status word of each I/O device to determine which one caused the interrupt. The figure shows the flow of an interrupt service program for two I/O devices. The interrupt status bit indicates whether or not a device has generated an interrupt request, and it is checked for each device. The device status word is read into the status register of the microprocessor. If the bit is set, a jump is then made to the device service program.

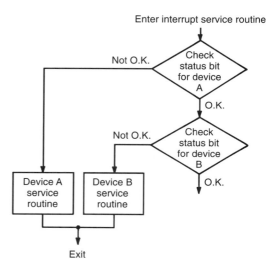

Device polling with separate status bits

I/O error count In the NetWare File Server Environment, the number of times I/O errors have occurred on the disk since the server was brought up.

I/O executive A modular programming technique for peripheral input/output device management and support. The executive program can free the user from time-dependent service routines and provide a well-defined protocol system.

I/O instructions Microprocessor instructions that handle the transfer of data between the CPU and external devices or peripherals. The transfer can involve status and control signals as well as data. The input/output operations must reconcile any timing differences between the CPU and the peripherals, format the data properly, and handle the status and control signals.

I/O interface A typical input/output interface might incorporate two input/output channels, a process input/output (*PIO*) channel, and a direct memory access (*DMA*) channel. The PIO channel interfaces with the process via the data input bus and provides simplex character-oriented data transfer capability. The DMA channel interfaces directly with the memory, via the data input bus, and provides high-speed, record-oriented data transfer capability at rates of up to 500,000 or more words per second. *Also see* DMA.

I/O M Abbreviation for *input/output multiplexer*.

I/O mapped system A system in which the processor uses control signals to indicate that the present cycle is for input or output and not for memory. Fewer address lines are used to select the I/O ports, since normally the system needs fewer ports than memory locations. One advantage to an I/O mapped system is that because separate I/O instructions are used, they can be distinguished from a memory reference instruction for ease in programming. Also, with the shorter addressing, less hardware is required for decoding, and instructions are shorter and usually faster. The disadvantages are the loss of processing power and the necessity of using two control pins for I/O read and I/O write. This technique is not used with most microprocessors; the 8080 is an exception to this rule.

I/O memory addresses It is almost always possible to use memory addresses for I/O devices. I/O ports are considered as if they were RAM locations; an input is performed by reading memory and an output by writing into it. The program may seem somewhat more obscure, because I/O operations become more difficult to find if the program isn't properly documented. This technique allows a greater number of I/O devices, limited only by the size of the memory that can be addressed by the microprocessor.

I/O module *See* I/O CARD.

I/O ports As shown in the figure, a simple I/O port requires the following:

- An input latch to hold external information until the system can read it
- An output latch to hold data from the system until required
- Bus buffers to receive and drive the data bus

There should also be an internal status register to indicate if there is data to be read, or if the data is to be output.

ion Any atom or molecule that has an electric charge due to loss or gain of valence electrons.

ion beam A directed stream of ions moving in the same direction with similar speeds, usually produced by some form of accelerating machine.

ion cluster A group of molecules loosely bound by electrostatic forces to an ion in a gas.

ion counter A tubular chamber for measuring the ionization of air.

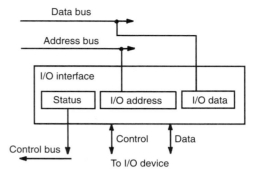

I/O port requirements

ionic Pertaining to or associated with gaseous or electrolytic ions. *Ion* is frequently used interchangeably with *ionic* as an adjective, as in *ion(ic) conduction*.

ionic radius The approximate limiting radius of ion crystals, ranging for common metals (including carbon) from a fraction to several angstroms.

ion implantation A method of introducing impurities into semiconductors that uses high-energy ion impingement on the silicon surface. Ion implantation allows shallow emitter junctions with a high degree of control. Ion implantation is used in CMOS circuits, shift registers, semiconductor memories, solar cells, and even resistors.

ionization heat The increase in heat necessary for complete ionization of a gram molecule of a substance.

IOP Abbreviation for *input/output processor*, a secondary processor used to transfer operations to and from the main memory. A typical IOP unit performs bidirectional data transfer between main memory and the peripheral devices. Up to 32 devices can be attached to the IOP, but the high data transfer rates may allow only one device to operate at a given time in some microcomputers.

IOPS Abbreviation for *input/output programming system*.

IOR Abbreviation for *input/output register*, a register used to temporarily hold input and output data.

I/O request words Control words used for input/output requests that are stored in the message reference block until the I/O operation is completed. *Also see* IRQ.

I/O switching Refers to the connection of input/output devices to more than one channel by using channel switching.

I/O table A plotting machine that generates a function representing the input device plotted against the output.

I/O test program A special PROM containing a program, which plugs into and checks input/output circuit boards.

IOU Abbreviation for *immediate operational use*.

IP **1.** Abbreviation for *initial point*. **2.** Abbreviation for *Internet protocol*.

IP address The 32-bit address defined by the Internet Protocol in STD 5, RFC 791. It is usually represented in dotted decimal notation.

IPC **1.** Abbreviation for *industrial process control*. **2.** Abbreviation for *information processing center*.

IPE Abbreviation for *interpret parity error*.

I phase A carrier phase separated by 57 degrees from the color subcarrier. Also referred to as the *in-phase carrier*.

IPL Abbreviation for *initial program loader*, a program that reads the supervisor into main storage and then transfers program control to the supervisor.

IPOS cycle Refers to a four-step, computer-related process consisting of

- Input (information being put into the computer)
- Processing (the computer acting on information)
- Output (the results of the processing becoming available)
- Storage (the results placed on magnetic media for later use)

ipot Acronym for *inductive potentiometer*, a variable resistor that uses a metallic resistive element such as nickel-chromium wire rather than deposited carbon.

IPS **1.** Abbreviation for *interpretive programming system*. **2.** Abbreviation for *inches per second*.

IPX Abbreviation for *internetwork packet exchange*; one of the two protocols used by NetWare (the other is SPX). IPX packets do not require a response from the recipient. Most packets transmitted on a LAN will result in a response from the recipient due to the nature of the request. Although IPX packets do not require a response, most will cause the recipient to respond to the request.

IPX major version In NetWare, the IPX major version installed on a node.

IPX minor version In NetWare, the IPX minor version installed on a node.

IPX not my network In NetWare, a count of packets received that were destined for the B, C, or D side drivers.

IPX workspace In NetWare Communication Services, a field reserved for IPX whenever it is using an ECB (event control block). When IPX is not using the ECB, an application may use this field.

IR Abbreviation for *instruction register*, which holds the instruction during the instruction decode-and-execute phase of microprocessor operation until it can be decoded. The bit length of the instruction register is the bit length of the basic instruction for the computer. Some computers use two instruction registers so they can save one instruction while executing the previous one; this is often called *pipelining*. The programmer can seldom access the instruction register.

IRAN Acronym for *inspect and repair as necessary*.

iraser A laser having an infrared output frequency.

IRC Abbreviation for *Internet Relay Chat*, a worldwide "party line" protocol that allows one to converse with others in real-time. IRC is structured as a network of servers, each of which accepts connections from client programs, one per user.

IRMA A system that provides a direct link between a PC and an IBM 3270 coax network. IRMA includes a circuit board that fits into a full-sized slot in a PC, along with software containing the 3278 emulator and two file-transfer utilities. IRMA fits into existing 3270 networks by attaching directly to 3278/9-configured IBM controller ports. The file transfer utilities run under VM/CMS and MVS/TSO. IRMA includes support for IBM keyboards through keyboard charts and decals that fit on the actual keys.

IRP Abbreviation for *initial receiving point*.

IRQ Abbreviation for *interrupt request signal*, a hardware feature that lets a peripheral device interrupt the CPU when the peripheral needs the CPU's attention. The processor waits until the current instruction is completed before recognizing the request. Then, if an interrupt mask bit in a condition register is not set, the interrupt sequence begins:

1. The contents of the index register, program counter, accumulator, and condition code register are stored in the stack.
2. The CPU sets an interrupt mask bit so that no additional interrupts could occur.
3. An address is loaded, which allows the CPU to branch to the interrupt routine.

In the IBM PC/AT architecture, each interrupt has its own signal trace in the motherboard to the expansion slots, so no two devices plugged into these slots may use the same interrupt channel. In IBM's Micro Channel machines, multiple devices can use the same interrupt because the device ID is also a part of the interrupt signal.

irreversible process A device or mechanism that does not return to its original state after a disturbance is removed.

ISA Abbreviation for *industry standard architecture*, IBM's original bus design found in XTs, ATs, and compatibles. The ISA bus comes in two versions: the 8-bit and 16-bit bus.

ISAM Abbreviation for *indexed-sequential access method*, a commonly used data storage and retrieval method which employs a Btree structure and an index of key fields.

IS **1.** Abbreviation for *internal signal*. **2.** Abbreviation for *information separator*, the character used to identify the boundary of information in a message.

ISAL Acronym for *information system access line*.

ISDN Abbreviation for *Integrated Services Digital Network*, a telecommunications concept and series of standards that allows one universal, digital-transmission network to carry computer data, voice, still and moving pictures, and high-fidelity sound. ISDN is in the process of being implemented by telephone companies worldwide.

ISM equipment The Federal Communications Commission designation for industrial, scientific, and medical equipment capable of causing interference.

ISN Abbreviation for *Information Systems Network*, AT&T's packet-switched network that can integrate voice and data.

ISO 1. Abbreviation for *International Standards Organization*, an international standards-making body responsible for the OSI (Open System Interconnect) network architecture. **2.** Abbreviation for *individual system operation*.

ISO 3309 and 4335 The international standards that defines the procedural elements used in the HDLC (hierarchical data link control) bit-oriented protocol.

ISO 6159 and 6256 The international standard that defines the procedural elements to be used in unbalanced and balanced operating configurations, respectively.

isochronous communications Communications in which the transmitter and the distant receiver use data clocks that have the same nominal rate, but are not truly synchronous.

isochronous TDM Time-division multiplexing in which the individual user terminals each generate their own clock. These clocks are not mutually synchronized, but they run at the same nominal rate. The isochronous multiplexers provide buffering and rate smoothing to compensate for the slight differences in the user clock rates. *Also see* TDM.

isolated digital output module A unit that provides an output interface along with electrical isolation between the microcomputer and a process control or peripheral device. Isolation is typically 1500V, and outputs of up to 50V can be provided.

isolated expansion multiplexer A board that allows the expansion of any analog input to 4 channels. They can supply cold junction compensation for thermocouple inputs; shunt terminals are provided for current measurements. An expansion multiplexer allows isolated inputs to be connected to an analog input board.

isolating diode A diode that passes signals in one direction through a circuit but blocks signals and voltages in the opposite direction.

isolation amplifier An amplifier used in those application conditions that require an actual galvanic isolation of the amplifier's input circuit from the output and the power supply. Typical applications include the following:

- High common-mode voltages between input and output
- Medical electronics equipment
- Two-wire inputs with no ground return for bias currents
- High CMRR (common-mode rejection ratio) required with a large source unbalance

isoplanar oxide isolation An isolation technique applicable to all bipolar processes. The oxide isolation technique primarily results in high packing densities and slightly higher speeds, and is accomplished by using silicon oxide to isolate the various components. Bipolar processes other than isoplanar also achieve electrical isolation of the circuit elements with reversed biased P-N junctions, but these junctions occupy more space and have higher capacitance.

isotron A device in which pulses from a source of ions are synchronized with a deflecting field. This separates isotopes, since their acceleration varies with mass.

isotropic Used to describe a medium with physical properties that do not vary with direction.

isotropic dielectric A dielectric insulator material with electrical properties that are independent of the direction of the applied field.

ISR Abbreviation for *information storage and retrieval*.

ISR offset In NetWare Value-Added Process Services, the offset of an interrupt.

ISR segment In NetWare Value-Added Process Services, either a real-mode segment value or a protected-mode segment descriptor, depending upon the processor mode in use.

IT Abbreviation for *ideal terminal*, a VT-100 and VT-52 terminal emulator and communications program for PCs. IT can communicate via Hayes Smartmodem-compatible modems with a dial-up host. IT can also auto-dial with such modems. You can use IT at 9600 baud with a host's screen editor such as EDT, EVE, or RAND for screen updates at a 9600 baud rate. IT is small (35K), loads fast, and can do file transfers between the PC and the host using two error-checking protocols (Xmodem and Kermit). IT can also send and receive ASCII files unchecked to and from hosts that have no Xmodem or Kermit services.

ITB Abbreviation for *intermediate block character*, a transmission control character that terminates an intermediate block. A block check character (*BCC*) usually follows. Use of ITBs allows for error-checking of relatively small transmission blocks.

item A unit of information relating to a single object, such as a set of one or more fields, or a collection of data characters that are treated as a unit. For example, a record may contain a number of items (fields), and a file may contain a number of items such as records.

item advance A technique used for the grouping

of records by operating successively on different records in storage.

item design A specification that contains the fields that make up an item, the order in which the fields are to be recorded, and the number of characters to be allocated to each field.

item size The magnitude of an item expressed in words, characters, or blocks.

iterate To repeat a loop or a series of steps in a program or routine.

iterative impedance The impedance of a four-terminal network when a large number of identical networks are cascaded.

iterative process A process for calculating a desired result by repeating a cycle of operations, each of which comes progressively closer to the result. For example, the square root of a number may be approximated by an iterative process using addition, subtraction, and division.

ITI Abbreviation for *interactive terminal interface*, a Telenet product.

ITT Abbreviation for *invitation to transmit*, the name for the token packet in an ARCnet network.

I^2L *See* INTEGRATED INJECTION LOGIC.

I^2L microprocessor The user of an I^2L microprocessor is able to adjust the injection current, allowing a trade off between speed and power consumption. When injection current is low, power consumption is low, but the speed of operation is reduced. Higher injection currents permit higher speed operation with an increase in power consumption. I^2L circuitry may be powered with a supply voltage as low as 0.8V. Since the performance characteristics are controlled by the injection current, the voltage/resistance combination can be used to an advantage, and the low power consumption make this an ideal technology for the consumer market. I^2L has not yet achieved the speed characteristics of TLL devices, but one advantage is the high-integration level that may be achieved. I^2L microprocessors are important for portable applications. *Also see* INTEGRATED INJECTION LOGIC.

IVDT Abbreviation for *integrated voice-data terminal*, a device combining both a telephone and a data terminal or PC in one piece of equipment. IVDTs are not widely used yet.

IXL A software product whose name stands for *induction on extremely large databases*. It finds previously unknown rules, patterns, and correlation in existing databases. The analysis of IXL may be shaped by the user towards a specific task, or IXL can roam freely through the database. The system outputs rules that characterize the data. IXL is made up of a built-in query processing module and database interface, a built-in statistical module for data analysis, and a discovery and induction module for rule generation.

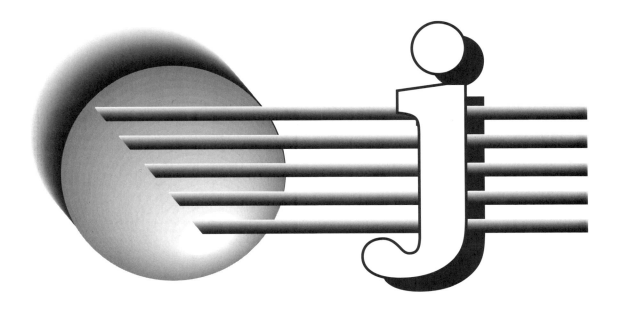

J Abbreviation for *joule*.

JA Abbreviation for *jump address*.

jabber A stream of incoherent bits on a communications channel. Defective communications devices, such as LAN adapter cards, can jabber. The communication channel slows down while error-handling protocols sort the good data from the garbage.

jabber frame A frame that exceeds 1,518 bytes in the data field and violates the IEEE 802.3 specifications.

jack A connecting device into which the wires of a circuit or device are attached.

jack panel An assembly of a number of jacks mounted on a board or panel.

jack part Refers to an electrical connector at the end of a wire designed to fit into a hub or other connecting device.

Jackson method A software design method in which the program is viewed as the means by which the input data is transformed into output data, as shown in the figure that follows. Paralleling the structure of the input data and the output report ensures a well-designed system. Some other assumptions of this method are that the resulting data structure will be compatible with a rational program structure, that only serial files will be used, and that the user of the method knows how to structure the data.

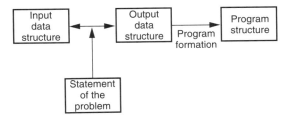

The Jackson methodology of software design

Jacquard, Joseph Marie Developer of punched cards to identify weaving patterns on a loom.

jaggies In computer graphics, the rough, jagged edges of curved and slanting surfaces caused by constructing images out of straight horizontal and vertical lines.

jam A short encoded sequence emitted by a transmitting node overriding other colliding packet signals. Ethernet uses this method.

JCL Abbreviation for *job control language*, a programming language specifically used to code job control statements.

Jetscript A PostScript controller upgrade for the LaserJet series of laser printers.

JetSet A LaserJet printer utility for 1-2-3 and Symphony. It has a Lotus-like menu for access to the HP laser printer's setup commands. You can select the font, typesize, paper orientation, margins, and number of copies.

J-FETS pair Refers to matched FET (field effect transistor) pairs for differential amplifiers. These general-purpose FETs are utilized for low- and medium-frequency differential amplifiers requiring low-offset voltage, drift, noise, and capacitance.

JIC Acronym for *joint industry conference*.

jitter A distortion caused by shifts in the time or phase position of pulses, which can cause difficulty in synchronization and detection.

jitter budget The allowed range for signal distortion on a LAN.

jittering A technique for reducing the effects of aliasing by randomly displaying samples from a uniform distribution.

J-K flip-flop A flip-flop with two inputs, J and K, as shown in the following diagram. A J-K flip-flop has the following features:

- A clock pulse will not cause a transition if either input is enabled.
- If both inputs are enabled, the output will change states.
- No indeterminate conditions are allowed.

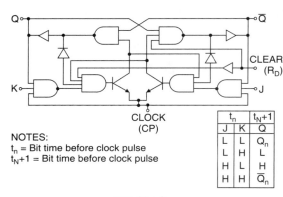

NOTES:
t_n = Bit time before clock pulse
t_N+1 = Bit time before clock pulse

J-K flip-flop

Jlaser A family of laser printer cards from Tall Tree Systems for the PC that allow faster, sharper printing. Jlaser provides its own laser printer connector, freeing up a port on the PC. A scanner port is also provided.

job A group of tasks prescribed as a unit of work for the computer. A job consists of one or more steps and may include programs, linkages, files, and instructions for the operating system.

job control flags In NetWare Queue Services, flags that indicate the status of a job. Typical bits in the field are set as follows: When the Services Auto-Start flag is set, the job will be serviced if a job server connection is broken, even if the client has not explicitly started the job. When the Service Restart flag is set, the job remains in the queue (in its current position) after a job server has aborted the job. When the User Hold flag is set, the job continues to advance in the queue, but cannot be serviced until the client who placed the job, or the operator, clears the flag. The Operator Hold Flag prevents the job from being serviced, as does the User Hold flag, but only operators can clear or set the Operator Hold flag.

job control language *See* JCL.

job control program A program called into storage to prepare each job or step to be run. It may assign I/O devices and set switches for program use.

job control statement A statement used in identifying a job or describing its requirements to the operating system.

job count The number of job entries in a print or job queue.

job entry In NetWare Queue Services, a number assigned by the Queue Management System to a job when the job first enters a queue.

job entry time In NetWare Queue Services, the time when the job entered the queue, according to the system clock of the file server.

job file handle In NetWare Queue Services, a handle created by the Queue Management System for a corresponding job entry.

job file name In NetWare Queue Services, the name of a file created by the Queue Management System for a corresponding job entry.

job input stream The input that is first sent to the operating system. The job input stream may contain the beginning of job indicators, directions, and programs.

job number In NetWare Queue Services, an array contains the job entry numbers the Queue Management System assigned to jobs when they entered the queue, listed according to their positions in the queue.

job position The job entry's position within a print or job queue.

job processing control That portion of a program that starts job operations, assigns I/O operations, and controls the transfer from one job to another.

job queue A method of holding multiple requests for a resource. The requests are allowed to queue up, as in the case of a print queue.

job scheduling executive A program that sequences the loading and execution of programs as directed by the user via system commands to the executive. Users can enter instructions, or commands may be supplied with the user program.

job step The execution of that portion of a program identified by a job control statement. Most jobs have several job steps.

Jobs, Steve One of the founders of Apple Computer, along with Steve Wozniak.

job stream The set of computer jobs in an input queue waiting for initiation and processing.

job turnaround The elapsed time from when a job is given to the computer system until its printed output reaches the person who submitted the job. The term applies to batch work only.

job type In NetWare Queue Services, a number specifying the type of a job entry.

jog A function that provides for the momentary operation of a drive for the purpose of accomplishing a small movement of the driven machine.

Johnson noise The electrical noise across the terminals of a resistor when it has no current flowing through it. It is caused by the thermal motion of charge and is greater for larger resistances, higher temperatures, and wider bandwidths.

join **1.** To form the logical sum or union. **2.** In DOS 3.0 and later, a command that treats a disk drive as a subdirectory. **3.** A database command that merges portions of multiple files into one file.

joint denial A logical operation that has a true output only if all inputs are false.

joint denial gate A circuit or device that provides a true output only if all inputs are false.

Josephson junction A thin-film junction that uses a tunneling mechanism for current flow.

Josephson junction memory A type of memory cell that contains two Josephson junctions and a sensing junction. A write current temporarily changes the magnitude of the current flowing and allows the sensing device to determine the current's original magnitude and direction: clockwise signifies a one and counterclockwise a zero. Experiments show that very fast and very low-power memories may be provided using this technique.

Josephson ratio A frequency-voltage ratio symbolized by $2e/h$ and equal to $4.835\ 939 \times 10^{14}$ Hz per volt.

joule The unit of energy (symbol J) that describes the work performed when the point of application of one newton is displaced a distance of one meter in the direction of force.

joule effect The production of heat due to current flow in a conductor.

joule magnetostriction The effect that causes the length of an iron core to increase when subjected to a longitudinal magnetic field.

JOVIAL A computer language used for command and control applications that is a version of the international algebraic language, an early version of ALGOL. JOVIAL contains facilities for numerical computations along with some data processing.

joystick A remote-control device for a computer that looks like a car's gearstick, as shown in the figure. It is used in video and arcade games and in some interactive video applications.

joystick dead zone A small area normally used to allow for drift in the joystick's center position. The relationship of cursor velocity to joystick displacement is generally not linear, as illustrated.

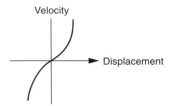

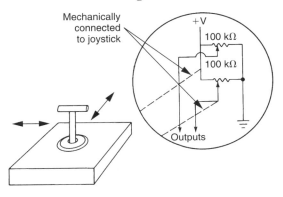

A displacement joystick with potentiometers used to sense movement

Nonlinear joystick characteristic

JPEG Abbreviation for *Joint Photo Experts Group*, an image-compression standards committee.

JPW Abbreviation for *job processing word*.

jumbogroup In frequency-division multiplexing, a number of voice channels (generally 3,600) composed of six mastergroups.

jump A departure from the normal sequence of executing instructions. Jumps usually differ from branches in that they do not use the relative addressing mode. Also called *transfer*.

jump and loop instructions Instructions that allow the microprocessor to move about nonsequentially within the program. For example, a program might contain three tasks, A, B, and C, with each being a complete section of code or a subroutine. The microprocessor can be directed to perform them in any order. The program flow is controlled using the jump or branch instructions as shown in the following program.

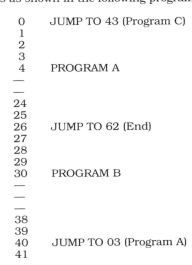

```
42
43
44     PROGRAM C
—
—
57
58
59     JUMP TO 29 (Program B)
60
61
62     END OF PROGRAM
```

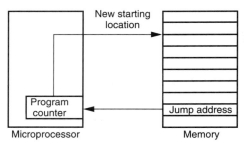

Jump instructions change the program counter

jumper A small black plastic connector that contains metal contacts, used to select one of two options. A jumper usually connects two of three metal pins. Options are selected by placing it on either the left two pins or the right two pins. Some of the jumpers on some circuit boards may have only two pins. You can disable the jumper by removing it or placing it on a single pin. Also called a *shunt*.

jump routine A routine designed to have the computer depart from the regular sequence of instructions and shift to another routine or program, as shown in the following diagram. For example, the following sequence in the 8080 microprocessor calls the ZZZ routine:

```
YYY
       .
       .
       .
CALL ZZZ    ; (call routine for ZZZ)
RET         ;(return to caller of YYY)
```

A better way of performing the same task uses a jump routine, as follows:

```
YYY
       .
       .
       .
JMP ZZZ    ;(go to ZZZ then return)
```

junction A connection between two or more conductors, flow paths, metals, or semiconductors.
junction box An enclosure used for connecting different runs of cable in a raceway or conduit.
junction circuit A circuit connecting two exchanges that are closer than those found in trunk lines or circuits.
junction diode A two-terminal device with a single-crystal structure that permits current flow in only one direction. Also called a *junction rectifier*.
junction summing A technique used in computing amplifiers and control systems in which various signals are connected to a common point at the input of the amplifier or control unit.
junction transistor 1. Bipolar transistor. **2.** Field-effect transistor without an insulated gate.
junk A term used for unintelligible signals, especially those received from a communications channel. Also called *garbage* and *hash*.
justification *See* PULSE STUFFING.
justify 1. To adjust the printing positions of characters on a page such that the rightmost edge of each line is flush with all other lines. **2.** To shift the contents of a register such that the least significant bit is at a desired position.

K **1.** Symbol (on drawings) to indicate the presence of an electromechanical relay. **2.** Symbol for *cathode*. **3.** Nonstandard but often used symbol for *kilohm*. **4.** Abbreviation for *Kelvin*. **5.** In microcomputer usage, the abbreviation for *kilobyte*, which is 1024 bytes (2^{10}).

k **1.** The SI prefix for *kilo-*, meaning thousand. **2.** The symbol for *constant*. **3.** The symbol for *coupling coefficient*.

Karnaugh map A chart or table that shows the combination of logical functions and tends to eliminate duplicate logical expressions by listing all of the similar functions. As shown in the following figure, A Karnaugh map is drawn as a rectangular diagram of variables with overlapping subrectangles such that the intersection of the subrectangles represents a unique combination of variables, and such an intersection is shown for all logical combinations.

kayser (*o.t.*) The obsolete unit for wave number, which is the reciprocal for wavelength. The SI unit for wave number is *reciprocal meter*.

KB Alternative abbreviation for *kilobyte*. Also see K, 5.

Kbps Abbreviation for *thousand bits per second*.

kc Abbreviation for *kilocycle*, one thousand cycles per second.

KCS An abbreviation for *thousand characters per second*, a generally accepted measurement of data transmission speed.

KEDIT A general-purpose text editor compatible with XEDIT, IBM's VM/CMS text editor. It also contains many PC-based editor features and supports multiple files, multiple windows, block operations, and string-based search and change.

keep alive message A message sent over a network link during periods when there is no traffic between users. The message tells the remote node that this computer is still in operation.

keep together In word processing, an instruction to keep together all of the specified text (usually a paragraph or table), creating a page break if necessary rather than splitting it between pages.

Kelvin ampere-balance A laboratory instrument for measuring current. The force between two coils carrying the current to be measured is balanced by the force of gravity on a weight sliding along a beam.

Kelvin effect A property of high-frequency currents in which most of the current flow concentrates near the surface. Also called *skin effect*.

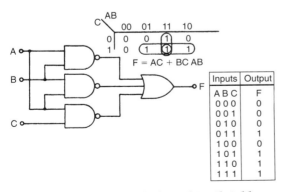

Karnaugh map with logic and truth table

264 Kelvin temperature • keyboard circuits

Kelvin temperature Temperature expressed on the Kelvin thermodynamic scale, in which measurements are made from absolute zero.

Kermit A communications protocol that allows file transfers between different types of computers, usually using a modem.

kerning In desktop publishing, reducing the amount of space between characters so that words are easier to read and the line of text looks better. Most page layout programs (such as PageMaker) and some word processors have a kerning feature.

kernel 1. A software product sold with the understanding that it must be modified by the buyer before it can be used on a specific machine. The kernel is usually, but not always, accompanied by other programs that facilitate customization. **2.** Sometimes used in the sense of a nucleus, the central and indispensable portion of a computer operating system.

key 1. A group of characters used to identify an item or record. **2.** A marked lever or switch used for entering a character or command into the system. A key is shown in the following figure.

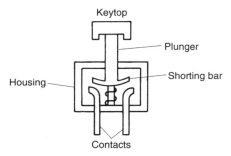

Typical keyswitch construction

keyboard A unit containing keys for entering data or information into a system, as shown in the following figure. Keyboards may be alphanumeric (as used for word processing, text processing, and data processing) or numeric (as used for touch-tone telephones, accounting machines, and calculators).

keyboard circuits The IBM PC family and its clones use a separate encoded keyboard which is connected to the system unit. The encoded keyboard for the IBM personal computer has five connections on the output plug. Two of these provide the power (+5 volts and ground). The other three provide the interface between the keyboard and the system board.

In the IBM keyboard, a key depression causes the encoded circuits to generate the ASCII code for the key. The keyboard feeds its ASCII output to the system unit. The keyboard uses a

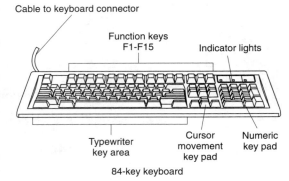

Typical PC keyboard layout

keyboard processor, an 8048 microprocessor chip. The 8048 chip is an 8-bit processor and contains 2K bytes of ROM. The ROM is preloaded with a character code known as a *scan code*.

The processor uses a row-scanning technique to monitor the keyboard matrix. Each key makes a connection at one of the row-column intersections when depressed. The 8048 processor scans the rows for keystrokes by sending a high-level logic signal to each of the columns, one at a time. It scans the matrix once every 5 milliseconds. The 8048 receives a high-level logic signal from each row if a key in that row has not been pressed. The signals are stored in the scanning buffer resister in the 8048.

If a key is pressed, then the intersection connection is made and a low-level signal is re-

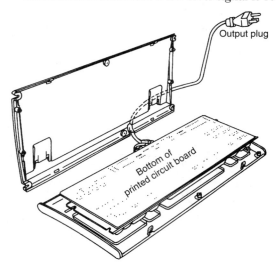

Keyboard with bottom removed

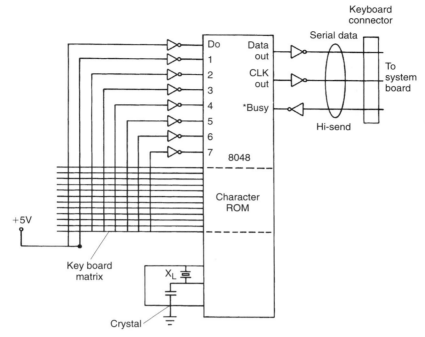

Electronic components inside the keyboard

ceived. The 8048 matches the column which is being scanned with the row that changed state. This sets the intersection point. The 8048 then looks up the character for this key in its character ROM. The coded bit pattern for the character is then sent out through the keyboard cable to the system board.

Inside the keyboard is a printed circuit board with the row-column matrix along with some electronic components, including the IC chips and supporting discrete parts. The main 8048 circuit chip has internal clock circuits that generate the timing for the processor, which is also sent to the system board. The clock output synchronizes the keyboard timing with the system board. See the following figures.

keyboard control keys Switches used in terminals to control and move the cursor on CRT displays, to change the terminal application, or to change the communications mode.

keyboard diagnostics Diagnostic programs like IBM Advanced Diagnostics (a segment of which is shown in the following figure), useful for troubleshooting keyboard problems on IBM ATs and compatibles. However, since keyboards are not identical in their electronics, this program may sometimes generate a keyboard error when none exists. If you use IBM Advanced Diagnostics, be prepared for this problem.

A
```
TESTING - KEYBOARD INTERNAL
END KEYBOARD TEST
PRESS "ENTER"...
```

B
```
TESTING - KEYBOARD INTERNAL
XX:XX:XX LOOP COUNT = XX
3XX XXXXXX
END KEYBOARD TEST
PRESS "ENTER"...
```

C
```
PRESS EACH KEY, HOLD FOR TYPEMATIC TEST
IF OK PRESS "Y THEN ENTER"
IF NOT OK PRESS "N THEN ENTER"
```

Typical keyboard tests: (A) normal end, (B) error message, (C) typematic test menu

keyboard display Refers to keyboards that offer possible interpretive operations; a particular

266 keyboard display • key field

job is assigned by the computer program, and the keys for that job are identified by removable overlays.

keyboard encoder A circuit or device that identifies each key function and produces a word corresponding to that function. Some encoders allow the use of custom encoding with the use of PROMs, and error detection for simultaneous key depressions.

keyboard function key *See* FUNCTION KEY.

keyboard lock A device that connects to and deactivates the keyboard, allowing you to keep your terminal accessible to network communication or job processing without interference from unwanted users.

keyboard processing In keyboard processing, the encoded keyboard signals are sent to the system board as shown in the figure. The keyboard output is a serial data signal that is sent to the system board circuits. A busy signal is used to control when the keyboard can send keyboard bits to the system board. The keyboard bits are sent in a serial format, with the least significant bit sent first and the most significant bit of the data byte sent last.

The serial data is sent to a serial-to-parallel 74LS322 register, which changes the serial format to parallel. The 74LS322 is also connected to a dual-D flip-flop, the 74LS74. The latched clock signal from the keyboard is sent from the 74LS175 to the serial/parallel register and the 74LS74 to synchronize these chips with the keyboard. The 74LS74 flip-flop is used to generate an interrupt request to the 8259 programmable interrupt controller. This chip generates an output signal which interrupts the main processor (CPU). The 74LS322 shift register sends its parallel bits to one of the ports of the 8255 I/D chip. The parallel bits are then sent to the system data bus.

These bits, which hold the keyboard characters, are then read by the CPU and stored in the video RAM section of memory. They can then be used by the video display system and sent to the monitor or to the printer for hardcopy output.

keyboard template A plastic template that fits on a keyboard. It can save time by providing a quick reference directly on the keyboard for needed commands, options, formats, symbols, functions, prompts, and printer setups.

key code In word processing, one or two characters you can use to assign a format or style to selected text. In addition to built-in key codes, you can define new key codes in style sheets.

key field In database management, a field in each record of a file that uniquely identifies that record. Also called a *key*.

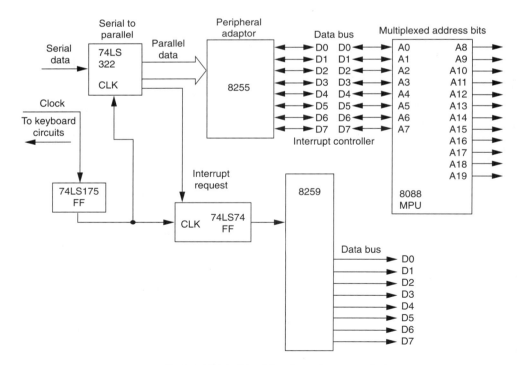

System board and keyboard processing

keying In a video-processing system, the process of inserting one picture into another picture under spatial control of another signal called the keying signal.

keypad A small keyboard or section of a keyboard containing a smaller number of keys, generally those used on simple calculators. These 10-, 20-, or 16-key units are often the simplest input devices to microcomputers, or they function as an extension of an ASCII keyboard to permit more extensive computational capability.

keyswitch debouncing The mechanical contact that occurs when you strike a key that is not perfect. As you press the key and the key closes the metallic connection, there is a condition of oscillation for a few milliseconds until the connection is finalized. During this time, the key-switch voltage is unstable and bounces between the two switching voltages. The same type of oscillations occur when you release the key.

In nonencoded keyboards, a resistor and capacitor are connected as a filter to reduce the oscillations and bouncing effect. In the encoded keyboards typical in most microcomputer systems, a delay of a few milliseconds is used before the keystrike is encoded. The delay is accomplished with a programmed loop that inserts the delay. This inhibiting of the key action during the switch bouncing is called *debouncing*. The 8048 microprocessor performs this debouncing in a PC keyboard by generating an interrupt during the time the keyboard voltage is bouncing.

keyword A significant word in the title, abstract, or text that can be used alone or with other significant words to describe a document. A keyword or set of keywords may describe a document's contents, label the document, or assist in identifying or retrieving the document.

keyword-in-context *See* KWIC.

Keyworks A DOS-based macro generator that lets you replace multiple keystrokes with a single command and also allows you to replace a program's original commands with menus and prompts. To make macros easier to use, Keyworks allows your macro to include a message at each pause to explain what the user must do next. For example, a message might read, "Move cursor to end of paragraph and press Return." A menu-builder allows you to set up a main menu for initiating programs or DOS functions. You can also run selected DOS functions from within an applications program. The package includes a full-screen macro editor that lets you edit all your macros in one session. You can also copy part of a macro into a new macro.

k-factor The ratio of effective to true earth radius.

kHz Abbreviation for *kilohertz* (1,000 cycles per second).

kill The command to erase a disk file in certain operating systems.

kilo Prefix indicating multiplication by a factor of 10^3; thousand.

kilobauds One thousand bauds, used to define the capacity of data channels.

kilobyte The microcomputer term for 1,024 bytes or characters, which is 2^{10}. This roughly corresponds to one-half of a typewritten page.

kilocycle *See* KC.

kilomega A prefix meaning one billion; a *kilomegacycle* is one billion cycles (same as *billicycle* and *gigacycle*), and a *kilomegabit* means one billion bits (same as *gigabit*). Also called *giga*.

kilomegacycle Also called *gigacycle*; one billion cycles per second.

kilometer One thousand meters, or 3,281 feet. The kilometer is the unit of measuring distance in most of the world.

kilovolt-ampere A unit of apparent electrical power equal to 1000 volt amperes.

kilowatt A unit of electrical power equal to 1,000 watts.

kilowatt hour The equivalent energy supplied by a power of 1,000 watts for one hour.

Kipp relay An alternative term for an *electromechanical one-shot* or *monostable multivibrator*, a circuit that has a stable and an unstable state, and goes through a complete cycle in response to a single triggering action.

Kirchhoff's laws Laws of electrical circuits that state the following:

- The current flowing to a given point in a circuit is equal to the current flowing away from that point.
- The algebraic sum of the voltage drops in any closed path in a circuit is equal to the algebraic sum of the electromotive forces in that path.
- At a given temperature, the emissive power of a body is the same as its radiation-absorbing power for all surfaces.

kit A set of parts and software assembled by the user for a specific application or specification. Microcomputer kits allow the user a cost-effective system without special hardware design. Kits are available as complete standalone systems for writing, debugging, and executing programs on the microprocessor. They include not only the processor and memory, but also a low-cost set of peripherals.

kludge A slang term for a quick-fix circuit or device. Also refers to a hastily formed interface between devices.

knowledge base The database of an expert system, containing the rules, decisions, and knowledge which the expert uses.

knowledge-based system *See* EXPERT SYSTEM.

knowledge engineering *See* EXPERT SYSTEM.

KnowledgeMaker An induction system that reads examples in text or Lotus 1-2-3 files and creates rules. The output can be in English or the syntax required by KnowledgePro, Micro-Expert,

M.1, or the system's own inference engine written in Borland's Turbo Prolog.

KnowledgeMan A database manager that is relational and procedural much like dBASE. The advantage of this package over other procedural relational database managers is that it adds spreadsheet analysis and statistical analysis to the other usual tools such as ad hoc inquiries, screen management, and printed forms management.

KnowledgeMan's data is organized into tables rather than forms. It allows up to 255 fields per record, multiple tables open at a time, indexed access, virtual fields, security, and a data dictionary. The ad hoc inquiry mode allows the query of multiple tables with a single command in the SQL syntax, multi-field control breaks, dynamic sorting, wildcard conditions, and output graphics.

KnowledgeMan's screen management functions include error checking and special effects such as inverse video and freeform field placement. The structured language for advanced users includes procedures such as if-then-else, while-do, and test-case structures. Parameterized procedures are supported with no limit on nesting levels.

KnowledgePro A high-level language for building applications in DOS. It lets the user create tutorials and explain complex procedures or regulations using a combination of object-oriented programming, expert systems, and hypertext techniques. The environment is a symbolic language and a programming paradigm called the *topic*. Topics are chunks of knowledge containing rules, calculations, hypertext commands, or graphics. It can read external files, call external programs, and access routines written in other languages.

Kodak PhotoCD Developed by Kodak Corporation, a technique of multisession recording of images onto CD-ROM.

KPSI A unit of tensile strength expressed in *thousands (k) of pounds per square inch*.

KSR Abbreviation for *keyboard send/receive*. A teletypewriter transmitter and receiver unit that has transmission capability from the keyboard only.

kurtosis A statistical quantity that expresses the peakedness of a distribution.

KWIC Acronym for *keyword-in-context*, a program-title index based upon the use of keywords for programs. The keywords are listed in alphabetical order for identification.

Kwikstat A graphics-oriented program for scientific statistical analysis. It can import ASCII and dBASE files, as well as building its own databases. It is entirely menu-controlled. There is a tutorial with the program, but the program assumes knowledge of statistics. The program modules allow for the creation of histograms, scatterplots, box plots, 3-D bar charts, comparative statistics, T-tests, and one-way analysis of variance (ANOVA) on independent or repeated observations.

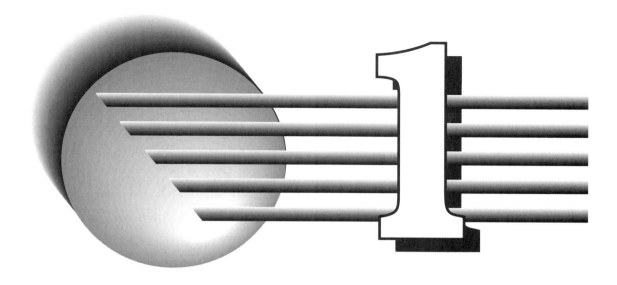

L Abbreviation for *label*.

LAA Abbreviation of *locally administered address*, an adaptor address that the user can assign to override the universally administered address (*UAA*).

label 1. A set of symbols that identify or describe an item, record, message, or file. **2.** A code name that classifies a name, term, phrase, or document.

Label Matrix Formally called Label Master, a program that prints any size label or form with bar codes, variable size text, lines, and PCX graphics. It supports over 200 models of printers, and can read from dBASE, spreadsheet, ASCII, and DIF files.

Labtech Acquire A menu-driven software package designed for using the PC as a data logger. The package allows up to four channels of time-stamped data to be written to disk, and one channel for digital input. The user can control start-up, data rates, run duration, and display and file writing parameters from a single menu.

Labtech Notebook An integrated DOS-based software package for data acquisition, monitoring, and real-time control. Labtech Notebook operates with a hardware analog/digital interface, but insulates the user from the low-level instructions the interface usually requires. It replaces laboratory notebooks and the rekeying of data in the same way that spreadsheet programs such as Lotus 1-2-3 replaced paper spreadsheets in business offices. Data samples are acquired in background mode, then read from Notebook's RAM memory buffers directly into spreadsheet, statistical data analysis, database management, and display programs.

LAC Acronym for *load accumulator*.

lag The relative difference between two events, states, or mechanisms.

Lamura Data Dictionary A centralized source for information about databases. It allows structures and relations to be prototyped and tested before any code is written. It assists database design, normalization, data and referential integrity, and prevents circular references. It supports dBASE, FoxBase, FoxPro, Clipper, and Arago.

LAN Acronym for *local area network*, an in-house data communications system, usually within a single building, connecting a number of microcomputers together. A LAN often includes a large mainframe computer as well, thus permitting the microcomputers to act both in a stand-alone mode and as terminals. Microcomputers can share devices and files using the LAN, so that equipment costs are reduced by pooling such resources as printers and hard disks.

LAN adapter card The circuit card added to a microcomputer that controls its access to the network. The LAN adapter card frames outgoing data into the format the network requires. It also performs checksum (CRC) functions.

LAN administrator The person responsible for the ongoing maintenance of the network. The LAN administrator adds and removes users and application software. The LAN administrator in a NetWare environment is called a *supervisor*.

LAN Automatic Inventory A configuration system that automatically creates a LAN equipment database including both hardware configuration and software application information for workstations and file servers. It detects the software titles on local and network hard drives and identifies specific software versions. It keeps track of the number of copies of each software package and allows users to customize additional software titles. It supports consolidation of data from multiple servers and sites with both PC and MAC hardware and software products.

LAN board status In NetWare, the following conditions are used to indicate the status of a LAN board:

- The board is alive and running.
- The board does not exist.
- The board is dead.

LAN card *See* LAN ADAPTER CARD.

land The reflective area between two adjacent non-reflective pits on a CD-ROM. In CD-ROM coding, a binary one represents the transition from pit to land and from land to pit, and two or more zeros represent the distances between transitions.

LAN description In NetWare, a null-terminated text string listing the LAN hardware supported by a driver.

landscape orientation Refers to printing across the length of the page. The term *landscape* is derived from pictures of landscapes, which are usually horizontal in format. *Contrast with* PORTRAIT ORIENTATION.

language A system for representing and communicating information or data between people or different types of machines. A language consists of a carefully defined set of characters and rules for combining the characters into larger units, such as words or expressions. There are also rules for word arrangement and usage in order to achieve specific meanings. Most computer languages have the following features:

- Data objects or structures with descriptions, corresponding to nouns and adjectives in natural languages
- Operations and commands that act upon the data objects, corresponding to verbs and adverbs in a natural language
- Control structures to specify the sequence of operations, corresponding to phrasing and forming paragraphs in natural languages

language assembler A development-oriented system that is used to assemble source code and convert it into binary output, which is then loaded and executed on the CPU. Input to the assembler is usually prepared with the aid of an assembler program.

language interpreter A processor, assembler, or other routine that accepts statements in one language and produces equivalent statements in another language. *Also see* INTERPRETER.

language translator A program or routine that converts statements in one language to equivalent statements in another language. The languages may be computer or machine languages, or natural languages such as English.

LAN hardware ID In NetWare, a code in the Master Configuration Table that uniquely identifies the LAN hardware. The OEM/Driver Support Group Manager at Novell assigns this ID.

LAN Manager An OEM LAN operating system developed by IBM, Microsoft, and 3Com. Microsoft licenses it to other vendors, who add their own features. OS/2 is its underlying operating system on the file server. However, workstations do not have to use OS/2. It is sometimes called *LAN MAN* for short.

LAN mode In NetWare, this is a one-byte field with the following bits:

bit 0   OFF (0): Place-holding dummy driver
         ON (1): Real driver
bit 1   OFF: Not 100% guaranteed driver
         ON: 100% guaranteed driver
bit 7   OFF: Driver does not use DMA
         ON: Driver uses DMA; no receive block straddles 64K physical address boundary

LAN probe A network diagnostic tool that allows you to examine a LAN and monitor traffic.

LAN Server *See* IBM LAN SERVER.

LAN shell A configurable menu interface that acts as an umbrella to the entire LAN system, making DOS and network command syntax transparent to users. Once the LAN shell is installed, users work faster because shared resources—files, printers, communications and applications software, file servers, and electronic mail—are accessible from a single interface.

LAN Support Center A real-time maintenance and alerting system for LAN managers. It gives access to user and hardware information, making it easier to answer support calls. You can track support efforts with relational databases that combine equipment records, user records, alerts, and trouble tickets.

Laplace's law The differential form of Ampere's law for the magnetic field produced by a current carrying conductor. In vector notation

$$dH = \frac{I\,(dl \times r)}{r^3}$$

where dl is an element of the conductor, I the current, and r the vector drawn from the element to the point at which the field component dH is required.

lapping The final abrasive polishing of a quartz crystal to adjust its operating frequency; also, the smoothing of the surface of crystalline semiconductors.

laptops Small, sleekly designed, lightweight, portable microcomputers. A typical laptop with DOS in ROM can weigh less than five pounds. With hard and floppy disk drives and seven hours of battery power, a laptop weighs less than seven pounds. Also called *notebooks*.

LARAM Acronym for *line-addressable random-access memory*.

large-scale integration *See* LSI.

Larmor frequency The angular frequency of precession for the spin vector of an electron acted on by an external magnetic field.

Larmor precession The motion experienced in a small uniform magnetic field by a charged particle (or system of charged particles) when subjected to a central force that is directed towards a common point.

Larmor radius Radius of the circular or helical path followed by a charged particle in a uniform magnetic field.

lase To undergo laser operation.

laser Once an acronym for *light amplification by stimulated emission of radiation*, the term has become legitimized as a word describing an amplifier and generator of a narrow and coherent beam of energy in the visible light spectrum.

laser cartridge replacement To determine when a laser cartridge needs to be replaced, look at the color of the print capacity indicator, visible through the window. As the drum rotates, the color of the indicator will change to indicate the usable service life of the cartridge, as shown in the figure.

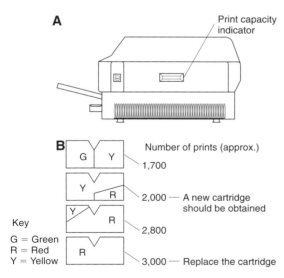

Laser toner replacement indicators: (A) indicator location, (B) typical print capacity indicator

laser disk A very high-capacity disk storage on which bit patterns are burned, as small holes, onto the disk surface using a laser beam.

laser emulsion storage Various types of digital data storage media that use a controller laser beam to expose very small areas on a photosensitive surface, producing the desired information patterns.

Laser FX A PostScript font enhancer for the Mac that can be used to apply more than 30 special effects to any PostScript font. Laser FX is compatible with most page layout programs, including Quark XPress and PageMaker. It reads and saves MacPaint, PICT, and EPS files.

LaserMaster Controller A full-length PC compatible board that accelerates the printing of Ventura, AutoCAD, Windows, GEM, and other software packages. It adds a high-speed video interface to your laser printer. Font-based special effects include rotation and custom fills.

LaserMenu A control program for HP laser printers. It supports resident, cartridge, and soft fonts; precise formatting; and fast font downloading. You can use it to overlay text output with boxes, lines, and shading. LaserMenu supports macros that control access to all of the functions of any printer, spooler, or switchbox, and can redirect printer output to any port at any time.

LaserPaint A paint program for laser printers with professional graphic workstation capabilities. You can display, edit, combine, and retouch 24-bit color photos, do automatic four-color separations, and import and export Macintosh file formats. The package includes drawing, painting, writing, and layout capabilities. A PostScript drawing program is provided that supports Bezier curves, circles, squares, arcs, spirals, lines patterns, screens, and colors.

LaserPak A set of BASIC subroutines for controlling an HP or compatible laser printer. It allows BASIC programs to draw lines, boxes, circles, symbols, and fill patterns. Other capabilities include graph scales and grids, text labeling, and control over all of the LaserJet control sequences. There is also a symbol editor that can be used to design and manage logos, symbols, clip art, and custom fonts.

LaserPort A laser printer controller for PCs for enhancing photograph reproductions. It allows halftone pictures by expanding page memory to provide 300 dpi graphics and a set of advanced graphics commands. Halftone pictures can be printed using up to 100 line screens with 64 shades of gray.

laser printer A high-resolution printer that uses laser optics as shown in the following figure to produce images on paper. Light and dark image areas are represented by electrostatically charged areas on the paper. A powdered ink called *toner* is dusted on the paper. The toner adheres to the charged areas and is melted into the paper by the heat from the lasers.

laser printer memory upgrade Refers to a memory board that installs into the laser printer's

RAM expansion slot and provides additional megabytes. No special tools are usually required.

Laser-Ready A program that lets you print professional-quality letters and envelopes, business forms, newsletters, flyers, mailing labels, business cards, and other office documents. More than 30 fill-in-the-blank document templates and over fifty fonts are included.

laser spooler board A board lets you assign priority levels to print jobs sent from the computer, with a 250K of buffer dynamically allocated as printing jobs are sent. High-priority jobs are completed in typical FIFO (first-in-first-out) order, while low-priority jobs are interspersed with other jobs as time permits. The board includes software that runs in background mode on a PC for configuring timeouts, cancel functions, end print job functions, and form feeds.

LaserTalk A PostScript development environment for both the Macintosh and the PC. It is designed to be used for a laser printer with a PostScript interpreter. It has facilities for coding, testing, debugging, and printer control. An interactive window connects you directly with the PostScript executive so you can interact on a line-by-line basis and obtain immediate feedback from the interpreter. It also provides a complete programmer's editor, an integrated debugger that allows you to send code to the printer one line at a time, and a dictionary browser that gives you access to all the dictionaries currently available in the printer. Online documentation is based on the *Addison-Wesley PostScript Language Reference Manual*. This gives you a dictionary of specific operators and a hierarchical display of operators organized by class. A preview feature allows you to display the actual state of the PostScript page on the screen prior to printing.

LaserTORQ A buffer designed to save CPU time that would otherwise be sacrificed to printing. It is designed especially for laser printers and runs whatever printer it is attached to at the printer's highest potential speed. With many programs, print time can be cut in half.

lasons The ultrahigh energy produced by lasers.

lasso A graphics function that allows a user to encircle part of a drawing that must be moved or copied elsewhere.

last record seen In NetWare File Server Environment Services, indicates the last record seen.

LAT Abbreviation for *local area transport*, a protocol developed by DEC for communication between terminal servers and hosts on an Ethernet network.

latch An arrangement or circuit (as shown in the figure) used to hold data in a ready position until required, usually controlled by another condition or circuit. Also called *lock*.

latency The time required by a computer to deliver information from its memory. In a serial storage system, the latency time becomes the access

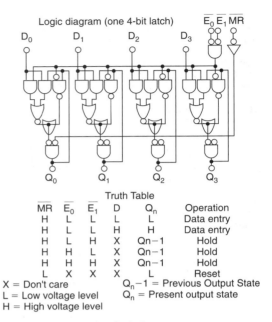

Latch

time minus the word time. In a rotational system, it becomes the time required for the desired location to appear at the heads.

latency buffer A token ring concept in which the buffer is maintained by the active monitor and is used to compensate for variations in the speed of data on the network.

lattice dynamics Refers to the mechanical properties of the thermal vibrations of crystal lattices.

lattice filter A wave filter composed of four branches connected together to form a mesh that functions as a section of the filter. The filter may have a single section, or it may be composed of several sections.

lattice network A circuit with four branches connected together to form a mesh, with the two non-adjacent junctions serving as inputs and the other two serving as outputs. Also called *bridge network*.

lattice spacing The length of an edge in a unit cell of a crystal.

lattice vibration The vibration of atoms or molecules in a crystal due to thermal energy.

lay The length of a turn of the helix of any helical element.

layer A part of the hierarchy of computing functions defined by a system's architecture.

layout The overall plan, structure, or design of a circuit, system, device, or document. The layout may include the arrangement of data, sequence, size, schematic diagrams, flow diagrams, and outlines of operation or procedure.

Layout A software tool that allows you to build programs without writing code, by arranging objects in a flowchart. It has objects for user interfaces (windows, menus, graphics, and buttons), mathematical functions, and program control, and works with hypertext databases. The flowchart can be transformed into C, Pascal, QuickBasic, or a ready-to-run EXE file. It supports Turbo Pascal, Microsoft C, Lattice C, QuickBasic, and Turbo C.

LB Abbreviation for *line buffer*.

LCB Abbreviation for *line control block*, an area of main storage used to hold control data for operations on communication lines.

LCD Abbreviation for *liquid-crystal display*, a display technique that uses segments of a liquid crystal solution in a sandwich of glass plates. The light-reflecting properties of the solution are controlled by an electric field.

LCL Abbreviation for *local*.

LCP method Abbreviation for *logical construction of programs*, a method of software design, as shown in the figure, that assumes the data structure is the key to software design. This method is procedure-oriented and has the following steps:

1. Identify and organize the input data in a hierarchical manner.
2. Define and note the number of times each element of the input file occurs and use variable names to note the ratio of occurrences, such as *N* records.
3. Repeat steps 1 and 2 for the desired output.
4. Obtain the program details by identifying the types of instructions required for the design using a specific order: read instructions, branches, calculations, output, and subroutine calls.
5. Using flowchart techniques, graph the logical sequence of instructions using *Begin Process*, *End Process*, *Branching*, and *Nesting* labels.

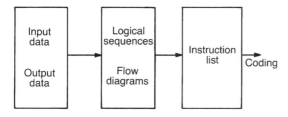

The LCP method for software design

LD Abbreviation for *load*.

LDS Abbreviation for *local distribution system*.

leader 1. A record that precedes a group of detailed records, giving information about the group that is not in the detailed records. 2. An unused or blank length of tape or film at the beginning of a reel. 3. In word processing, characters (usually dots or hyphens) that fill the space between columns to help draw the reader's eye across a line, as in a table of contents.

leading The amount of space between lines of type (pronounced "LED-ing"), usually referred to in terms of *point size*. The notation *10/12* or *10 on 12* means 10 point type in a 12 point space, which is the same as 10 point type with 2 points of leading between the lines.

leading zeros Zeros preceding the first nonzero integer of a number. Leading zeros may be employed in the numeric fields of some input blocks to indicate the position of the decimal point within the field.

Leadtools A 32-bit runtime library for compressing, decompressing, converting, resizing, rotation, flipping, and viewing of images. It compresses color and grayscale images to over a 200:1 ratio. It supports SPEG, LEAD CMP, TGA, TIFF, BMP, PCX, GIF, WMF, and EPS graphic file formats.

Leadview Software that can be used to compress, decompress, view, convert, and resize images. You can compress color or grayscale images with SPEG or LEAD to over 200 times smaller than original. Supported file formats include SPEL6 (FIF, JTIF, JPG), LEAD CMP, TGA, BMP GIF and PCX.

leakage Refers to undesired losses due to stray conductive paths in components and circuit boards.

leakage current Current flow due to undesirable conductive paths across or through insulating surfaces or barriers.

leakage radiation Spurious radiation in a transmitting system; radiation from other than the system itself.

leakage reactance The reactance represented by the difference in value between two mutually coupled inductances when their fields are aiding and then opposing.

leapfrog test A checking routine that copies itself using storage. A typical leapfrog routine might take the following steps:

1. Perform a series of operations on one group of storage locations
2. Transfer to another group of storage locations
3. Check the correctness of the transfer
4. Repeat the series of operations for the new locations
5. Continue transferring and repeating until all storage locations are occupied

learning bridge An intelligent device that interconnects two LANs with similar protocols.

leased line A private telephone line leased from the telephone company on a monthly basis. Leased lines offer an advantage over regular switched-line service in that they can be specially selected and conditioned to optimize them for data transmission.

leased-line modem A compact, economical, and reliable medium-speed modem that can perform on four-wire (full duplex), AT&T 3002, and M1040 leased lines and even on unconditioned lines. The modem can function in both point-to-point and multipoint modes, and is compatible with Bell 201 and CCITT V.26. The synchronizing time is only nine milliseconds, ensuring excellent performance in multidrop applications. A 1200 bps fallback speed is provided, for compliance with V.26 recommendations.

LED Acronym for *light-emitting diode*, a diode with a light-producing characteristic used as a low-cost, low-power indicator on panels and in displays. LEDs are available in several colors and operate at current levels of 5-10 mA.

left-justify 1. In word processing, to adjust the printing positions of characters on a page such that the left margin is aligned flush. **2.** To shift the contents of a register so that the most significant bit is at a specified position.

Legal Form Letter A program for contracts, employment applications, filings, and other correspondence. The program contains 100 forms for many different needs.

legend The patterns, markers, or colors (with accompanying labels) that identify the series in a bar/line, area, or high/low/close chart.

Lempel-Ziv coding A data encryption algorithm that provides an alternative to the Huffman encoding technique. *Also see* HUFFMAN CODING.

Lenz's law A current resulting from an induced electromotive force in such a direction as to oppose any change in the current that generates the EMF.

LEP Acronym for *lowest effective power*.

LET In BASIC, a statement allowing an internal value to be assigned to a variable name.

Letter Blitzer A mailmerge and letter-writing program for designing form letters and name/address databases. You can use the mailmerge facilities to create and send personalized letters for a mailing list. The program can also generate mailing labels for each letter created.

letter-quality printer A printer that uses a full-formed character to produce high-quality printouts like typewritten text or the text on this page. Also called *correspondence-quality printers* (because they are preferred for most business communications) or *full-character printers*.

letters shift A physical shift in a terminal using Baudot code, which enables the printing of alphabetic characters.

level 1. The absolute magnitude of a quantity. **2.** The degree of subordination in a hierarchy, as in the different levels in a nested loop.

level-enable signal A signal generated by the CPU for the purpose of changing the state of the level-enable flip-flop from 0 to 1.

Level 2 MPC *See* MPC LEVEL 2.

Level 3 MPC *See* MPC LEVEL 3.

LF 1. Abbreviation for *low frequency*, 30Hz to 300Hz. **2.** The line-feed character, a format effecter that causes the print to display position to be moved to the next line. In ASCII, the LF character generates a binary 10 (0000 1010), which is decoded to cause a line feed at the receiving terminal printer.

LG Abbreviation for *line generator*.

liar's dice A computer game based on the statistics of dice.

library software A collection of routines and subroutines available for many microcomputers. A typical microcomputer library includes the following:

- A loading and debugging program
- A text editor
- A resident assembler
- A cross assembler
- A floating point arithmetic program
- A PROM programming software
- A multiply/divide package

LIC Acronym for *line integrated circuit*.

life characteristic Operating life as a function of failure rate. The life characteristic is usually plotted showing three phases: an infant mortality or debugging phase, a normal operating phase, and a wearout phase.

lifecycle The organization of a system's development job into small, organized steps.

LIFMOP Acronym for *linearly frequency modulated pulse*.

LIFO Acronym for *last-in-first-out*, a queue technique in which the last item in is the first to be operated on. LIFO is used in pushdown stack operations. Also called *FILO*. *Contrast with* FIFO.

light-emitting diode *See* LED.

light pen A photosensitive device that is used with a CRT display for input to the system computer. The pen detects the CRT beam when pointed towards the screen and generates a narrow electrical pulse that can be fed to the computer as an interrupt signal. Most light pens also produce a signal that the user generates by pushing a button on the pen to signal the computer of the user's selection of a point, as shown in the figure. *Also see* LIGHT PEN FUNCTIONS.

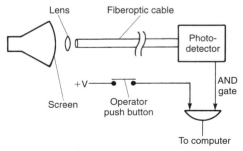

The basic light pen design using a lens with a fiber-optic cable

light pen attention An interrupt generated by a light pen when it senses light on the screen of a CRT display device.

light pen functions When the penlike device is pointed at information displayed on the screen, it detects light from the cathode ray tube (CRT) when a beam passes within its field of view. The pen's response is transmitted to the computer which in turn relates the computer action to the section of the image being displayed. In this way, light pens can be used to delete or add text, maintain control over the program, or choose from alternative courses of action. As the pertinent display information is selected by the operator, the pen signals the computer by generating a pulse. Acting upon this signal, the computer can instruct other points to be plotted across the tube face in accordance with the pen movement.

light sensitive Surfaces in which the electrical resistance, emission of electrons, or generation of a current depends on the incidence of light.

Lightyear A nonfinancial decision-modeling tool designed to help the user make better business decisions. It provides a structure for analyzing the variables that affect a complex decision and calculates an overall assessment of each of the alternatives. It can tell you why a particular alternative was ranked the way it was. This program is not related to spreadsheets, financial decision-making packages, or artificial intelligence.

Suppose, for example, a professional football team must analyze scouting reports on thousands of potential players each year. Players are rated in such categories as strength, durability, blocking ability, quickness, speed, aggressiveness, and intelligence. The importance of each characteristic depends on the position being considered. By matching the players' characteristics against the various criteria specified by the coaches, this program helps pick the best players for each position. To decide on the best player for a particular position, you define four items: alternatives (the players), criteria (the personal characteristics relevant to the position), weights (the relative importance of each characteristic), and rules (special constraints you want to incorporate into the decision, such as automatically rejecting a player weighing less than 190 pounds). After entering data on each of your alternatives (each player's scouting report), the program processes the information and presents an evaluation of your options (the best and worst candidates for the position). You can view the effect of changes on the results, a form of "what-if" analysis.

The program uses weighted values when measuring each alternative against the decision criteria. It allows you flexibility in assigning those weights; you can specify a weight numerically (by assigning a number), graphically (by positioning an x within a range), or verbally (by choosing the appropriate descriptive word).

The program is especially useful for group decisions (negotiations), because it allows the discussion to boil down to the criteria and thus takes the emotion out of the choice. It is also good for showing others how you arrived at a decision.

limited integrator An integrator that ceases to integrate when the output exceeds a specified limit.

limited process The restriction of the speed of the processing unit controls due to the processing time as contrasted with I/O limitations.

limiter 1. A transducer in which the output does not vary above a critical threshold value. **2.** A circuit that restricts amplitude to a specified level. **3.** In an FM receiver, a circuit that eliminates variations in amplitude to prevent AM components from being processed.

limiter tube An amplifier so biased that the output resulting from a large input voltage is substantially the same as that from a small one.

LIMM Abbreviation for *Lotus-Intel-Microsoft memory* specification. *Also see* EMS.

linac Acronym for *linear accelerator*.

lindemann electrometer A form of electrometer that uses a metal-coated quartz fiber located between an arrangement of electrodes to which the potentials are applied. The fiber is mounted on and perpendicular to a quartz torsion fiber that provides the controlling couple.

line A row of typing often used as a unit in work measurement. There is no universal standard, but a common definition sets a line at six inches of elite type, or 72 keystrokes.

linear A function that varies in direct proportion to the input.

linear amplifier A class A or AB amplifier that develops an output in direct proportion to the input signal.

linear control A rheostat or potentiometer having a uniform distribution of graduated resistance along the entire length of its resistance element.

linear displacement transducer A transducer that produces an output that is a direct function of position along a single axis.

linear distortion 1. Amplitude distortion in which the output and input signal envelopes are not proportionate, but no alien frequencies are involved. **2.** Distortion that results in the nonlinear response of a system, such as an amplifier, to the envelope of a varying signal, such as speech, without distorting (within acoustic perception) the detailed waveform.

linear energy transfer The linear rate of energy dissipation by particulate or electromagnetic radiation while penetrating absorbing media.

linear integer programming The use of linear programming models where only integer solutions are admissible. A special case of integer programming is selective programming. In this case, the variables in the solution can take only one of the preselected values.

linear interpolation In computer-integrated manufacturing, a mode of machine-tool control that uses the data contained in a block to produce constant velocities for two or more axes simultaneously.

linear magnetostriction The relative change of length of a ferromagnetic object in the direction of magnetization when the magnetization of the object is increased from zero to a specified value.

linear matrix transformation The process of transforming a group of n signals by combining the signals through addition or subtraction. It is used, for example, to convert RGB signals into YIQ.

linear modulation Modulation in which the amplitude of the modulation envelope is directly proportionate to the amplitude of the modulating wave at all audio frequencies.

linear network A circuit with electrical elements that remain constant in magnitude with varying currents.

linear optimization The set of procedures used to find maximum and minimum values of a linear function subject to specific constraints or conditions.

linear potentiometer A potentiometer in which the voltage at a movable contact is a linear function of the displacement of the contact.

linear power amplifier A power amplifier in which the output voltage is directly proportionate to the input voltage.

linear predictive coding A voice encoding technique based on the prediction of speed samples from a linear weighted sum of previously measured samples.

linear program An algorithmic program used to select one solution from a set of possible solutions to a given problem based on desired maximum or minimum requirements.

linear rectifier A rectifier with the same output current or voltage waveshape as that of the impressed signal.

linear resistor A resistor that obeys Ohm's law; under certain conditions, the current is always proportional to the voltage. Also called *ohmic resistor*.

linear selection An addressing technique that uses a line of the address bus to select a component. If a system requires a 4K memory, this implies that 12 bits of the address be reserved for this function. (2^{12} = 4K). The other four bits can be used as chip selects. One bit can be allocated to selecting ROM or RAM memory. In most cases, the RAM requirements are smaller than the ROM requirements. The 12 bits allocated for word selection will also provide the addressing for the RAM, when it is selected. This leaves a maximum of three bits available. Excluding one of the codes, such as 000, for memory selection, seven combinations of these three bits can be used to address the I/O devices. Any of the 12 address bits are reused to select locations within the devices.

line art Refers to an image with two shades, black and white. A scanner would use a one-bit-per-pixel gray level for recording the image.

linear variable differential transformer See LVDT.

line circuit A physical circuit path, such as a transmission or communication line.

line clipping A process in which points referenced outside a coordinate range become invisible in the viewing area. Any image crossing the viewing area (lying partially within and partially without) is cut off or clipped at the viewing area boundaries so that only points in range appear.

line code A single instruction contained on one line in a program. A line code may contain one or more addresses, or one or more operations. Also called *program line*. A line code for addition in the 6800 system is as follows:

```
ADD A 1, Y (Add Y + 1 to accumulator)
```

line conditioner and stabilizer A unit like the one shown, designed to protect equipment from ac line variations. *Also see* SURGE PROTECTOR.

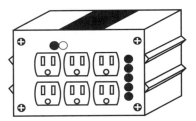

Line conditioner and stabilizer

line conditioning Extra-cost options on private telephone lines to allow higher speed or higher quality data transmission than an ordinary 3002 line.

line control block See LCB.

line discipline The procedures and rules used to adjust the operating values of transmission systems for the desired control. Line discipline includes considerations in polling and queuing priority.

line driver An amplifier used to transmit analog or digital signals over a transmission line or circuit, shown in the following figure.

line-feed character See LF, 2.

line graph A graphic that shows trends in the data. The graph usually has two scales. The bottom one might show the passage of time, while the side measures the quantity. Different trends can be shown as separate lines containing unique symbols.

line impedance The impedance of a transmission line. It is a function of the resistance, inductance, conductance, and capacitance of the line, and the frequency of the signal. Also called the *characteristic impedance*.

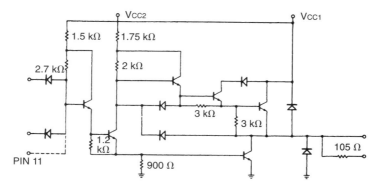

Line driver circuit

line integral A mathematical concept associated with vector fields. It is given by the summation along any path of the product of an element of the path and the component of the field vector parallel to it.

line number The number of the screen line counting from the last page break of text.

line number access A means of addressing points within a recorded text through codes that generally correspond to lines of the document, numbered sequentially.

line of flux or force Refers to a line drawn in a magnetic (or electric) field so that its direction at every point gives the direction of magnetic (or electric) flux (or force) at that point.

line-of-sight Radio propagation in the atmosphere along a path that is unobstructed by the earth or opaque objects.

line pairs A measure of resolution often used in film and print media. In television, only lines are used, which can create confusion when comparing film and video.

line printer A device that prints an entire line of characters at one time. The characters are typically contained on a series of continuously rotating disks, as shown in the following figure. The line printer stops the disks at the right characters and stamps a single line in a fraction of a second. High-speed line printers may operate at a rate of 1,000 lines per minute or more.

lines Refers to either scanning lines or lines of resolution. The latter are hypothetical lines alternating between white and black (or, in the case of chroma resolution, between complementary colors). The combined maximum number of black-and-white lines that might be perceived in a particular direction is the number of lines of resolution. *Vertical resolution* is measured with horizontal lines; *horizontal resolution* is measured with vertical lines. *Diagonal resolution* is measured with diagonal lines; current television systems or proposals do not favor one diagonal

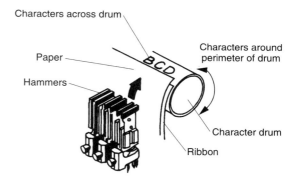

Line printer using drum technology

direction over the other, so diagonal resolution is not often used.

line spectrum An area in which the radiation is in narrow energy bands, called *lines*, which are characteristic of the atomic state.

line termination equipment *See* LT.

line turnaround The reversing of transmission direction from sender to receiver or from receiver to sender when using a half-duplex circuit.

lingering period The time interval during which an electron remains in its orbit of highest excitation before jumping to the energy level of a lower orbit. The difference in energy will be in the form of radiation.

link 1. A transmit-and-receive system for connecting two terminal locations. **2.** A connecting path between two units of switching apparatus, or that part of a subprogram that connects it with the main program. **3.** A one-bit register used as an extension of the accumulator in some systems. As a link register, the link is used in arithmetic operations and can be cleared, set, and complemented as part of the accumulator.

link address In NetWare Communication Services, a field maintained by IPX while an ECB (event control block) is in use and is available to the application when the ECB is not in use.

linkage A technique for providing connections for entry and exit of a closed subroutine from the main routine.

linkage editor 1. A utility program that edits the output of language translators and produces executable program phases. It relocates programs or program sections and links together separately assembled (or compiled) sections. **2.** A program that produces a load module by transforming object modules into a format that is acceptable to fetch; combining separately produced object modules and previously processed load modules into a single load module; resolving symbolic cross-references among them; replacing, deleting, and adding control sections automatically on request; and providing overlay facilities for modules requesting them.

link bit The single bit contained in the link register. The link bit can be used as an indicator for overflow from the accumulator or other diagnostic operations. *Also see* LINK, 3.

link control field A data field in an Ethernet packet used as part of the Internet protocol.

link editor A software system used to load and connect the object program output from a BASIC or Fortran compiler or an assembler into a main program.

linker Part of a program that links together object files that have been created by a compiler so that they form a single program.

link indicator An indicator used to display the contents of the link register.

linking loader A relocatable loader that completes memory address calculations that were partially processed by the relocatable assembler, allowing users to load and execute a program anywhere in memory.

LinkLoc An embedded systems linker/locator for the Intel 80 × 86 family of microprocessors. It is designed to link software written in assembly or high-level languages such as C and Pascal. It produces executable image files that can be downloaded for in-circuit emulators, ROM-based debuggers, and PROM programmers.

Linkstant An information management application designed for use by technical support and related departments to manage customer account communications. It is designed for high-speed processing of incoming customer telephone calls and allows users to create, access, and assimilate information, generate reports, and document activities.

link support layer An interface standard developed by Novell and Apple for interconnection of various data link device drivers and various network layers.

Linpack.h+ An advanced C++ interface with LU factorization for all Matrix.h++ types and Cholesky, QR, and singular value decompositions. Cholesky, QR, least-squares classes, and incremental least-squares classes (using Cholesky decompositions) allow over- and under-determined problems to be solved quickly and easily. Condition numbers and determinants are fully supported.

liquid crystal A type of display technology that uses segments of a liquid crystal solution between glass plates. An electric field at the plates causes the solution to change its light-reflecting properties selectively. Energizing the proper segments produces the desired display output. *Also see* LCD.

liquid drop model A model of the atomic nucleus using the analogy of a liquid drop in which such concepts as surface tension and heat of evaporation are employed.

liquid photoresists Photosensitive materials used for etching patterns through masks on semiconductor surfaces and thin films. Both negative and positive resists are available. In a *negative-resist* application, ultraviolet light is shone through a photomask onto a resist covered surface. The resist film beneath the clear areas of the photomask undergoes a physical and chemical change that renders it insoluble in the developing solution. In a *positive-resist* system, the identical action produces areas that are soluble in a developing solution. Most resist applications use the negative type.

LISP Acronym for *list processing*, an interpretive language designed for the handling of symbolic lists and recursive data. LISP can also be used for manipulation of mathematical and logical operations.

list An ordered set of items. A *pushdown list* is a set of items in which the last item entered is the first item of the list, and the position of the other items is pushed back by one. A *pushup list* has items entered at the end of the list, and the other items maintain the same relative position in the list.

LIST A printer-related utility program designed to aid programmers and others with simple document-printing requirements. The program controls printing of documents, providing automatic pagination, page numbering, titling, and printing of headers.

listen ECBs In NetWare Diagnostic Services, the number of times (since IPX was loaded) that applications have given IPX a listen-ECB.

listen packet requests In NetWare Diagnostic Services, the number of times (since SPX was loaded) that applications have given listen-ECBs to SPX.

listing A printed document that is a by-product of a program or operation. For example, an assembly listing would contain in logical instruction sequence the details of a routine with the coded and symbolic notation along with the actual notation established by the assembly routine. This listing is often useful in the debugging of a routine.

list processing A method of processing data in the form of lists. Chained lists are used to allow the order of items to be changed without altering their physical contents.

list-processing language A language such as LISP designed for symbol manipulation. List-processing languages are used mainly as research tools and have proved valuable in the design of compilers and problem-solving simulation. Other uses of list-processing languages include the following:

- Mathematical proofs
- Information retrieval
- Pattern recognition
- Algebraic programming
- Artificial intelligence

list-processing structure A technique in which list structures or sets of data items are used to organize the memory in computers. The memory is organized into several lists having symbolic names, headers, or starting records, and a number of entries. The header contains the first data entry address; each data entry contains one or more data items and the address of the next entry in the list.

listserv An automated mailing-list distribution system originally designed for the Bitnet/EARN network.

list structure A set of data items with each element containing the address of the successor item or element. It is relatively easy to insert or delete data items in a list structure, and such lists tend to reach the capacity of fixed storage systems.

literal A symbol that represents the value expressed rather than a reference to data. A literal in a source program is data, not a reference to data; for example, the literal 8 represents the value eight.

literal operand An operand that specifies precisely the value of a constant rather than an address where the constant is stored. Literal operands allow coding to be more concise than operands using data name references.

LiteSwitch A utility that allows DOS-based programs to become TSRs. You can call up the second program with a keystroke, and when you are finished with the second program, you are returned to the first program where you left off. You can use EMS, XMS, or the hard disk to save the current state of the first program.

lithium An element, atomic number 3, atomic weight 6.939, symbol Li, that melts at 186°C, boils at 1360°C, and has a specific gravity of 0.534. It is the lightest known solid, chemically resembling sodium but less active. It is used in alloys and in the production of tritium.

little-endian A format for storage or transmission of binary data in which the least significant byte (bit) comes first. *Contrast with* BIG-ENDIAN.

LiveWindows A combination video display/capture and image processing library that enables you to display live NTSC or PAL video images from laserdiscs, VCRs, and camcorders. LiveWindows has real-time scaling of live full-color video from $\frac{1}{64}$ to full-screen size. You can overlay VGA text and graphics, freeze video, and perform image-processing functions including brightness, contrast, sharpness, matrix conversion, histogram, and color and luminance masking. It supports TIFF-G, TIFF-R, Windows BMP, and TARGA file formats and has full TV tuner and audio support.

LLC *See* LOGICAL LINK CONTROL LAYER.

LLIST A BASIC command that prints the program code presently in memory.

LLL Abbreviation for *low-level logic*.

LLOPE Abbreviation for *linear low-density polyethylene* jacketing.

LLR Abbreviation for *load-limiting resistor*.

LMO Abbreviation for *lense-modulated oscillator*.

load The process of filling a storage unit in a computer. Loading includes the reading of the beginning of a program into virtual storage and the modifications necessary to the program for transfer of control for execution. Loading also includes the transfer of storage between memory units. A typical load operation transfers the contents of a memory byte and stores it in the accumulator. The memory is read bit by bit, and as each bit is read, the next sequential accumulator bit is set or reset to reproduce the status of the memory bit just read.

load-and-go A machine operation and compiling technique that uses pseudo-language for conversion directly into machine language. The program is then run without the need of an output machine language.

load balancing A technique to equalize the workload over peer and client network elements.

load capacitor A capacitor that tunes and maximizes the power to a load in induction or dielectric heating.

load coil The coil in an induction heater used to carry the alternating current, which induces the heating current in the object being heated.

load curve A curve of power versus time showing the value of a specified load for each unit in the period covered.

loaded impedance The impedance at the input of a transducer when the output load is connected.

loaded line A telephone line equipped with loading coils to add inductance in order to minimize amplitude distortion.

loader A program that operates as an input device to transfer data from offline memory to online memory. A loader usually performs the following functions:

1. Load a string of bytes into memory
2. Check each byte for correct transmission

3. Check each word to ensure that it is a valid instruction
4. Check the number of bytes read
5. Convert relocatable addresses to absolute addresses
6. Satisfy all external references and labels

loader routine A routine generated to perform program-loading operations. A loader routine usually includes printout of memory content upon request. Once a loader routine is in storage, it is able to bring other information into storage.

LOADHIGH A command in DOS starting with version 5 that loads TSR programs into high memory.

loading coil An induction device used in telephone local loops over 1,800 feet long that compensates for wire capacitance and boosts voice-grade frequency.

loading factor In a quantizer, the ratio of peak to rms (root mean square) amplitude for the input signal.

loading routine See LOADER ROUTINE.

load line On a set of characteristic curves for an active device, a line representing the load. It is straight if entirely resistive, elliptical if reactive.

load matching 1. As pertains to induction and dielectric heaters, adjustment of the load circuit impedance so that the desired energy will be transferred from the power source to the load. 2. Adjusting circuit conditions to meet requirements for maximum energy transfer to load.

load regulation Refers to the maximum change in the output of a power supply as the result of a specified change in output load current, usually from no load to full load.

lobe A section of cable from a MAU (multiple access unit) of hub to a node.

local 1. Limited in its effect to a single phase of the programs overall execution. 2. Attached directly to the computer system via house cable and treated by the system as a peripheral.

local allocation number In NetWare Communication Services, the number of outstanding packet receive buffers (posted listens) available for an SPX connection.

local area network See LAN.

local area transport See LAT.

local connection ID In NetWare, the number of the specified SFX connection from the local workstation's point of view.

local exchange The central or local exchange where the subscriber lines terminate.

local line A channel connecting the subscriber's equipment to the line-terminating equipment in the central office. Usually consists of a metallic circuit using either two-wire or four-wire cable. Also called a **local loop**.

local LPT device In NetWare Print Services, a flag that specifies which LPT device is the default. A 0 indicates LPT1, a 1 is LPT2, and a 2 is LPT3.

locally administered address See LAA.

LocalNet Sytek's broadband network product.

local oscillator The front-end oscillator in a superheterodyne circuit.

local repeater A device that lets you link two copper segments of your LAN. When used with an Ethernet transceiver, this unit allows connection between standard Ethernet segments. The local repeater transmits retimed data packets between each segment and performs the functions of regenerating preamble and extending collision fragments. It also performs automatic partitioning and reconnection functions in the event of a segment failure. Up to three Ethernet segments may be connected in series using two repeaters.

local socket In NetWare, the socket number that the local SPX is using to send and receive packets.

LocalTalk A data link developed for AppleTalk that uses ordinary twisted-pair cabling.

location A storage position that can store one word and is usually identified by an address.

location counter The control section of a computer that contains a register with the address of the instruction currently being executed. Synonymous with *instruction counter* and *program address counter*.

lock A control line used to prevent other processors from controlling the bus.

lock flag In NetWare, a part of File Server Environment Services that contains bit flags indicating the file's lock information.

lock-in amplifier A synchronous amplifier that is sensitive to variations in signal at its own frequency.

locking 1. The use of code extension characters to change the interpretation of a specified number of following characters. 2. Control of an oscillating circuit using a correction signal. 3. Latching.

locking directive In NetWare, directs the call to either log or log and lock the file.

locking key A key on the keyboard such as scroll lock, numlock, or capslock, that you turn on by pressing once and turn off by pressing again. Also called a *toggle key*.

lock manager A part of the operating system that ensures that multiple requests for the same data are not serviced in a way that will damage the integrity of the data.

lock status In NetWare, refers to the bit flags indicating a file's lock status.

lock type In the NetWare file server environment, a flag indicating the type of lock, if any, on a file, as follows:

1. Not Locked
2. Locked by a File Lock
3. Locked by Begin Share File Set

log The process of recording or collecting messages pertinent to a machine run, including

- Run identification
- Input/output identification
- Identification of stops and action taken
- A history of manual switch settings or key-ins

logarithmic A scale type for the X and/or Y axes that uses base-10 logarithms for the numeric divisions along the axes. The distance between divisions decreases as you go up the scale.

logarithmic amplifier An amplifier with an output that is a logarithmic function of the input signal, such as in decibel meters and some types of recorders. A logarithmic amplifier for data compression allows the encoding of signals that would ordinarily require a 20-bit data conversion to cover the dynamic range with a 12-bit converter. Also called a *log amp*.

logarithmic compression A technique that can be used in applications requiring a wide dynamic signal range. If the system is capable of tolerating a constant fractional error of 1% or less, a logarithmic amplifier for data compression can be used, as shown in the figure. Modest accuracy in a fixed ratio is substituted for extreme accuracy over the entire full-scale range. For many applications, this is acceptable. The data can be handled easily since it is to be processed digitally.

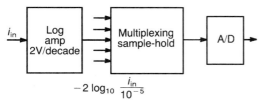

$$-2 \log_{10} \frac{i_{in}}{10^{-5}}$$

Logarithmic data compression

logarithmic decrement Relates a logarithm to the base of the ratio of the amplitude of successive oscillations that are diminishing through energy dissipation.

logic 1. The systematic scheme that defines the interaction of signals in data-processing systems. Logic includes the application of truth tables and the relationships between switching circuits involving arithmetic computation. **2.** The science dealing with the formal principles of reasoning and thought.

logical In data files, a way of indicating data without reference to physical details. Asking for data in a logical manner, for example, means not having to know where the data is located or how to get it.

logical add *See* OR OPERATION.

logical connection number In NetWare, the position of an attached workstation in the File Server Connection Table, or the logical connection involved in a transaction.

logical connective Any of the operators or words AND, OR, OR ELSE, IF-THEN, and EXCEPT, which make new statements from given statements.

logical construction of programs *See* LCP METHOD.

logical decision The choice between two alternatives based upon certain criteria pertinent to the application.

logical difference A relation in set theory that includes all members of one set that are not members of another. For example, if set A includes 1, 3, 5, 7, 9 and set B includes 2, 3, 5, 6, 7, then the logical difference is 1, 2, 6, and 9.

logical drive A unit that acts like a drive but does not exist as a separate physical piece of hardware. Also called *logical device*.

logical drive count In the NetWare File Server Environment, the number of logical drives attached to a server. If disks are mirrored, the logical drive count will be lower than the actual number of physical disks attached because a set of mirrored disks is considered to be on a logical drive. *Also see* MIRRORED DRIVE.

logical instructions Microprocessor instructions used for performing Boolean logic operations. A sample of these is shown in the following table.

Logical AND	The result of a logical AND of the accumulator and the contents of RAM currently addressed replace the contents of the accumulator.
Logical OR	The result of a logic OR of the accumulator and the contents of RAM currently addressed replace the contents of the accumulator.
Logical XOR	The result of a logic exclusive OR of the accumulator and the contents or RAM currently addressed replace the contents of the accumulator.
NOT Complement	Each bit of the accumulator is logically complemented and placed in the accumulator.

Typical logical instructions

Logical Link Control layer The upper portion of the data link layer, defined in the IEEE 802.2 standard. This protocol governs the exchange of frames between stations.

logical locks Locks created by assigning names to sections of data in the file which can be locked when the application accesses the data. Logical locks are not enforced by the operating system, but by the application software itself.

logical multiply The AND operator.

logical name A name that is assigned to a physical device to allow easier accessing to the device.

logical operator A BASIC symbol that indicates the type of comparison to be made in an IF-THEN statement.

logical record lock threshold In the NetWare Transaction Tracking System, the number of logical record locks that may be set before a transaction is begun.

logical relation A term used in assembler programming in which two expressions are separated by a relational operator such as EQ, GE, LE, LT, or NE.

logical shift A shift in which the sign is treated as another data position.

logical unit 1. In the IBM communications protocol, a device that is available to software interfaces. **2.** The device name for units attached to an SCSI controller in a PC.

logic analysis The determination of the specific steps required to produce the desired output or intelligence from given input data.

logic analyzer A device used to test and troubleshoot equipment containing digital logic. Logic analyzers can be used to trace logic states and timing, examine the activity on each line of a data bus by displaying that line on a CRT screen or using a string of light-emitting diodes, and design microprocessor-based products for examining the flow of command and data words on multi-line buses. Logic analyzers perform the first steps in locating the problem; from there, conventional instruments such as signal generators and oscilloscopes can be used.

logic bombs A type of computer virus that will infect a system and lay dormant until a particular event occurs (i.e., a particular date, time, accessing a particular file, and so on).

logic card A circuit board that contains components and wiring to perform one or more logic operations or functions.

logic circuit A set of elements connected or programmed to perform logic operations or represent logic functions such as AND, OR, and NAND.

logic coincidence element An operation defined by the equivalence operator. A logic coincidence element produces a true output when the two input signals are the same and a false output when they are different.

logic comparator A testing device that compares an in-circuit integrated circuit with a tested device. Any differences in the outputs are detected and displayed, usually by light-emitting diodes. A fault can be traced to a specific IC using a logic comparator.

logic design The specification of the operation of a system in terms of symbolic logic without primary regard to the hardware required to implement the system.

logic diagram A graphic representation of the logical elements and their interconnections without regard to construction details.

logic element The smallest part of a computer system that represents a function or operation of symbolic logic. Typical logic elements are flip-flops and gates.

logic error Programming code that is syntactically correct but produces incorrect or unintended results.

logic file A data set that is composed of one or more logical open records. A logic file may operate through the use of a file-definition macroinstruction.

logic flowchart A detailed solution of the work order or arrangement in terms of the logic for a specific machine or process. Symbolic notation is used to represent the information and describe the inputs and outputs, as well as the arithmetic and logical operations. Types of operations can be shown using block symbols.

logic gate A circuit or single component capable of performing a logic operation. A gate may have several inputs, but only one output.

logic high The voltage state furthest from zero in a two-state logic system, usually signifying a true, yes, on, or closed state. Also called *high level*.

logic instruction An instruction that executes an operation defined in symbolic logic.

logic level The voltage levels that represent binary conditions in a logic circuit.

logic low The voltage state nearest zero in a two-state logic system, usually signifying a false, no, off, or open state. Also called *low level*.

logic operation An operation in which logical quantities are expressed in ones and zeros to make comparisons, decisions, and extractions.

logic operator *See* LOGICAL CONNECTIVE.

logic probe A logic testing tool that provides a direct readout of logic levels by connecting to or placing over in-circuit ICs. The logic probe uses one or more lamps to indicate if a logic signal path is at logic 1 or logic 0 or toggling between these levels, as shown in the following figure. Some units use the relative brightness to indicate duty cycle, some rely upon blinking effects for frequency indication, and others are designed to be used in conjunction with a high-quality oscilloscope.

logic product The result obtained from the logical multiply operation (the AND operation).

logic pulser A testing tool that drives a logic path to a desired state for a short time to check for faults and short circuits.

LED States High Low Pulse	Signal Sensed	Explanation
○ ○ ○	No signal	Open circuit three-state
● ○ ○	5V ⎴₁ 0V	High level
○ ● ○	5V ⎵₀ 0V	Low level
● ○ ●	⊓⊓⊓⊓ 1	Negative pulses from high level
○ ● ●	⊔⊔⊔⊔ 0	Positive pulses from low level
○ ○ ●	⊓⊔⊓⊔⊓⊔	Square wave greater than 100 kHz
● ● ●	⊓⊔⊓⊔	Square wave less than 100 kHz

Typical logic probe signal-sensing states

logic shift A shift in which all bits are treated the same, with no special consideration given to the sign bit as in an arithmetic shift. A logic shift affects all positions.

logic swing The voltage difference between the two logic levels representing a zero and a one in a gate or circuit.

logic symbol A graphic character used to represent a logic operator.

logic, transistor-transistor *See* TTL.

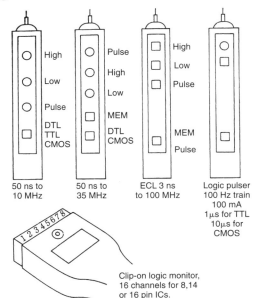

Logic probes, pulser, and monitor

logic testers Tools such as logic pulsers and probes, useful for checking logic levels on integrated circuits and helpful in isolating static or steady conditions. A quick indication is possible with a pulse; it will show that a signal is a 0, 1, or undetermined. The undetermined state usually indicates a problem unless it is a tristate floating output as shown in the figure. Several types of logic probes as well as logic pulsers and clip-on logic monitors are available.

login The process of identifying oneself to a computer system so that one can access the computer's resources. This process provides security for the system. Also, the name of the program used for this purpose in Novell's NetWare, found in the NetWare Login directory.

login enabled flag In the NetWare File Server Environment, indicates whether login is enabled or disabled.

login subdirectory name In NetWare Connection Services, an ASCII string containing the name of the subdirectory below Sys:Login where the file Login.exe can be executed.

login time In NetWare and other network operating systems, the time of login, given in the following form:

- Year (0 to 99, where a value of 94 = 1994, 95 = 1995, etc.)
- Month (1 to 12)
- Day (1 to 31)
- Hour (0 to 23)
- Minute (0 to 59)
- Second (0 to 59)
- Day (0 to 6, where a value of 0 = Sunday, 1 = Monday, etc.)

Logo A programming language developed chiefly for teaching young children the elements of computer programming. Logo is a simple and rather limited language oriented toward graphics. It is interactive, permitting children to learn quickly how to draw geometric patterns and pictures on the screen.

log sheet A document used to list such items as incoming and outgoing work.

Logshield A session-recording-and-playback library that can be linked to your application. It can be used for macro recording, automated regression testing, error recovery, and remote diagnostics. It can be linked with Windows applications to create self-running demos.

long directory/filename A part of AppleTalk Filing Protocol Services that returns the directory or filename of the specified directory or file.

longevity The period of time during which the failure rate of a group of components is basically constant.

long instruction format An instruction that occupies more than one standard length or position, such as a two-word instruction. The second word may be used for address modification or as an operand.

longitudinal current A current that flows in the same direction in both wires of a parallel pair, the earth being its return path.

longitudinal delay line Delay lines are often named according to a propagating medium, such as *mercury delay line*, *quartz delay line*, or according to vibrational modes such as longitudinal.

longitudinal magnetization A form of magnetization used in magnetic recording that is in a direction parallel to the line of travel.

longitudinal parity An error-detection scheme in which an extra character is added to each block of data. The value of each bit in this character is set so that the total number of 1 bits in each bit position is either always even or always odd.

longitudinal redundancy checking See LRC.

long-link comm set A set in which you connect the transmitter to your computer's parallel cable and the receiver to your printer. Standard modular telephone cable is used to send data to a remote printer in the warehouse, next office, or another building. One of the most popular uses is to put a noisy printer in a separate room to reduce noise in the work area. Data is sent at up to 7200 bps to keep up with the higher-speed line printers.

long packet A packet that exceeds the specified protocol length maximum.

look-ahead The ability of a CPU to mask an interrupt until the following instruction is completed.

look-ahead carry A logic characteristic resulting in machine-sensing that all carries required for addition are generated.

look-ahead-carry generator An adding circuit that anticipates carries to provide high-speed operations, as shown in the following diagram.

lookup A procedure for obtaining the value of a function from a table of values. If the values of the function are equally spaced, the locations of associated functions can be generated by a linear relationship. If the arguments are not equally spaced, the addresses can be separated using constants and a comparison operation.

lookup table A collection of data in a form suitable for ready reference, frequently stored in sequenced machine locations or in the form of rows and columns. The intersection of rows and columns can serve to locate specific items of data or information.

loop 1. A communications circuit between two private subscribers or a subscriber and the local switching center. **2.** A direction-finding antenna. **3.** A closed-circuit path within an electronic circuit or collection of circuits (such as a ground loop). **4.** A self-contained series of instructions in which the final instruction can modify itself, causing the process to be repeated until a terminal condition is reached. Productive instructions in the loop are used to manipulate operands, while housekeeping or bookkeeping instructions

Pin names

C_n	Carry input
$\bar{G}_0, \bar{G}_2$	Carry generate (active low) inputs
$\bar{G}_1$	Carry generate (active low) input
$\bar{G}_3$	Carry generate (active low) input
$\bar{P}_0, \bar{P}_1$	Carry propagate (active low) inputs
$\bar{P}_2$	Carry propagate (active low) input
$\bar{P}_3$	Carry propagate (active low) input
$C_{n+x}, C_{n+y}, C_{n+z}$	Carry outputs
$\bar{G}$	Carry generate (active low) output
$\bar{P}$	Carry generate (active low) output

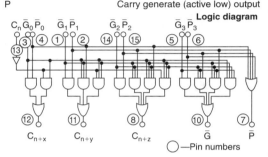

Look-ahead-carry generator

modify the productive instructions and keep track of the number of operations and repetitions. A loop may be terminated under a number of conditions. Loops are also used as return paths in control systems and other functions or operations requiring a feedback path.

loop approach A technique of distributed control that uses satellite microcomputers to perform a fixed number of functions. A single microcomputer could perform a single function in a number of different loops. Normally, a microcomputer is dedicated to a single loop, so a single failure will cause the loss of only one loop.

loopback A procedure for testing modems in which a transmission is sent back to the originating modem and compared to determine if the modem is transmitting and/or receiving the data correctly. Also called *loop checking*.

loopback plug A device that facilitates testing of I/O ports. The plug simulates a device attached to the port and provides feedback to the diagnostic program. Two common loopback plugs test the parallel and serial ports on a standard PC. Other types test Ethernet and RS-422 ports.

loop code Coding that uses a program loop for repetition of a sequence of instructions. Loop coding generally results in storage savings, but also requires more execution time compared to straight-line coding.

loop commands Commands that provide a method of executing loops for a specified number of iterations or until termination upon user-specified conditions. Using loop commands, spurious events can be trapped.

loop configuration The loop configuration shown in the figure is used in remote multiplexing. If a single link breaks, the nodes can still communicate. This is also called a *ring configuration*. The loop may begin and end at a *loop controller*, which is a computer that controls the communications. Messages between computers in the loop are handled as a string of words containing information on the originator and addressee. When a computer recognizes a message addressed to it, it accepts the message. Loops can be difficult to control, and the way that messages are sent past the computer requires higher data rates.

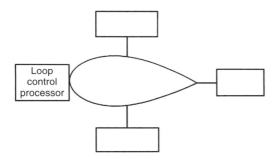

Loop network configuration

loop counter A counter used in assembly programming to prevent excessive looping during conditional processing.

loop error The error due to departure of the loop output signal from its desired value.

loop feedback The signal that is fed back to the input to produce the loop-actuating signal in a feedback control system.

loop gain The ratio of output to input amplitude in a control loop.

looping A repeating or recursive property of many programs and instructions used in microcomputers. Looping is often performed at delayed speeds, and many looped instructions are stored in ROM and then jumped to when required. Looping can also occur when the CPU is in a wait condition or as a result of errors and malfunctions.

loop initialization The instructions prior to a loop that set addresses and data to their initial values.

loop input Refers to an external signal applied to a feedback control loop in control system.

loop jump A jump instruction that causes a jump to itself.

loop output signal Refers to the output signal at a point in a feedback loop produced by an input signal applied at the same point.

loop program A series of instructions that are repeated until a terminal condition is reached.

loop test A series of instructions used to determine when a loop function has been completed.

loop transfer function The mathematical function representing the relationship between the output of a feedback loop control system and its input.

loop update The process of supplying the current parameters associated with a particular loop for use by the loop's control algorithm in calculating a new control output.

LOS Acronym for *loss of signal*.

loss The decrease in power of a signal as it is transmitted from one point to another, usually expressed in decibels.

loss angle A measure of the loss due to hysteresis in an imperfect dielectric, being the angular difference between its lead angle and 90°.

Lossev radiation The radiation due to the recombination of charge carriers injected into a p-i-n or p-n junction biased in the forward direction.

loss factor **1.** The characteristic that determines the rate at which heat is generated in an insulating material, equal to the dielectric constant of a material. **2.** The ratio of the average power loss to the power loss under peak loading.

lossy Pertaining to a material or apparatus that dissipates energy, such as a dielectric material or a transmission line with a high attenuation. The attenuation loss is expressed in decibels (dB), while the rate of loss in the dielectric is proportional to its loss factor, which is the product of the power factor and dielectric constant.

lost packets **1.** Packets that were sent but never received. **2.** In NetWare Diagnostic Services, the number of times (since IPX was loaded) that IPX has been unable to supply a receive-ECB for an incoming packet.

Lotus 1-2-3 A popular and long-lived spreadsheet program, simple enough to encourage the novice yet sophisticated enough for the expert. 1-2-3 combines a spreadsheet with simple information management and analytical graphics. These functions extend the usefulness of the basic spreadsheet. In addition to the standard spreadsheet functions of data entry, labeling, manipulation, and calculation, 1-2-3 has other features. For example, the program's automatic keystroke (macro) capability lets you write your own menu-driven applications. 1-2-3 shares data with most other popular applications programs. The product has constant screen prompts and context-sensitive help.

Lotus 1-2-3 macros A library of shortcuts, utilities, and keystroke savers that will work with a 1-2-3 worksheet. They eliminate repetitive operations and multiple menu steps, and allow manual input to be automated.

Lotus 1-2-3 templates Lotus 1-2-3-compatible sample spreadsheets for applications like loans, net worth, break-even analysis, rental income, and checking account balances.

Lovelace, Ada Augusta Mathematician who helped explain the theory of the analytical engine, which was an early mechanical calculator, and conceptualized the binary number system.

lower sideband In an AM signal, that band of frequencies adjacent to and immediately below the carrier and spaced from the carrier by 8, an amount equal to the frequency of the modulating wave. Since the sidebands (upper and lower) contain the intelligence, the carrier and one of the two sidebands may be discarded before transmission, so that only one of the two sidebands (upper or lower) is sent.

low frequency Electromagnetic radiation between 30 and 300 kHz.

low-level 1. The most negative voltage in binary logic systems. If the true level is most positive (as it is in positive logic or positive true logic), then the low level is the false or zero level. **2.** Characterized by a comparatively small value, as in *low-level signals*. **3.** Relatively crude or primitive when compared with other members of the same genre or class.

low-level format A process that creates (or overwrites) the data pattern on a hard or floppy disk.

low-level language A "primitive" language that resembles a machine code or has a one-to-one relationship with a machine code. *Contrast with* HIGH-LEVEL LANGUAGE.

low-level modulation Modulation at a point in a system when the power level is low compared to the power level at the output of the system.

low-level multiplexers The multiplexing of voltages in the millivolt range, up to 1V, requires low-level multiplexers. Low-level interference and thermal effects can be great, so lines are run in pairs, and differential techniques are commonly used to remove interference that is present as a common-mode signal. When high common-mode voltages are present, guarding techniques are used along with three-wire multiplexing of shielded input pairs.

lowlight The normal intensity of video display characters.

low loss A component or system with little power dissipation, such as a low-loss line.

low-order Refers to the weight or significance assigned to the digits of a number. For example, in the number 2,345,768, the low-order digit is 8.

low or high selector A device designed to automatically select either the highest or the lowest input signal from among two or more input signals. Also called a *high or low signal selector*.

low-pass filter A device or circuit that permits the passage of relatively low-frequency signals and attenuates high-frequency signals, shown in the following diagram.

low-performance equipment Equipment that has insufficient performance characteristics to allow its use in trunk or link circuits. This equipment

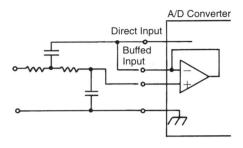

A/D input amplifier connected to low-pass filter

may be used in subscriber line circuits whenever it meets line circuit requirements.

low-power Schottky *See* LSTTL.

low record offset In NetWare, an unsigned long value that contains the offset from the beginning of the file where the record begins.

low-resolution graphics Refers to the display of graphic output by using a small number of pixels on a CRT screen. Low display quality becomes very noticeable when drawing curved lines.

low-speed storage Descriptive of storage devices that have long access times compared with the time required for arithmetic operations of the CPU, and low access times compared to other peripheral units.

low tension A term applied to the currents and voltages associated with low-voltage circuits.

LP Abbreviation for *linear programming*.

LPL Abbreviation for *list programming language*.

LPM Abbreviation for *line per minute*, used in measuring printer output speed.

LRC Abbreviation for *longitudinal redundancy checking*, a checking method that adds an additional block to the message. Each bit in this check block is obtained by performing an exclusive-OR on corresponding bits in the other blocks in the message. The receiving device calculates the contents of the check block from the data received. If the check block received is the same as the one calculated, the message has been received correctly.

LPRINT In BASIC, a statement that displays output on a printer.

LRU block dirty A part of NetWare File Server Environment Services that shows the number of times the least recently used cache-block allocation algorithm reclaimed a dirty cache block.

LSB Abbreviation for *least significant bit*.

LSI Abbreviation for *large-scale integration*, a name applied to integrated circuits with 1,000 or more functional units or gates on a single chip.

LSI board tester An automated tester designed for troubleshooting and repair stations. A typical system provides stored program capability, which permits the testing of boards, devices, and the entire module with the exact patterns timing necessary to do a functional test. With the stored program capability, testing of LSI boards and devices is possible.

LSTTL Abbreviation for *low-power Schottky TTL*, a variation of the Schottky TTL logic family. Low-power Schottky circuits allow smaller, less-costly power supplies, improved packing density, and less noise generation, along with simplified MOS-to-TTL interfaces.

LT Abbreviation for *line termination equipment*, defined by ISDN as equipment located within the local exchange company's or common carrier's network when lines must be extended beyond the normal range of a central office.

lug A device provided on the end of a conductor for inserting screws at terminal strips.

Lukaseiwicz notation See POLISH NOTATION.

luminance In an image, the brightness values of all the points in the image. A luminance-only reproduction is a black-and-white representation of the image. The human visual system is more sensitive to luminance detail than to chrominance detail.

luminance signal The portion of the video signal that controls the luminance of the picture. Also known as the *Y signal*.

lumped Circuit elements that are concentrated in discrete units rather than distributed over a transmission line or circuit path.

lumped loading Refers to the process of inserting uniformly spaced inductance coils along a line.

lumped parameter A circuit parameter that may be considered to be localized for the purpose of analysis.

lumped voltage A voltage formed by adding the sum of the products of a number of intermediate electrode voltages and the respective amplification factors associated with those electrodes. The total space current is a function of this quality.

LU 6.2 Abbreviation for *Logical Unit 6.2*. See APPC.

LU-LV session In SNA, a session between two logical units.

lurking Refers to passive participation on the part of a subscriber to an Internet mailing list, Usenet newsgroup, or other online service group. A person who is lurking is just listening to the discussion. Lurking is encouraged for beginners who need to get up to speed on the history of the group.

LVDT Abbreviation for *linear variable differential transformer*, which uses a movable core in a transformer configuration. Depending on the particular sensing element and linkage, transducers of this type can be sensitive to vibration and mechanical wear.

LWD Abbreviation for *larger word*.

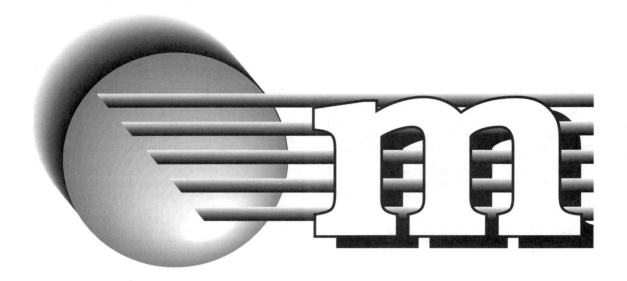

M 1. Abbreviation for *mega*, one million. **2.** When referring to memory, 2^{20}, or 1,048,576.
m Symbol for the empirically determined avalanche multiplication constant in transistors.
MA Abbreviation for *memory address*.
MAC 1. Acronym for *memory address counter*, a register used to point to the next location in memory for an instruction-fetch operation. The MAC may be a regular working register or a specially designed unit. **2.** Acronym for *message authentication code*. **3.** Acronym for *media-access control*, the last software-controlled sublayer before the physical signalling sublayer of the OSI model. The MAC sublayer constructs the frame from data supplied by the logical link control on an Ethernet (IEEE 802 standard) network. These two sublayers make up the data link layer of the OSI model. Other sublayers in the 802 standard include physical media attachment and the medium (physical wire). *Also see* OSI MODEL.
Mac Abbreviation for a Macintosh computer, a family of microcomputers produced by Apple and based on the Motorola 680x0 chip.
MacAccess An electronic mail package for the Macintosh from Action Technologies.
Mac-Art Library Twelve disks of clip art designed for professional desktop publishers. Images include animals, buildings, farm, flowers/trees/plants, geography, greeting cards, kitchen, people, sports, signs/symbols/borders, tools, and transportation.
MacAtlas Paint A library of map templates for the Macintosh. There are U.S. and world maps in MacPaint format, including maps of the states, and maps of the regions of the world by country. You can import maps into other documents using the Macintosh clipboard.
MacCalligraphy A type of graphics software that simulates the act of painting and writing. Included is a custom-touch editor that enables you to create a new brush shape using fatbits.
MacChuck A program that allows you to operate your PC from a Macintosh. You can transfer files, run DOS programs, use the Mac clipboard commands Copy and Paste with DOS programs, and copy PC files to and from your Macintosh. MacChuck allows you to connect a number of Macs to any PC on an AppleTalk network. You can communicate from Macintosh to PC via directline or AppleTalk. You can also run MacChuck in the background under MultiFinder to access programs on the PC.
MacDraft An object-oriented design/drafting program for the Macintosh. It can be used to create schematics, and construction, engineering, and scaled architectural drawings. MacDraft has 32 different scales; objects imported into the drawing are automatically adjusted to conform to the scale selected.
MacDraw Pro 1.5 A graphics design tool package for creating lines, rectangles, ovals, polygons, and bezigons (shapes made from BEZIER CURVES). Users can activate a grid while drawing. Word-processing features include a rule in each text block, and superscript and subscript modes. Opens and saves documents using PICT, PICT2, TIFF, EPSF formats.
Mace Utilities A set of DOS utilities for disk maintenance, data protection, and data recovery. This package can speed up performance, provide

protection, and enable the user to recover from most disk disasters. A pulldown menu system with optional user levels makes it easier to use.

MacGraphics A collection of large-format (8 × 10), bitmapped clip art in 13 different categories for 300 dpi images. The MacPaint files in FullPaint format are compatible with PageMaker, Quark Express, and most other Macintosh page layout applications.

machine A general term for a device such as a microprocessor or microcomputer that can store and process numeric and alphabetic information. The term *machine* is used to refer to both analog and digital computers, along with related data-processing equipment.

machine address *See* ABSOLUTE ADDRESS.

machine-check indicator A device that is switched on when programmed conditions are detected by the machine-checking circuits. The system is then programmed to run a diagnostic routine to find the cause of the interruption.

machine code An operation code that a machine is designed to recognize directly and without translation.

machine-code instruction The symbols that state a basic computer operation that is to be performed. The machine-code instruction is the combination of bits specifying the machine-language operator, which becomes a part of the instruction that designates the operation of logic.

machine cycle The shortest complete action or process that is repeated in order; also, the time required for this action or process. Typically, one machine cycle might be used to fetch the instruction, one or two more might be used for data access, and several more may be required for execution. Also called *microcycle*.

machine equation The equation that an analog computer is programmed to solve.

machine hardware The circuits contained in the five parts of the computer: input, output, control, storage, and arithmetic and logic sections.

machine ID In NetWare, the major version of a drive release.

machine infinity The largest number that can be represented in a computer's internal format.

machine instruction *See* MACHINE-CODE INSTRUCTION.

machine language A language that can be used directly by a microprocessor; a binary language. All other languages must be translated or compiled into binary code before entering the processor. Users generally write the program in coded instructions that are more meaningful to them. Then an assembly program translates the symbolic instructions into binary machine code. *Also see* OBJECT CODE.

machine learning The ability of a device to improve its performance based on its own prior experience.

machine length Refers to the working word length used by a device.

machine logic design Refers to the way a system is designed to do its operations, as well as what those operations are, and the type and form of data it will use internally.

machine-oriented language A language designed for interpretation and use by a specific machine or class of machine. The language may include instructions that define and direct machine operations along with any information to be acted upon by the machine during specific operations.

machine-readable The capability of being sensed or read by a specific device. Cards, drums, disks, and tapes are all machine-readable media.

machinery diagnostic expert *See* DXPERT.

machine unit The voltage used in an analog computer to represent one unit of the simulated variable.

machine variable Refers to the signal in an analog computer used to reproduce the variations of the simulated function.

machine word A word with the standard number of bits or characters that a computer normally handles in a register or during a transfer. Typical machine words in microcomputer systems are 4, 8, 16, or 32 bits long.

machining center A machine tool, usually numerically controlled, capable of automatically drilling, reaming, tapping, milling, and boring multiple faces of a part and often equipped with a system for automatically changing cutting tools.

Mac-In-DOS A program that allows a PC to read, write, and format Macintosh data files on disk. No cable or external hardware is needed.

Macintosh-compatible cable A cable designed for the standard Macintosh microcomputer. It has a DB9 connector on one end and an eight-pin mini din connector on the other.

Macintosh computer Refers to a microcomputer made by Apple, designed around the 680x0 microprocessor family. Macs are noted for their simplified user interface.

Macintosh Finder The portion of the Macintosh operating system that manages the Desktop.

Macintosh II A 68020 version of the original Mac, with six available expansion slots. The Nubus architecture used by Apple offered a 32-bit data path and 32-bit address space. This was larger than those of the PCs of its day, as shown in the following table.

Microcomputer	Address Lines	Data Lines
PC/XT and compatibles	20	8
AT and PS2 models 50 and 60	24	16
386 and PS/2 model 80	32	32
Macintosh II	32	32

Comparison of Mac and PC address lines

MAC-layer bridge A device that connects two or more similar data links in a way that is transparent to the user of the data link service (the network layer).

MacPaint A popular graphics program for the Macintosh. It allows the user to draw and create graphics.

macro **1.** A single instruction as written in source code, which may require a number of successive operational machine steps to execute, each step involving a machine instruction in microcode. *Also see* MACROINSTRUCTION. **2.** A group of frequently used instructions treated as a unit entity.

macroassembler A language processor that accepts words, statements, and phrases to produce machine instructions. A macroassembler allows segments of a large program to be created and tested separately. The full macro capability of a resident macroassembler eliminates the need to rewrite similar sections of code repeatedly and simplifies program documentation. *Also see* RESIDENT MACROASSEMBLER *and* TWO-PASS MACROASSEMBLER.

macro call A call for a subroutine jump to a macro command.

macro code **1.** That coding system that permits a macroinstruction to call upon a specified group of instructions for execution as if it were a discrete machine operation. **2.** Any instruction that results in a call for a jump to a routine that is not machine-peculiar, and which usually consists of a body of inseparable instructions. **3.** Collectively, the procedures used to provide code segments that are used frequently throughout a program.

macro command A command or statement used to bring a string or strings of frequently used instructions into operation.

macro cross-assembler An assembler that runs as a conversational program on a machine other than the target system. Many variations are available, including macro cross-assemblers that allow the use of a few simple pseudo-operations; that allow you to specify the radix of the assembler listing as octal, decimal, or hexadecimal; that number every statement; and that provide clear and extensive error messages.

macro definition The specification of a macro operation, including the name of the operations and the definitions of fixed and variable fields.

macro facility That feature of an assembler that allows it to produce a sequence of statements from a macro definition.

macro flowchart Refers to tables and charts utilized in designing the logic of a specific routine, in which the various segments and subroutines of a program are represented by blocks.

macro-generating program A program designed to construct a group of instructions in object code from a macroinstruction in the basic source language. Also called a *macro generator*.

macroinstruction An instruction in a source language that is equivalent to a specified sequence of machine instructions and requires several microcycles to execute. A macroinstruction is a powerful command that results from combining several operations into a single instruction. It may also generate a debugging routine to be used with a particular program.

A macroinstruction set may be register- or stack-oriented, and may be original or a copy from another machine. Lower cost and higher performance usually result when an original macroinstruction set is developed. If more than eight bits of operation code are used in a macroinstruction, the interpretation becomes complex and additional logic might have to be added to the hardware design, as shown in the following figure.

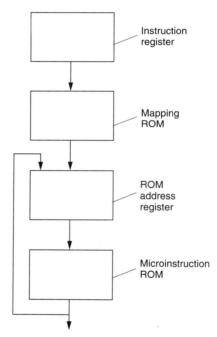

Macroinstruction decoding system

macroprogramming The procedure and methods used for writing machine statements in terms of macroinstructions.

macroscopic state A state described in terms of the overall second-statistical behavior of the discrete elements from which it is formed.

MAD **1.** Acronym for *Michigan algorithm decoder*. **2.** Abbreviation for *magnetic anomaly detection*.

MADT Acronym for *micro alloy diffused-base transistor*.

Magellan A DOS-based utility program from Lotus Development Corporation with a range of tools that lets users find information quickly. You can compress files to free up more hard disk space, recover deleted files, and check for corruption due to viruses. It is customizable, allowing users to rearrange function keys or create additional menus for individual needs.

magenta The color obtained by mixing equal intensities of red and blue light. It is also the correct name for the subtractive primary color sometimes called red.

Magic Fields A software package for creating Windows data-entry screens with intelligent input fields. It provides the data validation and range-checking found in high-end database packages. You can view, test, and modify fields without writing code or compiling. You can also visually define fonts and colors, and replace existing Windows edit controls without making source code changes. Magic Fields can be used with standard Windows dialog editors.

magnadur A ceramic material made from sintered oxides of iron and barium, used for permanent magnets and as an electrical insulator.

magnesium A metallic element, symbol Mg, atomic number 12, atomic weight 24.312, specific gravity 1.74, melts at 651°C, boils at 1120°C. A light metallic element, it is often alloyed with aluminum and used in constructing electronic components.

magnet A body that has the property of attracting iron; when freely supported in isolation from other bodies, it will tend to set in the north-south direction. Magnets occur naturally in stones containing magnetite, once known as a *lodestone*. Permanent magnets are made artificially from hardened steel that has been magnetized by a strong magnetic flux.

magnetic Descriptive of phenomena and devices depending essentially on magnetism.

magnetic analysis The separation of a stream of electrified particles by a magnetic field, in accordance with their mass, charge, or speed.

magnetic bias A steady magnetic field added to the signal field in magnetic recording. A magnetic bias can improve the linearity of response during recording.

magnetic bubble memory A technology that uses a single-crystal sheet with perpendicular magnetic fields to produce magnetic "bubbles." A pulsed field is used to break up and control the bubbles as groups of data bits. Densities of 10 million bits per square inch have been realized, and densities to one billion bits per square inch have been projected for this technology.

magnetic character reader *See* MICR.

magnetic circuit A closed path for magnetic flux.

magnetic coating The magnetic layer consisting of oxide particles held in a binder applied to magnetic recording materials such as tapes and disks.

magnetic code The specific manner in which data bits are represented on magnetic recording materials. A phase-encoding format records a one as a flux transition at the midpoint of the data cell toward the level representing erased tape. A zero is recorded as a flux reversal in the opposite direction.

magnetic core A memory device in which information is represented by the magnetic polarity of a wire-sensed permeable ring. Small rings called *cores* are used to represent bits 0 and 1, as shown in the following figure. The cores are made of ferrites; variations of the ring form include tapes, rods, and thin-film configurations. The cores are usually arranged in the form of a matrix.

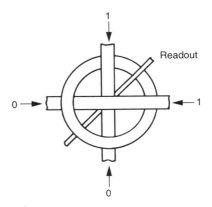

Magnetic core

magnetic cycle The sequence of changes in magnetization of an object corresponding to one cycle of alternating current.

magnetic damping The damping of motion of a conductor by induced eddy currents in it when moving across a magnetic field. It is particularly applicable to moving parts of instruments and integrating meters.

magnetic delay line A delay medium that uses magnetic material to slow the propagation of magnetic or sound waves.

magnetic disk A storage device or medium that uses a coated disk for storing information. The data is stored in the form of magnetic spots representing binary data and is arranged in circular tracks around the disks. The tracks are accessed by movable read and write heads that are positioned to the desired disk, and then to the desired track. The information is obtained sequentially as the disk rotates.

magnetic drum A storage device that uses a rotating cylindrical drum surfaced with a magnetic coating. The data is stored as magnetized spots on closed tracks that circle the drum. A read-write head is used for each track, and the proper head is selected by switching. Data is read or written sequentially as the drum turns.

magnetic energy The product of flux density and field strength for points on the demagnetization curve of a permanent magnetic material; this product enables researchers to measure the energy established in the magnetic circuit. It is normally required to be the maximum possible for the amount of magnetic material used.

magnetic ferrite A ceramic-type material that possesses strong magnetic properties along with good insulating qualities.

magnetic field A modification of space near a magnetic body or a current carrying body. The forces due to the magnetic body or current can be detected in this area of space. It is associated with electric currents and the motions of electrons in atoms.

magnetic field intensity The magnitude of the field strength vector in a medium; the magnetic strain produced by neighboring magnetic elements or current carrying conductors. The MKSA (meter-kilogram-second-ampere) unit is the *ampere-turn/meter*, and the CGS (centimeter-gram-second) unit is the *oersted*. Also called *magnetic field strength, magnetic intensity, magnetizing force.*

magnetic field interference Interference induced in the circuits of a device due to the presence of a magnetic field. It often appears as common-mode or normal-mode interference in the measuring circuits.

magnetic flip-flop A bistable amplifier that uses magnetic amplifiers. The two stable states are determined by changes in the control voltage or current. *Also see* FLIP-FLOP.

magnetic hysteresis loop A closed curve that shows the relation between the force and the induction in a magnetic substance when the field or force is determined for a complete cycle.

magnetic induction The vector associated with the mechanical force exerted on a current-carrying conductor located in a magnetic field.

magnetic ink An ink containing magnetic particles that can be detected by magnetic sensors.

magnetic-ink character recognition *See* MICR.

magnetic instability The property of magnetic material on tape that causes variations to occur from temperature, aging, and mechanical strain. Magnetic instability is a function of particle size and magnetization.

magnetic keyboard A device that records keystrokes and editing changes on a magnetic medium.

magnetic leakage That part of the magnetic flux in a system that is lost for most practical purposes; it may be a nuisance that affects nearby apparatus.

magnetic media Any of a wide variety of disks or tapes coated or impregnated with magnetic material for use with the appropriate equipment and on which data or information are recorded and stored.

magnetic memory The use of magnetic materials for registering and recovering information in the form of bits. In magnetic memory technology, bits are represented by the presence or absence of magnetism at a certain spot or region on a magnetic medium that can be mechanically scanned. Mechanical scanning puts some limitations on the speed and convenience of such memory, but the low cost per bit and the high capacity of such memories has produced a high market demand that continues to grow.

magnetic mirror A device based on the principle that ions moving in a magnetic field tend to be reflected away from high magnetic fields.

magnetic moment 1. A vector such that its product with the magnetic induction gives the torque on a magnet in a monogenious magnetic field. **2.** The dipole moment of an atom or nucleus associated with electron orbitals and/or electron and nuclear spin.

magnetic oxides Oxides that are ferromagnetic, used to fabricate permanent magnets and coat tapes and other media.

magnetic path Refers to the track or route followed by magnetic flux lines; a closed line that involves all media through which the lines of flux pass, such as the interior of a ferrite toroidal core.

magnetic potential A continuous mathematical function; the value of which at any point is equal to the potential energy, relative to infinity, of a theoretical unit north-seeking magnetic pole placed at that point.

magnetic potentiometer A flexible solenoid used with a ballistic galvanometer to explore the distribution of magnetic potential in a field.

magnetic quantum numbers Numbers that determine the components of orbital and spin angular momentum in the direction of the applied field.

magnetic recording The registering of data on a magnetic medium such as a tape or disk, as shown in the following figures. Magnetic recording parameters include tape or disk speed, transfer rate, and packing density. *Speed* refers to the speed or velocity at which the tape or disk moves past the recording head, and is usually expressed in inches or centimeters per second. *Transfer rate* is a measure of how fast data can be handled by the recording system and is expressed in bits or bytes per second, or in baud. *Packing density* refers to the number of bits per unit length stored on the disk or tape.

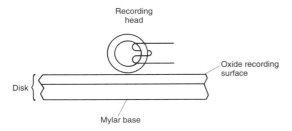

Magnetic recording on a magnetic oxide disk

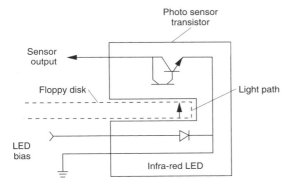

Photosensing circuit used for indexing

magnetic resonance line width The width of the absorption lines depends upon the interaction of the spins with each other and with the crystal lattice. It is measured by the random fluctuating magnetic field (H) that is exerted on a spin by its neighbors; $\Delta H = \mu/d^3$, where μ is the magnetic moment of each spin and d is the interatomic spacing.

magnetic rigidity A measure of the momentum of a particle. It is given by the product of the magnetic intensity perpendicular to the path of the particle and the resultant radius of curvature of this path.

magnetic saturation The limiting value of magnetic induction in a medium when magnetization is complete.

magnetic shield Any surface of magnetic material that reduces the effect on one side of a magnetic field on the other side. A shield is used to protect some instruments from errors arising from external alternating magnetic fields.

magnetic shift register A shift register in which the pattern of a row of magnetic cores is moved one step along the row by each new pulse.

magnetic spectrometer An instrument in which the distribution of energies among a beam of charged particles is investigated by means of magnetic focusing techniques.

magnetic susceptibility The amount by which the relative permeability of a medium differs from unity: positive for a paramagnetic medium and negative for a diamagnetic one.

magnetic tape A flexible oxide-coated tape on which data can be stored by selective polarization of portions of the surface. One side is usually coated with a uniform layer of dispersed magnetic material. The tape can be used for audio, video, or binary data recording.

magnetic tape diagnostic A routine used to check tape-controller and tape-transport operations.

magnetic tape reader *See* TAPE DRIVE.

magnetic thin film A layer of magnetic material used for logic and storage elements, as shown in the following figure. Thin films are usually less than one micrometer (micron) thick.

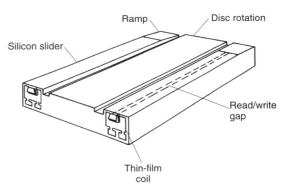

Thin-film recording head

magnetic units *Ampere-turn, gauss, gilbert, line of force, maxwell, oersted*, and *unit magnetic poles* are some examples of magnetic units that are used in measuring magnetic quantities.

magnetic wire A wire composed of or coated with a magnetic material and used for recording.

magnetism 1. The science covering magnetic fields and other magnetic phenomena. **2.** A property of devices or bodies due to the unbalanced spin of electrons in atoms.

magnetoelectric The property of certain materials, such as chromium oxide, of becoming magnetized when placed in an electric field. Conversely, they are electrically polarized when placed in a magnetic field. Such materials can be used for measuring pulsed electric or magnetic fields.

magnetohydrodynamics The study of the motion of electrical conducting fluids in the presence of a magnetic field.

magneto-ionic The components of an EM wave passing through an ionized region and divided into ordinary and extraordinary waves due to the magnetic field of the earth.

magneto-optical disk *See* MO DISK.

magnetoresistance The resistivity of a magnetic material in a magnetic field, when carrying an electric current, depends on the direction of the current with respect to the field. If they are parallel to one another, the resistivity increases, but if they are mutually perpendicular it decreases.

magnetostriction A phenomenon in which certain materials increase in length in the direction of a magnetic field and return to their original length when the field is removed.

magnetostriction transducer A device that uses the property of magnetostriction to convert electrical energy to mechanical energy, or vice versa.

magnetostrictive delay line A delay device that uses the magnetostrictive effect to convert electrical signals to sonic waves or sonic waves to electrical signals. Also called *magnetostrictive acoustic delay line*.

magnetron A UHF diode oscillator containing its own cavity resonator in which electrons assume a circular path due to the magnetic field.

mailbox 1. A set of locations in a common RAM storage area reserved for data addressed to specific peripherals and other microprocessors located in the immediate area. The mailbox arrangement helps the coordinator microprocessor and the supplementary microprocessors transfer data among themselves with minimal hardware. **2.** A particular user's area in an e-mail system.

mail bridge A mail gateway that forwards electronic mail between two or more networks while ensuring that the messages it forwards meet certain administrative criteria. A mail bridge is simply a specialized form of mail gateway that enforces an administrative policy with regard to what mail it forwards.

MAILbridge Server/MHS A software product used for connecting Action Technologies' MHS to other message-handling environments.

mail gateway A machine that connects two or more electronic mail systems (including dissimilar mail systems) and transfers messages between them. Sometimes the mapping and translation can be quite complex, and it generally requires a store-and-forward scheme whereby the message is received from one system completely before it is transmitted to the next system, after suitable translations.

Mail List Manager A full-featured mail list manager that stores names, addresses and other information about clients, customers, members, and associates. You can print mailing labels for all U.S. addresses from its directory.

mailmerge In word processing, a function that allows the user to send out personalized letters to the names on a mailing list. The list to be merged can be constructed with the word-processing program or taken from a database management system. In some programs, the mailmerge feature allows the user to enter variable data interactively, and has the ability to select paragraphs for a form letter based on the information in the database.

mail server A software program that distributes files or information in response to requests sent via e-mail. Internet examples include Almanac and netlib.

mail slots An application interface that is part of the LAN Manager software for the development of electronic mail applications.

main command menu The list of command names that appears at the top or bottom of the screen when a program like Word is ready for you to choose a main command.

main document In a mailmerge operation, contains standard text that is the same for all copies of a form document, plus special fields where a program like Word inserts varying text from another document (the data document).

mainframe 1. The heart of a computer system, which includes the CPU and ALU. **2.** A large computer, as opposed to a mini- or microcomputer, often used in large organizations such as insurance companies, banks, and government agencies. These computers deal with large files of data and heavy-duty mathematical or scientific calculations. With mainframes, many magnetic disks and tapes are connected to the computer in order to store data, so the input/output scheduling can become a major task. Microcomputers can be made to act as terminals connected to mainframes.

main memory The central storage through which information passes to and from peripheral units and CPU. Main memory is usually accessed directly by the operating registers and may be the fastest storage device in the computer, since it is used to execute all instructions. Also called *main storage*.

maintenance Activity used to eliminate faults and keep hardware and programs in satisfactory working condition. Maintenance may include tests, measurements, replacements, repairs, and adjustments.

maintenance control panel A panel of indicators and switches used to display a sequence of routines for repair checks.

Maintenance Manager A program designed to automate the preventive and corrective maintenance of HVAC (Heating, Ventilation, and Air Conditioning) equipment. It can be used for other types of equipment as well. You can perform three basic types of maintenance; preventive maintenance (PM) for assetable equipment, corrective maintenance (CM) for assetable equipment, and corrective maintenance (CM) for nonassetable equipment. Maintenance Manager helps perform the maintenance by automatically printing work orders and recording the maintenance activity in the Equipment History Records. If parts are necessary to perform the maintenance, the program updates the facility parts inventory.

maintenance processor A processor used to remotely check a microprocessor through the checking of memory or register contents. The maintenance processor can also be used to single-step the clock of the microprocessor in order to search out faulty register contents. Other circuitry could be checked in a similar manner.

maintenance time Time used for hardware repair, including corrective and preventive operations.

major control data The various high-priority items of data used to select, execute, or modify another data value, routine, record, file, or operation.

major cycle The time interval between successive appearances of a given storage element. Usually, it is the time of one rotation of a recirculating storage element and is composed of a number of minor cycles.

majority The logic operator having the property of unanimity: if P, Q, R are statements, then the majority of P, Q, R is true if more than half the statements are true, and false if more than half the statements are false.

majority carrier The predominant type of current carrier in a semiconductor region. For npn transistors, the majority carrier is the *electron*; for pnp it is the *hole*.

majority decision gate A device or circuit used to implement the majority logic operator. Also called a *majority gate*.

majority element Related to a threshold element or a decision element: if the weights are equal to 1 and the threshold is equal to (n + 1)/2, the element is called a majority element.

major state A basic control state in a computer, such as fetch, defer, or execute. Major control states are used to determine and execute instructions. During any one instruction, a state lasts for one cycle.

major state logic generator The logic circuits of the CPU that are used to establish the major state for each computer cycle. The major state logic generator determines the machine state as a function of the current instruction, the current state, and the conditions of the peripheral units.

major version In NetWare, the major version of a driver release.

makeup time 1. The part of available time that is used for reruns due to malfunctions and mistakes from a previous operating time. 2. The unproductive time required to prepare a system to perform a specific task.

male connector In electronics, plugs and connectors are commonly referred to as male and female. The male connector has protruding pins.

malformed listen ECBs In NetWare, the number of times (since SPX was loaded) that application has given malformed ECBs to SPX. An ECB is malformed if the value in its Fragment Count field is 0, if the value in its first Fragment Descriptor Field's Size field is less than 42, or if the listen socket is not open.

malfunction A failure in the operation of a computer system.

malfunction routine A routine used to locate a malfunction in a computer or as an aid in locating mistakes in the program. Also called *diagnostic routine*.

MAN Abbreviation for *metropolitan area network*, a network designed to link together diverse local networks into a city-wide network.

management information system *See* MIS.

Managing Your Money A program for PCs designed to manage your checkbook and budget, and understand the tax laws. It can be used to manage stocks and bonds, real estate, taxes, loans and mortgages, capital gains, tax shelters, and insurance.

Manchester coding *See* BIPHASE CODING.

manganese A grey-pink, hard, brittle metallic element: atomic number 25, atomic weight 54.9380, symbol Mn, specific gravity 7.2, melts at 1260°C. Alloyed with other nonferromagnetic elements of copper and aluminum, it forms a ferromagnetic material. The element is used in some primary batteries.

manganin A copper-base alloy containing 12 percent manganese and 4 percent nickel, used for making resistor wire because of its low temperature coefficient and low contact potential.

manipulated variable The quantity or condition that is altered by the computer to initiate a change in a regulated process.

mantissa For a number expressed in floating-point notation, the numeral that is not the exponent.

manual data input *See* MDI.

manual feedrate override A device enabling the operator to reduce or increase the feedrate.

manual input The entry of data by hand.

manual input generator A device that accepts manual input data and holds the contents for sensing by the computer or controller.

manual part programming The manual preparation of data in machine control language to define a sequence of commands for use on a numerical control machine.

ManualWriter A program for creating software manuals by using the functionality of each component of your application as you are designing it. It details menus, submenus, forms, and reports down to the field level and creates a table of contents and indexes.

manuscript A form used by a part programmer for listing detailed manual or computer part programming instructions.

MAP Acronym for *manufacturing automation protocol*, developed by General Motors for manufacturing control.

map A graphic portrayal of the correspondence between the elements of one set and the elements of another set, such as a listing that relates data names to addresses.

MapMaker A set of programs designed for making computer-plotted maps. This program allows the user to turn statistical data based on area into a form representing the data displayed as a map.

MAP token-passing bus The token-passing bus specified by the MAP protocol In the manufacturing environment.

MAR Acronym for *memory address register*, a register used to hold the address of a data word to be read from or written into memory. The MAR can also be used as an internal register for microprogram control during data transfers to and from the memory and peripherals.

margin The area between the edges of the page and the edges of the text, excluding indents.

marginal check A preventive maintenance technique that uses the variation of operating conditions such as voltages and frequency to detect and locate incipient defective components.

marginal test A built-in check system that uses resistor networks and variable voltages. All working registers are usually displayed on the console panel.

marginal voltage check A means of testing a unit by reducing the power supply voltage. The theory is that if there is a marginal circuit, it will fail at the reduced voltage.

mark A sign or symbol used to signify or indicate an event in time or space. Examples include end-of-message marks, file marks, and end-of-tape marks. Also called a *marker* or *flag*.

marking distortion A bias distortion in which received marks appear longer than received spaces.

MARK I (*o.t.*) A computer having mechanical counters controlled by electrical devices, developed in 1944.

Markov chain A probabilistic model in which the probability of an event is dependent only on the event that preceded it.

mark reader A device used to detect pencil marks on documents.

mark sensing The electrical detection of manually recorded conductive traces on a nonconductive surface such as paper.

M-ary A term used to refer to devices and operations with more than two states or conditions.

mask 1. A machine word that specifies by selective inhibition the parts of another machine word that is to be operated on. 2. A thin sheet with open and closed portions used in device photo-processing.

mask bit A specific bit used with a pattern of bits to extract selected bits from a string.

masking The process of extracting certain bits or sensing certain binary conditions while ignoring others by inhibition. One technique of masking uses zeros in bit positions of no interest and ones in positions to be sensed.

mask PROM A type of programmable read-only memory that is programmed during the final steps of manufacture. The surface of the wafer is coated with a layer of aluminum that is selectively etched to give the desired interconnecting pattern. The devices are fabricated up to this step of manufacture and then held in storage until a customer's data pattern is defined. Then the chips are mask-programmed and delivered to the user.

MASM Acronym for Microsoft's *Macro Assembler*, a program that reduces coding time and simplifies code maintenance by including intuitive, high-level language constructs and language extensions. The Microsoft Programmer's Workbench includes an editor, an assembler, a source-browsing facility, and a project management utility for writing programs in assembly language.

Massey formula A formula giving the probability of secondary electron emission when an excited atom approaches the surface of a metal.

mass spectrometer An instrument in which charged particles of different atoms are separated by their mass-to-charge ratios. Separation takes place in a high vacuum to eliminate collision with other molecules. A sample is admitted and ionized under reduced pressure by an electron beam. The charge particles pass through a magnetic field to determine the mass-to-charge ratios. Space collectors pass the charges to an electrometer where they are amplified into voltages proportional to the compositions. A closed-loop control system compensates for any changes in sensitivity. The use of a microcomputer makes the system self-calibrating and able to operate without human attention.

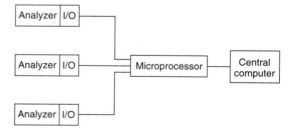

Microprocessor-controlled gas chromatography system

A central computer can be used with a microprocessor that scans all the analyzer units and converts and stores the signals for use as required. A block diagram of the system is shown.

mass storage A mechanical, nonvolatile memory device. Mass storage units include magnetic tape and disks, video tape and disks, and CD-ROMs.

mass-storage device A device with a large storage capacity such as a magnetic disk.

mass-storage dump A program used to transfer a specified area of memory to a mass-storage device. If an autoloadable format is used, the accuracy of the dumped program is automatically verified.

mass store *See* RAM.

master boot record The first physical sector on a PC hard disk (track 0, head 0, sector 1). It contains partition descriptors for each partition. The descriptors tell the operating system whether the partition is bootable and how to access it.

master clock The primary source of all timing signals in a digital computer. Most master clocks use a crystal to provide a stable source. The clock pulses are then used for precision time-triggering of events.

master control interrupt A signal that transfers control of the computer to the master control program. It may be generated by input/output devices, operator error, or processor request.

master control program A program designed to direct all phases of the operation of the system. The master control program usually is designed for minimum human intervention and may provide the following functions:

- Schedule programs to be processed
- Control input/output operations
- Allocate memory
- Direct compiling operations
- Provide error-detection and correction
- Provide printed instructions
- Adjust operation according to system environment

master control routine **1.** A part of a program used to control linking of other routines and subroutines, or calling selected program segments into memory. **2.** A routine used to control the operation of hardware.

mastergroup In frequency-division multiplexing, a number of voice channels, typically 300 or 600, consisting of five or ten super-groups. *Also see* FDM.

master scheduler A control program that allows the operator to initiate special actions designed to override the normal functions of the system.

master-slave A configuration in which one device or function, the *master*, always has control over another device or function, the *slave*. In a computer system, the master computer schedules and transmits tasks to the slave, which performs the computations as directed. Bus control can also be under a master-slave relationship. The processor is the master when fetching an instruction from memory, which is the slave.

master-slave multiprogramming A system designed to guarantee that one program cannot damage or access another program sharing memory.

master-slave network In the simplest form, a host processor connected by one line to a satellite processor. The communication line between the processors is referred to as a *link*. A link may be any communications channel, such as a coaxial cable or telephone line. Each device in a network is referred to as a *node*.

master slice Silicon wafers containing 30 or more clusters of components. These elements can be interconnected with paths of aluminum to form desired circuits. The wafer is then diced to form single devices.

master station A station that controls access of the stations on a LAN. The master station on a token ring LAN determines which PC can transmit next.

master synchronizer The primary source of timing signals in some systems. A typical configuration uses a ring counter synchronized by a crystal-controlled oscillator.

master unit Various units that handle a variety of jobs being executed simultaneously and have the capability of regrouping several units together to control a complete processing system or job independently.

match A check to determine identity, similarity, or agreement between items of data. A match is similar to a merge, except that instead of producing a sequence of items from the input, sequences are matched against each other on the basis of a key.

matching A technique used to verify coding. Individual codes can be compared by machine

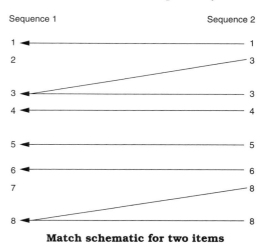

Match schematic for two items

against master codes to detect any that are invalid, as shown in the figure.

matching impedance The impedance value that must be connected to the terminals of a signal-voltage source of matching.

material control A technology concerned with the counting, sorting, and identification of raw materials and manufactured parts.

material dispersion In an optical fiber, the dispersion caused by the variation in propagation velocity with the wavelength of light. Also called *intramodial dispersion*.

material implication A Boolean operation defined by the following truth table:

Operands		Result
A	B	C
0	0	1
1	0	0
0	1	1
1	1	1

materials requirements planning *See* MRP.

math coprocessor A specialized chip that can be added onto a PC's system board. A math coprocessor unloads the CPU from involved mathematical calculations.

mathematical check A check that uses mathematical relationships. Also called *arithmetic check*.

mathematical control mode The control mode or control action used in a control system, such as proportional, integral, or derivative.

mathematical model The mathematical representation of a process, device, or system.

mathematical programming A procedure used in operations research for locating the maximum or minimum values of a function subject to specified conditions.

Math.h++ A set of C++ classes designed to improve the performance and reliability of numerics code. The class structure allows the manipulation of vectors and matrices. There are classes for linear algebra (via LU factorization), random numbers, statistics, linear regression, vectors, and general matrices.

Math Pak A series of BASICA programs that teach and help accelerate some math operations. It serves as a tutorial that covers basics to advanced math.

matrix An array of quantities or elements in a prescribed form. A matrix is usually capable of being subject to a mathematical operation using an operator or another matrix. For example, a matrix of circuit elements can be capable of performing functions such as code conversion. The matrix elements may be diodes, transistors, magnetic cores, or other binary devices.

matrix printer *See* DOT MATRIX PRINTER.

matrix storage A storage system with elements arranged such that access to any location requires the use of two or more coordinates, as shown in the following figure. Examples are magnetic-core storage and CRT storage.

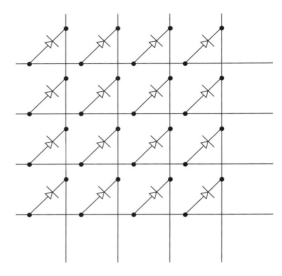

Matrix of diodes

matrix switch An array of circuit elements used to perform a specific function as interconnected. Functions include word translation, encoding, and number-system transformation. Elements include switches, transistors, diodes, and relays.

MAU Abbreviation for *multiple access unit*, the name IBM and other vendors use to refer to their hubs used to connect PCs in a token ring LAN.

Mauchly, John W. Codeveloper with J. Presper Eckert of the ENIAC (first all electronic computer) and the UNIVAC (first commercial computer).

Mavica Acronym for *magnetic video camera*.

Maxi Magic EMS A card designed to boost an IBM PC/XT/AT system to 2M of expanded memory. It is compatible with the LIMM specification and coexists with LIMM-compatible products. It allows you to create and use databases and spreadsheets that require more than 640K of RAM. *Also see* EMS.

maximum characters In NetWare Print Services, a flag that specifies the maximum characters per line, up to 65,535.

maximum data size In NetWare Diagnostic Services, the maximum size of a packet's data portion for the target driver. It is always 64 bytes less than the packet size for the LAN board.

maximum EGA resolution Specification used for boards that support an enhanced EGA mode.

maximum frequency operation The maximum repetition or clock rate at which the circuits will perform reliably under continuous worst-case conditions.

maximum lines in NetWare Print Services, a flag that tells the maximum lines per page, up to 65,535.

maximum number of servers In NetWare Queue Services, the maximum number of connections to be returned.

maximum open connections In NetWare Diagnostic Services, the maximum number of SPX connections that have been open simultaneously since IPX was loaded.

maximum open sockets In NetWare Diagnostic Services, the maximum number of sockets that have been open simultaneously since IPX was loaded.

maximum possible connections In NetWare Diagnostic Services, the maximum number of SPX connections possible on the target node. This value is configurable.

maximum possible sockets In NetWare Diagnostic Services, the maximum number of open sockets possible on a target node. This value is configurable.

maximum resolution Refers to the number of horizontal by vertical pixels that compose an image. The greater the resolution, the better the clarity of the picture.

maximum rights mask In NetWare Directory Services, a byte containing bit fields specifying privileges such as the following:

- Read files
- Write to files
- Open files
- Create files
- Delete files
- Create or delete subdirectories, and trustee rights can be granted or revoked
- Search directory
- Change file attributes

maximum SPX connections supported In NetWare Communication Services, the maximum number of SPX connections set up in the SHELL.CFG file.

maximum timeout In NetWare workstation Services, the most clock ticks a Receive Timeout is allowed.

maximum used dynamic space In the NetWare File Server Environment, the maximum amount of memory in the dynamic memory area that has been in use since the server was brought up.

maximum VGA resolution Specifies the highest resolution displayable by extended VGA adapters. These adapters offer higher screen resolutions than standard VGA mode while maintaining the capability of displaying 256 colors onscreen out of a color palette of 256,000. At high-resolution modes, extended VGA adapters can display broadcast-quality images.

maxwell In the CGS (centimeter-gram-second) system, the unit of magnetic flux. One maxwell is equal to 10^{-8} webers.

Maxwell's circulating current Refers to a cyclic current inserted in closed loops in a complex network for analytical purposes.

Maxwell's law A law stating that a movable portion of a circuit will always travel in the direction that gives maximum flux linkages through the circuit.

MBC-BASIC A version of BASIC offering programming features not available in other versions. MBC-BASIC syntax is virtually 100% compatible with GWBASIC and BASICA. For the programmer used to more structured languages such as C, MBC-BASIC offers the capability to create organized programs which use procedures and functions. Variables may be declared as local (within a procedure) or global (external). Many other forms of BASIC do not allow this type of structure.

In MBC-BASIC, an argument list can be declared as follows:

```
ARGUMENT PASSING
INTEGER ARG:X
STRING ARG: A$
KEYWORD ARG: K1 ON OFF
```

This argument list would require three arguments to be passed when calling the procedure/function. They would be referred to as X, A$, and K1. The first must be a numeric, which MBC-BASIC would convert to an integer if one were not given. The second argument is a string (A$), and the third is a keyword that must be either ON or OFF. If ON is given, K1 will have a value of 1; if OFF is given, K1 would have a value of 2.

MBC-BASIC allows the definition of up to five windows. Each window includes independent scrolling, borders, titles, foreground color, background color, and character attributes. Windows may display up to eight colors on the screen at a single time. Here are a few examples describing MBC-BASIC's use of windows:

```
10 DEFINE WINDOW 1 5,10,20,60 RED ON BLACK
20 FRAME WINDOW 1 CYAN ON RED
30 HEADER 1, "THIS IS WINDOW 1" WHITE ON BLACK
   BLINKING
40 Color CYAN ON BLUE
```

Line 10 defines window 1 with its upper-left corner at row 5, column 10, and its lower-right corner at row 20, column 60. Any outputting to this window will result in red-on-black characters. Line 20 will place a frame around window 1 with a foreground color of cyan and a background color of red. Line 30 will place a header in the window, centered on the first line of the window in blinking white-on-black characters.

Line 40 will set the window colors as cyan on blue.

MBC-BASIC also provides for the creation of libraries. This ability to create reusable code allows programmers to store pretested, error-free procedures for repeated use in different programs. MBC-BASIC allows programmers to use the entire 640K memory space available to DOS. Dimensioning and operating on large arrays and vectors are not limited by having to co-exist with the actual program, all within 64K as in some other implementations of BASIC.

MB Abbreviation for *megabyte*.

Mbps Abbreviation for *million bits per second*.

MBR Abbreviation for *memory buffer register*, a register used to store words as they come from memory (read operation) or prior to entering memory (write operation).

MCA Abbreviation for *Micro Channel Architecture*, IBM's bus design introduced with the PS/2. It is a 32-bit bus (low-end PS/2s have a 16-bit MCA bus) designed to allow more than one CPU in a single machine.

MCB Abbreviation for *message control block*, the format used by a packet transmitted by the Redirector to the NetBIOS interface.

MCD Abbreviation for *master clerical data*.

MCP 1. Abbreviation for *master control program*. 2. Abbreviation for *Microsoft Certified Professional*, a general term used to describe someone certified by Microsoft in one of these three areas: product specialist, systems engineer, or trainer.

MCPS Abbreviation for *Microsoft Certified Product Specialist*, a person certified by Microsoft to possess specific skills in the application product and operating systems areas. In most cases, the MCPS is responsible for the end user training, product installation, application-related problem-solving, and other non-network related tasks.

MCSE Abbreviation for *Microsoft Certified Systems Engineer*, a person certified by Microsoft to possess specific skills in the operating system, database management, and network areas. In most cases, this person performs consulting, development, network administrator, systems integration, or other network-related tasks.

MCT Abbreviation for *Microsoft Certified Trainer*, a person certified by Microsoft who provides training to others in the certified professional program. This person must provide proof that they possess the knowledge required to teach others about Microsoft-related products.

MCTE Abbreviation for *multiple console terminal eliminator*, a unit that eliminates the need for multiple terminals when several devices or systems are in use that normally require their own terminal. The MCTE allows one terminal to be used for up to eight devices or systems such as computers, data loggers, data concentrators, data PABXs, network management systems, and intelligent data test sets or analyzers.

MCU Abbreviation for *microprogram control unit*, a functional unit used in bipolar microprocessors to maintain and generate microprogram addresses. It is also used to control carry and shift operations, and with an interrupt control unit, to set the interrupt structure. The MCU uses the next address field rather than a program counter. The microprogram addresses are arranged in a two-dimensional array or matrix. Each microinstruction is selected by its row and column address.

MD A command starting in DOS 2.0 that makes a directory; same as MKDIR.

MDA An abbreviation for *monochrome display adapter*, the original IBM standard for text display on a monochrome monitor.

MDDS Abbreviation for *microcomputer disk development system*, a hardware development aid that generally features self-diagnostic capability and a comprehensive repertoire of software for error-free data. Software development on this system has several advantages, one of which is that during the assembly process, the entire program listing need not be printed to find assembly errors. Instead, the system prints out only those statements that contain assembly errors.

m-derived filter An electric filter element derived from the constant-k element by transformation.

MDF Abbreviation for *main distribution frame*.

MDI Abbreviation for *manual data input*, a means of inserting data manually into the control system.

MDPE Abbreviation for *medium-density polyethylene*, a jacketing for wire and cable.

MDR Abbreviation for *memory data register*, a register that holds the last data word read from or written into the memory location addressed by the contents of the memory address register. See the following figure.

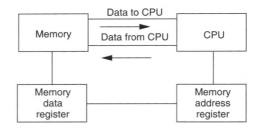

Memory data and address registers

mean repair time The average repair time per failure. The mean repair time, if taken over a given performance period, can be used to assess reliability of the equipment.

mean-time-between-failure See MTBF.

mean-time-between-outages See MTBO.
mean-time-to-failure See MTBF.
mean-time-to-repair See MTTR.
mean-time-to-service-restoral See MTSR.
measurand A specific physical quantity, condition, or property that is to be measured. Common measurands include pressure, temperature, rate of flow, thickness, and speed. Also called *measured variable*.
Measure A software package from Lotus that adds a powerful, easy-to-use data acquisition capability to the popular Lotus 1-2-3 program. It measures interfaces directly connected to analog input signals and can be interfaced to a variety of RS-232 or RS-422 instruments with serial communication boards. Measure allows experimental data to be acquired, transformed, and stored directly in a 1-2-3 worksheet. Reduction, analysis, and graphic display of the data is possible using 1-2-3's mathematics and graphics functions. The program is menu-driven with the same menu formats as 1-2-3.
measured signal Usually refers to the analog of the measured variable produced by a transducer; a measured signal concerns various electrical, pneumatic, mechanical, or other variables applied to the input of the device.
measured variable See MEASURAND.
measurement error Anticipated deviations in a measurement due to one or more of the following:

• Sampling variability
• Sample preparation variations
• Stability variations or lack of precision

measurement reproducibility The degree of agreement between repeated measurements under the same operating conditions over a given period of time.
mechanical dictionary A language-translating machine used to provide a word-for-word substitution from one language to another. The mechanical dictionary is used in automatic searching systems for encoding.
mechanical differential A device used in analog computers to provide a mechanical rotation equal to the difference of two input rotations.
mechanical interface Refers to the mechanical mounting and interconnections between system elements.
mechanical splicing The joining of two fibers together by mechanical means to enable a continuous signal path in a fiber-optic cable.
media The material on which data is stored, such as floppy and hard disks, magnetic tape, and CD-ROMs.
Media Developer An application-development tool for integrating multimedia into applications that were created with a development environment that supports DLL calls. It includes control for multimedia peripherals including analog devices. It supports animation, audio, video, and graphics formats.
median The average of a series of values, or that value for which there are an equal number of items with lesser magnitudes and greater magnitudes.
MediOrganizer A multimedia information-management system that can be used to organize, retrieve, and display multimedia data. It includes control for multimedia peripherals including analog devices and support of animation, audio, video, and graphics formats.
media protocols Protocols that govern the type of physical connection made on the network.
MediSoft A patient-accounting program that includes accounts receivable, insurance billing, multiple fee schedules, patient recall, and extended search capabilities. Reports include a day-sheet, practice analysis, HCFA-1500 insurance form, superbill, patient statements, aged accounts receivables, insurance aging, ledger, and the capability to export data to spreadsheets, word processors, and databases.
MediSoft ECS An electronic claim-submission program that integrates with MediSoft packages. It can transmit insurance claims with Hayes-compatible modems.
medium 1. The physical substance upon which data is recorded, such as magnetic tape or disk. **2.** Any carrier of any commodity, especially data.
medium-access control The bottom half of the OSI data link layer. *Also see* OSI MODEL.
medium frequency Radio frequencies from 300 kHz to 3 MHz, sometimes called *hectometric waves*.
medium-scale integration See MSI.
meet A Boolean operator that gives a true output only when both variables connected by the operator are true.
Meg Abbreviation for *megohm*.
mega Prefix denoting one million, abbreviated *M*.
megabit A unit equal to one million bits.
megabyte One million bytes, actually 2 to the 20th power (1,048,576), abbreviated *M* or *MB*.
megacycle A million (10^6) cycles per second, abbreviated *Mc*.
megahertz A unit of frequency equal to one million cycles per second, abbreviated *MHz*.
MegaLink four-port buffer A combination of buffer, automatic switch, and interface converter. It will accommodate up to three computers to allow the most effective use of resources. Two of the ports are parallel (one input, one output) and the other two are serial (independently changeable for input or output). Because of the flexibility of the serial ports, MegaLink can be configured in many ways:

• Inline buffer between one serial or parallel computer and one serial or parallel printer (any combination of serial and parallel)

- One serial and one parallel computer to one serial or parallel printer with inline buffer (automatic or manual A/B switching)
- One serial and one parallel computer to one serial and one parallel printer with inline buffer (automatic or manual cross-over switching)
- One parallel computer to one parallel and one or two serial printers with inline buffer automatic or manual selection of printer
- One parallel and two serial computers to one parallel printer with inline buffer (automatic or manual A/B/C switching)

Meissner circuit An oscillating circuit in which the resonant circuit is inductively coupled to two coils included in the anode and grid circuits.

Meissner effect The apparent expulsion of lines of magnetic induction from a superconductor when cooled below superconducting transition temperature in magnetic field.

MEM A command in DOS versions 4.0 and higher that displays the amount of used and free RAM.

member name In NetWare Bindery Services, the name of an object in a Property Name set.

membrane keyboard A keyboard with pressure-sensitive keys that have very little movement when touched.

memory A basic component of a computer that stores information for future use. The terms *memory* and *storage* are often used interchangeably.

A memory is used to accept and hold binary numbers until required. To be effective, a computer must be able to store the data that will be operated on as well as the program that directs what operations are to be performed. Memory units are designed to store large amounts of information and must allow rapid access to any desired part of that information in time of need. These two requirements tend to increase the cost of the memory. Various types of memory in use include disk, tape, CD-ROM, and semiconductor (RAM and ROM). See the following figure.

memory address In NetWare Diagnostic Services, identifies the address of a block of memory address space to be decoded by a LAN board.

memory address counter *See* MAC, 1.

memory address driver A device or circuit used to supply signal requirements over transfer lines in memory systems.

memory address register *See* MAR.

memory and device control unit A unit that provides the external signals to communicate with peripheral devices, switch registers, and other memories.

memory buffer register *See* MBR.

memory bus The circuit path for communication between the CPU and memory. A memory bus may actually consist of three buses that are time-shared over a single bus:

- Memory address bus
- Memory-to-CPU data bus
- CPU-to-memory data bus

memory cache A memory system that uses a limited but very fast semiconductor memory along with a slower but larger capacity memory. The overall effect of a larger and faster memory is achieved at reduced cost. Look-ahead procedures are used to locate and deposit the right information into the fast memory when it is needed.

memory chip density A fundamental measure semiconductor memory that typically gives the bits in a package per square inch.

Memory Commander A memory manager for conventional, high, and extended RAM. VGA graphics applications get up to 800K and text applications 920K of conventional DOS they can use. A video accelerator speeds DOS functions up to 200%. It is Windows-compatible.

memory cycle The operation and the time required for reading from and writing into memory.

memory data register *See* MDR.

memory diagnostic A routine used to check all memory locations for proper operation with a set of worst-case pattern tests.

memory dump An operation that causes a microcomputer to produce a listing of the contents of a storage device. A *dynamic* memory dump is concerned with only certain sections of memory under program control as a main routine is executed. A *differential* memory dump is concerned with only those words and bits that have been changed during execution of a routine.

memory expansion board An expansion board that gives your computer more extended or expanded memory for additional functions and applications.

memory extender A unit designed to provide powered channels for additional memory modules. A power-fail recovery system is also available that will support a memory system for a minimum of hours in the event of a total power failure.

memory fill The placing of patterns of bits in memory registers not in use in order to stop the computer if the program seeks instructions from these registers.

memory interleaving A method like caching for speeding access to the computer's memory. RAM is divided into two banks or pages, enabling the microprocessor to access one bank while the other is being refreshed. *Also see* CACHE.

memory latency time The time required for the memory control hardware to move the memory medium to a position where it can be read.

memory management The control and addressing scheme used for the total memory system. In some microcomputers, the memory manage-

,

CS = RAM block number BU = RAM number
BM = Row = register location BL = Columns = digit location

 The PPS special instruction SAG provides access to these 164-bit words on the next cycle time without altering the RAM address register. This feature allows indexed moves of data from any register to this register.

 The LB and LBL insturctions address any of the words of RAM 0.

/3\ RAM 1 through RAM 15 require a LBUA instruction for selection.

Memory organization—hexadecimal addresses

ment system controls the operation of user programs in a multiprogram environment.

memory management software Software that provides memory management capabilities for extended RAM. Often includes a high memory manager for TSRs. Many packages are able to extend standard DOS memory usage.

memory-mapped I/O The use of memory-type instructions to access the I/O devices. A memory-mapped system allows the processor to use the same instructions for memory transfers as it does for input/output transfers. An I/O port is treated as a memory location.

The advantage is that the same instructions used for reading and writing memory may be used to input and output data, as shown in the following diagrams. The traditional computer usually had many more memory instructions than I/O instructions. In a memory-mapped I/O computer, arithmetic can be performed directly on an input or output circuit or register without having to transfer the contents in and out of temporary intermediate registers.

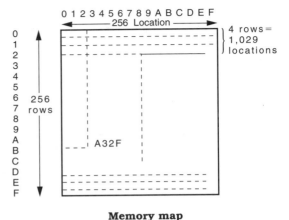

Memory map

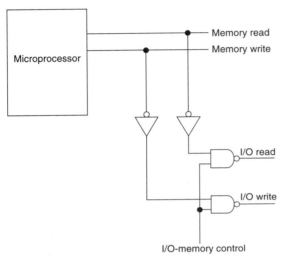

Memory-mapped I/O configuration

One disadvantage is that for each I/O port used this way, there is one fewer location available for memory. If all memory locations are needed as memory, memory-mapped I/O cannot be used. Also, instructions that operate on the memory may require three bytes to address the location of the port, but some I/O instructions may need only one byte to specify a port. Memory-mapped I/O instructions can also take longer to execute than I/O instructions because of the extra bytes. This problem can be solved by using short addressing modes.

memory map A list of the memory assignments made for the program, as shown in the following diagram. Memory maps prevent different routines from interfering with each other and help in determining the amount of memory needed as well as in finding the locations of subroutines and tables. Memory mapping is important to conserve memory, to manage addresses assigned as part of the hardware design, and to know the precise locations of parameters that may have to be changed.

memory, metal oxide semiconductor See MOS MEMORY.

memory module A semiconductor memory unit; one typical module is the SIMM (single inline memory module).

memory overlay In many systems, the monitor remains resident in lower memory at all times. Object programs are loaded into memory, starting at the end of the monitor. The program loader resides in upper memory. Object programs cannot be loaded into the loader area. This area can be overlaid by common storage. Part of the loader can also be overlaid by library subroutines. In addition, programmers can specify that sections of their own program may overlay each other when needed. *Also see* OVERLAY.

memory paging The process of moving memory in sections called *pages*.

memory parity Refers to a procedure that generates and checks parity on each memory transfer and provides an interrupt if an error is detected.

memory protect A CPU option that protects the system from accidental modifications. The memory is set up into two segments, separating the operating system from user programs. If the user program attempts to modify the system, an interrupt occurs and the system takes control.

memory, read-only *See* ROM.

memory receive Refers to a fax machine that can receive incoming faxes to memory when out of paper.

memory register A register used in all data add instruction registers between memory, the arithmetic unit, and the control register. The memory register may be involved in all transfers of data and instructions in either direction between memory and the ALU. The contents may be added to or subtracted from and are usually available until cleared. Also called *distributor*, *high-speed bus*, *arithmetic register*, *auxiliary register*, and *exchange register*.

memory-resident A program that, once started, occupies memory until it is unloaded. *Also see* TSR.

memory scan An option that provides a rapid search of any part of memory for any word. With a memory-scan option, any block of locations may be searched using a single instruction.

memory scratchpad Refers to the central, high-priority, small, immediate-access memory area of the CPU, with a significantly faster access time than the larger main store. This is normally used by the hardware and/or operating system for storing frequently used operands or instructions.

memory timing generator Circuits used in multiple-memory systems to determine where addresses should be written, which words should be sent to the CPU, and in what order they should be sent, as shown in the diagram.

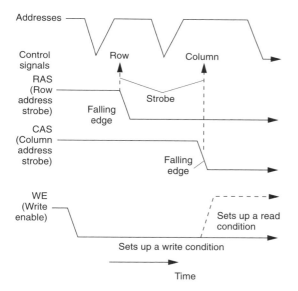

Timing diagram for 4164 control signals

memory unit A memory unit is specified by the number of words (m) it contains and the number of bits in each word (n), as shown in the figure. The address selection lines select a particular word out of all the m words. Each word is assigned an identification address, starting from zero and continuing up to $m-1$.

The selection of a specific word inside the memory is done by placing its address value on the selection lines or address bus. A decoder in the memory accepts this address and connects the paths required to select the word specified. Thus, k address bits will select one of $2^k = m$ words. Microprocessor memories may range from 1024 words, requiring an address of 10 bits, up to 1,048,576 (2^{20}) words or more, requiring an address of 20 bits. The number of words in a memory are referred to in terms of K ($1024 = 2^{10}$) or M ($1,048,576 = 2^{20}$) words; thus 640K = 655,360 words.

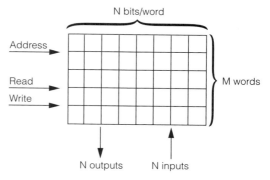

Typical memory card layout

memory window A portion of the file server's RAM set aside to run end-user DOS programs on a nondedicated file server. NetWare assigns 640K of the file server's RAM to this area.

Menabrea, L.F. Wrote a paper disseminating Babbage's theories on development of a computing machine.

menu in an interactive program, a list of choices from which to choose an action of the program.

Menuet A GUI toolkit implemented as a callable function library with over 500 high-level function calls. It has horizontal bar and pulldown menus, dialog boxes, icons, buttons, scrollable lists, and movable and resizable windows.

Menu-Master A DOS menu utility designed to access up to 12 applications and DOS functions on a hard disk. Commonly used applications are defined in terms that are meaningful to the user. The configuration program features context-sensitive help, and the configuration page may be password protected to avoid unauthorized changes. The menu name itself is user-defined, as is the submenu.

menu standards A major benefit of Windows is the fact that all menus are arranged the same way. Not all applications need exactly the same menu items, but to the extent that they do have common functions, you will find them in the same place. The first menu choice in most Windows programs is File. Pull down the File menu and you get the choices New, Open, Move, Copy, Delete, and Exit. Some programs will have other choices mixed in with these, but Exit is always the last one. Thus, once you know how to exit from any Windows program, you know how to exit from all of them. Similar standards apply to other menus, such as Edit and Help. So, once you learn your way around the menus of one fullscale Windows application, you have learned most of the menus of any Windows program.

mercury A metallic element; atomic number 80, atomic weight 200.59, symbol Hg, melts at 39°C, boils at 357°C; used in arc rectifiers and switches.

mercury delay line A delay circuit or system in which mercury is used as the medium of sound transmission.

mercury storage A storage system that uses the acoustic properties of mercury to store data.

mercury tank A container of mercury holding one of more delay lines.

mercury vapor tube 1. Any device in which an electric discharge takes place through mercury vapor. **2.** A triode with mercury vapor, which is ionized by the passage of electrons and reduces the space charge and the anode potential necessary to maintain a given current.

merge See MAILMERGE.

mesa A type of transistor in which one electrode is made smaller than the other to control bulk resistance. The base and emitter are raised above the collector.

mesh A set of branches forming a closed path in a network.

mesh network A mesh formed from a number of impedances in series.

message 1. A transported item of information or a group of words that is transported as a unit. **2.** The message authentication code, abbreviated *MAC*, a cryptographic checksum on the end of each message or data record.

message blocking The linking of several messages into a single transmission or record. Message blocking results in lower transmission overhead by reducing the delays due to changing the transmission direction of the communications link.

message control program The top-priority program that controls the sending and receiving of messages to and from remote terminals.

message exchange A device placed between a communication line and a computer to free the computer for other functions.

message control block See MCB.

Message Handling Service See MHS.

message length In NetWare, specifies the character length of the message to be displayed. If message length is greater than the actual length of the message, the remaining spaces will be filled with blanks.

message line The next-to-last line on the screen, where messages are displayed.

message mode In NetWare, tells whether attached file servers store or reject messages sent to a workstation, and whether a workstation should be notified of messages.

message routing The function of selecting the path or the alternate path by which the message will proceed to the next point in reaching its destination.

message store In standard X 4.00, a storage system to take delivery of messages addressed to a specific user.

message switching The operation in which a message is received at a central location and stored on a direct-access device until the proper outgoing circuit is available for transmission to its destination.

message transfer agent The portion of a message-handling system responsible for getting the message to its final destination.

metacompiler A compiler for a language that is used for writing other, usually syntax-oriented, compilers. A special-purpose metacompiler language is not very useful for writing general programs.

MetaDesign A flowcharting tool to help users plan and produce diagrams, flowcharts, and organizational charts. Its hierarchical structure allows the transfer of detail to subpages, logically linking specific graphics throughout longer documents. Palettes can be imported, exported, and custom-designed.

meta stepwise refinement A software design method that uses the philosophy that the more times one does something, the better the final result is. The designer assumes a simple solution to the problem and then gradually builds in detail until a final solution is derived. Several refinements at the same level of detail are used by the designer each time the additional detail is required, as shown in the figure. The best of these refinements is used for building more detailed versions.

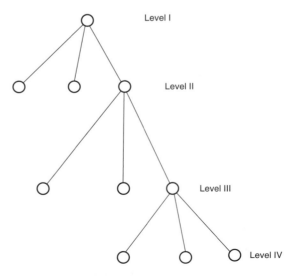

The MSR method for software design

metalanguage A language used to describe a language.

metal ceramic An alloy of a ceramic and a metal that retains its useful properties at very high temperatures.

metallic bond A bond in which the valence electrons of the constituent atoms are free to move in the periodic lattice.

metallic film resistor A resistor formed by coating a high-temperature insulator, such as mica, ceramic, glass, or quartz, with a metallic film.

metal-oxide semiconductor See MOS.

metal-oxide-semiconductor memory See MOS MEMORY.

MetraBus A family of industrial control and monitoring standards. The MetraBus can be used for a wide variety of process control and monitoring systems.

MetraBus boards The MetraBus concept involves plugging a driver board into a PC, MicroVAX, VME-Bus rack, or an Apollo DN3000. A single cable then connects to between one and 32 I/O boards mounted in a 19-inch rack or a NEMA enclosure. Field wiring is connected to the detachable screw terminals on the I/O boards.

These boards are suited for use in production test, incoming inspection, and other applications. A complete system consists of four main parts:

1. A host computer. A serial interface board allows any microcomputer with RS-232 or RS-422 communications capability to serve as a host computer.
2. A driver board. An intelligent driver board allows the MetraBus to operate as an independent control system. In some cases, it can eliminate the need for a host computer.
3. One or more I/O interface cards. There are I/O boards with relay outputs, analog inputs, high voltage digital inputs and analog outputs. The boards operate independently and allow the system to be customized for the application.
4. A cable connecting the driver boards and all of the I/O interface boards. Each driver board can interface up to 512 digital or 256 analog I/O points to the controlling computer. Large systems can be configured by using additional driver boards. The driver boards offer a parallel architecture that can transfer data in excess of 100 Kbaud.

MetraBus driver board A driver board can interface the MetraBus system to a microcomputer such as a PC. It allows a single PC expansion slot to control up to 64 external I/O boards. The board generates all required timing and control signals. It is a half-slot board with a 50-pin connector that extends out the rear of the PC and connects to the MetraBus cable. This cable connects the interface boards and power supply to the driver board. The cable carries data, address, and control signals as well as distributing power. Ground conductors are interleaved between all signal lines to increase the system noise immunity. The system allows cable lengths up to 100 feet. Applications that require communication at distances greater than 100 feet can use a remote driver card.

metric prefixes A group of symbols used to indicate powers of ten; for example, 1,000 is written as 1K.

Metro ImageBase Logically grouped clip art images stored in a compressed format to minimize disk space requirements. Selections are organized in a printed image index. Topics include Art Deco, Exercise and Fitness, Team Sports, Weekend Sports, People, Borders and Boxes, Computers and Technology, Business Graphics, Travel, and Food.

metropolitan area network See MAN.

MF Abbreviation for *medium frequency*, 300 kHz to 3 MHz.

MFB Abbreviation for *mixed functional block*.

MFC Abbreviation for *Microsoft Foundation Classes*.

MFC C++ A code-generation module that allows WindowsMAKER Professional users to generate optimized C++ source code for the MFC C++ class libraries (Microsoft Foundation Classes). Each module contains a knowledgebase for generating code for a specific platform. It supports Microsoft C/C++ and higher. Applications may be migrated across platforms and languages.

MFLOPS Acronym for *million floating-point operations per second*, a measure of computing power usually associated with large computers.

MFM Abbreviation for *mixed functional module*.

MFS Abbreviation for *magnetic-tape field scan*.

MHS Abbreviation for *Message Handling Service*, Action Technologies' product for message handling, which is bundled into Novell networks as NetWare MHS. This can be contrasted with the generic message handling service, which includes X4.00 and other standards.

MHz Abbreviation for *million hertz* or *million cycles per second*. A computer that operates at 4 MHz has a clock cycle time of 25 billionths of a second.

MIC Abbreviation for *microwave integrated circuit*.

mica A naturally occurring mineral that may be sheared into very thin sheets. In the very clear form it is an extremely good insulator even at very high temperatures and is used in capacitors. It is also employed as an insulator for high temperature connections.

MICR Abbreviation for *magnetic-ink character recognition*, a code for the machine-recognition of characters printed using magnetic inks developed for the American Bankers Association. It uses a set of 10 numeric symbols along with four special symbols; the characters are visually readable through the use of magnetic sensing heads in various types of sensing equipment.

micro 1. Prefix for one-millionth (10^{-6}). 2. A microcomputer, a microprocessor, or the system built using either.

microampere (µa) Equal to 10^{-6} ampere.

microATF Testing and support software for client support and programming staff. It captures and plays back keystrokes and records screen images. Editable keystroke files allow for special playback commands and provide automatic and manual screen image benchmark checking. It runs standalone or through the API protocol.

microbending Refers to minute curvatures in an optical fiber caused by external forces. Because the principle of total internal reflection is not fully satisfied at such bends, additional loss in the fiber is introduced.

Micro Channel The standard interface used in IBM PS/2 Model 50, 60, and 80 computers. It allows you to software-select I/O addresses, memory addresses, and interrupts.

Micro Channel Architecture *See* MCA.

Micro Channel ARCnet card A card that lets you connect IBM PS/2 Model 50, 60, and 80 computers to an ARCnet LAN.

Micro Channel card A card that lets you connect IBM PS/2 Model 50, 60, and 80 computers to a LAN or other interface application.

Micro Channel flags A part of NetWare Diagnostic Services that describe Micro Channel support for different configurations. The following options are defined:

- The configuration does not use Micro-channel.
- The configuration uses Microchannel but cannot be combined with other configurations that do not use Microchannel.
- This configuration uses Microchannel and can be combined with other configurations regardless of whether they use Microchannel.

microcircuit A circuit fabricated from integrated elements in such a way as to make the elements inseparable and the circuit miniaturized.

microcircuit isolation The electrical insulation of circuit elements from the electrically conducting silicon wafer. The two main techniques are *oxide isolation* and *diode isolation*.

microcode The microprocessor operational instructions that cause the device to respond to user-programmed instructions. A single user-programmed instruction may involve many microcode instructions, and each microcode instruction occurs during a microcycle. Some microcodes are user-programmable, allowing a microprocessor to be tailored to fit a particular language, making it competitive with larger machines that do not allow modifications of their basic structure.

microcommand A command issued in microcode used to specify elementary machine operations or microcycles that are to be performed within a basic machine cycle.

Microcom Network Protocol *See* MNP.

microcomputer A complete, computing system consisting of hardware and software. The hardware includes the microprocessing unit, memory, auxiliary circuits, power supply, and control panel, as shown in the following diagram. The main processing blocks are typically fabricated with LSI circuit packages.

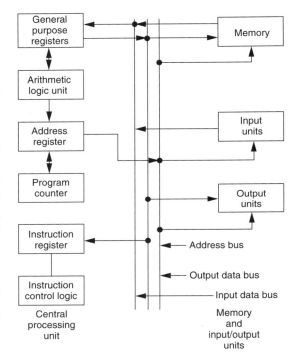

Microcomputer structure

Dramatic decreases in the costs of microcomputer hardware, achieved in the 1980s through a high level of circuit integration, opened up new applications for computers. These include consumer and control applications in which low-cost programmable logic is required. Microcomputers have been applied to games, controllers, terminals, and instruments with considerable success.

A typical microcomputer has the CPU on a single chip or circuit board; the system also contains ROM, storage for programs and data, clock circuits, input and output units, selector registers, and control circuits. The control devices typically include an alphanumeric keyboard and a display screen. Software includes assemblers, loaders, source editors, debugging and diagnostic routines, and cross-assemblers.

All microcomputers can use assemblers and most are supported by cross-assemblers on commercial time-sharing networks, which allow the user to develop and debug the software using a high-level operating system.

Despite their many advantages, microcomputers do have some disadvantages. They are not as efficient for high-speed applications such as data acquisition and communications as minicomputers and larger machines. Because of the high level of integration, testing is difficult and sometimes places a burden on the user in trying to develop effective diagnostics during product development.

microcomputer application Refers to a task that is small, relatively fixed, not too demanding of input/output paths, and requiring fast, efficient arithmetic.

microcomputer control section Refers to the area of a microcomputer that determines control action for the microprograms. The control section is similar to a processor within a processor; actions are usually determined by a microprogram stored in ROM, the control store. Instructions usually are very basic, and control is at a detailed level with a very short execution time.

microcomputer control system In a typical input/output system, four chips are required, as shown in the figure. A 4040 microprocessor, a 4201 clock chip, a 4002 RAM for read/write I/O capabilities, and a 4308 I/O chip for the program storage and I/O capabilities are used in this arrangement.

In most designs, it is desirable to reduce the number of components, so chips that incorporate both memory and I/O facilities are used when available. In a larger system, where expansion capability would be essential, the memory and I/O chips would be separate. The 4002 and the 4308 chips allow both memory and I/O facilities. Each has 16 lines of I/O. The basic I/O controller provides input facilities through the keyboard and display facilities through a four-digit display. It also communicates with an external microcomputer using a 16-bit bus. The program is contained in the 4308 ROM. A scratchpad area for storing temporary data and for intermediate computations is contained in the 4002.

Of the 16 lines of I/O functions provided by the 4308, four pins connect the columns of a 16-key keyboard, four pins collect the data from the four keyboard rows, four pins connect the LED display (three lines would be used for seven-segment LEDs), and the remaining four bits are used for a control panel or for communicating with the host computer.

microcomputer development system A prototyping system of hardware and software that allows the user to design, debug, and modify programs, shown in the following diagram. These systems can create programs; emulate the CPU, memory, and input/output units; and automate all debugging operations. Errors in the programs can be detected before masks are made, and implementation of high-level languages is allowed. Many systems operate in parallel with the standard instruction set. A typical development system includes the following:

- Console or panel for control and monitoring functions
- Processor card or board

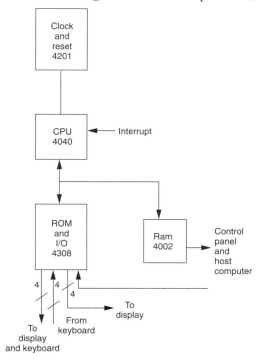

Basic microcomputer control system

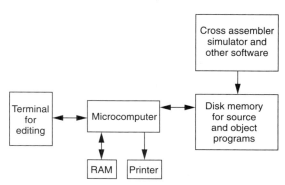

Microcomputer development system

- RAM card
- PROM card
- Input/output ports
- Printer interface
- PROM programmer
- Self-contained enclosure with power supplies

Software includes a debug program, editor, assembler, and PROM programmer. Standard documentation consists of instruction books and programming manuals.

microcomputer disk development system See MDDS.

microcomputer execution cycle The microcycles required for a microcomputer to execute an instruction. A typical microcomputer execution cycle involves the following:

1. Fetch instruction from memory
2. Store in instruction register
3. Decode instruction
4. Execute operation defined by instruction

microcomputer hydraulic system When the microcomputer control concept is extended to hydraulic motors, it works as follows: an electric machine is used to create hydraulic pressure that will drive the hydraulic motor. A control valve, arranged between the hydraulic pressure generator and the hydraulic motor, is opened or closed depending upon the motor's status. The microcomputer can be used to activate the valve.

microcomputer instrument A scientific instrument that uses microcomputers to control the collection, conversion, and recording of data. Examples include spectrometers and interferometers.

microcomputer interfacing kit A set of hardware designed to permit user interfacing of peripherals. A typical kit has a prewired card frame that will accommodate from 6 to 18 modules. The user selects the proper modules and wires in the mating system connector.

microcomputer kit A set of hardware or software or both that allows the user to configure a microcomputer system to a particular product application. A kit can be a collection of logic modules assembled by the user to a prewired system unit. Kits that allow the processor to communicate with a variety of peripherals are available. Provisions included allow interrupts at a hard-wired priority level and conversion of analog monitoring voltages.

Many kits are complete enough so that they can be wired for the user's configuration and used immediately. They include all the components needed, as well as full documentation. Many have enough input/output and memory capacity to implement an instrument controller, a point-of-sale terminal, a communications interface, an industrial robot, or a sophisticated game. Kits contain the microprocessor, RAM, EPROM, input/output ports, and support circuitry including a master clock, interrupts, DMA control, control panel circuits, and display.

Software usually includes a monitor, an editor, and an assembler program. The programs can be run directly on the CPU. System capabilities include the following:

- Program load and dump on disk
- Debug commands
- Display and store memory
- Display, set, and clear breakpoints
- Display and set contents of all registers
- Manual interrupt for program start and restart
- Execute programs from memory
- Memory protect

microcomputer kit assembler A software package used to generate object programs from a source program written in symbolic assembly language. Some assemblers process the source program in two passes. In the first pass, the assembler reads the source program and generates a symbol table for storage in the memory. During the second pass, the symbolic instructions from the symbol table are converted into binary data. This system allows a number of options during the second pass, such as the following:

- Generate a listing on the CRT display
- Generate a listing for the printer
- List only lines with errors
- Generate an object program

microcomputer machine control Microcomputers used as machine controllers. Besides economical considerations, other important features to be considered are the space a microcomputer takes compared to relays, the reliability of the integrated circuits, and the noise immunity level. Programmable controllers take very little space; the components are extensively tested, and excellent noise immunity is accomplished through the use of high threshold logic.

microcomputer POS A *point-of-sale* system in which the cash register is a special-purpose computer terminal. The POS system can monitor and record transactions directly in the store's data files, perform credit checks, and handle other marketing and inventory functions.

microcomputer prototyping system A hardware and software kit that allows the user to develop a prototype system to his or her own specifications. The system includes a chassis, control panel, power supplies, and one or more RAMs in addition to the processor cards.

microcomputer support device See PERIPHERAL.

microcomputer terminal A terminal that uses a microcomputer for intelligence. Microcomputer terminals usually have formatting and error-correction capability and can act as standalone data collection centers.

microcomputer timing modules Circuits used to clock the microcomputer. The real-time clock module, the resettable clock module, the pulse accumulator, and the time-of-day module are considered special timing modules.

microcomputer traffic control A microcomputer at each intersection allows a master traffic control system to know the traffic flow at each intersection. The intersection microcomputer can implement light changes operating on its own information, in conjunction with a group of intersections, or under central master control. This multimode control is now practical with microcomputers and has become low in cost.

microcontroller A device or instrument that controls a process with a high degree of resolution; it typically consists of a microprocessor, memory, and appropriate interfaces. A microcontroller is distinguished from a data-processing microcomputer by its shorter word length and inability to accommodate some types of arithmetic operations.

microcontroller design system A system that provides resources to aid in design implementation. Emphasis is placed on the designer's application knowledge rather than a knowledge of component design. Software support is usually provided to facilitate programming and minimize errors during the design. In addition, resources are available to the designer to operate and diagnose a system in real time at the hardware level.

microcontroller interface A microcontroller used as a tool for the designer to use to implement a programmable logic design. The capability exists in the system to store and execute control sequences. A typical interface uses a uniform method of input/output connection that accepts variable field length sizes; additional, expensive, custom circuitry for I/O is often not required. The programmed microcontroller becomes the controlling subsystem in the overall specified system.

microcycle *See* MACHINE CYCLE.

micro data switches A data switch shown in the following figure that can be mounted on a monitor, under a work surface, on the side of a desk, or even on a desk. These switches work with 25-pin RS-232 serial, 25-pin IBM parallel, and 36-pin Centronics parallel interfaces. They switch the 16 lines appropriate to the interface used.

microdiagnostic A test routine used to exercise the microprocessor and detect faults. Microdiagnostics are usually controlled by the microprocessor control store, which may be a RAM to allow writing capability. On most systems, microdiagnostics can detect a problem in a few seconds.

microdiskette A 3.5-inch floppy disk.

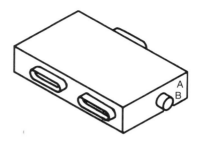

micro data switches

microelectronics The technology of fabricating functional circuits using subassemblies comprised of integrated-circuit packages.

micro enhancer A chip set for EGA applications that extends the EGA resolution beyond 640 × 350, to 640 × 480 and 752 × 410. You can have 16 colors out of 64 to choose from to display the picture. It is a short card that runs regular CGA software on an EGA monitor in 132 columns with 256K video memory. Also, Hercules 720 × 348 mode may be displayed on the same EGA monitor. A parallel printer port is included that can be configured as LPT1, LPT2, or LPT3. The port can also be disabled if desired.

microfiche A sheet of film, usually 4 × 6 inches, used to store printed or graphic material that has been reduced 12 to 38 times by photographic methods.

microfilm A film in the form of a strip, used to hold a photographic record of printed or graphic material that may be enlarged for viewing or reproduction.

Micro Focus Personal COBOL An integrated program development system for PCs. It includes a full-screen text editor, source-code generator for screens and forms, syntax checker, automatic file handling, and an interactive source-code-level debugging and maintenance facility. It is a good package for the student learning COBOL programming.

microfunction decoder An MSI (medium-scale integration) arithmetic logic function especially useful in microcomputer systems. Microfunction decoders perform lookahead operations for carry and shift functions, usually in a single microcycle.

Micrografx Designer A program designed to create technical illustrations, medical diagrams, logos, architectural designs, mechanical drawings, electrical schematics, and other detailed drawings. It has a color palette, WYSIWYG text editing, and a Windows-compatible PostScript driver. You can prepare color separations and design with color in standard and custom gradient shapes. It features text-on-a-curve, up to 64 layers, WYSIWYG, batch printing, and import/export to word processing, graphics, and desktop publishing programs.

microinstruction The microcode required for a machine cycle. Microinstructions are stored within a microprogram; they specify the sequential operations of individual computing elements. *Also see* MICROCODE *and* MACHINE CYCLE.

microinstruction decoder The logic used to interpret the microinstructions and provide signals to control data transfers, arithmetic operations, and sequences.

microinstruction display A display that can be implemented in binary, octal, or hexadecimal. During a single step execution, it is useful to display the current microinstruction being executed; with the help of the display, errors can be more quickly identified and corrected.

microinstruction sequence The series of microinstructions that the microprogram control unit selects from the microprogram to execute a single macroinstruction or command.

microkit A microcomputer system kit that usually consists of a CPU, keyboard, CRT display, and disk drive units.

micrologic cards Circuit boards that provide a logic family for use in wired or programmable logic systems. Typical micrologic cards include flip-flops, arithmetic functions, counters, converters, timing circuits, analog and digital converters, line and lamp drivers, motor controls, signal shapers, and input/output isolation circuits.

MicROM A read-only memory integrated circuit containing microcode.

micro MAV A transceiver device that converts standard, coaxial Ethernet to 10BASE-T twisted pair.

microminiaturization The production and use of circuits and components with very small dimensions, especially with regard to the scaling down of already-miniature circuits. An example of microminiaturization is the development of LSI (large-scale integration) chips that perform the functions once performed by circuit cards containing several MSI (medium-scale integration) chips.

micromodule A small electronic device capable of performing one or more circuit functions, and possessing the feature of replaceability as a (usually) plug-in element.

micron A unit of length equal to one millionth of a meter. The term has recently been supplanted in the International System of Units (SI) by *micrometer*.

micro print spooler A spooler that stores up to 64K of data and feeds it to a printer, modem, or other device, freeing the host computer for other tasks.

microprocessing unit *See* MPU.

microprocessor The large-scale integration (LSI) equivalent of a computer's central processing unit, designed to work as a sequential computational or control unit by executing a defined set of instructions contained in memory. In a microcomputer with a fixed instruction set, the microprocessor may consist of an arithmetic logic unit and a control logic unit. For a microcomputer with a microprogrammed logic set, it may contain an additional control memory unit. The microprocessor determines what devices should have access to data based upon timing requirements. It also correlates the activities of the memory and input/output units.

All microprocessors use LSI technology; some feature a single-chip construction, while others use several chips. The division or partitioning of functions is based on considerations of word length, flexibility, and performance.

Programmability can be obtained on one or two levels. The *microinstruction* level provides a very detailed level of control. The microinstructions can be combined to obtain a *macroinstruction* set which is then used to write control programs.

Control programs can sometimes be written in microcode to provide increased execution speed and more detailed control at the expense of more difficult programming. Microprocessors that are not microprogrammable use fixed, general-purpose instruction sets, which are usually adequate for most applications.

Key features of individual microprocessors include word length, architecture, speed, and programming flexibility. Word length depends on the requirements for resolution, accuracy, and the width of parallel inputs and outputs.

Microprocessors are structured for fixed word lengths or for modular expansion using the bit-slice approach. In some microprocessors, the word lengths used for addresses are greater than those used for instructions. Longer word lengths for either instructions or addresses provide higher system throughput and more powerful memory addressing; shorter word lengths can require less hardware and smaller memories.

Architecture can include general-purpose registers, stacking, interrupts, interface structure, and some integral memory. General-purpose registers may be used for addressing, indexing, and status. They can simplify programming and reduce memory by eliminating memory buffering. Stacking permits subroutine nesting and temporary storage of data when programs are placed in ROM. Stacks consist of RAM memory locations maintained by software or stack register hardware.

The interface structure should be simple to use and not too costly for the application. Separate buses for addressing, data, and memory are usually the best solution.

Memories can be a major portion of hardware cost. PROMs are used for program storage in many systems, while RAMs are used for variable data storage and program storage during development. The modular concept tends to reduce overall costs while allowing the most efficient system to be determined during development.

Programming flexibility can be determined from the nature of the instruction set. Multiple addressing modes conserve memory, simplify programming, and increase processing speed. Indexing and pointer addressing can be used to access tables stored in ROM or PROM. Custom instructions using microprogramming can improve overall performance by optimizing the microprocessor structure. Other features that aid programming include bit and byte manipulation, microprogram emulation, multiply and divide instructions, and double-precision arithmetic capability.

A typical microprocessor has an ALU and a number of registers to provide temporary storage, as shown in the figure. The accumulator is usually the one essential general-purpose register. It can serve as both a source and a destination register for operations involving another register, the ALU, or memory. Other general-purpose registers are used to store intermediate data and operands.

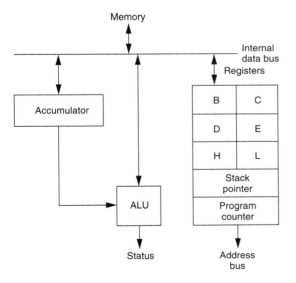

Typical microprocessor structure

The program counter is a dedicated register used to count and track the program instructions by maintaining the address of the next instruction in memory. Each time that the microprocessor fetches an instruction, it increments the program counter so that it always indicates the following instruction. The fetched instruction, in the form of an operation code, is sent to the instruction register to be decoded.

microprocessor alarm systems A system based on light, sound, and temperature, that uses various transducers and sensing devices to measure the required variables and provide inputs to a multiplexer. The microprocessor scans these input points at operator-selected time intervals by supplying a point address to the multiplexer. The data is read, processed, and checked against alarm limits.

Critical deviations from normal operating conditions are detected, and alarms are sent to the control/acknowledgment terminal. The terminal formats and routes the alarm data to operator's display panel. The operator observes the detected alarm and takes the necessary steps to correct the problem. Some alarms can be detected directly by limit switches or continuity breakage, or by manually pressing a button. Examples include spills, fire, burglary, or accident alarms. These crisis conditions require immediate attention and would therefore be implanted as prioritized vector interrupts in the monitor. Fast response and quick operator notification may require the sounding of an audible alarm.

microprocessor analyzer An instrument used for designing, troubleshooting, and testing both hardware and software in systems that use microprocessors. The analyzer is used with an oscilloscope and can display data related to a selected instruction cycle. Some types interface to the system using a connector that clips directly onto the microprocessor.

microprocessor assembler simulator A program that accepts microprocessor assembly language, edits the text, and then allows the user to debug the software on a simulation of the microprocessor. A microprocessor assembler simulator provides about 60% to 80% assurance that the final software product will work.

microprocessor cache memory A storage area used in addition to the main memory. A typical cache memory contains a cluster of bipolar devices in four blocks of four words each. When addressing memory, the CPU checks the cache and the main memory. If the cache is full, data is transferred to the main memory. A cache system can save CPU time when checking for errors.

microprocessor card A circuit board that contains a microprocessor or microprocessing elements. A 144-pin edge connector is used for interfacing to other units.

microprocessor chip The single piece of doped silicon upon which the microprocessor CPU is fabricated.

microprocessor chip set A group of LSI (large-scale integration) semiconductors that can be connected to form a microcomputer.

microprocessor code assembler Assembler programs for microcodes. The code assembler can also test the microprogram and is generally written in Fortran for running on a large computer system.

microprocessor compiler A program that translates the source program into machine language. Compiler programs can be run on medium to large computers, and are available from time-sharing service firms.

microprocessor components The hardware parts of a particular microprocessor configuration such as the ALU, control logic, and register array, as shown in the following figure.

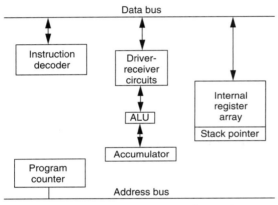

Typical microprocessor configuration

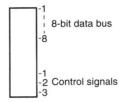

Microprocessor control signals

microprocessor controller See MICROCONTROLLER.

microprocessor control signals (o.t.) Some of the early microprocessors used the PMOS process and 18-pin packages. Eight pins were used for the 8-bit bidirectional date bus along with two clock signals. Three lines were used to indicate the state of the microprocessor to external circuitry:

1. A SYNC output indicated the beginning of a new machine cycle when information can be sent out.
2. A READY line was used to temporarily stop the operation of the microprocessor.
3. An interrupt input was used to change the execution sequence of the program.

Address information was multiplexed over the 8-bit bidirectional data bus, as shown in the figure. At the beginning of a machine cycle requiring a read from or write to memory, the address information was put on the data bus, after being saved or latched by external circuitry.

The address word was 14 bits long, so the eight low-order bits were sent out and latched and then the six high-order bits were sent out and latched. This multiplexing of address information reduced performance. The next microprocessors used an 8-bit bidirectional data bus for transferring data and an address of 16 bits. Some microprocessors used the data bus to propagate status information during a certain state of each machine cycle by multiplexing the data bus externally. This required a system chip called the *system controller*.

microprocessor data logging Data logging systems with integral microprocessors. With a wide variety of available peripherals, the microprocessor can analyze the data, and perform computations, limit tests, and averages. It can also record the entire data set or only portions or summaries. Most systems provide internal processing of the data by the microprocessor, replacing the online analyzing previously performed by a minicomputer. In addition, the microprocessor can perform functions such as the linearization of thermocouple curves.

microprocessor debugging program A program that resides in microprocessor memory and is used during system development to assist in debugging operations. A typical debugging program has the following capabilities:

- Load contents of external storage
- Write contents of memory
- Inspect memory
- Move and set program breakpoints
- Start program printout
- Modify memory

microprocessor economic feasibility The crossover point between fixed and programmable logic depends on the application, but economics tends to favor the microprocessor when the number of ICs required to implement the control of a dedicated logic system approaches thirty or forty. The improving cost/performance ratio, however, makes the programmable approach attractive for many less-complex circuits, especially when product line continuity is important.

microprocessor educator system A microprocessor-based communications terminal used for program development. A typical system contains the following:

- Keyboard
- CRT display
- Printer
- Composite video output for remote display

microprocessor-equipped traffic control This system uses a standard microprocessor plus the required interface and program, illustrated in the figure. A microprocessor-based board provides the memory, I/O, and CPU facilities. Two modules are shown on the top of the illustration: the real-time clock for precise timing of external events, and the power-fail restart unit for restarting the system after a power failure and for preserving data when a power failure is detected. Sensing and control are based on the information provided by the vehicle detectors. A rectangle is cut in the pavement and two or more loops of wire are deposited inside the groove. The loop is connected to an RC oscillating circuit. The frequency of oscillation will depend on the impedance of the loop. The presence of a large magnetic mass, such as a car, over part or all of the loop causes a change in inductance and oscillating frequency.

microprocessor evolution The microprocessor evolution began in the late 1960s when semiconductor manufacturers begin defining chips with high gate-to-pin ratios and regular cell structures. This marked the beginning of semiconductor memory market. These early semiconductor RAMs, ROMs, and shift registers were used in many calculator and CRT terminal products.

Like other computer components, microprocessors have gone through several generations. The first generation of microprocessors was ushered in by the Intel 4004 and 8008. These calculator product chips had limited instruction sets and were based on p-channel MOS technology.

The second generation began with the 4040 and 8080. These chips used larger instruction sets with up to 80 instructions and employed the faster n-channel MOS technology. The third generation began with the Intel 8086 that used a more sophisticated instruction architecture and improved high-density MOS technology.

microprocessor instruction set The basic instruction set for most microprocessors falls into four groups:

- *Transfer instructions* tell the CPU where in memory to load or access the instructions or data.

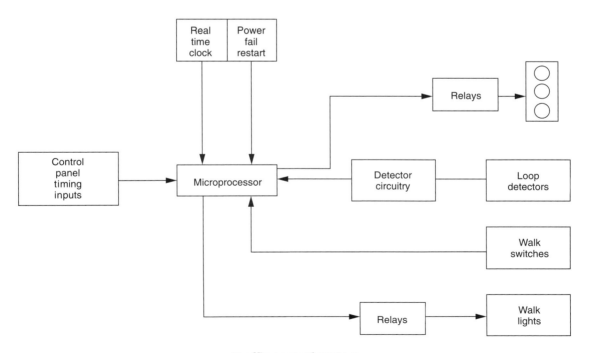

Traffic control system

- *Arithmetic and logic instructions* perform the number data manipulation.
- *Input and output instructions* allow the processor to communicate with the external environment.
- *Jump and branch instructions* modify the contents of the program counter so that the CPU modify the flow of the program.
- *Data transfer instructions* perform operations on the data or program memory such as setting up data addresses and returning from subroutines. They also allow the nesting of subroutines and may contain an arithmetic or logic function to complete the memory reference.

For example, see the table below. The first three of these instructions may be used to modify the transfer addresses for the next instruction if required by the program. To replace the contents of an address in RAM, the LDA instruction is followed by an XDSA instruction. To exchange the contents of two addresses in RAM the LDA instruction would be followed by EXA and XDA instructions.

microprocessor instrument A scientific instrument that contains a microprocessor for calculations and error corrections due to drift and other variations.

microprocessor intelligence The control program used to guide the microprocessor through the various operations it must perform.

microprocessor language assembler A software package used to assemble source code on a minicomputer and convert it into binary output for loading into the microprocessor.

microprocessor language editor A software set used primarily for creating and modifying source programs. Once in memory, the program text can be changed, deleted, and reformatted.

microprocessor maintenance console A diagnostic tool that interfaces with some types of microprocessors. The maintenance console can display and simulate the contents of any memory location and register in the microprocessor system. It can also display outputs and simulate inputs.

microprocessor monitor A system monitor gives users complete control over the operation of the system. All necessary functions for program loading and execution are provided, while additional commands implement extensive debugging facilities. These facilities include the capability to examine and modify memory or CPU register contents, set program breakpoints, and initiate program execution at any given address. Users can dynamically reassign system peripherals via monitor commands through calls to the system monitor's I/O subroutines.

microprocessor register See REGISTER.

microprocessor ROM programmer A program that is used to load, verify, and modify programs in a PROM device.

microprocessor slice The building-block approach of a 2- or 4-bit microprocessor that can be ganged to build 8-, 16-, 24-, or 32-bit systems. A longer word length provides higher throughput and easier programming, while shorter word lengths require less hardware and smaller memories.

microprocessor system analyzer An instrument used to design, troubleshoot, and test both programs and hardware in microprocessor systems. A system analyzer can test programs and hardware either together or individually and can be connected or disconnected in a short time using clip-type connectors.

microprocessor timing See CLOCK SIGNALS.

microprocessor training aid A hardware unit designed to help the user master the software of 4- and 8-bit microprocessors. The training aid contains memory circuits for program and data storage, with a front panel for display and control of addressing and CPU status. It gives the student training in the use of the instruction set and provides software solutions to hardware problems.

microprogram A program of instructions that do not reference the main memory. The microprogram is constructed from the basic subcommands, and it is sometimes a sequence of pseudo-commands that are translated into machine commands by hardware. A microprogram tends to obtain maximum utilization of the subcommands by directly controlling the operation of each functional element in the microproces-

Instruction	Result
LDA Load accumulator	The contents of RAM currently addressed are placed in the accumulator
EXA exchange	Same as an LDA except the accumulator and contents of the accumulator are memory, also placed in the currently addressed RAM location
XDA exchange	Same as an EXA except the RAM accumulator and address in the transfer memory and register are further modified by decrementing this register by one

Data transfer instruction examples

sor by using microcode. The microprogram can be used to implement a higher-language program by storing the microinstructions in ROM. *Also see* BIPOLAR MICROPROGRAM.

microprogram control unit *See* MCU.

microprogram display A special board used on some systems for display and debug operations. It can be used to trap, latch, and display the control signals from the microprogram for interface into the machine operations.

microprogram emulation process Sequential logic circuits using ROM, which within some time constraints can be used to simulate the performance of any sequential logic network. The ability of the device to emulate effectively is determined to a great degree by the address selection or sequencing portion of the unit. In microprogrammed devices with short microinstruction words, the design usually involves combining a program counter technique with a global branch instruction format. In larger systems, truncated addressing schemes are more frequent.

microprogram indexing A technique used to locate data within a memory and count the number of times an operation is performed in a microprogram. Indexing can be used to point to a data item in a list of words or count the number of times an inner loop in an instruction is used.

microprogrammable instruction An instruction that does not reference main memory and may have several shift, skip, or transfer commands to be performed.

microprogrammable processor A processor in which the instruction set is not firmly fixed, but can be tailored to specific needs by the programming of ROMs or other memory units. The instruction set is defined in memory, which is fetched to control the data paths of the machine. Since the contents and interpretation are defined in memory, the meaning and effect of the instruction can be changed by changing the contents of the memory.

microprogrammed sequencer A device that generates, increments, and stores addresses. It can branch anywhere in memory, perform a subroutine, and then return.

microprogrammed subroutine A program designed to be used by other routines to accomplish a particular purpose. These routines can be called from several points within the main body of the program. Subroutines are used in microprogramming because many microprograms contain similar or identical sections of code. For example, many memory-reference instructions in a computer system all use the same logical sequence in generating the address for an instruction; therefore, this sequence could be a subroutine called from within a body of code that executes the addressing algorithm.

microprogramming The techniques of modifying an instruction set by building higher-level instructions from basic elemental operations. The higher-level instructions can then be directly programmed. For example, if a machine has basic instructions for addition, subtraction, and multiplication, an instruction for division could be defined by microprogramming. Microprogramming adds flexibility to the microcomputer. Compared to conventional programming, the distinctive feature is the storage associated with the control unit. In microprogramming, a user instruction determines an address in control memory that provides the starting point for executing the microprogrammed steps.

The development of inexpensive semiconductor memory resulted in a wider use of microprogramming techniques. Microprogramming enhances flexibility by allowing the machine to optimize its control memory for specific applications. This ability to adjust can greatly simplify programming. Microprogramming is generally slow, since each user instruction requires that a sequence of programmed steps be executed. Control-storage ROM must be fast enough to allow the use of a separate clock that is five to ten times faster than that used for main memory.

In *monophase microprogramming*, each microinstruction requires a clock pulse period for execution, while in *polyphase microprogramming*, the microinstruction requires more than a single clock period. A monophase operation involves shorter instructions and a shorter instruction set. A polyphase operation needs fewer instructions and is faster, but is more complex to implement.

Microprogramming can aid system testing. Checking all data paths is difficult at the machine-language level, but microdiagnostics can check each path to isolate faults by checking functions rather than combinations of functions, as with conventional diagnostics. Microprogramming is not, however, without its disadvantages:

- Expensive compared to writing programs
- Tends to be application- and machine-peculiar
- Relatively slow
- High debugging costs

Microprogramming techniques have been implemented in terminals, calculators, peripheral controllers, processors, and instruments with success.

microprogramming parameterization A technique that uses stored parameters to characterize the state of the program. These parameters can be stored as program status words that are then tested to determine what actions should be initiated.

microsecond A time period equal to 10^{-6} second (one millionth of one second).

Microsoft The largest software publisher, founded by Bill Gates and Paul Allen in 1975. It publishes, among other products, MS-DOS, the operating system used on most PCs.

Microsoft BASIC Professional Development System Software to help you create high-performance BASIC applications. It supports EMS (expanded memory specification) and runtime overlays for creating large-scale programs and small, fast executables. It includes ISAM database functions, Excel-style spreadsheet features, and routines for presentation graphics, matrix math, and user interfaces. It supports math coprocessors and comes with Microsoft QuickBasic.

Microsoft C/C++ Development System for Windows A C/C++ development system for creating Windows-based applications. Foundation classes help you achieve increased productivity with object-oriented programming while generating tight code in a PC-based compiler. The foundation classes are a set of reusable object classes for non-GUI-based applications. An object-aware browser lets you navigate through your project.

Microsoft Certified Product Specialist See MCPS.

Microsoft Certified Professional See MCP.

Microsoft Certified Systems Engineer See MCSE.

Microsoft Certified Trainer See MCT.

Microsoft Chart A DOS-based business graphics package. It provides eight chart types in a total of 45 standard formats, and each one is pictured in a series of illustrated menus called the gallery. First you choose your chart type from the gallery, then you choose the exact format for the type of chart you have selected. Each chart type has from five to eight standard formats.

You can switch between formats until you find the one that best conveys the information you wish to present. Once you find the appropriate format, you can tailor your chart to meet your needs. Microsoft Chart lets you improve the clarity of a chart by changing any of its four components: axes, data, labels, or legend. Text can be tailored to your chart by varying the font, size, location, or amount of text. You can change size, colors, pattern, position, or frame. The program offers automatic scaling, spacing, and centering for all elements of the chart.

Microsoft Chart offers a direct interface to Multiplan and allows data input from Lotus 1-2-3, dBASE, or any other program that can output data in ASCII or DIF files. The program also has an editor for the input and correction of data directly from the keyboard.

Microsoft COBOL Development System A development environment for COBOL programmers. It includes the Programmer's WorkBench which is an integrated development environment, with tools that allow you to edit, build, compile, debug and browse DOS and OS/2 applications. Integrated utilities use pulldown menus and dialog boxes to set compiler options.

Microsoft Excel A Windows-based spreadsheet package; a competitor to Lotus 1-2-3 for Windows.

Microsoft Fortran Optimizing Compiler A Fortran development environment that can be used on a personal computer, minicomputer, or mainframe. There are VAX and ANSI extensions. The CodeView source-level debugger, programmable editor, and incremental linker provide a powerful development environment.

Microsoft Macro Assembler See MASM.

Microsoft Pascal Microsoft's implementation of the Pascal language with large symbol table and support for OS/2. There is a CodeView Debugger and editor for efficient program development. You can use data up to the limit of available memory, then link in separate modules and use overlays. Microsoft Pascal comes with the ECD and floating-point math libraries, including IEEE floating-point emulation and math coprocessor support. It supports direct inter-language calling to modules written in Microsoft C, Fortran, or Macro Assembler.

Microsoft PowerPoint A Windows-based presentation graphics program that features Microsoft's "wizards" that walk you step-by-step through the creation of a presentation, even suggesting content based on your stated needs.

Microsoft Professional Toolkit for Visual Basic A set of tools and controls for creating Visual Basic applications in Windows, including support for pen computing and multimedia. There are tools like the Windows Help Compiler, online Windows API reference, and over 150 articles from Microsoft development support.

Microsoft Project A project aid for job scheduling, resource planning, and cost analysis and control for the general business manager who has not been trained in project management or computer-based scheduling. It is based on the spreadsheet technique, and the layered structure makes "what if" analysis especially easy.

It works cooperatively with other members of the Microsoft family, such as Excel and Word. A conversion utility that allows it to send data to other applications such as Lotus 1-2-3 and dBASE.

Microsoft Publisher A Windows-based desktop publishing program. While lacking some features of high-end programs like PageMaker (notably color separations), it is easy for the beginner to use.

Microsoft QuickBasic A fast, easy way to program in a modern, structured way. Line numbers and GOTOs are gone. Features include DO/WHILE, CASE, recursion, subprograms with local variables, and user-defined datatypes (records). QuickBasic runs virtually all old GWBASIC/BA-

SICA programs at higher speed. Program lines are compiled at over 15,000 lines per second.

Microsoft Test for Windows Software that can be used to automate the testing of Windows applications. It makes testing easier and reduces the cost. You can validate the quality of software as you write it and produce better Windows applications in less time. It includes the tools necessary to create and run automated test scripts. The test scripts can simulate keyboard and mouse input, intercept events such as unrecoverable application errors (UAEs), automatically check for correct results, and log results of tests.

Microsoft Windows A GUI that provides multitasking capability and a windowing environment for 286 and higher PCs. You can have any number of DOS and Windows applications running at the same time, limited only by total system memory. Each DOS application runs in its own 640K 8086 environment, including memory-resident programs. Each can run in the background regardless of what else might be running. Pasting and copying of selected data between applications is supported. Applications may use the entire screen or execute in windows. The graphical user interface is consistent with OS/2's Presentation Manager.

Microsoft Word A word processor with versatile formatting capabilities, useful for sophisticated text layouts. Standard formats for contracts, tables, newsletters, annual reports and other complex documents can be stored on style sheets. Once a style sheet has been designed for a particular type of document, all documents of that type will automatically be in the standard format. If you later modify the style sheet, you automatically change the document.

The latest version includes formatting and correcting errors on the fly. It can capitalize the first letter of sentences automatically, but it does not capitalize the first letter in a new paragraph. It can also correct words you commonly misspell without slowing you down. It will also capitalize the names of days and automatically expand abbreviations.

Other features include the ability to quickly format table, a "sounds like" search capability, and 100 levels of undo. However, Word is slow at saving files, and requires more system resources than less-complex word processors.

MicroSTEP QS A visual programming tool for creating and maintaining database applications. It can be used to create high-performance client/server applications. It supports Btrieve, dBASE, ASCII, and NetWare SQL files.

Micro-Track A utility that monitors the use of a PC to determine whether more hardware is necessary, charge individual users for PC usage, determine how much time is spent on each application, or to plot a histogram of system usage. It will report usage by one or several users. Information is presented in tabular and graphical format, and reports are easy to interpret. It has the ability to gather information on a central database for up to 10,000 PCs. While this program is not a security device, it can be used for some limiting of access to the system.

MicroVAX A series of DEC microprocessors often used as workstations or small servers.

microwave Electromagnetic wavelengths shorter than 300 cm (frequencies above 1 GHz).

MICR reader An input device that reads the magnetic ink characters at the bottoms of checks. Also known as an *MICR scanner*. *Also see* MICR.

MIDI Acronym for musical instrument digital interface (pronounced "mid-ee"). A standard connection between computers and electronic musical instruments that allows them to communicate. The information is a stream of digital data, as opposed to an audio signal, sent at 31,250 bps. Up to 16 channels of information can be sent on a single MIDI channel.

midpoint equalization A combination of post-equalization and preequalization used at intermediate points in a circuit.

midsplit A broadband cable system in which the cable bandwidth is divided between transmit and head-end (reverse direction) at approximately 5 to 100 MHz; and away from the head-end (forward direction), approximately 160 to 300 MHz. The guard band between the forward and reverse directions (100 to 160 MHz) provides isolation from interference.

migration The movement of atoms within a metal or among metals in contact, such as the problem of the movement of atoms during plating of one metal over another. Migration can occur during the production of stinted circuit boards and often prevents one metal from performing its function as a protective coating.

MIIS Acronym for *metal-insulation-insulation-semiconductor*, a semiconductor "sandwich" that uses stored charges between two layers of insulation for nonvolatile memory. MIIS is used with the silicon-on-sapphire process to produce a memory that is independent of the external power supply.

mil A unit of length equal to 10^{-3} inches used in measurements of small thicknesses, such as thin sheets.

Miller-Pierce oscillator A crystal-stabilized oscillator in which a quartz crystal is connected between the grid and cathode of a triode, a parallel resonant circuit being formed in series with the anode.

million-bit CCD A memory of a charge-coupled device (CCD) that has a storage density of one million bits per board. One board contains 64 memory devices plus the logic and drive circuits to operate it as a complete memory system or as a plug-in subsystem of a larger memory. At maximum operating speed, the million bits of data on the card can be read out in 64 milliseconds, which represents a system data rate of 32 million bits per second.

millisecond A thousandth of a second. (One section of 1,000 milliseconds.) Abbreviated *ms* or *msec*.

miniaturization The reduction in size of components and circuits to increase packing density and reduce power dissipation and signal propagation delays.

mini-bundle cable A Siecor fiber-optic cable in which the buffer tube contains three or more fibers.

minicartridge A magnetic tape holder that is smaller than a cassette. A typical minicartridge holds 140 feet of tape, 54% less than a cassette. The drive unit records on a single track at 800 bpi with storage for 115 kilobytes. The minicartridge is expected to outlast the life of a cassette by a factor of six or seven.

minicomputer A general-purpose computer that has more computing power than a microcomputer, but less than a full-scale mainframe computer.

minimal latency coding A method of programming in which the access time for a word depends upon its location; the location is chosen to reduce or minimize the access time. Also called *minimum delay coding* or *optimum coding*.

minimum access code A coding system in which the effects of delays for the transfer of data or instructions between storage and other sections is minimized. Also called *minimum latency code*.

minimum access programming Programming aimed at minimizing the waiting time required to obtain information from storage. Also called *minimum latency programming*.

minimum access routine A routine coded such that the *actual* random access time is less than the *expected* random access time. Also called *minimum latency routine*.

minimum shift keying *See* MSK.

Minitel An asynchronous communications program for DOS that can receive or transmit files in Xmodem, Modem7 (batch) or Telink modes. It is menu-driven with all commands accessible by two keystrokes, and error-handling is simple.

minor cycle The time interval between the appearance of corresponding parts of successive operations used to provide serial access in a storage device. A major cycle usually contains several minor cycles.

minority carriers Nondominant charge carriers in a semiconductor device.

minuend The quantity from which another quantity is subtracted or is to be subtracted.

minus zone The bit positions in a code or coding that represent the algebraic minus sign.

M/IO A control line that distinguishes a memory cycle from an I/O cycle.

MIPS Acronym for *million instructions per second*, a measure of the speed of a CPU.

MIR Acronym for *memory information register*.

MIRROR A DOS command starting with version 5.0 that records data for UNDELETE and UNFORMAT.

mirrored drive A disk drive is mirrored when two identical copies of the data are kept on two different disk drives. If one fails, the other can keep on operating.

MIS Abbreviation for *management information system*, an organized assemblage of management activities performed with the aid of automatic data processing. One example is a data-processing system that provides management with the information required to manage or supervise a particular organization or function. Another example is a communications data-processing system in which data is recorded and processed for operational purposes. The problems are isolated for different levels of decision-making, and information is fed back to upper management to reflect the progress made in achieving objectives.

miscellaneous flags In NetWare, a one-byte field with the following bits defined:

bit 4   OFF (0): NonEthernet or non-configurable board drive
ON (1): Configurable Ethernet board driver
bit 0   OFF: IEEE 802.3 protocol
ON: Ethernet protocol
bit 2   OFF: Driver can run in protected mode
ON: Driver runs only in real mode on 286-based machines

miscellaneous function An off-on function of a machine such as fan or a coolant device.

mistake A human action that produces an unintended result such as faulty arithmetic, an incorrect formula, or incorrect instructions. Mistakes are sometimes called *gross errors* to distinguish them from rounding and truncation errors. In the strict sense of the word, humans make mistakes and do not malfunction, while computers malfunction and do not make mistakes.

MIT Abbreviation for *Massachusetts Institute of Technology*, developers of the X/Windows system.

MITRE Acronym for *Massachusetts Institute of Technology Research and Engineering*.

mixed-base notation A positional representation in which the ratios of significances for all pairs of adjacent digits are not the same. For example, let three digits represent hours, tens of hours, and minutes. The significances, taking one minute as a unit, are

    60, 10, 1

The radixes of the second and third digits are 6 and 10. The ratio of the significances must be an integer. Also called *mixed-radix notation*.

MK Abbreviation for *master clock*.

MKSA Abbreviation for the *meter-kilogram-second-ampere* system of measurement used by the European community.

MKS LEX Software that works with YACC as compiler construction tools for PC. Together they act as a program generator that takes descriptive input and writes a program module, giving fast, compact, portable code. MKS LEX is a scanner generator that takes a stream of characters as input and outputs a stream of tokens. YACC is a parser generator that can take any language specification as input and create output of straight C, C++, and/or Pascal code, which will compile and run with standard C, C++, and Turbo Pascal compilers.

MKS Make Software that offers users an efficient way to automate the production and maintenance of projects. It automatically regenerates the desired program by understanding the interdependencies among all of the components. It saves time and reduces errors in recompiling. User-defined meta-rules allow you to handle large object libraries and remotely access files over a network. It includes a UNIX-compatible AR object-code librarian that can be used with libraries generated with Microsoft LIB.

MKS system The meter-kilogram-second system, used in preference to the CGS (centimeter-gram-second) version of the metric system.

ML Abbreviation for *machine language*.

MLB Abbreviation for *multilayer board*, a printed circuit board that has two or more layers of circuit tracks. Multilayer boards increase logic speed and packing density, and cut electrical crosstalk.

MLI Abbreviation for *multiple link interface*, the bottom portion of the Link Support Layer standard from Novell and Apple. This interface specifies how device drives interact with the Link Support Layer.

MLID Abbreviation for *multiple link interface driver*, a network device driver that conforms to the Link Support Layer specification.

mnemonic 1. A word-like symbol used in assembly languages to code a computer to execute an instruction whose description resembles the word symbol. For example, the term *MOV A, B* is a mnemonic for "move the contents of register B into arithmetic register A." 2. Descriptive of any technique involving memorization of simple words and elements to recall complex words, rules, names, etc.

mnemonic address code An address code that uses an easy-to-remember abbreviation related to the destination, such as LAX for Los Angeles International Airport.

mnemonic operation code Refers to an operation code in which the names of operations are abbreviated and expressed in mnemonic terms to aid programmers. Examples include the folllowing:

- ADD for addition
- CLR for clear
- SQR for square root
- MPY for multiply

Source statements are usually written using mnemonic operation code for translation by an assembler into machine code, which consists of only ones and zeros.

MNOS memory A memory that utilizes MNOS transistors with thresholds that are altered by applying a large gate voltage. Erase time is between 10 and 100 milliseconds, and write time is between 1 and 10 milliseconds. Devices may use word-, row-, or chip-erasable configurations. Serial addressing and output is also available.

MNOS memories have not been widely used. Although a variety of devices has been available, problems in data retention and high cost due to the complex manufacturing process has limited their application.

MNP Abbreviation for *Microcom Network Protocol*, an industry-standard error-correction protocol for modems. MNP standards of class (or level) 3 and higher send data between two modems synchronously, speeding up the transfer of data over asynchronous communications. MNP class 5 adds data compression and advanced error-handling.

MO Abbreviation for *master oscillator*.

mobile systems Computer, radio, and other complex systems that are to be installed on ships, planes, or motor vehicles.

mobility Refers to the characteristics of the movement of charge carriers in vacuum or in materials.

MOD Acronym for *moving-domain memory*, a type of memory that can be batch-fabricated using conventional microcircuit techniques. Moving-domain memories are nonvolatile, like core memories, but much smaller; they operate reasonably fast, and need no external magnetic bias to form and hold the domains, as do bubble memories. Some MOD units have densities of 128k per substrate.

mode Any of the various methods of operation in a system, or the most frequent value in a series of values. Examples of modes in a system include the following:

- Access mode
- Interpretive mode
- Binary mode
- Alphanumeric mode
- Byte mode
- Conversation mode

Also see BURST MODE, BYTE MODE, *and* CONVERSATIONAL MODE.

model A characterization, usually involving mathematical terms, of a process, device, concept, or system. A model may be a schematic representation of a system or process. It usually allows some manipulation of variables to enable a study of the system or process under various conditions or modifications.

modem An electronic device that performs the modulation and demodulation functions required for communications, as shown in the following diagram. A modem can be used to connect computers and terminals over telephone circuits. On the transmission end, the modulator converts the signals to the correct codes for transmission over the communications line. At the receiving end, the demodulator reconverts the signals for communication to the computer using the computer interface unit.

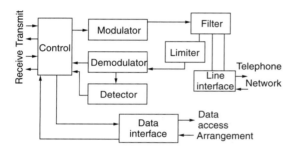

Modem

Modems may be designed to operate in three modes:

- Simplex, with data transmitted in only one direction
- Half-duplex, in which data transmitted in only one action at a time, but that direction can be reversed
- Full-duplex, in which data can be transmitted in both directions simultaneously

An *external modem* is a separate small box that attaches to the wall outlet with a power cord, to your telephone system with a telephone modular jack, and to a serial port on your PC with a serial cable. An *internal modem* is a card that fits into an expansion slot in the computer and connects directly to a modular phone jack. Also called a *data set*. Also see DIGITAL MODEM.

modem chip An LSI (large-scale integration) chip that can be used to build a standalone modem unit. A modem chip can be used to develop full-duplex, half-duplex, simplex, automatic answer, automatic disconnect, answer only, or answer/originate configurations. All that is required for a complete unit that can perform all supervisory functions, including handshaking routines, is an input filter, output buffer, and threshold amplifier.

modem control devices A device to help control the interface of signal lines, either dial-up or dedicated, with computer equipment. These devices can control such functions as error control and timeouts.

modem eliminator A device that interfaces between local terminals that normally require a modem, as shown in the following figure. It functions as an imitation modem in both directions.

Modem eliminator

modem multiplexer diagnostic A device that tests all data and control functions of an asynchronous modem multiplexer.

modem 103 An intelligent Bell 103-compatible auto-dial modem. A command menu displayed at the terminal uses simple, one-letter commands. It is useful for bulletin boards, electronic mail, Telex II (TWX), and remote printer interfaces.

modem splitter A passive device that attaches to a modem allowing multiple terminals or monitors to be interconnected, as shown. Diode circuits are provided to isolate the most useful leads of the RS-232 interface. Leads 2, 4, and 20 are all isolated to the three DB25S (female) connectors. A fourth BD25S (female) connector is provided for connection to the modem.

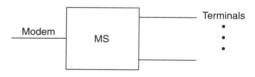

Modem splitter

modem surge protector A unit that protects sensitive equipment, ac lines, and dial-up telephone lines from damage due to transients, surges, and spikes. It can prevent garbled or lost data at critical moments. The unit provides 5,000 watts of suppression between line and ground. The modem surge protector is a two-receptacle, solid-state device, as shown in the figure, that employs avalanche diodes to handle high energy levels. When a surge, spike, or transient is detected, the unit reacts in less than one nanosecond and automatically resets itself.

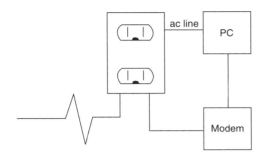

Modem surge protector (ac)

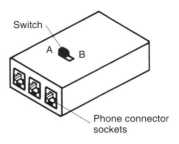

Modular A/B switch

modem 212 A Bell 212A-compatible, auto-dialing modem. Baud rate and parity are automatically sensed and selected by the modem 212.

moderating ratio The ratio of the slowing-down power of a moderator to the macroscopic absorption cross-section.

modes In NetWare, refers to the settings a printer can use. Printer modes are defined using the NetWare PRINTDEF program.

modification loop A group of instructions that form a closed path to alter or change instruction addresses or data.

modified duobinary A form of duobinary coding whose spectral shape has no dc component.

modifier A quantity used to alter the normal interpretation and execution of an instruction, such as an index tag or indirect address tag.

modify To alter a portion of an instruction or subroutine so that its interpretation and execution is different from its usual interpretation and execution. The modification may permanently change the instruction or affect only the current execution. A typical modification is the changing of effective address through the use of index registers.

MO disk Abbreviation for *magneto-optical disk*, a form of rewritable storage that can record data an almost unlimited number of times on the same disc before wearing out. MO disks are slower than standard hard drives, and come in 3.5-inch and 5.25-inch formats. The 3.5-inch disk can hold from 120M to 130M of data.

modular Possessing a building-block capability, whereby standard replaceable components can be grouped to form a variety of configurations of subassemblies, assemblies, or systems.

modular A/B switch A compact switch that makes it easy to share RJ-11 telephone company lines, MUX ports, and modems, shown in the following figure.

modular cable testers Test units used to identify and test telephone company and data cables. LEDs show data or voice configuration as well as continuity in a simple go/no-go plug-in test. One model tests RJ-11 cables while another tests RJ-45.

modular connector An electrical connector with sections that are used like building blocks or modules.

modular construction Refers to the special positioning of modules or functional units within a hardware item, or groups of information within a program.

modular converter A data conversion unit that can be interconnected to form data acquisition systems and subsystems. Modular converters are available in epoxy-encapsulated form for analog-to-digital and digital-to-analog conversion, along with sample-and-hold circuits and multiplexers.

modular design A design concept based on the breaking down of a big problem into smaller problems. Some examples of typical modules are a program to read a keyboard for key closures and a program that divides two signed decimal numbers.

There are several advantages in using program modules. The modules can be run and tested separately before they are linked into the main program. They can also be designed open-ended to allow changes without affecting the other parts of the program. Modular programming is based on techniques in which the program's modules are written, tested, and debugged in small units that are then combined. Top-down design may use modular programming, but modular programming is more common and older, and it is often used independently of any other techniques.

The modules are often divided along functional lines. In microprocessor systems, this division is most useful, since the modules can be used to form a library of programs for use in other designs. By partitioning the program into small, interconnecting modules, it is possible to create larger, complex programs rather easily.

The modular programming technique limits the size of programs that need to be debugged and tested at any one time. It also provides basic programs that may be reused and allows a division of functional tasks.

The disadvantages of modular design include the additional program interfacing that is required and the extra memory needed to transfer control to and from the modules. The need for separate testing of modules can also be more time-consuming without duplicate facilities. Modular programming can be difficult to apply if the structure of the data is critical and cannot be modified. Still, modular program design coupled with the proper documentation tools is a simple but effective design technique.

modular junction panels Junction panels used to centrally locate cables from terminals or computer ports, or as patch panels to transfer connection.

modular system A microcomputer that allows the user to plug in additional boards and to build up progressively to a bigger system.

modular tap A tap between two 50-pin telco connectors into the line that does not disturb ordinary line traffic. The modular tap comes in two RJ-11 models; one has five 4-wire ports, the other has five 6-wire ports. The RJ-45 model has five 8-wire ports.

modulate To vary the amplitude, frequency, or phase of a carrier wave (such as light or a radio signal) proportionally with intelligence (such as speech), for transmission and ultimate demodulation.

modulated carrier A wave whose magnitude, frequency, phase, or other characteristic has been varied according to the intelligence to be conveyed.

modulating electrode An electrode in which a voltage is applied to control the size of electron beam current.

modulating signal The signal that causes a corresponding variation in the characteristics of the carrier wave.

modulation The variation of any wave or parameter in direct correspondence with an intelligence-bearing signal. *Also see* DIPOLE MODULATION *and* FOUR-PHASE MODULATION.

modulation code The code used to cause variations in a signal in accordance with a predetermined scheme.

modulation index A measure in a frequency-modulated wave; the ratio of the frequency deviation to the maximum modulation frequency.

modulation meter A meter placed in shunt with a communication channel, giving an indication of the changing power level due to varying the modulation current.

modulation rate A measure of the reciprocal of the unit interval measured in seconds, expressed in bauds.

Modula-2 Abbreviation for *modular language 2*, a descendant of Pascal. The name refers to its most important feature, the module, and for the modular design of the programs that are written with it.

modulator-demodulator *See* MODEM.

module A software or hardware device that is of standardized design for easy replaceability or system expandability.

module board Interchangeable circuit boards that may contain a complete or partial functional circuit for building up a microcomputer system.

module extender boards The connecting boards that, when inserted between a modular circuit board and its receptacle, permit access to the circuit without breaking the existing electrical connections. Module extender boards are used during system testing and maintenance operations.

modulo check A checking operation that anticipates a remainder when the processed number is divided by a number carried through with data during the process.

modulo-n A ring of integers derived from the set of all integers. Let n be an integer greater than one, and A and B two other integers; if n is a factor of $A - B$, then A is congruent to B modulo-n.

modulo-n check A check that makes use of a check number equal to the remainder of the desired number when divided by n. For example, if $n = 4$, the check number will be 0, 1, 2, or 3 and the remainder of A must equal the check number B divided by 4. Sometimes called a *residue check*.

moire A wavy pattern on the screen, usually caused by interference.

MOL Acronym for *machine-oriented language*.

molar conductance The electrical conductance between electrodes that are 1 cm apart in an electrolyte having one mole of solute in one liter of solution.

mole The amount of any defined chemical substance that weighs its molecular weight in grams, symbol *mol*. Also called a *gram molecule*.

molecular beam A directed stream of ionized molecules issuing from a source and depending only on their thermal energy.

molecular bond The bond in which the linkage pair of electrons are provided by one of the bonding atoms; the atomic bond.

molecular volume The volume occupied by one mole of a substance in gaseous form at standard temperature and pressure.

molecule The smallest part of an element or compound that exhibits all the properties of that specific compound or element.

mole electronics The technique of growing solid-state crystals to form transistors, diodes, and resistors in one mass for microminiaturization. Also called *molecular electronics*.

mon Abbreviation for *monitor*.

monadic Boolean operator A Boolean operator with only one operand, such as the NOT operator.

monadic operation An operation on one operand, such as negation. Sometimes called *unary operation*.

monitor **1.** To supervise and verify the correct operation of a program during its execution. **2.** Software, hardware, or a human that observes, supervises, controls, or verifies the operation of a system or process. **3.** A unit in a computer that prepares machine instructions from a source code. It may use built-in compilers for one or more program languages. The machine instructions are sequenced into the processing unit once compiling is complete. **4.** A CRT.

monitor bit A token ring concept in which the monitor bit is changed by the active monitor to prevent a frame of priority greater than 0 from circulating continuously.

monitor program A computer software routine used to check for error conditions that may occur when the program is being executed. These error conditions may consist of numerical overflow, infinite loops, or attempts to access protected areas of memory. The monitor attempts to provide error recovery along with diagnostics.

monitor system The hardware and software used to control computer system functions. The monitor system can simulate the processor, maintain continuity between jobs, observe and report on the status of input/output devices, and provide automatic accounting of jobs.

A time-sharing monitor system usually remains permanently in memory to provide overall coordination and control of the total operating system. It allows several user programs to be loaded simultaneously into memory and prevents one user's program from interfering with another's during execution and control of all input/output devices.

monochromator A device for converting a heterogeneous beam of radiation (electromagnetic or particulate) to a homogeneous beam by the absorption or refraction of unwanted components.

monochrome connector A 9-pin connector, as shown in the figure. The functions of the pins are as follows:

- Pin 1: Ground
- Pin 2: Ground
- Pin 3: Not used
- Pin 4: Not used
- Pin 5: Not used
- Pin 6: Intensity
- Pin 7: Video
- Pin 8: Horizontal sync
- Pin 9: Vertical sync

monochrome CRT A screen display with a single-color phosphor, usually green, amber, or white. At the other end of the cathode-ray tube is the electron gun. It sends a beam of electrons to the face of the tube that lights up the phosphor and causes it to glow. The beam lights up only a small dot on the screen at any one time.

monolithic Refers to fabrication on a single silicon chip.

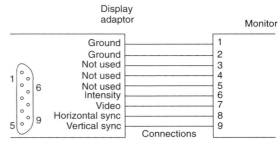

Monochrome monitor connections

monolithic integrated circuit An integrated circuit in which both active and passive elements are simultaneously formed in a single, small wafer of silicon by diffusion techniques. Metallic stripes are then evaporated onto the oxidized surface of the silicon to interconnect the elements.

monolithic microcircuit A semiconductor microcircuit in which circuit elements are not readily identified as individual components. Also called *molecular electronics* or *monolithic circuit*.

monolithic storage A computer memory made up of monolithic integrated circuits.

MONOS Abbreviation for *monitor out of service*.

monostable circuit **1.** A circuit that has one stable state. A monostable circuit repeats one complete cycle of operation for each trigger pulse. **2.** A one-shot multivibrator.

monostable multivibrator A one-shot device that provides a single output pulse for each input trigger pulse. The circuit provides a single signal of proper form and time from a varying shaped, randomly timed signal. Upon receiving a trigger signal, it assumes another state for a specified length of time, at the end of which it returns, of its own accord, to its original state.

Monte Carlo generator A random-number generator or program for obtaining a random number.

Monte Carlo method **1.** A trial-and-error method of obtaining a solution to a problem by repeated calculations. **2.** Any technique for generating a number that is truly random.

MOP Acronym for *Maintenance Operation Protocol*, a special-purpose DECnet protocol used for remote booting on the node and attaching a console onto a station remotely.

MORE A command in DOS and OS/2 that displays one screen of information at a time. When you press any key, the next screen of information appears.

more properties In NetWare Bindery Services, a flag that indicates if more properties exist for this object.

more segments In NetWare Bindery Services, a flag set to true (FFh) if there are more 128-byte value segments for a property.

morph A computer graphic technique that creates a series of images that transition one image to another.

MOS Acronym for *metal-oxide semiconductor*, a basic technology for fabricating integrated active devices employing FETs (field-effect transistors) in any of a variety of different configurations, as shown in the following figure. MOS devices tend to have a high capacitance, which makes them slower than their bipolar counterparts; however, MOS devices achieve a higher functional density with fewer process steps, so fabrication costs are lower.

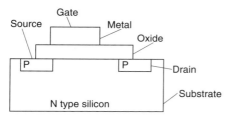

MOS structure

To make a MOS circuit, a single crystal of silicon must be grown. This crystal is then cut into thin circular slices called *wafers*. The crystal must be cut in a specific direction of the crystal lattice. Several hundred chips can be made from a wafer. These chips may be used for microprocessors, memory, or other functions. MOS devices employ field-effect transistors in one of three functional configurations: NMOS, PMOS, and CMOS (for negative, positive, and complementary).

Mosaic A graphical Internet interface.

mosaic A photoelectric pattern composed of a large number of photoemissive granules on an insulating support.

mosaic detector A detector containing a number of active elements arranged in an array. It is generally used as an imaging device.

MOS character generator An LSI (large-scale integration) device that uses MOS circuitry to generate the voltage patterns required to form numbers, letters, and symbols for visual displays.

MOS DMOS A double-diffused MOS (metal-oxide semiconductor) device. The second diffusion process results in a product capable of handling higher voltages and currents with very little parasitic capacitance and low noise.

MOS (DMOS) transistors An insulated gated FET in which the insulating layer between each gate electrode and the channel is an oxide material or an oxide and nitride material. Double-diffused MOS transistors that have been used in a noninvasive, nonradiating imaging system for observing the body's internal organs. Operating prototypes of this ultrasonic imaging system have been used by cardiologists to observe human heart action in real time. A two-dimensional 10 × 10 array of piezoelectric transducers are sequentially excited by bursts of energy at about 3 MHz. Each element transmits an ultrasound pulse into the region of interest in the body. Echoes from tissue interfaces are focused back to the array, are time-gated out, and undergo the appropriate signal processing. When the array is scanned in time periods much shorter than the cardiac cycle, real-time images of heart movement can be displayed.

MOSFET Acronym for *metal-oxide-semiconductor field-effect transistor*, a field-effect transistor made from a sandwich of metal and oxide layers.

MOSFET multiplexer A multiplexer with reversed biased diodes that protect the input channels from being damaged by overvoltage signals. The input channels are protected for up to 20 V beyond the supplies and can be increased by adding series resistors (Ri) to each channel. This input resistor limits the current flowing through the protection diodes to 10 mA. See the diagram that follows.

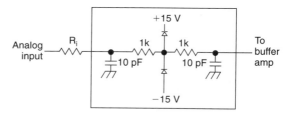

MOSFET equivalent circuit

MOS memory A computer storage medium that uses MOS LSI devices rather than devices such as disks.

MOS ROM Acronym for *metal-oxide-semiconductor read-only memory*, a storage medium that uses MOS transistor cells to store binary ones and zeros.

MOST Acronym for *metal-oxide-semiconductor transistor*.

MOS technology 6500 (*o.t.*) A family of 8-bit microprocessors produced using n-channel MOS with silicon gate processing. Ten CPU devices were available, with various options including addressable memory (4K to 65K), interrupts, and on-chip oscillators, and drivers. These ten

CPU devices were software-compatible among themselves and bus compatible with the 6800 series.

MOS transistor *See* MOSFET.

most significant bit *See* MSB.

motherboard The main board in a computer into which the circuits are plugged.

motor control system applications Microcomputers find many uses in stepping motor controls. The microcomputer can be used with hardwired logic to advance the motor by a step when an output appears from a state generator.

The logic sequence can also be stored in memory, and one bit sent out at a time. A step counter can be used to ensure that the motor goes through the correct number of steps. Two modes of operation may be used: constant speed operation and automatic acceleration and deceleration. In the constant speed mode, the motor covers the steps at a constant rate. The acceleration-deceleration mode uses progressively decreasing time delays between steps to increase the stepping rate.

Motorola DMA controller A cycle-stealing DMA controller, shown in the figure below.

Motorola 6800 (*o.t.*) An 8-bit NMOS single-chip microprocessor made by Motorola. A typical microprocessor like the 6800 has eight pins to which wires are attached for the movement of data into and out of the device. These eight wires constitute the data bus, and information can flow in both directions along the bus (during different times). This technique is called *multiplexing*. In addition to the data bus, microprocessors like the 6800 have a group of 16 pins to which wires can be attached that move binary words called *addresses*; together they are called the *address bus*. The address bus carries information outward only from the microprocessor to memory and input/output chips. The sig-

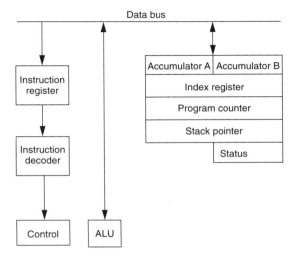

6800 architecture

nals on the address bus are used to select a certain part of memory or I/O section. The architecture of such chips as the 6800 is shown in the following figure.

There is also a group of assorted control signals that enter and leave the microprocessor. Some of these may carry control signals back and forth between the microprocessor and the memory and I/O chips. They are usually grouped together and called the *control bus*.

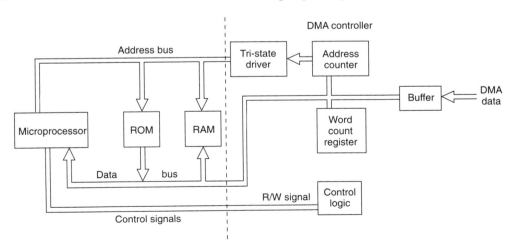

6800 DMA controller operation

Other wires may go back and forth between the microprocessor and support chips. No connection is made directly to the registers, the ALU, or other internal components.

Motorola 6800 interfacing (*o.t.*) The 6800 used the 6820 PIA (peripheral interface adapter) to interface with I/O equipment. The control bus channeled the data flow in the PIA's data bus, and the address bus let the 6800 read or write into the PIA's registers, which were divided into two independent sections, each with a control data and address register.

Motorola 6800 UART (*o.t.*) In the 6800, the UART (universal asynchronous transmitter-receiver) chip is an *asynchronous interface adapt-er*, or *ACIA*. The ACIA operates by placing the eight-bit byte into a shift register. Then the bits are shifted one bit at a time each time the register is shifted. The shifting is done in synchronism with a clock pulse, which comes from the device or was generated locally.

The ACIA also has a data register to accept the eight-bit byte from the microprocessor data bus and store it until the shift register is ready for it. This tends to smooth out the transmission rate of the bits. While the shift register is shifting, the data register can accept the next eight bits. When the shift register is finished, the movement of data from the data register to the shift register is done by the chip to keep the flow of bits uninterrupted.

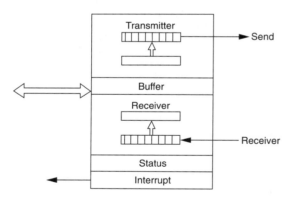

ACIA functions

Motorola 6801 (*o.t.*) A chip containing 2,048 bytes of mask-programmable ROM, 128 bytes of RAM, a 16-bit counter/timer, a UART (universal asynchronous transmitter-receiver), 31 parallel I/O lines, and an expanded instruction set of the 6800. It was expandable to 64k words.

The basic architecture of the 6801 microcomputer is shown in the following figure. In addition to the 6800 CPU, the program memory,

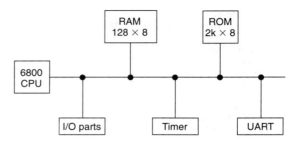

6801 microcomputer

scratchpad memory, counter, clock oscillator, UART, and I/O ports are on the microcomputer chip.

Motorola 6802 (*o.t.*) A second version of the 6800 including all of the features of the 6800 along with an on-chip clock oscillator and 128 bytes of RAM.

Motorola 6803 (*o.t.*) A chip similar to the 6801 except that it did not have on-chip ROM storage, and some of the port lines were used as a multiplexed data and address bus. The 6803 had a 16-bit counter/timer, 13 parallel I/O lines, UART, clock, and a 128-byte RAM.

Motorola 6809 (*o.t.*) A 16-bit internal version of the 6800. It used an extended 6800 instruction set with instructions like 8-by-8 bit multiply; it had 16-bit modes with the same mnemonics as the 6800. The 6809 also had a number of long branch instructions, which were absent in the 6800.

An additional addressing mode in the 6809 was auto-increment addressing. This capability improved the software in sequential indexing applications since index updating commands were not required. A new SYNC instruction stopped the processor until an interrupt occurred to resume processing. This instruction could be used to synchronize the processor to real-time events in a system.

Motorola 6820 control register (*o.t.*) A control register of the format shown in the following figure. Bit 7 indicates a transition of the CA1 input, and is used as an interrupt flag. Bit 6 monitors the CA2 input. Bits 5, 4, and 3 estab-

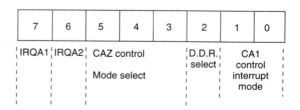

6820 control register

lish the eight different modes of the device and the function of the CA2 pin. Bit 2 indicates if the direction register or data register is to be selected. Bits 1 and 0 are the interrupt enable/disable control bits.

Motorola 6820 PIA (*o.t.*) A double I/O chip with two sets of eight lines, as shown in the figure. Each 6820 PIA (peripheral interface adapter) had two data registers, or peripheral registers, as they are called. One was used for each set of input/output lines. There were also two other registers used with each peripheral register, resulting in a total of six for each PIA.

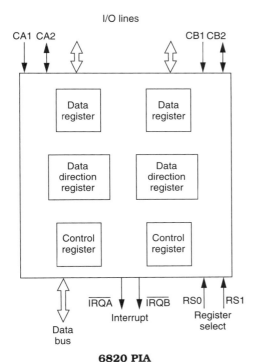

6820 PIA

Motorola 10800 The Motorola 10800 4-bit slice uses emitter-coupled logic (ECL) to achieve high-speed performance. A 48-pin quad inline package is used and both lateral and vertical expansion are allowed. Lateral expansion can be used to increase the bit length in increments of 4 bits and vertical expansion can be used to increase throughput by pipelining.

The 10800 arithmetic logic unit is combined with a microprogram control unit, a timer unit, and a memory interface unit for the microprogrammed system. The memory and register file complete the configuration.

The ALU components include a 4-bit adder, which uses a shift network and accumulator for arithmetic operations. A latch and multiplex system are used to control data flow within the ALU, and bus control logic is used to control the flow of data over the input and output busses.

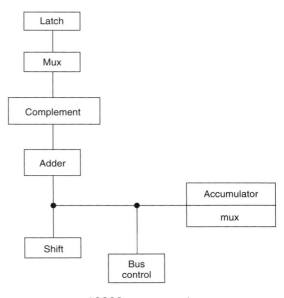

10800 components

Motorola 10801 A microprogram control unit designed as a component for the 10800 microprocessor system, but which may also be used as an independent device for controller applications. The 10801 contains bit-control registers expandable to any number of bits. It also contains a control memory address register and a 4-bit, 4-deep LIFO stack register for subroutine nesting. Sixteen address control functions are used for jumps, which may be conditional or unconditional, and for subroutine control. This chip also has an internal instruction register, a repeat register, and a 4-bit status register.

A single 10801 allows addressing of 256 words using row and column jumps. Two chips allow addressing for 65,536 words. A two-chip system also allows eight-way branching for three separate branch inputs. Multiple chip operation uses the extender bus.

Motorola 10802 A timer unit that contains a four-phase counter with a start synchronizer for ECL circuit chips. The phases, as well as the phase time, are programmable. One control function allows the microprocessor to be stepped through a routine for diagnostic testing.

Motorola 10803 An ECL memory interface unit used as an interface between memory and processor for generating memory addresses and routing data. It contains an ALU for generating memory addresses, which also may be used as the primary ALU in a simple system. It contains the memory address register, the memory data register, and a set of four 4-bit register files for minimum systems. The 10803 can perform 17 transfer or store operations for data manipulation and 12 register/bus/ALU functions.

Motorola 68000 A 16-bit microprocessor with an external 16-bit bus that is multiplexed from the 32 bits inside. A 32-bit ALU is used. The sixteen 32-bit registers of the 68000 are partitioned into eight data registers and seven address registers. An eighth address register exists as a stack pointer. The data registers can be addressed as byte, word, or double-word registers. The address registers are used for 32-bit base addressing, 32-bit software stack operations, and word or long word address operations. The stack pointers are used for the 32-bit base addressing and word or long word address operations.

The 68000 structure has the CPU centered around the microprogram-controlled execution unit. Control-store area size is minimized by the use of a two-level control structure. First, machine instructions are produced by sequences of microinstructions in the microcontrol program. (These microinstructions are actually addresses to nanoinstructions in the nanocontrol program.) This memory contains a set of machine state words to control the executing unit. Information that is timing-independent bypasses the control programs and is transmitted directly to the execution unit. About 22.5K bits of control memory is used, 50% less than required for a one-level implementation.

Since the two-level structure increases access time, an effort has been made to reduce this effect by a pipelined architecture, in which the instruction fetch, decode, and execute cycles are overlapped.

Motorola 68010 A variation of the 68000 microprocessor.

Motorola 68020 A variation of the 68000 used in the Apple Macintosh personal computer.

Mott scattering formula A formula that gives the differential cross-section for the scattering of identical particles arising from a coulomb interaction.

mount Term used in the Network File System for making a remote file system appear as if it were a local disk drive.

mouse A remote-control pointing device, originally popularized by the Macintosh computer, that moves the cursor across the screen as it is moved by hand across a flat surface. Commands are executed by clicking one of the buttons on the mouse. A mouse might have one, two, or three buttons, and come with software that enables a user to design popup menus for use with other programs. A typical mouse design is shown in the figure.

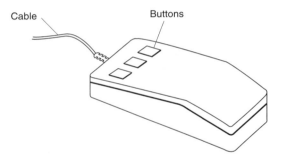

Typical mouse

An *optical mouse* has no moving parts and provides an accurate tracking of movement. The movement is read by an electronic sensor on a special surface rather than by a rolling ball.

MouseWrapper.h++ A software partner to View.h++, supplying the Model and View components of a Model-View-Controller architecture. It includes a variety of graphics primitives such as circles, polygons, and rectangles. All objects are full persistent, using Tools.h++'s powerful store/retrieve architecture. It includes a presentation system for managing object picks, drags, and rubber banding.

move A command used to change data from one position to another.

moving-domain memory See MOD.

MPC Abbreviation for *multimedia PC*.

MPC Level 2 A multimedia standard requiring a Windows-based PC with at least a 25-MHz, 486SX processor, 4M of RAM (8M recommended);

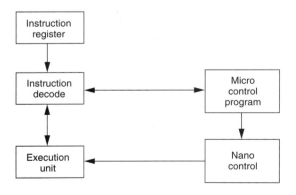

68000 structure

a 16-bit video card (65,000 colors) at 640 × 480 resolution; a 160M hard disk; a double-speed CD-ROM drive (400-ms seek time, 300Kbps transfer rate) that is multisession compatible; and a 16-bit, 44-kHz, MIDI-compatible sound card.

MPC Level 3 A multimedia standard requiring a Windows-based PC with a minimum 50 MHz 486 CPU with 8M of RAM, a hardware-accelerated video card, and a hard disk at least 240M. The hard disk should have an average access time below 20 ms. DSP-based audio cards or those that employ wavetable synthesis (where the sounds are sampled from real instruments) are also part of this standard.

Video requirements vary. If the user plans on working with 24-bit graphics (a 16.8 million color palette), 16-bit audio or digital video, bigger disks are always best. VESA or PCI cards are best since they utilize the faster bus speeds. If photo CDs are used, 24-bit video card ensures photorealistic quality.

MPI Abbreviation for *multiple protocol interface*, the upper portion of the Link Support Layer standard from Novell and Apple. This interface describes how transport service providers interact with the Link Support Layer.

MPR Abbreviation for *multiport repeater*, a unit that can be used to connect Ethernet LAN segments. The repeaters carry out preamble regeneration, fragment extension, and signal regeneration. Automatic partitioning and reconnection are provided so that a faulty segment can be isolated from the network.

MPS Abbreviation for *microprocessor system*.

MPT Abbreviation for *multiport transceiver*, several Ethernet transceivers built into one device. It can operate as a concentrator on a cable or as a standalone Ethernet (known as "Ethernet in a can").

MP tandem A 20 million volt particle accelerator used for neutron research.

MPU Abbreviation for *microprocessor unit*, the main part of the hardware for a microcomputer. The MPU consists of the microprocessor, the main memory, input/output ports, and the clock circuit. It does not contain power supplies, enclosure, or control panel, and it is usually on a single circuit board. The level of complexity of the microcomputer is a direct function of the MPU.

MQ Abbreviation for *multiplier quotient*.

MRP Abbreviation for *materials requirements planning*, computer applications where current inventory and production schedules determine the purchase and delivery of raw materials.

ms Abbreviation for millisecond.

MSB Abbreviation for *most significant bit*, the leftmost bit in a word. The MSB contributes the most weight to the numerical value of the word in most codes.

MS-DOS *See* DOS.

MS-DOS.SYS One of MS-DOS's system files. It must be part of each bootable disk.

MSI Abbreviation for *medium-scale integration*, that level of active-device integration that yields more than 100 but less than 1,000 active devices on a single substrate.

MSK 1. Abbreviation for *minimum shift keying*, a type of digital modulation that uses offset quadrature phase-shift keying (QPSK) with sinusoidal pulse shaping. **2.** A special case of frequency-shift keying (FSK) in which continuous phase is maintained at symbol transitions.

MS-NET An operating system developed by Microsoft that runs under MS-DOS to provide execution of the top three layers of the OSI network model. *Also see* OSI MODEL.

MTBF Abbreviation for *mean-time-between-failures*, the average time between failure taken as a function of the operating time. The MTBF represents the expected failure-free operating time for the equipment. Also called *mean-time-to-failure (MTTF)*.

MTBO Abbreviation for *mean-time-between-outages*, for a specific interval, the ratio of total operating time to the number of outages in the same interval.

MTL Abbreviation for *merged transistor logic*, a type of logic that uses multicollector transistors. *Also see* INTEGRATED-INJECTION LOGIC.

MTSR Abbreviation for *mean-time-to-service-restoral*, the mean time to restore service following system failures that result in a service outage. The time to restore includes all time from the occurrence of the failure until the restoral of service.

MTTF *See* MTBF.

MTTR Abbreviation for *mean-time-to-repair*, the total corrective-maintenance time divided by the total number of corrective-maintenance actions during a given period of time.

MU Abbreviation for *machine unit*.

mu-circuit The part of a feedback amplifier in which the vector sum of the input signal and that of the feedback portion of the output is amplified.

mu-factor The voltage amplification factor of grid to anode (or another grid), the current, and all other voltages being constant.

multiaccess Descriptive of a system that permits several users to interact with a single central computer using a number of online terminals. Access points are connected to the central processor by data transmission lines from remote terminals. Most multiaccess systems operate in a conversational mode with a fast response time.

multiaddress An instruction format that contains more than one address part.

multiaspect Descriptive of searches or systems that allow more than one facet of information to be used to identify and select operations.

multibus The bus structure for interfacing Intel's 8080/8586 products. It supports a 1M address space. The 8289 bus arbiter controls accesses by multiple processors. The control lines use a master/slave concept: a master processor takes control of the bus, then the slave device (I/O or memory) acts upon the command provided by the master. An asynchronous handshaking protocol allows units of different speeds to use the bus.

multicast The technique of sending messages to a defined group of users on the network.

multichannel A system that divides the frequency spectrum of a signal into a number of bands that are separately transmitted and then recombined.

multichannel current loop/EIA interface converter A unit that performs bidirectional conversion between EIA RS-232 and current loops. It is available in 4-, 8-, 12-, and 16-channel units. It is an economical approach to multichannel conversions.

multichip IC An integrated circuit that uses two or more semiconductor chips in a single package.

multidrop Refers to a communication bus that supports several devices that branch off of the bus. The *drop* is a branch off of the bus. A multidrop configuration, shown in the following figure, is also called a *data bus, data highway,* or *multipoint* configuration. The host controls the flow of data between any two nodes. Any satellite can communicate with the host or any other satellite at any one time.

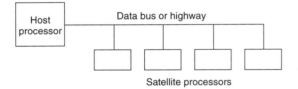

Multidrop network configuration

Multi-Edit-Lite An editor developed for environments where disk space may be limited, like a laptop. It has macro and mouse support, multiple windows, and dialog boxes. You can edit 25 files at once. It supports EMS/XMS with auto-error location for most compilers.

multifiber cable An optical cable that contains two or more fibers, each of which provides a separate information channel.

multifunction drive A drive that can handle write-once media (WORM) as well as rewritable media. *Also see* WORM.

multifunction lamination A technique that makes it possible to combine materials with different mechanical and electrical properties into a single, easy-to-handle sub-assembly. Designers can reduce the cost of assembling electronic products by replacing separate vibration dampers, electrical contacts, insulators, and EMI/RFI shields with laminated components.

multifunction TDR A time-delay relay that combines the functions and ranges of many different timers into one timer. It features five operating logics and time ranges from 50 ms to over 16 hours.

multilayer board *See* MLB.

multilevel address *See* INDIRECT ADDRESS.

multimedia cards A card that plugs into a microcomputer to provide video I/O. Better compression techniques, either hardware- or software-based, results in fluidity to motion video and fewer visual flaws, called *artifacts*. JPEG is the most common; Indeo, DVI, and Video 1 are newer schemes. Image quality is also rising. Color depth, a function of the number of colors captured, has improved with 16 bits per pixel providing 32,000 to 64,000 colors and 24 bits providing millions of hues. The resolution offered by cards can go up to 1,024 × 678, for full-screen, full-motion at acceptable quality you need 640 × 480.

A frame rate of 30 fps (frames per second) is required, although some cards feature 60 fields per second, which is true broadcast quality. For most multimedia purposes, 30 fps is more than adequate and is the rate found on CD-ROM based video clips.

Many cards offer extra features like audio capture and video overlay. International applications need a card that supports SECAM broadcast video input in addition to PAL and NTSC. Output to NTSC/PAL is vital to those who wish to save their finished material onto videotape via a VCR.

multimedia networks Systems that include video servers, CD-ROM networks, and media-on-demand. The simplest network is one that accesses a CD jukebox. CD-ROM caching and data prefetch may also be used. Since the access time for a CD-ROM drive may average 20 times slower than that of a hard disk, caching is used to store recently and frequently used instructions and data in high-speed, extended memory for faster retrieval. *Data prefetch* monitors data requests and learns to predict what data will be asked for, storing it in a memory buffer. The result is a much more responsible CD-ROM network.

Companies like DEC and Novell offer video-server software products. Fiber is best, since it offers the bandwidth and speed to handle future applications and technologies, but it is expensive. Hybrid systems use fiber-optic backbones or trunks linked to coax or copper lines to feed the signals into regional or individual sites.

multimedia programming A trend in GUI programming. In multimedia programming, computers add animation and sound to their graphic interface.

multimode device A machine that is able to emulate several other machines or adapt its functions to a wide variety of situations.

multimode dispersion In an optical fiber, the dispersion resulting from the different arrival times of optical rays that follow different paths.

multimode fiber A fiber that supports propagation of more than one mode at a given wavelength.

multipath fading The fading that results when signals reach a receiving antenna by two or more paths.

multiphase program A program in absolute form that requires more than one fetch or load operation to complete the execution.

multiple access unit See MAU.

multiple address code An instruction code in which an instruction word may specify more than one address to be used during the operation. Examples include the *two-address* code and the *four-address* code. In a typical instruction of a *four- address* code, the addresses specify the following:

- The location of the two operands
- The location where results are stored
- The location of the next instruction

multiple base pages In multiuser systems, each user can have a complete base page while the system also maintains a base page. The large space for base page links or direct addressing for both user and system allows users to write large programs without linking or common area limitations.

multiple bus structure A bus structure in which any memory module may send or receive information from several processors operating concurrently.

multiple channel system A system in which parts of the data acquisition chain are usually shared by two or more input sources. The sharing may occur in a number of ways, depending on the desired specifications of the system. Large systems might combine several different types of multiplexing and perhaps even use cascaded tiers of the same type.

multiple console terminal eliminator See MCTE.

multiple device Two or more semiconductor chips in a single package, connected together to function as a single unit.

multiple instruction-multiple data A form of parallel processing architecture that uses several processors, each following its own instructions and working on its own problems.

multiple interrupts In systems with several sources of interrupt, one or more interrupt requests may occur during the servicing of an earlier request. In simple systems, the interrupt mask bit is set when the first request is recognized. Subsequent requests are placed in a queue, waiting until the service of the first interrupt is complete before they are recognized and serviced. The order in which the queued interrupts are recognized determines the time delay before service. This order, or priority, is dictated either by software or by hardware with software priority. After recognizing an interrupt request, the service program can poll the devices in an order that determines the interrupt priority of each device. The devices polled first are serviced first.

multiple link interface See MLI.

multiple link interface driver See MLID.

multiple modulation A modulation technique that uses a succession of modulation processes in which the wave from one stage becomes the modulating wave for the next stage. For example, PPM-AM is a system where pulse-position modulation is used to amplitude-modulate a carrier.

multiple-precision The use of two or more words to represent a quantity or numeral, resulting in increased accuracy for computation.

multiple programming Programming that allows two or more logic or arithmetic operations to be executed simultaneously.

multiple protocol interface See MPI.

multiple system A computer system that contains two or more CPUs with I/O devices and other hardware units that are related and interconnected for simultaneous operation.

multiplex data terminal A device that transfers data from units operating at low transfer rates to units operating at high transfer rates in such a way that the high-speed devices are not required to wait for the low-speed units.

multiplexed operation Refers to simultaneous operations that share the use of a common unit in such a way that they are considered independent operations.

multiplexed sampling S/D converter A circuit like the one in the figure, in which a pair of sample-holds are switched from input to input, where each is sampled and its value held during conversion, which takes less than one carrier cycle. The sampling is done at the peak of the carrier cycle.

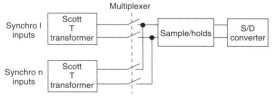

Multiplexed sampling S/D converter system

multiplexer A device that samples a number of channels and produces data that is the composite of all sampled channels, for transmission over a single channel. On reception, *demultiplexing* recreates all original channels. When more than one channel of data requires analog to digital conversion, it is necessary to use time-division or multiplex the analog inputs to a single converter, or to provide a converter for each input and then combine the converter outputs by digital multiplexing. See the following figure.

multiplexer channel A channel designed to operate with a number of devices simultaneously. A multiplexer channel allows several devices to transfer records at the same time by interleaving items of data. The multiplexer channel acts as a communications coordinator in many complex system configurations.

multiplexer polling A method of polling that allows each remote multiplexer to query the terminals connected to it. Multiplexer polling is usually more efficient than polling from a central computer, since it involves fewer control messages.

multiplexer settling time The time required for the analog signal to settle to within its error budget, as measured at the input to the converter. In a 12-bit system, with a ±10-V range, the multiplexer units typically settle within one microsecond, and a typical conversion time might be 20 microseconds.

multiplexing The process of transmitting more than one signal at a time over a single channel, usually by sequentially sampling all signals and coding them into a single data stream. Frequency-division multiplexing (*FDM*) allows a

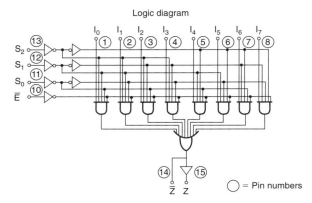

H = HIGH voltage level
L = LOW voltage level
X = Level does not affect output.

Multiplexer

number of devices to share a link by dividing its frequency spectrum into a number of subchannels. Time-division multiplexing (*TDM*) assigns a time slot into which each device may place information. *Also see* FDM *and* TDM.

multiplication 1. The secondary emission of electrons due to impact of primary electrons on a surface. It varies from zero for graphite, to 1.3 for nickel, and up to 12.3 for nickel-beryllium alloys. 2. The ratio of neutron flux in a subcritical reactor to that supplied by the neutron source alone. It is equal to $1(1 - k)$, where k is the multiplication constant. 3. The logic operation that makes use of the logical product and is given by the following table. It is the same as the AND operation.

Multiplier	Multiplicand	Logical Product
0	0	0
1	0	0
0	1	0
1	1	1

multiplication shift A shift that results in multiplication of the number by a positive or negative integral power of the radix.

multiplication time The time required to perform a multiply operation. In most binary operations, it is equal to the total of all addition times and shift times.

multiplier A device that generates a product from two numbers. A digital multiplier generates the product from two digital numbers by additions of the multiplicand in accordance with the value of the digits in the multiplier. It then shifts the multiplicand and adds it to the product if the multiplier digit is a one, or shifts without adding if the digit is a zero. This is done for each successive digit of the multiplier.

multiplier-quotient register A register in which the multiplier for multiplication is placed, and the quotient for division is developed.

multiply-divide instruction An instruction or set of instructions that allow multiply and divide operations directly. Multiply and divide instructions are standard or optional on some microcomputers.

multiply-divide package A collection of subroutines that perform single- and double-precision multiplication and division for signed and unsigned binary numbers. The multiply-divide package is usually supplied in the form of a source program with an assembly listing for the specific microcomputer.

multiplying D/A converters A special class of digital-to-analog converters with the capability of handling variable reference sources. Their output value is the product of the number represented by the digital input code and the analog reference voltage, which may vary from full scale to zero, and in some cases, to negative values.

multipoint line A single communications line or circuit interconnecting several stations. The use of this type of line usually requires some kind of polling mechanism to address each terminal with a unique address code.

multipoint network A type of network with multiple slaves. In this network, a single processor has control and determines which slave computer shall operate on a task. Communications between slave computers is under control of the master. After it is assigned a task, the slave proceeds asynchronously with respect to the master until completion of the task, or until it requires services from the meter. *Also see* MASTER-SLAVE NETWORK.

multipole moments Magnetic and electric measures of charge. These static multipole moments determine the interaction of the system with weak external fields. There are also transition multipole moments that determine radiative transitions between two states.

multiport register A register that is capable of reading two locations while writing one location. A typical 8-bit multiport register uses two sets of eight latches for address selection, as shown in the figure on page 336.

multiport repeater *See* MPR.

multiport transceiver *See* MPT.

multiprocessing The use of more than one independent processor and the processing of several programs or program segments concurrently. Each processor is active on only one program at any one time, while operations such as I/O transfers are performed in parallel on the programs. The processor can address adjacent storage modules in an odd or even fashion to reduce storage access conflicts in a multiprocessing system. Modules 0, 2, 4, and 6 would be referenced for even addresses, while modules 1, 3, 5, and 7 are referenced for odd addresses.

Multiprocessing microcomputer systems can be used to provide increased computing power, but hardware and software costs can outweigh the advantages compared to larger computers. *Also see* INTERLEAVING MULTIPROCESSING.

multiprocessor operating modes Multiprocessor systems may use a number of operating modes. The processors may cooperate in solving a problem that requires more computing speed than a single processor provides. Each processor can control a portion of the process. The necessary coordination may be effected through the interconnection.

multiprocessor systems Systems that use more than one CPU in the system configuration.

multiprogramming The concurrent execution of two or more programs. Multiprogramming generally uses overlapping or interleaving techniques to allow more than one program to time-share machine components. *Also see* MASTER-SLAVE MULTIPROGRAMMING.

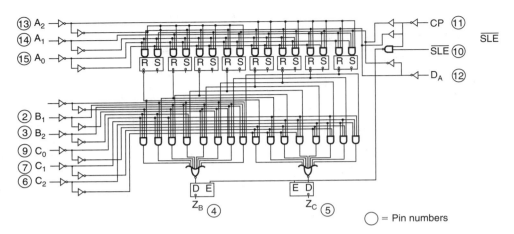

Multiport register

multiprogramming executive A software block that provides the operating system for concurrent execution of more than one program. A typical multiprogramming executive includes a priority scheduler along with memory allocation and deallocation.

multiprotocol router A device used to connect two LANs together. A regular router moves signals from one LAN to the other, while the multiprotocol router can move signals between dissimilar LANs. For example, a multiprotocol router can move data between a token ring LAN and an Ethernet LAN.

multiscanning monitor A monitor that can read more than one frequency. Some multiscanning monitors can read frequencies for both analog and digital signals, others can read frequencies for analog signals only. They are sometimes mistakenly referred to as "multisync monitors," but multisync is a specific type of multiscanning monitor manufactured by NEC.

multisegment Ethernet Several segments of Ethernet connected together with repeaters. All signals broadcast on a multisegment Ethernet are received by all other nodes. This is in contrast to the extended Ethernet, where the MAC-layer bridge forwards only those packets designated for the other Ethernet.

multistage 1. A control system that uses several levels of gain or amplification. **2.** A tube in which the electrons are progressively accelerated by anode rings held at increasing potentials.

multistatement transaction Several different interactions with a database grouped into a single transaction. If any one of the operations is not carried out because of a user abort or system crash, the entire transaction is rolled back. In a multistatement transaction, all or none of the operations are carried out.

multistate noise Refers to noise that is found occasionally in transistors and more often in diodes. It consists of erratic switching that is generated within the device at various sharply defined levels of applied current.

Multi-Tags A hypertext-style source code locator and browser for Multi-Edit. It scans the source code and builds databases of functions, structures, types, and objects (depending on language). Features include a database browser that lets you view, navigate through, and maintain databases, support for multiple-tag databases, and support for C/C++, CMAC, Turbo Pascal, ASM, Paradox, Quick-Pascal, Modula-2, dBASE, Clipper, and FoxBase.

multitasking The procedures in which several separate but interrelated tasks operate within a single program identity. Multitasking differs from multiprogramming in that common routines and disk files may be used. Multitasking may or may not involve multiprocessing.

multitasking operating system An operating system desirable in applications that have a significant number of random, asynchronous inputs, as shown in the following figure. Most of these applications have sections that are functionally similar and an overall organization that is structurally similar.

multithread A section of a program that can have more than one logical path through it executed simultaneously.

multitrace oscilloscope A device used to check the timing between critical chips such as the microprocessor and the memory.

multiuser The ability to have more than one person using the resources of the computer at one time.

multivariable control A control technique that uses built-in intelligence to simultaneously

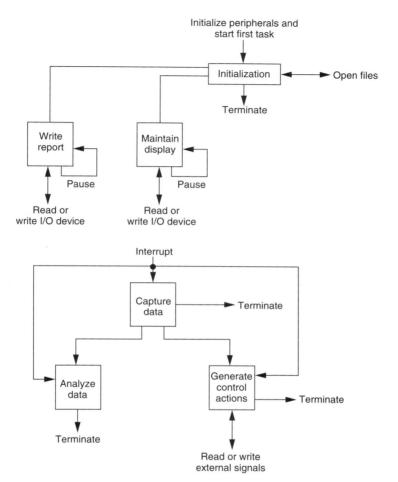

Multitasking operating systems

monitor many variables and to choose, based on the situation, the optimum of several programmed control strategies.

multivibrator An electronic switching circuit with two distinct states. When the device alternates rapidly between the two states, with no external crystal for frequency control, it is said to be *free-running*. When it is crystal-controlled, it is usually called an *oscillator*. When one of the two states is stable, it is called a *one-shot*. When both states are stable, it is called a *flip-flop*. In the free-running or crystal-controlled state, the multivibrator is said to be *astable*. As a one-shot, it is said to be *monostable*. As a flip-flop, it is considered *bistable*.

multiwire PC board process A wiring process that involves a customized pattern of insulated wires

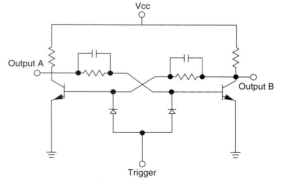

Multivibrator

laid down on an adhesive coated substrate. Multiwire competes with multilayer boards (MLB) in two areas: packaging density and as an interconnection method for high-speed bipolar logic. Some multiwire boards with an etched ground and powerplane and signal layers on each side are the equal of a six-layer MLB. Equivalents of a 12-layer MLB are also available.

MUMPS Acronym for *Massachusetts General Hospital Utility Multi-Programming System*, a high-level interactive programming language developed for use in hospitals to manage databases and develop medical application programs.

MUSE A manuscript tracking program.

MUSIC A program that provides keyboard access to the PC's built-in Play command. It allows you to enter one note at a time and lets you select the note on a regular music-sheet type display.

musical instrument digital interface See MIDI.

muting Refers to the suppression of an electronic signal to improve the signal/noise ratio.

mutual inductance The generation of an electromotive force in one conductor by a variation of current in another conductor that is linked to the first conductor by magnetic flux.

mutual synchronization A network synchronizing arrangement in which each clock in the network exerts some degree of control on all others.

MUX Abbreviation for *multiplex, multiplexing,* or *multiplexer.*

MVPEGA Multiple display requirements for EGA resolution applications can be satisfied with this display adapter. Each attached monitor may be set up for different display modes utilizing the individual RAM areas of the board. Display updates may be targeted towards selected monitors by writing a single byte to an I/O channel or by "hot key" selection. Two boards may be installed for eight-display capability.

MVPVGA An adapter that offers two or four SVGA-compatible video channels on a single card. Each channel is addressed through application programs to provide four independent displays for complete applications. Switching channels is accomplished by writing a single byte to an I/O channel. Attached monitors may have different display modes assigned. Monitors may be selected individually, or in combinations, for updating the displays. Two boards may be installed for eight display capability.

MVS/TSO Abbreviation for *multiple virtual storage/time sharing option*. MVS is an IBM operating system. TSO is the interactive subsystem, as opposed to a system used for batch processing.

MXR Abbreviation for *mask index register.*

Mylar Tradename for a type of polyester film widely used as a base for magnetic tape and for the dielectric of capacitors.

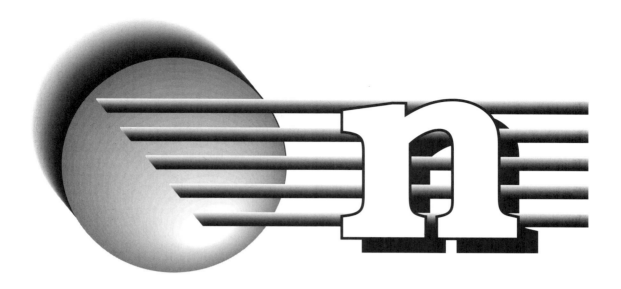

n A notation describing depletion layer behavior in transistors.

NA **1.** Abbreviation for *not assigned.* **2.** Abbreviation for *numerical aperture,* a number that expresses the light-gathering characteristics of an optical fiber, expressed by the sine of the maximum angle (with respect to the fiber axis) at which an entering ray will experience total internal reflection.

NACS Abbreviation for *NetWare asynchronous communications server,* server software that allows a workstation to use outside asynchronous resources such as hosts or modem pools.

NAK Abbreviation for *negative-acknowledge character,* a communication-control signal sent by the receiver as a negative response to the sender. An NAK indicates that the previous block was unacceptable and the receiver is now ready to accept a transmission.

Name Binding Protocol *See* NBP.

named mail slots A quick way for two processes to communicate without a full-duplex channel. The slots are accessed by name.

named pipes A process-to-process protocol that allows a full-duplex communication path to be maintained. The pipe is the endpoint of the communication path, through which a process gains entry to the function. Names are maintained and registered on the network, allowing a pipe to access services.

namespace The collection of names in a computing environment. A data dictionary in a database is an example of a namespace.

NAND flip-flop A flip-flop, such as the R-S type, that can be constructed from NAND gates.

NAND gate The use of an AND gate followed by an inverter, as shown in the figure. If all the inputs

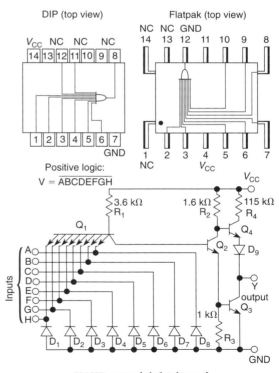

NAND gate (eight-input)

have a value of 1, the output is 0, and if any of the inputs have a value of 0, the output will be 1. This is the opposite of an AND gate. Also called *interval AND*, *negated AND*, and *NOT AND* gate. *Contrast with* AND GATE.

n- and p-channel MOS capacitance When a voltage is applied to the metal gate of a MOS device, a finite amount of time is required to charge the capacitance due to the oxide insulation between the gate and channel. The time taken to charge this capacitance represents the gate settling time. Just as the oxide layer between gate and channel presents a capacitance, the metal oxide substrate formations also present a capacitance, referred to as parasitic capacitance.

nano Prefix for 10^{-9} (a billionth) times a specified unit.

nanocircuit An integrated microelectronic circuit in which each component is fabricated on a separate chip or substrate for maximum high-speed performance.

nanometer A unit of measurement equal to one billionth of a meter.

nanoprocessor A processor that operates with a cycle time in the nanosecond range.

nanosecond An amount of time equal to 10^{-9} second. Abbreviated *ns*.

nanosecond circuit A circuit that processes pulses or waveforms with rise and fall times measured in billionths of a second or less.

Nantucket An extension library for Clipper 5.0. It is optimized to support professional developers and offers solutions that previously required C and assembler expertise.

NAPCAD/3D for Windows A 3D CAD program for Windows, complete with C++ source. It allows advanced surface creation and has editing tools for drawing complex objects. It supports lines, cubic spline curves, circles, polygons, spheres, 3D surface patches, sweeps, and extrusions. It also supports multiple viewpoints, 3D text, hidden surface removal with multiple light sources, and layers.

narrowband Description of the communications channel whose bandwidth is restricted to some specified value less than originally allocated for such channels.

narrowband coder A voice coder with a transmission rate that can be accommodated by 3-kHz telephone channels using modems.

narrowband FSK A form of frequency-shift keying in which the modulation index is much less than one. *Also see* FSK.

NASI See *NetWare Asynchronous Services Interface*.

National Electrical Code *See* NEC.

National Semiconductor IMP 5750 (*o.t.*) The National IMP 5750 register and arithmetic logic unit (RALU) was a microprocessor element utilizing p-channel enhancement-mode, silicon-gate technology. It provided a 4-bit slice of the register and arithmetic portion of a general purpose controller/processor. RALUs could be stacked in parallel for longer word lengths. Each RALU provided 96 bits of storage in the form of four bits in each of seven general registers, a status register, and a 16-word LIFO stack. The ALU performed ADD, AND, OR, and exclusive-OR operations.

National Semiconductor INS8900 The NMOS INS8900 is architecturally similar to the PACE PMOS microprocessor. This NMOS processor is recommended for all applications instead of the PACE. The microprocessor uses an on-chip 10-word stack, indirect addressing, 8- or 16-bit data operation, memory-mapped I/O, four accumulators, and vectored interrupts.

The architecture shown for the INS8900 and PACE provides the 10-word stack as well as four general-purpose registers and a 16-bit status and control flag register. A minimal system consists of the CPU, the clock, and memory.

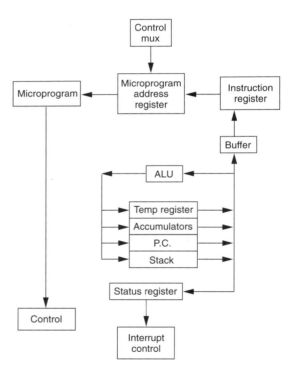

8900 architecture

National Semiconductor NS16000 family In the NS16000 microprocessor chip family, the 16008 and 16016 chips are 8080 code-compatible. The 16008 is designed for eight-bit systems while the 16016 has a 16-bit data bus. The 16032 has an internal 32-bit ALU bus and a direct address range of 16M using 24-bit address pointers. Unlike the 16032 and 16016, the 16008 cannot be used with an MMU to increase the address space beyond 64K.

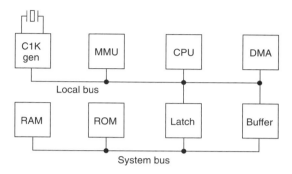

16000 system structure

The 16000 family offers symmetric addressing, including top of stack, memory relative, external, and scaled. This provides modular software capabilities, permitting a user to develop software packages independent of other packages and without regard to individual addressing. This can provide flexibility in system design and lower programming costs.

National Semiconductor SC/MP (*o.t.*) The National Semiconductor SC/MP (simple, cost-effective microprocessor) was an 8-bit PMOS processing unit that used a 16-bit memory bus for addressing up to 64K of memory with four address pointer registers. A preprogrammed, programmable logic array (PLA) was used for instruction decoding.

The instruction set for the SC/MP was smaller than that for most 8-bit microprocessors, with 40 basic instructions. Addressing modes in SC/MP included indexed addressing, auto in-

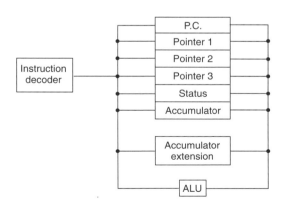

SC/MP architecture

dexed addressing, immediate addressing, and extension register addressing.

native language A communication language or coding between machine units or modules that is peculiar to or usable for a particular class or brand of equipment.

native mode The mode of operation where a device is itself and not emulating another device.

Native NetWare The version of the NetWare operating system marketed by Novell for 80386 and later PCs. Contrast with Portable NetWare, which is a guest on another operating system.

natural binary The most common digital code. In a natural binary code of bits, the most-significant bit has a weight of ½ (2^{-1}), the second bit has a weight of ¼ (2^{-2}) and so on to the least-significant bit, which has a weight of 2^{-n}. The value of the binary number represented is obtained by adding up the weights of the nonzero bits. A 4-bit representation is shown in the following table with the binary weights and the equivalent numbers shown as both decimal and binary fractions.

Decimal Fraction	Binary Fraction	Digital code			
		MSB (× ½)	Bit 2 (× ¼)	Bit 3 (× ⅛)	Bit 4 (× 1/16)
0	0.0000	0	0	0	0
1/16 = 2^{-4} (LSB)	0.0001	0	0	0	1
2/16 = ⅛	0.0010	0	0	1	0
3/16 = ⅛ + 1/16	0.0011	0	0	1	1
4/16 = ¼	0.0100	0	1	0	0
5/16 = ¼ + 1/16	0.0101	0	1	0	1

natural frequency The frequency of free oscillation; thus, the frequency of resonance of any device or circuit.

natural function generator An analog hardware unit or a software program used to solve differential equations using methods based upon physical laws.

natural language A language whose rules reflect and describe current usage rather than prescribed usage.

natural language processor A program within a DBMS (database management system) that allows input of English-language search requests, instead of special commands.

natural noise Noise caused by natural phenomena such as thermal emission or electrical storm static.

NAU Abbreviation for *network-addressable unit*, an SNA component that has an address and can send and receive data to the host, includes logical units (LUs), physical units (PUs) and system service control points (SSCPs).

NBP Abbreviation for *Name Binding Protocol*, the AppleTalk protocol for mapping logical names to network addresses. Similar to SAP in NetWare. *Also see* SAP.

NC 1. Abbreviation for *numerical control*, a system

that uses prerecorded intelligence prepared from numerical data to control a process or machine. **2.** Abbreviation for *normally closed*, used to describe a relay, switch, or solid-state switching device such that the circuit is completed when no input power is applied. **3.** Abbreviation for *no connection*, usually written adjacent to a depicted contact or conductor on a schematic to show that the absence of another conductor is not an inadvertent omission.

n-channel A semiconductor material with n-type dopants, used for the conduction channel in MOS field-effect devices. N-channel MOS devices have several advantages over p-channel types. In particular, the majority carriers are electrons rather than the holes, as in p-channel devices; thus, the mobility is increased, thereby allowing a theoretical improvement in speed. Also, threshold voltages are lower than with p-channel devices, which allows circuits to operate at lower supply voltages. The lower voltages result in fewer parasitic effects and permit tighter packing densities.

Compared to bipolar devices, n-channel MOS offers lower power consumption for the same speed, but bipolar offers higher speed if power is not a consideration.

n-channel enhancement mode A MOSFET (metal-oxide semiconductor field-effect transistor) device that features low switching voltages, fast switching times, low drain source resistance, and low reverse transfer capacitance. Manufactured using the silicon nitride press.

n-channel JFET A junction-type discrete field-effect transistor that uses an n-doped conduction channel. N-channel JFETs are characterized by high gain and low noise.

n-channel modem A modem that uses n-channel MOS circuits. N-channel modems operate from a single power supply and are fully TTL-compatible.

n-channel MOS *See* NMOS.

NCP Abbreviation for *network control program*, a communication system involving VTAM (the virtual telecommunications access method).

NCPMUX Abbreviation for *NetWare core protocols multiplexer*, a software module in Portable NetWare that maintains connections between a single NetWare engine and several clients.

NCR paper The NCR company's brandname for carbonless copying paper; 3M company's Action Paper is another brand.

ND Abbreviation for *no detect*.

NDR Abbreviation for *nondestructive read*, a read operation that does not result in erasure of the data in the source.

NDRO Abbreviation for *nondestructive readout*, a storage medium that cannot be erased and reused.

NDX In some filenaming schemes, an extension indicating an index file associated with a database. Also called *IDX*.

near-end crosstalk Crosstalk that is propagated in a channel in the direction opposite to the direction of propagation of the circuit. The receiving terminals of the disturbed channel and the energized terminals of the disturbing channel are usually near each other in the circuit.

near letter quality *See* NLQ.

NEC Abbreviation for *National Electrical Code*, a code that defines the building restrictions for network cable, as well as the flammability requirements.

negate To perform the logical operation of reversing a signal, condition, or state to its alternate or opposite state.

negation element A device, circuit, or gate capable of reversing a two-state signal, condition, or event into its alternate or opposite state. Also called a *negation gate*.

negative 1. Less than zero, the opposite of positive. **2.** Having surplus of electrons (negative charges). **3.** The minus terminal of a battery or power supply. **4.** The NOT function. A negative-OR gate is the same as a NOT OR or NOR gate; a negative-AND is a NOT AND or NAND.

negative-acknowledge character *See* NAK.

negative bias A potential, negative with respect to ground, applied as a constant voltage to an electronic circuit element for the purpose of keeping the circuit element in a ready-to-operate state. A negative bias on an amplifier input electrode, for example, establishes the operating point of that stage.

negative conductance The use of hot electrons in some form of a two-terminal negative conductance, forming the basis of both avalanche transit time devices and those devices relating to the Gunn effect. In the former, the negative conductance arises from a phase shift (greater than 90° and preferably near to 180°) between current and voltage. In the Gunn devices, it arises within the GaAs crystal in a strong electric field, the local current density decreasing whenever the local electric field exceeds a certain threshold. Other materials showing the Gunn effect are InP, InAs, CdTe and ZnSe.

negative conductor A conductor or cable connected to the negative terminal of a voltage source.

negative crystal A solid-state crystal structure in which the velocity of the extraordinary ray is greater than that of the ordinary ray.

negative electricity The phenomenon in a body due to effects associated with excess of electrons.

negative electrode 1. The anode of a primary cell; the electrode by which conventional current returns to the cell. **2.** The cathode of a tube or voltmeter connected to the negative side of the power supply.

negative feedback A circuit or system in which a part of the output signal is fed back out of phase and summed with the input for control purposes. Negative feedback decreases amplification and distortion because of polarity-difference signal cancellation. Also called *degeneration, inverse feedback,* and *stabilized feedback.*

negative impedance A condition occurring in electronic devices in which an increasing voltage at some point begins to produce a proportionate decrease in current.

negative impedance converter An active network for which a positive impedance connected across one pair of terminals produces a negative impedance across the other pair.

negative ion An atom with more electrons than normal; thus, it has a negative charge.

negative pulse stuffing In time-division multiplexing, the controlled deletion of bits from channel inputs so that the rates of the individual channel inputs correspond to a rate determined by the multiplex equipment. The deleted information is transmitted via a separate overhead channel. *Also see* TDM.

negative resistance *See* NEGATIVE IMPEDANCE.

negative transconductance A property of tubes in which an increase in positive potential on one electrode accompanies a decrease in current flowing to another electrode.

negatron A four-electrode thermionic tube for obtaining negative resistance, comprising an anode and grid on one side of a cathode, and an anode on the other.

NEMA Acronym for *National Electrical Manufacturers Association.*

nesistor A type of transistor that operates as a result of a bipolar field effect.

nest 1. To store subroutines or other data within subroutines or data of a different hierarchy such that the different levels can be accessed or executed recursively. **2.** To store subroutine addresses or general register data in such a fashion that the most recent stored data must be accessed first, and all subsequent data accessed in that same order (the reverse order of storage). **3.** A program technique of enclosing subroutines within program subroutines; the blocks of data or subroutines in the inner "ring" or loop are not necessarily part of the outer ring or loop.

nesting level The relative hierarchical level at which a term or subexpression appears in an expression in assembler programming, or the level at which a macro definition containing an inner macro instruction is processed by an assembler.

nesting loop A loop of instructions that can also include inner loops, nesting subroutines, outer loops, and rules and procedures relating to the in and out procedures for each type.

NET NetBIOS Sniffer Analyzer abbreviation for NetBIOS packets.

NetBEUI The protocol program used by IBM's PC Network LAN software for accessing the network.

NetBIOS Abbreviation for *Network basic input/output system,* an applications programming interface (API) that allows applications programs to communicate with each other. NetBIOS was originally developed for IBM's PC LAN and has become a standard for network communications, with networks using either NetBIOS itself or NetBIOS-compatible emulators. In the OSI model, NetBIOS provides communications at the session layer.

NetBIOS broadcast was propagated In the NetWare File Server Environment, a count of NetBIOS packets propagated through the network.

NetBIOS emulation program One of the components of the NetWare workstation shell files, a program called NETBIOS.EXE. This emulation program allows applications that use the IBM NetBIOS protocols to run with NetWare's IPX/SPX protocols.

NetBIOS propagate count In NetWare Diagnostic Services, the number of times the bridge has received NetBIOS broadcasts since it was initialized.

netiquette A pun on *etiquette,* referring to proper behavior on a network such as the Internet.

NetLib A networking function library that allows the Clipper programmer to do common networking tasks in a multiuser environment. These functions include binary access, directory rights information, user ID, reading and setting drive mapping, semaphore locks, locked-records, log-in/logout, and print capturing. There is support for Novell, Banyan Vines, and NetBIOS networks (some functions are network-specific). The library also provides functions useful in nonnetworked environments, like scatter/gather, transparent DBF encryption, and access to read-only files.

net lines Refers to finished lines of typing of final documents. Also called *net output.*

net loss The sum of gains and losses between two terminals of a device, circuit, or system.

Net/One A family of LAN products from Ungermann-Bass.

NetOptimizer Ontrack Computer software for organizing the file server, reducing access time and improving data recoverability. It can defragment files, arrange them into zones, and protect network data while reorganizing.

NETremote+ Network support software that lets you view users' screens on your screen and control their PCs with your keyboard. It provides diagnostic capabilities that let you check on server connections, LAN adapter and IPX statistics, programs in memory, and other data. It has both dial-in and on-LAN PC control.

NETRJE Abbreviation for *network remote-job entry protocol* in ARPANET.

NETRJS Abbreviation for *network remote-job entry service* developed by UCLA for ARPANET.

Netserial A high-speed interface between serial peripherals and AppleTalk networks. Devices with the standard RS-232 connection can be accessed by each Macintosh on the network.

net station A network workstation designed to operate on a network and use memory and programming functions from the network.

NETUTILS A DOS-based program that allows you to scan through your data, walk through your disk partition-by-partition, and scroll through the sectors, heads, and cylinders.

NetView An IBM network management tool that can collect data from non-IBM, non-SNA devices with NetView/PC.

NetWare A proprietary network, as well as a software operating environment used on top of other vendors' LANs. There are several versions of NetWare for various hardware configurations; the NetWare/S-Net is a star-based baseband network connecting up to 24 microcomputers using dual twisted-pair cable, as shown in the following figure.

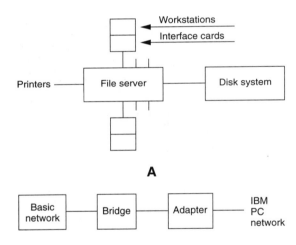

Novell Netware/S networks, basic (a) and advanced (b)

NetWare access server A server that allows dial-in asynchronous access from a workstation to a NetWare network.

NetWare Administrator A program that allows you to set up filters to restrict certain network packet flows. Filters may be selected by address, network segment, or protocol type, such as DECnet or XNS. The software also lets you create and control multiple data paths, permitting fault-tolerant networks. Monitor functions include address parameters display, node filters display, node parameter display, network parameter display, node statistics display, and network statistics display.

NetWare asynchronous communications server See NACS.

NetWare asynchronous services interface An API (application programming interface) that allows a program to control the function of the NetWare asynchronous communications server (NACS).

NetWare core protocols Protocols used to obtain the core services offered by a NetWare file server. These include facilities such as file access, locking, printing, and job management.

NetWare for VMS A program for DEC's VMS operating system that makes the VAX look like a NetWare server; the ancestor of Portable NetWare.

NetWare loadable module See NLM.

NetWare MHS Novell's product name for Action Technologies' Message Handling Service.

NetWare name service A distributed naming service introduced by Novell in 1990 to replace the bindery mechanism.

NetWare SQL requester Software for a NetWare server to allow it to service incoming SQL requests from clients.

NetWare support encyclopedia See NSE.

NetWare 3270 LAN workstation software Software that resides on a workstation and emulates an IBM 3270 terminal. The workstation uses the services of an SNA gateway.

NetWare 286 The NetWare Operating System for the 80286-based computer.

NetWare 386 The NetWare Operating System for the 80386-based computer.

NetWare version Refers to the version of NetWare running on the default server.

Netwise Maker of the Netwise RPC Tool, remarketed as NetWare RPC by Novell.

network 1. An interconnected combination of computers, terminals, and peripherals used to provide communications between two or more points. 2. An assemblage of components usually containing many similar elements and devoted to a common function, as shown in the figure. 3. Any system of interrelated circuit elements.

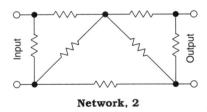

Network, 2

network access control Refers to the components on the LAN adapter card that control when the workstation can access the LAN.

network address The number of the network that the user is on. Each network (data link) in an internetwork has a number assigned to it. The full address of a station is the network address plus the local address of the node on that network.

network-addressable unit *See* NAU.

network administrator A program or person controlling a computer network's administrative details.

network analysis The process of calculating the transfer characteristic and other properties of a usually passive circuit from its configuration, elements, voltages, etc.

network analyzer 1. A group of circuit elements that can be interconnected to form a model of a network or system. Electrical measurements can then be used to determine desired quantities in the simulated system. Also called a *network calculator*. **2.** An electronic test-equipment item designed to make qualitative tests on specific network quantities.

network architecture The structure and protocols a network uses.

Network Assistant A program for selecting a printer on a network. With this package, there is no exiting and re-entering a program while you wait for a job to complete printing. Instead, you choose printers and print commands with a few simple keystrokes.

network bridge A unit that gives you intelligent internetworking, local routing, and wide-area bridging. A high-performance CPU and communication engine, the bridge may receive packets from local or remote interpreter modules. You may internetwork standard Ethernet, twisted-pair Ethernet, fiber-optic, Starlan, T1, and 56 Kbps links in any combination you choose. The bridge is also protocol-independent and may process TCP/IP, DECnet, XNS, TOP, OSI, and IPX data packets without discrimination. As a result, protocol migration is independent of your hardware network.

The bridge requires no internetwork setup or special commands from users because it learns automatically where packets have been routed successfully; without assistance, the bridge can build address tables. The addition of new devices, as well as relocation of existing devices, is also handled automatically. Because it knows where to route appropriate packets, the network bridge minimizes network traffic and facilitates the construction of large networks.

network buffer A storage device used to compensate for a difference in the rate of flow of data received and transmitted in a computer communications system. The buffer has memory and control circuits for storing incoming messages and holding outgoing messages that must be delayed because of busy lines.

network calculator *See* NETWORK ANALYZER, 1.

network configuration plan A plan that states current equipment status, network problem areas, fixes for those problems, and future upgrades. The plan can appear in either tabular or outline format, and should fully answer the questions users have about network equipment status. The plan normally includes a map as well.

network constant Any one of the resistance, inductance, mutual inductance, or capacitance values in a circuit or network. When these values are constant, the network is said to be *linear*.

Network Courier An e-mail package with popup windows that let you read and respond to incoming messages without leaving your current application. You are not limited to any particular message length. Network Courier lets you attach files of any type or size to your messages.

Network File System A distributed file system developed by Sun Microsystems and used on TCP/IP systems.

network gone count In NetWare Diagnostic Services, the number of times (since the shell was activated) that the shell has received a packet from a file server indicating the target network is gone. Only a 68000 file server can generate this type of packet.

network interface card *See* NIC.

network interface controller A communications device that allows the interconnection of information-processing devices to a network.

network layer The portion of the ISO-OSI model that is concerned with the routing of data from the source terminal to the destination terminal. *Also see* OSI MODEL.

network library A software module that comes with the Netwise RPC tool. The network library is added to the code generated by the RPC compiler to form a complete program. The library masks access to network communications from the rest of the program.

Network Management Protocol *See* NMP.

network management system *See* NMS.

Network Management Vector Transport *See* NMVT.

network model A database organization in which there is a connection of related data, similar to a hierarchical model but with additional pathways. The network model allows several routes, in both directions, for accessing a data item.

network monitor A device that displays information on network operations.

network number In NetWare, a server's four-byte network address.

network operating system *See* NOS.

network relay A relay used for the protection and control of alternating current networks.

network service A multiuser computer service. Typical network services include highly systematized programs and databases.

Network Services Protocol The DECnet transport layer protocol.

network shell program A set of programs that provides the interface between the user's workstation PC and the rest of the network. The set is made up of various individual components that perform different tasks to allow a workstation to communicate with the file server or other workstations in the network. *Also see* NOS.

network stabilization Relates to techniques used to shape the transfer characteristics in order to eliminate or minimize oscillations when feedback is provided.

network synthesis The process of formulating a network with specific requirements.

network topology Network topologies can be centralized or distributed. *Centralized* networks are those in which all nodes connect to a single node. The alternative topology is the *distributed* network, in which (in the pure sense of the term) each node is connected to every other node; however, the term *distributed* is commonly applied to topologies approaching this full connectivity.

network transfer function The ratio of output to input in a network, usually expressed in incremental units over a specific time period.

Neumann principle States that the physical properties of a crystal are never of lower symmetry than the symmetry of the external form of the crystal. The tensor properties of a cubic crystal, such as elasticity or conductivity, must have cubic symmetry, and the behavior of the crystal is isotropic.

Neural/Query Software that uses neural networks and fuzzy technology to generate answers to inexact queries. It finds partial matches and provides best guesses with the help of a concept dictionary. Human-like thought patterns can be incorporated into queries based on the users' weighting and definition.

neuron network simulation The study and duplication of neuron cells and networks in order to build multipurpose systems using analogous electronic components. Also called *neural network*.

neuron simulation The study of neuron cells and networks using electronic devices and systems.

neutral A conductor, device, or contact with no net charge or voltage with respect to another similar element in the same system, or with respect to ground.

neutral conductor The conductor nearest in potential to a neutral point in a polyphase power system.

neutralization The nullifying of inadvertent feedback within a device, circuit, or system for the purpose of preventing generation of spurious signals and unwanted radiation.

neutralizing capacitor A capacitor, usually variable, employed in a receiving or transmitting circuit to provide a feedback path for a portion of the signal voltage.

neutral state A condition of a ferromagnetic material when completely demagnetized. Also called *virgin state*.

neutral temperature The temperature for a thermocouple at which the EMF curve has a turning value; for CuFe, it is 270°C.

neutral zone 1. An area in space-time in which no control action takes place. **2.** A period between words used for switching or other operations. Also called *dead band*.

neutron An uncharged subatomic particle with a mass approximately equal to that of a proton. It is a part of the structure of atomic nuclei and interacts with matter primarily by collisions.

NEW A BASIC command that clears the program and data from the computer's memory.

new-AFP-entry ID An AppleTalk Filing Protocol entry ID that points to the newly created AFP directory.

newBASE A menu-driven database manager for mailing lists, name and address lists, sales reports, expense account maintenance, and budget preparation and maintenance..

NewFont Software for Ventura Publisher users that creates special effects on fonts, such as outline, shadow, gray, rotate, tilt, and stretch. The fonts created are directly accessible in Ventura Publisher from the font-selection menu. You can also use it create fractional point sizes such as 9.6 point Helvetica.

new input queue A group of new messages in a system awaiting processing. The main scheduling routine will scan them along with the other queues for processing at the right time.

new line character *See* NL.

NeWS for Microcomputers A windowing system platform that provides a hardware- and operating-system-independent environment on which diverse windowing systems, applications, and user interfaces can be built and coexist. NeWS is based on the PostScript language and imaging model.

newton The unit of force in the MKS system, being the force required to impact, to a mass of one kilogram, an acceleration of one meter per second.

NEXT Acronym for *near-end crosstalk*, crosstalk that is propagated in a channel in the direction opposite to the direction of propagation of the circuit. The receiving terminals of the disturbed channel and the energized terminals of the disturbing channel are usually near each other in the circuit.

NEXT coupling loss For near-end crosstalk, the ratio of power in the disturbing circuit to the induced power in the disturbed circuit.

NeXT computer A now-discontinued 68030-based desktop workstation developed by Apple cofounder Steve Jobs, widely praised for its elegant graphical interface and object-oriented development environment, which survives on several other platforms as the NeXTStep operating system.

next-higher assembly Designates an assembly of the next-higher order in the breakdown of a system.

next set starting point In NetWare Diagnostic Services, a point set to 0 for the first call for all known networks or servers. If that call returns a full set of 128, the application will set this field to 128 for the next call, 256 for the one after that and so on.

nexus A connection or interconnection; a tie or link.

NFB Abbreviation for *negative feedback*.

NFS Abbreviation for *network file system*, a Sun Microsystems network service that provides transparent access to file systems on the network.

nibble A set of four or five binary digits or bits. Usually refers to four bits.

NIC 1. Acronym for *not in contact*. **2.** Acronym for *network interface card*, an add-on board that is installed in a PC's expansion slot, allowing it to communicate as part of a local area network.

nichrome A nickel-chromium alloy used for heating resistance elements because of its high specific resistance and its ability to withstand high temperatures.

nickel A silver-white metallic element: atomic number 28, atomic weight 58.71, symbol Ni, melts at 1450°C, boils at 3000°C, electrical resistivity at 20°C, 10.9 microhm/cm. It is magnetostrictive, showing a decrease in length in an applied magnetic field. In the form of wire, it has been used in computers, in which data is circulated and extracted when required.

nickel delay line A delay line utilizing the magnetic and/or magnetostrictive properties of nickel.

nickel-iron secondary cell An alkali cell that uses potassium hydroxide electrolyte. It is lighter and more durable than lead cells and has an EMF of 1.2 V. Also known as an *Edison cell*.

nines' complement The radix-minus-one complement in decimal notation.

Nixie tube Trade name for a gas-discharge tube used as a visual alphanumeric display unit.

NJCL Abbreviation for *network job control language*.

NL Abbreviation for *new line* character, a format effector that causes the printing or display position to be moved to the first position of the next pointing or display line.

n-level logic A collection of gates connected in such a way that no more than n gates appear in series.

NLM Abbreviation for *NetWare loadable module*, a program that is loaded and run on a NetWare file server. NLMs are used to provide utility, communication, and disk services to the file server.

NLQ Abbreviation for *near letter quality*, refers to dot-matrix printing that approach, but do not equal, typewriter-quality characters.

NLQ print buffer The microprocessor-controlled unit that enables an NLQ printer with a Centronics interface to produce better-quality type in a number of print styles. It is equipped with a 128K buffer that stores the graphic codes, eliminating the waiting and delays associated with software packages sold as print upgraders.

Once the NLQ print buffer is placed between the computer and printer, it receives standard data from the computer software and converts it into a series of complex graphics instructions. These instructions are then forwarded to the printer to generate a high-quality printout.

NLS Abbreviation for *no lead speed*.

NMOS Abbreviation for *n-channel metal-oxide semiconductor*, a semiconductor technology that uses MOS devices with n-channel regions for field-effect conduction. Such devices tend to be faster and use less semiconductor real estate than p-channel units.

NMOS driver A circuit used to interface NMOS memories with emitter-coupled logic. A typical NMOS driver has a propagation time of 10 ns and a transition time of 20 ns with a 400 pF load.

NMOS EAROM A completely nonvolatile-bit ROM with moderate access speed. Memory contents can be electrically erased and altered externally from the device leads with no restrictions. The output can be either TTL or MOS compatible. Using the EAROM, a single hardware design can be applied to multiple product lines. The required programming for individual applications can be done on-site. Conventional ROMs require the development of different chip masks for each application. The EAROM eliminates such duplication, providing significant savings, especially in applications using only a few devices.

NMOS 40-pin package A package that permits separate data and address buses, thereby eliminating most external control circuitry and reducing the required interface circuitry.

NMOS RAM A random-access memory that uses NMOS technology for many high-speed cache applications. A typical NMOS RAM has the following features:

- Access time of less than 100 ns
- Maximum power dissipation of less than 600 mW
- Fully static operation
- Single 5V supply
- Standard 16-pin package

NMOS technology The most widely used technology for microprocessors today. The first NMOS microprocessor was the 8080. The original 8080 was designed for a maximum clock frequency of 2 MHz. Advances in n-channel technology now permit NMOS microprocessors to use clock rates upwards of 60 MHz. An important feature of MOS microprocessors is that the load resistors are MOS transistors that are used as resistors.

MOS transistors can also be classed as depletion-mode or enhancement-mode devices. *Depletion mode* transistors are normally on and require a gate voltage in order to be turned off. *Enhancement mode* devices are normally off and require a gate voltage in order to be turned on. The early NMOS microprocessors (such as the

8080) used enhancement-mode transistors for load resistors. This required a separate power supply to provide the gate voltage for the loads. Newer MOS microprocessors use depletion-mode loads, eliminating the need for the extra power supply voltage. These processors operate from a single 5-volt supply using circuits as shown.

Because NMOS is faster than PMOS, and newer versions such as HMOS and VMOS give excellent density, NMOS is the most popular technology used to implement microprocessors today.

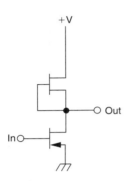

NMOS-FET amplifier with depletion mode load

NMP Abbreviation for *Network Management Protocol*, a set of protocols based on CMIP and used by AT&T in its Unified Network Management Architecture.

NMS Abbreviation for *network management system*, a system that manages and controls a network and provides features such as network configuration, alerts, and traffic analysis.

NMVT Abbreviation for *Network Management Vector Transport*, the protocol by which LANs can communicate with NetView.

n-n junction A junction in a semiconductor device produced between two n-type regions having different electrical properties.

NO Acronym for *normally open*, the designation applied to the contacts of a switch, relay, or solid-state switching device such that the circuit is not completed until power is applied.

no-address instruction An instruction specifying an operation that the computer can perform without referring to its storage or memory unit.

no backoff error A transmission state that occurs when a transceiver transmits when there is no carries and does not wait for the necessary delay.

node A terminal common to two or more branches in a network or system, as shown in the diagram. Also called *junction point, branch point, nodal point*, and *vertex*.

node address In NetWare, a server's six-byte node address or the six-byte node address of a LAN

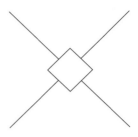

Node

board installed in a workstation. The node address uniquely identifies the driver and board on the network.

node address type In NetWare Diagnostic Services, indicates who records a node address in a driver to match the node address setting of the LAN board and how and when the node address is recorded. The following values are defined:

- The drive dynamically reads and records the node address by calling driver initialize.
- The developer hard codes the node address in the driver code master configuration table.
- A configuration utility assigns the node address.

no ECB available count In NetWare Diagnostic Services, specifies the number of packets the driver has received (since the last reset or initialization) for which there was no listening ECB.

noise Any unwanted disturbance in a system, such as random variations in voltage or current, or bits or words that are extra and must be removed before the data is used. *Steady-state* noise may consist of Gaussian noise, thermal noise, white noise, and random noise. *Impulse* noise is characterized by peaks of large amplitude and pulses of short duration. This type of noise can block out data signals and cause errors, especially in high-speed systems where more bits are affected in a given time period. *Also see* BACKGROUND NOISE, DELTA NOISE, IMPULSE NOISE, GAUSSIAN NOISE, and SYSTEM NOISE.

noise diode 1. A standard electrical-noise source consisting of a diode operated at saturation. The noise is due to the random emission of electrons. **2.** A diode operated as a noise generator under temperature-limited conditions.

noise-equivalent bandwidth The useful bandwidth of a thermistor bolometer for different frequencies in the input radiation. Normally equal to ¼ t, where t is the time constant of the bolometer.

noise immunity Refers to the insensitivity of a circuit or device to spurious signals or noise. CMOS logic offers a noise margin of 1.5 V compared to a noise margin of 0.4 V for TTL circuits.

noise level The strength of extraneous signals in a circuit or system.

noise margin The difference in potential between a signal and either the noise existing when the signal is removed or the threshold level of the device being rated.

noise ratio The ratio of the noise level to the signal level, usually expressed in decibels.

noisy digit A digit (usually zero) that is produced during the normalizing of a floating-point number and inserted during a left-shift operation into the fixed-point part.

noisy mode The mode during the normalization of a floating-point number in which digits are inserted with a left-shift operation into low-order positions.

no listen ECBs In NetWare Diagnostic Services, the number of times (since SPX was loaded) that SPX was forced to discard an inbound SPX connection packet because it lacked a corresponding SPX-listen-for-connection ECB.

no listen failures In NetWare Diagnostic Services, the number of times (since SPX was loaded) that SPX failed to send a packet because a target station had not allocated a receive buffer.

NOMA Acronym for *National Office Management Association*.

nominal bandwidth The band of frequencies, including guard bands, assigned to a channel.

nominal impedance The impedance of a circuit or device under normal conditions, usually specified for a specific frequency. For example, a loudspeaker with a nominal impedance of 8 Ω is considered to have an 8 Ω impedance when the speaker's input signal is a 1,000 Hz sine wave.

nonarithmetic shift A shift in which the digits dropped off at one end are returned at the other in an end-around carry operation. If a register holds 23456789, a nonarithmetic shift of two bits produces 45678923. Also called *end-around, ring shift*, or *cyclic shift*.

noncoherent detection Any form of detection that does not require a phase reference.

nonconductor An insulator through which no current can flow.

noncontention A network condition in which workstations do not have to contend for the right to use the network. A token bus or token ring are examples of a noncontention network.

Nondedicated Advanced NetWare A package that lets NetWare file servers and PCs operate concurrently as both file server and workstation. Nondedicated Advanced NetWare operates in protected mode and supports both expanded and extended memory. File-server functions can then execute in up to 14M of extended memory without affecting DOS applications running in real mode. The workstation keeps the full 640K of real memory space to itself.

nondestructive read *See* NDR.

nondestructive readout *See* NDRO.

nondissipative network A network in which the inductances and capacitances are assumed to be free of power dissipation, since they are constructed as components with minimum losses.

nonembedded command A program instruction that effects an immediate change in the data to be processed, such as a command to delete a given line.

nonequivalence element A two-input logic element that furnishes a *true* output only when its two input signals are different.

nonequivalence operation A logical operation applied to two operands that produces a 1 for those bits that are different, and a 0 for those bits that are the same:

Operands	Result
110110	101100
011010	

nonexclusive A type of lock on a file that permits other users to read information but prevents any write operations.

nonexecutable statement Program code that the computer does not act upon. It is used as a note to the programmer.

nonimpact printer A mechanism that produces text output on plain or special paper without contact between the printing mechanism and the paper. *Contrast with* IMPACT PRINTER.

noninductive capacitor A capacitor designed to have its inherent inductance reduced to a minimum.

noninductive circuit A circuit in which effects arising from associated inductances are negligible.

nonisolating error A token ring error that does not initialize a beacon, claim token, or other protocol-based error-recovery sequence.

nonlinear capacitor A capacitor that has a nonlinear mean charge characteristic or peak charge characteristic.

nonlinear distortion Distortion that is caused by a deviation from a linear relationship between the input and output of a system or device.

nonlinearity A relationship between the output and input that cannot be represented by direct proportioning.

nonlinearity monotonicity **1.** The ability to include all digital code numbers in a conversion operation. **2.** The amount by which the plot of output versus input deviates from a straight line.

nonlinear network A network of circuit elements that cannot be specified with linear variables such as differential equations or functions.

nonlinear programming A procedure used in operations research for locating the maximum and minimum of a function subject to nonlinear constraints.

nonlinear resistance A resistance with a nonproportionality between the potential difference and the electrical current.

nonlinear system A control system model that cannot be represented by linear equations.

nonloading lines Cable pairs or transmission lines with no added inductive loading.

nonmaskable interrupt An interrupt that allows the processor to complete the current instruction. Then, the contents of the index register, program counter, accumulator, and condition code register are stored in the stack. Next, an address is loaded to allow the CPU to branch to the nonmaskable interrupt, which is not affected by the condition code register.

nonnumerical data processing Refers to specific languages developed using symbol manipulation, used primarily as research tools rather than for actual data processing. These have proved valuable in the construction of compilers and in the simulation of human problem-solving. Other uses include the generalization and verification of mathematical proofs, pattern recognition, information retrieval, algebraic manipulation, heuristic programming, and the exploration of new programming languages.

nonoperable instruction An instruction whose only effect is to increment the instruction index counter, usually written as *continue*.

nonpersistent binding A style of binding in remote procedure calls where the connection is set up and torn down every time the remote procedure is called.

nonpolarized return-to-zero recording A recording method in which the reference condition is the absence of magnetization. Ones are represented by a specified condition of magnetization, and zeros are represented by the absence of magnetization.

nonpowered port-sharing device See NPPS.

nonpowered short-haul modem A modem that eliminates the need for an RS-232 transmission line and is powered by host or terminal equipment. It can transmit over three miles at 9600 bps. There are two models available, one for use with customer-owned twisted pairs and the other for use over telco private-line metallic circuits.

nonrecursive filter A filter that uses only the input to the filter to determine the output signal. The figure shows how a microprocessor is applied to a recursive digital filter. The microprocessor and ROM replace the coefficient generator, multipliers, and address of a hardwired digital filter. The three microprocessors in this example are synchronized and connected by the I/O interface along with a common data bus. The recursive data is applied to the three microprocessors as shown in the right part of the diagram where particular parts of the circuit assume functional values $f(n)$, $f(n-1)$, and $f(n-2)$.

nonreturn-to-change recording A recording method in which ones are represented by a specified condition of magnetization and zeros are represented by another condition. *Also see* NRS.

nonreturn-to-reference recording See NRZ.

nonreturn-to-zero See NRZ.

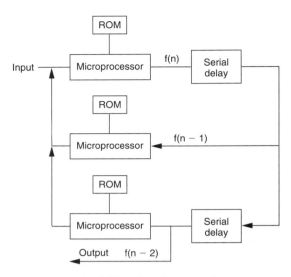

Digital filter implementation

nonswitched line A service or connection between a remote terminal and a computer that does not have to be established by dialing.

nonsynchronous Not related in speed, frequency, or phase to other quantities in a device or circuit. *Contrast with* SYNCHRONOUS.

nonvolatile Descriptive of a memory or storage medium that retains data in the absence of power so that the data is available upon restoration of power. A magnetic memory is nonvolatile; most semiconductor read/write memories are volatile. PROMs and EAROMs remain intact after they are programmed if power is removed and then reapplied.

NO OP A *no-operation* instruction, which causes the computer to do nothing except proceed to the next instruction in sequence. Also called *NOP*.

NOR A logical operation that has a true output only if all inputs are zero; the negative-OR operation.

NOR circuit *See* NOR GATE.

no receive buffers count In NetWare Diagnostic Services, the number of times (since the bridge was initialized) that the bridge could not receive inbound packets because of inadequate buffer space. These packets are lost.

NOR element A gate circuit having multiple inputs and one output that is energized only if all inputs are zero.

NOR gate A circuit or gate that has a true output only if all inputs are false, as shown in the following figure. Also called *NOR circuit*.

normal contact A contact that in its normal position closes a circuit and permits current to flow.

normal direction flow A flow in a direction from left to right or top to bottom in a flowchart.

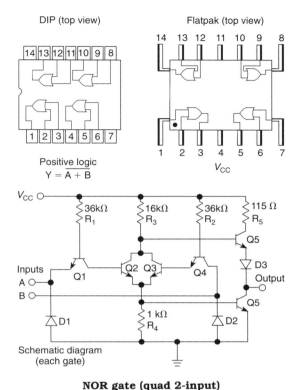

NOR gate (quad 2-input)

normal failure period That period of time during which an essentially constant failure rate exists.

normalization The multiplication of a variable by a numerical coefficient to make it assume a desired value. Also called *scaling*.

normalization routine A floating-point arithmetic operation related to the normalization of numerals in which digits other than zero are developed in the lower order or less-significant positions during a left shift.

normalization signal The generation or restoration of signals that comply with specified requirements in amplitude, shape, and timing. Such signals are often generated from another signal, and the requirements are often conventions or rules of specific computer systems.

normalized form A form used in a floating-point number adjusted so that its mantissa lies in a specified range. Also called *standard form*.

normalized frequency The ratio between the actual frequency and its nominal value.

normally closed *See* NC, 2.

normally open *See* NO.

normal magnetization The locus of the tips of the magnetic hysteresis loops obtained by varying the limits of the range of alternating magnetization.

normal state The condition of operation in a computer in which instructions are concerned with conventional aspects of computation such as adding, subtracting, and data transfer.

no router found count In NetWare Diagnostic Services, the number of times (since the shell was activated) that the shell has tried and failed to find a route to a destination node. The shell attempts to reroute a packet when a connection seems to fail and the user requests a retry.

Norton's theorem A theorem that states that any linear network of impedances and sources, if viewed from any two points in the network, can be replaced by an equivalent impedance in shunt with an equivalent current source.

Norton Utilities A set of programs that let you do or undo things to enhance the utility of your PC. You can recover erased files and scrambled data, recover from damaged disks, browse through files, and patch disks, among other things. You do not have to be a programmer to need and use these utilities, but they should not be used by the novice.

NOS Abbreviation for *network operating system*, a set of programs that control a local area network. The NOS controls multiple users who are accessing shared resources such as disk drives and their files, printers, and other output devices. The servers may also be used as a workstation. A portion of the NOS, referred to as the *LAN shell*, runs on the workstations attached to the network. The shell interfaces the PC to the LAN adapter card and also interfaces DOS to the NOS. The workstation shell is sometimes called a *re-director* because it passes some functions or commands to DOS for processing and routes others to the NOS for processing on the file server. Banyan's Vines, Novell's NetWare, and Microsoft's LAN Manager are examples of network operating systems.

no space for service count In NetWare Diagnostic Services, the number of times (since the bridge was initialized) that the bridge has received internetwork packets that it could not accommodate because the router did not have enough space in its DGroup area to copy the packets. These packets are lost.

NOT A logic operator having the property that if P is a statement, then the NOT of P is true if P is false; it is false if P is true. The NOT operator is represented by an overline.

NOT AND gate *See* NAND GATE.

notation The act, process, or method used to represent technical facts or quantities. In computer practice, the term typically describes the number radix, as follows:

Notation	Radix
Binary	2
Ternary	3
Quaternary	4
Quinary	5

Notation	Radix
Decimal	10
Duodecimal	12
Hexadecimal	16
Duotricenary	32
Biquinary	25

notational system Any of the various number systems used to indicate radix values, such as binary, decimal, or hexadecimal. *Also see* NOTATION.

NOT gate A circuit or gate that has a true output when the input is false, and a false output when the input is true. Also called *NOT circuit*.

NOT if-then gate A gate that performs the *A AND NOT B* and *B AND NOT A* operations.

NOT operation A Boolean operation that specifies that the output will always be the inverse of the input. A circuit or device that performs the NOT operation is called an *inverter*.

NOT OR *See* NOR.

Novell Maker of NetWare software for networks.

Novell NetWare *See* NETWARE.

Novell Wide Area Network Interface Module A Novell hardware board that allows several asynchronous connections to be maintained at the same time.

NOW A program that accelerates reading from and writing to hard disks and diskettes. This can add life to hard and floppy disks. It makes the most of extended or expanded memory by eliminating redundant disk activity and can be adapted to special needs.

NP Abbreviation for *new program*.

npin transistor A transistor that has an intrinsic (undoped) layer between the base and collector to extend the high-frequency range.

npip transistor A transistor that has an intrinsic layer between two p regions.

np junction The region in a semiconductor where the n-doped and p-doped areas meet. It is characterized by a high resistance in one direction and a low resistance in the other.

n-plus-one address instruction A multiple address instruction in which one address serves to specify the location of the next instrument in the normal sequence of execution.

npn transistor A junction transistor with a thin slice of p-type material forming the base between two pieces of n-type semiconductor, which form the collector and emitter. Such transistors are characterized by electrons as majority carriers (rather than holes).

NPPS Abbreviation for *nonpowered port-sharing device*, which allows two modems to share a computer or a multiplexer port in a polled environment. Data is transmitted simultaneously to both modems at rates up to 19.2 Kbps.

N(R) Receive sequence number, an LLC field that indicates the sequence number of the last packet received.

NRZ Abbreviation for *nonreturn-to-zero*, a recording technique in which the current through the write head does not return to zero after the write pulse. Also called *nonreturn-to-reference recording*.

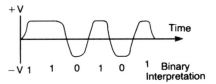

Nonreturn-to-zero recording

NRZI Format Converter NFC An NFC is placed into an NRZ system when foreign terminals, which do not conform to the NRZ format, are to be used. These terminals must conform to the protocol, as the NFC performs NRZI-NRZ conversion only. In synchronous mode, the modem clock is derived from pins 15 or 17 on the RS-232 interface.

NRZO Abbreviation for *nonreturn to zero one*.

ns Abbreviation for *nanosecond*.

N(S) Send sequence number, an LLC field that indicates the sequence number of the packet being sent.

NSE Abbreviation for *NetWare support encyclopedia*, files containing a complete set of Novell manuals along with articles and other information that the certified individual requires. The professional version of the product also contains a wide variety of product patches. Most of this additional material is also available on the NetWare forum of CompuServe.

NSF Abbreviation for *National Science Foundation*.

NSFnet Abbreviation for *National Science Foundation network*, a research network established by the NSF to give access to supercomputer and other computing facilities.

NSIA Abbreviation for *National Security Industrial Association*.

NSP Abbreviation for *Network Services Protocol*, the DECnet transport layer protocol.

NSV Abbreviation for *nonautomatic self-verification*.

NTSC Abbreviation for *National Television Standards Committee*, an advisory group established in the U.S. in the 1940s. In 1953, it was responsible for establishing the present color standards used in TV in the U.S. and Japan. The abbreviation *NTSC* is used to designate signals that conform to these standards. The NTSC standard uses a 525-line, 60-field/30-frame-per-second format. NTSC is defined primarily in the FCC Part 73 technical specifications. Many of it characteristics are defined in EIA-170A.

n-type conductivity The conductivity associated with conduction electrons in a semiconductor.

n-type semiconductor Refers to a semiconductor that is doped with small amounts of an impurity to provide excess electrons. Because electrons are negative particles, the material is called n-type, and conduction is primarily by electrons as the majority carriers.

NUL 1. A testing device of a disk operating system. **2.** A control character that serves to accomplish media-fill or time-fill functions. For example, in ASCII, the null character is a string of zeros. Null characters can be inserted or removed without affecting the meaning of a sequence, but control of equipment or the format may be affected.

null A balanced condition that results in zero output from a circuit, device, or system.

null character See NUL.

null cycle The time required to cycle through a program without introducing data. The null cycle represents the lower boundary for processing time.

null indicator A device that indicates when a parameter is zero.

null matrix A matrix of values in which every element is zero. Also called *zero matrix*.

null modem A device as shown in the figure that connects two DTE (data terminal equipment) devices directly by emulating the physical connections of a DCE (data communication equipment) device.

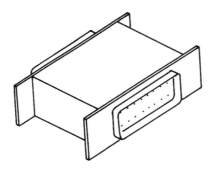

Null modem adapter

null modem adapter A unit that eliminates the use and cost of two modems. It is used primarily when connecting a local asynchronous terminal directly to the CPU's EIA interface.

null modem cable A serial cable that has pins 2 and 3 transposed so that a computer can be connected on each end. The computers can communicate with each as if they were using modems.

null set A set that contains no numbers. Also called the *empty set*.

null suppression The bypassing of all null characters in a data string to reduce the number of characters transmitted. Also called *data compaction*.

number A mathematical entity that indicates quantity or amount of units; a numeral.

number cruncher A computer designed to perform large numbers of scientific calculations. The ALU of a number cruncher may perform as many as twelve million arithmetic operations per second.

number of custom variables In NetWare Diagnostic Services, a field that specifies the number of custom variables that will follow.

number of known routes In NetWare Diagnostic Services, the number of routes between the source bridge and the destination network or server.

number of local drives In NetWare Connection Services, a number used to determine the workstation drive ID to assign to a server's SYS volume.

number of offspring In the AppleTalk Filing Protocol Services, a field that returns the number of files and subdirectories contained within the specified directory.

number of operator retries In NetWare Diagnostic Services, the number of times (since the shell was activated) that the user has instructed the shell to retry an operation.

number of packets In NetWare and other networks, the total number of packets to be sent to a destination node during a diagnostic test.

number of servers In NetWare Diagnostic Services, shows how many server types and name combinations the call is returning in the current set.

number of service processes In the NetWare File Server Environment, the number of service processes in the server. A service process handles incoming service requests.

number system See NOTATION SYSTEM.

numeral A discrete representation of a number using a single-digit symbol. For example, the number 12 is composed of two numerals. Also see DOUBLE-LENGTH NUMERAL.

numeral system A system for representing numbers by agreed sets of symbols according to agreed rules. Also called *numeration*.

numeric 1. Pertaining to numerals or representation by means of numerals. **2.** A set of numerals with an established meaning within a given context. For example, *10-4* is a communications numeric for "okay."

numerical Pertaining to numerals or representations using numerals.

numerical analysis The study of methods for obtaining useful quantitative solutions to problems that have been expressed mathematically. Numerical analysis also includes the study of errors and the bounds of errors in obtaining these solutions.

numerical aperture See NA, 2.

numerical control The automatic control of a machine or a process using numerical data as input. Most numerical-control devices have limited logical capability, and they rely on the input medium for detailed guidance.

A computer is generally used to prepare the control media. Direct numerical control uses a system of numerically controlled machines that are connected to a common memory. Direct numerical control systems may have provisions for collection and display of data along with limited editing and operator instruction capabilities.

Other types of numerical control systems may use methods with interchangeable connections for modifying the control sequence. *Also see* HAND-WIRED NUMERICAL CONTROL.

numerically controlled machine A machine that is under the control of numerical data.

numerical data Data in which information is expressed by a set of numbers that can assume only discrete values or configurations.

numeric code A code that consists only of number symbols and associated special characters.

numeric coding A system of abbreviation in which all information is reduced to numerical quantities, in contrast to alphabetic coding.

numeric constant A term that is treated as an octal or decimal number, depending upon the conversion mode in effect at the time.

numeric sort The ordering of numeric text, which includes digits and the following characters commonly associated with digits: dollar sign, percent sign, minus sign, comma, opening parenthesis, closing parenthesis, and decimal point.

numeric variable name A variable name in BASIC consisting of one or two letters or a letter and a number that identifies numeric data.

numeric word A word composed of characters from a numeric code. For example, in the Dewey-decimal classification system, 621.39 is a numeric word used to identify a specific class of literature.

Nusselt number The significant nondimensional parameter in convective heat loss problems, defined by $Qd/k/O$, where Q is the rate of heat loss from a solid body, O is the temperature difference between the body and its surroundings, k is the thermal conductivity of the surrounding fluid, and d is the significant linear dimension of the solid.

Nutrient A program that analyzes an individual's food intake for nutrient adequacy. After inputting the diet, chosen from a 700-food database that can be expanded, the program lists the average daily nutrient intake of 27 nutrients, including alcohol and cholesterol, and compares them to the Recommended Daily Allowance. It also generates personal graphs of the results.

NVT Abbreviation for *network virtual terminal*.

NWG Abbreviation for *Network Working Group*, a committee drawn from members of ARPANET which designed the higher-level protocols for ARPANET.

nylon A generic term for any long-chain synthetic polymeric amide that has recurring amide groups in an integral part of the main polymer chain and that is capable of being formed into a filament in which the structural elements are oriented in the direction of the axis.

Nyquist bandwidth As first described by Nyquist, the minimum channel bandwidth required for transmission without intersymbol interference.

Nyquist rate The maximum rate at which code elements can be resolved in a communication channel of limited bandwidth.

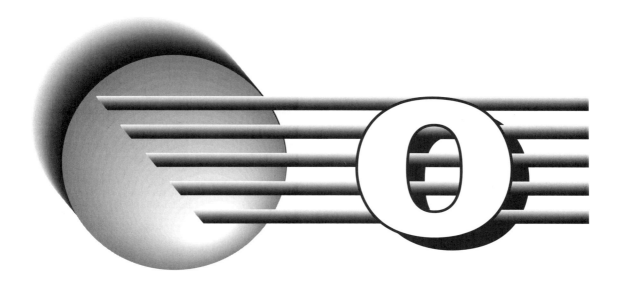

object A single line, block of text, geometric shape, or symbol created with an object-oriented graphics program.

object code The output from a compiler or assembler that is itself executable machine code or is suitable for processing to produce executable machine code. A line of object code might be a 16-bit string of ones and zeros whose combination is the machine-language equivalent of an instruction.

object file A set of information created by a compiler from language source code. An object file must be linked before it can be executed. Object files have .OBJ as their filename extension. *Also see* COMPILER.

object language The language that is the output of an automatic coding routine. Object language and machine language may be the same; however, if the coding routine is done in a series of steps, the object language of one step may serve as the source language for the next step.

Object-Menu Jr. A program that creates a graphics user interface for DOS applications. Menu elements include dialog boxes, buttons, and icons. It supports Borland C++ and Microsoft C/C++ compilers.

object name In NetWare Bindery Services, a string up to 47 uppercase characters long with only printable ASCII characters 21h through 7Dh. Excluded are control characters, spaces, slashes, backslashes, colons, semicolons, commas, asterisks, question marks, and tildes.

object name length In NetWare Bindery Services, the number of characters in a bindery object's name.

object-oriented graphic *See* VECTOR GRAPHIC.

object-oriented programming *See* OOP.

ObjectPM A C++ class library that provides the means for creating object-oriented applications, geared specifically for OS/2 and its Presentation Manager. ObjectPM provides over 120 classes of objects, encapsulation windows, controls, graphic tools, forms, and threads.

Object Professional An object-oriented library for Turbo Pascal. It provides over 100 high-level object types with over 2,000 methods for user-interface design, data manipulation, and low-level system access.

object program A source program that has been translated into machine language, or the final or target program which is the end result of processing. Typically, translator modules are used to translate the user-generated code into executable machine code; other operating modules add the utility routines to generate the executable object program.

object security In NetWare Bindery Services, a single byte with the high-order four-bit nibble defining write privileges and the low-order nibble defining read privileges.

object type In NetWare Bindery Services, a two-byte value that is set to 0 if the object's type is now known or set to –1 (wild) when scanning for an object whose type is unknown or not relevant.

ObjectVision A development tool that combines features from spreadsheets, databases, forms products, and front-ends into a WYSIWYG application for Windows users and developers. Features include direct access to data in Paradox, dBASE, Btrieve, and ASCII formats; DLL support; and customizable menus. It is useful for applications such as order processing, inventory management, call tracking, and equipment diagnosis.

OCAL Acronym for *online cryptanalytic aid language*.

OCLC Abbreviation for *online computer library catalog*, a nonprofit membership organization offering computer-based services to libraries, educational organizations, and their users. The OCLC network connects more than 10,000 libraries worldwide.

OCP 1. Abbreviation for *optional character printing*. **2.** Abbreviation for *output control pulse*.

OCR Abbreviation for *optical character recognition*, the recognition by machines of printed or written characters using optical sensing devices. OCR includes characters of all fonts or types.

octal A number system whose radix is 8, composed of the digits 0 through 7.

octet A networking term for eight bits, used instead of *byte* because some systems have bytes that are not eight bits long.

ODBC Abbreviation for *Open Database Connections*, a Microsoft API allowing for SQL access to servers via DBMS drivers.

odd-even check *See* PARITY CHECK.

odd-even interleaving The splitting of memory into several sections and independent paths with the odd and even addresses in alternate sections. Odd-even interleaving allows additional segmenting over normal memory interleaving.

odd-parity A parity-checking scheme in which the parity bit is set so that the total number of ones in the block is always odd.

odd-parity check A check in which the sum of all binary digits in a word is odd. An additional character position permits insertion of a one when the total is even, and insertion of a zero when the total is odd.

ODLI Abbreviation for *open data-link interface*, another way of referring to data link devices that conform to Novell's Link Support Layer specification. ODLI is synonymous with the multiple link interface driver (MLID). Also abbreviated *ODI*. *Also see* MLID.

OEM Abbreviation for *original equipment manufacturer*.

oersted A unit of field strength in the EEU system, such that 2 oersted is the field produced at the center of a circular conductor, 1 cm in radius, carrying 1 abampere (10 amperes). In the MKSA system, the measurement is given by the following equation:

$$1 \text{ oersted} = \frac{1000}{4} \text{ ampere-turns/meter}$$

off emergency A console or control panel switch that can be used to disconnect all power in the event of an emergency situation.

office automation Networking office equipment together to facilitate applications like word processing, electronic mail, and electronic filing.

Office Works A productivity software package that works as a fully integrated system and supports the essential business activities surrounding telephone messages, document control, and database maintenance.

OfficeWriter (*o.t.*) A basic word-processing program for the PC that emulates the Wang dedicated word processor.

offline 1. Equipment that is not under direct control of the CPU. **2.** Terminal equipment not connected to a transmission line. *Contrast with* ONLINE.

offline operation An operation that is independent of the system's operating time base. Offline operation usually refers to the operation of peripheral units independent of the CPU.

offset For a zero input, the extent to which the output deviates from zero, usually a function of time and temperature.

offset amplifier Current offset (or bias current) multiplied by the feedback resistor produces an output error. This effect can be minimized by using the differential offset (the difference in offset currents for the two inputs) when the resistance seen from both inputs to ground are equal.

offset binary code A three-bit-plus-sign code similar to natural binary for four bits, but more compatible with microcomputer inputs and outputs since it is easily changed to the more common two's complement. It also has a single, unambiguous code for zero.

offset quadrature phase-shift keying *See* OQPSK.

off-the-shelf Refers to items that are available from current stock, or software that can be used as purchased.

OFHC Abbreviation for *oxygen-free high conductivity*, a grade of electrolytic copper wire.

OG *See* OR GATE.

ohm The unit of electrical resistance.

ohm-cm The COS unit of resistivity.

ohmic contact A contact in which the potential drop is proportional to the current across the contact.

ohmic drop The voltage drop over a part of a circuit because of current passing through resistance.

ohmic loss The power dissipation in a circuit due to pure resistance losses.

ohmic resistor *See* LINEAR RESISTOR.

ohmmeter A portable battery-operated instrument for measuring electrical resistance and determining electrical continuity, as shown in the following diagram.

Ohm's law 1. A law formulated by B. S. Ohm in 1827 that states that in metallic conductors at a constant temperature and zero magnetic field, the resistance is independent of the current. **2.** A law stating that the voltage across an element of a circuit is equal to the current in amperes

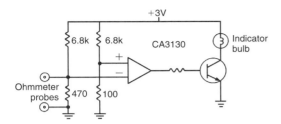

Voltage limiter for ohmmeter

through the element, multiplied by the resistance of the element in ohms. Expressed mathematically as $E = I \times R$ or $I = E/R$ and $R = E/I$.

O/L Abbreviation for *operations/logistics*.

OLE Acronym (pronounced "OH-lay") for *object linking and embedding*, a Windows extension offering a framework for the creation of object-oriented applications. OLE provides a standard object-technology model with broad appeal. One of the goals of OLE is to provide an environment that mirrors the way users work. In object technology, code and data are encapsulated in self-contained, easy-to-manipulate, interchangeable objects. You can rearrange them as you would building blocks, constructing complex, custom applications that can be easily modified to meet changing needs.

While the code for such an environment is complex, most of it remains hidden, so you can concentrate on manipulating data in a document. Microsoft calls this approach *document-centric*, because you can perform most editing and other operations on objects within a single document rather than having to switch to another application to access the appropriate editing tools.

OLE is in some respects the descendent of *DDE* (dynamic data exchange), an earlier attempt at Windows-based object-oriented computing. DDE proved to be awkward and limited by its *IPC* (interprocess communications) mechanism, designed to allow applications to communicate with each other during execution. IPC was fragile; links between applications were easily broken as files were moved or application software was updated.

OMR Abbreviation for *optical mark recognition*, the ability of a scanner to read a pencil mark. The most common application is an answer sheet.

ONC Abbreviation for *open network computing*, a marketing term used by Sun for the family of protocols that include the Network File System.

on-condition Any occurrence that could cause a program interruption. It can be the detection of an unexpected error, or of an occurrence that is expected, but at an unpredictable time.

one In binary code, the representation of an off, no, or false state. The complement to zero.

one-address A system of instructions such that each complete instruction explicitly describes one operation and one storage location. The instruction code of a single-address computer may include both zero and multiaddress instructions as special cases.

one-cell switching Refers to an array of magnetic cells and the selective switching of one cell in the array by the application of selected drive pulses.

one-digit adder A binary adding circuit that adds one digit at a time.

one-for-one A term used with assembly routines where one source-language instruction is converted into one machine-language instruction.

one-level storage A concept that treats all online storage as having one level of appearance to the user. One-level storage makes all online storage appear as main storage.

one-plus-one address An instruction that contains one operand address and one control address.

ones' complement The radix-minus-one complement in binary notation.

OneShot A DOS program that lets you select information from any downloaded text file and put it directly into your software. The user interface for OneShot is modeled after Lotus 1-2-3 and uses artificial intelligence concepts to learn how to convert the data.

one-shot 1. Any circuit or device having only one stable state. 2. *See* MONOSTABLE MULTIVIBRATOR.

one-step operation A method of operating a computer manually in which a single instruction or part of an instruction is performed in response to a single manual control operation. One-step operation is generally used for debugging procedures.

one-to-zero ratio The ratio of a one output level to a zero output level.

1-2-3 *See* LOTUS 1-2-3.

1-2-3 macros *See* LOTUS 1-2-3 MACROS.

online 1. Equipment, devices, and systems in direct interactive communication with the CPU. 2. Descriptive of terminal equipment connected to a transmission line. 3. Refers to communicating with a bulletin board system or similar service through the use of a modem.

online computer library catalog *See* OCLC.

online data processing Data processing in which all changes to records and accounts are made at the time that each transaction or event occurs.

online debugging The debugging of a program while sharing its execution with an online process program. Online debugging must be accomplished in such a way that any attempt by the program being debugged to interfere with the process program will be detected and inhibited.

online diagnostics The running of diagnostics while the system is online, but off peak to save time and to take corrective action without shutdown of the system.

Online Help A program that allows you to integrate help windows into your applications. One part of this two-system program is invoked via a call from your program, allowing you to control which help window is displayed and the action to be taken when the help window is cleared. The second system is a memory-resident version invoked by hot keys; no calls from your program are necessary. Both systems restore the original screen when the help window is cleared and give you control over the help window content, size, location, and color.

online service A type of bulletin-board system, usually commercial, with which subscribers communicate with one another and transfer files using modems. CompuServe, America Online, and Prodigy are a few of the larger online services.

online storage Storage devices under direct control of the computing system.

online system 1. A system in which the input data enters the computer directly from the point of origin and the output data is transmitted directly to where it is used. 2. A system that has no need for human intervention between the source of data and the processing by the CPU.

online test facilities Test facilities including line-loop tests, error-recovery procedures, checkpoint, restarts, and the collection of traffic and error statistics while directly connected to the CPUs.

on-off keying A form of modulation that involves switching the carrier off and on in a pattern corresponding to the sequence of data bits.

ONSPEC A software package for modeling systems on a personal computer. Online displays for status, trend analysis, and management may be planned and implemented.

On Stage Test Librarian A test librarian manager that enables QA developers and programmers to visually build, document, and execute large software test libraries. You can build and select tests by product, title, author, description, and keyword. On Stage supports a graphical desktop that lets users focus on one test or zoom out to see the bit picture. ANSI/IEEE Software Engineering Standards are online and help users document test libraries.

on-state drain current The current into the drain terminal of a MOS device with a specified forward-gate source voltage applied to bias the device to the on state.

oop Abbreviation for *object-oriented programming*, a type of programming that ties an object, such as an onscreen button that the user presses, to an action, such as exiting the word-processing program.

ooui Abbreviation for *object-oriented user interface*.

op Abbreviation for *operation*.

OPAL Acronym for *optical platform alignment linkage*.

op amp Abbreviation for *operational amplifier*, a usually integrated amplifier with high gain and wide bandwidth that can be used to perform mathematical operations.

open architecture A computer system like the IBM PC that can support a wide variety of components from many different vendors because its technical information and design is widely available and understood. An open architecture provides direct access to the system bus, so the owner/user can add expansion cards and special interfaces to the basic computer. Also called an *open system*. Contrast with CLOSED ARCHITECTURE.

op codes Operation codes that are decoded to serve as instructions in microcomputer systems. An op code usually contains source statements that are used to generate machine instructions after assembly.

open circuit The nondelivery of current from a source that is not loaded.

open circuit impedance The input or driving impedance of a line or network when the output is open circuited and not grounded or loaded.

open code In assembler programming, the portion of a source module that lies outside of any source macro definitions that may be specified.

open count In the NetWare Locking and File Server Environment, the number of stations that have opened a semaphore. This number is incremented when the station uses Open Semaphore and decremented when the station calls Close Semaphore.

open data-link interface See ODLI.

open-loop 1. A control system in which there is no self-correcting action and no feedback path. 2. A family of control units, which may include computers, linked together manually by operator action.

open-loop control system A control system without feedback, in which the output is directly controlled by the system input.

open-loop follower sample-hold An open-loop follower circuit is shown in the figure. As the switch is closed, the capacitor charges exponentially to the input voltage, and the amplifier's output follows the capacitor voltage. As the switch is opened, the charge and voltage level remain on the capacitor. The capacitor's acquisition time depends on the series resistance and the current available. Once the charge is complete to the desired accuracy, the switch can be opened, even though the amplifier may not have settled, without affecting the final output value or the set-

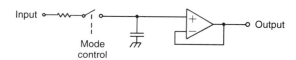

Basic open-loop follower sample-hold

tling time greatly, because the amplifier's input stage should not draw any appreciable current. (The switch is typically a field-effect transistor and the amplifier has a FET input.)

open-loop gain The ratio of the change in the return signal to the change in the corresponding error signal at a specified frequency.

open-loop response The response of a closed-loop system with the feedback path interrupted for test purposes.

open network computing *See* ONC.

Open Plan A DOS-based project management system.

open routine A routine that can be directly inserted into a larger routine with a linkage or calling sequence.

open shop The operation of a computer facility in which most of the problem programming is performed by the problem originator rather than by a group of programming specialists.

open socket failures In NetWare Diagnostic Services, the number of times (since IPX was loaded) that applications have unsuccessfully called the IPX Open Socket call. IPX cannot open a socket if the socket table is full or if the socket is already open.

open software A general term for software that is made available to users on terms other than conventional sales. *Also see* PUBLIC-DOMAIN SOFTWARE *and* SHAREWARE.

open subroutine A subroutine that is directly inserted into the linear operational sequence where it is used. It does not require a jump and must be recopied at each point where it is needed in the routine.

open system *See* OPEN ARCHITECTURE.

open systems interconnection *See* OSI MODEL.

operand 1. The fundamental quantity on which a mathematical operation is performed. A statement usually consists of an operator and an operand; in an add instruction, the operator is addition, and the operand indicates what is to be added. 2. A result, parameter, or the address portion of an instruction.

operand call syllable A specific syllable that calls for an operand to be brought from the stack either directly from the program reference table or indirectly using a descriptor.

operating conditions The various conditions, such as ambient temperature, ambient pressure, and vibration, to which a device is subjected. Operating conditions do not include the variable measured by the device.

operating procedure Rules that users follow to turn the computer on and off and accomplish standard functions, such as those for maintaining files.

operating system The basic group of programs for supervising the sequencing and processing operations in a computer system, sometimes abbreviated OS.

Operating systems typically provide scheduling, debugging, accounting, compilation, input/output control, storage assignment, data management, and other services, as shown in the diagram.

Popular microcomputer operating systems include DOS, Windows NT, Macintosh System 7.x, and OS/2.

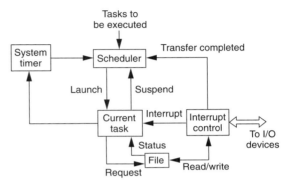

Basic tasks of an operating system

operating system, supervisor *See* SUPERVISOR OPERATING SYSTEM.

operation A defined action, usually specified by a single instruction or pseudo instruction. An operation may be arithmetic, logical, or transferal; it may be executed under the direction of a subroutine.

operational amplifier *See* OP AMP.

operational character A character used as a code element to initiate, modify, or stop a control operation. A typical operational character is the carriage return.

operational relay A relay controlled by an op amp or a relay amplifier.

operation code *See* OP CODE.

operation cycle *See* EXECUTION CYCLE.

operation decoder A device that selects one or more channels of operation according to the operation part of the machine instruction.

operation, dyadic Boolean *See* DYADIC OPERATOR.

operations analysis The use of analytic methods to provide criteria for decisions in systems involving repeatable operations. The usual objective is to provide management with a logical basis for making predictions and decisions. The following techniques may be used:

- Linear programming
- Probability theory
- Information theory
- Game theory
- Monte Carlo methods
- Queuing theory

operations manual A manual that contains instructions and specifications for a given application. Typically it includes the components of operator's manual and programmer reference manual; it may also include a log section.

operations personnel People involved in the day-to-day working and maintenance of computer equipment.

operations research Operations analysis (abbreviated *OR*).

operator 1. The mathematical symbol that represents the process to be performed on an associated operand. **2.** The portion of an instruction that indicates the action to be performed on the operands.

operator aborts count In NetWare Diagnostic Services, the number of times (since the shell was activated) that the user has aborted the shell-server connection by typing *A* in reply to a network error message.

operator indicator Any display light used to show conditions on a device. The operator indicators can usually be set, cleared, and tested under program control.

operator interrupt In some systems an operator interrupt trap is armed, and the fixed interrupt location is patched each time the monitor program receives control. When an operator interrupt occurs, control is given to a routine in the monitor.

operator intervention section That portion of the control equipment in which operators can intervene in normal programming operations.

op register A register used to hold the operation code of computer instructions.

optical character recognition *See* OCR.

optical computing A method of computing based on the propagation of light impulses rather than electrical impulses.

optical coupled isolation amplifier A common approach for obtaining electrical isolation, shown in the diagram. Optical coupling is effective for isolation, since it uses a portion of the electromagnetic spectrum that completely eliminates voltage, current, and magnetic flux for energy transmission.

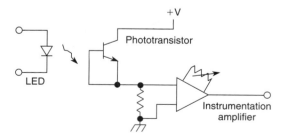

Optical-coupled isolation amplifier

optical coupler A photon-coupled amplifier used to isolate electrical outputs from inputs, as shown in the diagram. Optical couplers can operate at speeds of up to 10 MHz with isolation voltages as high as 5 kV. Also called *optocoupler* and *optoisolator*.

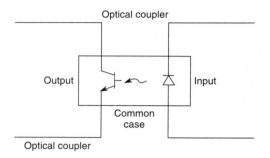

Optical coupler

optical disk A form of secondary storage that uses lasers.

optical fiber A thin cylinder having a central core of one transparent material of high refractive index surrounded with a cladding of another transparent material of lower refractive index, used to efficiently carry voice and data communications.

optical image chip An integrated circuit that converts optical images into electrical signals.

optical isolator *See* OPTICAL COUPLER.

optically isolated driver boards A board that plugs directly into an expansion slot within the PC to control or monitor up to 512 digital or 256 analog I/O points. A 50-conductor cable carries all data and control signals required by the system, as well as distributing power.

optical mark A mark made by a pencil on a designated area of paper, usually an answer sheet, that can be read by a scanner. *Also see* OMR.

optical mark recognition *See* OMR.

optical mouse A mouse that uses light instead of the ball-roller contact of the mechanical mouse. An optical mouse, as shown in the following figure, moves on a reflective pad with a grid of lines. As the mouse moves across the lines, the patterns of light breaks indicate the number of lines passed.

optical scanner A device that scans patterns of incident light and generates signals that are functions of the data represented. The data may be printed or written using a barcode or other representation.

optical sensor A device or transducer capable of detecting light and producing an electrical output.

optical shaft encoder A noncontacting, direct, rotary-to-digital converter. An optical shaft en-

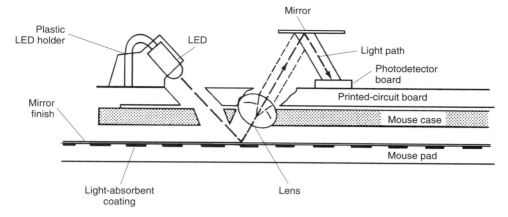

The optical mouse as it travels over a grid of lines on the mouse pad

coder uses light sources to deliver two-channel quadrature outputs from a single +5 V supply.

optical time-domain reflection An optical cable and network test method that uses a sequence of time-delayed light pulses.

optimize To rearrange instructions or data in storage such that a minimum number of jumps or transfers is required in the running of the program.

optimizing control action A type of control action that automatically seeks and maintains the most advantageous value of a specified variable, instead of maintaining it at a set value.

optimum code A computer code that is particularly efficient in regard to a specific aspect, such as

- Minimum time of execution
- Most efficient use of storage space
- Minimum coding time

optimum programming Programming in order to maximize efficiency with respect to some criterion.

optional stop A command similar to a program stop except that the control ignores the command unless the operator has previously actuated a manual selector to validate the command.

option board A circuit board family that allows users to implement certain basic system options. Typical option boards include real-time clocks, serial interfaces, and input/output circuits.

OptionWare A series of templates that allows you to put Lotus 1-2-3 to work quickly to handle various financial applications. The formulas in the templates can be viewed and modified to meet special requirements in the same manner as any other 1-2-3 formula.

OpTLINK/Compress A compressing overlay linker that permits storage of large programs on one floppy disk. Features include calling as many as 8,192 overlays, support of function pointers, EMS/XMS caching, and compression of the overlays.

optocoupler *See* OPTICAL COUPLER.

optoisolator *See* OPTICAL COUPLER.

optomechanical mouse A mouse that uses a rotating ball to drive two rollers that turn slotted disks, as shown in the figure. The disks turn between an LED and phototransistor combination. Optomechanical mice use an optically sensed spring-loaded plate to determine the direction and optically count the line crossings on a special mouse pad. This technique is low in cost, has a longer life than a mechanical mouse, and lets you track on any surface, but periodic cleaning is required.

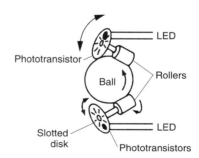

The rotating ball in an optomechanical mouse

OPTS-DOS A file conversion utility that translates documents from Unix troff, nroff, or mm macro formatting into DOS RTF form, compatible with word processors like Word or WordPerfect. It also converts from RTF to troff.

Opt-Tech Sort A high-performance sort/merge/select utility that can be used as a standalone or called as a subroutine to over 30 programming languages. It can sort, select, or merge on multiple key fields. Features include duplicate record elimination, reformatting records. and use of expanded memory.

OQPSK Abbreviation for *offset quadrature phase-shift keying*, a form of quadrature phase-shift keying (QPSK) in which the inphase and quadrature bit streams are offset in time by one bit-period. *Also see* QPSK.

OR A logic operator having the following property for logical quantities P and Q:

P	Q	P OR Q
0	0	0
0	1	1
1	0	1
1	1	1

The OR operator is represented in electrical and Fortran terminology by a plus sign.

OR circuit *See* OR GATE.

order **1.** The weight or significance assigned to a digit position in a number. **2.** To sequence or arrange in a series according to specified conditions.

ordering bias **1.** A check on the exactness of the order of alphabetic words or numerals. **2.** A unique characteristic of a sequence that keeps it away from or toward a needed, designed, or desired order. As a consequence, some degree of effort is required to achieve the desired order other than would normally be expected, say, from a random distribution.

order number In NetWare Workstation Services, this is a field that shows the order of the server's network/node address relative to the others in the table.

orderly shutdown The stopping of a system in such a way as to permit an orderly restart with no destruction of data. An orderly shutdown (or closedown) provides that all records and files are updated that should be updated, and no records or files are erroneously updated when the restart begins.

ordinary symbol A symbol used in assembler programming to represent an assembly time value when used in the name or operand field of an instruction. Ordinary symbols are also used to represent operation codes for assembly language instructions.

OR ELSE A logical operator that states that if P and Q are statements, then P OR ELSE Q is either true or false. The OR-ELSE operator is often represented by an inverted vee. Also called EITHER-OR.

organizational group A group that shares common data files. Most data files that are shared belong to groups already established by their roles or functions in the organization. The best way to handle the need for shared files in the network is to establish groups that correspond to these needs.

OR gate An electrical gate or mechanical device that implements the logical OR operator, as shown in the following figure. An output signal occurs whenever there are one or more inputs on a multichannel input. An OR gate performs the function of the logical inclusive-OR operator. Synonymous with *OR circuit*.

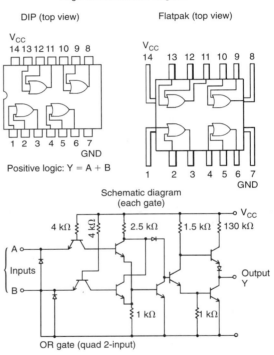

OR gate (quad 2-input)

origin The absolute storage address in relative coding to which addresses in a region are referenced.

origination Refers to the creating of a record in machine-sensible form, directly or as a by-product of a human-readable document.

origin counter The circuitry that develops the location of the start of the next instruction by adding the instruction word length to the initial value and to the running total after each instruction.

ORIN for Windows A RAD (rapid application development) system for relational databases from Oracle, Informix, DEC, and Ocelet. Features include an objective solutions graphical query system for window design and database access, application-wide data validation, formatting, triggers, and an object-oriented procedural language. Applications can operate in a client-server, standalone, or combination environment.

OR instruction A microprocessor instruction that causes the contents of the addressed memory location to be ORed to the contents of the accumulator. In the corresponding bit positions of the memory location and the accumulator, a single one will result in a one, and two zeros will result in a zero. This is shown in the following equation:

11001100 = Contents in accumulator
01100110 = Contents in memory location
11101110 = Logical OR result

OR operation A Boolean operation performed on two integers A and B such that if A and/or B equal one, the result is one; otherwise the result is zero. The OR operation is represented by a plus sign, $A \: OR \: B = A + B$, so the operation is also called a *logical add*.

OR operator The logical operator that produces an OR function.

orphan In word processing or desktop publishing, a layout problem in which a paragraph's first line appears alone at the bottom of a page or column, while the rest of the paragraph appears on the next page or column. Some programs will automatically scan for orphan lines. *Also see* WIDOW.

orthocode An arrangement of black-and-white bars resembling a piano keyboard that can be read by a photoelectric device.

orthoscanner An optical scanning device that reads coded information (orthocode) at the rate of 1,850 characters per second. Coupons, on which the code is typically printed, are read at the rate of 1,500 per minute.

orthotrack A complete row of orthocodes.

OR unit *See* OR GATE.

OS *See* OPERATING SYSTEM.

OSA Abbreviation for *Open System Architecture*, the reference model developed by ISO. *Also see* OSI MODEL.

OS bulk-storage diagnostic A diagnostic tool that tests and verifies the long-term reliability of operating system (OS) storage devices by continuously copying test files between devices.

oscillation The cyclic alternation of conditions (such as voltages and currents) in a circuit or system. *Also see* FREE OSCILLATION.

oscillation constant The square root of the product of inductance (henry) and capacitance (farad) of a resonant circuit.

oscillation frequency A frequency determined by the balance between the inertia reactance and the elastic reactance of a system that includes an open or short-circuited transmission line, a cavity, a resonant circuit, or a quartz crystal. Mathematically, this is given as frequency $f = 1/(2 \pi LC)m$ where C is capacitance and L is self-inductance or the circuit. In a mechanical oscillating system, $f = 2 \pi M/S$, where M is mass and S is the restoring force or unit displacement.

oscillator A low-current source of an alternating voltage at any frequency. Oscillators may be electrical, electronic, or mechanical. Most microcomputer systems use an oscillator with a piezoelectric crystal to provide a stable reference frequency for clocking. *Also see* ARMSTRONG OSCILLATOR, BLOCKING OSCILLATOR, COLPITTS OSCILLATOR, HARTLEY OSCILLATOR, *and* LOCAL OSCILLATOR.

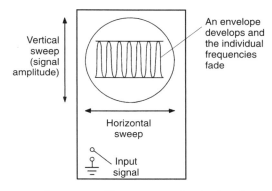

Using an oscilloscope to check signal amplitude and frequency

oscillatory discharge The discharge of a capacitor through an inductor when the resistance of circuit is sufficiently low; the current persists after the capacitor has discharged, so that it charges again in the reverse direction. This process is repeated until all initial energy is dissipated in the resistance.

oscilloscope A test instrument that uses a CRT to display graphic representations of pulses and waveforms, as shown in the following figure. Digital testing requires oscilloscopes with wide bandwidths and short rise times. Combining oscilloscopes with microprocessors and display units produces a high-performance troubleshooting unit. The microprocessor is used to calculate time intervals, compute voltage levels, convert time intervals to frequency, and calculate percentages.

OSI Abbreviation for *open systems interconnection*.

OSI model A network model designed by the International Standards Organization (ISO) that divides network communications into seven functional layers. The layers provide a communications relay from one system to the next, with each layer responsible for a different type of network service.

The OSI design is the standard for LAN product design. The layers are

1. Physical
2. Data link
3. Network
4. Application
5. Session
6. Presentation
7. Application

The first three layers are for data transmission and routing, the next two provide the interface between hardware and application, and the top three manage the application.

OSI-POSIX project Refers to a project by Berkeley to make its UNIX compatible with the OSI protocol.

OS text In NetWare Diagnostic Services, identifies the operating system.

OS/2 An operating system for PCs developed by Microsoft and IBM to take advantage of the features of the 80286 and later CPUs. It gives you the ability to run Windows, 16-bit, and 32-bit OS/2 applications concurrently from a single platform. It includes multitasking, a simplified user interface with a graphical installation procedure, an object-oriented workplace shell, and online context-sensitive help.

OS/2 Extended Edition IBM's proprietary version of OS/2. The standard edition of OS/2 is an OEM product licensed to other manufacturers. The extended edition includes features not found in the standard edition, such as a built-in SQL database manager and a communications manager for terminal emulation for connections to IBM mainframes.

OS/2 PM Switch-It A code-generation module that allows WindowsMAKER Professional to generate optimized C source code for OS/2's Presentation Manager. It contains a knowledgebase for generating code for a specific platform. The user's own code is not modified by the code generator and applications may be migrated across platforms and languages.

OS version text In NetWare Diagnostic Services, identifies the operating system version.

outage A condition in which a user is deprived of service due to failure in the communication system.

out-band signaling Telephone system signaling transmitted outside of the frequency band used for the voice signal.

outer macroinstruction A macroinstruction in assembler programming that is specified in open code.

outgoing packet discarded no buffer In the NetWare File Server Environment, the number of packets the server attempted to send that were lost because no routing buffers were available.

outlet expansion power strip *See* POWER STRIP.

outline font A character set in which each character is defined by a mathematical formula, so that it can be made as big or small as necessary without appearing distorted. *Contrast with* BITMAP FONT.

outline view As implemented in some word processors, a way of displaying a document so that the underlying structure of the document is shown. In an outline view, you can rearrange large amounts of text with just a few keystrokes. You can also raise and lower headings and subheadings and make text temporarily disappear and reappear.

out-of-band signalling A signal on an analog communications channel that uses a frequency just outside the data channel frequencies. Sometimes called *sideband*, it is used for controlling communications parameters.

Out of Controls Software designed to make Windows applications more powerful and intuitive. It includes CVA-compliant controls (multi-cell listbox, line-object editor, and spinbox), a text editor, and model-spawning libraries.

out-of-service testing A form of testing in which operational traffic is interrupted and replaced by a test pattern.

output 1. The produced signals used to drive peripheral terminals. **2.** Data delivered from a device or program, generally after processing.

output area A segment of internal storage reserved for output data. Also called the *output block* or *output working storage*.

output bus driver An amplifier used to drive the impedance loads used for the output lines in a system, as shown in the following figure.

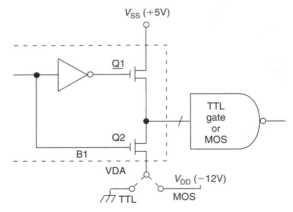

Output bus driver

output capacitance Refers to the capacitive component of the output impedance of a device or circuit.

output channel A path for conveying data from a device or logic element.

output device 1. A unit used for conveying data out from one area, block, or unit to another. 2. Equipment that provides the processed information to the user, such as printers or display screens.

output formatter A special program used to produce assembled microprocessor programs in formats compatible with available storage media. Output formatters are available for the following media:

- Mask-programmable ROM
- Laser-encodable ROMs
- Assemblers
- ROM emulators

output impedance 1. The idealized load impedance of a device producing signals for use in another system or another part of the same system. 2. An impedance measured at the output terminals of a transmission line, gate, or amplifier, under no load conditions.

output meter A meter that measures the output voltage of a circuit or line. It may be calibrated in volts or power level. In decibels, the zero power level is usually set at one milliwatt when the circuit is properly terminated.

output module valve A section of the computer that converts output data into analog control signals.

output ratings, amplifier See AMPLIFIER OUTPUT RATINGS.

output record The current record stored in the output area prior to being output, or a specific record written to an output device.

output register The register used to hold data until it can be output to an external device.

output regulation The variation of voltage with load current in a power supply.

output steering The sharing of one UART serial output among two separate serial output devices under program control. *Also see* UART.

output stream The messages and other output data issued by a system or program on the output device or devices activated by the operator. Also called *job output stream* or *output job stream*.

Outside-In A file-viewing and importing utility that adds clipboard-style cutting and pasting to DOS. You can view DOS files in their original format without the original software, select any part of the file, and insert the data into your current document. It supports more than 60 word-processing, spreadsheet, and database programs.

outside loop A program loop that executes the control parameters being held constant while the current loop is being carried through possible values. Outside loops are considered nested loops when loops within it are entirely contained.

outsourcing Disbanding one or more in-house computer operations and turning it over to be run by an external vendor.

overall loss A term adopted to represent the composite attenuation, the transducer loss, and the insertion loss of a circuit.

overcoupling A condition of two electrical circuits or mechanical systems tuned to the same frequency when there is sufficient interaction between them for the frequency response curve of the system to show two maxima, displaced to opposite sides of the maximum for either circuit alone.

overdamping Damping in excess of critical damping in a control system. Overdamping produces a slow nonoscillatory return to equilibrium following a disturbance.

overflow 1. The condition that occurs when the result of an arithmetic operation exceeds the capacity of the storage space alloted for it. 2. The digit or digits that occur from overflow conditions. Overflow develops when attempts are made to write longer fields into a location of specific length; for example, a 10-digit product will overflow an 8-digit accumulator.

overflow, arithmetic See ARITHMETIC OVERFLOW.

overflow indicator A device that changes state when an overflow occurs in the register it is monitoring. The overflow indicator can be interrogated and restored to its original state.

overflow operation An operation that exceeds the capacity of the storage device, leading to the generation of an overflow condition.

overflow position The extra position in a register used to hold an overflow digit.

overflow records Records that cannot be accommodated in assigned areas of a direct access file and must be stored in another area where they can be retrieved by means of a reference in the original assigned area.

overhead The distribution of operating time of the executive routine for checking, monitoring, and scheduling all jobs or tasks related to the total cost of the complete system, usually expressed in percentages or ratios.

overhead bit A bit other than a data bit, check bit, training bit, or parity bit.

Overhead Express A DOS-based program for making overhead transparencies and screen shows.

overlapping data channel A data channel that allows asynchronous operation of its I/O devices and processing by the CPU.

overlay A technique for bringing routines into high-speed storage from some other form of storage during processing, such that several routines will occupy the same storage locations at different times. Overlay is used when the total storage requirements for instructions exceed the available main storage. New information that is required is laid over information no longer needed. Usually the sets of information are not related, except that they are needed in the same program at different times. The use of the same data for successive cases is not an overlay. *Also see* MEMORY OVERLAY.

overlay module A software load module that has been divided into overlay segments and provided with the information to implement the desired loading of the segments when requested.

overlay path The segments in an overlay tree between a particular segment and the root segment of a program.

overlay program A program in which certain control sections can use the same storage locations at different times during execution.

overlay region An area of main storage where segments can be loaded independently of paths in other regions. Only one path within a region can be in main storage at any one time.

overlay supervisor A routine that controls the proper sequencing and positioning of segments in limited storage during execution.

Overlay Toolkit A set of overlay tools for programmers who use the overlay feature of Plink86+ or a compatible linker in their application programs. It analyzes the object modules to automatically design an overlay structure.

overlay tree A graphic representation showing the segments of an overlay program and their relationships.

overload A condition in a computing element that results in a substantial error in computation because of the saturation of one or more parts of the computing element.

overload capacity The excess capacity of a circuit or system over that of its rating.

overloading A capability available in some advanced programming languages that enables the computer to utilize two or more variables or subprograms with the same name. The compiler computes by references which specific entity is being referred to in each case.

overload module test A hardware test designed to detect substandard units by using operating conditions or parameters outside the normal.

overload recovery time The time required for the output to return to its proper value after an overload condition is removed.

overmodulation Amplitude modulation that exceeds 100 percent. Overmodulation can produce the loss of signal transmission for a fraction of the modulation cycle, along with considerable distortion.

overpunch A condition that occurs when data is transferred to or from a nonbuffered control unit operating with a synchronous medium, and the total activity initiated by the program exceeds the capability of the channel.

overscanning Displaying less than the complete area of an image to a viewer due to scanning beyond the visible area. All TV sets are overscanned at least slightly, so that viewers do not see blanking.

overshoot 1. The extent to which a control device or system carries the controlled variable or output past a final or desired value. **2.** The amount by which an output pulse exceeds a stabilized value momentarily.

overshoot rise time The measured time necessary for the output of a system (other than first order) to make the change from a small specified percentage (often 5 or 10) of the steady-state increment to a large specified percentage (often 90 or 95) either before overshoot or in the absence of overshoot.

oversized packet A packet that exceeds 1,518 bytes, including address, length, data, and CRC fields.

overview diagram Part of HIPO chart that details the input, processing, and output steps for the entire program.

overwrite The act of placing information in a location and destroying all previous information contained there.

Ovshinsky effect The switching action found in some types of glass semiconductors materials. The impedance of the device changes with an applied electric field and is independent of the polarity.

OWL Acronym for Borland's *ObjectWindows C++ library*.

OWL C++ Switch-It A code generator that allows WindowsMaker Professional to generate optimized C++ source code for OWL. Each module contains a knowledgebase for generating code for a specific platform. The user's code is not modified by the code generator, which also supports Borland C++. Applications may be migrated across platforms and languages.

owner object ID In NetWare, the bindery object identification of the user that created a file or directory.

oxide A chemical coating used in semiconductor devices, magnetic disks, and other electronic products.

oxide buildup The accumulation of magnetic residue on the surface of magnetic heads from repeated use. Oxide buildup causes a loss in output and accelerates wear.

oxide isolation The separation of elements on semiconductor chips using oxidized regions. Oxide isolation results in high packing density along with higher speeds. Without oxide isolation, the electrical isolation is achieved with reversed-biased junctions that occupy more space and have higher capacitance. *Also see* ISOPLANAR OXIDE ISOLATION.

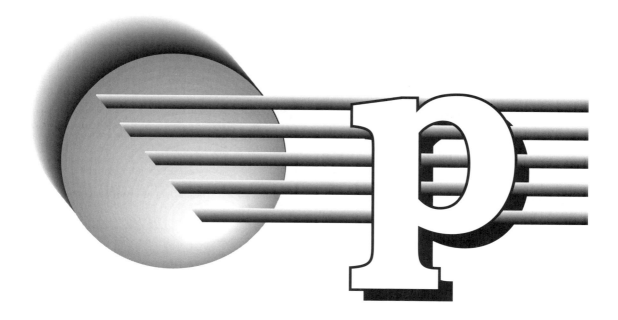

P 1. Symbol for *power*. 2. Symbol for **permeance** (webers per ampere). 3. Symbol for the prefix *peta* (10^{15}). 4. Abbreviation for *positive*.

p Symbol for the prefix *pico* (10^{-12}).

PABX Abbreviation for *private automatic branch exchange*, equipment that switches calls between the public telephone network and inside extensions.

PAC Abbreviation for *program address counter*. *Also see* PROGRAM COUNTER.

pack To compress data by taking advantage of known characteristics of the data in such a way that the original data can be recovered. Packing involves the use of bit or byte locations that would otherwise go unused and may be used to combine several fields of information into one machine word.

package The container used to house an active semiconductor device. Packages are available in plastic and ceramic housings with up to 40 pins.

Package size is important in many system designs, particularly those with cramped layouts. In general, microprocessors with fewer pins are easier to physically install, while those with larger numbers of pins are easier to interface with the rest of the equipment required for the microcomputer system. *Also see* CERAMIC PACKAGE, PLASTIC PACKAGE, SLAM PACKAGE, and TO PACKAGE.

packaged Descriptive of hardware or software that is complete and ready for use. *Also see* OFF-THE-SHELF.

packaging density *See* PACKING DENSITY.

packet A series of bits forming all or part of a data message (depending on its length) to be sent through a network. Each packet has a defined format, with some additional bits forming a "head" preceding the data and a "tail" following it. These carry information that the network needs to know about the packet, including its destination and source. The packets are formed by the controller in the sending data terminal equipment and the data is extracted and reassembled by the controller at the receiving end.

packet assembler/disassembler *See* PAD.

packet broadcasting A technique that uses the simultaneous transmission of a packet to several remote stations. Each remote station is equipped with decoding circuitry that decodes each incoming packet, determining if it is addressed to that station. Packet broadcasting is basically a radio broadcasting communication system. A packet broadcasting system can also be implemented by means of a satellite transmission network.

packet buffer A structure created in computer memory to build, disassemble, or temporarily store network data packets.

packet burst An overwhelming broadcast of packets requesting information or addresses, or indicating panic messages.

packet burst protocol A Novell enhancement protocol that helps to route information between different networks.

packet communications Communication based on the transmission of message packets. There are two forms of packet communications: packet switching and packet broadcasting.

packet data link interface In the functional diagram shown, the communication processor links the transmission lines with the buffer store, which is connected to the host processor. The

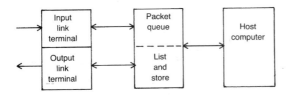

Packet data link interface

user interfaces with the host processor through a CRT terminal.

packet data link processor A system in which a microprocessor is connected to the control, address, and data buses that lead to the memory and interface units, as shown in the following figure. The microprocessor data link interface performs serial/parallel conversion, error checking, header and frame information encoding/decoding on outgoing and incoming data, assembling data into packets, and link and synchronization control.

The processor performs the packet-handling functions based on a protocol flowchart. From the information in the flowchart, the system designer will code the program that performs the desired operation. The program may then be stored in ROM to be called by system control or user command.

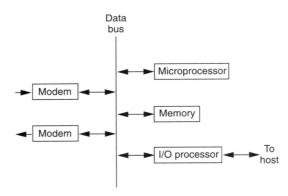

Packet data link processor

packet exchange protocol See PEP.
packet length The size of a packet sent through a network, usually measured in bits or bytes. Some LANs, such as the Cambridge Ring, have a fixed short packet length; others, including Ethernet, have a variable packet length, which facilitates the efficient transmission of long files.
packet radio A type of digital radio designed to handle multiple users who share a common high-speed channel and transmit data in bursts called *packets*.

packet Rx misc error count A part of NetWare Diagnostic Services that specifies the number of miscellaneous errors that have prevented the driver from receiving a packet (since the last reset or initialization).
packet Rx overflow count A part of NetWare Diagnostic Services that specifies the number of times (since the last reset or initialization) that the driver has received a packet larger than the buffer space allocated for the packet.
packet Rx too big count A part of NetWare Diagnostic Services that specifies the number of times (since the last reset or initialization) that the driver has received a packet over the maximum legal size.
packet Rx too small count A part of NetWare Diagnostic Services that specifies the number of times (since the last reset or initialization) that the driver has received a packet under the minimum legal size.
packets discarded unknown net A part of the NetWare File Server Environment Services that shows the number of packets discarded because their destination networks were unknown to the server.
packet sequence number A part of NetWare Workstation Services that contains the sequence ID number for the current request to the file server.
packet size Generally refers to the length of the packet. In NetWare, it refers to the size of the first packet to be sent, which must be between 30 and 512 bytes, inclusive. If the packet size shrinks below 30 bytes or grows beyond 512, IPX will automatically adjust the size to a valid value.
packets per send interval A part of NetWare Diagnostic Services that shows how many packets a source node should send to a destination mode as each send interval expires. For example, if the send interval is 3 and the packets per send interval is 5, a source node sends 5 packets every $\frac{3}{18}$ of a second.
packets received In NetWare and other networks, the number of point-to-point test packets that actually arrived at the destination node during a specified time period.
packets received during processing A part of NetWare File Server Environment Services that shows the number of times a new request was received while a previous request was still being processed.
packet switching The formation of messages into a packet or group with a predetermined length.
packet switching network A network that sends data in discrete blocks.
packets with bad request type A part of NetWare File Server Environment Services that shows a count of request packets containing invalid request types.
packet transmission The segmentation of messages and the subsequent transmission and re-

assembly at the destination. The separate routing of packets can be completely invisible to the host computers and terminals. The packets are typically stored in memory, and flow control procedures ensure that the storage does not become overloaded, while still maintaining loadings close to maximum. Packets can be checked for errors during transmission and retransmitted until they are correctly received. All messages can also be acknowledged from destination to source to ensure against their loss.

packet Tx misc error count A part of NetWare Diagnostic Services that specifies the number of miscellaneous errors that have prevented the driver from transmitting a packet (since the last reset or initialization).

packet Tx too big count A part of NetWare Diagnostic Services that specifies the number of times (since the last reset or initialization) that applications have asked the drive to send a packet over the maximum legal size.

packet Tx too small count A part of NetWare Diagnostic Services that specifies the number of times (since the last reset or initialization) that applications have asked the drive to send a packet under the minimum legal size.

packet type Refers to the type of service offered or required by the packet. In NetWare applications, Xerox has defined the following values:

- 0, unknown packet type
- 1, routing information packet
- 2, echo packet
- 3, error packet
- 4, packet exchange packet
- 5, sequenced packet protocol packet
- 16 through 31, experimental protocol
- 17, NetWare core protocol

pack field strength A limit of magnetizing forces associated with a magnetic field.

packing density The relative number of useful storage units or components per unit of dimension, such as the number of bits per inch on a magnetic tape, or the number of equivalent FETs on an LSI chip.

packing factor The number of words, bits, or characters that can be written or stored in a given length or volume of a device or medium.

PAD Acronym for *packet assembler/disassembler*, a processing unit on an X.25 network that allows asynchronous terminals to use the synchronous X.25 network by packaging asynchronous traffic into a packet. The PAD acts as an interpreter, allowing these disparate systems to talk to each other. The X.25 protocol extends to the lowest three levels of the OSI model. As an alternative, an asynchronous device may use a network interface module (NIM) to communication with an X.25 network.

pad 1. A device used to match or control impedance in a transmission line or between an rf generator and receiver terminals. **2.** To add capacitance in parallel with existing capacitors to alter the frequency of a tuned circuit. **3.** To add dummy records, words, or characters for the purpose of maintaining bit or timing integrity.

pad character A character inserted to fill a blank time slot in synchronous transmission or to fulfill the character count requirement for transmission of fixed block lengths.

page A segment of a computer program that has a virtual address and can be located in main storage or in auxiliary storage. A page can be moved into main memory by the operating system whenever the instructions of that subdivision need to be performed. A program can be divided into pages in order to minimize the total amount of main memory allocated to the program at any one time. Pages are normally stored on a fast-access store. Pages are typically a set of 4,096 consecutive bytes, with the first byte located at a storage address that is a multiple of 4,096.

page addressing A form of microprocessor addressing. Since the page memory is small, only a small address is needed. Also, a short address can be used with a base-plus-displacement addressing scheme. The high-order address byte can be stored in the processor while the low-order address byte is specified by a direct addressing instruction. This works well when most of the addresses to be accessed are located near each other (on the same page) so they have the same high-order address byte. In paging, one register is used to hold the page address, and there must be instructions to manipulate the register contents, such as increment or decrement commands.

page break Where one page of a printout ends and another begins.

Page One An add-on program for Word used for typesetting books. It controls kerning, widows, and orphans; hyphenates; and balances text on facing pages. It prepares the book for printing on any PostScript-compatible printer.

page orientation Orientation refers to the direction of print on the page. Printing across the width of a page is called *portrait orientation* printing. The word *portrait* refers to portraits of people, which are usually vertical in format. Printing across the length of a page is called *landscape orientation* printing. The term *landscape* is derived from paintings of landscapes, which are usually horizontal in format.

page printer A printer that sets up and prints entire pages at a time.

page protection The memory protection and control of page-mapped memories. The programmer may have control of read and/or write protection for each of the pages in memory. If the system and the user have independent memory maps, the programmer can specify a page of memory as unprotected for the operating system, but write-protected for the user. The result is a page of memory that can be altered by the operating system, but only read by the user.

pager A tiny pocketable receiver designed to receive personalized messages from a central dispatcher in a communication network.

page set-up Refers to how text is positioned on the page. Page set-up variables include the size of the paper to be printed, what margins will be used, and how many lines will be printed per inch.

page size The dimensions of the international page sizes used in laser printers are as follows:

- A3: 11.7 × 17"
- A4: 8.3 × 11.7"
- A5: 5.8 × 8.3"
- B4: 10.1 × 14.3"
- B5: 7.2 × 10.1"

pagination A word-processing feature that includes the placement of headers, footers, and page numbers.

paging 1. The procedure used to locate and transmit pages between main storage and auxiliary storage, or to exchange them with pages of the same program or other programs. Paging can be used to assist in the allocation of a limited amount of main storage among several concurrent programs. **2.** The process of calling a nontransmitter-equipped member of a communications network.

paintbrush A graphics function that allows the user to draw lines on the screen in a variety of widths.

paint program A graphics program such as Publisher's Paintbrush that produces bitmapped graphics. Paint programs have grown to the point where they are commonly employed to retouch images brought into the computer by a scanner. Another technique is replicating real media, such as airbrushes, chalk, oils, or acrylic paint. Some programs just do "watercolors," while others offer a full range of painting tools and also simulate various types of paper. *Contrast with* DRAW PROGRAM.

pair, binary *See* BINARY PAIR.

paired bars A bar chart that compares two series that apply to the same X-axis data.

paired cable A cable with two insulated conductors or with several sets of two conductors each.

PAL Abbreviation for *phase alteration line*, the color-television broadcast standard used in a number of European countries, including Germany and the United Kingdom. It is a common composite color transmission system (like NTSC) in which there are 625 scanning lines per frame and 25 frames per second. Brazil transmits PAL on a 525/30 system. *Also see* NTSC.

palette In computer graphics, the range of colors available.

PAM Acronym for *pulse-amplitude modulation*, a form of pulse modulation in which the amplitude of the pulses is varied in accordance with the modulating signal.

pancake A small, sealed package for a transistor.

panel The part of a computer or peripheral that provides an operator interface. A panel may be an interconnection unit with removable wires or plugs that allow specific functions to be changed by the operator. Other panels may show the relationship of system equipment using graphic indicators. *Maintenance and control panels* have indicator lights and switches on which are displayed a particular sequence of routines, and from which repairs can be determined.

PANEL Plus A user interface library with tools to design screen layouts and generate C or Fortran code for screen definitions. C applications can be ported between DOS, Windows, PS/2, Unix, and VMS with source changes.

pan-out unit A unit that gives a simple, flexible equipment interface to a LAN using only one transceiver. In applications where your LAN segment is short, a pan-out unit lets you get more people on the LAN than was possible without it. The unit can be used to create a stand-alone star network. In small areas, up to eight users can network to each other without a trunk cable.

The unit makes expansion of existing installations easy, permits a more economical use of the main network cable, and removes the need to snake the Ethernet cable in an area with a high density of equipment to be networked.

Acting as a transceiver multiplexer, the unit provides the full data rate of the network to each AUI connection. You can connect the pan-out unit to the network with a transceiver that compiles with IEEE 802.3 standards. Without the transceiver, the unit will operate in stand-alone mode and allow you to set up network diameters of up to 328.2 feet (100 meters).

Nine ports are used: eight for connecting external equipment and one for connecting an external transceiver. Each port implements transmit, receive, and collision functions, and can optionally support a heartbeat test when used with or without an external transceiver.

PAP Acronym for AppleTalk's *protocol for accessing printers*.

paper-checking exercise A technique used to check out a design on paper. It can be used to test the logical design of the program.

In a paper-checking exercise, you execute the program by hand, filling out entries in a table corresponding to the values of critical registers or outputs. This requires no development hardware, but it can be long and tedious. Paper checking is more often done at the flowchart level to verify the overall design. However, it might not result in a reasonable evaluation of actual performance.

paper feed guide The curved section directly beneath the EP cartridge in a laser printer. The guide directs paper past the cartridge to the fusing station. The surface of this guide may need occasional cleaning.

paper jam Refers to paper stuck somewhere along a printer's paper path.

paperless office Refers to offices where all mail, filing, and memos are done electronically.

paper park A feature of some dot matrix printers that allows fanfold paper to be loaded and ready while the printer works with single sheets.

paper refold basket A unit attached to the rear of a standard printer module or floor unit to catch and refold printout.

paper tape (*o.t.*) Long, narrow paper strips used to record and store information in the form of punched holes, partially punched holes, chemical impregnation, or magnetic-ink imprinting. Each character of information was punched in an established code across the width of the tape. Also called *punched paper tape* and *punched tape*.

parabola A plane curve generated by a point moving so that its distance from a fixed second point is equal to its distance from a fixed line.

parabolic interpolation A procedure used in the numerical control of a machine tool to control the centerline of a cutter path. The method uses parabolic segments defined by three programmed points.

Paradox A database manager where you can ask complex, ad hoc data questions with query-by-example (QBE). You can create multitable forms and reports, and export/import Quattro Pro spreadsheets. It uses PAL (Paradox Application Language), a development language for creating user applications.

PARAGON Control A software package in which the PC is used as a process control station. The user can configure the station for interactive process monitoring and control. The software package may also be used for diagnostics, simulation, and operator training.

paragraph In word processing, the text up to the point where the user pressed the Enter key. Paragraph attributes include line spacing, indentation, and justification.

paragraph mark In some word processors, a special code or character that identifies the point in the text where the user pressed the Enter key.

parallel Arranged in blocks for the simultaneous transmission, storage, or logical operation of items. *Contrast with* SERIAL.

parallel adder An adding circuit that processes all of the corresponding pairs of two numbers simultaneously.

parallel bidirectional bus driver/receiver A type of data bus buffer driver. The bidirectional bus driver has a high output drive capability for driving the system data bus. Use of this device reduces the number of components required to construct microcomputer systems.

parallel by character The handling of all characters of a machine word simultaneously in separate lines, channels, or storage units.

parallel circuit A circuit in which all elements are connected to two common points with the same applied voltage across all elements.

parallel connection The connection of two or more parts of a circuit to the same pair of terminals. Also called *shunt connection*.

parallel conversion A parallel 3-bit converter with Gray code output is shown in the figure. It has 2^{n-1} comparators, biased 1 LSB (least significant bit) apart and starting with +½ LSB. For zero input, all comparators are off. When the input increases, the number of comparators in the ON state increases. For any given bit position for the code, those comparator outputs that should give a logic 1 for a given input level are connected to the first NOR gate, and those that should be zero are connected to the next NOR gate, thus generating the correct code. Natural binary can be implemented in the same way.

In this approach, conversion occurs in parallel, with the speed limited only by the switching times of the comparators and logic gates. When the input changes, the output changes as a function of the switching times. This is the fastest approach to conversion, but the number of elements increases geometrically with the resolution. A 4-bit converter uses 15 comparators and seven 8-input gates. A 5-bit circuit requires 31 comparators and nine 16-input gates.

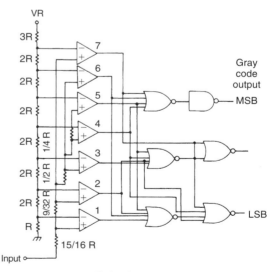

Parallel A/D controller

parallel conversion system A multichannel conversion system, such as the one shown in the diagram, with one converter for every analog source, in contrast to the conventional analog multiplexed system.

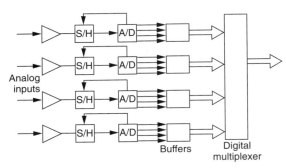

Parallel multichannel conversion system with digital multiplexing

parallel digital interface board A board that provides a means of interfacing a PC in any number of digital I/O applications. In addition to TTL/NMOS/CMOS-compatible data lines, it offers access to the PC's interrupt lines and external connection to the computer's power supplies.

parallel digital I/O card A card that provides TTL/DTL-compatible digital I/O lines, interrupt input, enable lines, and external connections to the PC's bus power supplies (+5, +12, −12, and −5 volt). It is a flexible interface for parallel I/O devices such as instruments, displays, and user-constructed systems and equipment.

parallel feed Refers to a connection using rc or lc coupling.

parallel input/output card A circuit board that has the necessary handshake flags for conventional parallel interfacing and contains all the required addressing circuitry.

parallel interface An interface that permits parallel transmission, or the simultaneous transmission of the bits making up a character or byte, over separate channels (wires) or different carrier frequencies of the same channel.

parallel operation The performance of several actions simultaneously using similar or identical devices for each action. Parallel operation can include the processing of all the digits of a word or byte by simultaneously transmitting each digit on a separate channel or bus. Parallel operation can save time over serial operation, but usually requires more equipment.

parallel-plate package A method of packaging circuits that uses a stacking arrangement to increase packing density.

parallel port An input/output plug that allows the entire bit pattern for a single character to be sent at one time, usually used to connect a printer to a computer.

parallel processing The processing of more than one program at a time using more than one active processor, in contrast to *multiprocessing*, where only one processor is active on one program at a time.

parallel processing system *See* PPS.

parallel processing system evaluation board A circuit designed for system development that usually contains a CPU, RAM, input/output ports, and a clock circuit.

parallel resonance In a circuit with inductance and capacitance connected in parallel, the steady state condition that exists when the current entering the circuit from the supply line is in phase with the voltage across the circuit.

parallel resonant circuit 1. A resonant circuit in which the applied voltage is connected across a parallel circuit formed by a capacitor and an inductor. **2.** An inductor and capacitor connected in parallel to furnish a high impedance at the frequency to which the circuit is resonant.

parallel search A memory-scanning and sensing operation in which the locations are identified by their contents rather than their addresses. A parallel-search memory allows fast interrogation for retrieving specific data elements.

parallel-series circuit A circuit in which several series strings of components are paralleled or in which several paralleled sets of components are series-strung. Also called *series-parallel*.

parallel storage Storage in which all characters, words, or bits are equally available. When words are in parallel, the storage is referred to as *parallel by word*. The use of parallel characters or bits implies a storage that is *parallel by character* or *parallel by bit*.

parallel system A system that uses two or more processors that may operate on two or more data streams in parallel, as shown in the following figure. The parallel system can also be configured to operate in parallel on a single data stream for high-reliability processing applications.

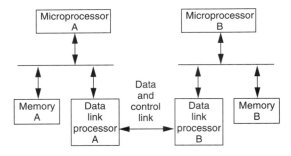

Parallel or linked multimicroprocessor system

parallel transfer Data transfer in which the characters of an element of information are trans-

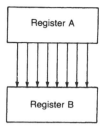

Parallel transfer

ferred simultaneously over a set of paths whose number equals the number of bits transferred at one time, as shown in the following figure.

parallel transmission The simultaneous data transmission of a number of signal elements over separate lines or communication channels.

parameter A variable that is usually given a constant value for a specific program or run. In a subroutine, a parameter may have different values when the subroutine is used in different main routines or in different parts of one main routine, but it usually remains unchanged throughout any one such use.

A *macro parameter* refers to the symbolic or literal elements in the operand part of a macro statement. The macro parameter is usually substituted into specific instructions in the incomplete routine to develop a complete open subroutine.

parameter and definition list A list that explains the function of each parameter and its meaning. The parameters can also be explained in the program.

parameter, macro *See* PARAMETER.

parameter potentiometer A potentiometer used to represent a parameter such as a coefficient or a scale factor. Also called a *scale-factor potentiometer* or *coefficient potentiometer*.

parametric amplifier A type of circuit that uses variable reactance elements to transfer energy from pumped power oscillators. There are many circuit arrangements, such as negative resistance amplifiers, up converters, and down converters.

parametric diode A diode in which the series capacitance can be varied by a biasing voltage.

parametric oscillator A type of oscillator that relies on the fact that certain nonlinear reactors, when driven by a pump or other source of frequency, f, may exhibit negative resistance at frequencies of $f/2, f/3, \ldots f/n$ where n is determined by the form the nonlinearity takes. If the reactor is an inductor, the device may be referred to as a *parametron*.

parametric potentiometer A potentiometer used to represent parameters such as coefficients or scale factors.

parametric subroutine A subroutine that involves parameters. The computer is expected to adjust and generate the subroutine according to the parametric values chosen.

parametron A device that uses two stable states of oscillation to store binary digits.

parasitic An undesirable radiation parameter in an electronic circuit, such as oscillation, which disappears when circuit operation ceases.

parasitic capacitance In MOS (metal-oxide semiconductor) devices, since most metal-oxide substrate formations are not at channels, parasitic or extraneous capacitance exists. Channel and parasitic capacitances slow down gate switching time because there is a threshold voltage (V^T) at which the channel starts to conduct; the time taken to reach this threshold voltage is increased by the presence of capacitance. Parasitic capacitance in MOS devices is caused by a current-carrying metal layer, a semiconductor layer, and a thin oxide isolating layer. SOS (silicon-on-sapphire) devices have the current-carrying metal separated from a conducting mounting by a thick, isolating sapphire base. The thickness of the sapphire base reduces the parasitic capacitance to negligible proportions.

parasitic oscillation Various types of desirable oscillation in an amplifier, or the oscillation of an oscillator at some frequency other than the resonant frequency. It is generally of high frequency and may occur during a portion of each cycle of the main oscillation. Also called a *spurious oscillation*.

parasitic stopper A device or component that attenuates or eliminates a parasitic condition.

parasitic suppressor A parallel resistance or a parallel combination of inductance and resistance that is used to suppress parasitic oscillations.

PARC Abbreviation for Xerox's *Palo Alto Research Center*.

parent A directory or group that includes one or more subdirectory or subgroup entries, called *child* directories or groups.

parent population A prototype or initial batch of articles or units under study or consideration.

parity The anticipated state (odd or even) of a set of binary digits. Parity is achieved by use of a self-checking code employing binary digits in which the total number of ones in each expression is deliberately kept odd or even by the addition of an extra digit whenever necessary. In ASCII, the leftmost digit is used as a parity bit.

parity bit In an even-parity system, a bit added to a group of bits whose total of ones would otherwise be odd; in an odd-parity system, an added bit to make an even number of ones total an odd number. The parity bit is error insurance; if odd parity is specified, an error condition will be flagged each time an even number of bits is counted with a parity bit present. In some systems, the transmission is specified as always odd or even so the parity bit does not change; in others the parity bit is added to make the sum of the bits odd or even when required. In ASCII, the leftmost bit is a parity bit added to character groups whose complement of ones is odd. Also see COLUMN PARITY.

parity check A check used to determine if the total number of ones or zeros in a word or byte is odd or even. This sum is checked against a previously computed parity digit. Also called *odd-even check*. Also see EVEN PARITY CHECK.

parity error A condition that occurs when a computed parity check does not agree with the parity bit; in an even-parity system, a parity error occurs when the total of bits (including the parity bit) is odd.

parity generator-checker A hardware unit used to generate and check parity conditions on data words, as shown in the following diagram. Available units can be used for either *odd* or *even* parity applications, and cascading allows expansion to any word length.

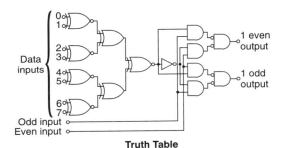

Parity generator-checker (eight bits)

parity interrupt An interrupt that occurs because of a parity error.

parity check A check using the number of binary ones that is always maintained as an odd or even number. If the ones in the data part of the word or character are even, the parity bit is zero; if they are odd, the parity bit is one.

parsing In language theory, the procedures for dividing components into structural forms.

part A discrete component in an electronic circuit or system.

part failure rate The anticipated or recorded number of occasions in a specified time period when a component will malfunction.

partial carry A technique used in parallel addition in which some or all of the carries are stored temporarily, rather than being allowed to propagate.

partial program A program that is incomplete by itself and generally a specification of only a process to be performed on data. It might be used at more than one point in any particular program, or it might be made available for inclusion in other programs. Often called a *subprogram* or *incomplete program*.

partial response A multilevel coding scheme that uses selected amounts of intersymbol interference to increase the transmission rate in a given bandwidth.

particle size The average volume of the magnetic particles used in magnetic memories.

partition 1. An area of fixed size in memory. In a multiprogram environment, memory can be divided into partitions, each containing a varying number of bytes. Each program is allocated a certain partition that it may use, and might be required to wait its turn for that partition to become available. Partition sizes are alterable by the user. **2.** To divide memory into partitions.

partition table A table of information stored at the beginning of a hard disk that identifies the location of the partitions of the disk.

part operation The part of an instruction that specifies the kind of arithmetic or logic operation to be performed, but not the address of the operands.

part programmer An operator who prepares the planned sequence of events for the operation of a numerically controlled machine tool.

parts family A set of closely related and compatible IC components, such as a clock and driver, microprocessor, RAM, ROM, and I/O chips. These parts are available as a kit and might be sold in single quantities by the manufacturer.

party line structure A bus structure in which each device is linked to a single bus through tristate buffers. The bus may be unidirectional, but more often, a bidirectional bus is used so the information can pass among the various sources and acceptors.

Pascal A structured, high-level language used in a wide variety of applications.

pass A complete cycle of reading, processing, and writing. Also called *machine run*.

pass element An automatic variable resistance device, such as a power transistor, placed in series with a source of dc power. The pass element is driven by the amplified error signal to increase its resistance when the output needs to be lowered or to decrease its resistance when the output must be raised. This technique is used in regulating power supplies.

passive device Any electrical device placed within a circuit that passes signals without altering them. This could be a connector or a signal monitor that observes the signals but does not change them.

passive hub An ARCnet hub for connecting up to four computers. *Contrast with* ACTIVE HUB.

passive star A topology in which cables branch out of a central block. There is no repeater function.

password A group of characters used to identify a user to a computer system so that he or she may gain access to the system or part of that system. Passwords are used to ensure the security of computer systems by regulating the amount of access freedom.

PAT Acronym for *program activity transmissions*, an electronic system for collecting manufacturing and accounting information.

patch 1. To insert corrected coding into a routine to correct a mistake or alter the routine. A patch does not have to be inserted into the routine sequence being corrected; it can be placed somewhere else with an exit to the patch and a return to the routine provided. **2.** A temporary repair to a malfunctioning system. **3.** A wired connection or set of wired connections used in place of switches, usually on a temporary basis.

patchboard A removable board containing terminals, into which patch cords (short wires) are connected that determine the different options for the machine. To change the options, the wiring pattern on the patchboard or the patchboard itself must be changed.

path A file system concept that indicates what set of folders or subdirectories a file is stored in. In DOS and similar operating systems, a *file path* specifies the full name of the target file. In NetWare, full paths may be specified as in SYS:USER\DJT\MYFILE.DAT, or paths may extend the default directory. Assuming the default directory is SYS:APPS, setting the file path to WP\TEST.DAT would make the target file SYS:APPS\WP\TEST.DAT.

path control layer The SNA layer that handles routing and flow control.

path profile A graphic representation of a communication propagation path showing the objects that might cause obstruction or reflection.

pattern 1. The waveform produced by a circuit or set of circuits (a pulse train, for example). **2.** The configuration of printed circuitry on a board or chip.

pattern recognition The identification of shapes, forms, or configurations by automated methods.

pattern-sensitive fault A fault that occurs in response to some particular pattern of data.

PAU Acronym for *position analog unit*, a unit that feeds back to an amplifier analog information corresponding to the position of a machine slide to be compared with the potential input information.

PAX Acronym for *private automatic exchange*.

PBX Abbreviation for *private branch exchange*. Loosely, this refers to a manual switchboard.

PC Abbreviation for *program counter* (the index address register), *programmable controller*, *process controller*, *printer controller*, and *personal computer*. Specifically, a (usually) DOS- or Windows-based microcomputer made by IBM or one of its competitors. An external view of a typical PC is shown in the following figure.

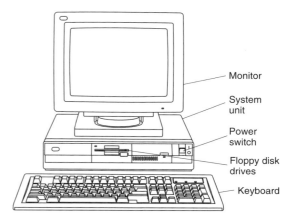

Typical IBM-compatible personal computer

pc Abbreviation for *printed circuit*.

PCA Abbreviation for *programmable communication adapter*, a versatile, microprocessor-based, data communication device. The PCA was designed to support a wide variety of data communications applications simply by changing the firmware (EPROM). The PCA architecture is structured around a microprocessor with two individually programmable asynchronous ports controlled by standard 8251 USARTs (universal synchronous/asynchronous receiver/transmitters). *Also see* USART.

PC Accounting A general-purpose business program useful for small businesses using the single-entry accounting method. It uses a process similar to that in the DOME accounting books and has several modules to calculate payroll, track expenses, calculate depreciation, and compare bank statements.

PC Album An integrated database package that allows users to include full-color images along with traditional database information. It is designed to utilize the latest image-compression and data-storage technologies. Images are captured from a video source, compressed, integrated with textual data records, and stored in a digital format.

pcANYWHERE A remote-access program that lets you operate your system from anywhere through a modem, as if you were using the host machine. You have complete access, including the ability to run programs remotely, or transfer files to and from the remote system. You can also connect a Macintosh to your PC and run your DOS programs remotely, transfer files, print on the Macintosh printer under DOS applications, or use the mouse to control DOS function keys.

PC-Art A multifunction drawing program that is not dependent upon having a mouse or light pen.

pc board Abbreviation for *printed-circuit board*, a board prepared from the printing of a chemically resistive ink.

pc board control point A contact area on a circuit board to make it easier to reconfigure the circuitry or conduct tests. There are two major methods for fabricating printed circuit boards: the *additive method* and the *subtractive method*. The subtractive method calls for the printing of a chemically resistive ink or paint in a type of stenciling operation on an insulating board with previously applied copper foil. Acid is used to selectively etch away unwanted metal to leave the desired pattern on the board. The additive method also employs a printing process, but the pattern covers only those areas where metal is not desired. Thus, selective plating can be performed on an unclad insulating board that has been treated to accept the plating metal.

pc board package *See* DIP.

pc board portable tester A tester with a built-in processor for field service use. These testers have the ability not only to test boards, but also to simulate peripherals. Some can exercise entire instruments and diagnose problems down to the component level.

pc board power shut-off A technique that is useful in LSI (large-scale integration) common bus circuitry on a board. A number of ROMs can be tied to a common bus. One ROM can be isolated from the influence of others by shutting off power to all but that ROM. Power shut-off can be controlled by means of a transistor switch or jumper wire. In either case, LSI circuitry or ROMs can be effectively isolated from one another.

pc board test language A language used in automatic pc board testing that is specifically designed for the requirements of testing complex boards containing microprocessors and other LSI components. A typical test language is capable of loading registers, transferring data between registers, generating repetitive routines, and performing limited tests.

pc board test point An area on a pc board used as a probe contact point during testing.

PC-Books An accounting package that helps you prepare journals, general ledgers, income statements, and balance sheets.

PCC Abbreviation for *program controlled computer*.

PC-Calc A simple spreadsheet program that is able to handle basic spreadsheet functions.

PC-Check A personal finance program that has a menu-driven checkbook and personal general ledger with printout and check-writing capabilities. It can sort data files, find payees, print checks, track income tax deductions, and list data by month, quarter, payee or ledger account.

PC cleaning kit A cleaning kit for personal computers that contains antistatic spray and supplies for disk drive head cleaning, CRT screen cleaning, and general surface cleaning.

PC-Deskteam A DOS-based all-in-one utility/accessory program. It includes an alarm clock, calculator, calendar, selected DOS commands, notepad, telephone dialer, printer control, typewriter mode, and an ASCII chart.

PC-DIAL A modem communications program that has the ability to create automatic logon scripts.

PC-DOS The operating system sold with IBM PC hardware. *See* DOS.

PC environmental considerations Because PCs were designed for the office environment, they are viewed as fragile. The floppy disk is not compatible with many environments. Dust or other particulates are a problem. Even industrial control rooms may tend to be dirty. Environmental concerns such as fumes can destroy floppy disk heads over time. Other electronic devices may also be degraded, but the disk drives appear to be the biggest concern. Moisture, dust, and corrosive chemicals are the main problems, but electromagnetic interference (EMI) can also be a problem, even if the power supply is conditioned properly. The plant floor is often electrically noisy. Shock and vibration are also hard on PCs, although these problems are generally easier to solve.

Some industrial PCs employ a cooling system where the air is drawn in through a filter and returned out through the disk openings. The opposite path is used in office machines. This can reduce the exposure of the internal components to corrosive materials and particulates. Another solution is to keep PCs out of harmful environments. This means installation in control rooms, enclosed offices, or someplace remote from the processes they are intended to monitor and/or control. It sometimes becomes a tradeoff between getting far enough away to keep the machine operating and being close enough for the machine to be able to get the data it needs, given the distance limitations of some of the communications schemes.

PCE2 ROMDISK A solid-state floppy drive emulator for the XT/AT compatible systems and 80386 AT compatible. It is capable of emulating single or dual diskette drives. In the single disk mode, EPROMs emulate a read-only disk with capacities up to 1.2M. With an SRAM version, a read/write disk of up to 1.44M can be emulated. In the dual disk mode, it can emulate two floppy disks or hard drives.

EPROMs are programmed by the on-board PROM burner. First, you prepare a floppy diskette with all the files and utilities and programs that you wish to have on your ROM disk. Next, you use the utility program to copy your floppy diskette to the EPROMs on the ROM disk. On-board BIOS ROMs interact with your system to emulate standard disk drives. Memory transfer can be set either for DMA channel 1 or through programmed I/O if DMA conflicts exist.

PC-File A popular database filing program that allows you to quickly retrieve data, change it, resequence it, perform queries, and prepare reports for display, printing, or subsequent retrieval.

PC/FOCUS A complete database and information management system for personal computers. Its design, function, and capabilities are identical to FOCUS, one of the leading information programs for mainframes. Code written for the PC version is transportable to and from the mainframe version. The facilities are among the most functional available on the PC. However, it was developed for a large system and uses up system resources.

PC-Font A program that enables an Epson dot matrix printer to print 243 of the 256 ASCII characters. These characters include those applicable for engineering, scientific, financial, and foreign language applications. Other capabilities include printing block graphic fonts and calling up one of 13 different fonts from the command line.

PC fortress An enclosure that locks out users.

PCF ROMDISK A solid-state peripheral storage device for PC/XT/AT and EISA bus computers. It allows systems to be assembled using solid-state nonvolatile memory without mechanical floppy and hard disk drives. These systems are up to 20 times more reliable than mechanical disk-based systems.

The unit can be erased and reprogrammed on a network from a remote terminal to eliminate service calls. Using flash technology and the Microsoft flash file system, the unit operates as a WORM (write-once, read-many) device that can add data to the memory until it is full. After the memory is full, it is bulk erased and reprogrammed.

PC-Fullback A DOS-based utility program for backing up, comparing, and restoring files between a hard disk and a floppy disk drive.

PC-General Ledger A program for accounting, finance, taxes and general management. The program has the controls necessary to make sure that everything is kept in balance and that a complete audit trail always exists. The program assumes a working knowledge of bookkeeping.

PC-GRAF A BASIC program to plot line graphs of data sets. Data entry is from the keyboard or from data files.

p-channel A p-type semiconductor region that functions as the conducting channel in n-gate FETs.

p-channel enhancement-mode MOSFET A metal-oxide field-effect transistor whose conducting channel between source and drain is doped with p-channel impurities.

p-channel metal gate (*o.t.*) The earliest successful MOS process. Although there were prior unsuccessful attempts by various manufacturers to develop a process and become established in the MOS business, not until 1967 was it proven that MOS integrated circuits were an economically and technologically viable product. Thus, the p-channel metal gate process became the basis for an entire MOS industry and stimulated the development of a multitude of other processes.

p-channel MOS Metal-oxide semiconductor devices that use a p-channel conduction mode. P-channel devices tend to be slower than n-channel units and also exhibit a lower gain.

p-channel technology (*o.t.*) The earliest microprocessors used p-channel technology. This, however, had two disadvantages. Holes have a lower mobility in silicon than electrons; as a result, PMOS transistors are slower than NMOS devices. Also, PMOS circuits provide an active pullup but require a passive pulldown of external loads. NMOS amplifiers provide an active pulldown, which is more effective for driving the TLL interface circuits common in microprocessors. PMOS is the older technology, which was better understood and thus more economical. It was used successfully in the first microprocessors. It provided good density then (up to 15,000 transistors per chip). It is, however, slower compared to newer technologies, such as NMOS with its many variations. Its main attraction to manufacturers today is that it is a well-understood process, and a complex device can be developed with a high probability of success at a lower cost than newer technologies. But, while p-channel MOS technology provided a low-cost approach to early microprocessor designs, it is not used in designs today.

PCI 1. Abbreviation for *peripheral command indicator*. **2.** Abbreviation for *program check interruption*. **3.** Abbreviation for *peripheral component interconnect*.

PCI bus The PCI (peripheral component interconnect) bus attempts to bring the PC's data-transmission technology up to the speed and capability of the microprocessors that provide the computing power. A bus is a collection of wires (or signal paths) and a standardized definition of each signal on each wire. The PCI bus defines the data and control signals that travel between the CPU and its peripheral devices, such as disk controllers or video graphics boards. The ISA (industry standard architecture) bus was introduced with the original IBM PC in 1981 and was upgraded to a 16-bit bus when the PC/AT was introduced in 1984. The ISA bus runs at 8MHz.

The architecture of the 486 microprocessor led to the 486 local bus and was standardized as the VESA (video electronic standards association) local bus and abbreviated VL-bus. The VL-bus allows peripheral to be connected directly to a high-speed 132M-per-second bus that is 32-bits wide for fast access to the CPU. The VL-bus was originally defined for video requirements. It requires a high chip count and is relatively costly to implement.

PCI is not a local bus that ties into the 1486 bus, it is an intermediate or mezzanine bus. It is generated from the high-speed bus, but not directly connected to it. Buffer chips provide the transfer of data to and from the PCI bus data and signal lines, which connect PCI peripheral devices, such as video cards and SCSI controllers. Another chip set can generate the ISA bus from the PCI bus system.

PCI has a 32-bit or 64-bit width. The VL-bus uses short connectors that are an extension of, and in the same line as, the two connectors for the ISA bus. PCI connectors are parallel with the ISA connectors. PCI and ISA slots are not incompatible, since the PCI connectors are smaller than the ISA connectors.

PC Illustrator A program that combines business graphics, word diagrams, freeform art, and slide presentations. PC Illustrator allows you to size, copy, move, and combine different types of charts. The slideshow feature organizes your pictures and charts, allowing you to replay them in three different ways with a variety of special effects. For example, you can dissolve one slide into another or lower and raise a curtain to reveal the next slide.

PC Imagescript The first full implementation of the PostScript page description language available for DOS. Output may be viewed either on the screen or from a hardcopy device such as a LaserJet or compatible laser printer.

PC industrial applications The major application of PCs in industrial plants is in configuring control systems. The next largest application is data acquisition, either as a front end to process controllers, or in direct connection to a process through I/O boards or I/O processors.

PC/Intercomm A program that turns a PC into a smart DEC VT100 terminal. PC/Intercomm includes full-screen cursor addressing, data to disk transfer, and transmission of ASCII and binary files at speeds up to 9600 baud. To facilitate uploading from a host computer, the program uses the Xmodem error-protection protocol. It is menu-driven, has XON/XOFF handshaking and line-feed deletion/addition. It stores specific terminal configurations and has programmable function keys.

PC keyboard video switch A device designed to give you dual access to a PC or compatible from any two workstations with a keyboard and monitor, as shown in the following diagram. It switches the keyboard and monitor simultaneously.

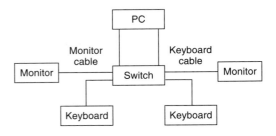

PC keyboard video switch

PCL Abbreviation for *process control language*, a language that resembles Fortran and is modeled after relay logic for arithmetic and logic commands. PCL allows a control program to be created in English, then converted into machine language for storage in a PROM. The following features should be a requirement for a powerful PCL:

- Compatibility with a major language
- Efficiency of overhead
- Simplicity
- Facility for running multiple tasks
- Inclusion of all common machine operations
- Interrupt capability
- Subroutine and compilation capability

PC-lint A diagnostic facility for C that can find bugs, glitches and inconsistencies that a compiler working on one module at a time will miss. It supports full K&R, ANSI, Microsoft, and Turbo C keywords, including file directories and indirect files. It can be used to find inconsistent declarations, argument/parameter mismatches, uninitialized variables, unaccessed variables, variables assigned but not used, suspicious macros, indentation irregularities, function inconsistencies, unusual expressions, and print-scan irregularities. It features automatic generation of declarations (prototypes) and wildcard support, and works with any C compiler or cross-compiler.

PCM Abbreviation for *pulse-code modulation*, the modulation of a pulse train using a specified code or code system.

PC MacTerm/Network A program that lets you control a PC through any Macintosh on an AppleTalk network. You can use it to transfer or copy files and run peripherals.

PCMCIA Abbreviation for *personal computer memory card industry association*, the standard used for the small PC card slots in notebook computers. These cards are about the size of a credit card and twice as thick. They fit into a slot in a notebook computer and attach to a 68-pin connector inside. PCMCIA cards are often used as portable modems, hard disk storage, and Ethernet interfaces. Most of the PCMCIA modems come with their own 16550A UARTs built in. Not all of the PC card slots are the same; some compatibility problems exist.

PC-NET (*o.t.*) IBM's initial DOS-based LAN operating system based on Microsoft's MS-NET OEM LAN operating system.

PC-Outline A program that gives users the capacity to outline and organize items by different categories. Features include hot-key definition and automatic numbering. It can interact with ProKey, SideKick, and other memory-resident programs.

PCP Abbreviation for *primary control program*.

PC Paint A DOS-based, mouse-driven color graphics program that lets you create and edit full-color pictures. It has a variety of applications, including the preparation of advertisements, promotional materials, architectural drawings and simple, one-screen flowcharts and organization charts. This program is well-suited for enhancing business presentations, because it can capture a graphics screen from another program such as 1-2-3 for modification into presentation material.

PC-Payroll A DOS-based, menu-driven payroll system for small to mid-sized companies. Reports include monthly, quarterly, and year-to-date summaries; federal tax reports (W2, W3, 941); and a pay period detail. Federal, state, and local taxes, FICA, pension/insurance withholding, and user-defined deductions are internally computed. Paychecks and stubs are printed according to several predefined formats.

PC printer switch A switch that interconnects a microcomputer, a modem, and an online transmit (or receive-only) serial printer, as shown in the following diagram.

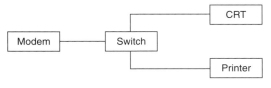

PC printer switch

PC Probe A software package for diagnostics, benchmarks, and utilities. You can test your system board, RAM, video, keyboard, COM ports, floppy drives, and hard drives. You can locate fading RAM and run tests in batch or single pass, remote or onsite. Utilities include virus protection, a CMOS editor, and a speed test.

PC Publisher Kit Software that turns a laser printer into a desktop publishing printer by allowing DDL and PostScript compatibility. It provides full scalable fonts, increased processing speed, multiple printing languages, HP-GL capabilities, rotatable fonts and graphics, arbitrary clipping, and a variety of typefaces.

PCs as operator interfaces PCs are often used as an operator interface for PLC (programmable logic controller) applications. The PC with the proper software can be used to replace control and graphic panels as well as annunciators.

PC Sell A point-of-sale (POS) system for the retail sales environment. It is an integrated program designed to assist retail management through inventory control, accounts receivable, and invoice production. Its 17 modules and five databases comprise a networkable POS system specifically designed for the retail industry.

PC serial modem cable The cable that connects the PC's DB25S (female) to the modem DB25P (male).

PC service kit A toolkit that contains 20 of the most common, demagnetized tools needed to maintain and enhance a PC or printer.

PCs in development work A major use of PCs is in development work, including the development of control applications for other devices as well as performing calculations in support of engineering. Personal computers are becoming part of a move to construct fully integrated data-handling systems. These generally parallel the physical processes being controlled. The PC is one of the fundamental building blocks in these systems.

pc testing, personality board See PERSONALITY CARD.

PC token card See TOKEN RING CARD.

PC Tools A collection of data recovery, hard-disk backup, DOS shell, and desktop management programs. It includes the DiskFix disk repair program and supports a wide variety of tape-backup systems.

PC-Write An easy-to-use DOS-based word processor that has been around for many years.

.PCX A filenaming extension that indicates a graphics file format used by PC Paint and other, faster, graphic-compatible applications.

PCX Toolkit A program that lets developers create applications to display, save, print, scroll, size, scale, capture, and manipulate PCX format images. It supports Turbo Assembler, Turbo C and C++, Turbo Pascal, Lattice C, Microsoft BASIC, Microsoft C/QuickC, Microsoft Fortran, Macro Assembler, Microsoft Pascal, QuickBasic, and Nantucket Clipper.

PC-ZAP A utility program that allows easy modification of any DOS file without the use of the DOS DEBUG command. PC-ZAP can dump a file, verify data in a file, and replace data in a file.

PD **1.** Abbreviation for *pulse driver*. **2.** Abbreviation for *pulse duration*.

PDL Abbreviation for *programmable digital logic*; refers to logic that can be changed by changing a program, in contrast to hardware logic that must be changed by changing connections. There are a number of economic advantages: the design costs are lower because the systematic approach to logic design is more efficient, and prototype modifications in software are quicker and less costly.

PDM Abbreviation for *pulse duration modulation*, the modulation of pulse data using varying widths of pulses to convey information.

PDQCOMM Software that adds serial communications to BASIC programs. It supports COM ports 1 through 4, and hardware and software handshaking. It uses syntax nearly identical to BASIC and features XMODEM and ASCII file transfers.

PDTE Abbreviation for *packet mode data terminating equipment*, equipment that generates packets, as opposed to characters.

PDU Abbreviation for *protocol data unit*, a layer that communicates with its peer by sending packets. Each packet has a header that contains the information the peer will work with, such as addresses or acknowledgment requests. It also contains data that is passed up to the client of the layer.

PE 1. Abbreviation for *phase encoding*. 2. Abbreviation for *polyethylene*, a type of plastic material used for cable jacketing. 3. *See* PORT EXPANDER.

peak 1. The maximum instantaneous value of a quantity. 2. A momentarily high amplitude occurring in electronic equipment.

peak amplitude Refers to the maximum deviation of a wave from its average position.

peak clipper A device that passes signals and cuts off peaks above a predetermined level without otherwise altering the waveform.

peak data transfer rate The maximum rate at which data is transmitted through a channel. The peak data transfer rate is usually measured in characters per second, discounting gaps between blocks and words.

peak distortion The worst-case displacement of wave components. Also called *jitter*.

peak follower A device composed of a sample-hold and a comparator circuit, as shown in the figure. Balancing the unknown input voltage against some form of internally produced reference, the comparator circuit responds to the polarity of the inequality between input and reference. The sample-hold output is biased by a few millivolts of hysteresis signal to avoid ambiguity problems during step inputs and reduce false triggering from noise. When the input is greater than the sample-hold output, the comparator's positive output forces the sample-hold to a track mode. When the input becomes less than the sample-hold output, the comparator causes the sample-hold to the hold state until the input once again becomes greater than the output. To reset the circuit, the control input is switched into sample, and a low level is applied at the input.

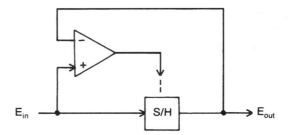

Peak follower with sample-hold

peak flux density A maximum magnetic condition of magnetic materials.

peak forward voltage The maximum instantaneous voltage in the forward now direction of an anode current as measured between the anode and cathode of a rectifier.

peaking circuit A circuit capable of converting an input signal into a peak waveform.

peaking network A circuit used to increase the amplification at the upper end of the frequency range for a system.

peak limiter A device that passes signals of average amplitude, but that compresses or otherwise restricts signal peaks to some established preset value. *Also see* PEAK CLIPPER.

peak load The maximum instantaneous rate of power consumption for a circuit, load, or system.

peak-to-peak amplitude The amplitude of an alternating quantity, measured from the positive peak to the negative peak.

peak transfer rate *See* PEAK DATA TRANSFER RATE.

peak value The maximum instantaneous value of a varying current, voltage, or power. For a sine wave, it is equal to 1.414 times the effective value of the sine wave. Also called the *crest value*.

peek-a-boo system (o.t.) An information retrieval system that uses small cards with drilled or punched holes. Also called *batten system* and *cordonnier system*.

peer network A configuration that uses mutually cooperating computers in which there is no defined master or slave relationship of one system over the other. The peer network requires that the operating system of each computer be aware of the status of the other computers in the network, and that a scheduling program provide the task distribution. As a job is passed to a computer in the network, the originating computer moves to a new task. A computer that is busy passes the task on to an available computer, which executes the task. The time response in a peer network is difficult to predict, since one computer does not know the workload of another and there is no master that can impose tasks.

Peer networks provide access to specialized

facilities not available on the originating computer, and the processors share the computing load for a more efficient use of the total facility. Also called *peer-to-peer network*.

peer-to-peer Refers to communication between two devices of the same general type.

peer-to-peer exchange The ability of different workstations to interconnect and communicate.

pel *See* PIXEL.

Peltier effect A phenomenon where heat is liberated or absorbed at a junction when current passes from one metal to another.

PEMDAS An acronym for the order of precedence in arithmetic operation for programming: parenthesis, exponentiation, multiplication, division, addition, and subtraction.

pending IO commands In the NetWare File Server Environment, the number of outstanding disk controller commands.

penetration A measure of the depth of the skin effect of eddy currents in induction heating or the depth of the magnetic field in super-conducting metals.

pen light A pen-like device with light and a photosensor on one end for communicating with a computer through a CRT device.

pentagrid A frequency-converting tube used in heterodyne receivers. The cathode and two grids form an oscillator, and the modulated electron stream is mixed with the incoming signal by the other grids and the anode acting as a pentode.

Pentium A microprocessor introduced by the Intel Corporation in March of 1993 as the successor to their i486. The Pentium is superscalar CISC-base microprocessor containing 3.1 million transistors. It uses a 32-bit address bus and a 64-bit data bus, a built-in floating point unit, memory management unit, and two 8KB internal caches.

pentode transistor A transistor designed for mixing, modulating, or switching, and containing four electrodes.

PEP Abbreviation for *packet exchange protocol*, an XNS transport protocol that requires each packet to be separately acknowledged. A PEP-like protocol forms the foundation of the NetWare Core Protocols.

PER Abbreviation for *program event recording*.

perfect dielectric A dielectric in which all the energy required to establish an electric field is returned when the field is removed. In practice, only a vacuum conforms to this, and all other dielectrics dissipate heat to varying extents.

performance Operation with some degree of effectiveness.

performance characteristic A characteristic measurable in terms of a useful denominator such as gain, power, or output.

performance requirements The set of values, conditions, and operating criteria that define the acceptable operation for a computer system and its subsystems. The computer system must fulfill minimum requirements for online response time, operating time, and record or file size.

perfusing Fusing with a low current to clean the fiber ends as a procedure to fusion splicing.

period 1. The time required for one complete cycle. 2. A specified time duration for the performance or evaluation of a procedure. 3. The reciprocal of frequency.

periodic Refers to a cycle that repeats regularly in time and form.

periodic current An oscillating current, the values that recur at equal time intervals.

periodic damping A damping in which the output of an instrument oscillates about the final position before coming to rest.

periodic pulse train A group of pulses that repeat at regular intervals in time sequence.

periodic quantity An oscillating quantity in which any value attained is repeated at equal, regular intervals.

periodic rating The electrical load that can be handled for alternate periods of load and rest without exceeding the specified heating limits for the equipment, or without significant degradation of circuit or system performance.

peripheral A device or piece of equipment distinct from the system unit, but which connects to the system usually by means of a bus and provides the processing unit with outside communication. Peripheral equipment includes all the auxiliary units that may be placed under the control of the computer, such as monitors, printers, modems, scanners, etc. Peripheral equipment may be used online or offline, depending upon the system job requirements and economic considerations.

peripheral bus The data direction register (DDR) of the peripheral bus is used to establish each individual peripheral bus line as either an input or an output. Each of the DDR's 8-bit positions corresponds to a peripheral data line; a zero or a one written into a bit position causes that line to function as an input or output, in some systems.

peripheral device control In order for a CPU to communicate with a peripheral device, the CPU must select the device and the mode of communication. During an I/O instruction, the CPU transmits the device address and control information to select a unique device in a specified mode. A PLA (programmed logic array) can be used to monitor the device address and control field bus to issue appropriate control signals to the devices. *Also see* PLA.

peripheral interface adapter *See* PIA.

peripheral interface channel The interface form that is designed or agreed upon so that two or more devices, systems, or programs may be easily joined or shared.

peripheral interface module The optional interface cards available for selected peripherals.

The modules or cards usually plug into a common chassis or card frame.

peripheral-limited Descriptive of a system whose processing speed or time is dictated by the limitations of the peripherals.

peripheral software driver The program that enables a user to communicate with and control peripheral devices.

peripheral subsystem A group of one or more peripheral units of the same type that are connected to an available I/O channel. A channel synchronizer-control unit interprets the control signals and instructions issued by the CPU and handles the transfer of data to and from the selected unit and the processor. It also indicates the status of the peripheral units and informs the CPU when errors or faults occur.

peripheral support computer A computer used for auxiliary operations in support of a large processing complex and compatible with the host computer only to the extent that data interchange is not required for auxiliary conversion.

peripheral transfer The process of transmitting data between two or more peripheral units.

Periscope/Remote A program that provides full-screen, source-level support for debugging Base and PM device drivers under OS/2. It runs at the systems level (ring 0) with minimal impact on the system being debugged. It offers easy access to any memory location in the system, and can coexist with an applications level (ring 3) debugger.

It requires two systems. The host system runs regular Periscope software in DOS and acts as the debugging system. The second system, the target, runs Periscope/Remote and the software you are debugging. The two systems are connected via a null-modem cable.

permalloy The group name for a class of high-permeability nickel-iron alloys.

permanent dynamic storage A form of dynamic storage in which the maintenance of the data stored does not depend on a flow of energy into the storage medium.

permanent error An error that is not eliminated by reprocessing.

permanent fault A repetitious failure in performance in the manner required or specified. Although they are repetitious, permanent faults may escape attention when they do not result in failure to perform some particular tasks.

permanent memory Stored data that remains intact when power is removed, such as a magnetic disk.

permanent storage Storage that is not altered by computer instructions, such as a magnetic core with a lockout feature. Also called *nonerasable storage, fixed storage*, and *read-only storage*.

permatron A hot cathode gas discharge diode, gated by an applied magnetic field.

permeability The ratio of magnetic field flux density to the magnetizing force.

permeability constant The inductance per unit area in a near-perfect vacuum or in free space, symbol μo. In the International System of Units, the value is $12.566\ 370\ 614 \times 10^{-7}$ henrys per meter.

permittivity The ratio of electric displacement to the electric field intensity in a material.

permittivity constant The capacitance per unit area in a near-perfect vacuum or in free space, symbol ϵo. In the International System of Units, the value is $8.854\ 187\ 818 \times 10^{-12}$ farads per meter. ϵo is the reciprocal of the product of free-space permeability and the speed of light squared.

permutation Any one of the total number of changes in position or form that are possible in a group.

permuted cyclic code A code in which words are represented by a fixed number of bits and arranged in sequence such that the signal distance between consecutive words is always one or unity.

permuted index An index developed by producing an entry for each word of interest, including those within the context of meaning. A permuted index is most often used only for title words.

Persona for Windows An integrated development environment that runs under Microsoft Windows. A programmer's editor provides both CUA and BRIEF emulations, multiple file buffers, multiple tiled windows, unlimited undo and redo, regular expression search, and selectable text fonts. There are compile, test, and debug facilities, as well as an error-tracking window.

personality card A PROM (programmable read-only memory) card that contains the specialized instructions for interfacing and programming that are unique for that particular PROM or family of PROMs. Personality cards may provide the proper timing patterns, voltage levels, and other requirements for the PROM. The output registers on most personality cards permit the generation of serial and/or parallel test patterns of various lengths; with the appropriate test-program control, these brands can also generate pseudo-random codes and other types of codes. Also called a *personality module*.

personal productivity software Refers to general-purpose programs that have wide appeal and work with words, numbers, graphics, and large groups of data.

Personal Rexx An implementation of the SAA Rexx procedure language for OS/2, DOS, and Windows. It supports batch files, prototyping, application script writing, and general personal programming. A number of functions for file system access, operating system control, and screen management are included.

PERT Acronym for *program evaluation and review technique*, a program or project management technique that uses critical path analysis for program and system performance evaluation.

PES Acronym for *photoelectric scanning*.

PFM Abbreviation for *pulse frequency modulation*, a modulation method in which the pulse repetition rate is varied in accordance with the amplitude and frequency of the modulating signal.

PFR Abbreviation for *power-fail recovery*, a system with charging and automatic switching circuitry that provides for computer restart without operator intervention after a power failure. A PFR system can maintain solid-state memory integrity for several hours after a power failure. *Also see* POWER-FAIL, AUTOMATIC RESTART.

PFS: First Choice An easy-to-use integrated software package for the first-time user. The package includes a word processor, a file manager to organize information, a spreadsheet for financial decisions, and a communications package to send or retrieve information.

PFS: First Publisher A page layout program that allows you to incorporate text and graphics into a single document.

PGL Toolkit A set of libraries allowing high-resolution printing of bitmap or vector images on many printers. It supports C, BASIC, Fortran, Pascal, Clipper, and assembly language. It is compatible with most DOS extenders and offers a device-independent programming environment with full printer control.

PGS Abbreviation for *program generation system*, a system that allows the user to output selected areas of memory in object-program format and load programs into memory. The PGS can load both programs it produced and those produced by the memory load builder or assembler.

phantom circuit A superposed circuit derived from suitably arranged pairs of wires, called *side circuits*, the two wires of each pair being effectively in parallel. *Also see* SIDE CIRCUIT.

phantom voltage The voltage differential (5Vde) maintained between the transmit and receive wire pairs in a 10BASE-T, twisted pair network.

phase The angular relationship between waveforms in ac circuits.

phase angle A measure of the time by which an output lags or leads an input.

phase-by-phase A modular build-up or growth of a system according to schedule "milestones."

phase delay In the transfer of a single-frequency wave from one point to another in a system, the time delay of the part of the wave that identifies its phase.

phase dictionary An abbreviated table of contents that contains the phase name and load addresses of the phases to be loaded for a given programming application.

phase difference The phase angle of the output minus the phase angle of the input using input and output at the same frequency.

phase discriminator A circuit preceding the demodulator in a phase modulation receiver. It converts the carrier to an amplitude modulated form.

phase frequency distortion A distortion that occurs when the phase shift is not directly proportionate to the frequency over the range required for transmission. Also referred to as *phase distortion*.

phase inverter A type of amplifier that supplies a positive and negative half-cycle of output for every half-cycle of input voltage.

phase jitter A type of undesirable random distortion that results in the intermittent shortening or lengthening of the observed signals.

phase library An ordered set of program phases processed and entered by a linkage editor for execution.

phase-locked loop *See* PLL.

phase-locked-loop motor control A motor control system using PLL techniques. With the combination of PLL control and a microprocessor, a single reference or clock can be used to provide high accuracy, and the microprocessor can be programed to provide flexible counting and to compare functions for tracking. *Also see* PLL.

phase-locked oscillator A type of parametric oscillator that can be made to oscillate in phases relative to the pumped frequency.

phase logic The general instructions that transfer the machine from one operational phase to another, such as *fetch* and *interrupt*. Combinatorial logic can be used to establish the current phase and the next phase. In some systems, a phase may be a microcoded subroutine.

phase modulation *See* PM.

phase-modulation recording A recording method in which each cell is divided into two parts and magnetized in opposite senses, with the sequence of the senses indicating if the bit represented is a one or a zero.

phase shift The change in the phase of a periodic waveform with respect to a reference point, usually occurring as a direct result of a connection of a component or circuit to the waveform-producing circuit or device.

phase shift keying *See* PSK.

phase splitter A technique of producing two or more waves that differ in phase from a single input wave.

phase transition Refers to a type of computer system conversion where part of the new system is implemented over the entire organization. When this part is operational, another part is implemented.

phase velocity The velocity at which a point of constant phase is propagated in a progressive wave.

phasing Causing two systems or circuits to operate in phase, or at some established phase difference.

phasing capacitor A capacitor used in a crystal filter circuit for neutralizing the capacity of the crystal holder.

PHIGS Acronym for *programmer's hierarchical interface to graphics*, a graphics standard developed by ANSI/ISO for three-dimensional graphics.

phone line protector Phone/communications transmission lines are subject to many of the same sources of surges as power lines. This unit monitors data lines continuously and absorbs surges before they can harm a modem, microprocessor-based telephone, or similar device.

PhoneNet An AppleTalk-compatible network that lets you use existing telephone wiring, connectors, and accessories to network Macintosh computers.

PhoneNET and CheckNET A device that makes it easy to keep track of network devices and identify their names, addresses, and types. It is a useful tool for setting up and debugging AppleTalk networks. Users can search to find other users or devices even across zones.

phosphor dots Elements in the screen of the CRT that glow in the three primary colors.

phosphorescence Refers to the property of emitting light for a period of time after the source of excitation is taken away. CRTs (cathode ray tubes) use this phenomenon to permit a trace on a screen to remain after a transient signal causing the signal is removed; it is thus a form of temporary storage.

phosphor trio Refers to the phosphor dots arranged in triangular groups accurately deposited in interlaced positions on the phosphor screen of the tricolor CRT. Each trio consists of a green-emitting dot, a red-emitting dot, and a blue-emitting dot.

Photo CD player A device that connects to a television monitor for playback of Photo CDs. A range of video connection options, stereo headphones, and remote control are offered. Features include enlarging an image, viewing pictures in any order, and programming the device to display specific images in a certain order.

photocell 1. A device that converts light into electricity. **2.** A device whose resistance changes with relative linearity according to the amount of light impinging on its surface.

photocell matrix In optical character recognition, a device capable of projecting an input onto a fixed two-dimensional array of photocells to develop a simultaneous display of the horizontal and vertical components of the character. The time necessary to scan the character is related to the response time of the photocells.

photocomposition A form of text production in which each character is exposed photographically on light-sensitive paper, which is then developed to become a reproduction proof.

photoconductive The specific electrical conductivity of some materials dependent upon the intensity and frequency of electromagnetic radiation incident upon the material.

photodiode A junction diode constructed to provide an electrical output under the influence of light. Photodiodes are widely used as optical sensing devices in data-processing equipment.

photoelasticity A phenomenon in which strain in certain materials results in colored fringes when under the influence of polarized light.

photoelectric effect Refers to any of the phenomena resulting from the absorption of photons by electrons, resulting in their ejection with a kinetic energy equal to the difference between the energy of a photon and the surface work function or an atomic binding energy (Einstein photoelectric equation). Among these phenomena are photoconductive, photovoltaic, photoemissive, and photoelectromagnetic effects. The emission of x-rays on the impact of high energy electrons on a surface is an inverse photoelectric effect.

photoelectric threshold The limiting frequency for which the quantum energy is just sufficient to produce photoelectric emission. It is given by equating the quantum energy to the surface work function.

photoelectric yield The proportion of incident quanta on a photosensitive surface that liberates electrons.

photoemissive The effect in which electrons are emitted from the surfaces of certain specific materials at particular threshold levels of frequency of incident electromagnetic radiation, such as visible, infrared, or ultraviolet light.

photoform A photo-imaging additive printed circuit process. Photoforming needs no resists and provides conductor definition as good or better than that of additive boards using dry-film resists. Since a catalytic image is formed photographically, line definition is potentially as good as the quality of the line work used on the photographic negative.

photographic storage Storage methods that use photographic processes, such as high-density storage on photographic disks, photographic data shown on CRT screens, or computer-output microfilm and facsimile systems.

photo-optic memory A memory or storage system that uses an optical medium such as a light beam to record on photographic film.

photoresist A substance that resists the erosion properties of an etchant when exposed to intense light. It is used in making printed circuits.

photoresist process The process used to remove, in a selective manner, portions of a light-exposed surface of a semiconductor chip or a circuit board. The photoresist is usually an organic material that polymerizes on exposure to intense light, which allows it to resist the etchant solution used to eat away nonconductive areas of the board or substrate.

Photoshop *See ADOBE PHOTOSHOP.*

physical address The unique address associated with each workstation on a network.

physical channel The actual wiring and transmission hardware needed to implement networking.

physical coordinate system The logical limits of the screen.

physical data Data representing environmental conditions such as light or sound.

physical device An item of hardware on a network or computer system.

physical disk channel In NetWare and other environments, refers to the disk unit that is attached.

physical drive count In NetWare and other environments, the number of physical disk units attached to a server.

physical drive type In NetWare and other environments, the type of drive used. NetWare uses the following types:

- 1: XT
- 2: AT
- 3: SCSI
- 4: disk coprocessor
- 5: PS/2 MFM controller
- 6: PS/2 ESDI controller
- 7: convergent technology SBIC
- 50 to 255: value-added disk drive

physical layer The portion of the ISO-OSI model concerned with defining the mechanical, electrical, functional, and procedural characteristics of the physical link between two communicating devices. *Also see* OSI MODEL.

physical lock In NetWare and other networks, locks a range of bytes on the file. This permits multiple users access to the file, but protects given records during an update process. Physical locks are enforced by the operating system.

physical media The cabling of a LAN: twisted pair, coax, or fiber.

physical node address In NetWare and other networks, the address of the workstation's LAN board.

physical read errors In NetWare, the number of times the cache software received an error from the disk driver on a read request.

physical read requests In the NetWare File Server Environment, the number of times the cache software issued a physical read request to a disk driver.

physical record lock count In the NetWare File Server Environment, a count of the number of physical record locks.

physical record lock threshold In the NetWare Transaction Tracking System, the number of logical record locks that may be set before a transaction is begun.

physical simulation system A computer system designed to represent or simulate physical systems for research and study.

physical unit *See* PU, 2.

physical write errors In the NetWare File Server Environment, the number of times the cache software received an error from the disk driver on a write request.

physical write requests In the NetWare File Server Environment, the number of times the cache software issued a physical write request to a disk driver.

PI **1.** Abbreviation for *programmed instruction.* **2.** Abbreviation for *performance index.*

PIA Abbreviation for *peripheral interface adapter*, a hardware unit for matching the I/O channels of a microprocessor with peripheral equipment, as shown in the following diagram. A typical PIA provides eight or 16 bits of external interface and four or more control lines at addressable locations in memory. Each interface bit is individually programmable to act as either an input or an output.

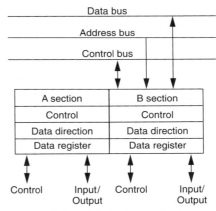

Peripheral inferface adapter

A typical PIA uses a data bus line for data flow between the microprocessor and the PIA. The direction of data flow is controlled by the microprocessor using the control bus. When more than one PIA is used, chip-select lines allow the selection of the desired PIA. The microprocessor can read or write into the data registers by addressing the unit over the address and control buses. The 8-bit outputs are bidirectional, and the control I/O lines can be used for interrupts.

Each half of the two symmetrical sections of the PIA has a control register, a data direction register, and a data register. The *data direction register* is used to establish the lines to the peripheral units as inputs or outputs. The *data register* stores the data on the data bus during a write command; during a read operation, data is transferred directly to the data bus from the peripherals. The *control register* establishes and controls the operating modes of control lines to the peripherals.

The functional configuration of the PIA is programmed by the microprocessor during system initialization. Each of the peripheral lines is programmed as an input or an output, and the control lines are also programmed at this time.

PIA bus interface The PIA in many systems is used to provide eight or 16 bits of external interface as well as control lines at addressable locations in the system memory. The I/O bits may be accessed in two words of eight bits each, but each I/O bit can be individually programmable to act as either an input or an output system memory. All operating characteristics of the interface can be established by writing from the processor to the data direction and control registers of the PIA. This is required at the time of system reset and permitted at other times in most systems.

PIA read-write A signal generated by the microprocessor unit to control data transfers on the data bus of the PIA (peripheral interface adapter).

pica 1. The larger of two common typewriter typeface sizes, the smaller being *elite*. Also called *10 pitch*. **2.** A unit of measure used in printing and the graphic arts, equal to 12 points or about one-sixth of an inch.

pickup Interference from a nearby circuit or system.

pickup value The minimum value that will energize the contacts of a relay, voltage, current, or power.

pico Prefix meaning 10^{-12}.

picofarad A capacitance value equal to 10^{-12} farad, abbreviated *pF*.

picoprocessor A self-contained high-speed miniature digital processor used in intelligent cable systems to provide controller functions for data transfer, control signaling, status monitoring, and interrupt generation. The picoprocessor is usually microprogrammed; because of its small size, it can be attached almost anywhere in the system.

picosecond A time period equal to 10^{-12} second, abbreviated *ps*.

picowatt One ten-thousandth of a microwatt.

PictureBase A program for organizing graphics files that uses libraries. For each image in the library, you enter a title and a list of keywords. You can then find the graphic documents you want by instructing PictureBase to search for the title or keywords. An accessory called PB Retriever lets you search and place images directly into applications, such as PageMaker.

PICU Acronym for *priority interrupt control unit*, a unit that is designed to simplify the interrupt system for a microcomputer. A typical unit can accept eight requesting levels, determine the highest priority, compare this priority with the current status register, and issue an interrupt along with vector data to identify the service routine.

PIE Acronym for *plug-in electronics*.

piezo Of or pertaining to a piezoelectric crystal, a crystal that changes its shape when an electrical signal is applied between its faces.

piezoelectric crystal A crystal transducer that converts mechanical pressure into an electrical signal or converts an electrical signal into mechanical pressure.

piezoelectric device A device that uses the conversion properties of a piezoelectric substance such as an oscillator crystal used as a frequency reference, or a crystal microphone that produces an electrical analog of the vibrations of a modulated diaphragm.

piezoelectric effect Electric polarization arising in some anisotropic (not possessing a center of symmetry) crystals (quartz, Rochelle salt, barium titanate) when subjected to a mechanical strain. Also called *piezoelectricity*.

piezoelectricity *See* PIEZOELECTRIC EFFECT.

piezoelectric transducer A transducer that depends upon a material with piezoelectric properties for its operation. Also called a *ceramic* or *crystal* transducer.

.PIF A filename extension that stands for *program information file*. It indicates a Windows configuration file that determines the environment provided to run a specific DOS application. Characteristics include video and memory limitations, as well as whether the application runs in windowed or full-screen mode.

piggybacked 1. Refers to hardware or software added onto an existing hardware or software unit or module. **2.** In communications, refers to protocols that require the acknowledgement of prior packets. The acknowledgment can be piggybacked into the same packet as data that is headed in that direction.

piggyback module A small printed circuit board that attaches to the main board, adding various features. Piggyback modules do not take up an extra expansion slot.

pigtail Fiber-optic cable that has connectors installed on one end.

PILOT Acronym for *program inquiry, learning or teaching*, a computer language created exclusively for use in preparing computer-aided instruction.

pilot operation Refers to a type of computer system conversion where all of the new computer system is implemented for only one operation or department in an organization. As the system proves successful, other operations or departments are included.

pilot, reference *See* REFERENCE PILOT.

pilot, synchronizing *See* SYNCHRONIZING PILOT.

pilot system A collection of file records and data obtained from a business over a period of time and used for simulation purposes.

PIM Acronym for *personal information manager*, a database management program that stores and

pin retrieves personal information such as notes, memos, names and addresses, and appointments.

pin 1. Any of the leads on an electrical device, such as a chip, that plug into a socket and connect it to a system. Each pin provides a function such as input, output, power, ground, or control. **2.** Acronym for *personal identification number*, a group of characters, as a word, entered on a keyboard as a secret code to gain access to functions in a computer system.

pinboard A type of control panel that uses pins rather than wires to control the operation of the computer. Some such systems allow the operator to change programs by removing one pinboard and inserting another.

pinch-off The cessation of channel (source-to-drain) current in FETs (field effect transistors) as a result of increased gate bias. This state is comparable to *cutoff* in bipolar-transistor and vacuum-tube operation.

pin-connect crystal A clock crystal that is connected to a microprocessor system with two separate external pins.

pin connection Connections made to the base of pins in a connector or socket.

pin contact A contact used to mate with a socket or connector.

pin diode A semiconductor diode with an intrinsic layer between the p and n junctions. The term *pin* is an acronym for *positive, intrinsic, negative*.

pine Mailer An electronic mail system used on the Internet with an easy menu interface. All the options available are displayed in the bottom portion of the screen. It allows you to read, send, reply, or print messages, create folders of saved messages, and create an address book of aliases (also called nicknames) to handle the Internet's e-mail ID addresses.

pin feed A term applied to printer platens having sprocket-like end pieces that help convey continuous forms through the unit.

ping A protocol request to poll a subset of network stations for an active status.

ping-pong A type of transport protocol that requires each packet be individually acknowledged. Before a node can send another packet, it must wait for an acknowledgment. PEP is an example of this type of protocol, as opposed to SPX, which allows a window of unacknowledged packets to be outstanding. *Also see* PEP.

PINO Acronym for *positive-input/negative-output*.

pinout Describes the order of the pin connections of a particular connector. Each connector pin is numbered in a standard way on the connector, and those numbers are used in a pinout.

PIO Acronym for *processor input/output*; refers to an I/O channel that interfaces with the process via the data input bus and provides simplex character-oriented data transfer capability. *Contrast with* DMA.

pip A spot of light on a CRT screen for display pointing or calibration.

pipe 1. A facility used so one program can talk to another. **2.** In DOS, the symbol ¦ added to some commands in combination with an option, such as type¦more.

pipeline An executed serial program using a register at the output of the microprogram memory. Pipelining can produce a faster configuration than a normal series mode of operation. Since only conditional instructions can test the results of previous instructions, the pipelined machine may require more memory. For example, a serial machine might execute ADD AND BRANCH IF ZERO as a single microinstruction, while the pipeline machine might require two microinstructions for the same operation.

pipe status list In NetWare Messages Services, a pipe status code is used for each connection number contained in the connection List field. The following codes are used:

- *Open* The message pipe is complete at both ends.
- *Incomplete* The target connection's half of the message pipe does not exist.
- *Closed* The calling client's half of the message pipe does not exist, or the connection number is not in use or is invalid.

PIT Acronym for *programmable interval timer*, an IC with several independent counters that can operate in input or output modes. In the output mode, one can measure the duration of external pulses. A counter register is loaded with the desired value in micro- or milliseconds. A status bit can be set or an interrupt generated when the counter reaches zero; thus, a signal is generated as the desired period of time has elapsed. In some applications, it is necessary to measure the elapsed time for input or output scheduling. Using microprocessor-looping techniques is a time-consuming task. The availability of a component frees the microprocessor for other tasks.

A PIT is usually required in all real-time operations. In a real-time system using interrupts, software counters cannot provide sufficiently accurate timing. An internal counter could be interrupted by external events, which would result in erroneous time measurements.

An external PIT means adding an extra chip to the system. Some microcomputer chips implement a PIT directly on the chip or included on one of the other 10 chips used in the system, such as a PIO or a UART.

pit 1. A microscopic depression in the reflective surface of a CD-ROM disc. The pattern of pits on the disc represents the data that is stored. The unpitted area between the pits is called a *land*. A tiny laser beam reads back the data reflected from the lands, but scattered by the pits. A typical pit is about the size of a bacterium 0.5

by 2.0 microns (millionths of a meter). **2.** Broadly, any type of data-carrying mark in optical media.

pitch The density of printed copy. It usually refers to the number of characters printed per horizontal inch, for example, "10 pitch" means ten characters per inch; however, it can also indicate the number of vertical rows.

pixel Abbreviation for *picture element*, a small graphic on a display screen representing the degree of brightness on that spot of the screen. Many pixels are used in combination to form characters or graphics.

pixel aspect ratio The width-to-height of a pixel, a function of the number of scan lines along the vertical axis and the number of scanning spots along the horizontal axis, along with the screen's physical aspect ratio.

pixel depth The number of bits stored for each pixel in a bitmapped image. The greater the pixel depth (the more bits per pixel), the wider the range of intensity levels or colors a bitmap can represent. The number of possible pixel values is two to the power of n, where n is the pixel length.

pixel doubling A method of changing the aspect ratio of a display by duplicating rows or columns of pixels.

pixel graphic *See* BITMAPPED GRAPHIC.

pixel operation The process of modifying a pixel value for some specific purpose.

PixelPaint A program with paint capabilities, color tools, and special effects. You can use it to paint with up to 256 colors from a palette of 16.8 million colors. A color editor allows you to customize the palette. An eyedropper tool lets you pick up a customized color from one area and use it in another.

PixelPrint A utility for printing a range of graphics file formats on over 200 printers. There is a built-in PCL command interpreter for use on HP and compatible printers.

pixellation In a digital image, an impairment in which the pixels are large enough to become visible individually.

pixel scan *See* SCANNER, 1.

pixel thinning A technique for reducing the bandwidth or changing the aspect ratio of an image by systematically discarding pixels.

pixel value A number or series of numbers that represent the color and luminance of a single pixel.

PLA Abbreviation for *programmed logic array*, an arrangement of logical AND and OR functions programmed for specific operations, as shown in the following diagram. PLAs are used for code conversion, instruction decoding, and command decoding. The output of a PLA is the sum of the products of the input address programmed by a masking step during manufacture. PLAs offer some advantages over random logic, but generally require more interconnections and board space. Compared to random logic equivalents, they are also slow and may cost more. PLAs have been used for correct sequencing of instructions in CPUs and to translate codes in microprogramming functions.

A PLA can be used efficiently in code-conversion applications where all possible combinations of a particular code are not used. The conversion from 12-level Hollerith code to eight-level ASCII provides such an example. In the standard solution to this problem, the 12-level Hollerith code is first reduced to eight levels, with logic before it is presented to a 256 × 8 ROM. All nonexisting input combinations are decoded as "don't care" output states in the ROM.

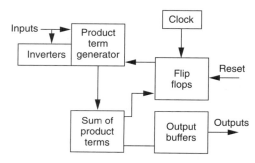

PLA block diagram

placement algorithm An algorithm designed to determine where internal storage segments should be placed prior to their use.

PLA instruction fetch During an instruction fetch, the instruction to be executed is loaded into the instruction register. A PLA (programmable logic array) can be used for the correct sequencing of the CPU for the appropriate instruction. The state of a priority network decides whether the machine is going to fetch the next instruction in sequence or service one of the request lines.

planar A semiconductor processing technology in which monolithic components extend below the surface of the substrate, but the plane surface remains relatively flat during fabrication.

planar integrated circuit An integrated circuit produced using the planar process.

planar network A network in which no branches cross when drawn on the same plane.

planar process A basic technology of silicon transistors, involving a combination of oxidation, selective oxide removal, and heating to introduce doping materials by diffusion. The introduction of the planar process in 1960 revolutionized the microelectronics field. Silicon, rather than germanium, emerged as the predominant semiconductor material. As applied to semiconductor devices, the term is used to mean that the monolithic components fabricated by this process extend below the surface of the silicon substrate. The plane surface of the semiconductor, however, remains relatively flat and unaltered through the sequence of different fabrication steps. Planar process technology is comprised of five independent processes: epitaxy, surface passivation, photolithography, diffusion, and thin-film deposition.

planar transistor A transistor constructed by etching a thin slice of semiconductor and characterized by a parallel plane protected by an oxidized surface.

Planck's constant A constant that has dimensions of energy × time. The present accepted value is $6.625 \cdot 10^{-27}$ erg. sec. *Also see* PLANCK'S LAW.

Planck's Law A law that states that the energy of electromagnetic waves is confined in indivisible packets or quanta, each of which has to be radiated or absorbed as a whole, the magnitude being proportional to frequency—the basis of quantum theory. If E is the value of the quantum expressed in energy units, and v is the frequency of the radiation, then $E = hv$, where h is known as Planck's constant.

plane Refers to a bitmap memory organization that contains a single bit for all of the pixels. One bit per pixel results in one plane, two bits per pixel results in two planes, etc.

PlanPerfect A spreadsheet package that is compatible with its word-processing forerunner, WordPerfect.

plantwide data acquisition configuration A configuration as shown in the following figure, in which a single computer performs supervisory control and process monitoring. The computer monitors the process by reading analog and digital data from the field via I/O equipment. It may change an analog controller's setpoint to perform supervisory controller. Analog signals such as flows or levels are used by both the computer and the analog panel instrumentation. Most peripheral equipment is connected to the I/O channel by interface circuitry. This hardware performs functions related to the operation of both the channel and the peripheral

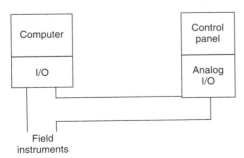

Plantwide data-acquisition configuration

device, such as address detection, decoding, timing, and error detection/correction.

PLA output latch A latch available in some microcomputer systems that allows the programmed logic array to be pipelined. The PLA output latch fetches the next control sequence while the CPU is executing the current sequence.

plasma An ionized gaseous discharge used in some laptop display units for screen illumination.

plasma display A display panel with supporting electronics that uses the plasma or gas-discharge effect.

plasma torch A heating device in which solids, liquids, or gasses are forced through an arc within a water-cooled tube, with consequent ionization; the deionization on impact results in very high temperatures. It is used for cutting and depositing carbides.

plasmatron A discharge tube in which anode current can be regulated by the control of a plasma, either by a grid or through the electron stream originating the plasma.

plastic deformation The changes in shape that solids undergo.

plastic integrated circuits ICs packaged in plastic. Ordinary plastic ICs may cause some worries about field failures. To counter this worry and provide reliability plus the economy and ruggedness of plastic, there are *gold chip ICs*, which have noncorroding gold metalization and leads and contain no aluminum with its potential problems. The chip itself is made hermetic and put in an advanced plastic package with proven reliability in the following areas: temperature/humidity/bias, operating life, thermal fatigue, pressure cooker, thermal shock, and temperature cycle.

plastic package Usually refers to a plastic dual-inline package (DIP), a widely accepted industry standard refined by manufacturers for MOS/LSI applications. Many packages use a silicon body that is transfer-molded directly onto the assembled lead frame and die. The lead frame is often Kovar or Alloy 42, with external pins tin-plated. Internally, some plastic packages use 50 microinch gold spot on each die-attach pad and on the bonding fingertips. Gold bonding wire is attached with the thermocompression gold-ball bonding technique.

Materials of the lead frame, the package body, and the die attach are all closely matched in thermal expansion coefficients to provide optimum response to various thermal conditions. During manufacture, every step of the process must be rigorously monitored to assure maximum quality of the plastic package. Generally, plastic packages are available in 14-, 16-, 18-, 22-, 24-, 40-, and 48-pin configurations.

plate 1. The principal electrode to which the electron stream is attracted in an electron tube. Preferably called the *anode*. 2. One of the conductive electrodes in a capacitor. **3.** One of the electrodes in a storage battery.

platen Refers to the roller that supports the paper as it moves through a printer.

plate neutralization A method of neutralizing an amplifier (preventing its oscillation) by shifting a part of the plate voltage and applying it to the cathode grid circuit with a neutralizing capacitor.

platinum A heavy, almost white metal that resists most acids and is capable of high temperatures. It is used in precision resistors. Sparking does not damage platinum as much as it does other metals, and a cleaner contact is assured with minimum attention. Platinum is chemically inert and not easily contaminated. It does not readily oxidize and can be used up to 1500°C. It is generally more expensive than other resistance temperature sensors, although some industrial grades are competitive.

platinum resistance thermometers The International Temperature Scale has been defined by a pure platinum resistance thermometer from the triple point of hydrogen (13.81 K) to the freezing point of antimony (630.74°C). The R/T relationship of platinum is well known, reproducible, and linear over a wide temperature range.

platter Refers to the hard disk where information is stored. The platter is similar to a floppy disk, but is made of rigid material, often aluminum. A hard disk may contain several platters.

PLA versus ROM The availability of low-cost ROMs and PLAs offers many possibilities in digital systems design. The PLA (programmed logic array) offers an alternative to ROM in some cases and allows regular design concepts to be used in situations where ROMs are impractical. The PLA concept is useful in combinational and sequential digital systems.

plesiochronous The relationship between two signals such that their corresponding significant instants or transitions occur at nominally the same rate, any variation in rate being constrained within a specified limit.

Plink86+ A linker with overlay capabilities that handles any compiler or assembly producing standard Intel or Microsoft OBJ files. Virtual memory management increases the capacity for symbol and common block names. It supports an unlimited number of modules and up to 4,095 overlays nested up to 32 deep. It merges object modules, caches, and overlays in extended memory and automatically reloads overlays.

PLL Abbreviation for *phase-locked loop*, a control circuit, usually integrated, which locks the phase of the controlled frequency with a reference frequency.

PLM Abbreviation for *pulse length modulation*.

PL/M+ A high-level compiler language developed as an assembly language replacement for microcomputer systems. PL/M is derived from PL/1, a high-level language that has some features of Fortran and some features of COBOL. Debug and checkout time with PL/M can be less than with an assembly language. Also, the PL/M structure allows the compiler to detect error conditions that could get past an assembler.

PL/1 programming language A computer programming language that has some features of Fortran and some features of COBOL, among others.

plotter A peripheral unit in which a dependent variable is graphed by an automatically controlled pen or pencil as a function of one or more variables. Any position on a two-dimensional area can be referenced, accessed, or written onto by precise control of both vertical and horizontal axes.

plotting board An output unit that graphs the curves of one or more variables as a function of its input variables.

plugboard 1. A board with removable connections for changing the wiring pattern. **2.** A board that can be removed and replaced to change the program or wired connections for a machine.

plug-compatible Two competing devices that can be exchanged without having to make other changes to accommodate their differences.

plugging A system of electric breaking by reversing the motor connections. A series resistance keeps the current at a safe value, and the circuit is opened when the motor stops so that it does not reverse.

plugging chart A diagram or chart that indicates where plugs, pins, or wires are to be placed on a plugboard.

plug-in Descriptive of devices in which connections are completed using conductors with pins, plugs, sockets, jacks, or other connectors that are readily removed.

plug-in unit A self-contained assembly that can be inserted or unplugged easily.

plug-in upgrades Refers to a modularity that permits you to, for example, reconfigure your system from an 80386 at 25 MHz to an 80486 at 50 MHz by changing modules or chips on your system board. These parts provide system upgrades without having to change the system board.

plug-PROM A ROM diode array that is programmed by inserting small plugs into edge connectors. After it is connected to the microcomputer system, programming consists of selecting the proper plugs (each representing a 4-bit hexadecimal value) and inserting them into the edge connector of the word being programmed. Changing a program requires only removing and replacing the plugs.

plug wire A flexible wire with a metal pin at each end for connecting to the sockets of a plugboard.

plus zone Those bit positions in a code that represent the algebraic plus-sign.

PM Abbreviation for *phase modulation*, a method of modulation in which the amplitude of the carrier remains the same, while the phase is changed as a function of the amplitude of the modulating signal. PM is used in most so-called FM two-way communications systems.

PMD Abbreviation for *post-mortem dump*.

PMOS Abbreviation for *p-channel metal-oxide semiconductor*, a FET (field-effect transistor) technology based on use of p-type material for the source-and-drain channel. Basic PMOS and NMOS circuits are shown in the following figure.

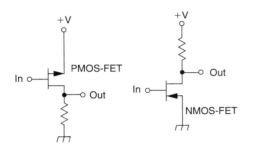

Basic PMOS and NMOS transistor amplifier circuits

PMOS transistor A transistor that uses n-type silicon doped with p-type impurities in order to create the source and the drain of the transistor. Typical doping agents are boron and phosphorus. The areas to be doped with impurities are defined by a mask, which is made by the photolithographic process or the electron beam process. The impurities are added to the exposed area of the wafer using thermal diffusion.

pn boundary The surface where the donor and acceptor concentrations are equal in the transition region between n and p zones in a semiconductor.

pneumatic crimp tool Benchstation and handheld tools used as an effective alternative to hand-crimping wires and terminals.

pneumatic interfacing Refers to the two basic methods of interfacing pneumatic instruments to the computer. One is to use P/I (pneumatic-to-current) and I/P (current-to-pneumatic) converters. In this type of system, the output of the converters are continuous. The other method replaces the P/I converters with a pneumatic multiplexer/converter. This can be accomplished with either a host or remote multiplexing configuration.

pnip transistor A transistor with a layer of intrinsic (undoped) material between the base and collector to extend the high-frequency range.

pn junction A region of transition between p and n semiconductor materials that has the properties of a diode. LED pn junctions use gallium arsenide or phosphide to provide visible or infrared LEDs (light-emitting displays).

pnp A transistor consisting of two p-type regions separated by an n-type region and characterized by a flow of holes as majority carriers (rather than the more mobile electrons).

pnpn A semiconductor switching device with three junctions.

pnpn-type switch A semiconductor device made up of three or more junctions, at least one of which is able to switch between reverse and forward voltage polarity.

pnp transistor See *pnp*.

pn-type junction A transition region between p and n (positive and negative) regions in semiconductor materials. The distributions and potential (voltage) gradients permit diode and transistor action.

POET An object-oriented database management system that runs on DOS, Windows, UNIX, and NeXT. The object database has a unique identity that supports the full inheritance and encapsulation of C++. Applications include complex models. A graphical browser allows you to use, navigate, analyze, and modify the structure of your database schemas.

point A typographic measure equal to 0.013837 inches or about $1/72$ of an inch, used chiefly for specifying type sizes and leadings.

point and shoot Refers to choosing what you want from a list by highlighting it using either a mouse or arrow keys, as opposed to typing character-based commands.

point contact 1. A pressure contact between the semiconductor body and a metallic point. 2. A condition in which current flow to a semiconductor is through a point of metal.

point contact diode A diode that obtains its rectifying characteristic from a point contact.

point contact rectifier A rectifier made with a metal point pressing onto a crystal of semiconductor.

point contact transistor A transistor having a base electrode and two or more point contact electrodes.

point effect The phenomenon in which a discharge will occur more readily at sharp points than elsewhere on an object.

pointer 1. The indicating needle of an analog meter. 2. The most recently stored word in a stack, which gives the address of another memory location; the word is taken temporarily from a register that is to be used for another purpose or from the program counter during subroutine jumps. The pointer is replaced following the temporary operation or jump.

point junction transistor A transistor having a base electrode and both point contact and junction electrodes.

point of presence See POP.

point-of-sale system An electronic system for automating the various functions of retail sales operations. Point-of-sale systems include inventory control using electronic cash registers, credit authorization via a reader terminal to a central computer, and electronic funds transfer using card-activated systems. Point-of-sale terminals are used in department store and other large retail outlets such as supermarkets. Also called *POS system*.

point-to-point A connection between two, and only two, devices.

point-to-point configuration A network configuration in which all processors have a direct access to every other processor in the network, as shown in the figure. For n processors, $n(n-1)/2$ interconnections are required. For example, with three processors, three communication links are required; with five processors, the number of links is ten; with 10 processors, the number of links is 45. The number of links quickly becomes excessive. The advantages of this configuration are faster response times, the ability to use lower-grade communications lines, and the ability to use alternate paths to allow messages to continue to be forwarded when some of the links are interrupted.

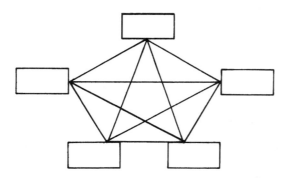

Point-to-point network configuration

POL Acronym for *problem-oriented language*.

polar **1.** A logic technique in which a binary one is represented by current flow in one direction and a zero by current flow in the opposite direction. **2.** Having poles (as a magnet). **3.** A type of plot showing coordinates over a two-dimensional plane, used to depict signal distribution from an antenna, the pickup field of a microphone, etc.

polar axes The fixed lines from which the angles made by radius vectors are measured in a polar coordinates system.

polar coordinates A system of coordinates in which a point is located by its distance and direction (angle) from a fixed point on a reference line called the polar axis.

polar crystals Crystals having a lattice composed of alternate positive and negative ions.

polar diagram A diagram in which the magnitude of a quantity is shown by polar coordinates.

polarity **1.** The orientation of any device that has poles or signed electrodes. **2.** The value established by the ungrounded electrode of any grounded dc system; for example, the polarity of most vehicle electrical systems is +12 volts. **3.** Electrical opposition.

polarized capacitor An electrolytic capacitor designed for operation only with fixed polarity. The dielectric film is formed only near one electrode; thus, the impedance is not the same for both directions of current flow.

polarized plug A plug constructed in such a manner that it can only be inserted into a socket with proper polarity.

polarizing slot A cutout in the edge of a circuit board to properly align certain types of connectors or to ensure that proper pin polarity is maintained.

polar mode **1.** A device that separates or breaks up a quantity, particularly a vector, into constituent parts or elements. **2.** A device for resolving a vector into its mutually perpendicular components.

polar molecule A molecule with unbalanced electric charges, usually valency electrons, resulting in a dipole moment.

polaron An electron in a substance that is trapped in a potential well produced by polarization charges on the surrounding molecules.

pole **1.** An electrode of an electrical device such as a battery, switch, or relay. **2.** Either of two opposite signs (positive or negative). **3.** One of the regions in a magnetized body where the magnetic flux density is concentrated.

policies and procedures document A set of written guidelines that the network user can refer to in case of emergency. This document outlines the network rules and regulations and contains the procedures for performing special network-related tasks.

Polish notation A system of expressing logical and arithmetic statements without using parentheses. In Polish notation, the expression *A plus B multiplied by C* would be represented by +ABC. Also called *Lukaseiwicz notation, parentheses-free notation*, and *prefix notation*. Also see REVERSE-POLISH NOTATION.

poll In communications, a systematic method for sampling the output of stations on a multipoint system. The computer contacts the stations according to an order specified by the user to determine if it requires servicing. Polling is also used to determine the source of multiple interrupt requests in multiprocessing systems. If several interrupts occur at the same time, the control program is used to make the decision as to the order of servicing. *Also see* TIME-SHARING POLLING.

polled I/O A technique in which I/O devices are

connected to the system bus. They may also have to be connected to some control lines. The principle is to implement a procedure for determining the next I/O device that requires service. The polling technique is a synchronous technique. The microprocessor periodically asks each device connected to the data bus if it requires service. Each device answers with a yes or no. When a no is received, the microprocessor proceeds to the next device and asks it. The microprocessor thus calls each I/O device successively to determine if service is required. In actual practice, a status flag is tested on the device or its interface. If the test is true, action is initiated. This is usually the transfer of a word or block of data to or from the device.

polling characters The characters used to identify a particular terminal during a polling operation. The characters also indicate to the computer whether or not the terminal has a message to send. *Also see* POLL.

polling interval The time between polling operations if no data is being transmitted from a polled station.

polling list A list containing control information and the order in which terminals are to be polled.

polling loop The software used to implement an I/O device-polling algorithm. The process of asking the device and receiving information in return is called *handshaking*. The communications protocol between one device and the next one on a link normally uses some form of handshaking. Before transmitting information to the device, a status bit is checked to test if the device is ready to accept data. Before reading a word from a device, a status bit is checked to test if the word is complete. The basic flowchart of a polling loop is shown in the following figure.

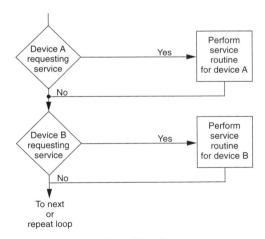

Basic polling loop

polygon A simple type of primitive surface composed of three or more vertices connected by straight edges.

PolyLibrarian A utility for creating and managing object module libraries, including OS/2 and Windows IMPORT libraries. It works with compilers and assemblers that produce object modules compatible with Microsoft linker, Plink86+, or other compatible linkers. It lets you add, delete, replace, and extract object modules to and from library files. PolyLibrarian timestamps each module in a library. Any identifier can be changed to prevent name conflicts, and the user can substitute modified versions of library routines.

polyline A line with more than one segment, including at least one angle or curve.

polymorphic Capable of existing in several different forms.

polymorphic system A system that can take on various forms for the problem at hand by altering its interconnections or functions. A polymorphic system may change its logic construction or operation in order to handle a variety of tasks.

polyphase 1. Having or utilizing several phases. For example, a polyphase motor operates from a power line having several phases of alternating current. **2.** A set of ac power-supply circuits carrying currents of equal frequency with uniformly spaced phase differences, nominally employing a common return conductor.

polyphase synchronous generator A generator with its ac circuits so arranged that two or more symmetrical, alternating electromotive forces with definite phase relationships to each other are produced at its terminals.

polystyrene A clear thermoplastic material with excellent dielectric properties, especially at very high frequencies.

polystyrene capacitor A capacitor with a polystyrene dielectric.

polyvalence The property of being interrelated in several ways.

polyvalent notation A method of describing characteristics in condensed form in which each character or group of characters represents one of the characteristics.

PoP Abbreviation for *point of presence*, an interface point in an LATA to the inter-LATA carriers.

pop The act of removing an item from a stack memory.

population The total collection of units being considered, sometimes referred to as the *universe*.

population inversion The reversal of the normal ratio of populations of two different energy states, such that fewer and fewer atoms occupy states of successively higher energies. It forms the basis of laser action.

port 1. A place of electrical or physical access to a system or circuit. The point at which an input or output is in contact with the CPU can be considered a port, along with any entrance or exit from a network or system. Each microprocessor can have a number of I/O ports. Some are associated with external system activity; others are for the information exchange with other system processors. In practice, ports are part of the I/O section of a processor. **2.** An opening of critical but controllable dimensions in a tuned enclosure (such as a cavity or loudspeaker cabinet).

portable battery pack A unit that typically has an 8 ampere-hour rechargeable battery in a water-resistant carrying case, used with inverters for portable computers. Sometimes called a *power brick*.

portable editor An editor unit with display and data entry keys to edit PROMs (programmable read-only memories) in machine language.

portable multimedia Refers to computer systems including CD-ROM drives and audio boards that are portable, although not particularly lightweight. Extra batteries are needed with this approach, and these batteries are heavy.

Portable NetWare Software that resides on a guest operating system and allows NetWare workstations to treat the host as a NetWare server.

Portable/REXX An implementation of REXX with all standard statements and built-in functions. Additional functions enable the user to maximize productivity in DOS. The product is useful for developing complex batch scripts, and the REXX parsing capabilities can be used for a wide range of file transformations. Variable interfaces are provided for exchanging data with Microsoft C and Borland C/C++ programs.

Portable Streams Environment *See* PSE.

portable uninterruptable power supply A self-contained, continuous power source used to protect equipment from power gaps, surges, brownouts, and blackouts. Some units use sealed, rechargeable gel-cell batteries with a life expectancy of three to four years. The battery status is constantly monitored by LEDs.

port expander A unit sometimes abbreviated *PE*, designed to add additional ports to connect to a local or remote synchronous device, as shown in the figure. The PE can operate in a polled environment, or each of the subordinate ports can be manually enabled or disabled using toggle switches on the front panel of the unit. The user can select either a DCE or DTE configuration for each of the subordinate ports, giving the PE built-in modem elimination for local applications. The PE is designed for a synchronous environment.

portrait orientation Refers to printing across the width of the page, letter-style. The term *portrait* is derived from portraits of people, which are usually vertical in format. *Contrast with* LANDSCAPE ORIENTATION.

POS 1. Abbreviation for *point-of-sale*. **2.** Abbreviation for *programmable option select*, a technique

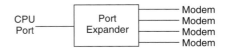

Port expander

in the IBM PS/2 Micro Channel Architecture. It refers to the fact that there are no DIP switches or jumper installations on any of the expansion boards; base address setting and interrupt level selection are performed by the software.

position In a string, each location that can be occupied by a character and identified by a number.

positional operand In assembler programming, an operand in a macroinstruction that assigns a value to the corresponding positional parameter, which is declared in the prototype statement of the called macro definition.

position code The established positions or sites in recording media in which data may be entered or recorded according to specific conventions adopted to standardize the locations for coding information.

position-dependent unfairness A situation common in LANs where some stations receive better service due to their proximity to other stations or a central location in a bus-structured LAN.

positioning/contouring system A type of numerical control system that has the capability of contouring in two axes, and the ability of positioning in a third axis for such operations as drilling, tapping, and boring.

position sensor A device for measuring a position and converting this measurement into a form convenient for data transmission.

position storage The storage media in a numerical control system containing the coordinate position.

positive charge An electrical charge with fewer electrons than normal.

positive electricity 1. A phenomenon in a body associated with a deficiency of electrons, such as when positive electricity appears on glass rubbed with silk.

positive electrode The conductor node that serves as the anode terminal of a polarized device such as a battery, an electrolytic capacitor, or a self-contained two-pole circuit.

positive feedback A system in which the amplification is increased at the cost of fidelity by returning a part of the output in phase with the input signal. An oscillator, for example, employs positive feedback to sustain self-amplification. Also called *regeneration*.

positive ion An atom that has lost one or more electrons and thus has an excess of protons, giving it a positive charge.

positive ion sheath A collection of positive ions that may block normal currents.

positive logic A logic convention in which the positive voltage is defined as a one and the more negative voltage is defined as a zero.

positive pulse stuffing In time-division multiplexing (TDM), the provision of a fixed number of dedicated time slots used to transmit either information from the individual channel inputs, or no information, according to the relative bit rates of the channel input and the TDM channel output signals. *Also see* TDM.

positive-zero-negative pulse stuffing A combination of positive and negative pulse stuffing, in which the two stuffing states are indicated by uniquely coded signals and the state of no stuffing is indicated by a third signal.

positron A positive electron of the same mass as a normal (negative) electron but with a charge that is of the opposite sign. It is produced in the decay of radioisotopes and in pair production by x-rays of greater than 1 MeV.

positron quadrapole A type of ion beam focusing magnet.

POST Acronym for *power-on self test*, a series of tests run by the computer when you first turn it on.

postedit To edit output data resulting from a previous computation.

postequalization The equalization of a circuit performed at the receiver.

postfix notation *See* REVERSE-POLISH NOTATION.

postinstallation evaluation An evaluation of a computer configuration to determine if it meets the objectives established at the time of acquisition.

post mortem 1. The analysis of a condition or malfunction after its completion. 2. Collectively, the routines and listings used to locate a malfunction or an error in the program or system. A post-mortem routine can automatically print information on the contents of registers and storage locations at the time the routine is stopped in order to assist in the location of a mistake in coding.

postponed AES Events In NetWare Diagnostic Services, the number of times (since IPX was loaded) that IPX has been unable to service an AES event on time. For example, IPX cannot send an outgoing packet to a driver that is busy with another packet.

PostPress A product that allows PostScript language output on inkjet, dot-matrix, and non-PostScript laser printers. PostPress offers a cost-effective alternative to expensive printers.

post processing When data is analyzed after it is acquired and stored in a file. *Concurrent processing*, on the other hand, provides immediate results.

PostScript A page-description language from Adobe Systems used on laser printers like the Apple LaserWriter, and in workstations from NeXT and Sun Microsystems. PostScript describes how to print a page blending text and graphics. A PostScript printer creates a font only when needed for printing rather than storing ready-made soft fonts on the hard drive.

PostScript font A font that is compatible with the PostScript language.

PostScript Library for Clipper Software that allows you to print to a PostScript printer from within a CA-Clipper application. You can print in any font, size, color, and orientation, as well as create barcodes and other graphics.

pot 1. A potentiometer or variable resistor. 2. To encapsulate a circuit or device into an inaccessible, usually epoxy, package. 3. Abbreviation for potential (as in *hi-pot*, for *high potential*).

potential The voltage between two points in a circuit, device, or system; electromotive force; electrical pressure.

potential difference The voltage existing between two points in a circuit or system.

potential gradient The differences in value of the potential per unit length along the conductor or through a dielectric.

potentiometer A usually circular or disk-type resistor with two fixed terminals and a third terminal connected to a variable contact arm.

potentiometer circuit A network arranged so that, when two or more potential differences are present in as many branches, the response of a suitable detecting device in any branch can be made zero by adjusting the electrical constants of the network.

potentiometer function generator A generator in which functional values of voltage are applied to points on a potentiometer, which becomes an interpolator.

potentiometer transducer A transducer in which a displacement is transmitted to the slider in a potentiometer, thus changing the ratio of output resistance to total resistance.

potentiometric input device Refers to one of several types of computer input devices that use potentiometers. For example, a set of rotary potentiometers may be mounted in a unit such as a joystick, as shown in the figure. In the figure, two controls are needed for two-axes positioning; the other controls could be used for fine and coarse positioning. Slide potentiometers, in

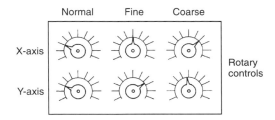

A set of controls used for screen positioning

which a linear movement replaces the rotation, are also used in some designs. Potentiometers are sampled by devices whose analog values are converted and stored in registers to be read by the microprocessor. The values read from the registers are then converted to equivalent numbers to be used by the program.

An analog-to-digital converter and a power supply can be used to determine the potentiometer's position by measuring the voltage as shown. The voltage is proportional to the amount of shaft rotation about the axis. When the converter is correctly adjusted, a zero position will correspond to a digital reading of all zeros and a fullscale position will correspond to all ones.

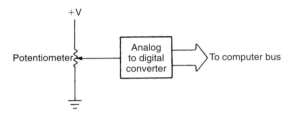

The potentiometer interface

potentiometric pressure transducers The potentiometric pressure transducer was first available in 1914, and is still used today due to low cost and connection simplicity. The potentiometric transducer consists of a resistance element either wirewound or deposited on conductive film, and a movable slider or wiper connected to the mechanical sensing element, as shown in the diagram. The motion due to a pressure change results in a resistance change. Depending on the design of the potentiometer, the output can be linear, sine, cosine, logarithmic, or exponential. These transducers can be used with ac or dc, and no amplification or impedance matching may be required.

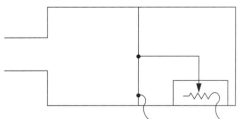

Potentiometric pressure transducer

powdered iron core A core consisting of fine particles of magnetic material mixed with a suitable bonding material and pressed into shape.

power amplifier 1. An amplifier intended for driving one or more speakers or transducers. **2.** A circuit designed to amplify both voltage and current.

power amplifier with gain A unit used to boost the signal-handling capability of an operational amplifier. The buffer output allows one to drive up to 50 mA output currents with 20V output swings.

PowerBase A fully relational, menu-driven database manager. On input, table validation provides automatic rejection of unmatched values and ensures that the data entered is valid. Lookup at entry time allows the retrieval of information from other files.

Reports are available using information from multiple files with up to five sort levels. Mailing labels can be custom designed on the screen. The program reads and writes ASCII, DIF, SYLK, WKS, PRN, and IMP files to link with online information services, mainframes, and spreadsheets. PowerBase is self-documenting; it provides a report that shows each file in detail and describes the relationships.

power check A sudden halt of a computer when a significant fluctuation in power occurs.

power console A power control where outlets are controlled individually or all at once by a master switch. Included are heavy-duty surge protection (140 Joules, 6,500 amps) to prevent catastrophic damage from power line disturbances and multistage filtering to block electromagnetic interference from scrambling the data in the computer.

power control center A protection device that guards against voltage spikes. It is equipped with suppression circuitry to protect a computer, monitor, printer, and auxiliary devices.

power derating The use of computed curves to determine the correct power rating of a device or component that is to be used above its reference ambient temperature.

Power Desk A business-productivity package that includes a word processor, database, autodialer, telephone log, calendar/reminder, calculator, label and envelope printer, and more.

power dissipation The dispersion of the heat generated within a device or component when a current flows through it. This is accomplished by convection to the air, radiation to the surroundings, or conduction.

powered enclosure A unit with a recessed frame and power supplies with connectors for specific microcomputers.

power factor correction The adding of capacitors to an inductive circuit to increase the power factor by making the total current more nearly in phase with the applied voltage.

power factor meter An instrument for measuring power factor with a scale graduated directly in power factor.

power fading A fading caused by anomalous propagation conditions characterized as slowly varying in time.

power fail 1. A usually temporary and inadvertent loss of power to an otherwise functioning machine. **2.** A specific interrupt that occurs when a loss of primary power is detected.

power-fail, automatic restart 1. A facility that provides a processor interrupt when a low-power signal is received from the primary power source. Sufficient time is then available to preserve the contents of the working registers in the memory. The automatic restart enables processing to resume at the point of interruption when power is restored. **2.** Refers to a specific power-fail interrupt that provides an interrupt when a loss of primary power is detected. A power-restart interrupt occurs when the power is applied and is up to normal operating levels.

power-fail detect module A unit designed to provide an interrupt or flag at least 500 microseconds before a low-power condition is detected and program execution is halted. Such a device can be used to prevent loss of data in memory for critical applications.

power-fail logic Logic circuits that protect a system in the event that primary power fails. The circuits automatically store the current operating parameters. When the power is restored, the circuits use this information to continue proper operation.

power-fail recovery *See* PFR.

power frequency The frequency in hertz at which electric power is generated and distributed.

power gain The ratio of output power to input power in an amplifier.

power ground A ground that is part of the circuit for the main source of power to or from various units.

Power Label A DOS-based label-printing program that prints any size label or form with barcodes and variable size text and lines. It supports background printing on up to four printers at a time.

power level The ratio of power at a point in the system to some arbitrary amount of power chosen as a reference. Power-level differences are usually expressed in decibels.

power-line monitor A device that observes and records levels of electrical power on a continuous basis. Some power-line monitors draw a continuous graph, while others only report on deviations from an established norm.

power lock A device that lets you lock your power switch in either the on or off position to prevent unauthorized use or power interruption. Typically, this device attaches to the back of your PC, guarding against board swapping as well as power interruption.

power loss The ratio of the power absorbed by the input circuit to the power delivered to a specified load under specified operating conditions.

PowerMac Macintosh computer built around the IBM/Apple/Motorola "PowerPC" RISC microprocessor, rather than the traditional Motorola 68000 series typical of earlier Macs.

power-on reset A signal used at power turn-on in some systems to initialize the CPU to a known state; it allows the proper sequence of events to occur. The power-on reset signal is generated external to the CPU, which receives the signal, sets the internal logic states, and produces a signal that can be used to initialize other circuits.

power pack 1. A unit for converting power from ac to dc or dc to ac for electronic devices. **2.** A battery of cells for powering electronic equipment.

PowerPoint A Windows-based presentation program from Microsoft designed to create overheads, flip charts, slides, or computer-based presentations. It provides audience handouts and note pages directly from your presentation. Also included is a full-featured word processor with spelling checker.

power problems Power transients can force too much power into the computer or deprive the computer of the necessary power. The first type of problem includes surges and spikes while the second includes sags, brownouts, and blackouts. Since spikes are rapid excursions of voltage with a large amplitude, they can propagate through the system and cause sensitive components to break down. Typical powerline problems are shown in the following figure.

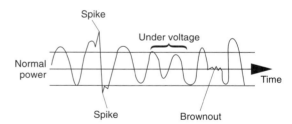

Powerline problems

power relay A relay that functions at some predetermined value of power. It may be an overpower relay, an underpower, or a combination of both.

power response The frequency response capabilities of an amplifier running at or near its full rated power.

power sag A short temporary drop in voltage.

Power Search A library of C functions designed to search for character strings or regular expressions in DOS and OS/2-based applications. It can generate custom machine code while your application program is running. It supports Turbo C, Turbo C++, Borland C++, and Microsoft C.

power semiconductors Semiconductors with ratings for a single transistor that are up to 750 volts at several amperes, with turn off times on the order of one microsecond. Slower devices may have turn off times of two to three microseconds, and ratings can run up to 600 V at 15 amperes.

power spike A short-term rise in voltage.

power strip Two-, four-, and six-receptacle models that feature a three-stage clamping circuit plus RFI/EMI noise filtering to withstand and dissipate more than 6,000 volts. Some use a metal enclosure, lighted master switch, and circuit breaker, as shown in the figure. A light indicates the circuitry is functioning, protecting your system.

Even minor power disturbances can cause permanent hardware and software damage. A voltage surge that lasts less than one-thousandth of a second can result in scrambled data and premature component failure. Utility companies have no effective way to control surges caused by unpredictable circumstances, but you can stop surges from affecting your hardware and software with a surge protector suited to your application.

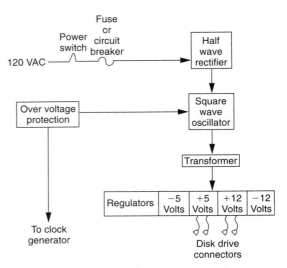

Typical switching power supply

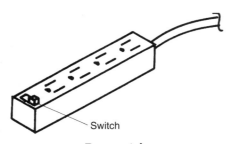

Power strip

power supply The system and circuitry for converting the ac line power into suitable dc voltages for the electronic equipment in a system, as shown in the following diagram. A basic power supply includes a transformer, rectifier, and filter. The power transformer steps up the voltage for high-voltage supplies or steps down for a low-voltage supply. The voltages at the transformer's secondary then goes through a rectifier system, where it is converted to pulsating dc. The filter system then smoothes out the pulsations to make the dc voltage at the supply's output appear more like the steady-state dc characteristic of batteries.

power switch 1. A mechanical switch used for high-current control applications or for application of operating voltages to equipment. 2. An electronic circuit that performs a switching action to deliver high-current voltages to equipment.

power-switch module A module used to drive solenoids, motor starters, and other such high-current devices.

power transformer 1. A transformer used for raising or lowering the supply voltage required by the load. 2. A transformer used to introduce the energizing supply into an instrument or system, distinct from a signal transformer.

power transistor A transistor capable of handling relatively heavy current loads.

P-P Abbreviation for *peak-to-peak*, the total difference between the most positive and most negative peaks of a waveform.

pp junction A region of transition between two regions having different properties in p-type semiconductor material.

PPM Abbreviation for *pulse position modulation*, a pulse modulation system in which the position of the pulse is a function of the modulating signal.

PPS Abbreviation for *parallel processing system*, a microcomputer system that uses a compatible set of LSI (large-scale integration) chips in order to achieve the capability of a parallel minicomputer, as shown in the following diagram.

pps Abbreviation for *pulses per second*.

PRA Abbreviation for *print alphamerically*.

PRD Abbreviation for *printer dump*.

preamble The 64-bit encoded sequence that the physical layer of Ethernet transmits before each frame to synchronize clocks and other physical layer circuitry at other nodes on the network transmission channel.

preamplifier A one- or two-stage amplifier required to strengthen the output of an electrical device so that it can drive a main amplifier.

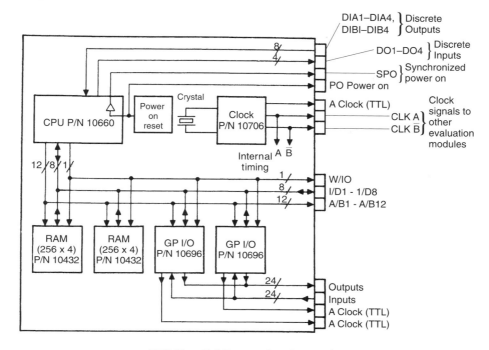

PPS (Parallel Processing System)

preanalysis An initial review of a computer task, for the purpose of increasing the efficiency of the computer for that task.

preassembly time The time used by an assembler to process macro definitions and perform conditional assembly operations.

precision The degree of exactness with which a quantity is defined. Precision is related to the number of distinguishable alternatives from which a representation is selected, such as the number of digits or bits in a number or word. *Double-length precision* pertains to words or operations with twice the normal length of a unit of data in a computing system. A double-length register would have the capacity to store twice as much data as a single-length or normal register; a double-length word would have twice the number of characters or digits as a normal or single-length word.

PreCursor A menu interface system that has unlimited menu selections, utilities, mouse support, menu cloning, and built-in password security. PreCursor is network-compatible and includes API support, computer usage reports, and screen blanking.

predictive control A control system that uses a computer for real-time repetitive comparison of pertinent parameters.

preedit A checking of application or operational programs before the test run. A preedit run can remove such problems as a disobedience to supervisory or segmentation rules.

preequalization The equalization of a circuit performed at the transmitter using a form of predistortion.

preferred values A series of resistor and capacitor values adopted by the EIA and military. In this system, the increase between any two steps is the same percentage as between all other steps.

prefix An add-on designator for the scheduling and transferring of control between programs.

prefix multiplier A scale or conversion factor for increasing a basic unit or quantity, as shown in the following table.

Prefix	Factor	Symbol
exa	10^{18}	E
peta	10^{15}	P
tera	10^{12}	T
giga	10^{9}	G
mega	10^{6}	M
kilo	10^{3}	k
hecto	10^{2}	h
deka	10^{1}	da
deci	10^{-1}	d
centi	10^{-2}	c
milli	10^{-3}	m
micro	10^{-6}	μ

(continued on page 400)

Prefix	Factor	Symbol
nano	10^{-9}	n
pico	10^{-12}	p
femto	10^{-15}	f
atto	10^{-18}	a

prefix notation *See* POLISH NOTATION.

preimaging Making a copy of a piece of data just before it is changed. The copy is stored on the disk in case the computer fails in the middle of the update operation and corrupts the file. The preimage is then used to return the data to its previous state.

preliminary review An examination or evaluation of matters related to processing procedures in an attempt to offer guidance in the preparation of plans, proposals, or designs previous to the installation of computer system equipment.

premastered tape A magnetic tape that contains all the data and control codes that are to be put on an optical disc via laser beam modulation.

premastering In a CD-ROM, a data formatting process performed on each block of user data. The process determines the sector address and adds synchronization information. For example, if the format is to be mode 1, then 288 bytes of error-detection and correction data are calculated. This data is added at the end of each sector to ensure the full recovery of user block data.

preprocessor A program that converts data from the format of an emulated system to the format accepted by an emulator.

preprogrammed CROM In some microcomputers, the definition of the instructions (the microinstructions) are stored in ROM as part of the control chip that makes up a part of the CPU. That chip is a CROM (*control read-only memory*). It can be bought preprogrammed, or the customer can define the contents. Since the microprogram is placed into the CROM by mask programming, the user must have a high volume to warrant the expenses involved in defining the contents.

prerecorded A term applied to material stored on media for repetitive use, such as programmed instructions or the standard paragraphs of form letters.

presentation graphics Refers to a type of productivity software package that is used to prepare line charts, pie charts, and other information-intensive images.

presentation layer The portion of the ISO-OSI model concerned with providing the necessary services to interface a variety of applications to the communications system without requiring modifications to the applications software. *Also see* OSI MODEL.

presentation syntax A standard method of representing data in a heterogeneous environment. ASN.1 (the abstract syntax notation 1) is an example of a presentation syntax.

preset An activity to set the contents of a storage location to an initial value or to establish the initial control value of a loop.

preset equalization A form of automatic equalization where a test sequence is used to fix the settings of the equalizer.

presettable I/O A set of switches that allow the programmer to verify microinstructions that perform input/output data transfers before actual peripherals are connected to the system.

pressure transducer Typically, an electrical output transducer that senses pressure using a mechanical sensing element. The elements are generally thin-walled elastic members, such as plates, shells, or tubes, such as those shown in the figure, that offer the pressure a surface area to act upon. When the pressure is not balanced by an equal pressure acting on the opposite surface, the element will deflect. The deflection is used to produce an electrical change in the transduction element.

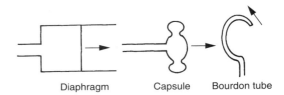

Pressure-sensing elements

presumptive address The address constant containing the absolute address of a memory location and a relative address; also called *base address*.

pretravel The distance or angle a plunger or actuator travels from the free position to the operating position.

preventive maintenance Precautionary measures designed to forestall system failures.

prewired external circuitry Connectors and cable systems that are prewired to extend the input/output system.

PRF Abbreviation for *pulse repetition/frequency*.

PRI Abbreviation for *primary*.

primary color In a tri-stimulus color video system, one of the three colors mixed to produce an image. In additive color systems, the primary colors are red, green, and blue. In subtractive color systems, the primaries are cyan, magenta, and yellow.

primary constants Refers to the capacitance, inductance, resistance, and leakance of a conductor, usually to earth (coaxial or concentric), or to return per unit length of line for a balanced conductor.

primary current The current flowing through the primary winding of a transformer. Changes in this current cause a voltage to be induced in the secondary winding of the transformer.

primary electrons 1. Electrons incident on a surface where secondary electrons are released. 2. Electrons released from atoms by internal forces and not by external radiation, as with secondary electrons.

primary emission Electron emission due to irradiation, including thermal heating, or by the application of a strong electric field to a surface.

primary flow The flow of carriers determined by the main properties of a device.

primary ionization In collision theory, the ionization produced by the primary particles, in contrast to total ionization, which includes secondary ionization.

primary key The most important field in a relational database. The primary key is a field such as social security number of employee ID number that is common to all or most of the files, the contents of which is unique to each record in a file.

primary registers Any general-purpose CPU register with an address in assembly language, where data can be loaded from memory, operated upon, and written back to memory using program instructions. A CPU normally reserves some registers for its exclusive use in controlling the computer that the program cannot directly utilize; these are excluded from the primary registers.

primary storage The main storage method in a computer system and the one from which instructions are executed, as contrasted with auxiliary or off-line storage.

primary task A task that receives priority processing from the CPU. The primary task usually controls the monitor and keyboard.

primitive Descriptive of the lowest level of a machine instruction or the lowest unit of language translation.

print A command to make a hardcopy of data or a document.

print buffer A segment of memory used to temporarily store data as it is transferred from the computer to the printer.

print chart A form used to determine the exact spacing and layout for printed output.

print density The relative darkness of print on the page. Very dense print appears totally black. Less-dense print looks lighter, and solid filled areas may not be totally black. You can adjust the print density in most laser printers.

printed circuit A circuit in which interconnecting wires have been replaced by conductive strips bound onto an insulating board.

printed circuit assembly 1. A printed circuit board to which separable components have been attached. 2. An assembly of one more printed circuit boards.

printed circuit board An insulating board (also called a *card*) onto which circuit paths have been printed or etched. Printed circuits boards may be single-sided, double-sided, or multilayer for high-density applications.

printed circuit breadboard A printed circuit board with pretinned holes arranged to accommodate standard integrated circuits for custom electronic designs in a modular microcomputer system. It is useful in prototyping. ICs may be inserted directly into the board, or sockets may be used.

printed circuit card *See* PRINTED CIRCUIT BOARD.

printed circuit, ceramic A material usually used only for very small printed-wiring applications, since large ceramic pieces tend to be brittle and are not as flexible as phenolic or glass epoxy. Ceramic material is used when dimensional stability is required at high temperatures.

printed circuit, double-sided A printed circuit in which great complexity is required and both sides of the insulating material contain the printed wiring pattern. The components are mounted only on one side. The connections between conductors of the two opposite sides may be made by the insertion of eyelets, rivets, or wire. For many applications, plated-through holes are used. In this process, conductive material is deposited inside the holes connecting the two printed-wiring patterns.

printed circuit epoxy coatings Coatings that offer excellent mechanical and thermal protection, as well as electrical insulation, but do not lend themselves to easy repair. Removal of the epoxy coating to gain access to a solder connection can be difficult.

printed circuit, glass epoxy laminate A widely used PC material, more translucent and stronger than phenolic material, with excellent temperature stability.

printed circuit, multilayer A printed-wiring technique that uses several layers of printed-wiring patterns, each mounted on a thin insulating material and carefully aligned and molded together. This technique almost always uses plated-through holes to provide the connection of conductors between the conducting layers.

printed circuit, phenolic A brown, board material used in commercial applications where temperature stability and strength are not critical.

printed circuit, polyvinyl fluoride A plating material that provides excellent insulating capability and can withstand extreme environmental conditions, but is difficult to repair. The polyvinyl fluoride material must usually be scraped away before soldering.

printed circuit, rhodium plating A plating material that is used because of its hardness and surface stability for extreme environmental and wear conditions. The fingers on printed circuit boards that mate with connector surfaces are usually rhodium-plated for long wear.

printed circuit, solder plating A mixture of tin and lead used on PC boards to improve solderability and prevent corrosion.

printed circuit switch A rotary switch that can be soldered in place directly onto a printed circuit board.

printed component A type of printed circuit component intended for electrical and/or magnetic functions other than point-to-point connections or shielding; examples include printed inductors and printed transmission lines.

printed contact That portion of a printed circuit that connects the circuit to a plug-in receptacle and performs the function of a plug pin.

printed element An element such as a resistor formed on a circuit board by deposition or etching.

printed wiring A conductive path formed on the surface of an insulating baseboard by plating or etching.

printed wiring substrate A conductive pattern printed on a substrate.

printer A typewriter-like machine that produces marks or impressions, usually on paper, in the form of graphic characters. A typical desktop printer produces anywhere between 25 lines and 10 pages per minute.

Printer Access Protocol An AppleTalk protocol for accessing printers.

printer card Usually refers to a parallel port expansion card.

printer commands Commands that change printing variables such as page orientation, margins, and font selection.

printer controller A device that contains the circuitry necessary to interface a printing unit to a microcomputer. Components are usually mounted on a card that plugs directly into the microcomputer chassis assembly.

printer description Refers to a file for each of the printers supported by a piece of software, usually containing a list of the fonts available on the printer and the dimensions of the characters in each font.

printer emulation Refers to the different printer languages that a printer can emulate. For example, a printer that can emulate an Epson FX-100 is compatible with any software designed to work with that printer. Some printers can be configured with a specific interface, for example, IBM or Epson compatibility.

printer fuse A fuse that, when open, will disconnect power from the printer, as shown in the figure.

printer reset buffer address In NetWare Print Services, a flag containing a long pointer to a buffer that holds the printer reset string.

printer setup buffer address In NetWare Print Services, a flag containing a long pointer to a buffer that holds a printer setup string.

printer sound enclosure A unit that can eliminate up to 95% of printer noise. Features include a clear Plexiglas shield that lets you see data and protects the printer, a cooling fan to prevent damaging heat buildup, thick convoluted foam for sound control, and a sound-absorbent base to muffle vibration.

printer stand A stand made of wire, plastic, or some other material that holds the printer and paper. A dot-matrix printer stand also controls the flow of forms from storage through the printer to a refold basket.

print flags In NetWare Print Services, a byte containing four bit fields that control a print job. The available options are

1. Print job is released to be printed if the capture is interrupted by a breach of connection with the file server.
2. Automatic form feed is suppressed after the document is printed.
3. Tabs are converted to spaces (and other control characters are converted). Tab size is specified in the next field.
4. Banners are printed before documents.

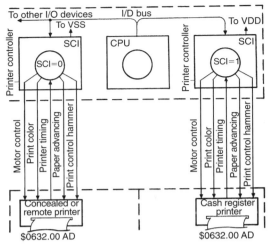

Printer controllers

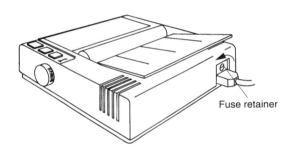

Printer fuse, often located near the power cord

print head On an impact printer, the unit where the printer makes its marks on the paper.

printing media Refers to any material that you can use to print on with a particular printer, such as envelopes, labels, or overhead film.

print job valid In NetWare Print Services, a flag set while a capture file is open to receive captured characters. When the capture is ended, canceled, or flushed, the flag is cleared.

printout refold basket A basket that clamps to the printer stand and receives and refolds fanfold printouts to keep the work area organized.

print queue In NetWare Print Services, a flag set when a job entry is placed in a print queue. When the capture is ended or canceled, the flag is cleared.

print queue ID In NetWare Print Services, a flag containing the bindery object ID (four bytes) of the print queue on the target server.

print server A device on a network that allows multiple users to share printers. Jobs sent to the printer are written to disk files and then sent to the printer as the printer becomes available. Most print servers have software to control the order in which the jobs are queued. Several third-party print servers are available for the Novell NetWare environment. They allow shared printers to be attached to local workstations rather than the file server.

print spooler A software program that accepts several jobs at once for printing. The spooler controls access to the printer and queues incoming jobs for execution.

PRINT USING A BASIC statement that outputs information to a screen, paper, or file in a format specified after the keyword USING.

print wheel (*o.t.*) The print head for daisywheel printers.

print zone In BASIC, the breakdown of a screen or paper into 14-column sections. Numeric values are displayed one-per-print-zone if no other printing format is used.

priority circuits Circuits of the control unit that grant memory access to the various units of the system in a sequence that enables each I/O device and the system's running time to be used most efficiently. Priority circuits receive, store, and grant requests for accesses to memory.

priority dispatching In multitasking, refers to the numbers assigned to tasks and used to determine precedence for the use of the CPU.

priority indicators Code signals that form a queue of data for processing in order of importance.

priority interrupt controller A controller that enables the programmer to selectively mask any interrupt level. The basic logic as shown in the figure gives the generation of the level vector but not the address vectoring. These devices typically accept eight interrupt levels, shown on the right of the diagram; each one will set a bit in the interrupt register.

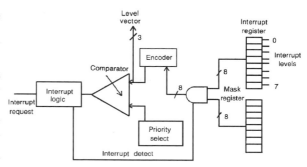

Priority interrupt controller

priority interrupt control unit *See* PICU.

priority interrupt module A device that acts as the monitor for a number of field contacts and notifies the computer when an external priority request has been made.

priority interrupt table A table that lists the priority sequence for handling and testing interrupts in systems without fully automatic interrupt capability.

priority ordered interrupts An interrupt capability that permits a terminal to be attached to more than one interrupt line. If the attached interrupts cover a range of priorities, by selectively arming and disarming the external interrupt lines, the executive program can change the relative priority of a terminal's attention requests, allowing different classes of service or response to be given.

priority scheme A technique that allows several devices to request service simultaneously. Assume that interrupt 0 is the highest priority, interrupt 1 the next, and so on to the lowest priority device. The microprocessor tests bit 0 of the interrupt register, then bit 1, and so on until it finds a 1. When it finds a 1, the corresponding interrupt line is serviced. Thus the highest level of interrupt is serviced first. After this interrupt is serviced, the microprocessor reads the contents of the interrupt register and services any other waiting interrupts. This is a software implementation of a priority interrupt scheme.

private automatic branch exchange *See* PABX.

private-key encryption A system in which the computer acts as a key distribution center to pass out keys to sender and receiver.

Private Line A selective calling system in two-way communications characterized by a continuously transmitted low-frequency tone during all station transmissions.

private line A channel furnished to a subscriber for exclusive use. Also called a *private wire* or *leased line*.

private wire The interconnection of a number of points by communication facilities.

privileged instructions Specialized restrictions to commands that prevent one subprogram from misusing another subprogram's I/O devices.

PRN Abbreviation for *print numerically*.

Pro Art Professional Art Library A three-volume clip art library with business, sports, and holidays illustrations for newsletters, business presentations, ads, and promotions.

probable error The amount of error that, according to the laws of probability, is most likely to occur during a measurement.

probe The terminal point at the end of a test equipment's input conductor.

problem board A removable panel with an array of terminals interconnected by short leads in patterns to simulate specific program problems. The entire problem board can be inserted or removed for different programs.

problem definition The act of compiling information in the form of logic diagrams and flowcharts to present a specific problem to the programmer in a clear and concise manner.

problem description A statement of a specific problem, which may include the method of solution, the solution, the transformations of data required, and the relationships of procedures, data, and constraints.

problem determination The process of identifying a hardware or software failure and determining responsibility and cause.

problem language The language used by a programmer in stating the definition of a problem.

problem-oriented language A programming language designed for the convenient expression for a given class of problems, usually a source language suited to describe procedural steps. A problem-oriented language is designed for the convenience of program specification in a general problem area, rather than for easy conversion to machine code.

procedural test A check of machine control and operation before processing. Procedural test data should cover all or most of the conditions that can occur during the run. Results can be compared against predetermined conditions.

procedure A systematic course of action to be used by people involved in working with a computer system.

procedure-oriented language A machine-independent language that describes how the process of solving a problem is to be carried out. The language should be designed for the convenient expression of procedures for problem solution, usually in terms of algorithms. Fortran, ALGOL, COBOL, and PL/1 are all examples of procedure-oriented languages. Fortran is oriented towards algebraic procedures, while COBOL is oriented toward business procedures and applications.

process bound *See* COMPUTE BOUND.

process control The control of industrial processes such as metal production, chemical refining, and other manufacturing operations. Process control usually implies a continuous operation or production. Some typical process control application areas are precious metals production, cement production, environmental control, chemical processes, and petroleum refining.

process control analog modules Signal conversion, sample-and-hold, amplifiers, multiplexers, and signal conditioning units designed especially for process control applications.

process control compiler A compiler used to program PROMs using a process control language or machine language. The compiler accepts keyboard entry of data, displays the data for verification and editing, compiles the program, and loads it into the PROM chips.

process control computer A computer designed for process control applications. It is generally limited in software requirements, instruction capacity, word length, and accuracy.

process control language *See* PCL.

process controller A computer that controls the process to which it is connected and executes machine-language programs to accomplish this control.

process control loop A complete process control system in which computers are used for the automatic control and regulation of industrial processes and operations, as shown in the diagram.

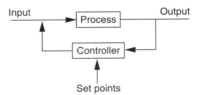

Process control loop

process ID In NetWare, the ID of a created process or a calling process.

processing section The portion of a computer that does the changing of input data into output data. The processing section usually includes the arithmetic and logic sections.

process loop test A check made to determine the need for loop operations.

process monitoring Refers to data acquisition in which the PC is directly connected to a process through I/O boards or I/O processors. Several may be interfaced to data highways in order to extract data from programmable controllers and distributed process control devices. Plug-in cards for PCs offer independent data paths for simultaneous analog input, analog output, and digital I/O.

processor A hardware data processor or a program that performs the functions of compiling, assembling, and translating for a specific language. Processor operations can involve registers, accumulators, program counters and stacks, I/O control, and internal instruction control.

processor basic instructions Instructions that can be functionally grouped into five categories: register operations, accumulator operations, program counter and stack control operations, I/O operations, and machine operations.

processor, bit-slice See BIT-SLICE PROCESSOR.

processor evaluation module A circuit card that contains all the necessary components of a microprocessor set, including the following:

- CPU
- RAM
- Clock generator
- Input/output circuits
- Power-on circuits

processor I/O channel A channel used to communicate with devices that are generally asynchronous in nature. Each item of data is transferred to or from an addressed device by executing an I/O instruction for each transfer. I/O instructions, in addition to transferring data, are also used to test the status of a device and to initiate input or output operations.

processor interface module A unit that connects the LSI processor to as many as eight I/O devices. It provides a common interface and standardized software for either serial or parallel operation.

processor interrupt An automatic procedure used to alert the system to conditions that might affect the sequence of instructions being executed.

processor module The circuit card that contains the microprocessor along with the logic and control circuitry necessary to operate as a processing unit. The processor support circuits consist of clock circuits, a multiplexer, bus control, I/O control, and interrupt logic.

processor slices See BIT-SLICE PROCESSOR.

processor status word See PSW.

processor transfer time The time required for data transfer before the processor acknowledges the data as input or output. Processor transfer time depends on the internal cycle time and the channel transfer rate of the processor.

Prodigy A joint offering of IBM and Sears, Prodigy is the most consumer-oriented of the big three online services. Prodigy stagnated in the early 1990s, losing ground to upstart AMERICA ONLINE. In early 1995, Prodigy showed signs of new life as it became the first service to offer access to the World Wide Web. It also debuted an innovative information retrieval service for students, Homework Helper.

ProDoc/ProDraft A software set for program development, documentation, and support software. It can be used with PC, MicroVAX, and Unix systems.

producer's risk Associated with an acceptance test; refers to the probability of rejecting an item or a lot that is, in fact, satisfactory.

production automation The automatic techniques used in such industrial applications as machine tool control, material handling, mixing of materials, inspection systems, and assembly operations.

production automation microcomputer A rugged, compact microcomputer system designed for industrial control and automation applications.

production automation system components These system modules include all the basic building blocks to configure a complete working microcomputer system: central processor modules and memories; analog, digital, and power switching modules; clocks, timers, and special modules; communication modules; peripheral, programming, test, and diagnostic equipment; and power supplies and mounting hardware.

Professional Clip Art Gallery A package containing some of the richest-detailed clip art available, compatible with nearly any PC-based word-processing or desktop publishing application.

Professional Masterkeys A collection of disk utilities that lets you manipulate and change your disks.

Professor DOS A training package designed to teach DOS. It concentrates on operating system concepts, DOS commands, and using DOS's editor.

profiler A tool to visibly explore where an application is using CPU, system, or network resources.

ProFont A program with 24 graphic screen fonts in six scalable typefaces. Fonts can be rotated, scaled, and precisely positioned at the pixel level.

program A set of instructions arranged in proper sequence for directing the computer in performing a desired operation, such as the solution of a mathematical problem or the sorting of data.

A program includes instructions for the transcription of data, coding for the computer, and plans for the absorption of results into the system. As each instruction is obeyed, the sequence of operations determines the overall task. Since programs are infinitely variable, the number of possible tasks is only limited by the ingenuity of those doing the programming.

Developing the program involves coding the algorithms into a programming language. Coding involves the translation of the program specifications into instructions. These instructions form the actual program or software product. The coding may be done using the assembly language for the particular microprocessor or, alternative, a higher-level language.

program address counter See PROGRAM COUNTER.

program address register A register that holds the instruction location to be transmitted to the control ROM.

program analyzer A development unit designed for

the convenient field service of microcomputer systems. It can be used for software debugging and troubleshooting in the field. The analyzer connects to the CPU and displays the contents of bus lines along with the processor state, including instructions and data.

program control unit A unit or section of the CPU for controlling the execution of computer instructions and their sequence of operation.

program conversion The controlled transition from an old system to a new one. It involves careful planning for the various steps that have to be taken and equally careful supervision of their execution.

program counter The counter or instruction pointer, sometimes abbreviated *PC* or *PAC*, that contains the address of the memory location containing the next instruction. The instruction cycle typically begins with the CPU placing the contents of the program counter on the address bus; the CPU fetches the first word of the instruction from memory and increments the contents of the program counter so that the next instruction cycle can fetch the next instruction in sequence from memory. When the instruction occupies more than one word of memory, the CPU increments the program counter each time it is used. In this way the CPU executes the instructions sequentially unless an instruction like JUMP or BRANCH changes the program counter. Thus, the program counter keeps track of the processor's progress through the program. Often the processor has other instructions to modify the way the counter behaves such as decrementing instead of incrementing and skipping a count. Also called *index address register* or *program address counter*.

program development system A development aid that allows users to make, simulate, and debug programs.

program documentation See DOCUMENTATION.

program, editor See EDITOR.

program error A mistake made in the program code by the programmer, compiler, or assembler.

program, executive See EXECUTIVE.

program file Refers to files that perform functions. On the PC, these files often have extensions such as EXE or COM.

program forms A convenient tool for describing program listings. The program form can provide several levels of communication between the designer and the hardware. The highest level is found in the comments and notation section, where the designer communicates in sequential form using a human language. This section is much like the flowchart and is essentially independent of the machine language. The program forms should also describe the subroutines, provide the purpose of the program, the form of the input and output data, the requirements for memory, and a description of the parameters.

program generation system See PGS.

program generator A program that permits other programs to be written automatically. A *character-controlled generator* operates like a compiler, examining control characters and altering instructions according to directions found in the control characters. A *pure generator* is a program that writes another program. Most assemblers are also compilers and generators. The generator in an assembler is usually a section of program that is called by the assembler to write one or more entries in another program.

program instruction The set of characters that may include one or more addresses that define an operation and cause the computer to operate on the indicated quantities.

program, internally stored A set or sequence of instructions, a program, or a routine that is stored within the computer (internal memory), as opposed to those programs which might be stored externally on magnetic disk or tape.

program library A collection of available computer programs and routines. A microcomputer library might include a text editor, loader, assembler, RAM test program, decimal addition, PROM programmer, A/D conversion, logic subroutines, and BCD-to-binary conversion.

program listing A step-by-step list of the program operation. The listing may be made up of the machine-language bit patterns or actual instructions.

programmable Capable of being set to operate in a specified manner or of accepting remote setpoint or other commands.

programmable A/D board Refers to one of the programmable gain analog/digital I/O expansion boards for the PC, full-length boards that install in an expansion slot and turn the computer into a fast, high-precision data acquisition and signal analysis instrument. The programmable gain amplifier has a fixed gain-bandwidth product so that its settling time increases at higher gain. This causes the maximum throughput rate to decrease as the gain increases.

programmable calculating oscilloscope A programmable instrument for the acquisition and manipulation of electronic data. This instrument combines an oscilloscope and a microprocessor in a single unit with the capability to calculate rise times, integrals, differentials, peak areas, averages, and many other values.

programmable calculator A calculating device that is programmed by a keyboard or simple storage devices. High-level programmable calculators may use BASIC keywords and can be used as elements in data communication networks, instrumentation, and peripheral controllers, or to perform remote job-entry functions.

programmable clock A system timing device that can be used to synchronize the CPU to external events, measure time intervals between events, and provide interrupts at preset intervals.

programmable communication adapter See PCA.

programmable communications interface See USART.

programmable controller A control unit designed as a direct replacement for a relay panel in industrial control applications. Programmable controllers are usually programmed directly from ladder diagrams or English-like logic statements. In general, programmable controllers sacrifice many of their data-handling capabilities for programming simplicity. Programmable controllers can be configured to handle as few as eight outputs or as many as 256, with or without timing or counting. They can also be used for arithmetic and shift register operations.

programmable data mover A custom-configured modular data acquisition and transmission device that can control the signal timing and conditioning for a wide variety of input and output signals. Typical programs can be written in about 20 minutes using a 16-pad keyboard and 32-character display.

programmable digital logic See PDL.

programmable interval timer See PIT.

programmable I/O channel Refers to the programmed control of information transfer between the central processor and an external device. The programmed input/output channel allows the data to be acted on immediately, thus eliminating the need for a memory reference by either the channel or the program.

programmable I/O device A programmable, parallel LSI input/output device that can perform the following functions: address decoding, data I/O buffering, multiplexing, establishing status signals for handshaking, and performing other control functions, as shown in the following figure.

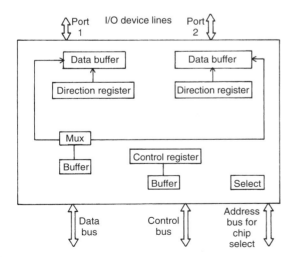

Programmable I/O device

programmable logic Devices and systems that provide logic functions that can be changed by the user. *Programmable logic devices* are relatively simple devices and, of themselves, do not comprise an entire computing system. Included in this category are FPLAs, PLAs, ROMs, EAROMs, RAMs, CAMs, and microprocessors. *Programmable logic systems* include microcomputers, programmable calculators, minicomputers, and mainframe computers.

programmable logic array A mask-programmable chip that provides functions from arrays of AND and OR gates.

programmable memory A memory with locations that are addressable by the program counter. A program within this memory may directly control the operation of the arithmetic and control unit.

programmable option select See POS, 2.

programmable peripheral interface An I/O device with individually programmable pins. The pins can be programmed either as inputs or outputs.

programmable point-of-sale terminal A terminal that has a read-only microprogram memory for retail sales applications.

programmable read-only memory See PROM.

programmable sharing device See PSD.

program maintenance procedures The checking and testing requirements designed to reduce machine malfunctions or human mistakes in programming.

programmed acceleration A controlled velocity increase to the programmed feedrate of a numerical control machine.

programmed check A check of machine functions performed by the machine in response to an instruction included in the program. The programmed check may be a sample problem with a known answer.

programmed data transfer Refers to data I/O performed with a minimum of hardware support. The maximum rate at which programmed data transfers may take place is limited by the CPU instruction rate. The data rate of the most commonly used peripheral devices, however, is much lower than that of maximum rate. The major drawback associated with programmed data transfer is that the CPU must stay in a waiting loop while the I/O device completes the last transfer and prepares for the next transfer. The technique permits easy hardware implementation and simple, economical interface design. For this reason, many devices rely heavily on programmed data transfer.

programmed dwell The ability to insert delays in program execution for a programmable length of time.

programmed learning An instructional method that uses expository material along with questions coupled to branching logic. Programmed learning has been applied in computers as computer-assisted instruction (CAI).

programmed logic A logic system that is alterable in accordance with a program that controls the equivalent connections of all the gating elements. In programmed logic, the instruction repertoire can be changed to match the machine capability to the problem.

programmed logic array See PLA.

programmed search The automatic finding of various segments of prerecorded material on media for output in some predetermined sequence.

programmer 1. A person involved in the writing and testing of programs. **2.** A device designed for program generation. For example, an EEPROM programmer is a unit that provides a means of programming an electrically erasable ROM.

programmer check A check procedure designed by the programmer and implemented specifically as a part of the program.

programmer-defined macro Refers to specific segments of coding that are used frequently throughout a program and are defined and referenced by a mnemonic code with parameters. This increases the coding efficiency and readability of the program.

programmer, EEPROM See EEPROM PROGRAMMER.

programmer's console diagnostic A routine that tests most of the console logic using an automatic loop-back test. It will also test all lights and switches under control of the operator.

programmer tools All hardware and software designed for generating a system's programs. Programmer tools include assemblers, simulators, editors, and assemblers. Some may run on timesharing systems, while others may be run on the microcomputer system itself.

program, micro See MICROPROGRAM.

programming The design, writing, and testing of programs. Programming may consist of the following steps:

1. Definition of problem
2. Preparation of flowchart
3. Listing of computer instructions
4. Selecting control modes

program, background See BACKGROUND PROGRAM.

programming language A language used for the preparation of programs. Languages that support programming efforts include Fortran, BASIC, COBOL, C and Pascal.

programming, machine language See MACHINE LANGUAGE.

programming module A discrete, identifiable set of instructions that is handled as a unit by an assembler, compiler, linkage editor, or loader.

programmable peripherals In many systems two distinct functions are relegated to the software: setting the data direction and control register patterns at the time of system initialization and handling interrupts. Setting the data direction and a control register pattern establishes the operating characteristics of the I/O device. Handling interrupts in a system is often a problem of software polling. A polling and corresponding program are required.

Such a polling approach is usually the lower-cost alternative for identifying interrupts, but may in some instances be too slow. For such applications, hardware may be added to the system to achieve priority encoding of the various interrupt requests. The encoded value of the interrupt request can then be used as a system address to transfer control to the appropriate response routine. This is referred to as *vectoring*.

program module An independent program, also called a *segment* or *overlay*, which performs a part of a longer routine within a larger program. In order for a program to be run with a minimum of storage, the program may be divided into program modules. When a module's task is over, it calls the next section, which replaces the previous section in storage. Certain parts of the program or data areas may remain common to all modules so that communication can take place between different parts of the program.

program name The name given to each program by which it is stored and retrieved.

program parameter See PARAMETER.

program-patching plugboard Refers to a relatively small, auxiliary plugboard patched with a specific variation of a portion of a program.

program redesign Altering a program by adding new features or meeting new requirements. The redesign process may involve making a program meet critical time or memory requirements. When increases of 25 percent or less in speed or reductions of the same order in memory are desired, the program can often be reorganized, but the program structure may have to be sacrificed. The redesign should follow the same paths as the previous design stages of software development.

program reference table See PRT, 1.

program register See PROGRAM COUNTER.

program run 1. The actual processing time of a computer program. **2.** Collectively, those steps performed by a computer as it executes all cycles of a program.

program scheduler A facility that permits use of the CPU unit among programs based in storage, depending upon priority requirements.

program segments The logically discrete units, such as subprograms, that comprise a complete program. Program segments consist of sequences of program statements that make up the main program. Control and data can be passed between segments as desired.

program-sensitive error An error arising from some unforeseen behavior of some circuits, discovered when a comparatively unusual combination of program steps occurred.

program, service See SERVICE ROUTINE.

program specifications Detailed listings of input,

processing, output, and storage requirements for a new program.

program stack A dedicated memory portion for providing multiple-level nesting capability. The stack nests subroutine addresses and program counter words for orderly return to the main program following subroutine calls. As new values are added to the stack, all previous values are pushed down, with the top level being the most recent entry.

program statement A basic unit used to construct programs. For example, a typical assembly language statement begins in character-position one of a source line and is terminated with a carriage return or a semicolon. A semicolon allows multiple statements to be coded on the same physical source line, as follows:

```
LOC 1 ADI 2; (add 2 to accumulator)
```

program status word See PSW.

program step A single operation or phase of one instruction or command in a sequence of instructions.

program stop instruction An instruction that is used to automatically stop the machine under certain conditions, such as reaching the end of processing or completing the solution of a problem.

program storage The section of internal memory reserved for the storage of programs, routines, and subroutines. Program storage areas are sometimes protected using various schemes to prevent the alteration of the contents.

program storage unit See PSU.

program testing time The time expended for the testing of a machine or system program to ensure that no malfunctions or faults are present. Program testing may include debugging and special diagnostic routines, or circuit and component testing to determine machine status.

program test system A checking system in which a sample problem with a known answer is run before running the program to solve the actual problem.

program, trace See TRACE PROGRAM.

ProKey A memory-resident macro generator that reduces typing time and makes other software easier to use. ProKey generates macro commands that allow you to type multiple keystrokes by pressing a single key. For example, suppose you want to periodically save a document with your word-processing program. To do so, the program requires you to exit to the main menu, enter a save command, then jump back to the end of the document to continue where you left off. With ProKey, you can store these commands in a macro that can be executed by pressing just one key.

PROLOG A high-level language used in artificial intelligence applications. Its name stands for *programming in logic*. PROLOG is used for developing expert systems because its main strength is in defining and working with logical relationships.

PROM 1. Acronym for *programmable read-only memory*, usually a semiconductor memory that is not programmed during fabrication and requires a physical or electrical operation to program it, such as deliberately blowing selected diodes or exposing them to ultraviolet light. Devices are also available for automatically copying master PROMs quickly and easily. See the following figure. **2.** A circuit board that contains the sockets for PROM along with the necessary address decoding, control, and timing circuits. The sockets allow PROM chips to be added or deleted to satisfy the system requirements. *Also see* PROM TECHNOLOGY.

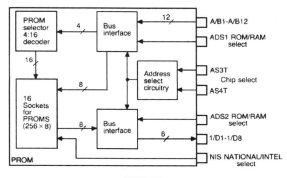

PROM

ProMath A collection of 150 mathematical functions and routines, including trigonometric, hyperbolic, factorial, gamma, error, beta, Fresnel, and Bessel functions.

PROM blaster A device for changing the protected read-only memory section found in some PROMs. The blaster allows the entire PROM to be changed by the user.

PROM decoder Refers to a fixed decoder internal to the device. The internal decoder selects a word by examining the address inputs. For a 512×8 PROM, one of 512 words are selected by examining nine address inputs.

promotional software A program available for little or no cost, showing the capabilities of commercial software but limiting the amount of data that can be used.

PROM programmer Erasable PROMs that plug into a unit for programming. One typical PROM programmer can copy PROMs in less than one minute using a control program. Operating as an online peripheral device to a microcomputer system, the unit can be a fully self-contained subsystem that will load and verify user-generated routines in individual PROM chips. Source data for loading PROMs is binary code, previously generated by an assembler or the debugging programs.

PROM programmer card A card that allows blocks of memory to be automatically programmed into PROM.

PROM programming system A system for low-cost microcomputer programming that uses PROMs. The system has four basic parts:

1. Prototype board
2. Microprogram control programs
3. Programmer for the PROM
4. Keyboard

PROM prompting A PROM programming system function that helps a user by requesting information such as operands necessary to continue processing.

prompt A message or symbol that appears on the screen, asking for information from the user.

PROM puller A device that helps prevent broken or bent pins that can occur during extraction from or insertion into an IC socket. A simple one-hand operation removes DIP ICs from printed circuit boards or sockets.

PROM simulator A device that uses RAM for testing and debugging operations prior to PROM programming.

PROM technology PROMs are an engineering development aid; they are a special form of semiconductor read-only memory. The PROM is similar in size and appearance to a ROM, but while the information in a ROM is written permanently during the process of fabrication, in a PROM, it is programmed after the chip is packaged using one of a number of built-in characteristics.

Programmable ROM devices fall into two basic categories: those that are erasable and those that are not, as shown in the following diagram. The nonerasable PROMs involve some form of fusing process in which a link or junction is fused open or closed, as shown in the figure. The process involves an action that is basically irreversible, thus making this type of PROM nonerasable.

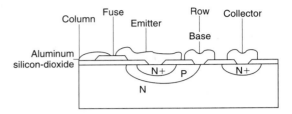

Fusible link PROM cell structure

PROM verifying Using a PROM programmer, data may be verified while writing a copy or reading a copy. With the verify switch on, data in the master is compared to data in the copy. Any difference in the data will light an error indicator, stop the programmer, and display the data in error.

ProNet A family of LAN products from Proteon Corporation.

proof listing A report (prepared by the processor) that shows the coding as originally written, with comments and machine-language instructions.

propagated error An error occurring in one operation and affecting data required for subsequent operations, so that the error is spread through much of the processed data.

propagation The traveling of waves or pulses through or along a transmission medium.

propagation constant A number expressed by the Greek letter P (rho) to indicate the effect in a transmission line of a wave propagating through it.

propagation delay The time required for a signal to travel from one point in a circuit or transmission path to another.

propagation velocity The rate at which a signal propagates on a wire.

property has value In NetWare Bindery Services, a flag that tells whether a property contains a value.

proportional control A type of control in which there is a continuous linear relation between the output and the input, as shown in the figure.

Proportional control

proportional control system A feedback control system that generates a correction signal that is a linear function of the error.

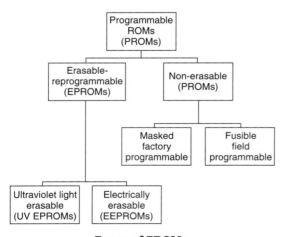

Types of PROMs

proportional gain The ratio of the change in output due to a change in input in a proportional control system.

proportionality That part of a linearity curve when it passes through a zero-error reference point or an origin.

proportional plus derivative controller A control action in which the output is proportional to the linear combination of the input and the time integral of the output.

proportional plus integral controller A controller that produces proportional plus integral (reset) control action.

proportional range A band or set of values of a specific condition being controlled that causes the controller to operate over a linear range.

proportional spacing A property of many fonts in which each letter takes up a different amount of space based on its shape. For example, an *i* takes less space than a *w*.

proportional-speed floating controller A unique single-action controller that produces integral control action only.

proposed response A response supplied by some programs in a command field, usually based on the most recent use of a command or the current status of the program. You can usually replace a proposed response with your own response.

proprietary LAN A LAN environment that can only use the devices from a single manufacturer.

proprietary program A program that is controlled by the owner through the legal right of possession and title.

proprietary slot An expansion slot that only accepts cards made specifically for that particular machine or that manufacturer's machines.

ProPrint Report Generator A report generator that supports Paradox, Btrieve, dBASE, ASCII, and binary data file formats. A full-screen interface allows users to create and run reports using WYSIWYG line and field formatting.

ProScreen A screen painter with color control. You can edit three screens at a time and up to 130 fields per screen. There are 19 predefined and user-defined masks.

Prospect Organizer A program designed for sales and marketing databases of prospect information. Its database can be used to retrieve and display selected prospect information by identifying criteria such as ZIP code, city, state, territory, or alphabetical listing. Telemarketing scripts can be created for questionnaires, surveys, or solicitations. Respondents' answers can be entered directly into the computer during the call to automatically update the prospect database.

Prospero A distributed file system that provides the user the ability to create multiple views of a single collection of files distributed across the Internet. Prospero provides a filenaming system, and file access is provided by existing access methods (e.g., anonymous FTP and NFS). The Prospero protocol is also used for communication between clients and servers in the Archie system.

Pro Struct A utility to unscramble and restructure older Fortran to F-77 or VAX Fortran. It converts IF-GOTO statements to IF-THEN-ELSE and DO-WHILE constructs, and DO.CONTINUE to DO.END DO statements.

protect To restrict access to or use of all, or part of, a data-processing system.

protected check A check prepared in such a manner as to prevent alterations.

protected location A storage location reserved for special purposes. Data to be stored in these locations is required to undergo a screening procedure. Protected locations may be block locations in main storage or in disk files where data may be read from, but not written into.

protected mode A mode of 80286 and higher CPU chips. In this mode, the CPU chip supports multitasking by protecting data segments in use by one program from access by another program. The memory is protected, so this mode is called protected mode. *Contrast with* REAL MODE.

protection key An indicator in the program status word that is associated with a task. It must match the storage keys of all storage blocks that it is to use.

protective gap A spark gap between conductors on an open transmission line or in sets of conductors, to protect the system against excessive high-voltage surges.

Proteus A program to create self-running or interactive software demos, tutorials, and prototypes. It includes video effects, pull-down menus, slide advance control, and mouse and screen grabber support.

protocol The set of conventions between communication lines and links to the messages to be exchanged, especially those conventions that set the precedence among messages. Protocols can be used to define a complex hierarchy for the various level of exchange encountered in information systems. At the lowest level, the *synchronous communications protocol* is used for the exchange of information between switching computers; next, a first level of protocol exists for the exchange of information between a host computer and its interface. The next level of protocol uses these two levels to control the flow of information between host computers. Level-three protocols are used to control the flow of information between processes, where a process may be a program or a terminal. Specific protocols are used to make initial connections in a link, for the transmittal of large files between computers, and for batch communication.

protocol analyzers An instrument that can be used to provide an independent, controlled network load on a LAN. The analyzer can be used to observe the effects on network performance parameters, as shown in the following figure.

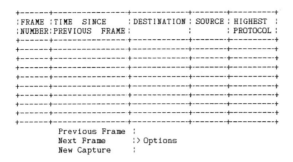

Protocol analyzer screen features

protocol converter A device for translating the data transmission code and/or the protocol of one network or device to the corresponding code or protocol of another network or device, allowing equipment with different conventions to communicate with one another.

protocol, database See DATABASE PROTOCOL.

protocol data unit See PDU.

protocol-level timer A timer within a communicating device that synchronizes and sets deadlines for protocol related activities. A protocol-level timer issues a high-priority interrupt.

protocol stack A set of functions, one at each layer of the protocol stack, that work together to form a set of network services. Each layer of the protocol stack uses the services of the module beneath it and builds on that service.

Pro3D/PC A 3D modeling and sculpting package for artists needing to create realistic renderings of three-dimensional scenes, and industrial designers who need to make prototypes and architectural renderings. Pro3D is available for Windows or DOS. It is compatible with PageMaker and Ventura Publisher.

ProtoGen A development program for code generation and prototyping Windows applications. You can develop the user interface for your application using visual prototyping methods. ProtoGen generates expert-level commented code for ANSI C, Microsoft MFC C++, Borland OWL C++, Turbo Pascal, and Microsoft Windows NT.

prototype An initial design system or package that usually is a model for additional development.

prototype board A circuit board used in development systems to evaluate new system concepts.

prototype development system A collection of modules and equipment used for software and firmware development and programming. A typical system includes the processor, control panel, keyboard, RAM, PROM programmer, and power supplies. Software includes an assembler, text editor, PROM programmer, debug programs, and control programs.

prototype statement An assembler statement that provides a name to a macro definition for a model or for the macroinstruction that is to call the macro definition.

prototyping The initial design and fabrication of a system on a trial basis for "shakedown."

ProtoView Screen Management A set of design tools, data-entry controls, and libraries that lets you create a use-friendly interface with data validation for Windows applications. A custom-control DLL provides built-in data validation, DDE links, and message handling. A second DLL contains high-level functions for file browsers, editors, and printing files and buffers under Windows, A PVDialog class lets you encapsulate the extended functionality of the two DLLs within the ObjectWindows library of the Microsoft Foundation Classes hierarchy.

proving time The time used in running a test program to check if a particular fault has been corrected.

proximity effect The redistribution of current brought about in a conductor by the presence of another current-carrying conductor.

prr Abbreviation for *pulse repetition rate*, the measure of the number of electric pulses per unit of time experienced by a unit in a computer; usually a factor of the standard pulse rate. Usually expressed in pulses per second (pps).

PRT 1. Abbreviation for *program reference table*, a table of the locations reserved for program variables, data descriptions, and other program information. When a program references a word in the PRT, the relative address is used rather than the absolute address. The relative address of any particular location is based upon its position relative to the start of the table. **2.** In many programs, an abbreviation for *print*.

ps Abbreviation for *picosecond*, one trillionth of a second (10^{-12} second). Also abbreviated *psec*.

PSD Abbreviation for *programmable sharing device*, a device that can be easily configured to act as a port-sharing unit, a modem-sharing unit, or a combination of the two. It is compatible with both asynchronous and synchronous equipment. Configuring the device is quick, there is a minimum of straps, and crossover cables are not required because all crossover connections are performed internally. The PSD is primarily designed for half-duplex operation in a polled system. The main channel transmits data to all subchannels in parallel. Subchannels contend to transmit to the main channel by activating RTS (request to send) or DCD (data carrier detect) signals, or by data transitions.

PSE Abbreviation for *Portable Streams Environment*, a generic version of Streams that is packaged into the source code for Portable NetWare.

PS ERROR An error system for CA-Clipper that is able to record both runtime and fatal errors to a log file when they occur. Its runtime error handler includes source code so you can customize it as needed. The fatal error handler can be customized through Clipper function calls.

pseudocode A code that requires translation prior to execution. Pseudocode is often used to link a subroutine into the main routine. It usually expresses programs in terms of source language by referring to locations and operations using symbolic names and addresses.

pseudoerror detector A bit error rate (BER) estimation technique that uses modified decision regions in a separate decision circuit to degrade the receiver margin intentionally and reduce the time required to estimate the BER.

pseudo-instruction A group of characters having the same general form as an instruction, but that is never executed as an actual instruction. Pseudo-instructions are used as symbolic representations in compilers, interpreters, and assemblers to designate groups of instructions for performing a particular task. Also called *quasi-instruction*.

pseudo-random code A digital code that has the appearance of a random sequence of finite length. Pseudo-random codes repeat themselves and are not truly random, but are useful for synchronization and sequence control.

pseudo-random-number generator A programmed sequence or function that accepts a *seed number* as input and produces an apparently random number as output. The resulting output always repeats after a given number of iterations for a specific seed. The number of iterations between repetitions depends on the complexity of the code used to create the generator. Some generators accept an output range as input; most, however, output a number in the range of $0 \leq x \leq 1$.

pseudo-random-number sequence A sequence of numbers that is considered random for a given purpose. The sequence may be used to approximate a particular distribution of parameters, such as a uniform distribution or a normal (Gaussian) distribution.

PSK Abbreviation for *phase-shift keying*, a form of digital modulation in which discrete phases of the carrier are used to represent a digital signal.

PS-Print A LAN printing utility that allows users to have access to all the printers on the LAN. This LAN printing system can improve printing speed on NetWare and simplifies printing access. It prints graphics more than 10 times faster than NetWare RPrinter.

PSR Abbreviation for *processor state register*.

PSS Abbreviation for *personal signalling system*.

PSTN Abbreviation for the *public switch telephone network*, the common dial network.

PS/2 driver board The board that interfaces IBM PS/2 models 50 through 80 and other Micro Channel compatible computers to an interface like the MetraBus. The MetraBus driver board allows a single expansion slot to control up to 64 external I/O boards. Power for the MetraBus must be supplied by a separate supply, as the IBM PS/2 design specifications limit the amount of power that can be drawn from Micro Channel bus. Due to space limitations in the PS/2 backplane, the standard 50-pin MetraBus interface connector is not used. The board uses a 37-pin "D" connector, which requires an adapter cable.

PS/2 interface Refers to a device's ability to connect to PS/2 model 50, 60, and 80 Micro Channel machines. PS/2 model 25 and 30 computers do not use the Micro Channel Architecture. Devices compatible with the PC/XT/AT series are also compatible for models 25 and 30.

PSU Abbreviation for *program storage unit*, an integrated circuit used for the storage of programmed instructions and nonvolatile data constants required for program execution. A PSU may interface directly with the CPU without the need for buffers; the chip may also include a program counter, stack register, interrupt control, and timing circuits.

PS View A program that allows you to view PostScript graphics and text onscreen before sending them to the printer. Thirty sample PostScript programs and over 1,000 outline fonts are included.

PSW Abbreviation for *program status word*, a word in main storage used to control the order in which instructions are executed and to hold and indicate the status of the computer in relation to a particular program. The PSW may include information on priority conditions of arithmetic or logic results.

p-type conductivity The conductivity in a semiconductor as expressed by the movement of holes.

p-type crystal rectifier A crystal rectifier in which forward current flows whenever the semiconductor region is more positive than the metal region.

p-type semiconductor A semiconductor in which the hole density exceeds the conduction electron density because the crystal material has been doped with small amounts of an impurity that will produce acceptor-type centers in the crystal lattice structure. Since the main current carriers are positive particles, the material is called p-type.

PU **1.** Abbreviation for *pick-up*. **2.** Abbreviation for *physical unit*, an SNA NAU (network-addressable unit) that performs control functions for the devices in which it is located as well as for any attached devices.

public-domain software Free programs without copyright or patent that are available to the general public.

public key encryption An encryption system that uses one key for encryption and a separate key for decryption. The encryption keys for a number of different users can be published in a public directory and used by anyone wishing to encrypt a message and send it to one of the listed users.

Each user has a different decryption key that is kept private to ensure that only the intended recipient can decrypt the message.

Publisher's PaintBrush A package from Z-Soft that provides curvilinear font technology to create characters in sizes up to 350 points without jaggedness. There are pull-down menus for colors, line widths, shapes, and patterns. Hollow or filled boxes, rounded boxes, and circles are some of the tools provided.

Publisher's Type Foundry A package from Z-Soft that integrates several modules, including Bitmap Editor and PaintBrush, into a complete system. You can build fonts from scratch; customize existing fonts, logos and special symbols; modify fonts to one-pixel resolution; and then download them to a laser printer. A Windows screen-font translator allows you to translate a font for display in a Windows application.

Publish-It! An integrated word-processing, page layout, and graphics software package. It includes typefaces with more than 1,200 type style combinations, sizes from 9 to 72 points, and automatic text flow and wordwrap. Typesetting functions include kerning and leading adjustment, international character sets, and WYSIWYG.

pull-down menu A menu that, when pointed to by keyboard or mouse, drops down to show the available options.

pulling by crystal Refers to the growing of both metal and nonmetal crystals by slowly withdrawing a seed crystal from a molten surface.

pull operation An operation in which operands are taken from the top of a pushdown stack in memory and placed in general registers. The operand remains in the stack unchanged; a pointer value is changed to indicate the current top of the stack.

pulse A variation in a quantity, such as a voltage, characterized by a rise and decay of finite duration.

pulse accumulator module A module with counters for accumulating pulses from several sources for frequency measurements. Input pulses can be accumulated and then held for interrogation by the CPU on the basis of jumpered or preselected intervals ranging from 100 microseconds to ten seconds.

pulse amplifier An amplifier with a wide bandwidth that can amplify pulses without excessive distortion.

pulse amplitude The level of a pulse or waveform of pulses.

pulse-amplitude modulation *See* PAM.

pulse bandwidth The frequency band occupied by the components of the pulse that have appreciable amplitude and that make an appreciable contribution to the actual pulse shape.

pulse carrier 1. A carrier consisting of a series of pulses, usually employed as subcarriers. **2.** A carrier wave comprised of a series of equally spaced pulses.

pulse code A code in which sets of pulses have been assigned particular meanings, such as in the Morse, Baudot, or binary codes.

pulse code modulation A form of pulsed modulation in which the signal is sampled periodically, and each sample is quantized and transmitted as a digital binary code.

pulse counter A device that gives an indication of or actually records the total number of pulses that has been received during a given time interval.

pulse-counting module A device to count and store pulse information and transmit this information to a computer upon command.

pulse decay time The amount of time required for the trailing edge of a pulse to decay from 90 percent to 10 percent of the peak pulse amplitude.

pulse delay time The time interval between the leading edges of the input and output pulses, measured at 10 percent of their maximum amplitude.

pulse detector A circuit designed for use with modulated pulse signals.

pulse digit A drive pulse corresponding to a logical one-digit position in some or all of the words in a storage unit. The pulse digit may be an inhibit pulse or an enable pulse in specific applications.

pulse discriminator A device that responds only to a pulse having some particular characteristic, such as a duration or period. The latter is also called a *time discriminator*.

pulse drive 1. A pulsed magnetomotive force applied to a magnetic core. **2.** A particular pulse of current in a winding inductively coupled to one or more magnetic cells, which produces a pulse of magnetomotive force.

pulse droop The exponential decay of amplitude often experienced with rectangular pulses of appreciable duration.

pulse duration The time interval between the leading and trailing edge of a pulse. Also called *pulse length*.

pulse duration modulation *See* PDM.

pulse equalizer A circuit that produces output pulses of uniform size and shape when driven by input pulses that may vary in size and shape.

pulse flatness deviation For a rectangular pulse that exhibits pulse droop, the difference between maximum and minimum amplitudes of the top of the pulse divided by the maximum amplitude.

pulse frequency modulation *See* PFM.

pulse, gating A pulse that permits the operation of a particular circuit.

pulse generator A device for generating a series of pulses of specific form, duration, and repetition rate for the purpose of special timing or gating. Also known as a *time-pulse generator*.

pulse interleaving A process in which pulses from two or more time-division multiplexers are systematically and alternately combined for transmission over a common path. *Also see* TDM.

pulse jitter A slight variation of the pulse spacing in a pulse train. It may be random or systematic depending on its origin, and it is generally not coherent with any regular pulse modulation characteristics.

pulse mode A coded group of pulses used to select a particular communication channel from a common carrier.

pulse modulation The modulation of pulses by a carrier. Pulse modulation includes pulse amplitude modulation (PAM), pulse position modulation (PPM), and pulse duration modulation (PDM).

pulse origin time The start of a pulse, defined as the time at which it first reaches some given fraction, such as 10 percent of full amplitude; this time is called the *time origin*.

pulse position modulation *See* PPM.

pulse ratio The ratio of the length of a pulse to its total period.

pulse regeneration The process of restoring a series of pulses to their original timing, form, and magnitude.

pulse repeater A device that receives pulses from one circuit and transmits corresponding pulses at another frequency or wavelength into another circuit. Also called a *transponder*.

pulse repetition frequency The rate at which pulses occur in a given unit of time. More correctly termed *pulse repetition rate*, since pulses are digital in character and "frequency" is generally applied to analog (ac) signals.

pulse repetition rate *See* PRR.

pulse resolution The minimum time separation, usually in microseconds or milliseconds, between input pulses that allows proper circuit or component response.

pulse shaping Intentionally changing the shape of a pulse.

pulse string A sequential group of pulses with similar characteristics, also called a *pulse train*.

pulse, strobe A pulse used to gate the output of a memory sense amplifier or similar circuit.

pulse stuffing A process for changing the rate of a digital signal in a controlled manner to a rate different from its own inherent rate, usually without loss of information. Also called *bit stuffing* or *justification*.

pulse-stuffing jitter The jitter caused by the removal of stuffed bits at the demultiplexer and the inability of a clock recovery circuit to eliminate completely the resulting gaps in the information signal.

pulse, sync *See* SYNC PULSE.

pulse time modulation Modulation in which the modulating wave is used to vary a time characteristic of the pulse carrier, such as in pulse duration modulation and pulse position modulation. *Also see* PDM and PPM.

pulse train generator A circuit or device that produces a fixed number of usually equally spaced pulses.

pulse transformer A transformer designed for pulses using square hysteresis loop material for the core or other techniques to maintain the output currents or voltages at the proper pulse levels.

pulse, width modulation *See* PDM.

pulse-width recording A method of recording in which each storage cell is made up of two regions magnetized in opposite senses with unmagnetized regions on each side. A zero bit is represented by a cell containing a negative region followed by a positive region.

pulse, write *See* WRITE PULSE.

pumping The use of electromagnetic radiation to raise the energy levels of electrons in devices such as lasers.

punch (*o.t.*) Refers to a perforation in a punched card or tape.

punchdown blocks A connection system that allows you to interconnect twisted-pair devices to existing in-house wire. Wires for up to 12 devices can be punched down to each of the two 50-pin Telco connectors wired on the sides of the block.

punched card (*o.t.*) A heavy paper material on which information was coded in the form of holes. The holes could be of many shapes and were punched either by machine or by hand.

PUP Acronym for *peripheral unit processor*.

PUR Abbreviation for *polyurethane*, a material used to manufacture a type of cable jacketing material.

pure generator A routine that is capable of writing another routine. The pure generator may be a section of a program in an assembler. It can then be called by the assembler to perform.

purge To erase a file.

purity Complete color saturation; freedom from white in CRTs.

push To add an item to the top of the stack memory.

pushdown list A list that uses the LIFO (last-in-first-out) system. The item to be retrieved is the most recently stored item in the list, and the last item entered becomes the first item retrieved from the list. Also called *pushdown queue*.

pushdown stack A segment of memory used to receive information from the program counter and store address locations of the instructions which have been pushed down during an interrupt. The pushdown stack can be used for subroutines; its size determines the level of subroutine nesting. When instructions are returned, they are "popped back" on a LIFO (last-in-first-out) basis, as shown in the figure. The stack tends to minimize register transfers, facilitate counter and sorting, and limit transfers to and from main memory.

push operation The operation in which operands from a general register are stored in the top location of a pushdown stack in memory.

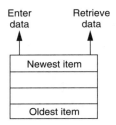

Pushdown stack

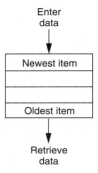

Pushup list

push-pull 1. A system in which one leg of a balanced circuit is driven by a periodic waveform, while the other leg is driven by the same waveform with the phase reversed. **2.** A term applied to soundtracks that carry sound recordings in antiphase. They are *class A* when each carries the whole waveform and *class B* when each carriers half the waveform; both halves are united optically using a push-pull photocell.

push-pull circuit A circuit containing two like elements that operate in 180° phase relationship to produce additive output components of the desired wave and the cancellation of certain unwanted products. Push-pull amplifiers and oscillators use such a circuit.

push-push amplifier An amplifier that uses two similar devices or transistors with their control electrodes in phase opposition but with their output electrodes parallel. Connected to a common load. By this means the even-order harmonics are emphasized.

pushup list A list that uses a FIFO (first-in-first out) order, in which the most recent arrival is placed at the end of the line and the item waiting the longest receives service first, as shown in the figure. Previous items maintain their same relative position in the list. *Contrast with* PUSHDOWN LIST.

pushup storage A method of storage in which the next item of data to be retrieved is the oldest and has been in the queue the longest.

put command A database command that allows input of data into fields determined by the create command.

PVC Abbreviation for *polyvinyl chloride,* a material used in the manufacture of a type of cable jacketing material.

PVR Abbreviation for *precision voltage reference.*

PW Abbreviation for *pulse width.*

PWC See *PWM.*

PWE Abbreviation for *pulse-width encoder.*

PWM Abbreviation for *pulse-width modulation,* a pulse modulation technique in which the modulating wave is used to vary the width of a pulse proportionally.

pyroelectricity Polarization developed in some hemihedral crystals by an inequality of temperature.

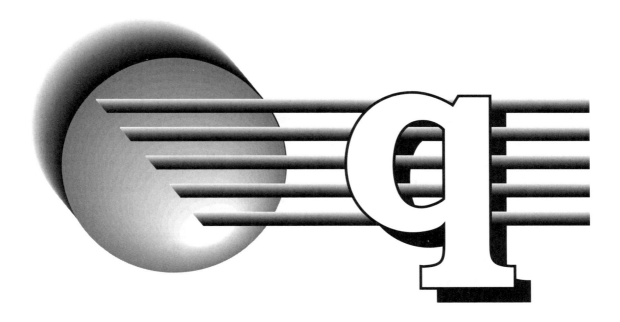

Q **1.** Symbol for electric charge. **2.** Schematic designation of active solid-state devices (usually followed by a numeral). **3.** Abbreviation for accumulator extension. **4.** In NTSC video, refers to the quadrature color difference signal. It is 90° out of phase with the color subcarrier.

QAM Abbreviation for *quadrature amplitude modulation*, the independent amplitude modulation of two orthogonal channels using the same carrier frequency.

Q&A An intelligent DOS-based database program that understands English-language queries like, "Which salespeople have sales greater than their quotas?"

Q&A Write A DOS-based word processor with some high-end features such as a fat cursor increases the size of the mouse arrow, fast formatting for copying the format from one section of text to another, and the ability to repeat the last command. It handles graphics and frames much like Ami Pro, but without options such as shadows.

QB *See* MICROSOFT QUICKBASIC.

QB Plus Software that expands the capabilities of QB and QBX environments. It allows any compile and link options to be specified and has a memory viewer and execution profiling (timing).

QCW A 3.58-MHz continuous-wave signal having Q phase. Generally restricted to reference the receiver local oscillator (3.85 MHz) and associated circuits in color TV.

Q+E database server A Windows and OS/2 query and editing tool to display, query, sort, search, join and edit relational data. It supports DDE and can access data from dBASE, Paradox, Oracle, DB2, SQL Server, Sybase, NetWare SQL, EE Database Manager, and Excel files.

QEMM-386 A program from Quarterdeck Office Systems that allows you to find memory-hogging DOS Resources, TSRs, and drivers and load them into high memory (the area between 640K and 1M). This extended and expanded memory manager is capable of performing on-the-fly memory conversions so you do not have to re-boot every time a change is needed. You can map ROM into other areas, gaining up to 211K of additional high memory.

QF Abbreviation for *quality factor*.

QIC drive Abbreviation for *quarter-inch cartridge drive*, a popular type of cassette tape drive used for backing up data. QIC drives are commonly used for low-end storage in the 20M to 525M range.

QIL Acronym for *quad-inline*, a dual-inline package (DIP) with four similar functional units or circuits. *Also see* DIP.

QISAM Acronym for *queued indexed sequential access method*.

QMS Abbreviation for *Queue Management Services*, part of the NetWare operating system used by programs to manage a queue of several incoming requests.

Q output The reference output of a flip-flop. The Q output corresponds to a one condition, and is inverted or a zero in the normal state.

QPARSER A tool for writing translators, compilers, assemblers, and other language-parsing programs.

Q phase A color television signal carrier phase separated by 147° from the color subcarrier, also referred to as the *quadrature carrier*.

QPL Abbreviation for *qualified products list*.

QPR Abbreviation for *quadrature partial response*,

the use of partial response filtering on the two orthogonal channels of a QAM system to increase the bandwidth efficiency.

QPSK Abbreviation for *quadrature phase-shift keying*, a form of phase-shift keying (PSK) in which four discrete phases, separated by 90 degrees, are used to represent two information-bits per signaling interval.

quad 1. A packaged integrated circuit containing four identical stages. **2.** Four-channel stereophonic sound. **3.** Containing four identical or nearly identical electrodes, terminals, or leads (as outputs).

Quadbase-SQL/Win A DLL that supports Windows development languages such as Visual Basic, C, C++, Toolbox and SQLWindows. It supports the ANSI level 2 standard plus extensions. It can support multiple instances and is designed to manage large amounts of data efficiently. Features include referential integrity, multiuser concurrency control, crash recovery, and transaction processing. It is useful for small to medium-sized LAN file server systems or standalone machines.

quadbit A symbol that contains four bits of information.

quad clock driver A driver circuit with four separate outputs. It is useful for driving the address, control, and supplementary timing circuits for various logic systems.

quad density A data-recording format on a floppy disk that allows four times the normal amount of data to be stored on the floppy disk.

quad MOS clock driver An IC used for supplying the voltage and current drive requirements for address, control, and timing inputs for MOS (metal-oxide semiconductor) devices. This device is usually configured as a quad NAND driver with two common enable inputs per gate pair, as shown in the following figure. It will operate on a wide variety of supply voltages.

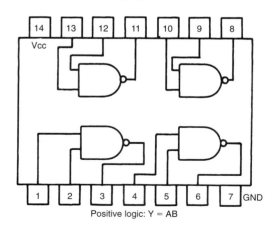

Quad NAND gate

Quadra Formerly Macintosh's top-of-the-line personal computer, the 68040-based Quadra has been superseded by the RISC-based PowerMac, which utilizes the IBM/Apple/Motorola "PowerPC" microprocessor.

quadrant Any of the four parts into which a plane is divided by the rectangular coordinant axes lying in that plane.

quadratic programming A type of nonlinear programming used in operations research in which the function to be maximized or minimized is a quadratic function and the constraints are linear functions.

quadrature Refers to a displacement of 90° in phase angle.

quadrature amplitude modulation See QAM.

quadrature component A reactive component of a current or voltage due to the inductive or capacitive reactance in a circuit or device.

quadrature partial response See QPR.

quadrature phase-shift keying See QPSK.

quad-tabulation A function that provides for the automatic alignment of a character or group of characters within a column.

QualBase A collection of C++ class libraries for persistency, multitasking, interrupts, arrays, strings, registers, stacks, binary trees, bit vectors, queuing, conversions, hash tables, graphs, and lists. It has an extendible persistent store manager, simple array execution, bounded array for quick debugging, and linked list modes for prototyping.

qualification 1. The testing of a program, equipment, or system prior to its delivery from the manufacturer to the user. **2.** In COBOL, a technique used to make a name or situation unique by adding IN or OF.

qualified name A data name accompanied by the class to which it belongs in a given classification system.

qualifier tester A benchtop system for testing DTL, TTL, and CMOS devices. This tester uses a microcomputer to control all internal test functions and can be used with RS-232C terminals.

quality diagnostic Software that verifies the proper operation of the CPU, memories, and input/output functions. Quality diagnostics include routines to check the instructions, memory, real-time clock, printer, keyboard, power-fail/restart, automatic loader, etc.

quality engineering An engineering program used to establish quality tests and acceptance criteria along with interpreting quality data.

quantity Any positive or negative number used to specify a value; it may be a whole number, a fraction, or a combination of both.

quantization The subdivision of an element or parameter into a finite number of distinct values such as occurs in analog-to-digital conversion and some forms of multiplexing.

quantization distortion A communications process in which the range of values of a wave is divided into a finite number of smaller subranges, each of which is represented by an assigned or quantized value within the subrange. *Quantized* is used as an adjective modifying various forms of modulation, such as *quantized pulse amplitude modulation*.

quantization noise An undesirable random signal caused by the error of approximation in a quantizing process.

quantization uncertainty Refers to a measure of the uncertainty, which may cause irretrievable information loss, that occurs as a result of the quantization of a function in an interval in which it is continuous.

quantize To subdivide an element or parameter into a number of distinct values.

quantizer *See* DIGITIZER.

quantizing distortion The distortion resulting from the process of quantizing.

quantum 1. A unit of processing time in a time-sharing system that may be allocated for operating a program during its turn in the computer. 2. A subrange in a quantization operation. 3. The smallest indivisible element of a quantized signal. 4. An indeterminate quantity; an amount. 5. The smallest increment into which an energy form can be described.

quantum clock The timing of an interval of processing according to developed priorities in a time-sharing system.

quantum efficiency 1. The number of electrons released in a photocell per unit of incident radiation. 2. The ratio of energy output to input in an energy-conversion system.

quantum electronics Refers to a branch of science concerned with the amplification or generation of microwave power in solid crystals, governed by quantum mechanical laws.

quantum number One number of a set describing the possible states of a magnitude when quantized.

Quark XPress A desktop publishing package for page layout/typography with integration of graphics and color. It has full-featured word processing capability; four color models (including PANTONE) for defining and editing colors; support for fonts from 2 to 500 points; and the ability to print color output, thumbnails, negative and mirror images, variable screen densities, collating, tiling, and registration marks.

quarter-inch cartridge drive *See* QIC DRIVE.

quartz A piezoelectric material used in the manufacture of crystals for oscillators. It may be natural or manufactured. Quartz exhibits a variety of predictable characteristics that vary according to the axis from which it is cut.

quartz clock A clock fabricated from quartz crystal.

quartz crystal A frequency-determining crystal cut to oscillate at some precise fixed frequency over a specified temperature range. It exhibits the properties of a resonant RLC circuit and is used in close-tolerance oscillators as a source for clock signals.

quartz plate A quartz crystal finished for a generalized frequency range but not trimmed to a specific frequency within that range. Also called a *blank*.

quartz pressure transducers A capacitive pressure transducer that utilizes quartz. The sensor consists of two thin quartz disks, each having a platinum electrode on its inner surface. The disks are fused at their periphery to form a capsule, with the electrodes separated by a 0.002-inch gap. When a vacuum is drawn inside the gap, absolute pressures of up to 30 psi are measured. Gauge pressures of up to 30 psi can also be measured with one port vented to the atmosphere.

quartz thermometer A transducer that determines temperature from the frequency difference between a temperature-dependent quartz oscillator and a temperature-independent one.

quasi-instruction *See* PSEUDO-INSTRUCTION.

QubeCalc A three-dimensional spreadsheet. As opposed to some two-dimensional spreadsheets that let you link cells of multiple spreadsheets together, QubeCalc may be thought of as a large cube with 262,144 cells arranged into 64 rows, 64 columns, and 64 pages. You may view, enter, or manipulate data from any of the six faces of the cube, providing a different perspective of the data stored within by turning columns into pages, pages into rows, etc.

quench Resistor or resistor-capacitor shunting used to reduce the high-frequency sparking when a current is broken in an inductive circuit.

quenched spark gap A spark gap in which the discharge takes place between cooled or rapidly moving electrodes.

quenching circuit A circuit that inhibits multiple discharges from an ionizing event by suppressing or reversing the voltage.

query language In database management systems, an alternative to conventional programming language that enables users without formal training in algorithmic thought to formulate ad hoc information-retrieval requests using English-like phrases.

query station A terminal or station that introduces requests for data or information while the system is computing or communicating.

query-type In NetWare, a parameter that can be set to one for a general service query or three for a nearest-server query.

queue The waiting line for items to be serviced. Queues may be LIFO (last-in-first-out) or FIFO (first-in-first-out).

queue, automatic *See* AUTOMATIC QUEUE.

queued content addressed memory Refers to an automatic memory structure that contains a series of parallel automatic queues. The front member of each queue is content-addressable.

queue control block A control block used for regulating the sequential use of a set of competing tasks.

queued access An access method that synchronizes the transfer of data between the program and I/O devices with minimal delays.

queue, direct-access See DIRECT-ACCESS QUEUE.

queue discipline The method used to determine the order of service in a queued system.

queued sequential access A method of sequential access in which queues are formed of input data blocks that are awaiting processing, and of output data blocks that have been processed and are awaiting storage or transfer to an output device.

queued telecommunications access method See QTAM.

queue ID In NetWare Queue Services, the bindery object ID of a queue.

Queue Management Services See QMS.

queue name In NetWare Queue Services, a name that can be 1 to 47 characters long.

queue, ready See READY QUEUE.

queue status In NetWare Queue Services, a byte with options set as follows:

1. The operator does not want new jobs added to the queue.
2. The operator does not want additional job servers attaching to the queue.
3. The operator does not want job servers servicing jobs in the queue.

queue type In NetWare Services, the bindery object type of a queue.

queuing list A list used for scheduling actions in real-time on a priority basis.

queuing theory See QT, 2.

queuing theory problems Conditions when a row of objects or data is bottlenecked at a particular servicing point; losses accumulate in the form of lost information, idle equipment, and unused labor. Minimizing such costs involved in waiting lines, or queues, is the object of queuing theory.

queuing time The time spent waiting to send or receive a message because of contention on the line.

quibinary code A binary-coded decimal system for representing decimal numbers in which each decimal digit is represented by seven binary digits.

quick-access memory See SCRATCHPAD.

quick break A characteristic of a switch or circuit breaker when it has a fast contact opening speed that is independent of the operator.

quickcharting A flowcharting technique that does not require knowledge of standard flowchart symbols.

Quickcode A code generator to aid users with little programming background in writing dBASE programs. Quickcode acts as a translator; you enter the appropriate data at the prompts, and Quickcode writes the dBASE program. The program includes Quickscreen, a facility that lets you create forms by drawing directly on the screen.

QuickComm A communications library that supports up to 16 serial ports simultaneously, including COM1 through COM4 generic boards. No TSR is required when QuickComm is linked with your programs. It supports Microsoft BASIC and QuickBasic compilers, Turbo C/C++, and Microsoft C/QuickC.

quick-configuration device A device that is inserted into a previously incompatible interface to reconfigure it for proper functioning.

quick-disconnect A type of connector that allows quick locking and unlocking of all contacts.

QuickDraw A utility that prints lines, addresses, and different types of barcodes onto any size label.

QuickForm Contracts An expert system for your PC that automates the drafting of nine categories of contracts most often needed by software developers and consultants. It prompts you with multiple-choice questions and then automatically assembles an agreement weighted to your side.

QuickHelp A system that lets you add pop-up help to any application. Features include indexed file access, user-definable hot key, and customized colors.

QuickMenu A DOS-based menu system with up to nine commands per menu, a full-screen command editor, and context-sensitive help. QuickMenu does not remain memory-resident while executing a program.

QuickPak Scientific Software that adds numerical methods to your programs, including routines for solving linear algebra, differential equations, curve fitting, complex numbers, statistics, vectors, matrices, integration and differentiation, fast Fourier transforms, and nonlinear equations.

QuickReport A DOS-based dBASE report generator that includes a simple word processor, as well as line-drawing characters. You can create multiline page headers and define individual headings for each break field. Reports may be sent to screen, printer, or disk.

Quick Screen Software that lets you create data-entry screens using a screen painter to draw the text and backgrounds and define the fields. It can manage screen libraries with dozens of screens in a single file. Features include routines for field-by-field editing with full data validation, online help, 17 field types, and automatic field calculations. You enter formulas using ordinary BASIC equations.

QuickShare A program for transferring data between a PC and a Macintosh. Any Macintosh with a SCSI port can use all or part of the PC's hard drive as a Macintosh volume. QuickShare also provides format translation so that you can convert most PC files into MacWrite or MacPaint files. You can also use this program with PC streaming drives for backing up.

QuickSilver/SQL Software used to compile dBASE application programs to run in combination with a SQL-based database server engine. Using invisible and embedded SQL, you can integrate the dBASE language and SQL. *Invisible SQL* automatically and transparently maps dBASE commands to a SQL database as needed. *Embedded SQL* allows SQL queries to be explicitly formulated within a dBASE application.

quick test *See* QT, 1.

QuickWindows Advanced A set of user-interface routines that work in text and graphics modes to create windows (exploding and shadowed), multitasking pop-up and pulldown menus, contact-sensitive help windows, pick lists, message boxes, and data-entry forms with picture fields and dialog boxes. There is a full-featured icon and font editor; no TSRs are required.

quiescence Refers to a device at rest, waiting for an input signal or command.

quiescent current The current in an amplifier or control device in the absence of a command or control signal.

quiescent push-pull amplifier An amplifier in which one side passes current for one phase and then the other side passes current for the other phase.

quiescing The process of bringing a device or system to a halt by the rejection of new jobs or new requests for work.

quiet cable Refers to a cable that can help reduce EMI/RFI in environments that must comply with FCC part 15 docket 20780. The cable has a twisted-pair construction covered with two shields: a shorted aluminum foil shield to attenuate high-frequency emissions, and a copper braid shield to attenuate low-frequency emissions, as shown in the figure.

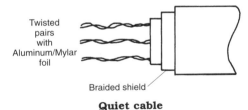

Quiet cable

quinary *See* BIQUINARY EDITING.

Quincke's method A technique for determining the magnetic susceptibility of a substance in solution by measuring the force acting on it in terms of the change of height of the free surface of the solution when placed in a suitable magnetic field.

quit A program function to leave the current program.

Qume (*o.t.*) The tradename for a typing mechanism that uses an interchangeable printwheel.

quoted string A character string used in assembler programming in which the string is enclosed by apostrophes to represent a value that can include blanks in a microinstruction operand.

QR Abbreviation for *quick reaction.*

QRAM A program from Quarterdeck Office Systems that loads TSRs, device drivers, and DOS resources into high memory (the area between 640K and 1M). You can save yourself up to 130K of memory and use the VIDRAM feature for a total savings of over 194K. It is compatible with Windows and is useful for increasing performance in a network environment.

QT 1. Abbreviation for *quick test,* an RS-232 test set that allows a quick look at your interface leads. You insert the set into the circuit and switch-select the lead you wish to monitor. The unit displays the condition of the monitored position with two LEDs (light-emitting diodes). One LED shows ON or HIGH (a space) and the other shows OFF or LOW (a mark). Both together indicate data or clock. 2. Abbreviation for *queuing theory,* a form of probability theory used in the study of delays or lines at servicing points. Queuing theory is concerned with minimizing these delays.

QTAM Abbreviation for *queued telecommunications access method,* a method used to transfer data between main storage and remote terminals. A macroinstruction is used to request the transfer, which is performed by a message control program that synchronizes transfer with minimum delays.

QWERTY keyboard The standard typewriter keyboard, named for the arrangement of the first six letters. *Contrast with* DVORAK SIMPLIFIED KEYBOARD.

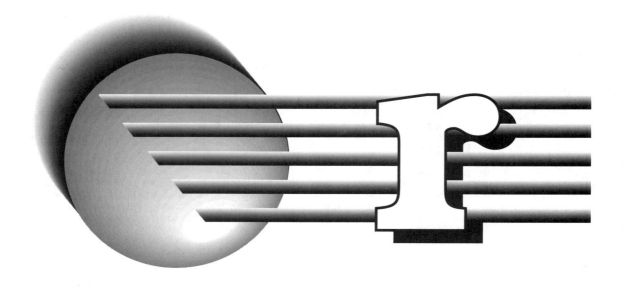

R Abbreviation for the rise time factor in transistors.

race In any multisignal logic system, a condition in which the timing between two coincident signals is unpredictable even though the system operation requires a specific timed sequence for proper operation.

rack A freestanding metal frame or cabinet into which panels of equipment may be installed.

rack-mounting Descriptive of a piece of equipment whose front panel is designed to fasten to a standard, usually 19-inch, rack (cabinet) in such a way that the equipment is contained within the rack, but the controls are accessible from the front.

RAD 1. Acronym for *rapid access disk*. 2. Acronym for *rapid application development*, a programming technique that depends on screen, report, and code generators to greatly decrease development time. This technique also uses third-party library routines to reduce coding and debugging times.

RADA Acronym for *random-access discrete address*.

radians A measurement of angles based on π (pi) rather than on degrees. A straight line (180° angle) has an angle of π (3.1425927 radians); a 90° angle is 1.5707963 radians, or half-π. Trigonometric functions in many high-level languages work in radians instead of degrees.

radiation The propagation of energy through space or a medium.

radio button An item in a dialog box that is part of a set of mutually exclusive options. In a particular set of radio buttons, one and only one item must be selected at all times.

radio circuit A communication system consisting of a radio link with a transmitter and antenna, the radio transmission path, and a receiving antenna and receiver.

radio frequency *See* RF.

radio-frequency interference *See* RFI.

radio-frequency switch A remote radio-frequency trigger relay that electrically switches sections of network wiring or coaxial cable and alters the network topology. Sometimes called an *isolation switch* or *firewall*.

radio refractivity One million times the amount by which the refractive index of the atmosphere exceeds unity.

radix The quantity of characters for use in each of the digital positions of a numbering system. Also called the *base*.

System	Characters	Radix
binary	0, 1	2
octal	0, 1, 2, 3, 4, 5, 6, 7	8
decimal	0, 1, 2, 3, 4, 5, 6, 7, 8, 9	10

radix complement A complement obtained by subtracting each digit from one less than its radix, adding one to the least-significant digit, and executing all carries required. Examples include ten's complement in decimal notation or two's complement in binary notation. Also called *true complement*.

radix-minus-one complement *See* DIMINISHED-RADIX COMPLEMENT.

radix notation A positional representation in which the significance of any two adjacent positions has an integral ratio which is the radix of the least-significant of the two positions. The permissible values of the digit in any position range from zero to one less than the radix of that position.

radix point The real or implied character that separates the digits associated with the integral part of a numeral from those associated with the fractional part.

RAID Acronym for *redundant array of inexpensive disks*, a scheme where data is written to several disk drives simultaneously and the parity data collected is sufficient to reconstruct data that is lost or corrupted.

raised-cosine filter A filter with a specific characteristic that produces no intersymbol interference at the sample times of adjacent signaling intervals.

RALU Acronym for *register and arithmetic logic unit*, a collection of logic elements such as accumulators, stacks, and that arithmetic logic unit, which provides data storage and processing functions. A typical RALU, shown in the following diagram, is designed so that up to eight units can be combined in parallel to allow the implementation of processors from four to 32 bits wide. All elements in the unit are tied together by a set of buses, and data flow can be defined using microprogramming (usually with a CROM chip).

Arithmetic and logic unit
Accumulator
Accumulator
Accumulator
Program counter
Memory address register
Memory address register

RALU

RAM Acronym for *random-access memory*, a mass store that provides fast access to any storage location by means of vertical and horizontal coordinates. Information is written in or read out using the same procedure. The memory cycle time is the same for any location addressed because there is no waiting or sorting time required, as there is when data items are stored sequentially.

A RAM system as shown in the following figure can be divided into three main sections:

- Address buffers, read-write logic, and chip-select logic
- Data bus buffers and memory array
- Refresh and control logic

RAM is the working memory of the computer. When you run a program, it is loaded from your hard disk into RAM and remains there while you use it. You have to save work onto a disk because whatever is in RAM gets erased when the computer is turned off. *RAM chips* are the physical components that contain the memory and are grouped in rows called *banks*.

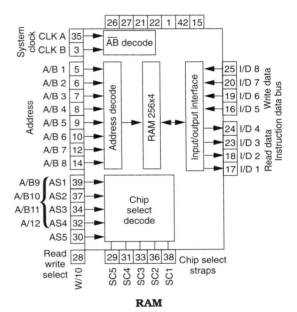

RAM

RAM address register A register that contains the address location to be accessed in RAM.

RAM alarm An alarm triggered when the data on a given channel in the memory system does not agree with alarm setpoint values. The microprocessor then prints out a complete data scan from memory, regardless of which channel is in alarm.

RAM cache *See* MEMORY CACHE.

RAM card system A complete RAM with control logic on a single circuit board or card.

RAM CCD cell A RAM array of two electrode CCD cells. Negative potentials produce a depletion-region potential well in the n-type layer beneath the electrodes. To write a logic 1 in the cell, the p-type channel is pulsed positive, thus allowing holes into the well. To write a logic 0, both electrodes are grounded, letting any holes recombine.

RAM circuit The circuit for a four-by-three RAM is shown in the following figure. It has four words

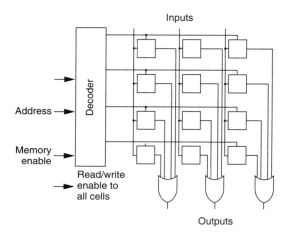

12-word RAM

of three bits each, for a total of 12 storage cells. Each cell contains the circuit of a binary cell. The address lines use a two-by-four decoder with a memory enable input.

When the memory enable is zero all the outputs of the decoder are false and none of the words is selected. When the memory enable input is one, one of the four words is selected, depending on the bit combination of the two address lines. With the read/write at one, the bits of the selected word go through the OR gates to the output. The nonselected cells produce zeros at the inputs of the OR gate, and thus have no effect on the outputs. When the read/write control is zero, the data at the input lines is transferred into the flip-flops of the selected word.

The nonselected cells in the other words are disabled by their address selection line so their previous values remain unchanged. An inhibited operation is obtained when the memory enable is zero. This condition leaves the contents of all words in memory as they were, regardless of the read/write control input. RAMs sometimes use cells with outputs that can be tied to form a wired-OR or a wired-AND function. Other RAMs may provide tristate outputs. These outputs are useful when a high impedance path is desired for isolation from the other integrated circuits in the microcomputer system.

RAM control memory Refers to the use of RAMs in a system's control memory, often referred to as *WCS* (writeable control storage).

RAM disk A part of random access memory set up by a program to behave like a disk drive. The computer reads and writes data from this section of RAM as though it were another disk drive, but much faster because it does not have to wait for the mechanical motions of the drive and heads. Data in RAM is lost when the computer is turned off. Also called an *electronic disk*.

RAM enable A RAM control line that allows new data to be written into the address field.

RAM 4000 A memory expansion board for IBM PS/2 models 50 and 60 with Micro Channel architecture. The board provides up to 4M of expanded or extended memory using 1M RAM chips. RAM 4000 is accompanied by EMM (the expanded memory manager), which manages the operation of all EMS memory, while EDISK lets you use RAM to simulate an extra-fast drive. There is also a print spooler that lets you print files while you edit others. RAM 4000 operates with no additional wait states on a model 50 or 60.

ramp A signal that increases in level linearly with time, as shown. Usually the ramp is repetitive, operating at a predetermined rate.

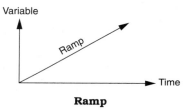

Ramp

RAMpage A memory expansion board and software that lets PCs run up to nine large programs at the same time. RAMpage places all nine programs in memory and allows you to view them in windows. For example, you can print a file, receive information over your modem, and sort a database at the same time, increasing the PC's productivity. RAMpage provides the extra memory necessary for multitasking, while DESQview supplies the multitasking operating environment.

RAM print-on-alarm An operation mode in which continuous scanning takes place but data is read out only when an alarm is interpreted by the CPU.

RAMPS Acronym for *resources allocation and multi-project scheduling*.

RAM refresh The periodic signals that must be applied to dynamic MOS RAMs to ensure that stored data is retained. The refresh operation consists of a specified number of write cycles (and sometimes a read cycle as well) on the least-significant address bits within a given period of time. The number of cycles may vary from 16 to 64 within a 2 millisecond period. The refresh requirement tends to increase system costs and reduce the overall memory system performance due to the additional required timing circuitry.

RAM refresh clock The source of the timing signals required for refreshing dynamic RAMs. A typical system uses a ripple counter to generate the sequential states and a multiplexer for gating these states with the CPU.

RAM refresh cycle The period required for dynamic RAM refresh.

RAM register simulator A program that simulates execution of microcomputer programs. Such simulators are interpretive and provide bit-for-bit duplication of instruction execution timing, register contents, and other functions.

RAM/ROM pattern processor A test system that can be used to check RAM and ROM patterns.

RAM save An option that prevents data in memory from being lost due to power outages. One type of system uses a custom-initialization ROM that restores the full program to the RAMs, restarts the clock, and begins data scanning. Other types use battery banks or other units to provide power for a certain number of minutes, or until external power is returned.

RAM test program A program that uses a PROM that plugs into prototyping boards for complete checkout.

RAM text editor A RAM-resident character-oriented text editor with search, substitute, insert, and delete commands that facilitate alternation.

RAN Acronym for *read around number*.

random-access 1. The process of obtaining information from or placing information into a storage system in which the time required for access is independent of the location of the formation most recently obtained or placed in storage. **2.** An access mode in COBOL in which specific logical records are obtained from or placed into a mass storage file nonsequentially.

random-access buffer memory system Refers to a static memory system designed to meet the reliability and cost requirements of random access buffer storage applications. The compact size of these systems makes them ideal for use as buffer storage for various computer peripheral applications. The memory systems can be easily modified to interface with most microprocessors.

random-access device A unit in which access time is independent of data location and system history.

random-access memory *See* RAM.

RAM, bipolar *See* BIPOLAR RAM.

random-access programming Programming without regard to the time for access to the information in the registers called for in the program.

random-access time The average time period between the end-of-readout of a word from storage at a randomly chosen address and the end-of-readout of another word from any other randomly chosen address. The readout operations are performed as fast as the microcomputer can carry them out, so no waiting period for the arithmetic and logic unit is included in this time. *Minimum random access time* is the time period between the end-of-readout of a word at any given address and the end-of-readout of the word in the most favorable other address in the storage unit.

random aloha A scheme in which stations transmit when they have something to transmit; they do not need to be polled.

random failure A failure whose occurrence at a particular time is unpredictable. Also called *chance failure*.

random logic Logic circuits that use discrete integrated circuits for individual functions. Random logic uses hardware gates to implement the logic equations. Design aids include Karnaugh maps, state diagrams, computer simulation, and breadboarding.

random logic devices The small-scale integration (SSI) and medium-scale integration (MSI) integrated circuits used to design random logic systems.

randomness A condition of equal chance for the occurrence of any of the possible outcomes.

random noise *See* WHITE NOISE.

random number A number in a series that is obtained completely by chance. Random numbers are considered to be free from bias and thus are used for statistical testing.

random-number generator *See* PSEUDO-RANDOM-NUMBER GENERATOR.

random, pseudo *See* PSEUDO-RANDOM-NUMBER SEQUENCE.

random pulsing Varying the repetition rate of pulses by noise modulation or continuous frequency change.

random variable A variable that may assume any one of a number of values, each having the same probability of occurrence. Also called a *variate*.

random walk A method used in problem analysis in which experiments with probabilistic variables are traced to determine if the results are significant.

range 1. The set of values between two limits that a quantity may assume. **2.** The usable operating sphere of a communications system.

range conversion A signal conditioning technique that uses a dc offset to bias odd ranges, such as 2.5 to 7 volts, to levels more compatible with standard converters, as shown in the following figure.

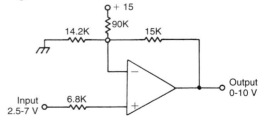

Range conversion

range, dead band See DEAD BAND.
range, error See ERROR RANGE.
RAP Acronym for *random-access program*.
rapid-access loop A section of storage that has a much faster access than the remainder of storage. Such loops are found in some disk, drum, and tape units. Sometimes called *revolver*.
rapid applications development See RAD.
RAR Acronym for *ROM address register*.
raser Acronym for *radio amplification by stimulated emission of radiation*.
RaSQL A program designed to give the CA-Clipper or FoxPro programmer access to Btrieve data files. Using this library, you can access both Btrieve files and dbf files in the same applications and transfer data between them. You use Clipper-like commands like n-xuse and n-xskip to access Btrieve data.
raster An illuminated gray cathode-ray screen without an image-forming video input.
raster count The number of coordinate positions addressable on a cathode-ray screen. The horizontal count gives the number of coordinate positions addressable across the width of the tube, while the vertical count gives the number addressable across the height of the tube.
raster graphic See BITMAPPED GRAPHIC.
raster image processing The process in which a printer controller converts text and graphic images from a computer into a grid of dots (the raster pattern) transferred to paper.
raster-op Abbreviation for *raster operation*.
raster scan A technique of generating a display image by a line-by-line sweep across the entire display screen, the way pictures are created on a television screen.
rated capacity The output of equipment, which can continue indefinitely, in conformity with some criterion such as heating, or distortion of signals or of waveform.
rated output The output power, voltage, or current at which a device is designed to operate under normal conditions.
rate gain The ratio of maximum gain resulting from proportional plus derivate control action to the gain due to proportional action alone.
rate-grown transistor A variation of the double-doped transistor, in which N- and P-type impurities are added to the melt. Also called a *graded-junction transistor*.
rate test A test in which problems are run with known solution times to determine if a computer is operating correctly.
rating A value that determines the limiting capacity or limiting conditions for a device. Ratings are determined for specified values of environment and operation.
rating system The set of principles upon which ratings are established and interpreted.
ratio, amplitude See AMPLITUDE RATIO.
ratio, noise signal See NOISE RATIO.

raw data Data that has not been processed.
ray tracing A complex approach to rendering high-quality, photo-realistic computer images by calculating the brightness, transparency level, and reflectivity of each point of every object in the scene. Attributes of each particular object are then used to calculate the color and intensity of each pixel on the display in relation to the viewer. As a consequence of such precision, ray tracing demands a tremendous amount of computer processing power.
RB 1. Abbreviation for *read buffer*. **2.** Abbreviation for *return to bias*, a mode of recording in which the state of the medium changes from a bias state to another state and then returns to record a binary one or zero.
R:base CLOUT A database query facility that helps you retrieve data from other software products, including 1-2-3 and dBASE. It uses expert systems theory and natural language techniques to simplify the retrieval of information. If you ask a question using an unfamiliar word or phrase, CLOUT will initiate a dialog with you until it understands, then add the new word or phrase to its dictionary and resume your inquiry.
R:base A relational database system that is similar to IBM's SQL. It has about the same power as dBASE, but uses mainframe terms such as relation (file) and attribute (field). R:base includes Application Express, a menu-driven application generator that leads you through the process of designing programs. A compiler is included, which can encrypt the code and protect program from unwanted changes. R:base also includes full report-writing capability and File Gateway, a subset of CLOUT.
RC 1. Abbreviation for *resistance-capacitance*. **2.** Abbreviation for *resistance-coupled*. **3.** Abbreviation for *remote control*.
RC amplifier An amplifier that uses resistance-capacitance coupling.
RCA 1800 family Refers to the RCA 1800 series of microprocessors, based on CMOS (complementary metal-oxide semiconductor) technology. The CMOS unit requires a minimal power supply and may be operated with unregulated supplies over a wide voltage range. Noise immunity is high, and there is compatibility with other logic families such as TTL and NMOS. The power requirements can be lowered at slower operating speeds to allow the use of small batteries in remote or isolated applications. The 1802 is an 8-bit silicon gate CMOS device that has an on-chip single-phase clock. Its architecture is shown in the following figure.
    The register file uses sixteen 16-bit registers that can be used as program counters, data pointers, or as scratchpad locations for holding data. When a register is used as the main program counter, its register number must be stored in the P register. Other registers in the array can

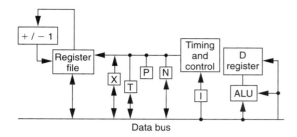

1802 architecture

then be used as subroutine program counters. When a call is required, the contents of the P register are changed by an instruction that allows the call to be made. A basic 1820 system with ROM, RAM, and I/O is configured as shown.

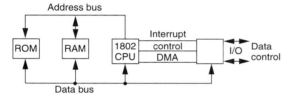

Basic 1820 architecture

RC circuit A circuit that uses resistors and capacitors to form a time constant.

RC network A circuit using resistors and capacitors to perform a particular function, such as filtering, timing, differentiation, or integration.

RC oscillator An oscillator circuit in which the frequency of oscillation is determined by resistor and capacitor elements.

RCTL Abbreviation for *resistor-capacitor-transistor logic*, a logic family that uses discrete transistors with RC coupling, as shown in the following diagram.

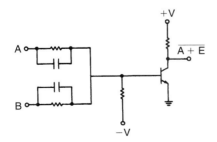

RCTL NOR gate

RD Abbreviation for *research and development*.

RDA Abbreviation for *remote data access*, an international standard for access to databases in a heterogeneous computing environment.

Rdb DEC's relational database management system.

RDBMS Abbreviation for *relational database management system*, a type of database management system that allows you to access and maintain multiple databases through a shared field.

RD CHK Abbreviation for *read check*.

RDR Abbreviation for *receive data register*. In some communications systems, data is automatically transferred to an RDR from a receiver deserializer register when it receives a complete character. This causes the receive data register's full bit in the status buffer to go high. Data may then be read through the bus by addressing the ACIA (asynchronous communications interface adapter) and selecting the RDR when the ACIA is enabled. When the register is full, the automatic transfer of data from the receiver shift register to the data register is inhibited.

RDT Abbreviation for *remote data transmitter*.

RE 1. Abbreviation for *real number*. **2.** Abbreviation for *reset*.

reactance chart A chart of logarithmic scales so arranged that it is possible to read directly the reactance of a given inductor or capacitance at any frequency.

reactance modulator In FM communications, a circuit that modulates the capacitive reactance of a stage in accordance with the applied signal amplitude.

reactive document A routine document that is rarely revised and infrequently proofread.

reactive mode A condition of communications between remote terminals and a host computer in which each entry causes an action of the host, sometimes without an immediate reply.

read To sense, acquire, or interpret information contained in some storage medium.

Readability Plus A computerized writing-style analyzer designed to complement a grammar checker. Unlike grammar checkers, this program assumes that what it is asked to analyze is mechanically correct. Rather than look for errors, it looks for sentences and words that are not appropriate for the writer's intended audience.

read-after-write verify A check for determining that information currently being written is correct as compared to the information source.

read-around ratio The number of times a location in a storage medium may be consulted before deterioration results in the loss of data.

read-back check A check in which the information that was transmitted to an output device is returned to the source and compared with the original information to ensure accuracy.

read beyond write In the NetWare File Server Environment, the number of times a file read request was made when file write requests had not yet filled the cache block.

reader A device for sensing information stored in memory and generating signals that represent such sensed data.

reader-interpreter A service routine that reads an input stream, stores program and data for later processing, identifies control information in the data stream, and stores this information in the proper control list.

read in 1. The act of placing data in storage at a specified address. **2.** To sense information contained in some source and transmit this information to internal storage.

reading rate The number of characters, words, or items that can be sensed by an input unit in a given time.

Read-It OCR A program that enables the Macintosh and any scanner to act as an OCR (optical character recognition) system. It reads most typeset material such as magazines, books, telephone books, and printed correspondence. It recognizes serif and sans serif type faces from 7 point to over 48 point.

read-only A type of access that allows data to be read but not modified.

read-only memory See ROM.

read-only memory, blastable See BLASTABLE ROM.

ROM programmer See PROM PROGRAMMER.

read-only storage See ROM.

readout An array of addressable display characters that collectively form numbers or words as the result of a machine operation; a display of alphabetical, numerical, or alphanumeric characters.

readout device A display.

read pulse A pulse applied to one or more binary storage cells to determine if a bit of information is stored there.

read queue server current status In NetWare, refers to the server status record of a job server attached to a queue.

read wire The wire used to couple read pulses into magnetic storage cells.

read-write A control line that signals the peripherals and memory devices when the microcomputer is in a read or write state.

read-write counter A device used to store the starting and current addresses being transferred by a read-write channel between the main memory and peripheral devices.

read-write head The electromagnetic device used for recording or erasing information on magnetic tapes or disks.

read-write memory A memory that can be altered at will, abbreviated *RWM*.

read-write memory module A circuit board that contains RAM along with all necessary timing, control, and decoding logic.

ready The status or condition of being prepared to run. A program or device that is in a ready condition needs only a start signal to begin operation.

ready condition Refers to a specification or circumstance of a job or task when all of its requirements for execution other than control of the central processor have been satisfied.

ready line A line on some processors designed to interface the processor to a slow memory or a slow I/O device.

ready queue A condition such that when a user task is in a ready status, it can be executed or resumed. Generally, a separate queue of ready tasks is maintained by the executive. When a processor is available, the executive activates the task at the head of the ready queue and changes its status to running.

Ready Set Go! A desktop publishing program that includes word processing, spell checking, global linking, glossaries, fractional point sizes and kerning, and letter spacing to $\frac{1}{1000}$ of an em.

ready status word A status word used to indicate that the remote computing system is waiting for entry from the terminal.

real address mode An address mode in 80286 and 80386 microprocessors where physical memory is a contiguous array. The selector portion of the pointer is interpreted as the upper 16 bits of a 20-bit address, and the remaining four bits are set to zero. This mode of operation is compatible with the 8088 and 8086. Segments in this mode are 64K in size and may be read, written, or executed. An interrupt may occur if data operands or instructions attempt to wrap around the end of a segment. In this mode, the information contained in the segment does not use the full 64K, and the unused end of the segment may be overlaid by another segment to reduce physical memory requirements.

Realia COBOL A program that compiles, tests, and executes IBM VS COBOL and COBOL II programs under OS/2 or DOS. It supports IBM VS, OS/VS, ANS, and SAA COBOL; EBCDIC; transactional file locking; networks; C and Pascal.

REALIZER An application development environment for Windows. It has a visual form designer and a structured superset of BASIC extended to access Windows object resources.

real mode When 80286s and higher CPUs work within DOS's 1M address limit, they are working in real mode. *Contrast with* PROTECTED MODE.

real time The actual time during which a physical process occurs. In a real-time system, the results of the computation can be used in guiding the physical process.

real-time BASIC satellites A technique used in some systems that combines the speed and ease of conversational real-time BASIC programming with the operation of a number of time-and-event scheduled tasks.

real-time clock 1. A device that provides interrupts at twice the line frequency and allows for the maintenance of an accurate time-of-day clock. **2.** A timed device that produces output signals that correspond exactly with actual time—usually in hours, minutes, seconds, and tenths of seconds—and which may be used to indicate cumulative elapsed time, elapsed time, or time of day.

real-time clock diagnostic A routine that tests for the proper functioning of a real-time clock.

real-time clock interrupt An interrupt that occurs when a present clock count in a unique memory location is incremented to zero. The clock count location is automatically advanced at each clock time. The real-time clock interrupt is enabled and disabled under program control.

real-time clock module A circuit board or unit that provides programmable time bases for real-time clocking.

real-time debug routine A program that allows the user to test, examine, and modify a program task while the real-time application is running.

real-time executive *See* RTE.

real-time guard A mode that results in an interrupt to an address in central store when any attempt is made to perform a restricted operation. The guard mode is terminated by the occurrence of an interrupt.

real-time information system The system that provides information fast enough for the process to be controlled by the operator using this information.

real-time I/O Signals that are accepted by the system as they occur, or output signals that are generated to control external devices in real-time such as required in industrial process control.

real-time interface An interface used for such tasks as controlling relays, solenoids, limit counters, and controllers.

real-time mode A mode of operation that provides answers when answers are needed and delivers data when the need for that data occurs. Real-time mode eliminates slow information-gathering procedures along with lax reporting techniques and slow communications. It ensures that facts within the system are as timely as the prevailing situation.

real-time monitor An operating and programming system designed to monitor the construction and execution of programs. An effective monitor will tend to optimize the utilization of hardware and to minimize programmer effort and operator intervention. The system is usually modular and tailored for a specific microcomputer and application.

real-time operating system *See* RTOS.

real-time operation Data processing that allows the machine to use information as it becomes available. Real-time operation is opposed to *batch operation*, which processes information at a time unrelated to when the information was generated.

real-time remote inquiry Online inquiry stations that allow users to interrogate computer files and receive immediate answers.

real-time trace A trace that shows the history of program execution after reaching a breakpoint. The previous memory cycles are stored. A real-time trace answers questions such as how a program got here or how a pointer miscalculation occurred. Many of the problems that only occur in real time, such as those due to interrupts, can only be found with real-time trace data.

real-time trigonometric-function generation An approach to synchro-to-digital conversion that uses a real-time trigonometric-function generator, as shown in the diagram.

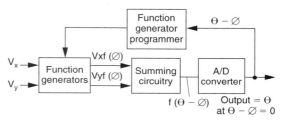

Real-time trigonometric function generator S/D converter

rear output tray A laser printer feature that allows the paper to exit the rear of the printer, coming out with the printed side facing up. This is a useful feature when printing on heavy stock or envelopes because it shortens the paper path and does not require the paper to roll over the final transport rollers. Also called a *pass-through tray*.

reasonableness check A test made on information in a computer system to ensure that the data is within a desired range of values.

receive data register *See* RDR.

received line signal detector *See* CARRIER DETECT.

receiver A device equipped for reception of incoming signals that are then transformed into a desired format.

receiver card A circuit board that accepts incoming data and translates it into some other usable form. A typical receiver card accepts ASCII data and translates it into parallel digital data.

receiver gating Refers to the application of gating voltages to one or more stages of a receiver, during the time when reception is desired.

receiver holding register A register that holds and then presents assembled receiver characters to the bus lines when requested by a read operation.

receiver isolation The attenuation between any two receivers in a system.

receiver register A register used to input received data into the system at a clock rate determined by the control register.

receiver throughput The receiver throughput depends on the number of characters identified in the control bytes as being special (interrupt generating) and the size of the message buffers for received characters. As a receiver interrupt is generated, the received characters may be accumulated in a FIFO (first-in/first-out) storage buffer until the interrupt is handled.

receiver/transmitter communication controller An asynchronous controller that can interface data sets to a microcomputer. The controller consists of timing and control interface circuits, a receiver, and a transmitter.

receive timeout In NetWare, the number of clock ticks the workstation will wait for a response from a file server before timing out. This field is used in the shell's retry-management procedure; it changes to adapt to differing traffic levels on the networks.

recirculating loop memory A section of magnetic memory in which stored information recirculates continuously to provide rapid access.

rec mark Abbreviation for *record mark*.

reconfiguration burst A term used in ARCnet. When a node wishes to initiate a network reconfiguration, it starts transmitting a long burst of data, which clears the network of any other data.

record A collection of related items of data that can be treated as a unit. For example, one line of an invoice might form a record, and a complete set of records might form a file.

recordable CD drive *See* CD-R.

record blocking The grouping of records into data blocks that can be read or written using magnetic tape in one operation, as shown in the figure. Record blocking allows for more efficient tape operation and reduces the time to read or write files.

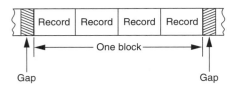

Record blocking

record format The design and organization of a record, usually a part of the program specification.

record gap An area on a data medium that indicates the end of a block or record. Also called *interrecord gap*.

recording density The number of bits in a single linear track measured per unit length of the recording medium.

recording head A transducer that accepts electrical variations and produces a corresponding field that selectively magnetizes a storage medium.

record layout The arrangement and structure of a data record, including the sequence and size of components. The record layout form is used by systems analysts and programmers to determine the field and record formats for a data file. Also called *record format*.

record length A measure of the size of a record, usually specified in characters or words.

record locking A scheme employed in multiuser systems and LANs to ensure data integrity when multiple users access a shared data file simultaneously. A user who locks a particular record in a data file can update it or prevent someone else from changing it. Different users may have record locks on different records and may change those records.

record offset Refers to a value containing the offset from the beginning of the file to the point where the record begins.

record separator *See* RS, 2.

records, overflow *See* OVERFLOW RECORDS.

record type A method used to differentiate various classes of records. In NetWare Accounting Services, for example, a type 1 indicates a charge and a type 2 is a note.

recoverable error An error condition that allows the continued execution of a program.

recoverable synchronization An operational feature that allows synchronization to be recovered or reestablished when upset.

recovery factor A measure of a thermocouple sensor's ability to indicate total temperature.

recovery from fallback The restoration of a system to full operation from a fallback mode of operation after the causes of the fallback have been removed.

recovery procedures Procedures designed to help isolate, and where possible, recover from errors in equipment. The procedures are often used in conjunction with programs that record the statistics of machine malfunctions.

recovery program A program that allows a computer system to continue functioning when certain equipment fails.

recovery time Specifies the time required for the output voltage of a power supply to return to a value within the regulation specification after a step load or line change. Recovery time, as opposed to response time, is a more meaningful way of specifying power supply performance since it relates to regulation specifications.

rectangular loop A magnetic hystersis loop that is not an S-shaped curve but tends to be square or rectangular in shape.

rectifier A device for converting alternating current into direct current by permitting the passage of signals in one direction only.

rectifier crystal A diode manufactured with a junction of crystalline elements, such as silicon or germanium.

rectifier diode A device intended for power rectification applications (as opposed to signal detection applications).

rectifier instrument An instrument that uses a rectifying device so alternating currents or voltages can be measured.

rectifying nonlinearity, Schottky diode The rectifying nonlinearity of a Schottky diode results from the presence of a potential barrier at the metal semiconductor interface. The carriers must surmount this barrier by thermionic emission before they can flow through the junction. The barrier potential can be reduced by a forward bias to increase the carrier flow from the semiconductor into the metal. Under reverse bias, the Schottky diode behaves similarly to a pn-junction diode; the reverse current is small and almost voltage-independent unless the breakdown voltage is exceeded. *Also see* SCHOTTKY DIODE.

recurrence coding A data-compression technique in which the sending system replaces strings of three or more identical characters with a character count and one of the original characters.

recursion 1. The continued repeating of the same operation or group of operations. **2.** The ability of an operation or group of operations to repeat or call itself.

recursive digital filter A filter that uses a feedback path to provide input signals from the previously calculated outputs.

recycling programs An organized arrangement in a computer where alternations have been made in one program that may change or have an effect on other programs.

Red Book A standard for audio CDs. *Also see* YELLOW BOOK.

red, green, blue *See* RGB.

redirection An operating system technique for receiving or sending data from a device other than the device the program expected. For example, DOS uses the > character to redirect output that usually is displayed on the monitor to a printer or file.

redirector program A program that intercepts all commands and function calls issued by the user or the application and decides whether DOS or the file server should process them. If the redirector decides that the command or function requires a resource located within the workstation, it passes it to DOS. If the redirector decides that the command or function requires network resources, it is bundled into a packet and sent to the file server.

red-tape operation An operation that is necessary to process data, but does not contribute to the final answer.

redundancy 1. That part of the information content that can be eliminated without loss of essential data. **2.** The employment of several devices to perform the same function in order to improve the reliability of a particular portion of a system.

redundancy check The systematic insertion of bits or characters in a message for error detection. The added bits are redundant, since they can be eliminated without the loss of message information. Parity checking is one form of redundancy checking.

redundancy-check character A character used for checking parity. It is usually the last character recorded in each block.

redundancy check, longitudinal *See* LRC.

redundancy check, vertical *See* VRC.

redundant array of inexpensive disks *See* RAID.

redundant code A self-checking code that uses an added check bit. Examples of redundant codes include the biquinary code and the two-out-of-five code.

reel tape A storage medium consisting of magnetic tape rolled onto a reel. Files stored on reel tape must be accessed sequentially.

reengineering The process of taking old systems and programs and, through a combination of software engineering tools and techniques, reworking them into more efficient and more modern systems.

reenterable A routine that can be shared by several tasks concurrently by calling itself or a program that then calls it.

reenterable load module A loading module that can be used repeatedly or concurrently by two or more jobs or tasks.

reference address The common address or address portion for a group of relative addresses.

reference block A block within a numerical control program identified by an *O* or *H* in place of the word address and containing sufficient data to enable resumption of the program following an interruption. This block should be located at a convenient point in the program that enables the operator to reset and resume operation.

reference-input signal A signal that is external to a control loop; it serves as the standard of comparison for the directly controlled variable.

reference listing A list printed by a compiler to indicate instructions as they appear in the final routine; the listing usually includes details of storage allocation.

reference noise The magnitude of electrical noise that will produce a reading equal to that produced by 10 watts of electric power at 1 kHz.

reference pilot A different type of wave from those that transmit the communication signals. It is used in carrier systems to facilitate maintenance and adjustment of the carrier transmission system.

reference point A terminal that is common to both the input and the output circuits.

reference program table A section of storage that is used as an index for operations, variables, and subroutines.

reference record A compiler output that lists the operations and their positions in the routine, along with information on the segmentation and storage allocation of the routine.

reference, D/A converter *See* D/A CONVERTER.

reference search The use of keywords to look up related items and articles in a library collection.

reference time In a computer, an instant chosen near the beginning of switching as an origin for time measurements. It is taken as the first instant at which the instantaneous value of the clock pulse reaches a specified fraction of its peak pulse amplitude.

reference voltage A voltage used as a comparison standard for various circuit operations.

reflected binary unit distance code A binary code in which sequential numbers are represented by expressions that are the same except in one place, and in that place, differ by one unit; thus in moving from one decimal digit to the next sequential digit, only one binary digit changes its value.

reflected impedance The impedance at the input terminals of a transducer, device, or circuit as a result of the impedance characteristics at the output terminals.

reflection 1. A phenomenon that occurs when a wave meets a surface of discontinuity between two media, and part of it has its direction changed so as not to cross this surface, in accordance with the reflection laws. **2.** A reduction of power from the maximum possible because a load is not matched to the source, and only a part of the energy is transmitted. The loss of power is usually measured in decibels below the maximum possible.

reflection gain The gain received in a load from a source due to the introduction of a matching network, such as a transformer; usually measured in decibels.

reflection loss The loss in power from a source as a result of an impedance mismatch between source and load.

reflectometer An instrument for measuring the ratio of energy of a reflected wave to that of an incident wave.

Reflex An analytic database that bridges the gap between spreadsheets and conventional database programs. You can group and summarize data in ways that quickly reveal interrelationships, trends, and deviations. Reflex will also calculate and chart the sum, average, count, standard deviation, variance, minimum or maximum of field values. Reflex is basically a flat (not relational) database, but it has many of the features found in a relational product.

REFLIST A program that makes lists of references, bibliographies, and footnotes. Easy-to-use and menu-driven, REFLIST consists of two programs and several files. One program reads through your own text file and formats references. The second program enters the references into a master catalog, maintained in the support files. Other files serve as reference formats from various journals for the formatting program to copy.

refold stand A printer stand for continuous-feed paper in which paper feeds from the middle shelf and refolds on the bottom shelf.

reformatting The changing in the representation of data from one format to another. Reformatting may include the translation of data values from one character set to another, such as from ASCII to EBCDIC.

refractive index *See* INDEX OF REFRACTION.

refresh To restore signals or data states in a volatile storage system such as a dynamic MOS RAM (metal-oxide semiconductor, random-access memory).

refresh rate The rate at which the electron beam of a CRT monitor scans the screen, thereby restoring an image or displaying a new one. A computer display typically refreshes the screen every 1/60 of a second.

reg Abbreviation for *register*.

regeneration 1. The process of restoring information or signals to specified requirements in amplitude or timing. **2.** Positive feedback in (usually) a single amplifier stage from the output in a circuit or system to the input such that it causes an increase in the output. Also called *regeneration feedback.*

regeneration signal A restoration of signals that comply with specified requirements for amplitude, shape, and timing. Such signals are often generated from other signals, and the requirements are often conventions or rules of specific computers or systems.

regenerative memory A memory or storage system that requires refreshing of the data to avoid loss of the contents.

regenerative read A read operation that automatically refreshes or rewrites the data back to the positions from which it was extracted.

register A set of flip-flops, shown in the following diagram, inside a microprocessor that helps to control and keep track of the various operations. It is used for temporary storage of subsets of data to facilitate arithmetic, logical, and transfer operations. Typical registers in microcomputers include the accumulator, index address register, instruction counter, and stack pointer, as shown. These registers should have good accessibility to the CPU.

Every microprocessor must have an accumulator register. The accumulator is the focal point for data manipulation. Here, numbers are added or subtracted. Shift operations and complementing can be done, as well as many Boolean operations. Most of today's microprocessors use more than one register for these functions.

The accumulators function as temporary storage registers during calculations. Since the computer may also use the accumulators in logical operations, shifts, and other instructions,

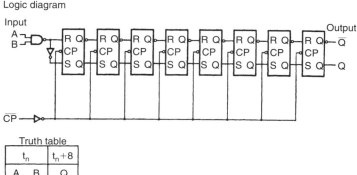

t_n		t_n+8
A	B	Q
L	L	L
L	H	L
H	L	L
H	H	H

NOTES:
t_n = Bit time before clock pulse.
t_{n+8} = Bit time after 8 clock pulse.

Register

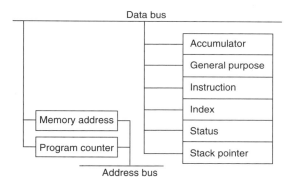

Microprocessor registers

accumulators are generally the most frequently used registers.

register, accumulator *See* ACCUMULATOR REGISTER.

register address An address where the operand lies in one of the general registers. For example, in the 8080 system, an instruction such as

```
ADDC ;(A = A + C)
```

will add the contents of C to the accumulator and then place the results in the accumulator.

register address field The part of a computer instruction that contains a register address.

register addressing Register addressing is used when the CPU has several possible registers that may be used for reference. Since the number of registers is usually small, only a few bits are necessary to select a register.

register and arithmetic logic unit *See* RALU.
register, arithmetic *See* ARITHMETIC REGISTER.
register arrangement Part of the microcomputer architecture, along with the addressing modes. Registers not dedicated to any specific function can be used as determined by the instruction that is decoded. They can contain the address of an operand, serve as pointers to the address of an operand, autoincrement or autodecrement, or serve as index registers for data and program access.
register, base *See* BASE REGISTER.
register, buffer *See* BUFFER.
register, external *See* EXTERNAL REGISTER.
register, input/output *See* IOR.
register, memory-address *See* MAR.
register, multiplier-quotient *See* MULTIPLIER-QUOTIENT REGISTER.
register, sequence control *See* SEQUENCE CONTROL REGISTER.
register, standby *See* STANDBY REGISTER.
register transfer module *See* RTM.
registration In desktop publishing, the accuracy of the positioning of color separations.
Regit Point-of-Sale A program that transforms a PC into a point-of-sale cash register for retail businesses. The program can control up to 12,000 products with product codes up to 16 characters long. There is support for UPC (uniform product codes).
rejection, common mode *See* COMMON MODE REJECTION.
rejection, normal mode *See* NORMAL MODE REJECTION.
relating coding To form or use a relative code.
relation The comparison of two expressions in a

program to determine if the value of one is greater than, equal to, or less than the other.

relational database A database that lets you retrieve information from two or more files using a common field to link the files.

relational database management system *See* RDBMS.

relational model A database model in which data are organized into tables. Rows represent records, while columns represent fields. Other tables are used to index the data tables, allowing access to single fields or records.

relative file A file organization where the desired record's key is translated into a disk location with a hashing routine.

relational operator An operator used in programming to indicate when a comparison is to be performed between different terms.

relative address An address that is to be altered to an absolute address at the time the program is being run.

relative address label A label used to identify the location of data by reference to its position with respect to some other location in the program.

relative addressing A type of addressing that shortens the address part of an instruction by allowing a reference within some range relative to a register. In some systems, a relative addressing instruction is formed by adding the second byte of the instruction to the op code plus two. Because the addition is in twos' complement arithmetic, the result is the original value plus 127 or minus 128, and the relative address lies between +129 and −126 of the current instruction. For example, the following instruction

```
BBC 12 ;(branch if carry clear)
```

transfers control to the current location plus 14 if the carry bit is cleared.

relative addressing mode An addressing mode that specifies a memory location in the program counter or another register for reference. The relative addressing mode can be used for branch instructions, in which case an op code is added to the relative address to complete the instruction.

relative code A code in which all addresses are specified or written with respect to an arbitrary position or represented symbolically in a computable form.

relative frequency A measure or calculation of the ratio of numbers of observations in a class or subset to the total number of observations or elements constituting a population, such as a universal subset.

relative frequency drift The frequency drift divided by the nominal frequency value. Also called *normalized frequency drift*.

relative magnitude Refers to the relationship or comparison of one quantity to another, most often related to a base magnitude and expressed as a difference from or a percentage of the base or reference.

relative path The path an operating system must use to get to a directory.

relative time clock *See* RTC.

relaxation oscillator An oscillator that operates by being driven to a regenerative state rapidly and repetitively. Upon reaching the saturated regenerative state, the device "relaxes" to return to its original state and is immediately driven again to saturation.

relay 1. An electromechanical switching device usually composed of a solenoid, a movable armature containing at least one contact point, and a set of fixed contact points. Applying a voltage to the solenoid sets up a magnetic field that attracts the armature, thus causing it to make or break a circuit completed by the touching contact points. **2.** A repeater system, usually automatically operated and controlled.

relay contacts The contacts that are closed or opened by the movement of a relay armature.

relay driver A circuit that produces an output powerful enough to drive relay solenoids when a low-current logic signal is applied.

relay, electromagnetic *See* ELECTROMAGNETIC RELAY.

relay input module A unit that connects relay coils to the computer. The contacts of the relays are presented to the processor's I/O bus.

relay output module A unit that provides a set of relay contacts that may be used to drive devices such as lamps.

relay tree A group of relays whose contacts are interconnected, but whose solenoids are independently driven, as shown in the figure; so called because each relay in the array has twice the contacts of the prior relay. Relay trees perform binary-to-decimal conversion (for driving seven-segment displays) and permit selection of a

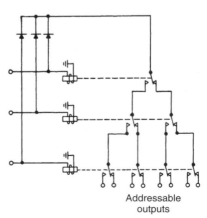

Relay tree

number of power-driving functions with only a few input signals.

release-guard signal A signal sent in response to a clear-forward signal that indicates that the circuit is free at the incoming end.

reliability The probability that a device will perform without failure for a specified time period under specified operating conditions.

reliability control The coordination and direction of reliability activities.

reliability index The figures of merit that are used to denote relative reliability.

reliability testing Tests that are designed to determine the anticipated failure-free performance or life expectancy of a product or system under specified conditions.

relocatability The ability to situate a program or data in an area of memory at different times without modification to the program. Relocatability allows flexibility in both designing the program modules and bringing them together into an executable program.

relocatable assembler An assembler that generates an object program with memory addresses entered as displacements from a relative program origin or as external references.

relocatable code Software code that can be loaded in any point in the program.

relocatable expression An assembly expression whose value is affected by program relocation. A relocatable expression may represent a relocatable address.

relocatable program loader A program that assigns absolute origins to relocatable subroutines, object programs, and data. It assigns absolute locations to each of the instructions or data, and modifies the reference to these instructions or data.

relocatable term A term in assembler programming whose value is affected by program relocation.

relocating object loader A program used to load and link object programs produced by assemblers. It satisfies external references between separate program segments, generates linkages as required, and loads only those segments required to satisfy external references.

relocation dictionary *See* RLD.

reluctance The opposition in a magnetic circuit to flux.

reluctive transducers Transducers that use the ratio of the reluctance of two coils. They are less sensitive to temperature effects than one-coil devices. Reluctive transducers use a small motion of 0.003 inch to yield an ac output voltage of about 100 mV.

REM 1. Acronym for *remote electronic mail*, an MCI Mail account used by companies that have several users. 2. A command in some languages that provides for remarks on a program line.

remanence A unit of measure for determining the magnetic flux density after removal of an applied magnetic force.

remirrored block In the NetWare File Server Environment, the block number that is being remirrored.

remirrored drive In the NetWare File Server Environment, the physical drive number of the disk currently being remirrored.

remote access The capability for communication with a processing facility by one or more stations that are distant from that facility.

remote acknowledge number In NetWare Communication Services, the sequence number of the next packet that the remote SPX expects to receive from the local SPX.

remote batch processing Batch processing where an input device is located at some distance from the main installation and has access through the communications system to the computer.

remote-boot ROM Devices that allow a workstation to boot up from the file server rather than using DOS on the workstation's own disk drives. PROMs are used in diskless workstations and those that have only floppy drives, since they eliminate the need for a boot diskette. When PROMs are used, the network interface card (NIC) must be configured for both their presence and the memory addresses used by the PROM.

remote connection ID In NetWare Communication Services, the number of the specified SPX connection from the remote workstation's point of view.

remote console A terminal located some distance from the processor.

remote control signals Signal lines that allow the microcomputer to be operated from a remote control panel. Remote control signals include REMOTE HALT, REMOTE LOAD, and REMOTE POWER-ON.

remote data access *See* RDA.

remote date concentration Communications processors that are used for the multiplexing of data from low-speed lines or terminals or low-activity lines or terminals onto one or more higher-speed lines.

remote debugging The use of remote terminals for the testing of programs.

remote inquiry The interrogation of the contents of a storage unit from a device displaced from the storage unit site. Remote inquiry stations allow the computer to be interrogated from various locations for immediate answers to inquiries.

remote job entry *See* RJE.

remote login Refers to a network user operating on a remote computer, using a protocol as though locally attached.

Remotely Possible/DIAL One of the first true Windows-based, dial-up, remote-control packages, it allows access as though the user were working directly on the remote PC. It supports a wide variety of modems and includes file transfer and chat mode, full mouse and keyboard support, data compression, and security features.

remote monitoring and control Refers to the use of a microcomputer as a programmable remote station to be addressed from a central computer. It can be given operating setpoints strategies or can send data from a number of sensors and then implement decisions based on complex combinations of conditions. In addition, distributed digital processing allows the central controller to receive refined status reports rather than raw data from remote stations. Since information is then exchanged only when established limits are exceeded or when remote units are specifically interrogated, communication burdens are reduced. By relieving the central computer from routine data manipulation and control tasks, the machine can do more computations and better optimize the control of the total system.

remote multiplexing system Remote multiplexing uses a configuration like that shown below. The remote multiplexers are located throughout the plant. Analog and digital signals are sent to the nearest remote multiplexer.

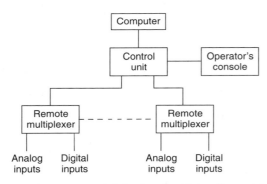

Remote multiplexing configuration

remote network In NetWare Communication Services, the number of the network on which the remote workstation resides.

remote node In NetWare Communication Services, the node address of the destination node.

remote procedure call *See* RPC.

remote real-time terminal A terminal with a sensor, instrument and control interfaces with discrete I/O lines, A/D converters, D/A converters, analog multiplexers, and a modem.

remote reset ROM *See* REMOTE-BOOT ROM.

remote serial driver board An interface board for connecting a MetraBus or other industrial control/data acquisition system to any standard RS-232 or RS-422 serial data port. The serial control information is brought in through a 25-pin (RS-232) or 9-pin (RS-422) connector.

remote socket In NetWare Communication Services, the number of the socket that the remote SPX is using to send and receive packets.

removable cartridge system A high-capacity storage system that can be removed from the PC. A removable cartridge system consists of a drive mechanism and the cartridges used to store data. The most well-known removable cartridge system is the Bernoulli Box by Iomega.

removable disk A hard disk module containing an access arm and read/write head in a protective case that can be removed from the drive.

removable random-access Storage devices like magnetic disk packs that can be physically removed because they are not permanently attached to the computer.

REN A DOS command to rename a file.

repeatability The closeness of agreement among a number of consecutive measurements of a constant signal approached from the same direction. Repeatability is expressed as maximum nonrepeatability in percent of span or counts of error.

repeat counter A counter used to control repeated operations, such as block transfer and search commands.

repeated addition multiplication A technique for multiplication that requires a counter, as shown in the following figure. The value of the multiplicand is loaded into its register, and the value of the multiplier is loaded into the multiplier counter.

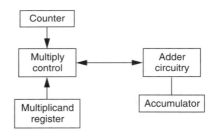

Multiplication using repeated addition

repeated subtraction division A method of division in which the number of subtractions that take place is loaded into the counter. The counter then holds the answer. The repeated subtraction technique of division is shown in the figure.

At the start, the dividend is loaded into the accumulator, and the divisor into the divisor register. As each subtraction takes place, the value in the accumulator becomes smaller and smaller, finally reaching zero (or some remainder); the value in the counter becomes larger and larger, finally yielding the correct quotient. The divider circuit does not stop when the accumulator reaches zero (or a remainder). The subtracter will try to continue subtracting beyond the point of zero remainder; when it does, the value in the accumulator becomes a negative quantity. The negative sign can be recognized with a *sign comparator*, which stops the divide process. The machine then adds-back the subtrahend and produces the correct positive remainder.

Often in dealing with large binary numbers, many of the arithmetic processes drop a few of the least significant bits in the answers. The final result may be in error, but it is usually more accurate than required.

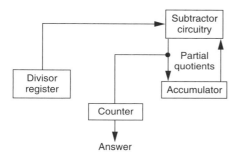

Division using repeated subtraction

repeater 1. A device that reconstitutes signals into standard or desired requirements. 2. A communications system that automatically retransmits received signals on a different fixed frequency within the same band.

repertoire The set of instructions that a processor is capable of performing or a coding system is capable of assembling.

repetition One of the three structured programming patterns. A sequence of instructions is repeated until a condition is met.

replies canceled In the NetWare File Server Environment, refers to the number of replies that were canceled because a connection was reallocated while a request was being processed.

report A presentation of data or information in tabular, graphic, narrative, or any other form.

report generator A routine or program that can be run to automatically produce a report with the desired content and arrangement. To use the report generator, the user prepares a set of parameters defining control fields and report lines. These parameters are used to produce a symbolic program. The assembled version of this program accepts the raw data as input, edits it, and generates the desired reports. *Also see* REPORT WRITER.

report program generator 1. A program used to generate object programs that produce reports from existing data. **2.** *See* RPG.

report writer A program that allows users to create hardcopy report formats for data output. Users can set up the format including margins, headers, and footers. The report writer may also perform calculations, such as totals and averages.

repository manager The database that holds network management information in IBM's SystemView.

representative calculating operation A method of evaluating the speed performance of a computer. One method is to use one-tenth of the time required to perform nine complete additions and one complete multiplication. A complete addition or a complete multiplication time includes the time required to procure two operands from high-speed storage.

reprocessed requests In the NetWare File Server Environment, the count of requests that were reprocessed by a server.

reproducibility The closeness of agreement among repeated measurements of the output for the same value of input made under the same operating conditions over a period of time, approaching from either direction.

reprogrammable associative ROM A term sometimes used for a programmable logic array. *Also see* PLA.

reprogrammable ROM *See* EPROM.

request bitmap An AppleTalk transaction protocol field used to keep track of the parts of a reply have been sent or received.

requested socket number In NetWare Communication Services, the socket to be opened.

Request For Comments The document series, begun in 1969, that describes the Internet suite of protocols and related experiments.

request for proposal *See* RFP.

request for repetition, automatic *See* ARQ.

request to send *See* RTS.

required hyphen *See* EMBEDDED HYPHEN.

rerun point One of a set of preselected points in a program that is used as a restarting point in the event of error detection.

rerun routine A routine that uses rerun points for restarting.

Rescue A program that can recover data from physically damaged floppies and hard drives. It bypasses DOS's inability to read bad disks and moves the drive heads directly; it will even read a floppy with a hole poked through it.

rescue dump A dump on magnetic tape of the entire memory, along with a starting point to allow the rerun from this point. Rescue dumps can prevent the rerunning of an entire program when the run is interrupted by an error or power shutdown.

research data Refers to data on an organization representing the analysis of past performance and future plans.

reservation field A field in token ring packets that allows a node to inform the active monitor that it has data of a certain priority to send.

reserve amount In NetWare Accounting Services, the amount that the account server expects to charge for a service it is about to provide.

reset To return a device such as a register to zero or to an initial or selected condition.

reset key A key or switch on the computer console to reset the error-detection system and restart the program after a power-down condition, such as an error, has been discovered. For a master reset, all registers are set to zero, the interrupt system is disabled, the input/output interface is initialized, and the program counter is set.

reset pulse A pulse used to set a flip-flop or a magnetic cell to its original state.

Resicalc A DOS-based, memory-resident calculator that can be popped-up whenever needed.

resident compiler A compiler that uses the computer itself to produce programs. A resident compiler may require several passes in a microcomputer system to reduce a source program to machine language.

resident font A type of hard font. Unlike soft fonts, which must be loaded before they can be used, resident fonts are always available to the printer. Resident fonts are permanently written at the factory on ROM memory inside a printer. Also called *internal font*. Also see HARD FONT.

resident macroassembler An assembler that enables users to translate an assembly language program into the appropriate machine language instructions. The macro capability eliminates the need to rewrite similar sections of code repeatedly and simplifies the user's program documentation. The conditional assembly feature of the macroassembler, which may vary from system to system, permits users to include or delete optional code segments.

resident module A module that keeps track of program execution status.

resident program A program that is permanently located in storage.

residual charge The charge remaining on the plates of a capacitor after a discharge.

residual current The vector sum of the currents in an electric circuit after the source of power is removed.

residual resistance The resistance persisting at temperatures near zero on the absolute scale, arising from crystal irregularities and impurities.

residue A number calculated by dividing it by the modulus, resulting in an integer and a remainder. The remainder is the residue. Residue codes can be used to detect or even correct errors from an arithmetic unit or faults produced by data transfers or memory operations.

residue check *See* MODULO-N CHECK.

resillator A miniaturized frequency standard combining a resonator and oscillator in a single package.

resist *See* PHOTORESIST.

resistance A property of conducting materials that determines the current produced by a given voltage. The unit of resistance is the ohm. The value of resistance of a given circuit component is equal to its voltage divided by its current.

resistance box 1. An assembly of resistors and the necessary switching or other means for changing the resistance connected across its output terminals by known, fixed amounts. **2.** A device containing carefully constructed and adjusted resistors, which can be introduced into a circuit by switches or keys. At high frequencies, there are disturbing inductive and capacitive effects that complicate measurements using resistance boxes. These are mitigated by suitable design techniques to make the boxes as nonreactive as possible.

resistance continuity tester A unit that lights up or buzzes if there is a complete circuit present. A low-voltage tester can use the circuit shown in the following figure.

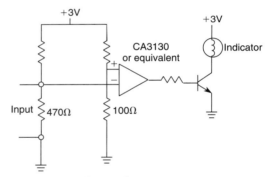

Low voltage tester

resistance drop The voltage drop occurring across two points on a conductor when current flows through the resistance between those points. Multiplying the resistance in ohms by the current in amperes gives the voltage drop in volts.

resistance ladder A network that uses a limited number of repeated values, with attenuation. One approach, as shown, uses a binary resistance quad consisting of the four values 2R, 4R, 8R, and 16R for each group of four bits, with an attenuation of 16:1 for the second quad and 256:1 for the third quad. The proper quad weights for BCD conversion can be achieved with an attenuation between quads of 10:1.

resistance lamp Refers to a lamp used to limit the current in a circuit.

resistance material A material used for the construction of resistance elements. Typical materials are nichrome wire and carbon.

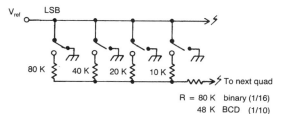

Quad resistance ladder

resistance sensor input boards Analog input boards used for a variety of variable resistance sensors. They are suited for the measurements of devices operated in a current excitation mode or in standard bridge configurations. Sensors included in these categories include two-, three-, or four-wire RTDs, thermistors, strain gauges, and variable potentiometer devices. Some are designed with all cold-junction compensation circuit boards for thermocouple measurements.

resistance temperature detector See RTD.

resist-etchant A material deposited onto a copper-clad base material to prevent the conductive area underneath from being etched away.

resistive component Refers to those parts of the impedance of an electrical system that lead to the absorption and dissipation of energy in the form of heat.

resistive coupling The use of resistors to connect or link two circuits or gates.

resistor A component with a specified resistance value designed to restrict the flow of current.

resistor-transistor logic See RTL.

resolution 1. The smallest incremental step in separating a value into constituent parts. **2.** The smallest inseparable part of a value.

resolver 1. A device that breaks up a quantity, such as a vector, into components or elements. **2.** A small section of storage that has much faster access than the rest of the storage.

resolver differential A device used to obtain zero shift or offset in control systems that use resolver feedback. It is connected between the reference and the feedback to furnish a signal to the position feedback unit.

resonance The sympathetic electrical vibration of a circuit or device to a signal.

resonant-gate transistor A type of field-effect transistor with a mechanically tuned input.

resonator A device exhibiting a sharply defined electric, mechanical, or acoustic resonance effect, such as a piezoelectric crystal.

resource Refers to items or devices utilized by the computer system.

resource allocation mapping The use of visual aids or maps to allow register, memory, or I/O space assignments as they are required by the computer or microprocessor, as shown in the following figure.

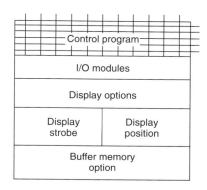

Resource allocation map

resource fork The second half of a file on a Macintosh file system. The resource fork contains the executable code, while the *data fork* has user data.

resource fork size In the AppleTalk Filing Protocol, the size of a target AFP file's resource portion. If the AFP directory/file path specifies an AFP directory, the resource fork size field is a zero.

resource set A term used in the NetWare ELSGEN and NETGEN programs when generating the NetWare operating system. A resource set has more than one resource item. Several items may be combined into a set for convenience. When you want to use all of these devices, the entire set can be selected with the menu option "Select Resource Sets."

Resource Workshop A Borland development tool that lets you create Windows-based programs visually, without writing code. Borland's Custom Controls include three-dimensional radio buttons and check boxes with the graphics and text, and dialog boxes with backgrounds that stand out. Each resource created within Resource Workshop can be tested without leaving the program. There is no need to exit and compile before testing a new icon or menu.

responses found In the AppleTalk Filing Protocol, indicates how many sets of information a call is returning.

response time The time elapsed between generation of an inquiry at a terminal and receipt of a response at that same terminal.

response type In the Service Advertising Protocol (SAP), a field set to 2 for general service or to 4 for nearest service when the server responds to the query packet. It is also set to 2 for initialization and periodic broadcasts.

restart To reestablish the execution of a routine by using a checkpoint.

restart procedure A procedure that allows processing to continue from the last checkpoint, rather than the beginning of the run. Restart procedures are used in machines with heavy scheduling, since complete reruns due to errors or interruptions cannot be tolerated.

restore 1. To return an index, address, word, or character to its initial state, sometimes by periodic recharge or regeneration. 2. To superimpose a dc level on an ac signal after loss of the original dc in a stage.

restorer generator A device that generates the signals required to restore specific conditions in a system.

restorer pulse generator A circuit designed to generate pulses for special timing or gating purposes. These pulses are used as inputs to gates to aid in pulse shaping and timing.

restrictions enforced In the NetWare File Server Environment, tells whether limits were placed upon use of disk resources when the network was installed.

result list In NetWare Message Services, a field that returns code for each connection number contained in the connection list field. The following results are defined:

1. *Successful.* The server stored the message in the target connection's message buffer. (It is the target connection's responsibility to retrieve and display the message.)
2. *Rejected.* The target connection's message buffer is already holding a message.
3. *Invalid.* The specified connection number is unknown.
4. *Blocked.* The target connection's message mode is set to block messages, or the target connection is not in use.

retentivity The degree or expression of the ability of a material to retain magnetic flux.

retransmission count In NetWare Communication Services, the number of times (since SPX was loaded) that SPX attempts to retransmit an unacknowledged packet before it decides that the remote SPX has become inoperable or unreachable.

retransmit error checking Communications channel may be sensitive to intermittent noise and signal failures, thus it is necessary to determine if the transmitted message is received without errors. One technique requires that the receiving station to retransmit the message received back to the transmitting device. The message must then be transmitted twice. This can be done for most applications.

retransmitted packets In NetWare Communication Services, the number of times (since SPX was loaded) that the local SPX has had to retransmit a packet on a connection before receiving the expected acknowledgment.

retrieve To load a previously existing document into the computer's memory.

retrofit Work done to an existing machine or system by simply adding special fixtures or modules.

retry count In NetWare Communication Services, specifies how many times SPX will resend unacknowledged packets before concluding that the destination node is not functioning properly.

retry TX Count In NetWare Diagnostic Services, specifies the number of times (since the last reset or initialization) that the drive resent a packet. For example, when the driver detects a collision, the driver resends a packet.

return address The part of a subprogram that connects it with the main program or routine. A return address can be used to unite two or more separately written, compiled, or assembled programs or routines into a single operational unit.

return from zero time The elapsed time between the end of a pulse at full strength and the start of the absent electrical flow or some lower level of electrical flow.

return to bias *See* RB, 2.

reverse bias A voltage applied to a pn crystal such that the positive terminal of the voltage is applied to the n section and the negative to the p section.

reverse-blocking pnpn switch A pnpn-type switch that exhibits a reverse-blocking state when its anode-to-cathode voltage is negative and does not switch in the normal manner of a pnpn-type switch.

reverse direction The direction of greater resistance to current flow through a diode or rectifier; that is, from the positive to the negative electrode. Also called *inverse direction.*

reverse gate current The direct current into the gate terminal of a MOS device with a reverse gate-source voltage applied.

reverse image Highlighting a character field or cursor by reversing its color and its background.

reverse interrupt *See* RVI.

reverse-Polish notation A system for expressing mathematical statements wherein the operators follow the numbers, and the answer appears without an equal (=) sign. *Also see* POLISH NOTATION.

reverse recovery time In a semiconductor diode, the time required for the current or voltage to reach a specified state after being switched instantaneously from a specified forward current condition to a specified reversed bias condition.

reverse scan An editing operation used to suppress zeros by replacing them with blanks.

reverse video The process of putting text into the opposite colors expected on a screen, such as black characters on a white background.

reversible capacitance For a capacitor, the limit, as the amplitude of the applied sinusoidal voltage approaches zero, of the ratio of the amplitude of the inphase, fundamental frequency component of transferred charge to the amplitude of the applied voltage, with a specified constant-bias voltage superimposed on the sinusoidal voltage.

reversible process A mechanism of flux change within a magnetic material where the flux returns to its initial state when the magnetic field is removed.

revision cycle The path of a document through a series of corrections after its initial release.

revoke rights mask In NetWare Directory Services, a field that contains the rights to be removed from a directory's maximum rights mask.

rewrite The restoring of information in storage writing. Also called *regeneration*.

RF Abbreviation for *radio frequency*, the term used for high-frequency transmission, usually in the megahertz range.

RF amplifier An amplifier capable of operation at radio frequencies.

RFFlow A Windows-based drawing tool for flowcharts and organization charts. It has 100 shapes with auto-adjust for size, auto-line routing, and rerouting.

RFI Abbreviation for *radio frequency interference*, the unwanted interference in a circuit or device caused by electromagnetic radiation from another circuit or device.

RF modem A high-frequency modem used to convert digital signals to analog signals.

RFP Abbreviation for *request for proposal*, a formal bidding procedure that can be used for an organization's new computer system: system specifications are sent to vendors, who send bids to the organization.

RGB Refers to output hardware that shows images in colors that contain, red, green, and blue pixels. The pixels are mixed in patterns to create the various colors.

RG-58 A type of coaxial cable having a nominal characteristic impedance of 50 ohms.

RG-59 A type of coaxial cable having a nominal characteristic impedance of 75 ohms.

rheostat An electric component in which the resistance introduced into a circuit is variable by a knob, handle, or mechanical means, such as an electric motor.

rhythm generator A circuit designed for electronic keyboards and other musical electronic instruments. One type contains an internal oscillator, a counter, and a ROM that drives the rhythm instruments and a seven-segment sequence count display. The oscillator frequency is determined by an external network.

RI Abbreviation for *reliability index*.

RIB Acronym for *ring indicator box*, a unit that allows the interconnection of an asynchronous terminal and a synchronous computer port. The RIB contains the appropriate switch options and indicators to effect a proper installation as well as simulate a ring on pin 22. An LED displays the presence of a data terminal ready (DTR) from the computer port.

right-justify To adjust the printing positions on a page such that the right margin is flush.

rights Rules that govern the activities a network user can perform in a directory. Some typical rights are read, write, create, delete, open, search, modify, supervisory, and file scan.

right shift An operation in which digits of a word are displaced to the right, as shown in the figure. A right shift has the effect of division if the word represents a binary number.

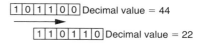

Right shift

ring A network topology with the cable configuration in the form of a circle. Data is sent around the circle loop from station to station in one direction, with each station acting as a repeater. LAN rings usually look like a star topology, however, because the stations are connected to a hub; the hub device makes the connections a ring. IBM's hub device is called a multiple access unit (MAU).

ring counter A loop of connected bistable elements in which one and only one is in a specified state at any one time; as input signals are counted, the position of this state moves in an ordered sequence around the loop.

ring indicator A modem interface signal defined in RS-232 that indicates to the attached data terminal equipment that an incoming call is present. *Also see* RIB.

ring indicator box *See* RIB.

ringing Refers to oscillations that occur after a level transition in a digital signal. Ringing is usually caused by an impedance mismatch or an improperly terminated signal line.

ring interface unit A device used in ring-topology LANs for interfacing a terminal to the ring. By using the properly designed ring interface unit, potentially unreliable terminals can be used without jeopardizing the entire network.

ring oscillator 1. An oscillator in which a number of devices feed each other in a circle or circuit. **2.** An oscillator in which the frequency is determined by a ring cut from a quartz crystal suspended at its nodes to minimize damping.

ring purge A token ring packet that clears the network of data, similar in function to the ARCnet reconfiguration burst.

ring topology A network model where each node is connected to two other computers in a ring formation. *Also see* RING.

ripple 1. The component arising from sources within a dc power supply. Ripple is the ratio, expressed in percent, of the root-mean-square value of the ripple voltage to the absolute values of the total voltage. **2.** The excursions above and below the average peak amplitude.

ripple counter A counting circuit in which flip-flops are connected in series, with one flip-flop affecting the next in sequence until the last flip-flop is triggered.

ripple factor The amount of ac voltage in the output of a rectifier after rectification. It is measured, in percent, by the ratio of the rms value of the ac component to the algebraic average of the total voltage across the load.

ripple filter A filter designed to reduce the ripple or ac variation produced by a rectifier circuit.

RISC Acronym for *reduced instruction set computer*, a type of parallel processing architecture that uses multiple processors each working on a part of a particular program simultaneously. *Contrast with* CISC.

riser Refers to a physical solution for indoor cables that pass between floors; it is normally a vertical shaft or space.

riser connector An expansion connector in some 386 and 486 machines. The connectors are horizontal and mounted on a rack, as shown in the figure.

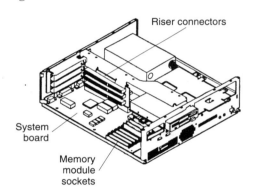

Riser connectors used in some 80386 and 80486 systems

rise time The time required for the leading edge of a pulse to rise from 10 to 90 percent of its final value. It is proportionate to the time constant and is a measure of the slope of the wavefront.

rise time, overshoot *See* OVERSHOOT RISE TIME.

risk analysis software Software that uses Monte Carlo simulation and statistical analysis to provide estimates of project completion dates and costs. It enables the user to see in advance the potential effect of variables (risks) and plan accordingly. The system generates a criticality index to identify the likelihood of individual activities becoming critical during the project.

RJE Abbreviation for *remote job entry*, the processing of stacked jobs over communication lines via terminals that are usually equipped with line printers. Small computers are also used to operate as RJE stations. A typical RJE station performs tasks such as data transmission, report transmission, file updating, and program compilation in Fortran or COBOL.

RJ-11 An interface between the telephone line and a customer's device consisting of a modular six-wire plug and jack. It is the standard modular telephone connection.

RJ-11 modular cables Cables used as extensions for plugging in a telephone or modem. They are complete with terminated male RJ-11 connectors at each end. RJ-11 cables have four 28-AWG, stranded-copper conductors and are nonshielded.

RJ-16 A six-wire jack for exclusion-key telephones (USOC 502 or 2502). This jack is used with modems that do not incorporate voice-data switches. The exclusion key of the telephone is the voice-data switching device. The modem plugs into the RJ-16 jack; the telephone company wires the two jacks together.

RJ-21 A 50-wire jack for up to 25 lines.

RJ-27 A programmable 50-wire jack for up to eight lines.

RJ-36 *See* RJ-16.

RJ-41 An eight-wire jack that has a fixed resistance, unless used with an exclusion-key telephone. It provides eight-decibel attenuation to provide a maximum output of –4 dBm. When programmable with an exclusion-key telephone, it is programmed by the telephone company to provide optimum conditions at the central office.

RJ-45 An interface between the telephone line and customer's devices consisting of an eight-wire modular plug and jack. The RJ-41 is physically similar.

RJ-45 cable A cable that has eight 28-AWG, solid-copper conductors (nonshielded) and is terminated with male RJ-45 connectors.

RJEP Abbreviation for *remote job-entry protocol*. *Also see* RJ3.

RLD Abbreviation for *relocation dictionary*, part of a program that contains the information necessary to change addresses when it is relocated.

RLL Abbreviation for *run length limited*, an enhanced version of the MFM format for hard disk drives that features 25 or 26 sectors per track. This format increases the capacity of a drive by 50%. The data transfer rate of an RLL formatted drive starts at 7.5M per second. Like MFM drives, RLL formatted drives use the ST-506 interface.

RLogin Mux Module A portion of Portable NetWare that allows multiple remote workstations to emulate a terminal in the host operating system.

RM/COBOL developer pack An RM/COBOL-85 development compiler/runtime system conforming to both ANSI COBOL 1974 and 1985 standards. RM/CO creates a menu-driven, windowed environment that keeps the operating system in the background. It has object, data file, and source portability.

RM/FORTRAN An implementation of ANSI Standard Fortran X3.9-1978 (Fortran-77) with no errors. It contains mainframe extensions from VAX, VS, and Fortran-66. A memory resource manager allows multiple program units to share the same memory. It includes a full-screen editor, an interactive symbolic debugger, a linker, library routines, and utilities to support IEEE floating-point arithmetic. RM/Fortran is available for DOS and OS/2, and runs on the 286 and higher processors.

RMM Abbreviation for *read-mostly memory*, a special type of ROM that can be programmed while it is in the computer. It is used to control the operation of the computer and is, therefore, used primarily for reading its program and is written upon only when a change is needed in the controlling program. The process of reading data from such a memory is performed much more quickly than writing data into it.

rms pulse amplitude Root-mean-square pulse amplitude, the square root of the average of the squares of the instantaneous amplitudes taken over the duration of the pulse.

RO Abbreviation for *read-only*, a device with no transmission capability.

RoboHELP Software that turns Microsoft Word for Windows into a hypertext authoring system. It has a customizable, visual tool palette (like PageMaker). Using RoboHELP, programmers and non-programmers can develop a help system under Windows.

robot **1.** A device or system that can detect input signals or environmental conditions and perform calculations for resultant actions of a control mechanism. Robots are being used for visual inspection and identity-and-attitude analysis. They have been used to determine the two-dimensional outline of an object, locate corners, find holes and grip points, separate multiple objects, and identify objects based on characteristics. **2.** A mechanical simulation of a human and a human's movements; an automaton.

robotics An area of artificial intelligence that deals with the development and use of robots.

Rockwell 6500/1 (*o.t.*) A microcomputer chip that combines the 6502 microprocessor with 2048 bytes of ROM, 64 bytes of RAM, 32 bidirectional I/O lines, four interrupts, and a 16-bit programmable counter/timer. The 6500/1 single-chip microcomputer has a separate pin for RAM power, which may be used to maintain data in the RAM on 10 percent of the total power for the chip. The programmable 16-bit counter/timer can operate as either an interval timer, pulse generator, or event counter.

ROI Abbreviation for *return on investment*.

rollback A programmed return to a prior checkpoint.

rollback snapshot A recording of data taken at periodic intervals in a program to allow the program to restart at the last recording after a system failure.

roll-in To restore to main storage the data that had previously been transferred from main storage to auxiliary storage.

roll-out To record the contents of main storage in auxiliary storage.

ROM Acronym for *read-only memory*, a memory whose contents are not alterable by computer instructions. A semiconductor ROM is programmed by a mask pattern as a part of the final manufacturing process. The organization of the storage cells determines the number of input and output lines required for a given ROM. The address pins are the means by which a specific word is accessed or selected, as shown in the figure. If the ROM is organized as 32 words of eight bits, then each word can be addressed using five input lines, since $32 = 2^5$.

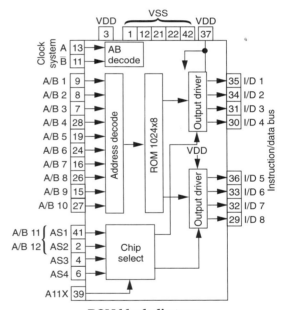

ROM block diagram

The number of output lines is determined by the number of bits in the word. ROMs can be used to store microprograms or fixed programs, depending upon the application. A ROM can be used to implement in one package the functions that previously took up to 50 TTL packages.

The size of a ROM varies with system requirements, and the maximum size is usually dictated by the addressing capability of the microprocessor. A ROM does not need any store control circuitry; instructions can be fetched from a ROM in half the time it would take with a RAM. However, programs must be correct, since a ROM gives no flexibility for changing the instruction sequence.

ROM address lines The lines or pins used to select a specific word in ROM.

ROM assimilator A self-contained microcomputer system with assembly and utility programs that can develop, debug, and simulate proposed ROM programs. The system includes a debug console and terminal interface for input and output. Proposed ROM programs are stored in RAM and modified directly from the terminal.

ROM bootstrap A ROM program that is used as a bootstrap loader. If everything in memory is wiped out, the bootstrap loader will allow the programmer to recreate a main memory load.

ROM chip Read-only memory that contains the commands a computer needs to get itself going. The ROM is nonvolatile; its contents are retained even when the power is off. The instructions in ROM allow the computer to get started when the power is turned on.

ROM chip enable Most types of ROMs have a pin labeled CE for *chip enable*. This permits the output to be isolated from the rest of the circuitry inside the IC. Thus, if a one is placed at CE (while the address is being changed), the outputs will be at logic-1 level.

ROM loader A loader program that is implemented in ROM. A typical ROM loader is contained on a printed-circuit card for plugging into the microcomputer system.

ROMON Acronym for *receive-only monitor*.

ROM-oriented architecture A system in which the microprocessor instruction set can be executed completely from ROM without the need for external RAM. This system requires an internal stack for subroutines and internal registers for indirect addressing operations. The instruction set needs logical instructions for bit manipulation.

ROM/RAM A circuit containing a mask-programmable MOS ROM as well as a RAM, as shown in the following figure. The ROM/RAM is designed for applications requiring only a small amount of ROM and RAM. One specific unit has a ROM section of 704 words of eight bits, and a RAM of 76 words of four bits.

ROM/RAM/CPU A chip for low-cost applications that contains a processor along with RAM and ROM memories.

ROM self-test To check the contents of a ROM, the microprocessor reads out every word in the ROM and performs a cumulative parity check, an exclusive-OR operation on each bit. At the end, the result should be a one in every bit position of the accumulating register. If the specific microprocessor's instruction set doesn't include an exclusive-OR instruction, it can execute the equivalent operation in a subroutine. This self-test always

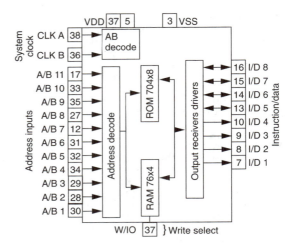

ROM/RAM

detects single errors, whole-word errors, data output lines stuck at one or zero, and address input lines stuck at one or zero. It sometimes detects address lines short-circuited to each other, output lines short-circuited to each other, and multiple random errors.

ROM simulator An instrument designed to replace ROM or PROM during program development and debugging. The instrument can be used to simulate PROM or ROM configurations and provide an inexpensive means of altering microprograms. The memory modules are loaded and verified through the ROM simulator or front-panel address and data switches. Simulation is achieved by extending control of the read-only function to the user's equipment using simulation cables.

root directory In many operating systems, the directory created on each disk or drive when it is formatted. Also called the "base" or "main" directory.

root segment The master or controlling segment of an overlay structure that resides in the main memory. The root segment is usually the first segment within the program, and it is always the first to be loaded at program initiation time.

ROS Abbreviation for *read-only storage*. See ROM.

rotate The process of moving each bit in a register in a circular manner, either to the right or the left. Each bit that leaves one end of the register enters the other end. Also called *circular shift*.

round The deletion of the least significant digits with or without modifications to reduce bias.

rounding error An error due to round-off.

round-off Deletion of the least significant digit or digits and adjustment of the part retained to reduce bias.

round-robin The cyclical multiplexing of a resource among jobs with fixed time slices.

roundtrip propagation time The worst-case bit time required for the transmitting node's collision-detect jam signal to propagate throughout the network. It is the two-way travel time because the transmitting node needs to receive acknowledgment from all the contending nodes. This delay is the primary component of slot time.

route hops In NetWare Diagnostic Services, the number of hops between the source bridge and the destination network or server of the most efficient route.

route 0 time In NetWare Diagnostic Services, the time it takes a packet to travel between the source bridge and the destination network or server on route 0.

router A hardware/software device that connects diverse networks such as token ring and Ethernet.

router hello A DECnet packet used by routers to let other nodes on the network know they are operating.

router 0 next board position In NetWare Diagnostic Services, indicates the position of the LAN board (inside router 0) that receives packets from the LAN board indicated in the preceding field.

router 0 node address In NetWare Diagnostic Services, the node address of the LAN board inside router 0 that receives packets from the source bridge.

route time In NetWare and other networks, the route time (between the source bridge and the destination network or server) of the most efficient route. The value in this field and the value returned in the NetWare "route 0 time" field are the same.

routine An ordered set of instructions used to direct the computer to perform one or more specific tasks or operations. A *closed routine* is one that is not entered as a block of instructions within the main routine, but entered by a linkage from the main routine. A *minimum-latency routine* operates in such a way that minimum waiting time is required to obtain information out of storage. A routine may be considered as a subdivision of a program with two or more instructions that are functionally related.

routine, correction *See* CORRECTION ROUTINE.

routine, floating-point *See* FLOATING-POINT ARITHMETIC.

routine, input *See* BOOTSTRAP.

routing The process for connecting data terminal equipment (DTE) and data communications equipment (DCE). It defines both the mechanical and electrical interfaces.

routing directory A database maintained by the network layer to determine which paths to use to get to particular networks.

Routing Information Protocol Protocol used in Novell's NetWare and Xerox's XNS to inform computers on a network of any changes in the topology of the network.

routing node In NetWare Workstation Services, the address of the preferred bridge to route through if a connection is not direct on the same network.

routing table maintenance protocol AppleTalk protocol for the maintenance of routing tables. Similar to RIP in Novell's NetWare and XNS.

routing tables A directory maintained by the network layer that contains the address of nodes on the internetwork and how to reach them.

row A horizontal arrangement of characters or other expressions.

RPC compiler A product sold by Netwise that allows programs written for a single computer to be distributed on the network.

RPC Abbreviation for *remote procedure call*, a set of network protocols that allow a node to call procedures that are executing on a remote machine. The Netwise RPC tool is an example of such a protocol.

RPC specification The information prepared by a programmer as input to the RPC compiler. The specification informs the compiler which procedures will be distributed.

RPC tool The RPC system sold by Netwise, including the RPC compiler.

RPG Abbreviation for *report program generator*, a problem-oriented language for commercial programming. Especially useful in smaller applications, RPG is like COBOL in having powerful and simple file manipulation capabilities, but it lacks algorithmic facility.

RR Abbreviation for *receive ready*, an LLC field indicating that the sending node is ready to receive data.

RS **1.** Abbreviation for *remote station*. **2.** Abbreviation for *record separator*, a control character used to separate and qualify data logically; it usually delimits a data item called a *record*.

R-S flip-flop A flip-flop consisting of two cross-coupled NAND gates and having two inputs, a *set* and a *reset*, as shown in the following diagram.

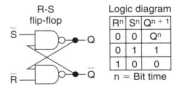

R-S flip-flop

R-S-T flip-flop A flip-flop that operates like an R-S flip-flop with an additional input (the trigger), which is used to cause the flip-flop to change states.

RS-232 cable test set A handheld cable tester suited to testing the 25-pin cables used on RS-232 interfaces, shown in the following figure. The graphic layout of the front panel mimics the physical layout of the actual connector to speed identification of pins. Fifty LEDs identify the active lines and continuity.

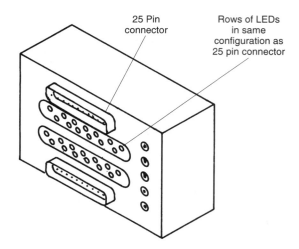

RS-232 cable test set

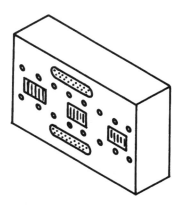

RS-232 interface test set

RS-232 compatible controller A module designed to interface a microcomputer system to most asynchronous modems. Baud rates include 2400, 4800, and 9600, with selectable words lengths from 5 to 8 bits and odd or even parity.

RS-232 fan-out unit A device constructed with two RS-232 connectors on a printed circuit board. All 25 pin positions or leads are exposed. Use of the fan-out enables data communication users to monitor or produce any or all RS-232 pin positions. These pin positions are available via test pin posts located along the PC board.

RS-232 interface 1. An interface standard designated by EIA and spelled out in *Standard RS-232*. RS-232 is an EIA standard applicable to the 25-pin interconnection of data terminal equipment (DTE) and data communications equipment (DCE) employing serial binary data exchange. RS-232 has been the most widely accepted interface in computer and data communications technology; it is essentially the same as the CCITT's V.24. *Also see* V.24. **2.** An interface used to connect a modem or printer with associated equipment that is standardized by EIA standard RS-232.

RS-232 interface test set An RS-232 test set (shown in the following figure) that allows configuring and testing of most interfaces without using any jumpers. Signal crossover and control substitution are available with a switch. Dedicated monitors for the 11 major RS-232 signals allow use for asynchronous and synchronous applications. Monitor LEDs are interface-powered to locate weak transmitter circuits.

RS-232 line drivers Used in pairs, these limited-distance modems are ideal for long RS-232 cable runs such as one end of the building to another, floor to floor, and building to building. They will operate up to 1½ miles at 19.2K baud and further at lower data rates. Powered entirely by your equipment interface, all you have to do is plug them in and flip the DTE/DCE switch to match your interface. They have 25-pin female connectors for the asynchronous RS-232 interface side and quick-connect screw terminals for the line side.

RS-232 line protector Data communications lines are often subject to harm from static shocks and induced voltage spikes. These are serious problems that can shorten the life of equipment. An RS-232 line protector uses 10 metal-oxide varistors, which clamp high voltage spikes to within safe levels. They install directly on the output ports of the equipment you are protecting.

RS-232/422 expansion board An I/O expansion board for the PC, designed to plug into one I/O slot. The board interfaces to the RS-422, RS-232, or current loop serial interface bus through a 25-pin (RS-232 and current loop) or 9-pin (RS-422) D connector. The RS-232 interface includes standard bus control protocols (data set ready, clear to send, data terminal ready and others).

RS-232/422 PS/2 interface board An I/O expansion board for the IBM PS/2 models 50 through 80 designed to plug into a Micro Channel bus slot. These boards can be configured to operate either as an RS-232 or as an RS-422 interface, but not both concurrently. The user can choose to use control protocols (data set ready, clear to send, data terminal ready for the RS-232, or clear to send and request to send for the RS-422) or to employ only the data transmit and receive lines. Applications include instrument interfaces, industrial controller interfaces, printer/plotter interfaces, and interfaces to networks.

RS-422 interface An interface standard, operating in conjunction with RS-449, that specifies electrical characteristics for balanced circuits with their own ground leads.

RS-422-232 interface adapter A unit that provides electrical and mechanical interconnection of RS-232 interface circuits with RS-422 interface circuits, shown in the following figure.

RS-422 interface adapter

RS-423 A standard, operating in conjunction with RS-449, that specifies electrical characteristics for unbalanced circuits using common or shared grounding techniques.

RS-449 A bus standard that accommodates data rates as high as 2M per second. It introduces a few more signals than RS-232 and uses two connectors: a 37-pin unit for the most frequently used signals and a 9-pin unit for a secondary channel. A single 37-pin connector is used in most applications. RS-449 is intended to replace RS-232C. In the meantime, new equipment conforming to the RS-449 standard will require an adapter to mate to RS-232 devices. Some applications may require cables with 36-, 9-, and 25-pin connectors to interconnect newer and older equipment. The RS-449 standard adapter requires resistors for the logic conversion.

RS-449 interface adapter A unit that performs the necessary adjustments between RS-449 and RS-232 to allow interconnection. Electrical, functional, and mechanical considerations are implemented in accordance with the EIA recommended procedure for interconnection between interface circuits using RS-449 and RS-232.

RS-449 interface family Another EIA standard along with RS-232, the RS-449 family of interfaces is applicable to the 37- and 9-pin interconnection of data terminal equipment (DTE) and data communications equipment (DCE) employing serial binary data interchange. RS-449 is comprised of two electrical standards, RS-422 and RS-423. The RS-422 interface facilitates balance transmission, while transmission is unbalanced on the RS-423 interface. Generally, the RS-422 interface provides for faster transmission over longer distances than the RS-423 interface.

RS-485 interface board A board that allows PCs to be networked over the RS-485 bus. Unlike the RS-422 bus, which allows multiple receivers but only a single transmitter on the bus, the RS-485 standard allows multiple transmitters and receivers to communicate over a two-wire bus, allowing a party-line type of network configuration. The board may be set up as a COM1 or COM2 standard serial interface port, or can be set at any base-address/interrupt-level combination desired.

RT Abbreviation for *research and technology*.

RTC Abbreviation for *relative time clock*, a clock system used to allow the executive to keep track of time and service interrupts. At every relative time-clock interrupt, the program control is returned to the executive, which determines the priority of action. *Also see* EXECUTIVE.

RTD Abbreviation for *resistance temperature detector*, sensors that operate on the principle that the resistance of a material to electric current flow is temperature-dependent. The resistance of metals used as sensing elements increases with increasing temperature, as shown in the figure, while most semiconductor materials decrease in resistance. One component of the total resistivity is due to impurities and is known as *residual resistivity*. It is lowest for the pure metals. The residual resistivity can change if the RTD is used at too high a temperature or if the wire is contaminated by the environment or materials in contact with the wire.

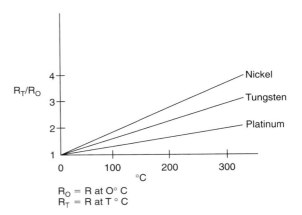

$R_O = R$ at $0°$ C
$R_T = R$ at $T°$ C

Temperature dependence of common RTD materials

RTE Abbreviation for *real-time executive*, a multitasking program system that can handle all aspects of priority scheduling, interrupt servicing, input/output control, intertask communications, and queuing functions. Executives are designed for operation with specific microcomputer systems. Tasks operating under executive supervision provide the mechanism to real-time events. The occurrence of an event typically results in the scheduling of a response task. This scheduling is performed using a priority structure that associates each task with a distinct priority level. A given task may be interrupted while in the process of execution and temporarily suspended while a higher-priority task is executed.

RTF Abbreviation for *radio telephone*.

RTL Abbreviation for *resistor-transistor logic*, a logic family that uses discrete transistors with resistive coupling.

RTM Abbreviation for *register transfer module*, a functional register unit designed for the construction of register logic systems.

RTM 1000 A menu-driven extension of DOS that allows a PC user to receive, display (digitally or in graphic form), and log (to disk or printer) data acquired from the MetraBus family of I/O boards. Acquisition, analysis, and display is performed in real time. The foreground/background capability of the package allows the operator to be using the computer for a task in the foreground while the process control, monitoring, and data logging continues in the background.

The package maintains a real-time database that is divided into columns referred to as *display cells* or *slots*. In addition to the current values, 15 cells of historical data are also maintained, and can be operated on by other cells or can be logged to disk or printer in case of an alarm condition.

RTMP Abbreviation for *routing table maintenance protocol*, the AppleTalk protocol for the maintenance of routing tables. RTMP is similar to RIP in Novell's NetWare and XNS.

RTOS Abbreviation for *real-time operating system*, a comprehensive software operating system designed to support the microcomputer in dedicated real-time applications. The system usually includes a system generation program, input/output routines, and analog-to-digital conversion routines.

RTS Abbreviation for *request to send*, one of the basic data set interchange leads defined in the EIA Standard RS-232. A DTE (data terminal equipment) sends an RTS signal requesting clearance to transmit.

rubidium clock An atomic clock using the element rubidium to produce a stable, accurate timing source.

ruly English A language based on English in which every word has one and only one meaning, and each concept has one and only one word to describe it.

run The performance of one computer program or several routines linked together so that they form an operating unit. Usually during a run, manual operations are minimal; a typical run may involve loading, reading, processing, and writing.

runaway A condition that arises when one of the parameters of a physical system undergoes a large, sudden, undesirable, and often destructive increase.

run book The material needed to document a computer application, including problem statement, flowcharts, and coding and operating instructions.

run indicator A device used to indicate that the processor is in a run mode.

run-length encoding A data-encoding method where the stripping of characters occurs if they appear three consecutive times. This is done to condense the data for transmission.

run switch A switch that allows the processor to begin instruction execution, beginning at the address contained in the program counter.

runtime The time required to complete a single, continuous execution of an object program.

runtime error A program error not detected in the process of translation, but which causes a processing error to occur during execution.

runt frame An Ethernet frame that is too short. A runt frame has fewer than the 60 bytes in the data fields required by the IEEE 802.3. If the frame length is less than 53 bytes, a runt frame indicates a normal collision. A frame less than 60 bytes, but at least 53 bytes, indicates a late collision.

RVI Abbreviation for *reverse interrupt*, a transmission control character sent by a receiving station to request termination of the current transmission because of a higher-priority message it must send.

RWI Abbreviation for *read or write initialize*.

RWM Abbreviation for *read-write memory*, a memory that can be altered at will.

R/W RAM refresh Dynamic read-write RAMs require refreshing. The refresh process can create problems in I/O-to-memory and CPU-to-memory interaction. The balancing of the CPU, asynchronous-memory refresh, and real-time semi-asynchronous I/O memory bandwidth demands must be solved in the system design.

R/W RAM volatility Refers to the volatility of the data in R/W semiconductor RAMs. While this problem can be overcome with a battery backup power subsystem, the cost, complexity, and inconvenience of such a subsystem can prohibit its use.

RX Abbreviation for *receiver*.

RX-Net Novell's version of ARCNet.

RY Abbreviation for *relay*.

RZ Abbreviation for *return to zero*.

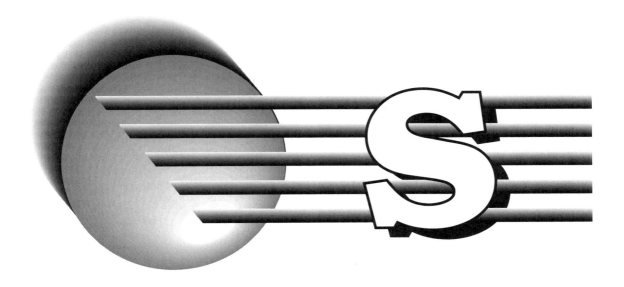

S **1.** Abbreviation for *store*. **2.** Abbreviation for *spool*.

SAA Abbreviation for *System Application Architecture*, IBM's product for a common programming interface between the IBM different operating systems.

SAC Abbreviation for *store and clear*.

safeguard timer A system for fault detection. A hardware timer is run continuously; it is periodically reset if nothing delays the main program within its appointed window of time. If an error causes the main program to be delayed, the timer is not reset, and an error is detected.

SAM Acronym for *status activity monitor*, a device that gives an indication of signal activity by monitoring leads with LEDs. Many SAM units have the ability to both monitor and modify an interface. This capability can be very useful when working with a known set of interface signals.

Samna Word (*o.t.*) A DOS-based word processor, the precursor to Ami Pro.

sample A measurement of a particular property at a specific point in time and/or space.

sampled data Data in which the information content can be, or is, ascertained only at discrete intervals of time.

sample-hold A circuit used to increase the interval during which a sampled signal is available by maintaining an output equal to the most recent input sample, as shown in the following diagram.

sample-hold acquisition time The time in a sample-hold from when the sample command is given to the point when the output enters and remains within a specified band around the input value. At the end of the acquisition time, the output is tracking the input.

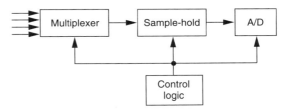

Data acquisition system with sample-hold

sample-hold amplifier An amplifier that can increase both the system data acquisition throughput rate and the highest frequency signal that can be encoded within the converter resolution. System throughput rate without the sample-hold is determined mainly by the multiplexer's settling time and the A/D conversion time.

sample-hold aperture time The time between the hold command and the point at which the sampling switch is completely open. Also called *turn-off time*.

sample-hold aperture uncertainty time The variation in the aperture time. The difference between the maximum and minimum aperture times.

sample-hold applications In data acquisition systems, sample-holds are used either to hold fast signals during conversion or to store multiplexer outputs while the signal is being converted and the multiplexer is seeking the next channel. In analog data-reduction, sample-holds are used to determine peaks or valleys, establish amplitudes, and allow computations involving signals obtained at different times.

sample-hold characteristics An ideal sample-hold, or *zero-order hold* as it is also called, takes a sample in zero time and then holds the value of the sample indefinitely with perfect accuracy. In practical devices, a sample is taken in a time period that is short compared to the holding time. During the holding time, there is some change in the output that might effect the system accuracy. The effect on a continuous analog input signal can be determined by finding the transfer function of the sample-hold, shown in the following figure.

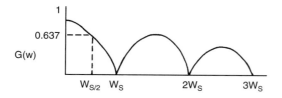

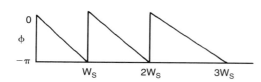

Sample-held transfer function

By use of the impulse response of the device and the Laplace transform method, the transfer function is found for the ideal sample hold:

$$G(jw) = \frac{2\pi}{w_s} \frac{\sin \pi w/w_s}{\pi w/w_s} e^{-j \pi (w/w_s)}$$

where T is the sampling period and w_s is the sampling frequency. The magnitude and phase of this function show that the sample-hold acts like a low-pass filter with a cutoff frequency of approximately $f^s/2$ and a phase delay of $T/2$, or half the sampling period.

sample-hold counting Counting that uses a DAC (digital-to-analog converter), an up-down counter, a comparator clock, and logic gates. The initial acquisition time can be very long, since the clock period (t^s) depends on the LSB (least-significant bit) settling time of the D/A converter, and the number of counts (n) depends on the resolution. For a fullscale step, the acquisition time is approximately $(2/n - 1)t^s$. Smaller, slower changes are followed rapidly. The system can also be converted into a peak follower by disabling the up-count function. The range of input signal levels and polarity will determine the choice of D/A converter. A BCD (binary-coded decimal) counter and BCD DAC can be used with a display for a maximum peak digital voltmeter.

sample-hold decay rate The change in output voltage with time in the hold mode.

sample-hold device A device with a signal input, an output, and a control input. It has two operating modes: the hold mode and the sample (or track) mode, in which it acquires the input signal and tracks it until commanded to hold, at which time it retains the value of the input signal at the time the control mode changed. Sample holds are also known as *track holds* if a large portion of time has been spent in the sample mode tracking the input. Sample holds normally have unity gain and are noninverting. The control inputs are usually TTL-compatible. Logic 1 is usually the sample command, and logic 0 is the hold command.

A sample-hold in its basic form consists of a switch and a capacitor. When the switch is closed, the unit is in the sampling or tracking mode and will follow the changing input signal. When the switch is opened, the unit is in the hold mode and retains a voltage on the capacitor for a period of time, depending on capacitor size and leakage resistance. Practical sample-hold circuits may also use input and output buffer amplifiers along with sophisticated switching techniques. The output buffer amplifier should be a low-input-current FET amplifier in order to have a small effect on leakage of the capacitor. The electronic switch used should also have a low leakage. *Also see* CURRENT-SOURCE SAMPLE HOLD.

sample-hold feedthrough The amount of input signal appearing at the output when the unit is in the hold mode. Feedthrough varies with signal frequency and is sometimes expressed as an attenuation in decibels.

sample-hold settling time The time from the command transition until the output has settled within a specified error band around the final value.

sampling 1. Obtaining the values of a usually analog function by making automatic measurements of the function at periodic intervals, as shown in the diagram. Each sample thus obtained becomes a digital value and is processed with digital circuitry. **2.** A representative value of a population of values.

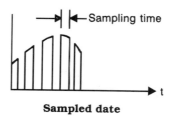

Sampled date

sampling gate A device activated by a selector pulse, usually to extract instantaneous-value information for a system.

sampling oscilloscope An oscilloscope in which the input waveform is sampled at successive points along the waveform instead of being monitored continuously.

sampling period The time between observations in a periodic sampling system.

sampling rate The clock frequency for sampling, or the number of samples per second.

sampling thermocouple A device for collecting samples of the gas stream at two or more locations and mixing the samples at the thermocouple junction so that an average temperature will be indicated.

sapphire A material used as a substrate for some types of integrated-circuit chips. Silicon-on-sapphire chips have reduced parasitics and permit tighter geometries for high-speed applications.

SAP 1. Abbreviation for *Service Advertisement Protocol*, the NetWare protocol for publicizing the current network address of services. **2.** Abbreviation for *service access point*, the address of the user of a service according to IEEE 802 specifications.

SAS Acronym for *statistical analysis system*, a trademark for an integrated system of programs written in PL/1, designed for extensive data analysis, including data modification, programming, report writing, statistical analysis, and file handling.

satellite computer 1. A computer connected to a larger computer and performing simple tasks or time-consuming operations, as shown in the diagram. A satellite computer is usually subordinate to the central processor, although sometimes independent. **2.** An earth-orbiting system consisting principally of a usually dedicated computer or processor.

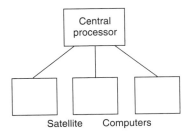

Satellite computer system, 1

satellite transmission A transmission path in which the data is transmitted to a satellite and relayed back to the receiving unit. Because of the vast distances involved, satellite transmission involves delays up to 800 ms receiving replies to handshaking signals, so modems have special options to work with satellites.

saturated color A color as far from white, black, or gray as possible; for example, vermilion rather than pink.

saturating integrator *See* INCREMENTAL INTEGRATOR.

saturation 1. In an amplifier, a condition in which an increase in the input signal no longer produces a significant change in the output. This is in contrast to the cutoff point, where usually negative-going signal inputs in excess of the cutoff-point value cause the amplifier to shut off momentarily. Linear amplifiers are operated in the relatively linear region between the two extremes. **2.** The condition of maximum signal-carrying ability in any medium.

saturation current The current that flows between the base and collector of a transistor when an increase in the emitter-to-base voltage causes no further increase in the collector current.

saturation limiting Limiting the maximum output of an active device by operating the device in the region of saturation. When the input signal increases, saturation occurs immediately and the output is held at approximately the value of saturation.

saturation noise 1. Extra bits or words that can be removed or ignored before the data is used without affecting the data represented. **2.** Errors introduced into a system due to disturbances occurring when the signal-carrying medium is at saturation. *Also see* NOISE.

save A command that copies the data in a computer's memory onto disk or tape.

save buffer In NetWare, a 16-byte buffer that contains information on the volume and directory pointed to by a directory handle.

sawtooth A triangular waveform consisting of a fairly linear voltage or current ramp of ascending value that returns abruptly to the original value.

sawtooth generator An oscillator-type circuit used to produce a sawtooth waveform (shown in the figure), usually at some specific frequency or within a specific frequency range.

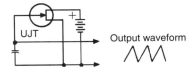

Sawtooth generator

sawtooth wave A signal composed entirely of a recurring sawtooth, such as the type used to establish the timebase in a cathode-ray oscilloscope. Also called *sawtooth waveform*.

SB386 A CPU in a plug-in format designed for use in industrial applications. The feature of a basic AT-compatible PC are included on the single-board design, centered around the Intel 80386DX chip and the VLSI/Intel 82340DX chip set. The SB386 fits into any passive backplane of the ISA configuration. All standard AT-compatible options and accessories may be used with the unit.

SC Abbreviation for *shift control*.

scalar Having a value that may be plotted on a graduated scale.

scalar product The product of two quantities that itself has magnitude but no direction. In the example *force × distance = work*, two vector quantities produce the scalar product, *work*.

scalar quantity A quantity that has magnitude without direction, such as a real number.

scale 1. A range of values usually dictated by the computer word length or the routine being processed. 2. To change the units of a variable so that the quantity may be measured by a system whose limits are in a different range. Scaling can bring the values of a variable within the bounds required by register size or other factors. 3. Any value range that permits identification of any incremental value within that range, such as a temperature scale.

scale factor A value used to convert the magnitude of a variable to a usable value in another range or to convert from one notation to another. Scale factors are often used to adjust the radix point so that the significant digits occupy specified positions in a word or register. *Also see* RADIX.

scaler 1. A unit that produces an output equal to the input multiplied by a constant. 2. A converter used at the input of a device (such as a frequency meter) to bring the quantity being measured to within the range of measurement of the instrument (a *frequency scaler*, for example).

scale span The algebraic difference between the values of the actuating electrical quantity that corresponds to the two ends of the scale of an instrument.

scaling 1. The changing of a quantity from one notation to another, or from one value range to another, using scale factors, as shown. 2. Refers to the uniform reduction or enlargement of dimensions in an image.

scamp Loose acronym for a *small cost-effective microprocessor*, in which addresses are generated by four 16-bit pointer registers with processor timing generated on the chip.

scan 1. To examine sequentially using a part-by-part technique. 2. The successive trace-and-flyback operation required to produce a raster or image on a screen, as shown in the following figures. A high scanning frequency produces more scanning lines and improves the resolution.

scan converters Units needed when resolving PC-to-video problems. Scan converters plug into the output of a computer's graphics adapter. These

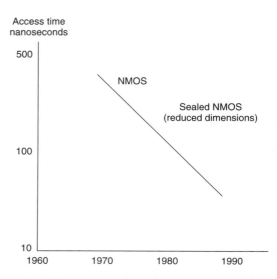

The effect of scaling on dynamic MOS RAM speed

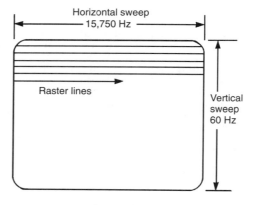

Horizontal sweep

devices help to display presentations on large monitors or record computer images to a VCR. External converters are available for DOS and Mac platforms. Some units automatically adapt to the timing of the Mac or DOS computer's output, converting it to composite and S-video signals. Computer images can be displayed simultaneously on a monitor and sent to a videotape recorder. Flicker filters are another feature. A typical unit supports resolutions to 1,024 × 768, magnification with panning, 24-bit RGB processing, and digital encoding.

scan line A complete horizontal row of pixels on the display surface.

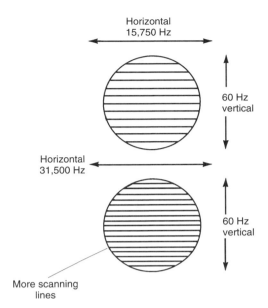

Scanning frequency

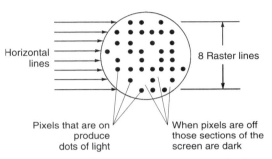

Closeup view of raster lines and pixels

scanner 1. A device that senses and interprets printed or handwritten symbols and converts the information into machine-language code. The scanner views images that are illuminated by a light. The brightness of the image is sampled at many points and digitized into data that are compatible with the computer. In a *pixel scan*, the display allows the analyst to observe the image being viewed and processed. A mouse or similar cursor controller allows the user to point to any pixel as a single bit.

Scanners are separated by type: flatbed, drum, handheld, and film. Flatbed scanners are medium-priced units usually operating at standards of 300 dpi to 1,200 dpi, with three-pass scanners offering better image quality than one-pass units. Drum scanners are high-performance units designed for professional publishing. Hand-held scanners are at the other end of the spectrum, with low cost and limited use. Film scanners are designed for slide-oriented needs. They can handle 35mm slides, transparencies, and normal-sized prints. The average price is about double that of flatbed scanners. **2.** A device that samples or interrogates the state of a process or processes, including files and physical conditions. It then may initiate action or cause another device to initiate action based upon the information obtained. A typical scanner might connect a specified sensor to measuring or monitoring equipment for transmission to the processor.

scanning frequency The scanning in the CRT takes place using the timing of the monitor's sweep circuits. A higher scanning frequency produces more scanning lines. The scanning must be in sync with the computer's clock.

scanning lines In a CRT, the beams scan the face of the tube line-by-line from the top down. As the scanning takes place, each dot is switched either on or off, as shown in the figure. This scanning is done by the video circuits that control or focus the beam.

scanning rate The speed per unit time at which a scanner operates. Also called *scan rate*.

scattering A phenomenon in which waves or particles are reflected or dispersed irregularly, such as in acoustic waves in an enclosure leading to a diffuse reverberant sound.

scattering loss The loss of energy from a beam of radiation as a result of various scattering processes arising either at a surface of discontinuity or in the medium traversed.

scatter load A method of loading a program into main memory such that each section occupies a single connected memory area without the sections being adjacent to one another. The sections are usually a page, and the system is usually implemented with a virtual memory structure. Also called *scatter read*.

SCE Abbreviation for *single cycle execute*.

scheduled maintenance Maintenance that is carried out in accordance with an established plan.

schema An organization plan that helps people view the logical setup of a database.

Schema Generator A program that provides pick lists that allow only certain data types and constraints for the selected target database. Several SQL options are supported, including the ability to specify a primary or foreign key and force uppercase or lowercase field types, names, and commands.

schematic A diagram that uses symbols to show components and their interconnections for a system or circuit. A schematic diagram permits tracing of circuit and flow paths for continuity.

Schmitt limiter A bistable pulse generator that gives a constant amplitude output pulse provided that the input voltage is greater than a predetermined value.

Schmitt trigger A monostable circuit (shown in the figure) that has a sensitive, accurate, and stable trigger level. It is often used to restore pulses and pulse information.

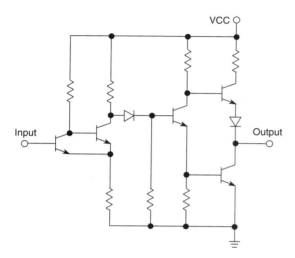

Schmitt trigger circuit

Schmoo plot A graphical representation of the relative output parameter failure condition resulting from varying two input parameters at the same time. This graph facilitates the establishment of an operating envelope within which input parameters may be varied without resulting in circuit or system failure due to parameter interdependence.

Schottky barrier 1. In a hot-carrier diode, the metal-semiconductor junction. 2. A hot-carrier diode junction incorporated into some TTL devices to increase switching speed (transit times) and reduce system noise.

Schottky bipolar TTL (transistor-transistor logic) devices that use a Schottky clamping diode to prevent transistor saturation and improve switching speeds. With the use of integrated Schottky diodes, the saturation delay normally encountered is avoided. The process is simple and does not have a significant effect upon manufacturing costs.

Schottky bipolar decoders Systems that use input ports, output ports, and memory components with active low chip-select input can be expanded with these bipolar decoders. When the unit is enabled, one of its eight or more outputs goes low, selecting a single row of a memory system. One unit has three chip-enable inputs on the decoder, which allows easy system expansion. In large systems, decoders can be used in sets, with each decoder driving eight or more other decoders for memory.

Schottky bipolar latch A latch circuit designed with the Schottky TTL process. It is used where high speed is important.

Schottky bipolar look-ahead carry A high-speed circuit capable of anticipating a carry across the central processing array. In systems with multiple arrays, the carry circuit can provide high-speed look-ahead capability for any word length.

Schottky bipolar memory A memory that uses Schottky barrier diodes to obtain fast switching speeds, as shown in the diagram. Their high speed makes them ideal for scratchpad applications.

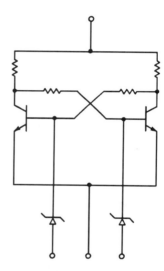

Schottky bipolar memory

Schottky bipolar microcomputer A set of bipolar chips designed with the Schottky bipolar process for high speed. A typical microcomputer set of this variety includes

- Central processing elements
- Bipolar PROM
- Microprogram control units

Schottky bipolar microcomputer chips can be much faster than MOS chips. The chips allow a design that is fast, but smaller and less expensive than equivalent designs using SSI or MSI integration. Schottky microcomputer chip sets have two major components—the microprogram control unit (MCU), and the central processing element (CPE). These can be combined with a bipolar memory to construct controller-processors using a minimum of auxiliary logic.

A programmable microcontroller can provide the best features of both program controllers and microprocessors. These systems can be used in high-speed instruments, control systems, and data-processing acquisition systems. A unit can be put on a single circuit board and can perform eight-bit binary or four-bit BCD arithmetic; it can test individual bits and perform data manipulation. A typical unit might have the following components:

- A 32-word by 8-bit register file
- A LIFO (last-in, fast-out) stack of 16 levels for nesting subroutines
- High-speed multilevel interrupt capability
- Parallel and serial input/output
- Field-programmable ROM of 1,000 words for program memory, expandable to 4,000 words

Available development aids include a control console for program development. A typical CPE can be used in an array of eight to construct a 16-bit controller-processor.

Schottky bipolar ROM A ROM manufactured using Schottky barrier-diode clamped transistors, which allows higher switching speeds than those devices made with a conventional gold diffusion process.

Schottky-clamped transistor A bipolar transistor that is limited by a Schottky diode to prevent saturation and improve switching speeds.

Schottky diode A hot-carrier diode that has a short recovery time and a low forward-voltage drop. It is formed by the metal-to-semiconductor contact at the surface of the crystal.

Schottky effect Refers to the increase of saturation with an increasing potential gradient near the cathode.

Schottky process The manufacturing process used to produce Schottky diodes in bipolar circuits. The process is simple and does not have significant effects upon manufacturing costs.

Schottky TTL Transistor-transistor logic devices that use Schottky diodes for improved speed performance.

Schottky II A TTL process that uses ion-implanted techniques and minimum geometry to extend the performance of Schottky devices into the one-nanosecond range. A Schottky II microprocessor chip set with a cycle time of 50 ns is available.

Schottky, Walter Rectifying metal semiconductor contacts were discovered and investigated by Ferdinand Braun in 1874. Despite many attempts to understand their current flow mechanism, the correct physical model was not discovered until half a century later by Walter Schottky. Researchers at Bell Labs in the late 1940s were investigating metal semiconductor interfaces when they accidentally discovered the transistor. From then on, most efforts in the semiconductor industry have been directed toward pn-junction devices. Only in the recent past have manufacturers gained the understanding of surface phenomena and developed the metalization techniques required to produce reliable Schottky barrier diodes.

scintillation In radio propagation, a random fluctuation of the received field about its mean value. The deviations usually are relatively small.

SC/MP Abbreviation for *simple cost-effective microprocessor*, a microprocessor developed by National Semiconductor. A simple SC/MP system can be constructed with three integrated circuit packages. The timing capacitor is connected to the CPU for clock timing; a ROM and RAM complete the system along with the power source. This system has three serial data input ports and four serial data output ports for applications like games, traffic controls, simple industrial controllers, appliances, and vending machines.

SC/MP expansion The input/output capability of the SC/MP unit may be increased by adding the three CMOS devices shown. To increase the number of serial data input and output ports, a hex D flip-flop, an eight-channel digital multiplexer, and a 1-to-8 demultiplexer are added.

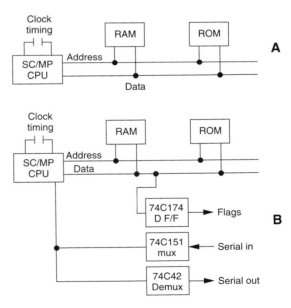

Basic (A) and expanded (B) SC/MP microcomputer system

This system has four latched control flags and can address 4K bytes of memory. It can be used to implement industrial controls with up to eight loops or complex traffic controllers.

SC/MP multiprocessing The SC/MP chip has two control lines that allow implementation of a multiprocessor system. The CPUs are tied together through two enable control lines. When a CPU requires the bus, it requests access to the bus and then waits for a bus enable signal. Until the CPU receives this signal, it waits with its address and data buses in the high impedance state. This provides the user with the flexibility of adding extra processors to achieve additional throughput without changing the processor or software.

SC/MP programmed delay A delay instruction that is useful in control interfaces for I/O, as shown. For this serial interface, SIN is the receive data line and SOUT the send data line. A single control word contains a start bit, data bits, and a stop bit. The delay instruction may be used to cause a delay of time according to the formula

$$\text{delay} = 13 + 2 \times \text{accumulator} + 514 \times \text{displacement}$$

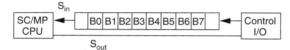

SC/MP programmed timing delay

SC/MP II An NMOS version of the original SC/MP PMOS microprocessor. Also called *INS8060 microprocessor*.

SCR Abbreviation for *silicon-controlled rectifier*, a three-junction rectifying device that is triggered by means of a voltage applied to a gate terminal. The SCR is a member of the *thyristor* family of devices, which includes diacs, triacs, and a variety of four-layer diodes.

scratchpad An area of computer memory used to hold temporary results or data in an intermediate state of computation. It is usually the fastest memory in the system. Also called *quick-access memory* or *temporary storage*.

screen 1. The face of a video monitor on which graphic or other visual material is displayed. **2.** To sift or cull a collection of data or data elements for the purpose of extracting only those of use in a subsequent process or operation.

screen layout form A form used by systems analysts and programmers to design the screen output.

screensaver A "slide show" displayed on a computer screen to reduce the potential of burn-in because a particular image has sat on the screen too long. Also called a *screenshow*.

screen size The diagonal width in inches of the monitor's display screen. Monitors are often categorized by screen size.

screw terminal accessory board A board that connects accessory boards to the system. Equipped with five-volt power, some accessory boards also have a small breadboard that lets you construct custom circuits.

scroll To move all or part of the screen material up or down, left or right, to allow new information to appear.

scrollbar A box at the side or a bar that lets you scroll using a mouse.

scrollbox A box in the scrollbar that indicates the position of the current page and can be dragged by the mouse to change pages. Sometimes called a *thumb*.

SCSI Abbreviation (pronounced "scuzzy") for *small computer system interface*, a specification for a popular type of peripheral controller. Apple Corporation was one of the first to use the SCSI disk controllers, and it is now widely available for most PCs. It allows you to easily add a number of drives and other peripherals.

SCSI board A board originally designed to provide high-speed data transfers for military or ruggedized environments. Typically used for applications requiring intensive real-time disk I/O activity with a minimum of bus loading. In some boards, an onboard processor manages all local resources, including DMA (direct-memory access) and SCSI control.

SCT Abbreviation for *subroutine call table*.

SD Abbreviation for *sample delay*.

SDA Abbreviation for *source data automation*, the recording of information in coded form on a medium that may be used again and again without rewriting to produce other records of the data.

S/D converter Abbreviation for *synchro-to-digital converter*.

SDLC Abbreviation for *synchronous data link control*, a standard protocol used in data transmission.

SDO Abbreviation for *source data operation*.

sealed circuits Circuits that use components that are sealed in place.

search A function in an application in which specific material is located in memory.

search algorithm An algorithm developed for minimizing the number of accesses needed to find an item in RAM. The time required to find an item in memory can be reduced if the stored data can be identified by the content of the data rather than the address.

search-and-replace A program facility that allows a user to enter a phrase or word to be found and a corresponding replacement text. In a *global replace*, all occurrences of the phrase are found and automatically replaced. In a *discretionary replace*, replacement of each occurrence of the word is decided by the user.

search attributes In NetWare File Services, a bit field that specifies the type of file, as follows:

1. Normal files
2. Normal and hidden files
3. Normal, hidden, and system files

search-bit map In the AppleTalk Filing Protocol, this determines what kinds of subdirectories and/or files to search for. The following bits are defined:

1. Low byte
2. Hidden files and directories
3. System files and directories
4. Subdirectories
5. Files

search index A method used in NetWare to keep track of the results of a request that returns more than one value. When one value is returned, as in the case of a directory search for filenames, the packet also contains a search index value. The search index value is submitted with the next search request, and the next filename will be returned.

search path A mechanism in DOS and other operating systems that allows a user to specify a command without knowing which directory it is stored in. The operating system will search each of the directories in the search path for the command until it finds the file.

search procedure The strategy for choosing a sequence of addresses, reading the content of memory at each address, and comparing the data read with the item being searched for until a match occurs.

SECAM Acronym for *sequential couleur avec memoire*, the color-television broadcast system of France, Russia, and other countries.

second The international unit of time and equal to the duration of 9,192,631,770 periods of the radiation corresponding to the transition between the two hyperfine levels of the ground state of the cesium-133 atom.

secondary **1.** Any output winding of any transformer that contains multiple windings. **2.** Relating to the second order in a string of ordinally identified functions or values.

secondary channel A logical channel using the same physical path as the main channel, but independent of it. It usually runs at a lower data rate and is used for control signals on HDX systems.

secondary constants Those constants for a transmission line that are derived from the primary constants. They are the characteristic impedance of the line and the propagation constants (attenuation and phase).

secondary grid emission The electrons released by bombarding electrons; dependent on the surface of the grid material.

secondary-level address That portion of an instruction that indicates a location where the address of the referenced operand is to be found. Multiple levels of addressing can be terminated by control or by a termination symbol.

secondary storage A general term for storage other than the computer's main memory; it usually has a large capacity, but a long access time. Disks and tapes are examples of secondary storage.

secondary winding See *secondary*.

second DMA channels used In the NetWare File Server Environment, a list of the DMA controllers a disk driver uses to control a disk channel.

second DMA channels used in flag In the NetWare File Server Environment, a flag for the DMA channels used field.

second-generation computer (*o.t.*) A computer developed in the late 1950s that used transistors as part of the processing hardware. It contained core memory, used an operating system, and was programmed in high-level programming languages.

second interrupt numbers used In the NetWare File Server Environment, this contains interrupt numbers a disk driver uses to communicate with a disk channel.

second interrupt numbers used in use flag In the NetWare File Server Environment, a flag for the second interrupt numbers used.

second IO address used In the NetWare File Server Environment, this contains addresses a disk driver uses to control a disk channel.

second IO address uses length In the NetWare File Server Environment, this contains the lengths of the addresses a disk driver uses to control a disk channel.

second-level addressing A type of addressing in which instructions use a referenced location for the address of the operand.

second-level protocol Sometimes called "line discipline" or "data link control," it is an orderly set of rules controlling the transmission of data between two physically connected devices.

second shared memory address In the NetWare File Server Environment, this is a field a disk driver uses to control a disk channel.

second shared memory address length In NetWare File Server Environment, this contains the length of a shared memory addresses.

second-source To manufacture a product designed, developed, and also produced by another manufacturer. Second-sourcing originated from the reluctance of the government to purchase devices available from only one maker.

section A length of coaxial cable that forms the transmission medium for a network. Sections are interconnected to form a *segment*.

sector The smallest addressable space on a disk's media. A sector is the evenly divided subsections on a track that hold the stored data or programs.

sector header A block of data that appears at the beginning of each sector on a disk. Information in the sector header lists the sector's physical address, including the track number, surface number, and sector number around the track.

sectors per block In NetWare Directory Services, the number of 512-byte sectors in each block of a volume.

sectors per track In the NetWare File Server Environment, this is the number of sectors on each disk track (1 sector = 512 bytes).

secure voice Refers to telephone communications that are protected through the use of an encryption system.

security The safeguarding of computer information or data.

security mailers A mailer for sensitive data diskettes with security seals that must be broken for access.

seek 1. The process of locating specific data in a random-access store. A seek refers to each memory location searched, and the number of seeks determines the total search time. 2. To search a memory array.

seek time The time required to locate data in a direct-access storage device, including the time needed to position the access mechanism.

segment 1. To divide a routine into parts, with each one capable of being completely stored in internal storage and containing the necessary instructions to jump to other segments. 2. A part of a routine short enough to be sorted entirely in the internal storage of a computer, yet containing the coding necessary to call in and jump to other segments. A segment can be placed anywhere in memory and addressed relative to a common origin. 3. One of the components of a single-character numeric or alphanumeric display. *Also see* SEVEN-SEGMENT DISPLAY.

segmentation overlays A segment of a program is that portion of memory that is defined by a single reference to the loader. Usually a segment overlays some other segment and may have within itself other portions, called *subsegments*, that in turn overlay one another. That part of a segment that is actually brought into memory when the loader is referenced is called the fixed part of a segment. Segments are built up from separate relocatable elements, common blocks, or other segments.

segmented instruction addressing An addressing technique used in microcomputers where the ROM is subdivided into pages and other segments. The size is determined by the number of bits that can be contained in the instruction word. For example, six bits could be reserved for the address within a page of 64 words.

segment number In NetWare Bindery Services, a counting field used with Read Property Value and Write Property Value.

segment registers Registers that extend the addressability of the memory beyond the instruction word limit. Extensions beyond the word length are accomplished by adding additional bits to the address. Special instructions may be dedicated to the manipulation of these registers. Some typical forms of these instructions for branching are as follows:

- Conditional, 8-bit immediate, relative
- Unconditional, 8-bit immediate, relative
- Unconditional, 16-bit immediate, absolute

For call instructions, instructions may take the following forms:

- Computed, 16-bits absolute
- Unconditional, 16-bit immediate, absolute

segment selector file A file used to reference segments such as the current module code segment, module data segment, and process stack segment.

segment size (*o.t.*) In a NetWare Value-Added Process, specified as 16-byte paragraphs.

segment value (*o.t.*) In a NetWare Value-Added Process, either a real-mode segment or a protected mode segment descriptor, depending on the mode at the time. If zero, no memory was available.

seising signal A signal that is often translated at the start of a message to initiate a circuit operation at the receiving end of a circuit.

select command A database command that retrieves only those records fulfilling user-dictated criteria.

selected configuration In NetWare Diagnostic Services, a value indicating which configuration in the hardware configuration table the driver is using.

selection One of the three structured programming patterns, in which a choice of instructions is made based upon certain criteria.

selection check A check that verifies the choice of devices in the execution of an instruction.

selective dump A dump of one or more desired storage locations. A selective dump is usually a library subroutine that is called when other programs are running and a dump is desired.

selective fading 1. Fading that unequally affects different frequencies within a specified band. 2. Fluctuation in which the components of a signal fade or decrease disproportionately, such as the rise and fall of only the high or low frequency components.

selectivity The degree of narrowness of a circuit's frequency-response bandwidth. High selectivity implies high Q, narrow bandwidth, and single-frequency sensitivity. Low selectivity implies low Q, broadband response, and relatively uniform sensitivity over the response frequency range.

selector 1. A switching operation based on previous processing, which allows a logical choice to be made in the program or system. 2. A mechanical multiposition switch. 3. The cursor.

selector circuit A circuit that selects a specified output, magnitude, waveform, amplitude, phase, or frequency.

selenium Atomic number 34, atomic weight 78.96, symbol Se, specific gravity 4.81, melts at 217°C, boils at 685°C. A nonmetallic element that is a semiconductor and exists in a number of allotropic forms. One form becomes electrically conducting when irradiated with light.

selenium rectifier A rectifier that uses a barrier layer of crystalline selenium on an iron base.

self-adapting The ability of a system to change its performance characteristics in response to environmental changes.

self-defining In assembler programming, a term with a value that is absolute and implicit in the specification of the term itself.

self-diagnosis The ability of a computer to identify and report its operational problems to the user.

self-discharge 1. The loss of capacity of a primary cell as a result of internal leakage. **2.** The loss of charge from a capacitor due to finite insulation resistance between the plates.

self-induction The property of an electric circuitor component by which it resists any change in the current flowing. *Also see* LENZ'S LAW.

self-instructed carry A carry process in which information is allowed to propagate to succeeding places as soon as it is generated, without requiring an external signal.

self-organizing machine *See* SOM, 1.

self-oscillation Usually unwanted oscillation that is generated in a circuit as a result of inadvertent positive feedback, such as through the interelectrode capacitance of an active device.

self-powered Containing an independent power source, such as a special voltaic cell or group of cells.

self-pulse modulation A modulation that uses an internally generated pulse.

self-relocating program A program that can be loaded into any area of main storage and that uses an initialization routine to adjust its address constants so that it can be executed at that location.

self-test techniques Testing methods that use the microcomputer in the system to test the system functions. Self-test employs time-outs, start-up routines, or other programs stored in a self-test ROM. Many simple products can easily be tested upon each reset or power-up. The self-test program can usually detect major faults in the system or its boards.

semantic error An error results from an ambiguous meaning in a program statement. Semantic errors are the responsibility of the programmer and can be removed by debugging prior to use of the program.

semantics The relationship between symbols and their intended meanings.

semaphore A synchronization mechanism used in NetWare and other operating systems.

semaphore handle In NetWare, a two-word value returned by the call Open Semaphore. It is used in all the subsequent semaphore calls.

semaphore value In the NetWare Locking and File Server Environment, the number of available openings in the semaphore.

semicompiled Descriptive of a program converted from source language to object language but not called by the source program.

semiconducting material Intrinsic or extrinsic material, such as germanium and silicon, used in the manufacture of active solid-state devices.

semiconductor 1. A material with a conductivity between a metal and an insulator. **2.** Any member of the class of devices constructed from a semiconductor. Semiconductors include diodes, transistors, and the complex integrated circuits that are fabricated from wafers of semiconducting material.

semiconductor contact The section of a semiconductor device where the interconnects for the leads are made.

semiconductor diode A two-terminal semiconductor device with a pn junction possessing a nonlinear voltage-current characteristic.

semiconductor doping The adding of impurities to semiconductor materials to produce desired conducting characteristics.

semiconductor functional blocks The functional blocks that are used in microcomputer design.

semiconductor integrated circuits Complex single-package circuits fabricated from semiconductor wafers.

semiconductor, intrinsic *See* INTRINSIC SEMICONDUCTOR.

semiconductor junction The region between p and n areas in a semiconducting material.

semiconductor LSI memory 1. Refers to semiconductor flip-flop circuits in the form of large-scale storage units. They were originally used primarily for microcomputer storage registers and computational logic units (such as the arithmetic logic unit). **2.** A memory whose storage medium is semiconductor circuits, the primary storage devices for most computers. A typical semiconductor memory is contained on a single circuit card and contains all refresh, control, and interface logic required to operate as a memory unit.

semiconductor, n-type *See* N-TYPE SEMICONDUCTOR.

semiconductor, p-type *See* P-TYPE SEMICONDUCTOR.

semiconductor RAMs A semiconductor memory is a collection of storage registers together with the circuits necessary for transferring information in and out of the registers. When the memory can be accessed for information as required, it is a random-access memory, or RAM. Sometimes these use a single line for the read/write control; one binary state specifies the read operation and the other state specifies the write operation. Enable lines are included in the IC to provide a means for accessing a single chip in a group of devices.

semiconductor strain-gauge elements Elements

that are usually bonded or deposited so that the semiconductor foil and diaphragm appear as a single part. Semiconductor types feature larger output than wire types, but tend to be more temperature-sensitive.

semiconductor trap The lattice defects in a semiconductor crystal that produce potential wells in which electrons or holes can be captured.

semimetals Material such as bismuth, antimony, and arsenic having characteristics between semiconductors and metals.

semistor A semiconductor resistor that uses the resistance of silicon.

send failures In NetWare Diagnostic Services, the number of times (since SPX was loaded) that SPX has been unable to send a packet across an SPX connection and receive acknowledgement. In such a case, SPX aborts a connection and informs the calling application.

send interval In NetWare Diagnostic Services, this indicates how often a source node should send a specified number of packets to a destination node. The send interval is measured in units of $\frac{1}{18}$ of a second.

send packet In NetWare Diagnostic Services, the number of times (since IPX was loaded) that applications have called IPX to send a packet.

send packet requests In NetWare Diagnostic Services, the number of times (since SPX was loaded) that applications have issued calls to SPX send sequenced packet.

sense The action required to examine or determine the arrangement of coded items; to read.

sense wire A wire that carries the output signal in a magnetic core unit.

sensing The process of determining the state or condition of an item.

sensing element The specific portion of a device that is directly responsive to the value of the measured quantity.

sensitive relay A relay requiring only a small current, such as those used in photoelectric circuits.

sensitivity The relative response of a device to an incoming signal or stimulus. The sensitivity of a receiver is the minimum input signal required to produce a specified output signal.

sensitivity analysis A test or trial of a range of values at the input to determine the response and interdependence of the output values. Sensitivity analysis can be conducted using parametric programming in which parameters are allowed to vary in order to determine the solution of a problem.

sensitivity ratio The measured ratio of the change in output to the change in input that causes it.

sensor A transducer or other device that can be used to provide a quantity whose value is a measure of some physical phenomenon.

sensor-based computer A computer designed to be used to receive real-time data from transducers or sensors that monitor a physical process. In a typical application, the computer might receive data from a pressure transducer or a flow meter, compare the data to required conditions, and then produce a signal to operate a control device.

sensor scan A type of sequential interrogation of lists of information or devices under process control. This develops a collection of data from process sensors by a computer for use in calculations, usually through a multiplexer.

sentinel A character or indicator used to mark some condition, such as the beginning or end of a word.

sentinel value The value that a program tests for in a decision module. Also called the *trailer value*.

separator A specific character used for the demarcation of the logical boundary between items that can be considered separate and distinct units.

sequence An orderly progression of items.

sequence checking A routine that checks every instruction executed and prints desired data. The printout may include coded instructions, the contents of registers, or transferred data.

sequence control register A register that is used to control the location of the next instruction to be processed. Also called the *sequence counter*.

sequenced packet exchange Novell implementation of the XNS Sequenced Packet Protocol.

Sequenced Packet Protocol The XNS protocol for the reliable transfer of data at the transport layer.

sequence number A number identifying the relative location of blocks or groups of blocks on a magnetic tape.

sequencer A device or circuit used to trigger a predetermined series of events as a result of a specific action. The circuit selects the order of occurrence in accordance with the action to which it responds.

sequence readout A display of the number of the block of tape being read by the tape reader.

sequencer register A counter that is reset following the execution of an instruction to form a new memory address for locating the next instruction.

sequence timer A succession of time-delay circuits arranged so that completion of the delay in one circuit initiates a delay in the following circuit.

sequential-access storage A form of storage, also called *serial storage*, in which the items of stored information are available in sequence regardless of the information desired. Storage in which words appear one after another is *serial-by-word*. Bits that must appear in time sequence are found in *serial-by-bit* systems.

sequential alarm A device that monitors a group of alarm contacts and signals a priority interrupt to the computer when an alarm condition occurs. The computer can then establish an alarm sequence based on current and previous information.

sequential computer A computer with built-in logic that executes instructions in a fixed sequence, which can usually be overridden or changed by another instruction.

sequential control A control mode in which instructions are set up in an ordered progression and fed into the machine consecutively during the solution of the problem.

sequential file A method of organizing data by putting all records in key field order; access can be slow.

sequential logic A logic methodology in which the output state is determined by the previous state of the input.

sequential power controller A remotely activated power switch for up to six pieces of equipment, shown in the following figure. It has an intelligent master socket that lets you use the power switch on your monitor or any other conveniently located switch to control the power to all your equipment. It also provides a three- to five-second time delay between activation of each socket to prevent harmful surges caused by one unit with others. This lets hard drives reach speed and printers initialize without interfering with each other.

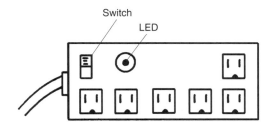

Sequential power controller

sequential sampling A type of sampling inspection in which the decision to accept, reject, or inspect another unit is made following the sampling of each unit.

serial The time-sequential handling of individual items, such as the processing of a sequence of instructions one at a time. Serial transmission uses a time sequence for words with the same facilities required for successive parts.

serial-access system A computer system in which the access time is dependent upon the location of the data most recently obtained or placed into storage.

serial adder A device that adds two binary words one bit-pair at a time. The least-significant digit is performed first, and the more-significant digits are added in succession with carries until the sum is formed. Serial adders require less hardware but are slower than parallel units.

serial cable kit A kit that allows you to construct your own serial (RS-232) cable. The kit consists of a shielded 10-foot, 25-pin cable. Each end is crimped with pins. There are two hoods, two 25-pin connectors, an insertion/extraction tool, and jumper cables.

serial data controller A unit that provides a flexible interface for full-duplex, synchronous or asynchronous serial communications. Both transmitter and receiver may be double-buffered; the device is capable of data rates up to 250 Kbps (synchronous) or 16 Kbps (asynchronous). Data formatting (bits per character, character framing, odd/even parity) is usually programmable under CPU control. Interrupt and/or direct memory access modes may also be selected.

serial interface An interface that requires serial transmission, in which the bits composing a character are sent sequentially. It implies only a single transmission channel.

serially reusable Descriptive of a reusable program that is not necessarily reenterable. The same copy of the routine or program can be used by another task after the current use has been concluded in main memory.

serial memory system Systems designed to meet the high-reliability and low-cost requirements of CRT refresh applications. These systems are available as self-contained memory units or as units that can be expanded to virtually any size in either word or bit length through the use of additional memory cards.

serial mouse See MOUSE.

serial-parallel The property of being partially serial and partially parallel, such as serial by character and parallel by bits that make up the character.

serial-parallel converter A unit designed for changing data in serial format to parallel format. A typical unit allows full-duplex operation between a CPU and a remote location. The modules are used in pairs, with one at the central processor and the other at the remote location.

serial-parallel register A shift register that can be used to perform serial-to-parallel data conversion, shown in the figure on page 462.

serial port An I/O port that allows only one bit to be sent at a time. It consists of two single-bit serial data buses linked to the serial input and serial output lines of a shift register, which is usually 16 bits long. The shift register is loaded or read via parallel input and output lines and shifted one bit at a time under software control. The serial port is often used as a simple asynchronous data communications interface. The shift register performs parallel-to-serial and serial-to-parallel code conversions under programs control.

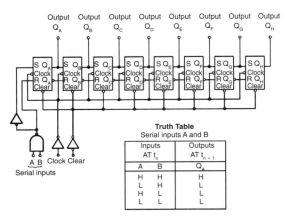

Serial-parallel register with truth table

serial printer A printer that outputs one character at a time.

serial processing Pertaining to the sequential or consecutive execution of two or more processes in a single device such as a channel.

serial programming Programming in such a way that only one arithmetic or logical operation can be executed at one time.

serial storage *See* SEQUENTIAL-ACCESS STORAGE.

serial transfer Data transfer in which the characters of information flow in sequence over a single path.

serial transmission A sequential transmission of characters or items of data over a single path.

serial work flow A system of operations in which each operation is performed singly, while no other task is being operated on.

series 1. The condition of being wired so that a single current flows through several devices sequentially. **2.** A set of related terms in a mathematical expression. **3.** A group or string of individual but related items or values.

series interface board A circuit board designed to allow custom interfaces to be used with different types of series memory systems.

series-parallel circuit *See* PARALLEL-SERIES CIRCUIT.

series-parallel network A network in which successive branches are connected in series and/or in parallel.

series resistor A resistor used for adapting an instrument or device so that it will operate on some designated voltage or voltages. It forms an essential part of the voltage circuit and may be either internal or external to the device.

server A processor that provides a specific service to the network. Servers can be classified as follows:

- Routing, which connects nodes and networks of like architecture
- Gateway, which connects nodes and networks of different architectures by performing protocol conversions
- Printer, which provides an interface between one or more printers and one or more nodes on the LAN
- File, which provide a central repository of files and programs

server address In NetWare Diagnostic Services, the destination server's 12-byte internetwork address.

server-based LAN A network in which data are processed at individual workstations but stored on a central, or dedicated, file server. Centralized networks are typically larger, more powerful, and more expensive per unit than distributed networks. Also called a *centralized network*.

server-client model *See* CLIENT-SERVER MODEL.

server control procedure Program used in Netwise RPC.

Server for DOS LANs Software that prints forms designed with JetForm Design in multiuser and network applications. You can merge variable length data for any client LAN. One request can print multiple forms on multiple printers.

server ID In NetWare Bindery and Accounting Services, the bindery object ID of a server.

server ID list In NetWare Queue Services, the object IDs of job servers servicing a queue.

server ID number In NetWare Queue Services, the ID number of a job server servicing a job.

server name In the NetWare Service Advertising Protocol, a 48-byte, null-terminated string that is the server's unique name within the internetwork.

server order number In NetWare Connection Services, indicates the order number (one through eight) assigned to the corresponding server. The lowest order number indicates the server with the lowest network/node address, and the second-lowest number indicates the second-lowest address.

server printer In NetWare Print Services, a flag holding the number of the printer to which a job will be sent.

server/requester programming interface *See* SRPI.

server station In NetWare Queue Services, the station number of the job server servicing a job.

server status record In NetWare Queue Services, a 64-byte field that can contain information useful to job servers and queue users.

server stub A piece of software generated by the RPC tool. The server stub emulates the calling application program to the remote procedure on the server.

server task number In NetWare Queue Services, the task number of the job server servicing a job.

server type In NetWare Diagnostic Services, the

object type of the server. In the Service Advertising Protocol, it is the type of server that should respond to a query. A file server's object type is 0004h. A print server's object type is 0003h. FFFh is wild and causes all server types to respond. The wildcard is used only for general service queries.

server utilization percentage In the NetWare File Server Environment, the current server utilization percentage (zero to 100). The field is updated once a second.

service access point *See* SAP, 2.

service address point A data link status value contained within the logical link control field of each frame data field that initiates, maintains, and terminates any communication.

Service Advertisement Protocol *See* SAP, 1.

service bureau A company that specializes in providing data-processing or desktop publishing services for other organizations.

service organization A company that offers contract maintenance and operation of computers.

service point A location for the management of non-SNA resources.

service routine A routine in general support of the operation of a computer. Service routines are designed to assist in the maintenance and operation of the computer as well as for the preparation of programs. They include monitoring and supervisory routines and are generally standardized to meet the needs at a particular installation for a wide variety of programs.

service technician Person responsible for repairing and installing computer equipment.

service type In NetWare Accounting Services, specifies the type of service for which a charge is being made.

servo A system in which electrical signals are used to produce mechanical movement in a remote device, wherein the rate and direction of motion are represented by specific signal characteristics.

servo link A mechanical power amplifier that permits low-strength signals to operate control mechanisms that require larger power.

servomechanism A feedback control system in which at least one of the system signals represents a mechanical motion.

servomotor A motor in a servo system that is controlled by a corrective electric signal. Its controller is a microcomputer-based unit that accepts commands in ASCII format. The microcomputer reads an encoder on the motor and calculates motor speeds and positions, allowing precise control with programmable variables.

servo multiplier An analog device capable of multiplying several different variables by a single variable or constant.

session A series of interactions (conversations) that take place between application programs.

Session Control Protocol The DECnet session layer protocol.

session layer The portion of the ISO-OSI model that is concerned with providing file management and bookkeeping functions needed to support intersystem communications. *Also see* OSI MODEL.

set 1. To place a storage device into a desired state. **2.** A collection of values or items, such as all even numbers or positive integers. **3.** An equipment system.

set breakpoint A command that causes a breakpoint to be set in a specified location.

set point The value of a variable to which specific control actions, such as alarms or process changes, are desired.

set symbol A variable symbol used in assembly programming to communicate values during conditional assembly processing.

set theory The mathematical study of groups, sets, and elements.

settling time The time required for a signal to attain a final value of full scale.

set-up diagram A graphic representation showing how a computing system should be prepared and the arrangements to be made for its operation.

set-up utility menu A menu used to configure or set up the computer system, like the one shown in the following figure.

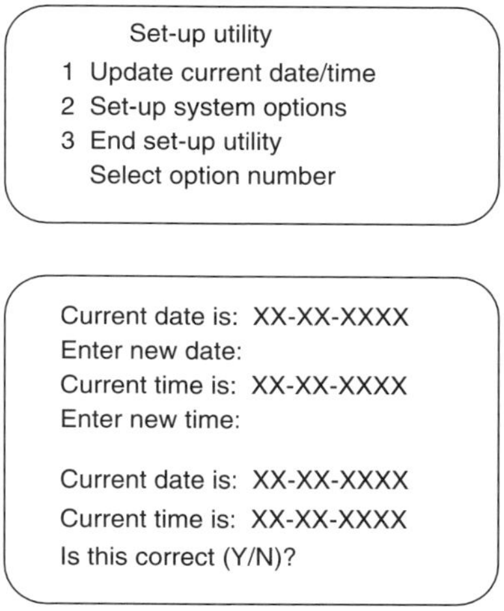

```
         Set-up utility
1  Update current date/time
2  Set-up system options
3  End set-up utility
   Select option number
```

```
Current date is:  XX-XX-XXXX
Enter new date:
Current time is:  XX-XX-XXXX
Enter new time:

Current date is:  XX-XX-XXXX
Current time is:  XX-XX-XXXX
Is this correct (Y/N)?
```

Set-up utility menus

seven-segment display A single-character readout with seven individually addressable segments that are illuminated selectively to form numerals and other symbols. A calculator uses such a display.

sexadecimal notation *See* HEXADECIMAL NOTATION.

SF 1. Abbreviation for *shift forward.* **2.** Abbreviation for *signal frequency*. **3.** Abbreviation for *skip flag*.

SFM Abbreviation for *semiconductor functional module*.

SFT Abbreviation for *system fault tolerant*, used to describe computer systems that have special reliability features designed to minimize the downtime due to hardware or software faults. For example, Novell has a version of NetWare called SFT NetWare with special features designed to minimize file server downtime as well as time lost restoring data files when a transaction has been interrupted.

SFT error table In the NetWare File Server Environment, a 60-byte table containing SFT internal error counters.

SFT level In the NetWare File Server Environment, the SFT level offered by the file server. SFT level 1 offers hot disk-error fix, level 2 has disk mirroring and transaction tracking, and level 3 offers physical file-server mirroring.

SG Abbreviation for *symbol generator*.

shaft encoder A simultaneous data converter in which all bits appear at once and can be read in parallel at any one time. There is an equivalent form of simultaneous A/D converter having a Gray code output. It uses a chain of biased comparators and the outputs provide a quantized indication of the analog input level. All comparators above are zero, and all comparators below are one. Logic gates are used to obtain the parallel Gray code output. Such converters are fast—being capable of 10 million conversions per second. However, they require a number of comparisons that is a geometric function of the required resolution, as well as large numbers of logic gates. *Also see* GRAY CODE.

Shannon equation An expression in information theory that gives a theoretical limit to the rate of transmission of binary digits with a given bandwidth and signal/noise ratio.

shaped card potentiometer A function generator for functions of one variable, in which the input variable sets the angular position of a potentiometer shaft.

shareable lock count In the NetWare File Server Environment, the number of logical connections that have a shareable lock.

shared logic Refers to a system in which several terminals simultaneously use the memory and processing powers of a single CPU.

shared storage The ability to share main storage between two processors. In shared storage, either machine can insert information into storage, and either machine can access the data and use it.

shareware Software "on the honor system." Shareware is usually freely distributed outside retail channels, but the author requests a fee if it is used. For this fee, the user is registered as the legitimate owner of his or her copy of the software,

and might also receive updates and printed manuals.

sharing 1. The use of a device for two or more purposes during the same time interval. **2.** The apportionment of time intervals for different tasks by interlacing or interleaving.

sharpness Apparent image resolution. High sharpness can be the result of high resolution, or it can be an illusion caused by image enhancement or by visible edges in a display, such as the vertical stripes of an aperture-grille CRT such as the Trinitron. Visible scanning lines can actually increase perceived sharpness.

sheath 1. An excess of positive or negative ions in a plasma, giving a shielding or space charge effect. **2.** The covering on a cable.

Sheffer stroke *See* NAND GATE.

Sheffield Pascal/386 A 32-bit extended-memory ISO Pascal compiler. It has a fast compile-time speed with diagnostics at both compile and runtime. It includes a DOS extender, virtual memory manager, disk cache, linker, coprocessor emulation, full-screen debugger, and an extensive runtime graphics library.

shell 1. A shell-like magnet in which the magnetization is always normal to the surface and inversely proportional to the thickness. The strength of the shell is the product of magnetization and thickness of shell. **2.** A program that replaces the basic prompt screen of an operating system or application (such as DOS or the Internet) with a graphic interface and adds functions not available from the command prompt.

shell requests count In NetWare Diagnostic Services, the number of times (since the shell was activated) that the shell has made requests to a file server.

SHF Abbreviation for *superhigh frequency*: 3,000 to 30,000 megahertz.

shield *See* SHIELDING.

shielded-conductor cable A cable in which the insulated conductor or conductors are enclosed in a conducting envelope or envelopes, with almost every point on the surface at ground potential or at some predetermined potential with respect to ground.

shielded line A transmission line enclosed in a conducting material to protect it from inadvertent signal pickup from stray radiation, or to protect adjacent circuits from radiation of the line.

shielded pair A balanced pair of transmission lines within a screen used to mitigate interference from outside.

shielded twisted-pair Pairs of 22-26 gauge wire clad with a metallic shield.

shielding 1. The protection of circuits, components, and conductors from radiated interference by enclosing them with conducting material. **2.** The physical barriers placed within the confines of a chassis to minimize interaction between separated stages or circuits.

shift To move digits or characters in a register to the right or left, either transferring the information or performing an arithmetical operation. For example, if a register holds the following eight digits:

23456789

a shift to the right produces

12345678

shift-in character *See* SI, 1.
shift instruction A computer instruction that causes the contents of an accumulator register to shift to the right or the left. A right-shift instruction is equivalent to dividing by two; a left-shift instruction is equivalent to multiplying by two, or adding the contents of the register to itself.
shift out To move information within a register toward one end to clear the register.
shift-out character *See* SO.
shift pulse A pulse that initiates the shifting of characters in a register.
shift register A register for the short- or long-term storage of serial or parallel data in which data may be shifted to the right or left, shifted out, and shifted in. A typical shift register, as shown, operates at a speed of 5 MHz from standard TTL voltage levels. It is composed of a series of flip-flops connected in tandem. Registers may be connected together to form larger memory units.
Shockley, William Inventor of the transistor along with Bardeen and Brattain, and winner of the 1956 Nobel Prize in physics.
short-circuit A direct resistance-free connection between two points in a circuit or system that normally are not connected or are not intended to be connected. Also called a *short*.
short-circuit impedance The input impedance of a device when the output or voltage source is short-circuited.
short-circuit parameters In an equivalent circuit of a device, the resultant parameter when independent device terminals are shorted.
shorted directory/file name In the AppleTalk Filing Protocol Services, a field that returns the NetWare directory or filename of the specified directory or file.
shorted-junction devices Technology that consists of two semiconductor junctions that appear as a high-impedance circuit of back-to-back diodes, as shown. Generally, an npn double-diffused transistor structure is used, with only the emitter and collector contacts metalized. The base is left open, forming the back-to-back diodes, D^1 and D^2. This structure is the result of an irreversible process that occurs on the migration of aluminum through silicon to the diffused junction.

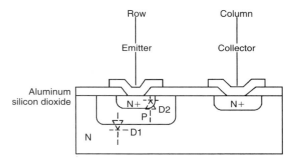

Shorted junction of AIM PROM cell structure

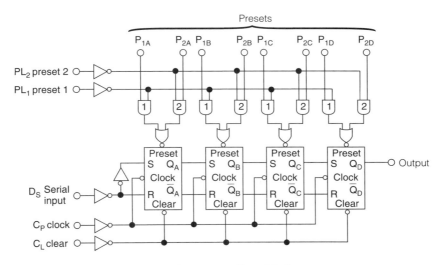

Shift register (four bits)

D^2 is reverse biased, and the large flow of electrons in the reverse direction causes aluminum atoms from the emitter contact to migrate through the emitter to the base, causing an emitter-to-base short. The remaining junction is thus usable as a forward-based diode and represents a programmed data bit. The avalanche technique requires a higher voltage and current than the fuse technique. Shorted-junction devices are also referred to as *AIM* (avalanche-induced migration) technology.

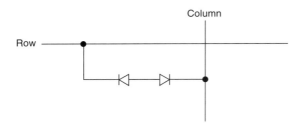

Shorted junction of AIM PROM cell

shorted out Made inactive by connecting a wire or other low resistance path around a device or portion of a circuit.

short-haul modem A signal converter that conditions a digital signal to ensure reliable transmission over continuous private-line metallic circuits.

short-haul modem hub A unit that enables data communication users to transmit and receive data using one computer port and several remote terminals, as shown in the following diagram. The hub also provides an RS-232 extension port for local connection to the CPU.

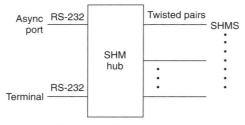

Short-haul modem hub

short instruction The standard one-word instruction format, as opposed to a multiple-word instruction.

short stack A stack of only a few bytes used to allow the monitor program to store flags temporarily when interrupts occur. The short stack improves the interrupt-handling capability of the microprocessor at minimal cost.

shot noise Noise that is generated as a result of the random passage of discrete carriers across a barrier or discontinuity such as a semiconductor junction. *Also see* NOISE.

Showcase An image database with virtual imaging and animation display capabilities. It can handle images to 1024 × 768 × 256 and Autodesk Animator FLI sequences. It is suitable for management of SVGA, photorealistic, scanned, or video-captured pictures.

Show Partner Software to create and show dynamic presentations using color, graphics, animation, special effects, and sound. It has interactive capabilities, branching, and an advanced memory management system.

shunt 1. A precision low-value resistor placed across the terminals of a device to increase its range. **2.** Any part connected in parallel with some other part; also the act of connecting such a part. **3.** In an electric circuit, a branch the winding of which is in parallel with the external or line circuit. **4.** The addition of a component to divert current in a known way. *Also see* JUMPER.

shunt leads The leads that connect the circuit of an instrument to an external shunt. The resistance of these leads must be taken into account when the instrument is adjusted.

SI 1. The *shift-in* character, a code-extension character used to return a register to its prior state before shifting operations. **2.** Abbreviation for *International System of Units.* **3.** Abbreviation for *superimpose*: refers to the process that moves data from one location to another, superimposing bits or characters on the contents of specified locations.

sidebands The frequency bands on both sides of the carrier frequency. The frequencies of the wave produced by modulation fall within these bands. During amplitude modulation with a sine-wave carrier, the upper sideband includes the sum (carrier plus modulating) frequencies, and the lower sideband includes the difference (carrier minus modulating) frequencies.

side circuit A circuit arrangement for deriving a phantom circuit. In four-wire circuits, the two wires associated with the on-channel form one side circuit, and those associated with the return-channel form another.

side circuit repeating coil A repeating coil designed to function as a transformer at a side circuit terminal. Often used as a means for superimposing one side of a phantom channel on that circuit.

Sidekick A DOS-based memory-resident, personal organizer that resides in memory while you are using other programs. It includes a notepad, calendar, auto-dialer, and calculator.

Sideways A program that rotates wide printouts on the page without modifying the original file. Sideways allows you to modify margins, spacing, density, and size of font. It can write across the perforations on continuous-feed paper to give output whatever the width. It is compatible with any program that creates an ASCII output file, as well as Lotus 1-2-3.

SIE Abbreviation for *single instruction execute*.

SIG Acronym for *special-interest group*.

Sigma NetBIOS Engine Software that contains C functions to access the NetBIOS API standard from Windows or DOS programs. You can access the network name, datagram, and session services directly. It supports NetBIOS wait, no-wait, and post-driven requests, and includes NCB and data transfer buffer functions.

sign 1. A symbol that distinguishes negative from positive quantities. 2. A flag.

signal The intelligence, message, or effect to be conveyed from one point to another; it may be electrical, visual, or audible.

signal conditioning Refers to changing or modifying a signal with electronic circuitry, as shown in the following figure.

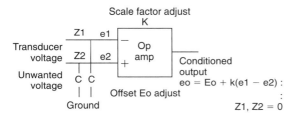

Differential amplifier used as a signal conditioner

signal constellation Refers to the signal magnitudes and phases of a digital modulation scheme when displayed by a phasor diagram.

signal converter A transducer that converts from one type of transmission signal to another.

signal distance *See* HAMMING DISTANCE.

signal element The part of a signal that occupies the shortest interval of the signaling code.

signal frequency noise Noise that lasts for a significant time period and is highly localized in frequency about some common reference. *Also see* NOISE.

signal generator An oscillator used to provide a test voltage (usually from one volt to less than one microvolt) over a wide range of frequencies; used for testing equipment. It may be amplitude-, frequency-, or pulse-modulated.

signal injector A tool applied in conjunction with a time-domain reflectometer, optical time-domain reflectometer, transceiver tester, ring scanner, or cable tester for analyzing the integrity and performance of a LAN. The signal injector creates a signal that mimics the electrical or optical characteristics of the transmission medium.

signal interphasing A technique of overlapping multiple transmission signals to improve transmission rates.

signal level The magnitude of a waveform's or pulse train's voltage amplitude, either absolute or with respect to a reference value. Often expressed in decibels.

signal line protector A unit designed to protect signal/data lines from transient over-voltages caused by lightning, heavy machinery, elevator motors, generators, and other sources. The protectors interface between the signal lines and the sensitive circuit to provide a sophisticated high-speed voltage limiting and protection. The signal line protectors recover automatically in preparation for further protection.

signal power An expression of the absolute signal strength at a specific point in a circuit.

signal processor A device that performs complex processing of waveforms for analysis and transmission. A typical signal processor is used with a host computer to provide the functions of a fast Fourier transform processor, array processor, display processor, and voice processor.

signal pulse repetition The basic frequency or pulse repetition rate of a signal has no intrinsic intelligence until it is modulated by another signal that does have intelligence. A signal may be amplitude, phase, or frequency modulated; for example, an 8-MHz sound wave carrier can be amplitude or pulse modulated by a 1-MHz pulse code signal; the presence or absence of a pulse determines whether a one or a zero is present in the binary number being represented.

signal quality error heartbeat A signal from the transceiver to the node peripheral indicating that the transceiver is functioning properly.

signal strength The strength of the signal produced by a transmitter or other device at a particular location, usually expressed in millivolts per meter.

signal-to-distortion ratio The ratio of the amplitude of the desired signal to the amplitude of the distortion.

signal-to-noise ratio The ratio of the magnitude of the signal to the magnitude of the noise at the same point when the signal is removed, usually expressed in decibels.

signal tracing The methodological following of a signal path in hardware or on diagrams in order to locate faults.

signal transducer A transducer designed to convert one standard transmission signal to another.

signature analysis A testing technique that uses a test mode or pattern to exercise a digital system. Four hex digits can be used to represent a pattern for 16 bits. A test sequence uses these signatures within a certain window of time at a desired clock rate to detect timing-related faults.

There are several basic methods that can be used for isolating faults using digital signatures. In one, the signal can be traced from the point of application to the output. As the test point moves, the signature will change at a particular point. The faulty component is then one of the devices connected to the point at which the signature change appears.

sign bit A binary digit occupying the sign position in a word to give the value direction.

sign-control flip-flop A specific flip-flop used to store the algebraic sign of numbers. *Also see* FLIP-FLOP.

sign digit A character used to designate the algebraic sign of a number.

Signetics 2650 (*o.t.*) A single-chip, eight-bit microprocessor that has 576 bits of ROM and about 250 bits of registers, as shown.

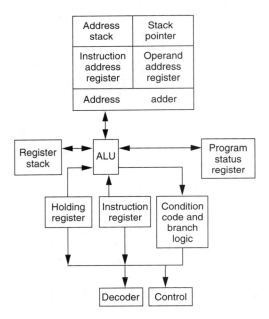

2650 architecture

significance The weighting factor in positional representations, which is dependent on the digit place and by which a digit is multiplied to obtain its additive contribution in the representation of a number.

sign-magnitude bipolar D/A conversion A type of digital-to-analog conversion in which the converter's current output can be inverted, and circuitry controlled by the MSB (most-significant bit) determines if the output amplifier's input is direct or through the current inverter. One technique is shown in the following figure.

sign position In an array of binary digits, the position that contains an indication of the algebraic sign of a number.

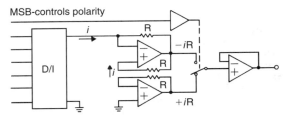

Sign magnitude bipolar D/A converter

Sign Studio A Macintosh product that allows you to create signs by choosing from hundreds of typestyle and thousands of color and insert combinations.

SIL Abbreviation for *speech interference level*.

silica gel A moisture-absorbent chemical used for dehydrating wave guides, coaxial lines, pressurized components, shipping containers, and other equipment.

silicon A nonmetallic element having semiconducting properties; it is widely used in the manufacture of active electronic devices.

silicon-controlled rectifier *See* SCR.

silicon diode A rectifying device that uses silicon as the semiconducting material.

silicon dioxide In MOS device manufacturing, the layer used to insulate the metal gate from the p or n regions.

silicon-gate CMOS A complementary MOS technology that allows high packing density with good speed performance and noise immunity along with low power dissipation. The internal logic structure for a microprocessor using this technology is fully static, which allows the clock to be stopped between instructions, cycles, and minor cycles. It requires only a single supply, and all signals are TTL-compatible.

silicon-link PROMs PROMs that use notched strips of polycrystalline silicon material. Programming of these polysilicon fuses involves melting the links using a mechanism similar to that in metal fuses. During programming, a current of 20 to 30 mA is used to blow the fuse link. This current generates heat estimated at 1400°C. At this temperature, the silicon oxidizes, forming an insulating material around the open link. The use of silicon results in the absence of contact problems or difficulties caused by the use of a dissimilar material. Additionally, it eliminates the existence of conductive materials in the open gap between the formerly linked polysilicon fuse ends. Thus, growback is greatly reduced, although not completely eliminated.

silicon-nitride passivation A semiconductor manufacturing process that involves the use of a layer of silicon nitride to protect the surface of devices from ionic contamination. The silicon nitride layer is covered with a layer of phosphorous silicon dioxide. The double layer prevents both mechanical and ionic damage and enhances device reliability.

silicon-on-sapphire *See* SOS.

Silicon Press A Macintosh printing utility that allows you to create and print labels, forms, cards, envelopes and stickers. You can import data from most Macintosh database programs with the merge-printing capabilities.

silicon processing Refers to the basic techniques of forming a dielectric layer on a semiconductor surface by thermally oxidizing a silicon surface. The low diffusion coefficients of most dopants in the resulting silicon dioxide and the task of etching without attacking the silicon itself are key factors in silicon processing. The silicon dioxide is not often a sufficient final passivation. Silicon nitride is often used because of its properties.

silicon rectifier One or more silicon rectifying cells or cell assemblies.

silicon resistor A resistor of silicon material that has an almost constant positive temperature coefficient, making it suitable as a temperature sensing element.

silicon solar cell A photovoltaic cell that consists of a thin wafer of specially processed silicon designed to convert light energy into electrical energy.

silicon steel Steel containing three to five percent silicon. Its magnetic qualities make it desirable for use in the iron cores of transformers and other ac devices.

silicon transistor A transistor formed from a silicon crystal, as opposed to a germanium transistor.

SilverClip Library An interrupt-driven asynchronous communications package for CA-Clipper. It allows simultaneous access to an unlimited number of communications ports with baud rates to 115K, background timers, and terminal emulation for ANSI, TTY, VT 100 and VT 52. You can do file transfers with Xmodem, Ymodem (batch), 1K-modem-G, Ymodem-G (batch), and ASCII. It supports Smartmodem as well as high-level remote inputs.

SilverComm C Async Library 3.1 An interrupt-driven asynchronous communication library with baud rates up to 115K, an unlimited number of ports, device event monitors, background times, model queues, direct video functions, table-driven design, and terminal emulation.

silver mica capacitor A high-stability, low-power-factor fixed capacitor prepared by the vacuum deposition of silver on thin mica sheets.

sim Abbreviation for *simulated*.

SimCGA Software that allows you to run many programs that require a color graphics adapter on a monochrome system.

SimGauss 386 A fully interactive, nonlinear simulation module written in the Gauss programming language. It provides a quick way to simulate nonlinear differential equations and state-space systems, such as vehicle dynamics, biological systems, and economic models.

SIMM Abbreviation for *single inline memory module*, a memory add-in board that increases the RAM available on a PC. Most 386 and 486 systems have at least 2M of factory-installed memory. By adding SIMMs, you can usually increase the system-board memory to at least 16M. However, if you have the maximum of RAM on the system board, you cannot add a memory add-in board.

SIMMs are installed on the system board in sets of sockets called *banks*. Bank 0 is always the first bank. Each bank may hold 256K, 1M, 4M, 8M, 16M, or 32M SIMMs. The table below shows some typical valid SIMM configurations for a system with two SIMMs in each bank.

Before handling SIMMs or other components, discharge any static electricity by touching a ground surface, such as a metal portion of your computer's chassis. You must fill the banks in sequence: first install SIMMs in bank 0, then bank 1, and then bank 2. Do not mix SIMMs; you cannot put a 1M SIMM in one socket of a bank and a 4M SIMM in the other. Also, both sockets of a bank must be either full or empty. Some 30-pin SIMMs are taller than others and may interfere with the lower adapter card slot. The lower adapter card must not touch the SIMM module.

SIMM Configurations

Total Memory	Bank 0		Bank 1		Bank 2	
	SIMM0	SIMM1	SIMM2	SIMM3	SIMM4	SIMM5
2 MB	1 MB	1 MB	Empty	Empty	Empty	Empty
3 MB	256 KB	256 KB	256 KB	256 KB	1 MB	1 MB
4 MB	1 MB	1 MB	1 MB	1 MB	Empty	Empty
4.5 MB	1 MB	1 MB	1 MB	1 MB	256 KB	256 KB
6 MB	1 MB	1 MB	1 MB	1 MB	1 MB	2 MB
8 MB	4 MB	4 MB	Empty	Empty	Empty	Empty
9 MB	256 KB	256 KB	256 KB	256 KB	4 MB	4 MB
12 MB	1 MB	2 MB	1 MB	1 MB	4 MB	4 MB

To remove existing SIMMs and replace them, you must pull the retaining clips away from the edge of the last SIMM installed. (You might need a small pencil screwdriver to grasp the edges.) Then push the SIMM slightly forward and pull the SIMM out of its socket.

To install a SIMM, slide it into the empty socket on the system board. Push carefully until it is fully seated. (Sometimes you have to work one end of the SIMM in, and then the other end.) Then, push the SIMM back until it snaps into place.

Most systems treat all system-board memory above 1M as extended memory. When you install a memory board, you might need to allocate its memory as extended or expanded, depending on the board's type and the operating system you use.

Simple Mail Transfer Protocol *See* SMTP.
Simple Network Management Protocol *See* SNMP.
simplex A communications system or channel that is not capable of simultaneous transmission and reception. *Contrast with* DUPLEX.
simplex circuit A communications circuit derived from an existing two-wire circuit by the use of a center-tapped repeating coil. This additional circuit must use another conductor or ground return to complete its path.
simplex transmission Data transmission in one direction only.
Simscript A high-level language specifically designed for simulation applications.
Simterm A package that provides Hewlett-Packard (HP) terminal simulation to Unix systems. Simterm creates a PC simulation of an HP-like terminal to the Unix system. It does not require the asynchronous communications software support package.
SIMULA Abbreviation for *simulation language*.
simulate 1. To employ one system to duplicate the principle operational characteristics of another, using software to effect the simulation so that the imitating system accepts the same data, executes the same instructions, and performs the same operations. 2. To represent physical systems using computers and models.
simulation language A language designed for the simulation of systems using computers. Simulation languages include *Simscript* and *GPSS* (general-purpose simulation system). They tend to have more comprehensive diagnostics than general-purpose languages such as Fortran or PL/1. Both Simscript and GPSS have an event monitor that tracks events and can be used for clocking.
simulator A program that can be used to emulate or imitate the operation of a given microprocessor. They are designed to execute object programs generated by a cross assembler on a machine other than the one being worked on. A simulator offers a powerful and flexible design support

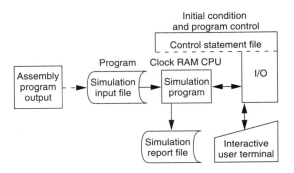

Simulator

system that can reduce development time and allow products to get to market sooner.

A hardware simulator is a program usually stored in RAM that is used to simulate the execution of a test program, tracing its progress and detecting errors. It allows the user to interact with and modify the program in order to simplify the debugging process. A typical hardware simulator for a microprocessor comes complete with all timing details, breakpoints, and debug commands, as shown. Direct user control over RAM and register contents, interrupts, and input/output data is usually provided.

simulator/debug utility A program or routine that allows microcomputer programs to be simulated and debugged on other computers or prototype systems.
simultaneous access 1. Immediate access. 2. Parallel access.
simultaneous computer A computer that contains a separate unit to perform each portion of the computation concurrently. The units can be interconnected in a manner determined by the run.
simultaneous I/O Generally refers to computers that can handle other operations concurrently with input and output operations, most often using buffers that temporarily hold I/O data and information as it arrives, while other operations are executed by the CPU. Thus, the computer need not wait for data from the slower I/O units and may instead take it from the buffer in larger quantities.
simultaneous I/O bus interface Input/output bus interfaces generally consist of drivers and receivers of the I/O bus. In many systems, the I/O command register can simultaneously contain the I/O commands to control devices and buffer memories.
simultaneous multichannel system A data acquisition system in which a shared A/D converter with a multiplexer is used for switching among the outputs of a number of sample-

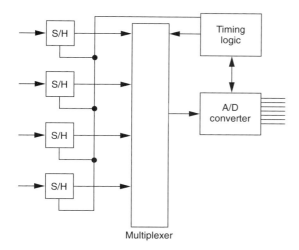

Simultaneous multichannel system

holds. As shown in the figure, this is used in situations in which the sample-holds must be updated rapidly or even simultaneously, and then read out in some sequence. It is usually a high-speed system, in which items of data indicating the state of the system must do so as at the same approximate time. Typical applications that use this approach include wind tunnel measurements, seismographic experiments, and the testing of radar or fire control systems. Usually the event is a one-time phenomenon, and the information is required at a critical time during the event, for example, when a ground shock or air blast hits the test specimen.

simultaneous sample-hold S/D converter A circuit in which each input has its own pair of sample-holds, and all samples are taken at the carrier peak as shown in the configuration.

sine law The law that states that the intensity of radiation in any direction from a linear source varies in proportion to the sine of the angle between a given direction and the axis of the source.

sine potentiometer A dc voltage divider (potentiometer), the output of which is proportionate to the sine of the shaft angle position.

sine wave A wave that is the sine of a linear function of time or space; a sinusoidal waveform.

single and multiple passes A single-pass program generates the desired end result in one computer run. A multiple-pass program generates intermediate outputs that require additional processing or loops to obtain the end result.

single-bus operation A microcomputer system that uses a single path or bus for all data transfers. Any device transmitting data can become bus master, while any device receiving data becomes a bus slave. Any master can transmit data to any slave without CPU intervention.

single card connector Usually refers to a 144-pin, two-piece connector, mounted in a sheet metal plate to simplify chassis mounting and to provide mechanical rigidity. The connector includes plastic alignment ears that simplify card insertion and provide some support for a circuit board.

single-card IEEE 488 bus interface A board that links directly to the microcomputer bus, relieving the microcomputer of some of the detailed transactions required to transfer blocks of data.

single channel system The simplest data acquisition system, which uses a single A/D converter that performs repetitive conversions at a free running rate, as shown. It has an analog signal input, and its outputs are a digital coded word with an over-range indication, polarity information if necessary, and status output to indicate when the output is valid. One example of this system is a digital panel meter, which consists of an A/D converter and a numeric display.

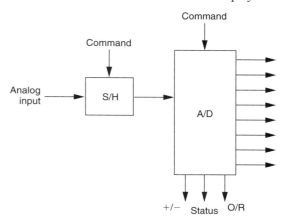

Single-channel system with sample hold

single-chip microcomputers The first true microcomputer to have all of its functions implemented in a single chip was the 3870, a modification for the two-chip F8. The major use for these chips was embedded, low-cost industrial and consumer applications. Other single-chip devices appeared in the 8048 from Intel and the Z-8 from Zilog. The 8048 architecture is derived from the 8080, but is not compatible with it. The 8048 also has its own instruction set. One version of the 8048, the 8748, uses a UV-erasable EPROM instead of ROM which can be erased with ultraviolet light and then reprogrammed.

single-ended A unit or system designed for use with unbalanced signals, having one input and one output terminal permanently earthed.

single inline memory module *See* SIMM.

single instruction multiple data A type of parallel processing architecture that uses one instruction to operate on several pieces of data at a time.

single-loop memory An architecture used for magnetic bubble memories. Single-loop memories are simple to operate, since they require the minimum number of current loop functions and have a higher data access time. However, a single defective location in the loop makes the entire memory inoperative.

single mode fiber An optical fiber with a core radius close to a wavelength of light, so that only one mode can be propagated.

single pass Refers to a program that generates the desired end result in one computer run.

single pole Refers to a switch or relay in which connections to only one circuit can be made. A single-pole single-throw switch is a basic on-off switch.

single precision In the representation of numbers, the degree of accuracy that requires the use of one computer word. In single precision, seven digits are stored and up to seven digits are printed. *Contrast with* DOUBLE PRECISION.

single ramp A/D converter An A/D converter that uses a reference voltage of opposite polarity to the signal, which is integrated while the counter tracks clock pulses until the integrator output is equal to the signal input. At this time, called Δt, the output of the integrator is $VR\ \Delta t/RC$. The number of counts is proportional to the ratio of the input to the reference. This circuit has the disadvantage that its accuracy depends on the capacitor and the clock frequency. The multiple ramp types provide increased compensation.

single-sideband A method of amplitude-modulated communications in which either the lower or upper sideband-frequency signals produced as a result of modulation are retained and transmitted, and the carrier itself is suppressed. The signals are detected at the receiver by heterodyning them with an oscillator whose output is a modulated beat-frequency tone.

single-step debug A debugging method that uses short routines to set up system states for checking the response of a microprocessor.

single-step operation A method of operating a computer manually in which a single instruction or part of an instruction is performed in response to a single operation of the manual control. Single-step operation is usually initiated to detect mistakes in programming. Each step displays the instruction to be executed as well as the next several instructions. A window can be defined to display user-defined data after each single step.

single-throw circuit breaker A circuit breaker in which only one set of contacts needs to be moved to open or close the circuit.

single-tuned circuit A circuit that may be represented by a single inductance and capacitance, together with their resistances.

single-word instruction An instruction format that requires only one memory location. A single-word instruction format is typical of microcomputer systems.

sink 1. A device that drains off power or energy from a system. **2.** A place where power or energy from several sources is collected or drained away.

sintering Refers to the formation of a solid from powders.

sinusoidal field A field in which the magnitude of the quantity at any point varies as the sine or cosine of an independent variable such as time, displacement, or temperature.

sinusoidal wave *See* SINE WAVE.

SIP Acronym for *single inline package*.

SiteLock A program that provides software license metering, virus protection, and software execution control for NetWare LANs. It limits concurrent use of software to ensure compliance with license agreements and locks users out when all legal copies of software are in use. It also verifies protected files before allowing execution by performing bit-by-bit check against a registered copy of the file. It prevents altered, unauthorized, or possible infected software from running and is compatible with Microsoft Windows.

SI units The modern Scientific International system of units, identical to the electric MKSA system, but more general, using six fundamental units.

SixPack An expansion unit that puts 64 384K bytes of parity-checked memory, one serial port, one printer port, two clock calculators, and one optional game adapter port on a single card. It combines expanded memory for multitasking and added memory for extra-large spreadsheets and databases.

16-bit microprocessors The first 16-bit microprocessors appeared in 1974, with the National Pace unit. The Pace used PMOS technology and it was comparatively slow. During this same period several faster NMOS microprocessors were designed for a variety of minicomputers. The Data General MN601 implemented on a single chip most of the slowest NOVA minicomputer architecture. Most of the early 16-bit microprocessors were targeted at the minicomputer market. The later ones would establish new markets.

6800 microprocessor *See* MOTOROLA 6800.

6531-KBD A unit that provides a standard PC keyboard in a RTMA 19-inch rack mount. A drawer is one rack-unit high (1.75 inches). It is useful for rack installations where rack space is at a premium, since the mounted keyboard takes up so little space.

6531-PRC3 A type of rack mounting for standard office printers. The platform area of the unit will accept many standard printers like Citizen, Panasonic, NEC, HP, and Okidata. There is a 3-inch paper storage area below the printer and a paper take-up area for fanfold paper provided behind the printer platform.

6200-EV An industrial chassis that provides an environmental cocoon for 386 PCs. The computer is shock-mounted for use in high-vibration environments.

skeletal coding Routines or programs in which some addresses and operations are coded while other parts remain undetermined.

skeleton table A macro assembly program table that contains all the prototypes of the macro definitions in a program.

skew The presentational differences between the input and output signals of a propagation system when the response of the processing circuits is not linear over the full signal range.

skewness A statistical measure of the asymmetry in a distribution.

skin effect An effect that occurs when metallic conductors are used to carry high-frequency currents, which are limited to a surface layer equal in thickness to the skin depth; it produces a large value for the high-frequency resistance of the conductor.

skip An instruction that directs the program to proceed to the next instruction. Also called a *blank* instruction or a *no op*.

skip bus A CPU bus that is shared by I/O interfaces, used to test devices associated with each interface and provide conditional branching of the program as a result of the testing.

skip flag A flag produced by a one-bit register to represent the true or false condition with respect to the instruction being executed by the processor.

skip test A microinstruction designed for conditional operations based on the state of readiness of devices or conditions in a register.

sky noise Noise produced by radio energy from stars.

slab A relatively thick crystal from which blanks are cut.

slack The space at the end of a cluster that is not used by a file.

SLAM package Acronym for *single layer metalization*, a DIP (dual-inline package) that offers a low-cost alternative to three-layer ceramic packages. The package uses the same basic materials as a ceramic unit, but is constructed in a simpler manner. It uses a 96% alumina base, one basic metallization layer, an alumina passivation layer, and brazed-on Kovar leads. The leads are suitable for either socket insertion or soldering. Either a glazed ceramic or a Kovar lid is used to hermetically seal the package. The glazed ceramic lid is attached with a low-temperature controlled devitrified glass frit sealant; a gold silicon eutectic solder is used for Kovar lids. It is available in various 14- to 40-pin configurations. *Also see* CERAMIC PACKAGE.

slave A unit or device that is under the control of another unit or device. At any time, there is one device that has control of the communication bus—the *bus master*. The bus master may in turn communicate with any other device, which is called the *slave*.

slaved tracking A system of interconnecting two or more regulated power supplies in which one (the master) operates to control the others (the slaves). The output voltages of the slave units may be equal or proportional to the output voltage of the master unit. The slaved output voltages track the master output in a constant ratio.

slave mode A mode of computer system operation in which most of the basic controls affecting the state of the computer system are protected from outside interference.

slew rate 1. The rate at which a device can be driven from limit to limit over the dynamic output range. **2.** The maximum rate at which a circuit, device, or system can be cycled through its operational states.

slice architecture A microcomputer architecture that uses a section of the register file and ALU in one package. Each end of each two- or four-bit register is accessible through the chip's edge to allow registers (slices) to be cascaded together to form larger word lengths. A slice system can handle large amounts of data at high speed. Typical applications for slice systems include high-speed instrumentation, communications processors, and real-time analysis.

slice latch/mask The device that controls data to one input port of an arithmetic slice unit. A holding latch is used to provide temporary storage for data entering through the output bus port. The latch-clock input controls the latch operation. When not latched, data ripples through the latch and need not be clocked. By using mask-select lines, it is possible to mask data on the output bus.

slice look-ahead A circuit that allows high-speed look-ahead arithmetic operations in bit-slice systems.

slice memory An interface device that connects the slice packages to a main memory system. The chip contains the data and address storage and logic along with the logic for the more complex addressing methods required for the slice configuration.

SlickEdit A programmable editor that can simultaneously edit Mac, Unix, and DOS ASCII format files. It has undo/redo, multiple windows, the ability to handle multiple files up to 1G, online help, multiple clipboards, compiler error-message processing, procedure tagging, a typeless REXX-style macro language, and a programmable file manager. It is available for DOS, OS/2, Windows NT, Sun SPARC 4, SCO Unix 386, and

Xenix 386. The code is compatible across all platforms.

slide A chart produced by a graphics program and incorporated in a slide show.

slide show A list of charts, templates, and other graphics used to create batch output, practice cards, or a screenshow on a graphics program.

slip The irretrievable loss or gain of a set of consecutive bits without loss of alignment. Also called *timing slip*.

slope The essentially linear portion of the characteristic curve of a vacuum tube or solid-state amplifying device. This is where the operating point is chosen for linear amplification.

slope overload distortion In quantization, the distortion that results when the slope of the input signal exceeds the slope of the quantizer.

slot 1. Refers to the cells under a set of heads at one time in a magnetic memory. 2. A port or interface.

slot in use In NetWare Connection Services, indicates whether a slot in the connection ID table is in use.

slotted Aloha A scheme where stations transmit whenever they have something to transmit as long as it is within a time slot boundary.

slotted ring An access control scheme sometimes used in LANs with ring topologies. A number of tokens, separated by fixed-length slots for data packets, circulate continuously around the ring. The fixed spacing between the tokens eliminates the need for complex token-recognition hardware.

slot time A mulitpurpose parameter used to describe the contention behavior of the data link layer of the OSI reference model. It is defined in Ethernet as the propagation delay of the network for a minimum-size packet (64 bytes). Slot time in token-based protocols is either the waiting time for a token or the maximum token-hold time (for the longest packet). Slot time indicates an upper limit on the collision vulnerability of a given transmission and on the size of the frame fragment from the collision run frame, and the scheduling time for collision retransmission.

slow death A term used to describe the gradual deterioration of semiconductor devices, usually due to contamination of surfaces.

SLR Abbreviation for *storage limits register*.

SLT Abbreviation for *solid logic technology*.

slug 1. A heavy metal ring or short-circuit winding used on a relay core to delay operation of the relay. 2. A metallic core that can be moved along the axis of a coil for tuning purposes. 3. A thick copper band on a relay that, through induced eddy currents, retards the operation and fall-off of the relay.

small-signal current gain The output current of a transistor with the output circuit shorted divided by the input current. The current components are understood to be small enough that linear relationships hold.

small-signal power gain The ratio of signal power delivered to the load, to the signal power delivered to the input. Usually expressed in decibels.

Smalltalk/V Windows A popular object-oriented programming environment with complete access to Windows-specific features like DDEs and DLLs. It allows incremental program development with a push-button debugger to simplify application development.

smart actuator An actuator that can be used for position indication, memory, logic, or electronic sensing. It provides inherent intelligence for control applications.

smart card A credit-card-sized unit containing a processor and memory chip that is used to store and update records. For example, smart cards are used in some electronic funds-transfer systems.

Smartcom A menu-driven communications package designed to provide the ability to communicate with mainframe computers as well as other PCs. When you boot up Smartcom it checks the Smartmodem unit to see if the switches are set correctly; if not, it will tell you so. Smartcom has auto-dial and auto-answer features as well as a directory service and a simple text editor.

SmartDRV.SYS DOS's disk cache driver.

SmartHeap for Windows A memory-management library and debugging toolkit for C and C++. It supports heaps and free lists and detects double-freeing, memory overwrites, and leakage.

Smartmodem A series of popular internal and external modems for the PC. The Smartmodem series can be used to access virtually any time-sharing network, information service, electronic mail network, minicomputer or mainframe system that supports asynchronous terminals.

smart printer buffer A printer buffer that allows you to use your computer while it is printing, shown in the following figure. It also will accept data from, or output data to, most other computer-related devices, such as modems, scanners, multiplexers, and terminals. Both serial and parallel versions can store up to 256K of text (approximately 128 pages) and then release it to your printer while you go on to other projects.

SmartSlot architecture In multiuser environments where several users access the disk drive simultaneously, the SmartSlot Advanced Disk Controller manages disk input and output independent of the CPU. The overall result is lower overhead and optimization of overall system throughput.

Smart Software A DOS-based, integrated package system with natural information flow among programs (no reformatting or translations) and a consistent instruction set throughout. The series includes three stand-alone programs: a word processor, database, and spreadsheet with graphics. The database is fully relational and the

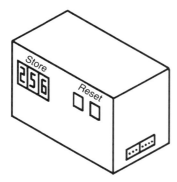

Smart printer buffer

large spreadsheet has many functions. Each of these programs includes a communications capability.

smart terminal A terminal in which part of the processing is done using a microcomputer in the terminal itself. Sometimes called an *intelligent terminal*, the unit allows the user to program the terminal for his or her application.

SMD Abbreviation for *surface-mount device*, an integrated-circuit chip package that uses solder pads to enable chips to be mounted on both sides of the board. *Also see* IC CHIP PACKAGES.

SMDS Abbreviation for *switched multimegabit data service*, a regional Bell operating company service that provides high-speed switched data transmission.

smear An analog artifact in which vertical edges in the display show a spreading to the left or right. It is typically caused by midfrequency distortions in an analog system.

SMI 1. Abbreviation for *static memory interface*. 2. Abbreviation for *structure of management information*, a set of rules that defines the basic identification and formats of the network management for OSI.

smooth contact A socket or pin contact that has a significantly smooth profile with a flush surface.

smileys Tiny cartoons done entirely with the keyboard, as shown in the following table. They can be included in E-mail messages to help indicate your mood or tone of voice. All smileys need to be viewed with the head tilted left. Also called *emoticons or baudy language*.

:-)	Happy, just kidding	;-)	A wink, really kidding
8-:	Surprise!	:{	How sad!
;->	Sardonic incredulity;	:-(	Good grief!
:->	Sarcasm	:-O	Yawn
:*	Kisses	:-\	Undecided
:-x	My lips are sealed		

smoother A combination of capacitors and inductors for removing the ripple from a rectifier supply.

SMP 1. Abbreviation for *sampler*. 2. The *standby monitor present* packet sent out by a standby monitor every seven seconds to advertise its presence.

SMTP Abbreviation for *Simple Mail Transfer Protocol*, a mail service available in TCP/IP. *Also see* TCP/IP.

SNA Abbreviation for *Systems Network Architecture*, IBM's standard protocol between its virtual telecommunication access method (VTAM) and the network control program (NCP/VS).

snail mail Slang term for the traditional postal service, as opposed to e-mail.

SNAP Acronym for *simplified numerical automatic programmer*, a two axis, point-to-point technique or program for numerical control or CAD systems.

snapshot debugging A type of diagnostics and debugging technique in which the programmer specifies the start and end of program segments for which he or she wants to examine the contents of various registers and accumulators. The snapshot tracing may indicate the contents not only of the various accumulators and registers but also of specified memory locations.

snapshot dump A dynamic partial printout during computing at breakpoints and checkpoints, or selected areas of storage. It provides a "snapshot" of the system at a particular point.

Snapshot Storage Scope A menu-driven digital storage oscilloscope package for PC compatibles. It is designed for users whose primary needs are real-time collection, display, and storage of analog data. It can both acquire and display data in virtual real-time up to the maximum sampling speed of the boards.

snapshot system A system that plants unconditional transfer orders to the system at arbitrary points in another program, executes dumps of specified registers and storage locations at these points during the running of the program, and then returns control to the program in such a way that the program is unaffected.

Sniffer network analyzer A Network General product used to monitor many different upper- and lower-layer network protocols.

SNMP Abbreviation for *Simple Network Management Protocol*, a protocol originally designed for the Internet to manage devices from different vendors.

SNOBOL Acronym for *string-oriented symbolic language*, a programming language used mainly for advanced string manipulation. Some examples of this are in artificial intelligence, compiler construction, and text preparation. It was developed by Bell Laboratories.

snowflake A LAN configuration in which a number of star-configured subsystems are interlinked.

This topology has particular application in fiber-optic networks.

SNR Abbreviation for *signal to noise ratio*.

SO Abbreviation for the *shift-out* character, a code-extension character that can be used to replace one set of characters in a register with another set, or the null set.

SOA Abbreviation for *state-of-the-art*.

socket 1. In the NetWare Service Advertising Protocol, a socket number allows a value-added server to accept queries and deliver services. **2.** A slot for the installation of a memory module. *Also see* SIMM.

socket longevity flag In NetWare Communication Services, this specifies how long a socket should remain open. You can set this field to specify that the socket will remain open until closed with the IPX close socket call, or until the application is terminated. You can also set the socket to remain open until it is explicitly closed with the IPX close socket.

socket number In NetWare, the number of the socket on which a server will receive requests, or the socket associated with an ECB.

soft boot *See* WARM BOOT.

soft break 1. A page or line break that is determined by page or line layout. Soft breaks may change after further editing of the document. *Contrast with* HARD BREAK. **2.** A phenomenon in RAM where a memory location is altered due to background radiation or other electrical interference. The soft break rate in most RAM memory is once in every several trillion memory accesses. Most soft breaks occur in unused memory locations and are not noticed. Also called a *soft drop*.

softcopy A name for output to a monitor. *Contrast with* HARDCOPY.

soft font A font located on a disk and loaded into the RAM of the printer when needed. Soft fonts are lost from the printer's memory when the power is turned off.

soft limited A limiting action with an appreciable tolerance in the limiting value.

SoftProbe A source-level remote target debugger for 386 and higher embedded systems applications. It accepts executable files in boot-loadable formats and allows downloading programs from the host PC and debugging on the actual target system. The debugger has a multiwindow user interface and concurrently displays registers, sources, and command dialogs.

soft return A carriage return entered into a document when hyphenation help or word wrap is used.

soft-sectored disk A floppy disk on which records are placed by the drive to mark the boundaries of each sector before the disk is initially used.

Softerm PC Software that allows a PC to communicate with hosts and dial-up services. It also gives multitasking capabilities that allow you to interrupt any program and make your connection by pressing a key.

soft error An intermittent error on a computer system or network that may cause data to be transmitted more than once in order to be received.

Soft/3270 A software product designed for PC-to-IBM-mainframe access. It allows asynch 3270 emulation, mainframe file transfer, and remote print software for a PC.

Soft-touch A memory-resident program that allows keys to be reprogrammed. It operates as a type of computer shorthand, allowing you to speed through often-repeated commands or entries.

software The programs, routines, languages, and procedures used in a computer system. Software items include assemblers, generators, subroutines, compilers, operating systems, and applications. Off-the-shelf software continues to grow in variety and sophistication, providing relief from the high cost of in-house software development. Word processors and spreadsheets are the most widely used of these packages, although database and graphics packages are also common.

software compatibility Refers to the ability of software to work on a given configuration of hardware and operating programs. Many problems in compatibility can be minimized by using a standard operating system and BIOS. In some cases, however, users may already have a mix of different machines. Extra effort may be needed to make such a variety of brands and models work together for a particular application.

software cross assembler *See* CROSS ASSEMBLER.

software development Refers to the development of a mathematical model of the process or task the microcomputer is to solve and the interpretation of the model into a set of control programs. A typical software development process includes the following:

- Problem statement
- Design of algorithms
- Flowchart construction
- Program coding
- Preparation of source code
- Translation to object code
- Loading of object code
- Checkout and debugging
- Documentation

software documentation *See* DOCUMENTATION.

software documents Written or printed material associated with the microcomputer, including manuals, diagrams, and listings.

software evaluation and development modules A system of modules that gives a means of building up and testing a proposed microcomputer system before committing the design to hardware. First the functional specifications and programs are established, then the ROM program is assembled and simulated on a time-shared system, using the software modules.

software house A company that offers software support services to users, including consulting and programming.

software integrity The software's reliability.

software interrupt An interrupt instruction that can be used for debugging purposes. The instruction usually saves the current value of the program counter and then branches to a specified memory location. This memory location may be used as the starting point for a debugging program that then lists or displays selected status information. *Also see* INTERRUPT.

software interrupt instruction *See* SWI.

software library The collection of programs used by an operating system. A microcomputer software library may include a machine-language assembler, Teletype operating system, tape editor, simulator, cross assembler, map generator, and utility and diagnostic programs.

software modularity The degree of flexibility in the programming and operating aids furnished with systems. Most types of programs in the software library are offered in several versions to run in system configurations of different sizes and compositions. Most software written for large systems are designed to take advantage of the increased internal and I/O processing capacities of these systems.

software package The programs or sets of programs used in a particular application or function. Many software packages include diagnostic programs for verifying processor and memory operation.

software priority interrupts Refers to interrupt priorities that are defined and controlled by the microprocessor. After an interrupt request occurs, it is transmitted to the microprocessor and the address is compared with a multibit interrupt-enabling mask. If the address is equal or less than the mask, the request is recognized. The mask is forced to one less than the address and servicing begins. If the address is greater than the mask, the request is queued. In this scheme, only interrupts from a device with an address lower than that of the device being serviced are recognized. The lower the address, the higher the priority, as shown in the following figure. The interrupts are nested for rapid service of high-priority interrupts even when they occur while a low-priority interrupt is being serviced.

software simulator A major aid to the programming of a microcomputer system, useful to check out central processor coding, and sometimes peripherals or input/output equipment. However, a programming problem can be related to the timing and quality of the signal on a computer input or output or can be related to an external device fault, which can be difficult to isolate with only a simulator.

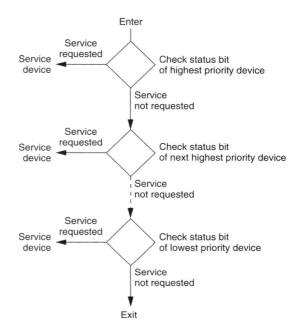

Software priority interrupt system

software stack register A status register that sometimes provides latched flag outputs and accepts sense inputs. It can be tested under program control. The status register may contain the interrupt enable flag as well as arithmetic carry and overflow flags. The carry flag can also be used as a link for multiple byte shift and rotate instructions. The provision of the interrupt input means that the processor does not have to use valuable computing time looping through a scan or polling sequence.

software test set A set of programs used to support the development of custom programs and to verify the design under actual operating conditions prior to release of the ROM pattern to manufacturing. The software set usually consists of a cross assembler, simulator, and test-program generator.

software tools Programs that assist the programmer during the development cycle. Software tools include editors, assemblers, compilers, loaders, linkage editors, debuggers, and simulators.

SOH The *start-of-heading* character, a communications control character used as the first character of a heading in a message. In ASCII, it is designated as a seven-bit binary one.

SOL Abbreviation for *simulation-oriented language*.

solder A tin-lead alloy used for making electrical connections. In use, molten solder is applied to conductor joints. When the solder cools, it solidifies to hold the conductors permanently in place.

solder-covered wire Copper wire coated with solder instead of tin, used to facilitate connections between components in electrical and electronic equipment.

solderless breadboard A circuit breadboard that contains sockets and socket pins to allow temporary solder-free connections during test or debugging operations.

solderless connector A device for clamping two wires together without the use of solder.

solderless wrap A method of connection in which a solid wire is wrapped around a metal terminal using a special hand or power tool. Also called *wire wrap*.

solder short A circuit or component defect that occurs when solder forms a short-circuit path between two or more conductors.

solder socket-type pins Pins for insertion into the crimp-type connector shell after being soldered to the cable conductor.

solder sucker A type of soldering iron designed for desoldering chips; for resoldering you need a regular low-wattage iron. The solder sucker has a small rubber bulb that is used to take up melted solder, as shown in the figure.

When the DIP is desoldered, the iron is heated and the bulb is squeezed while the tip of the hot iron is placed on the bottom of the board under the first plated through-pin. (It helps to have a bright light on the bottom of the board.) The bulb is held closed while the solder melts. When the solder is liquid, the bulb is released. The solder at the heated pin is sucked into the bulb. The solder is removed from the bulb by squeezing it. This is repeated until all the pins are free and the chip can be removed.

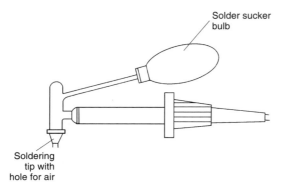

Solder sucker

solder track An electrical conductor on a printed circuit board, made by applying molten solder to the board.

solenoid A current-carrying iron-core coil of wire typically used as a controllable magnet for opening or closing mechanical contacts or valves.

solicit successor frame A frame sent on a token bus network, designed to determine the next user of the network.

solid conductor A wire or conductor composed of a single strand.

solid-state Descriptive of circuits or systems constructed with active devices other than vacuum tubes.

solid-state component A component that depends upon the control of electrical or electromagnetic phenomena in a solid material; thus, a transistor, diode, or integrated circuit.

solid-state I/O accessory board A board used to accommodate different power loads. Separate modules let you control loads ranging from 24 to 140 VAC and 60 VDC at 3A, as well as sense voltages of 90 to 140 VAC and 10 to 32 VDC. Up to eight modules can be added to the board.

solid-state integrated circuit The class of integrated circuit components in which only solid-state materials are used.

solid-state memory A memory constructed entirely of circuits employing semiconductor devices.

solid-state physics The branch of physics that studies the properties of solid materials, especially conduction in semiconductors and metals.

SOM 1. Abbreviation for *self-organizing machine*, a machine in which the internal organization is conducted by the machine itself, without external intervention. 2. Abbreviation for *start of message*.

SONET Acronym for *synchronous optical network*, a common-carrier fiber optic transmission link providing bandwidth in blocking units of 50 Mbits per second. Multiple streams can support bandwidths up to 18 billion bits per second.

sonic delay line A device for simulating the acoustical delay of a long transmission line and used to emulate the effect of reverberation, or for providing phase changes to input signals under controlled conditions.

SOP Acronym for *standard operating procedure*.

sophisticated vocabulary An advanced and elaborate set of instructions.

sort To rearrange or segregate usually listed items into groups according to a specified order. For example, a list of subjects in a book can be entered in order of page number, then sorted to be listed in alphabetical order.

sort command A database command that places data into order by a key field identified by the user.

sorter A device or routine used as the basis for determining the sequential order of the items in a set and for producing the list in that order.

sort key A key used as the basis for determining the sequential arrangement of items in a set.

SOS Abbreviation for *silicon-on-sapphire*, a semiconductor process that uses a sapphire base to "grow" silicon for the production of MOS transistors. SOS devices achieve bipolar speeds, provide radiation protection for military applications, and are well-suited for CMOS designs. SOS technology can be applied in memories, microprocessors, high-speed counters, and multiplexers.

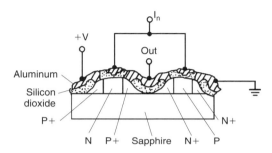

SOS structure

SOS CMOS Abbreviation for *silicon-on-sapphire complementary metal-oxide semiconductor*, a low-power, high-speed MOS device.

SOS RAM Abbreviation for a type of random access memory that uses the silicon-on-sapphire technology. A typical unit uses the SOS MOS technology for a 1024-bit memory that operates with +4.5 to 6 volts and consumes only 4 mW of power. The unit is static, with no requirement for refreshing, clocking, or pulsing circuitry.

SOS transistor Abbreviation for *silicon-on-sapphire* transistor, an active device on a sapphire substrate that is electrically isolated from all others on the substrate.

sound card An audio card used for multimedia. Most are 16-bit, although the originals were 8-bit cards. Newer cards have features like DSP (digital signal processing), data compression, 3D sound, onboard fax/modems, voice mail, and voice recognition. Sampling rates are critical to the quality of a sound card. The benchmark is the basic sample rate of CD audio: 44KHz. The higher the rate, the more accurately a card can record and playback sounds. However, better quality also means bigger files; a one-minute file at 44-KHz stereo can take up 10M of disk space. For this reason, many cards use ADPCM data compression.

Synthesis is another important topic. FM (frequency modulation) is a common technique in inexpensive cards, but wavetable synthesis produces better sound because it uses digital recordings of actual instruments. Many cards use FM with wavetable as an option.

For Windows-based applications, compatibility with Sound Blaster or AdLib is needed for most software. This can be accomplished by using an FM synthesis chip, as on the original cards, or by emulation.

To be most useful, a sound card also needs an onboard mixer. Sources may include CD-ROM audio, synthesizer, digitized sound, the computer's internal speaker, and a microphone.

In a sound card, the interfaces are important. CD-ROM interfaces are common. Proprietary interfaces limit the drive types, while SCSI and SCSI-2 can connect a large range of CD-ROM drives along with tape drives, scanners, and hard disks. A MIDI interface is also useful to connect the computer to a synthesizer keyboard or external module.

sound synthesizer Output hardware that generates recognizable sounds such as warnings and music.

source 1. A circuit or device that serves as a distributor (of voltage, data, timing pulses, etc.) to other devices. **2.** An element in a circuit which serves as the starting point for an energy pulse of a given polarity (a charged capacitor, for example). **3.** An originator.

source address The part of a data message that indicates the message's origin.

source code Program statements, arguments, and codes generated by keyboard inputs to a system.

source-code instruction An instruction used as a pointer in microprogrammed systems to emulate a particular instruction set being executed.

source connection ID In NetWare Communication Services, a number assigned by SPX at a packet's source.

source data Data generated in the course of research, design, and development.

source data automation See SDA.

source document A form on which data are collected for computer input.

source editor A program that allows the entry and modification of source code into the system for later translation or storage.

source-explicit forwarding A security feature provided by a router or gateway that allows only packets from a specified list to be forwarded to another network.

source file editor A line-oriented editor that operates on programs in a sequence determined by their assembler-produced statement line numbers. The editor produces an updated file while preserving the original master file.

source impedance The impedance presented to the input of a device by the source.

source language The original language in which a program is prepared prior to translation for processing by the machine.

source-language translation The translation of a program to a target program, such as from Pascal to machine language.

source-level debugging A form of debugging that can show you what is happening with high-level

source code in contrast to only assembly language code.

source library A collection of programs (compiler or assembler) for a specific machine.

source module A set of statements in a source language recorded in machine-readable form and suitable for input to an assembler or compiler.

source network In NetWare Communication Services, the network number of a station sending an IPX packet. NetWare network numbers are four-byte values given to servers on the same network segment.

source node In NetWare Communication Services, this is set by IPX as the physical address of the source node.

source program A program that can be translated automatically into machine language to become an object program. Source programs are usually written in a language designed for ease of expression. A generator, assembler, translator, or compiler routine is used for translation into the object program in machine code.

Sourcer A commenting disassembler that automatically converts COM files, EXE files, device drivers, overlays, RAM, and ROM into commented assembly code. It has built-in code and data analyzers with code simulation. It disassembles 8080 through 80486, real and protected code, and includes automatic indexed call/jump analysis with descriptive labeling for BIOS areas.

source socket In NetWare Communication Services, this is set by the IPX and is the socket address of the process sending a packet.

source statement A statement written in other than machine language. Source statements are written in symbolic terms for translation to machine code.

source utility A program that aids in the preparation and modification of symbolic assembly-language programs.

space 1. A site intended for the storage of data, such as a specific position on a page in memory. 2. A unit of area equal to a single character on a line. 3. To advance a reading or display position in order to create a desired format.

space character 1. A nonprinting character used to separate words. 2. A format effector that controls the printing or display position in a system, sometimes abbreviated *SP*.

space diversity A method of radio transmission employed to minimize the effects of fading by the simultaneous use of two or more antennas spaced apart.

spacing distortion A bias distortion in which received spaces appear longer than received marks.

spacing A typographic term for the proportionality of a particular font. All fonts are designed with either fixed or proportional spacing. Using *fixed spacing*, all characters are the same width, as they are on a typewriter. Using *proportional spacing*, character width depends on the character size, so i takes up less space on a line than w.

spark The result of the breakdown of insulation between two conductors when the potential is sufficient to cause ionization and rapid discharge.

spark absorber A resistor and/or capacitor placed across a break in an electrical circuit to damp any possible oscillatory circuit that would tend to maintain an arc or spark when the current is interrupted.

Sparkle Software that lets you use any NetBIOS LAN workstation as a LAN terminal. You can connect to any async host, either local or remote, from anywhere on the LAN and use any modem or serial port on your LAN from any other workstation. You can then move files to and from almost any computer (even a minicomputer host). You can also take control of a remote PC equipped with Sparkle, exchange files with that PC, or give it dial-up access to your LAN and share your workstation remotely.

SPC Abbreviation for *silver-plated copper*.

spec Shortened form (pronounced "speck") of *specification*.

special character A graphic symbol that is neither a letter, a numeral, nor a space character.

special-function keys *See* FUNCTION KEY.

special-purpose bus interface A bus system that may use one or more integrated circuits to link the microprocessor to a particular I/O device. In addition to the basic bus interface circuits, the interface may contain circuits for specific functions peculiar to the I/O device. For example, a keyboard interface would require matrix encoding and perhaps parity-generating functions. A printer interface would require message formatting, character storage, and print heat control and timing functions. A communications interface might require serial-to-parallel/parallel-to-serial conversion, parity generation, message formatting, and modem control.

special-purpose computer A computer designed to handle a restricted class of problems.

specific address An absolute address.

specific code An absolute code.

specific conductivity The conducting ability of a material in ohms per cubic centimeter. It is the reciprocal of resistivity.

specific dielectric strength The dielectric strength per millimeter of thickness of an insulating material.

specific gravity The weight of a substance compared with the weight of the same volume of water at the same temperature.

specific magnetic moment The value of the saturation moment per unit weight of a magnetic material, expressed in *emu/gm*. The specific magnetic moment is a convenient quantity in which to express the saturation magnetization of fine particle materials. For example, the specific magnetic moment of pure gamma ferric oxide is approximately 75 emu/gm at room temperature.

specific resistance The resistance of a conductor, expressed in ohms per unit length per unit area.

specific routine A routine used to solve a particular arithmetic, logic, or data-handling problem in which each address refers to explicitly stated registers and locations.

spectrometer 1. A test instrument that determines the frequency distribution of the energy generated by a source and displays all components simultaneously. **2.** An instrument used for the measurement of wavelength or energy distribution in a heterogeneous beam of radiation.

spectrum 1. The arrangement of components of a complex color or sound in order of frequency of energy, thereby showing the distribution of energy or stimulus among the components. A mass spectrum is one showing the distribution in mass or in mass-to-charge-ratio of ionized atoms or molecules. **2.** The range of electromagnetic waves to the shortest cosmic rays. Light, the visible portion of the spectrum, lies about midway between the two extremes. **3.** A graphical representation of the distribution of the amplitude (and sometimes phase) of the components of a wave as a function of frequency. A spectrum may be continuous or contain only points corresponding to certain discrete values.

spectrum analysis A technique that measures signal frequencies to ascertain that the signal meets the requirements.

speech generator Output hardware that generates recognizable human speech.

speech interpolation A voice-multiplexing scheme in which the gaps and pauses occurring in one voice channel are filled with speech bursts from other voice channels to reduce the bandwidth or transmission rate.

speed-matching buffer A small memory that adjusts speeds between two devices operating at different data-transfer rates. The first machine writes into the buffer at its own rate and then signals the second machine that a message is waiting. The second machine reads the message at its own rate and replies by writing a message into the buffer.

spelling checker A part of some word-processing packages that finds possible spelling errors in text and may display a suggested correction.

SpinRite A program designed to eliminate the cause of DOS errors such as Sector Not Found, Boot Failure, Bad Sector Error and other data-related Abort, Retry, and Ignore problems. It identifies, diagnoses, and repairs hard drive that use standard DOS partitions. It uses worse-case data pattern testing on all drive types, including IDE and SCSI. It finds disk surface flaws, moves endangered data to safety, and prevents flawed areas from being used again. It optimizes the sector interleave to deliver the maximum hard disk data transfer rate and also restores the drive's low-level format.

splice closure A container used to organize and protect spliced cable trays.

splice tray A container used to organize and protect spliced fiber cables.

splicing The permanent joining of fiber cable ends to identical or similar fibers, without the use of a connector.

spike A sudden surge of electricity.

spindle The part of a disk drive that rotates the disk.

spin out An effect that occurs when a relay is subjected to high inrush currents of relatively long duration.

split screen A mode of operation on a display screen in which the screen is subdivided into zones, each containing a different file or portion of a file, or with one zone displaying output and the other reserved for prompts and input.

spool A memory or storage area for a fast device (such as a software program) to leave data for later processing on a slow device (such as a printer).

spooler enhancement switch A switch that expands the configuration possibilities of a serial-to-parallel print spooler or mini-spooler, as shown. The switch has three DB25S (female) connectors, three female Centronics-type connectors, and two switch settings, A and B. The A setting connects serial ports 1 and 2 together and parallel ports 1 and 2 together. The B setting connects serial ports 2 and 3 together and parallel ports 2 and 3 together. By connecting this spooler across any combination of a serial port and a parallel port, a wide variety of system utilizations can be achieved.

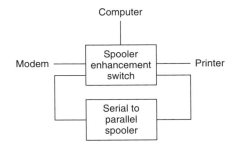

Spooler enhancement switch

spooling A procedure of temporarily storing data on disk until the CPU is ready for additional processing of the information.

spool time In NetWare Print Services, this indicates when a job was spooled to a print queue.

sporadic Intermittent.

sporadic fault Intermittent failures to perform in the manner required under specified conditions.

spraypaint A method of spreading color or a pattern over a large area in a drawing or paint program. As with a can of paint, the color or pattern gets darker the more the spraypaint function is used over an area.

spreadsheet A program for managing numbers, particularly useful in accounting and related applications. A spreadsheet program allows the user to input rows and columns of data analogous to the traditional ledger sheet, which can be manipulated and updated through use of spreadsheet functions and commands. When you change the values of numbers in the grid, the program automatically calculates what effect, if any, there is on all the other numbers. The spreadsheet can provide answers within seconds to all sorts of financial and statistical "what-ifs."

Spreadsheet Auditor A utility for spreadsheet users that can be used to locate and correct errors in your spreadsheet and to document a spreadsheet so that it can be used by those other than the person who designed it.

Typical spreadsheet errors include specifying the wrong ranges in a formula, entering data on top of a formula, copying a formula incorrectly, entering an otherwise correct formula with an incorrect reference. The Spreadsheet Auditor displays formulas in a two-dimensional grid that exactly matches the layout of your spreadsheet. All formulas are shown with column letters and row numbers.

spread-spectrum technology A technology that spreads a data signal across a wide range of frequencies.

spring-finger action The operation of electrical contact that permit a stress-free spring action to develop contact pressure. These contacts are used in sockets of printed circuits and in many types of connectors.

sprites Screen images movable under program or manual control through an input device. Sprites may be characters, cursor shapes, or specific patterns and are normally smaller than full screen size.

SPS Abbreviation for *series-parallel-series*.

SPSS Abbreviation for *Statistical Package for the Social Sciences*, an integrated system of programs combined in one program, designed for the analysis of social science data.

spurious oscillation *See* PARASITIC OSCILLATION.

spurious pulse A pulse not purely generated or directly due to circuit or system operation.

spurious pulse mode An unwanted pulse mode that may be formed by the chance combination of two or more pulse modes. It may be indistinguishable from a normal pulse mode or reply.

SPX Abbreviation for *sequenced packet exchange*, Novell's implementation of the XNS Sequenced Packet Protocol. SPX is the part of the NetWare shell that guarantees delivery of a message sent from one node to another.

SPX installation flag In NetWare Communication Services, a flag that indicates whether SPX is installed.

SPX major revision number In NetWare Communication Services, this indicates which SPX revision is installed.

SPX major version In NetWare Diagnostic Services, the SPX major version installed on a responding node.

SPX minor revision number In NetWare Communication Services, this indicates which SPX revision is installed.

SPX minor version In NetWare Diagnostic Services, the SPX minor version installed on a responding node.

SPX packet header In NetWare Diagnostic Services, a 42-byte field containing information specific to SPX.

SPX watchdog In NetWare Communication Services, a flag that monitors an SPX connection, ensuring that the connection is functioning properly when traffic is not passing through the connection. The application should initialize the this flag.

SQA A tool for the quality-assurance and testing process of software development. It allows developers to automate test planning, tracking and management. It includes standard IEEE, DOD, and MILSPEC test plan templates and comprehensive reports for relational databases, e-mail, and spreadsheets.

SQL Abbreviation for *structured query language* (pronounced "es-cue-el" or "sequel"), a database query language IBM developed for its mainframe databases. SQL is implemented in many PC database software applications to allow a more standard method of accessing data across both mainframe and PC platforms.

square loop A hysteresis loop that is not like an S-shaped curve but is square or rectangular in shape.

squareness ratio The ratio for a magnetic material in a symmetrically cyclically magnetized condition of the residual magnetic flux density, or the flux density at zero magnetizing force, to the maximum flux or density.

square pixels Pixels generated on a monitor or tel-evision having the same horizontal and vertical resolution. There is some evidence that a large mismatch between horizontal and vertical resolution prevents the higher resolution from being fully perceived by the human visual system. NTSC was created with square pixels with a resolution of approximately 330 by 330 lines.

square wave A pulse with very rapid (theoretically infinite) rise and fall times, and a pulse duration equal to half period of repetition.

SR 1. Abbreviation for *study requirement*. **2.** Abbreviation for *shift register*. **3.** Abbreviation for *send-receive*.

SRAM Abbreviation for *static RAM*, a type of RAM that holds its contents as long as the power is on. In contrast, *DRAM* (dynamic RAM) has to be refreshed many times a second. However, SRAM suffers from a lack of circuit density because it uses transistor-only construction, rather than the capacitor-transistor construction of DRAM. This same construction technique makes SRAM more expensive per memory unit.

SRC Sniffer analyzer abbreviation for the source data link address.

SRPI Abbreviation for *server/requester programming interface*, a programming interface that allows mainframe computers to be accessed like a file server on a network.

SS 1. Abbreviation for *single-sided*, referring to the use of one side of the floppy disk for recording information. **2.** Abbreviation for *solid state*. **3.** Abbreviation for *single side-band*.

SSAP Abbreviation for *source service access point*, the address of the user of a service.

SSB Abbreviation for *single side-band*.

SSCP Abbreviation for *system service control point*, a device in an SNA network. *Also see* NAU.

SSI Abbreviation for *small-scale integration*.

SSS Abbreviation for *server session socket*, the AppleTalk Session Protocol field that contains the socket number to which session-level packets are sent.

stability The freedom from undesirable deviation, used as a measure of process controllability.

stable 1. A system not exhibiting sudden changes. **2.** The incapability of following a stated mode of spontaneous change. **3.** The state of an amplification or control system when it satisfies a stability test such as the Nyquist criterion, either conditionally or unconditionally.

stable oscillation A condition in which amplitude and/or frequency will remain constant indefinitely. A *statically stable* system may be dynamically unstable and follow a divergent oscillation when subjected to a disturbance. *Dynamically stable* means that an induced oscillation will be convergent, with a decreasing amplitude.

stable state In a digital circuit, a phase that will continue each time the circuit is restarted, until the circuit is switched to the opposite state or phase by another input signal.

stable trigger A circuit with two binary states, each state requiring a trigger signal for transition from one state to another. Also known as *binary pair*, *trigger pair*, and *R-S-T flip-flop*.

stack A block of successive memory locations accessible from one end and coordinated with a stack pointer that keeps track of storage and retrieval of each word in the stack, as shown in the figure. A pushdown stack operates as a LIFO (last-in- first-out) buffer; as data is added, the stack moves down with the last item occupying the top position. The stack hardware is a

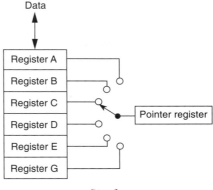

Stack

collection of registers with a counter that indicates the most recently loaded register. The registers are unloaded in the reverse order in which they were loaded.

The major use of the stack is to store subroutine return addresses. Each jump-to-subroutine instruction moves a return address from the program counter to the stack, and each return instruction fetches a return address from the stack and places it in the program counter. Thus, the program can trace its path through the subroutine by using the stack.

Some microprocessors use a dedicated stack to save the program counter. These systems have a minimum of status information and are limited in the calling subroutines or serving polled inputs and interrupts. When the stack is in RAM for saving return address, certain locations of the data memory are assigned as the stack. These bytes provide the locations that permit stacking. A counter will point initially to the first location. A call instruction increments this counter by one and a return decrements it by one. This configuration usually has a fixed depth. The stack register may also be used as conventional data memory.

stack architecture Descriptive of a microcomputer that uses a stack for part of its internal memory. Stack architecture reduces the number of registers required for temporary storage and can decrease the number of steps required in a program. Multilevel interrupts can easily be handled with a stacked system, since system status can be saved when an interrupt occurs and restored after the interrupt.

stack control The ability to process stacked service requests and status words. The type of stack control used is important in reducing processor time.

stacked bar chart A graphics bar chart in which each bar represents more than one measurement, each in a different color or pattern.

stacked job processing A procedure of automatic job-to-job transitions with little or no operator intervention.

stack manipulation Refers to a system with instruction addressing modes that allow temporary data storage structures for the convenient handling of data that is frequently processed. The register used to keep track of stack manipulation is called the *stack pointer*. Stack manipulation is often used in microcomputers to offset the shortcomings of their relatively small instruction sets.

stack pointer A register that contains the address of the top of a stack. The stack is the LIFO (last-in-first-out) buffer used for memory referencing. In most computer stacks, the stored elements do not actually move; the only change that occurs is in the stack pointer. The CPU adds data to the stack by placing the data in the memory location addressed by the stack pointer and then incrementing the stack pointer. It removes data from the stack by decrementing the stack pointer and obtaining the data from the memory location addressed by the stack pointer.

The stack may be composed of read/write memory or a register array. The main idea behind the use of a stack is that data can be added up to the capacity of the stack without disturbing the data that is already there. If this data were stored in a memory location or register, the previous contents would be lost. The stack can be used over and over since its previous contents are automatically saved. Also, the CPU can quickly transfer data to or from the stack since the address is in the stack pointer and the stack instructions can be very short.

stack register See STACK POINTER.

STALO Acronym for *stable local oscillator*.

stand-alone program A program that operates independently of system control. It is generally either self-loaded or loaded by another stand-alone program.

stand-alone system A system that is self-contained and performs its specified functions without being connected to other equipment.

standard An established unit of measurement, or a reference instrument or component, suitable for use in the calibration of other instruments. Basic standards are those possessed or set by national or international laboratories or institutes.

standard component A component that is regularly produced by one or more manufacturers and supplied by one or more distributors.

standard dictionary Provides for spelling of common words in a word processor. Most standard dictionaries contain over 100,000 words. Spell checks are made against this dictionary first, although the user may create additional, specialized dictionaries. Also called the *main dictionary*.

standard form See NORMALIZED FORM.

standard interface An interface that allows several units or systems to be easily interconnected.

Standard-Micro Systems The makers of ARCnet hardware.

standard mode A Windows operating mode that supports the capabilities of the 80286 processor. This means that Windows will use any extended memory found in the workstation by using the processor's protected mode. You can also load more than one application at a time (up to the limits imposed by physical RAM). This mode does not support virtual memory or page-swapping. It also does not support the multitasking features available starting with the 80386.

standard refraction The refraction resulting from a gradient of radio refractivity equal to –40 N/km. Also corresponding to atmospheric refraction, with k equal to $\frac{4}{3}$.

standards converter A device for converting signals from one standard to another. Converting between different color schemes with the same scanning structure is called *transcoding*. Converting between different scanning structures requires line and field interpolation, which usually introduces artifacts. Conversion is performed regularly between 525 and 625 scanning-line signals.

standard subroutine A subroutine applicable to a specific class or set of problems.

standby 1. A nonoperating-but-ready condition of equipment, which allows resumption of operation when permitted. **2.** A duplicate set of equipment used when the primary equipment malfunctions.

standby application An application where two or more machines are tied together as a part of the system design and stand ready for activation and processing of system inquiries.

standby monitor present A packet sent out by a standby monitor every few seconds to advertise its presence.

standby register A register in which information is stored for rerun in the event of a mistake in the program or a malfunction in the machine.

standby time The time between inquiries in a system, or the time two or more computers are connected for a standby application.

standby UPS An uninterruptible power supply that stands by in case of a power failure. It has an electronic converter to provide the ac power needed.

standing-on-nines carry A high-speed carry in which a carry input to a given digit place is bypassed to the next digit place if the current sum in the given digit place is nine.

star configuration A network configuration in which the host processor is the center of the system and each processor communicates with the host, as shown. Communication between satellite processors is through the host, so this configuration lends itself to control by the host. More than one satellite can talk to the host at the same

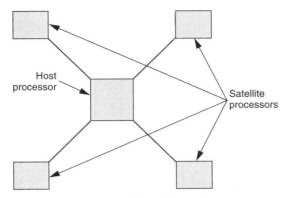

Star network configuration

time, and the host may be burdened with supervising data flow between satellites. Also known as a *radial* or *centralized* configuration.

Starlan A network noted for its low cost per user and its flexible star topology. Starlan is easy to install; you can use star topologies, daisychains, or both, and set up modular workgroups appropriate to your environment. Starlan uses CSMA/CD access and operates over two twisted pairs (unshielded, 24 or 26 gauge). Throughput is 1 mb/sec.

Starlan local module A local module for AT&T or Western Digital Starlan networks. You can use a module to upgrade your existing Starlan network or to interconnect with other modules. You can also connect it to an Ethernet local module to access an Ethernet backbone.

start bit In asynchronous transmission, the first bit or element in each character, normally a space, which serves to prepare the receiving equipment for the reception and registration of the character.

starter voltage drop Refers to the voltage drop across the starter gap in a glow-discharge, cold cathode tube, after conduction is established there.

starting block In NetWare Directory Services, the number of the first block of a volume.

start-of-heading character See SOH.

start-of-text character See STX.

start-top multivibrator A type of multivibrator that has one stable state and one unstable state and goes through a complete change cycle. The circuit provides a single signal of the proper form and time from a varying shaped, randomly timed signal. Upon receipt of a trigger signal, it assumes another state for a specified length of time, at the end of which it returns of its own accord to its original state.

star topology A LAN topology in which links to all of the other stations radiate from a central hub station.

statement A meaningful expression or generalized instruction in a program.

state-of-the-art A phrase that implies being up-to-date in technology, including current hardware, software, and methods of operation. Sometimes abbreviated *SOA*.

static 1. Nonmovable or nonrotating; for example, a transformer or rectifier is a static converter. 2. Electrostatic. 3. An electrical disturbance that arises through electrostatic induction, particularly from lightning flashes.

static behavior The behavior of a control system or a unit under fixed conditions; as contrasted with dynamic behavior, which occurs under changing conditions.

static charge The accumulated electric charge on an object.

static CMOS memory A group of memory cells that use a flip-flop arrangement in which the transistors function as the loads are combined into a complementary circuit. The static CMOS (complementary metal-oxide semiconductor) memory allows low power dissipation with less density than the standard metal-oxide semiconductors (MOS). It is also compatible with TTL logic for easy interfacing.

static-column page mode-RAM A RAM where the chip's address is made up of two parts, the column and row addresses. Since both of these are not always needed, reads and writes are faster.

static dissipating unit A unit that absorbs and dissipates harmful static charges at a rate of 20,000 volts in less than two seconds. It consists of two coiled leads, one attached to the screen and one to the keyboard, that plug into a static collector with an attached ground wire. They channel the static charges to ground.

static drain-source on-state resistance The dc resistance between the drain and source terminals with a specified gate source voltage applied to bias the device to the on state.

static dump A dump that is performed at a specific time in a machine run, usually at the end of the run.

static eliminator A device that fills the air with a stream of positive and negative ions. The static charges are continuously neutralized at the source.

static error An error that is independent of time.

static forward-current transfer ratio The ratio, under specified test conditions, of the dc output current to the dc input current in a transistor.

static gain The gain of a device under steady-state conditions.

static input resistance The ratio of the dc input voltage to the input current in a transistor.

static interface A menu that does not automatically change to reflect the current machine configuration or operating system environment.

staticizer A storage device for converting serial or

time-sequential information into parallel static data.

static magnetic cell A storage cell in which the two values are represented by different patterns of magnetization.

static magnetic storage Storage of information bits on a medium that holds the data in place so that it is available at any time, such as in a core cell.

static memory A memory device that contains no mechanical moving parts or one that contains fixed information. Also refers to memory chips that do not need to be refreshed or clocked. *Also see* STATIC STORAGE.

static memory card A circuit board that contains a semiconductor memory.

static MOS Metal-oxide semiconductor memory circuits that are cross-coupled bistable units for storing information in one of two stable states.

static MOS RAM A read-write memory that stores data in integrated flip-flops, shown in the following figure.

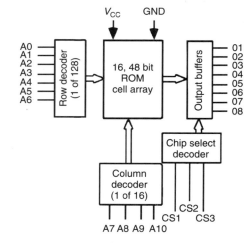

Static MOS ROM

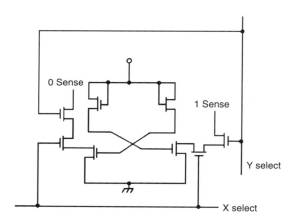

Basic static MOS RAM cell

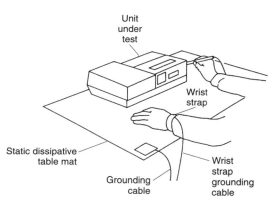

Shorting static electricity to ground with a static mat and wrist strap

static MOS ROM A static read-only memory based on metal-oxide semiconductor technology, as shown. Static MOS ROMs offer low cost, simple interfacing, and high performance for applications requiring large capacity. Applications include microprogramming, table lookup, code conversion, and character generation. Inputs and outputs are usually TTL (transistor-transistor logic) compatible.

static pad *See* ANTISTATIC DEVICES.

static protection Refers to the use of table pads, floor mats, and other devices made of a semiconductive vinyl, as shown in the figure. The semiconductive material provides discharging for static effects but prevents shorting of circuit board pins. A floor mat works best for leather-soled shoes; other types of soles will be insulated from the mat.

static read/write memory A memory in which clocks or refreshing are not needed. A typical static N-channel MOS memory is designed and organized to be compatible with various microprocessors. Its data, address, and control line organization and functions match those of the microprocessor, and all signal levels are TTL compatible.

static storage A memory that requires no refresh logic since data does not degenerate or leak away as long as power is applied to the memory elements. *Contrast with* DYNAMIC STORAGE.

static subroutine A subroutine involving no parameters other than the addresses of the operands.

station Refers to hardware set up to perform a computer operation, for example, a PC station.

stationary gap A device used in conjunction with

a pulse-forming line to form short-period high-voltage pulses for modulating microwave oscillators.

station doubler A unit that allows a second keyboard, monitor, and mouse alternative access to one PC. Access to either station can be locked out with a privacy switch.

station line protector *See* SIGNAL LINE PROTECTOR.

station protector A device installed at each end of a twinaxial or coaxial cable to provide protection from lightning and electrical damage, as shown. A pair of these units should be installed on all outside lines.

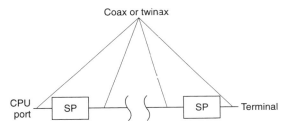

Station protectors

statistical concentrators A category of devices usually involved in the optimization of line usage by allowing more than one set of data to be carried on a single line. This can be done by one of the following:

- Interleaving variable-length (channel-activity dependent) blocks from several channels (a concentrator/statistical multiplexer)
- Interleaving constant-length blocks from several channels (a channel splitter/time-division multiplexer)
- Splitting the voice bandwidth into subfrequencies, each carrying a set of data (a frequency division multiplexer)

statistical error An error arising in measurements of random events, as a result of statistical fluctuations in the data.

statistical multiplexing A form of concentration in data multiplexing in which time slots are allocated to whichever terminals are active at any one time.

statistical package Application software that uses a series of mathematical equations to allow the user to analyze numerical data.

statistics version In NetWare Diagnostic Services, a field that returns a major and minor version number that a developer assigns and updates each time the driver diagnostic table is changed.

statistical universe A complete set of items that are similar or related in certain respects.

STATMAP A statistical, marketing, and demographic mapping package. With it you can transform data into maps suitable for analysis or presentation. Some of its applications are to measure sales performance versus population, map sales territories, investigate locations for expansion, target promotional and advertising campaigns, and prepare maps for presentation.

STAT MUX A statistical multiplexer.

status activity monitor *See* SAM.

status bit A bit used in many systems to designate interrupt conditions. The status bit is tested by the program to check for the presence of an internal interrupt condition. The status bit can be used to check for a console interrupt, DMA termination, clock interrupt, power-fail/restart interrupt, and other changes. Microprograms can be shortened with the use of status bits. Branches can be made after the status bits are set to eliminate premature branching and reduce the number of microinstructions required.

status information 1. In a microprocessor, the condition of registers, masks, flags, and other internal controls. **2.** In the NetWare File Server Environment, this refers to information about the lock state of the connection.

status line A line of the screen, usually at the bottom, where an application may display information such as page and division numbers, line and column numbers, the memory status, and the status of various keys.

status message A control-panel display that keeps you informed of a device's current operating condition.

status register A register used to hold information about communication errors, data register status, and communication device status. Some systems use several status registers and exchange data between the registers to allow limited nesting capability.

status word 1. A word used to resume processing after the servicing of an interrupt. **2.** A word used to indicate the status of an internal or external device. The status word may provide information on the sign of a number, overflow conditions, carry bits, accumulator conditions, and interrupts.

status word, device *See* DSW.

status word register A group of binary numbers that informs the user of the present condition of the microprocessor. In some systems, the status register may provide the plus or minus sign, overflow indication, carry bit, all zeros in the accumulator, and interrupt bit status.

STDM Abbreviation for *synchronous time-division multiplexing*, a multiplexer that shares a synchronous data line by scanning and interleaving bits into frames of the incoming data stream.

STE 1. Abbreviation for *special test equipment*. **2.** Abbreviation for *segment table entry*.

steady-state A condition in which all values remain essentially constant or recurring in a cyclic manner.

steady-state deviation The difference between the final value assumed by a specified variable after the expiration of transients and its ideal value.

steady-state oscillation Oscillation in which the motion at each point is a fixed periodic quantity.

STEP In BASIC, part of a FOR...NEXT statement that identifies the value by which the counter will be incremented.

step-by-step switch *See* STEPPER.

step counter A counter used in the arithmetic unit to count the steps in a process such as multiplication, division, or a shift operation.

step-down amplifier An amplifier that is used to reduce an input signal.

step-down transformer An electrical transformer that provides the transfer of energy from a high to a low voltage.

step function A function that is zero preceding time zero, and then has a constant value after time zero, as shown.

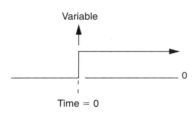

Step function

step index fiber An optical fiber that has an abrupt change in refractive index at the boundary of the core and cladding.

stepper A device or relay that has a particular number of discrete conditions and advances from one condition to the next each time it receives an input pulse. Also called a *stepper switch* or *step-by-step switch*.

stepper motor A motor in which rotation occurs in a series of discrete steps that can be controlled by pulses. It is controlled from the computer by a board on which each stepper channel uses an intelligent chip that can execute a variety of motion-control commands. Once a command has been loaded, the host computer is not involved in controlling the motion, but it may monitor the status.

stepping switch *See* STEPPER.

step response The response of a device to an instantaneous change in the input.

step-up transformer An electrical transformer with more secondary than primary turns. It thus transforms low to high voltages and matches low to high impedances.

ST-506 A hard drive interface, also known as the ST-506/412, developed by Seagate Technology and first used on the Seagate ST-412 drive.

sticking relay A relay that makes (closes) when dc current passes through the operating coil and continues to operate on the cessation of current, thereby saving current. It may be released with a reversed current.

STIL Abbreviation for *statistical interpretive language*.

still-frame compression multimedia adapter A frame compressor that can compress from 8:1 to 75:1. It saves disk space, reduces file retrieval time, and uses a JPEG algorithm. It requires SVGA video (at least 640 × 480), a 16-bit expansion slot, and 2M of RAM.

still-video format An analog video-production system that stores fields or frames of video information on 2-inch floppy disks.

STL Abbreviation for *synchronous transistor logic*.

stochastic An operation in which the element of chance cannot be avoided or excluded from consideration.

stochastic noise Noise that maintains a statistically random distribution. *Also see* NOISE.

stochastic process A process characterized by a family of random variables.

stochastic simulation A simulation of the random variables and the properties of the system, rather than the system itself.

Stock Trader A program for tracking selected stock performances and generating buy and sell signals according to trends over user-selected periods of time. Stocks may be added and deleted, and the DOW performance, or other accepted market average, is also displayed.

stop-and-wait ARQ A technique where a node waits for an acknowledgement that a data unit was received correctly before beginning to transmit again.

stop bit The last element of a character in start-stop asynchronous serial transmission. The stop bit is used to ensure recognition of the next start element. Also called *stop element*.

stopper **1.** A resistance used to reduce high-frequency potentials and the consequent build up of parasitic oscillations. **2.** A resistor-capacitor combination for decoupling supply circuits, in order to prevent oscillation or motorboating in amplifiers.

stop/reset switch A switch that allows the user to stop and start the system. It is often used when troubleshooting.

storage A device or medium on or into which data can be entered, held, and retrieved later; memory. Storage may use electrostatic, magnetic, acoustic, optical, electronic, or mechanical methods.

storage allocation The assignment of sections of data to a specific cell or group of cells in memory.

storage area The section or space in memory used for specific data.

storage capacity The amount of information that can be retained in a storage device, usually expressed in bits or words. Also called *memory capacity*.

storage cell The elemental unit of storage in a storage system.

storage cycle The sequence of events required when information is transferred to or from the storage device of a computer. The storage cycle may include storing, sensing, and regeneration.

storage cycle time The time required for a complete storage cycle.

storage device The medium or device in which data can be inserted, retained, and retrieved. Mass-storage devices are used to collect, organize, and retrieve large volumes of data. Examples include tape and disk drives.

storage element A unit of memory capable of storing a single bit of information.

storage flip-flop A bistable storage device that stores binary data as states of flip-flop elements. *Also see* FLIP-FLOP.

storage fragmentation The sectionalizing of memory required as a result of the inability to assign actual storage locations to virtual addresses when the available spaces are smaller than the page size.

storage key A special set of bits associated with every word or character in some block of storage; it allows tasks with matching sets of key bits to use that block of storage.

storage medium Media (disk or tape) used to save data for later processing.

storage module A usually add-on circuit card or package that functions as auxiliary memory for the storage and retrieval of data. A typical module uses a 4,096-word RAM with two stack pointers. The processor accesses the memory using transfer instructions that reference the addresses assigned to the stack pointers.

storage oscilloscope An oscilloscope in which the displayed trace of an extremely short-duration phenomenon is retained as long as desired. It is used for observation of nonrecurring pulses, periodic repetitive pulses, and transients.

storage, primary *See* PRIMARY STORAGE.

storage protection An arrangement for preventing access to storage for reading, writing, or both. Storage protection usually operates with a programmed protection key that prevents one program from destroying or covering another by protecting a specific area of storage.

storage switch A switch provided on the console to allow the operator to read the contents of selected registers.

storage tube A CRT-type tube capable of retaining a trace resulting from a nonrecurring phenomenon.

storage, virtual *See* VIRTUAL MEMORY.

storage volatility The inability of a storage device to retain data when power is removed.

store **1.** Memory. **2.** To enter or retain information in a storage device for later retrieval.

store-and-forward Communication systems in which messages are received at intermediate routing points and recorded (stored). They are then retransmitted to a further routing point or to the ultimate recipient. Also known as the *packet concept*.

stored I/O method A diagnostic technique in which a truth table with the input/output responses is stored in memory and executes the system. Most automatic functional test systems use some variation of this method. The principal differences are in the mechanization of the hardware or software. A major disadvantage in many systems is cost because thousands of digital states must be generated to provide the stimulus.

stored program A set of instructions in a computer memory that specify the operations to be performed and the location of the data on which the operations are to be performed.

stored-program computer A computer controlled by internally stored instructions that are used to synthesize, store, or modify data or other instructions.

stored upstream address A token ring concept in which each node on the token ring stores the address of the neighbor from which it receives data.

Stork A set of onscreen design tools to assist in each step of a product installation. It allows a customized menu interface, auto-check of target system hardware, auto-edit of AUTOEXEC.BAT and CONFIG.SYS, and customized target directory structure. There are also simulation mode facilitates for testing.

STR Abbreviation for *synchronous transmit/receive*, a transmission mode used in communications.

straight-line coding Coding in which loops are avoided by explicitly writing the instructions for repetition of parts of the coding when required. Straight-line coding can require less execution time and more space than loop coding. A generator is usually required if the number of repetitions is large, since the coding is limited by the variable number of instructions required as well as the space available.

strain The dimensional change in a medium when subjected to a stress.

strain gauge A transducer that detects changes in pressure of mechanical stress and delivers a corresponding electrical analog of that pressure.

strain gauge pressure transducer A transducer that converts a pressure change into a change in resistance due to a mechanical strain. Usually four or sometimes two arms of a Wheatstone bridge are used for temperature compensation. The pressure-sensing element can be a flat or corrugated diaphragm or a straight tube, because the deflection required is small. The strain gauges can be mounted right on the tube, which is sealed at one end.

strategic decision A long-term decision made by top management.

streaking An analog artifact in which bright objects in the picture cause a shifting of level that extends horizontally all the way across the picture. Typically caused by distortions to the frequency components below the horizontal line frequency.

stream head The entry point to a stream, a series of software modules connected with the STREAMS mechanism. *Also see* STREAMS.

streaming A condition that occurs particularly in polling systems where one device monopolizes the line because a fault keeps it sending spurious signals.

stream-oriented A type of transport service that allows its client to send data in a continuous stream. The transport service will guarantee that all data will be delivered to the other end in the same order as sent, and without duplicates. Also known as a *reliable transport service*.

STREAMS An AT&T mechanism developed for the Unix operating system and adopted by Novell for NetWare. STREAMS is a way of connecting a series of software modules and letting them send messages to each other.

Street Talk A distributed database under VINES that provides a sophisticated resource-naming service.

STRESS Acronym for *structural engineering system solver*, a language used in civil engineering for solving structural analysis problems.

string A linear sequence of items grouped in series according to certain rules. For example, a string may be a set of records grouped in ascending or descending sequence according to a key contained in the records.

string length In NetWare, this specifies the character length of a string to be printed.

string manipulation The process of creating strings for the control of groups of items.

string variable A string value that can change each time a program is run.

string variable name A variable name in BASIC consisting of one or two letters or a letter and a number that identifies string data. It is always followed by a dollar sign.

stripe pitch The measurement between horizontal scans of a display, in millimeters (mm).

stripe recording A magnetic recording in which a stripe of magnetic material is deposited on a document or card.

striping The method of data storage used with RAID (redundant array of inexpensive disk) drives. Each drive in the set contains one or more bits of the data word. Striping allows the system to recover from a single drive fault by reconstructing the missing bits from the contents of the remaining drives and the parity bit drive.

strobe 1. The detailed examination of a designed phase or epoch of a recurring waveform or phenomenon. **2.** The enlargement or intensification of a part of a waveform. **3.** The process of viewing vibrations with a stroboscope; colloquially the stroboscope itself. **4.** The selection of a desired point or position in a recurring event or phenomenon, such as a wave, or the device or circuit used to make the selection or identification of the selected point.

strobed I/O Refers to input/output ports that use a strobed enable signal. As shown in the figure, these ports can be built from SSI devices and other components; they are also available in lower-cost higher-integration packages.

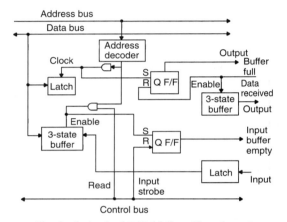

Typical strobed I/O bidirectional port

strobe pulse A pulse used to gate the output of a circuit or device.

stroboscope An aperture-producing device that gives the appearance of slow or zero motion when a vibrating or rotating object is intermittently illuminated by short flashes from a xenon or neon gas discharge tube or other source, at a suitable integral or frequency.

stroke A straight line or arc used as a segment of a graphic character in character recognition.

stroke centerline A line midway between the two stroke edges.

stroke edge The line of discontinuity between the side of a stroke and the background, obtained by averaging the irregularities between the printing and detecting processes.

stroke weight Refers to a bold, medium, or light print density, or darkness.

stroke width The distance between two stroke edges.

structured design A development technique in which the system is assumed to be composed of processes, divided into modules that implement the functions. This is shown in the figure.

Structured design utilizes measures, analysis techniques, and guidelines in order to control the flow of data through the system, which in turn is used to formulate the program design. The data flow is traced by charting each data transformation, each transforming process, and the order of occurrence. A system specification is then used to produce a data flow diagram, and the diagram is used to develop a structure chart. The structure chart is then used to develop the data structure, and these results are used to reinterpret the system specification. The process is iterative, but the order of iteration is not rigid.

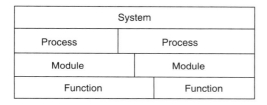

System partitioning

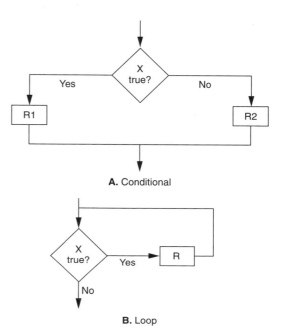

A. Conditional

B. Loop

Logic structures used in structured programming

structured programming Programming that tends to use only simple logic structures, including sequential structures, conditional structures, and looping structures. When sequential structures are used, the instructions or routines are executed in the order written. Conditional structures can be of the IF-THEN-ELSE type, while loop structures can be of the DO-WHILE type, as shown. Many users of structured programming do not use GO TO statements, which cause unconditional transfer of program control.

Structured programs are usually slower and require more memory than unstructured programs. In large programs, however, execution time and memory usage are not as critical as the time required for program development, and structured programs can make the debugging, testing, and maintenance stages of software development much simpler. The simpler flow of control produces clearer, more reliable, and more easily traced programs. The results of structured programming in various applications has been rewarding, especially in large programming projects.

structured programming languages Languages that contain the structures of structured programming, including high-level languages based on PL/1. Structured programming could be used in the design stage and then translated to assembly language.

Structured Query Language *See* SQL.

structured walkthrough A step-by-step review of program design by programmers other than the creators of the program.

structure of management information *See* SMI, 2.

STRUDL Acronym for *structural design language*, an extension of the STRESS language for the analysis and design of structures.

stub network A network that only carries packets to and from local hosts. Even if it has paths to more than one other network, it does not carry traffic for other networks.

stub testing The testing of one program module at a time, then combining it with other working modules until the entire program is tested.

stunt box The unit that controls the nonprinting functions of a printing terminal or the response of stations to selective calling signals in a communications terminal.

STX The *start-of-text* character, a control character that indicates the beginning of text and the end of the heading. In ASCII, it is designated as a seven-bit binary two.

Style A general-purpose class library that provides high-level object management for C++. It allows the implementation of associations and links among objects to become transparent. It removes many of the details of C++ programming.

style A named set of formatting instructions. Each style can produce a specific appearance in the text. With styles, you can not only apply many formats at one time to text, you can standardize your document by applying the same style to all text you want to appear in the same format. Styles are created and revised in a *style sheet*.

SUB 1. Abbreviation for *subtract*. 2. Abbreviation for the *substitution* character, an accuracy-control character used to replace a character that has been determined to be invalid or in error.

subaddress An order code that allows access to an I/O device. For example, in a disk system, the subaddress might be the module number.

subcommand Refers to a portion of an I/O device that is accessible through an order code. For disk storage units, the module number is the subaddress.

subdirectory Any directory contained in the root directory list or within another subdirectory list.

subdirectory name In DOS, a regular file or directory name: up to an eight-character name and three-character extension, separated by a period.

subminiaturization The technique of packaging miniaturized parts using methods to obtain increased densities.

submodulator A low-frequency amplifier that immediately precedes the modulator in a transmitter.

subnet A portion of a network that may be a physically independent network segment, but which shares a network address with other portions of the network and is distinguished by a subnet number. A subnet is to a network what a network is to an internet.

subprogram A segment of a program that can perform a specific function. Subprograms can reduce programming time when a specific function is required at more than one point in a program. If the required function is handled as a subprogram, the statements for that function can be coded once and executed at the different points in the program. Subroutines, functions, and macroinstructions may be used to provide subprograms, and they may be linked in one of the two ways:

- The subprogram reference is replaced by a jump to the desired procedure.
- The subprogram reference is replaced with the actual statements for the desired procedure.

subrefraction Refraction for which the refractivity gradient is greater than that for standard refraction. Also corresponds to atmospheric refraction with k < 1.

subroutine A routine that can be part of another routine, as shown in the following diagram. A subroutine may be used to perform a specific task for many other routines and may be distinguished from a main routine in that it requires a location specifying where to return to the main program after its function has been accomplished.

A *closed* subroutine may obtain control from a master routine and then return control to the master routine upon concluding its function by branching or jumping.

subroutine address stack A stack register used to save the program return address for subroutines.

subroutine call instruction Some microprocessors use a subroutine call instruction for restarts (RST). This instruction is the same as *call i*, where *i* is the restart number. The difference between a restart call and its equivalent subroutine call is that the subroutine call can use three bytes of memory, while the restart call (RST) may use only one byte.

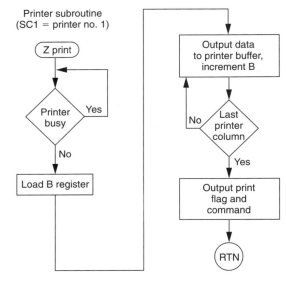

Printer subroutine (SC1 = printer no. 1)

	TM	PRINT	
Z PRINT	: IOL	P BUSY	PRINTER BUSY?
	ADI	8	
	T	Z PRINT	YES, WAIT
	LBL	PRBUF	LOAD B WITH PRINTER BUFFER ADDRESS
LOAD PB	LD		
	IOL	PLPD	LOAD PRINTER BUFFER
	INCB		
	SKBI	11	PRINT COMPLETE?
	T	LOAD PB	NO, GO BACK
	LBL	PRFLG	LOAD B WITH PRINT FLAG ADDRESS
	LD		
	IOL	PRNT	GET PRINT COMMAND DATA PRINT LINE
	RTN		

AUXILIARY INFORMATION

PRINT	PTR	ZPRINT	SUBROUTINE ENTRY POINTER
PBUSY	EQX	EE	
PLPD	EQX	E6	SEE TABLE 1
PRNT	EQX	E9	
PRBUF	EQX	13	RAMO, REGISTER 1, WORD 3
PRFLG	EQX	12	RAMO, REGISTER 1, WORD 2

Subroutine

subroutine library A set of standard, proven subroutines that are kept on file for use at any time in various programs. For example, a subroutine library for floating-point operations might include decimal-to-floating conversion, addition, subtraction, multiplication, division, fixed-point-to-floating-point conversion, and floating-point-to-fixed-point conversion.

subschema A detailed plan of a part of a database available to a particular user.

subscript 1. Integer numerals or symbols attached to a quantity to indicate its location in an array such as a matrix. They are often used below a set name to identify a particular element or elements of that set. 2. An indexing notation for elements of a set, an equation, or other expression.

subsequent counter An instruction counter designed to step through or count micro operations or parts of larger programs.

SUBSET A DOS command that substitutes a string for a path name.

substitute character *See* SUB.

substrate The base material upon which or in which a transistor or integrated circuit is fabricated.

subsystem A secondary or subordinate system, which may be a self-contained portion of a major system. A subsystem may be used to provide one of the major system functions, with only minimal interaction with other portions of the system.

subtask A task that is started by another, logically related task of higher priority.

subtract 1. In a microprocessor, a command that performs subtraction between two digital numbers. 2. In a database, a command that compares two files and creates a third containing data they do not have in common.

subtracter A device used to perform the subtraction operation. Subtracters may use parallel or serial configurations.

subtracter-adder An element designed to act as an adder or subtracter depending on the control signal or command issued to it.

subtracter instrumentation amplifier An amplifier whose drift, linearity, and noise-rejection capability makes it useful for extracting and amplifying low-level signals in the presence of high common-mode-noise voltages. They are used as transducer amplifiers for thermocouples, strain-gauge bridges, and biological probes. As preamplifiers, they can be used for extracting small differential signals superimposed on large common-mode voltages. Subtracter instrumentation amplifiers require high-precision feedback networks.

The figure shows a simple subtracter that uses one operational amplifier. It has a problem with source unbalance characteristics with its low-input impedance since CMRR depends on resistance matching. When a FET-input amplifier is used with very large values of resistance, noise and bandwidth problems can also occur.

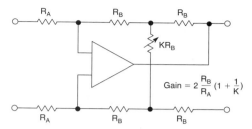

Subtracter instrumentation amplifier

$$\text{Gain} = 2\frac{R_B}{R_A}\left(1 + \frac{1}{K}\right)$$

subtractive color system Color reproduction by mixing appropriate amounts of the subtractive primary pigments: cyan, magenta, and yellow.

subtrahend The number or quantity subtracted from another number (the minuend).

subvector Portion of a MAC frame in a token ring network. For example, the token ring command to request initialization on the ring contains subvectors with the adapter software level, upstream neighbor address, and several other fields.

successive-approximation A/D converter A technique that consists of comparing an unknown input against a precisely generated internal voltage at the output of a D/A converter. The input of the D/A converter is the digital output number of the A/D converter. The conversion process is similar to a weighing process with a set of n binary weights.

When the conversion command is applied, the converter has been cleared, and the D/A converter's MSB (most significant bit) output (half fullscale) is compared with the input. If the input is greater than the MSB, it remains on and the next bit is tested. If the input is less

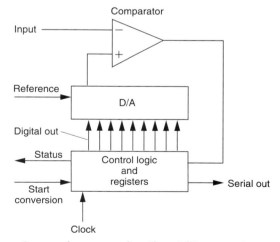

Successive-approximation A/D converter

than the MSB, it is turned off, and the next bit is tested. If the second bit doesn't have enough weight to exceed the input, it is left on, and the third bit is tested. If the second bit exceeds the input, it is turned off, and the third bit is tested. The process continues until the last bit has been tested. When the process is completed, the status-line changes to indicate a valid conversion. The output register now holds the digital code corresponding to the input signal.

successive-approximation conversion interface In the successive-approximation converter, each bit is compared with the analog input voltage, and the bit is left on by the register if less than this voltage or turned off if greater than the input. If the register is part of the microprocessor, this converter can be implemented with only a comparator and digital-to-analog converter as shown. The comparison operation is repeated for each bit-related position in the register until a close approximation of the input voltage is completed. The successive approximation method is fast and does not require a large amount of hardware. This method tends to be sensitive to temperature and voltage drifts. It is normally used only when high-speed conversions are required.

successive-approximation system A successive approximations type of converter that uses a sample-hold (S/H) device at its input. Between conversions, the S/H acquires the input signal. Just before conversion takes place, it is in hold, where it remains throughout the conversion. If the S/H responds quickly and accurately enough, the converter will convert the changes from the preceding sample accurately at a speed up to the conversion rate.

sudden death A term used to define an abrupt failure of a working device or system.

Suitcase A program designed to access the Macintosh system's fonts, sounds, function keys, and desk accessories. You can select suitcase files to be opened automatically when your Mac starts up, or open any desk accessory using keyboard or mouse.

sum check A check developed when groups of digits are summed. The check is usually made without regard to overflow, and this sum is compared with a previously computed sum to verify that no digits have changed since the last summation. Also called *summation check*.

summary report A report that lists totals and trends of data contained in a file, rather than each record.

summary sheet A collection of descriptive information about a document such as author, title, and operator.

summing junction A junction used in computing amplifiers and operational amplifiers to sum voltages and currents for computation, as shown in the figure.

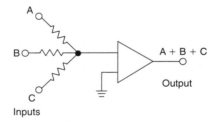

Summing junction

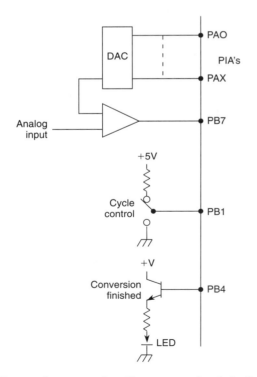

Successive-approximation conversion interface

summing point A point in a circuit or system at which signals are added algebraically.

Sun workstation A powerful RISC-based desktop computer manufactured by Sun Microsystems, typically running the SunOS or Solaris variety of Berkeley UNIX. Extremely popular in scientific, engineering, and graphics applications.

Sunshow An image converter program that is menu-driven and raster-based. It has a control panel interface, 3D buttons, and mouse point-and-click. It supports importing and conversion of most eight-bit formats up to 1024 × 768.

super band The frequency band from 216 to 600

MHz, used for fixed and mobile radios and additional television channels on a cable system.

SuperCalc One of the original spreadsheet programs.

supercomputer An extremely fast computer that can process both scalar and vector quantities, perform thousands of operations at once and do billions of additions a second.

superconductivity **1.** The decrease in resistance of certain materials such as lead, tin, and thallium as their temperature is reduced to nearly absolute zero. When the critical (transition) temperature is reached, the resistance will be almost zero. **2.** The physical characteristic displayed by certain materials whose resistance to the flow of electric current becomes zero below a specified temperature.

SuperFax Fax communications software that supports EIC Class 2 and CAS boards. The software allows users to fax directly from Windows applications. It has DDE capability that lets users establish direct communication with their application.

super video graphics adapter See SVGA.

supergroup In frequency division multiplexing, a number of voice channels, typically 60, occupying a 240-kHz bandwidth and composed of five groups.

superheterodyne A receiver in which carrier frequencies at the forward end are reduced through heterodyning.

SuperKey A utility that allows you to store keyboard macros so that frequently used functions can be called up with only a single keystroke. A privacy mode allows you to have the screen turn off and the keyboard lock when an unauthorized user tries to access the system.

supermastergroup In frequency-division multiplexing, a number of voice channels, typically 900, occupying a 3872-kHz bandwidth and composed of three 300-channel mastergroups.

SuperPaint A paint package that combines both painting and drawing capabilities. It offers the control of a bitmap program with object-oriented flexibility.

superposed circuit An additional channel obtained from one or more circuits normally provided in such a manner that all channels can be used simultaneously, without interference.

superrefraction Refraction for which the refractivity gradient is less than that for standard refraction.

superscript Text that appears slightly higher in a line than the text around it. For example, a footnote reference mark.[1]

Super 3D A Mac-based three-dimensional graphics and animation program that can be used to construct detailed, realistic models and lifelike animations. Its speed is provided by math coprocessor support. You begin by creating a two-dimensional object, then produce a three-dimensional view instantly using the revolve, extrude, or sweep commands. Objects can be viewed as wireframe or with solid surfaces.

Super Video Windows A program that can be used to create full-motion video in a window. It accepts and digitizes input from NTSC or PAL cameras, VCR, Videodisc, or still-frame video cameras.

supervising system See EXECUTIVE.

supervisor **1.** The network manager on a NetWare network. **2.** See EXECUTIVE.

supervisor mode A mode of operation in which certain operations, such as memory protection instructions and input/output operations, are permitted.

supervisor operating system An operating system that consists of a supervisory control program, system programs, and system subroutines. It may include a symbolic assembler and macroprocessor, a compiler, and debugging aids. A library of general utility programs may also be provided.

supervisor overlay A routine that controls fetching of overlay segments using information recorded in the overlay module by the linkage editor.

supervisory control action A mode in which control loops operate independently, subject to intermittent corrective action.

supervisory program See EXECUTIVE.

super-voltage A voltage of over one million volts used in x-ray tubes or accelerators.

supply voltage **1.** The steady-state dc potential required to operate an electronic system. **2.** The ac line voltage required to power the circuits that produce system operating potentials.

support Refers to hardware, software, and personnel available to aid the user of a system. Support often means the difference between the success or failure of a project.

support system A collection of programs, hardware, and skills used to develop, operate, and maintain a data-processing system.

suppressed packets In NetWare, this occurs when the local SPX has received and discarded a packet because the packet was a duplicate of a previously received packet or because the packet was out-of-bounds for the current receive window.

suppression **1.** The elimination of any component of an emission, such as a particular frequency or group of frequencies. **2.** The reduction or elimination of noise generated by a motor or generator.

suppressor A resistor or other component used in a circuit to reduce or prevent oscillation or the generation of unwanted signals.

surface barrier The potential barrier across the surface of a semiconductor junction due to the diffusion of charge carriers.

surface leakage The leakage along the surface of a nonconducting material or device. It can vary widely with contamination and humidity.

surface lifetime The lifetime of current carriers in the surface layer of a semiconductor where recombination takes place.

surface mount device *See* SMD.

surface resistivity The resistance between opposite sides of a unit square inscribed on the surface of a material. Its reciprocal is the surface conductivity.

surge A sudden current or voltage change in a circuit.

surge protector A unit that provides protection by filtering noise and clamping voltage transients down to safe levels. The unit can react within five nanoseconds and resets automatically. It can absorb up to 160 joules (160 kilowatts for one millisecond). An LED (usually green) monitors activity to indicate the equipment is safe.

surge strip An outlet strip that clamps dangerous voltages to 55 volts over the ac peak in less than five-billionths of a second, shown in the following figure.

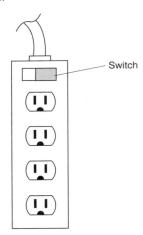

Surge protector strip

surge voltage (or current) A large, sudden change of voltage (or current), usually caused by the collapse of a magnetic field or by a shorted or open circuit element.

SVGA Abbreviation for *super video graphics adapter*, a DRAM-based VGA adapter that supports both monochrome and color high-resolution graphics and provides extended resolutions of usually 1024 × 768.

swamping resistor A resistor used to minimize the effects of undesirable variations in a circuit or device parameter.

swap **1.** To write the main storage image of a job to auxiliary storage and read the image of another job into main storage. **2.** A type of memory multiplexing in which jobs are transferred between auxiliary and main storage. Swapping is usually found in time-sharing applications.

swap file A temporary file established to buffer data access and improve display and file processing.

sweep circuit A circuit used to guide the movement of an electron beam in a CRT.

SWI Loose abbreviation for *software interrupt instruction*, an interrupt used in some Motorola microprocessors to decrease memory requirements. This instruction uses the subroutine address that is stored in memory locations FFFC and FFFD. It is quite similar to a restart except that its address is not fixed, since it comes from the memory. SWI can be used to simulate hardware interrupts in order to allow debugging without special hardware.

SWIFT Acronym for *society for worldwide interbank telecommunications*.

swish noise The noise produced by convection currents in a gas surrounding certain control or sensing elements.

swiss cheese A technique of circuit fabrication using a thin board containing a lattice of holes into which dot type circuit elements are dropped. Also referred to as *imitation 2D*.

switch **1.** To make or break a connection between two stations or points. In message switching applications, the computer can be used to accept messages and route them over trunk lines to remote switching devices, while providing an audit trail along with the error control. **2.** The mechanical or electronic device that makes or breaks the circuit between two points. **3.** A multivibrator (bistable, astable, or monostable).

switchboard loop panel A patch panel with rows of jacks for access to local loops.

switch bounce routine In applications in which switches are used to control the inputs to the microprocessor, it may be desirable to have a delay in the program to allow for switch bounce. A mechanical switch can cause on and off transients for as long as 40 milliseconds. A sequence like the following can be used to ensure that the processor does not sample this input until the transients have settled.

```
        LDX     #5000       ;load index
                            register, 3
                            cycles
LOOP    DEX                 ;decrement index
                            register, 4 cycle
        BNE     LOOP        ;branch to LOOP,
                            4 cycles
```

switched circuit A circuit that can be temporarily established at the request of one or more of the connected stations.

switched message network A communications service that allows customers to communicate among themselves. Switched message networks include the TELEX and TWX systems.

switched multimegabit data service *See* SMDS.

switched network A dial-up telephone network. A telephone switching system provides communication links between lines in response to subscriber requests. Systems range in size from small PABXs (private automated branch exchanges) with under 100 lines to central office or tandem systems with tens of thousands of lines. Block diagram of a central office switching system are shown in the following figures. The diagram shows the main elements of the system—the switching network and the processor. The switching network allows for selectively interconnecting the two wire paths by internal junction circuits. The interconnections allow a path between a subscriber station and a trunk that connects to other central offices.

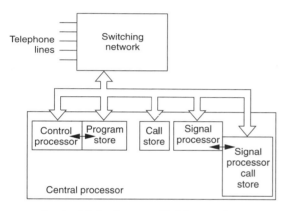

Central telephone switching system

switched system 1. An array of processors connected by crossbar switches that directly couple any one processor to any other processor. 2. A telephone switching system.

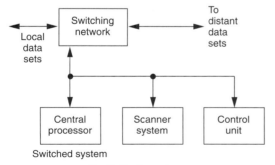

Switched system

switching circuit A circuit that can be used to perform a switching function, such as the connection of two or more inputs. Switching circuits include gates and the logic devices made from them.

switching device A device or mechanism that can be electrically placed in a desired state or condition.

switching diode A diode designed for high-speed switching applications.

switching module A module used to provide isolated output voltages for driving solenoids and other high-power devices.

switching time The time required for switching action to be completed from reference level to a final level, usually a fraction or percentage of the peak value.

switch matrix An array of circuit elements interconnected to perform a specific function. The array elements may be transistors, diodes, or gates for functions such as encoding, decoding, transformation, code conversion, or word translation.

switch register An array of switches that can be used to manually alter the contents of the accumulator, program counter, or memory data register. The switch register can also be read under program control.

switch-type function generator A function generator that uses multitap switch rotated in accordance with the input and has its taps connected to suitable voltage sources.

SWR Abbreviation for *standing wave ratio*.

syllabic companding A form of companding in which the step sizes are controlled by the syllabic rate of human speech. *Also see* COMPANDING.

symbol A graphic representation of a concept or item, such as a letter representing a quantity in a formula. Although a symbol usually consists of a single character, in some computer systems a symbol may consist of up to eight letters. Symbols may be used to express statements or equalities in these systems. The value of the symbol, when defined as a statement label, is the value of the location counter at the time the symbol is encountered. When used as an equality, the symbol is defined by the value of the expression.

symbol cross-reference table A table of all identifiers or entry points used in program modules. The identifiers can be listed in alphabetical order followed by the name of the module in which they are defined as well as the modules referencing them.

Combined with the assembler cross-reference listings, this table can provide good traceability of the identifiers and their references, as shown in the following table.

Identifier	Address	Defined	Referenced
ADD	016B	ARITH	MAIN
DIVIDE	01A6	ARITH	MAIN
MULTIPLY	028B	ARITH	MAIN
SUBTRACT	0270	ARITH	MAIN

symbolic address An address expressed in symbols convenient to the programmer, as shown. Also called a *floating address*, the symbolic address is used as a label to identify a particular word, function, or other item that is independent of the location of the information within the routine. If the programmer can refer to memory locations by symbolic name rather than numeric addresses, the assembler can translate these as well as the instructions. The assembler requires less time than manual translation, so fewer coding errors result.

Label	Mnemonic	Operand
XO	PTR	LXO
CLRX	LB	XO

Symbolic addresses

symbolic assembler A programming system that translates mnemonic instructions into binary machine-readable form.

symbolic assembly system The use of an assembler to translate mnemonic instruction into machine format. A symbolic assembly system provides the means of entering linkages, mapping common data, and using address modifiers.

symbolic code A code used to express programs in source language. The symbolic code allows the programmer to refer to storage locations and machine operations by symbolic names and addresses independent of their hardware-determined labels and addresses.

symbolic coding A coding system that uses symbols rather than actual machine addresses and instructions.

symbolic concordance A program used to produce a cross-referenced list of all the symbolic names in a program. Symbolic concordance programs are used for debugging and modification of larger programs.

symbolic debugging A capability that gives the programmer access to the variables which have been passed by the compiler or assembler to the linker and symbol table. This capability allows the display and changing of variables symbolically.

symbolic language A language that expresses addresses and codes in terms convenient to humans (rather than in machine form). A program prepared in any coding other than a machine language uses a symbolic language, which requires assembly or compiling.

symbolic logic The study and discipline of formal logic using expressions that seek to avoid the ambiguity and inadequacy of ordinary language and expressions.

symbolic name A label used in programs written in source language to reference data elements, peripherals, or instructions.

symbolic parameter A variable symbol used in some programming languages to call a macro definition. The symbolic parameter is usually assigned a value from the corresponding operand in the macroinstruction that calls the definition.

symbolic programming The use of symbols to represent addresses in order to facilitate programming. An assembly program is used to translate the symbolic program and assign instruction locations.

symbolic unit A designation used to refer to an external storage area or I/O device during coding. The actual location or device to be used is determined later.

symbol set A unique sub-grouping of all the available characters in a font. Each symbol set is defined for a specific set of applications. For example, the IBM-US symbol set was defined to support PC applications.

symbol string A string of characters consisting entirely of symbols.

symbol variable A symbol used in macro assembly processing that can assume any of a given set of values.

symmetrical Refers to circuits, networks, or transducers for which the impedance level (image impedance or iterative impedance) is the same in both directions.

symmetrical transistor A transistor in which the collector and emitter are identical, so either can be used interchangeably.

symmetry The measure of a device's ability to provide corresponding outputs on each side of zero when the polarity of the applied energy is reversed.

symmetry-breaking effects Effects that violate the invariance of a given symmetry.

Symphony An integrated program compatible with Lotus 1-2-3 that includes a database, communications module, and word processor.

sync 1. Synchronous operation. **2.** To synchronize.

sync character A character used to establish character synchronization in communications systems. When the receiving station recognizes the sync character, the station is in synchronization with the transmitting station and communication can begin.

synchro A rotary position indicator consisting of an induction machine with a stator and a rotor.

synchro differential generator A shafted device with rotor and stator coils that normally produce a three-terminal output signal equal to the sum or difference of an input signal and an input shaft rotation.

synchronization The matching or coordinating of two systems, devices, or functions, such as synchronizing the operations of a computer to clock pulses.

synchronization of oscillators A phenomenon that occurs when two oscillators having nearly equal frequencies are coupled together. When the degree of coupling reaches a certain point, the two suddenly pull into step and appear to be synchronized.

synchronization pulse 1. Pulses introduced to keep all components operating in order or step. **2.** Timing pulses sent to a master clock to keep all logic gates operating in synchronous order.

synchronizer A device or unit used to maintain synchronism between two devices or systems. Synchronizers include buffers or storage devices that are used to compensate for differences in the rate of flow of data or occurrence of events between devices or systems.

synchronizing pilot A reference pilot for the purpose of either maintaining the synchronization of oscillators of a carrier system, or comparing the frequencies and/or the phases of the currents generated. *Also see* REFERENCE PILOT.

synchronous Having a constant time interval between bits, characters, and events in a circuit or system.

synchronous capacitor A rotating machine running without mechanical load and designed so that its field excitation can be varied in order to draw a leading current (like a capacitor) and thereby modify the power factor of the ac system or influence the load voltage through such a change in the power factor.

synchronous channel splitter A unit that attaches to most synchronous modems and splits the channel into two synchronous subchannels, as shown. Each of the resultant channels must operate at half the modem data rate; for example, two 2400-baud channels can be derived from one 4800-baud modem.

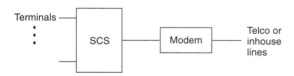

Synchronous channel splitter

synchronous clock A system in which events are controlled by signals from a clock generator at a desired rate or frequency.

synchronous communication Data communication that uses constant intervals between data bits and characters. Each end synchronizes itself to standard signals using clock timing to regulate data, rather than using start and stop bits. This results in fewer bits being transmitted and therefore less time used than by asynchronous transmission. *Contrast with* ASYNCHRONOUS COMMUNICATION.

synchronous communications interface An interface for providing two-way communications between devices in a synchronous mode. Programmable functions include parity checking, special character recognition, and synchronization modes.

synchronous computer A computer in which all operations and events are controlled by equally spaced pulses from a clock. *Contrast with* ASYNCHRONOUS COMPUTER.

synchronous data Data that usually contain a specified bit pattern for synchronization. The pattern is defined by the protocol.

synchronous data line control *See* SDLC.

synchronous data transmission A system in which timing is derived by synchronizing characters at the beginning of each message.

synchronous detection *See* COHERENT DETECTION.

synchronous gate A gate that is controlled by time pulses and that in turn may be used to synchronize other operations in the computer system.

synchronous idle A transmission control character used by a synchronous transmission system in the absence of any other character (the idle condition), to provide a signal.

synchronous idle character *See* SYN REGISTER.

synchronous input An input that allows data to be entered only when a clock pulse is present.

synchronous machine A machine that has an average speed exactly proportionate to the frequency of the system to which it is connected.

synchronous-mode comparator The comparator that is used in the synchronous mode to compare the assembled contents of registers. The comparator output allows character synchronization following successive matches of data.

synchronous modem eliminator The unit that provides strapping options to emulate dial-up or direct-connect (dedicated) service, as shown. Diagnostics include LEDs for online monitoring and a loopback switch for system diagnostics. External switches allow the selection of loopback, ring-indicate, and data-set-ready control.

Synchronous modem eliminator

synchronous operation A mode of operation in which each event is timed by a signal generated by a clock.

synchronous preprocessor A device used for interfacing synchronous lines to computers. It is designed to reduce the overhead for the computer by handling most of the interrupt processing and character manipulation.

synchronous receiver A receiver that assembles characters from serial communications lines and asserts a flag as each character is received.

synchronous serial data adapter A device that converts parallel data to serial, or serial data to parallel in a synchronous system. The adapter usually provides error detection and correction during transmission and reception.

synchronous speed A speed value related to the frequency of an ac power line and the number of poles in the rotating equipment. Synchronous speed in revolutions-per-minute is equal to the frequency in hertz divided by the number of poles, with the result multiplied by 120.

synchronous time-division multiplexer *See* STDM.

synchronous transmission A mode of transmission that uses a timed stream of bits or characters. *Contrast with* ASYNCHRONOUS TRANSMISSION.

sync information In television, this refers to the part of the video signal designed to move the display scanning in synchronism with the camera scanning.

sync pulse A pulse used by all system elements as a reference point for operational timing. Especially, a pulse transmitted to a circuit by a master unit in order to operate the slave in synchronism with the master.

syndetic 1. Connections or interconnections. **2.** Pertaining to a document or catalog with cross-references.

synergetic A combination of every unit in a system that, when combined, develop a total larger than their arithmetic sum. Also called *synergistic*.

SYN register Abbreviation for *synchronous idle character register*, a communication control character used in synchronous transmission to provide a signal so that synchronism can be achieved between devices. This register is used in some systems to hold the synchronous character code used for receiver-character synchronization.

syntactic error An error due to incorrect structure or symbols. Syntactic errors include typographic errors, incorrect punctuation, mixed-mode expressions, illegal statements, illegal transfers, and references to nonexistent statement numbers. Also called *syntax error*.

syntax The relationship among characters and groups of characters and their structure in a language.

syntax checker A program that tests source statements in a programming language for violations of syntax.

syntax error list A linked list of syntactic errors provided so the program can be scanned to locate the errors.

syntax transducer A subroutine designed to recognize the phase class in an artificial language, normally expressed in Backus normal form.

synthesis 1. The act of combining parts to form a desired result based on the performance requirements, such as the formation of an analog signal by a rapid series of digital pulses. **2.** The process of generating any one of a variety of fixed- frequency signals using special electronic techniques and devices.

synthetic language A pseudocode or symbolic language; a fabricated language.

.SYS In DOS, the filename extension for a file that is installed via CONFIG.SYS. *Also see* SYSTEM FILE.

syscode An ARCnet concept that indicates which network-layer user the packet is intended for.

sysgen Abbreviation for *system generation*, the process of modifying the generalized operating system received from the vendor into a tailored system meeting the unique needs of the user.

sysin Abbreviation for *system input*.

syslib Abbreviation for *system library*.

sysop Abbreviation for *system operator*, the operator of an electronic bulletin-board system, usually responsible for answering questions and reinforcing the rules of bulletin board.

Systat A program that provides a number of statistical procedures and is especially appropriate for multivariate analysis. It also provides some flexibility in manipulating data. Users of the SAS, BMDP, or SPSS-X mainframe statistics packages will find many of the data and statistical procedures familiar.

system A collection of methods, devices, programs, equipment, or other items united by some form of regulated interaction to create an organized whole. A system could be a collection of routines for providing sequencing control or debugging operations, or it could be an overall relationship between hardware, programs, procedures, and management at a particular computer installation.

systematic drift Frequency drift in an oscillator resulting from slowly changing physical characteristics and causing frequency changes that, over a long period of time, tend to be in one direction.

systematic inaccuracies Inaccuracies due to limitations in equipment design.

systematic noise A class of noise, as opposed to random or periodic noise. Systematic noise is a form of noise found in imperfect equipment. For example, if the signal for the character *u* were always replaced by the signal for the character *s* in a message because of some failure, it would be a case of systematic noise.

system attribute An indicator stored in a file's directory entry that prevents the file from being changed or deleted and limits access to the file.

system board The main circuit board in the computer, which can be divided into two sections or functional areas. One contains the CPU (central processing unit) circuitry, including the microprocessor, arithmetic processor (if used), clock generator, bus controller, and buffers. The other section contains the peripheral I/O devices, RAM, and analog circuits.

system check A performance check based on external program tests other than built-in hardware circuits.

system check module A device that monitors a system for power failure or deviations from desired performance, and when necessary, initiates emergency actions.

system command executive An executive program that accepts and interprets commands by a user. Typical commands include

- Log in, log out
- Save or restore program
- Compile, execute
- Interrupt, terminate
- Edit, list
- Request status

system configuration tests Typically, tests run in single-pass, multiple-pass, or batch mode for isolating intermittent errors. Results can be logged to a disk file, display, serial port, or printer. Tested components include the system board, RAM, video board and display, keyboard and mouse, parallel and serial ports, floppy controller, and disk drives. See the following figure.

```
           LOADING
   Investigation system configuration

Local        — Check for remote operation
(Standard)   — Identify BIOS manufacturer
Complete     — Determine system components
Complete     — Look for RAM (Base, extended, expanded)
Not present  — Look for math co-processor
Not present  — Look for mouse

System configuration checks complete
        Press any key to continue
```

System configuration display

system controller and bus driver A single-chip unit that generates all signals required to interface RAM, ROM, and I/O devices to the microcomputer system.

system data bus A bus designed for communications between all external units and the CPU. A typical bus transfers information between any two devices connected to the bus by granting access through a priority network for bus control.

system design The specification of the working relationship between all parts of the system, in terms of their characteristic actions.

system design aids Hardware and software support items used in design of the various types of equipment encountered in microcomputer applications. Systems design aids include the following:

- Evaluation modules and support hardware
- Development and test equipment
- System design documentation and manual
- Support software

system diagnostic A program used to detect overall system malfunctions rather than isolate errors or faults.

system drive (*o.t.*) On a two-disk-drive computer system, the drive where the operating system files reside.

system elapsed time In NetWare Directory Services, the file server's interval marker, a count of the number of ticks (18 per second) on its clock at the time of a call. This field can be used to measure time between calls.

system engineering An engineering approach in which all aspects of the system are considered in arriving at a solution.

system fault tolerant *See* SFT.

system file A file with the system attribute; in DOS, the two files IO.SYS and MSDOS.SYS.

system firmware *See* FIRMWARE.

system gain The difference, in decibels, between the transmitter output power and the minimum receiver signal level required to meet a given performance objective.

system gamma The overall light-in/light-out characteristic of a television system, from camera through receiver. In an ideal system, the gamma should be one. In practice, it is 1.4.

system handbook A document that provides a concise reference of all the major characteristics of the microcomputer system. The system handbook contains operation codes, addressing modes, device status details, interfaces, timing diagrams, and data flow.

system interface Any device, usually a circuit board or card, that connects support hardware to the microprocessor. Interfaces are available for such peripherals as printers, power switchers, analog transducers, and communications devices in parallel or serial modes.

system loader A supervisory routine used to retrieve program phases from an image library and load them into main storage.

system log A set of records containing all job-related information, such as descriptions of unusual occurrences, and all commands and messages from or to the operator.

system multiplex To interleave sequentially and transmit two or more messages on a single data channel.

System Network Architecture See SNA.

system noise 1. The extra bits or words that must be removed from the data before it is used. **2.** Any disturbance tending to interfere with the normal operation of the system by creating signals that can be read as pulses. *Also see* NOISE.

system-oriented Descriptive of applications that use a common bus system for all data and communications within the microcomputer system itself.

systems analysis The examination and study of an activity, method, technique, procedure, or business operation to determine what operations must be accomplished and how they should be accomplished. The examination is usually aimed at achieving the maximum result at minimum cost and may include feasibility studies, identification of areas for study and correction, identification of requirements for information, assessment of costs and benefits, and definition of purpose and objectives.

systems analyst One who defines the applications problem, determines system specifications, recommends equipment changes, designs procedures, and devises data verification methods. She or he also prepares block diagrams and record layouts from which programmers prepare flowcharts, and may assist in or supervise the preparation of flowcharts.

systems and support software The wide variety of software that includes assemblers, compilers, subroutine libraries, operating systems, and application programs.

systems approach The examination of an overall situation or problem with the aim of devising a total solution, as opposed to dealing with the separate functions that constitute the whole.

systems development project The design, development, and implementation of a system, usually done in organized steps called a *lifecycle*.

system software Operating system programs that control computer activity.

systems programmer A person who writes systems programs for an organization.

systems programs Programs written to control the computer and related equipment, for example, programs that start and stop tasks or find data on disk or tape.

system specification A determined listing of the exact requirements for new systems hardware and software. Also called a *spec*.

system support Generally refers to the support furnished by the manufacturer to simplify the application of the microprocessor and the design and development of the microcomputer system. System support may include manuals, literature, field and factory engineering specialists, prototyping hardware, and development software.

system support program A program that contributes directly to the use and control of the system and the production of end results. System support programs include linkage editors, job control processors, and utility packages.

system test A running or simulation of the total connected set of components of a system to obtain test data and check the adequacy of the design.

system tester A test device used to check modules in modular industrial control systems.

system timing A typical processor instruction cycle might consist of five states, two states in which an address is sent to memory, one state for the instruction or data fetch, and two states for the execution of the instruction. If the processor is used with slow memories, a READY line may synchronize the processor with the memories. When the memories are not available for either sending or receiving data, the processor may go into a WAIT state. Instructions for some systems require one, two, or three machine cycles or states for complete execution. The first cycle is usually an instruction fetch cycle. The second and third cycles are often data reading, data writing, or I/O operations. The processor controls the use of the data bus and determines whether it will be sending or receiving data. State signals inform the peripheral circuitry of the state of the processor. Many of the multicycle instructions do not require the two execution states. As a result, these states are omitted when they are not needed, and the system operates asynchronously with respect to the cycle length.

system unit The unit that contains the power supply, the system board, disk drives, a fan, and the system power switch, as shown. This unit can be designed to be placed horizontally on a disk or vertically on the floor.

The components of the system unit should be designed to make installation of options and maintenance of components easy. The system unit's cover is secured by screws at the rear of the system box. The disk drives and power supply can be removed by disconnecting their cables and removing their mounting screws. The system chassis has connectors in it for mounting the disk controller, memory extension options, and other options. The connectors for peripheral devices are usually at the back of the system unit, as shown.

System View IBM's network management architecture that includes integrating management information from Unix as well as SNA, TCP/IP, OS/2, and others.

system unit • System View

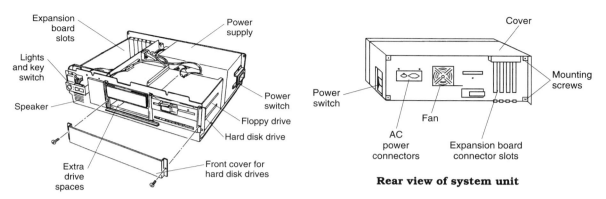

Typical PC system unit, front view

Rear view of system unit

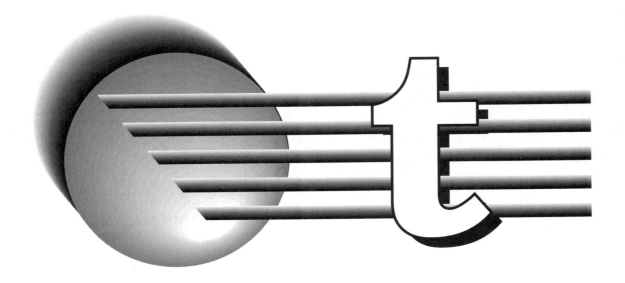

T Abbreviation for *tera*, a prefix for the numerical quantity of 10^{12} as in, for example, *tera ohm*.

tab 1. A nonprinting spacing action on a typewriter or other preparation device whose code is used to separate words or groups of characters in a sequential format. **2.** A tabulate switch.

Tabin A software product from Corel Systems that scans a standard ASCII text file that contains a table and replaces the spaces between columns with tabs. You can import spreadsheet files into a desktop publishing or word-processing program, then print using proportionally spaced fonts such as Times Roman and still have the columns of data line up.

table A graphically arranged collection of data in which each item is uniquely identified by a label or position relative to other items. The items are usually laid out in rows and columns for reference or stored in memory as an array.

A *decision table* contains all contingencies that are to be considered in the solution of a problem, including all the actions to be taken. Decision tables can be used in place of flow charts for problem description.

A *lookup table* can be used to obtain a derived value of a variable which corresponds to an argument or table address.

table lookup instruction An instruction that allows a reference to stored data arranged in tabular form. The instruction usually directs the computer to search for a named argument and to locate and retrieve a desired value. This operation is performed in place of a calculation.

tabletop mounting Refers to enclosing a microcomputer in a tabletop cabinet. There are several types of tabletop mountings available, including a single row for single-rack mounting and a double row for double-rack mounting. Rear cable panels are available for internal and external connections.

tab sequential format A means of identifying a word by the number of tab characters preceding the word in a block. The first character of each word is usually a tab character.

tab size In NetWare Print Services, a flag holding a number from one to 18 that determines how many spaces each tab contains. The default is eight.

Tabsol Software for the structuring of table solutions to problems involving multiple sequential decisions such as those in manufacturing planning, engineering design, and inventory control.

tab stop The position at which text is aligned in columns by using tab characters. A tab command is used to set and clear tap stops.

tabulate 1. To format data into an array or table. **2.** To print out the totals of a section of storage.

tactical decision A decision about short-term managerial problems, made by middle-level management.

tactile keyboard A pressure-sensitive keyboard with conductive sheets.

taffeta weave A plain, fairly tight weave, in which the warp and filling yarns cross each other at each row in both directions; used in semiconductor clean rooms.

tag *See* FLAG.

tail circuit A feeder circuit or an access line to a network node.

tandem transistor Two transistors in one package that are internally connected together.

tap A connection to the main transmission line in a LAN.

tape A storage device consisting of metallic or plastic tape coated with magnetic material. Binary data are stored as small, magnetized spots arranged in column form across the width of the tape. A read-write head is usually associated with each row of magnetized spots so that one column can be read or written at a time as the tape is moved relative to the head. Tape is often used for backup purposes in a microcomputer system.

tape and disk eraser A powered eraser that restores magnetic qualities to reels and disks.

tape cable A type of cable that contains flat ribbon conductors embedded side-by-side with an insulating material separating them.

tape cartridge A self-contained continuous loop of magnetic tape in a plug-in package. A typical tape cartridge can store over one hundred million bytes.

tape conversion program *See* TCP.

tape drive A device that contains a tape drive unit along with reading and writing heads and associated control circuitry. Also called *tape deck* or *magnetic tape reader*. Tape drives offer high recording speed and high density storage. Disadvantages include relatively slow retrieval speeds and vulnerability to dust, temperature, and humidity.

tape-drive controller A unit designed to interface one or more tape drive units to a microcomputer. The controller usually provides error checking and may provide buffering.

tape format The method the tape drive uses to record data on the tape. *Also see* QIC.

tape leader The front or lead portion of a tape.

tape load point The position on a magnetic tape where reading or writing can begin.

tape track One of several parallel areas on a track holding a single bit for a byte of data.

tape trailer The trailing end of a tape.

tape transport *See* TAPE DRIVE.

tapped line A delay line having more than two terminal pairs associated with a single delay channel.

tapped potentiometer function generator A technique used for generating functions of one variable in which the input variable sets the angular position of a potentiometer shaft. A number of taps along the potentiometer are positioned to represent the table of values for the function.

target 1. A processor or memory element for which code or data is being written or processed. 2. In an assignment statement, a variable whose value is being set.

target execution time In NetWare Queue Services, the earliest a job can be serviced.

target job type In NetWare Queue Services, the job type a station will accept for service.

target language The language into which a program is to be translated.

target phase The time when a number of target statements comprising a target program are run, usually during compiling operations.

target program *See* OBJECT PROGRAM.

target server ID number In NetWare Queue Services, the bindery object ID of a queue server that can service a job.

TASI Acronym for *time assignment speech interpolation*, a form of speech interpolation typically used with analog voice transmission to increase the capacity of telephone cables.

task An assigned piece of work.

task data sheet A record of jobs by time period, usually for a day or week.

tasking A capability in a system that allows the handling of several tasks during the same time interval using task-scheduling commands.

task management A set of functions in the control program for allocating the hardware and software resources of the system by tasks.

task number In the NetWare File Server Environment, refers to the task within a logical connection that is involved in a transaction.

task queue A waiting line or list of all the task control blocks that are in the system at any one time.

task state In the NetWare File Server Environment, the state of the task for which information is to be returned, as follows:

1. TTS explicit transaction in progress
2. TTS implicit transaction in progress
3. Shared file set lock in progress

task swapper A program that lets you run more than one program at a time and switch among them.

task switching The capability of Windows and OS/2 to manage several programs at the same time, using "windows" (boxes on the screen that overlap each other). You can also minimize a window to a small icon at the bottom of the screen, which in most cases temporarily suspends its operation. Another window takes precedence, and its program gets most or all of the computer's attention. When you want the first program back, you click on its icon; it zooms back up to an open window and takes precedence.

Taskx A system used for vibration analysis of structures. Taskx uses a mathematical model of desired performance and compares the model online, in real time, with actual test data. It then automatically analyzes the two sets of data to determine how close the test object is to design performance parameters.

Tax-File A tax recordkeeping system written for dBASE. It enables a person to collect financial records throughout the year and then print several reports. The system keeps personal and business records for most types of deductions and income. The program makes use of the menu approach for entering and editing data and has several built-in reports.

T-BASE A library that enables CA-Clipper, dBASE, FoxPro, and C users to add pictures and documents to their applications. You can display images in any location, display images with existing text, and scroll images in a window.

TbxSHIELD A library of software objects that enables you to add toolboxes to applications. These toolboxes let users select a tool, operational mode, or option from an array of graphical selectors. Toolboxes can be 3D, and selectors can be bitmaps, metafiles, animation, and icons. Developer-defined procedures can be linked to each control.

TC 1. Abbreviation for *tinned copper*. **2.** Abbreviation for *time to computation*. **3.** Abbreviation for *transmission controller*. **4.** Abbreviation for *thermocouple*.

TCAM Acronym for *telecommunications access method*, a communication subsystem designed to exchange information between a communications network and a set of message queues. The exchange is carried out according to information contained in the control blocks and headers. The control program is coded for each particular installation using a set of system macroinstructions.

TCP 1. (*o.t.*) An abbreviation for *tape conversion program*, a program for duplicating paper tapes and converting from one tape format to another. The program can be used to convert from hexadecimal to binary format, or binary to hexadecimal format. **2.** An abbreviation for *transmission control protocol*, the transport protocol in TCP/IP used for the reliable delivery of data. It is similar to Novell's SPX.

TCP/IP Abbreviation for *Transmission Control Protocol/Internet Protocol*, a communications protocol designed by the Department of Defense's ARPA (Advanced Research Projects Agency). It deals with the physical layer of the OSI model, while TCP resides in the transport layer. TCP/IP is designed to work across a wide range of computer types. It is widely used in government agencies, and is often associated with Ethernet, 802.3 LANs, and Internet.

TCP workstation A single-user alternative to a gateway, allowing independent PCs to concurrently utilize TCP/IP and NetWare services without rebooting. Large volumes of data can be exchanged with dissimilar TCP/IP hosts.

TCS Abbreviation for *terminal control system*, a control program designed to handle multiterminal operations in a computer system. The program schedules the use of hardware and all input/output processing.

TDM Abbreviation for *time-division multiplexing*, a multiplexing method that transmits two or more coincident signals over a common path using a sampling technique for sensing each signal alternately.

TDR 1. Abbreviation for *time-domain reflectometry*, the study or measurement of phenomena associated with signal propagation along wires or other related media. **2.** Abbreviation for *transmit data register*, a register used in ACIA transmission systems to hold data ready to be transmitted out. *Also see* ACIA.

Technical and Office Protocol A set of protocols developed by Boeing and based on the OSI model. It was developed for engineering, graphics, accounting, and marketing support functions in a manufacturing-oriented company. *Also see* OSI MODEL.

technical manual A manual explaining how equipment is built and repaired.

technical writer A person who writes and edits technical manuals, reports, and documentation.

Teflon Tradename for fluorinated ethylene propylene, a nonflammable material used for cable foam and jacketing.

Teknowledge A program for the PC family for designing, building, and running knowledgebased systems.

telco Abbreviation for *telephone company*; also called *common carrier*.

Telecommn Toolkit Software routines for Xmodem, Modem7, and Ymodem batch file transfer. It includes VT52, VT100, and ANSI-BBS terminal emulation with baud rates up to 15,200 bps, a command processor, script language, dialing directory, autodialing, pop-up menus, and status windows.

telco line bridge *See* TLB.

telecommunications The communication of information in written, verbal, or pictorial form by electrical means using wire or radio waves.

telecommunications access method *See* TCAM.

telecommuting Refers to an employee who does work at home and communicates electronically with the office, rather than being onsite.

teleconference A conference between persons linked together by a telecommunications system.

telemeter To transmit or cause the transmission of analog or digital data such as measurement results from a remote fixed or moving station to a control or recording station using radio waves.

telemeter service A metered telegraph service between paired telegraph instruments over a time-shared circuit.

telemetry The remote sensing of systems using transmitted electrical signals coded using a suitable modulation method.

Telenet A virtual terminal service offered under TCP/IP's protocols. *Also see* TCP/IP.

Telepathy A serial communications library for CA-Clipper that supports most common file-transfer protocols, allows background communication, and enables the direct use of serial devices like barcode wands. Terminal emulators include TTY, PC ANSI, and VT102.

telephone dialer A circuit that converts pushbutton closures or stored information into dial pulses compatible with standard telephone systems. The circuit might also store the last number dialed for automatic redialing.

telephone line controller A device that intercepts a call and determines whether it is coming from a fax, modem, or telephone.

telephone wire The unshielded twisted-pair copper wire used in most telephone applications. It is usually number-24 single-strand, copper twisted approximately 20 turns per foot.

teleprinter A communications terminal that includes a printing device.

teleprinter interface A serial interface that makes the computer system compatible with a teleprinter. In typical use, data is fed to the teletypewriter and stored for later transmission or fed to the computer and printed out at the same time. Standard output for the interface is a two-wire 20 mA current loop, with simplex operation at 10 characters per second.

teleprocessing A term for describing systems that transmit data from one point to another during the course of processing the information.

Teletype Trade name for a terminal with a typewriter-printer used to send or receive messages by wire or radio.

Teletype controller A device that contains parallel-to-serial and serial-to-parallel conversion circuitry to interface a Teletype terminal to a computer for asynchronous operation.

Teletype/CRT utility A package of programs for performing the most common input/output functions for a Teletype or CRT terminal.

Teletype exchange Exchange services such as TELEX or TWX, which provide direct-dial point-to-point connections using Teletype equipment. Facilities are also available to allow computers to interface through these services.

Teletype modification kit A kit that contains the circuitry for converting TTL signals to 20-mA loop currents for Teletype units. It also contains incremental control circuits for the tape reader.

Teletype network A system of points connected together by private telegraphic channels. Typically, up to 20 channels time-share a single circuit.

teletypewriter A teleprinter that is part of a communications terminal.

teletypewriter exchange service *See* TWX.

Telex The international network of teleprinter subscribers.

TeliSolar A program that provides the user with a quick method of evaluating energy-saving alternatives for hot water usage, building heating/cooling loads, and solar collector design.

Telix A communications package that allows adjustable baud rates from 300 to 115,200 and includes all popular file-transfer protocols like Xmodem, Ymodem, Zmodem, and Kermit. It provides automatic redial, dialing directory, shelling out to DOS, and usage log scripts.

TELNET A telecommunications network, the ARPANET virtual terminal protocol.

Telpak A leasing service of wideband channels for communications.

temp Abbreviation for *temporary register*, a register used as a latch to avoid race conditions. It can also be used as an internal register for microprogram control.

temperature influence The change in an indication due solely to a change in ambient temperature from a specified reference temperature.

temperature rating 1. The maximum temperature at which insulating material may be used continuously without breaking down. **2.** The maximum temperature at which a device or unit may be operated without overheating.

Tempest Macintosh A unit that protects sensitive data from electronic eavesdropping, while supporting the Hypercard and MultiFinder software. The unit consists of an extended keyboard, Macintosh CPU with RAM, monitor, and disk drive.

template An electronic form developed for specific software applications, such as creating a fax cover sheet or creating a loan payment schedule.

temporary register *See* TEMP.

temporary storage *See* WORKING STORAGE.

temporary storage area *See* SCRATCHPAD MEMORY.

temporary text delay *See* TTD.

10BASE2 A reference to the Ethernet standard Cheapernet and Thinnet variations. The number designates that these networks are baseband networks with transmission rates of 10 Mbits per second, with maximum contiguous coaxial segment lengths of 2×100 meters (200 m).

10BASE5 A reference to the Ethernet standard. The number scheme designates that these networks are baseband networks with transmission rates of 10 Mbits per second, with maximum contiguous coaxial segment lengths of 5×100 meters (500 m).

10BASE-T A reference to the Ethernet standard supplemental definition. It applies to twisted-pair wiring and connectors and twisted-pair variations. The number scheme designates that these networks are baseband networks with transmission rate of 10 Mbits per second. The maximum contiguous cable segment lengths are usually limited to 100 meters because of the signal interference on the unshielded cabling, although 200 meters is supported for distances between a concentrator (hub) and a workstation.

There are two versions of 10BASE-T. One supports bidirectional signaling with dual-pair (four-wire) telephone wiring, thus allowing the hardware to sense collisions. The other version uses a single pair to support daisy-chaining of multiple workstations. Signal repeaters are required for the dual-pair twisted-pair wire to boost signal between the concentrator (hub) and the workstations.

TenKey A software calculator for the PC that uses the numeric keyboard. The program is concurrent, which means that it runs alongside any other application program and allows you to transport final totals to your application.

ten-pitch A term applied to typewriter spacing of 10 characters per horizontal inch. Also known as *pica spacing*.

tera *See* T.

terabyte A measurement of computer memory or disk capacity equal to one trillion bytes.

terminal A point in a system or communications network at which data can be entered or retrieved. In systems where computers must communicate with each other, asynchronous and synchronous interfaces are used with modems for communications. A complete terminal facility includes a keyboard, display, microprocessor, memory, printer, modem, and adapters, as shown in the following diagram.

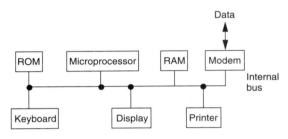

Terminal block diagram

terminal area In a printed circuit, the portion of the conductive pattern to which electrical connections are made.

terminal block A connection strip for attaching cable wires.

terminal controller A unit that contains the circuitry to interface a teletypewriter or data terminal to a microcomputer. It contains a receiver that converts incoming serial data in parallel format with parity, framing, and overrun detection. The internal transmitter converts outgoing parallel data into serial format with start and stop bits.

terminal control system *See* TCS.

terminal dependent Software that allows the attached terminal to utilize its screen-formatting capabilities. The attributes supported may vary depending on the asynchronous terminal used.

terminal display mode The manner in which points are to be displayed on the CRT screen. Terminal display modes include vector, increment, characters, point, or vector continue.

terminal emulator A program that allows a microcomputer to emulate a terminal. The computer thus appears as a terminal to the host.

terminal equipment The equipment at the end of a communications channel used for the reception and transmission of messages. Terminal equipment may include telephone and teletypewriter switchboards in which communications circuits are terminated.

terminal fan-out The number of circuits designed to be supplied with input signals from an output terminal.

terminal forward-gate current The direct current into the gate terminal with a forward gate-source voltage applied.

terminal impedance The impedance of a specific device such as a transmission line, gate, or amplifier, under no-load conditions.

terminal interface The connections, voltage levels, and impedance matching circuitry between data-processing equipment and data communication equipment.

terminal line-sharing interface *See* TLSI.

terminal locking device *See* TLD.

terminal security device *See* TSD.

terminal server A unit that lets you connect up to eight RS-232 async devices to one Ethernet connection. Because it establishes virtual circuits (electronic paths that logically connect otherwise incompatible devices), it can handle communications between terminals, PCs, printers, ports, and modems, simplify wiring, and automatically manage contention for scarce resources.

terminate and stay resident *See* TSR.

terminated line A transmission line with a resistance/impedance attached across its far end equal to the characteristic impedance of the line, so that there is no reflection and no standing waves when an input signal is placed at the near end.

termination 1. The connection or load at the end of a propagating medium. 2. The end of a program or program run.

termination expression In the NetWare RPC Tool, the expression included in a data structure when there is less data than the structure could have held. The termination allows the RPC mechanism to send only the real data instead of transmitting blank cells for unused portions of the data structure.

terminator A resistive device on each end of a high frequency cable to prevent reflections.

ternary 1. The characteristic involving a selection or choice in which there are three possibilities. 2. A number system with a base of three.

ternary incremental representation An incremental representation in which the value of the increment is rounded to one of three values.

Terranova Network Version An AT&T product that allows you to use a PC as part of a StarLAN network and communicate with other computers that are not part of the same network. The network version has all of the features of Terranova DOS, with additional capabilities to act as a gateway through a UNIX-based LAN server.

tertiary A separate output winding on a multi-winding transfer, but not the principal output for which the transformer is designed.

test bench Equipment designed specifically for making overall bench tests on equipment using a particular test set-up under controlled conditions.

test card A card that can be used to test all input and output functions and simulate regular and DMA controllers. The card includes special-purpose test logic for a complete test of every I/O bus signal. Connections typically are provided to check the power-failure restart system and to test automatic loaders.

test data The data developed to check the adequacy of the run or computer system; including data from previous runs and data created from simulated runs for test purposes.

tester devices and adapters The various devices that allow you to test the various types of chips used in systems. A functional test is usually performed on each chip. Some testers provide fast, thorough, automatic testing of devices in a dynamic mode.

testing nominative A standard of performance established for quantitative and qualitative testing.

testing to destruction The intentional operation of equipment to stress levels within design limits until failure occurs. Accelerated tests to destruction require that an item is subjected to stress levels beyond design limits to induce early failure.

test instruments Open conductors and incorrect voltages are among the most common circuit problems. They are also the easiest to detect. An ohmmeter can be used to check for opens and shorts, and a DVM (digital voltmeter) or VOM (volt-ohm-milliampmeter) can be used to check voltages and currents, as shown. Other test equipment, such as LCR meters, digital capaci-

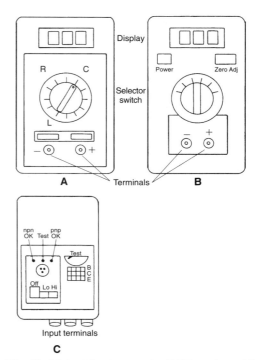

Handheld test instruments: LCR meter with LCD display (A), digital capacitance meter (B), transistor tester with LEDs (C)

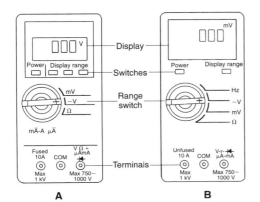

Two examples of handheld digital VOMs

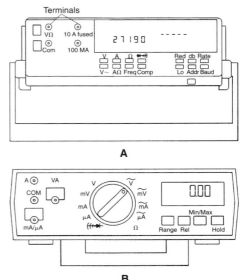

Bench-type multimeters for testing frequency (A) and voltage (B)

tance meters, transistor testers, and multimeters, is needed for diodes and transistors to measure the actual device characteristics.

test macro An ordered set of software and hardware designed for the testing of LSI (large-scale integration) devices. The total system includes a conditioning module, a memory, and a programmable clock generator with the associated software package.

test message A message indicating the test being executed with a pass/fail indicator, as shown in the figure.

```
Other          Floppy Test          Pass    Comm Port Test        Pass
Messages       RAM Tests            Pass    RAM Arbitration       Pass
               RAM Test             Pass    System Test           Pass
               Video Test           Pass    Keyboard Self-Test
               Number of Drives to be Tested? select 2 or 4
               Remove Diagnostic Disk and Insert Formatted Disks
               Warning Contents of Diskettes are Destroyed???
               Number of Tests - 1
               Test 1  - Internal Register Test
               Test 2  - Head Load Test
               Test 3  - Loopback Test
               Test 4  - Restore Test
               Test 5  - Step Test
               Test 6  - Motor Test
               Test 7  - Seek Test
               Test 8  - Forced Write Errors Test
               Test 9  - Write Sectors Test
               Test 10 - Forced Read Errors Test
Error          Error:  Drive A, Failure
Messages       Status: Testing
& Status
```

Test messages with pass/fail indicators

test program package A collection of test and diagnostic programs for microcomputers and peripheral devices. A typical package might consist of the following:

- Processor exerciser
- Interface test
- Interrupt test
- RAM

test to failure See TESTING TO DESTRUCTION.

tetrad A group of four pulses used to express a digit.

tetrode A four-electrode active device, especially a vacuum tube, which contains cathode, control grid, screen grid, and anode.

tetrode field-effect transistor See FET.

tetrode transistor A transistor with four electrodes.

Texas Instruments 9900 (o.t.) A single-chip 16-bit CPU available in a NMOS silicon gate version or an I^2L equivalent. The basic architecture of the 9900 was similar to some minicomputers. There were no general-purpose registers in the CPU itself; instead, the general registers are found in memory. All data went directly from memory to the ALU or to special-purpose registers for interrupts or data status and then back to memory again.

The chip's ALU is shown in the following figure. Three internal registers were accessible to the user: The program counter (PC) contained the address of the next instruction. This address was referenced by the processor for fetching the next instruction from memory; it was then incremented. The status register contained the previous state of the processor including the interrupt mask level and information pertaining to the instruction operation. The 16-bit workspace pointer register held the address of the first general register in memory.

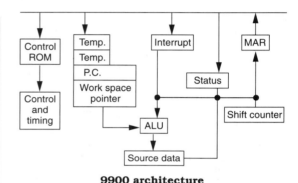

9900 architecture

Texas Instruments 9940 (o.t.) A microcomputer designed to be compatible with the 9900 family of microprocessors. It copied the memory-oriented architecture of this family. Program memory was a 1K-by-16 ROM, which was not expandable.

The 9940 provided an extensive I/O structure for a single-chip device. It had 32 general-purpose I/O lines and provisions for expansion to 256 additional lines.

Texas Instruments 99000 (o.t.) A microprocessor that used n-channel, silicon-gate scaled MOS (SMOS) circuitry and ran at 6 MHz.

Texas Instruments SBP 0400 A four-bit slice microprocessor that uses nonisolated I^2L technology. SBP stands for *semiconductor bipolar processor*. It is microprogrammable with up to 512 microinstructions and uses a single-phase clock. The 4-pin package draws 200 ma at 0.85 volts, and the current drain can be adjusted to be as low as 1 µa.

This processor contains about 1,450 logic gates, which would be equivalent to 30 or 40 standard TTL packages. It contains the functions required for four-bit parallel processing except for sequence controls. The architecture of the 0400 is organized as shown. The ALU has 16 functions with full carry-look-ahead logic. It receives inputs from a multiplexed A port and a multiplexed B port. The eight general-purpose registers have access to the A port, while the data-in bus has access to the A or B ports or the working registers. The output from the ALU is multiplexed and transferred out or along the data bus to the general registers or the working register and its extension. The eight-word general register file includes a program counter and incrementer; the working register and extension can handle either single or double length operations.

A PLA (programmable logic array) is used to define the instruction set desired by the user. Up to 512 operations can be programmed into this on-chip array compared to 50 to 100 instructions for the typical fixed-instruction-set microprocessor. The user can define an instruction set that is unique to a particular application, allowing greater system security and integrity. The PLA is programmed at the factory and would be difficult to copy the software instruction set; thus the developed software remains proprietary with the developers. The PLA technique also allows emulation of larger systems.

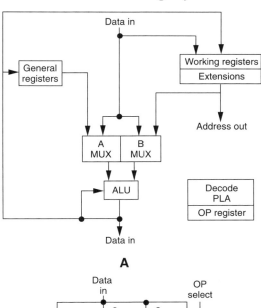

A

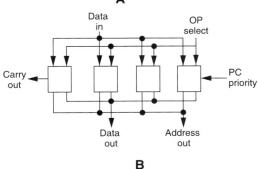

B

SBP 0400 architecture (A) and circuit (B)

Texas Instruments TMS 1000 family (o.t.) A series of four-bit devices that used PMOS technology and included the ALU, ROM, and RAM on a single semiconductor chip. The user's application determined the ROM pattern, which was produced during manufacture.

The architecture for the 1000 series is shown. The ROM held the program used to control data input, processing, storage, and output. All data processing was done by the ALU with temporary storage in the 4-bit accumulator. Data storage in the 256-bit RAM was organized as 64 four-bit words, are grouped into four 16-bit files, and addressed by a two-bit register.

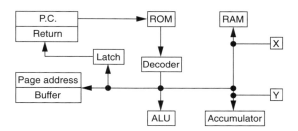

1000 microcomputer architecture

text A sequence of several characters treated as an entity.
text area The window in which the text of a document appears as you type.
text box The area, usually delineated by a rectangular box, in which you type text, particularly in response to a query by the system.
text delimiter In NetWare Diagnostic Services, marks the end of the text fields.
text description In NetWare Diagnostic Services, a null-terminated text string of not more than 69 bytes summarizing configuration information in preceding fields.
text editing A facility designed into a program to allow the keyboard entry of text or copy without regard to the final format. After the copy has been placed in storage, it can be edited by specifying the desired format.
text file A file of letters and/or numbers that is displayed in the form of conventional text for reading, without graphics. Text files are common in word processing and other programs where text is used.
text job description In NetWare Queue Services, a null-terminate ASCII description of the content or purpose of a job. The client creating the queue job must supply this field.
text mode The display mode in which a word processor shows character formats on screen in different colors or hues.

text processing A term generally synonymous with word processing, though often applied specifically to applications dealing with lengthy documents, such as articles or books for publication, which may go through several editing cycles.

text stringing Placing text in different columns and continuing them onto different pages.

text string search A machine function that allows a user to access a point or points within a document by keying in a set of unique characters identifying the locations.

Textures Typesetting software for the Macintosh that lets you design formats and automatically typeset large, structured documents, complex technical reports, books, proposals, and documents that include math and scientific notation.

text wrap In word processing, the ability of a program to sense when a margin is reached and automatically move to the next line.

T flip-flop A flip-flop that has only one input electrode that causes the device to be triggered (to change from one state to another). T flip-flops are used in ripple counter applications.

TFM Abbreviation for *thin film memory*, a memory made up of plates or disks of thin-film magnetic layers deposited on a nonmagnetic base.

TFT Abbreviation for *thin film transistor*.

TG-2D A 2D CAD/CAM/CAE developers kit with over 300 geometric and graphic routines. It includes curves of the following types: NURBS, Bezier, B-spline, Catmull-ROM, quadratic, and conic sections. It allows intersection unions and differences of polygons, composite 2D transformations (rotate, scale, shear, translate, and mirror), surface area calculations, and vector computations.

thermal agitation 1. The movement of the free electrons in a material. In a conductor, they produce minute pulses of current. When these pulses occur at the input of a high-gain amplifier in the conductors of a resonant circuit, the fluctuations are amplified together with the signal currents and heard as noise. **2.** The minute voltages arising from random electron motion, which is a function of absolute temperature expressed in degrees Kelvin. Also called *thermal effect*.

thermal noise The electromagnetic noise due to thermal agitation in a material. Also called *Johnson noise*.

thermal printer An output device that uses chemically treated paper that darkens when exposed to heat. The resistor pins on the print head (shown in the following figure) are heated, which creates the character's dots on the paper. Thermal printers have print heads that are often composed of dozens or hundreds of resistor elements and are used widely in office equipment such as facsimile machines.

thermal runaway A condition in semiconductor devices where increased temperature results in increased power dissipation, which accordingly

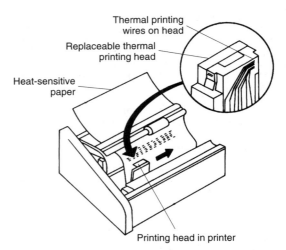

Nonimpact thermal printing

increases the temperature until ultimate destruction occurs.

thermal shock An abrupt temperature change.

thermal traverse A plot of measurements made to determine the time necessary for components of greatest thermal inertia to stabilize at a new temperature under controlled heat-transfer conditions.

thermionic conduction The conduction that arises through electrons being liberated from hot bodies.

thermistor A temperature-sensitive device whose resistance varies with temperature. Its temperature coefficient of resistance is usually high, typically nonlinear, and either positive or negative, as shown in the graph.

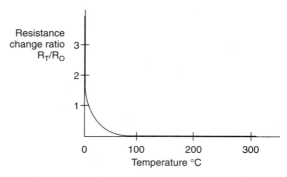

Thermistor temperature characteristics

thermocouple A junction of two dissimilar metals, which produces a voltage as shown in the graph by virtue of the difference in the response of the

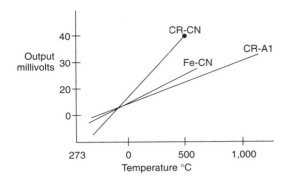

Typical thermocouple temperature characteristics

atoms in the two metals to applied heat. The EMF developed is typically very small and must be amplified or conditioned before use.

thermocouple linearization A technique for correcting errors in a thermocouple measurement system and compensating for the known nonlinearity. Linearization can be accomplished using ROMs, with a specific ROM for each calibrated thermocouple.

thermoelectric effect The phenomenon whereby a small EMF is produced by the difference in temperature between two junctions of dissimilar metals in a circuit.

thermographic printer A nonimpact printer that creates images through heat impressions.

thermonic relay Three (or more) electrode valves in which the on-off potential applied to one electrode controls the current flowing to another, usually without any loss of energy at the control electrode.

thick-film circuit A usually integrated circuit in which layers of appropriate conducting paths and components are deposited on an insulating substrate.

thickwire Another name for the 10Base5 standard for coaxial cables and Ethernet. Also called *thicknet*. Also see 10BASE5.

thin Ethernet RG-58 coaxial cable used in place of the more expensive, larger, and heavier Ethernet cable. Also called *cheapnet*, *cheapernet*, and *10Base2*. Also see 10BASE2.

thin-film capacitor Refers to a capacitor formed by the evaporation of two conducting layers and an intermediary dielectric film, such as silicon monoxide, on an insulating substrate.

thin-film integrated circuits Microminiature circuits produced on a passive substrate. Terminals, interconnections, resistors, and capacitors are formed by depositing a thin film of various materials on the substrate. Microsize active components are then inserted separately to complete the circuit. Also called *two-dimensional circuitry*.

thin-film magnetic module A storage cell that uses thin films of magnetic alloys for switching action. The thin-film cells allow fast switching speeds and miniaturization of magnetic storage units.

thin-film memory *See* TFM.

thin-film microelectronics Circuits that use thin-film technology to achieve miniaturization.

thin-film processing Refers to processes involving conducting layers that are a few hundred angstroms thick and are important in the reliability of integrated circuits. There are a number of important limitations in the techniques used. For example, electromigration in aluminum conductors can cause problems that result in a reduction in aluminum thickness at the oxide steps.

thin-film resistor A high-stability resistor that is formed by a conducting layer a few hundred angstroms thick on an insulating substrate.

ThinNet *See* THIN ETHERNET.

thinwire *See* THIN ETHERNET.

third generation The period of technology in computer design utilizing integrated circuits, advanced programming concepts and time sharing.

third-generation computer A computer utilizing solid-state electronic logic blocks in the form of integrated circuits.

third-party lease An arrangement whereby a vendor sells equipment to a buyer, often a leasing company, who in turn leases it to a user.

THOR Acronym for *tape-handling option routine*.

Thoughtware A series of computer-based training courses designed to improve management skills and the effectiveness of an organization. The program analyzes personal characteristics and helps translate the results to an action plan for improved effectiveness.

thrashing count In the NetWare File Server Environment, the number of times a cache block was not available when a cache allocation was requested.

three-address An instruction format that contains three address parts.

three-card connector cage A case that consists of a U-shape bracket with edge connectors mounted along the bottom and card-guide ridges formed in the sides. The connector spacing is made to allow the mounting of three wire-wrapped circuit boards.

three-D process A triple-diffusion process for complementary integrated-circuit structures.

3+ An implementation of MS-NET that provides options to allow the use of PS/2s on an Ethernet or token ring LAN, or Macs on an Ethernet or AppleTalk LAN.

three-plus-one address An instruction that contains three operand addresses and one control address.

three-wire system A system of electrical supply using three conductors; one of these (the neutral wire) is maintained at a potential midway between that of the other two, which are called the *outer conductors*.

threshold 1. The point at which an effect is first observed or measured. 2. A logic operator having the property if P, Q, and R are statements, then the threshold of P, Q, R is true if at least n statements are true; it is false if less than n statements are true. In this context, n is a nonnegative integer called the *threshold condition*.

threshold element A device that performs the logic threshold operation in which the truth of each input statement contributes to the output determination.

throughput The rate at which work can be handled by a system. Throughput is a measure of system efficiency, and it relates to the speed at which problems, programs, or routines are performed. It can be measured as the total information processed in a specified time period, including input time, processing time, and output time. Speed can increase the throughput, but greater processing volume is also attained by increasing information paths.

thru-put Alternate spelling of *throughput*.

thumb Term sometimes used for the small mark in a scrollbar that marks your position in a document. For example, if the thumb is in the middle of the vertical scrollbar, you are in the middle of the document.

thyristor A semiconductor device for bistable switching. There are various pnpn types using silicon that provide a phase-controlled rectifier. Voltage ratings of up to 600 V are common, while current handling capability can be on the order of 50 A.

tickle An AppleTalk packet that is sent periodically to keep a connection alive.

Tics Realtime Multitasking Kernel Software that allows the development of realtime multitasking programs under DOS or as standalone products on an embedded target. Features include preemption, nonpreemption, and time slicing in any combination.

TIE Abbreviation for *time interval error*, the error in time that accumulates when a frequency source is used as a clock.

TIF Acronym for *tagged image file*, an image file format common in scanners and desktop publishing.

tight buffer A type of cable construction where each fiber is tightly buffered by a protective thermoplastic coating to a diameter of 900 microns. This provides high tensile strength and durability and allows ease of handling and connection.

tiling Setting aside separate areas on a display screen of a computer that runs more than one program concurrently. Each area is a viewport to a different program, where that program displays its output. Tiling is similar to windowing except that program areas do not overlap.

tilt Input-to-output waveform differences when the processing circuits are not fully linear; skew.

TIME A DOS command that displays and sets the system time.

Time Accountant A timekeeping and billing system for professionals who charge for their time and expenses. The program automates the process of recording hours, reviewing performance, and billing for professional services.

time accuracy The degree to which a clock agrees to a specified standard.

time assignment speech interpolation See TASI.

time charge occurs In NetWare Accounting Services, a field that contains the half-hour during which a charge rate takes effect.

time constant In an RC circuit, the product of R (ohms) and C (farads) expressed in seconds, which is the time required for an uncharged capacitor to charge to 63.2% of the applied voltage. After five such periods, the capacitor is considered to be fully charged (except in pulse circuits, where seven periods are considered necessary to completely charge the circuit).

When voltage is removed from an RC circuit, the time constant describes the complementary arrangement: the amount of time required for the capacitor to lose 63.2% of its charge (drop to the 36.8% voltage level). In an RL circuit, the time constant in seconds is equal to L/R (in henrys and ohms) and follows the same charge and discharge curves.

time-constant chart A chart showing universal charge and discharge curves for RC and RL circuits, where voltage or current is shown as a decimal fraction of one.

time, cycle See CYCLE TIME.

time-delay circuit A circuit or device that provides either electrical contact after a specified time, the breaking of electrical contact after a specified time, or the delayed transmission of input signals.

time delay reflectometer An incorrect reference to a device called a *time domain reflectometer*.

time discriminator Refers to a type of circuit with an output proportional to the time difference between two pulses; its polarity reverses if the pulses are interchanged.

time-division multiplexing See TDM.

time-domain measurements Frequency measurements taken on clocks, timed devices, and circuits and compared over a period of time.

time-domain reflectometer Test equipment that performs time-domain reflectometry.

time-domain reflectometry See TDR.

time interval error See TIE.

TimeLine A program that allows you to plan and manage projects. Workgroup facilities include multi-project-control that lets you create a network-wide project management system and resource calendars to schedule vacations and equipment downtime. You can also account for inflation and productivity changes with varying resource cost rates and availability.

time of next charge In NetWare Accounting Services, the time of the next charge, measured in minutes since January 1, 1985.

time of previous charge In NetWare Accounting Services, the time of the previous charge, measured in minutes since January 1, 1985.

time origin A start of a pulse defined as the time at which it first reaches some given fraction, such as 10 percent of its full amplitude.

timeout limit In NetWare, the time the program will wait for a file to become available if another station has it locked. It is measured in *clock ticks*, where a tick is an eighteenth of a second.

timeouts count In NetWare Diagnostic Services, the number of times (since the shell was activated) that the shell has sent a request to a server and then timed out without receiving a reply.

time-pulse generator *See* PULSE GENERATOR.

time-schedule controller A controller whose actions adhere automatically to a predetermined time schedule.

time series Refers to a discrete or continuous sequence of quantitative data assigned to specific moments in time, usually studied with respect to their distribution in time.

time-share To use a device or system for two or more interleaved purposes. Time-sharing programs are available for several microprocessors, and time-sharing services are available from a number of service organizations. Time-sharing allows a microcomputer system to be developed on a pay-as-you-go basis, since there is not normally a fixed overhead charge.

time-shared BASIC An enhancement of BASIC that is used as a conversational language to provide access to a computer system for a maximum number of users.

time-shared computer A computer system that allows usage by a large number of subscribers, usually through data communication subsystems. Certain data and programs may be shared by all users, while other data and programs may only be provided and used by certain subscribers. Documentation for general programming on the system is available with the time-sharing service, which provides system-dependent operating instructions. The user may be assigned a work area in the system for storing programs that can be edited using the system editor.

time-sharing polling Polling is a technique for controlling the use of lines by an agreed protocol between devices that share a common transmission path. The devices are controlled (so that only one of them sends information along a line at any instant) by an exchange of signals or messages. Sometimes polling is governed by the CPU, which sends a control message to each terminal in turn, inviting it to transmit a message. The terminal replies either with such a message or with a message indicating it has nothing to report.

time slice A designated interval of time during which a job or task uses a resource without being preempted.

time-slicing **1.** The allocation of time slots to terminal jobs in timesharing systems. **2.** A feature in some systems which prevents a task from monopolizing CPU time and delaying other jobs or tasks.

time stamp In NetWare Accounting Services, the date and time the server submitted the charge.

time to loss of frame alignment After proper frame alignment occurs, the time-to-loss-of-frame synchronization, usually specified as a function of the bit error rate (BER).

timing clock The source of timing signals or clock pulses required for sequencing computer operation. This source usually consists of a clock generator and a cycling unit to derive the sets of pulses required at specific intervals. Sometimes called *timing master*.

timing signals The electrical pulses that are required at specific intervals to ensure synchronization in processors. The synchronous logic used in most machines is based on a clock signal to trigger operations on pulses of a fixed period. Instruction times are based on the maximum clock frequency of the microprocessor, and other lower-frequency signals may be desired to optimize other functions, such as memory access time.

timing slip *See* SLIP.

TIMM Acronym for *thermionic integrated micromodule*.

tinkertoy Refers to one of the early attempts at modularization in which wafers with one more component parts printed or mounted on them were stacked vertically with interconnecting wiring stiff enough to provide support running through holes around the periphery of the wafer. The multiplatform-like appearance of the stacked wafers and support wiring inspired the name of the technique which, with modifications, is still employed for some high-density packaging.

TIP Acronym for *terminal interface processor*, an ARPANET switch that allows terminals to be connected to the network.

TL Abbreviation for *transmission line*.

TLB Abbreviation for *telco line bridge*, an active bridge that enables data communication users to transmit and receive data over multiple telephone channels (four-wire) using only one computer port and a single modem. Multiple terminals can

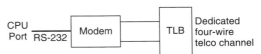

Telco line bridge

use the TLB to share a single telephone channel, as shown.

TLD Abbreviation for *terminal locking device*, a switch that prevents anyone other than the keyholder from using a terminal or printer. Both standalone and wallmount models are equipped with a high security lock packaged in a tamper-resistant enclosure. The units are small in size and easy to install. Each of the units has two rear-mounted DB25S (female) connectors. All 25 leads of the RS-232 interface are supported.

TLI Abbreviation for *transport level interface*, an AT&T-developed specification for the interface between the transport layer and upper-layer users. *Also see* OSI MODEL.

T-LIB A version control system for source code, documentation, and binary files. It creates and maintains annotated libraries containing all past and current versions of each file and a complete revision history including date, author, and comments for each version.

TLSI Abbreviation for *terminal line-sharing interface*, an active modem-sharing unit that supports synchronous or asynchronous operation and may be cascaded to attach more terminals. Terminals may operate as if the modem were dedicated.

TMP file A temporary file for revisions to a document.

TMS 5501 (*o.t.*) A chip that has a PIO with an eight-bit input port, an eight-bit output port, an asynchronous serial line, two interrupts, and five programmable interval timers to interface to the 8080.

TNC A threaded type of connector used on coaxial cable.

TNF Abbreviation for *transfer on no overflow*.

TN3270 A variant of the Telenet program that allows you to attach to IBM mainframes and use the mainframe as if you had a 3270 or similar terminal.

TNZ Abbreviation for *transfer on nonzero*.

toggle A bistable trigger circuit such as a flip-flop, which switches between two stable states.

toggle key *See* LOCKING KEY.

toggle switch A circuit or switch that holds one of two states until changed.

token A distinguishable unit in a sequence of characters.

token bus A medium access method where nodes are not allowed to transmit until they receive a token. The token is broadcast on the medium, as in Ethernet, and gives each successive node permission to use the medium.

token passing A popular access control technique used in LAN switch-ring topologies.

token rotational time The time for a token to circulate once around the network.

token ring A LAN technology developed by IBM to be used with an IBM cabling system. The token-ring physical-star/logical-ring topology allows for flexible expansion of even very large networks, as shown in the diagram. There is a high fault tolerance in the token-ring design; breaks in the ring are handled with redundant circuits and loopbacks.

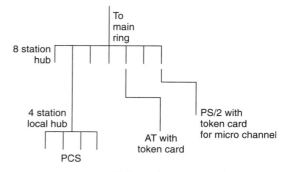

Token ring

token-ring card A card that allows diverse PC environments to be connected to a token-ring network.

tolerance A permissible deviation from a specified value. A frequency tolerance is expressed in cycles or as a percentage of the nominal frequency; a temperature tolerance is expressed in degrees centigrade.

T-1 carrier A digital transmission carrier AT&T developed to transmit data across a WAN (wide area network) at 1.554 million bits per second. A single T-1 channel can carry 24 simultaneous voice communications encoded at 4,000 bits per second.

tone-burst generator A circuit for producing pulses of short duration.

toner A dry, powdered substance used in the laser printing process. A low-powered laser inside the laser printer is used in conjunction with an electrical corona to impart an electrical charge on the surface of a revolving drum. The toner is attracted to this charge, which is in the exact representation of the printed image. The toner is then transferred to the surface of the paper and melted (or fused) in place. The toner supply for most laser printers is contained inside a disposable cartridge.

toolbar A set of graphic images used to represent the utility functions of a program. For example, a painting program may provide a toolbar offering such functions as "fill," "line," "rectangle," "circle," and so on.

ToolBook A program that allows you to build custom applications for Windows for such uses as computer-based training, flat-file databases, database front-ends, prototypes, simulations, and interactive presentations. It includes an object-oriented language with custom functions along with DDE and DLL support.

toolbox A graphics package feature that contains a variety of tools to let the user manipulate what is on the screen.

ToolBox A set of tools for developing applications with the development ease and speed of a 4GL and the execution speed and efficiency of C. Features include prototype generation, data dictionary, dynamic resource swapping, screen management, overlapped windows, file restructuring, runtime portability, menu management, variable length record support, index key compression, dynamic file space reclamation, variable length key fields, and high-speed B+ trees.

ToolQube A utility that allows you to create floating toolbars for Windows instructions to perform destructive tasks.

Tools.h++ A set of C++ foundation classes designed to make programming easier. It includes collection classes modeled after the Smalltalk-80 environment. It can be compiled as a Windows DLL. All classes support isomorphic persistence, making it possible to restore a collection on a different operating system.

ToolsKan A development toolkit for Windows, compatible with Microsoft C/C++, Borland C/C++, Turbo Pascal for Windows, and Quick C.

too many hops count In NetWare Diagnostic Services, the number of times (since the bridge was initialized) that the bridge has received packets on their fifteenth hop across an internetwork bridge. These packets are discarded.

TO package A standard metal-can package for small lead count chips. The package generally consists of a Kovar body, a pure nickel lid, and Kovar leads, brazed in with a glass seal. The lid is sealed onto the body by cold welding to assure hermeticity of the package.

top-down design A technique based on the philosophy that a problem can be broken down into smaller tasks or sections that can become modules. In top-down design, the testing and integration can occur along the way rather than at the end; thus some problems may be discovered early. Testing can be done closer to the actual system environment instead of using driver programs. The top-down design technique tends to combine the design, coding, debugging, and testing stages.

For example, in the top-down design for an analog-to-digital conversion, the flowchart is written as shown in the figure. The program initially calls the A/D input routine, which is a program stub, and then calls the other routines or program stubs if the input data is not zero; it then returns to reading the A/D input.

The routine that reads the A/D input is expanded, the input from the converter consists of three BCD digits that the CPU fetches

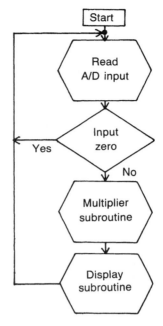

A/D general flowchart for top-down design

one at a time. The expansion results in the following tasks:

1. Send a START CONVERSION signal to the A/D converter.
2. Check the CONVERSION COMPLETE line. Wait if the conversion is not complete.
3. Fetch a digit.
4. Check the digit for zero.
5. Repeat steps 3 and 4 three times.
6. If all the digits are zero, repeat starting with step 1.
7. Check if the converter has reached the final value by waiting and then repeating steps 1 through 6.
8. If the inputs are not equal, repeat step 7 until equal within the converter accuracy requirement.
9. Save the final input value.

top octave synthesizer A frequency synthesizer designed to generate the highest frequencies used in electronic organs. They are applicable to any electronic musical instrument based on the equal tempered scale. These products facilitate the design of instruments that never require tuning and offer automatic transposition. The outputs contain both odd and even harmonics and do not jitter or produce undesirable subtones.

topology The layout or configuration of a network.

The principal network topologies are star, bus, ring, and snowflake.

TOPS An expansion board and related software for the PC that gives it access to networked AppleTalk printers. To connect the TOPS network, use any low-cost twisted-pair cable or existing RJ telephone wiring.

TopView Software that provides a multitasking operating environment that allows you to switch from one program to another. To run an application under TopView the user must set up a PIF (program information file) for that product. A PIF requires that you specify information about the program's operating characteristics such as data file locations, minimum and maximum memory constraints, and range of software interrupt vectors swapped. This information is readily available for popular programs, but for others it must be gotten from the software vendors or through trial and error.

TopView Programmer's Toolkit A set of tools designed to aid programmers in writing applications compatible with TopView's multitasking and windowing environment.

total blocks In NetWare Directory Services, the total number of blocks on the volume.

total cache writes In the NetWare File Server Environment, the total number of cache buffers written to disk.

total capacitance The capacitance between a given conductor and all other conductors in a system.

total changed FATS In the NetWare File Server Environment, the number of FAT sectors the file system has modified since it was brought up.

total directory slots In NetWare Directory Services, the maximum number of slots on a volume. These slots correspond to entries in the directory table. A new file will take up space as well as a directory slot.

total dynamic space In the NetWare File Server Environment, the amount of memory in the dynamic memory area.

total file service packets In the NetWare File Server Environment, the number of request packets serviced by a file server.

total files opened In the NetWare File Server Environment, a field that contains the number of files the server has opened since the server was brought up.

totalizing Registering a precise total count from a mechanical, electromagnetic, or electronic device.

total multiplexing A system that allows both analog and digital signals to flow either to or from a central control and the remote multiplexers.

total other packets In the NetWare File Server Environment, a count of all packets received that are not requests for file services.

total packets routed In NetWare Diagnostic Services, the total number of packets that the router actually routed.

total read requests In the NetWare File Server Environment, the number of file read requests a server has received since it was brought up.

total request packets In the NetWare File Server Environment, the number of request packets a logical connection has sent to a server since the workstation attached.

total routed packets In NetWare Diagnostic Services, a count of all packets routed by the server.

total Rx packet count In NetWare Diagnostic Services, the number of packets the driver has successfully received and passed into the system since the last reset or initialization.

total server memory In the NetWare File Server Environment, the total amount of memory the server has installed (in 1K units).

total transactions performed In the NetWare File Server Environment, the number of transactions performed by the server since it was brought up.

total transition time The time interval between the point of 10 percent input change and the point of 90 percent output change. It is equal to the sum of the delay time and rise or fall time.

total Tx packet count In NetWare Diagnostic Services, the number of packets the driver has successfully transmitted since the last reset or initialization.

total unfilled backout requests In the NetWare File Server Environment, the number of backouts that failed because transaction tracking was disabled.

total write requests In the NetWare File Server Environment, the number of write requests the server has received since it was brought up.

total write transactions performed In the NetWare File Server Environment, the number of transactions that required the file server to track file changes. If a workstation requests a transaction but does not actually modify (write) a file during the transaction, the transaction-tracking software will ignore the transaction.

touch control A device that adjusts the pressure required to operate a keyboard.

touch screen A video screen constructed to sense when one is touching it, and to be able to furnish a computer with precise information as to exactly where on the screen the touch occurred. Touch screens are used with software that uses the information provided by the screen touch to respond to user requests. The most common implementation of touch-screen capability is to equip a video screen with a grid of discrete light beams that are located extremely close to the glass of the screen. When something touches the screen, it breaks one or more beams of light, allowing coordinates for the touch to be determined. Also called a *touch-sensitive screen*.

Touchtype A set of program designed for gaining skill on the keyboard.

townsend avalanche A multiplication process in which a single charged particle that is accelerated by a strong field causes a large increase in ionized particles through collisions.

townsend criterion A relationship expressing the minimum requirement for breakdown in terms of the ionization coefficients.

TPI Abbreviation for *tracks per inch*, a measure of disk recording capacity. The higher the TPI, the more information the media can record.

TPM Abbreviation for *tape preventive maintenance*.

trace 1. An interpretive diagnostic method that provides an analysis of each executed instruction and writes it on an output device as each instruction is executed, as shown in the following figure. A selective trace may be used to trace instructions which satisfy certain specific criteria such as instruction type or data location. 2. The graphic representation of a waveform on a CRT screen. 3. To troubleshoot a circuit or system by monitoring signals at various points along the signal route.

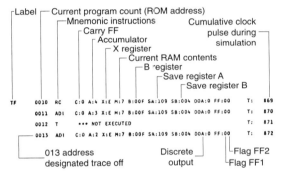

Trace, 1

trace command A command that displays the previous *n* cycles of real-time program execution before the break condition was achieved. The trace shows assembled op codes and operands, data transferred during execution cycles, stack operations, I/O operations, bus operations, and interrupt cycles. Program symbols in the trace data make the identification of program operation easier to understand.

trace program A diagnostic program used to perform a check on another program. A complete trace program instructs the CPU to provide the status of all registers and memory locations affected by each instruction each time the instruction is executed. Unlike many debug routines that instruct the computer to halt at certain selected breakpoints, trace programs allow users to command the computer to print the contents of any selection of registers in memory and then resume program execution automatically.

track 1. The path along which information is recorded on a storage medium such as a tape. 2. To properly follow a master control signal or control element.

trackball A pointing device that looks somewhat like an upside-down mouse, shown in the following figure. Unlike a mouse, a trackball remains stationary; as you move the ball in the center with your finger or palm, sensors detect movement and cause the onscreen cursor to move.

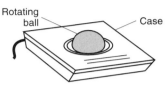

Trackball

tracking converters A tracking synchro converter is shown in the following figure. Three-wire synchro-angle data are sent to a Scott-T transformer, isolated from ground and translated into two signals, the amplitude of one being proportional to the sine of θ and the other proportional to the cosine of θ. These amplitudes are the carrier amplitudes at the reference frequency. The cosine wave is cos θ cos wt; the carrier term, cos wt, is removed in the demodulator. The tracking converter acts as a closed-loop servomechanism (continuously attempting to null the error to zero) with two lags, since there are two integrators in series.

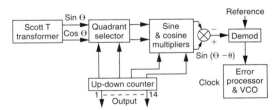

Tracking S/D converter

track-to-track speed The speed in milliseconds that it takes a disk drive head to move from one track to the next adjacent track of data. Also known as the *minimum access time*.

traffic A measure of network load that usually refers to the transmission rate.

TrafficWatch A LAN utility that lets the user monitor who is talking to whom, and how often, as well as detect errors on the network. Once data is recorded, TrafficWatch will automatically save it in Microsoft Excel-readable files. TrafficChart and TrafficFormat macros convert data into meaningful charts.

trailer label A special record indicating the end of a disk or tape file.

trailing Located at the end of a string or number. For example, the number 1000 has three trailing zeros.

training time The time necessary to train an operator or user to operate a piece of equipment or software.

transaction An exchange of value, usually recorded as data.

transaction cycle The input, processing, output, and storage of a single transaction.

transaction disk space In the NetWare File Server Environment, the number of disk blocks being used by the transaction-tracking software. (A block is equal to 4,096 bytes.)

transaction FAT allocations In the NetWare File Server Environment, the number of blocks that have been allocated for FATs of files being tracked since the server was brought up.

transaction file size changes In the NetWare File Server Environment, the number of times files being tracked changed their sizes within transactions since the server was brought up.

transaction files truncated In the NetWare File Server Environment, the number of times files being tracked have been truncated within a transaction since the server was brought up.

transaction log A report detailing the transmissions (faxes, e-mail messages, etc.) sent and received, as well as the status of those transmissions, including errors.

transaction processing A database process that measures the integrity of files during adds and deletes.

transaction tracking A technique where the file server groups together all files associated with a transaction. Only when all these files are updated is the transaction complete.

transaction tracking supported In the NetWare File Server Environment, a field that tells whether the server supports TTS. If this field is zero, the server does not support TTS and the rest of the fields are undefined.

transaction tracking system *See* TTS.

transaction volume number In the NetWare File Server Environment, identifies the volume used for the transaction work file.

transceiver A terminal device that can be used to transmit and receive signals. A typical asynchronous transceiver provides a data communications interface for operation in full- or half-duplex modes. The unit accepts parallel data words from a computer or terminal and converts the data into asynchronous serial format. Received information is converted into parallel data for transmission to the computer or terminal. Baud rates, bits per character, parity mode, and number of stop and start bits are typically selectable by control signals or jumper leads.

transceiver cable A cable of up to 50 meters between the transceiver and the Ethernet controller.

transceiver tester A test tool that verifies the integrity and performance of Ethernet transceivers and transceiver attachment cables. It activates the built-in functions of the transceiver, including the loop-back test. Also called a *transceiver exerciser.*

transcoder A device that performs direct digital-to-digital conversion between two different voice-encoding schemes without turning the signals to analog form.

transcribe To copy, with or without translating, between storage media or between computers and storage media.

transcriber The equipment used for translating data recorded in one format to another format, and recording this data for later use elsewhere.

transducer A device that converts one form of energy into another form. The energy may be electrical, mechanical, acoustical, thermal, etc.

transducer-coupling system efficiency The power outputs at the point of application divided by the electrical power input into the transducer.

transducer, expander *See* EXPANDER TRANSDUCER.

transducer, feedback *See* FEEDBACK TRANSDUCER.

transducer loss A ratio of the power from the source to the power that the transducer delivers to the load under specified operating conditions.

transducer pulse delay The interval of time between a specified point on the input pulse and on its related output pulse.

transducer translating device A device for converting the error of the controlled member of a servomechanism into an electrical signal that can be used for correcting the error.

transfer **1.** To jump or cause to jump. **2.** To transmit or copy information from one device to another.

transfer admittance The ratio of the current at a pair of terminals of an electrical device to the voltage applied between another pair, with all terminals being terminated in a specified manner.

transfer check **1.** A check to determine if a transfer or jump operation was successfully completed. **2.** A verification of data by temporarily storing, retransmitting, and comparing. The transfer check can be implemented by comparing each character with a copy of the same char-acter transferred at a different time or by another route.

transfer circuit A circuit that connects two or more communications networks to transfer the traffic between the networks.

transfer corona wire A very fine, steel wire used in laser printers to impart a negative electrical charge to the surface of the paper, causing the toner to move from the photosensitive drum to the paper's surface. Occasionally, excess particles of toner might need to be cleaned from the surface of this wire.

transfer command An instruction that changes control from one part of the program to another by indicating a remote instruction.

transfer current The current in a gas tube control electrode required for ionization and gas discharge.

transfer function The expression relating the output of a control system to its input.

transfer impedance In a network, the ratio of the potential difference between a pair of terminals to the resultant current at another pair of terminals, with all terminals being terminated in a specified manner.

transfer rate The rate at which information is transferred between various units in a system. It is limited by the transfer capabilities of the memory itself and of the memory bus. The transfer rate is sometimes called the *memory bandwidth* and measured in words or bits per second.

transfer ratio The ratio of transfer of a parameter such as power or current in a circuit or transducer at a specified frequency.

transfer table A table that contains a list of all transfer instructions of programs in main memory. The transfer table allows the transfer of control between programs.

transfer time The time required to complete a transfer operation in a computer.

transform To change the form of data according to a specific procedure, usually leaving some feature of the data unchanged. The structure or composition may be changed, but the meaning or value is not significantly altered.

transformer An inductive electrical device that uses electromagnetic energy to transform voltage and current levels in a circuit.

transformer-coupled isolation amplifier Isolation amplifiers, employing transformer coupling, offer total galvanic isolation, a low capacitance of greater than 10 pF between input and output ground circuits, a CMR of 115 dB at 60 Hz, and common-mode voltage ratings to 5 kV. Capable of transmitting millivolt signals with unity or adjustable gain, these devices are used, for example, in medical applications where an ECG waveform is the input to isolate patients from ground-fault currents.

Like instrumentation amplifiers, these amplifiers use committed gain circuits with internal feedback networks and can operate from dc to 2 kHz. They are designed in two parts: an isolated amplifier section and an output section. The amplifier section includes a fixed-gain op amp, a modulator, and a dc regulator enclosed in a floating guard-shield. The output section contains the demodulator, filter, and power supply oscillator circuit, operating from a single supply. Operating power is transformer-coupled into the shielded input circuits and capacitively or magnetically coupled to the output demodulator circuit. A typical ECG application in a medical electronics data acquisition system is shown in the following figure.

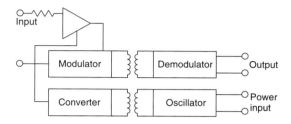

Transformer-coupled isolation amplifier

transformer step-down A transformer in which the output voltage is less than the input voltage.

transformer step-up A transformer in which the output voltage is greater than the input voltage.

transient A sudden pulse in a signal; it is usually of extremely short duration and may be difficult to detect, but it often causes problems because it may be read by the system as a signal element. High-voltage transients can be destructive to unprotected components in a system.

transient analyzer A device used for the study and observation of transient electrical phenomena in circuits and systems.

transient distortion A distortion due to the inability of a system to reproduce transients linearly.

transient motion Any motion that has not reached or has ceased to be a steady state.

transient oscillation A momentary oscillation that may occur in a circuit during switching.

transient response The fidelity with which a circuit responds to step voltages, pulses, or waveforms with extremely fast rise times.

transient wave A wave-pulse that results from changes in the current amplitude and/or frequency. The effects decay rapidly but are propagated along transmission lines.

transistor A usually three-terminal active solid-state device that can be used for amplification and switching. Some two-terminal transistors have no input lead and are controlled by incident light.

transistor action Refers to the physical mechanism of amplification in a transistor.

transistor amplifier An amplifier that uses one or more transistors.

transistor and diode automatic test system A computer-operated system for the testing of transistors and other semiconductor devices, including diodes, SCRs, and FETs.

transistor, binary counter See BINARY COUNTER TRANSISTOR.

transistor current gain The slope of the output current against input current characteristics for a constant output voltage. In a common-base circuit it is somewhat less than unity, but in a common-emitter circuit it may be relatively large.

transistor, depletion-type field-effect See FET.

transistor, drain cutoff current The direct current that goes into the drain terminal of a depletion transistor with a specified reverse gate-source voltage applied to bias the device to the off state.

transistor, dual-gate field-effect See FET.

transistor flip-flop A flip-flop consisting of two cross-connected transistors.

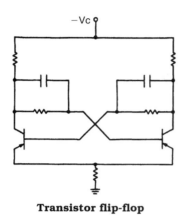

Transistor flip-flop

transistor, insulated-gate field-effect See FET.

transistorized Fabricated using transistors for active signal processing functions.

transistor logic Circuits that use transistors with other components for performing logic functions.

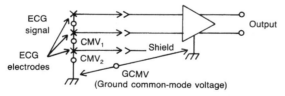

ECG amplifier

transistor, metal-oxide semiconductor See MOS (DMOS) TRANSISTOR.

transistor NAND circuit In diode logic circuits, the input and output signals are of the same polarity, but if transistors are used instead of diodes, it is possible to invert the polarity and perform the logic function in a single stage. It is therefore simple to change the AND circuit into a circuit in which there is a one output only when both inputs are not one. Since this circuit has an output only in the NOT AND condition, it is called a NAND circuit.

transistor oscillator An oscillator that uses at least one transistor to produce its output signal.

transistor power-pack A power supply unit that uses transistor inverters or converters.

transistor seconds Refers to transistors from a production run that do not meet the primary manufacturing specifications, but that are functioning units suitable for less rigorous applications than specified.

transistor tetrode A transistor designed to operate at high frequencies, having an emitter, collector, and two base connections.

transistor-transistor logic See TTL.

transistor width to ratio length An important dimension-related design parameter of the transistor channel, this ratio determines the total resistance of the channel and is one determinant of speed. It also relates to the overall size of the transistor and thus affects the final chip size.

transit angle The product of delay or transit time and the angular frequency of operation. In a velocity-modulated tube, the transient time corresponds to the time taken for an electron to pass through a drift space.

transitional coding A coding scheme used to convert asynchronous data to synchronous transmission by transmitting the data values and data transition times.

transit network A network that passes traffic between networks in addition to carrying traffic for its own hosts. It must have paths to at least two other networks.

transit time 1. The time taken by an electron to go from cathode to anode of a tube. 2. The time necessary for injected charge carriers to diffuse across the barrier region in a semiconductor device.

translate To change information from one form of representation to another without significantly affecting the meaning of the data. For example, a translation converts a source program in Fortran or COBOL to a target program in machine language.

translator 1. A device or program that converts programs or data from one form to another. Translators include code converters, assemblers, compilers, and interpreters. Translators allow the user to express data or write programs using codes or languages that are convenient to humans. 2. An automatic radio relay station (repeater) that receives an entire frequency band and retransmits it in another frequency range.

transliterate To convert the characters of one alphabet to the corresponding characters of another alphabet.

transmission 1. The sending or conveying of electrical energy or data along a path between locations of recipients. Transmission methods and systems include telemetering, telephony, broadcasting, facsimile, and television. **2.** A message conveyed by wire or radio.

transmission control protocol *See* TCP.

transmission deferred Refers to the act of not transmitting when such transmission would create an Ethernet collision. This is sometimes called *avoidance of contention*.

transmission error A general term for a CRC (cyclic redundancy check) error; it might be caused by undersized or oversized packets.

transmission media The physical carrier used for transmitting data. It describes the type of wiring or cabling used to connect a LAN.

transmission preprocessor A unit designed to remove a part of the processing overhead from the central processor in a system. A typical preprocessor handles protocol modes and performs block checks for redundancy.

transmission system The collection of elements that are capable of functioning together for the transmission of signals and information.

transmission technology The means for transmitting signals. In telephone communications, this refers to the grade of the line (low-speed, voice, or broadband) and the type of line (private, switched, or WATS).

transmit data register *See* TDR, 2.

transmit errors In NetWare Diagnostic Services, the number of errors that occur during the transmission of diagnostic packets.

transmitter The equipment used to generate and amplify carrier signals for the transmission of information.

transmitter card A circuit board that converts parallel digital data into asynchronous serial data in ASCII format. It contains a transmitter module, a clock module, and conditioning circuitry.

transmitter-distributor A device used in a teletypewriter terminal to make and break the transmission line in timed sequence.

transmitter holding register A register used to hold parallel transmitted data transferred from the data access lines by a write operation.

transmitter-receiver serial/parallel module A unit used to convert parallel data for serial transmission and received serial data into a parallel format.

transmitter register A register used to serialize data for the transmitted data output section. It may accept data from a holding register or the SYN register.

transmultiplexer A device that transforms frequency-division multiplexed signals (group or supergroup) into corresponding time-division multiplexed signals that have the same structure as those derived from PCM multiplexing. This type of equipment also carries out the inverse function. *Also see* FDM and TDM.

transparent Refers to communications in which the input data is conveyed accurately to the correct output, with action being needed by the sender, or receiver, to monitor or direct the means by which this occurs.

transphasor An optical switch through which multiple light beams pass through simultaneously. This is like a transistor except that it uses light instead of electricity. It is the interference between streams of light that creates the switching action in the transphasor. Also called an *optical transistor*.

transponder *See* PULSE REPEATER.

transponder efficiency For a given deployed transponder, the ratio of the number of replies to the number of interrogations.

transponder suppressed time delay The overall fixed delay between the reception of an interrogation and the transmission of a reply.

transport control In NetWare Communication Services, this is used by internetwork bridges. IPX sets this field to zero before transmission.

transport layer The portion of the ISO-OSI model that is concerned with the interface between the hardware-oriented lower layers and the software-oriented upper layers. *Also see* OSI MODEL.

Transport Level Interface *See* TLI.

transport protocols The rules for moving data packets from one node on the network to another.

transport time In NetWare Diagnostic Services, a value indicating the speed of the LAN associated with a target driver and board. Speed is measured by the amount of time it takes a 576-byte packet to travel from one node on the LAN to another node. The time is measured in units of $\frac{1}{18}$ of a second.

transposition An interchange of the positions of the conductors of a circuit, the characters in a printed word, or the data in a stream or block.

transputer A parallel high-speed computer based on RISC-based architecture and noted for its parallel processing abilities.

transversal filter An equalizer that uses a tapped delay line with weighting coefficients at each tap to reduce intersymbol interference.

trap 1. A form of a conditional breakpoint activated by hardware or operating conditions. Traps are usually set by unexpected or unpredictable occurrences that cause an automatic transfer of control or jump to a known location. In some systems, the program can only set or clear a trap bit by popping a new program status word off the stack. When set, a processor trap will occur through a specific location at the completion of the current instruction execution, and a new processor status word will be loaded from another specific location. This is useful in debugging programs because it is an efficient method of installing breakpoints. **2.** A device to selectively filter a single frequency or a small frequency band.

trapped flux The magnetic flux linked with a closed superconducting loop in a material in the superconducting state.

trapped instruction An instruction that is executed by a software routine when the hardware is unavailable.

trapping A feature in which an unscheduled jump is made to a predetermined location in response to a machine condition. Trapping is used by monitor routines to provide automatic checking.

trapping mode A method used for program diagnostic procedures. If the trapping mode flip-flop is set and the program includes a certain instruction of a set, the instruction is not performed, but the next instruction is taken from a specified location.

trap setting Establishment of conditions to control interrupt signals when using trapping methods.

TREE A DOS command that displays directories and filenames.

Tree86 A file-management tool that is network-compatible. Options accessed with pulldown menus and the directories are displayed in a graphic format. Files can be sorted in 10 different ways; the program handles 16,000 files in 2,000 subdirectories and works across drives.

tree structure A pyramid system such as a file- or data-addressing structure that selects an element by fan-in cascading, or all the members of a set by fan-out cascading.

tree topology An interconnection scheme used to connect stations on a LAN where there can be more than one backbone cable and the backbone cables are interconnected in a treelike fashion.

Treeview A hard disk and file maintenance utility system that can be used for operations such as copying, renaming, erasing, and backing up files. The files are displayed in a tabular format that is continually updated as you make changes.

trend line chart A line chart in which a straight line, determined by a best-fit, passes through the graphing area.

triac A thyristor equivalent to a solid-state three-terminal ac relay; it is the structural equivalent to reverse-parallel connected SCRs, and can be gated by signals of either polarity.

triad A group of three bits or three pulses, usually in sequence on one wire or simultaneously on three wires.

tribit A data element that contains three bits.

trifurcated Having three electrical contacts in series, all closed by the same mechanical switch so that if two fail, the switch still works.

Trigger A management control program that monitors business performance. Whenever an element being monitored falls outside its acceptable performance range, the program issues action memos and makes sure those actions are taken. Managers can set guidelines for any measurable activity. Typical applications include sales performance, manufacturing processes, staffing levels, retail sales, customer service effectiveness, and personnel performance.

trigger 1. To start a circuit action. **2.** The pulse used to start a circuit action. **3.** The electrode on which a start pulse is applied. **4.** The circuit that initiates an action as a result of a signal change, as a Schmitt trigger.

trigger action The instantaneous initiation of current flow by a smaller controlling impulse in a circuit or device.

trigger, bistable *See* FLIP-FLOP.

triggering circuits The circuits used for triggering flip-flops or registers in a system.

trigger level The minimum input required to cause an output.

trigger pair A circuit that has two stable states and requires a trigger to cause a transition from one state to the other.

trigistor A bistable pnpn semiconductor that acts as an R-S-T flip-flop, or bistable multivibrator.

trigonometric conversion A synchro-to-digital conversion technique in which the synchro signals are applied to trigonometric function generators (either tangent bridges or sine/cosine nonlinear multipliers). By manipulating the generator outputs in accordance with trigonometric identities, an analog voltage proportional to the difference between θ and the function-generator setting θ, is developed. The integral of this voltage is digitized, and this digital value is fed back, as ϕ to drive (θ − ϕ) to null; then θ equals the shaft angle θ.

trimmer capacitor A small variable capacitor usually associated with another capacitor and used for fine adjustment of the total capacitance of the combination. Also called a *trimmer*.

trinistor A three-terminal semiconductor device that operates like a thyratron for controlling large amounts of power.

triode A three-electrode electronic device that is active, such as a vacuum tube or transistor, and can be used as an amplifier.

triode FET A field-effect transistor having a gate, a source, and a drain. Also called a *field-effect triode*.

triode pnpn-type switch A pnpn type switch having an anode, a cathode, and a gate terminal.

triple diffusion A semiconductor process in which three impurity depositions are prepared on the substrate.

tripler A circuit or device that multiplies an input frequency or voltage by three.

triple-state gates The bus buffers that control the direction of information flow are shown. The control input of each triple-state buffer controls its output. When the control input is enabled, the output of the gate is equal to its input value. When the control input is disabled, the output of the buffer may be disabled regardless of the input condition. By controlling the selection lines, the data bus lines are placed in an input or output status. The selection lines can also be used to inform external modules of the status condition in which the data bus is at a particular time.

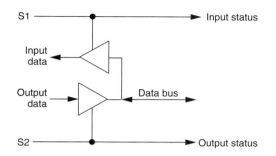

S1	S2	
0	0	Bus disabled
0	1	Input status
1	0	Output status
1	1	Not allowed

Using triple state gates for the bidirectional data bus

TRL Abbreviation for *transistor-resistor logic*.

Trojan horse A program that appears harmless but contains hidden instructions to perform destructive tasks. *Also see* VIRUS.

TROLL A language for the implementation and testing of models using systems of linear and nonlinear equations. Capabilities include the following:

- Continuous simulation
- Regression methods
- Statistical analysis
- Vector transformations

trouble-location problem A test problem that supplies information on the location of a fault. It is usually applied after a check problem has been used to show that a fault exists.

troubleshoot To search for the cause of a failure for the purpose of isolating the responsible stage or device and correcting the problem. Components, software, and noise can all cause problems to occur. Some basic methods of troubleshooting typical problems are shown in the following figure.

Most hardware tools tend to be specialized testers. A large number of logic state, trace, and test capabilities, as well as the ability to display the various states of the computer's operations, are features of these units.

true complement *See* RADIX COMPLEMENT.

TrueType An outline font technology introduced by Apple Computer as a means of including high-quality fonts with the Apple Macintosh and Microsoft Windows operating systems. The design of TrueType fonts allows them to be scaled over a wide range with no reduction in quality.

truncate **1.** To terminate a computational process in accordance with some procedure or rule. **2.** To

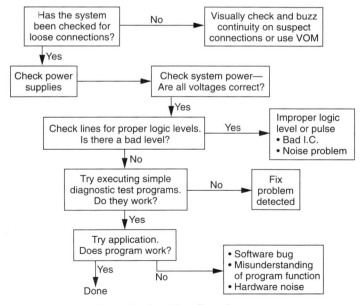

Troubleshooting flowchart

intentionally drop digits of a word or series, thus reducing precision. For example, 3.141 592 653 may be truncated to 3.1415, but 3.1416 would be the rounded-off value.

truncation error The error resulting from a truncation operation.

trunk 1. A single message circuit between two points, both of which are switching centers and/or individual message distribution points. **2.** A communications channel between two different offices or between groups of equipment within the same office.

trunk cable A term used to distinguish the coaxial Ethernet cable (the trunk) from the attachment to the individual node (the transceiver cable).

trustee A NetWare security concept in which certain individual users or groups of users called *trustees* have specified privileges for file access, in contrast to the general public.

trustee assignment Rights explicitly granted to a user or group in NetWare.

trustee object ID In NetWare Directory Services, the bindery object identification of the trustee that will be placed in the directory's trustee list with the rights specified in its trustee rights mask.

trustee path In NetWare Directory Services, the path of a directory for which a trustee access mask applies.

trustee rights mask In NetWare Directory Services, contains the rights a user or users may enjoy in a directory if the maximum rights mask concurs.

truth table A table that describes a logic device or function by listing all possible logic-state combinations with the appropriate output values.

truth table generator A technique that uses a microprocessor to develop the truth table from a diagnostic written in the microprocessor machine code or assembly language.

TSD Abbreviation for *terminal security device*, a device that protects a computer from unauthorized access to the terminals on its dial-up lines. The TSD provides a password protection scheme that presents the would-be intruder with a one-in-10^{30} chance of presenting the proper password randomly. The TSD is located between the modem and its associated computer port, as shown in the diagram. In its normal mode, all RS-232 leads are passed directly through the TSD with the exception of the receive data lead (RXD), which is blocked by a normally open reed relay. Upon sensing carrier detect (CD) from the modem, the TSD starts a timer and begins to monitor character input until a carriage return is received or until 16 characters have been entered; there is no prompting for the password. The TSD then compares the input string to the programmed password and rejects or accepts the password accordingly. The unit allows three unsuccessful password attempts, then blocks all access attempts on the line for fifteen minutes. If the password is correct, the RXD lead is closed and the caller is allowed access to the protected computer port.

The TSD places a 1 ms pulse on pin 9 of the programming connector each time an invalid entry is detected. This pulse can be used to generate a signal to operations personnel. The TSD is programmed with any standard ASCII terminal through the programming port. The unit has a nonvolatile memory capable of storing 25 passwords of up to 16 characters each.

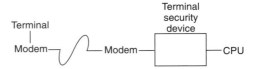

Terminal security device

TSHELL A visual shell for DOS that includes callable help screens and customization files.

TSMT Abbreviation for *transmit*.

TSO Abbreviation for *time-sharing option*.

TSO command language The set of commands, subcommands, and operands recognized under the time-sharing option for a machine.

TSR Abbreviation for *terminate and stay resident*, a program that is always running in the background, ready to be activated by a specific keystroke. Borland's Sidekick is an example of a TSR.

TSRific Software that lets you write terminate-stay-resident (TSR) programs that automatically swap DOS memory with another program. It requires a single function call and uses only 14K or less of RAM. It can swap to XMS, EMS, or disk and has a user-definable hot-key. It supports Borland C/C++, Turbo C/C++, Borland Turbo Pascal, Microsoft C/Quick C, Microsoft Quick, Basic, dBASE, FoxPro, and CA-Clipper.

TSS Abbreviation for *time-sharing system*.

T switch An electrical switch that connects one machine to either of two other devices. The switched device is terminated at the lower end of the stem and the alternatives are at the ends of the top bar. You can switch a microcomputer port between a low-speed, high-quality and a high-speed, low-quality printer.

TTD Abbreviation for *temporary text display*, the control sequence (STX ENQ) sent by a sending station in message transfer state when it wants to retain the line but is not ready to transmit.

T-test A comparison test of two units of quantitative data for the determination of which is greater.

T3 1. A word-processing program for preparing scientific documents. It can be used for documents with complex chemical structures and complex mathematical expression that requires a large number of fonts. It has a chemical-structures library and font editors for both screen and printers. Up to 25 levels of superscript and subscript are supported. **2.** A term for a digital carrier facility used to transmit a DS-3 formatted digital signal at 44.746 megabits per second.

TTL Abbreviation for *transistor-transistor-logic*, a bipolar integrated-circuit logic that uses transistors with multiple emitters. The circuit for a TTL NAND gate is shown. This circuit uses four transistors and four resistors.

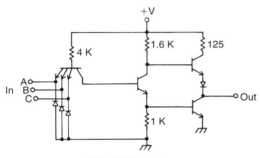

TTL NAND gate

TTL is a saturated form of logic; during turn-on both the emitter-base and collector-base junctions are forward biased, causing an accumulation of charged carriers in the base region. As the device is turned off, this charge must be discharged through the collector. The time required for this discharge results in a delay in turning the transistor off. All saturated logic experiences this storage-time delay. There are other versions of the TTL gate. Five versions are listed, together with propagation delay, power dissipation, and the product of these two parameters which serves as a figure of merit.

The standard TTL gate was the original version of the TTL family. Improvements were made as TTL technology matured. In the low-power version, the propagation delay was sacrificed to reduce power dissipation. In the high-speed version, power dissipation is increased to reduce the propagation delay. Schottky TTL increases the speed of operation without an excessive increase in dissipated power. The low-power Schottky version sacrifices some speed for reduced power dissipation. It compares with the standard TTL in speed but requires less power. The fan-out of TTL gates is 10 when the standard loads of the same circuit version are used. The noise margin is greater than 0.4 volt, with a typical value of about 1 volt.

The multi-emitter transistors are easy to fabricate, requiring only a single isolated collector region upon which a single base region and then the several emitter regions are diffused. Operation is simple, but complex configurations require a lot of components or chip area with high power dissipation in comparison to other logic types. Noise immunity can also be a problem in some applications.

TTL character generator A device that furnishes the correct drive to character displays from a coded set of inputs.

TTL compatibility The capability of being directly interfaced with TTL circuits.

TTL dual D/A converter A digital-to-analog converter subsystem that incorporates the circuitry necessary to interface two analog output channels to the microcomputer. It consists of a dual-channel D/A converter with intensity control for point-plotting applications, a digital input group, and a buffered digital output group. The subsystem accepts digital data from the processor and produces analog output signals having full-scale ranges of 0 to +10 V.

TTL I/O A standard module that provides an interface with TTL-compatible processor peripheral devices. A typical unit contains 16 bits of digital input and 16 bits of digital output with flag and interrupt capabilities. Data outputs are fully buffered, allowing output data to be stored on the module.

TTL-level clock Many CPUs operate directly from a high-frequency crystal with a single-phase, TTL-level clock.

TTL logic Two dc flips-flops are used with one single-phase clock pulse to control the logic steps in a classic master-slave relationship.

TTL PDC A parallel data controller that provides a flexible programmable interface between peripherals and the microcomputer. A typical PDC includes full handshaking under CPU control, and a direct memory-access function for data rates to 256,000 bps, along with four interrupt inputs.

TTL, Schottky *See* SCHOTTKY TTL.

TTS Abbreviation for *transaction tracking system*, Novell software to maintain the integrity of file operations in the case of system failures.

TTTL A modified TTL configuration in which a third transistor is added to the output of the TTL gate to increase drive and improve noise immunity. *Also see* TTL.

TTY Abbreviation for *teletypewriter*.

TTY controller A unit that provides the 20 mA loop transfer currents and control between low- and medium-speed serial devices such as teletypewriters and microcomputers. Typical transmit and receive speed is about 2400 baud.

TU 1. Abbreviation for *tape unit*. **2.** Abbreviation for *timing unit*.

tuned circuit A circuit consisting of inductance and capacitance that can be adjusted for resonance at the desired frequency.

tuning The adjustment of coefficients governing the various modes of control of a circuit.

tuning capacitor A variable capacitor for adjusting the natural frequency of an oscillatory or resonant circuit.

tunnel diode A pn diode to which a large amount of impurity material has been added. Its operation is based on the tunnel effect of quantum mechanics. As the voltage across this diode increases, the current first increases, then decreases, and finally increases again. The region where the current falls as the voltage rises is called the *negative-resistance region*. This negative resistance is useful in microwave amplifier oscillators and converters. Also called an *Esaki diode*.

tunnel effect The probability that a particle of given potential energy can penetrate a finite barrier of higher potential.

tuple A term used in relational database systems. A tuple is the equivalent of a record in a file management system and corresponds to one row of data in a table.

TurboCAD A CAD (computer-aided design) system giving the user accuracy and performance similar to that available on more costly systems.

Turbo C Tools A set of tools for writing applications, including windowing systems with virtual stackable menus and windows with optional borders and drop shadows. Full mouse support is integrated within the windowing and menu systems. Routines for building TSRs are provided.

Turbo Pascal A Pascal compiler with fast compilation speed and low cost. The compiler generates machine code (COM) files in one pass so that no linking is necessary; thus, the compilation is fast. This package has a built-in full-screen editor that interacts with the compiler. When an error is detected during compilation, a message is displayed, the editor is invoked, and the cursor is positioned at the location of that error. If you want to customize the commands to the editor, you can do so through the installation program. Turbo Pascal also includes Turtle graphics, which allows the programmer to manipulate a "turtle" to draw a line rather than specifying coordinates.

Turbo Vision Development Toolkit A set of utilities and object libraries designed for Turbo Pascal's object-oriented, event-driven framework, Turbo Vision. It includes a resource editor for interactively creating or changing dialog boxes and other resources, a utility to convert Turbo Vision resources into Windows resource script files, and an object library to extend Turbo Vision's capabilities.

Turing machine A mathematical model of a machine that changes its internal state and reads from, writes on, and moves an infinite tape, providing a computer-like model. The behavior of the machine is specified by listing an alphabet of symbols for the control of tape motion and read-write operations.

turnaround time The total time between the submission of a job to a computer and the return of the results.

turnkey front panel A panel that eliminates all controls except the one that restarts the processor. It is used in a number of applications in which it is desirable to eliminate the possibility of having an operator affect the contents of the memory or the computing cycle. An example might be a sophisticated intruder-detection system in which the only control provided for the operator is essentially on/off.

turnkey system A dedicated computer system whose hardware and software have been fully debugged before installation. The user's responsibility is then reduced to the task of learning the essential operational instructions only.

turn-off delay time The time interval from a point 90 percent of the maximum amplitude on the trailing edge of the input pulse to a point 90 percent of the maximum amplitude on the trailing edge of the output pulse. This corresponds to the storage time for a bipolar transistor.

turn-on delay time The time interval from a point 10 percent of the maximum amplitude on the leading edge of the input pulse to a point 10 percent of the maximum amplitude on the leading edge of the output pulse. This corresponds to delay time for a bipolar transistor.

turn-on power controller An intelligent power controller that provides unattended remote access to a microcomputer. When the telephone rings at the powered-down PC, the controller automatically powers up the computer and peripherals, puts a program in operation, and leaves a visual signal that remote activation has occurred. The software permits automatic recording of every incoming call by user ID, identifies which program the user executed and the time and date of the call. Other application software can be run or files transferred between PCs all from a remote location.

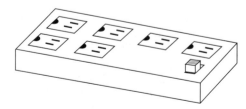

Turn-on power controller

tutorial light An indicator that is used on a terminal to show the transaction history or provide indications of keyboard action.

TValue A loan amortization and compound interest program that solves for loan amount, payment amount, interest rate, or number of payments, and produces customized reports. It handles multiple loans, APR computations, yields on investments, leases, and graduated rate mortgages.

TWAIN A communication standard allowing scanners to communicate with application software through a single interface, thus eliminating the traditional proliferation of device drivers needed for various scanner products.

twelve-pitch A term applied to typewriter-style character spacing of 12 characters per horizontal inch. Also known as *elite spacing*.

twinaxial cable A shielded cable consisting of one or more twisted pair cables.

twin check A continuous computer check that uses a duplication of hardware and a comparison of results.

twill weave A weave in which the filling yarns are interlaced with the warp yarns in such a way as to form diagonal ridges across the fabric, which is used in clean rooms.

twin crystal The imperfect growth of crystals whereby two lattices have a common face, leading to a double resonance and unsuitability for oscillator use.

twinning 1. The intergrowth of crystals of near symmetry such that, for quartz, the piezoelectric effect is not sufficiently determinate. *Also see* TWIN CRYSTAL. **2.** One of two defects that occur in quartz crystals. Either defect results from structural misgrowth of otherwise perfect crystals, yet it cannot be seen in ordinary light. *Optical twinning* is the presence of both right and left hand quartz in the same crystal. *Electrical twinning* is the presence of adjacent regions of quartz having electrical axes of opposite poles.

twip A unit of measurement used in some applications, especially Microsoft products. It equals $1/1440$ of an inch or $1/20$ of a point. Most applications use it to position text or graphics for printing.

twisted-pair cable A communication cable consisting of two insulated conductors twisted together to minimize the effects of inductance.

twisted-pair Ethernet An Ethernet implementation on two 24-AWG solid-copper twisted pairs. It lets the user install voice and data with the same type cable and in the same wiring closet.

twisted-pair local module A module that permits attachment of a twisted-pair Ethernet segment to the network bridge via a twisted pair RJ-45 connector. You can use an Ethernet or fiber-optic local module to allow a twisted pair workgroup access to a copper or fiber backbone.

twisted-pair wiring Refers to two wires that are twisted to cancel out electromagnetic induction.

twist-lock connector A power plug and receptacle used for terminals and other electrical devices that could cause catastrophic effects if accidentally powered off because the plug was knocked loose. To make contact, the plug is twisted after it is inserted, thus locking it in place.

two-address An instruction format that includes an operation and specifies the location of two registers, one for the operand and the other for the result of the operation.

two-chip microprocessor A microprocessor whose complete architecture is developed using only two integrated-circuit chips.

two-dimensional circuitry *See* THIN-FILM INTEGRATED CIRCUITS.

two-level subroutine A subroutine that contains another subroutine within its own structure.

two-out-of-five code A positional notation in which decimal digits are represented by five binary digits of which two are one kind (zeros or ones) and the others are another kind.

two-pass macroassembler An assembler used on some computers that is available with subprogram, literal, and macro facilities. Some can be directly processed by debugging programs; these can provide symbol tables for program checkout in terms of the source language symbols.

two-plus-one address An instruction that contains two operand addresses and one control address.

two's complement The radix complement in binary notation. All positive numbers are the same as in standard binary, while negative numbers are the reverse of the negative standard binary number plus one. *Also see* RADIX COMPLEMENT.

two's complement code A binary code for positive magnitude with a zero-sign bit and the two's complement of each positive number to represent its negative equivalent. The two's complement is formed by complementing the number and adding one LSB (least significant bit). The two's complement of 3/8 (binary 0011) is the complement plus the LSB: 1100 + 0001 – 1101. Two's complement is easy to work with since it may be thought of as a set of negative numbers. Thus, addition can be used instead of subtraction. To subtract 3/8 from 5/8, one adds 5/8 to –3/8, or 0100 to 1101. The result is 0001, or 1/8, neglecting the extra carry.

two-valued variable A variable that assumes values in a set of two elements, usually symbolized as one or zero. Also called *binary variable* or *two-state variable*.

two-way memory interleave A technique in which a computer accesses one bank of RAM chips while another bank is being refreshed.

two-wire circuit A circuit formed by a pair of metallic conductors that are insulated one from the other and that, in turn, feed a load in one direction at a time.

TWX Abbreviation for *teletypewriter exchange service*, a subscriber service for teletypewriter interconnections with communication rates of up to 100 words per minute.

.TXT 1. In DOS and some other operating systems, a filenaming extension that indicates an

ASCII (or pure) text file. It is not an extension attached to a specific program. The extension *.ASC* is sometimes used for the same purpose. **2.** In Windows, a filenaming extension that indicates a file created with the Windows Notepad applet.

TYPE A DOS command to display the contents of an ASCII text file.

type error A packet that is improperly labeled with protocol information.

typeface A synonym for *font*, although it is sometimes used to designate the specific hardware component, such as a typing element, that produces text in a given font.

typematic key A key that repeats as long as you hold it down. Also called a *repeating key*.

type-3 cable An unshielded twisted pair that meets IBM token ring specifications.

Typing Tutor A typing program that provides an effective way to learn to type on a computer. The program adjusts itself to the user's level automatically, giving custom-designed lessons that test strengths and weaknesses.

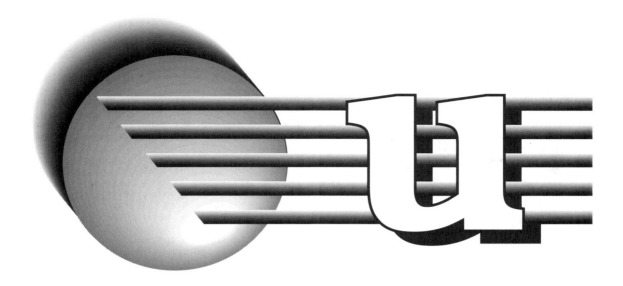

U Abbreviation for *temporary accumulator*.

UA 1. Abbreviation for *unnumbered acknowledgment*, a datalink control command used in establishing a link and in answering the receipt of logic link control frames. **2.** Abbreviation for *user agent*, defined by X.400 recommendations as the component providing the X.400 envelope, including the necessary headers and addresses, before forwarding a message to a message transfer agent (MTA).

UAA Abbreviation for *universally administered address*. Also see LAA.

UADS Abbreviation for *user attribute data set*.

UAE Abbreviation for *unrecoverable application error*.

UAM Abbreviation for *User Authentication Method*, the method in an AppleTalk network by which users are identified to a file server before they can access resources.

UART Abbreviation for *universal asynchronous transmitter-receiver*, a device used to interface a parallel controller or data port to a bit-serial communications network. An asynchronous port can be connected to a UART, which converts the parallel data inputs into a serial stream for communications, or converts received serial data input into parallel format. A typical UART is a single-chip MOS LSI device, as shown in the following figure. It will transmit or receive words of five, six, seven, or eight bits.

Options allow the generation and checking of odd or even parity, which is automatically added to the word for transmission. UARTs use double buffering, which allows one character to be read from a buffer as a shift register receives

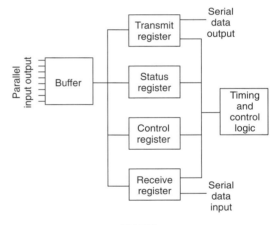

UART

another. The UART has separate clock input pins for the receiver and transmitter sections, so that receiving rates can be different from transmitting rates. This allows different rates to be used between terminals than from terminals to a microcomputer. The receiver in the UART has priority on simultaneous interrupts. *Also see* USART.

UART controller In an asynchronous serial port, data input and data output lines are connected to a universal asynchronous receiver transmitter (UART) circuit, which converts a serial bit stream to 8 bits of parallel data. An 8-bit character is transferred off the data input lines to a buffer memory area for processing. Error conditions are tested to ensure the character integrity, and finally a receive flag is cleared, indicating that the previous character has been transferred.

UART functions Standard UARTs have three sections: a receiver, a transmitter, and a control section, as shown in the figure. The receiver takes the serial input and a clock, and supplies a parallel 8-bit output. The transmitter receives an 8-bit parallel input along with a clock and supplies a serial output. The control section receives the control signals from the microprocessor and implements the required operations. It also supplies the status and control outputs to the microprocessor.

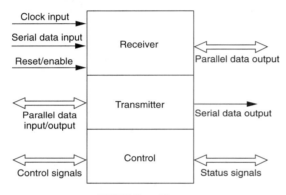

UART functions

UART simulator A program that simulates UART operation in the microcomputer system. The UART has a complexity comparable to a 4-bit microprocessor, and its functions can be transformed for execution into an 8-bit microcomputer. The program passes characters to the UART simulator as if it were a hardware device.

UBC Abbreviation for *universal buffer controller*.

UC Abbreviation for *uppercase*.

U-contact A type of contact and connector system that pierces the insulation of conductors without cutting them, compressing them in a firm connector grip.

U-contacts, cable A system for the transition from flexible cables to rigid printed-circuit boards that simplifies the harness assembly. Flat-ribbon cable/connectors are used in many areas, such as peripherals and readout devices. This connector system accurately spaces conductors for termination in a U-contact connector, which assures a firm contact between flexible cables and the connectors on printed circuit boards.

UCS Abbreviation for *universal character set*.

UDP Abbreviation for *User Datagram Protocol*, part of the TCP/IP protocol suite. UDP operates at the transport layer and, in contrast to TCP, does not guarantee the delivery of data.

UHF Abbreviation for *ultrahigh frequency*, the range of frequencies from 300 to 3000 MHz.

UID Abbreviation for *user identification*, a code that identifies a user to a network during log-on.

UI2 A development environment that includes an editor for designing screens and reports, a data dictionary, and a template-driven applications generator. It includes a set of templates that generate dBASE, Clipper, FoxBase+, FoxPro, QuickSilver, dBXL, and C programs.

UL Abbreviation for *Underwriters Laboratories, Inc.*, a U.S.-based company that tests the standards of products for safety and reliability. Manufacturers pay to have their equipment tested to acquire a UL stamp of approval.

ULSI Abbreviation for *ultra large scale integration*.

ultrafiche A sheet of film containing images or frames that have been reduced more than 100 times by photographic means.

ultrastrip A film, usually 1.5 inches by 7 inches, containing images or frames which have been reduced 150 times by photographic methods.

ultraviolet *See* UV, 2.

ultraviolet erasable PROM *See* UV EPROM TECHNOLOGY.

ultraviolet erasing lamp A lamp designed for erasable PROMs. One model can be mounted for a constant height from the work surface, or moved over the PROMs as a portable hand unit. Typical erasing time ranges from 5 to 10 minutes.

ultraviolet safety goggles Shortwave ultraviolet light can cause sunburning of the eyes and skin. Operators should never look directly into the lighted lamp. Long-sleeved clothing and gloves should be worn. Due to the high intensity of the lamps, UV safety goggles are essential in protecting the eyes from shortwave exposure and avoiding eyestrain.

UMB Abbreviation for *upper memory block*, a block of memory in a PC between 640K and 1M not used for add-in adapters or controllers. Users can gain access to this memory by using a memory manager. Expanded memory resides within UMB. *Also see* EXPANDED MEMORY.

umbilical cord A cable for interconnecting a piece of equipment with a system, which contains vital functions for system operation; because of this, it may be given special requirements or precautions.

unacknowledged connectionless service A type of service where the LLC (logical link control) and MAC layers do not provide any acknowledgment that data has been received, nor are flow-control or error-recovery services offered.

unallowable digit A character or digit combination that is not accepted as a valid representation by the program or computer.

unary operation An operation on one operand, such as negation.

unary operator An arithmetic operator having only one term, such as the negation operator.

unavailability The probability or fraction of time that a system is down.

unbalanced 1. A circuit having one side grounded. 2. A line, circuit, or network in which the impedances measured from corresponding points on opposite sides are unequal.

unbalanced instrumentation amplifier system An unbalanced system does not use symmetry in the configuration. As shown in the figure, a major application of instrumentation amplifiers is in eliminating the effects of ground-potential differences in these single-ended systems.

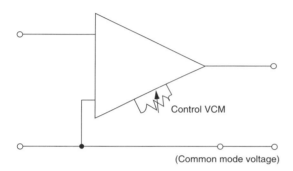

Unbalanced system

unbalanced transmission A method for the transmission of baseband data in which each signal circuit consists of one signal conductor and a ground return.

unbonded strain-gauge elements Unbonded wire elements are stretched and unsupported between a fixed and a moving end. The wire is usually looped one or more times over supporting posts. They tend to have high sensitivity, but are unusually sensitive to vibration.

unbundling The separate pricing of software items from total equipment costs. *Contrast with* BUNDLING.

uncommitted storage list A list of blocks of storage that are not allocated for any particular use.

unconditional branch An instruction that switches the normal sequence of control to a specified location. Also called *unconditional jump* and *unconditional transfer of control.*

unconditional control transfer An instruction that always causes a jump.

uncorrectable error An error in which the intent of the programmer cannot be determined. The CPU usually rejects the statement and continues processing.

undelete To recover the data in a file that was previously deleted.

undercarpet ribbon A special coaxial cable intended for use in walkways and undercarpet applications. This cable is best used for lengths not to exceed 5 feet.

undercut In a printed circuit board, the reduction of the cross-section of a metal-foil conductor due to the removal of metal from beneath the edge of the resist by the etchant.

underdamped A circuit in which the value of resistance is lower than the critical resistance and the response is oscillatory or the output level momentarily exceeds the input level.

underflow A condition that occurs when a computation yields a result that is smaller than the smallest possible quantity capable of being stored.

undermodulation In an AM system, a modulation percentage substantially below 100%. In an FM system, modulation insufficient to permit full carrier deviation to channel limits on amplitude peaks.

underscoring In word processing, the automatic underlining of designated words and phrases.

undershoot 1. The tendency of a numerical-control machine to round off corners of a programmed path as a result of servo lag. 2. A mechanical or electrical system lag due to the inability of the system to react at the same speed as the input or driver.

undersized packet A packet that contains less than 64 bytes, including address, length, data, and CRC fields.

undo To reverse the most recent editing or formatting changes with a command.

unformat To recover the directories and files on a disk that was reformatted.

unformatted capacity The base storage capacity of a disk before it is formatted for use with a particular computer. Some manufacturers list only the unformatted capacity.

unichassis A memory chassis designed for mounting memory and control cards in a rack panel.

UNICOM Acronym for *universal integrated communication system.*

unidirectional Characterized by operation in one principal polarity or direction.

unidirectional bus A bus over which signals are permitted to pass in one direction only.

unidirectional current A direct current that is always positive or always negative and never alternating.

unidirectional pulses Single-polarity pulses that always rise in the same direction.

unidirectional transducer A transducer that can only be actuated by signals at its input; there is no response at the input if the signal is applied to the output terminals. Also called a *unilateral transducer.*

UNIFORTH An assembler, video editor, and software for floating-point arithmetic. It supports the FORTH-83 standard with a few exceptions.

unijunction transistor A three-terminal semiconductor that exhibits stable negative-resistance characteristics. It is used in relaxation oscillators and trigger circuits.

unilateral impedance Any electrical or electromechanical device in which power can be transmitted in one direction only.

unilateralization The neutralization of feedback so that a transducer or circuit has a unilateral response (responds only in one direction). Many vacuum-tube circuits were inherently unilateral, but most equivalent transistor circuits require external neutralization.

uninterruptible power supply See UPS.

union A logical operator such that if P and Q are statements, then the union of P and Q is true if either P or Q is true; it is false if both P and Q are false.

unipolar devices Devices that use charge carriers of only one polarity, such as field-effect transistors made with MOS technology. The transistors are created on the surface of a small piece of silicon, called the *substrate*.

unipolar FET A field-effect transistor structure containing a semiconductor current path, the resistance of which is modulated by applying a transverse electric field, shown in the following diagram.

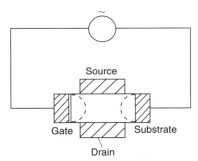

Unipolar field-effect transistor

unipolar transistor A transistor in which the charge carriers are of only one polarity.

unit 1. A portion or subassembly of a system, usually one piece, which provides the means of accomplishing a specific operation or function. **2.** The standard qualitative element by which a quantity is measured; for example, the ohm is the internationally accepted unit for measuring resistance, impedance, and reactance. **3.** A whole, as one. **4.** A digit in the least significant position of a whole number.

unit approach A control technique in which a separate control system is used for each unit in a plant, with a microcomputer assigned to each unit. For example, a microcomputer might be assigned to the control of a milling machine.

United Network Management Architecture See UNMA.

uniterm 1. A word, symbol, or number used as a descriptor for the retrieval of information from a collection, especially from one using a coordinate indexing system. **2.** The selecting of words or parts of words that are considered descriptive of the contents of an item. The selected words or phrases are then included in a *uniterm index*.

uniterm indexing An indexing system that uses uniterm descriptors.

uniterm system A data-recording system based on classifying keywords in a coordinate indexing array.

units, absolute Those units derived directly from the fundamental units of a system and not based on arbitrary numerical definitions, such as the internationally adopted fundamental units of the meter and the second.

unit separator The information separator (abbreviated *US*) intended to identify a boundary between units of information.

unit string A string with only one entity.

unitunnel diode A diode similar to a tunnel diode, but characterized by peak reverse currents in the microampere region while providing high forward conductance at low voltage levels. *Also see* TUNNEL DIODE.

unity gain Exhibiting a voltage amplification of one or less, as applied to follower circuits.

unity gain frequency The frequency at which open loop gain of an amplifier is equal to one. The input signal must be restricted in amplitude such that the maximum rate of change of output (slew rate) is not exceeded.

Univac (*o.t.*) Blending of *Universal Automatic Computer*, the first commercial computer, developed in 1950 by John W. Mauchly and J. Presper Eckert.

universal asynchronous receiver-transmitter See UART.

universal cable adapter A 25-conductor ribbon cable with both male and female DB25 connectors on both ends. This cable is helpful in solving connection and cabling problems.

universal data buffer A print and data spooler compatible with virtually all RS-232 and Centronics interfaces. The unit will interface between computer and printer, computer and plotter, or two computers, and will transfer data in any serial-parallel mode of operation.

universal negotiation and statistical duplexing A protocol under which two modems begin transmission at the lowest transmission speed and then negotiate higher rates of transmission.

universal printer stand A front-access stand that can accommodate any printer regardless of size. Adjustable brackets allow you to match the exact width and depth of any printer. An open-leg design keeps paper feeding into the printer evenly, and a built-in steel wire basket catches and stacks up to 60 pounds of continuous-form paper.

Universal Product Code *See* UPC.

universal PROM programmer A device that allows users to program and verify PROMs using commands from the system console. The PROMs are programmed by plugging personality cards into the programmer card sockets.

universal synchronous-asynchronous transmitter-receiver *See* USART.

universal synchronous receiver-amplifier *See* USRT.

universal terminator board A single-height, standard-length etched and drilled module that can be used for mounting user-selected and user-supplied discrete components to provide a variety of termination or voltage-source circuits. Each signal pin can have two components connected to ground and one component connected to a common tie point.

universal transistor A theoretical, common transistor for specific applications categories. Such a transistor would not break down under any practical reverse voltage, would have a high beta and a high frequency response, would be free from internal noise and immune to external noise with little or no internal capacitances, and could operate at several amperes of current. No universal transistor exists because the design criteria to maximize certain transistor characteristics are diametrically opposite to the optimization of others. Thus, it takes a variety of transistor designs to meet the wide spectrum of performance requirements.

universal Turing machine A Turing machine that can simulate any other Turing machine. *Also see* TURING MACHINE.

Unix An operating system developed by Bell Laboratories for minicomputers, and adapted for both mainframe computers and larger microcomputers. Unix permits several programs to run concurrently and contains many aids for program development. It is considered one of the most powerful general-purpose operating systems and is easily transportable from one system to another.

UnkelScope A general-purpose data acquisition and control package for the PC. It is divided into two levels. One level allows the personal computer to emulate an oscilloscope, a chart recorder, or an X-Y plotter. The other level provides the capability to acquire, display, print, and store up to four analog inputs simultaneously. UnkelScope is menu-driven and can produce data files that can be read by most major spreadsheet and data-reduction packages such as Lotus 1-2-3.

UnkelScope Junior A low-cost data acquisition tool for use with a PC and an analog input board. It supports sampling on up to four channels, with a sample size of up to 1024 points each. It can also be set to acquire 4096 points from two channels, or 8192 points from a single channel scan.

unknown error count In NetWare Diagnostic Services, the number of times (since the shell was activated) that the shell has received a packet containing an undefined error value.

unknown network count In NetWare Diagnostic Services, the number of times (since the bridge was initialized) that the bridge has received packets bound for an unknown network. These packets are discarded.

UNMA Abbreviation for United Network Management Architecture, an AT&T network architecture using NMP (the network management protocol). *Also see* NMP.

unmodulated signal A signal with no modulation. *Contrast with* MODULATING SIGNAL.

unnumbered acknowledgment *See* UA, 1.

unpack To separate or decompose combined items or packed information into a sequence of items, words, or elements.

Unpacker A program designed to assist with the debugging and disassembly analysis of software. It converts packed programs into runnable, unpacked programs. It also allows the separation of attached overlay programs. Multi-segment .COM programs can be converted back into real .EXE-type programs. There are also utilities to simplify the viewing of interrupt vectors and for testing video operations.

unshielded twisted-pair cable Two separate wires twisted together to form a cable, commonly known as *telephone wire*.

unstructured program A program that does not follow the standard guidelines for structuring. It may be difficult to follow and modify.

unused disk blocks In the NetWare File Server Environment, the number of remaining blocks the bindery object can allocate.

unwind To code in full all the operations of a cycle in order to eliminate red-tape operations in the final coding. Unwinding is performed during assembly, generation, or compilation of programs. *Also see* RED-TAPE OPERATION.

UOC Abbreviation for *ultimate operating capability*.

UPC Abbreviation for *Universal Product Code*, a symbol of the supermarket industry that provides automated reading of product information in point-of-sale systems. The UPC symbol contains 10 digits of information divided into two 5-digit fields. The data in the fields are also represented as numerals below the symbol. In a specific representation, the left 5-digit field contains the characters 1 through 5, and the right 5-digit field contains the characters 6 through 0. In the retail industry, the left five digits identify the manufacturer of the product, while the right five digits identify the product.

The representation of a specific digit in the UPC symbol is shown in the figure below. Each character position consists of a region of seven bar positions. A dark bar represents a 1, while a light bar represents a 0. Thus the code represented by the character shown has bits 1000100, which indicates the decimal value 7.

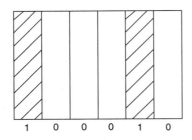

UPC character

update 1. To put into a master file changes required by current transactions. **2.** To modify an instruction so that the address numbers it contains are increased by a desired amount each time the instruction is performed.

up-down counter A binary counting unit that can change its counting mode from up to down or vice versa without disturbing the count stored up to that time, shown in the following diagram.

up-down counter module A module used to provide event counting for a microcomputer system. The module is capable of detecting count overflows and setting up flags for this condition. Count parameters are fully programmable, along with reset conditions.

upload 1. To transfer data in a microcomputer to a storage device in a larger computer. **2.** To transfer files to a bulletin board system or online service. *Contrast with* DOWNLOAD.

upper memory block *See* UMB.

UPS Abbreviation for *uninterruptible power supply*, a power supply designed to provide power in the event of commercial power failure, shown in the following figure.

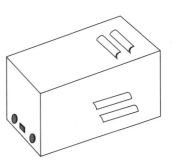

Uninterruptible power supply

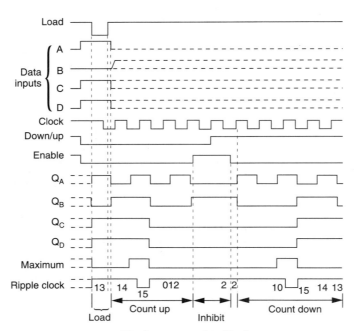

Up-down counter timing

UpShot A utility that allows users to construct large-scale online help files, such as manuals, reference books, and dictionaries. The manuals have a table of contents, index, and numbered pages. UpShot's access engine can be installed and left resident as a TSR or can be run from the command line as a standard program. The utilities allow you to build manuals, print manuals on LaserJet printers, and capture text screens.

upsizing The process of linking stand-alone PCs together into a LAN. Upsizing usually results when a business grows beyond the capacity to use a "sneaker net" for exchanging files. Upsizing can require the addition of a mainframe or minicomputer for storage or data manipulation purpose when using database management applications.

uptime The time during which equipment is operating free of failure or is available for such operation. *Contrast with* DOWNTIME.

upward reference A reference made in an overlay system from one segment to another segment higher in the same path and closer to the root segment.

US *See* UNIT SEPARATOR.

USART Acronym for *universal synchronous-asynchronous transmitter-receiver*, a chip designed as a peripheral device for data communications shown in the following figure. It is programmed by the CPU to operate in a desired serial data mode. The chip accepts data from the CPU in parallel and converts the data into a continuous serial stream for transmission. It also converts received serial data into parallel format for the CPU. The USART signals the CPU when it can accept new characters for transmission, or when it has new data for the CPU. The CPU can check the status of the USART at any time. The USART may operate in the synchronous or asynchronous mode.

The Intel 8251 is a USART. The organization of the 8251 device appears below. The functional blocks shown are the transmitter section, the receiver section, and the control section. The data bus buffer communicates with the other sections. The connections to the microprocessor are on the left side; the connections to the peripherals are on the right side. There are two signals per I/O function: a data line and clock signal. There is also a synchronization line for the synchronous mode. Most USARTs are TTL-compatible, operate from a single 5-V power supply, and have a single clock. Also sometimes called *programmable communications interface*.

USART application A typical application of the 8251 USART in asynchronous mode is shown in the figure that follows. In this system, the USART reads serial information from a keyboard and sends display information to a CRT. A baud-rate generator is used to supply the clock pulses. The slowest mode of operation is nor-

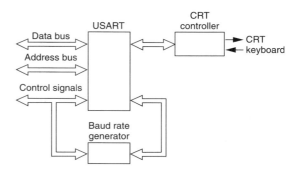

USART CRT control

mally 110 baud, where a baud is a bit per second. Most CRT controllers use a baud-rate generator, where the rate may be selected from 110 baud to 9600 baud. The main applications for the USART are for communications with devices such as a printer or a modem connected to a telephone line.

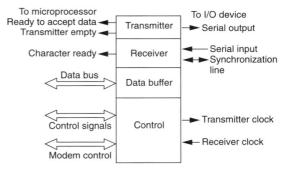

8251 USART

USASCII *See* ASCII.

USASI (*o.t.*) Acronym for *United States of America Standards Institute*, a former name of the American National Standard Institute (ANSI).

use count In the NetWare File Server Environment, the number of logical connections that have used a logical record, or the number of tasks that have opened or logged a file.

used directories In the NetWare File Server Environment, the number of directories owned by a bindery object.

used files In the NetWare File Server Environment, the number of files created by a bindery object.

use, joint Refers to the simultaneous use of a communications or computer system by more than one user.

Usenet A collection of thousands of topically named newsgroups, the computers which run the protocols, and the people who read and submit Usenet news. Not all Internet hosts subscribe to Usenet and not all Usenet hosts are on the Internet.

user Anyone who requires the use of services or products from a computing system or facility.

user agent *See* UA, 2.

User Authentication Method *See* UAM.

User Datagram Protocol *See* UDP.

user-developer Users who design and write programs for their own applications.

user dictionary In word processing, a dictionary you can create and expand as you review the spelling in documents. This dictionary is useful if you have special terminology that you use often in your documents, such as legal terms or medical terms.

user-friendly A buzzword meaning easy-to-use and suitable for nondata-processing professionals.

user interface A protocol (or set of standard programs) that allows a person to communicate with a computer. DOS is an example of a character-based user interface, while Windows is a graphical user interface. Both translate commands from the user into the machine code the computer understands.

user library A basic library of general-purpose software furnished by manufacturers to perform most common jobs; to this, the user can add developed programs and routines.

user-microprogrammed processors Refers to microprogrammable processors having a variety of microinstruction sequencing capabilities. A primary use of microprograms is as an alternative to hardwired control sequencers in the implementation of the control function in computers with conventional instruction sets. These microprograms are used to implement tasks that have a relatively simple logical structure. Microprograms can also be used to support special-purpose architectures, with instruction sets chosen to simplify the programming of certain classes of algorithms. These microprograms may be used to implement tasks that have a relatively complex logical structure.

user program A group of programs, subprograms, or subroutines that have been written by the user, as contrasted with manufacturer-supplied programs.

user questionnaire A set of questions designed to help the user think about his or her needs and express them in a way that the network administrators and corporate management can understand.

user-selected default Default for printing that can be selected using the printer control panel.

user group An organization made up of users of specific hardware or software who share knowledge, exchange programs, and jointly influence vendor support policy. Members of the users group are encouraged to submit programs they have created. User groups often have newsletters that contain updates on hardware and software developments, programming tips, and other useful information.

user's manual 1. A book of instructions outlining procedures for proper operational use of equipment or software. 2. A guide for programming and data-processing procedures that sets forth the other documents, style, and standards used in the organization or system.

user-supported software *See* SHAREWARE.

USOC Abbreviation for *Universal Service Ordering Code*, for telephones.

USOC-500 A standard telephone, rotary-dial.

USOC-502 A rotary-dial telephone with an exclusion key, which is a voice/data switch and is normally one of the buttons on which the handset rests. It is pulled up to be activated. There are two ways to wire a 502 telephone:

- The telephone can control the line, and a call is made or answered by lifting the handset. The exclusion key must be pulled to go into the data mode.
- The modem can control the line, and the exclusion key is used to originate or answer a voice call. The modem is in the data mode when the telephone is hung up, so if the modem is the auto-answer type, it can answer a call without any action by an operator.

USOC-2500 A standard telephone, touch-tone.

USOC-2502 A touch-tone telephone with an exclusion key. *Also see* USOC-502.

USRT Abbreviation for *universal synchronous receiver-transmitter*, a single-chip LSI device that provides serial-to-parallel and parallel-to-serial conversion to interface a parallel controller or terminal with a serial, synchronous communication network. The device consists of separate receiver and transmitter sections with independent clocks, status, and data lines. The transmitter and receiver have common word lengths and parity modes. Data is transmitted and received at a rate equal to the clock frequency. Data messages are transmitted in a data stream, which is bit-synchronous with the clock and character-synchronous with respect to the framing or sync characters that start and stop each message. The receiver compares the contents of the sync register with the incoming data, and when a match is made, the receiver becomes character-synchronous using a 5-, 6-, 7-, or 8-bit character.

utility A program or group of programs that adds functions missing from the program or operating system it is designed to supplement.

utility debug A design-aid program for the testing and debugging of utility functions. The utility debug may allow memory and register changing, selecting breakpoints, and searching memory.

utility routine A routine used to assist in the operation of the computer. Utility routines may include conversions, sorting, printout operations, tracing, mathematical functions, read and write for all peripherals, and text generation for teletypes, CRTs, or other terminal devices. The utility routines may involve a large package for a variety of operations, but only those required for the application need to be loaded into memory.

UV 1. The chrominance components of the PAL color-television system. **2.** Abbreviation for *ultraviolet*, electromagnetic radiation with frequencies higher than visible light and with wavelengths from about 200 to 4000 angstroms.

UV EPROM technology A type of programmable read-only memory (PROM) that can be erased for reprogramming by using concentrated ultraviolet light. The device package, shown in the figure, has a quartz "window" that is transparent to ultraviolet light, with a floating silicon gate inside that isolates the memory. The technique for erasing UV EPROMs is to direct an ultraviolet lamp that has a wavelength of 2537 A through the quartz window. The UV lamp is placed at a distance of 2 or 3 cm from the window, and the radiation is allowed to fall on the element for 10 to 45 minutes, depending on the type of device and source. The UV radiation raises the conductivity of the silicon dioxide and allows the floating-gate charge to leak away.

The erasing process is not selective and results in the resetting of all cells in the device. Also, it may be necessary to check the UV source periodically, since it may age with time, and its intensity may diminish.

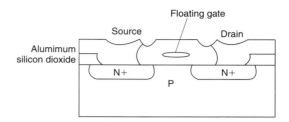

UV EPROM structure

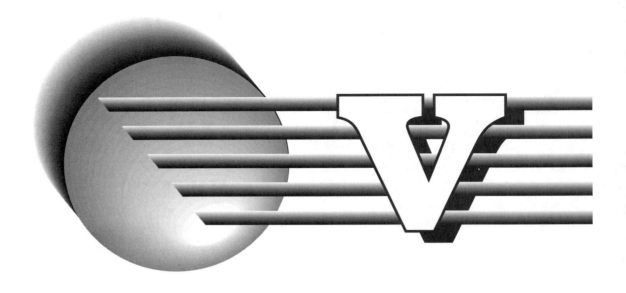

VA 1. Abbreviation for *value analysis*. 2. Abbreviation for *video amplifier*.

VAB Acronym for *voice answer-back*, an audio response unit that can link a computer system to a telephone network and provide voice responses to inquiries made from telephone terminals. The audio response is composed from a vocabulary prerecorded on a disk.

vaccine An analyzer program that performs virus checks on your computer using various virus-checker and virus-protection utilities. *Also see* VIRUS.

vacuum tube (*o.t.*) A glass tube containing electrodes, which was the processing basis for first-generation computers.

valid Legitimate; permissible; operationally acceptable.

validity Correctness; especially the degree of closeness by which iterated results approach the correct result.

validity check A check based on limits related to a specific problem. Data records are checked for range, valid coding, illogical bit combinations or storage addresses, and similar factors. For example, in a validity check, a computed time of day would be rejected if greater than 24 hours.

valid memory address An output line that indicates to peripheral devices that there is a valid address on the address bus.

value In presentation graphics, the quantity or percent contributed by one element of a pie or column chart to the whole.

Value-Added Process (*o.t.*) An optional program for older versions of NetWare. It was replaced by the Network Loadable Module in NetWare 386.

value-added reseller *See* VAR.

VAP *See* VALUE-ADDED PROCESS.

VAR Acronym for *value-added reseller*, a company that sells complete computer systems, both hardware and software. Typically, a VAR buys the hardware and software from other companies, then loads the software and installs the system for a client. VARs also provide after-sale training and support.

varactor diode The pn junction reverse-biased diode types that are used in voltage-controlled parametric amplifiers and multipliers.

variable A quantity that can assume any of the numbers of some set of numbers, or a condition, transaction, or event which changes or may be changed as a result of processing data.

variable address An address that is to be modified by an index register or similar device. Also called an *indexed address*.

variable area meters Flowmeters that use a float in a tapered section of tubing (called a *rotameter*), a spring-restrained plug, or a spring-restrained vane. The displacement of these items causes the area of flow passage to vary while the differential pressure or head remains constant. The displacement is measured to provide an output proportional to the flowrate.

variable block format The format that allows the number of words in successive blocks to vary.

variable capacitance diode A semiconductor diode, abbreviated VCD, in which the junction capacitance has been accentuated. An appreciable change in the thickness of the junction-depletion layer and a corresponding change in the capacitance occur when the dc voltage applied to the diode is changed.

variable capacitor A capacitor that changes its capacitance by varying the useful area of its plates, as in a rotary capacitor, or by altering the distance between them, as in some trimmer capacitors.

variable connector 1. The collective instructions that cause a logical chain to take one of several paths. **2.** The device inserting such instructions. **3.** A flowchart symbol representing a connection that is not fixed, but which can be varied by the program or procedure.

variable-cycle operation Computer action in which any cycle or operation may be of a different time length. Variable-cycle operation computer operation is characteristic of asynchronous machines.

variable expenses A category in many accounting and tax programs for costs that change over time and are more under the control of the individual, such as food and entertainment. *Contrast with* FIXED EXPENSES.

variable field A field in which the vectors at any point can change during the time under consideration.

variable field-length In database management, a data field that can have a varying number of characters from record to record.

variable function generator A function generator that operates using a set of values of the function that are preset within the device with or without interpolation between these values.

variable-length record In database management, a file that contains records that are not uniform in length.

variable master clock A clock that provides frequencies from 100 kHz to 1 MHz for evaluation of microcomputer system components.

variable-point representation A positional notation in which the position of the radix point is indicated by a character at that position. *Contrast with* FLOATING-POINT CALCULATION.

variable-reluctance pressure transducer In the diaphragm-type of variable-reluctance pressure transducer, a diaphragm of magnetic material is supported between two symmetrical inductance assemblies. The diaphragm deflects when there is a difference in pressure between the two input ports. This tends to increase the gap in the magnetic flux path of one core and decreases the gap in the other. The reluctance varies with the gap. The overall effect is a change in inductance of the two coils. The inductance ratio is usually measured in a bridge circuit to produce a voltage proportional to the pressure difference.

Most manufacturers of reluctive transducers offer dc-to-ac-to-dc conversion circuitry in separate or integral packaging. Reluctive transducers with dc excitations of 28 and 5 V are available for absolute, gauge, and differential pressure measurements. The typical range is 1 inch of water to 12,000 psi.

The performance of reluctive transducers, with or without dc-to-dc converters, is comparable in most respects to the best available versions of other transducer types. Static-error is typically ±0.5 percent, with nonlinearity producing the major portion. Errors due to hysteresis and nonrepeatability can be below 0.2 percent. Proof pressure ratings of greater than six times range are available. Errors can be introduced by stray magnet and electric fields.

Most ac transducers operate at a carrier frequency in the range of 60 Hz to 30 kHz. When dc conversion is used, the internally generated carrier frequency may be much higher, permitting smaller coils and capacitors in a smaller package. Temperature effects are minimized by similar sensing-element and coil materials. Temperature errors are typically one or two percent to 100°F. Pressure transducers without dc conversion operate over a wide temperature range, with an upper limit of 350°F. The solid-state components of dc converters may limit the operating temperature of this transducer to less than the ac version. Frequency response is flat from 50 to 1000 Hz, but depends on the particular design.

variable resistance pickup A transducer whose operation depends on the variation of resistance, such as a thermistor or strain-gauge element.

variable-resistance transducer A transducer that produces an electrical analog of the resistance value of its input device.

variable resistor A wirewound or composition resistor, the resistance of which may be changed. *Also see* POTENTIOMETER.

variable symbol 1. A symbol used in assembly programming that does not have to be declared since it is assigned a read-only value. **2.** A symbol used to denote a variable quantity.

variable word-length A computer in which the number of characters addressed is not a fixed number, but is varied by the data or instruction.

variance In statistics, the sum of the squared difference between sample values and the sample average.

variant In desktop publishing or graphics, a variation of a font or stylesheet identified by a number or a special name.

varistor A silicon, carbon, or selenium device used for surge suppression or contact protection. Its resistance is a function of the applied voltage.

varying text In word processing, the text that changes from copy to copy of a form document.

VAX A popular and quite powerful minicomputer produced by Digital Equipment Corporation.

VBLite A program that controls printers, access communication, sorts, and search arrays. You can also use it to write a database application using btree indexing.

VCD *See* VARIABLE CAPACITANCE DIODE.

VCRDBASE A program for keeping track of the movies in a video library. Written in Turbo Pascal, it can be used to keep records of a video library by movie name, publisher, star, and style.

VCScreen An interactive screen painter and code generator for use with the Vitamin C function library. It allows you to draw your input forms and windows using the interactive WYSIWYG design editor. Objects like input fields, output fields, headers, and windows may be created, deleted, repositioned, and modified. Configurable templates allow code generation for DOS or OS/2.

Vdc Abbreviation for *voltage direct current*. Voltages are either alternating current (ac) or direct current (dc). Standard power outlets are ac. Integrated circuits such as those in a computer run off dc. As a result, most computers have a power supply that converts ac power to the proper dc voltages.

VDI Abbreviation for *virtual device interface*, a standard that defines how a computer communicates with a graphic device to produce output. *Also see* CGI.

VDP Abbreviation for *video display processor*, a custom chipset that provides the video circuits for a computer.

VDT Abbreviation for *visual display terminal*, a device that permits inputs to a computer system through a keyboard or other manual input device such as a light pen, and whose primary output is visual through a CRT unit or other type of display. The terminals allow keyboarding, verification, editing, correction, and reformatting of material. They may be user-programmable using parameter designations or data entry languages.

VDU Abbreviation for *visual display unit*. *See* VDT.

vector 1. A symbol for a directed quantity. 2. A quantity that has direction, magnitude, and sense, and which can be expressed graphically as a line segment referred to other coordinate line segments.

vector algebra The manipulation of symbols representing vector quantities according to the laws of addition, subtraction, multiplication, and division.

vector diagram An arrangement of vectors showing the relationships between the representative quantities.

vectored interrupt system An interrupt system in which the microprocessor recognizes the interrupting device, since each I/O device is assigned a unique interrupt address. This address is then used to generate an interrupt trap address for the device. The trap addresses are usually located sequentially in program memory to form the interrupt vector. Each location contains the starting address of a device-service program. The contents of the interrupt vector are loaded into the program counter, and program control is transferred to the correct device-service program.

Some vectored systems, instead of transmitting an address, use an I/O device to transmit a single byte instruction to the microprocessor after the request has been acknowledged. The interrupt-control logic loads the instruction code into the instruction register. Normal operation continues after this instruction is executed. Vectoring is achieved by a single-byte jump instruction that derives the jump address from a part of the instruction code. A unique jump address is defined for each I/O device in the system.

vectored priority interrupt An interrupt that automatically determines priority.

vector feedrate A programmed motion at a specified rate over a given distance in a given direction.

vector field In a given region of space, the total value of some vector quantity that has a definite value at each point of the region, such as the distribution of magnetic intensity in a region surrounding a current-carrying conductor.

vector function A function that has both magnitude and direction, such as the magnetic intensity at a point near an electric circuit.

vector graphic In graphics and desktop publishing, the most common type of graphic, composed of lines and curves drawn point-to-point and layered one on top of another. The resulting shapes can be resized, moved, or altered independently of each other. Also called a *draw* or *object-oriented graphic*. Contrast *with* BITMAPPED GRAPHIC.

vector impedance The ratio of the complex harmonic potential difference to the corresponding complex current.

vector instruction An instruction that can accept an interrupt and branch to the correct routine or device.

vectorize To convert a bitmapped image to a vector graphic.

vector potential The resultant phase angle of a power circuit where a pure resistance circuit has a phase angle of 0°, a pure capacitive circuit has a phase angle of 90°, and a pure inductive circuit has a phase angle of –90°. The phase angle of the incoming power affects overall circuit efficiency where a phase angle of 0° is the most efficient. The phase angle is normally affected by motors or other devices attached to the power line. A vector potential is normally associated with an inductive circuit.

vector power A vector quantity equal to the square root of the sum of the squares of the active and reactive powers. The unit is the vector-ampere.

vector quantity A quantity with magnitude, sense, and direction.

vector ratio A ratio between two complex quantities in which both the amplitudes and phases are expressed as vectors.

vector transfer table A transfer table used to communicate between two or more programs. The transfer vector provides the communication linkage between the programs.

VEDIT A full-screen editor useful for program editing. Every key except the Enter key is programmable, so you can customize the editor to meet your needs. It has useful split and merge file capabilities, a command mode that speeds repetitive tasks, macro support, an Undo key, and line and column status displays. It does not have print formatting or proportional spacing. It is a virtual editor; the file being edited can be stored on disk, so you are limited in document size only by disk capacity.

VEGA Deluxe A high-resolution graphics adapter for the IBM PC, XT, and AT designed to be compatible with the IBM Enhanced Graphics Adapter (EGA). It emulates the following video-display standards:

- IBM EGA, 640 × 350 and 640 × 480 resolutions
- IBM CGA, 640 × 200 and 320 × 200 resolutions
- IBM monochrome display, 640 × 350 resolution
- Hercules graphics card, 720 × 348 resolution

V86 mode Virtual 8086 mode, a submode of the protected operating node in 80386 and later chips. When using the V86 mode, the 386 is able to simulate 8086 systems operating in real mode.

Veitch diagram A graphical technique used for the solution of problems arising in digital circuit design.

velocity 1. A vector quantity that includes both magnitude (speed) and direction in relation to a given frame of reference. **2.** The rate of motion in a given direction. **3.** In a wave, the distance travelled by a given phase divided by the time taken. It is a vector quantity such that it has a magnitude and a direction expressed relative to some frame of reference.

velocity of propagation The speed of a wave within a media such as a cable. This speed is usually compared with the same wave in free space.

Venn diagram A diagram in which each region represents an individual parameter. Sets are represented by the overlapping of regions, as shown in the figure. Basic logic relations, operations, and propositions are illustrated and defined by the inclusion, exclusion, and intersection of the regions.

Ventura Publisher A desktop publishing package that performs page composition in real time, selects and builds pages, and imports text and graphics from over 500 programs. It adds typographic refinements and illustrations, as well as the final annotations and captions. Documents can contain up to 128 chapters of some 300 pages each, with an automatically generated index, table of contents, and list of Illustrations.

VER 1. Acronym for *vision electronic recording.* **2.** A DOS command that gives the DOS version in use.

verbs, processor Refers to verbs that specify to the processor the procedures by which a source program is to be translated into an object program.

C = A AND B

C = A AND NOT B

C = NOT A AND B

Venn diagrams

verification The process of checking the results of one data transcription against those of another.

verification mode A mode of operation in time-sharing systems in which all edit subcommands are acknowledged and text changes are displayed as they are made.

verifier A device on which a record or data can be compared or tested for identity, character by character, with a retranscription of copy as it is being prepared.

verify To make a certain determination that a computer operation has been accomplished accurately.

Vermont Views A user-interface development system that includes an interactive designer and C-language libraries. There are over 500 functions for creating and managing menus, windows, data entry, help systems, and error-handling routines. Each system is developed as a separate resource, and allows an application to read in and use designer forms and menus or generated source-code equivalents. Hooks and low-level functions are provided for customized processing.

vernier capacitor A variable capacitor placed in parallel with a larger tuning capacitor and used to provide a fine adjustment.

Veronica An Internet utility for browsing files.

version A different edition of a program, numbered so that the most current form can be recognized. Also called *release number.*

vertical blanking When the electron beam of a CRT finishes writing information on the screen at the end of a display refresh cycle, the beam must return to the top of the screen. The beam is turned off during the interval so that it does not write incorrect information to the screen; this is known as vertical blanking.

vertical CPU stand A stand that adjusts to accommodate vertically positioned CPUs, as shown in the following figure.

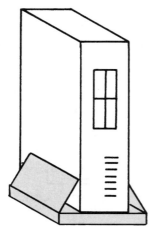

Vertical CPU stand

vertical delta encoding Delta encoding in the vertical direction. *Also see* DELTA ENCODING/DECODING.

vertical parity check A check in which the binary digits of a character column are added and the sum is checked against a previously computed parity digit to test whether the number of ones is odd or even.

vertical polarization The state of an electromagnetic wave when the electric component lies in the vertical plane and the magnetic component in the horizontal plane.

vertical redundancy checking *See* VRC.

vertical resolution The specification of display resolution in the vertical direction, meaning the ability to reproduce closely spaced horizontal lines. Also, the amount of detail that can be perceived in the vertical direction, or the maximum number of alternating white-and-black horizontal lines that can be counted from the top of the picture to the bottom. It is not the same as the number of scanning lines.

vertical-scan frequency Refers to the speed at which the screen image is refreshed by the monitor. It is an indication of the stability of the image displayed. A monitor with a higher vertical-scan frequency will display less flicker than an equivalent monitor with a lower vertical-scan frequency.

vertical scroll To move vertically within a document that is longer than the window, so that parts of it formerly above or below the window come into view.

vertical tabulation character *See* VT.

very high frequency *See* VHF.

very large-scale integration *See* VLSI.

very low frequency *See* VLF.

vestigial sideband The incomplete suppression of one sideband in an AM system to reduce the total signal bandwidth without degradation of information content.

vestigial-sideband transmission A method of communication in which frequencies of one sideband, the carrier, and only a portion of the other sideband are transmitted.

VFax A two-board, single-line, fax-on-demand kit that runs on AT-compatible computers. It provides unattended distribution of literature by document number via fax machine. The caller responds to voice messages with touchtone responses. Features include one-call and call-back document delivery, security codes, user account control, reports, and remote document entry.

vf band Abbreviation for *voice-frequency band*, that frequency range between 600 and 3000 Hz that is adequate for transmission of speech with good intelligibility.

V.15 CCITT Recommendation by the CCITT (Consultative Committee for International Telegraphy and Telephony) for the use of acoustic coupling for data transmission.

V.50 CCITT Standard units for transmission quality of data transmission.

V.52 CCITT Recommendation for characteristics of distortion and error-rate measuring apparatus for data transmission.

V.53 CCITT Recommendation for limits on the maintenance of telephone circuits used for data transmission.

V.54 CCITT Recommendation for loop-test devices for modems.

V.55 CCITT Specification for an impulsive-noise measuring instrument for telephone-type circuits.

V.56 CCITT Recommendation for comparative tests for modems for use over telephone-type circuits.

V.57 CCITT Recommendation for a comprehensive data test set for high data-signaling rates.

V.5 CCITT Recommendation by the CCITT (Consultative Committee for International Telegraphy and Telephony) for the standardization of modulation rates and data signaling rates for synchronous data transmission in the switched network.

VFO Abbreviation for *variable frequency oscillator*.

V format A data record format with records of variable length. Each record begins with a record-length indicator.

V.41 A CCITT recommendation for code-independent error-control systems.

V.42 bis A CCITT standard for modem communication.

VFT Abbreviation for *voice frequency terminal*.

VGA Abbreviation for *Visual Graphics Adapter*, the color graphics provided in the IBM PS/2 series of computers and compatibles.

VGA card A card that provides the features found in the IBM PS/2 display adapter.

VGA Plus Card A card that provides the features found in the IBM PS/2 display adapter plus faster performance. You can also display up to 132 columns of text.

VGA Professional Card A card that gives the compatibility and extra features of the VGA Plus Card and additional modes, such as the ability to display 256 colors onscreen at 640 × 480 resolution or display 16 colors onscreen at 800 × 600 resolution. The VGA Professional Card provides up to 1024 × 768 on high-resolution multisynchronous monitors.

VHD Abbreviation for *video high density*. A video disc system in competition with Philips's laser reading (VLP) system and RCA's grooved capacitance (CED) video.

VHF Abbreviation for *very high frequency*, those frequencies between 30 and 300 MHz.

VHP Abbreviation for *very high performance*.

vibrator *See* MULTIVIBRATOR.

Victor Image-Processing Library A grayscale and color image-processing library with brightness, contrast, sharpen, outline, resize, rotate, flip, overlay, and matrix conversion features. It has color reduction and can process multiple, single, or partial images of any size, with support for expanded, extended and conventional memory. You can convert 24-bit RGB to SVGA/VGA/EGA images in TIFF/PCSGIF/TGA file formats.

VIDAT Abbreviation for *visual data acquisition*.

video card An expansion board that allows the computer to send the correct signals to the monitor, as shown in the following figure. The card must match the type of monitor being used. On the card is a video output chip, usually a 6845 CRT controller. It is the main chip for the conversion of digital bits from the computer to the image on the monitor. There are other support chips on the board, including, for example, 4K of static RAM and an MK-36000 character ROM. This RAM is a part of the system memory map. It acts as the video RAM.

video circuits The computer sends horizontal and vertical sync signals to the sweep circuits to lock the horizontal and vertical oscillators in step with the computer's operating frequencies, as shown in the figures.

video coprocessor A separate CPU for video functions, which operates in parallel with the main system CPU.

videodisc The video counterpart of the phonograph record; it stores visual and audio matter that can be displayed on the television set through a special turntable. It is being developed in three different, incompatible formats: LV (LaserVision—MCA/Phillips' reflective laser optical system), CED (RCA's capacitance electronic disc), and VHD (the Japanese video high-density system).

videodisc players Players used in multimedia to read videodiscs. Industrial laser disc players will play 12-inch and 8-inch LaserVision discs as

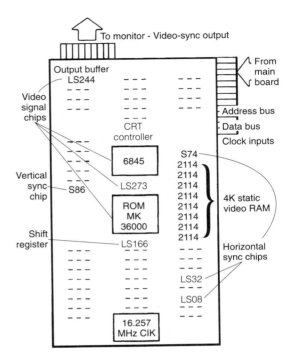

Monochrome video adapter layout

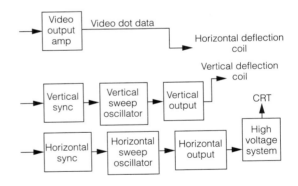

Video system block diagram

well as 3-inch and 5-inch audio CDs and CDV (CD-video) discs. Some external drives provide 600KBps data transfer rates, which makes them well-suited for playing discs with plenty of animation.

The 3-inch optical disks are known as *electronic books*; one disc stores over 100,000 pages of text, 32,000 graphics, six hours of audio, or

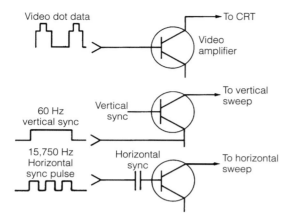

Video signal characteristics

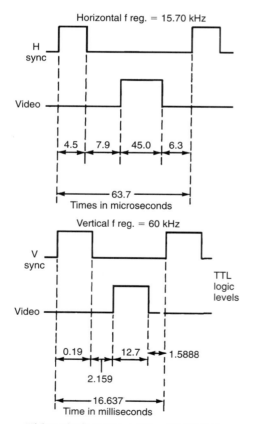

Video timing chart fH = 15.70 kHz

any combination of these. A one-pound player integrates a built-in speaker, a QWERTY keyboard, and a 4-inch diagonal LCD screen.

video-display adapter In the IBM PCs, the plug-in board that provides the video display circuitry for the system.

video display processor See VDP.

video display terminal See VDT.

video editors Programs such as the Macintosh QuickTime editor for providing finished videos. Entry-level video-editing programs capture and play back video, and offer basic editing functions such as cut, copy, and paste. Mid-level programs add special effects, transitions, and titles using a timeline upon which icons are dragged and dropped, in sequence. Separate tracks are supplied for audio, video, effects, and superimposed elements such as titles; tracks may overlap. Some programs also support plug-ins and DVE (digital video effects) add-on packages.

For integrated special effects, advanced chroma key, and compositing capabilities, a higher level of digital video editors is offered, which is distinguished by 60-field editing. Broadcast video is interfaced, two fields per frame, reflecting the odd and even horizontal TV scan lines, which at 30 frames per second equals 60 fields.

video RAM See VRAM.

video signal Part of a TV signal that conveys all the information (intensity, color, and synchronization) required for establishing the visual image on a monochrome or color TV.

video standards Refers to the display characteristics for monochrome/color cards that support text and Hercules graphics on a monochrome monitor, or CGA on a color monitor. Other standards are available with EGA or VGA compatible cards.

view A database construct that makes a collection of one or more tables appear as a single database table.

viewing ratio In video displays, the ratio between the viewer's distance from the screen and the height of the display screen.

viewport In computer graphics, a directed line segment; a one-dimensional array.

View232 A product that turns your PC into a communications dataline monitor, allowing data to be displayed in different formats, and the system configuration to be controlled and saved.

View Workstation Software A package that provides a real-time, menu-driven, multitasking software link to data loggers.

VIG Acronym for *video interface group*.

Vines Acronym for *Virtual Networking System*, a networking system by Banyan Systems based on UNIX but supporting DOS-based applications.

VIPS Acronym for *voice interruption priority system*.

virtual Conceptual rather than actual, but possessing the essential characteristics of a real function.

virtual address A symbol or word that can be used as a valid address part, but does not necessarily refer to an actual memory location.

virtual address mode A mode in the 80286 that uses 32-bit pointers consisting of a 16-selector and offset components. The selector specifies an index into a memory-resident table, and the 24-bit base address of the desired segment is obtained from the memory table. A 16-bit offset is added to the segment base address to form the physical address. The microprocessor automatically references the tables whenever a segment register is loaded with a selector. Instructions that load a segment register will refer to the memory-based tables without additional program support. The memory-based tables contain 8-byte values called *descriptors*.

virtual address space In a virtual storage system, the storage area assigned to a job, user, or task.

virtual circuit A circuit or function that is established in a computer operation.

virtual device A software entity that defines the interface characteristic of a specific physical device, such as a video display.

virtual earth A terminal of a device such as an amplifier that remains approximately at earth potential although not connected to earth.

virtual 8086 mode *See* V86 MODE.

virtual image The apparent spatial position of a reflection in a mirror.

virtual machine A system that uses multiple copies of another computer's hardware and software to create a machine environment that can be used to test software and hardware designs. The virtual machine allows a large memory capacity through the use of virtual memory, and provides simplified software and improved development reliability. The technique maps the memory plus the instructions; when instructions are executed, the machine traps and implements them directly.

virtual memory A memory technique that transfers information one page at a time between primary and secondary memory, and adds only the page-swapping time to the operating time. This technique permits a program to be larger than main memory, and with the use of a pointer arrangement, software demands can be much less than other types of segmentation systems.

Virtual memory systems have been used in large system-development programs, allowing programmers to write programs as if memory capacity were unlimited. The operating system keeps the pages of the program on disk and out of use until required. Each page is loaded into the system when called for by the program.

virtual memory pointer A pointer used to keep track of the parts of programs and data scattered between main memory and auxiliary storage in a virtual memory system. The pointer system is usually transparent to the user.

Virtual Memory System *See* VMS.

virtual memory, user-coded A virtual memory that can be provided by a user-determined form of code segmentation. This approach permits a program to be larger than the main memory while avoiding problems that may result when segmentation is totally machine determined.

virtual reality Abbreviated *VR*; refers to a computer-based simulation system, usually involving special equipment, designed to fool the user's senses into reacting as if the simulated environment were real. By putting on a helmet, sliding on a special glove, and pressing a few computer keys, you are transported into a colorful, synthetic, computer-generated world. The virtual world may be simulated by two tiny television screens build into a helmet's visor. One screen is positioned in front of each eye, each displaying a scene at a slightly different angle. The brain combines the two, producing the illusion of being in the scene. This is called *stereoscopic viewing*.

virtual storage system *See* VIRTUAL MEMORY.

virtual telecommunications access method *See* VTAM.

virtual terminal A DECnet protocol that allows a user on one DECnet node to emulate a locally attached terminal on a remote node.

virtual terminal network A network that allows the user to select the type of terminal to be used at each location independently. A computer supporting the network has the capability to handle a wide range of terminal types without additional software.

virtual unbundling A marketing concept in which manufacturers sell as much or as little computer hardware as the applications require. The user needs may call for a complete computer system, subsystem, boards, kit parts, or components, which are all furnished by one manufacturer.

Virt-Win A program that gives you virtual windowing and display power. It lets you write complex displays to memory, take partial screen snapshots, and cut and paste screen segments. The windowing system allows an unlimited number of overlapping windows that can move, resize, shadow, and explode.

virus In just a few years, the computer virus phenomenon has grown from a theoretical threat to a real and deadly danger. Mainframes, minicomputers, engineering workstations, and computer networks have all been successfully attacked. As evident in the recent attack that spread through the Internet communication network, every organization is vulnerable to the threat of viruses. In the past, viruses have attacked IBM, DEC, AT&T, Hewlett-Packard, Apple Computer, MIT, Stanford, Harvard, Lehigh, Georgetown, NASA, Aldus Corporation, SRI International, and Arco, to name but a few.

A typical computer virus is a simple program that reproduces and buries itself inside other programs. When infected programs are run, they spread the virus to other programs and computers with which they are in contact. Once hidden in a computer's software, viruses can wipe out program files, destroy data, alter numerical values in a spreadsheet, reformat hard disks, or perform other damage programmed by their creator. Viruses often go unnoticed while causing significant damage.

Viruses circumvent normal controls even in the most secure environment; long-trusted security systems like RACF, ACF2, and TOP SECRET have proven useless as viral defenses. For example, in just two hours, 500,000 copies of a virus spread through IBM's worldwide computer network, bringing operations to a halt. Aftershocks affected hundreds of users over the next eight weeks.

In another example, the Pakistani Brain virus infected and destroyed a reporter's files at the Providence *Journal-Bulletin* and spread to floppy disks throughout the newspaper's system. Over 100,000 copies of the virus were detected in six months at businesses and universities worldwide. Vaccines, strict backup procedures, and careful monitoring of computer use provide the best protection against viruses. *Also see* VACCINE.

VisiCalc (*o.t.*) A popular early spreadsheet program for PCs.

visual acuity The amount of detail perceptible by the human visual system. It depends on many factors, including brightness, color, orientation, and contrast.

visual display A unit that can display characters of information, such as tables, graphs, charts, or the lines and curves of drawings. Computer console displays may indicate the next instruction, parity, the contents of any memory location, or the status of interrupts in the system.

visual display interface The circuitry required to connect the results of a measurement or computation to a display device for observing and recording.

visual display station An input/output unit that allows the interrogation of a CPU using a CRT or similar display.

visual display terminal *See* VDT.

Visual Interface A class library that lets you design graphical user interfaces with movable windows and mouse-driven menus in Clipper. It provides all of the elements of graphical user interfaces.

Visual Librarian Software that provides a flowchart-based, point-and-click approach to managing libraries for Microsoft QuickBasic or Professional Development System. It allows you to create or modify libraries by including object modules, link libraries, function names, and by scanning BASIC source code. It will also resolve external references and search all link libraries for specific procedures. Features include context-sensitive help, formatted reports, mouse support, and object module extraction.

Visual SQL A prototyper and C source-code generator for creating Windows SQL database applications. It offers the performance of compiled C code and the development speed of 4GL, building database access into your application as you visually design it with the screen painter. You can interactively make changes to your prototype before compiling. It generates source code for simultaneous access to many different databases, including ORACLE, SQL Server, SQL Base, Integra SQL, and dBASE.

visual table of contents *See* VTOC.

visual terminal A unit that allows the interrogation of a processor along with the input of data using a visual display technology. Visual terminals use cathode-ray tubes, magneto-optics, light-emitting diodes, and gas-discharge displays.

Vitamin C A program with professional C functions for development. Features include multiple, overlapping, virtual, parent, and child windows; input fields; push and radio buttons; check and list boxes; and scrollbars. The open architecture has hooks and provides easy customization and extensibility.

VLF Abbreviation for *very low frequency*, electromagnetic radiation between 3 and 30 kHz. Sources of this form of radiation normally occur in computer monitors. Some medical experts claim VLF radiation produces adverse effects in the human body. Many countries have laws that severely restrict the amount of radiation a computer component can produce.

VLR Abbreviation for *very long range*.

VLSI Abbreviation for *very large-scale integration*, a concept whereby a complete system function is fabricated as a single microcircuit. In this context, a system, whether digital or linear, is considered to be one that contains 1000 or more gates, or circuitry of similar complexity.

VMOS Abbreviation for *vertical metal-oxide semiconductor*, a MOS transistor technology in which devices are formed using a vertical structure, which permits high power-dissipation capability. *Also see* MOS.

VMS Abbreviation for *Virtual Memory System*, a DEC proprietary operating system for VAX computers.

VMT Abbreviation for *virtual memory technique*; *see* VIRTUAL MEMORY.

V.19 CCITT Recommendation by CCITT for modems regarding parallel data transmission using telephone signaling frequencies.

VOC Abbreviation for *voice-operated circuit*.

vocoder A voice encoder.

voice answer-back *See* VAB.

voice channel A circuit of sufficient bandwidth to allow a data transfer of 2400 bits per second.

voice grade A classification for a communication line used in normal telephone service that is capable of handling speech data without significant degradation of signal regardless of path length.

voice-operated device See VOX BOX.

voice-over-data local multiplexer A frequency-division multiplexer that employs the unused high-frequency bandwidth of in-house wiring for data transmission. The data signals are then removed by the MUX (multiplexing) central unit and routed over separate interface cables to the data PABX (private automatic branch exchange) or computer. At the same time, the voice transmissions are routed back to their normal destination, the voice PABX. The MUX data-modulating frequencies are well above the range of human audibility and are transparent to normal telephone conversations.

voice recognition device Input hardware that accepts spoken words as data.

VOL A DOS command that displays the disk volume label.

volatile Refers to memory units that lose stored information with time or when the power is turned off. Integrated circuit memories are volatile because their cells require power to maintain the stored information. A nonvolatile memory unit such as a magnetic disk retains its stored information after power is removed, since the stored information is determined by the direction of magnetization, which is retained when power is off. Microcomputers with volatile memories may use backup batteries or power supplies that continue to provide power for some time after a power interruption occurs.

volatile dynamic storage A type of dynamic storage that depends upon the supply of power along with refresh circuitry to maintain stored information. Without such circuitry, stored data would be lost with the removal of power.

Volkswriter Deluxe An older, DOS-based word processor similar to WordStar features such as true proportional spacing, page orientation, and footnotes, and comes with a notepad feature so that the user can jot down a thought and file it for future reference. Foreign language, engineering, and scientific symbols can be used by assigning them a keystroke. Files can be freely interchanged with other programs; a special routine reads WordStar files.

volt The international unit of electromotive force (abbreviated V), equal to the product of current and resistance.

voltage The measure of electromotive force that forces current through a circuit.

voltage comparator A device that can compare two voltages and issue output that is a function of the comparison.

voltage direct current See VDC.

voltage doubler A power-supply circuit in which both half-cycles of an ac supply are rectified, and the resulting dc voltages are added in series.

voltage, drain gate The dc voltage between the drain and gate terminals.

voltage, drain gate breakdown The dc breakdown voltage between the drain and gate terminals with the source terminal open.

voltage, drain source on-state The dc voltage between the drain and source terminals with a specified forward gate source applied to bias the device to the on state.

voltage, drain-substrate The dc voltage between the drain and substrate terminals.

voltage drop The reduction of voltage along a conductor or through a device as a result of the conductor's (or device's) resistance.

voltage, forward gate-source The dc voltage between the gate and source terminals of such polarity that an increase in its magnitude causes the channel resistance to decrease.

voltage gain The ratio of the output to input voltage in a circuit or device.

voltage, gate-source The dc voltage between the gate and source terminals.

voltage, gate-source threshold The forward gate source voltage at which the magnitude of the drain current of a field-effect transistor has been increased to a specified low value.

voltage jump An abrupt discontinuity in voltage drop across a device, normally associated with a marked change in the device characteristic.

voltage level The value of the voltage at any point in a network expressed relative to a specified reference level.

voltage multiplier A circuit for obtaining a high dc potential from a low-voltage ac supply. A ladder of half-wave rectifiers charges successive capacitors connected in series on alternate half-cycles. It is effective only when the load current is small, such as for the anode supply to a CRT.

voltage regulation The degree to which a power source maintains a stable output under varying load conditions, usually expressed as a percentage.

voltage regulation/load The change in output voltage of a power source for a specified change in the load. This is often expressed as the percentage ratio of the voltage change.

voltage regulator A circuit or device, such as the one shown, used in conjunction with a power

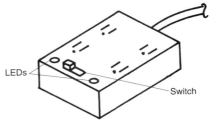

Voltage regulator

supply to maintain a stable voltage under different load and environmental conditions. Voltage regulators protect equipment and data by maintaining a constant power level during brown-outs and surges.

voltage regulator diode A diode that is used as a stable reference source in a voltage regulator application.

voltage, reverse gate-source The dc voltage between the gate and source terminals of such polarity that an increase in its magnitude causes the channel resistance to increase.

voltage, source-substrate The dc voltage between the source and substrate terminals.

voltage spike A sudden surge of electricity on a power or communications line, usually of extremely short duration.

voltage stabilizer The use of a zener or stabilizer diode to reduce the voltage across a device.

voltage standard An accurately known voltage source, such as a standard cell, that is used for comparison with or for the calibration of other voltages.

voltage supply drain The current drain, shown in the specifications for a module, that is consumed by the circuit in its worst-case state. This is usually the maximum specified current from all voltage sources simultaneously.

voltage-to-frequency converter A device for changing an input voltage into a proportional frequency that can then be counted by a digital device or processor.

voltaic cell A device with an *electrolyte* (ionized chemical compound in water) and two differing electrodes that are used to establish a difference of potential.

voltaic couple A contact with two dissimilar metals, resulting in a contact potential difference.

voltaic pile A voltage source consisting of alternate pairs of dissimilar metal discs separated by moistened pads, which form a number of elementary primary cells in series.

volt-ammeter An instrument designed to read both voltage and current.

volt ampere 1. The product of actual voltage (in volts) and actual current (in amperes) in a circuit, abbreviated *VA*. **2.** A unit of apparent power in an ac circuit containing reactance. It is equal to the potential in volts multiplied by the current in amperes, without considering phase.

volt-ampere hour The MKSA unit of apparent power, equivalent to the watt-hour.

volt-ampere meter An instrument for measuring the apparent power in an alternating current circuit. Its scale is graduated in volt-amperes or kilovolt-amperes.

Volta's law When two dissimilar conductors are placed in contact, the same contact potential is developed between them, whether the contact is direct or through one or more intermediate conductors.

voltmeter An instrument for measuring voltage (potential difference), usually in any of a number of voltage ranges.

voltohmmeter A portable instrument for measuring voltage and resistance.

voltohmmilliammeter A generally portable instrument for measuring voltage, sub-ampere current levels, and resistance.

volume hash A RAM index to the directory of the volume NetWare uses to quickly locate directory entries.

volume is cached In NetWare Directory Services, this shows whether a volume is cached. Caching is the process of storing the most recent reads and writes to memory so that subsequent requests may read from memory instead of the drive. It is used to improve performance on the drive.

volume is hashed In NetWare Directory Services, this shows whether a volume's directory table is stored in file server memory, which improves performance.

volume is mounted In NetWare Directory Services, this tells whether a volume is mounted in the file server.

volume is removable In NetWare Directory Services, a bit field for the flag showing whether a volume can be physically removed from the file server, such as in a removable hard disk cartridge-type drive.

volume name This refers to the name of the volume in a directory. In NetWare and other operating services, this must be no longer than 16 characters and must not contain spaces, asterisks, question marks, colons, backslashes, or forward slashes.

volume number In NetWare Directory Services, this refers to a volume's offset into the volume table.

voluntary interrupt An interrupt caused by an object program's deliberate use of a function known to cause an interrupt.

VOM *See* VOLTOHMMETER (or VOLTOHMMILLIAMMETER).

von Neuman bottleneck An inefficiency inherent in the design of all digital computers. In order to process information, data must be moved from memory to the CPU, worked on, and the results sent back to memory, Thus, the computer spends most of its time moving data instead of working on it. Named after the mathematician John von Neuman (1903-1957) who laid down the basic design for digital computers.

VOR Acronym for *VHF omnidirectional range*.

VOX Acronym for *voice-operated device*.

VOX box A modular device for interconnection to a tape recorder, radio transmitter, etc. that allows the presence of an audio signal to initiate a desired operation or function.

VP-Info A high-speed database management system that is data-file compatible with dBASE and allows users to use files from both products together without conversion. With its built-in compiler, VP-Info runs applications 2 to 10 times faster than most other interpretive data-base programs.

VR 1. *See* VOLTAGE REGULATOR. 2. *See* VIRTUAL REALITY.

VRAM Abbreviation for *video random access memory*, a variation of dynamic RAM that has two ports: the usual random-access port for access by a CPU, and a separate serial port that can output or input a serial stream of data at high rates independent of the activity on the random-access port. It is designed to reduce the conflict between trying to draw into the frame buffer while having to read the frame buffer to display the image on the CRT.

VRC Abbreviation for *vertical redundancy checking*, a type of error-checking that adds a parity bit to each block of data. *Also see* LRC.

VRR Abbreviation for *visual radio range*.

VS Abbreviation for *virtual storage*.

VSB Abbreviation for *vestigial sideband*.

V.6 Same as V.5, for leased telephone circuits.

V.16 CCITT Recommendation by CCITT for modems regarding the transmission of analog data.

VSW Abbreviation for *very short waves*.

VSWR Abbreviation for *voltage standing wave ratio*.

VT The vertical tabulation character, a format effecter that causes the printing or display position to be moved up or down a predetermined number of lines.

VTAM 1. Acronym for *virtual telecommunications access method*, a set of programs to control communication between nodes and application programs in SNA. 2. Acronym for *vortex telecommunications access method*, a software package designed to simplify the data communications programming required to serve remote user stations with a host computer.

V.32 A standard drafted by the CCITT in 1984 for dial-up 9600 bps modems. Standardization allows 9600 bps modems from different manufacturers to compatibly communicate.

V.35 CCITT Recommendation for data transmission at 48 Kbps using 60–108 kHz group band circuits.

V.35 BERT A unit that performs the three industry-accepted error rate tests: bit error rate (BERT), block error rate (BLERT), and errored second tests. You select the level of accuracy you want with selectable test lengths. Rate calculations are made internally and are indicated by a four-digit LCD display.

V.35 interface The CCITT standard for data transmission; facilitates high-speed transmission at speeds up to 56 Kbps. The interface supports only synchronous equipment, and is typically used on data terminal equipment or data communication equipment interfacing with a high-speed digital carrier such as AT&T's Dataphone Digital Service.

V.36 CCITT Modem recommendation for synchronous data transmission using 60 to 108 kHz group band circuits.

VTOC 1. Acronym (pronounced "vee-tock") for *volume table of contents*, also called directory. On a disk pack, a list of all the programs and where to find them on the device (track addresses). 2. Acronym for visual table of contents, part of a HIPO chart containing an abbreviated hierarchy chart with reference numbers and descriptions for each module. *Also see* HIPO CHART.

VTP Abbreviation for *vertical terminal protocol*.

V.21 Recommendation by CCITT defining standards for modems operating asynchronously to 200 or 300 bps, full-duplex, on the dial network. Similar to Bell 103.

V.22 A 1200 bps, full-duplex, two-wire modem standard by CCITT for use in the switched telephone network. Similar to Bell 212.

V.23 CCITT Recommendation defining standards for modems operating asynchronously at 600 bps or 1200 bps, half-duplex on the dial network, and full-duplex on a leased four-wire line. Similar to Bell 202.

V.24 A list of CCITT definitions for interchange circuits between data terminal equipment (DTE) and data communication equipment (DCE). It is effectively the same interface as RS-232, accepted internationally on the recommendation of the CCITT. *Also see* RS-232 INTERFACE.

V.25 CCITT Recommendation for automatic calling and/or answering equipment on the switched telephone network.

V.26 CCITT Recommendation defining standards for modems operating synchronously at 2400 bps, half-duplex on the dial network and full-duplex on a leased four-wire line. Similar to Bell 201.

V.27 CCITT Recommendation defining standards for modems operating synchronously at 4800 bps, half-duplex on the dial network and full-duplex on a leased four-wire line. Similar to Bell 208.

V.28 CCITT Recommendation defining electrical characteristics for interchange circuits defined in CCITT V.24. Similar to, and operationally compatible with, the EIA's RS-2132C standard.

V.29 CCITT Recommendation defining standards for modems operating synchronously at 9600 bps, full-duplex, on a leased four-wire line. Similar to Bell 209.

Vuwriter A word processing program that provides a wide range of characters to facilitate the creation of scientific and multilingual documents. There are nearly 500 characters in a wide variety of languages, including both Eastern and Western languages, Russian and Greek, Old English, international phonetic characters, Teletex, and classical Greek. Characters can be modified with an interactive editor.

W Symbol for *watt*.

WAC Acronym for *write address counter*.

WACK *Wait before transmit*, a character sequence that allows a receiving station to indicate a temporary not-ready-to-receive condition to the transmitting station.

wafer package Transistor or IC chips. The wafer is supplied unscribed, and except for the aluminum bonding pads, the chips are completely covered with silicon dioxide to minimize damage due to handling. They are 100 percent tested to electrical specifications. When the wafers are ordered, diced elements that fail the electrical test are inked out. Extra dice may be included to cover possible breakage and/or rejects. *Also see* DICED ELEMENT.

WAIS Abbreviation for *Wide Area Information Servers*, a distributed information service that offers simple natural language input, indexed searching for fast retrieval, and a "relevance feedback" mechanism that allows the results of initial searches to influence future searches.

waiting list A queue of unprocessed data or programs.

waiting state The state of an interrupt level that is armed and has received an interrupt signal, but has not yet been allowed to become active.

waiting-time jitter In a pulse-stuffing multiplexer, the jitter occurring because of the delay between the time pulse-stuffing is needed and the prescribed times that stuffing is allowed. *Also see* PULSE-STUFFING.

wait time The time interval during which a processing unit is waiting for information. This time interval may occur while information is being retrieved from a serial access file or located by a search.

wall energy The energy per unit area stored in the domain wall bounding two oppositely magnetized regions of a ferromagnetic material.

wall-less ionization chamber A chamber in which, due to the use of a guard ring, the collecting volume is defined by the applied field.

wall plates Plates like the one shown that mount directly to the wall with molly bolts or to regular, single or double electrical wall outlet boxes. Wall plates are an integral part of a flexible system installation, permitting the user to place connector outlets throughout a building to facilitate equipment moves. Wall plates are available for all DB-type connectors.

Wall plate

Wall Street A menu-driven portfolio management package for stock and bond investors. The program can be updated with information on changes in a position or current prices as needed. You can see how much the value of a holding has increased or decreased since the purchase date, the current value of any holding or the entire portfolio, the total or annualized rate of return, and commissions. This information can be viewed in chart form or graphed in color.

wallpaper A feature of Windows that allows a graphic image (typically a 16-color image in the BMP file format) to be used as a background(as opposed to standard light gray), which can be seen when all Windows functions (including the Program Manager) are reduced in size or minimized completely.

WAN Acronym for *wide area network*, a telecommunication network that covers a large area. The operation may include voice, video, packet-switching, and public data.

wander *See* DRIFT.

Wang Maker of some of the first and most-popular dedicated word-processing systems.

warm boot To reload or reinitialize a computer's operating system in such a way that the flow of electricity through the hardware is not cut off. In DOS, this is accomplished by holding down the Ctrl and Alt keys, then tapping the Delete key. Also called a *soft boot*. *Contrast with* COLD BOOT.

warm-up time The time required for a device to reach a stable state after application of power.

wasted server memory In the NetWare File Server Environment, this is the amount of memory in the server that is not being used in 1K units. The wasted server memory will normally be zero. If it is not zero, the file server has more memory installed than can be used. Usually all extra memory is used for cache blocks.

waste instruction An instruction which specifically instructs the processor to do nothing but process the next instruction in sequence. Also called a *blank*, *skip*, or *no-op*.

Watchdog One of several security packages available for limiting access to a PC. It protects against unauthorized viewing or copying files, running programs, or formatting the hard disk. It provides several levels of security, including ID and password protection.

The first level of security is access control. In order to access the files on the PC, the user must first enter an ID number, then a password, and finally a project ID number. Watchdog checks the information, then allows access to the system.

Once the user is granted access to an area, the audit trail feature keeps track of how much time the user spends in each area. The audit trail tracks the ID, password, and project ID, as well as the date and time spent in each area so that it can generate reports based on any of the information.

Another feature is the *automatic data encryption* of files, a security measure that prevents files from being read even if they are accessed by coding them into a format that is not comprehensible; *decryption* decodes the files into a readable format. Encrypted files can also be stored on floppy disks to transfer them to another hard disk or for backup purposes. The encryption/decryption process takes no more than three seconds for a 100K file and is transparent to the user. Watchdog also includes a text editor and a confidential mail facility so that users can exchange password-protected messages.

watchdog-destroyed connections In NetWare Diagnostic Services, this is the number of times (since SPX was loaded) that the watchdog process destroyed a connection because the connection was no longer valid. *Also see* SPX.

watchdog is on In NetWare Communication Services, this field indicates that the watchdog process is monitoring local SPX proceedings. *Also see* SPX.

watchdog program A program, not associated with a user, that watches for specific events. A typical watchdog program in a network looks for idle workstations and logs the user off.

watchdog timer In utilizing duplexed processors, one must consider when the backup processor should be activated to take over. The primary processor can set a watchdog timer in the backup unit on a periodic basis. Failure to set the timer causes the backup to assume control and disable the primary unit.

WATCOM A program to develop and debug 32-bit applications for extended DOS and Windows. It is a 32-bit C development package with tools for 32-bit applications, including DOS/4GW, components from Microsoft Windows SDK, a compiler, a protected-mode linker, an interactive debugger, an execution profiler, and runtime compatibility with Fortran 77/386.

water-chilled Refers to an electronic device that is cooled by a liquid that runs through small pipes to carry off heat.

WATFOR Software for Fortran 77 program development that integrates the compiler, editor, and debugger. Compile time is optimized by compiling the source code directly into memory, automatically linking, and executing. The integrated editor allows a program to be edited, compiled, and executed directly without leaving the environment. It supports the full ANSI Fortran X2.1978 language as well as enhancements. The IBM PC version also includes a library of ANSI standard (level 0a) routines to create graphical images.

WATS Acronym for *wide-area telephone service*, a telephone-subscriber service that permits a customer to make calls to other telephones in distant zones on a flat-fee rather than a toll-call basis.

watt The international unit of electric power (abbreviated W), equal to the product of voltage and current in dc circuits.

wattage rating The maximum power that a device can safely handle.

watt-hour The MKSA unit of electrical energy, being the work done by one watt acting for one hour, and equal to 3600 Joules.

.WAV In DOS and Windows filenaming schemes, an extension that indicates a popular type of digitized sound file.

wave 1. A single cycle of a periodic propagated disturbance such as a radio wave, a sound wave, or a carrier wave for transmitting data signals. 2. A graphic representation of a recurring cyclic signal; a waveform.

wave amplitude The maximum change from zero characteristic of a wave.

wave analyzer An instrument used to measure the amplitude and frequencies of the components of an electrical wave.

wave angle The angle at which a wave is propagated from one point to another.

wave band The band of frequencies assigned to a particular function or application.

wave carrier The basic frequency or pulse-repetition rate of a signal bearing no intrinsic intelligence until it is modulated by another signal that does bear intelligence. A carrier may be amplitude-, phase-, or frequency-modulated. In a pulse-coded signal, the presence or absence of a pulse determines whether a one or a zero is present in the binary number being represented.

waveform The graphic representation of the shape of a wave, showing the variations in amplitude with time.

waveform analyzer An instrument that measures or displays the components in an electrical waveform, usually with a variable-timebase capability.

waveform generator A circuit used to produce a desired waveform in a system.

waveform influence The change in indication, caused solely by a change in waveform from a specified waveform, of the applied current and/or voltage.

wave function In a wave equation, a point function that specifies the amplitude of a wave.

wave guide 1. A system of material boundaries capable of guiding electromagnetic waves. 2. A transmission line comprising a hollow conducting tube within which electromagnetic waves are propagated on a solid dielectric or dielectric-filled conductor. 3. A hollow metal conductor within which VHF energy can be transmitted efficiently in one of a number of modes of electromagnetic oscillation. Dielectric guides, consisting of rods or slabs of dielectric, can also be used, but these normally have higher losses.

wave interference A phenomenon that results when waves of the same or nearly the same type and frequency are superimposed. It is characterized by variations in the wave amplitude that differ from that of the individual superimposed waves.

wavelength 1. The distance between two similar and successive points on a periodic wave. 2. The approximate length in meters (abbreviated Λ) of any signal wave within a given band, used to express the approximate range of frequencies represented. The 6-meter band, for example, refers to frequencies between 50 and 54 MHz.

The formula for wavelength is $\Lambda = c/f$ where c is the propagation speed of the wave (300 million meters per second) and f is the frequency of the wave in hertz.

waveshape The graphic representation of one cycle of a wave, usually referenced against time. Principal waveshapes are sine, triangle, and square.

wave theory The explanation of diffraction, interference, and optical phenomena, as in electromagnetic waves, predicted by Maxwell and verified by Hertz for radio frequency waves.

WC Abbreviation for *write and compute*.

WCS Abbreviation for *writeable control store*, the control portion of a read-write memory (RAM) that allows the user to microcode a specialized instruction set for the system application. This technique is especially suited for some communications and signal-processing applications where a few well-designed algorithms are inquired.

wear-out failure A failure due to normal deterioration or mechanical wear, the probability of which increases with use.

weber The MKSA unit of magnetic flux. The weber is also used as the MKSA unit of magnetic pole strength.

weed To discard currently undesirable or needless items from a file.

weight In desktop publishing, refers to the thickness of characters. Each weight is considered a separate font. Thus, 9pt Palatino Bold is a different font from 9pt Palatino.

weighted average An average adjusted to give a different significance to each item according to its importance to the problem being studied. This technique can be used in selecting hardware and software for a particular application. One can analyze a number of issues, both technical and nontechnical, weight them accordingly, and the optimum choice can be computed.

WetPaint A set of disks containing Macintosh clip art for newsletters, brochures, flyers and brochures. The styles range from modern line art to antique images. You can automatically browse multiple files, present slideshows, scale selections (between 12% and 400%), invert, flip, or rotate the largest paint images, copy picture to the clipboard, or place them directly into any Macintosh-compatible page-layout program.

WF Abbreviation for *write forward*.

WFW *See* WINDOWS FOR WORKGROUPS.

Wheatstone bridge A basic circuit for measuring electrical resistance by the null method, comprising two parallel resistance branches, each branch consisting of two resistances in series. It is the basic prototype of other bridge circuits that can be used for measuring other electrical parameters.

Whirlwind I (*o.t.*) A very early, large computer which used ferromagnetic cores in its main memory. It was built at M.I.T.

whisker resistance Refers to the resistance of a catwhisker element in a semiconductor device.

white balance A means of adjusting, either manually or automatically, the color balance of a camera by shooting a white object and adjusting for a white image on the monitor. With a still video-camera, white balance is achieved instantly as the subject is photographed.

white noise Noise that has equal energy at all frequencies, as opposed to *pink noise*, which has equal energies within a specified band and very little energy elsewhere. Also called *fluctuation noise* and *random noise*.

white-stripe laser problems If white or light lines or stripes appear on the printout, check the print-capacity indicator on the toner cartridge. If it indicates a low condition, usually red, replace the cartridge. If the indicator is not completely red, you can distribute the toner by rocking the cartridge.

Whitewater Resource Toolkit A toolkit that provides C or Actor programmers a way of interactively customizing Microsoft Windows applications. This toolkit lets you draw dialog boxes, color bitmaps, cursors, and icons simply by selecting from a palette. It can create menus, keyboard accelerators, and string resources. It is compatible with all Windows resource file formats.

wicking The flow of solder up under the insulation on a covered wire.

wide-area bridge A MAC-layer bridge that works on wide-area communications links such as T1 and dial-up lines. *Also see* MAC-LAYER BRIDGE.

wide area network *See* WAN.

wideband coder A voice coder with a transmission rate that exceeds the rate that can be accommodated by 3 kHz telephone channels using modems.

wideband FSK A form of frequency-shift keying (FSK) in which the modulation index is much greater than one.

widow In word processing or desktop publishing, a layout problem in which a paragraph's last line appears alone at the top of a page or column, while the rest of the paragraph appears on the next page or column. Some programs will automatically scan for widow lines. *Also see* ORPHAN.

width, pulse modulation The duration of a pulse in the time interval between the points of the leading and trailing edges at which the instantaneous value bears a specified relation to the pulse amplitude.

wildcard A character that can represent one or more other characters, numbers, or symbols. The wildcards in DOS are the question mark (?), which matches any single character, and the asterisk (*), which matches any number of characters.

Williams tube A cathode-ray tube designed by F. C. Williams of the University of Manchester, England, for the electrostatic storage of information.

Wiltalk File Transfer Software that allows the IBM PC, XT, AT or compatible to upload and download files to and from a mainframe IBM 3X host. In both local and remote applications, the PC will emulate the IBM 5251 Model II workstation. There is no need for a communications port on the IBM System 3X or an 5251 emulation card in the PC.

winchester disk *See* HARD DISK.

winding drive A pulse of current in a winding, such as a drive wire or drive winding, that is inductively coupled to one or more magnetic cells; also, the pulse of magneto-motive force produced.

window In a graphical user interface, a defined area in the world coordinate system. *Also see* GUI.

windowing The division of a single display screen into several viewports, each showing a different program or file running concurrently. The windows may overlap each other in the same sense that papers on a desk may overlap, partially concealing the papers underneath. Windowing allows the user to work with more than one file or program at a time.

Windows *See* MICROSOFT WINDOWS.

Windows for Workgroups An extended version of Microsoft Windows that contains limited, built-in networking capabilities, a more full-featured Clipboard, and other additions. Sometimes abbreviated *WFW*. *Also see* MICROSOFT WINDOWS.

WindowsGENERATOR An automatic C code generator for developing user interfaces for Windows applications. It uses a high-level language to specify the elements that make up the Windows environment such as application windows, child windows, dialog boxes, messages boxes, and icons. The C code generated contains hooks which are indicated by comments, where users can insert their codes.

Windows NT A much-expanded version of Microsoft Windows that incorporates an operating system, multitasking, security features, and built-in networking capabilities, for use on computers that can support 32-bit programs. *Also see* MICROSOFT WINDOWS.

Windows Teach An interactive system that teaches Windows programming with tutorials, hypertext, and stepwise source-code annotations and explanations. A range of Windows applications are explained, including event-based programming, icons, hypermedia, device-independent graphics, and multi-document interfaces.

Windows Workstation A group of utilities designed to manage Windows on the network. It provides icon-based menus, centrally managed printing, a scripting language, network and standalone, security and metering of Windows applications.

WinGEN An object-oriented WYSIWYG source code generator/data-entry design tool for Windows-based versions of dBASE, Paradox, C/C++, and Turbo Pascal. WYSIWYG text, buttons, colors, and other object properties enable the creation of advanced, interactive Windows database applications. OLE and DDE links are supported.

WIN.INI A Windows ASCII initialization file used to define characteristics of the Windows environment.

Winstall A Windows utility that uses DDE to add a program to the Program Manager. It will also modify .INI files and add groups and icons to the Program Manager. It will find and execute Windows if it is not already running, and will run a text-mode installation if it cannot run under Windows.

wire A solid or stranded group of solid cylindrical conductors having a low resistance to current flow, together with any associated insulation.

wired-AND The stringing together of a number of circuits or functions such that when all circuits are at a logic 1, a desired connection point is a logic 1.

wired-OR The connecting of separate circuits or functions such that the combination represents an OR function or operation; the point at which the separate circuits are wired together will be a 1 if any of the wired-together circuits are a 1, as shown in the diagram.

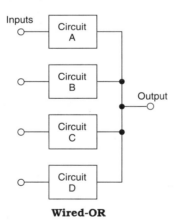

Wired-OR

wired-program computer (*o.t.*) A computer in which a majority of the instructions are determined by the placement of interconnecting patch-cords or pins using a device such as a plug or patchboard. If the wires are permanently soldered, the computer is a *fixed-program machine*.

wire harnesses, U contact The handling that allows mass termination of individual wires in connectors originally designed for flat cable. During assembly, the conductors of multiple-conductor cable harnesses must be aligned with the U contacts in the connector. The conductors in flat cable are accurately spaced during cable manufacture, but those in a twisted-pair woven cable must be separated and accurately spaced before they can be terminated in a U-contact type of connector.

wire-in Components that are too small to be plugged safely into a connector or holder.

wire printer stand *See* PRINTER STAND.

wirewrap An alternative to soldering connections in which a number of turns of a stripped solid conductor are wrapped around a metal post by special tools. With the proper technique, a good metal-to-metal contact results with enough corrosion resistance, mechanical stability, and conductivity to be used in military equipment. Wirewrap offers ease of design, freedom of layout, ease of design change, and good densities for logic designs.

wirewrap board A board that allows users to adapt portions of a microcomputer system for special applications or changes during the development process.

wirewrap module A module designed to fit into a microcomputer system that has wirewrap pins along with IC sockets for easy circuit modifications.

wirewrapped panel A panel designed to accommodate RAM chips along with the ROM chip and CPU required for a microcomputer system. A typical panel has 200 to 300 input or output pins for wirewrap connections.

wirewrapped socket board A board containing sockets and wirewrap pins for maximum flexibility of design of the microcomputer system. The sockets will accept components with 14 to 40 pins.

wirewrap tool The hand or power tool used to accomplish prototype or production wirewrapping. Tools are available with electrical ac power, battery power, or air power.

wiring diagram A circuit diagram that indicates the physical layout of equipment and the point-to-point distribution and interconnection of conductors.

wiring harness A group of wires that are gathered and held together by straps.

wiring hub The central wiring concentrator for a series of nodes.

wiring pencil A prototype aid that contains a replaceable spool or wire and a pencil-like tip to guide and cut the wire. The wire is wrapped around the terminal and cut. Heat from a soldering iron melts the insulation and completes the connection as the solder bond is made.

wiring-system service kit A kit that provides all the necessary tools, application instructions, and tool selection charts to support a complete wiring system. All of this is organized and packaged in a durable case or cabinet. Service kits are available for many military and commercial systems including all types of aircraft, weapon systems, ground vehicles, and marine equipment.

.WK1 A filename extension indicating a spreadsheet file created with a newer version of Lotus 1-2-3.

.WKS A filename extension indicating a spreadsheet file created with an older version of Lotus 1-2-3.

WO Abbreviation for *write out*.

word **1.** An ordered set of characters occupying one storage location and treated as a unit. Usually a word is treated by the control unit as an instruction, and by the arithmetic unit as a quantity. Word lengths may be fixed or variable, depending on the system configuration. **2.** A byte containing as many bits as the word-length capacity of the machine permits.

word address format The order of appearance of the character information within a word, as shown.

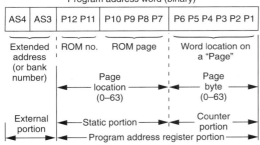

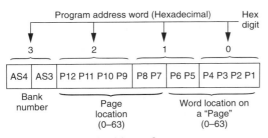

Word address format

word and byte addressing Some systems provide both word and byte addressing for most memory-reference instructions. This means that users can deal directly with either bytes or full words, as the application requires, without the complications required in microcomputers without both types of addressing.

word comparator time Circuitry that compares a word-time counter with the specified word time at the moment of the coincident pulse. This is done in order to verify that the correct word is being read.

word count The number of words in a record or other data item.

word-count register A register that holds the transfer word count during block transfer operations, used to keep track of input/output transfers. In a typical application, the word-count register is loaded at the start of an operation with the number of data words to be transferred, and then decremented after each transfer. When the register reaches zero, it signals the completion of the operation by generating an interrupt.

Word for Windows *See* MICROSOFT WORD.

word generator A circuit or device for providing words and sequences for testing and checkout. Many units are interactive and respond to levels or pulses from the device under test. Some word generators can perform program loops, generate serial or parallel data, generate data from selected locations in memory, and generate data continuously or in single words.

A word generator can be used to test logic states in a system. With the generator supplying the desired signals, operation of the circuit or system is checked using an oscilloscope or logic state analyzer. It may also be used to test serial devices such as shift registers, disk memories, and terminal hardware.

word interleaving *See* CHARACTER INTERLEAVING.

word length A measure of the size of a word specified in characters or bits. Longer word lengths in a microcomputer system increase efficiency and accuracy, but add to the system complexity and cost. For greater precision and memory access, multiple-word operands and instructions are used, although they increase execution time and complexity. In a fixed-point arithmetic system, a double-length word is stored in two registers.

word-length, double Many arithmetic instructions produce two-word results. With fixed-point multiplication, a double-length product is stored in two registers of control storage for integer and fractional operations. Integer and fractional division can be performed upon a double-length dividend; the remainder and the quotient will be retained in the registers.

word-length, I/O compatibility The efficient handling of 8-bit words is important in communications processing, in which 8-bit ASCII characters are typical; 8-, 16-, or 32-bit machines with good byte-handling capabilities are required in such applications. Incompatible I/O word lengths increase the difficulties encountered in interfacing computers with communication lines and peripherals.

word mark An indicator used to signal the beginning or end of a word.

Word, Microsoft *See* MICROSOFT WORD.

word-organized storage A type of magnetic storage in which each word of storage has a winding common to all the magnetic cells of the word.

word pattern The smallest meaningful language unit recognized by a machine. It is usually composed of a group of syllables and/or words.

WordPerfect The most-popular DOS-based word-processing package. It was originally function-key based, but now includes a menu-driven GUI interface. The program comes with a color-coded key template telling which of four commands is performed by each function key when it is pressed alone or in combination with the Shift, Alt, or Ctrl keys.

WordPerfect uses embedded codes to control features such as fonts, margins, and footnotes. One feature is the ability to search for and change these codes. Other features of the most recent version include the following:

- Advanced envelope-printing that allows you to save return addresses, add postal bar codes, and adjust margins
- The ability to create hypertext links to take the user between areas of the same document or to a different document
- Support for up to nine documents open at one time
- A built-in grammar checker
- The ability to print watermarks in the background, such as a light-gray "Confidential"

WordPerfect for Windows The Windows version of the popular WordPerfect word processor. Features of the most recent version include advanced mailmerge capabilities and built-in modules for creating text art, object-oriented graphics, and charts.

WordPerfect Library A DOS shell that permits the user to quickly switch between programs and share the data with different programs. Included is a collection of programs that are fully compatible with WordPerfect: a calendar for appointments and schedules, a file manager, and a notebook. The Macro Editor lets the user edit WordPerfect macros.

word processing The preparation of printed material for publication using computers.

word processor Any one of a category of programs that allows an operator to edit or otherwise manipulate text.

word-select, memory section The word-select steering technique used for memory addressing. An important consideration for dynamic memories is nondestructive readout with positive, automatic restoration that prevents an accidental loss of memory information.

word size *See* WORD LENGTH.

WordStar One of the first popular DOS-based word processors, first introduced in 1979. It is considered difficult to learn, but if used often, the user can become comfortable with it. Many other programs, including file and database managers and other word processors, are compatible with this program. Variations include WordStar 2000 and WordStar Professional (which adds mailmerging, grammar checking, and indexing).

word time The amount of time required to transport a word past a given point, or from one storage device to another.

word, trap The storage location used to store the instruction counter and trap identification data.

wordwrap The ability of word-processing programs to automatically place a word on the next line. When the right margin or indent is reached, the word processor checks to see if the last word typed fits completely on the active line. If not, it places the whole word on the next line.

work area A section of storage where data items may be processed or temporarily stored. The work area is used to retain intermediate results of a calculation, especially those results that do not appear as output in the program.

work distribution center A consolidation of tasks and activities that a particular department does, with each station in the center fitting into the department's overall activities.

workgroup Refers to people who work together on the same project or document. Several computers may be isolated on a small network, known as a *workgroup network*.

workgroup concentrator A concentrator that provides a wiring-closet solution when cabling LAN with twisted pairs. If AT&T specification wire is already in place, or the installation is new, using the same cable for all voice and data needs makes sense. Network setup can be as simple as patching cable to a telco splice block. The workgroup concentrator has integral retiming circuitry that amplifies and retimes received signals and transmits those signals to the attached host device or concentrator. The concentrator corrects network collisions and provides a diagnostic LED indication of network activity.

working register A register reserved for data on which operations are being performed. Working registers can be specified using fewer bits than working-storage memory locations, and execution time can be faster.

working storage A portion of storage reserved for data upon which operations are being performed. Working storage can be used in a microcomputer as buffer storage or for storage of intermediate program data.

work output queue A list of data that is output, but is stored temporarily in an auxiliary medium until a printer or other output device is available.

workstation Any terminal or computer in a local area network that is not a server. Sometimes abbreviated *WKS*.

WORLD A menu-driven database of statistical and demographic information about the nations of the world. Through the main menu, the user can select information about the names, capitals, geography, population, per capita income, mortality rates, and sovereignty of more than 100 countries.

world coordinate system A coordinate system not bounded by any limits—unlimited space in graphics.

World Wide Web A hypertext-based, distributed information system created by researchers at CERN in Switzerland. Users may create, edit, or browse hypertext documents. Also called *W3* and *WWW*.

WORM Abbreviation for *write-once read-many*, refers to a type of optical memory disk that can only be written to once, and cannot be erased or reformatted.

worm A potentially harmful computer program that replicates itself and is self-propagating. Worms, as opposed to viruses, are meant to spawn in network environments.

WOROM Abbreviation for *write-only read-only memory*.

worst-case circuit analysis A type of circuit analysis in which the worst possible effects are determined due to all possible combinations of circuit parameters.

worst-case design A conservative design approach in which the circuit is designed to function assuming the worst possible combination of operating characteristics.

worst-case noise pattern The noise appearing in a magnetic storage system when half of the selected cores are in a logic 1 state and the other half are in a logic 0 state.

Wozniak, Steve Started the Apple Computer company with Steve Jobs by building and marketing the Apple computer. Later, they formed Apple Corporation to produce Apple and Macintosh computers.

wp Abbreviation for *word processing*.

WPM Abbreviation for *words per minute*, a measure of user speed in various word-processing systems.

WR A control line used to indicate a write operation to memory or an output port.

wraparound The continuation of an operation such as

- A change in the storage location from the maximum addressable location to the first addressable location
- The shift of a register address from the highest address to the lowest
- A shift in a read or cursor movement from the last character position to the first position

wrapping 1. A procedure where an FDDI (fiber distributed data interface) network activates its second ring to bypass and isolate a failed node. 2. *See* WORDWRAP.

WR CHK Abbreviation for *write check*.

wrist strap A band that goes around your wrist to carry away the electrostatic charge when working on circuitry before it builds up. As shown in the figure, these lightweight wrist straps have a coiled cord, which acts as the grounding cable and connects to earth ground.

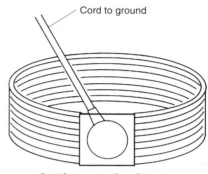

Static-control wrist strap

It is best to use the wrist strap on the same hand that is used to hold a probe or soldering iron. The closer the strap is to the hand that works on the chips, the safer the chips will be.

When wearing a wrist strap, you have to be especially careful not to touch any electrical lines. Since you are now grounded to earth, you would provide a short circuit path to ground! Two things are done to reduce this danger: the outside of the wrist strap is insulated, and a 1-megohm resistor is connected in series with the ground line at the wrist strap connection. This resistor prevents the current through the ground line from exceeding 0.5 milliamps for voltages up to 220 volts.

write To transfer, record, or copy, usually from one storage device to another. The information may be recorded in a register or any other storage location or medium.

writeable control store *See* WCS.

write addressing To direct or control a write operation in a device, such as with a binary counter, in which the first location address contains all zeros, and each successive address is incremented by one bit, such as shown in the table.

FIRST WRITE ADDRESS	00000000
SECOND WRITE ADDRESS	00000001
THIRD WRITE ADDRESS	00000010

write error count In NetWare Diagnostic Services, the number of times (since the shell was activated) that the driver has been unable to send a request to a file server (after repeated retries). In this case, the shell displays the message "Error writing to network" on the workstation screen.

write head Magnetic-tape recording head.

write lock Also known as an *exclusive lock*; prevents others from reading or writing the locked data.

WriteNow A fast word processor. You get up to four columns on the screen with WYSIWYG. Embedded graphics can be proportionally or nonproportionally resized. Other features include full mailmerge support; automatic footnote numbering; and character, word, and paragraph counting.

write operation, cache memory Typically, a logical address is sent from the CPU to the memory-cache subsystem. A page address is presented to a CAM memory for a presence check. If the page is present in the cache, a match occurs and a signal is sent to the control logic, indicating that the page is in the cache; the memory access is then made from the cache. If the operation is a write, the field changes to indicate a write has taken place on that page. If the page is not present, the control logic transfers the desired page from main memory to the cache, completing the memory request in the process.

write-protect The action of a user or manufacturer to prevent the erasure or overwriting of a program or data. On a 5¼-inch floppy disk, write-protection is done by covering up the cut-out notch on the side of the disk. On a 3½-inch floppy, write-protection is done by pushing up the write-protect tab on the corner of the disk so the hole is uncovered.

write pulse A drive pulse or the sum of several simultaneous drive pulses that, under suitable conditions, can write into a memory cell or set a circuit, usually to a one condition.

write-read 1. An operation in which a block of data is read in while simultaneously processing the previous block and writing out the results of that block. **2.** Possessing the capability of both read and write operations.

write-read process To read in one block of data while simultaneously processing the previous block and writing out the results of the preceding block.

Writer's Toolkit A set of tools to improve your writing, including grammar, style, and spelling checkers; a dictionary; a thesaurus with definitions; a quotation reference; and an abbreviation program.

writing analyzer Word-processing software that checks text for reading level, length of sentences, misuse or overuse of certain words, and other style indicators.

writing rate The maximum speed at which the spot on a cathode-ray tube can move and still produce a satisfactory image.

writing speed The rate of registering signals on a storage device.

WRU The "who-are-you" character.

WS *See* WORKING STORAGE.

W-shaped plugboard A plugboard with a W cut that allows easier insertion than conventional plugboards.

WSI Abbreviation for *wafer scale integration*, integrated circuits consisting of wafers instead of separate chips.

WSS Abbreviation for *Workstation Session Socket*, an AppleTalk session protocol field for the socket on the workstation that will receive session-level packets.

W3 *See* WORLD WIDE WEB.

WTS Abbreviation for *word terminal synchronous*.

Wullenweber A type of directional antenna array. A large Wullenweber is operated by the University of Illinois. It consists of 960 reflecting wires arranged in a 995 foot circle. The receivers are in the 5 to 15 MHz range, and it is used for studies of signals reflected from the ionosphere.

WWW *See* WORLD WIDE WEB.

Wylbur/AT A reproduction of the IBM mainframe version of WYLBUR for PCs. It provides the same editing environment for the MVS programmer, and enables EXEC programs to be ported from the mainframe to the PC with little or no change. Other features provide serial communication for automated script files, direct program execution under DOS, data entry panels, and indexed database creation.

WYSIWYG An acronym for "what you see is what you get" (pronounced "wiz-ee-wig"); refers to the match between the display and the printed copy. If a piece of software produces WYSIWYG displays, what you see on the computer screen in terms of fonts, graphics, and enhancements is what you will get on the printed copy.

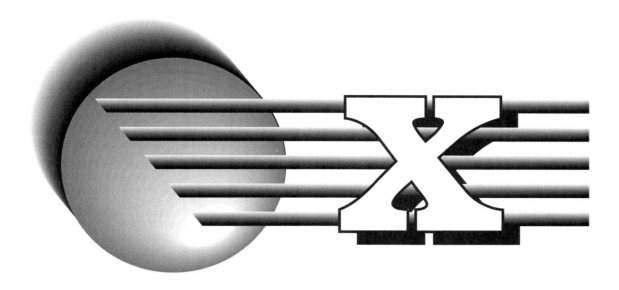

X The horizontal deflection on a CRT.

xasers A family of giant pulse lasers.

x-axis 1. The horizontal axis, as on a CRT screen, graph, printer, or plotter. *Contrast with* Y-AXIS. **2.** The reference axis of a quartz crystal.

Xbase Any of several database products that use the dBASE language or a derivative of it. Most Xbase products offer either an interpreted or a compiled environment; some, like FoxPro, offer both.

X_c Abbreviation for *capacitive reactance*, the reactance or opposition that a capacitor offers to an AC current flow.

XCOPY An expanded version of the DOS COPY command.

XDASM A software product that produces assembler-ready source code for Cross-16/32 from an Intel, Motorola, or binary hex file. The processor families it supports are 4004, 64180, 6502, 6800, 6805, 6809, 68HC11, 7BC10, 8048, 8051, 8085, 8096, 89700, COP400, COP800, SUPER8, Z8, and Z80. It is user-configurable for other 8-bit processors.

XEC An instruction to execute register contents. This instruction allows the programmer to load the binary machine-code representation into a working register and then have the CPU treat the contents of a working register as an instruction. If the programmer wishes to include optional features in a ROM program, he or she can include an XEC instruction in the ROM, then select and load the appropriate instruction code into the working register before branching to the ROM program.

xerographic printer *See* LASER PRINTER.

xerography A dry copying process in which light is used to discharge an electrostatically charged plate, which is then dusted with a dielectric powder to make the image visible. Fixing is usually done by heat directly after the dusting.

Xerox Tradename for a particular line of xerographic equipment.

Xerox Network System *See* XNS.

Xerox Palo Alto Research Center The Xerox research laboratory that did much of the early research that led to the development of many current technologies including PostScript, Apple Macintosh Interface and Ethernet.

X.500 A directory services protocol drafted by the CCITT and ISO to provide a global distributed directory for connected LANs.

X.4 CCITT specification defining the general structure of signals of the International Alphabet No. 5 code for data transmission over public data networks.

X.400 An international communications standard for e-mail that allows dissimilar e-mail systems to communicate. E-mail services including MCI Mail and CompuServe have accepted it as a standard.

XGA Abbreviation for *extended graphics array*, a video graphics specification promoted by IBM initially in their PS/2 model 90 series of computers. It supports 1024 × 768 resolution.

XIO Abbreviation for *execute input/output*.

X_l Abbreviation for *inductive reactance*, the reactance or opposition that an inductor offers to an AC current.

XLISP A programming language combining some features of LISP with an object-oriented extension capability. It is written in C and is easily extended with user-written, built-in functions and classes. It assumes some knowledge of LISP and object-oriented programming.

Xmodem A communications program that imposes no restrictions on the contents of the data being transmitted. Any kind of data may be sent, such as binary or ASCII.

Xmodem CRC In telecommunications, a type of Xmodem protocol that uses a complex polynomial equation to calculate a 16-bit cyclical redundancy check on the Xmodem 128-byte packet.

Xmodem protocol An 8-bit error-checking protocol widely used in computerized bulletin board systems. It sends information over the modem in packets of 128 bytes along with a checksum that is calculated by adding all of the ASCII values in the block, dividing by 256, and throwing away the remainder. Once received, the receiver calculates this checksum again on the received packet. If the two checksums match, the receiver sends an affirmative acknowledgment (ACK) character and the next block of data is sent; otherwise, a negative acknowledgment (NAK) character is sent back, causing the sender to retransmit the packet.

XMT Abbreviation for *transmit*.

XMTR Abbreviation for *transmitter*.

X.95 CCITT recommendation for network parameters in public data network.

X.96 CCITT recommendation for call-progress signals in public data networks.

XNS Abbreviation for *Xerox Network System*, the network architecture that forms the basis for Novell's NetWare.

XNS Mail Transport Protocol Message-handling service in XNS.

XOFF Indicates *transmitter off*, a shut-off signal sent by a receiving machine to a transmitter telling it to stop sending if it is sending, or not to send if it is preparing to do so.

XON Indicates *transmitter on*, a ready signal sent by a receiving machine to a transmitter telling it to start sending if it has anything to send.

X.1 CCITT recommendation for international user classes of service in the public data network.

XOR Abbreviation for *exclusive-OR*.

XQL Abbreviation for *Xtructured Query Language*, Novell's subset of the SQL standard.

XQLM Abbreviation for *XQL manager*, a high-level library of calls to Novell's XQL.

XQL relational-primitives Low-level library of calls to Novell's XQL.

Xray/beta-particle sensor, nuclear gauging A combination sensor that uses two isotopes, one of which emits low-energy x-rays and the other mid-energy beta particles. It has been developed to gauge foil laminates and magnetic films. Designed for online monitoring, the sensor takes advantage of the preferential x-ray absorption of metallic coatings.

XREF Abbreviation for *cross-reference*.

X.75 An international communications standard, developed by CCITT, for intranetwork communication. X.75 is based upon and includes extensions to X.25. It supports internetwork signaling, satellite usage, and multiple physical circuits.

Xsupport A database administration tool for Novell's XQL data dictionaries. It can create tables, Btrieve files, or modify existing data structures. All parameters for underlying Btrieve files are supported. It builds Btrieve/XQL dictionaries compatible with ObjectVision, R&R, Forest & Trees, and Novell's Xtrieve.

X-switch A crossover switch for reversing compatible devices; two pairs of devices can be switched, as shown in the diagram. For example, with an X-switch, one microcomputer can be printing letters on a printer while another microcomputer is transmitting on a modem, then switch the dial to have the first microcomputer communicate via the modem while the other prints out a report. A rotary switch does all of the reversing.

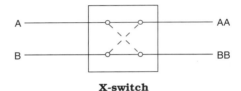

X-switch

XTAL Abbreviation for *crystal*.

X.3 CCITT recommendation defining PADs.

Xtrieve Plus Novell's menu-driven relational data access system with a flexible report writer. It allows users to define and modify databases created with Btrieve and with XQL (Novell's subset of SQL). It can access front-end applications that are compatible with Btrieve and XQL, including PC accounting packages, spreadsheets, and project management systems. It can be used to create custom displays and reports without programming, or to write Command File macros. It is available for the DOS and OS/2 environments, and can be configured to operate with NetWare Btrieve, the DOS or OS/2 client-only version of Btrieve, or with any version of XQL.

X.20 CCITT recommendation for the interface between data terminal equipment (DTE) and data circuit-terminating equipment (DCE) for synchronous services on public data networks.

X.21 CCITT recommendation for the interface between DTE and DCE devices for synchronous operation on public data networks.

X.21 interface Identical to the RS-422 interface, except that the X.21 interface is applicable to the 15-pin interconnection of DCE and DTE equipment employing serial binary data exchange. *Also see* RS-422 INTERFACE.

X.24 CCITT definitions of interchange circuits between DTE and DCE devices on public data networks.

X.25 CCITT recommendation that defines the interface between a packet-mode DTE and a packet-mode DCE.

X.25 interface A specification establishing standards for connection of communicating devices to an HDLC (hierarchical data link control) packet-switching network.

X-25 switch X-switch models for the RS-232 interface equipped with four DB25S (female) connectors. They are used for crossover switching of RS-232 devices.

X.28 CCITT recommendation that defines the interface between a start/stop mode DTE and PAD.

X.29 CCITT recommendation that defines the interfaces between a packet-mode DTE and the PAD.

X.2 CCITT recommendation for international user facilities in public data networks.

XY address The intersection of XY coordinates.

XY coordinates The specification of a location (address) by the use of graphing. A plane is delineated into horizontal units of measurement (the X-axis) and vertical units (the Y-axis). The location of any point can then be expressed by identifying its x and y coordinates. In data processing, XY coordinates are often used as cursor addresses on a display screen (corresponding to column and row numbers), as subscripts of an array element, and for other indexing.

X-Y plotter A device used to plot coordinate points in the form of a graph.

X-Y recorder A recorder that traces the relationship between two variables on a chart or graph. The chart or graph may move such that one of the variables becomes time-dependent.

X-Y switch A type of switch in which the wipers are moved first in one direction and then in the other.

XyWrite III Plus A word-processing program for large, complex documents that can run on almost any PC, even an 8088 with no hard disk drive. It includes a spelling checker and thesaurus, as well as up to 10 columns on a page with automatic justification, hyphenation, and wordwrap with each column; sort; red-lining; hidden, foot-, and endnotes; and a fully user-definable keyboard.

XyWrite for Windows 4.1 A word-processing program popular among writers and editors. The user can view and edit documents in four different modes: Fast Draft, Formatted Page/Line, Expanded View, and WYSIWYG, includes a programmable button bar that allows users to arrange icon menus, and provides drag-and-drop capabilities, along with graphics input and TrueType fonts.

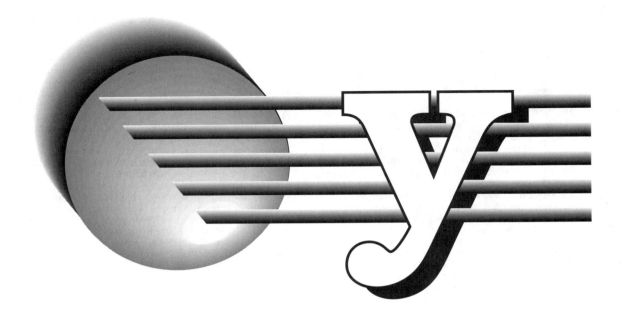

Y **1.** The vertical deflection on a CRT. **2.** In color video, the abbreviation for *luminance signal*, so named because it is the Y-axis of the chart of the spectral sensitivity of the human visual system.

Y-axis The vertical axis, as on a CRT screen, graph, printer, or plotter. *Contrast with* X-AXIS.

Y cable A cable in the form of a Y that doubles the use of a single cable, shown in the following figure.

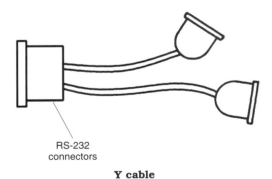

Y cable

Y-circuit A star-connected three-phase power circuit, so called because of its resemblance to the letter Y. Also called a *wye circuit* or *delta circuit*.

Yellow Book A CD-ROM standard.

yellow pages A Sun Microsystems management TCP/routing table.

yig Acronym for *yttrium-iron-garnet*, a crystal used in tuning devices in microwave circuits.

yig device A device using a yig crystal with a magnetic field for functional applications in wideband circuits. Yig devices include filters, discriminators, and multiplexers.

yig filter A filter that uses a yig crystal in a magnetic field provided by an electromagnetic coil.

yig oscillator A microwave oscillator that uses a yig filter in a tunnel-diode oscillator circuit.

Ymodem protocol A telecommunications protocol that uses 1024 blocks. Ymodem sends its first packet labeled 0. This packet contains the time and date stamp of the file being sent, along with its filesize and filespec. Ymodem may operate in batch mode; if implemented, this allows the receiver to specify more than one file to be transferred in a session.

yoke 1. A piece of ferromagnetic material that connects two cores or heads for reading or writing operations. **2.** A coil assembly used to provide electromagnetic deflection in a CRT.

YUV color system A color-encoding scheme for natural pictures in which the luminance and chrominance are separate. The human eye is less sensitive to color variations than to intensity variations, so YUV allows the encoding of luminance (Y) information at full bandwidth, and chrominance (UV) information at half bandwidth.

Z Abbreviation for *impedance*.

ZA Abbreviation for *zero and add*.

zap 1. To modify machine-language instructions in a program while the program is in memory and either executing or preparing to execute. **2.** To apply a change to the executable copy of a program without recompiling the program. **3.** To erase permanently. (As slang, usually implies accidental erasure.)

zApp A library of C++ classes to simplify the creation of DOS text-mode applications with a Window-like GUI. It provides an event-driven model, Windows, menus, dialog boxes, mouse support, transparent MDI support, message handling, forms, and automatic background-tasking in DOS text mode. It gives single-source code compatibility with Microsoft Windows, OS/2 Presentation Manager, and Unix X/MOTIF.

zata-code indexing *See* COORDINATE INDEXING.

z-axis 1. The longitudinal or optical axis of a quartz crystal slab, perpendicular to both the X and Y axes. **2.** In CAD and virtual reality systems, the axis representing depth, along which an object usually moves.

zener A semiconductor diode with a high ratio of reverse to forward resistance until breakdown occurs. The voltage drop after breakdown remains essentially constant, and the current is limited mainly by the circuit in which the device is connected. The zener is commonly used as a voltage regulator, reference, and ac clipper.

zener breakdown The avalanche of a semiconductor device due to field emission of charge carriers in the depletion layer.

zener current The current produced in an insulator by electrons that have been raised in energy from the valence bond to the conduction bond through the use of a strong electric field.

zener diode A diode that exhibits a sharp increase of reverse current at a certain negative potential, which is called the *zener* or *breakdown voltage*.

zener diode coupling A method of coupling circuits using zener diodes to provide a high degree of noise rejection.

zener diode regulator A power or voltage regulator that uses one or more zener diodes as the basic regulating element.

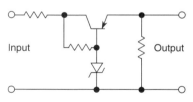

Zener diode regulator

zener effect A reverse-current breakdown due to the presence of a high electric field at the junction of a semiconductor or insulator.

zener voltage The negative breakdown voltage of a zener diode, which remains essentially constant over a wide range of current values.

zero 1. A numeral denoting lack of magnitude. Some machines may have distinct representations for +0 or −0. **2.** The bit or state representing false or off in a two-state logic system.

zero-access storage A method of storage in which waiting time is negligible and information is immediately available.

zero address instruction An instruction consisting of an operation that does not require an address in the usual sense. For example, the instruction

```
@Code:SHIFT LEFT 0002
```

has in its address portion the amount of shift desired.

zero adjust A control for setting the reading of a device to the zero mark in the absence of any signal.

zero beat The condition in which two signals, combined in a nonlinear element, are brought to the same frequency by nulling the element's output as a result of shifting the frequency of one of the two signals.

zero bit A bit used in the program counter to indicate that the accumulator has been cleared.

zero-bit insertion/deletion A technique used in bit-oriented protocols to separate six or more contiguous runs so they are not mistaken for flags or aborts.

zero compression A method of data compression in which all nonsignificant leading zeros are eliminated.

zero-cut crystal A crystal cut at such an angle to the axes as to have a zero frequency/temperature coefficient. Such a crystal can be used for a frequency standard.

zero error 1. The error on any instrument when indicating zero. **2.** The residual time delay that has to be compensated for in determining readings of range.

zero-error reference A constant ratio of incremental cause and effect. Proportionality is a special case of linearity in which the straight line passes through the origin. Zero-error reference of a linear transducer is a selected straight-line function of the input from which output errors are measured. *Zero-based linearity* is transducer linearity defined in terms of a zero-error reference, where zero input coincides with zero output.

zero fill To fill in characters with the representation of zeros without changing the meaning or content.

zero-forcing equalizer An equalizer in which the weighting coefficients of a transversal filter are selected to force the equalizer output to zero at sampling instants on either side of the desired signal.

zero-gate voltage drain current The direct current into the drain terminal when the gate source voltage is zero. This is an on-state current in a depletion type device, and an off-state current in an enhancement-type device.

zero-gate voltage source current The direct current into the source terminal when the gate-drain voltage is zero. This is an on-state current in a depletion-type device and an off-state current in an enhancement type device.

zero gradient synchrotron An atomic accelerator capable of accelerating protons with 12.5 billion electron volts of energy.

zero level 1. The usually arbitrary reference point for measuring signal levels in decibels. **2.** In audio and telephone systems, a reference level established by a power of 1 mW across a 600-Ω line; the decibel value is abbreviated *dBm* to specify the reference point.

zero-level address *See* IMMEDIATE ADDRESS.

zero page addressing A page-addressing method that uses only the second byte of an instruction and assumes a zero address byte. This technique is used in some systems with an index register in which the second byte is added to the contents of the register to produce an effective address.

zero paging A microprocessor addressing technique used for small memory spaces. A single, implied base register is assumed to contain the value zero. The address is then a displacement from this zero base. The number of bits used in the instruction for addressing within the zero page will be small. For example, an 8-bit address will give a zero page of 256 words. Above the zero page size, an additional mode of addressing must be provided that takes the address out of the zero page.

zero potential The potential of a point at infinite distance, such as used for defining capacitance.

zero power level An arbitrary power level for referring to other power levels, either in decibels or nepers. Zero power level in the U.S. is now defined as 1 mW, for a standard 600 ohm impedance.

zero stability The drift in the no-signal output level of an amplifier or device, either with time or with the operating conditions.

zero suppression The elimination of nonsignificant zeros, usually before printing or display.

zero transmission-level reference point An arbitrarily chosen point in a circuit to which all relative transmission levels are referred. The transmission level at the transmitting switchboard is frequently taken as the zero transmission-level reference point.

zero wait states A hardware configuration that permits data transfer between the CPU and memory every cycle.

ZIF Acronym for *zero insertion force*.

zigzag line chart A line chart in which straight lines connect the data in each series.

Zilog Z8 (*o.t.*) The Z8 single-chip microcomputer provided an on-chip ROM of 2048 bytes, a RAM of 124 bytes, 32 I/O lines, two counter/timers, and a programmable UART. Up to 64K of external memory could be addressed by the processor, which also contained a 64-byte ROM test memory.

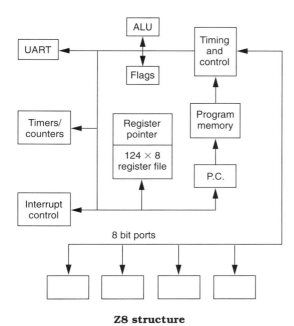

Z8 structure

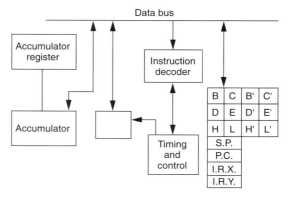

Z80 architecture

Zilog Z80 (*o.t.*) The first Z80 appeared in April 1976. By using a depletion mode load and n-channel MOS fabrication, only a single 5-volt power supply was required for this microprocessor. The Z80 did not multiplex status information on the data bus, as did the 8080, but it contained in the same 40-pin DIP used for the 8080.

The Z80 architecture is shown in the figure. An accumulator register was used to store data from the accumulator. This additional register tended to improve response time during interrupts. The temporary registers W and Z were replaced with a set of temporary registers that served as the general registers B, C, D, E, H, and L. This set of temporary registers also improved the interrupt response time. The Z80 microprocessor had four 16-bit registers, a program counter that provided the same functions as in the 8080, a stack pointer like one in the 8080 to hold the address of the next available location in the last-in-first-out (LIFO) stack stored in RAM, and two index registers X and Y.

A clock generator was on the CPU chip, along with circuitry for dynamic RAM refreshing and a special register for controlling interrupts. This allowed the microprocessor to operate in a mode in which an indirect call to memory could occur from an interrupt. The added special purpose register could be used to hold the upper 8 bits of the indirect address, while the lower 8 bits was furnished by the interrupting device.

Zilog Z8000 The Z8000 is a 16-bit microprocessor with an instruction set based on an expanded Z80 instruction set. Z80 users must use a translator to convert programs to the Z8000. Although the Z8000 uses a different architecture, both processors are register-oriented, and the addressing modes of the Z80 are a subset of the Z8000 modes. The Z8000 has a greater addressing space, and a larger number of instructions,

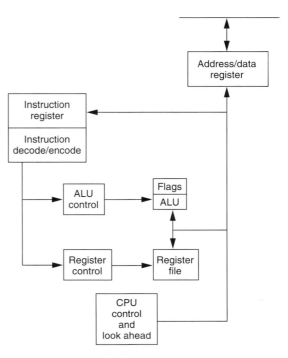

Z8000 structure

which are more powerful than those found in the Z80 instruction set.

The Z8000 is a random-logic-based CPU; its structure is shown in the figure. An internal 16-bit data bus is used for internal addressing and data communication. Instructions are fetched over the bus interface and executed by the instruction control unit. Throughput is enhanced by lookahead pipelining, which allows prefetching of the next single-word instruction or the first word of the next multiword instruction.

The Z8000 is available either in a 40-pin package or a 48-pin package. The 40-pin Z8000 is able to address 64K of memory, while the 48-pin device will address 8M of memory. In the Z8000 units, addresses are expressed in bytes. Single bytes are read and written using the byte/word output line. The 8M of directly addressable memory is split up into 128 segments, each of 64K. The CPU generates information that enables the address range to be increased by separating code, data, and stack spaces. External logic is used for this extension.

Zince Interface Library Software that lets you develop object-oriented applications for Windows and DOS with one set of source code. It uses platform-independent persistent objects to let you interactively design and save application screens.

ZIP 1. Refers to a popular file-compression system for PCs, named for the filename extension, *.ZIP*, that the compressed, or *zipped*, files have. To use a zipped file, it must be decompressed, or *unzipped*. **2.** Acronym for *Zone Information Protocol*, the AppleTalk protocol for the maintenance of zones.

ZipCode/Clip A database of zipcodes, with cities, states and counties. The database can be accessed from dBASE, Clipper, FoxBase, FoxPro or other dBASE-compatible applications.

ZIP RATE A program that computes motor freight or UPS shipping costs between your location and any three-digit ZIP code area in the continental United States. ZIP RATE uses a database of ICC class rates and UPS rates. The database includes rates for all weight breaks and standard product classes, bureau and tariff authorities, rate base numbers, and effective dates. The program is furnished for the user's particular zipcode.

Zmodem protocol A telecommunications protocol that uses a 32-bit CRC (cyclic redundancy check) character to detect transmission errors. It allows for batch transfer of more than one file, along with time and date stamping. Zmodem does not wait for the receiver to acknowledge receipt of an error-free packet; it continues sending until the receiver sends a packet NAK (negative acknowledgement), which causes the sender to resend that one bad packet. This lack of turn-around time speeds up Zmodem transfers.

zone A portion of storage allocated for a particular purpose or function.

zone bit 1. A bit in a group of positions used to indicate a specific class of items. **2.** A bit used as a key to a code.

zone digit A digit used as a key to a section of code. Zone digits can be used independently of other markings for control significance in a system.

Zone Information Protocol *See* ZIP, 2.

zone leveling A process carried out during the manufacturing of semiconductors in order to distribute impurities evenly.

zoo event Refers to a radio signal from space that has no known source or cause, so called because the enormous variety and number of possible sources of the signal are comparable to the number and variety of animals in a zoo.

zoom In many WYSIWYG programs, the ability to switch back and forth between a close-up and far-away rendering of the subject or image.

Zortech C++ A program for developing applications for DOS and Windows. It includes Windows development tools that allow developers to create Window applications without the Windows SDK. A library converts DOS command-line programs to Windows applications.

z-parameters The open circuit impedance parameters of a transistor.

ZPR Abbreviation for *zero power reactor*.

zulu time Greenwich meridian time, the international reference point for the time of day.

zwitterion A dipolar ion, such as an electrically neutral molecule that has a dipole moment. Many amino acids form such dipolar ions.

ZyINDEX An information search and retrieval program that allows you to locate your data files on your PC. The first step in using ZyINDEX is to run each of the files on a disk through the program's indexing routine, which creates a full-text index for handling search requests. To locate files pertinent to a particular subject, you enter a search request in the form of keywords. ZyINDEX then searches through its index to identify the files with contents that match the search request.